A New History of Western Philosophy

A NEW HISTORY OF WESTERN PHILOSOPHY

In Four Parts

ANTHONY
KENNY

CLARENDON PRESS · OXFORD

OXFORD
UNIVERSITY PRESS

Great Clarendon Street, Oxford OX2 6DP

Oxford University Press is a department of the University of Oxford.
It furthers the University's objective of excellence in research, scholarship,
and education by publishing worldwide in

Oxford New York

Auckland Cape Town Dar es Salaam Hong Kong Karachi
Kuala Lumpur Madrid Melbourne Mexico City Nairobi
New Delhi Shanghai Taipei Toronto

With offices in

Argentina Austria Brazil Chile Czech Republic France Greece
Guatemala Hungary Italy Japan Poland Portugal Singapore
South Korea Switzerland Thailand Turkey Ukraine Vietnam

Oxford is a registered trade mark of Oxford University Press
in the UK and in certain other countries

Published in the United States
by Oxford University Press Inc., New York

© Sir Anthony Kenny 2010

The moral rights of the author have been asserted
Database right Oxford University Press (maker)

First published 2007
First published in paperback 2008
This volume published 2010

British Library Cataloguing in Publication Data

Data available

Library of Congress Cataloging in Publication Data

Data available

Typeset by SPI Publisher Services, Pondicherry, India
Printed in Great Britain
on acid-free paper by
Clays Ltd., Elcograf S.p.A.

ISBN 978–0–19–965649–3

11

To the memory of Georg Henrik von Wright

CONTENTS

us today. But people who say that do not understand the reason why it has to be so. The reason is that our language has remained the same and always introduces us to the same questions. . . . I read 'philosophers are no nearer to the meaning of "reality" than Plato got'. What an extraordinary thing! How remarkable that Plato could get so far! Or that we have not been able to get any further! Was it because Plato was *so* clever? (MS 213/424)

The difference between what we might call the Aristotelian and the Wittgensteinian attitude to progress in philosophy derives from two different views of philosophy itself. Philosophy may be viewed as a science, on the one hand, or as an art, on the other. Philosophy is, indeed, uniquely difficult to classify, and resembles both the arts and the sciences.

On the one hand, philosophy seems to be like a science in that the philosopher is in pursuit of truth. Discoveries, it seems, are made in philosophy, and so the philosopher like the scientist has the excitement of belonging to an ongoing, cooperative, cumulative intellectual venture. If so, the philosopher must be familiar with current writing, and keep abreast of the state of the art. On this view, we twenty-first-century philosophers have an advantage over earlier practitioners of the discipline. We stand, no doubt, on the shoulders of other and greater philosophers, but we do stand above them. We have superannuated Plato and Kant.

On the other hand, in the arts, classic works do not date. If we want to learn physics or chemistry, as opposed to their history, we do not nowadays read Newton or Faraday. But we read the literature of Homer and Shakespeare not merely to learn about the quaint things that passed through people's minds in far-off days of long ago. Surely, it may well be argued, the same is true of philosophy. It is not merely in a spirit of antiquarian curiosity that we read Aristotle today. Philosophy is essentially the work of individual genius, and Kant does not supersede Plato any more than Shakespeare supersedes Homer.

There is truth in each of these accounts, but neither is wholly true and neither contains the whole truth. Philosophy is not a science, and there is no state of the art in philosophy. Philosophy is not a matter of expanding knowledge, of acquiring new truths about the world; the philosopher is not in possession of information that is denied to others. Philosophy is not a matter of knowledge; it is a matter of understanding, that is to say, of organizing what is known. But because philosophy is all-embracing, so universal in its field, the organization of knowledge that it demands is something so difficult that only genius can do it. For those of us who are not geniuses, the only way in which we can hope to come to grips with philosophy is by reaching up to the mind of some great philosopher of the past.

Though philosophy is not a science, throughout its history it has had an intimate relation to the sciences. Many disciplines that in antiquity and in the Middle Ages were part of philosophy have long since become independent sciences. A discipline remains philosophical as long as its concepts are unclarified and its methods are controversial. Perhaps no scientific concepts are ever fully clarified, and no scientific methods are ever totally uncontroversial; if so, there is always a philosophical element left in every science. But once problems can be unproblematically stated, when concepts are uncontroversially standardized, and where a consensus emerges for the methodology of solution, then we have a science setting up home independently, rather than a branch of philosophy.

Philosophy, once called the queen of the sciences, and once called their handmaid, is perhaps better thought of as the womb, or the midwife, of the sciences. But in fact sciences emerge from philosophy not so much by parturition as by fission. Two examples, out of many, may serve to illustrate this.

In the seventeenth century philosophers were much exercised by the problem of which of our ideas are innate and which are acquired. This problem split into two problems, one psychological (what do we owe to heredity and what do we owe to environment?) and one epistemological (how much of our knowledge depends on experience and how much is independent of it?). The first question was handed over to psychology; the second question remained philosophical. But the second question itself split into a number of questions, one of which was 'is mathematics merely an extension of logic, or is it an independent body of truth?' This was given a precise answer by the work of logicians and mathematicians in the twentieth century. The answer was not philosophical, but mathematical. So here we had an initial, confused, philosophical question that ramified in two directions—towards psychology and towards mathematics—leaving in the middle a philosophical residue that remains to be churned over, concerning the nature of mathematical propositions.

An earlier example is more complicated. A branch of philosophy given an honoured place by Aristotle is 'theology'. When we read what he says of it today, it seems to us a mixture of astronomy and philosophy of religion. Christian and Muslim Aristotelians added to it elements drawn from the teaching of their sacred books. It was when St Thomas Aquinas, in the thirteenth century, drew a sharp distinction between natural and revealed theology that the first important fission took place, removing from the philosophical agenda the appeals to revelation. It took rather longer for the astronomy and the natural theology to separate out from each other. This example shows that what may be sloughed off by philosophy need not be science but may be a humanistic discipline such as biblical studies. It shows also that the history of philosophy contains examples of fusion as well as of fission.

Philosophy resembles the arts in having a significant relation to a canon. A philosopher situates the problems to be addressed by reference to a series of classical texts. Because it has no specific subject matter, but only characteristic methods, philosophy is defined as a discipline by the activities of its great practitioners. The earliest people whom we recognize as philosophers, the pre-Socratics, were also scientists, and several of them were also religious leaders. They did not yet think of themselves as belonging to a common profession, the one with which we claim continuity. It was Plato who in his writings first used the word 'philosophy' in a sense close to our own. Those of us who call ourselves philosophers today can genuinely claim to be the heirs of Plato and Aristotle. But we are only a small subset of their heirs. What distinguishes us from their other heirs, and what entitles us to inherit their name, is that—unlike the physicists, the astronomers, the medics, the linguists, and so on—we philosophers pursue the goals of Plato and Aristotle only by the same methods as were already available to them.

If philosophy lies somewhere between the sciences and the arts, what is the answer to the question 'is there progress in philosophy?'

There are those who think that the major task of philosophy is to cure us of intellectual confusion. On this, modest, view of the philosopher's role, the tasks to be addressed differ across history, since each period needs a different form of therapy. The knots into which the undisciplined mind ties itself differ from age to age, and different mental motions are necessary to untie the knots. A prevalent malady of our own age, for instance, is the temptation to think of the mind as a computer, whereas earlier ages were tempted to think of it as a telephone exchange, a pedal organ, a homunculus, or a spirit. Maladies of earlier ages may be dormant, such as the belief that the stars are living beings; or they may return, such as the belief that the stars enable one to predict human behaviour.

The therapeutic view of philosophy, however, may seem to allow only for variation over time, not for genuine progress. But that is not necessarily true. A confusion of thought may be so satisfactorily cleared up by a philosopher that it no longer offers temptation to the unwary thinker. One such example will be considered at length in the first part of this history. Parmenides, the founder of the discipline of ontology (the science of being), based much of his system on a systematic confusion between different senses of the verb 'to be'. Plato, in one of his dialogues, sorted out the issues so successfully that there has never again been an excuse for mixing them up: indeed, it now takes a great effort of philosophical imagination to work out exactly what led Parmenides into confusion in the first place.

Progress of this kind is often concealed by its very success: once a philosophical problem is resolved, no one regards it as any more a matter of philosophy. It is like treason in the epigram: 'Treason doth never prosper, what's the reason? | For if it prosper, none dare call it treason.'

The most visible form of philosophical progress is progress in philosophical analysis. Philosophy does not progress by making regular additions to a quantum of information; as has been said, what philosophy offers is not information but understanding. Contemporary philosophers, of course, know some things that the greatest philosophers of the past did not know; but the things they know are not philosophical matters but the truths that have been discovered by the sciences begotten of philosophy. But there are also some things that philosophers of the present day understand that even the greatest philosophers of earlier generations failed to understand. For instance, philosophers clarify language by distinguishing between different senses of words; and, once a distinction has been made, future philosophers have to take account of it in their deliberations.

Take, as an example, the issue of free will. At a certain point in the history of philosophy a distinction was made between two kinds of human freedom: liberty of indifference (ability to do otherwise) and liberty of spontaneity (ability to do what you want). Once this distinction has been made the question 'Do human beings enjoy freedom of the will?' has to be answered in a way that takes account of the distinction. Even someone who believes that the two kinds of liberty in fact coincide has to provide arguments to show this; he cannot simply ignore the distinction and hope to be taken seriously on the topic.

It is unsurprising, given the relationship of philosophy to a canon, that one notable feature of philosophical progress consists in coming to terms with, and interpreting, the thoughts of the great philosophers of the past. The great works of the past do not lose their importance in philosophy—but their intellectual contributions are not static. Each age interprets and applies philosophical classics to its own problems and aspirations. This is, in recent years, most visible in the field of ethics. The ethical works of Plato and Aristotle are as influential in moral thinking today as the works of any twentieth-century moralists—this is easily verified by taking any citation index—but they are being interpreted and applied in ways quite different from the ways in which they were used in the past. These new interpretations and applications do effect a genuine advance in our under-standing of Plato and Aristotle, but of course it is understanding of quite a different kind from that which is given by a new study of the chronology of Plato's early dialogues, or a stylometric comparison between Aristotle's various ethical works. The new light we receive resembles rather the enhanced appreciation of Shake-speare we may get by seeing a new and intelligent production of *King Lear*.

The historian of philosophy, whether primarily interested in philosophy or primarily interested in history, cannot help being both a philosopher and a historian. A historian of painting does not have to be a painter, a historian of medicine does not, qua historian, practise medicine. But a historian of philosophy cannot help doing philosophy in the very writing of history. It is not just that someone who knows no philosophy will be a bad historian of philosophy; it is equally true that someone who has no idea how to cook will be a bad historian of cookery. The link between philosophy and its history is a far closer one. The historical task itself forces historians of philosophy to paraphrase their subjects' opinions, to offer reasons why past thinkers held the opinions they did, to speculate on the premises left tacit in their arguments, and to evaluate the coherence and cogency of the inferences they drew. But the supplying of reasons for philosophical conclusions, the detection of hidden premises in philosophical arguments, and the logical evaluation of philosophical inferences are themselves

CONTENTS OF PART ONE

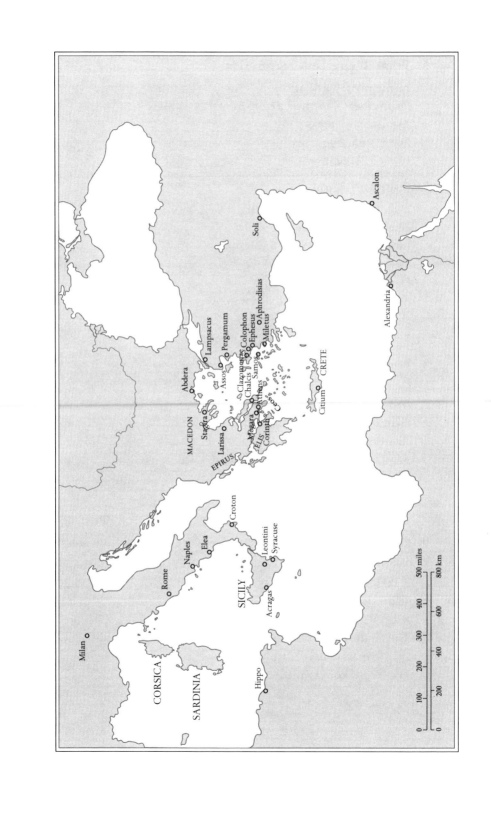

Milan

CORSICA

SARDINIA

Rome

Naples

Elea

Hippo

Acragas

SICILY

Leontini

Syracuse

Croton

EPIRUS

MACEDON

Larissa

Stagira

Abdera

Assos

Lampsacus

Pergamum

Clazomenae Colophon

Chalcis Ephesus

Samos Aphrodisias

Megara Miletus

Athens

Elis

Corinth

Citium

CRETE

Soli

Ascalon

Alexandria

0   100   200   300   400   500 miles

0   200   400   600   800 km

INTRODUCTION TO PART ONE

Not only ancient philosophy, but philosophy's whole history, is dominated by Plato and Aristotle. No later philosopher, ancient, medieval or modern, has surpassed the genius of these two colossi.

It is not too much to say that Plato invented the subject of philosophy. To be sure, he was preceded by hardy speculators such as Pythagoras, impressive gurus like Heraclitus, and eccentric geniuses like Parmenides. But what these men presented were philosophical problems rather than philosophical insights. It was Plato who formulated the methods for their solution. He had to invent, from whole cloth, the basic technical concepts that have been the tools of philosophy ever since. Of course, he acknowledged an enormous debt to his teacher Socrates, in whose mouth he places many of his own original ideas. But, as Socrates himself left no writings, the man who has ever since been revered as the patron saint of philosophy is the Socrates of Plato.

If Plato can be said to have invented philosophy, Aristotle can claim to be the founder of science. Like Plato, he had predecessors of great distinction, such as the evolutionist Empedocles and the atomist Democritus. But Aristotle, besides being himself a distinguished logician and biologist, was the first to identify and classify different scientific disciplines, and the first to create a research institute for empirical inquiry.

But if Plato and Aristotle deserve a central place in the history of ancient philosophy, scholars in recent decades have shown that there is much to be learnt from their successors in late antiquity, such as the Stoics and Epicureans during the Hellenistic period, and the Neoplatonists in the latter days of imperial Rome. The writings of the first great Christian philosopher, St Augustine of Hippo, was the channel through which Platonic ideas travelled to the Middle Ages, and the date of his conversion, which terminates the present part, provides a hinge between the ancient and the medieval world.

In accordance with the strategy outlined in the general introduction I offer in the first section of this part a conventional chronological tour from Pythagoras to Augustine, and in the second section a more detailed treatment of topics where I believe we have still much to learn from our predecessors in classical Greece and imperial Rome. The topics of these thematic sections have been chosen partly with an eye to the development of the same themes in the parts that are yet to come.

1

Beginnings:
From Pythagoras to Plato

T he history of philosophy does not begin with Aristotle, but the historiography
of philosophy does. Aristotle was the first philosopher who systematically
studied, recorded, and criticized the work of previous philosophers. In the first
book of the *Metaphysics* he summarizes the teachings of his predecessors, from his
distant intellectual ancestors Pythagoras and Thales up to Plato, his teacher for
twenty years. To this day he is one of the most copious, and most reliable, sources of
our information about philosophy in its infancy.

The Four Causes

Aristotle offers a classification of the earliest Greek philosophers in accordance
with the structure of his system of the four causes. Scientific inquiry, he believed,
was above all inquiry into the causes of things; and there were four different kinds
of cause: the material cause, the efficient cause, the formal cause, and the final
cause. To give a crude illustration of what he had in mind: when Alfredo cooks a
risotto, the material causes of the risotto are the ingredients that go into it, the
efficient cause is the chef himself, the recipe is the formal cause, and the satisfaction of the clients of his restaurant is the final cause. Aristotle believed that a
scientific understanding of the universe demanded an inquiry into the operation
in the world of causes of each of these kinds (*Metaph. A* 3. 983^{a}24–^{b}17).

Early philosophers on the Greek coast of Asia Minor concentrated on the
material cause: they sought the basic ingredients of the world we live in. Thales
and his successors posed the following question: At a fundamental level is the
world made out of water, or air, or fire, or earth, or a combination of some or all of
these? (*Metaph. A* 3. 983^{b}20–84^{a}16). Even if we have an answer to this question,
Aristotle thought, that is clearly not enough to satisfy our scientific curiosity. The

ingredients of a dish do not put themselves together: there needs to be an agent operating upon them, by cutting, mixing, stirring, heating, or the like. Some of these early philosophers, Aristotle tells us, were aware of this and offered conjectures about the agents of change and development in the world. Sometimes it would be one of the ingredients themselves—fire was perhaps the most promising suggestion, as being the least torpid of the elements. More often it would be some agent, or pair of agents, both more abstract and more picturesque, such as Love or Desire or Strife, or the Good and the Bad (*Metaph. A* 3–4. 984^{b}8–31).

Meanwhile in Italy—again according to Aristotle—there were, around Pythagoras, mathematically inclined philosophers whose inquiries took quite a different course. A recipe, besides naming ingredients, will contain a lot of numbers: so many grams of this, so many litres of that. The Pythagoreans were more interested in the numbers in the world's recipe than in the ingredients themselves. They supposed, Aristotle says, that the elements of numbers were the elements of all things, and the whole of the heavens was a musical scale. They were inspired in their quest by their discovery that the relationship between the notes of the scale played on a lyre corresponded to different numerical ratios between the lengths of the strings. They then generalized this idea that qualitative differences might be the upshot of numerical differences. Their inquiry, in Aristotle's terms, was an inquiry into the formal causes of the universe (*Metaph. A* 5. 985^{b}23–986^{b}2).

Coming to his immediate predecessors, Aristotle says that Socrates preferred to concentrate on ethics rather than study the world of nature, while Plato in his philosophical theory combined the approaches of the schools of both Thales and Pythagoras. But Plato's Theory of Ideas, while being the most comprehensive scientific system yet devised, seemed to Aristotle—for reasons that he summarizes here and develops in a number of his treatises—to be unsatisfactory on several grounds. There were so many things to explain, and the Ideas just added new items calling for explanation: they did not provide a solution, they added to the problem (*Metaph. A* 5. 990^{b}1 ff.).

Most dissertations that begin with literature searches seek to show that all work hitherto has left a gap that will now be filled by the author's original research. Aristotle's *Metaphysics* is no exception. His not too hidden agenda is to show how previous philosophers neglected the remaining member of the quartet of causes: the final cause, which was to play a most significant role in his own philosophy of nature (*Metaph. A* 5. 988^{b}6–15). The earliest philosophy, he concluded, is, on all subjects, full of babble, since in its beginnings it is but an infant (*Metaph. A* 5. 993^{a}15–17).

A philosopher of the present day, reading the surviving fragments of the earliest Greek thinkers, is impressed not so much by the questions they were asking, as by the methods they used to answer them. After all, the book of Genesis offers us answers to the four causal questions set by Aristotle. If we ask for the origin of the first human being, for instance, we are told that the efficient cause was God, that the material cause was the dust of the earth, that the formal cause was the image and likeness of God, and that the final cause was for man to have dominion over the fish of the sea, the fowl of the air, and every living thing on earth. Yet Genesis is not a work of philosophy.

On the other hand, Pythagoras is best known not for answering any of the Aristotelian questions, but for proving the theorem that the square on the hypotenuse of a right-angled triangle is equal in area to the sum of the squares on the other two sides. Thales, again, was believed by later Greeks to have been the first person to make an accurate prediction of an eclipse, in the year 585 BC. These are surely achievements in geometry and astronomy, not philosophy.

The fact is that the distinction between religion, science, and philosophy was not as clear as it became in later centuries. The works of Aristotle and his master Plato provide a paradigm of philosophy for every age, and to this day anyone using the title 'philosopher' is claiming to be one of their heirs. Writers in twenty-first-century philosophy journals can be seen to be using the same techniques of conceptual analysis, and often to be repeating or refuting the same theoretical arguments, as are to be found in the writings of Plato and Aristotle. But in those writings there is much else that would not nowadays be thought of as philosophical discussion. From the sixth century BC onwards elements of religion, science, and philosophy ferment together in a single cultural cauldron. From our distance in time philosophers, scientists, and theologians can all look back to these early thinkers as their intellectual forefathers.

The Milesians

Only two sayings are recorded of Thales of Miletus (c.625–545 BC), traditionally the founding father of Greek philosophy. They illustrate the mélange of science and religion, for one of them was 'All things are full of gods', and the other was 'Water is the first principle of everything'. Thales was a geometer, the first to discover the method of inscribing a right-angled triangle in a circle; he celebrated this discovery by sacrificing an ox to the gods (D.L. 1. 24–5). He measured the height of the pyramids by measuring their shadows at the time of day when his own shadow was as long as he was tall. He put his geometry to practical use: having proved that triangles with one equal side and two equal angles are congruent, he used this result to determine the distance of ships at sea.

Thales also had a reputation as an astronomer and a meteorologist. In addition to predicting the eclipse, he is said to have been the first to show that the year contained 365 days, and to determine the dates of the summer and winter solstices. He studied the constellations and made estimates of the sizes of the sun and moon. He turned his skill as a weather forecaster to good account: foreseeing an unusually good olive crop, he took a lease on all the oil mills and made a fortune through his monopoly. Thus, Aristotle said, he showed that philosophers could easily be rich if they wished (*Pol.* 1. 11. 1259ᵃ6–18).

If half the stories current about Thales in antiquity are true, he was a man of many parts. But tradition's portrait of him is ambiguous. On the one hand, he figures as a philosophical entrepreneur, and a political and military pundit. On the other hand, he became a byword for unworldly absent-mindedness. Plato, among others, tells the following tale:

> Thales was studying the stars and gazing into the sky, when he fell into a well, and a jolly and witty Thracian servant girl made fun of him, saying that he was crazy to know about what was up in the heavens while he could not see what was in front of him beneath his feet. (*Theaetetus* 174a)

An unlikely story went around that he had met his death by just such a fall while stargazing.

Thales was reckoned as one of the Seven Sages, or wise men, of Greece, on a par with Solon, the great legislator of Athens. He is credited with a number of aphorisms. He said that before a certain age it was too soon for a man to marry; and after that age it was too late. When asked why he had no children, he said 'Because I am fond of children.'

Thales' remarks heralded many centuries of philosophical disdain for marriage. Anyone who makes a list of a dozen really great philosophers is likely to discover that the list consists almost entirely of bachelors. One plausible list, for instance, would include Plato, Augustine, Aquinas, Scotus, Descartes, Locke, Spinoza, Hume, Kant, Hegel, and Wittgenstein, none of whom were married. Aristotle is the grand exception that disproves the rule that marriage is incompatible with philosophy.

Even in antiquity people found it hard to understand Thales' adoption of water as the ultimate principle of explanation. The earth, he said, rested on water like a log floating in a stream—but then, asked Aristotle, what does the water rest on? (*Cael.* 2. 13. 294ᵃ28–34). He went further and said that everything came from and was in some sense made out of water. Again, his reasons were obscure, and Aristotle could only conjecture that it was because all animals and plants need water to live, or because semen is moist (*Metaph. A* 3. 983ᵇ17–27).

It is easier to come to grips with the cosmology of Thales' junior compatriot Anaximander of Miletus (d. *c.*547 BC). We know rather more about his views, because he left behind a book entitled *On Nature*, written in prose, a medium just beginning to come into fashion. Like Thales he was credited with a number of original scientific achievements: the first map of the world, the first star chart, the first Greek sundial, and an indoor clock as well. He taught that the earth was cylindrical in shape, like a stumpy column no higher than a third of its diameter. Around the world were gigantic tyres full of fire; each tyre was punctured with a hole through which the fire could be seen from outside, and the holes were the sun and moon and stars. Blockages in the holes accounted for eclipses of the sun and phases of the moon. The celestial fire which is nowadays largely hidden was once a great ball of flame around the infant earth; when this ball exploded, the fragments grew tyres like bark around themselves.

Anaximander was much impressed by the way trees grow and shed their bark. He used the same analogy to explain the origin of human beings. Other animals, he observed, can look after themselves soon after birth, but humans need a long nursing. If humans had always been as they are now, the race would not have survived. In an earlier age, he conjectured, humans had spent their childhood encased in a prickly bark, so that they looked like fish and lived in water. At puberty they shed their bark, and stepped out onto dry land, into an environment in which they could take care of themselves. Because of this, Anaximander, though not otherwise a vegetarian, recommended that we abstain from eating fish, as the ancestors of the human race (KRS 133–7).

Anaximander's cosmology is more sophisticated than Thales' in several ways. First of all, he does not look for something to support the earth: it stays where it is because it is equidistant from everything else and there is no reason why it should move in any direction rather than any other (DK 12 A11; Aristotle, *Cael.* 2. 13. $295^{b}10$).

Secondly, he thinks it is an error to identify the ultimate material of the universe with any of the elements we can see around us in the contemporary world, such as water or fire. The fundamental principle of things, he said, must be boundless or undefined (*apeiron*). Anaximander's Greek word is often rendered as 'the Infinite', but that makes it sound too grand. He may or may not have thought that his principle extended for ever in space; what we do know is that he thought it had no beginning and no end in time and that it did not belong to any particular kind or class of things. 'Everlasting stuff' is probably as close a paraphrase as we can get. Aristotle was later to refine the notion into his concept of prime matter.[1]

Thirdly, Anaximander offered an account of the origin of the present world, and explained what forces had acted to bring it into existence, inquiring, as Aristotle would say, into the efficient as well as the material cause. He saw the universe as a field of competing opposites: hot and cold, wet and dry. Sometimes one of a pair of opposites is dominant, sometimes the other: they encroach upon each other and then withdraw, and their interchange is governed by a principle of reciprocity. As Anaximander put it poetically in his one surviving fragment, 'they pay penalty and render reparation to each other for their injustice under the arbitration of time' (DK 12 B1). Thus, one surmises, in winter the hot and the dry make reparation to the cold and the wet for the aggression they committed in

---

[1] See Ch. 5 below.

summer. Heat and cold were the first of the opposites to make their appearance, separating off from an original cosmic egg of the everlasting indeterminate stuff. From them developed the fire and earth which, we have seen, lay at the origin of our present cosmos.

Anaximenes (fl. 546–525 BC), a generation younger than Anaximander, was the last of the trio of Milesian cosmologists. In several ways he is closer to Thales than to Anaximander, but it would be wrong to think that with him science is going backwards rather than forwards. Like Thales, he thought that the earth must rest on something, but he proposed air, rather than water, for its cushion. The earth itself is flat, and so are the heavenly bodies. These, instead of rotating above and below us in the course of a day, circle horizontally around us like a bonnet rotating around a head (KRS 151–6). The rising and setting of the heavenly bodies is explained, apparently, by the tilting of the flat earth. As for the ultimate principle, Anaximenes found Anaximander's bound-less matter too rarefied a concept, and opted, like Thales, for a single one of the existing elements as fundamental, though again he opted for air rather than water.

In its stable state air is invisible, but when it is moved and condensed it becomes first wind and then cloud and then water, and finally water condensed becomes mud and stone. Rarefied air became fire, thus completing the gamut of the elements. In this way rarefaction and condensation can conjure everything out of the underlying air (KRS 140–1). In support of this claim Anaximenes appealed to experience, and indeed to experiment—an experiment that the reader can easily carry out for herself. Blow on your hand, first with the lips pursed, and then from an open mouth: the first time the air will feel cold, and the second time hot. This, argued Anaximenes, shows the connection between density and temperature (KRS 143).

The use of experiment, and the insight that changes of quality are linked to changes of quantity, mark Anaximenes as a scientist in embryo. Only in embryo, however: he has no means of measuring the quantities he invokes, he devises no equations to link them, and his fundamental principle retains mythical and religious properties.[2] Air is divine, and generates deities out of itself (KRS 144–6); air is our soul, and holds our bodies together (KRS 160).

The Milesians, then, are not yet real physicists, but neither are they myth-makers. They have not yet left myth behind, but they are moving away from it. They are not true philosophers either, unless by 'philosophy' one simply means infant science. They make little use of conceptual analysis and the a priori argument that has been the stock-in-trade of philosophers from Plato to the present day. They are speculators, in whose speculations elements of philosophy, science, and religion mingle in a rich and heady brew.

---

[2] See J. Barnes, *The Presocratic Philosophers*, rev. edn. (London: Routledge, 1982), 46–8.

The Pythagoreans

In antiquity Pythagoras shared with Thales the credit for introducing philosophy into the Greek world. He was born in Samos, an island off the coast of Asia Minor, about 570 BC. At the age of 40 he emigrated to Croton on the toe of Italy. There he took a leading part in the political affairs of the city, until he was banished in a violent revolution about 510 BC. He moved to nearby Metapontum, where he died at the turn of the century. During his time at Croton he founded a semi-religious community, which outlived him until it was scattered about 450 BC. He is credited with inventing the word 'philosopher': instead of claiming to be a sage or wise man (*sophos*) he modestly said that he was only a lover of wisdom (*philosophos*) (D.L. 8. 8). The details of his life are swamped in legend, but it is clear that he practised both mathematics and mysticism. In both fields his intellectual influence, acknowledged or implicit, was strong throughout antiquity, from Plato to Porphyry.

The Pythagoreans' discovery that there was a relationship between musical intervals and numerical ratios led to the belief that the study of mathematics was the key to the understanding of the structure and order of the universe. Astronomy and harmony, they said, were sister sciences, one for the eyes and one for the ears (Plato, *Rep.* 530d). However, it was not until two millennia later that Galileo and his successors showed the sense in which it is true that the book of the universe is written in numbers. In the ancient world arithmetic was too entwined with number mysticism to promote scientific progress, and the genuine scientific advances of the period (such as Aristotle's zoology or Galen's medicine) were achieved without benefit of mathematics.

Pythagoras' philosophical community at Croton was the prototype of many such institutions: it was followed by Plato's Academy, Aristotle's Lyceum, Epicurus' Garden, and many others. Some such communities were legal entities, and others less formal; some resembled a modern research institute, others were more like monasteries. Pythagoras' associates held their property in common and lived under a set of ascetic and ceremonial rules: observe silence, do not break bread, do not pick up crumbs, do not poke the fire with a sword, always put on the right shoe before the left, and so on. The Pythagoreans were not, to begin with, complete vegetarians, but they avoided certain kinds of meat, fish, and poultry. Most famously, they were forbidden to eat beans (KRS 271–2, 275–6).

The dietary rules were connected with Pythagoras' beliefs about the soul. It did not die with the body, he believed, but migrated elsewhere, perhaps into an animal body of a different kind.[3] Some Pythagoreans extended this into belief in a three-thousand-year cosmic cycle: a human soul after death would enter, one after the other, every kind of land, sea, or air creature, and finally return into a human

---

[3] See Ch. 7 below.

body for history to repeat itself (Herodotus 2. 123; KRS 285). Pythagoras himself, however, after his death was believed by his followers to have become a god. They wrote biographies of him full of wonders, crediting him with second sight and the gift of bilocation; he had a golden thigh, they said, and was the son of Apollo. More prosaically, the expression 'Ipse dixit' was coined in his honour.

Xenophanes

The death of Pythagoras, and the destruction of Miletus in 494, brought to an end the first era of Presocratic thought. In the next generation we encounter thinkers who are not only would-be scientists, but also philosophers in the modern sense of the word. Xenophanes of Colophon (a town near present-day Izmir, some hundred miles north of Miletus) straddles the two eras in his long life (c.570–c.470 BC). He is also, like Pythagoras, a link between the eastern and the western centres of Greek cultures. Expelled from Colophon in his twenties, he became a wandering minstrel, and by his own account travelled around Greece for sixty-seven years, giving recitals of his own and others' poems (D.L. 9. 18). He sang of wine and games and parties, but it is his philosophical verses that are most read today.

Like the Milesians, Xenophanes propounded a cosmology. The basic element, he maintained, was not water nor air, but earth, and the earth reaches down below us to infinity. 'All things are from earth and in earth all things end' (D.K. 21 B27) calls to mind Christian burial services and the Ash Wednesday exhortation 'remember, man, thou art but dust and unto dust thou shalt return'. But Xenophanes elsewhere links water with earth as the original source of things, and indeed he believed that our earth must at one time have been covered by the sea. This is connected with the most interesting of his contributions to science: the observation of the fossil record.

Seashells are found well inland, and on mountains too, and in the quarries in Syracuse impressions of fish and seaweed have been found. An impression of a bay leaf was found in Paros deep in a rock, and in Malta there are flat shapes of all kinds of sea creatures. These were produced when everything was covered with mud long ago, and the impressions dried in the mud. (KRS 184)

Xenophanes' speculations about the heavenly bodies are less impressive. Since he believed that the earth stretched beneath us to infinity, he could not accept that the sun went below the earth when it set. On the other hand, he found implausible Anaximenes' idea of a horizontal rotation around a tilting earth. He put forward a new and ingenious explanation: the sun, he maintained, was new every day. It came into existence each morning from a congregation of tiny sparks, and later vanished off into infinity. The appearance of circular movement is due simply to the great distance between the sun and ourselves. It follows from this theory that there are innumerable suns, just as there are innumerable days, because the world lasts for ever even though it passes through aqueous and terrestrial phases (KRS 175, 179).

Though Xenophanes' cosmology is ill-founded, it is notable for its naturalism: it is free from the animist and semi-religious elements to be found in other Presocratic philosophers. The rainbow, for instance, is not a divinity (like Iris in the Greek pantheon) nor a divine sign (like the one seen by Noah). It is simply a multicoloured cloud (KRS 178). This naturalism did not mean that Xenophanes was uninterested in religion: on the contrary, he was the most theological of all the Presocratics. But he despised popular superstition, and defended an austere and sophisticated monotheism.[4] He was not dogmatic, however, either in theology or in physics.

> God did not tell us mortals all when time began
> Only through long-time search does knowledge come to man.
>
> (KRS 188)

Heraclitus

Heraclitus was the last, and the most famous, of the early Ionian philosophers. He was perhaps thirty years younger than Xenophanes, since he is reported to have been middle-aged when the sixth century ended (D.L. 9. 1). He lived in the great metropolis of Ephesus, midway between Miletus and Colophon. We possess more substantial portions of his work than of any previous philosopher, but that does not mean we find him easier to understand. His fragments take the form of pithy, crafted prose aphorisms, which are often obscure and sometimes deliberately ambiguous. Heraclitus did not argue, he pronounced. His delphic style may have been an imitation of the oracle of Apollo which, in his own words, 'neither speaks, nor conceals, but gestures' (KRS 244). The many philosophers in later centuries who have admired Heraclitus have been able to give their own colouring to his paradoxical, chameleon-like dicta.

Even in antiquity Heraclitus was found difficult. He was nicknamed 'the Enigmatic One' and 'Heraclitus the Obscure' (D.L. 9. 6). He wrote a three-book treatise on philosophy—now lost—and deposited it in the great temple of Artemis (St Paul's 'Diana of the Ephesians'). People could not make up their minds whether it was a text of physics or a political tract. 'What I understand of it is excellent,' Socrates is reported as saying. 'What I don't understand may well be excellent also; but only a deep sea diver could get to the bottom of it' (D.L. 2. 22). The nineteenth-century German idealist Hegel, who was a great admirer of Heraclitus, used the same marine metaphor to express an opposite judgement.

---

[4] See Ch. 9 below.

When we reach Heraclitus after the fluctuating speculations of the earlier Presocratics, Hegel wrote, we come at last in sight of land. He went on to add, proudly, 'There is no proposition of Heraclitus which I have not adopted in my own Logic.'[5]

Heraclitus, like Descartes and Kant in later ages, saw himself as making a completely new start in philosophy. He thought the work of previous thinkers was worthless: Homer should have been eliminated at an early stage of any poetry competition, and Hesiod, Pythagoras, and Xenophanes were merely polymaths with no real sense (D.L. 9. 1). But, again like Descartes and Kant, Heraclitus was more influenced by his predecessors than he realized. Like Xenophanes, he was highly critical of popular religion: offering blood sacrifice to purge oneself of blood guilt was like trying to wash off mud with mud. Praying to statues was like whispering in an empty house, and phallic processions and Dionysiac rites were simply disgusting (KRS 241, 243).

Again like Xenophanes, Heraclitus believed that the sun was new every day (Aristotle, *Mete.* 2. 2355^{b}13–14), and, like Anaximander, he thought the sun was constrained by a cosmic principle of reparation (KRS 226). The ephemeral theory of the sun is indeed in Heraclitus expanded into a doctrine of universal flux. Everything, he said, is in motion, and nothing stays still; the world is like a flowing stream. If we step into the same river twice, we cannot put our feet twice into the same water, since the water is not the same two moments together (KRS 214). That seems true enough, but on the face of it Heraclitus went too far when he said that we cannot even step twice into the same river (Plato, *Cra.* 402a). Taken literally, this seems false, unless we take the criterion of identity for a river to be the body of water it contains rather than the course it flows. Taken allegorically, it is presumably a claim that everything in the world is composed of constantly changing constituents: if this is what is meant, Aristotle said, the changes must be imperceptible ones (*Ph.* 8. 3. 253^{b}9 ff.). Perhaps this is what is hinted at in Heraclitus' aphorism that hidden harmony is better than manifest harmony—the harmony being the underlying rhythm of the universe in flux (KRS 207). Whatever Heraclitus meant by his dictum, it had a long history ahead of it in later Greek philosophy.

A raging fire, even more than a flowing stream, is a paradigm of constant change, ever consuming, ever refuelled. Heraclitus once said that the world was an ever-living fire: sea and earth are the ashes of this perpetual bonfire. Fire is like gold: you can exchange gold for all kinds of goods, and fire can turn into any of the elements (KRS 217–19). This fiery world is the only world there is, not made by gods or men, but governed throughout by Logos. It would be absurd, he argued, to think that this glorious cosmos is just a piled-up heap of rubbish (DK 22 B124).

---

[5] *Lectures on the History of Philosophy*, ed. and trans. E. S. Haldane and F. H. Simpson (London: Routledge, 1968), 279.

'Logos' is the everyday Greek term for a written or spoken word, but from Heraclitus onwards almost every Greek philosopher gave it one or more of several grander meanings. It is often rendered by translators as 'Reason'—whether to refer to the reasoning powers of human individuals, or to some more exalted cosmic principle of order and beauty. The term found its way into Christian theology when the author of the fourth gospel proclaimed, 'In the beginning was the Logos, and the Logos was with God, and the Logos was God' (John 1: 1).

This universal Logos, Heraclitus says, is hard to grasp and most men never succeed in doing so. By comparison with someone who has woken up to the Logos, they are like sleepers curled up in their own dream-world instead of facing up to the single, universal truth (S.E., M. 7. 132). Humans fall into three classes, at various removes from the rational fire that governs the universe. A philosopher like Heraclitus is closest to the fiery Logos and receives most warmth from it; next, ordinary people when awake draw light from it when they use their own reasoning powers; finally, those who are asleep have the windows of their soul blocked up and keep contact with nature only through their breathing (S.E., M. 7. 129–30).[6] Is the Logos God? Heraclitus gave a typically quibbling answer. 'The one thing that alone is truly wise is both unwilling and willing to be called by the name of Zeus.' Presumably, he meant that the Logos was divine, but was not to be identified with any of the gods of Olympus.

The human soul is itself fire: Heraclitus sometimes lists soul, along with earth and water, as three elements. Since water quenches fire, the best soul is a dry soul, and must be kept from moisture. It is hard to know exactly what counts as moisture in this context, but alcohol certainly does: a drunk, Heraclitus says, is a man led by a boy (KRS 229–31). But Heraclitus' use of 'wet' also seems close to the modern slang sense: brave and tough men who die in battle, for instance, have dry souls that do not suffer the death of water but go to join the cosmic fire (KRS 237).[7]

What Hegel most admired in Heraclitus was his insistence on the coincidence of opposites, such as that the universe is both divisible and indivisible, generated and ungenerated, mortal and immortal. Sometimes these identifications of opposites are straightforward statements of the relativity of certain predicates. The most famous, 'The way up and the way down are one and the same', sounds very deep. However, it need mean no more than that when, skipping down a mountain, I meet you toiling upward, we are both on the same path. Different things are attractive at different times: food when you are hungry, bed when you are sleepy (KRS 201). Different things attract different species: sea-water is wholesome for fish, but poisonous for humans; donkeys prefer rubbish to gold (KRS 199).

---

[6] Readers of Plato are bound to be struck by the anticipation of the allegory of the Cave in the *Republic*.

[7] See the discussion in KRS 208.

Not all Heraclitus' pairs of coinciding opposites admit of easy resolution by relativity, and even the most harmless-looking ones may have a more profound significance. Thus Diogenes Laertius tells us that the sequence fire–air–water–earth is the road downward, and the sequence earth–water–air–fire is the road upward (D.L. 9. 9–11). These two roads can only be regarded as the same if they are seen as two stages on a continuous, everlasting, cosmic progress. Heraclitus did indeed believe that the cosmic fire went through stages of kindling and quenching (KRS 217). It is presumably also in this sense that we are to understand that the universe is both generated and ungenerated, mortal and immortal (DK 22 B50). The underlying process has no beginning and no end, but each cycle of kindling and quenching is an individual world that comes into and goes out of existence.

Though several of the Presocratics are reported to have been politically active, Heraclitus has some claim, on the basis of the fragments, to be the first to produce a political philosophy. He was not indeed interested in practical politics: an aristocrat with a claim to be a ruler, he waived his claim and passed on his wealth to his brother. He is reported to have said that he preferred playing with children to conferring with politicians. But he was perhaps the first philosopher to speak of a divine law—not a physical law, but a prescriptive law, that trumped all human laws.

There is a famous passage in Robert Bolt's play about Thomas More, *A Man for All Seasons*. More is urged by his son-in-law Roper to arrest a spy, in contravention of the law. More refuses to do so: 'I know what's legal, not what's right; and I'll stick to what's legal.' More denies, in answer to Roper, that he is setting man's law above God's. 'I'm not God,' he says, 'but in the thickets of the law, there I am a forester.' Roper says that he would cut down every law in England to get at the Devil. More replies, 'And when the last law was down, and the Devil turned round on you—where would you hide, Roper, the laws all being flat?'[8]

It is difficult to find chapter and verse in More's own writings or recorded sayings for this exchange. But two fragments of Heraclitus express the sentiments of the participants. 'The people must fight on behalf of the law as they would for the city wall' (KRS 249). But though a city must rely on its law, it must place a much greater reliance on the universal law that is common to all. 'All the laws of humans are nourished by a single law, the divine law' (KRS 250).

What survives of Heraclitus amounts to no more than 15,000 words. The enormous influence he has exercised on philosophers ancient and modern is a matter for astonishment. There is something fitting about his position in Raphael's fresco in the Vatican stanze, *The School of Athens*. In this monumental scenario, which contains imaginary portraits of many Greek philosophers, Plato and Aristotle, as is right and just, occupy the centre stage. But the figure to which one's eye

---

[8] Robert Bolt, *A Man for All Seasons* (London: Heinemann, 1960), 39.

is immediately drawn on entering the room is a late addition to the fresco: the booted, brooding figure of Heraclitus, deep in meditation on the lowest step.[9]

Parmenides and the Eleatics

In Roman times Heraclitus was known as 'the weeping philosopher'. He was contrasted with the laughing philosopher, the atomist Democritus. A more appropriate contrast would be with Parmenides, the head of the Italian school of philosophy in the early fifth century. For classical Athens, Heraclitus was the proponent of the theory that everything was in motion, and Parmenides the proponent of the theory that nothing was in motion. Plato and Aristotle struggled, in different ways, to defend the audacious thesis that some things were in motion and some things were at rest.

Parmenides, according to Aristotle (*Metaph.* A 5. 986^{b}21–5), was a pupil of Xenophanes, but he was too young to have studied under him in Colophon. He spent most of his life in Elea, seventy miles or so south of Naples. There he may have encountered Xenophanes on his wanderings. Like Xenophanes, he was a poet: he wrote a philosophical poem in clumsy verse, of which we possess about 120 lines. He is the first philosopher whose writing has come down to us in continuous fragments that are at all substantial.

The poem consists of a prologue and two parts, one called the path of truth, the other the path of mortal opinion. The prologue shows us the poet riding in a chariot with the daughters of the Sun, leaving behind the halls of night and travelling towards the light. They reach the gates which lead to the paths of night and day; it is not clear whether these are the same as the paths of truth and opinion. At all events, the goddess who welcomes him on his quest tells him that he must learn both:

> Besides trustworthy truth's unquaking heart
> Learn the false fictions of poor mortals' art.

(KRS 288. 29–30)

There are only two possible routes of inquiry:

> Two ways there are of seeking how to see
> One that it is, and is not not to be—
> That is the path of Truth's companion Trust—
> The other it is not, and not to be it must. (KRS 291. 2–5)

---

[9] The figure traditionally regarded as Heraclitus does not figure on cartoons for the fresco. Michelangelo is said to have been Raphael's model, though R. Jones and N. Penny, *Raphael* (London: Yale University Press, 1983) 77, doubt both traditions.

(I must ask the reader to believe that Parmenides' Greek is as clumsy and as baffling as this English text.) Parmenides' Way of Truth, thus riddlingly introduced, marks an epoch in philosophy. It is the founding charter of a new discipline: ontology or metaphysics, the science of Being.

Whatever there is, whatever can be thought of, is for Parmenides nothing other than Being. Being is one and indivisible: it has no beginning and no end, and it is not subject to temporal change. When a kettle of water boils away, this may be, in Heraclitus' words, the death of water and the birth of air; but for Parmenides it is not the death or birth of Being. Whatever changes may take place, they are not changes from being to non-being; they are all changes within Being. But for Parmenides there are not, in fact, any real changes at all. Being is everlastingly the same, and time is unreal because past, present, and future are all one.[10]

The everyday world of apparent change is described in the second part of Parmenides' poem, the Way of Seeming, which his goddess introduces thus:

> I bring to an end my trusty word and thought,
> The tale of Truth. The rest's another sort—
> A pack of lies expounding men's beliefs.   (KRS 300)

It is not clear why Parmenides feels obliged to reproduce the false notions that are entertained by deluded mortals. If we took the second part of his poem out of its context, we would see in it a cosmology very much in the tradition of the Ionian thinkers. To the normal pairs of opposites Parmenides adds light and darkness, and he is given credit by Aristotle for introducing Love as the efficient cause of everything (*Metaph.* A 3. 984^{b}27). The Way of Seeming in fact includes two truths not hitherto generally known: first, that the earth is a sphere (D.L. 9. 21), and secondly, that the Morning Star is the same as the Evening Star. Parmenides' disowned discovery was to provide philosophers of a later generation with a paradigm for identity statements.[11]

Parmenides had a pupil, Melissus, who came from Pythagoras' island of Samos and who was said to have studied also with Heraclitus. He was active in politics, and rose to the rank of admiral of the Samos fleet. In 441 BC Samos was attacked by Athens, and though Athens was finally victorious in the war Melissus is recorded as having twice inflicted defeat on the fleet of Pericles (Plutarch, *Pericles* 166c–d; D.L. 9. 4).

Melissus expounded the philosophy of Parmenides' poem in plain prose, arguing that the universe was unlimited, unchangeable, immovable, indivisible, and homogeneous. He was remembered for drawing two consequences from this monistic view: (1) pain was unreal, because it implied (impossibly) a deficiency of being;

---

[10] A detailed examination of Parmenides' ontology will be found in Ch. 6 below.

[11] The 19th-century philosopher Gottlob Frege used the example to introduce his celebrated distinction between sense and reference.

(2) there was no such thing as a vacuum, since it would have to be a piece of Unbeing. Local motion was therefore impossible, for the bodies that occupy space have no room to move into (KRS 534).

Another pupil of Parmenides was Zeno of Elea. He produced a set of more famous arguments against the possibility of motion. The first went like this: 'There is no motion, for whatever moves must reach the middle of its course before it reaches the end.' To get to the far end of a stadium, you have to run to the half-way point, to get to the half-way point you must reach the point half-way to that, and so ad infinitum. Better known is the second argument, commonly known as Achilles and the tortoise. 'The slower', Zeno said, 'will never be overtaken by the swifter, for the pursuer must first reach the point from which the fugitive departed, so that the slower must necessarily remain ahead.' Let us suppose that Achilles runs four times as fast as the tortoise, and that the tortoise is given a forty-metre start when they run a hundred-metre race against each other. According to Zeno's argument, Achilles can never win. For by the time he reaches the forty-metre mark, the tortoise is ahead by ten metres. By the time Achilles has run those ten, the tortoise is still ahead by two and a half metres. Each time Achilles makes up a gap, the tortoise opens up a new, shorter, gap, so he can never overtake him (Aristotle, *Ph.* 5. 9. 239^{b}11–14).

These and other similar arguments of Zeno assume that distances and motions are infinitely divisible. His arguments have been dismissed by some philosophers as ingenious but sophistical paradoxes. Others have admired them greatly: Bertrand Russell, for instance, claimed that they provided the basis of the nineteenth-century mathematical renaissance of Weierstrass and Cantor.[12] Aristotle, who preserved Zeno's puzzles for us, claimed to disarm them, and to re-establish the possibility of motion, by distinguishing between two forms of infinity: actual infinity and potential infinity.[13] But it was not for many centuries that the issues raised by Zeno were given solutions that satisfied both philosophers and mathematicians.

Empedocles

The most flamboyant of the early philosophers of Greek Italy was Empedocles, who flourished in the middle of the fifth century. He was a native of Acragas, the town on the south coast of Sicily which is now Agrigento. The town's port today bears the name Porto Empedocle, but this testifies not to an enduring veneration of the philosopher, but to the Risorgimento's passion for renaming sites in honour of Italy's past glories.

---

[12] *The Principles of Mathematics* (London: Allen & Unwin, 1903), 347.   [13] See Ch. 5 below.

Empedocles came of an aristocratic family which owned a stud of prizewinning horses. In politics, however, he is reputed to have been a democrat; he is said to have foiled a plot to turn the city into a dictatorship. The grateful citizens, the story goes on, offered to make him king, but he refused the office, preferring his frugal life as a physician and counsellor (D.L. 8. 63). If free of ambition, however, he was not devoid of vanity, and in one of his poems he boasts that wherever he goes men and women throng to him for advice and healing. He claimed to possess drugs to ward off old age, and to know spells to control the weather. In the same poem he frankly professed himself to have achieved divine status (D.L. 8. 66).

Different biographical traditions, not all chronologically possible, make Empedocles a pupil of Pythagoras, of Xenophanes, and of Parmenides. Certainly he imitated Parmenides by writing a hexameter poem *On Nature*; this poem, dedicated to his friend Pausanias, contained about 2,000 lines, of which we possess about a fifth. He also wrote a religious poem, *Purifications*, of which less has been preserved. Scholars do not agree to which poem should be attached the many disjointed citations that survive; some, indeed, think that the two poems belonged to a single work. Further pieces of the textual jigsaw were recovered when forty papyrus fragments were identified in the archives of the University of Strasbourg in 1994. As a poet, Empedocles was more fluent than Parmenides, and also more versatile. According to Aristotle, he wrote an epic on Xerxes' invasion of Greece, and according to other traditions he was the author of several tragedies (D.L. 8. 57).

Empedocles' philosophy of nature can be regarded, from one point of view, as a synthesis of the thought of the Ionian philosophers. As we have seen, each of them had singled out some one substance as the basic or dominant stuff of the universe: Thales had privileged water, Anaximenes air, Xenophanes earth, and Heraclitus fire. For Empedocles all four of these substances stood on equal terms as the fundamental ingredients, or 'roots' as he put it, of the universe. These roots had always existed, he maintained, but they mingle with each other in various proportions in such a way as to produce the familiar furniture of the world and also the denizens of the heavens.

> From these four sprang what was and is and ever shall:
> Trees, beasts, and human beings, males and females all,
> Birds of the air, and fishes bred by water bright;
> The age-old gods as well, long worshipped in the height.
> These four are all there is, each other interweaving
> And, intermixed, the world's variety achieving.   (KRS 355)

What Empedocles called 'roots' were called by Plato and later Greek thinkers *stoicheia*, a word earlier used to indicate the syllables of a word. The Latin translation *elementum*, from which our 'element' is derived, compares the roots not to syllables, but to letters of the alphabet: an *elementum* is an LMNtum. Empedocles' quartet of elements was assigned a fundamental role in physics and chemistry by philosophers and scientists until the time of Boyle in the seventeenth century. Indeed, it can be claimed that it is still with us, in altered form. Empedocles thought of his elements as four different kinds of matter; we think of solid, liquid, and gas as three states of matter. Ice, water, and steam would be, for Empedocles, specific instances of earth, water, and air; for us they are three different states of the same substance, H_2O. It was not unreasonable to think of fire, and especially the fire of the sun, as a fourth element of equal importance. One might say that the twentieth-century emergence of the science of plasma physics, which studies the properties of matter at the sun's temperature, has restored Empedocles' fourth element to parity with the other three.

Aristotle praised Empedocles for having realized that a cosmological theory must not just identify the elements of the universe, but must assign causes for the development and intermingling of the elements to make the living and inanimate compounds of the actual world. Empedocles assigns this role to Love and Strife: Love combines the elements, and Strife forces them apart. At one time the roots grow to be one out of many, at another time they split to be many out of one. These things, he said, never cease their continual interchange, now through love coming together into one, now carried apart from each other by Strife's hatred (KRS 348).

Love and Strife are the picturesque ancestors of the forces of attraction and repulsion which have figured in physical theory throughout the ages. For Empedocles, history is a cycle in which sometimes Love is dominant, and sometimes Strife. Under the influence of Love the elements combine into a homogeneous, harmonious, and resplendent sphere, reminiscent of Parmenides' universe. Under the influence of Strife the elements separate out, but when Love begins to regain the ground it had lost, all the different species of living beings appear (KRS 360). All compound beings, such as animals and birds and fish, are temporary creatures that come and go; only the elements are everlasting, and only the cosmic cycle goes on for ever.

To explain the origin of living species, Empedocles put forward a remarkable theory of evolution by survival of the fittest. First flesh and bone emerged as chemical mixtures of the elements, flesh being constituted by fire, air, and water in equal parts, and bone being two parts water to two parts earth and four parts fire. From these constituents unattached limbs and organs were formed: unsocketed eyes, arms without shoulders, and faces without necks (KRS 375–6). These roamed around until they chanced to find partners; they formed unions, which were often, at this preliminary stage, quite unsuitable. Thus there arose various monstrosities: human-headed oxen, ox-headed humans, androgynous creatures with faces and breasts on front and back (KRS 379). Most of these fortuitous organisms were fragile or sterile; only the fittest structures survived to be the human and animal species we know. Their fitness to reproduce was a matter of chance, not design (Aristotle, *Ph.* 2. 8. 198^{b}29).

Aristotle paid tribute to Empedocles for being the first to grasp the important biological principle that different parts of dissimilar living organisms might have homologous functions: e.g. olives and eggs, leaves and feathers (Aristotle, *GA* 1. 23. 731^{a}4). But he was contemptuous of his attempt to reduce teleology to chance, and for many centuries biologists followed Aristotle rather than Empedocles. Empedocles had the last laugh when Darwin saluted him for 'shadowing forth the principle of natural selection'.[14]

Empedocles employed his quartet of elements in giving an account of sense-perception, based on the principle that like is known by like. In his poem *Purifications* he combined his physical theory with the Pythagorean doctrine of metempsychosis.[15] Sinners—divine or human—are punished when Strife casts their souls into different kinds of creatures on land and sea. A cycle of reincarnation held out a hope of eventual deification for privileged classes of men: seers, bards, doctors, and princes (KRS 409). Empedocles, of course, had a claim to identify himself with all these professions.

In his writing, Empedocles moves seamlessly between an austerely mechanistic mode and a mystically religious one. He sometimes uses divine names for his four elements (Zeus, Hera, Aidoneus, and Nestis) and identifies his Love with the goddess Aphrodite, whom he celebrates in terms anticipating Schiller's great 'Ode to Joy' (KRS 349). No doubt his own claim to divinity can be deflated in the same way as he demythologizes the Olympian gods. But it caught the attention of posterity, especially in the legend of his death.

A woman called Pantheia, the story goes, given up for dead by the physicians, was miraculously restored to life by Empedocles. To celebrate, he offered a sacrificial banquet to eighty guests in a rich man's house at the foot of Etna. When the other guests went to sleep, he heard his name called from heaven. He hastened to the summit of the volcano, and then, in Milton's words,

> to be deemed
> A god, leaped fondly into Aetna flames.
>
> (*Paradise Lost* III. 470)

Matthew Arnold dramatized this story in his *Empedocles on Etna*. He places these verses in the mouth of the philosopher at the crater's rim:

> This heart will glow no more; thou art
> A living man no more, Empedocles!
> Nothing but a devouring flame of thought—
> But a naked, eternally restless mind!

---

[14] Appendix to 6th edn. of *The Origin of Species*, quoted in A. Gottlieb, *The Dream of Reason: A History of Western Philosophy from the Greeks to the Renaissance* (London: Allen Lane, 2000), 80.

[15] See Ch. 7 below.

To the elements it came from
Everything will return
Our bodies to earth,
Our blood to water,
Heat to fire,
Breath to air.
They were well born, they will be well entomb'd—
But mind?

(lines 326–38)

Arnold gives the philosopher, before his final leap, the hope that in reward for his love of truth his intellect will never wholly perish.

Anaxagoras

If Empedocles achieved a kind of immortality as a precursor of Darwin, his contemporary Anaxagoras is sometimes regarded as an intellectual ancestor of the currently popular cosmology of the big bang. Anaxagoras was born around 500 BC in Clazomenae, near Izmir, and was possibly a pupil of Anaximenes. After the end of the wars between Persia and Greece, he came to Athens and was a client of the statesman Pericles. He thus stands at the head of the distinguished series of philosophers whom Athens either bred or welcomed. When Pericles fell from favour, Anaxagoras too became a target of popular attack. He was prosecuted for treason and impiety, and fled to Lampsacus on the Hellespont, where he lived in honourable exile until his death in 428.

Here is his account of the beginning of the universe: 'All things were together, infinite in number and infinite in smallness; for the small too was infinite. While all things were together, nothing was recognizable because of its smallness. Everything lay under air and ether, both infinite' (KRS 467). This primeval pebble began to rotate, throwing off the surrounding ether and air and forming out of them the stars and the sun and the moon. The rotation caused the separation of dense from rare, of hot from cold, of dry from wet, and bright from dark. But the separation was never complete, and to this day there remains in every single thing a portion of everything else. There is a little whiteness in what is black, a little cold in what is hot, and so on: things are named after the item that is dominant in it (Aristotle, *Ph.* 1. 4. 187^{a}23). This is most obvious in the case of semen, which must contain hair and flesh, and much, much more; but it must also be true of the food we eat (KRS 483–4, 496). In this sense, as things were in the beginning, so now they are all together.

The expansion of the universe, Anaxagoras maintained, has continued in the present and will continue in the future (KRS 476). Perhaps it has already generated worlds other than our own. As a result of the presence of everything in everything, he says,

men have been formed and the other ensouled animals. And the men possess farms and inhabit cities just as we do, and they have a sun and a moon and the rest just like us. The earth produces things of every sort for them to be harvested and stored, as it does for us. I have said all this about the process of separating off, because it would have happened not only here with us, but elsewhere too. (KRS 498)

Anaxagoras thus has a claim to be the originator of the idea, later proposed by Giordano Bruno and popular again today in some quarters, that our cosmos is just one of many which may, like ours, be inhabited by intelligent creatures.

The motion that sets in train the development of the universe is, according to Anaxagoras, the work of Mind. 'All things were together: then Mind came and gave them order' (D.L. 2. 6). Mind is infinite and separate, and has no part in the general commingling of elements; if it did, it would get drawn into the evolutionary process and could not control it. This teaching, placing mind firmly in control of matter, so struck his contemporaries that they nicknamed Anaxagoras himself the Mind. It is difficult, however, to assess exactly what his doctrine, though it greatly impressed both Plato and Aristotle, actually meant in practice.

In Plato's dialogue *Phaedo*, Socrates, in his last days in prison, is made to express his gradual disillusionment with the mechanistic explanations of natural science to be found in the early philosophers. He was pleased, he said, when he heard that Anaxagoras had explained everything by *nous*, or mind; but he was disappointed by the total absence of reference to value in his work. Anaxagoras was like someone who said that all Socrates' actions were performed with his intelligence, and then gave the reason why he was sitting here in prison by talking about the constitution of his body from bones and sinews, and the nature and properties of these parts, without mentioning that he judged it better to sit there in obedience to the Athenian court's sentence. Teleological explanation was more profound than mechanistic explanation. 'If anyone wants to find out the reason why each thing comes to be or perishes or exists, this is what he must find out about it: how is it best for that thing to exist, or to act or be acted upon in any way?' (*Phd.* 97d).

Anaxagoras speaks about his Mind in ways appropriate to divinity, and this could have made him vulnerable to a charge, in the Athenian courts, of introducing strange gods. But in fact the charge of impiety seems to have been based on his scientific conjectures. The sun, he said, was a fiery lump of metal, somewhat larger than the Peloponnesus. This was taken to be incompatible with the veneration appropriate to the sun as divine. In exile in Lampsacus, Anaxagoras made his final benefaction to humanity: the invention of the school holiday. Asked by the authorities of the city how they should honour him, he said that children should be let off school in the month of his death. He had already earned the gratitude of students of science by being the first writer to include diagrams in his text.

The Atomists

The final and most striking anticipation of modern science in the Presocratic era was made by Leucippus of Miletus and Democritus of Abdera. Though they are always named together, like Tweedledum and Tweedledee, and considered joint founders of atomism, nothing really is known about Leucippus except that he was the teacher of Democritus. It is on the surviving writings of the latter that we principally depend for our knowledge of the theory. Democritus was a polymath and a prolific writer, author of nearly eighty treatises on topics ranging from poetry and harmony to military tactics and Babylonian theology. All these treatises are lost, but we do possess a copious collection of fragments from Democritus, more than from any previous philosopher.

Democritus was born in Abdera, on the coast of Thrace, and was thus the first significant philosopher to be born on the Greek mainland. The date of his birth is uncertain, but it was probably between 470 and 460 BC. He is reported to have been forty years younger than Anaxagoras, from whom he took some of his ideas. He travelled widely and visited Egypt and Persia, but was not over-impressed by the countries he visited. He once said that he would prefer to discover a single scientific explanation than to become king of Persia (D.L. 9. 41; DK 68 B118).

Democritus' fundamental thesis is that matter is not infinitely divisible. We do not know his exact argument for this conclusion, but Aristotle conjectured that it ran as follows. If we take a chunk of any kind of stuff and divide it up as far as we can, we will have to come to a halt at tiny bodies which are indivisible. We cannot allow matter to be divisible to infinity: for let us suppose that the division has been carried out and then ask: what would ensue if the division was carried out? If each of the infinite number of parts has any magnitude, then it must be further divisible, which contradicts our hypothesis. If, on the other hand, the surviving parts have no magnitude, then they can never have amounted to any quantity: for zero multiplied by infinity is still zero. So we have to conclude that divisibility comes to an end, and the smallest possible fragments must be bodies with sizes and shapes. These tiny, indivisible bodies were called by Democritus 'atoms' (which is just the Greek word for 'indivisible') (Aristotle, *GC* 1. 2. 316^{a}13–^{b}16).[16]

Atoms, Democritus believed, are too small to be detected by the senses; they are infinite in number and come in infinitely many varieties, and they have existed for ever. Against the Eleatics, he maintained that there was no contradiction in admitting a vacuum: there was a void, and in this infinite empty space atoms were constantly in motion, just like motes in a sunbeam. They come in different forms: they may differ in shape (as the letter A differs from the letter N), in order (as AN differs from NA), and in posture (as N differs from Z). Some of them are concave and some convex, and some are like hooks and some are like eyes. In their

---

[16] For Aristotle's counter to this argument, see Ch. 5 below.

ceaseless motion they bang into each other and join up with each other (KRS 583). The middle-sized objects of everyday life are complexes of atoms thus united by random collisions, differing in kind on the basis of the differences between their constituent atoms (Aristotle, *Metaph. A* 4. 985^{b}4–20; KRS 556).

Like Anaxagoras, Democritus believed in plural worlds.

> There are innumerable worlds, differing in size. In some worlds there is no sun and moon; in others there is a larger sun and a larger moon; in others there is more than one of each. The distances between one world and the next are various. In some parts of space there are more worlds, in others fewer; some worlds are growing, others shrinking; some are rising and some falling. They get destroyed when they collide with one another. There are some worlds devoid of animals or plants or moisture. (KRS 565)

For Democritus, atoms and the void are the only two realities: what we see as water or fire or plants or humans are only conglomerations of atoms in the void. The sensory qualities we see are unreal: they are due to convention.

Democritus explained in detail how perceived qualities arose from different kinds and configurations of atoms. Sharp flavours, for instance, originated from atoms that were small, fine, angular, and jagged, while sweet tastes were produced by larger, rounder, smoother atoms. The knowledge given us by the senses is mere darkness compared with the illumination that is given by the atomic theory. To justify these claims, Democritus developed a systematic epistemology.[17]

Democritus wrote on ethics as well as physics. Many aphorisms have been preserved, a number of which are, or have become, commonplace. But it is a mistake to think of him as a sententious purveyor of conventional wisdom. On the contrary, as will be shown in Chapter 8, a careful study of his remarks shows him to have been one of the first thinkers to have developed a systematic morality.

The Sophists

In the lifetime of Democritus, a younger compatriot from Abdera, Protagoras, was the doyen of a new class of philosopher: the sophists. Sophists were itinerant teachers who went from city to city offering expert instruction in various subjects. Since they charged fees for imparting their skills, they might be called the first professional philosophers if it were not for the fact that they offered instruction and services over a much wider area than philosophy even in the broadest sense. The most versatile, Hippias of Elis, claimed expertise in mathematics, astronomy, music, history, literature, and mythology, as well as practical skills as a tailor and shoemaker. Some other sophists were prepared to teach mathematics, history, and geography; and all sophists were skilled rhetoricians. They did brisk business in mid-fifth-century Athens, where young men who had to plead in law courts, or

---

[17] See Ch. 4 below.

who wished to make their way in politics, were willing to pay substantial sums for their instruction and guidance.

The sophists made a systematic study of forensic debate and oratorical persuasion. In this pursuit they wrote on many topics. They started with basic grammar: Protagoras was the first to distinguish the genders of nouns and the tenses and moods of verbs (Aristotle, *Rh*. 3. 4. 1407^{b}6–8). They went on to list techniques of argument, and tricks of advocacy. As interpreters of ambiguous texts, and assessors of rival orations, they were among the earliest literary critics. They also gave public lectures and performances, and set up eristic moots, partly for instruction and partly for entertainment (D.L. 9. 53). Altogether, their roles encompassed those in modern society of tutors, consultants, barristers, public relations professionals, and media personalities.

Protagoras first visited Athens as an ambassador for Abdera. He was held in honour by the Athenians and invited back several times. He was asked by Pericles to draw up a constitution for the new pan-Hellenic colony at Thurii in southern Italy in 444 BC. He gave his first public performance in Athens in the house of the tragedian Euripides. He read aloud a tract entitled *On the Gods*, whose opening words were long remembered: 'About the gods, I cannot be sure whether they exist or not, or what they are like to see; for many things stand in the way of the knowledge of them, both the opacity of the subject and the shortness of human life' (D.L. 9. 51). His most famous saying, 'Man is the measure of all things', encapsulated a relativist epistemology which will be examined in detail later in this book.[18]

Protagoras seems to have been prepared to argue on either side of any question, and he boasted that he could always make the worse argument the better. This may simply have meant that he could coach a weak client into the best presentation of his case; but by critics as different as Aristophanes and Aristotle he was taken to mean that he could make wrong seem right (Aristophanes, *Clouds* 112 ff., 656–7; Aristotle, *Rh*. 2. 24. 1402^{a}25). Protagoras' enemies liked telling the story of the time when he sued his pupil Eualthus for non-payment of fees. Eualthus had refused to pay up, saying he had not yet won a single case. 'Well,' said Protagoras, 'if I win this case, you must pay up because the verdict was given for me; if you win it, you must still pay up, because then you will have won a case' (D.L. 9. 56).

Another sophist, Prodicus from the island of Ceos in the Aegean, came to Athens, like Protagoras, on official business of his home state. He was a linguist, but more interested in semantics than grammar: he can perhaps be regarded as the first lexicographer. Aristophanes and Plato teased him as a pedant, who made quibbling distinctions between words that were virtually synonymous. In fact, however, some of the distinctions credited to him (such as that between two

---

[18] See Ch. 4 below.

Greek equivalents of 'want', *boulesthai* and *epithumein*; Plato, *Protagoras* 340b2) were later of serious philosophical importance.

Prodicus is credited with a romantic moral fable about the young Heracles choosing between two female impersonations of Virtue and Vice. He also had a theory of the origin of religion. 'The men of old regarded the sun and the moon, rivers and springs, and whatever else is helpful for life, as gods, because we are helped by them, just as the Egyptians worship the Nile' (DK 84 B5). Thus, the worship of Hephaestus is really the worship of fire, and the worship of Demeter is really the worship of bread.

Gorgias, from Leontini in Sicily, once a pupil of Empedocles, was another sophist who came to Athens on an embassy, to seek help in a war against Syracuse. He was not only a persuasive orator, but a technician of rhetoric who categorized different figures of speech, such as antithesis and rhetorical questions. His style was much admired in his own day, but was later regarded as excessively florid. Of his writings there have survived two short works of philosophical interest.

The first is a rhetorical exercise defending Helen of Troy against those who slander her, arguing that she deserves no blame for running off with Paris and thus sparking off the Trojan war. 'She did what she did either because of the whims of fortune, the decisions of the gods and the decrees of necessity, or because she was abducted by force, or persuaded by speech, or overwhelmed by love' (DK 82 B11, 21–4). Gorgias goes through these alternatives in turn, arguing in each case that Helen should be held free from blame. No human can resist fate, and it is the abductor, not the abductee, who merits blame. Thus far, Gorgias has an easy task: but in order to show that Helen should not be blamed if she succumbed to persuasion, he has to engage in an unconvincing, though no doubt congenial, encomium on the powers of the spoken word: 'it is a mighty overlord, insubstantial and imperceptible, but it can achieve divine effects'. In this case, too, it is the persuader, not the persuadee, who should be blamed. Finally, if Helen fell in love, she is blameless: for love is either a god who cannot be resisted or a mental illness which should excite our pity. This brief and witty piece is the ancestor of many a philosophical discussion of freedom and determinism, *force majeure*, incitement, and irresistible impulse.

Gorgias' work entitled *On What is Not* contained arguments for three sceptical conclusions: first, that there is nothing; secondly, that if there is anything it cannot be known; thirdly, that if anything can be known it cannot be communicated by one person to another. This suite of arguments has been handed down in two forms, once in the pseudo-Aristotelian treatise *On Melissus*, and once by Sextus Empiricus.

The first argument trades on the polymorphous nature of the Greek verb 'to be'. I shall not spell out the argument here, but I shall endeavour in Chapter 6 to sort out the crucial ambiguities involved. The second argument goes like this. Things that have being can only be objects of thought if objects of thought are things that have being. But objects of thought are not things that have being; otherwise everything one thinks would be the case. But you can think of a man flying or of a chariot driven over the sea without there being any such things. Therefore, things that have being cannot be objects of thought. The third argument, the most plausible of the three, argues that each individual's sensations are private and that all we can pass on to our neighbours is words and not experiences.

The arguments of this famous sophist for these distressing conclusions are indeed sophisms, and were no doubt dismissed as such by those who first encountered them. But it is easier to dismiss a sophism than to diagnose its nature, and it is harder still to find its cure. The first sophism was disarmed essentially by Plato in his dialogue appropriately named *The Sophist*.[19] The second sophism involves a fallacious form of argument that sometimes occurs in Plato himself. Aristotle's logic, however, made clear to subsequent thinkers that 'Not all As are B' does not entail 'No B is an A'. The third argument, from the privacy of experience, was not given its definitive quietus until the work of Wittgenstein in the twentieth century.

Beside Protagoras, Hippias, Prodicus, and Gorgias there were other sophists whose names and reputations have come down to us. There was Callicles, for instance, the champion of the doctrine that might is right; and Thrasymachus, the debunker of justice as the self-interest of those in power. There were Euthydemus and Dionysidorus, a pair of logic choppers who would offer to prove to you that your father was a dog. These men, however, and even the better-known sophists whom we have considered, are known to us primarily as characters in Plato's dialogues. Their philosophical contentions are best studied in the context of those dialogues. Searching for the historical truth about the sophists is no more rewarding than trying to discover what King Lear or Prince Hamlet were like before Shakespeare got hold of them.

We shall say goodbye, therefore, to these sophists and turn to consider Socrates, who, according to one view, was the greatest of the sophists, and according to another, was a paradigm of the true philosopher at the opposite pole from any kind of sophistry.

Socrates

In the history of philosophy Socrates has a place without parallel. On the one hand, he is revered as inaugurating the first great era of philosophy, and therefore, in a sense, philosophy itself. In textbooks all previous thinkers are lumped together in textbooks as 'Presocratics', as if philosophy prior to his age was somehow prehistoric. On the other hand, Socrates left behind no writing, and

---

[19] See Ch. 6 below.

there is hardly a single sentence ascribed to him that we can be sure was his own utterance rather than a literary creation of one of his admirers. Our first-hand acquaintance with his philosophy is less than with that of Xenophanes, Parmenides, Empedocles, or Democritus. Yet his influence on subsequent philosophy, down to our own day, has been incomparably greater than theirs.

In antiquity many schools of thought claimed Socrates as a founder and many individuals revered him as a paragon philosopher. In the Middle Ages his history was not much studied, but his name appears on the page whenever a logician or metaphysician wishes to give an example: 'Socrates' was to scholastic philosophers what 'John Doe' long was to legal writers. In modern times Socrates' life has been held up as a model by philosophers of many different kinds, especially by philosophers living under tyranny and risking persecution for refusal to conform to unreasoned ideology. Many thinkers have made their own the dictum that has as good a claim as any to be his own authentic utterance: 'the unexamined life is not worth living'.

The hard facts of Socrates' life do not take long to tell. He was born in Athens about 469 BC, ten years after the Persian invasions of Greece had been crushed at the battle of Plataea. He grew up during the years when Athens, a flourishing democracy under the statesman Pericles, exercised imperial hegemony over the Greek world. It was a golden age of art and literature, which saw the sculptures of Phidias and the building of the Parthenon, and in which Aeschylus, Sophocles, and Euripides produced their great tragedies. At the same time Herodotus, 'the father of history', wrote his accounts of the Persian Wars, and Anaxagoras introduced philosophy to Athens.

The second half of Socrates' life was overshadowed by the Peloponnesian War (431–4), in which Athens was eventually forced to cede the leadership of Greece to victorious Sparta. During the first years of the war he served in the heavy infantry, taking part in three major engagements. He acquired a reputation for conspicuous courage, shown particularly during the retreat after a disastrous defeat at Delium in 422. Back in Athens during the last years of the war, he held office in the city's Assembly in 406. A group of commanders was tried for abandoning the bodies of the dead after a sea victory at Arginusae. It was unconstitutional to try the commanders collectively rather than individually, but Socrates was alone in voting against the illegality, and the accused were executed.

In 404, after the war had ended, the Spartans replaced Athenian democracy with an oligarchy, 'the Thirty Tyrants', long remembered for a reign of terror. Instructed to arrest an innocent man, Leon of Salamis, Socrates took no notice. He refused to accept illegal orders, but seems to have taken no part in the revolution that overthrew the oligarchy and restored democracy. His uprightness had by now given both democrats and aristocrats a grievance against him, and the restored democrats remembered also that some of his close associates, such as Critias and Charmides, had been among the Thirty.

An aspiring democrat politician, Anytus, with two associates, caused an indictment to be drawn up against Socrates in the following terms: 'Socrates has committed an offence by not recognizing the gods whom the state recognizes but introducing other new divinities. He has also committed the offence of corrupting the young. Penalty demanded: death' (D.L. 2. 40). We have no record of the trial, though two of Socrates' admirers have left us imaginative reconstructions of his speech for the defence. Whatever he actually said failed to move a sufficient number of the 500 citizen jurors. He was found guilty, albeit by a small majority, and condemned to death. After a delay in prison, due to a religious technicality, Socrates died in spring 399, accepting a poisonous cup of hemlock from the executioner.

The allegation of impiety in the indictment of Socrates was not something new. In 423 the dramatist Aristophanes had produced a comedy, *The Clouds*, in which he introduces a character called Socrates, who runs a college of chicanery which is also an institute of bogus research. Students at this establishment not only learn to make bad arguments trump good arguments, but also study astronomy in a spirit of irreverent scepticism about traditional religion. They invoke a new pantheon of elemental deities: air, ether, clouds, and chaos (260–6). The world, they are told, is governed not by Zeus, who does not exist, but by Dinos (literally 'Vortex'), the rotation of the heavenly bodies (380–1). Much of the play is burlesque that is obviously not meant to be taken seriously: Socrates measures how many flea-feet a flea can leap, and explores the clouds in a ramshackle flying machine. But the allegation that astronomy was incompatible with piety, if it was a joke, was a dangerous one. After all, it was only in the previous decade that Anaxagoras had been banished for asserting that the sun was a fiery lump. At the end of the play Socrates' house is burnt down by an angry crowd of people who wish to punish him for insulting the gods and violating the privacy of the moon. To those who recalled Aristophanes' comedy, the events of 399 must have seemed a sorry case of life imitating art.

Some of Socrates' traits in *The Clouds* are attributed to him also by other, more friendly writers. There is general agreement that he was pot-bellied and snub-nosed, pop-eyed and shambling in gait. He is regularly described as being shabby, wearing threadbare clothes, and liking to go barefoot. Even Aristophanes represents him as capable of great feats of endurance, and indifferent to privation: 'never numb with cold, never hungry for breakfast, a spurner of wine and gluttony' (414–17). From other sources it appears that he was a spurner of wine not in the sense of being a teetotaller, but as having an unusual ability to hold his liquor (Plato, *Smp.* 214a). Socrates married Xanthippe, with whom he had a son, Lamprocles; a stubborn, but perhaps ill-founded, tradition represents her as a shrew (D.L. 2. 36–7). According to some ancient writers he had two other sons by an official concubine, Myrto (D.L. 2. 26). In antiquity, however, he was best known for his attachment to the flamboyant aristocrat Alcibiades, some twenty years his junior: an attachment which, though passionate, remained, in the terminology of a later age, platonic.

The Socrates of Xenophon

On more important issues, there is little that is certain about Socrates' life and thought. For further information we are dependent above all on the two disciples whose works have come down to us intact, the soldierly historian Xenophon, and the idealist philosopher Plato. Both Xenophon and Plato composed, after the event, speeches for the defence at Socrates' trial. Xenophon in addition wrote four books of memoirs of Socrates (*memorabilia Socratis*) and a Socratic dialogue, the *Symposium*. Plato, besides his *Apology*, wrote at least twenty-five dialogues, in all but one of which Socrates figures. Xenophon and Plato paint pictures of Socrates which differ from each other as much as the picture of Jesus given in the gospel of Mark differs from that in the gospel of John. While in Mark Jesus speaks in parables, brief aphorisms, and pointed responses to questions, the Jesus of the fourth gospel delivers extensive discourses that resonate at several levels. There is a similar contrast between Xenophon's Socrates, who questions, argues, and exhorts in a workmanlike manner, and the Socrates of Plato's *Republic*, who delivers profound metaphysical lectures in a style of layered literary artifice. Just as it was John's presentation of Jesus that had the greatest impact on later theological development, so it is the Socrates of Plato whose ideas proved fertile in the history of philosophy.

According to Xenophon, Socrates was a pious man, punctiliously observant of ritual and respectful of oracles. In his prayers he let the gods decide what was good for him, since the gods were omnipresent and omniscient, knowing everyone's words, actions, and unspoken intentions (*Mem.* 1. 2. 20; 3. 2). He taught that the poor man's mite was as pleasing to the gods as the grand sacrifices of the rich (*Mem.* 1. 3. 3). He was a decent, temperate person, devoid of avarice and ambition, moderate in his desires, and tolerant of hardship. He was not an educator, though he taught virtue by practice as well as exhortation, and he discouraged vice by teasing and fable as well as by reproof. He was not to be blamed if some of his pupils went to the bad in spite of his example. Though critical of some aspects of Athenian democracy, he was a friend of the people, and totally innocent of crime and treason (*Mem.* 1. 2).

Xenophon's major concern in his memoirs was to exonerate Socrates from the charges made against him at his trial, and to show that his life was such that conservative Athenians should have revered him rather than condemned him to death. Xenophon is also anxious to place a distance between Socrates and the other philosophers of the age: unlike Anaxagoras he had no futile interest in physics or astronomy (*Mem*. 1. 1. 16), and unlike the sophists he did not charge any fees or pretend to expertise that he lacked (*Mem*. 1. 6–7).

Xenophon's Socrates is an upright, rather wooden person, capable of giving shrewd, commonsensical advice in practical and ethical matters. In discussion he is quick to resolve ambiguities and to deflate cant, but he rarely ventures upon philosophical argument or speculation. In a rare case when he does so it is, significantly, in order to prove the existence and providence of God. If an object is useful, Socrates argues, it must be the product of design, not chance; but our sense-organs are eminently useful and delicately constructed. 'Because our sight is delicate, it has been shuttered with eyelids which open when we need to use it, and close in sleep; so that not even the wind will damage it, eyelashes have been planted as a screen; and our foreheads have been fringed with eyebrows to prevent harm from the head's own sweat' (*Mem*. 1. 4. 6). Such contrivances, and the implantation of the instincts for procreation and self-preservation, look like the actions of a wise and benevolent craftsman (*demiourgos*). It is arrogant to think that we humans are the only location of Mind (*nous*) in the universe. It is true that we cannot see the cosmic intelligence that governs the infinite multitudinous universe, but we cannot see the souls that control our own bodies either. Moreover, it is absurd to think that the cosmic powers that be have no concern for humans: they have favoured humans above all other animals by endowing them with erect posture, multi-purpose hands, articulate language, and all-year-round sex (*Mem*. 1. 4. 11–12).

Despite this anticipation of the perennial Argument from Design, there is little in Xenophon's work that would entitle Socrates to a prominent position in the history of philosophy. Several of the Presocratics would be more than a match for Xenophon's Socrates in scope, insight, and originality. The Socrates who has captured the imagination of succeeding generations of philosophers is the Socrates of Plato, and it is he with whom we shall henceforth be concerned.

The Socrates of Plato

It is, however, an oversimplification to speak of a Platonic Socrates, because Plato's dialogues do not assign a consistent role or personality to the character called Socrates. In some dialogues he is predominantly a critical inquirer, challenging the pretensions of other characters by a characteristic technique of question and answer—*elenchus*—which reduces them to incoherence. In other dialogues Socrates is quite willing to harangue his audience, and to present an ethical and metaphysical system in dogmatic form. In yet other dialogues he plays only a minor part, leaving the philosophical initiative to a different protagonist. Before going further, therefore, we must digress to consider when and where the dialogues can be taken to be presenting Socrates' actual views, and when and where the character Socrates is acting as a mouthpiece for Plato's own philosophy.

In recent centuries scholars have sought to explain these differences in chronological terms: the different role assigned to Socrates in different dialogues represents the development of Plato's thought and his gradual emancipation from the teaching of his master. The initial clue to a chronological ordering of the dialogues was given by Aristotle, who tells us that Plato's *Laws* was written later than the *Republic* (*Pol.* 2. 6. 1264^{b}24–7). There is indeed a tradition that the *Laws* was unfinished at Plato's death (D.L. 3. 37). On this basis nineteenth-century scholars sought to establish a grouping of the dialogues, beginning from the final stage of Plato's life. They studied the frequency in different dialogues of different features of style, such as the use of technical terms, preferences between synonymous idioms, the avoidance of hiatus, and the adoption of particular speech rhythms.

On the basis of these stylometric studies, which by the end of the nineteenth century had covered some 500 different linguistic criteria, a consensus emerged that a group of dialogues stood out by its similarity to the *Laws*. All scholars agreed on including in the group the dialogues *Critias*, *Philebus*, *Sophist*, *Statesman*, and *Timaeus*, and all agreed that the group represented the latest stage of Plato's writing career. There was no similar consensus about ordering within the group: but it is notable that the group includes all the dialogues in which Socrates' role is at a minimum. Only in the *Philebus* is he a prominent character. In *Laws* he does not appear at all, and in the *Timaeus*, *Critias*, *Sophist*, and *Politicus* he has only a walk-on part while the lead role is given to another: in the first two to the protagonist named in the dialogue's title, and in the latter two to a stranger from Parmenides' town of Elea. It seemed reasonable, therefore, to regard the dialogues of this group as expressing the views of the mature Plato rather than those of his long-dead teacher.

In dividing the earlier dialogues into groups, scholars could once again follow a clue given by Aristotle. In *Metaph.* M 4. 1078^{b}27–32 he sets out the prehistory of Plato's Theory of Ideas, and assigns the following role to Socrates: 'Two things may fairly be attributed to Socrates: inductive arguments and general definitions; both are starting points of scientific knowledge. But he did not regard the universal or the definitions as separate entities, but [the Platonists] did, and called them Ideas of things.' Expositions of the Theory of Ideas are placed in the mouth of Socrates in several important dialogues, notably *Phaedo*, *Republic*, and *Symposium*. In these dialogues Socrates appears not as an inquiring questioner, but as a teacher in full possession of a system of philosophy. By stylometric criteria these dialogues are closer than other dialogues to the late group already described. It is reasonable, therefore, to treat them as a middle group in the corpus, and to regard them as representing Plato's own philosophy rather than Socrates'.

A third group of dialogues can be identified by a set of common features: (1) they are short; (2) Socrates appears as an inquirer, not an instructor; (3) the Theory of Ideas is not presented; and (4) stylometrically they are at the greatest remove from the late group first identified. This group includes *Crito, Charmides, Laches, Lysis, Ion, Euthydemus,* and *Hippias Minor.* These dialogues are commonly accepted as those most likely to be presentations of the philosophical views of the historical Socrates. Here too belongs the *Apology,* in which Socrates is the sole speaker, on trial for his life, and which in philosophical content and stylometric features resembles the other dialogues of the group. The first book of the *Republic,* too, in both content and style, resembles this group more than it resembles the remaining books of the dialogue: some scholars suppose, with good reason, that it first existed as a separate dialogue, perhaps under the title *Thrasymachus.* It is difficult to assign a chronology within this early group, though some authors place the *Lysis* first and assign it before 399, on the basis of an ancient anecdote that it was read to Socrates himself, who said, 'what a load of lies this young man tells about me' (D.L. 3. 35).

In my view there is good reason to accept the general consensus that thus divides the Platonic dialogues into three groups, early, middle, and late. The division results from the striking coincidence of three independent sets of criteria, dramatic, philosophical, and stylometric. Whether we focus on the dramatic role given to Socrates, or the philosophical content of the dialogues, or tell-tale details of style and idiom, we reach the same threefold grouping. Twentieth-century developments in stylometry, with much more refined statistical techniques, and with vast amounts of new data obtained from computerized texts, have essentially done little more than confirm the consensus achieved in the late nineteenth and early twentieth century.[20]

A number of dialogues, however, do not fall clearly into one of the three groups, because the three criteria do not so happily coincide: the most important such cases are *Cratylus, Euthyphro, Gorgias, Meno, Phaedrus, Parmenides, Protagoras, Theaetetus.* Here more recent stylometric studies have thrown new light on the problems.[21] There is no space here to enter into the detailed arguments for assigning each of these dialogues to a particular period, so I will simply state the chronology that appears to me most probable after an examination of the three sets of criteria.

Gorgias, Protagoras, and *Meno* seem to belong between the first and second group. Though the Theory of Ideas is absent from the discussion, the role of Socrates is closer to the didactic philosopher of the middle dialogues than to the agnostic inquirer of the early dialogues. The order suggested by philosophical considerations is *Protagoras, Gorgias, Meno;* the order that emerges from stylometric studies is *Meno, Protagoras, Gorgias.* The *Cratylus* in style is close to these three, but is difficult to

---

[20] The consensus has been significantly questioned only in respect of the *Timaeus* and its appendix, the *Critias.* The debate here will be examined later when I discuss Plato's Theory of Ideas.

[21] See L. Brandwood, *The Chronology of Plato's Dialogues* (Cambridge: Cambridge University Press, 1990); G. Ledger, *Re-counting Plato: A Computer Analysis of Plato's Style* (Oxford: Clarendon Press, 1989); J. T. Temple, 'A Multivariate Synthesis of Published Platonic Stylometric Data', *Literary and Linguistic Computing,* 11/2 (1996), 67–75.

place precisely. The *Euthyphro* is generally considered an early dialogue, but it contains a hint of the Theory of Ideas, and stylistic indicators place it close to the *Gorgias*. Accordingly, I would place it in this intermediate group.

The *Phaedrus* was sometimes thought in antiquity to be the earliest of Plato's dialogues (D.L. 3. 38), but on both doctrinal and stylistic grounds the dialogue fits reasonably well into the middle group. The case is not the same with two other very important dialogues that in style are close to the *Phaedrus*, namely the *Parmenides* and *Theaetetus*. In content these works stand at some distance from the classical Theory of Ideas, which is ignored in the *Theaetetus* and subjected to severe criticism in the *Parmenides*. In structure the *Parmenides* differs from all other dialogues; the *Theaetetus* resembles the dialogues of the early group. Internal references in the *Theaetetus* look backwards to the *Parmenides* (183e) and forwards to the *Sophist* (210d). On balance it seems sensible to place these two dialogues between the middle and the later dialogues, but a discussion of the problems in giving a coherent statement of Plato's philosophical position at this period will have to wait until we have given an account of the Theory of Ideas.

Socrates' Own Philosophy

It was necessary to establish a plausible chronology for the Platonic texts in order to indicate to what extent it is safe to rely on Plato as a source of information about the historical Socrates. Having done this, we can give an account of Socrates' own philosophy as it is presented in the early dialogues of his pupil. In the *Apology* Plato is anxious, like Xenophon, to defend Socrates from the charge of atheism. He points to the inconsistency between the two charges, that he is an atheist and that he introduces strange divinities, by distancing him from the secular physicism of Anaxagoras. The denial in the *Apology* that he had ever discussed physics (19d) does not ring altogether true, even though it is echoed later by Aristotle (*Metaph. A* 6. 987^{b}2). If Socrates had never shown any interest in issues of cosmology, Aristophanes' mockery would have been so wide of the mark that the jokes would have fallen very flat. Moreover, Plato himself in his *Phaedo* represents Socrates as confessing that he at one time shared Anaxagoras' curiosity about whether the earth was flat or round and whether it was in the middle of the universe, and what was the reason for the motion and speed of the sun and moon and other heavenly bodies (*Phd.* 97b–99a).

It may have been Socrates' disillusionment with Anaxagoras that made him give up scientific inquiry and concentrate on the issues which, according to the *Apology* and Aristotle, dominated the latter part of his life. According to both Plato and Xenophon, another factor that directed his interest was an oracle uttered in the name of Apollo by the entranced priestess in the shrine at Delphi. When asked if there was anyone in Athens wiser than Socrates, the priestess replied in the negative. Socrates professed to be puzzled by this response, and began to question different classes of people who claimed to possess wisdom of various kinds. It soon became clear that politicians and poets possessed no genuine expertise at all, and that craftsmen who were genuine experts in a particular area would pretend to a universal wisdom to which they had no claim. Socrates concluded that the oracle was correct in that he alone realized that his own wisdom was worthless (23b).

It was in matters of morality that it was most important to pursue genuine knowledge and to expose false pretensions. For according to Socrates virtue and moral knowledge were the same thing: no one who really knew what was the best thing to do could do otherwise, and all wrongdoing was the result of ignorance.[22] This makes it all the more absurd that he should be accused of corrupting the young. Anyone would obviously prefer to live among good men than among bad men, who might harm him. He cannot, therefore, have any motive for corrupting the young on purpose; and if he is doing so unwittingly he should be educated rather than prosecuted (26a).

Socrates, in the *Apology*, did not claim to possess himself the wisdom that is sufficient to keep a man from wrongdoing. Instead, he said that he relied on an inner divine voice, which would intervene if ever he was on the point of taking a wrong step (41d). So far from being an atheist, his whole life was dedicated to a divine mission, the campaign to expose false wisdom which was prompted by the Delphic oracle. What would really be a betrayal of God would be to desert his post through fear of death. If he were told that he could go free on condition that he abandon philosophical inquiry, he would reply, 'Men of Athens, I honour and love you; but I shall obey God rather than you, and while I have life and strength I shall never cease from the practice and teaching of philosophy' (29d).

The early dialogues of Plato portray Socrates carrying out his philosophical mission. Typically, the dialogue will be named after a personage who claims knowledge of a certain subject or who can be taken to represent a certain virtue: thus the *Ion*, on poetry, is named after a prizewinning rhapsode (a reciter of Homer), and the *Laches*, on courage, is named after a distinguished general. *Charmides* and *Lysis*, on passion, temperance, and friendship, are named after two bright young men who commanded a circle of aristocratic admirers. In each dialogue Socrates seeks a scientific account or definition of the topic under discussion, and by questioning reveals that the eponymous protagonist is unable to give one. The dialogues all end with the ostensible failure of the inquiry, confirming the conclusion in the *Apology* that those who might most be expected to possess wisdom on particular topics fail, under examination, to exhibit it.

---

[22] For a fuller discussion of this remarkable doctrine, 'the Socratic Paradox', see Ch. 8 below.

The search for definitions serves different purposes in different dialogues: a definition of justice is sought in *Republic* 1 in order to determine whether justice benefits its possessor, and a definition of piety is sought in the *Euthyphro* in order to settle a particular difficult case of conscience. But Aristotle was right to pick out the search as a notable feature of Socratic method. The method has sometimes been criticized as involving the fallacious claim that we cannot ever know whether some particular action is or is not, say, just or pious unless we can give a watertight definition of justice and piety. Such a claim would be inconsistent with Socrates' regular practice in the course of his *elenchus* of seeking agreement whether particular actions (such as returning a borrowed knife to a madman, or carrying out a strategic retreat in battle) do or do not exhibit particular virtues such as justice and courage. Socrates' method involves only the weaker claim that unless we have a general definition of a virtue we will not (*a*) be able to say whether the virtue universally has a particular property, such as being teachable, or being beneficial, or (*b*) be able to decide difficult borderline cases, such as whether a son's prosecuting his father for the manslaughter of an accused murderer is or is not an act of piety.

The other feature of Socrates' method emphasized by Aristotle, namely the use of inductive arguments, does in fact presuppose that we can be sure of truths about individual cases while still lacking universal definitions. Plato's Socrates does not claim to have a watertight definition of *techne*, or craft; but over and over again he considers particular crafts in order to extract general truths about the nature of a craft. Thus, in *Republic* 1 he wishes to show that the test of a good craftsman is not whether he makes a lot of money, but whether he benefits the objects of his craft. To show this he runs through the products of different crafts: a good doctor produces healthy patients, a good captain delivers safe navigation, a good builder constructs a good house, and so on. How much money these people make is not relevant to their goodness at their craft; it tells us only how efficient they are at the quite different craft of moneymaking (*Rep.* 1. 346a–e).

The two procedures identified by Aristotle are, in Socrates' method, closely related to each other. The inductive argument from particular instances to general truths is a contribution to the universal definition, even though the contribution in these dialogues is forever incomplete, never leading to an exception-proof definition. In the absence of the universal definition of a virtue, the general truths are applied to help settle difficult borderline cases of practice, and to evaluate preliminary hypotheses about the virtue's properties. Thus, in the *Republic* case, the induction is used to show that a good ruler is one who benefits his subjects, and therefore justice is not (as one of the characters in the dialogue maintains) simply whatever is to the advantage of those in power.

In these early dialogues about the virtues, in spite of Socrates' profession of ignorance, a number of theses emerge both about knowledge and about virtue.

These will be explored in greater detail in later chapters on epistemology and ethics. For the moment we may notice that the issues converge on the question: Can virtue be taught? For if virtue is knowledge, then surely it must be teachable; and yet it is difficult to point to any successful teachers of virtue.

In Athens, however, there was no lack of people claiming to have the relevant expertise, namely the sophists. At the end of the early period, and before the central period of Plato's writing career, we find a series of dialogues named after major sophists—Hippias, Gorgias, Protagoras—which address the question whether virtue can be taught and which deflate the pretensions of the sophists to possess the secret of its teachability. The *Hippias Minor* sets out a serious difficulty for the idea that virtue is a craft that can be learnt. A craftsman who makes a mistake unknowingly is inferior to a craftsman who makes a mistake deliberately; so if virtue is a craft, one who sins deliberately is more virtuous than one who sins in ignorance (376b). The *Gorgias* argues that rhetoric, the main arrow in the sophist's quiver, is incapable of producing genuine virtue. The *Protagoras* seems to suggest—whether seriously or ironically—that virtue is indeed teachable, because it is the art of calculating the proportion of pleasure and pain among the consequences of one's actions.[23]

From Socrates to Plato

Whether or not this is Socrates' last word on the teachability of virtue, a reader of the dialogues soon finds a quite different answer being given, in the *Meno* and the *Phaedo*. Virtue, and the knowledge of good and evil, which according to Socrates is identical with virtue, cannot be taught in the present life: it can only be recovered by recollection of another and better world. This is presented not as a particular thesis about virtue, but as a general thesis about knowledge. In the *Meno* it is claimed that a slave-boy who has never been taught geometry can be brought, by suitable questioning, to recall significant geometrical truths (82b–86a). In the *Phaedo* it is argued that though we often see things that are more or less equal in size, we never see a pair of things absolutely equal to each other. The idea of absolute equality cannot therefore be derived from experience, but must have been acquired in a previous life. The same goes for similar ideas such as that of absolute goodness and absolute beauty (74b–75b).

The *Meno* and the *Phaedo* therefore introduce two doctrines—the Theory of Ideas, and the thesis of recollection—which by the common consent of scholars belong to Plato, and not to the historical Socrates. They effect the 'separation', of which Aristotle spoke, between the universal definitions sought by Socrates and the empirical entities of our everyday world.

[23] See Ch. 8 below.

The *Phaedo* also contains Plato's account of the last days of Socrates in prison. Socrates' friend Crito has (in the dialogue named after him) failed to gain acceptance of a plan for escape. Socrates has rejected the proposal, saying that he owes so much to the laws of Athens, under which he was born and bred and lived contentedly, that he cannot now turn his back on his covenant with them and run away (51d–54c). The arrival of a ship from the sacred isle of Delos marks the end of the religious stay of execution, and Socrates prepares for death by engaging his friends in a long discussion of the immortality of the soul.[24] The discussion ends with Socrates' narrating a series of myths about the journeys in the underworld of the soul after it survives death.

Crito asks whether Socrates has any instructions about his burial; he is told to remember that he will be burying only the body, and not the soul, which is to go to the joys of the blessed. After his last bath Socrates says farewell to his family, jokes with his gaoler, and accepts the cup of hemlock. He is represented (with a degree of medical improbability) as composing himself serenely as sensation gradually deserts his limbs. His last words, like so many in his life, are puzzling: 'Crito, I owe a cock to Aesculapius [the god of healing]. Please remember to pay the debt.' Once again we ask ourselves whether he means his words literally or is employing his unique form of irony.

It is perhaps no coincidence that it is in one and the same dialogue that Plato records the last hours of Socrates and introduces clearly for the first time his own characteristic Theory of Ideas. As well as the physical death of Socrates, we witness the demise of his personal philosophy, to be reincarnated henceforth in the more metaphysical and mythical form of Platonism.

When Socrates died, Plato was in his late twenties, having been his pupil for about eight years. A member of an aristocratic Athenian family, Plato would have been just old enough to have fought in the Peloponnesian War, as his brothers Glaucon and Adeimantus certainly did. His uncles Critias and Charmides were two of the Thirty Tyrants, but he himself took no part in Athenian political life. At the age of 40 he went to Sicily and became an associate of Dion, the brother-in-law of the reigning monarch, Dionysius I; during this visit he made the acquaintance of the Pythagorean philosopher Archytas. On his return to Athens he founded a philosophical community, the Academy, in a private grove beside his own house. Here a group of thinkers, under his direction, shared with each other their interests in mathematics, astronomy, metaphysics, ethics, and mysticism. When 60 years old he was invited back to Sicily by Dion's nephew, who had now succeeded to the throne as Dionysius II; but his visit was not a success because Dion and Dionysius quarrelled with each other. A third visit as a royal adviser was equally abortive, and Plato returned home disillusioned in 360. He died peacefully at a wedding feast in Athens, himself unmarried, in the year 347, being aged about 80.

---

[24] The philosophical content of this discussion is analysed below in Ch. 7.

Writers in antiquity wove many stories around Plato's life, few of which deserve credence. If we wish to put flesh around the bare bones of his biography, we do best to read the Letters that have traditionally been included in his works. Though some, if not all, are the composition of other authors, they contain information that is much more plausible than the anecdotes to be found in the Life of Plato by Diogenes Laertius. They profess to be from the last two decades of Plato's life and principally concern his involvement in the government of Syracuse and his attempt to convert a tyranny into a constitution embodying his own political ideals.

Plato's works as handed down to us amount to some half a million words. Though probably some of the works in the corpus are spurious, there are no written works attributed to Plato in antiquity that have not survived today. However, later writers in antiquity, in addition to making copious citations of his dialogues, from time to time attach importance to an oral tradition of his lectures in the Academy.

Because Plato chose to write in dialogue form, and never himself appears in them as a speaker, it is difficult to be sure which of the varied philosophical theses expounded by his characters were ones to which he was himself committed. We have seen this par excellence in the case of his Socrates, but similar caution must be exercised in attributing to him the doctrines of the other main interlocutors in the dialogues, Timaeus, the Eleatic Stranger in the *Sophist* and *Statesman*, and the Athenian Stranger in the *Laws*. The dialogue form enabled Plato to suspend judgement about difficult philosophical issues, while presenting the strongest arguments he could think of on both sides of the question (cf. D.L. 3. 52).

The Theory of Ideas

The best known of the doctrines to be found in Plato's dialogues is the Theory of Ideas. In the central dialogues, from the *Euthyphro* onwards, the theory is more often alluded to, taken for granted, or argued from, than explicitly stated and formally established. The clearest short statement of the theory is found not in the dialogues but in the seventh of the Letters traditionally attributed to Plato, which is largely devoted to a defence of his activities in Sicily. The authenticity of this letter has often been rejected in modern times. There is, however, no better ground for rejecting Plato's Seventh Epistle to the Syracusans than there is for rejecting Paul's Second Epistle to the Corinthians (which it resembles in several ways). Certainly there is no good stylometric reason for calling it into question.[25] If

---

[25] Ledger, *Re-counting Plato*, 148–50, 224, regards the Seventh Letter as authentic, and close in time to the *Philebus*, the first dialogue of the final period.

it is not authentic, then it is one of the clearest and most authoritative statements of the theory to be found in all the secondary literature on Plato. Hence it provides a useful starting point for the exposition of the theory.

The letter states the following as a fundamental doctrine that Plato has often expounded:

For each thing that there is three things are necessary if we are to come by knowledge: first, the name, secondly, the definition, and thirdly, the image. Knowledge itself is a fourth thing, and there is a fifth thing that we have to postulate, which is that which is knowable and truly real. To understand this, consider the following example and regard it as typical of everything. There is something called a circle; it has a name, which we have just this minute used. Then there is its definition, a compound of nouns and verbs. We might give 'The figure whose limit is at every point equidistant from its centre' as the definition of whatever is round, circular, or a circle. Thirdly, there is what we draw, or rub out, or rotate, or cancel. The circle itself which all these symbolize does not undergo any such change and is a quite different thing. In the fourth place we have knowledge, understanding, and true opinion on these matters—these, collectively, are in our minds and not in sounds or bodily shapes, and thus are clearly distinct from the circle itself and from the three entities already mentioned. Of all these items, it is understanding that is closest to the fifth in kinship and likeness; the others are at a greater distance. What is true of round is also true of straight, of colour, of good and beautiful, and just; of natural and manufactured bodies; of fire, water, and the other elements; of all living beings and moral characters; of all that we do and undergo. In each case, anyone who totally fails to grasp the first four things will never fully possess knowledge of the fifth. (342a–d)

If I follow Plato, then, I will begin by distinguishing four things: the word 'circle', the definition of circle (a series of words), a diagram of a circle, and my concept of a circle. The importance of being clear about these four items is to distinguish them from, and contrast them with, a fifth thing, the most important of all, which he calls 'the circle itself'. It is this that is one of the Ideas of which Plato's celebrated theory treats. The theory is a wide-ranging one, as is clear from the list that ends the paragraph of the fields in which the theory applies. In his other writings Plato uses many other expressions to refer to Ideas. 'Forms' (*eide*) is probably the most common, but the Idea or Form of X may be called 'the X itself', 'that very thing that is X', or 'Xness', or 'what X is'.

It is important to note what is absent from Plato's list in the Seventh Letter. He does not mention, even at the lowest level, actual material circular objects such as cartwheels and barrels. The reason for his omission is clear from other passages in his writings (e.g. *Phd.* 74a–c). The wheels and barrel we meet in experience are never perfectly circular: somewhere or other there will be a bend or bump which will interfere with the equidistance from the centre of every point on the circumference. This is true too, for that matter, of any diagram we may draw on paper or in the sand. Plato does not stress this point here, but it is the reason why he says that the diagram is at a greater distance from the circle itself than my concept is. My subjective concept of the circle—my understanding of what 'circle' means—is not the same as the Idea of the circle, because the Idea is an objective reality that is not the property of any individual mind. But at least the concept in my mind is a concept *of a perfect circle*; it is not merely an imperfect approximation to a circle, as the ring on my finger is.

In the passage I have cited, Plato arrives at the Idea of circle after starting from a consideration of the word 'circle' as it occurs in the subject-place of a sentence such as

> A circle is a plane figure whose circumference is everywhere equidistant from its centre.

However, he sometimes introduces the Idea of X by reflection on sentences in which 'X' appears not in subject-place, but as a predicate.

Consider the following. Socrates, Simmias, and Cebes are all called 'men'; they have it in common that they are all men. Now when we say 'Simmias is a man' we may wonder whether the word 'man' names or stands for something in the way that the name 'Simmias' stands for the individual man Simmias. If so, what? Is it the same thing as the word 'man' stands for in 'Cebes is a man'? In order to deal with questions of this kind, Plato introduces the Idea of Man. It is that which makes Simmias, Cebes, and Socrates all men; it is the prime bearer of the name 'Man'.

In many cases where we would say that a common predicate was true of a number of individuals, Plato will say that they are all related to a certain Idea or Form: where A, B, C, are all F, they are related to a single Form of F. Sometimes he will describe this relation as one of imitation: A, B, C, all resemble F. Sometimes he will talk rather of participation: A, B, C all share in F, they have F in common between them. It is not clear how universally we are to apply the principle that behind common predication there lies a common Idea. Sometimes Plato states it universally, sometimes he hesitates about applying it to certain particular sorts of predicate. Certainly he lists Ideas of many different types, such as the Idea of Good, the Idea of Bed, the Idea of Circle, the Idea of Being. He is prepared to extend the theory beyond single-place predicates such as 'is round' to two-place predicates like 'is distinct from'. When we say that A is distinct from B and when we say that B is distinct from A, although we use the word 'distinct' twice, each time we are applying it to a single entity.

We may state a number of Platonic theses about Ideas and their relations to ordinary things in the world.

(1) *The Principle of Commonality.* Wherever several things are F, this is because they participate in or imitate a single Idea of F (*Phd.* 100c; *Men.* 72c, 75a; *Rep.* 5. 476a10, 597c).

(2) *The Principle of Separation.* The Idea of F is distinct from all the things that are F (*Phd.* 74c; *Smp.* 211b).

(3) *The Principle of Self-Predication.* The Idea of F is itself F (*Hp. Ma.* 292e; *Prt.* 230c–e; *Prm.* 132a–b).

(4) *The Principle of Purity.* The Idea of F is nothing but F (*Phd.* 74c; *Smp.* 211e).

(5) *The Principle of Uniqueness.* Nothing but the Idea of F is really, truly, altogether F (*Phd.* 74d, *Rep.* 5. 479a–d).

(6) *The Principle of Sublimity.* Ideas are everlasting, they have no parts and undergo no change, and they are not perceptible to the senses (*Phd.* 78d; *Smp.* 211b).

The Principle of Commonality is not, by itself, uniquely Platonic. Many people who are unhappy with talk of 'participation' are content to speak of attributes as being 'in common' among many things which have them. They may say, for instance, 'If A, B, and C are all red, then this is because they have the property of being red in common, and we learn the meaning of 'red' by seeing what is common among the red things.' What is peculiar to Plato is that he seriously follows up what is implied if one uses the metaphor of 'having in common'.[26] For instance, there must be only a single Idea of F, otherwise we could not explain why the F things have something in common (*Rep.* 597b–c).

The Principle of Separation is linked with the notion of a hierarchy between Ideas and the individuals that exemplify them. To participate and to be participated in are two quite different relationships, and the two terms of these relationships must be on a different level.

The Principle of Self-Predication is important for Plato, because without it he could not show how the Ideas explain the occurrence of properties in individuals. Only what is hot will make something hot; and it is no good drying yourself with a wet towel. So, in general, only what is itself F can explain how something else is F. So if the Idea of Cold is to explain why snow is cold, it must itself be cold (*Phd.* 103b–e).

The Idea of F is not only F, it is a perfect specimen of an F. It cannot be diluted or adulterated by any element other than Fness: hence the Principle of Purity. If it were to possess any property other than being F, it would have to do so by participating in some other Idea, which would surely have to be superior to it in the way that the Idea of F is superior to all the non-ideal Fs. The notion of stratified relationships between Ideas opens up a Pandora's box which Plato, when presenting the classical Theory of Ideas in his central dialogues, preferred to keep closed.

The Principle of Uniqueness is sometimes stated in a misleading way by commentators. Plato frequently says that only Ideas really are, and that the non-ideal particulars we encounter in sense-experience are between being and not being. He is often taken to be saying that only Ideas really exist, and that tangible objects are unreal and illusory. In context, it is clear that when Plato says that only Ideas really

---

[26] I owe this point to G. E. M. Anscombe, *Three Philosophers* (Oxford: Blackwell, 1961), 28.

are, he does not mean that only Ideas really exist, but that only the Idea of F is really F, whatever F may be in the particular case. Particulars are between being and not being in that they are between being F and not being F—i.e. they are sometimes F and sometimes not F.[27]

For instance, only the Idea of Beauty is really beautiful, because particular beautiful things are (*a*) beautiful in one respect but ugly in another (in figure, say, but not in complexion), or (*b*) beautiful at one time but not another (e.g. at age 20 but not at age 70), (*c*) beautiful by comparison with some things, but not with others (e.g. Helen may be beautiful by comparison with Medea, but not by comparison with Aphrodite), (*d*) beautiful in some surroundings but not in others (*Smp.* 211 a–e).

An important feature of the classical Theory of Ideas is the Principle of Sublimity. The particulars that participate belong to the inferior world of Becoming, the world of change and decay; the Ideas that are participated in belong to a superior world of Being, of eternal stability. The most sublime of all Ideas is the Idea of the Good, superior in rank and power to all else, from which everything that can be known derives its being (*Rep.* 509c).

The problem with the Theory of Ideas is that the principles that define it do not seem to be all consistent with each other. It is difficult to reconcile the Principle of Separation with the Principles of Commonality and of Self-Predication. The difficulty was first expounded by Plato himself in the *Parmenides*, where he gives an argument along the following lines. Let us suppose that we have a number of particulars, each of which is F. Then, by (1) there is an Idea of F. This, by (3), is itself F. But now the Idea of F and the original particular Fs make up a new collection of F things. By (1) again, this must be because they participate in an Idea of F. But by (2) this cannot be the Idea first postulated. So there must be another Idea of F; but this in turn, by (3), will be F, and so on *ad infinitum*. If we are to avoid this regress, we must abandon one or other of the principles that generate it. To this day scholars are divided as to how seriously Plato took this difficulty, and which, if any, of his principles he modified in order to solve it. I shall return to the question when we engage in a fuller discussion of Plato's metaphysics.[28]

Plato applied his Theory of Ideas to many philosophical problems: he offered them as the basis of moral values, the bedrock of scientific knowledge, and the ultimate origin of all being. One problem to which Plato offered his theory as an answer is often called the problem of universals: the problem of the meaning of universal terms such as 'man', 'bed', 'virtue', 'good'. Because Plato's answer turned out to be unsatisfactory, the problem was to remain on the philosophical agenda.

[27] I first learnt this from Vlastos's article 'Degrees of Reality in Plato', in R. Bambrough (ed.), *New Essays on Plato and Aristotle* (London: Routledge & Kegan Paul, 1965).

[28] See p. 208ff. below.

In succeeding chapters we shall see how Aristotle handled the issue. The problem had a continuing history through the Middle Ages and up to our own time. A number of notions that occur in modern discussions of the problem bear a resemblance to Plato's Ideas.

Predicates. In modern logic a sentence such as 'Socrates is wise' is considered as having a subject, 'Socrates', and a predicate, which consists of the remainder of the sentence, i.e. ' . . . is wise'. Some philosophers of logic, following Gottlob Frege, have regarded predicates as having an extra-mental counterpart: an objective predicate (Frege called it a 'function') corresponding to ' . . . is a man' in a way similar to that in which the man Socrates corresponds to the name 'Socrates'. Frege's functions, such as the function *x is a man*, are objective entities: they are more like the fifth items of the Seventh Letter than like the fourth items. They share some of the transcendental properties of Ideas: the function *x is a man* does not grow or die as human beings do, and nowhere in the world can one view or handle the function *x is divisible by 7*. But functions do not conform to the Principles of Self-Predication or Uniqueness. How could one ever imagine that the function *x is a man*, and only that function, was really and truly a human being?

Classes. Functions serve as principles according to which objects can be collected into classes: objects that satisfy the function *x is human*, for instance, can be grouped into the class of human beings. Ideas in some way resemble classes: participation in an Idea can be assimilated to membership of a class. The difficulty in identifying Ideas with classes arises again over the Principle of Self-Predication. The class of men is not a man and we cannot say in general that the class of Fs is F. However, it seems at first sight as if there are, indeed, some classes that are members of themselves, such as the class of classes. But just as Plato was to find that the Principle of Self-Predication led him into serious problems, so modern philosophers discovered that if one was allowed total freedom to form classes of classes one would be led into paradoxes. Most notorious is the paradox of the class of all classes that are not members of themselves. Bertrand Russell pointed out that if this class is a member of itself it is not a member of itself, and if it is not a member of itself then it is a member of itself. It is no accident that Russell's paradox bears a striking resemblance to Plato's self-criticism in the *Parmenides*.

Paradigms. It has more than once been suggested that Platonic Ideas might be looked on as paradigms or standards: the relation between individuals and Ideas might be thought to be similar to that between metre-long objects and the Standard Metre by which the metre length was formerly defined.[29] This notion fits well the way in which for Plato particulars imitate or resemble Ideas: to be a

---

[29] The idea originated with Wittgenstein. See P. T. Geach, 'The Third Man Again', in R. E. Allen (ed.), *Studies in Plato's Metaphysics* (London: Routledge & Kegan Paul, 1965).

metre long was, precisely, to resemble the Standard Metre, and if two things were each a metre long it was in virtue of their common resemblance to the paradigm. However, such paradigms fail the Principle of Sublimity: the Standard Metre was not in heaven but in Paris.

Concrete universals. Philosophers have sometimes toyed with the notion that in a sentence such as 'Water is fluid' the word 'water' is to be treated as the name of a single scattered object, the aqueous portion of the world, made up of puddles, rivers, lakes, and so on. This would give a clear sense to Plato's principle that particulars participate in Ideas: this particular bottle of water is quite literally a part of all-the-water-in-the-world. Moreover, water is undoubtedly water, and nothing that is not water is really and truly water. This notion also suits Plato's preference (not often shared by his commentators) for referring to Ideas by a concrete mode of speech (e.g. 'the beautiful') rather than an abstract one (e.g. 'beauty'). However, concrete universals fail the Principle of Sublimity and the Principle of Purity: the water in the universe can be located and can change in quantity and distribution, and it has many other properties besides that of being water.

None of these notions do full justice to the many facets of Plato's Ideas. If one wants to see how his six principles seemed plausible to Plato it is better to consider, not any modern logician's technical concept, but some more unreflective notion. Consider the points of the compass, north, south, west, and east. Take the notion, say, of the east as one might conceive it by naive reflection on the various idioms we in Britain use about the east. There are many places that are east of us, e.g. Belgrade and Hong Kong. Anything thus eastward is part of the east (participation) and is in the same direction as the east (imitation). That is what makes whatever is east of us east (1). The east, however, cannot be identified with any point in space, however eastward it may be (2). The east is of course east of us (3), and the east is nothing but east (4): if we say 'The east is red' we only mean that the eastern sky is red. Nothing but the east is unqualifiedly east: the sun is sometimes east and sometimes west, India is east of Iran but west of Vietnam, but in every time and place the east is east (5). The east has no history in time, and it cannot be seen, handled, or parcelled out (6).

I am not, of course, suggesting that points of the compass will supply an interpretation of Plato's principles that will make them all come out true: no interpretation could do that since the principles form an inconsistent set. I am merely saying that this interpretation will make the theses look prima facie plausible in a way that the interpretations previously considered will not. Functions, classes, paradigms, and concrete universals all raise problems of their own, as philosophers long after Plato discovered, and though we cannot go back to the classical Theory of Ideas, we have yet to give a fully satisfactory answer to the problems it was meant to address.

Plato's Republic

In Plato's most famous dialogue, the *Republic*, the Theory of Ideas is put to use not only for the logical and semantical purposes that we have just been considering, but also to address problems in epistemology, metaphysics, and ethics. These ramifications of the theory will be considered in later chapters. But the *Republic* is best known to the world at large not for its manifold exploitation of the theory, but for the political arrangements that are described in its central books.

The official topic of the dialogue is the nature and value of justice. After several candidate definitions for justice have been examined and found wanting in the first book (which probably originally existed as a separate dialogue), the main part of the work begins with a challenge to Socrates to prove that justice is something worthwhile for its own sake. Plato's brothers Glaucon and Adeimantus, who are characters in the dialogue, argue that justice is chosen as a way of avoiding evil. To avoid being oppressed by others, Glaucon says, weak human beings make compacts with each other neither to suffer nor to commit injustice. People would much prefer to act unjustly if they could do so with impunity—the kind of impunity a man would have, for instance, if he could make himself invisible so that his misdeeds passed undetected. Adeimantus supports his brother, saying that among humans the rewards of justice are the rewards of seeming to be just rather than the rewards of actually being just, and with regard to the gods the penalties of injustice can be bought off by prayer and sacrifice (2. 358a–367e).

We shall see in Chapter 8 how Socrates responds, through the remaining books of the dialogue, to this initial challenge. Now, in the interests of setting out Plato's political philosophy, we should concentrate on his immediate response. To answer the brothers he shifts from the consideration of justice, or righteousness, in the individual person to the larger issue of justice in the city-state. There, he says, the nature of justice will be written in bigger letters and therefore easier to read. The purpose of living in cities is to enable people with different skills to supply each other's needs by an appropriate division of labour. Ideally, if people were content as they once were with the satisfaction of their basic needs, a very simple community would suffice. But in the modern luxurious age citizens demand more than mere subsistence, and this necessitates more complicated political arrangements, including a well-trained professional army (2. 369b–374d).

Socrates now presents a blueprint for a city with three classes. Those among the soldiers best fitted to rule are selected by competition to form the upper class, called guardians; the remaining soldiers are described as auxiliaries, and the rest of the citizens belong to the class of farmers and artisans (2. 374d–376e). How are the working classes to be brought to accept the authority of the ruling classes? A myth must be propagated, a 'noble falsehood', to the effect that members of the three classes have different metals in their soul: gold, silver, and bronze respectively.

Citizens in general are to remain in the class in which they were born, but Socrates allows a limited amount of social mobility (3. 414c–415c).

The rulers and auxiliaries are to receive an elaborate education in literature (based on a bowdlerized Homer), music (provided it is martial and edifying), and gymnastics (undertaken by both sexes in common) (2. 376e–3. 403b). Women as well as men are to be guardians and auxiliaries, but this involves severe restraints no less than privileges. Members of the upper classes are not allowed to marry; women are to be held in common and all sexual intercourse is to be public. Procreation is to be strictly regulated on eugenic grounds. Children are not to be allowed contact with their parents, but will be brought up in public creches. Guardians and auxiliaries may not own property or touch money; they will be given, free of charge, adequate but modest provisions, and they will live in common like soldiers in a camp (5. 451d–471c).

The state that Socrates imagines in books 3 to 5 of the *Republic* has been both denounced as a piece of ruthless totalitarianism and admired as an early exercise in feminism. If it was ever seriously meant as a blueprint for a real-life polity, then it must be admitted that it is in many respects in conflict with the most basic human rights, devoid of privacy and full of deceit. Considered as a constitutional proposal, it deserves all the obloquy that has been heaped on it by conservatives and liberals alike. But it must be remembered that the explicit purpose of this constitution-mongering was to cast light on the nature of justice in the soul, as Socrates goes on to do.[30] Plato, we know from other dialogues, delighted in teasing his readers; he extended the irony he had learnt from Socrates into a major principle of philosophical illumination.

However, having woven the analogy with his classbound state into his moral psychology, Plato in later books of the *Republic* returns to political theory. His ideal state, he tells us, incorporates all the cardinal virtues: the virtue of wisdom resides in the guardians, fortitude in the auxiliaries, temperance in the working classes, and justice is rooted in the principle of the division of labour from which the city-state took its origin. In a just state every citizen and every class does that for which they are most suited, and there is harmony between the classes (4. 427d–434c).

In less ideal states there is a gradual falling away from this ideal. There are five possible types of political constitution (8. 544e). The first and best constitution is called monarchy or aristocracy: if wisdom rules it does not matter whether it is incarnate in one or many rulers. There are four other inferior types of constitution: timocracy, oligarchy, democracy, and despotism (8. 543c). Each of these constitutions declines into the next because of the downgrading of one of the virtues of the ideal state. If the rulers cease to be persons of wisdom, aristocracy gives place to timocracy, which is essentially rule by a military junta (8. 547c). Oligarchy differs from timocracy because oligarchic

---

[30] See Ch. 7 below.

rulers lack fortitude and military virtues (8. 556d). Oligarchs do possess, in a rather miserly form, the virtue of temperance; when this is abandoned oligarchy gives way to democracy (8. 555b). For Plato, any step from the aristocracy of the ideal republic is a step away from justice; but it is the step from democracy to despotism that marks the enthronement of injustice incarnate (8. 576a). So the aristocratic state is marked by the presence of all the virtues, the timocratic state by the absence of wisdom, the oligarchic state by the decay of fortitude, the democratic state by contempt for temperance, and the despotic state by the overturning of justice.

Plato recognizes that in the real world we are much more likely to encounter the various forms of inferior state than the ideal constitution described in the *Republic*. Nonetheless, he insists that there will be no happiness, public or private, except in such a city, and such a city will never be brought about unless philosophers become kings or kings become philosophers (5. 473c–d). Becoming a philosopher, of course, involves working through Plato's educational system in order to reach acquaintance with the Ideas.

The Laws *and the* Timaeus

Later in his life Plato abandoned the idea of the philosopher king and ceased to treat the Theory of Ideas as having political significance. He came to believe that the character of the ruler was less important to the welfare of a city than the nature of the laws under which it was governed. In his late and longest work, the *Laws*, he portrays an Athenian visitor discussing with a Cretan and a Spartan the constitution of a colony, Magnesia, to be founded in the south of Crete. It is to be predominantly agricultural, with the free population consisting mainly of citizen farmers. Manual work is done largely by slaves, and craft and commerce are the province of resident aliens. Full citizenship is restricted to 5,040 adult males, divided into twelve tribes. The blueprint for government that is presented as a result of the advice of the Athenian visitor stands somewhere between the actual constitutional arrangements of Athens and the imaginary structures of Plato's ideal republic.

Like Athens, Magnesia is to have an assembly of adult male citizens, a Council, and a set of elected officials, to be called the Guardians of the Laws. Ordinary citizens will take part in the administration of the laws by sitting on enormous juries. Various appointments are made by lot, so as to ensure wide political participation. Private property is allowed, subject to a highly progressive wealth tax (5. 744b). Marriage, far from being abolished, is imposed by law, and bachelors over 35 have to pay severe annual fines (6. 774b). Finally, legislators must realize that even the best laws are constantly in need of reform (6. 769d).

On the other hand, Magnesia has several features reminiscent of the *Republic*. Supreme power in the state rests with a Nocturnal Council, which includes the wisest and most highly qualified officials, specially trained in mathematics, astronomy, theology, and law (though not, like the guardians of the Republic, metaphysics). Private citizens are not allowed to possess gold or silver coins, and the sale of houses is strictly forbidden (5. 740c, 742a). Severe censorship is imposed on both texts and music, and poets must be licensed (7. 801d–2a). Female sex police, with right of entry to households, oversee procreation and enforce eugenic standards (6. 784a–b). In divorce courts there must be as many women judges as men (9. 930a). Women are to join men at the communal meals, and they are to receive military training, and provide a home defence force (7. 814a). Education is of great importance for all classes, and is to be supervised by a powerful Minister of Education reporting direct to the Nocturnal Council (6. 765d).

Substantive legislation is set out in the middle books of the dialogue. Each law must have a preamble setting out its purpose, so that citizens may conform to it with understanding. For instance, a law compelling marriage between the age of 30 and 35 should have a preamble explaining that procreation is the method by which human beings achieve immortality (4. 721b). The duties of the many administrative officials are set out in book 6, and the educational curriculum is detailed, from playschool upward, in book 7; the *Laws* itself is to be a set school text. Book 9 deals with forms of assault and homicide and sets out the procedure relating to capital offences such as temple robbery. Elaborate provision is made to ensure that the accused gets a fair trial. In civil matters the law goes into fine detail, laying down, for instance, the damages to be paid by a defendant who is shown to have enticed away bees from the plaintiff's hive (9. 843e). Hunting is to be very severely restricted: the only form allowed is the hunting of four-legged animals, on horseback, with dogs (7. 824a).

From time to time in the *Laws* Plato engages in theoretical discussion of sexual morality, though actual sexual legislation is restricted to a form of excommunication for adultery (7. 785d–e). In a way that has been very common during the Christian era, but was rare in pagan antiquity, he bases his sexual ethics on the notion that procreation is the natural purpose of sex. The Athenian says at one point that he would like to put into effect 'A law to permit sexual intercourse only for its natural purpose, procreation, and to prohibit homosexual relations; to forbid the deliberate killing of a human offspring and the casting of seed on rocks and stone where it will never take root and fructify' (8. 838e). He realizes, however, that it will be very difficult to ensure compliance with such a law, and instead he proposes other measures to stamp out sodomy and discourage all forms of non-procreative intercourse (8. 836e, 841d). We have reached a point in Plato's thinking far distant from the arch homosexual banter which is such a predominant feature of the Socratic dialogues.

One of the most interesting sections of the *Laws* is the tenth book, which deals with the worship of the gods and the elimination of heresy. Impiety arises, the Athenian says, when people do not believe that the gods exist, or believe that they exist but do not care for the human race. As a preamble to laws against impiety, therefore, the lawgiver must establish the existence of the divine. The elaborate argument he presents will be considered in a later chapter on philosophy of religion.

In the *Timaeus*, a dialogue whose composition probably overlapped with that of the *Laws*, Plato sets out the relationship between God and the world we live in. He returns to the traditional philosophical topic of cosmology, taking it up at the point where Anaxagoras had, in his view, left off unsatisfactorily. The world of the *Timaeus* is not a field of mechanistic causes: it is fashioned by a divinity, variously called its father, its maker, or its craftsman (*demiourgos*) (28c).

Timaeus, the eponymous hero of the dialogue, is an astronomer. He offers to narrate to Socrates the history of the universe, from the origin of the cosmos to the appearance of mankind. People ask, he says, whether the world has always existed or whether it had a beginning. The answer must be that it had a beginning, because it is visible, tangible, and corporeal, and nothing that is perceptible by the senses is eternal and changeless in the way that the objects of thought are (27d–28c). The divinity who fashioned it had his eye on an eternal archetype, 'for the cosmos is the most beautiful of the things that have come to be, and he is the best of all causes' (29a). Why did he bring it into existence? Because he was good, and what is good is utterly free from envy or selfishness (29d).

Like the Lord God in Genesis, the maker of the world looked at what he had made and found that it was good; and in his delight he adorned it with many beautiful things. But the Demiurge differs from the creator of Judaeo-Christian tradition in several ways. First of all, he does not create the world from nothing: rather, he brings it into existence from a primordial chaos, and his creative freedom is limited by the necessary properties of the initial matter (48a). 'God, wishing all things to be good and nothing, if he could help it, paltry, and finding the visible universe in a state not of peace but of inharmonious and disorderly motion, brought it from disorder into an order that he judged to be altogether better' (30a). Secondly, while the Mosaic creator infuses life into an inert world at a certain stage of its creation, in Plato both the ordered universe and the archetype on which it was patterned are themselves living beings. What is this living archetype? He does not tell us, but perhaps it is the world of Ideas which, he concluded belatedly in the *Sophist*, must contain life. God created the soul of the world before he formed the world itself: this world-soul is poised between the world of being and the world of becoming (35a). He then fastened the world on to it.

The soul was woven all through from the centre to the outermost heaven, which it wrapped itself around. By its own revolution upon itself it provided a divine principle of unending and rational life for all time. The body of the heaven was made visible, but the soul is invisible and endowed with reason and harmony. It is the best creation of the best of intelligible and eternal realities. (36e–37a)

In contrast to those earlier philosophers who spoke of multiple worlds, Plato is very firm that our universe is the only one (31b). He follows Empedocles in regarding the world as made up of the four elements, earth, air, fire, and water, and he follows Democritus in believing that the different qualities of the elements are due to the different shapes of the atoms that constitute them. Earth atoms are cubes, air atoms are octahedrons, fire atoms are pyramids, and water atoms are icosahedrons. Pre-existent space was the receptacle into which the maker placed the world, and in a mysterious way it underlies the transmutation of the four elements, rather as a lump of gold underlies the different shapes that a jeweller may give to it (50a). In this Plato seems to anticipate the prime matter of Aristotelian hylomorphism.[31]

Timaeus explains that there are four kinds of living creatures in the universe: gods, birds, animals, and fish. Among gods Plato distinguishes between the fixed stars, which he regards as everlasting living beings, and the gods of Homeric tradition, whom he mentions in a rather embarrassed aside. He describes the infusion of souls into the stars and into human beings, and he develops a tripartite division of the human soul that he had introduced earlier in the *Republic*. He gives a detailed account of the mechanisms of perception and of the construction of the human body.[32] This construction, he tells us, was delegated by God to the lesser divinities that he had himself made personally (69c). A full description is given of all our bodily organs and their function, and there is a listing of diseases of body and mind.

The *Timaeus* was for centuries the most influential of Plato's dialogues. While the other dialogues went into oblivion between the end of antiquity and the beginning of the Renaissance, much of the *Timaeus* survived in Latin translations by Cicero and a fourth-century Christian called Chalcidius. Plato's teleological account of the forming of the world by a divinity was not too difficult for medieval thinkers to assimilate to the creation story of Genesis. The dialogue was a set text in the early days of the University of Paris, and 300 years later Raphael in his *School of Athens* gave Plato in the centre of the fresco only the *Timaeus* to hold.

---

[31] See Ch. 5 below.   [32] See Ch. 7 below.

2

Schools of Thought:
From Aristotle to Augustine

The fourth century saw a shift in political power from the city-states of classical Greece to the kingdom of Macedon to the north. In the same way, after the Athenians Socrates and Plato, the next great philosopher was a Macedonian. Aristotle was born, fifteen years after Socrates' death, in the small colony of Stagira, on the peninsula of Chalcidice. He was the son of Nicomachus, court physician to King Amyntas, the grandfather of Alexander the Great. After the death of his father he migrated to Athens in 367, being then 17, and joined Plato's Academy. He remained for twenty years as Plato's pupil and colleague, and it can safely be said that on no other occasion in history was such intellectual power concentrated in a single institution.

Aristotle in the Academy

Many of Plato's later dialogues date from these decades, and some of the arguments they contain may reflect Aristotle's contributions to debate. By a flattering anachronism, Plato introduces a character called Aristotle into the *Parmenides*, the dialogue that contains the most acute criticisms of the Theory of Ideas. Some of Aristotle's own writings also belong to this period, though many of these early works survive only in fragments quoted by later writers. Like his master, he wrote initially in dialogue form, and in content his dialogues show a strong Platonic influence.

In his lost dialogue *Eudemus*, for instance, Aristotle expounded a conception of the soul close to that of Plato's *Phaedo*. He argued vigorously against the thesis that the soul is an attunement of the body, claiming that it is imprisoned in a carcass and capable of a happier life when disembodied. The dead are more blessed and happier than the living, and have become greater and better. 'It is best, for all men and women, not to be born; and next after that—the best option for humans—is, once born, to die as quickly as possible' (fr. 44). To die is to return to one's real home.

Another Platonic work of Aristotle's youth is his *Protrepticus*, or exhortation to philosophy. This too is lost, but it was so extensively quoted in later antiquity that some scholars believe they can reconstruct it almost in its entirety. Everyone has to do philosophy, Aristotle says, for arguing against the practice of philosophy is itself a form of philosophizing. But the best form of philosophy is the contemplation of the universe of nature. Anaxagoras is praised for saying that the one thing that makes life worth living is to observe the sun and the moon and the stars and the heavens. It is for this reason that God made us, and gave us a godlike intellect. All else—strength, beauty, power, and honour—is worthless (Barnes, 2416).

The *Protrepticus* contains a vivid expression of the Platonic view that the soul's union with the body is in some way a punishment for evil done in an earlier life. 'As the Etruscans are said often to torture captives by chaining corpses to their bodies face to face, and limb to limb, so the soul seems to be spread out and nailed to all the organs of the body' (ibid.). All this is very different from Aristotle's eventual mature thought.

It is probable that some of Aristotle's surviving works on logic and disputation, the *Topics* and *Sophistical Refutations*, belong to this period. These are works of comparatively informal logic, the one expounding how to construct arguments for a position one has decided to adopt, the other showing how to detect weaknesses in the arguments of others. Though the *Topics* contains the germ of conceptions, such as the categories, that were to be important in Aristotle's later philosophy, neither work adds up to a systematic treatise on formal logic such as we are to be given in the *Prior Analytics*. Even so, Aristotle can say at the end of the *Sophistical Refutations* that he has invented the discipline of logic from scratch: nothing at all existed when he started. There are many treatises on rhetoric, he says, but

on the subject of deduction we had nothing of an earlier date to cite, but needed to spend a long time on original research. If, then, it seems to you on inspection that from such an unpromising start we have brought our investigation to a satisfactory condition comparable to that of traditional disciplines, it falls to you my students to grant me your pardon for the shortcomings of the inquiry, and for its discoveries your warm thanks. (*SE* 34. 184^{a}9–^{b}8)

It is indeed one of Aristotle's many claims on posterity that he was logic's founder. His most important works on the subject are the *Categories*, the *de Interpretatione*, and the *Prior Analytics*. These set out his teaching on simple terms, on propositions, and on syllogisms. They were grouped together, along with the two works already mentioned, and a treatise on scientific method, the *Posterior Analytics*, into a collection known as the *Organon*, or 'tool' of thought. Most of Aristotle's followers thought of logic not as itself a scientific discipline, but as a propaedeutic art which could be used in any discipline; hence the title. The *Organon*, though shown already in antiquity to be incomplete as a system of logic, was regarded for two millennia as providing the core of the subject.[1]

While Aristotle was at the Academy, King Philip II of Macedon, who succeeded his father in 359, adopted an expansionist policy and waged war on a number of Greek city-states, including Athens. Despite the martial eloquence of Aristotle's contemporary Demosthenes, who denounced the Macedonian king in his 'Philippics', the Athenians defended their interests only half-heartedly. After a series of humiliating concessions they allowed Philip to become, by 338, master of the Greek world. It cannot have been an easy time to be a Macedonian resident in Athens.

Within the Academy, however, relations seem to have remained cordial. Later generations liked to portray Plato and Aristotle embattled against each other, and some in antiquity likened Aristotle to an ungrateful colt who had kicked his mother (D.L. 5. 1). But Aristotle always acknowledged a great debt to Plato, whom on his death he described as the best and happiest of mortals 'whom it is not right for evil men even to praise'. He took a large part of his philosophical agenda from Plato, and his teaching is more often a modification than a repudiation of Plato's doctrines. The philosophical ideas that are common to the two philosophers are more important than the issues that divide them—just as, in the seventeenth and eighteenth centuries, the opposing schools of rationalists and empiricists had much more in common with each other than with the philosophers who preceded and followed them.

Already, however, during his period at the Academy, Aristotle began to distance himself from Plato's Theory of Ideas. In his pamphlet *On Ideas* he maintained that the arguments of Plato's central dialogues establish only that there are, in addition to particulars, certain common objects of the sciences; but these need not be Ideas. He employs against Ideas a version of an argument that we have already encountered in Plato's own dialogues—he calls it the 'Third Man argument' (Barnes, 2435). In his surviving works Aristotle often take issue with the theory. Sometimes he does so politely, as where, in the *Nicomachean Ethics*, he introduces a series of arguments against the Idea of the Good with the remarks that he has an uphill task because the Forms were introduced by his good friends. However, his duty as a philosopher is to honour truth above friendship. In the *Posterior Analytics*, however, he dismisses Ideas contemptuously as 'tarradiddle' (1. 22. 83ª33).

More seriously, in his *Metaphysics* he argues that the theory fails to solve the problems it was meant to address. It does not confer intelligibility on particulars, because immutable and everlasting forms cannot explain how particulars come into existence and undergo change. Moreover, they do not contribute anything

---

[1] Aristotle's logic is considered in detail in Ch. 3.

either to the knowledge or to the being of other things (A 9. 991ᵃ8 ff.). All the theory does is to bring in new entities equal in number to the entities to be explained: as if one could solve a problem by doubling it (A 9. 990ᵇ3).

Aristotle the Biologist

When Plato died in 347, his nephew Speusippus became head of the Academy, and Aristotle left Athens. He migrated to Assos on the north-western coast of what is now Turkey. The city was under the rule of Hermias, a graduate of the Academy, who had already invited a number of Academicians to form a new philosophical institute there. Aristotle became a friend of Hermias, and married a close relation of his, Pythias, with whom he had two children. In 343 Hermias met a tragic end: having negotiated, with Aristotle's help, an alliance with Macedon, he was treacherously arrested and eventually crucified by the Great King of Persia. Aristotle saluted his memory in an 'Ode to Virtue', his only surviving poem.

During his period in Assos, and during the next few years, when he lived at Mytilene on the island of Lesbos, Aristotle carried out extensive scientific research, particularly in zoology and marine biology. These researches were written up in a book later known, misleadingly, as the *History of Animals*, to which he added two shorter treatises, *On the Parts of Animals* and *On the Generation of Animals*. Aristotle does not claim to have founded the science of zoology, and his books contain copious citations of earlier writers, accompanied by a judicious degree of scepticism about some of their wilder reports. However, his detailed observations of organisms of very various kinds were quite without precedent, and in many cases they were not superseded until the seventeenth century.

Though he does not claim to be the first zoologist, Aristotle clearly saw himself as a pioneer, and indeed felt some need to justify his interest in the subject. Previous philosophers had given a privileged place to the observation of the heavens, and here was he prodding sponges and watching the hatching of grubs. In his defence he says that while the heavenly bodies are marvellous and glorious, they are hard to study because they are so distant and different from ourselves. Animals, however, are near at hand, and akin to our own nature, so that we can investigate them with much greater precision. It is childish to be squeamish about the observation of the humbler animals. 'We should approach the investigation of every kind of animal without being ashamed, for each of them will exhibit to us something natural and something beautiful' (*PA* 1. 5. 645ᵃ20–5).

The scope of Aristotle's researches is astonishing. Much of his work is taken up with classification into genus (e.g. *Testacea*) and species (e.g. sea-urchin). More than 500 species figure in his treatises, and many of them are described in detail. It is clear that Aristotle was not content with the observation of a naturalist: he also practised dissection like an anatomist. He acknowledges that he found dissection distasteful, particularly in the case of human beings: but it was essential to examine the parts of any organism in order to understand the structure of the whole (*PA* 1. 5. 644^{b}22–645^{a}36).

Aristotle illustrated his treatises with diagrams, now sadly lost. We can conjecture the kind of illustrations he provided when we read passages such as the following, where he is explaining the relationship between the testicles and the penis.

In the accompanying diagram the letter A marks the starting point of ducts leading down from the aorta; the letters KK mark the heads of the testicles and the ducts that descend to them; the ducts leading from them through the testicles are marked $\Omega\Omega$, and the reverse ducts containing white fluid and leading to the testicles are marked BB; the penis Δ, the bladder E, and the testicles $\Psi\Psi$. (*HA* 3. 1. 510^{a}30–4)

Only a biologist could check the accuracy of the myriad items of information that Aristotle offers us about the anatomy, diet, habitat, modes of copulation, and reproductive systems of mammals, birds, reptiles, fish, and insects. The twentieth-century biologist Sir D'Arcy Thompson, who made the canonical translation of the *History of Animals* into English, constantly draws attention to the minuteness of his detailed investigations, coupled with vestiges of superstition. There are some spectacular cases where Aristotle's unlikely stories about rare species of fish were proved accurate many centuries later.[2] In other places Aristotle states clearly and fairly biological problems that were not solved until millennia had passed. One such case was the question whether an embryo contained all the parts of an animal in miniature form from the beginning, or whether wholly new structures were formed as the embryo develops (*GA* 2. 1. 734^{a}1–735^{a}4).

The modern layman can only guess which parts of passages like the following are accurate, and which are fantasy.

All animals that are quadrupedal, blooded, and viviparous are furnished with teeth; but, to begin with, some have teeth in both jaws, and some do not. For instance, horned quadrupeds do not; for they have not got the front teeth in the upper jaw; and some hornless animals, also, do not have teeth in both jaws, as the camel. Some animals have tusks, like the boar; and some have not. Further, some animals are saw-toothed, such as the lion, the leopard, and the dog; and some have teeth that do not interlock, as the horse and the ox; and by 'saw-toothed' we mean such animals as interlock the sharp-pointed teeth. (*HA* 2. 1. 501^{a}8 ff.)

With such fish as pair, eggs are the result of copulation, but such fish have them also without copulation; and this is shown in the case of some river-fish, for the minnow has eggs when quite small—almost, one might say, as soon as it is born. These fishes shed their eggs, and, as is stated, the males swallow the greater part of them, and some portion of

[2] See G. E. R. Lloyd, *Aristotle: The Growth and Structure of his Thought* (Cambridge: Cambridge University Press, 1968), 74–81.

them goes to waste in the water; but such of the eggs as the female deposits in suitable places are saved. If all the eggs were preserved, each species would be vast in number. The greater number of these eggs are not productive, but only those over which the male sheds the milt; for when the female has laid her eggs, the male follows and sheds its milt over them, and from all the eggs so besprinkled young fishes proceed, while the rest are left to their fate. (*HA* 6. 3. 567^{a}29–^{b}6)

It is easier to form a quick judgement about Aristotle's attempts to link features of human anatomy to traits of character. He tells us, for instance, that those who have flat feet are likely to be rogues, and that those who have large and prominent ears have a tendency to irrelevant chatter (*HA* 1. 11. 492^{a}1).

Despite an admixture of old wives' tales, Aristotle's biological works must strike us as a stupendous achievement, when we remember the conditions under which he worked, unequipped with any of the aids to investigation that have been at the disposal of scientists since the early modern period. He, or one of his research assistants, must have been gifted with remarkably acute eyesight, since some of the features of insects that he accurately reports were not again observed until the invention of the microscope. His inquiries were conducted in a genuinely scientific spirit, and he is always ready to confess ignorance where evidence is insufficient. With regard to the reproductive mechanism in bees, for example, he has this to say:

The facts have not yet been sufficiently ascertained. If ever they are, then we must trust observation rather than theory, and trust theories only if their results conform with the observed phenomena. (*GA* 3. 10. 760^{b}28–31)

The Lyceum and its Curriculum

About eight years after the death of Hermias, Aristotle was summoned to the Macedonian capital by King Philip II as tutor to his 13-year-old son, the future Alexander the Great. We know little of the content of his instruction: the *Rhetoric for Alexander* that appears in the Aristotelian corpus is commonly regarded as a forgery. Ancient sources say that Aristotle did write essays on kingship and colonization for his pupil, and gave him his own edition of Homer. Alexander is said to have slept with this book under his pillow; and when he became king in 336 and started upon his spectacular military career, he arranged for biological specimens to be sent to his tutor from all parts of Greece and Asia Minor.

Within ten years Alexander had made himself master of an empire that stretched from the Danube to the Indus and included Libya and Egypt. While Alexander was conquering Asia, Aristotle was back in Athens, where he established his own school in the Lyceum, a gymnasium just outside the city boundary. Now aged 50, he built up a substantial library, and gathered around him a group of brilliant research students, called 'Peripatetics' from the name of the avenue (*peripatos*) in which they walked and held their discussions. The Lyceum was not a private club like the Academy; many of the lectures given there were open to the general public without fee.

Aristotle's anatomical and zoological studies had given a new and definitive turn to his philosophy. Though he retained a lifelong interest in metaphysics, his mature philosophy constantly interlocks with empirical science, and his thinking takes on a biological cast. Most of the works that have come down to us, with the exception of the zoological treatises, probably belong to this second Athenian sojourn. There is no certainty about their chronological order, and indeed it is probable that the main treatises—on physics, metaphysics, psychology, ethics, and politics—were constantly rewritten and updated. In the form in which they have survived it is possible to detect evidence of different layers of composition, though no consensus has been reached about the identification or dating of these strata.

In his major works Aristotle's style is very different from that of Plato or any of his other philosophical predecessors. In the period between Homer and Socrates most philosophers wrote in verse, and Plato, writing in the great age of Athenian tragedy and comedy, composed dramatic dialogue. Aristotle, an exact contemporary of the greatest Greek orator Demosthenes, preferred to write in prose monologue. The prose he wrote is commonly neither lucid nor polished, though he could compose passages of moving eloquence when he chose. It may be that the texts we have are the notes from which he lectured; perhaps even, in some cases, notes taken at lectures by students present. Everything Aristotle wrote is fertile of ideas and full of energy; every sentence packs a massive intellectual punch. But effort is needed to decode the message of his jagged clauses. What has been delivered to us from Aristotle across the centuries is a set of telegrams rather than epistles.

Aristotle's works are systematic in a way that Plato's never were. Even in the *Laws*, which is the closest to a textbook that Plato ever wrote, we flit from topic to topic, and indeed from discipline to discipline, in a disconcerting manner. None of the other major dialogues can be pigeon-holed as relating to a single area of philosophy. It is, of course, anachronistic to speak of 'disciplines' when discussing Plato: but the anachronism is not great because the notion of a discipline, in the modern academic sense, is made very explicit by Aristotle in his Lyceum period.

There are three kinds of sciences, Aristotle tells us in the *Metaphysics* (E 1. 1025^{b}25): productive, practical, and theoretical sciences. Productive sciences are, naturally enough, sciences that have a product. They include engineering and architecture, with products like bridges and houses, but also disciplines such as strategy and rhetoric, where the product is something less concrete, such as victory on the battlefield or in the courts. Practical sciences are ones that guide behaviour, most notably ethics and politics. Theoretical sciences are those that have no product and no practical goal, but in which information and understanding is sought for its own sake.

There are three theoretical sciences: physics, mathematics, and theology (*Metaph. E* 1. 1026ᵃ19). In this trilogy only mathematics is what it seems to be. 'Physics' means natural philosophy or the study of nature (*physis*). It is a much broader study than physics as understood nowadays, including chemistry and meteorology and even biology and psychology. 'Theology' is, for Aristotle, the study of entities above and superior to human beings, that is to say, the heavenly bodies as well as whatever divinities may inhabit the starry skies. His writings on this topic resemble a textbook of astronomy more than they resemble any discourse on natural religion.

It may seem surprising that metaphysics, a discipline theoretical *par excellence*, does not figure in Aristotle's list of theoretical sciences, since so much of his writing is concerned with it, and since one of his longest treatises bears the title *Metaphysics*. The word, in fact, does not occur in Aristotle's own writings and first appears in the posthumous catalogue of his works. It simply means 'after physics' and refers to the works that were listed after his *Physics*. But he did in fact come to recognize the branch of philosophy we now call 'metaphysics': he called it 'First Philosophy' and he defined it as the discipline that studies Being as Being.[3]

Aristotle on Rhetoric and Poetry

In the realm of productive sciences Aristotle wrote two works, the *Rhetoric* and the *Poetics*, designed to assist barristers and playwrights in their respective tasks. Rhetoric, Aristotle says, is the discipline that indicates in any given case the possible means of persuasion: it is not restricted to a particular field, but is topic-neutral. There are three bases of persuasion by the spoken word: the character of the speaker, the mood of the audience, and the argument (sound or spurious) of the speech itself. So the student of rhetoric must be able to reason logically, to evaluate character, and to understand the emotions (1. 2. 1358ᵃ1–1360ᵇ3).

Aristotle wrote more instructively about logic and character in other treatises, but the second book of the *Rhetoric* contains his fullest account of human emotions. Emotions, he says, are feelings that alter people's judgements, and they are accompanied by pain and pleasure. He takes each major emotion in turn, offering a definition of the emotion and a list of its objects and causes. Anger, for instance, he defines as a desire, accompanied by pain, for what appears to be revenge for what appears to be an unmerited slight upon oneself or one's friends (2. 2. 1378ᵃ32–4). He gives a long list of the kinds of people who make us angry: those who mock us, for instance, or those who stop us drinking when we are thirsty, or those who get in our way at work.

[3] See Ch. 5 below.

Also those who speak ill of us, and show contempt for us, in respect of the things we most care about. Thus those who seek a reputation as philosophers get angry with those who show disdain for their philosophy; those who pride themselves upon their appearance get angry with those who disparage it, and so on. We feel particularly angry if we believe that, either in fact or in popular belief, we are totally or largely lacking in the respective qualities. For when we are convinced that we excel in the qualities for which we are mocked, we can ignore the mockery. (2. 2. 1379^{a}32–^{b}1)

Aristotle takes us on a detailed tour of the emotions of anger, hatred, fear, shame, pity, indignation, envy, and jealousy. In each case his treatment is clear and systematic, and often shows—as in the above passage—acute psychological insight.

The *Poetics*, unlike the *Rhetoric*, has been very widely read throughout history. Only its first book survives, a treatment of epic and tragic poetry. The second book, on comedy, is lost. Umberto Eco, in *The Name of the Rose*, wove a dramatic fiction around its imagined survival and then destruction in a fourteenth-century abbey.

To understand Aristotle's message in the *Poetics* one must know something of Plato's attitude to poetry. In the second and third books of the *Republic* Homer is attacked for misrepresenting the gods and for encouraging debased emotions. The dramatic representations of the tragedians, too, are attacked as deceptive and debasing. In the tenth book the Theory of Ideas provides the basis for a further, and more fundamental, attack on the poets. Material objects are imperfect copies of the truly real Ideas; artistic representations of material objects are therefore at two removes from reality, being imitations of imitations (597e). Drama corrupts by appealing to the lower parts of our nature, encouraging us to indulge in weeping and laughter (605d–6c). Dramatic poets must be kept away from the ideal city: they should be anointed with myrrh, crowned with laurel, and sent on their way (398b).

One of Aristotle's aims was to resolve this quarrel between poetry and philosophy. Imitation, he says, so far from being the degrading activity that Plato describes, is something natural to humans from childhood. It is one of the features that makes men superior to animals, since it vastly increases their scope for learning. Secondly, representation brings a delight all of its own: we enjoy and admire paintings of objects which in themselves would annoy or disgust us (*Po.* 4. 1448^{b}5–24).

Aristotle offers a detailed analysis of the nature of tragic drama. He defines tragedy in the following terms.

A tragedy is a representation of a grand, complete, and significant action, in language embellished appropriately in the different parts of the work, in dramatic, not narrative form, with episodes arousing pity and fear so as to achieve purification (*katharsis*) of these emotions. (6. 1449^{b}24 ff.)

No one is quite sure what Aristotle meant by *katharsis*, or purification. Perhaps what he wanted to teach is that watching tragedy helps us to put our own sorrows and worries into perspective, as we observe the catastrophes that have overtaken people who were far superior to the likes of ourselves. Pity and fear, the emotions to be purified, are most easily aroused, he says, if the tragedy exhibits people as the victims of hatred and murder where they could most expect to be loved and cherished. That is why so many tragedies concern feuds within a single family (14. 1453^{b}1–21).

Six things, Aristotle says, are necessary for a tragedy: plot, character, diction, thought, spectacle, and melody (6. 1450^{a}11 ff.). It is the first two of these that chiefly interest him. Stage setting and musical accompaniment are dispensable accessories: what is great in a tragedy can be appreciated from a mere reading of the text. Thought and diction are more important: it is the thoughts expressed by the characters that arouse emotion in the hearer, and if they are to do so successfully they must be presented convincingly by the actors. But it is character and plot that really bring out the genius of a tragic poet, and Aristotle devotes a long chapter to character, and no less than five chapters to plot.

The main character or tragic hero must be neither supremely good nor supremely bad: he should be a person of rank who is basically good, but comes to grief through some great error (*hamartia*). A woman may have the kind of goodness necessary to be a tragic heroine, and even a slave may be a tragic subject. Whatever kind of person is the protagonist, it is important that he or she should have the qualities appropriate to them, and should be consistent throughout the drama (15. 1454^{a}15 ff.). Every one of the dramatis personae should possess some good features; what they do should be in character, and what happens to them should be a necessary or probable outcome of their behaviour.

The most important element of all is plot: the characters are created for the sake of the plot, and not the other way round. The plot must be a self-contained story with a clearly marked beginning, middle, and end; it must be sufficiently short and simple for the spectator to hold all its details in mind. Tragedy must have a unity. You do not make a tragedy by stringing together a set of episodes connected only by a common hero; rather, there must be a single significant action on which the whole plot turns (8. 1451^{a}21–9).

In a typical tragedy the story gradually gets more complicated until a turning point is reached, which Aristotle calls a 'reversal' (*peripeteia*). That is the moment at which the apparently fortunate hero falls to disaster, perhaps through a 'revelation' (*anagnorisis*), namely his discovery of some crucial but hitherto unknown piece of information (15. 1454^{b}19). After the reversal comes the denouement, in which the complications earlier introduced are gradually unravelled (18. 1455^{b}24 ff.).

These observations are illustrated by constant reference to actual Greek plays, in particular to Sophocles' tragedy *King Oedipus*. Oedipus, at the beginning of the play, enjoys prosperity and reputation. He is basically a good man, but has the fatal flaw of impetuosity. This vice makes him kill a stranger in a scuffle, and marry a bride without due diligence. The 'revelation' that the man he killed was his father and the woman he married was his mother leads to the 'reversal' of his fortune, as he is banished from his kingdom and blinds himself in shame and remorse.

Aristotle's theory of tragedy enables him to respond to Plato's complaint that playwrights, like other artists, were only imitators of everyday life, which was itself only an imitation of the real world of the Ideas. His answer is given when he compares drama with history.

From what has been said it is clear that the poet's job is to describe not something that has actually happened, but something that might well happen, that is to say something that is possible because it is necessary or likely. The difference between a historian and a poet is not a matter of prose v. verse—you might turn Herodotus into metre and it would still be history. It is rather in this matter of writing what happens rather than what might happen. For this reason poetry is more philosophical and more important than history; for poetry tells us of the universal, history tells us only of the particular. (9. 1451^b5–9)

What Aristotle says here of poetry and drama could of course be said of other kinds of creative writing. Much of what happens to people in everyday life is a matter of sheer accident; only in fiction can we see the working out of character and action into their natural consequences.

Aristotle's Ethical Treatises

If we turn from the productive sciences to the practical sciences, we find that Aristotle's contribution was made by his writings on moral philosophy and political theory. Three treatises of moral philosophy have been handed down in the corpus: the *Nicomachean Ethics* (*NE*) in ten books, the *Eudemian Ethics* (*EE*) in seven books, and the *Magna Moralia* in two books. These texts are highly interesting to anyone who is interested in the development of Aristotle's thought. Whereas in the physical and metaphysical treatises it is possible to detect traces of revision and rewriting, it is only in the case of ethics that we have Aristotle's doctrine on the same topics presented in three different and more or less complete courses. There is, however, no consensus on the explanation of this phenomenon.

In the early centuries after Aristotle's death no great use was made of his ethical treatises by later writers; but the *EE* is more often cited than the *NE*, and the *NE* does not appear as such in the earliest catalogues of his *Works*. Indeed there are traces of some doubt whether the *NE* is a genuine work of Aristotle or perhaps a production of his son Nicomachus. However, from the time of the commentator Aspasius in the second century AD it has been almost universally agreed that the *NE* is not only genuine but also the most important of the three works. Throughout the Middle Ages, and since the revival of classical scholarship, it has been treated as *the* Ethics of Aristotle, and indeed the most generally popular of all his surviving works.

Very different views have been taken of the other works. While the *NE* has long appealed to a wide readership, the *EE*, even among Aristotelian scholars, has never appealed to more than a handful of fanatics. In the nineteenth century it was treated as spurious, and republished under the name of Aristotle's pupil Eudemus of Rhodes. In the twentieth century scholars have commonly followed Werner Jaeger[4] in regarding it as a genuine but immature work, superseded by an *NE* written in the Lyceum period. As for the *Magna Moralia*, some scholars followed Jaeger in rejecting it as post-Aristotelian, whereas others have argued hotly that it is a genuine work, the earliest of all three treatises.

There is a further problem about the relationship between the *NE* and the *EE*. In the manuscript tradition three books make a double appearance: once as books 5, 6, and 7 of the *NE*, and once as books 4, 5, and 6 of the *EE*. It is a mistake to try to settle the relationship between the *NE* and the *EE* without first deciding which was the original home of the common books. It can be shown on both philosophical and stylometric grounds that these books are much closer to the *EE* than to the *NE*. Once they are restored to the *EE* the case for regarding the *EE* as an immature and inferior work collapses: nothing remains, for example, of Jaeger's argument that the *EE* is closer to Plato, and therefore earlier, than the *NE*. Moreover, internal historical allusions suggest that the disputed books, and therefore now the *EE*, belong to the Lyceum period.

There are problems concerning the coherence of the *NE* itself. At the beginning of the twentieth century the Aristotelian Thomas Case, in a celebrated article in the eleventh edition of the *Encyclopaedia Britannica*, suggested that 'the probability is that the *Nicomachean Ethics* is a collection of separate discourses worked up into a tolerably systematic treatise.' This remains highly probable. The differences between the *NE* and the *EE* do not admit of a simple chronological solution: it may be that some of the discourses worked up into the *NE* antedate, and others postdate, the *EE*, which is itself a more coherent whole. The stylistic differences that separate the *NE* not only from the *EE* but also from almost all Aristotle's other works may be explicable by the ancient tradition that the *NE* was edited by Nicomachus, while the *EE*, along with some of Aristotle's other works, was edited by Eudemus. As for the *Magna Moralia*, while it follows closely the line of thought of the *EE*, it contains a number of misunderstandings of its doctrine. This is easily explained if it consists of notes made by a student at the Lyceum during Aristotle's delivery of a course of lectures resembling the *EE*.[5]

---

[4] *Aristotle: Fundamentals of the History of his Development*, trans. R. Robinson (Oxford: Clarendon Press, 1948).

[5] The account here given of the relationship between the Aristotelian ethical treatises is controversial. I have expounded and defended it in *The Aristotelian Ethics* (Oxford: Clarendon Press, 1978) and, with corrections and modifications, in *Aristotle on the Perfect Life* (Oxford: Clarendon Press, 1992).

The content of the three treatises is, in general, very similar. The *NE* covers much the same ground as Plato's *Republic*, and with some exaggeration one could say that Aristotle's moral philosophy is Plato's moral philosophy with the Theory of Ideas ripped out. The Idea of the Good, Aristotle says, cannot be the supreme good of which ethics treats, if only because ethics is a practical science, about what is within human power to achieve, whereas an everlasting and unchanging Idea of the Good could only be of theoretical interest.

In place of the Idea of the Good, Aristotle offers happiness (*eudaimonia*) as the supreme good with which ethics is concerned, for, like Plato, he sees an intimate connection between living virtuously and living happily. In all the ethical treatises a happy life is a life of virtuous activity, and each of them offers an analysis of the concept of virtue and a classification of virtues of different types. One class is that of the moral virtues, such as courage, temperance, and liberality, that constantly appeared in Plato's ethical discussions. The other class is that of intellectual virtues: here Aristotle makes a much sharper distinction than Plato ever did between the intellectual virtue of wisdom, which governs ethical behaviour, and the intellectual virtue of understanding, which is expressed in scientific endeavour and contemplation. The principal difference between the *NE* and the *EE* is that in the former Aristotle regards perfect happiness as constituted solely by the activity of philosophical contemplation, whereas in the latter it consists of the harmonious exercise of all the virtues, intellectual and moral.[6]

Aristotle's Political Theory

Even in the *EE* it is 'the service and contemplation of God' that sets the standard for the appropriate exercise of the moral virtues, and in the *NE* this contemplation is described as a superhuman activity of a divine part of ourselves. Aristotle's final word here is that in spite of being mortal we must make ourselves immortal as far as we can. When we turn from the *Ethics* to their sequel, the *Politics*, we come down to earth. 'Man is a political animal', we are told: humans are creatures of flesh and blood, rubbing shoulders with each other in cities and communities.

Like his work in zoology, Aristotle's political studies combine observation and theory. Diogenes Laertius tells us that he collected the constitutions of 158 states—no doubt aided by research assistants in the Lyceum. One of these, *The Constitution of Athens*, though not handed down as part of the Aristotelian corpus, was found on papyrus in 1891. In spite of some stylistic differences from other works, it is now generally regarded as authentic. In a codicil to the *NE* that reads like a preface to the *Politics*, Aristotle says that, having investigated previous

---

[6] Aristotle's ethical teaching is explained in detail in Ch. 8 below.

writings on political theory, he will inquire, in the light of the constitutions collected, what makes good government and what makes bad government, what factors are favourable or unfavourable to the preservation of a constitution, and what constitution the best state should adopt (*NE* 10. 9. 1181^{b}12–23).

The *Politics* itself was probably not written at a single stretch, and here as elsewhere there is probably an overlap and interplay between the records of observation and the essays in theory. The structure of the book as we have it corresponds reasonably well to the *NE* programme: books 1–3 contain a general theory of the state, and a critique of earlier writers; books 4–6 contain an account of various forms of constitution, three tolerable (monarchy, aristocracy, polity) and three intolerable (tyranny, oligarchy, and democracy); books 7 and 8 are devoted to the ideal form of constitution. Once again, the order of the discourses in the corpus probably differs from the order of their composition, but scholars have not reached agreement on the original chronology.

Aristotle begins by saying that the state is the highest kind of community, aiming at the highest of goods. The most primitive communities are families of men and women, masters and slaves. He seems to regard the division between master and slave as no less natural than the division between men and women, though he complains that it is barbaric to treat women and slaves alike (1. 2. 1252^{a}25–^{b}6). Families combine to make a village, and several villages combine to make a state, which is the first self-sufficient community, and is just as natural as is the family (1. 2. 1253^{a}2). Indeed, though later than the family in time, the state is prior by nature, as an organic whole like the human body is prior to its organic parts like hands and feet. Without law and justice, man is the most savage of animals. Someone who cannot live in a state is a beast; someone who has no need of a state must be a god. The foundation of the state was the greatest of benefactions, because only within a state can human beings fulfil their potential (1. 2. 1253^{a}25–35).

Among the earlier writers whom Aristotle cites and criticizes Plato is naturally prominent. Much of the second book of the *Politics* is devoted to criticism of the *Republic* and the *Laws*. As in the *Ethics* there is no Idea of the Good, so in the *Politics* there are no philosopher kings. Aristotle thinks that Platonic communism will bring nothing but trouble: the use of property should be shared, but its ownership should be private. That way owners can take pride in their possessions and get pleasure out of sharing them with others or giving them away. Aristotle defends the traditional family against the proposal that women should be held in common, and he frowns even on the limited military and official role assigned to women in the *Laws*. Over and over again he describes Plato's proposals as impractical; the root of his error, he thinks, is that he tries to make the state too uniform. The diversity of different kinds of citizen is essential, and life in a city should not be like life in a barracks (2. 3. 1261^{a}10–31).

However, when Aristotle presents his own account of political constitutions he makes copious use of Platonic suggestions. There remains a constant difference between the two writers, namely that Aristotle makes frequent reference to concrete examples to illustrate his theoretical points. But the conceptual structure is often very similar. The following passage from book 3, for instance, echoes the later books of the *Republic*.

The government, that is to say the supreme authority in a state, must be in the hands of one, or of a few, or of the many. The rightful true forms of government, therefore, are ones where the one, or the few, or the many, govern with a view to the common interest; governments that rule with a view to the private interest, whether of the one, or the few, or the many, are perversions. Those who belong to a state, if they are truly to be called citizens, must share in its benefits. Government by a single person, if it aims at the common interest, we are accustomed to call 'monarchy'; similar government by a minority we call 'aristocracy', either because the rulers are the best men, or because it aims at the best interests of the state and the community. When it is the majority that governs in the common interest we call it a 'polity', using a word which is also a generic term for a constitution . . . Of each of these forms of government there exists a perversion. The perversion of monarchy is tyranny; that of aristocracy is oligarchy; that of polity is democracy. For tyranny is a monarchy exercised solely for the benefit of the monarch, oligarchy has in view only the interests of the wealthy, and democracy the interests only of the poorer classes. None of these aims at the common good of all. (3. 6. 1279^{a}26–^{b}10)

Aristotle goes on to a detailed evaluation of constitutions of these various forms. He does so on the basis of his view of the essence of the state. A state, he tells us, is a society of humans sharing in a common perception of what is good and evil, just and unjust; its purpose is to provide a good and happy life for its citizens. If a community contains an individual or family of outstanding excellence, then monarchy is the best constitution. But such a case is very rare, and the risk of miscarriage is great: for monarchy corrupts into tyranny, which is the worst of all constitutions. Aristocracy, in theory, is the next best constitution after monarchy, but in practice Aristotle preferred a kind of constitutional democracy, for what he called 'polity' is a state in which rich and poor respect each others' rights, and in which the best-qualified citizens rule with the consent of all the citizens (4. 8. 1293^{b}30 ff.). The corruption of this is what Aristotle calls 'democracy', namely, anarchic mob rule. Bad as democracy is, it is in Aristotle's view the least bad of the perverse forms of government.

At the present time we are familiar with the division of government into three branches: the legislature, the executive, and the judiciary. The essentials of this system is spelt out by Aristotle, though he distributes the powers in a somewhat different way from, say, the US constitution. All constitutions, he tells us, have three elements: the deliberative, the official, and the judicial. The deliberative element has authority in matters of war and peace, in making and unmaking alliances; it passes laws, controls the carrying out of judicial sentences, and audits the accounts of officers. The official element deals with the appointment of ministers and civil servants, ranging from priests through ambassadors to the regulators of female affairs. The judicial element consists of the courts of civil and criminal law (4. 12. 1296^{b}13–1301^{a}12).

Two elements of Aristotle's political teaching affected political institutions for many centuries: his justification of slavery and his condemnation of usury. Some people, Aristotle tells us, think that the rule of masters over slaves is contrary to nature, and is therefore unjust. They are quite wrong: a slave is someone who is by nature not his own but another man's property. Slavery is one example of a general truth, that from their birth some people are marked out for rule and others to be ruled (1. 3. 1253^{b}20–3; 5. 1254^{b}22–4).

In practice much slavery is unjust, Aristotle agrees. There is a custom that the spoils of war belong to the victors, and this includes the right to make slaves of the vanquished. But many wars are unjust, and victories in such wars entail no right to enslave the defeated. Some people, however, are so inferior and brutish that it is better for them to be under the rule of a kindly master than to be left to their own devices. Slaves, for Aristotle, are living tools—and on this basis he is willing to grant that if non-living tools could achieve the same purpose there would be no need for slavery. 'If every instrument could achieve its own work, obeying or anticipating the will of others, like the statues of Daedalus . . . if the shuttle could weave and the plectrum pluck the lyre in a similar manner, overseers would not need servants, nor masters slaves' (1. 4. 1253^{b}35–54^{a}1). So perhaps, in an age of automation, Aristotle would no longer defend slavery.

Though not himself an aristocrat, Aristotle had an aristocratic disdain for commerce. Our possessions, he says, have two uses, proper and improper. The proper use of a shoe, for instance, is to wear it: to exchange it for other goods or for money is an improper use (1. 9. 1257^{a}9–10). There is nothing wrong with basic barter for necessities, but there is nothing natural about trade in luxuries, as there is in farming. In the operation of retail trade money plays an important part, and money too has a proper and an improper use.

The most hated sort of wealth-getting is usury, which makes a profit out of money itself, rather than from its natural purpose, for money was intended to be used for exchange, not to increase at interest. It got the name 'interest' (*tokos*), which means the birth of money from money, because an offspring resembles its parent. For this reason, of all the modes of getting wealth this is the most unnatural. (1. 10. 1258^{b}5–7)

Aristotle's hierarchical preference places farmers at the top, bankers at the bottom, with merchants in between. His attitude to usury was one source of the prohibition, throughout medieval Christendom, of the charging of interest even at a modest rate. 'When did friendship', Antonio asks Shylock in *The Merchant of Venice*, 'take a breed for barren metal of his friend?'

One of the most striking features of Aristotle's *Politics* is the almost total absence of any mention of Alexander or Macedon. Like a modern member of Amnesty International, Aristotle comments on the rights and wrongs of every country but his own. His own ideal state is described as having no more than a hundred thousand citizens, small enough for them all to know one another and to take their share in judicial and political office. It is very different from Alexander's empire. When Aristotle says that monarchy is the best constitution if a community contains a person or family of outstanding excellence, there is a pointed absence of reference to the royal family of Macedon.

Indeed, during the years of the Lyceum, relations between the world-conqueror and his former tutor seem to have cooled. Alexander became more and more megalomaniac and finally proclaimed himself divine. Aristotle's nephew Callisthenes led the opposition to the king's demand, in 327, that Greeks should prostrate themselves before him in adoration. He was falsely implicated in a plot, and executed. The magnanimous and magnificent man who is the hero of the earlier books of the *NE* has some of the grandiose traits of Alexander. In the *EE*, however, the alleged virtues of magnanimity and magnificence are downgraded, and gentleness and dignity take centre stage.[7]

Aristotle's Cosmology

The greater part of Aristotle's surviving works deal not with productive or practical sciences, but with the theoretical sciences. We have already considered his biological works: it is time to give some account of his physics and chemistry. His contributions to these disciplines were much less impressive than his researches in the life sciences. While his zoological writings were still found impressive by Darwin, his physics was superannuated by the sixth century AD.

In works such as *On Generation and Corruption* and *On the Heavens* Aristotle bequeathed to his successors a world-picture that included many features inherited from the Presocratics. He took over the four elements of Empedocles, earth, water, air, and fire, each characterized by the possession of a unique pair of the properties heat, cold, wetness, and dryness: earth being cold and dry, air being hot and wet, and so forth. Each element had its natural place in an ordered cosmos, and each element had an innate tendency to move towards this natural place. Thus, earthy solids naturally fell, while fire, unless prevented, rose ever higher. Each such motion was natural to its element; other motions were possible, but were 'violent'. (We preserve a relic of Aristotle's distinction when we contrast natural with violent death.)

In his physical treatises Aristotle offers explanations of an enormous number of natural phenomena in terms of the elements, their basic properties, and their

---

[7] See my *The Aristotelian Ethics*, 233.

natural motion. The philosophical concepts which he employs in constructing these explanations include an array of different notions of causation (material, formal, efficient, and final), and an analysis of change as the passage from potentiality to actuality, whether (as in substantial change) from matter to form or (as in accidental change) from one to another quality of a substance. These technical notions, which he employed in such an astonishing variety of contexts, will be examined in detail in later chapters.

Aristotle's vision of the cosmos owes much to his Presocratic precursors and to Plato's *Timaeus*. The earth was in the centre of the universe: around it a succession of concentric crystalline spheres carried the moon, the sun, and the planets in their journeys around the visible sky. The heavenly bodies were not compounds of the four terrestrial elements, but were made of a superior fifth element or quintessence. They had souls as well as bodies: living supernatural intellects, guiding their travels through the cosmos. These intellects were movers which were themselves in motion, and behind them, Aristotle argued, there must be a source of movement not itself in motion. The only way in which an unchanging, eternal mover could cause motion in other beings was by attracting them as an object of love, an attraction which they express by their perfect circular motion. It is thus that Dante, in the final lines of his *Paradiso*, finds his own will, like a smoothly rotating wheel, caught up in the love that moves the sun and all the other stars.

Even the best of Aristotle's scientific work has now only a historical interest. The abiding value of treatises such as his *Physics* is in the philosophical analyses of some of the basic concepts that pervade the physics of different eras, such as space, time, causation, and determinism. These are examined in detail in Chapter 5. For Aristotle biology and psychology were parts of natural philosophy no less than physics and chemistry, since they too studied different forms of *physis*, or nature. The biological works we have already looked at; the psychological works will be examined more closely in Chapter 7.

The Aristotelian corpus, in addition to the systematic scientific treatises, contains a massive collection of occasional jottings on scientific topics, the *Problems*. From its structure this appears to be a commonplace book in which Aristotle wrote down provisional answers to questions that were put to him by his students or correspondents. Because the questions are grouped rather haphazardly, and often appear several times—and are sometimes given different answers—it seems unlikely that they were generated by Aristotle himself, whether as a single series or over a lifetime. But the collection contains many fascinating details that throw insight into the workings of his omnivorous intellect.

Some of the questions are the kind of thing a patient might bring to a doctor. Ought drugs to be used, rather than surgery, for sores in the armpits and groin? (1. 34. 863^{a}21). Is it true that purslane mixed with salt stops inflammation of the gums? (1. 38. 863^{b}12). Does cabbage really cure a hangover? (3. 17. 873^{b}1). Why is it difficult to have sex under water? (4. 14. 878ª35). Other questions and answers make us see Aristotle more in the role of agony aunt. How should one cope with the after-effects of eating garlic? (13. 2. 907ᵇ28–908ª10). How does one prevent biscuit from becoming hard? (21. 12. 928ª12). Why do drunken men kiss old women they would never kiss when sober? (30. 15. 953ᵇ15). Is it right to punish more seriously thefts from a public place than thefts from a private house? (29. 14. 952ª16). More seriously, why is it more terrible to kill a woman than a man, although the male is naturally superior to the female? (29. 11. 951ª12).

A whole book of the *Problems* (26) is devoted essentially to weather forecasting. Other books contain questions that simply reflect general curiosity. Why does the noise of a saw being sharpened set our teeth on edge? (7. 5. 886ᵇ10). Why do humans not have manes? (10. 25. 893ᵇ17). Why do non-human animals not sneeze or squint? (Don't they?) (10. 50. 896ᵇ5; 54. 897ª1). Why do barbarians and Greeks alike count up to ten? (15. 3. 910ᵇ23). Why is a flute better than a lyre as an accompaniment to a solo voice? (19. 43. 922ª1). Very often, the *Problems* ask 'Why is such and such the case?' when a more appropriate question would have been '*Is* such and such the case?' For instance, Why do fishermen have red hair? (37. 2. 966ᵇ25). Why does a large choir keep time better than a small one? (19. 22. 919ª36).

The *Problems* let us see Aristotle with his hair down, rather like the table talk of later writers. One of his questions is particularly endearing to those who may have found it hard to read their way through his more difficult works: Why is it that some people, if they begin to read a serious book, are overcome by sleep even against their will? (18. 1. 916ᵇ1).

The Legacy of Aristotle and Plato

When Alexander the Great died in 323, democratic Athens became uncomfortable even for an anti-imperialist Macedonian. Saying that he did not wish the city that had executed Socrates 'to sin twice against philosophy', Aristotle escaped to Chalcis, where he died in the following year. His will, which survives, makes thoughtful provision for a large number of friends and dependants. His library was left to Theophrastus, his successor as head of the Lyceum. His own papers were vast in size and scope—those that survive today total around a million words, and it is said that we possess only one-fifth of his output. As we have seen, in addition to philosophical treatises on logic, metaphysics, ethics, aesthetics, and politics, they included historical works on constitutions, theatre and sport, and scientific works on botany, zoology, biology, psychology, chemistry, meteorology, astronomy, and cosmology.

Since the Renaissance it has been traditional to regard the Academy and the Lyceum as two opposite poles of philosophy. Plato, according to this tradition, was idealistic, utopian, other-worldly; Aristotle was realistic, utilitarian, commonsensical.

Thus, in Raphael's *School of Athens* Plato, wearing the colours of the volatile elements air and fire, points heavenwards; Aristotle, clothed in watery blue and earthy green, has his feet firmly on the ground. 'Every man is born an Aristotelian or a Platonist,' wrote S. T. Coleridge. 'They are the two classes of men, besides which it is next to impossible to conceive a third.' The philosopher Gilbert Ryle in the twentieth century improved on Coleridge. Men could be divided into two classes on the basis of four dichotomies: green versus blue, sweet versus savoury, cats versus dogs, Plato versus Aristotle. 'Tell me your preference on one of these pairs', Ryle used to say, 'and I will tell you your preference on the other three.'[8]

In fact, as we have already seen and will see in greater detail later, the doctrines that Plato and Aristotle share are more important than those that divide them. Many post-Renaissance historians of ideas have been less perceptive than the many commentators in late antiquity who saw it as their duty to construct a harmonious concord between the two greatest philosophers of the ancient world.

It is sometimes said that a philosopher should be judged by the importance of the questions he raises, not the correctness of the answers he gives. If that is so, then Plato has an uncontestable claim to pre-eminence as a philosopher. He was the first to pose questions of great profundity, many of which remain open questions in philosophy today. But Aristotle too can claim a significant contribution to the intellectual patrimony of the world. For it was he who invented the concept of Science as we understand it today and as it has been understood since the Renaissance.

First, he is the first person whose surviving works show detailed observations of natural phenomena. Secondly, he was the first philosopher to have a sound grasp of the relationship between observation and theory in scientific method. Thirdly, he identified and classified different scientific disciplines and explored their relationships to each other: the very concept of a distinct discipline is due to him. Fourthly, he is the first professor to have organized his lectures into courses, and to have taken trouble over their appropriate place in a syllabus (cf. *Pol.* 1. 10. 1258ª20). Fifthly, his Lyceum was the first research institute of which we have any detailed knowledge in which a number of scholars and investigators joined in collaborative inquiry and documentation. Sixthly, and not least important, he was the first person in history to build up a research library—not simply a handful of books for his own bookshelf, but a systematic collection to be used by his colleagues and to be handed on to posterity.[9] For all these reasons, every academic scientist in the world today is in Aristotle's debt. He well deserved the title he was given by Dante: 'the master of those who know'.

---

[8] Preference for an item on the left of a pair was supposed to go with preference for the other leftward items, and similarly for rightward preferences.

[9] See L. Casson, *Libraries in the Ancient World* (New Haven: Yale University Press, 2001), 28–9.

Aristotle's School

Theophrastus (372–287), Aristotle's ingenious successor as head of the Lyceum, continued his master's researches in several ways. He wrote extensively on botany, a discipline that Aristotle had touched only lightly. He improved on Aristotle's modal logic, and anticipated some later Stoic innovations. He disagreed with some fundamental principles of Aristotle's cosmology, such as the nature of place and the need for a motionless mover. Like his master, he wrote copiously, and the mere list of the titles of his works takes up sixteen pages in the Loeb edition of his life by Diogenes Laertius. They include essays on vertigo, on honey, on hair, on jokes, and on the eruption of Etna. The best known of his surviving works is a book entitled *Characters*, modelled on Aristotle's delineation in his *Ethics* of individual virtues and vices, but sketching them with greater refinement and with a livelier wit. He was a diligent historian of philosophy, and the part of his doxography that survives, *On the Senses*, is one of our main sources for Presocratic theories of sensation.

One of Theophrastus' pupils, Demetrius of Phaleron, was an adviser to one of Alexander's generals, Ptolemy, who made himself king of Egypt in 305. It is possible that it was he who suggested the creation in the new city of Alexandria of a library modelled on that of Aristotle, a project that was carried out by Ptolemy's son Ptolemy II Philadelphus. The history of Aristotle's own library is obscure. On Theophrastus' death it seems to have been inherited not by the next head of the Lyceum, the physicist Strato, but by Theophrastus' nephew Neleus of Skepsis, one of the last surviving pupils of Aristotle himself. Neleus' heirs are said to have hidden the books in a cave in order to prevent them from being confiscated by agents of King Eumenes, who was building up a library at Pergamon to rival that of Alexandria. Rescued by a bibliophile and taken to Athens, the story goes, the books were confiscated by the Roman general Sulla when he captured the city in 86 BC, and shipped to Rome, where they were finally edited and published by Andronicus of Rhodes around the middle of the first century BC (Strabo 608–9; Plutarch, *Sulla* 26).[10]

Every detail of this story has been called in question by one or another scholar,[11] but if true it would account for the oblivion that overtook Aristotle's writings between the time of Theophrastus and that of Cicero. It has been well said that 'If

---

[10] Puzzlingly, our best ancient catalogue of the Andronican edition appears to have been made by a librarian at Alexandria. Is it possible that Mark Antony acquired the corpus from an heir of the proscribed Sulla and shipped them off to Cleopatra to fill the gaps in her recently destroyed library, just as her earlier lover Julius Caesar had pillaged the Pergamum library for her benefit?

[11] See J. Barnes, in J. Barnes and M. Griffin, *Philosophia Togata*, vol. ii (Oxford: Clarendon Press, 1997), 1–23.

Aristotle could have returned to Athens in 272 BC, on the fiftieth anniversary of his death, he would hardly have recognized it as the intellectual milieu in which he had taught and researched for much of his life.'[12]

It was not that philosophy at that date was dormant in Athens: far from it. Though the Lyceum under Strato was a shadow of itself, and the Platonic Academy under its new head Arcesilaus had given up metaphysics in favour of a narrow scepticism, there were two flourishing new schools of philosophy in the city. The best-known philosophers in Athens were members neither of the Academy nor of the Lyceum, but were the founders of these new schools: Epicurus, who established a school known as The Garden, and Zeno of Citium, whose followers were called Stoics because he taught in the Stoa, or painted portico.

Epicurus

Epicurus was born into a family of Athenian expatriates in Samos, and paid a brief visit to Athens in the last year of Aristotle's life. During early travels he studied under a follower of Democritus, and established more than one school in the Greek islands. In 306 he set up house in Athens and lived there until his death in 271. His followers in the Garden included women and slaves; they lived in seclusion and ate simple fare. He wrote 300 books, we are told, but all that survive intact are three letters and two groups of maxims. His philosophy of nature is set out in a letter to Herodotus and a letter to Pythocles; in the third letter, to Menoecus, he summarizes his moral teaching. The first set of maxims, forty in number, has been preserved, like the three letters, in the life of Epicurus by Diogenes Laertius: it is called *Kyriai Doxai*, or major doctrines. Eighty-one similar aphorisms were discovered in a Vatican manuscript in 1888. Fragments from Epicurus' lost treatise *On Nature* were buried in volcanic ash at Herculaneum when Vesuvius erupted in AD 79. Painstaking efforts to unroll and decipher them, begun in 1800, continue to the present day. But for most of our knowledge of his teachings, however, we depend on the surviving writings of his followers, especially a much later writer, the Latin poet Lucretius.

The aim of Epicurus' philosophy is to make happiness possible by removing the fear of death, which is the greatest obstacle to tranquillity. Men struggle for wealth and power so as to postpone death; they throw themselves into frenzied activity so that they can forget its inevitability. It is religion that causes us to fear death, by holding out the prospect of suffering after death. But this is an illusion. The terrors held out by religion are fairy tales, which we must give up in favour of a scientific account of the world.

---

[12] Introd. to LS, 1.

This scientific account is taken mainly from Democritus' atomism. Nothing comes into being from nothing: the basic units of the world are everlasting, unchanging, indivisible units or atoms. These, infinite in number, move about in the void, which is empty and infinite space: if there were no void, movement would be impossible. This motion had no beginning, and initially all atoms move downwards at constant and equal speed. From time to time, however, they swerve and collide, and it is from the collision of atoms that everything in heaven and earth has come into being. The swerve of the atoms allows scope for human freedom, even though their motions are blind and purposeless. Atoms have no properties other than shape, weight, and size. The properties of perceptible bodies are not illusions, but they are supervenient on the basic properties of atoms. There is an infinite number of worlds, some like and some unlike our own (Letter to Herodotus, D.L. 10. 38–45).

Like everything else, the soul consists of atoms, differing from other atoms only in being smaller and subtler; these are dispersed at death and the soul ceases to perceive (Letter to Herodotus, D.L. 10. 63–7). The gods too are built out of atoms, but they live in a less turbulent region, immune to dissolution. They live happy lives, untroubled by concern for human beings. For that reason belief in providence is superstition, and religious rituals a waste of time (Letter to Menoecus, D.L. 10. 123–5). Since we are free agents, thanks to the atomic swerve, we are masters of our own fate: the gods neither impose necessity nor interfere with our choices.

Epicurus believed that the senses were reliable sources of information, which operate by transmitting images from external bodies into the atoms of our soul. Sense-impressions are never, in themselves, false, though we may make false judgements on the basis of genuine appearances. If appearances conflict (if, for instance, something looks smooth but feels rough) then the mind must give judgement between these competing witnesses.

Pleasure, for Epicurus, is the beginning and end of the happy life. This does not mean, however, that Epicurus was an epicure. His life and that of his followers was far from luxurious: a good piece of cheese, he said, was as good as a feast. Though a theoretical hedonist, in practice he attached importance to a distinction he made between different types of pleasure. There is one kind of pleasure that is given by the satisfaction of our desires for food, drink, and sex, but it is an inferior kind of pleasure, because it is bound up with pain. The desire these pleasures satisfy is itself painful, and its satisfaction leads to a renewal of desire. The pleasures to be aimed at are quiet pleasures such as those of private friendship (Letter to Menoecus, D.L. 10. 27–32).

To his last, Epicurus insisted that for a philosopher pleasure, in any circumstances, could outweigh pain. On his deathbed he wrote the following letter to his friend Idomeneus: 'I write this to you on the blissful day that is the last of my life. Strangury and dysentery have set in, with the greatest possible intensity of pain. I counterbalance them by the joy I have in the memory of our past conversations'

(D.L. 10. 22). He lived up to his conviction that death, though inescapable, is, if we take a truly philosophical view of it, not an evil.

Stoicism

Stoics, like Epicureans, sought tranquillity, but by a different route. The founder of Stoicism was Zeno of Citium (334–262 BC). Zeno was born in Cyprus, but migrated to Athens in 313. He read Xenophon's memoir of Socrates, which gave him a passion for philosophy. He was told that the nearest contemporary equivalent of Socrates was Crates the Cynic. Cynicism was not a set of philosophical doctrines, but a way of life expressing contempt for wealth and disdain for conventional propriety. Its founder was Diogenes of Sinope, who lived like a dog ('cynic' means 'dog-like') in a tub for a kennel, wearing coarse clothes and subsisting on alms. A contemporary of Plato, for whom he had no great respect, Diogenes was famous for his snub to Alexander the Great. When the great man visited him and asked, 'What can I do for you', Diogenes replied, 'You can move out of my light' (D.L. 6. 38). Crates, impressed by Diogenes, gave his wealth to the poor and imitated his bohemian lifestyle; but he was less misanthropic, and had a keen sense of humour that he expressed in poetic satire.

Zeno was Crates' pupil for a time, but he did not become a cynic and drop out of society, though he avoided formal dinners and was fond of basking in the sun. After some years as a student of the Academy, he set up his own school in the Stoa Poikile. He instituted a systematic curriculum of philosophy, dividing it into three main disciplines, logic, ethics, and physics. Logic, said his followers, is the bones of philosophy, ethics the flesh, and physics the soul (D.L. 7. 37). Zeno studied under the great Megarian logician Diodorus Cronos, and was a fellow pupil of Philo, who laid the ground for a development of logic which marked, in some areas, an improvement on Aristotle.[13] He himself, however, was more interested in ethics.

It may seem surprising that a moralist like Zeno should give physics the highest place in the curriculum. But for Zeno, and later Stoics, physics is the study of nature and nature is identified with God. Diogenes Laertius tells us, 'Zeno says that the whole world and heaven are the substance of God' (7. 148). God is an active principle, matter is an active principle; both of them are corporeal, and together they constitute an all-pervasive cosmic fire (LS 45G).

Zeno's writings do not survive: the most famous of them in antiquity was his *Republic*. This combined Platonic utopianism with some cynic elements. Zeno rejected the conventional educational system, and thought it a waste of effort to build gymnasia, law courts, and temples. He recommended community of wives,

---

[13] On Diodorus and Philo, see Ch. 3 below.

and thought that men and women should wear the same, revealing, clothing. Money should be abolished and there should be a single legal system for all mankind, who should be like a herd grazing together nurtured by a common law (LS 67A).

In spite of these communistic proposals, which many of his own later disciples found shocking, Zeno in his lifetime was held in honour by the Athenians, who gave him the freedom of the city. King Antigonus of Macedon invited him to become his personal philosopher, but Zeno pleaded old age and sent to court instead two of his brightest pupils.

After Zeno's death his place as head of the Stoa was taken by Cleanthes (331–232), a converted boxer of a religious bent. Cleanthes wrote a hymn to Zeus, later quoted by St Paul in a sermon in Athens, which exalted the Stoic active principle in terms that were appropriate enough for Judaeo-Christian monotheism. The underlying Stoic conception of God is very different, however, from that of the biblical religions. God is not separate from the universe but is a material constituent of the cosmos. In his prose writings Cleanthes expounded in detail the way in which the divine fiery element provided the vital power for all the living beings in the world (Cicero, *ND* 2. 23–5).[14]

Cleanthes was succeeded as head of the school by Chrysippus of Soli, who governed it from 232 to 206. Chrysippus had been Cleanthes' pupil, but he seems to have had no great respect for his teacher. 'You tell me your theorems', he is said to have told him, 'and I'll supply them with proofs.' He spent some time as a student at the Academy, inoculating himself against scepticism. He was the most intelligent and the most industrious of the Hellenistic Stoics. His literary output was prodigious: his housekeeper reported that he wrote at a rate of 500 lines a day, and he left 705 books behind. Nothing but fragments survive. But it is clear that it was he who rounded Stoicism into a system; it used to be said, 'If there had been no Chrysippus, there had been no Stoa' (D.L. 6. 183).

It is difficult to separate out precisely the contributions of the three early Stoics, since their works have all been lost. However, there is little doubt that Chrysippus deserves the main share of the credit for the significant advances in logic that will be examined in detail in the next chapter. In physics he substituted breath (*pneuma*) for Cleanthes' fire as the vital principle of animals and plants. He accepted the Aristotelian distinction between matter and form, but as a good materialist he insisted that form too was bodily, namely *pneuma*. The human soul and mind are made out of this *pneuma*; so too is God, who is the soul of the cosmos, which, in its entirety, constitutes a rational animal. If God and the soul were not themselves bodily, Stoics argued, they would not be able to act on the material world.

The fully developed Stoic physical system can be summarized as follows. Once upon a time, there was nothing but fire; gradually there emerged the other

---

[14] On Cleanthes' theology, see Ch. 9 below.

elements and the familiar furniture of the universe. Later, the world will return to fire in a universal conflagration, and then the whole cycle of its history will be repeated over and over again. All this happens in accordance with a system of laws which may be called 'fate' (because the laws admit of no exception), or 'providence' (because the laws were laid down by God for beneficent purposes). The divinely designed system is called Nature, and our aim in life should be to live in accord with Nature.

Chrysippus was also the principal author of the Stoic ethical system, which is based on the principle of submission to Nature. Nothing can escape Nature's laws, but despite the determinism of fate human beings are free and responsible. If the will obeys reason it will live in accordance with Nature. It is this voluntary acceptance of Nature's laws that constitutes virtue, and virtue is both necessary and sufficient for happiness.[15]

The Stoics all agreed that because society is natural to human beings, a good man, in his aim to be in harmony with Nature, will play some part in society and cultivate social virtues. But Chrysippus had a number of ethical and political views that marked him out from other Stoics. Like Zeno, he wrote a *Republic*, in which he is alleged to have defended incest and cannibalism (LS 67F). Chrysippus differed from some of his fellows in insisting that a philosopher need not devote himself to scholarship: for a Stoic it was acceptable, indeed praiseworthy, to take part in public life (LS 67w).

Scepticism in the Academy

During the latter part of the third century Stoic doctrine came under attack from the Academy. The academic heirs of Plato began to take their inspiration from Plato's questioning master, Socrates, and turned to a form of scepticism. The leader of the Academy from 273 to 242 was Arcesilaus, a pupil of Pyrrho of Elis, a man often regarded as the founder of philosophical scepticism. Pyrrho, an older contemporary of Epicurus, who had served as a soldier in Alexander's army, taught that nothing could be known and, accordingly, wrote no books. It was Arcesilaus and another of Pyrrho's pupils, Timon, who brought scepticism to Athens in the early years of the third century. Timon denied the possibility of finding any self-evident principles to serve as the foundation of sciences. In the absence of such axioms, all lines of reasoning must be circular or endless.

The scepticism of Timon and Arcesilaus came to fruition, in a modified and more sophisticated form, with the work of Carneades, who headed the Academy from 155 to 137. Like Pyrrho, Carneades left no writings, but his arguments were

---

[15] The Stoic ethical system is considered in greater detail in Ch. 8 below.

recorded by a pupil who attended his highly popular lectures. They have come down to us principally through the good offices of Cicero, who was once taught by Carneades' pupil Philo. In 155 Carneades was sent by Athens, along with a Stoic and a Peripatetic philosopher, on an embassy to Rome. During this embassy he displayed his rhetorical skill by arguing on successive days for and against justice. Cato the Roman Censor, who heard his performance, sent him packing as a subversive influence (LS 68M).

Arcesilaus criticized the Stoics because they had claimed to found their search for truth upon mental impressions incapable of falsehood: there were, he argued, no such impressions. Carneades too attacked Stoic epistemology, and taught that probability, not unattainable truth, should be the guide to life. Though not himself an atheist, he ridiculed mercilessly both the traditional pantheon and Stoic pantheism. His arguments against the Stoic theory of divination were adopted and skilfully developed by Cicero.[16]

Lucretius

No philosopher of the second century was as intelligent or persuasive as Carneades, and in the first century primacy in philosophy passed from Greek to Latin authors. Latin philosophy, like Greek philosophy, began in verse and only later turned to prose. The first complete Latin philosophical work that has reached us is a long and magnificent poem in hexameter verse, *On the Nature of Things*, by Lucretius.

Almost nothing is known of Lucretius' life: we can conjecture the rough dating of his poem by noting that it was read by Cicero in 54, and was dedicated to one C. Memmius, who stood for the consulship in 53. Lucretius was an adoring admirer of Epicurus, and the six books of the poem set out the Epicurean system in verse which, as Cicero observed, always displays great artistry and sometimes shows flashes of genius. Lucretius himself described his poetic skill as honey to disguise the wormwood of philosophy (1. 947). Parts of the poem were translated into English by John Dryden. Had he completed the task, his version would have been a worthy rival of Pope's *Essay on Man.*

Lucretius begins his poem by praising the bravery of Epicurus in throwing off the fear of religion. People cannot stand up to the tyranny of priests, because they fear eternal punishment; but that is only because they don't understand the nature of the soul. In his first book Lucretius sets out Epicurean atomism: nature consists of simple bodies and empty void, bodies perceived by sense, and void established by reason. Bodies are made out of atoms as words are made out of

---

[16] The debate between Stoics and Sceptics is considered in detail in Ch. 4 below.

letters: the words 'ignis' and 'lignum' are made up of almost the same letters, just as the things they signify, namely fire and wood, are made up of almost the same atoms (1. 911–14).

In a famous passage early in the second book Lucretius describes the philosopher looking down, from the heights of virtue, on the petty struggles of mankind. He extols the Epicurean pursuit of simple pleasures and avoidance of unnecessary desires.

> O wretched man! in what a mist of life
> Enclosed with dangers and with noisy strife
> He spends his little span; and overfeeds
> His crammed desires, with more than nature needs!
> For nature wisely stints our appetite
> And craves no more than undisturbed delight;
> Which minds unmixed with cares and fears obtain;
> A soul serene, a body void of pain.
> So little this corporeal frame requires,
> So bounded are our natural desires,
> That wanting all, and setting pain aside,
> With bare privation sense is satisfied.　　　　　(2. 16–28)

The third book sets out the Epicurean theory of the soul and the mechanisms of sensation. Once we understand the material nature of the soul, we realize that fears of death are childish. A dead body cannot feel, and death leaves no self behind to suffer. It is those who survive who have the right to grieve. Give up fear of death, Lucretius tells his patron,

> For thou shalt sleep, and never wake again,
> And, quitting life, shalt quit thy living pain.
> But we, thy friends, shall all those sorrows find
> Which in forgetful death thou leav'st behind;
> No time shall dry our tears, nor drive thee from our mind.
> The worst that can befall thee, measured right,
> Is a sound slumber, and a long goodnight.　　　　　(3. 90–6)

Even Epicurus had to die, though his genius shone so brightly in comparison with other thinkers that he reduced them to nothing just as the rising sun puts out the stars (3. 1042–4).

Lucretius' fourth book, on the nature of love, is full of lively description of sexual activity, as well as atomistic explanations of the underlying physiology. No doubt it was the content of this book that gave rise to the legend, reported by St Jerome and dramatized by Tennyson, that Lucretius wrote the poem in the lucid intervals of a madness brought on by over-indulgence in an aphrodisiac.

St Jerome also preserves a tradition that the poem was left unfinished and edited, after the poet's death, by Cicero. This seems unlikely, for Cicero, having expressed his admiration on first reading of the poem, never mentions it in his own philosophical writing, even though he devotes considerable attention to the Epicurean system.

Cicero

Cicero himself was eclectic in his philosophy, which is a boon to the historian, since his writings provide information about a variety of philosophical tendencies. He made his first acquaintance with the different philosophical schools when he studied in Athens in his late twenties. Later he studied at Rhodes under the Stoic Posidonius. He was greatly influenced by Philo of Larissa, the last head of the Academy, who came to Rome from Athens in 88 BC. He kept in his house, as personal guru, the Stoic Diodotus until his death in 60.

For a long time Cicero's busy life in politics and in the courts did not leave him much leisure for any philosophy except political philosophy. In the late 50s he imitated Plato by writing a *Republic* and a *Laws*, which have survived only in part. He withdrew from public life, however, when Julius Caesar came to supreme power after a civil war in which he himself had taken the opposite side. Cicero spent much of Caesar's dictatorship in literary activity, and after the death of his only daughter, Tullia, in February 45 he wrote ever more frantically so as to forget his grief. Most of his philosophical works were written in the years 45 and 44.

The two first in the series are now lost, a *Consolatio* on the death of Tullia, and the *Hortensius*, an exhortation to the study of philosophy that was to play a dramatic part in the life of St Augustine. Ten other works, however, survive, impressive in their range and eloquence.

Cicero set himself the task of creating a Latin philosophical vocabulary, so that Romans could study philosophy in their own language. Many, indeed, of the philosophical terms of modern languages derive from his Latin coinages. In his own opinions, he took elements from different philosophical tendencies. In epistemology he favoured the moderate sceptical opinion that he had learnt from Philo: he presents the academic system and its variants in his *Academica*, which appeared in two different versions. In ethics he favoured the Stoic rather than the Epicurean tradition. He looked to moral philosophy for consolation and reassurance. In his *de Finibus* and *Tusculan Disputations* he writes, often with great passion and beauty, on the relation between emotion, virtue, and happiness. His works *On the Nature of the Gods* and *On Fate* contain interesting discussions of philosophical theology and the issue of determinism, and his *On Divination* puts to good use arguments he had learnt, at a remove, from Carneades.[17]

Cicero wrote philosophy without profundity, but his arguments are often acute, his style is always elegant, and he is capable of great warmth. His essays

---

[17] See Ch. 9 below.

on friendship and old age have been popular throughout the ages. His final work on moral philosophy, *On Duties* (*de Officiis*), was addressed to his son shortly after the assassination of Julius Caesar in March 44. It was, during various periods of history, regarded as an essential item in the education of a gentleman.

After Caesar's death Cicero returned to politics with a series of bitter attacks on the Caesarian consul Mark Antony. After Antony went into partnership with Caesar's adopted son Octavian, Cicero was executed in the putsch that they jointly organized. He did not live to see the quarrel between the two that led to Antony's defeat at Actium in 31. He was dead before Octavian became the first Roman emperor, changing his name to Augustus.

Judaism and Christianity

For the long-term development of philosophy the most important event in the first century of the Roman Empire was the career of Jesus of Nazareth. The impact of his teaching on philosophy was, of course, delayed and indirect, and his own moral doctrine was not without precedent. He taught that we should not render evil for evil; but so had Plato's Socrates. He urged his hearers to love their neighbours as themselves; but he was quoting the ancient Hebrew book of Leviticus. He told us that we must refrain not just from wrong deeds, but from wrong thoughts and desires; Aristotle too had said that the really virtuous person is one who never even wants to do wrong. Jesus taught his disciples to despise the pleasures and honours of the world; but so, in their different ways, did the Epicureans and the Stoics. Considered as a moral philosopher, Jesus was not a great innovator: but that, of course, was not at all how he and his disciples saw his role.

The framework of Jesus' teaching was the world-view of the Hebrew Bible, according to which the Lord God Yahweh had created, by mere fiat, heaven and earth and all in them. The Jews were God's chosen people, uniquely privileged by their possession of the divine law revealed to Moses. Like Heraclitus and other Greek and Jewish thinkers, Jesus predicted that there would be a divine judgement on the world, amid cosmic catastrophe. Unlike the Stoics, who placed the cosmic denouement in the indefinite and distant future, Jesus saw it as an imminent event, in which he would himself play a crucial role as the Messiah.

Around the time of Jesus' crucifixion (c. AD 30) Jewish ideas were gaining a hearing in Rome. Since the Hebrew Scriptures had been translated into Greek in Alexandria in the time of the first Ptolemys, there had been a substantial Greek-speaking Jewish diaspora. In the first century AD the outstanding representative of Hellenistic Jewish culture was Philo, who led a delegation to the emperor Caligula in 40 to protest against the persecution of the Jews in Alexandria and the imposition of emperor-worship. He wrote a life of Moses and a series of commentaries on the

Pentateuch designed to make the Hebrew Scriptures intelligible and palatable to those educated in Greek culture.

In its early days Christianity spread through the empire via the Greek-speaking diaspora, but it soon came into contact with Gentile philosophy. St Paul, preaching the gospel in Athens, held a debate with Epicurean and Stoic philosophers, and the sermon against idolatry placed in his mouth in the Acts of the Apostles is skilfully crafted, and shows an awareness of matters at issue between the philosophical sects. Taking his cue from the altar of the unknown God, Paul undertook to show the philosophers the god whom they worshipped in ignorance.

[God] is not far from every one of us. For in him we live, and move, and have our being; as certain also of your own poets have said, for we are also his offspring. Forasmuch then as we are the offspring of God we ought not to think that the Godhead is like unto gold or silver or stone, graven by art and man's device. (Acts 17: 27–9)

The 'poet' Paul quoted was Cleanthes, the second head of the Stoa. Later legend imagined Paul in philosophical discourse with the Stoic philosopher Seneca. The story was no doubt untrue, but it was not wholly fanciful. Paul once appeared in court before Seneca's brother Gallio, and he had friends in the palace of Seneca's master Nero.

The Imperial Stoa

Seneca was the most significant philosopher of the first century. Born in Spain, at Cordoba, at the beginning of the Christian era, he was in 49 made tutor to the 12-year-old Nero. When Nero came to the throne in 54 he became a senior adviser, and guided the emperor through a period of comparatively good government, which came to an end in the year 59 when Nero murdered his own mother. Seneca lost all influence on Nero after 62 and gradually withdrew from public life. In 65 he was forced to slit his veins for alleged participation in a plot against the tyrant, and died a Socratic death.

Seneca wrote a number of tragedies, and left a scrapbook of questions on physical phenomena, but his reputation as a philosopher rests on his ten ethical dialogues, and his 124 moral epistles, mostly written during the period of his retirement. Seneca's style is more exhortatory than argumentative; he prefers preaching to debate. He was not interested in logic, and he had a philistine attitude to the liberal arts: he compared a person over-learned in literature to a man with an over-furnished house (Ep. 88. 36). He had a certain interest in the physical sciences, and wrote a treatise *On Natural Questions*, but he likes to draw a moral from natural phenomena, and of the three branches of Stoic philosophy it is ethics that is his main concern.

He urges us to strive towards liberation from the passions. In the longest and best known of his dialogues, *On Anger*, he insists on the crucial difference between bodily turmoil on the one hand, and the false judgements which were the essential element from which we need purification. On this issue, earlier Stoics had not spoken with a single voice. 'None of those things that strike the mind fortuitously should be called passions: they are not things the mind causes but things that happen to it. It is not passion to be affected by the appearances of things that present themselves; passion consists in surrendering oneself to them and following up this fortuitous impact' (2. 3. 1). Weeping, turning pale, sudden intakes of breath, and sexual arousal are not passions, but mere bodily phenomena: it is what happens in the mind that matters. Seneca is able to conduct the Stoic crusade against the passions with greater clarity and energy once this distinction has been made.

Seneca was a materialist, accepting the Stoic doctrine that the human mind was a material part of a material divine world-soul (Ep. 66. 12). But he often writes about the relation between soul and body in a manner that is distinctly other-worldly. 'The human heart is never more divine than when it meditates on its own mortality, and realises that a human being is born in order to give up life, and that this body is not a home but a short-term hostelry which one must leave as soon as one sees one is becoming a burden on one's host' (120. 14). Seneca recognizes the difficulty of the Stoic path to virtue. He distinguishes between three stages in moral progress. There are those who have given up some vices but not all—they are without avarice, but not without anger; without lust but not without ambition; and so on. Then there are those who have given up all passions but are not yet safe from relapse. The third class, the closest approximation to wisdom, consists of those who are beyond relapsing, but have not yet acquired secure self-confidence in their virtue (Ep. 75. 8–14).

Seneca also made popular the distinction in Stoicism between doctrines and precepts. The doctrines provided the general philosophical framework; the precepts enabled the true concept of the highest good to find expression in specific prescriptions to individuals (Ep. 94. 2). This distinction enabled Stoics to counter the allegation that their system was too elevated to be of any practical use, and justified the philosopher in giving the kind of pastoral advice of which Seneca's own letters are full.

Many, in both ancient and modern times, have regarded Seneca as a hypocrite: a man who praised mercy but was implicated in a tyrant's crimes; a man who preached the worthlessness of earthly goods but piled up a gigantic fortune. In his defence it can be said that he acted as a restraining influence on Nero, and that in his last years he sought genuine detachment from the world. He was under no illusion that he lived up to Stoic standards. 'I am a long way, not only from perfection, but from being a halfway decent person,' he wrote (Ep. 57. 3).

Seneca was the founding father of the Imperial Stoa. Two other prominent members of the school show how wide was the appeal of Stoicism under the empire: the slave Epictetus and the emperor Marcus Aurelius. The Stoics of the imperial period were far less interested in logic and physics than their predecessors in Hellenistic times, and like Seneca both Epictetus and Marcus are remembered principally for their moral philosophy.[18]

Epictetus' dates are uncertain, but we know that he was banished from Rome, along with other philosophers, by the emperor Domitian in AD 89. Freed from slavery, though permanently lamed, he set up a school in Epirus; his admirer Arrian published four books of his discourses and a handbook of his main teachings (*enchiridion*). Epictetus is one of the most readable of the Stoics, and has a rugged and jocular style, making constant use of cross-talk with imaginary interlocutors. Because of this, many people beside philosophers have found him attractive. Matthew Arnold lists him, along with Homer and Sophocles, as one of three men who have most enlightened him:

> He, whose friendship I not long since won,
> That halting slave, who in Nicopolis
> Taught Arrian, when Vespasian's brutal son
> Cleared Rome of what most shamed him.

Typical of Epictetus' style is the following passage on suicide, where he imagines people suffering from tyranny and injustice addressing him thus:

Epictetus, we can no longer endure imprisonment in this bodikin, feeding it and watering it and resting it and washing it, and being brought by it into contact with so-and-so and such-and-such. Aren't these things indifferent, indeed a very nothing, to us? Death isn't an evil, is it? Aren't we God's kin, and don't we come from him? Do let us go back where we came. (1. 9. 12)

He responds as follows:

Men, wait for God. When he gives the signal and releases you from this service, then you may go to him. For the time being, though, stay at the post where he has stationed you.

Rather than seek refuge in suicide, we should realize that none of the world's evils can really harm us. To show this, Epictetus identifies the self with the moral will (*prohairesis*).

When the tyrant threatens and summons me, I answer, 'Who is it that you are threatening?' If he says, 'I will put you in chains,' I respond, 'It is my hands and my feet he is threatening.' If he says, 'I will behead you,' I respond, 'It is my neck he is threatening.' . . . So doesn't he threaten *you* at all? No, not so long as I regard all this as nothing to me. But if I let myself fear any of these threats, then yes, he does threaten me. Who then is left for me to

---

[18] J. Barnes, *Logic and the Imperial Stoa* (Leiden: Brill, 1997) has made a gallant case for the logical competence of Epictetus.

fear? A man who can master the things in my own power?—There is no such man. A man who can master the things that are not in my power?—Why should I trouble myself about him? (Disc. 1. 29)

In many periods Epictetus' writings have been found comforting by those who have had to live under the rule of tyrants. But in his own time the person who was most impressed by them was himself the ruler of the Roman world. Marcus Aurelius Antoninus became emperor in 161 and spent much of his life defending the frontiers of the Roman Empire, now at its furthest extent. Though himself a Stoic, he founded chairs of philosophy at Athens for all of the major schools, Platonic, Peripatetic, and Epicurean. During his military campaigns he found time to make entries into a philosophical notebook, which has been known in modern times as the *Meditations*. It is a collection of aphorisms and discourses on themes such as the brevity of life, the need to work for the common good, the unity of mankind, and the corrupting nature of power. He sought to combine patriotism with a universalist viewpoint. 'My city and country,' he says, 'so far as I am Antoninus, is Rome; but so far as I am a man, it is the world.' He hails the universe as 'Dear City of Zeus'.

One of Marcus Aurelius' friends was the medical doctor Galen, who came to Rome after being physician to the gladiators of Pergamum. His voluminous writings belong rather to the history of medicine than to that of philosophy, though he was a serious logician and once wrote a treatise with the title *That a Good Doctor Must Be a Philosopher*. He corrected Aristotle's physiology on an important point which was crucial for a true appreciation of the mind–body relationship. Aristotle had believed that the heart was the seat of the soul, regarding the brain as a mere radiator to cool the blood. Galen discovered that nerves arising from the brain and spinal cord are necessary for the initiation of muscle contraction, and hence he regarded the brain, and not the heart, as the primary seat of the soul.

Early Christian Philosophy

With Marcus Aurelius, Stoicism took its last bow, and Epicureanism was already in retirement. Among the schools of philosophy to whom the emperor assigned chairs in Athens, one was conspicuous by its absence: Christianity. Indeed, Marcus instituted a cruel persecution of Christians, and dismissed their martyrdoms as histrionic. One of those who was executed in his reign was Justin, the first Christian philosopher, who had dedicated to him an *Apologia* for Christianity.

It was at the end of the second century that Christians first made substantial attempts to harmonize the religion of Jesus and Paul with the philosophy of Plato and Aristotle. Clement of Alexandria published a set of Miscellanies (*Stromateis*), written in the style of table talk, in which he argued that the study of philosophy was not only permissible, but necessary, for the educated Christian. The Greek thinkers were pedagogues for the world's adolescence, divinely appointed to bring it to Christ in its maturity. Clement enrolled Plato as an ally against dualist Christian heretics, he experimented with Aristotelian logic, and he praised the Stoic ideal of freedom from passion. In the manner of Philo, he explained away as allegorical aspects of the Bible, and especially the Old Testament, which repelled educated Greeks. In this he founded a tradition that was to have a long history in Alexandria.

Clement was an anthologist and a popularizer; his younger Alexandrian contemporary Origen (185–254) was an original thinker. Though he thought of himself primarily as a student of the Bible, Origen had sat at the feet of the Alexandrian Platonist Ammonius Saccas, and he incorporated into his system many philosophical ideas which mainstream Christians regarded as heretical. He believed, with Plato, that human souls existed before birth or conception. Formerly free spirits, human souls in their embodied state could use their free will to ascend, aided by the grace of Christ, to a heavenly destiny. In the end, he believed, all rational beings, sinners as well as saints, and devils as well as angels, would be saved and find blessedness. There would be a resurrection of the body which (according to some of our sources) he believed would take spherical form, since Plato had decreed that the sphere was the most perfect of all shapes.

Origen's eccentric teaching brought him into conflict with the local bishops, and his loyalty to Christianity laid him under the ban of the empire. He was exiled to Palestine, where, against his pagan fellow Platonist Celsus, he used philosophical arguments to defend Christian belief in God, freedom, and immortality. He died in 254 after repeated torture in the persecution of the emperor Decius.

The Revival of Platonism and Aristotelianism

While Christian philosophy was in its infancy, and while Stoicism and Epicureanism were in decline, there had been a fertile revival of the philosophy of Plato and Aristotle. Plutarch (c.46–c.120) was born in Boeotia and spent most of his life there, but he had studied at Athens and at least once gave lectures in Rome. He is best known as a historian for his parallel lives of twenty-three famous Greeks paired with twenty-three famous Romans, which in an Elizabethan translation by Sir Thomas North provided the plot and much of the inspiration for Shakespeare's Roman plays. But he also wrote some sixty short treatises on popular philosophical topics, which were collected under the title *Moralia*. He was a Platonist and commented on the *Timaeus*. He wrote a number of polemical treatises against the Stoics and Epicureans which contributed to the decline of those systems: they bear parallel titles such as *On the Contradictions of the Epicureans* and *On the Contradictions of the Stoics* or *On Free Will in Reply to Epicurus* and *On Free Will in Reply to the Stoics.* One of the longest of his surviving essays bears the title *That Epicurus Actually Makes a Pleasant Life Impossible,* and another is an attack on an otherwise unknown work by Colotes, one of Epicurus' earliest disciples. Though his works are not often read by philosophers for their own sake, they have long been quarried by historians for the information they provide about their targets of attack.

More important, initially, than the incipient revival of Platonism was the beginning of a tradition of scholarly commentary on the Aristotelian corpus. The oldest surviving commentary on a text is the second-century work of Aspasius on the *Ethics,* which inaugurates the custom of treating the *Nicomachean Ethics* as canonical. At the end of the century Alexander of Aphrodisias was appointed to the Peripatetic chair in Athens, and he produced extensive commentaries on the *Metaphysics,* the *de Sensu,* and some of the logical works. In pamphlets on the soul, and on fate, he presented his own developments of Aristotelian ideas. Aristotle had spoken, obscurely, of an active intellect that was responsible for concept formation in human beings. Alexander identified this active intellect with God, an interpretation that was to have a great influence on Aristotle's later Arab followers, while being rejected by Christians, who regarded the active intellect as a faculty of each individual human being.

Plotinus and Augustine

It was Plato, however, not Aristotle, who was to be the dominant philosophical influence during the twilight of classical antiquity. Contemporary with the Christian Origen, and a fellow pupil of Ammonius Saccas, was the last great pagan philosopher, Plotinus (205–70). After a brief military career Plotinus settled in Rome and won favour at the imperial court. He toyed with the idea of founding a Platonic republic in Campania. His works were edited after his death in six groups of nine treatises (Enneads) by his disciple and biographer Porphyry. Written in a taut and difficult style, they cover a variety of philosophical topics: ethics and aesthetics, physics and cosmology, psychology, metaphysics, logic, and epistemology.

The dominant place in Plotinus' system is occupied by 'the One': the notion is derived, through Plato, from Parmenides, where Oneness is a key property of Being. The One is, in a mysterious way, identical with the Platonic Idea of the Good: it is the basis of all being and the standard of all value, but it is itself beyond being and beyond goodness. Below this supreme and ineffable summit, the next places are occupied by Mind (the locus of Ideas) and Soul, which is the creator of time and space. Soul looks upward to Mind, but downward to Nature, which in turn creates the physical world. At the lowest level of all is bare matter, the outermost limit of reality.

These levels of reality are not independent of each other. Each level depends for its existence and activity on the level above it. Everything has its place in a single downward progress of successive emanations from the One. This impressive and startling metaphysical system is presented by Plotinus not as a mystical revelation but on the basis of philosophical principles derived from Plato and Aristotle. It will be examined in detail in Chapter 9 below.

Plotinus' school in Rome did not survive his death, but his pupils and their pupils carried his ideas elsewhere. A Neoplatonic tradition throve in Athens until the pagan schools were closed down by the Christian emperor Justinian in 529. But it was Christians, not pagans, who transmitted Plotinus' ideas to the post-classical world, and foremost among them was St Augustine of Hippo, who was to prove the most influential of all Christian philosophers.

Augustine was born in a small town in present-day Algeria in 354. The son of a Christian mother and a pagan father, he was not baptized as an infant, though he received a Christian education in Latin literature and rhetoric. Most of what we know of his early life comes from his own autobiography, the *Confessions*, a portrait, by a biographer nearly as gifted as Boswell, of a mind more capacious than Johnson's.

Having acquired a smattering of Greek, Augustine qualified in rhetoric and taught the subject at Carthage, a city which he described as 'a cauldron of unholy loves'. At the age of 18, reading Cicero's *Hortensius*, he was fired with a love of Plato. For about ten years he was a follower of Manichaeism, a syncretic religion which taught that there were two worlds, one of spiritual goodness and light created by God, and one of fleshly darkness created by the devil. The distaste for sex left a permanent mark on Augustine, though for several years in early manhood he lived with a mistress and had with her a son, Adeodatus.

In 383 he crossed the sea to Rome and quickly moved to Milan, then the capital of the western part of the now divided Roman Empire. There he became friends with Ambrose, the bishop of Milan, a great champion of the claims of religion and morality against the ruthless secular power of the emperor Theodosius. The influence of Ambrose, and of his mother, Monica, turned Augustine in the direction of Christianity. After a period of hesitation he was baptized in 387.

For some time after his baptism Augustine remained under the philosophical influence of Plotinus. A set of dialogues on God and the human soul articulated a Christian Neoplatonism. *Against the Academics* set out a detailed line of argument against Academic Scepticism. In *On Ideas* he presented his own version of Plato's Theory of Ideas: the Ideas have no extra-mental existence, but they exist, eternal and unchangeable, in the mind of God. He wrote *On Free Choice* on human freewill, choice, and the origin of evil, a text still used in a number of philosophy departments. He also wrote a donnish Platonic tract, the *83 Different Questions*.

He also wrote six books on music, and an energetic work *On the Teacher*, reflecting imaginatively on the nature and power of words.

All these works were written before Augustine found his final vocation and was ordained as a priest in 391. He became after a short period bishop of Hippo in Algeria, where he resided until his death in 430. He had a prodigious writing career ahead of him, including his masterpiece *The City of God*, but the year 391 marks an epoch. Up to this point Augustine showed himself the last fine flower of classical philosophy. From then onwards he writes not as the pupil of the pagan Plotinus, but as the father of the Christian philosophy of the Middle Ages. We shall follow him into this creative phase in the next volume of this work.

Augustine did not see himself, in his maturity, as a philosophical innovator. He saw his task as the expounding of a divine message that had come to him from Plato and Paul, men much greater than himself, and from Jesus, who was more than man. But the way in which succeeding generations have conceived and understood the teaching of Augustine's masters has been in great part the fruit of Augustine's own work. Of all the philosophers in the ancient world, only Aristotle had a greater influence on human thought.

3

How to Argue: Logic

Logic is the discipline that sorts out good arguments from bad arguments. Aristotle claimed to be its founder, and his claim is no idle boast. Of course, human beings had been arguing, and detecting fallacies in other people's arguments, since human society began; as John Locke said, 'God did not make men barely two legged and leave it to Aristotle to make them rational.' None the less, it is to Aristotle that we owe the first formal study of argumentative reasoning. But here as elsewhere, there is first of all a debt to Plato to be acknowledged. Following the lead of Protagoras, Plato made important distinctions between parts of speech, distinctions that form part of the basis on which logic is built. In the *Sophist* he introduces a distinction between nouns and verbs, verbs being signs of actions, and names being signs of the agents of those actions. A sentence, he insists, must consist of at least one noun and at least one verb: two nouns in succession, or two verbs in succession, will never make a sentence. 'Walks runs' is not a sentence, nor is 'Lion stag'. The simplest kind of sentence will be something like 'A man learns' or 'Theaetetus flies', and only something with this kind of structure can be true or false (*Sph.* 262a–263b). The splitting of sentences into smaller units—of which this is only one possible example—is an essential first step in the logical analysis of argument.

Aristotle left a number of logical treatises, which are traditionally placed at the beginning of the corpus of his works in the following order: *Categories, de Interpretatione, Prior Analytics, Posterior Analytics, Topics, Sophistical Refutations*. This order is neither the one in which the works were written nor the one in which it is most fruitful to read them. It is best to begin with the consideration of the *Prior Analytics*, the most substantial and the least controversial of his contributions to the discipline of logic which he founded.

Aristotle's Syllogistic

The *Prior Analytics* is devoted to the theory of the syllogism, a central method of inference that can be illustrated by familiar examples such as

> Every Greek is human.
> Every human is mortal.
> Therefore, Every Greek is mortal.

Aristotle sets out to show how many forms syllogisms can take, and which of them provide reliable inferences.

For the purposes of this study, Aristotle introduced a technical vocabulary which, translated into many languages, has played an important part in logic throughout its history (1. 1. 24^{a}10–^{b}15). The word 'syllogism' itself is simply a transliteration into English of the Greek word 'syllogismos' which Aristotle uses for inferences of this pattern. It is defined at the beginning of the *Prior Analytics*: a syllogism is a discourse in which from certain things laid down something different follows of necessity (1. 1. 24^{b}18).

The example syllogism above contains three sentences in the indicative mood and each such sentence is called by Aristotle a *proposition* (*protasis*): a proposition is, roughly speaking, a sentence considered in respect of its logical features. The third of the propositions in the example—the one preceded by 'therefore'—is called by Aristotle the *conclusion* of the syllogism. The other two propositions we may call *premisses*, though Aristotle does not have a consistent technical term to differentiate them.

The propositions in the above example begin with the word 'every': such propositions are called by Aristotle *universal* propositions (*katholou*). They are not the only kind of universal propositions: equally universal is a proposition such as 'No Greeks are horses'; but whereas the first kind of proposition was a universal *affirmative* (*kataphatikos*), the second is a universal *negative* (*apophatikos*).

Contrasted with universal propositions there are *particular* propositions (*en merei*) such as 'Some Greeks are bearded' (a particular affirmative) or 'Some Greeks are not bearded' (a particular negative). In propositions of all these kinds, Aristotle says, something is *predicated* of something else: e.g. mortal is predicated of human in one case, and horse of Greek in another. The presence or absence of a negative sign determine whether these predications are affirmations or negations respectively (1. 1. 24^{b}17).

The items that enter into predications in propositions are called by Aristotle *terms* (*horoi*). It is a feature of terms, as conceived by Aristotle, that they can either figure as predicates themselves or have other terms predicated of them. Thus, in our first example, human is predicated of something in the first sentence and has something predicated of it in the second.

Aristotle assigns the terms occurring in a syllogism three distinct roles. The term that is the predicate of the conclusion is the *major* term; the term of which the major is predicated in the conclusion is the *minor* term; and the term that appears in each of the premisses is the *middle* term (1. 4. 26ᵃ21–3).[1] Thus, in the example given 'mortal' is the major term, 'Greek' the minor term, and 'human' the middle term.

In addition to inventing these technical terms, Aristotle introduced the practice of using schematic letters to bring out patterns of argument: a device that is essential for the systematic study of inference and which is ubiquitous in modern mathematical logic. Thus, the pattern of argument we illustrated above is set out by Aristotle not by giving an example, but by the following schematic sentence:

If A belongs to every B, and B belongs to every C, A belongs to every C.[2]

If Aristotle wishes to produce an actual example, he commonly does it not by spelling out a syllogistic argument, but by giving a schematic sentence and then listing possible substitutions for A, B, and C (e.g. 1. 5. 27ᵇ30–2).

All syllogisms will contain three terms and three propositions; but given that there are the four different kinds of proposition Aristotle has distinguished, and that there are different orders in which the terms can appear in the premisses, there will be many different syllogistic inference patterns. Unlike our initial example, which contained only affirmative universal propositions, there will be triads containing negative and particular propositions. Again, unlike our example in which the middle term appeared in the first premiss as a predicate and in the second as a subject, there will be cases where the middle is subject in each premiss and cases where it is predicate in each premiss. (By Aristotle's preferred definition, the conclusion will always have the minor term as its subject and the major as its predicate.)

Aristotle grouped the triads into three figures (*schemata*) on the basis of the position occupied in the premisses by the middle term. The first figure, illustrated by our initial example, has the middle once as predicate and once as subject (the order in which the premisses are stated is immaterial). In the second figure the middle term appears twice as subject, and in the third figure it appears twice as predicate. Thus, using S for the minor, M for the middle, and P for the major term, we have these figures:

---

[1] Aristotle's use of these terms in the *Prior Analytics* is not consistent: the account given here, from which he departs in considering the second and third figures of syllogism, has been accepted as canonical since antiquity (see W. C. Kneale and M. Kneale, *The Development of Logic* (Oxford: Clarendon Press, 1962), 69–71).
[2] Note that beside being cast in schematic form, Aristotle's exposition of syllogisms follows the pattern 'If *p* and *q*, then necessarily *r*' rather than '*p, q* therefore *r*'.

	(1)	(2)	(3)
	S–M	M–S	S–M
	M–P	M–P	P–M
Therefore,	S–P	S–P	S–P

Aristotle was mainly interested in syllogisms of the first figure, which he regarded as alone being 'perfect', by which he probably meant that they had an intuitive validity that was lacking to syllogisms in other figures (1. 4. 25^{b}35).

Predication occurs in all propositions, but it comes in different forms in the four different kinds of proposition: universal affirmative, universal negative, particular affirmative, particular negative. Thus the predication S–P can be either 'All S is P', 'No S is P', 'Some S is P', or 'Some S is not P'. Within each figure, therefore, we have many possible patterns of inference. In the first figure, for instance, we have, among many possibilities, the two following.

Every Greek is human.   Some animals are dogs.
No human is immortal.   Some dogs are white.
No Greek is immortal.   Every animal is white.

Triads of these different kinds were, in later ages, called 'moods' of the syllogism. Both of the given triads exemplify the pattern of a syllogism of the first figure, but there is obviously a great difference between them: the first is a valid argument, the second is invalid, having true premisses and a false conclusion.[3]

Aristotle sets himself the task of determining which of the possible moods produces a valid inference. He addresses it by trying out the various possible pairs of premisses and asking whether any conclusion can be drawn from them. If no conclusion can be validly drawn from a pair of premisses, he says that there is no syllogism. For instance, he says that if B belongs to no C, and A belongs to some B, there cannot be a syllogism; and he gives the terms 'white', 'horse', 'swan' as the test instance (1. 3. 25^{a}38). What he is doing is inviting us to consider the pair of premisses 'No swan is a horse' and 'Some horses are white' and to observe that from these premisses no conclusion can be drawn about the whiteness or otherwise of swans.

His procedure appears, at first sight, to be both haphazard and intuitive; but in the course of his discussion he is able to produce a number of general rules which, between them, are adequate to determine which moods yield a conclusion and which do not. There are three rules which apply to syllogisms in all figures:

(1) At least one premiss must be universal.
(2) At least one premiss must be affirmative.
(3) If either premiss is negative, the conclusion must be negative.

---

[3] No valid argument has true premisses and a false conclusion, but of course there can be valid arguments from false premisses to false conclusions, and invalid arguments for true conclusions.

These rules are of universal application, but they take more specific form in relation to particular figures. The rules peculiar to the first figure are

(4) The major premiss (the one containing the major term) must be universal.
(5) The minor premiss (the one containing the minor term) must be affirmative.

If we apply these rules we find that there are four, and only four, valid moods of syllogism in the first figure.

Every S is M	Every S is M	Some S is M	Some S is M
Every M is P	No M is P	Every M is P	Every M is not P
Every S is P	No S is P	Some S is P	Some S is not P

Aristotle also offers rules to determine the validity of moods in the second and third figures, but we do not need to go into these since he is able to show that all second- and third-figure syllogisms are equivalent to first-figure syllogisms. In general, syllogisms in these figures can be transformed into first-figure syllogisms by a process he calls 'conversion' (*antistrophe*).

Conversion depends on a set of relations between propositions of different forms that Aristotle sets out early in the treatise. When we have particular affirmative and universal negative propositions, the order of the terms can be reversed without alteration of sense: Some S is P if and only if some P is S, and no S is P if and only if no P is S (1. 2. 25^{a}5–10). (By contrast, 'Every S is P' may be true without 'Every P is S' being true.)

Consider the following syllogism in the third figure: 'No Greek is a bird; but all ravens are birds; therefore no Greek is a raven'. If we convert the minor premiss into its equivalent 'No bird is a Greek' we have a first-figure syllogism in the second of the moods tabulated above. Aristotle shows in the course of his treatise that almost all second- and third-figure syllogisms can be reduced to first-figure ones by conversion in this manner. In the rare cases where this is not possible he transforms the second- and third-figure syllogisms by a process of *reductio ad absurdum*, showing that if one premiss of the syllogism is taken in conjunction with the negation of its conclusion as a second premiss, it will yield (by a deduction in the first figure) the negation of the original second premiss as a conclusion (1. 23. 41^{a}21 ff.).

Aristotle's syllogistic was a remarkable achievement: it is a systematic formulation of an important part of logic. Some of his followers in later times—though not in antiquity or the Middle Ages—thought that syllogistic was the whole of logic. Immanuel Kant, for instance, in the preface to the second edition of his *Critique of Pure Reason*, said that since Aristotle logic had neither advanced a single step nor been required to retrace a single step.

In fact, however, syllogistic is only a fragment of logic. It deals only with inferences that depend on words like 'all' or 'some', which classify the premisses and conclusions of syllogisms, not with inferences that depend on words like 'if' and 'then', which, instead of attaching to nouns, link whole sentences. As we shall see, inferences such as 'If it is not day, it is night; but it is not day; therefore it is night' were formalized later in antiquity. Another gap in Aristotle's syllogistic took longer to fill. Though it was concerned above all with words like 'all', 'every', and 'some' (quantifiers, as they were later to be called), it could not cope with inferences in which such words occurred not in subject place but somewhere in the grammatical predicate. Aristotle's rules would not provide for assessing the validity of inferences containing premisses such as 'Every boy loves some girl' or 'Nobody can avoid every mistake.' It took more than twenty centuries before such inferences were satisfactorily formalized.

Aristotle may perhaps, for a moment, have thought that his syllogistic was sufficient to deal with every possible valid inference. But his own logical writings show that he realized that there was much more to logic than was dreamt of in his syllogistic.

The de Interpretatione *and the* Categories

The *de Interpretatione* is principally interested, like the *Prior Analytics*, in general propositions beginning with 'every', 'no', or 'some'. But its main concern is not to link them to each other in syllogisms, but to explore the relations of compatibility and incompatibility between them. 'Every man is white' and 'No man is white' can clearly not both be true together: Aristotle calls such propositions *contraries (enantiai)* (7. 17^{b}4–15). They can, however, both be false, if, as is the case, some men are white and some men are not. 'Every man is white' and 'Some man is not white', like the earlier pair, cannot be true together; but—on the assumption that there are such things as men—they cannot be false together. If one of them is true, the other is false; if one of them is false, the other is true. Aristotle calls such a pair *contradictory (antikeimenai)* (7. 17^{b}16–18).

Just as a universal affirmative is contradictory to the corresponding particular negative, so too a universal negative contradicts, and is contradicted by, a particular affirmative: thus 'No man is white' and 'Some man is white'. Two corresponding particular affirmatives are neither contrary nor contradictory to each other: 'Some man is white' and 'Some man is not white' can be, and in fact are, both true together. Given that there are men, the propositions cannot, however, both be false together. This relationship was not given a name: later followers called it the relationship of subcontrariety.

The relationships set out in the *de Interpretatione* can be set out, and have been set out for centuries by Aristotle's followers, in a diagram known as a square of opposition.

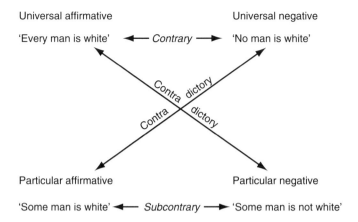

The propositions that enter into syllogisms and into the square of opposition are all general propositions, whether they are universal or particular. That is to say, none of them are propositions about individuals, containing proper names, such as 'Socrates is wise'. Of course, Aristotle was familiar with singular propositions, and one such, 'Pittacus is generous', turns up in an example in the final chapter of the *Prior Analytics* (2. 27. 70ᵃ25). But its appearance is incongruous in a treatise whose standard assumption is that all premisses and conclusions are quantified general propositions. In the *de Interpretatione* singular propositions are mentioned from time to time, principally to point a contrast with general propositions. It is a simple matter, for instance, to form the contradictory of 'Socrates is white': it is 'Socrates is not white' (7. 17ᵇ30). But to find a systematic treatment of singular propositions we must turn to the *Categories*.

Whereas the *Analytics* operates with a distinction between propositions and terms, the *Categories* starts by dividing 'things that are said' into complex (*kata symploken*) and simple (*aneu symplokes*) (2. 1ᵃ16). An example of a complex saying is 'A man is running'; simple sayings are the nouns and verbs that enter into such complexes: 'man', 'ox', 'run', 'win', and so on. Only complex sayings can be statements, true or false; simple sayings are neither true nor false. A similar distinction appears in the *de Interpretatione*, where we learn that a sentence (*logos*) has parts that signify on their own, while on the other hand there are signs that have no significant parts. These simple signs come in two different kinds, names (*Int.* 2. 16ᵃ20–ᵇ5) and verbs (*Int.* 3. 16ᵇ6–25): the two are distinguished from each other, we learn, because a verb, unlike a noun, 'signifies time in addition', i.e. has a tense. But in the *Categories* there is a much richer classification of simple sayings. In the fourth chapter of the treatise Aristotle has this to say:

Each one signifies either substance (*ousia*), or how big, or what sort, or in relation to something, or where, or when, or posture, or wearing, or doing, or being acted on. To give a rough idea substance is e.g. human, horse; how big is e.g. four-feet, six-feet; what sort is e.g. white, literate; in relation to something is e.g. double, half, bigger than; where is e.g. in the Lyceum, in the forum; when is e.g. yesterday, tomorrow, last year; posture is e.g. is lying, is sitting; wearing is e.g. is shod, is armed; doing is e.g. cutting, burning; being acted on is e.g. being cut, being burnt. (4. 1^b25–2^a4)

This compressed and cryptic passage has received repeated commentary and has exercised enormous influence over the centuries. These ten things signified by simple sayings are the *categories* that give the treatise its name. Aristotle in this passage indicates the categories by a heterogeneous set of expressions: nouns (e.g. 'substance'), verbs (e.g. 'wearing'), and interrogatives (e.g. 'where?' or 'how big?'). It became customary to refer to every category by a more or less abstract noun: substance, quantity, quality, relation, place, time, posture, vesture, activity, passivity.

What are categories and what is Aristotle's purpose in listing them? One thing, at least, that he is doing is listing ten different kinds of expression that might appear in the predicate of a sentence about an individual subject. We might say of Socrates, for example, that he was a man, that he was five feet tall, that he was wise, that he was older than Plato, and that he lived in Athens in the fifth century BC. On a particular occasion his friends might have said of him that he was sitting, wearing a cloak, cutting a piece of cloth, and being warmed by the sun. Obviously, the teaching of the *Categories* makes room for a variety of statements much richer than the regimented propositions of the *Prior Analytics*.

The text makes clear, however, that Aristotle is not only classifying expressions, pieces of language. He saw himself as making a classification of extra-linguistic entities, things signified as opposed to the signs that signify them. In Chapter 6 we shall explore the metaphysical implications of the doctrine of the categories. But one question must be addressed immediately. If we follow Aristotle's lead, we shall easily be able to categorize the predicates in sentences such as 'Socrates was pot-bellied', 'Socrates was wiser than Meletus'. But what are we to say about the 'Socrates' in such sentences? Aristotle's list seems to be a list of predicates not of subjects.

The answer to this is given in the succeeding chapter of the *Categories*.

Substance—strictly so called, primarily and *par excellence*—is that which is neither said of a subject nor is in a subject, e.g. such-and-such a man, such-and-such a horse.

Second substances are the species and genera to which the primary substances belong. Thus, such-and-such a man belongs in the species human, and the genus of this species is animal; so both human and animal are called second substances. (5. 2^a11–19)

When Aristotle speaks of a subject in this passage, it is clear that he is talking not about a linguistic expression, but about what the expression stands for. It is the man Socrates, not the word 'Socrates', that is the first substance. The substance that appeared first in the list of categories, it now emerges, was second substance: so the sentence 'Socrates was human' predicated a second substance (a species) of a first substance (an individual). When Aristotle in this passage contrasts a first substance with things that are *in a subject*, what he has in mind as being in a subject are the items signified by predicates in the other categories. Thus, if 'Socrates is wise' is true, then Socrates' wisdom is one of the things that are in Socrates (cf. 2. 1ᵃ25).

Aristotle goes through the categories, discussing them in turn. Some, such as substance, quantity, and quality, are treated at length; others, such as activity and passivity, are briefly touched on; yet others, such as posture and vesture, pass into oblivion. Detailed logical points are made in order to mark the distinctions between different categories. For example, qualities often admit of degrees, while particular quantities do not: one thing can be darker than another, but cannot be more four-foot-long than another (7. 6ᵃ19; 8. 10ᵇ26). Within individual categories, further subclasses are identified. There are, for instance, two types of quantity (discrete and continuous) and four types of quality, which Aristotle illustrates with the following examples: virtue, healthiness, darkness, shape. The criteria by which he distinguishes these types are not altogether clear, and the reader is left in doubt whether a particular item can occur in more than one of these classes, or indeed in more than one category. Aristotle's commentators through the ages have laboured to fill his gaps and reconcile his inconsistencies.

The *Categories* contains more than the theory of categories: it deals also with a mixed bag of other logical topics. It is clear that the treatise we have was not written as a single whole by Aristotle, though there is no need to question, as some scholars have done, that it is his authentic work.[4]

One cluster of topics discussed is that of homonymy and synonymy. These words are transliterations of the Greek words Aristotle uses; but whereas the English words signify properties of bits of language, the Greek words as he uses them signify properties of things in the world. Aristotle's account can be paraphrased thus: if A and B are called by the same name with the same meaning, then A is synonymous with B; if A and B are called by the same name with a different meaning, then A is homonymous with B. Because of peculiarities of Greek idiom, we have to tweak Aristotle's examples in English, but it is clear enough what he has in mind. A Persian and a tabby are synonymous with each other because they are both called cats; but they are only homonymous with the nine-tailed whip that is also called a cat. The difference between homonymous and synonymous things, Aristotle says, is that homonymous things have only the name in common, whereas synonymous things have both the name and its definition in common.

Aristotle's distinction between homonymous and synonymous things is an important one which is easily adapted—and was indeed later adapted by himself— into a distinction between homonymous and synonymous bits of language, that is to say between expressions that have only the symbol in common and those that have also the meaning in common.

---

[4] With the exception of 8. 11ᵃ10–18, an editorial insertion to link together two of the disparate elements and to explain gaps in the treatment of the later categories.

The study of homonymy was important for the treatment of fallacies in arguments that are due to the ambiguity of terms used. It is undertaken for these purposes in the *Topics*, and Aristotle gives rules for detecting it. 'Sharp', for instance, has one meaning as applied to knives, and another as applied to musical notes: the homonymy is made obvious because in the case of knives the opposite of 'sharp' is 'blunt', whereas in the case of notes the opposite is 'flat' (*Top.* 1. 15. 106ᵃ13–14). In the course of his studies Aristotle came to draw a distinction between mere chance homonymy (as in the English word 'bank', which is used both for the side of a river and for a moneylending institution) and homonymy of a more interesting kind, which his followers called 'analogy' (*NE* 1. 6. 1096ᵃ27 ff.). His standard example of an analogical expression is 'medical': a medical man, a medical problem, and a medical instrument are not all medical in the same way. However, the use of the words in these different contexts is not a mere pun: medicine, the discipline that is practised by the medical man, provides a primary meaning from which the others are derived (*EE* 7. 2. 1236ᵃ15–22). Aristotle made use of this doctrine of analogy in a variety of ethical and metaphysical contexts, as we shall see.

In Aristotle's logical writings we find two different conceptions of the structure of a proposition and the nature of its parts. One conception can trace its ancestry to Plato's distinction between nouns and verbs in the *Sophist*. Any sentence, Plato there insisted, must consist of at least one verb and one noun (262a–263b). It is this conception of a sentence as constructed from two quite heterogeneous elements that is to the fore in Aristotle's *Categories* and *de Interpretatione*. This conception of propositional structure has also been paramount in modern logic since the time of Gottlob Frege, who made a sharp distinction between words that name objects, and predicates that are true or false of objects.

In the syllogistic of the *Prior Analytics* the proposition is conceived in quite a different way. The basic elements out of which it is constructed are *terms*: elements that are not heterogeneous like nouns and verbs, but that can occur indifferently, without change of meaning, either as subjects or as predicates.[5] To be sure, two terms in succession (like 'man animal') do not compose a sentence: other elements, a quantifier and a copula, such as 'is', must enter in if we are to have a proposition capable of occurring in a syllogism, such as 'Every man is an animal'. Aristotle shows little interest in the copula, and his attention now focuses on the quantifiers and their relations to each other. The features that differentiate subjects from predicates drop out of consideration.[6]

---

[5] Cf. 43ᵃ25–31. Instead of a distinction between noun and verb we here have a distinction between proper names (which are not predicates but of which things are predicated) and terms (which are both predicates and predicated of).

[6] Modern admirers of Frege naturally regard the theory of terms as a disaster for the development of logic. Peter Geach has written, 'Aristotle was logic's Adam; and the doctrine of terms was Adam's fall' (*Logic Matters* (Oxford: Blackwell, 1972), 290).

One of the dysfunctional features of the doctrine of terms is that it fosters confusion between signs and what they signify. When Plato talks about nouns and verbs, he makes quite clear that he is talking about signs. He clearly distinguishes between the name 'Theaetetus' and the person Theaetetus whose name it is; and he is at pains to point out that the sentence 'Theaetetus flies' can occur even though what it tells us, namely the flying of Theaetetus, is not among the things there are in the world. It takes him some trouble to bring out the distinction between signs and signified, because of the lack of inverted commas in ancient Greek. This valuable device of modern languages makes it easy for us to distinguish the normal case where we are using a word to talk about what it signifies, and the special case in which we are mentioning a word to talk about the word itself, as in ' "Theaetetus" is a name'. The doctrine of terms, on the other hand, makes it all too easy to confuse use with mention.

Take a syllogism whose premisses are 'Every human is mortal', 'Every Greek is human'. Shall we say, as Aristotle's language sometimes suggests (e.g. *APr.* 1. 4. 25^{b}37–9), that here mortal is predicated of human, and human is predicated of Greek? This does not seem quite right: what occurs as a predicate is surely a piece of language, and so perhaps we should say instead: 'mortal' is predicated of human and 'human' is predicated of Greek. But then we seem to have four terms, not three, in our syllogism, since ' "human" ' is not the same as 'human'. We cannot remedy this by rephrasing the first proposition thus: 'mortal' is predicated of 'human'. It is human beings themselves, not the words they use to refer to themselves, that are mortal. There is no doubt that Aristotle sometimes fell into confusion between use and mention; the wonder is that, given the quicksand provided by the doctrine of terms, he did not do so more often.

Aristotle on Time and Modality

A feature of propositions as discussed in the *Categories* and the *de Interpretatione* is that they can change their truth-values. At *Cat.* 1. 5. 4^{a}24, when discussing whether it is peculiar to substances to be able to take on contrary properties, he says 'The same statement seems to be both true and false. If, for example, the statement that somebody is sitting is true, after he has stood up that same statement will be false.' According to a common modern conception of the nature of the proposition, no proposition can be at one time true and at another false. A sentence such as 'Theaetetus is sitting', which is true when Theaetetus is sitting, and false at another time, would on this view be said to express a different proposition at different times, so that at one time it expresses a true proposition, and at another time a false one. And a sentence asserting that 'Theaetetus is sitting' *was true* at time *t* is commonly treated as asserting that the proposition that ascribes *sitting at time t* to

Theaetetus is true timelessly. On this account, no proposition is significantly tensed, but any proposition expressed by a tensed sentence contains an implicit reference to time and is itself timelessly true or false.

Aristotle nowhere puts forward such a theory according to which tensed sentences are incompletely explicit expressions of timeless propositions. For him uttered sentences do indeed express something other than themselves, namely thoughts in the mind; but thoughts change their truth-values just as sentences do (*Cat.* 1. 5. 4ª26–8).[7] For Aristotle, a sentence or proposition such as 'Theaetetus is sitting' is significantly tensed, and is at some times true and at others false. It becomes true whenever Theaetetus sits down, and becomes false whenever Theaetetus ceases to sit.

There is, for Aristotle, nothing in the nature of the proposition as such that prevents it from changing its truth-value: but there may be something about the content of a particular proposition that entails that its truth-value must remain fixed.

Logicians in later ages regularly distinguished between propositions that can, and propositions that cannot, change their truth-value, calling the former *contingent* and the latter *necessary* propositions. The roots of this distinction are to be found in Aristotle, but he speaks by preference of predicates, or properties, necessarily or contingently belonging to their subjects. In both the *de Interpretatione* and the *Categories* he discusses propositions such as 'A must be B' and 'A can be not B': propositions later called by logicians 'modal propositions'.

In the *de Interpretatione* he introduces the topic of modal propositions by saying that whereas 'A is not B' is the negation of 'A is B', 'A can be not B' is not the negation of 'A can be B'. A piece of cloth, for instance, has the possibility of being cut, but it also has the possibility of being uncut. However, contradictories cannot be true together. Hence the negation of 'A can be B' is not 'A can be not B' but rather 'A cannot be B'. In the straightforward categorical statement, whether we take the 'not' as going with the 'is' or the 'B' makes no practical difference. In the modal statement, whether we take the 'not' as going with the 'can' or the 'B' makes a great difference. Aristotle likes to bring out this difference by rewriting 'A can be B' as 'It is possible for A to be B', rewriting 'A can be not B' as 'It is possible for A to be not B', and rewriting 'A cannot be B' as 'It is not possible for A to be B' (*Int.* 12. 21ª37–b24). This rewriting allows the negation sign to be unambiguously placed, and brings out the relationship between a modal proposition and its negation.

Modal expressions other than 'possible', such as 'impossible' and 'necessary', are to be treated similarly. The negation of 'It is impossible for A to be B' is not 'It is impossible for A not to be B' but 'It is not impossible for A to be B'; the negation of 'It

---

[7] The truth-value of a proposition is its truth or its falsity, as the case may be.

is necessary for A to be B' is not 'It is necessary for A to be not B' but 'It is not necessary for A to be B' (*Int.* 13. 22ª2–10).

These modal notions are interrelated. 'Impossible' is obviously enough the negation of 'possible', but more interestingly 'necessary' and 'possible' are inter-definable. What is necessary is what is not possible not to be, and what is possible is what is not necessary not to be. If it is necessary for A to be B, then it is not possible for A not to be B, and vice versa. Moreover, if something is necessary, then a fortiori it is possible, and if it is not possible, then a fortiori it is not necessary. Aristotle arranges the different cases in a square of opposition similar to that I exhibited above for categorical propositions.

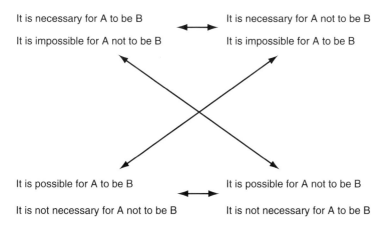

In each corner of this diagram the pairs of propositions are equivalent to each other: this brings out the interdefinability of the modal terms. The operators 'necessary', 'possible', and 'impossible' in this square of opposition are related to each other in a way parallel to the quantifiers 'all', 'some', and 'no' in the categorical square of opposition. As in the categorical case, the propositions in the upper corners are contraries: they cannot both be true together, but they can both be false together. Propositions in one corner are the contradictories of propositions in the diagonally opposite corner. The pair of propositions in the upper corners entail the pair of propositions immediately below them, but not conversely. Propositions in the lower corners are compatible with each other: they can both be true together, but they cannot both be false together (*Int.* 13. 22ª14–35).

In this scheme all necessary propositions are also possible, though the converse is not true. There is, however, as Aristotle remarks, another use of 'possible' in which it is contrasted with 'necessary' and inconsistent with it. In this other use, 'It is possible that A is not B' is not just consistent with 'It is possible that A is B' but actually follows from it (*Int.* 12. 21ᵇ35). In this use 'possible' would be equivalent to 'neither necessary nor impossible'. There is another word, 'contingent' (*endechomenon*), which is available to replace 'possible' in this second use, and Aristotle often uses it for that purpose (e.g. *Apr.* 1. 13. 32ª18–21; 15. 34ᵇ25). Thus propositions can be divided into three classes: the necessary, the impossible, and between the two, the contingent (i.e. those that are neither necessary nor impossible).

One of the most interesting passages in Aristotle's *Organon* is the ninth chapter of the *de Interpretatione*, in which he discusses the relation between tense and modality in propositions. He begins by saying that for what is and what has been, it is necessary that the affirmation or the negation should be true or false (18ª27–8). It transpires that he is not saying simply that if '*p*' is a present- or past-tense proposition, then 'Either *p* or not *p*' is necessarily true: that is something that holds of all propositions, no matter what their tense (19ª30). Nor is he saying just that if '*p*' is a present- or past-tense proposition, it is either true or false: it turns out later that he thinks this is true also of future-tense propositions. What he is saying is that if '*p*' is a present- or past-tense proposition, then '*p*' is a necessary proposition. The necessity in question is clearly not logical necessity: it is not a matter of logic that Queen Anne is dead. The necessity is the kind of necessity that is expressed in the proverbs that what's done cannot be undone, and that it is no use crying over spilt milk (cf. *NE* 6. 2. 1139ᵇ7–11).

The central part of *de Interpretatione* 9 is an inquiry into whether this kind of necessity that applies to present and past propositions applies also to all future propositions. There are, no doubt, universally necessary truths that apply to the future as well as to the present and to the past: but Aristotle's attention focuses on singular propositions such as 'This coat will be cut up before it wears out', 'There will be a sea-battle tomorrow'. The truth or falsity of such propositions is not, on the face of it, entailed by any universal generalization.

However, it is possible to construct a powerful argument to the effect that such a proposition about the future, if it is true, is necessarily true. If A says that there will be a sea-battle tomorrow, and B says that there will not be, then one or other will be speaking the truth. Now there are relations between propositions in different tenses: for instance, if 'Socrates will be white' is now true, then 'Socrates will be white' has been true in the past, and indeed was always true in the past. So—the argument goes—

If it was always true to say it is or will be, then it is impossible for that not to be or to be going to be. But if it is impossible for something not to come about, then it cannot not come about. But if it cannot not come about, then it is necessary for it to come about. Therefore everything that is going to come about is, of necessity, to come about. (9. 18ᵇ11–25)

The argument that Aristotle is considering began by supposing that someone says, for example, 'There will be a sea-battle tomorrow' and someone else 'There will not be a sea-battle tomorrow' and pointing out that one or the other is speaking truly. But, he goes on, a similar prediction might have been made long ago, 'There will be a sea-battle ten thousand years hence', and this too, or its contradictory, will be true. Indeed, it makes no difference whether any prediction has ever been made. If in the whole of time either the proposition or its contradictory has been the truth, it was necessary for the thing to come about. Since of whatever happens 'It will happen' was always previously true, everything must happen of necessity (9. 18ᵇ26–19ᵃ5).

It will follow, Aristotle says, that nothing is a matter of chance or happenstance. Worse, there will be no point in deliberating and choosing between alternatives. But in fact, he says, there are many obvious examples of things turning out one way when they could have turned out another, like a cloak that could have been cut up but wore out first. 'So it is clear that not everything is or happens of necessity, but some things are a matter of happenstance, and the affirmation is not true rather than the negation; and with other things one is true rather and for the most part, but still it is open for either to happen and the other not' (9. 19ᵃ18–22).

How then are we to deal with the argument to the effect that everything happens of necessity? Because Aristotle says that in some cases 'the affirmation is not true rather than the negation', some have thought that his solution was that future contingent propositions lack a truth-value: not only are they not necessarily true or false, they are not true or false at all. However, this can hardly be what he means; for at 18ᵇ17 he says that it is not open to us to say that neither 'It will be the case that *p*' nor 'It will not be the case that *p*' is true. One reason he gives for this is that it is obviously impossible that they should both be false; but that does not rule out their both having some third value. His argument to rule this out is not altogether clear, but it appears to be something like this: if neither 'There will be a sea-battle tomorrow' nor 'There will not be a sea-battle tomorrow' is true today, then neither 'There is a sea-battle today' nor 'There is not a sea-battle today' will be true tomorrow.

At the end of the discussion it seems clear that Aristotle accepts that future contingent propositions can be true, but that they are not necessary in the way that present and past propositions are. Everything is necessary-when-it-is, but that does not mean it is necessary, period. It is necessary that there should or should not be a sea-battle tomorrow, but it is not necessary that there should be a sea-battle and it is not necessary that there should not be a sea-battle (9. 19ᵃ30–2).

What is less clear is how Aristotle disarms the powerful argument he built up in favour of universal necessity. The distinction just enunciated is not sufficient by itself to do so, for it does not take account of the appeal to the past truth of future contingents that was part of the argument. Since on his own admission the past is necessary, past truths about future events must be necessary, and therefore the future events themselves must be necessary. The solution must come through an analysis of the notion of past truths: we must distinguish between truths that are stated in the past tense, and truths that are made true by events in the past. 'It was true ten thousand years ago that there was going to be a sea-battle tomorrow', for all its past tense, is not really a proposition about the past. But this solution is nowhere clearly enunciated by Aristotle, and the problem he set out recurred in many different forms in later antiquity and in the Middle Ages.[8]

In the *Prior Analytics* Aristotle explores the possibility of constructing syllogisms out of modal propositions. His attempt to construct a modal syllogistic is nowadays universally regarded as a gallant failure; and even in antiquity its faults were realized. His successor Theophrastus worked on it and improved it, but even so it must be regarded as unsatisfactory. The reason for the lack of success has been well explained by Martha Kneale: it is Aristotle's indecision about the best way to analyse modal propositions.

If modal words modify predicates, there is no need for a special theory of *modal* syllogisms. For these are only ordinary assertoric syllogisms of which the premises have peculiar predicates. On the other hand, if modal words modify the whole statements to which they are attached, there is no need for a special modal *syllogistic*, since the rules determining the logical relations between modal statements are independent of the character of the propositions governed by the modal words.[9]

The necessary basis for a modal logic, she concludes, is a logic of unanalysed propositions such as was developed by the Stoics. This statement needs qualification. It is true that the flowering of modal logic in the twentieth century depended on just such a propositional calculus. But there were also significant developments in modal logic in the Middle Ages within an Aristotelian context, when Aristotle's own modal syllogistic was superseded by much more sophisticated systems. Again, not all propositions in which words such as 'can' and 'must' occur within the predicate can be replaced by propositions in which the modal operator attaches to an entire nested proposition. 'I can speak French', for instance, does not have the same meaning as 'It is possible that I am speaking French'. Aristotle makes a distinction between two-way possibilities (such as a man's ability to walk, or not to walk, as he chooses) and one-way possibilities (fire can burn wood, and if it has wood placed on it, it *will* burn it, and there are no two ways about it) (*Int.* 22^b36–23^a11). The logic of the two-way abilities exercised in human choice has not, to this day, been adequately formalized.

---

[8] This passage of the *de Interpretatione* has also been the subject of voluminous discussion in modern times. My interpretation owes a lot to that of G. E. M. Anscombe, whose 'Aristotle and the Sea-Battle' of 1956 (*From Parmenides to Wittgenstein* (Oxford: Blackwell, 1981)) is still, nearly fifty years on, one of the best commentaries on the passage. For a carefully argued alternative account, see S. Waterlow, *Passage and Possibility: A Study of Aristotle's Modal Concepts* (Oxford: Clarendon Press, 1982), 78–109.

[9] Kneale and Kneale, *The Development of Logic*, 91.

Stoic Logic

In the generation after Aristotle modal logic was developed in an interesting way in the school of Megara. For Diodorus Cronos a proposition is possible iff it either is or will be true, is impossible iff it is false and will never be true, and is necessary iff it is true and will never be false.[10] Diodorus, like Aristotle, accepted that propositions were fundamentally tensed and could change their truth-values; but unlike Aristotle he does not need to make a sharp distinction between actuality and potentiality, since potentialities are defined in terms of actualities. Propositions, on Diodorus' definitions, change not only their truth-values but also their modalities. 'The Persian Empire has been destroyed' was untrue but possible when Socrates was alive; after Alexander's victories it was true and necessary (LS 38E). For Diodorus, as for Aristotle, a special necessity applies to the past.

It is a feature of Diodorus' definition of possibility that there are no possibilities that are forever unrealized: whatever is possible is or will be one day true. This appears to involve a form of fatalism: no one can ever do anything other than what they in fact do. Diodorus seems to have supported this by a line of reasoning that became known (we know not why) as the Master Argument. Starting from the premiss (1) that past truths are necessary, Diodorus offered a proof that nothing is possible that neither is nor will be true. Let us suppose (taking an example used in ancient discussions of the argument) that there is a shell in shallow water, let us call it Nautilus, which will never in fact be seen. We can construct an argument from this premiss to show that it is impossible for it to be seen.

(2) Nautilus will not ever be seen.
(3) It has always been the case that
    Nautilus will not ever be seen.   (a plausible consequence of (2))
(4) It is necessary that Nautilus will
    not ever be seen.   (from (4) and (1))
(5) It is impossible that Nautilus
    will ever be seen.   (necessarily not = impossible that)

Though we do not know the precise form of Diodorus' proof, it is easy enough to generalize this line of argument to show that only what will happen, can happen.

The argument is obviously akin to one that we met in discussing Aristotle's treatment of future contingents. Diodorus' argument appears to be flawed by an ambiguity in the premiss that past truths are necessary. What is a past truth? If it

---

[10] 'Iff' is a logician's abbreviation for 'if and only if'.

means a true proposition in the past tense, then there is no guarantee that it is necessary. To see this, we have only to think of a negative proposition in the past tense, such as 'The Persian Empire has not been destroyed.' This proposition was true in the time of Socrates, but it was not necessary: it was about to change its truth-value from true to false. On the other hand, if a past truth is a proposition that is made true by an event in the past, then past truths are indeed necessary; but a proposition such as (4) is not a past truth and hence does not entail (5).[11]

Diodorus' pupil Philo abandoned his master's modal definitions, and explained possibility in terms of the internal properties of a proposition rather than in terms of its truth-values over time. We do not know how his explanation went, but we know that on his account a piece of wood would be capable of being burnt even if it was never burnt and even if it spent its whole existence on the bed of the ocean (LS 38B).

Philo's major contribution to logic was his definition of the conditional. 'If p, then q', he said, was false in the case in which p was true and q false, and true in the three other possible cases. The truth of a conditional proposition, on this view, does not depend at all on the content of the antecedent or the consequent, but only on their truth-values. Thus, 'If it is night, it is day' will be true whenever it is daytime, and on the assumption that the atomic theory is true, 'If there are no atoms, there are atoms' is true. In treating the conditional in this way Philo anticipated the truth-functional definition of material implication used in modern propositional logic. However, the truth-values that determine the truth or falsity of his conditionals are changeable truth-values. This has disadvantages for the formulation of logic, since 'If p, then p' is no longer a logical law: 'If I am sitting, I am sitting' comes out false, as a Philonian conditional, if I rise to my feet between the antecedent and the consequent.

Nonetheless, Philo's definition seems to have been adopted by the Stoic logicians who were the first to offer a formalization of propositional logic. Where Aristotle used letters as variables in his logical texts, the Stoics used numbers; this is a trivial difference, but more importantly, where Aristotle's variables stood in for terms, Stoic variables stood in for whole sentences, or rather for elements that are capable of being whole sentences. In 'If the stars are shining, it is night' neither the antecedent, 'the stars are shining', nor the consequent, 'it is night', are complete sentences, but each set of words is capable of standing on its own as a complete sentence.

Stoic propositional logic was embedded in an elaborate theory of language and signification. The Stoics made a distinction between sound (*phone*), speech (*lexis*), and saying (*logos*). The roar of a beast or of the sea is a sound, but only articulate sound counts as speech. Not all speech, however, is meaningful: humans can utter nonsense words like 'hey nonny no'. Only meaningful speech counts as saying

---

[11] See A. N. Prior, *Time and Modality* (Oxford: Clarendon Press, 1957), 86–7; Jonathan Barnes in *CHHP* 89–92.

anything (D.L. 7. 57). The sounds and speech of a Greek can be taken in by a non-Greek-speaking barbarian, but the meaning is understood only by someone who knows the language (S.E., *M* 8. 11–12).

The word 'logos', which I have translated 'saying', is a Greek word of very wide meaning: in different contexts it can mean 'word', 'sentence', 'language', 'reason'. It is a noun connected with the common verb 'legein', meaning 'to say'. The Stoics coined a new word from this verbal root, 'lekton'. This means literally 'thing said', but I will leave the word as an untranslated technicality, since there is no exact English equivalent.

The *lekton* plays an important part in the Stoic treatment of the distinction between signs and what they signify. Consider a sentence such as 'Dion is walking', a proposition which may be true or false. Sextus Empiricus, discussing some such sentence, tells us this:

> The Stoics said that three items are linked together, the signification, the signifier, and the topic (*tunchanon*). The signifier is a sound, such as 'Dion', the signification is the matter that is portrayed (*deloumenon*) by it. . . . and the topic is the external object such as Dion himself. Of these three items two, the sound and the topic, are material, but one is intangible, the matter signified, i.e. the *lekton*, which is what is true or false. (S.E., *M* 8. 11–12)

The *lekton* is what is said by the sentence, namely *that Dion is walking*. This, as Sextus says, is not a tangible entity like Dion himself, or the name 'Dion', or the whole sentence 'Dion is walking'. Dion, the man, is the topic of the sentence, that is to say, what the sentence is *about*. Whether the sentence is true or false depends on whether the *matter* it portrays[12] obtains or not, i.e. on whether Dion is or is not walking. On the basis of passages such as this, then, we can say that a *lekton* is the content of a sentence in the indicative (cf. Seneca, Ep. 117. 13).

Two qualifications need to be made, however, to this definition of *lekton*.

First, Diogenes Laertius tells us that the Stoics distinguished between self-standing and defective *lekta*. He offers 'active and passive predicates' as a gloss on 'defective *lekton*', and explains that a defective *lekton* is one that has a linguistic expression that is incomplete, such as 'is writing', which evokes the question 'Who?' A defective *lekton*, therefore, would be what is said by a predicate, e.g. we may say of someone *that he is writing*. Such a *lekton* remains defective until we make clear who we are talking about, thus specifying a topic, e.g. Socrates (D.L. 7. 63).

Secondly, indicative sentences are not the only ones whose contents provide examples of *lekta*. There are also interrogative sentences, which come in two kinds: the questions that can be answered by 'yes' or 'no', such as 'Is it day?', and the questions that need more complicated answers such as 'Where do you live?' Again,

---

[12] The customary translation of *deloumenon* as 'revealed' is unsatisfactory since you can only reveal what is in fact the case. If the sentence is false, there is no matter to be revealed.

there are commands, like 'Take a bath' and exclamations like 'Isn't the Parthenon beautiful!' (D.L. 7. 66–7).

In fact, the definition I offered of *lekton* as the content of a sentence in the indicative really fits only one particular, though most important, kind of *lekton*. This is what the Stoics called an *axioma*. Several definitions of *axioma* are offered. 'An *axioma* is what is true or false, a complete matter capable of assertion in and by itself.' 'An *axioma* is something which can be asserted or denied in and by itself, such as "it is day" or "Dion is walking" ' (D.L. 7. 65). While an *axioma* is capable of being a self-standing assertion, it need not be asserted. Neither of the two quoted *axiomata* are asserted in 'If Dion is walking, then it is day'. Hence some authors translate the word as 'assertable'.[13] The translation is accurate, but cumbrous, and instead I shall use 'proposition' to render *axioma*, since the meaning of the Greek word, as explained, is close to one of the standard meanings of the English word. It is important to remember, however, that a Stoic proposition is unlike an Aristotelian proposition in that it is not a sentence itself, but something abstract that is said by a sentence; and that it is unlike a proposition as discussed by modern logicians since it is something that can change its truth-value over time.

The Stoics distinguished between simple and non-simple propositions. Simple propositions are constantly illustrated by 'It is day' and 'It is night'; but they include three kinds of subject–predicate propositions, which differ depending on whether their subject is a demonstrative, a proper name, or a pronoun functioning as a quantifier. 'That one is walking' they called a definite proposition, 'Someone is walking' an indefinite proposition, and 'Socrates is walking' an intermediate proposition. Non-simple propositions are those that are compounded out of different propositions by means of one or more connectives (*sundesmoi*). Examples are 'If it is day, it is light', 'Since it is day, it is light', 'Either it is day or it is night' (D.L. 7. 71).

It is in their treatment of non-simple propositions that the Stoics approached most nearly to the modern propositional calculus based on truth-functional operators.[14] A number of differences, however, need to be marked.

In the modern calculus the negation sign is treated as a truth-functional operator, on a par with binary connectives such as 'and', 'or', and 'if'. The Stoics, by contrast, classified negative propositions as simple propositions. They did, however, recognize the possibility of negating a proposition by attaching a negative sign to the entire proposition and not just to the predicate, the procedure that is essential to the operation of the propositional calculus. Thus, they preferred 'Not: it is day' to 'It is not day'. They recognized further that negation could be applied to

---

[13] e.g. Suzanne Bobzien in *CHHP* 93 ff.

[14] A logical operator (i.e. a symbol that forms a new proposition out of one or more other propositions) is truth-functional iff the truth-value of the new proposition depends only on the truth-value of the original propositions, and not on their content.

complex as well as simple propositions; and they realized that in such a case care needed to be exercised in order to sort out genuine from spurious contradictories. 'It is day and it is light' was not the contradictory of 'It is day and it is not light'. The contradictory must be formed by attaching the negation sign at the beginning so that it governs the entire proposition. Thus the notion of *scope* enters into the history of logic (S.E., *M*. 8. 88–90).

Another difference between Stoic logic and modern propositional logic comes out in the treatment of individual connectives. 'Or' in modern propositional logic is treated by convention as an inclusive connective: this is to say, '*p* or *q*' comes out true if *p* and *q* are both true and not just when only one of them is true. The Stoics seem to have been undecided between this view and the exclusive interpretation according to which '*p* or *q*' is true if and only if one and only one of the constituent propositions is true. Moreover, the Stoics allowed among the connectives that form complex propositions some that are not truth-functional. Whether a proposition of the form 'Since *p* then *q*' is true is determined not simply by the truth-values of the constituent propositions.

With regard to the conditional connective 'if', there is some uncertainty how far the Stoics accepted Philo's truth-functional interpretation of it, according to which 'If *p* then *q*' is true in every case except when '*p*' is true and '*q*' is false. Sextus Empiricus roundly attributes this view to them in the following passage:

A sound conditional is one that does not have a true antecedent and a false consequent. A conditional may have a true antecedent and a true consequent, e.g. 'If it is day it is light'. It may have a false antecedent and a false consequent, e.g. 'If the earth flies, the earth has wings'. It may have a true antecedent and a false consequent, e.g. 'If the earth exists, the earth flies'. Or it may have a false antecedent and a true consequent, e.g. 'If the earth flies, the earth exists'. Of these they say that only the one with the true antecedent and the false consequent is unsound, all the others are sound. (S.E., *P*. 2. 104–6)

The examples given here support Sextus' assertion that the Stoics interpreted the conditional truth-functionally. It is characteristic of such an interpretation that the truth of a conditional does not demand any link between the content of the antecedent and the content of the consequent. While 'If the earth flies, the earth has wings' may be linked by the thought that whatever flies has wings, no such link connects 'the earth exists' with 'the earth flies'. Of course, the conditionals in which the Stoics were most interested were ones in which such a link did exist; as in an example given by Sextus shortly afterwards: 'If she has milk, she has conceived'. But the same would be true of most of the examples in a modern textbook even though the logic it expounds is firmly based on a truth-functional interpretation of the basic form of conditional.

On the other hand, there are passages suggesting that at least some Stoics took a different view of the truth-conditions of conditional propositions. Chrysippus is reported as saying that in 'If *p* then *q*' the connective declared that *q followed from p*. This was glossed, by himself or by another Stoic, in the following way:

A conditional is true when the contradictory of its consequent conflicts with its antecedent. For instance, 'If it is day, it is light' is true because 'It is not light', the contradictory of the consequent, conflicts with 'It is day'. A conditional is false when the contradictory of its consequent does not conflict with the antecedent, such as 'If it is day, Dion is walking' because 'Not: Dion is walking' does not conflict with 'It is day'. (D.L. 7. 73)

Here it seems clear that 'conflict' must refer to some kind of incompatibility of content between antecedent and consequent, and not just a difference of truth-value. But the exact nature of the incompatibility (is it logical? is it discovered empirically?) remains unclear.

It is, fortunately, not necessary to resolve these uncertainties in order to present and evaluate the Stoic theory of inference. Whereas Aristotle had indicated each of his syllogisms by listing the conditional necessary truths corresponding to them, the Stoics present their arguments in the form of inference schemata, sometimes using numbers as variables and sometimes using standard examples, and sometimes a mixture of the two as in 'If Plato is alive, Plato is breathing. But the first, therefore the second.' An inference, most Stoics said, must consist of a first premiss (*lemma*), a second premiss (*proslepsis*), and a conclusion (*epiphora*). It was a minority view that an inference might sometimes have only a single premiss (D.L. 7. 76).

The criterion for the invalidity of an inference was analogous to the one Chrysippus offered for the truth-value of a conditional. An inference was valid (*perantikos*) if the contradictory of the conclusion conflicted with the conjunction of the premisses; if it did not conflict, then the inference was invalid. A typical invalid inference was 'If it is day, it is light. But it is day. Therefore Dion is walking' (D.L. 7. 77). Nowadays we are accustomed to distinguish between valid inferences and sound inferences. An inference may be valid but unsound if one or more of its premisses is untrue. The Stoics made a similar distinction, but used the Greek word for 'true', *alethes*, to correspond to 'sound' and 'false' to correspond to 'unsound'. An inference was unsound, they said, if either it was invalid or it contained some falsity in its premisses (D.L. 7. 79).

Inferences came in various forms, called 'moods'. Chrysippus listed five basic forms of valid inference, or 'indemonstrable moods' (D.L. 7. 79). They may be set out as follows, using cardinal numbers rather than ordinals.

(A) If 1 then 2; but 1; therefore 2.
(B) If 1 then 2; but not 2; therefore not 1.
(C) Not both 1 and 2; but 1; therefore not 2.
(D) Either 1 or 2; but 1; therefore not 2.
(E) Either 1 or 2; but not 2; therefore 1.

All valid inferences, Chrysippus believed, could be reduced to these primitive forms, and in his many lost works he seems to have proved many theorems which reduced more complex and derivative moods to these simple patterns. Thus, if we take

(F) If 1, then if 1 then 2; but 1; therefore 2,

we can show this is a valid inference schema by deriving from the two premisses in accordance with (A) 'If 1 then 2', and then using (A) once more to derive, from this conclusion and the second premiss '2' (S.E., *M* 8. 234–6).

On the face of it, Chrysippus' five primitive schemata form neither a complete nor an irreducible basis for deductions within the propositional calculus. There is no primitive proposition to justify the inference of '*p*' from 'both *p* and *q*'; this, no doubt, is because of the reluctance to consider inferences with only a single premiss. The fourth primitive schema is valid only if 'or' is given its exclusive interpretation; but if it is, then it is not needed, since any inference that it validates will already have been validated by (C).

In late antiquity Aristotelian logic and Stoic logic were regarded as rivals, and while the Stoics' own writings have not survived, we have much evidence of polemics between supporters of the two systems. With the hindsight of millennia we can see that the systems were not in general incompatible with each other, but were formulations of different areas of logic, each of them precursors of different, but complementary, modern developments, in the propositional and predicate calculus.

4

Knowledge and its Limits: Epistemology

There is a branch of philosophy nowadays called epistemology: the inquiry into what can be known, and how we can know it. We all have many beliefs on many topics; which, if any of them, can count as real knowledge? What is the mark of genuine knowledge and how does it differ from mere belief? Is there a reliable way to acquire knowledge of the truth and to eliminate false beliefs that are mere seemings? These questions occupied the attention of Greek thinkers from an early stage.

Presocratic Epistemology

Parmenides might well claim to be the founder of epistemology: at least he is the first philosopher to make a systematic distinction between knowledge and belief. At the beginning of his great poem a goddess promises that he will learn all things, both reliable truth and the untrustworthy opinions of mortals. The poem is in two parts: the way of truth and the way of seeming. The way of truth sets out Parmenides' theory of Being, which we will consider in Chapter 6 on metaphysics. The way of seeming deals with the world of the senses, the world of change and colour, the world of empty names. Mortals who do not accept the way of truth, sunk in metaphysical error, know nothing at all. Deaf, dazed, and blind, they can be called 'two-headed' because of the internal inconsistencies of their beliefs (KRS 293).

A sharp contrast between reality and appearance also appears in the writing of a very different philosopher, Democritus. For him, atoms and the void are the only two realities and the qualities perceived by the senses are mere appearances. To show that sense-appearances cannot be the truth about things, he argues that they conflict with each other. The sick and the healthy do not agree about the taste of things, men disagree with other animals, and sensory properties appear different even to the same individual at different times (Aristotle, *Metaph* Γ 5. 1009^{b}7). Sense-appearances lead only to belief, not to truth. 'By convention sweet,' he is quoted as saying, 'by convention bitter; by convention hot, by convention cold; by convention colour, but in reality atoms and void' (KRS 549). To say that a proposition such as 'The wind is cold' enunciates a false belief seems not quite the same as saying that it enunciates something that is true only by convention; but whatever exactly Democritus meant, it is clear that he maintained that the senses did not deliver truths about an independent reality.

If I stand in the same wind as you and pronounce it hot, while you pronounce it cold, Democritus would say that neither of us is speaking the truth. The sophist Protagoras took up a quite opposite position: he claimed that each of us is speaking the truth (Plato, *Tht.* 151e). 'Man is the measure of all things,' he famously said; 'both of things that are that they are, and of things that are not that they are not' (KRS 551). Whatever appears true to a particular person *is* true for that person. All beliefs, therefore, are true: but they have only a relative truth. There is no such thing as the independent, objective truth that Democritus sought, and failed to find, in sense-appearance. Democritus objected that Protagoras' doctrine was self-refuting. If all beliefs are true, then among true beliefs is the belief that not every belief is true (DK 68 A114).

Protagoras might have tried to counter this objection by restricting his claim to the case of sense-perception. The expression 'It appears to me that . . . ', and its equivalent in Greek, can cover either sense-impressions or opinions, and this fact is exploited by Democritus in his refutation. Historically, however, Protagoras did not take this route of escape: his interests extended far wider than the realm of sense-perception. Diogenes Laertius tells us that he said that there were two opposed accounts of every matter, and Seneca that he claimed that on every issue one could argue equally well on either side.[1] If A offers arguments for *p*, and B offers arguments for not-*p*, and both sets of arguments are equally good, how should I decide between them? Protagoras appears to suggest that I should not decide, but accept both. But does not this involve accepting both sides of a contradiction? On the contrary, Protagoras denied that contradiction was possible (D.L. 9. 53). What is really accepted is not '*p*' and 'not-*p*' but ' "*p*" is true for A' and ' "not-*p*" is true for B'.

For Protagoras, all truth is relative, and not just truth about obviously subjective matters such as the feel of the wind. For this thesis, so far as we know, he did not offer any argument, merely the analogy between sense-appearances and beliefs, and a personal claim to be able to match any argument pro with an argument contra. But the thesis does give him an escape from Democritus' trap. He can accept 'Some beliefs are false' as true—but true *for Democritus*. He can

---

[1] D.L. 9. 51; DK 80 A20. See J. Barnes, *The Presocratic Philosophers*, rev. edn. (London: Routledge, 1982), ii. 243.

continue to believe that 'No beliefs are false' is true—true, of course, for himself, for Protagoras. There has to be some other way of sorting out the issue between the two of them—a way which Plato, as we shall see, attempted to provide.

Protagoras is sometimes described as a sceptic. In one way this is an odd description. A sceptic is someone who thinks the discovery of truth is difficult, perhaps impossible. For Protagoras it is all too easy: you only have to frame a belief and, hey presto, it is true. But from the point of view of someone like Democritus, the replacement of a universal, objective concept of truth with a relative one is itself a very deep form of scepticism. The only kind of truth really worth seeking is, for a relativist, impossible to discover because it does not exist.

Democritus himself, however, was in no strong position to reject scepticism. He claimed that there were two kinds of knowledge, one through the senses and one through the intellect. Only intellectual knowledge is legitimate knowledge; the five senses deliver only a bastard version (S.E., *M.* 7. 130–9). There is, however, a problem: the intellectual knowledge expressed in the atomic theory is based in part on empirical evidence: and this comes from the cheating senses. Galen, quoting the dictum about the conventionality of sense-properties, says, 'Having slandered appearances, [Democritus] makes the senses address the intellect thus: "Mind, you wretch! You take your evidence from us and then you throw us over! Our overthrow is your downfall too"' (KRS 552).

Logically, then, perhaps Democritus should have ended up not as an atomist but as a sceptic. One of his pupils, Metrodorus of Chios, is known to have made an extreme statement of scepticism: 'None of us knows anything, not even whether we know or do not know, nor even what knowing and not knowing are' (DK 70 B1). But this was at the beginning of a book of atomistic physics, so it is hard to know how seriously to take this manifesto. The sophist Gorgias, on the other hand, offered an argument to show that knowledge of reality was impossible. It went like this. If objects of thought (*ta phronoumena*) are not real (*onta*), then what is real is not an object of thought. But objects of thought are not real; for if any of them are, all of them are, just as they are thought. But just because someone thinks of a man flying or chariots running on the sea, that does not mean that there is a flying man or chariots running on the sea. Hence it is not the case that what is thought of is real; and therefore what is real is not an object of thought (DK 82 B3).

We do not know whether Gorgias meant this argument seriously or not. We need not question that if no object of thought is a reality, then no reality is an object of thought. The weak point in the argument seems to be the claim that if some object of thought is real, then all objects of thought are real. The very choice of examples suggests that we can distinguish between those cases where an object of thought is not real and those cases where it is real (i.e. when the thought has a reality corresponding to it).

Socrates, Knowledge, and Ignorance

Protagoras and Gorgias were sophists, and it was a regular complaint against the sophists that they were purveyors of scepticism. Some thought that Socrates was tarred with the same brush. Socrates certainly went round puncturing other people's claims to knowledge, and prided himself on his awareness of his own ignorance. But he never challenged claims to knowledge when made by craftsmen and experts in their own particular fields. Indeed, over and over again, in Plato's Socratic dialogues, we are given a run through half a dozen arts and crafts—shoemaking, shipbuilding, navigation, cookery, medicine—to provide a paradigm of knowledge against which to test and find wanting the pretensions of those who claim moral and political knowledge. If Socrates was a sceptic, his scepticism was of a limited and contingent kind. It was only of certain important things that knowledge was unavailable; and it was not necessarily unavailable to human beings, it was just not to be found in the Athens of the day.

But in order to evaluate Socrates' epistemology, and still more in order to understand the epistemological theses that Plato in his dialogues puts in Socrates' mouth, it is necessary to discuss the different Greek words that correspond more or less to the English word 'knowledge'. The word 'epistemology' itself is derived from the Greek word 'episteme', a word that is often used to indicate knowledge of a rather grand kind, so that one of its English equivalents is 'science'. Besides the verb 'epistamai' which goes with this noun, there are humbler words for more everyday knowledge and acquaintance. Hence, someone who denies the possibility of *episteme* in a particular area is not necessarily a sceptic ruling out the possibility of all knowledge.

The Delphic oracle pronounced that no one was wiser than Socrates. After interrogating those who had a reputation for wisdom (*sophia*), Socrates came to the conclusion that he was wiser than them in that he did not falsely believe he knew matters that he did not know. Questioning the politicians and the poets, he concluded that they did not have any real knowledge of the areas in which they had made their reputation. When he went to the craftsmen, however, he did find that they had knowledge (*episteme*) of many things where he was ignorant, and to that extent they were wiser than he was. The problem was that on the basis of their particular expertise, they foolishly thought themselves wise on totally different, and more important, topics. Socrates decided that he was better off than they, lacking both their wisdom and their ignorance (*Apol.* 22d–e).

In Plato's Socratic dialogues there is always someone who claims knowledge in a particular area; typically, a character will claim to know the nature of a particular virtue or craft. Thus, Euthyphro claims to have knowledge of piety and impiety (*Euthphr.* 4e–5a), Meno is happy to accept that he knows what virtue is (*Men.* 71d–e), and even the modest Charmides thinks he knows what modesty is. Socrates then questions such a character in order to get the knowledge expressed in a definition. As each definition is produced, he declares it deficient, either producing counter-examples or revealing ambiguities in its terms. Counter-examples can take two forms: they can show either that the definition covers more than it should, or that it covers less than it should. Thus, when Cephalus in *Republic* 1 says that justice is telling the truth and returning what is borrowed, Socrates complains that returning a borrowed weapon to a mad friend is not just (*Rep.* 331c–d). On the other hand, when Laches, in the dialogue called after him, says that courage is standing at one's post without running away, Socrates points out that tactical retreat can be an expression of courage (191c). Sooner or later, the alleged expert has to admit that his definition breaks down; and the failure to be able to produce a satisfactory definition is taken to show that the claim to knowledge was unjustified.

The questioning Socrates, in Plato's dialogues, is never satisfied with being offered a list of items falling under a certain concept such as *virtue* or *knowledge*. Meno tells him that there are many different kinds of virtue: one for males, one for females, one for children; one for slaves and one for freemen; one for the young and one for the old. Socrates says that this is no use: it is like telling someone who wants to know what a bee is that there are many different kinds of bee. Bees of different kinds, Socrates says, do not differ from one another in so far as they are bees; and what we want to find out is that very thing in which they are all the same and do not differ from one another (*Men.* 72c). So too with virtue. Socrates, we might say, is looking for the *essence* of virtue.

Knowledge of the essence of something is clearly a very special kind of knowledge: and ever since Plato's Socrates it has been for many philosophers a paradigm of knowledge. Other philosophers, in recent times, have criticized Socratic insistence on knowledge of essences. Wittgenstein pointed out that among the items that most interest philosophers some may not have such an essence at all. He denied, for instance, that everything we call language possesses one feature in common which makes us use the same word for all. Rather, these phenomena are related to one another in many different ways, just as different members of the same family will resemble each other in different features such as build, gait, colour, temperament, and so on.[2] Even where X does have an essence, being able to define that essence or to articulate an exceptionless criterion for distinguishing Xs from not Xs is not a necessary condition for being genuinely able to tell an X when one sees one. Thus, I can know that a computer is not alive without being able to produce a watertight criterion to separate life from non-life.[3]

[2] L. Wittgenstein, *Philosophical Investigations* (Oxford: Blackwell, 1958), 1. 66–7.
[3] The denial of this is called by Peter Geach 'the Socratic Fallacy' (*God and the Soul* (London: Routledge, 1969), 40).

We can agree that knowledge, in the everyday sense of the English word, can be present in the absence of the power to define and delimit. It might well be thought, however, to be the special task of the philosopher to seek for essences, or, as the case may be, to lay out the family resemblances between different applications of a concept. The goal of this special task is to reach a level of knowledge, or at least understanding, that is superior to that possessed by the ordinary informal employer of a concept. And it was for this level of insight that Plato, in his mature dialogues, came to reserve the Greek word 'episteme'.

Knowledge in the Theaetetus

One of the richest of Plato's dialogues, the *Theaetetus*, is devoted to the question: What is knowledge (*episteme*)? (145e). This dialogue, though not an early one, has the structure usual for a Socratic dialogue: the protagonist (in this case a brilliant young mathematician) offers a series of definitions, all in turn are rejected by Socrates, and the drama ends with a proclamation of ignorance. The young Theaetetus, at the beginning of the dialogue, is pregnant with a reply to the question, 'What is knowledge?' Socrates offers himself as midwife to bring it to birth (149a–151d); but the pregnancy turns out to be imaginary, with only a phantom offspring.

Theaetetus' first proposal is that knowledge consists of things like geometry and astronomy, on the one hand, and shoemaking and carpentry on the other (146d). This will not do: Socrates is never happy with a list, and he says that if we tried to define geometry and carpentry the word 'knowledge' itself would turn up in the definition. Theaetetus next suggests that knowledge is perception: to know something is to perceive it with the senses (151e). Socrates observes that since only what is true can be known, knowledge can be sense-perception only if such perception is always correct. But this can only be the case if we accept the thesis of Protagoras that whatever seems to a particular person is true for him.

With regard to momentary sensations, Protagoras' thesis may be given plausibility by the thesis of Heraclitus that the world is in constant flux. The colours we see are not stable objects: when my eye encounters a piece of marble, the whiteness of the marble and my vision of that whiteness are two momentary items, twins begotten together by the encounter of the parent eye and the parent marble (156c–d). If, then, on a particular occasion I say 'This is white', I cannot be wrong: no one else is in a position to contradict me. The same is true of other kinds of sense-perception (157a).

Let us suppose we concede to Protagoras that, in such a case, what the perceiver says goes. Still, Socrates insists, there are many other kinds of case where it would be absurd to make such a claim. We have dreams in which we think we are flying; a man may go mad and think he is a god. Surely these are cases where what seems to a person is not true? And even the ordinary cases, where the perception is not erroneous, cannot be cases of real knowledge. For how can we be sure that we are not dreaming? Half our life is spent abed, and it is a commonplace that it is impossible to prove that one is awake and not asleep (158c–e).

At this point Socrates offers Theaetetus (and Protagoras) a response—rather a feeble response, since it deals with the case not of dreamers or madmen, but of sick people whose senses are affected by their disease. Suppose Socrates falls ill, and sweet wine begins to taste sour to him. On the Heraclitean account, the taste of the wine is the offspring of the wine and the taster. Socrates sick is a different taster from Socrates healthy, and with a different parent naturally the offspring differs. It may not be true that the wine is sour, but it is, in his sickness, sour for Socrates. So we do not have here a case of erroneous perception, and the equivalence of knowledge and perception is not yet defeated.

Socrates in the dialogue moves on to different terrain. There are cases of perception without knowledge: we can hear a foreign language spoken, and yet not know the language (163b). There are cases of knowledge without perception: when we shut our eyes and recall something we have seen, we know what it looks like and yet are no longer seeing it (164a). But if knowing = perception, then both these must be cases of simultaneously knowing and not knowing, and surely that is an absurdity? But even now, Socrates is willing to allow Protagoras a way out. It is easy to have cases of simultaneous perception and non-perception: if you wear an eyepatch you see something with one eye but not with the other. So if perception = knowledge, it is no surprise that you can both know and not know at the same time (165c).

In discussing Theaetetus' identification of knowledge and perception, Plato's Socrates gives Protagoras a surprising amount of rope. But he is, in the end, confident that Protagoras hangs himself on Democritus' hook. It seems to all men that some men know better than others: if so, that must—according to Protagoras—be true for all men. It seems to most people that Protagoras' thesis is false; if so, his thesis must be, on his own account, more false than true, since the unbelievers outnumber the believers (170b–171d). But his thesis can be attacked more directly. However plausible it may be if applied to sense-perception, it cannot apply to medical diagnosis or political prediction. Even if each man is an authority on what he senses *now*, he is not the measure of what he *will* feel or perceive: a physician knows better than a patient whether the patient will later feel hot or cold, and a vintner will know better than a drinker whether a wine, come next year, will taste sweet or dry (178c).

The final argument by which Socrates leads Theaetetus to abandon the proposal that knowledge is perception is this. The objects of the senses are delivered to us through different channels: we see with our eyes and hear with our ears. Colours are not the same as sounds; we cannot hear colours and we cannot see sounds. But what of the judgement 'Colours are not the same as sounds'? Where does that piece of knowledge come from? It cannot come from the eyes, since they cannot see sounds; it cannot come from the ears, since they cannot hear colours. Moreover, there are no organs for detecting sameness, in the way that there are organs for seeing and hearing. It is the soul itself that contemplates the common terms that apply to the deliverances of all of the senses (184b–185d).

Theaetetus, in response to this argument, moves to a second proposed definition of knowledge. Knowledge is not perception (*aesthesis*); it is thought (*doxa*), and thought is an activity of the soul by itself. When the mind is thinking, it is as if it were talking to itself, asking and answering questions, and silently forming opinions. Knowledge cannot be identified outright with thought, because there are false thoughts; but perhaps we can say that knowledge is true thought (187a5).

Socrates, after an interesting diversion in which he points out that the notion of 'false thought' is not without its problems, offers an objection to this definition. There are cases where people have true thoughts, and form true opinions, without having actual knowledge. If a jury is persuaded by a clever attorney to bring in a certain verdict, then if the verdict accords with the facts, the jurors will have formed a true opinion. But do their true thoughts amount to knowledge? Not really, says Socrates: only an eyewitness is in a position really to know what happened in a case of alleged assault or robbery. So knowledge cannot be defined as true thought.

Socrates showed earlier that knowledge is not perception by giving an example of a piece of knowledge for which perception was insufficient. He has now shown that knowledge is not true opinion by giving an example of a piece of knowledge for which perception was necessary. It might be expected that Theaetetus might have responded by offering an account of knowledge embracing both perception and thought in some relation to each other. Instead he offers an elaboration of his second definition. Knowledge, he now suggests, is true thought plus a *logos*; and he proposes three forms that the *logos* may take (206c).

'Logos', as has been remarked, is a difficult word to translate because it corresponds to many different English words: 'word' itself, 'sentence', 'discourse', 'reason'. In the present context it is clear that for Theaetetus a true thought with a *logos* is a thought that is somehow articulated in a way that a thought without a *logos* is not: but I shall leave the word untranslated while explaining the different kinds of articulation he has in mind.

One way in which one can give a *logos* of a thought is by expressing it in words. But being able to articulate a thought in this sense cannot be what makes the difference between true thought and knowledge, since anyone who is not dumb is capable of doing so (206d–e).

More plausibly, a *logos* may be a kind of analysis. To know what X is to be able to analyse it into its elements. Thus one can exhibit knowledge of a word by spelling it out in letters. If that is what knowledge is, then knowledge of reality must be exhibited in analysing it into the ultimate elements of which it is composed. But the analogy with spelling places us in a difficulty. The word 'Socrates' can be analysed into its elements, such as the letter S. But the letter S cannot be further analysed; unlike the word 'Socrates', the letter S has no spelling. So if knowledge involves analysis, the ultimate, unanalysable elements of the universe cannot be known. And if the elements of a complex cannot be known, how can the complex itself be known? Moreover, a mere listing of the elements of a complex is insufficient for knowledge unless the elements are put together in the correct way (207b).

Theaetetus' final account of giving a *logos* of an object is giving a description that is uniquely true of it: thus one might give a *logos* of the sun by saying that it is the brightest of the heavenly bodies. But does this amount to real knowledge of the sun? Surely, being able to offer some definite description of X is a necessary condition of having any thought at all about X; it is not sufficient to turn a true thought about X into a piece of genuine knowledge.

At this point Theaetetus gives up. The thoughts he has delivered with the aid of Socrates' midwifery turn out to be mere wind-eggs. We are far from having reached a definition of knowledge; and hence all the use of words like 'know' and 'not know' throughout the dialogue turns out to have been illegitimate (196e).

Perhaps Theaetetus gave up too soon. If he had offered a fourth account of 'logos' as meaning something like 'justification', 'reason', or 'evidence', then his definition of knowledge as true belief plus *logos* would have been found satisfactory by many a philosopher during the subsequent millennia of philosophy. But Plato's Socrates was a hard man to satisfy, and Plato himself, in the sixth and seventh books of his *Republic*, has his Socrates present quite a different epistemology in quite a different style.

Knowledge and Ideas

The presentations in the two dialogues differ above all because the *Republic* appeals, as the *Theaetetus* does not, to Plato's Theory of Ideas. Common to both dialogues is the principle that what is known must be true; knowledge can only be of what *is*. The Ideas are relevant in the *Republic* because Plato is committed to the thesis that only the Ideas really *are*: that is to say, everything other than an Idea is what it is only in a qualified sense. Beautiful things other than the Idea of Beauty, for instance, are beautiful only at one time and not another, or beautiful only in one part and not in another. Nothing except the Idea of Beauty is just beautiful, period (*Smp.* 211a). The Ideas make their first appearance in the *Republic* in the fifth book, where Plato is describing the philosopher. He describes him as the lover of truth, and distinguishes him from the mere dilettante, the lover of sights and sounds.

The non-philosopher does not know the difference between beautiful objects and beauty itself: he is living in a dream, mistaking an image for reality (*Rep.* 476c–d). For the state of mind (*dianoia*) of such a person, Plato uses the word 'doxa', which in the *Theaetetus* was used for thought, or belief. He contrasts it with the knowledge that belongs to the philosopher—here called *gnome*. If knowledge must be knowledge of what *is*, and only an Idea utterly *is*, then knowledge must be knowledge of Ideas. If there is anything at the opposite pole from an Idea, something that utterly *is not*, that is totally unknowable. But most things that are F are partly F and partly not F, F in one respect and not in another. They are set in between what is utterly F and what is utterly not F. These are the objects of *doxa*.

At this point a fundamental difference emerges between the *Republic* and the *Theaetetus*. In the *Theaetetus* we sought to locate the essential characteristic of knowledge as a feature of the state of mind of the knower: is it a matter of sensation? must it include a *logos*? But in the *Republic* the difference between knowledge and belief is a difference between objects: between *what* is known and *what* is thought of. This point is made quite explicitly. Knowledge and thought, Plato says, are *powers* (*dynameis*), just as sight and hearing are powers. Powers do not have colours or shapes by which we can tell one from another. 'In the case of a power I look only at what it is concerned with and what it does to it, and by reference to that I call each the power it is' (477d). Sight is a power to discriminate colour, and hearing a power to discriminate sound: it is the difference between the objects, colour and sound, that distinguishes these two powers from each other. Similarly, Plato proposes, the difference between knowledge and belief is to be determined by noting the differences between the two kinds of object with which they deal (478b6 ff.).

In book 6 Plato takes this line of argument further, and subdivides *gnome* and *doxa*. *Doxa*, or thought, has the visible world as its realm, but it comes in two different forms that have different objects. One form is imagination (*eikasia*), whose objects are shadows and reflections; another form is belief (*pistis*), whose objects are the living creatures about us and the works of nature or of human hands. The realm of *gnosis*, of knowledge, is likewise divided into two. Knowledge *par excellence* is *noesis*, or understanding, whose object is the Ideas that are the province of the philosopher. But there is also another kind of knowledge, typical of the mathematician, to which Plato gives the name *dianoia* (509c5 ff.). The abstract objects of the mathematician share with the Ideas the characteristic of eternity and unchangeability: they belong to the world of being, not of becoming. But they also share a characteristic with ordinary terrestrial objects, namely they are multiple and not single. The geometer's circles, unlike the Ideal Circle, can intersect with each other; and the arithmetician's twos, unlike the one and only Idea of Two, can be added to each other to make four (cf. 525c–526a).

Plato distinguishes between the mathematician and the philosopher on the basis not only of the different objects of their disciplines, but also of the different methods of their investigation. Mathematicians, he complains, start from hypotheses which they treat as obvious and do not feel called upon to give an account of. The philosopher, however, though starting likewise from hypotheses, does not, like the mathematician, immediately move down from hypotheses to conclusions, but ascends first from hypotheses to an unhypothetical principle, and only then redescends from premiss to conclusion. Philosophical method is called by Plato 'dialectic'; and dialectic, he says, 'treats its assumptions, not as first principles, but literally as hypotheses, like stepping stones or starting points on a journey up to an unhypothetical first principle'. Having grasped this principle, dialectic 'goes into reverse, and, keeping hold of what follows from the principle, finally comes down to a conclusion' (511b). The upward path of dialectic is described again in book 7 as a course of 'taking up what has been laid down and travelling up to the first principle of all'. 'Taking up what has been laid down' is equivalent to unhypothesizing the hypotheses, which in a particular case may mean either abandoning a hypothesis, or placing it on an unhypothetical foundation (533c).

Scholars have not been able to reach agreement on the precise nature of dialectic, as envisaged by Plato, but in broad outline we can say that the dialectician operates as follows. He takes a hypothesis, a questionable assumption, and tries to show that it leads to a contradiction. When he reaches a contradiction, he abandons the hypothesis and goes on to test the other premisses used to derive the contradiction, and so on until he reaches a premiss that is unquestionable. The procedure can be illustrated in the *Republic* itself.

In book 1 three characters in the dialogue, Cephalus, Polemarchus, and Thrasymachus, each offer definitions of justice, which are shown by Socrates to be unsatisfactory. Cephalus' proposal that justice is telling the truth and returning what is borrowed is refuted because, Socrates claims, it is not just to return a weapon to a mad friend (331c). But this refutation depends on an implicit definition of justice as doing good to one's friends and harm to one's enemies. When this definition is made explicit by Polemarchus (332b ff.), it is refuted on the grounds that it is never just to harm any man at all. This refutation, in its turn, depends on the premiss that justice is human goodness: it is surely preposterous to think that a good man could exercise his goodness in making others less good. But Thrasymachus leaps in to challenge this premiss: justice is not goodness, but weakness and foolishness (338c). Eventually, Thrasymachus too is refuted, when he is forced to agree that the just man will have a better life than the unjust (354a). His surrender is exacted by a number of hypotheses that are themselves questionable and most of which are questioned elsewhere in the *Republic*.

For instance, one hypothesis assumed against Thrasymachus is that it is the soul's function to direct the person whose soul it is. This hypothesis is reviewed when, in book 4, Socrates divides the soul into three parts: this directing function belongs not to the whole soul but only to reason. In establishing the trichotomy Socrates appeals to the following principle: it is not the case 'that the same thing can ever act or be acted upon in two opposite ways, or be two opposite things, at the same time, in respect of the same part of itself, and in relation to the same object' (437a). This, which seems at first to be a harmless principle of non-contradiction, turns out to be, in Plato's eyes, a hypothesis that is not true of anything except the Ideas. So the dialectician on his upward path has to move into the realm of Ideas.

The path to a full understanding of the nature of justice would go through the different degrees of cognition identified by Plato on book 6. The first degree is what Plato calls imagination. Someone who reads the poets and watches dramatic spectacles (provided the texts are of an approved kind) will have seen justice triumphing on the stage and will have learnt that the gods are unchanging, good, and truthful (382c). From this he will proceed to true belief about justice: this will be equivalent to competence in the human justice that operates in the law courts. But to learn what ideal justice is, and to see how it takes its place in the system of Ideas which is presided over by the supreme Idea, the Idea of Good, will be the task of dialectic. Sadly, as he approaches the end of the upward path of dialectic, to learn from goodness itself the first principles of law and morality, the Socrates of the *Republic*, like Moses on Mount Sinai, disappears into a cloud. He can talk only in metaphor, and cannot give even a provisional account of goodness itself (506d).

The obscurity of the Theory of Ideas, and in particular of the Idea of the Good, means that there is a hole at the centre of the epistemology of the *Republic*. What it is to have knowledge of an Idea, and how such knowledge is acquired, is never there explained. Other dialogues—the *Phaedo*, the *Meno*—put forward a startling suggestion to fill this gap. Knowledge of Ideas is essentially recollection: recollection of acquaintance in an earlier, more spiritual life. This proposal, more metaphysical than epistemological, will be considered in a later chapter.

Aristotle on Science and Illusion

In epistemology, as in other matters, Aristotle's agenda was set by Plato. He accepted Plato's distinction between the senses and the intellect, and attached great importance to it, often attacking earlier thinkers, such as Empedocles and Democritus, for failing to appreciate the distinction between sensation and thought (e.g. *Metaph. Γ* 5.1009^{b}14 ff.). With the *Theaetetus* in mind, he addressed once again the Protagorean question of the reliability and fallibility of the senses. Finally, he took over and developed the Platonic catalogue of different intellectual states; and set out criteria for the attainment of the highest such state, namely scientific knowledge.

Plato frequently emphasized the unstable and confusing nature of sense-experience. For instance, in the tenth book of the *Republic* he wrote, 'Things look crooked when seen in water and straight when seen out of it; things can look both concave and convex because colours mislead the eye; and all kinds of similar confusion are manifest in our souls' (602c–d). He contrasted this with the constancy of the results of the calculations and measurements carried out by the reasoning part of the soul.

Aristotle considers the epistemic status of the senses in the course of defending the principle of contradiction against Protagorean arguments in *Metaphysics Γ* (5. 1009^{b}1 ff.). The problem arises from the occurrence of conflicting sense-impressions. We have these four propositions.

(1) Sense says that *p*.
(2) Sense says that not-*p*.
(3) What Sense says is true.
(4) Not both *p* and not-*p*.

This is an inconsistent quartet: any three of the propositions can be used to prove the falsity of the fourth. This possibility is used in different ways by different protagonists to the debate that Aristotle is addressing. Democritus and Plato, followed by sceptics ancient and modern, accept (1), (2), and (4) as showing the falsity of (3). Aristotle's Protagoreans accept (1), (2), and (3) as showing the falsity of (4). In modern times some philosophers have sought to defend (3) and (4) by qualifying (1) and (2) and introducing the notion of sense-data. Sense, according to these philosophers, does not really say that the stick is straight and that the stick is not straight; it says that here and now there is a visual non-straight-looking sense-datum, and here and now there is a tactile straight-feeling sense-datum.

Aristotle, like the sense-datum theorists, deals with the inconsistent quartet by qualifying (1) and (2). But he does not do so by altering the content of *p*. The senses do tell us about external realities and not about an alleged purely mental entity such as a sense-datum. He solves his problems by focusing on Sense. Wherever we have an apparent case of Sense saying that *p*, and Sense saying that not-*p*, we really have a case of one sense S1 saying that *p*, and another sense S2 saying that not-*p*. Not all that the senses tell us is true, and if S1 and S2 tell us different stories we can give reasons for making a choice between them.

It is an essential part of the Protagorean contention that where two judgements of sense conflict, there should be no reason for preferring the one to the other in regard of truth. But someone might say that in the case of the conflict of tastes between healthy and sick, we are to prefer the report of the healthy, since this is the opinion of the majority. The reply to this that Aristotle offers Protagoras is that we cannot treat majority opinion as the criterion of truth. If a worldwide epidemic broke out, those now called healthy might be outnumbered, and there would no longer be reason to accept as true their opinion that honey is sweet (*Metaph. Γ.* 5. 1009^{a}1–5).

Aristotle can agree that the reason for preferring healthy perception to diseased perception must be something other than statistical. But he counters the

Protagorean conclusion by saying that everyone does in fact grade appearances and no one treats them as all equally trustworthy. If you doze off in Libya and dream you are in Athens, you do not, on waking, set off for the Athens theatre (*Metaph.* Γ. 5. 1010^{b}11). Aristotle offers a number of criteria for ranking sense-appearances when it is necessary to choose between them, the most important of which is that a sense has priority when it is judging its proper object.

The proper object of each sense is defined in the *de Anima* (2. 6. 418^{a}12) as being that which cannot be perceived by another sense, and that about which it is impossible to be deceived: colour is the proper object of sight, sound of hearing, and flavour of taste. Aristotle's first point is clear enough: we cannot taste a colour, hear a flavour, or see a sound. But what is meant by saying that a sense cannot be deceived about its proper object? Aristotle is quick to explain that if I see something white, I can be mistaken about whether it is a man or something else, but not about whether it is white or not (3. 6. 430^{b}29). This makes it look as if he is saying simply that if when you use your eyes, and confine yourself to making statements about how things look to you here and now, then you cannot go wrong. But this cannot be what he means, for he clearly envisages there being genuine conflicts between two deliverances of a single sense, and he offers rules for sorting them out: in the case of sight, for instance, prefer a closer glimpse to a more distant one.

So the infallibility of the senses about their proper objects, for Aristotle, does not mean that whatever appears to a particular sense within its own competence is true. Not all statements made about colour on the basis of using our eyes are true: what appears to be red may not be red. Statements such as 'That is red' made on the basis of visual experience are not incorrigible. What is special about them is that they can be corrected only by a further use of the same sense. If we are not sure whether a thing really is the colour it looks from here to me now, we check by having a better look, by looking closer, by looking in a better light. Against the verdict of any particular look an appeal lies; but where what is in question is colour, the appeal can never go to a court higher than that of sight. With qualities proper to other senses, or senses perceptible by more than one sense (the 'common sensibles'), sight does not have the final verdict (*Metaph.* Γ. 5. 1010^{b}15–18). So, generalizing: each sense is the final judge in the case of its proper object, though it has to get into the right condition and position to judge. Where S1 and S2 tells us different things about sensory properties, S1 is to be preferred over S2 if S1 is the proper sense, and S2 is the alien sense, for the property in question. Between two verdicts of the proper sense, we are to choose the one delivered in optimum conditions: near, not far; healthy, not ill; awake not asleep; and so on.

It is thus that Aristotle seeks to avoid both Protagoras' phenomenalism and Plato's intellectualism. He insists that our knowledge depends on the senses both for the concepts we employ and for the unproved premises from which we start.

131

We form concepts thus: first there is sensation and then there is memory; memories build up into experience and out of individual experience we form a universal concept, which is the basis of both practical skill (*techne*) and theoretical knowledge (*episteme*) (*APo.* 19. 100ᵃ3). It is for experience, Aristotle says in the *Prior Analytics* (1. 30 46ᵃ17–22), to provide the principles of any subject. Astronomers begin with their experience of the heavens, and only after mastering astronomical phenomena do they go on to seek causes and offer proofs. A similar method should be adopted in the life sciences (*APr.* 1. 1. 639ᵇ7–10, 640ᵇ14–18).

Science begins, but does not end, with experience, and, like Plato, Aristotle has an elaborate classification of cognitive and intellectual states. Both philosophers regard moral virtue and intellectual excellence as two species of a particular genus; but whereas Plato (no doubt under the influence of Socrates) tended to treat virtue as if it was a special kind of science, Aristotle treats science as a special kind of virtue. The Aristotelian counterpart of Plato's anatomy of knowledge occurs in one of the common books of the *Ethics* (*NE* 6, *EE* 5) where he is dealing with intellectual virtues. The Greek word 'arete' corresponds to both 'virtue' and 'excellence'; so I shall leave it, in the present context, untranslated.

The nature of the *arete* of anything depends upon its *ergon*, that is to say its job or characteristic output. The *ergon* of the mind and all its faculties is the production of true and false judgements (*NE* 6. 2. 1139ᵃ29). That, at least, is its *ergon* in the sense of its characteristic activity, its output whether it is working well or ill; its activity when it is working well and doing its job, and therefore its *ergon* in the strict sense, is truth alone (2. 1139ᵇ12). The intellectual *aretai*, then, are excellences that make an intellectual part of the soul come out with truth. There are five states of mind that have this effect—*techne*, *episteme*, *phronesis*, *sophia*, *nous*—which we may translate as skill, science, wisdom, understanding, and insight (3. 1139ᵇ16–17).

Skill and wisdom are both forms of practical knowledge: knowledge of what to do and how to bring things about. Skills, such as architecture or medicine, are exercised in the production (*poiesis*) of something other than their exercise, whether their output is concrete, like a house, or abstract, like health. Wisdom, on the other hand, is concerned with human activity (*praxis*) itself rather than with its output: it is defined as a ratiocinative excellence that ascertains the truth concerning what is good and bad for human beings (4. 1140ᵇ5, ᵇ21).

It is characteristic of the wise man to deliberate well about goods attainable by action: he is not concerned with things that cannot be other than they are (7. 1141ᵇ9–13). Thus wisdom differs from science and understanding, which are concerned with unchanging and eternal matters. The rational part of the soul is divided into two parts: the *logistikon* that deliberates and the *epistemonikon* that is concerned with the eternal truths. Each of these parts has its proper *arete*: wisdom for the former and understanding for the latter. Other intellectual virtues turn out to be parts of either *phronesis* or *sophia*: *sophia*, for instance, consists of *nous* plus *episteme* (7. 1141^{b}3–4).

Sophia, Aristotle tells us, has as its subject matter divine, honourable, and useless things: it is what was practised by famous philosophers such as Thales and Anaxagoras. What *nous* is, is not immediately clear: it is a word often used for the whole human intellectual apparatus, for the cognitive as opposed to the affective part of the mind (cf. 1. 1139^{a}17, 2. 1139^{b}5). Here, however, it appears to mean insight into the first principles of theoretical science: the understanding of unproven necessary truths which is the basis of *episteme* (6. 1140^{b}31–41^{a}9). It is this which, in conjunction with *episteme*, constitutes *sophia*, the highest human intellectual achievement.

The *Ethics* does not spell out what is involved in *episteme* or science. That is laid out, explicitly and at length, in the first six chapters of *Posterior Analytics* 1. Aristotle accepts that to know something is the case is to be genuinely acquainted with the explanation of its being the case and to be aware that it cannot be otherwise. If that is what knowledge is, Aristotle says, 'It is necessary for demonstrative knowledge to depend on things that are true and primitive and immediate and better known than the conclusion, to which they must also be prior and of which they must be explanatory' (*APo.* 1. 2. 70^{a}20–2). A body of scientific knowledge is built up out of demonstrations. A demonstration is a particular kind of syllogism: one whose premisses can be traced back to principles that are true, necessary, universal, and immediately intuited. These first, self-evident principles are related to the conclusions of science as axioms to theorems.

There is an unsolved problem about the account of science in the *Posterior Analytics*: it bears no resemblance to the substantial corpus of Aristotle's own scientific works. Generations of scholars have tried in vain to find in his writings a single instance of a demonstrative syllogism. To be sure, the *Posterior Analytics* is not a treatise on scientific method, but a set of guidelines for scientific exposition.[4] But Aristotle's treatises are themselves expository, not methodological, and they do not even approximate to the pattern of the *Posterior Analytics*.

It is not only the Aristotelian corpus that lacks an Aristotelian science: the whole history of scientific endeavour contains no perfect instance of any such science. Many of the examples given by Aristotle are drawn from arithmetic or geometry, and his thought was clearly influenced by the mathematicians of his time. When, after Aristotle's death, Euclid presented his axiomatized geometry, it looked as if the scientific ideal of the *Posterior Analytics* had been fulfilled: but after more than two millennia it was discovered that one of Euclid's axioms lacked the necessary self-evidence. A similar fate, in the twentieth century, overtook Gottlob Frege's project of axiomatizing logic and arithmetic. Spinoza's seventeenth-century attempt to

---

[4] See J. Barnes, 'Aristotle's Theory of Demonstration', in J. Barnes, M. Schofield, and R. Sorabji (eds.), *Articles on Aristotle*, i: *Science* (London: Duckworth, 1975).

axiomatize philosophy itself served only to show that the ideal held up in the *Posterior Analytics* was a will-o'-the-wisp.

Epicurean Epistemology

In the Hellenistic period epistemology came to occupy a more fundamental position in philosophy than it had done for either Plato or Aristotle. It was Epicurus who first gave it a name as a separate branch of philosophy. He called it 'canonic', from the Greek word 'kanon', meaning a rule or measuring rod. More often than 'canon' Epicurus and other Hellenistic philosophers made use of the word 'criterion'. According to Epicurus the three criteria of truth are sensations, concepts (*prolepseis*), and feelings.

Sensation is the foundation of knowledge for Epicurus, and he held a strong form of the thesis that the senses are infallible with regard to their proper objects. This is set forth elegantly by Lucretius:

> Truth's very notion from the senses came.
> What witness, then, to challenge them can claim?
> Against the senses' faith to win the day
> What greater truth can chase the false away?
> What right has reason sense to criticize
> When from false sense that reason took its rise?
> If what the senses tell us is not true
> Then reason's self is naught but falsehood too.
> Can ears deliver verdict on the eyes?
> Can touch convict the ears, or taste the touch, of lies?

> (4. 478–87)

Lucretius, like Aristotle, points out that one sense cannot be corrected by another with regard to its proper object. But the Epicureans go further than Aristotle in claiming a sense cannot even correct its own impressions: each impression is of equal reliability and hence whatever appears to a sense at any time is true (Lucretius 4. 497–9; D.L. 10. 31).

By treating all appearances as on a par, instead of grading them in terms of reliability, Epicureans rule out Aristotle's method of dealing with conflicting impressions, such as that of a tower that looks round from a distance but square close up. Instead, they claim that in such a case we have two equally valid impressions, but impressions of different objects. Sextus Empiricus explains how Epicurus would deal with the problem, by invoking his atomistic explanation of sight as an encounter with a stream of images flowing from an object of vision.

I would not say that sight is deceived when from a great distance it sees a tower as small and round, and from nearby as large and square. Rather, it is quite correct. When what is perceived appears small and so-shaped, it really is small and shaped like that, because the edges of the images have been rubbed off as a result of their journey through the air. And when it appears big and of a different shape, once again it really is big and of that shape. But the two are not the same. (*M.* 7. 208)

Our common impression that these are two glimpses of the same thing, Epicurus says, is due not to perception but to 'distorted belief'. He deals in a similar way with other objections to the infallibility of sensation, such as dreams and delusions. When Orestes thought he saw the Furies, his sight was not deceived because there were genuine images present; it was his mind that erred in taking them as solid bodies (S.E., *M.* 8. 63). We must distinguish sharply between a sense-impression (*phantastike epibole*) and an accompanying, but distinct, belief (D.L. 10. 51).

Sensations, therefore, the first criteria of truth, in spite of their infallibility, provide only a rather slender base for the structure of our knowledge. We need to turn to the second set of criteria, namely concepts. Epicurus' word 'prolepsis' is often translated 'preconceptions', but that is misleading, partly because it suggests prejudice, partly because it suggests something that would be expressed by a whole proposition, while most of the examples we are given are expressed by single words, such as 'body', 'man', 'cow', 'red'. A concept is a general notion of what kind of thing is signified by such a word (which may, of course, be expressed in a sentence of paraphrase, such as 'A cow is an animal of such-and-such a kind'). The 'pro' in 'prolepsis' is meant to indicate that a concept of X is not a set of infor- mation about X derived from experience, but rather a template by which we recognize in advance whether an individual presented in experience is or is not an X. Concepts are not things that have to be proved: they are themselves employed in any proof (D.L. 10. 33, 38). It remains obscure, in both Epicurus and his followers, whence concepts originate. They cannot all be the result of experience, since they provide the means by which we sort sensations, which are the basis of experience. But some of them do seem to be the result of experience—perhaps misinterpreted experience, like the concept of God (Lucretius 5. 1169–71).

Sensations and concepts, for Epicurus, are both 'evident' (so too are feelings, but they will be considered in a different context). It is on these evident elements that we must base our beliefs in what is not evident. We start with the senses, he said, and then must infer the non-evident by reasoning from their testimony (D.L. 10. 39). Conjectures and theories are false if the senses bear witness against them (D.L. 10. 50–1). A conjecture is true if it is confirmed by the senses; a theory is true if it is not impugned by the senses (S.E., *M.* 213). The latter claim seems surprising: may not more than one incompatible theory be consistent with the evidence? The Epicureans accepted this possibility; thus Lucretius accepts that there may be different explan- ations of the movements of the stars, just as there may be different hypotheses about the cause of death of a corpse on a slab (6. 703–11). In such a case they should all be accepted: each of them is likely to be true in one or other of the many worlds in the universe, even if we do not know which is true in our world (5. 526–33).

Stoic Epistemology

The early Stoics shared with the Epicureans a number of assumptions about the nature of knowledge. Like them, they believed it must have a dual basis of infallible sense-impressions and primitive and acquired concepts. On the topic of concepts they are more informative than the Epicureans, and they give an account of their origin that closely resembles Aristotle's. When a man is born, his mind is like a blank sheet of paper, and as he develops towards the use of reason, concepts are written on the page. The earliest concepts come from the senses: individual experiences leave behind memory, and memory builds up experience. Some concepts are acquired from teaching or devised for a purpose; others arise naturally and spontaneously, and it is these that deserve the name 'prolepsis' (LS 39E). Concepts of this kind are common to all humans: disagreement arises only when they are applied to particular cases, as when the same action is described by one man as courageous and by another as lunatic (Epictetus 1. 22. 3).

The Stoics developed a more elaborate classification of mental states than ever the Epicureans did. They wanted to propound an epistemology that would withstand sceptical challenge. In addition to the two states of knowledge (*episteme*) and belief (*doxa*) that had been contrasted since Plato, they introduced a third state, cognition (*katalepsis*).[5] The Stoics, Sextus Empiricus tells us,

> say there are three things connected to each other, knowledge and belief and located between them cognition. Knowledge is cognition that is sound and firm and unchangeable by argument; belief is weak and false assent, and cognition is in between the two: it is assent to a cognitive appearance. (*M* 7. 150–1)

A new element is here added to the definition of knowledge: knowledge is unchangeable by argument. This seems a sound insight. If I claim to know that *p*, I am claiming, among other things, that no one is going to (rightly) argue me out of believing that *p*. This is unlike the case where I believe that *p* but am open to conviction that not-*p*. This latter is what is meant by saying that belief is weak assent. It is also (possibly) false: there is nothing absurd in saying 'X believes that *p*, but it is false that *p*' as there is in saying 'X knows that *p*, but it is false that *p*'. But the most interesting point in this passage is the definition of cognition in terms of cognitive appearance (*phantasia kataleptike*).

'Appearance' is a broad term, including not only what appears to the senses but candidates for belief of other kinds. Cognitions, likewise, may result from the senses or from reason (D.L. 7. 52). An appearance is not the same thing as a belief: belief involves an extra item, namely assent; assent, unlike appearance, is a

---

[5] This translation is now standard, being used by Long and Sedley (LS 254) and Frede (*CHHP* 296 ff.). I use it with reluctance, since the word 'cognition' is associated with much confusion in modern philosophy of mind.

voluntary matter. An appearance is cognitive if it is worthy of assent. Cognition is between knowledge and belief in that, unlike belief, it is never false, and unlike knowledge, it does not involve the resolution never to change one's mind.[6]

A cognitive appearance, we are told, is 'that which arises from what is and is stamped and impressed exactly in accordance with what is' (D.L. 7. 46; Cicero, *Acad.* 2. 77). Well and good: clearly such an impression (as we may call it) is worthy of assent. A wise man will have no mere beliefs, Zeno said (Cicero, *Acad.* 2. 77); and no doubt this can be achieved if the wise man assents only to cognitive appearances. But how do I know whether an appearance is cognitive or not? Is it a matter of an appearance being so clear and distinct that it actually forces my assent, so that I cannot help but believe? Or does it have certain features that I can use as a criterion by which I decide to confer an assent that I might have withheld? Our evidence is not totally clear, but we are given some indications by the examples that survive.

First, we are told that the impressions of the insane are not cognitive. (Sometimes, indeed, the Stoics denied that they were genuine impressions, calling them instead 'phantasms'; D.L. 7. 49.) They 'arise purely externally and fortuitously, so that they are often not positive about them and do not assent to them' (S.E., *M.* 7. 248). But suppose they do assent to them: clearly that does not make them cognitive, since they are not true and only a true appearance can be cognitive. But what epistemological rule have the insane violated? Well, perhaps they have not examined the degree of detail in their impression: for a second piece of information we are given is that a cognitive impression must be highly comprehensive, so that all the characteristics of its original are reproduced. 'Just as the seals on rings always stamp their features accurately on the wax, so those impressions that create cognition of objects should incorporate all their peculiarities' (S.E., *M.* 2. 750). However, if cognitive impressions are ones that are fully comprehensive in detail, they must be very few and far between.

Perhaps, we might conjecture, cognitive impressions have a specially persuasive quality that marks them out. The Stoics did indeed classify impressions in terms of their persuasiveness into four classes:

(1) Persuasive; e.g. 'It is day', 'I am talking'.
(2) Unpersuasive; e.g. 'If it is dark, it is day'.
(3) Persuasive and unpersuasive; e.g. philosophical paradoxes.
(4) Neither persuasive nor unpersuasive; e.g. 'The number of all the stars is odd'.

However, persuasiveness is not a guarantee of truth: the bent appearance of an oar in water is persuasive enough, but is a false impression for all that. No doubt a man who is wise will resist the temptation to accept all persuasive

---

[6] So Frede, *CHHP* 296 ff.

appearances, and will restrict his assent to appearances that are not only persuasive but reasonable. Thus, Posidonius tells us, in addition to offering cognitive impressions as the criterion of truth, some older Stoics identified the criterion as being right reason (D.L. 7. 54).

However, the matter is further complicated. In addition to cognitive impressions there are reasonable impressions. A Stoic, trapped by King Ptolemy Philopator into taking wax pomegranates for the genuine article, replied that he had given his assent not to the proposition that they were pomegranates, but to the proposition that it was reasonable (*eulogon*) to believe that they were. A reasonable impression, he said, was compatible with falsehood (D.L. 7. 177) If so, it seems, the assessment of whether an appearance is or is not cognitive cannot be a matter of reason. The early Stoics give us no further assistance in determining the identifying feature of cognitive impressions.

The weakness of the Stoic position was exposed by Arcesilaus, the head of the New Academy during the latter part of the third century. He challenged the Stoic definition of a cognitive impression as 'something stamped and impressed from something that is, exactly as it is'. Could there not be, he asked, a false impression indiscernible from a true one? Zeno agreed that if an impression was such that there could be a false one exactly like it, then (even if true) it could not be a cognitive impression. Accordingly he modified the definition, adding 'and of such a kind that it could not arise from what is not' (Cicero, *Acad.* 2. 77; S.E., *M.* 7. 251). But it is not clear how the Stoics were to establish in which cases such unmistakable distinguishing marks were to be found, or respond to a sceptical claim that wherever there was a true appearance a false indiscernible replica could be imagined.

Academic Scepticism

It is not surprising that Stoic epistemology should be challenged from a sceptical angle. It was surprising, however, that the challenge should come from the Academy, from the heirs of Plato. Surely the Platonic corpus contains some of the most dogmatic philosophy ever to be devised. The leaders of the later Academy, however, Arcesilaus and his successor, Carneades, traced their ancestry further back. They appealed to Socrates, whose question and answer technique so famously punctured false claims to knowledge (Cicero, *Fin.* 2. 2). Socrates himself claimed no philosophical knowledge, and left no philosophical writings; and Arcesilaus and Carneades followed him in both respects. But they went further than Socrates in commending a much more radical scepticism: a suspension of belief not only on philosophical but also on the most everyday topics.

Though Arcesilaus and Carneades left no writings, we are reasonably well informed about their philosophical teachings because Cicero, who had been taught by Carneades' pupil Philo, was much attracted to Academic Scepticism, and left a lively account of the to and fro of sceptical debate in his *Academica*. From him and other sources we learn that the Academics presented a battery of arguments to show that there could be no infallible impressions.

There is no true impression arising from sensation that cannot be paired with another impression, indistinguishable from it, which is non-cognitive. But if two impressions are indistinguishable, it cannot be the case that one of them is cognitive and the other not. Therefore no impression, even if true, is cognitive. To illustrate this argument, consider the case of identical twins, Publius Geminus and Quintus Geminus. If someone looking at Publius thinks he is looking at Quintus, he has an impression that corresponds in every detail to the one he would have if he were in fact looking at Quintus. Hence, his impression is not a cognitive one: it does not answer to the final clause of Zeno's definition: 'of such a kind as could not arise from what is not' (Ciccro, *Acad.* 2. 83–5).

In reply, the Stoics seem to have denied the possibility of any pair of objects resembling each other in every respect. They propounded the thesis later known as the identity of indiscernibles: no two grains of sand, no two wisps of hair, were totally alike. The Academics complained that the thesis was gratuitous; but it is surely no more gratuitous than their own claim that true impressions are *always* liable to be confused with false replicas.

In fact, the Stoic reply seems to be either unnecessary or insufficient, depending on how we interpret the sceptical challenge. If only a genuine possibility of a mistake prevents an impression from being cognitive, then in order to preserve cognitive impressions the Stoic need not claim that in all cases a true impression will be irreplaceable by a false one: he need only claim that there are some cases in which this is so. On the other hand, if the mere imaginability of a deceptive replica is sufficient to undermine the cognitivity of an impression, then the identity of indiscernibles will not restore it. I may be as certain as I am of anything that I am talking to you: but isn't it imaginable that you have an identical twin, quite unknown to me, and that it is he whom I am addressing?

There are various degrees of scepticism. A sceptic may simply be someone who denies the possibility of genuine knowledge (in some, or all, areas of inquiry). Such a sceptic need have no objection to the holding of beliefs on various topics, provided that the person holding them does not claim that those beliefs have the status of knowledge. He may very well have a set of beliefs himself, including the belief that there is no such thing as knowledge. There is no inconsistency here, provided he does not claim to *know* that there is no knowledge. Arcesilaus went so far as to reprove Socrates for claiming to know that he knew nothing (Cicero, *Acad*. 1. 45).

A more radical sceptic, however, may question not only the possibility of knowledge but also the propriety of belief. He may recommend abstinence from not only the resolute assent characteristic of certainty, but also the tentative assent characteristic of opinion. Arcesilaus appears to have been a sceptic of this kind: he maintained, Cicero tells us (*Acad*. 1. 44; LS 68A), 'no one should assert or affirm anything or offer it assent; instead we should curb our rashness and hold it back from any slip. It would be rash indeed to approve something false or unknown, and nothing is more disgraceful than to allow assent and approval to outrun cognition.' Arcesilaus made a practice of offering arguments pro and con every thesis, so as to facilitate the suspension of assent that he recommended (*Fin*. 5. 10). Scholars are uncertain whether his arguments were all purely *ad hominem* or whether he did (inconsistently) assert as true his own sceptical philosophical position.[7]

According to some of our ancient sources, Carneades was a sceptic of the less radical kind who, while rejecting the possibility of knowledge, accepted that the wise man could legitimately hold mere belief. The two Academics focus their attack on Zeno at different points. Zeno held that no wise man would hold mere belief, but if he relied only on cognitive impressions his assents would all count as knowledge. Arcesilaus and Carneades agree with each other that there are no cognitive impressions and therefore no knowledge, but the former concludes that the wise man will give no assent, while the latter concludes that the wise man will hold mere belief (Cicero, *Acad*. 2. 148).

On another account, however, in evaluating Carneades' position we need to make a more subtle analysis of the mental phenomena studied by the epistemologist. Instead of simply distinguishing between an appearance and assent to the appearance, we have to introduce a new notion of impulse (*hormē*). While assent is voluntary and can be withheld, appearance, we know, is outside our control. But appearance is inevitably followed by impulse, and it is possible to follow this without the mental assent in which truth is to be found and falsehood to be avoided (Plutarch, *adversus Coloten* 1122 LS 69A; Cicero, *Acad*. 2. 103–4 LS 69I).

This distinction appears to have been introduced in order to answer a common objection to radical scepticism: if the sceptic suspends judgement, how can he live a normal life. How can he get into a bath if, for all he knows, it is a chasm? The answer is that he does not judge, rashly, that it really is a bath; but he is swept along by his bath-entering impulse. In non-philosophical discussions a wise man may even follow his impulses so far as to give the answers 'yes' and 'no' to questions.

---

[7] See Schofield, in *CHHP* 334.

Pyrrhonian Scepticism

In the first century BC there grew up a new fundamentalist school of scepticism which regarded the Academics as having watered down scepticism in unacceptable ways. The founder of this school was Aenesidemus, but he and his followers described their version of scepticism as Pyrrhonism, after Pyrrho of Elis, a soldier in the army of Alexander the Great, whom they regarded as their founding father. Aenesidemus wrote a lost book of Pyrrhonian discourses that set out his differences with Academic Scepticism. He collected together sceptical arguments of the kind that we have encountered in this chapter, and grouped them under ten headings, which achieved fame as the Ten Tropes of Aenesidemus. Our knowledge of them, as of much else in ancient scepticism, derives from the writings of Sextus Empiricus, a Pyrrhonian sceptic of the second century AD.

Sextus left three books of *Outlines of Pyrrhonism* and eleven books *Against the Professors*. In these books appear almost all the sceptical arguments from illusion that appeared in the later literature, and many that no one cared to use again. We find in him the yellow look of jaundice, the after-image on the book, vision distorted by pressure on the eyeball, concave and convex mirrors, wine which tastes sour after figs and sweet after nuts, ships apparently stationary on the horizon, oars bent in water, smells more pungent in the bathroom, the fleeting flashes of colour on the necks of pigeons, and, of course, our old friend the tower that looks round from afar and square close at hand.

Sextus' own version of scepticism turns out not to be as different from Academic Scepticism as he would have us believe. Sceptics, without giving assent to anything, still seem, for him, to be able to have views, not only about perceptual matters of everyday life, but even on philosophical issues. Sextus' works are of value to us, not because they give a new turn to the sceptical discussion, but because they are a treasury of information about the reasoning of earlier and more original sceptics. He brought to an end the sceptical tradition he chronicled.

The study of ancient epistemology can teach us much about the nature of knowledge and the limits of scepticism. Several insights became part of the patrimony of all future philosophy: knowledge can only be of what is true; knowledge is only knowledge if it can appeal implicitly or explicitly to some kind of support, whether from experience, reasoning, or some other source; and one who claims knowledge must be resolute, excluding the possibility of being rightly converted, at a later stage, to a different view.

However, ancient epistemology is bedevilled by two different but related fallacies. Both of them are generated by a misunderstanding of the truth that whatever is knowledge must be true. One of the fallacies haunts classical epistemology, up to the time of Aristotle; the other fallacy haunts Hellenistic and imperial epistemology.

The first fallacy is this. 'Whatever is knowledge must be true' may be interpreted in two ways.

(1) Necessarily, if *p* is known, *p* is true

or

(2) If *p* is known, *p* is necessarily true.

(1) is true but (2) is false. It is a necessary truth that if I know you are sitting down, then you are sitting down; but if I know you are sitting down it is not a necessary truth that you are sitting down; you may get up at any moment. Plato and Aristotle, over and over again, seem to regard (2) as indistinguishable from (1). Given the necessary connection between knowledge and truth, they seem to think, only what is necessary can be known. From the acceptance of (2) there flows the construction of the theory of eternal and immutable Ideas, and there flows the impossible ideal of Aristotelian science.

If whatever is knowledge must be true, then it may seem that knowledge must be the exercise of a faculty that cannot err. This is the form that the fallacy takes in Hellenistic times. The Epicureans and Stoics, unlike Plato and Aristotle, are prepared to countenance knowledge not just of eternal truths, but of mundane contingencies such as that Dion is now walking. But this, they claim, is possible only if we have faculties—whether sense or reason—that are capable of infallible operation. This Hellenistic fallacy is just the mirror image of the classical fallacy. Let F stand for some faculty. Then it is true that

It is impossible, if F knows that *p*, that F has gone wrong.

But that is not the same as, nor is it true that,

If F knows that *p*, then it was impossible for F to go wrong.

The epistemological fallacy, both in its classical and in its Hellenistic form, would cast long shadows through philosophy's history.

5

How Things Happen: Physics

In earlier chapters we saw how Greek thinkers, from Thales to Plato, developed an elaborate picture of the universe we live in. Though of great historic interest, their physical theories have been superseded by the progress of science, and can no longer offer us enlightenment about the world. The same is true of Aristotle's world-picture; but in addition to physical speculation, Aristotle offered, to a much greater extent than any of his predecessors, a philosophical examination of underlying concepts that are basic to physical explanation of many different kinds. His philosophy of physics, unlike his physical system itself, contains much that remains of abiding interest.

The second of Aristotle's categories is the category of quantity: this is the one that answers to the question 'how big?', and Aristotle has in mind answers such as 'four feet long', 'six feet high' (*Cat.* 4. 1^{b}28). There are two kinds of quantities, he tells us, discrete and continuous. A discrete quantity would be, for example, an army of a thousand men (cf. *Metaph.* Δ 13. 1020^{a}7); as examples of continuous quantities, we are given lines, surfaces, bodies, time, and place (*Cat.* 6. 4^{b}20 ff.). Aristotle's treatment of the continuum and of continuous quantities is fundamental to his philosophy of physics, and the first part of this chapter will be devoted to these topics.

The Continuum

At the beginning of book 6 of the *Physics* Aristotle introduces three terms to indicate different relationships between quantified items: they may be successive (*ephexes*), adjacent (*hama*), or continuous (*syneches*). Two items are successive if between them there is nothing of the same kind as themselves. Thus, two islands in an archipelago are successive if there is only sea between them; two days are successive if there is no day, but only night, between them. Two items are adjacent, Aristotle says, if they have two boundaries in contact with each other, and they are continuous if there is only a single common boundary between them (231[a]18–25). He uses these definitions to base an argument that a continuum cannot be composed of indivisible atoms.

A line, for instance, cannot be composed of points that lack magnitude. Since a point has no parts, it cannot have a boundary distinct from itself: two points therefore cannot be either adjacent or continuous. If you say that the boundary of a point is identical with the point itself, then two points that were continuous would be one and the same point. Nor can points be successive to each other: between any two points on a continuous line we can always find other points on the same line (231[a]29–[b]15).

Similar reasoning, Aristotle says, applies to spatial magnitude, to time, and to motion: all three are continua of the same kind. Time cannot be composed of indivisible moments, because between any two moments there is always a period of time; and an atom of motion would in fact have to be a moment of rest.

Divisibility, indeed, is a defining feature of quantity or magnitude, and is so used in Aristotle's lexicon of philosophical terms in *Metaphysics* Δ (1020[a]7): 'We call a quantity whatever is divisible into two or more constituent parts of which each is of a kind to be a single individual entity.' We shall have to explore later what 'being of a kind to be an individual' amounts to.

Points or moments, therefore, which were indivisible would lack magnitude, and zero magnitude, however often repeated, could never add up to any magnitude. By another route, therefore, we reach the conclusion that a continuous quantity is not composed of indivisible items. If a magnitude can only be divided into other magnitudes, and every magnitude must be divisible, it follows that every magnitude is infinitely divisible.

Aristotle's notion of infinite divisibility is not easy to grasp, and he was fully aware of this. In *On Generation and Corruption* he spells out at length a line of objection to his thesis, and suggests that it was the line of argument that led Democritus to espouse atomism. The argument goes like this.

If matter is divisible to infinity, then let us suppose that this division has been carried out—for if matter is genuinely so divisible, there will be nothing incoherent in this supposition. How large are the fragments resulting from this division? If they have any magnitude at all, then, on the hypothesis of infinite divisibility, it would be possible to divide them further; so they must be fragments with no extension, like a geometrical point. But whatever can be divided can be put together again: if we saw a log into many pieces, even pieces as small as sawdust, we can put them together again into a log of the same size. But if our fragments have no magnitude, then how can they ever have added up to make the extended chunk of matter with which we began? Matter cannot consist of mere geometrical points, not even of an infinite number of them, so we have to conclude that divisibility comes to an end, and the smallest possible fragments must be bodies with sizes and shapes (1. 2. 316ª14–317ª3).

Aristotle in several places sets out to answer this difficulty (*Ph.* 3. 6. 206ª18–25; 7. 207ᵇ14). 'Divisible to infinity', he insists, means 'unendingly divisible', not 'divisible into infinitely many parts'. However often a magnitude has been divided, it can always be divided further. It is infinitely divisible in the sense that there is no end to its divisibility. The continuum does not have an infinite number of parts; indeed Aristotle regarded the idea of an actually infinite number as incoherent. The infinite, he says, has only a potential existence (3. 6. 206ª18).

This is a sound answer to the Democritean argument: but Aristotle goes on to gild the lily. He offers a distinction between different kinds of potentiality. A block of marble has the potentiality to become a statue: when this is realized, the statue will be there, all of it at once. But the parts into which a temporal period or series can be divided have a different kind of potentiality. They cannot be all there at once: when I wake up, the day ahead contains both morning and afternoon, but they cannot both occur at once.

This seems an injudicious move, on several counts. First of all, Aristotle is defending a thesis about the continuum in general: it seems perverse to defend it by appealing to a property which may be peculiar to a particular form of continuum, namely time. Secondly, the argument for the infinite divisibility of the continuum is not concerned with the process of division. Democritus, in the argument Aristotle offers him, says that if something is infinitely divisible, it does not matter whether the division can be carried out simultaneously, the question is whether the result of the division is something coherently conceivable (*GC* 1. 2. 316ª18). Thirdly, the contrast with the potentiality of producing a statue is a false trail.

In one of his sonnets Michelangelo gives a powerful evocation of the potentialities inherent in a block of marble.

> There's not a concept in an artist's mind,
> However great, but in a marble block
> It's hidden there for someone to unlock
> Whose intellect can teach his hand to find.[1]

The simultaneous actualization, from a single block of marble, of all the concepts of all the greatest artists would be just as impossible as the simultaneous actualization of all the parts of the continuum. In general, it is a fallacy to argue from

---

[1] Non ha l'ottimo artista alcun concetto
Ch'un marmo solo in sè non circoscriva
Col suo soverchio, e solo a quello arriva
La man che ubbidisce all'intelletto.

(1) It is both possible that p and possible that q

to

(2) It is possible that both p and q,

and to see this one has only to look at the case where 'q' is 'not p'. Hence, in order to answer Democritus, Aristotle does not need to introduce his distinction between powers that are, and powers that are not, simultaneously actualizable. It is sufficient to point out (as he does; *GC* 1. 2. 317ª8) that there is a difference between saying that whatever is continuous can be divided at *any* point and saying that whatever is continuous can be divided at *every* point.

But we should look more closely at the sonnet. While the hand and intellect of Michelangelo were unsurpassed at realizing the potentialities of marble, it may be questioned whether his poem shows an adequate philosophical grasp of the nature of potentiality. Clearly, he thinks of potential statues as shadowy realities, already present there in some mysterious way within the uncut marble. If one conceives of potentialities as shadow actualities, then it seems that one can count them and quantify over them. Whatever is infinitely divisible, in that case, would have an infinite number of parts. But the temptation to think of potentialities in this way must be resisted, whether in Michelangelo or in Democritus.

Aristotle on Place

The fifth of Aristotle's categories is place, the answer to the question 'where?', of which a typical answer is 'in the Lyceum' (*Cat.* 4. 2ª1). We are not told anything further about this category in the *Categories*, but the fourth book of the *Physics* contains six chapters on place (a difficult topic, he tells us, on which he has found no help from his predecessors; 4. 1. 208ª32–3). Every body, prima facie at least, is in some place, and can move from place to place. The same place can be occupied at different times by different bodies, as a flask can contain first water and then air. So place cannot be identical with the body that occupies it (4. 1. 208ᵇ29–209ª8). What, then, is it?

The answer that Aristotle eventually reaches is that the place of a thing is the first motionless boundary of whatever is containing it. Thus, the place of a pint of wine is the inner surface of the flask containing it—provided the flask is stationary. But suppose the flask is in motion, on a punt perhaps floating down a river? Then the wine will be moving too, from place to place, and its place has to be given by specifying its position relative to the motionless river banks (4. 5. 212ᵇ15). So too with a tree in a stream, surrounded by rushing water: its place is given by the unmoving bed in which it is rooted.[2]

---

[2] See W. D. Ross, *Aristotle*, 86; id., *Aristotle's Physics* (Oxford: Clarendon Press, 1936), 575.

As is clear from these examples, for Aristotle a thing is not only in the place defined by its immediate container, but also in whatever contains that container. Thus, just as a child may write out his address as 1 High Street, Oxford, England, Europe, The Earth, The Universe, so Aristotle says, 'You are now in the universe because you are in the atmosphere and the atmosphere is in the universe; and you are in the atmosphere because you are on the earth, and you are on the earth because you are in your own particular place.' The universe is the place that is common to everything.

If to be in place is to be within a container, it follows that the universe is not in place at all: and this is a conclusion that Aristotle himself draws. 'The universe is not anywhere; for whatever is somewhere must not only exist itself, but also have something alongside it in which it is and which contains it. But there is nothing outside the entire universe' (*Ph.* 4. 5. 212^{b}14–17). And if the universe is not in place, it cannot move from place to place.

It is clear that place as described by Aristotle is quite different from space as often conceived since Newton as an infinite extension or cosmic grid. Newtonian space would exist whether or not the material universe had been created. For Aristotle, if there were no bodies there would be no place; there can, however, be a vacuum, a place empty of bodies, but only if the place is bounded by actual bodies (4. 1. 208^{b}26). His concept of place, therefore, can avoid the difficulties that have led philosophers such as Kant to deny the reality of space. However, he adds to his basic concept a significant element that is irredeemably anachronistic: the notion of natural place.

In an ordered cosmos, Aristotle believed, each of the four elements, earth, air, fire, and water, had a natural place, which exercised a causal influence: air and fire were by nature carried upward, water and earth were carried downward. Each such motion was natural to its element; other motions were possible, but were 'violent'. In the universe as we find it, these natural motions are hindered by various factors, so that few things are actually in their natural place; but the actual distribution of the elements is to be explained *inter alia* by their tendency to seek their natural place, the place where it is best for them to be (4. 1. 208^{b}9–22). We preserve a relic of Aristotle's distinction between natural and violent motions when we contrast natural with violent death. But none of Aristotle's modern admirers defends this rather class-bound vision of the universe, in which each element knows its place and is happiest to be in the station to which nature has assigned it.

Aristotle on Motion

Aristotle's fundamental account of motion, however, is not vitiated by the antiquated theory with which it was conjoined: indeed it was one of the most subtle components of his philosophy of physics. 'Motion' (*kinesis*) was for him a broad term, including changes in several different categories, such as growth in size or change in colour (*Ph.* 3. 1. 200^{b}32). Movement from place to place, however, local motion, provides a paradigm which can be used to expound his theory.

The definition of motion that Aristotle offers in the third book of the *Physics* is not, at first glance, very illuminating. 'Motion', he says, 'is the actuality of what is in potentiality, in so far as it is in potentiality.' Let us spell this out. If a body X is to move from point A to point B, it must be able to do so: when it is at A it is only potentially at B. When this potentiality has been realized, then X is at B. But it is then at rest, and not in motion. So motion from A to B is not simply the actualization of a potential at A for being at B. Shall we say that it is a partial actualization of that potentiality? That will not quite do, either, because a body stationary at the mid-point between A and B might be said to have partially actualized that potentiality. We have to say that it is an actualization of a potentiality that is still being actualized: and that is what Aristotle's definition amounts to. While at A, the body has in fact two different potentialities: a potentiality to be at B, and a potentiality to move to B. Aristotle illustrates the point with other examples of *kinesis*: the gradual heating of a body, the carving of a statue, the healing of a patient, the building of a house (3. 1. 201^{a}10–15).

Motion, he says, is a notion difficult to grasp, and this is because it is as it were halfway between straight potentiality and straight actuality. He sums up his account in a slogan, saying that motion is an incomplete or imperfect actuality of an imperfect potentiality (3. 2. 201^{b}31). Being at B would be the perfect actuality; moving to B is the imperfect actuality. The potentiality for being at B is the perfect potentiality; the potentiality for moving to B is the imperfect potentiality.

Motion is a continuum: a mere series of positions between A and B is not a motion from A to B. If X is to move from A to B, it has to pass through any intermediate point between A and B; but passing through a point is not the same as being located at that point. Aristotle argues that whatever is moving already has been moving. If X, travelling from A to B, passes through the mid-point K, it must already have passed through an earlier point J halfway between A and K. However short the distance between A and J, that too is divisible, and so on ad infinitum. At any point at which X is moving, there will be an earlier point at which it was already moving (cf. *Ph.* 6. 5. 236^{b}33–5). It follows that there is no such thing as a first instant of motion.

Aristotle's account of motion is embedded within a careful analysis of the semantic properties of Greek verbs. English, unlike Greek, has a special continuous form of each tense. The difference between 'He runs' and 'He is running' is clear enough in English. So too is the difference between 'Whatever moves has moved before' (which is doubtful) and 'Whatever is moving has been moving before' (which is true). In Greek Aristotle has to go to some pains to make clear that he is talking not about whatever moves, but whatever is moving. He does, however, maintain not just that whatever is moving has been moving before, but that whatever is moving *has moved* before (*Ph.* 5. 6. 237^{b}5).

For Aristotle, there are some verbs that signify *kineseis* (motions) and some that signify *energeiai* (actualities) (*Metaph. θ* 6. 1048^{b}18–36). *Kinesis*, as has been said, includes not only motion but many different kinds of change and production: Aristotle gives as examples learning something, building a particular house, walking to a particular place. As examples of *energeiai* he gives seeing, knowing, and being happy. He distinguishes between his two classes of verbs by means of subtle linguistic points.

Verbs of the first kind signify activities that are imperfect in the following sense: if I am φing, then I have not yet φd (if I am still building this house, I have not yet built it, and so on). The activities they signify are activities that take time (*NE* 10. 4. 1174^{b}8). Activities or achievements of the second kind, however, do not *take* time, but rather *last* or continue over time. A *kinesis* can be faster or slower, and can be completed or interrupted; not so an *energeia*. I may learn something quickly, but I cannot know it quickly; I may be interrupted while learning, but not while knowing (*NE* 10. 4. 1173^{a}33; *Metaph. Θ* 6. 1048^{b}19).

Energeiai such as knowing are states. Besides states such as knowledge, there are secondary *energeiai*, or actualities that are the exercise of such states. Thus, we have a triadic sequence: I learn Greek, I know Greek, I speak Greek. Secondary actualities have some of the features of motions and some of the features of activities: speaking Greek is not an imperfect process towards a terminus, in the way that learning Greek is; on the other hand it can be interrupted in a way that knowing Greek cannot.

Aristotle's classifications can be looked on as a study in what grammarians call the *aspect* of verbs, which, in Greek rather more than in English, often gets entangled with the *tense* of verbs. We still use Aristotle's terminology in distinguishing, for instance, between the imperfect tense (which tells was what *was happening*) and the perfect tense (which tells us what *has been done*). We have already encountered Aristotle's treatment of tense, when in Chapter 3 we studied his treatment of past- and future-tense propositions in the *de Interpretatione*. It is now appropriate to look at his formal treatment of the topic of time in the *Physics* (4. 10–14).

Aristotle on Time

For Aristotle extension, motion, and time are three fundamental continua, in an intimate and ordered relation to each other. His paradigm of change is local motion, motion over distance: motion acquires its continuity from the continuum of spatial extension. Time, in its turn, derives its continuity from the continuity of motion (*Ph.* 4. 11. 219^{a}10–14). Thus Aristotle's account of time is parasitic on his account of motion: his formal definition, indeed, is this: time is the number of motion in respect of before and after (4. 11. 219^{b}1).

Clearly motion and time are closely linked; but might not one question the priority that Aristotle thus gives to motion? Motions, and changes of any kind, are clearly impossible without time. If X is to move from A to B, it must *first* be at A and *then* be at B, and any change must involve an *earlier* state and a *later* state. But is time impossible without motion? Can we not conceive of a static, or indeed empty, universe enduring over a longer or shorter period of time?

Aristotle believed not: where there was no motion there was no time (4. 11. 219^{a}1). Not that time is identical with motion: motions are motions of particular things, and different kinds of changes are motions of different kinds, but time is universal and uniform. Motions, again, may be faster or slower; not so time. Indeed it is by the time they take that the speed of motions is determined (4. 10. 218^{b}9; 14. 223^{b}4). Nonetheless, Aristotle says, 'we perceive motion and time together' (4. 11. 219^{a}4).

We tell how much time has passed by observing the process of some change. We, nowadays, find out what the time is by finding out what point the fingers of the clock have reached in their journey round the clock face. Analogous points can be made about whatever processes are being used as clocks in hourglasses or clepsydras. More importantly, for Aristotle, we measure days and months and years by observing the sun and moon and stars upon their celestial travels.

The part of a journey that is nearer its starting point comes before the part that is nearer its end. This spatial relation of nearer and further underpins the relation of before and after in motion; and this is the 'before' and 'after' that appears in Aristotle's definition of time. It is the *before* and *after* in motion that provides the *earlier* and *later* in time. Thus temporal order is, on Aristotle's view, derived from the ultimately spatial ordering of stretches of motion.

When Aristotle says that time is the number of motion, this ordering is no doubt one of the things he has in mind: we can list parts of the motion as first, second, third, and so on. But he may well have in mind cardinal as well as ordinal numbering, since time has a metric as well as a topological element. We can often say not only that A came before B, but also *how long* before. This seems implicit when Aristotle explains that when he speaks of 'number' he means what is counted, not the unit of counting (*Ph.* 4. 11. 219^{a}9). To make it explicit he might have added to his definition that time is numbering not only in respect of before and after, but also in respect of faster and slower. For as a proof of the universality of time he offers the fact that any change whatever can be measured in terms of velocity (*Ph.* 4. 13. 222^{b}30).

What is the relationship between time as it appears in Aristotle's definition (the earlier–later series) and time as expressed by tense (past, present, and future)? Aristotle links the two by his concept of 'the now' (*to nun*).

We say 'earlier' and 'later' with reference to distance from the now; and the now is the boundary between the past and the future...But 'earlier' is used in opposite ways in respect to past time and future time: in the past we call earlier that which is further from the now, and later that which is nearer to the now; in the future we call earlier that which is nearer to the now, and later that which is further away. (*Ph.* 4. 14. 223ᵃ5–14)

Aristotle frequently talks of the 'now'. He seems to use it for two different purposes: one, the most natural usage, to indicate present time; another, more technical one, in which it seems to mean 'instant' or 'moment'. In this second use one can speak of earlier and later nows (*Ph.* 4. 10. 218ᵇ24; 11. 220ᵃ21). In the passage just quoted he appears to be amalgamating the two uses, to mean 'the present instant'. This is unfortunate, because *the present instant* is an incoherent notion. 'Present' is an adjective applicable only to periods, such as the present year or the present century. Instants are the boundaries of periods, and future periods are bounded by future instants, and past intervals by past instants. But present periods are bounded not by present instants, but by two instants, one of which is past and the other future. There is no instantaneous present.[3]

The thesis that the present is an instant sorts ill with another thesis to which Aristotle attaches considerable importance, namely his claim that there can be no motion at an instant. If now is an instant, and there is no motion at an instant, then nothing is in motion now. This argument can be repeated at any time whatever; so it seems that motion must be forever unreal. But what, in any case, are we to make of this second thesis in its own right?

We can readily agree that no object can move at an instant. There cannot be movement between *t* and *t*, any more than there can be movement from A to A. But it does not follow from that that no object can *be moving* at an instant, any more than that no object can be moving at a point. Aristotle, however, is not just making a fallacious inference from one acceptation of the Greek present tense to another; as we have seen, he is well capable of steering his way through any possible semantic confusion of this kind. He offers an argument for the stronger conclusion, based on the premiss we have already seen: that whatever is moving has already been moving. But the correct conclusion to draw from this argument is not that nothing can be moving at a moment, but that nothing can be moving for a single moment only.

The truth that lies behind Aristotle's claim is that we can only talk of X moving at time *t* if *t* is a moment within a period of time, *t'* to *t''*, during which X is in movement; just as we can only talk of X moving at point *p* if *p* is a point on a track between *p'* and *p''* along which X is in movement. The notion of velocity at a point is then a derivative (which may be simple or complex, depending on the

---

[3] G. E. L. Owen ('Aristotle on Time', in J. Barnes, M. Schofield, and R. Sorabji (eds.), *Articles on Aristotle*, iii: *Metaphysics* (London: Duckworth, 1975), 151) suggests that the confusion here originates in Plato's *Parmenides* 152a–e and is not dispelled until Chrysippus.

movement's uniformity or lack of it) from the length of time, t' to t'', that X takes to get from p' to p''.

Aristotle on Causation and Change

In his philosophical lexicon in *Metaphysics* $\varDelta$, and also in *Physics* 2. 3 (194^b16–195^b30), Aristotle distinguishes four types of cause, or explanation. First, he says, there is that of which and out of which a thing is made, such as the bronze of a statue and the letters of a syllable. This is called the material cause. Secondly, he says, there is the form and pattern of a thing, which may be expressed in its definition: his example is that the proportion of the length of two strings in a lyre is the cause of one note being an octave away from the other. The third type of cause is the origin of a change or state of rest in something; Aristotle's followers often called it the 'efficient cause'. Aristotle gives as examples a person reaching a decision, a father who begets a child, a sculptor carving a statue, a doctor healing a patient, and in general anyone who makes a thing or changes a thing. The fourth and last type of cause is the end or goal, that for the sake of which something is done; it is the type of explanation we give if someone asks us why we are taking a walk, and we reply 'In order to keep healthy'. This last kind of cause became known as the 'final cause'.

In modern philosophy causation is standardly thought of as a relation between two events, one being cause and the other effect. Clearly, Aristotle structures causation rather differently. He does occasionally speak of events causing events (the Athenian expedition to Sardis caused the war with Persia; *APo.* 2. 11. 94^a36), but none of the causes he mentions in his canonical list are episodic events. Most are substantial entities, human beings, for instance, or chunks of bronze; some are enduring states, such as the proportion between the strings of the lyre, or the skill of the sculptor (which is the more immediate cause of the statue; *Ph.* 2. 3. 195^a6). Effects, too, as he describes them, may be in many categories: states, actions, and products. The effects of the third type of cause, efficient causes, as stated include substances (a child), artefacts (a statue), and events (the healing of a patient). But it would not do violence to Aristotle's concept to say that, in the case of efficient causation, what is brought about is always an event, either a change in something (the recovery of the patient) or the coming into being of something (the procreation of the child, the fabrication of the statue).

The difference between Aristotelian and modern notions of cause is so notable that some scholars reject the traditional translation of *aitia* as cause; they prefer other terms such as 'explanation', or speak of the four becauses rather than the four causes. Aristotle himself tells us that they are four types of answer to the question 'why?'

The ultimate answer to a 'why' may take us, in the case of unchanging things like mathematics, to the 'what' (to the definition of straight, or commensurable, or the like); or it may take us to the originating change (why did they go to war? because there had been a raid), or to the purpose (so as to come into power) or, in the case of things that come into being, to the matter. (*Ph.* 2. 7. 198ª14–21)

Here we meet the same four items, but in the order: formal, efficient, final, material.

When listing his four causes, Aristotle gives mathematical examples of formal causes. But the forms whose causation interests him most are the forms or natures of living beings: it is these that provide the internal explanation for the life-cycles and characteristic activities of plants and animals. In these cases, formal and final causes coincide: the mature realization of natural form being the end to which the activities of the organism tend. But he was also interested in the explanation of interchanges between non-living substances, of which he would give as an example the turning of water into steam. In such cases he uses the formal and material causes as explanatory principles.

Change, for Aristotle, could take place in many different categories: growth, for instance, was change in the category of quantity, and a change in a quality (e.g. of colour) was called an alteration (*GC* 1. 5. 320ª13). Local motion, as we have seen, is change in the category of place. But change in the category of substance, where there is a change from one kind of thing into another, was a very special kind of change. When a substance undergoes a change of quantity or quality, the same substance remains throughout, with its substantial form. But if one kind of thing turns into another, does anything remain throughout? Aristotle answers: matter.

We have a case of alteration when the subject of change is perceptible and persists, and merely changes its properties ... A body, for instance, while remaining the same body, is now healthy and now ill; some bronze may be now circular and now angular, and yet the same bronze. But when nothing perceptible persists in its identity as a subject of change, and the thing changes as a whole (when e.g. semen becomes blood, or water changes into air, or air totally into water), such an occurrence is a case of one substance coming to be and another substance ceasing to be ... Matter, in the most proper sense of the term, is to be identified with the underlying subject which is receptive of coming-to-be and passing away. (*GC* 1. 4. 319ᵇ8–320ª2)

What is the nature of this matter that underlies substantial change? Aristotle constantly explains the relationship of matter to form in living things (e.g. in the formation of a foetus, as he archaically described it above) by analogy with artefacts. 'As the bronze is to the statue, the wood is to the bed, or the formless before receiving form is to the formed object, so is the underlying nature to the substance' (*Ph.* 1. 7. 191ª9–12). The analogy is not easy to grasp. What is the underlying nature that remains through substantial change in the way in which wood remains wood before and after being made into a bed? Surely the reshaping of wood or bronze is an example of an accidental, not a substantial change.

Things do not yet get any clearer when Aristotle tells us,

By matter I mean what in itself is neither of any kind nor of any size nor describable by any of the categories of being. For it is something of which all these things are predicated, and therefore its essence is different from that of all the predicates. All the other categories are predicated of substance, but substance of matter. Therefore the ultimate subject is of itself neither of any kind or any size nor anything else. (*Metaph.* Z 3. 1029ᵃ21–5)

An entity that is not of any kind or any size or any shape, and of which nothing at all can be said, appears to be highly mysterious. But that is not what Aristotle is inviting us to accept. His ultimate matter (he sometimes calls it prime matter) is not *in and of itself* of any kind. It is not in and of itself any particular size, because it can grow or shrink; it is not in and of itself water, and it is not in and of itself steam, because it is each of these in turn. This does not mean that there is any time at which it is not of any size, or any time in which it is neither water nor steam nor anything else.

How then is a chunk of matter to be identified? Well, in everyday life we are familiar with the idea that one and the same parcel of stuff may be first one kind of thing, and then another kind of thing. A bottle containing a pint of cream may be found, after shaking, to contain not cream but butter. The stuff that comes out of the bottle is the same stuff as the stuff that went into the bottle: nothing has been added to it and nothing has been taken from it. But what comes out is different in kind from what goes in. It is from cases such as this that the Aristotelian notion of matter is derived.

The Stoics on Causality

The Stoic account of causes is both simpler and more complex than the Aristotelian one. It is simpler in that the Stoics do not count the material, formal, and final causes as causes properly so called, and they mock Aristotle's followers' 'crowd of causes' (Seneca, Ep. 65. 4). Their treatment of efficient causes, however, is more complex, in that they adopt a canonical form for the description of causation, and they offer a rich classification of different kinds of cause. Most importantly, unlike Aristotle, they offer a law of universal causation, which needs to be spelt out and defended.

The Stoics' standard analysis of causation was of the following form: A brings it about that B is F. A, the cause, must be a body, and so must B; but the effect, B's being F, is not a body but an abstract entity, a *lekton*. This is explained by Sextus:

The Stoics say that every cause is a body that becomes for another body a cause of something non-bodily. For instance a scalpel, which is a body, becomes for the flesh, another body, a cause of the non-bodily predicate *being cut*. Again a fire, which is a body, becomes for the wood, another body, a cause of the non-bodily predicate *being burnt*. (*M*. 9. 211)

While A and B are both material entities, the Stoics used the term 'matter' specially to refer to B, the passive element in causation (Seneca, Ep. 65. 2 LS 55ᴇ). So in Stoic causation we have a triad of cause, matter, and effect.

The Stoics introduced the notions of joint causes (*sunaitia*) and auxiliary causes (*sunerga*). Two oxen are joint causes of the movement of the plough if neither of them can pull it alone; I am an auxiliary cause if I help you lift a load which you can, at a pinch, manage by yourself (LS 55ɪ). The recognition of joint and auxiliary causes was important, because it shows that it can often be misleading to speak of *the* cause of a particular state or event. Causes form not a chain, but a network.

For the Stoics it is not only changes and beginnings of existence that need causes: there are also sustaining causes (*aitiai synektikai*) that bring it about that things continue in existence. Bodies of all kinds, for instance, are held together by an active and tenuous fluid called *pneuma*, literally 'breath', which is responsible for the cohesion of the universe. Living bodies are kept alive by the soul, which is their sustaining cause. It is characteristic of such causes that if they cease to operate, their effects cease to obtain.

Zeno, indeed, stated this characteristic as a feature of all causes (LS 55ᴀ); but other Stoics seem to have allowed another category of antecedent (*prokatarktikai*) causes, whose effect remained after they had been removed (LS 55ɪ). It seems obvious enough that a house may remain in existence long after the builder has ceased working. What Zeno seems to have had in mind were sustaining causes that sustained something other than existence or life: it is prudence, for instance, that brings it about that a man is prudent, and he is prudent only for so long as his prudence lasts. Prudence, it must be remembered, was for Stoic materialists a physical ingredient of a person (LS 55ᴀ).

The way in which the existence of antecedent causes is to be reconciled with Zeno's theory of sustaining causes seems to have been this: an antecedent cause brings it about that an object possesses an internal feature that is itself a sustaining cause simultaneous with the effect to be explained. This, certainly, was the form the theory took when it was employed to underpin medical practice: when a patient catches a chill, the coldness of the air is an antecedent cause, and the patient's fever is the internal and enduring state that is the sustaining cause of his symptoms.[4]

Chrysippus was famous for using the illustration of a garden roller or a child's spinning top. The top will not move unless the child strikes it: but once struck it will continue to spin 'of its own force and nature' (Cicero, *Fat*. 43). The crack of the

---

[4] See texts in Hankinson, *CHHP* 487–91.

whip is an antecedent cause, but the top's internal force is the principal cause. Likewise the roller, once pushed, will continue to roll of its own accord. This illustration was used in an attempt to reconcile the Stoic theory of causality with the possibility of human responsibility.

Causation and Determinism

The Stoics believed not just in universal causation, that is to say, the thesis that everything has a cause; they believed also in universal causal determinism, that is to say, that everything has a cause by which it was determined. Alexander reports them thus:

Nothing in the world is or comes about without a cause, because nothing of what it contains is independent from, or isolated from, all that has gone before. For the world would be torn apart and shattered, and no longer remain a unity under the governance of a single order and policy, if any uncaused motion were introduced. That would be the case unless all the things that are and come about have preceding causes from which they follow of necessity. (Alexander of Aphrodisias, *Fat.* 191. 30 LS 55N)

Note the extreme position of the Stoics. They claim not just that every beginning of existence has a cause, but that everything that happens has a cause. Further they claim that every cause is a necessitating cause: given the cause, the effect cannot but happen. They maintain not just universal causation, but universal determinism. This doctrine, which was to be hugely influential henceforth, is a Stoic invention. It lurks no doubt in ancient atomism (Cicero, *Fat.* 23), but Democritus does not spell it out with anything like Stoic clarity. Neither of the Stoics' causal claims was accepted by Aristotle, and the Epicureans, while accepting the universality of causation, did not accept the universality of necessity.

This unified, successive, inescapable series of necessitating causes was called, by the Stoics and their critics, Fate (LS 55F). The doctrine of fate was immediately subjected to philosophical criticism from several quarters, and Cicero's *On Fate* gives a lively account of arguments levelled against it and Stoic responses to those arguments. One famous argument was called the Lazy Argument (*argos logos*); its purpose was to show that if determinism was true, there was no point in doing anything whatever.

The argument imagines someone addressing a Stoic patient on his sickbed. 'If it is fated that you will recover from this illness, then whether or not you call a doctor you will recover; likewise, if it is fated that you will not recover from this illness, then whether or not you call a doctor you will not recover. One or the other is your fate: so there is no point in calling a doctor' (*Fat.* 29 LS 55s0). Obviously, an argument of the same kind can be applied to any of the normal actions of life: another source imagines it being used to persuade a boxer that there is no point in putting up his guard.

In response, Chrysippus made a distinction between simple and complex facts. 'Socrates will die on such and such a day' may be true whatever Socrates does; but 'Laius will beget Oedipus' cannot be true unless Laius copulates with his wife. If the patient's recovery is a complex fact linked to calling a doctor, then calling the doctor will be no less fated than the eventual recovery.

If the history of the world is a single tissue of interconnected events, it is not clear how far Chrysippus is entitled to make his distinction between simple and complex facts: perhaps Socrates' death is co-fated (to use Chrysippus' term) with several of his actions, such as his behaviour when on trial. Indeed, perhaps everything is co-fated with everything else.

Nonetheless, Chrysippus is entitled to reject the Lazy Argument. Consider the propositions

(1) If I call the doctor, I will recover.
(2) If I do not call the doctor, I will recover.

If I am fated to recover, then the consequent of each of these propositions is true; and if we interpret each of the propositions truth-functionally, in the manner of Philo, each of them will on that supposition be true. In that sense it will be true that whether or not I call the doctor I will recover. But as these propositions are normally used in guiding behaviour, they must be understood not simply truth-functionally, but also as supporting the corresponding counterfactuals

(3) If I called the doctor, I would recover.
(4) If I did not call the doctor, I would recover.

But a Stoic has no reason to accept (4).[5]

Determinism and Freedom

More serious was the argument that if determinism is true, human responsibility for action evaporates, and praise and blame become pointless. This argument was mounted both by Epicureans and by Academics. Necessity is accountable to no one, Epicurus said, and what depends on us, what attracts blame and its converse, must be free of the overlordship of fate (LS 20A). To reconcile this freedom with their own atomistic system, Epicureans hypothesized that atoms engaged in unpredictable swerves. Thus Lucretius:

---

[5] The Lazy Argument appears across the centuries in many different contexts, e.g. in John Milton's de Doctrina Christiana in an argument against Calvinist predestination.

> Lest mind should suffer from compulsive force
> And helpless trace a predetermined course
> A travelling atom deviates a space
> And swerves at no fixed time and no fixed place.   (2. 290)

Neither in antiquity nor in modern times has it been clear how such a random quantum jerk would be a sufficient condition for human freedom; and not only Stoics, but Academics too, considered the swerve not only insufficient but unnecessary.

Carneades, Cicero tells us,

> showed that the Epicureans could defend their case without this fictitious swerve. They taught that some voluntary motion of the mind was possible, and a defence of this doctrine was better than the introduction of the swerve, especially as they could assign no cause to it. By defending it they had an answer to Chrysippus: they could agree that no motion lacks a cause without conceding that everything that happens is a result of antecedent causes. For there are no external antecedent causes of the operation of our will. (*Fat.* 33)

Voluntary motion, by its intrinsic nature, is in our power and obedient to us; and it is this intrinsic nature that is its cause.

Carneades is here offering the Epicureans an answer to Chrysippus; yet Chrysippus is reported as stating his own position in a way very similar to that of Carneades. Chrysippus, as I remarked earlier, was fond of using the examples of the spinning top and the garden roller to explain causation; and he uses them to make room for responsible action. Our assent to any proposition or proposal is triggered by external stimuli, as the top begins to spin only when the child whips it. But the actual assent is in our power, and this preserves responsibility without violating fate. 'If something could be brought about without an antecedent cause, it would be false that everything happens through fate; but if it is probable that there is an antecedent cause for whatever happens, what possible reason is there for denying that all things happen through fate?' (Cicero, *Fat.* 43).

The difference appears to be this. Carneades denies that voluntary actions have an external antecedent cause; Chrysippus affirms that they have, but appears here to deny that they are necessitated by it. How is this to be reconciled with the universal determinism the Stoics maintained elsewhere? To answer this question we must look more closely at the analogy with the top. The top is set in motion by the whip, but it moves in the way it does (a way different from the motion, say, of a garden roller) because of its own nature. Similarly, the mind's assent, when a stimulus is presented to it, is given because of its own nature. The assent falls under the overarching rule of fate if it is the only possible outcome of the joint causes, the external stimulus and the agent's own nature. But it is not necessitated by the external, antecedent cause, and in this sense Chrysippus can deny that it is necessary.

Many philosophers in later ages have claimed that if a human agent is responsible for an action X, it must have been possible for her, at the moment of action, both to do and not to do X. Such freedom of alternative choice was later given the technical name of 'liberty of indifference'. Chrysippus is not claiming that liberty of indifference is compatible with fate: he is interested rather in what later philosophers called 'liberty of spontaneity'. An agent enjoys liberty of spontaneity if he does X because he wants to do X. Chrysippus' humans do enjoy liberty of spontaneity, because they do X because they assent to X, and they assent to X because of their own nature and character. The responsibility that he defends is the autonomy of the agent to act unforced by external causes and stimuli.

From the time of Chrysippus up to the present day philosophers have debated how far it is possible to reconcile determinism and freedom. One of the most interesting contributions in the ancient world was made by St Augustine, in his work on the freedom of the will, written in the year of his conversion to Christianity. However, since he locates his discussion in an ethical and theological context, we shall wait to consider it until Chapter 8.

6

What There Is:
Metaphysics

The central topic of metaphysics is ontology: the study of Being. The word
'ontology' derives from the Greek word 'on' (in the plural 'onta'), which is
the present participle of 'einai', the verb 'to be'. In Greek, as in English, a definite
article can be placed in front of a participle to mark out a class of people or things:
as when we talk of the living or of the dying, meaning all the people who are now
living or all the people who are now dying. The founder of ontology was
Parmenides, and he defined his topic by placing the definite article 'to' in front
of the participle 'on'. 'To on', literally 'the being', on the model of 'the living',
means: all that is. It is customary to translate the expression into English as 'Being'
with an initial capital. Without a capital, the English word 'being' has, in philosophy, two uses, one corresponding to the Greek participle and one to the Greek
infinitive. A being, we can say, using the participle, is an individual that is; whereas
being (using the verbal noun) is, as it were, what any individual being is engaged
in. The totality of individual beings make up Being.

These rather tedious grammatical distinctions need making, because neglect of
them can lead, and has led, even great philosophers into confusion. In order to
understand Parmenides, one further important distinction has to be made:
between being and existence.

'To be' in English, and its equivalent in Greek, can certainly mean 'to exist'.
Thus, Wordsworth tells us, 'She lived unknown, and few could know | When Lucy
ceased to be.' In English the use is largely poetic, and it is not natural to say such
things as 'The pyramids are, but the Colossus of Rhodes is not', when we mean
that the pyramids are still in existence, while the Colossus is not. But analogous
statements would be quite natural in ancient Greek, and this sense of 'be' is
certainly involved in Parmenides' talk of Being. All that there is, all that exists, is
included in Being.

However, the Greek verb 'to be' occurs not only in sentences such as 'Troy is no more' but also in sentences of many different kinds, such as 'Helen is beautiful', 'Aphrodite is a goddess', 'Achilles is brave', and so on through all the different modes that Aristotle was to dignify as categories. For Parmenides, Being is not just that which exists, but that of which any sentence containing 'is' is true. Equally, being is not just existing (being, period) but being anything whatever: being hot or being cold, being earth or being water, and so on. Thus interpreted, Being is a realm both richer and more puzzling than the totality of existents.

Parmenides' Ontology

Let us now look in detail at some of Parmenides' mysterious claims, expressed in his rugged verse, which I have tried to render in an equally clumsy translation.

> What you can call and think must Being be
> For Being can, and nothing cannot, be.   (DK 28 B6)

The first line (literally: 'What is for saying and for thinking must be') expresses the universality of Being: whatever you can call by any name, whatever you can think of, must be. Why so? Presumably because if I utter a name or think a thought, I must be able to answer the question 'What *is* it that you are talking about or thinking of?' The message of the second line (literally 'It is for being be but nothing is not') is that anything that can be at all must be something or other; it cannot be just nothing.

The matter becomes clearer when Parmenides, in a later fragment, introduces a negative notion to correspond to Being.

> Never shall this prevail, that Unbeing is;
> Rein in your mind from any thought like this.   (DK 28 B7, 1–2)

My 'Unbeing' represents the negation of Parmenides' participle (*me eonta*). I use the word instead of some formula such as 'not-being' because the context makes clear that Parmenides' Greek expression, though a perfectly natural one, is meant to designate a polar opposite of Being. If Being is that of which something or other, no matter what, is true, then Unbeing is that of which nothing at all is true. And that, surely, is nonsense: not only can it not exist, it cannot even be thought of.

> Unbeing you won't grasp—it can't be done—
> Nor utter; being thought and being are one.

If we understand 'Unbeing' as meaning that to which no predicate can be attached, then it is surely correct to say that it is something unthinkable. If, in answer to your question 'What kind of thing are you thinking of?', I say that it isn't any kind of thing, you will be puzzled. If, further, I cannot tell you what it is like, or indeed tell you anything at all about it, you may justly conclude that I'm not thinking of anything, indeed not really thinking at all. If we understand Parmenides in this sense, we can agree that to be thought of and to be go together.

But granting this much, we may still want to protest against the sweeping claim that being thought and being are one. It may be the case that if I am to think of X I must be able to attach, in thought, some predicate to X. But it is not the case that any thought I have about X must be true: I can think that X *is* P when X *is not* P. If we take the dictum in that way, then it is false: being thought and being true are two very different things.

Again, we can agree that Unbeing cannot be thought of without agreeing that what does not exist cannot be thought of. We can think of fictional heroes and chimerical beasts who never existed. If it were true that what does not exist cannot be thought of, we could prove that things exist simply by thinking of them. Did Parmenides believe we could? Given the contortions of his language, it is hard to be sure. Some scholars claim that he confused the 'is' of predication (involved in the true claim that Unbeing cannot be thought of) with the 'is' of existence (involved in the false claim that the non-existent cannot be thought of). It is, I think, more helpful to say rather that Parmenides always treats 'to be'—in any of its uses—as a fully fledged verb. That is to say, he thinks of 'being water' or 'being air' as related to 'being' in the same way as 'running fast' and 'running slowly' is related to 'running'. In a sentence of the form 'S is P', instead of thinking of the 'is' as a copula and the 'P' as a predicate, he thinks of the 'is' as a verb and the 'P' as analogous to an adverb. A person who first runs fast and then runs slowly is running all the time. Similarly, for Parmenides, stuff which is first water and then air goes on be-ing all the time. Change is never from not-being to being, or vice versa; the most there can ever be is variation of being.

Interpreting Parmenides in this way helps us to understand how he draws some very remarkable conclusions from the theses of the universality of Being and the inconceivability of Unbeing.

> One road there is, signposted in this wise:
> Being was never born and never dies.
> Four-square, unmoved, no end it will allow.
> It never was, nor will be; all is now,
> One and continuous. How could it be born
> Or whence could it be grown? Unbeing?—No—
> That mayn't be said or thought; we cannot go
> So far ev'n to deny it is. What need,
> Early or late, could Being from Unbeing seed?
> Thus it must altogether be or not.

> (DK 28 B8. 1–11)

From the principle 'Nothing can come from nothing' many philosophers of different persuasions have drawn the conclusion that the world must always have existed. Other philosophers, too, have offered as a supporting argument that there could be no sufficient reason for a world to come into existence at one moment rather than another, earlier or later. But Parmenides' claim that Being has no beginning and no end takes a much more sweeping form. Being is not only everlasting, it is not subject to change ('four-square, unmoved') or even to the passage of time (it is all now, and has no past or future). What could differentiate past from present and future? If it is no kind of being, then time is unreal; if it is some kind of being, then it is all part of Being. Past, present, and future are all one Being.

By similar arguments Parmenides seeks to show that Being is undivided. What could separate Being from Being? Being? In that case there is no division, but continuous Being. Unbeing? In that case any division is unreal (DK 28 B8. 22–5). We might expect him to argue in a parallel fashion that Being is unlimited. What could set limits to Being? Unbeing cannot do anything to anything; and if we imagine that Being is limited by Being, then Being has not yet reached its limits. Some of Parmenides' followers argued thus (Aristotle, *GC* 1.8. 325^{a}15), but this is not how Parmenides himself seems to have seen matters. When he comes to sum up his teaching, starting from premises that are by now familiar he reaches a rather startling conclusion.

> To think a thing's to think it is, no less.
> Apart from Being, whate'er we may express
> Thought does not reach. Naught is or will be
> Beyond Being's bounds, since Destiny's decree
> Fetters it whole and still. All things are names
> Which the credulity of mortals frames—
> Birth and destruction, being all or none,
> Changes of place, and colours come and gone.
> But since a bound is set embracing all
> Its shape's well rounded like a perfect ball.

(DK 28 B8, 34–43)

It is not at all clear how the concept of the universe as a perfect sphere is either coherent in itself or reconcilable with the rest of Parmenides' teaching. However that may be, there is a more pressing question. If this is the nature of Being, uniform, unchanging, immobile, and timeless, what are we to make of the multiplicity of changing properties that we normally attribute to items in the world on the basis of sense-experience? These, for Parmenides, belong to the Way of Seeming. If we want to follow the Way of Truth, we must keep our minds fixed on Being.

While Parmenides and his disciples, in Greek Italy, were stressing that only what is utterly stable is real, Heraclitus, across the seas in Greek Asia, was stressing that what is real is in total flux. Heraclitus was given to speaking in riddles: to express his philosophy of universal change he used both fire and water as images. The world is an ever-living fire, now flaring up, now dying down; fire is the currency into which everything can be converted just as gold and goods are exchanged for each other (DK 22 B30, B90). But the world is also an ever-flowing river. If you step into a river, you cannot put your feet twice into the same water. Getting rather carried away by his metaphor, Heraclitus went on to say—if Plato reports him honestly—that you cannot step twice into the same river (*Cra.* 402a). However that may be, he seems undoubtedly to have claimed that all things are in motion all of the time (Aristotle, *Ph.* 8. 3. 253^{b}9). If we do not notice this, it is because of the defects of our senses. For Heraclitus, then, it is change that is the Way of Truth, and stability that is the Way of Seeming.

Plato's Ideas and their Troubles

Parmenides and Heraclitus laid out a battlefield for centuries of philosophical warfare. Much of Plato's most energetic philosophizing was devoted to the task of reconciling, or disarming, these two champions. One of his characters tells us that the true philosopher must refuse to accept either the doctrine that all reality is changeless, or the doctrine that reality is everywhere changing. 'Like a child who wants to have his cake and eat it he must say that Being, the sum of all, is both at once—all that is unchangeable, and all that is in change' (*Sph.* 249c–d).

Aristotle tells us that Plato began to philosophize under the influence of Heraclitean ideas, and retained them well on in life (*Metaph. A* 6. 987^{a}31–3). In the *Theaetetus* Plato offers a theory of perception that endeavours to preserve the truth in Heraclitus' insights without accepting the universal flux. We will consider this in Chapter 7, concentrating for the present on his treatment of Parmenidean problems.

During his life Plato made three systematic attempts to cope with the metaphysical issues raised by the two giants. The first is the Theory of Ideas, as presented in the *Symposium*, *Phaedo*, and *Republic*. Very crudely, one can say that in this phase Plato's Socrates divided the realm of philosophy in two, and handed over the intelligible universe of the Ideas to Parmenides, and the perceptible universe of the senses to Heraclitus. In the second phase Parmenides himself, in the dialogue named after him, is represented as exposing for Socrates some unacceptable consequences of the Ideal theory. In the final phase, in the *Sophist*, a third protagonist, an unnamed stranger from Elea, leads us to disown not only Parmenides and Heraclitus, but also Plato's own Theory of Ideas, in favour of an elaborate solution that will supersede all three and enable us to have our metaphysical cake and eat it.

As we have seen, the Ideas, as represented in the early middle dialogues, belong in an eternal world that is as unchanging as the Being revealed by Parmenides' way of Truth. The entities that inhabit the empirical world, on the other hand, are in a Heraclitean flux, constantly flitting between being and non-being. Plato is not, however, even-handed between the two protagonists: the Parmenidean world is far superior to the Heraclitean one; the unchanging world of Ideas is more real, and contains more truth, than the flickering world of experience. Only intellectual insight into Ideas gives knowledge; the senses can provide nothing better than true belief.

But while the realm of the Ideas is unchanging, it is not uniform or homogeneous like Parmenides' Being. Being is undifferentiated and single, whereas there are many different Ideas in some kind of relation to each other. They appear to be hierarchically ordered, under the Idea of Good, which appears to trump any notion of Being (*Rep.* 6. 509b). No doubt the other Ideas owe it to the Idea of Good that they are Ideas at all: a bed is a Perfect or Ideal Bed because it participates in Perfection and is the best possible bed. But the relations between the different subordinate ideas are not at all spelt out; there is certainly no suggestion that they are all one with each other in some sublime Parmenidean sphere.

It is not surprising, then, that when Plato comes to place a critical evaluation of the Theory of Ideas in the mouth of Parmenides, it is the One, the Idea of Unity, that is the focus of discussion.

The *Parmenides* is the most difficult of Plato's dialogues to interpret, and many scholars have confessed themselves baffled by it. It falls into two parts. The first part resembles one of the earlier Socratic dialogues in which a self-styled expert is shown to be unqualified to hold forth on the topic of his alleged expertise. The startling thing is that the usual roles are reversed. Instead of the inquiring Socrates puncturing the pretensions of some famous sophist, it is the young Socrates himself who is put to the question, and the topic of the quiz from which he emerges humiliated is none other than the Theory of Ideas. Parmenides, who is the successful inquisitor, tells Socrates that he is insufficiently trained in dialectic, and needs further exercise. The second part of the dialogue purports to illustrate the kind of exercise that Socrates needs. Starting from a pair of hypotheses about One and Being, which appear between them to exhaust the possibilities, Parmenides shows by a series of tight but often implausible arguments that whichever arm of the contradiction we accept we are led to wholly unpalatable conclusions.

Scholars disagree about both the nature of each of the two parts and their relation to each other. Are the criticisms of the Ideas in the first part regarded by Plato as seriously damaging to his theory? If so, does he have a remedy to propose, or is he just candidly confessing his perplexity? Are the proofs in the second part meant as jokes or as serious arguments? If the latter, did Plato mean us to detect fallacies in them, or did he himself regard them as valid? Either way, what is the relevance of the second part to the assault on the Ideas in the first part?[1]

Before outlining the main problems for the Theory of Ideas that are put forward in the first part, it is worth repeating at this point the six principles that we identified in Chapter 1 as constituting the core of the classical Theory.

(1) *The Principle of Commonality.* Wherever several things are F, this is because they participate in or imitate a single Idea of F (*Rep.* 5. 476a).

(2) *The Principle of Separation.* The Idea of F is distinct from all the things that are F (*Phd.* 74c).

(3) *The Principle of Self-Predication.* The Idea of F is itself F.

(4) *The Principle of Purity.* The Idea of F is nothing but F (*Phd.* 74c).

(5) *The Principle of Uniqueness.* Nothing but the Idea of F is really, truly, altogether F (*Phd.* 74d; *Rep.* 5. 479a–d).

(6) *The Principle of Sublimity.* Ideas are everlasting, they have no parts and undergo no change, and they are not perceptible to the senses (*Phd.* 78d).

The problems set out in the first part of the dialogue are as follows.

1. According to the theory, particular Fs are F because they participate in the Idea of F. But what does 'participation' mean? Does a particular F share only a part of the Idea, or does it contain the whole of the Idea? There are difficulties either way. If a particular large thing L has the whole Idea of Large, then the Idea seems to be scattered and lack the unity of an Idea; but if L shares only a part of the Large, then it is large by something which is itself small, because being only a part it must be smaller than the Large (131a ff.).

2. It is essential to the theory that wherever several things are F they derive this from some other entity which is the Idea of F. Thus, the several large things derive their largeness from the Idea of Large. But if we put together the original set of large things plus the Idea, we have a new set of large things, which must derive their largeness from some other entity. 'So another form of largeness will appear, alongside the Idea of Large and the things that participated in it, and then another again over all of these'—so that we are set off on an infinite regress (132b). This line of thought much impressed Aristotle, who, substituting 'man' instead of 'large' for F in the original premiss, named it the Third Man argument, after the Man who would appear as a Super-idea, after (*a*) the men in the world and (*b*) the Ideal Man.

3. There is a special difficulty with relational predicates. Suppose I am a slave. According to the theory, that must be because I resemble the Ideal Slave. But who is the Ideal Slave's owner? Surely, the Ideal Owner. But I am not a slave of the

---

[1] In what follows I am indebted to Constance C. Meinwald's *Plato's Parmenides* (New York: Oxford University Press, 1991), though I differ from her on important points of interpretation.

Ideal Owner but of whoever is my terrestrial slave-owner. So the relationships between entities in the world cannot be explained by relationships between the Ideas (133e).

These difficulties are genuine problems for the Theory of Ideas, and surely Plato means us to realize this. At the very least they demand substantial modification of the theory, and in other dialogues Plato undertakes such modification. In the *Parmenides*, however, he does not explicitly present the necessary modifications. We might expect, though, that the second part of the dialogue offers some guidance over the lines the modification needs to take.

A major problem with the second part is that it is not clear exactly what is the pair of hypotheses from which Parmenides starts his argument (137b). He describes the hypotheses as hypotheses about the One itself, but the Greek in which they are stated can be rendered in several ways. The two following pairs are the most promising translations:

(1) If the One is   v.   If the One is not.
(2) If it is one   v.   If it is not one.

(2) is the reading that best fits the Greek of the received text of this passage of the dialogue, where no definite article occurs before the word 'one' (*hen*). Indeed, even the most enthusiastic partisans of the first reading agree that it can only be sustained if one amends the text at this point. On the other hand, (1) seems to be a better fit not only to the immediately preceding wording, but to the whole series of subsequent arguments, which quite frequently unambiguously refer to the One, with a definite article. Moreover, anyone who accepts reading (2) has to answer the question what the 'it' stands for.

On my view, there is no need to amend the text. The second reading, which is the most natural translation, can easily be reconciled with the subsequent argument. There are two ways to do this.

The first is to take the 'it' in question to be the same as the 'it' which is the subject of the Way of Truth in the poem of the historical Parmenides: namely, Being. The references to the One in the course of the subsequent arguments are easy to account for. They occur in the course of following out the hypothesis that 'It (sc. Being) is One'. If that hypothesis is true, then there is one pre-eminent subject to which the predicate 'One' applies, namely Being itself. This subject can quite naturally be referred to as 'the One', and it is proleptically so referred to by Parmenides at 137b3. However, this interpretation becomes harder to sustain when Parmenides proceeds to examine the negative hypothesis, which on this account would be 'that Being is not one'.

A second interpretation, therefore, is preferable. The 'it' should be read as 'the One'. In that case, the two hypotheses are 'The One is one' and 'The One is not one'. Initially, this may seem a very implausible reading: surely the second hypothesis rules itself out instantly as being self-contradictory. But if we reflect, we see that this is not so. Some of the major problems with the Theory of Ideas that were laid out in the first part of the dialogue derived from the principle of self-predication, namely that the Idea of F is itself F (see p. 167 above). It is appropriate that the second part of the dialogue should not take self-predication for granted, but explore the consequences, in the case of one pre-eminent Idea, of its denial as well as of its affirmation.

The dialectic begins with the protagonist Parmenides inquiring what predicates attach to the One, and what predicates attach to other things, on the basis of the first hypothesis. If the One is one, then the One is not a whole with parts (137d). It is without limit and without place (138b). It is unchanging, but it is also not at rest (139b). It is neither different from, nor the same as, itself or another (139e), and it is neither like nor unlike itself or anything else (140b). It is neither greater nor less than itself or anything else (140d). It is not situated in time, and since it does not belong in the past, present, or future, it cannot have any share in being at all. The conclusion is this:

> Therefore the One in no way is. Therefore it is not in such a way as to be one, because in that case it would be a being and a partaker of being. But, as it seems, the One is not one and is not at all, if we have to trust this argument. But if something is not, then nothing can belong to it or be about it. So it has no name, no sentence or thought can be about it, and there can be no sensation or knowledge of it. (142a)

We are pretty clearly not intended to accept this conclusion as a true statement about the One. Parmenides' interlocutor in the dialogue, Aristotle (no relation), who is commonly a complete yes-man, interposes a rare note of dissent when asked if this conclusion is possible. If it were true, it would cut the ground from under the arguments that lead to it, since they all purport to speak about the One, which according to this conclusion cannot be done. The dialectic up to this point must be intended as a *reductio ad absurdum*: but a *reductio* of what? Surely of the hypothesis that the One is one *and nothing but one*. But of course an important part of the Theory of Ideas was the Principle of Purity: that the Idea of F was F and nothing but F. So the dialectic, to this point, is a recantation of an important element in the theory.

At this point Parmenides makes a fresh start from the hypothesis that the One is one and proves that the One is a whole with ever so many parts (142b, 143a), bounded and shaped (145b), located both in itself and elsewhere, both in motion and at rest, both the same as and different from itself and from other things (146b), both like and unlike itself and other things (148c), simultaneously equal to, greater than, and less than itself and other things (151b). It is and becomes older and younger than itself and other things, but equally it neither is nor becomes older or younger than itself nor other things (155c). It belongs to past, present, and future, and it partakes in being, though being and oneness are not the same (if they were, Plato argues, 'is one' would mean the same as 'one one') (142c). So there is no problem in naming it, speaking of it, and arguing about it (155e).

There is clearly a close parallel between these two first sections of the dialectic. At each stage of each argument we are presented with a pair of opposite predicates (e.g. in motion, at rest). In the first section Parmenides argues that neither of these predicates apply to the One. In the second section he argues that both of these predicates apply to the One. Between them, the two sections throw a damaging light on the Theory of Ideas. The first section shows the folly of holding that the Idea of F is nothing but F (the Principle of Purity). The second section shows the falsehood of holding that nothing but the Idea of F is F (the Principle of Uniqueness).

But the two sections are not meant to be on all fours with each other. The conclusion of the first section is, as we have seen, self-stultifying and the whole argument can only be taken seriously as a *reductio ad absurdum*. The second section, however, leads to a conclusion that, though it may be surprising, can be understood in a way which is in no way self-refuting.

Summing up the results of this section, Parmenides says that the One sometimes partakes of being and sometimes does not. His words echo the complaint made in the *Republic* about the ordinary objects of sense-perception, namely that they roll about between being and non-being. But now it is a form that displays this pattern, whereas in the heyday of the theory what marked off Ideas from common or garden objects was that they did not roll about. The Idea of F was not sometimes F and sometimes not F, nor was it F in one respect and not F in another respect. What is now said about the One marks a very significant departure from the original Theory of Ideas.

In the case of the sensible particulars, we could specify the times, respects, relations, and so forth that made them—without any violation of the principle of non-contradiction—both F and not F. What we now have to do is to draw appropriate distinctions to see how both a predicate and its opposite can be true in different respects, of the One, and by implication, of other Forms. It is to be noted that the subjects of all Parmenides' predications are Ideas, or at least they are all items referred to by universal terms, not individual names: the expressions for them are things like 'the same', 'the other', not 'Callias', or 'Dio'.

In order to resolve some of the problems about Ideas, Plato introduces a distinction between two types of predication. Using a terminology which belongs to a later period, we can say that he makes a distinction between predication per se and predication *per accidens*. The difference between the two can be brought out thus: S is P per se if being P is part of what it is to be S. Thus, an oak is a tree per se. (If we allow improper as well as proper parts of what it is to be S, then an oak is oak per se.) S is P *per accidens*, on the other hand, if S is as a matter of fact P, but it is no part of being S to be P. Thus, if oaks are as a matter of fact plentiful in a certain area, 'plentiful' is predicated only *per accidens*.[2]

We have seen that Plato, in the *Parmenides*, abandoned the Principles of Purity and Uniqueness. With respect to the Principle of Self-predication he makes use of his distinction between types of predicate. The Large is indeed large: being large is an improper part of what it is to be large. But other things are not large per se. If my house is large, that is not because being large is part of what it is to be a house. Hence 'large' is not predicated in the same way of large things and of the Large; and hence the Large and the other large things cannot be grouped together to form a set as they have to be in order to generate the regress nicknamed the Third Man.

Similarly, the Slave belongs per se to the Owner: for belonging to an owner is part of what it is to be a slave. But the relations between human slaves and human owners, and the relations between both and the Ideal Slave and the Ideal Owner are not per se but *per accidens*. Both sets of relationship, relationships between individuals and between forms, can function side by side without conflict.

Finally, we can revisit the notion of participation. A major difficulty in understanding how many things can share in a single Idea was that this seemed to divide an Idea into parts. We can now say that a Form is one per se if it is part of what it is to be a Form that it should be single and unique: otherwise it will not achieve the purpose for which it was invented, to mark what is common to things bearing the same name. But if there are many individuals instantiating the Form, then it will be many *per accidens*.

The common thread that runs through the dialectical arguments and the suggested solutions to the Parmenidean difficulties about the Theory of Forms is this: nothing can be predicated in the same way of individuals and of the Forms in which the individuals partake. One modern analogue of the Platonic notion of participation is that of class membership: if *x* participates in the Form of F, *x* is a member of the class of Fs. Equally, a modern analogue of the message of the *Parmenides* is that one cannot simply predicate of classes what one predicates of individuals. The paradox that results if we talk of the class of all classes that are not members of themselves is the lineal descendant of the paradoxes of the *Parmenides*.

The adaptation of the Theory of Ideas into a Theory of Forms is carried out further in the dialogue the *Sophist*. The official purpose of the dialogue is to find a definition of a sophist. The definition eventually offered is clearly intended as a joke. What the search for the definition is meant to illustrate is a method of definition that is still popular in parlour games. In such games the respondent thinks of an object that it is the questioner's task to identify by putting a series of questions offering a dichotomy. Is it living or non-living? If living, is it an animal or

---

[2] The Latin terms are meant to correspond to, though they are not translations of, Plato's Greek terms *pros heauto* (with respect to itself) and *pros alla* (with respect to others).

a plant? If an animal, is it human or non-human? And so on. In the course of the dialogue Plato examines the metaphysical presuppositions of such a style of definition.

What the pursuit of a definition by division will reveal, if it is carried out in a serious manner, is a tree structure in which species will appear under genera, and narrower genera under broader genera: human under animal, animal under living being, and so on. This tree structure is related to the predication per se which we found an important feature of the *Parmenides*. For anything that appears above F in a genus–species tree structure will be something that is predicated per se. Thus, being an animal is part of what it is to be human; being a living thing is part of what it is to be an animal.

On the way to the definition of the sophist we have to address the problem of false thought and false discourse. One cannot distinguish the fraudulent sophist from the true philosopher without discussing the nature of falsehood. But how can we talk about falsehood without falling into the traps set out by the historical Parmenides in his poem (237a)? To say what is false is to say what is not. But what is not is surely Unbeing, and Unbeing is nonsense for reasons that Parmenides gave (238e). It seems to be impossible, therefore, to say what is false without talking nonsense. Shall we revise our account, then, and maintain that to say what is false is to say that what is, is not, or that what is not, is? Will this avoid Parmenides' censure?

To deal with this problem we have to disarm Parmenides by forcing him to agree that what is not, in some respect is, and what is, in a manner is not (241d). Motion, for instance, is not rest, but that does not mean that motion is not anything at all (250b). There are many things that even Being is not: for instance, Being is not motion and Being is not rest (250c–e).

In the *Sophist* as in the *Parmenides* Plato is interested in the relationships between different Forms. Here, he describes this topic as 'the interweaving of Forms', which he says is what underpins language (259e). We dig a pit for ourselves if we assume either that no Forms can combine with each other or that all can (251e–252e). Clearly, some can and some cannot, and we need to inquire which Forms can combine with which other Forms. Being (*to on*) here occupies the central role in this inquiry that the One (*to hen*) occupied in the *Parmenides*. But in addition to Being four other forms—motion, rest, sameness, and difference—are considered and their interrelations explored.

Difference turns out to have a crucial relationship to Being (256d–e). When we speak of what is not, we are not talking of Unbeing, the contrary of Being: we are speaking simply of something that is different from one of the things there are (257b). The non-beautiful differs from the beautiful and the unjust differs from the just; but the non-beautiful and the unjust are no less real than the beautiful and the just (257e–258a). If we lump together all the things that are non-something, or unsomething, then we get the category of non-being, which is just as real as the category of Being. So we have blown open the prison into which Parmenides had confined us (258c).

We are now in a position to give an account of falsehood in thought and speech. The problem was that it was not possible to think or say what was not, because Unbeing was nonsense. But now that we have found that non-being is perfectly real, we can use this to explain false thoughts and false sentences.

A typical sentence consists of a noun and a verb, and it says something about something (262a–e). 'Theaetetus is sitting' and 'Theaetetus is flying' are both sentences about Theaetetus, but one of them is true and one false (263b). They say different things about Theaetetus, and the true one says a thing about him that is among the things that he is, while the false one says a thing about him that is among the things that he is not. Flying is not Unbeing, it is a thing that is—there is quite a lot of it about—but it is a thing that is different from the things that Theaetetus is, the things that can truly be said of Theaetetus (263b).

From time to time in the *Sophist* Plato describes the controversy over the nature of Being in terms of a battle between groups of philosophical adversaries. In one place it is a battle between giants and gods, giants being materialists who think there is nothing but bodies, and gods being idealists who accept non-bodily Forms as described in the Theory of Ideas (246a ff.). Elsewhere the materialists appear, under the leadership of Heraclitus, as the proponents of universal flux (since all bodies are constantly changing) while the chief of the friends of Forms appears to be Parmenides, with his doctrine that all reality is changeless. Finally we are told that the true philosopher must turn a deaf ear to Heraclitus, and also reject the doctrine that all true reality is changeless, whether put forward by the champion of a single Form (Parmenides) or the champion of many Forms (the Plato of the theory).

The *Sophist* shows us the way to have our cake and eat it and say that Being encompasses all that is unchangeable and all that is in change (271d).

Aristotelian Forms

Aristotle was a severe critic of the Theory of Ideas. Sometimes he criticizes it respectfully (e.g. *NE* 1. 6. 1096^{a}11 ff.: Plato is my friend, but truth is a greater one), and sometimes contemptuously (e.g. *APo.* 1. 22. 83^{a}28: farewell to such tarradiddle). His critique, whether rude or civil, always seem directed to the theory as presented in the middle dialogues, and not to the developments of the Theory of Forms in the *Parmenides* and the *Sophist*. He does, however, often tacitly make use of Plato's later thoughts in his own writings, in particular when developing his own theory of forms in *Metaphysics* Z. There, he treats on equal terms problems with Plato's theory and difficulties in his own. The book is dense and difficult, and the account of it I now give can only claim to be one possible thread to guide us through its labyrinth.

The difference between Aristotelian forms and Platonic Forms is that for Aristotle forms are not separate (*chorista*): any form is the form of some actual individual. As we have seen in our account of Aristotelian physics, form is paired with matter, and the paradigm examples of forms are the substantial or accidental forms of material substances. Aristotle cannot avoid, however, the questions for which Plato sought a solution in his theory. He must, for instance, provide his own answer to someone who asks what is common to the many things that are called by the same name or fall under the same predicate. He must, that is, offer an account of universal terms.

In *Metaphysics Z* Aristotle discusses the relationships between being, substance, matter, and form. He there works to relate the teaching of the *Categories* on substance and predication with the teaching of the *Physics* on matter and form, and he combines the two together, with modification and amplification, into a treatise on Being. 'The question that was asked of old, and is asked now, and always will be asked and always will be a problem is "what is Being?" And this is the question; "what is substance?" ' (*Z* 1. 1028^{b}2–4).

The reason he gives for eliding the two questions recalls the *Categories*. Whatever there is must be either a substance or something that belongs to a substance, such as a quantity or a quality of it. When we are listing the things that there are, we may count, if you like, health and goodness; but any actual health is someone's health, and any actual goodness is the goodness of something or other. If we ask, in such cases, what really and truly is, the answer will be: this healthy person, this good dog (*Z* 1. 1028^{a}24–30).

So Aristotle can regard it as obvious that material entities like animals and plants and earth and water and the sun and the stars are substances (*Δ* 8. 1017^{b}8; *Z* 3. 1028^{b}8). He puts on one side, for later treatment that we have no space to follow, a number of further questions. Are surfaces, lines, and points substances? Are numbers substances? But he addresses right away, though in a roundabout manner, the great Platonic question: Are there separate substances of any kind, distinct from those we can perceive with our senses? (*Z* 3. 1028^{b}8–32).

Essence and Quiddity

We saw that in the *Parmenides* Plato introduced a form of predication per se: S is P per se if being P is part of what it is to be S. Aristotle is keenly interested in this form of predication. In the *Categories* it is predication in the category of (second) substance. In the *Metaphysics* it is predication that answers the question what kind of thing something is (*ti esti*). Sometimes Aristotle speaks of the 'what-is-it?' of a thing; and in the context of the present discussion he often uses an almost untranslatable expression, *to ti en einai*, composed of the definite article, the question 'what-is-it?' and the infinitive of the verb 'to be'. This translates literally as 'the what-is-it to be' of a thing, i.e. the type of being that answers the question 'What is it?'

Latin commentators on Aristotle sometimes used the word 'quidditas' to correspond to this Greek expression; the Latin question 'Quid est?' corresponds to the Greek question 'Ti esti'. Many English scholars use 'essence'as a translation. That is quite possible; but I shall take my cue from the Latin and use the word 'quiddity'. 'Essence' is, of course, itself a Latinism, deriving from the Latin verb for being, 'esse', just as the Greek 'ousia' derives from the Greek word for being. There is good reason, however, to stick with the traditional translation 'substance' for 'ousia'. We can then use the word 'essence' to cope with another crabbed Aristotelian construction. We can speak, for example, of the essence of gold where Aristotle would speak of 'the for-gold being', using the infinitive after the Greek dative case, meaning 'what it is for gold to be gold'. This last construction, again, is descended from Plato's concern with questions about what is and what is not part of what being gold involves. For most purposes, 'quiddity' and 'essence' can be treated as synonyms.

With these preliminaries, we can state the agenda that Aristotle sets for himself at the beginning of the central section of *Metaphysics Z*. 'Substance', he says, has four principal meanings: the quiddity, the universal, the genus, and the subject. He treats of each of these four items in later chapters: the subject in chapter 3, the quiddity in chapters 4 and 5, the genus not until chapter 12, and finally the universal in chapter 14.

The subject (*to hypokeimenon*) turns out to be the same as the first substance of the *Categories*: it is that of which everything is predicated and which is itself predicated of nothing. Such first substances, we are told, are composites of matter and form; in the way that a statue is related to its bronze and its shape ($1029^{a}3$–5): so much is familiar to us from the *Physics*. But matter is not substance (because pure matter cannot exist alone; $1029^{a}27$), and if we are to discover whether form is substance, we have to investigate its relation to quiddity.

In treating of quiddity Aristotle makes use of a distinction he drew in his lexicon in *Metaphysics Δ* ($1017^{a}7$) between being per se (*kath'auto*) and being *per accidens* (*kata sumbebekos*). I have already used these expressions in giving an account of the *Parmenides*, though Plato's Greek expressions are not quite the same. The Latin phrases are simply transverbalizations of Aristotle's Greek expressions. It is futile to seek to render them into English, since the meaning of any English equivalents, as of the Latin and Greek phrases, would have to be gleaned from the contexts in which they occur. The phrases are used in various contexts, for instance in that of causation. A builder is a per se cause of a house: he builds it *qua* builder. But if the builder happens also to be blind, then the headline 'Blind man builds house' gives not the per se but the *per accidens* cause of the house.

The distinction is applied to the case of being in the following way. Entities in all ten of the categories, he tells us, are examples of per se beings: a thing's colour or shape is as much a per se being as the thing itself (Δ 7. 1017^{a}22). Clearly, the distinction between per se and *per accidens* is not the same as that between substance and accident. Accidents, confusingly, are per se beings. It is a substance-qualified-by-an-accident that is a *per accidens* being. So while the wisdom of Socrates is a per se being, wise Socrates is not; he is a being *per accidens*.

Aristotle uses his definition in defining quiddity: a quiddity is what a thing is said to be per se. You may be a scholar, but you are not a scholar per se as you are a person per se (Z 4. 1029^{b}15). 'The scholar Theophrastus' names a *per accidens* being. However, 'the man Theophrastus' names a per se being, and 'Theophrastus is a man' is a per se predication. Being a man is the quiddity or essence of Theophrastus.

A quiddity, we are further told, is what is given by a definition. This is puzzling, for surely not only per se beings have definitions. No doubt, for Aristotle, a postman would be a *per accidens* being: but can we not define 'postman' as 'man who brings the post' (cf. 1029^{b}27)? Aristotle responds that we do not always have a definition of X when we have a series of words equivalent to 'X': otherwise the whole epic would be a definition of the word 'Iliad' (Z 4. 1030^{a}9). A definition must be in terms of species and genus, and only such a definition will generate a quiddity (Z 4. 1030^{a}12).

Accidents as well as substances can be defined in this way: we can ask what 'triangular' means as well as asking what a horse is. To allow for this Aristotle is willing to soften his original strict account of definition. 'Definition', he says, like 'being', 'quiddity', and 'essence', are all analogous terms: all four of them belong primarily only to substances, just as 'health' is predicated primarily of patients and only secondarily of medicines and instruments. Secondarily, they can be applied to accidents, and thirdly even to *per accidens* beings (Z 4. 1030^{b}1; 5. 1031^{a}9).

Aristotle next asks: what is the relation between a thing and its quiddity? His answer is that they are identical: and this takes us by surprise, since a thing is surely concrete and a quiddity is surely abstract. His initial justification of his surprising claim is that a thing is surely the same substance as itself, and a thing's quiddity is called its substance. The *Categories* seems to offer a fairly straightforward way of sorting out the mystery here: Socrates, for example, is identical with a first substance, and his quiddity is his second substance. But here in *Metaphysics Z* Aristotle is looking for the answer to the question, what is really meant by 'second substance'? In 'Socrates is human' what does 'human' signify?

The first answer Aristotle considers is that of Plato: it stands for a Humanity that is something distinct from Socrates. Aristotle uses a variant of the Third Man argument to show that this will not do. If a horse was distinct from its quiddity, the horse's quiddity would have its own distinct quiddity, and so on for ever. The chapter ends with the remark, 'It is clear then that for things that are primary and spoken of per se the thing and its essence are one and the same' (Z 6. 1032^{a}8).

What this seems to mean is this. In a sentence such as 'Socrates is wise' the word 'wise' signifies an accident, the wisdom of Socrates, which is distinct from Socrates. But in 'Socrates is human' the word 'human' does not signify anything distinct from Socrates himself. We need to distinguish between Socrates and his wisdom because they have two different histories: as Socrates gets older, Socrates' wisdom may increase or perhaps evaporate. But Socrates and his humanity do not have two different histories: to be Socrates is to be human, and if Socrates ceases to be a human being he ceases to exist.

But is there not still the difference between concrete and abstract to be taken account of ? Aristotle helps us with this in his discussion of coming-into-being in chapters 7 and 8, where he makes the point that when a thing comes into being, neither its form nor its quiddity begins to exist. Using his long-overworked analogy, he says that if I manufacture a bronze sphere, I do not thereby make either the bronze or the spherical shape. He goes on to generalize:

What comes into existence must always be divisible, and there must be two identifiable components, one matter and the other form. . . . it is clear from what has been said that the part which is called form or substance does not come into existence; what comes into existence is the composite entity which bears its name. (Z 8. $1033^{b}16$–19)

He goes on to draw an anti-Platonic conclusion: if everyday enmattered forms do not come into existence at all, there is no need to invoke separate, Ideal, Forms to explain how forms come into existence (Z 8. $1033^{b}26$).

We do not even need to invoke Forms to explain how an individual substance gets its form. Human beings derive their form not from an Ideal Human, but from their parents (Z 8. $1033^{b}32$). The father (plus the mother, though Aristotle was ignorant of this) is responsible for introducing form into the appropriate matter. 'The final product, a form of such-and-such a kind in this flesh and these bones, is Callias or Socrates. What makes them distinct is their matter, which is distinct; but they are the same in form (for that is not subdivided)' (Z 8. $1034^{a}8$). In this passage Aristotle enunciates a thesis that was to have a long history, namely the thesis that matter is the principle of individuation. According to this thesis, however different two things may be from each other, it is not the differences between their properties or characteristics that make them distinct from each other. For it is possible for things to resemble each other totally without being identical with each other. Two peas, for instance, however alike they are, are two peas and not one pea because they are two different parcels of matter.

In some places Aristotle identifies form and quiddity (e.g. Z 7. $1032^{a}33$) and he goes on to say that in the case of humans and other animals, the form and the quiddity are to be identified with the soul (Z 10. $1035^{b}14$). This presents a problem: if the soul is the quiddity, and the quiddity is the same as what has the quiddity, does this mean that Socrates is identical with Socrates' soul? Aristotle seems briefly ready to contemplate this possibility (Z 11. $1037^{a}8$), but that is not his considered opinion, and he goes on to qualify his identification of soul, form, and quiddity. 'Man and horse and whatever is predicated universally of individuals are not substance. Substance is the composite of this definition and this matter taken universally' (Z 10. 1035^{b}27). That means that having flesh and blood is indeed part of being human; but having *this* particular flesh and blood is not part of being human. It is part, however, of being Socrates.

We may wonder what is the relationship between the pair matter–form and the pair body–soul. Aristotle at Z 11. 1037^{a}5 says that an animal is composed of body and soul, and he clearly identifies body with matter, but at that point he says not that the soul is form, but that it is first substance. He goes on shortly afterwards to say that the primary substance is the form inherent in the thing, and that substance (of another kind) is the composite of this and the matter (Z 11. 1037^{a}29). To make this cohere with his earlier teaching, we have to assume that he is here calling 'first substance' what in the *Categories* he called 'second substance'!

We are left, however, with a serious problem. In studying an earlier passage of the *Metaphysics* we had good reason to conclude that Aristotle was teaching that in 'Socrates is human' the predicate 'human' signified nothing other than Socrates. Now it seems to be suggested that it signifies Socrates' form or soul: it is that which provides the definition of Socrates, and it is here being distinguished from Socrates' matter. Socrates' body is clearly part of Socrates: but is it part of Socrates' definition or quiddity?

Some light is thrown on this by Aristotle's treatment of definition. Definitions have parts, and the substances they define also have parts: Aristotle takes a chapter to explain that if A is a part of X this does not always mean that the definition of A has to be part of the definition of X. (You don't have to mention an acute angle in defining a right angle; just the reverse, in fact; Z 11. 1035^{b}6.) The definition has to mention parts of the form, but not parts of the matter. Parts of the form are to be identified by the method of definition by division, into genus and species, that we met in Plato's later dialogues.

We can now see why it is misguided to ask whether Socrates' body is part of his quiddity. Body and soul are parts of Socrates (parts of a rather special kind, as will be explained in the next chapter). Being rational and being animal are parts of the quiddity of Socrates, and being animal includes having a body (an organic body of a particular kind). But *having a body* is not at all the same as a body. To ask whether Socrates' body is part of his quiddity is to fall into the confusion of concrete and abstract of which we were earlier tempted to accuse Aristotle himself. On the other hand, we must say something similar about soul. The soul cannot simply be identified with the quiddity, as Aristotle sometimes incautiously suggests: to be human is to have a soul of an appropriate kind incarnate in an organic body.

We have done our best to make sense of the doctrine of substance in the *Metaphysics*. The topic was introduced by Aristotle as a method of answering the fundamental question, What is being? It is now time to address that question frontally.

Being and Existence

It is clear that Aristotle uses the expression *to on* in the same manner as Parmenides: Being is whatever is anything whatever. Whenever Aristotle explains its meaning he does so by explaining the sense of the Greek verb 'to be' (e.g. *Δ* 7. 1017ᵃ6 ff.; *Z* 2. 1028ᵃ19 ff.).

Being contains whatever items can be the subjects of true sentences containing the word 'is', whether or not the 'is' is followed by a predicate. Both 'Socrates is' and 'Socrates is wise' tell us something about Being. Predicates in all the categories, Aristotle tells us, signify being, because any verb can be replaced by a predicate that will contain the copula 'is': 'Socrates runs', for instance, can be replaced by 'Socrates is a runner'. Every being in any category other than substance is a property or modification of substance. That is why the study of substance is the way to understand the nature of Being.

With Aristotle, as with Parmenides, it is a mistake to equate being with existence. In the dictionary entry for 'being' in the philosophical lexicon *Metaphysics Δ* existence is not even mentioned as one of the senses of the word. This is surprising, for from time to time in his logical works he seems to have identified it as a special sense. Thus in *Sophistical Refutations* he makes the point that 'to be something is not the same as to be, period', i.e. to be and to be F are not the same (5. 167ᵃ2). He uses this principle to dissolve fallacious inferences such as 'What is not is, because what is not is thought of' or 'X is not, because X is not a man'. He makes a similar move in connection with the being F of that which has ceased to be: e.g. from 'Homer is a poet' it does not follow that he is (*Int.* 11. 21ᵃ25).

In a famous passage of *Posterior Analytics* (11. 7. 92ᵇ14) Aristotle says 'to be is not part of the substance (*ousia*) of anything, because what is (*to on*) is not a genus'. This can be taken as saying that existence is not part of the essence of anything: i.e. *that there is* such a thing is not *what* anything is. If that is what it means, then it deserves the compliment paid by Schopenhauer when he said that with prophetic insight Aristotle forestalled the Ontological Argument.[3] But it is not clear that this is the only sense that can be given to the passage.

The premiss that *to on* is not a genus need not mean that there is no such kind of thing as *the things that there are*, true though that may be. Aristotle elsewhere argues that being is not a genus because a genus is differentiated into species by differences

---

[3] See G. E. M. Anscombe, in Anscombe and P. T. Geach, *Three Philosophers* (Oxford: Blackwell, 1961), 20–1.

that are distinct from it, whereas any differentia is a being of some kind (Metaph. *B* 3. 998^{b}21). The clearest case where 'be' must mean 'exist' is when it is attached to 'entia per accidens': when he says 'wise Socrates is' and distinguishes it from 'Socrates is wise' he can hardly mean anything else than that wise Socrates exists, and is among the things that there are. It is much more difficult to decide, when Aristotle writes simply 'Socrates is', whether this means that Socrates exists or that Socrates is a subject of predication: we cannot pin him down to the distinction that seems so clear to us between the copula 'is' and the 'is' of existence.

When 'is' does occur as a copula, joining subject and predicate, we may ask what it signifies. Two possible accounts are suggested by the Aristotelian texts. One is that it has no signification: it is an incomplete symbol, not to be construed by itself, but to be taken with the predicate-term that follows it, so that '...is white' is to be taken as standing for the accidental form being 'white'. There will then be no general answer to the question what 'is' denotes, but there will in general be an answer to the question what '...is P' denotes, namely an entity in one of the ten categories.

The other, which is easier to fit to the texts, is that it stands for *being*, where 'being' is to be taken as a verbal noun like 'running'. If we say this, it seems that we must add that there are various types of being: the being that is denoted by 'is' in the substantial predicate '...is a horse' is substantial being, whereas the being that is denoted by 'is' in the accidental predicate '...is white' is accidental being of a kind corresponding to the category of quality. Further, more detailed, difference can be drawn between different kinds of being and therefore different senses of 'is'.

A passage that strongly supports this reading is the second chapter of *Metaph. H.* Here Aristotle says that there are many ways in which things differ from each other. Sometimes it is because there are different ways in which their components are combined: sometimes these are mingled, as in a punch, sometimes they are tied together, as in a sheaf, sometimes they are glued together, as in a book. Sometimes the difference is one of position: a stone block may be a threshold or a lintel according as it is above or below a door. Time makes the difference between breakfast and supper, and direction makes the difference between one wind and another. He goes on to say that 'is' is said in as many different senses. A threshold *is* because it is placed in such and such a position, and so its being is to be so placed. For ice to be is for it to be solidified in such and such a way (*H* 3. 1043^{b}15 ff.).

While it is a mistake to look to Aristotle's treatment of being for an account of existence, it would be wrong to think that he is unaware of the issues that have exercised philosophers in this area. When philosophers ask themselves which things really exist and which do not, they may be worrying about the contrast between the concrete and the abstract (e.g. Socrates v. wisdom, Socrates v. humanity), or the contrast between the fictional and the factual (e.g. Pegasus v. Bucephalus), or the contrast between the extant and the defunct (the Great Pyramid v. the Pharos of Alexandria). In different places Aristotle treats of all three problems.

We have seen at length how Aristotle deals with abstractions by introducing the categories. Accidents are modifications of substance, so that statements about abstractions, such as colours, actions, and changes, are analysable into ones about first substances. Predicates in the category of substance, on the other hand, do not involve the existence of any entity—such as a Form of Humanity—distinct from the individual substance of the appropriate kind.

Aristotle provides himself with the means to deal with the problems about fictions by introducing a sense of 'is' in which it means 'is true' (Δ 7. 1017ᵃ31). A fiction *is* a genuine thought, but it *is not*, i.e. is not true. With regard to the extant and the defunct, Aristotle solves problems about things that come into existence and go out of existence by means of the doctrine of matter and form. To exist is to be matter under a certain form, to be a thing of a certain kind. Socrates ceases to exist if he ceases to possess his form, that is, if he ceases to be a human being.

We have still not explicitly considered the most important of Aristotle's contributions to metaphysics, namely the doctrine of actuality and potentiality. If we consider any item, from a pint of milk to a policeman, we shall find a number of things true of that item and a number of other things which, though not at that time true of it, can become true of it at some other time. Thus, the pint of liquid *is* milk, but it *can be* turned into butter; the policeman *is* fat, prone, and speaks only English, but if he wants to he *can* become slim, start mowing the lawn, and learn French. The things that something currently is, or is doing, are called by Aristotle its actualities (*energeiai*); the things that it can be, or can do, are its potentialities (*dynameis*). Thus the liquid is actually milk but potentially butter; the policeman is actually fat but potentially slim; and so on. Potentiality, in contrast to actuality, is the ability to undergo a change of some kind, whether through one's own action or through the action of other agents upon oneself. A change from fat to slim is an accidental change: in such a case a substance has the potentiality to be now F and now not F. A change, however, from milk to butter would be, for Aristotle, a substantial change. It is not the substance, but the matter, that has the potentiality to take on different substantial forms.

Of course in studying the pairs matter–form and substance–accident, we have in fact become acquainted with particular types of potentiality and actuality. The importance of the analysis in the history of metaphysics is that Aristotle saw it as a way of disarming the challenges of Parmenides, Heraclitus, and Plato. The early metaphysicians had spelt out the paradoxes that could be generated either by saying that being came from being, or that being came from non-being. Aristotle wants to cut between the two by saying that actual being comes from potential being. This, of course, is not a magic formula that will dissolve all philosophical puzzlement: but it is an appropriate template in which to insert detailed analyses of different types of possible change.

Aristotle did not call his own investigations 'Metaphysics'; that name initially just meant 'After Physics' and was given it by his editors to mark the text's place in the corpus. He does, however, say that there is a discipline 'which theorizes about Being *qua* being, and the things which belong to Being taken in itself' (Γ 1. 1003ᵃ21). This discipline is called 'first philosophy', and it interests itself in first principles and supreme causes. Aristotle seems to give two conflicting accounts of its subject matter: one that, unlike the special sciences, it deals with Being as a whole; the other that it deals with a particular kind of being, namely divine, independent, and immutable substance (for this reason he sometimes calls it 'theology'). Are we to say that these are two different accounts of Being *qua* being?

No: there is no such thing as Being *qua* being: there are only different ways of studying Being. You can study Being *qua* being, but that is not to study a mysterious object but rather to undertake a particular sort of study. This study, like all Aristotelian sciences, is an inquiry into causes: and when we study Being *qua* being we are looking for the most universal and primary causes. Contrast this with the other disciplines: when we study human physiology, we study humans *qua* animals, that is to say we study the structures and functions that humans have in common with animals. But of course there is no such entity as a human *qua* animal.

To study something as a being is to study it in virtue of what it has in common with all other things. (Precious little, you might think: and Aristotle himself says, as we have seen, that nothing can have being as its essence or nature.) But a study of the universe *as being* is to study it as a single overarching system embracing all the causes of things coming into being and remaining in existence. At the supreme point of the hierarchy of Aristotelian causes—as we shall see more fully in Chapter 9—are the heavenly moved and unmoved movers that are the final causes of all generation and corruption. When Aristotle says that first philosophy studies the whole of Being, he is assigning to it the field it is to explain; when he says that it is the science of the divine, he is assigning to it its ultimate principles of explanation. Thus Aristotle's first philosophy is both the science of Being *qua* being, and also theology.

Epicureans and Stoics devoted little attention to the ontological questions that preoccupied Plato and Aristotle. One development, however, deserves a brief remark.

In one of his letters Seneca writes to explain to a friend how things are classified by species and genus: man is a species of animal, but above the genus *animal* there is the genus *body*, since some bodies are animate and others (e.g. rocks) are not. Is there a genus above *body*? Yes: there is the genus of what there is (*quod est*): for of the things there are, some are bodily and some are not. This, according to Seneca, is the supreme genus.

The Stoics want to place above this yet another, more primary genus. To these Stoics the primary genus seems to be 'something'—let me explain why. In nature, they say, some things are and some things are not, and nature includes even those things that are not—

things that enter the mind, like Centaurs, giants and whatever other delusory fictions take on an image although they lack substance. (Ep. 58. 11–15)

Here, we can see clearly identified a use of the verb 'to be' in the sense of 'exist' without any of the complications dating from Parmenides.[4] This is a great advance. On the other hand, in treating the existent and the non-existent as two species of a single supreme ontological genus, namely 'something' (*ti, quid*), the Stoics sowed the seed of centuries of philosophical confusion. We shall meet the fruits of this confusion in later volumes. Its most elaborate product is the ontological argument for the existence of God; its most fashionable offspring is the distinction between worlds that are actual and worlds that are possible.

Despite the significance of this Stoic development, it is not until we come to the Neoplatonists that metaphysics resumes its importance in the ancient world as the prime element of philosophy. But in an author such as Plotinus, metaphysics has taken such a theological turn that his teaching is best considered in Chapter 9 devoted to the philosophy of religion.

[4] See LS i. 163.

7

Soul and Mind

The soul is much older than philosophy. In many places and in many cultures human beings have imagined themselves surviving death, and the ancient equivalents of the world 'soul' first appear as an expression for whatever in us is immortal. Once philosophy began, the possibility of an afterlife and the nature of the soul came to be one of its central concerns, straddling the boundary between religion and science.

Pythagoras' Metempsychosis

Pythagoras, often venerated as the first of philosophers, was also renowned as a champion of survival after death. He did not, however, believe as many others have done that at death the soul entered a different and shadowy world; he believed that it returned to the world we all live in, but it did so as the soul of a different body. He himself claimed to have inherited his soul from a distinguished line of spiritual ancestors, and reported that he could remember fighting, some centuries earlier, as a hero at the siege of Troy. Such transmigration (which need not continue for ever) was quite different from the blessed immortality of the gods, altogether exempt from death (D.L. 8. 45).

Souls could transmigrate in this way, according to Pythagoras, not only between one human and another, but also across species. He once stopped a man whipping a puppy because he claimed to have recognized in its whimper the voice of a dead friend (D.L. 8. 36). Shakespeare was struck by this doctrine, and refers to it several times. Malvolio, catechized about Pythagoras in *Twelfth Night*, tells us that his belief was

> That the soul of our grandam might haply inhabit a bird.
>
> (iv. ii. 50–1)

And when Shylock is abused in *The Merchant of Venice*, the possibility is raised of migration in the reverse direction.

> Thou almost mak'st me waver in my faith
> To hold opinion with Pythagoras
> That souls of animals infuse themselves
> Into the trunks of men.   (IV. i. 130–3)

Pythagoras did not offer philosophical arguments for survival and transmigration; instead he claimed to prove it in his own case by identifying his belongings in a previous incarnation. He was thus the first of a long line of philosophers to take memory as a criterion of personal identity (Diodorus 10. 6. 2). His contemporary Alcmaeon seems to have been the first to offer a philosophical argument in this area, claiming, by a dubious inference from an obscure premiss, that the soul must be immortal because it is in perpetual motion like the divine bodies of the heavens (Aristotle, *de An.* 1. 2. 405^{a}29–^{b}1).

Empedocles adopted an elaborate version of Pythagorean transmigration as part of his cyclical conception of history. As a result of a primeval fall, sinners such as murderers and perjurers survive as wandering spirits for thrice ten thousand years, incarnate in many different forms, exchanging one hard life for another (DK 31 B115). Since the bodies of animals are thus the dwelling places of punished souls, Empedocles told his followers to abstain from eating living things. In slaughtering an animal you might even be attacking your own son or mother (DK 31 B137). Moreover, transmigration is possible not only into animals but also into plants, so even vegetarians should be careful what they eat, avoiding in particular beans and laurels (DK 31 B141). After death, if you had to be an animal, it was best to become a lion; if a plant, best to become a laurel. Empedocles himself claimed to have experienced transmigration not only as a human but also in the vegetable and animal realm.

> I was once in the past a boy, once a girl, once a tree,
> Once too a bird, and a silent fish in the sea.

> (DK 31 B117)

In this early period, inquiry into the nature of the soul in the present life seems to have been subsequent to speculation on its location in an afterlife. All the earliest thinkers seem to have taken a materialist view: the soul consisted either in air (Anaximenes and Anaximander) or fire (Parmenides and Heraclitus). It took some time, however, for the problem to be addressed: how does a material element, however fine and fluid, perform the soul's characteristic functions of feeling and thought?

Heraclitus offers only a splendid simile:

As a spider in the middle of its web notices as soon as a fly damages any of its threads, and rushes thither as though grieving for the breaking of the thread, so a person's soul, if any part of the body is hurt, hurries quickly thither as if unable to bear the hurt of the body to which it is tightly and harmoniously joined. (DK 22 B67a)

This paragraph is the ancestor of many philosophical attempts to explain the capacities and behaviour of humans as the activities of a tiny animal within— though later philosophers were more inclined to view the soul as an internal homunculus than as an internal arthropod.

Perception and Thought

Empedocles was the first philosopher to offer a detailed account of how perception takes place. Like his predecessors he was a materialist. The soul, like everything else in the universe, was a compound of earth, air, fire, and water. Sensation takes place by a matching of each of these elements, as they occur in the objects of perception, with their counterparts in our sense-organs. Strife and Love, the forces that in Empedocles' system operate upon the elements, also have their part in this matching procedure, which is governed by the principle that like is perceived by like.

> We see the earth by earth, by water water see,
> The air of the sky by air, by fire the fire in flame,
> Love we perceive by love, strife by sad strife, the same.

(DK 31 B109)

The process seems to take place like this. Objects in the world give off an effluence that reaches the pores of our eyes; sound is an effluence that penetrates our ears. If perception is to take place, the pores and the effluences have to match each other (DK 31 A86). This matching must, of course, take place at the level of the elements, the fundamental principles of explanation in Empedocles' system. In some cases this is simple: sound is carried by air, which is echoed by the air in the inner ear. In the case of sight it is more complicated, and must be a matter of the proportions of each of the elements, as suggested in the fragment above. The most complex mixture of all the elements is blood, and as the blood churns round the heart this produces thought. The refined nature of the blood's constitution is what explains the wide-ranging nature of thought (DK 31 B105, 107).

The crude nature of Empedocles' materialism made him easy game for later philosophers of mind. Aristotle complained that he had not distinguished between perception and thought. Others pointed out that other things besides eyes and ears had pores: why then were sponges and pumices not capable of perception? The atomist Democritus offered an answer to this question. The visual image was the product of an interaction between effluences from the seen object and effluences from the person seeing: this image or impression was formed in the intervening air, and then entered the pupil of the eye (KRS 589). But Democritus, like Empedocles, was unable to offer any remotely convincing account of thought, and so, like him, fell foul of Aristotle's criticism.

The Presocratic whom later Greeks revered as a philosopher of mind was Anaxagoras. Anaxagoras believed that the universe began as a tiny complex unit which expanded and evolved into the world we know, but that at every stage of evolution every single thing contains a portion of everything else. This development is presided over by Mind (*nous*), which is itself outside the evolutionary process.

Other things have a portion of everything, but Mind is unlimited and independent and is unmixed with any kind of stuff, but stands all alone by itself. For if it was not by itself, but was mixed with anything else, it would have a share in every kind of stuff, since as I said earlier in everything there is a portion of everything. The things mixed with it would prevent it from controlling everything in the way it does now when it is alone by itself. For it is the finest and purest of all things, and it has all knowledge of and all power over everything. All things that have souls, the greater and the lesser, are governed by Mind. (KRS 476)

Anaxagoras distinguishes between souls, which are part of the material world, and a godlike Mind, which is immaterial, or at least is made of a unique, ethereal, kind of matter. Whereas for Empedocles like was known by like, Anaxagoras' Mind can know everything only because it is unlike anything. There is not only the one grand cosmic Mind: some other things (presumably humans) have a share in mind, so that there are lesser minds as well as greater (KRS 476, 482).

Immortality in Plato's Phaedo

Among those influenced by Anaxagoras was Socrates; but it is difficult to be sure what the historic Socrates truly thought about the soul and the mind. Socrates in Plato's *Apology* appears to be agnostic about the possibility of an afterlife. Is death, he wonders, a dreamless sleep or is it a journey to another world to meet the glorious dead? 'We go our ways, I to die and you to live: which is better, only God knows' (40c–42a). The Platonic Socrates in the *Phaedo*, however, is a most articulate protagonist of the thesis that the soul not only survives death, but is better off after death (63e).

The starting point of his discussion is the conception of a human being as a soul imprisoned in a body. True philosophers care little for bodily pleasures such as food and drink and sex, and they find the body a hindrance rather than a help in philosophic pursuits (64c–65c). 'Thought is best when the mind is gathered into itself, and none of these things trouble it—neither sounds nor sights nor pain, nor again any pleasure—when it takes leave of the body and has as little as possible to do with it' (65c). So philosophers in pursuit of truth keep their souls detached from their bodies. But death is the separation of soul from body: hence a true philosopher has throughout his life in effect been craving for death (67e).

Socrates' interlocutors, Simmias and Cebes, find his words edifying: but Cebes feels obliged to point out that most people will reject the idea that the soul can survive the body. They believe that at death the soul ceases to exist, vanishing into nothingness like a puff of smoke (70a). Socrates agrees that he needs to offer proofs that after a man's death his soul still exists.

First he offers an argument from opposites. If two things are opposites, each of them comes from the other. If you go to sleep, you must have been awake; if you wake up, you must have been asleep. If A becomes larger than B, A must have been smaller than B; if A becomes better than B, A must have been worse than B. So opposites like *larger* and *smaller*, *better* and *worse*, come into being from each other. But death and life are opposites, and the same holds here. If death comes from life, must not life in turn come from death? Since life after death is not visible, it must be in another world (70c–72e).

Socrates' next argument sets out to prove the existence of a non-embodied soul not after, but before, its life in the body. He argues first that knowledge is recollection, and then that recollection involves pre-existence. We often see things, he says, that are more or less equal in size; but we never see any two things in the world absolutely equal to each other. Our idea of equality, therefore, cannot be derived from experience. The approximately equal things we see are simply reminders of an absolute equality we have encountered earlier. But this encounter did not take place in our present life, nor by means of the senses: it must have taken place in a previous life and by the operation of pure intellect. What goes for the Idea of absolute equality must work also for other similar Ideas, like absolute goodness and absolute beauty (73a–77d).

Thirdly, Socrates argues from the concepts of dissolubility and indissolubility. Whatever can disintegrate, as the body does at death, must be composite and changeable. But the Ideas with which the soul is concerned are unchangeable, unlike the visible and fading beauties we see with our eyes. Within the visible world of flux, the soul staggers like a drunkard; it is only when it returns within itself that it passes into the world of purity, eternity, and immortality in which it is at home. If even bodies, when mummified in Egypt, can survive for many years, it is hardly credible that the soul dissolves at the moment of death. Instead, provided it is a soul purified by philosophy, it will depart to an invisible world of bliss (78b–81a).

In response to these arguments, Simmias offers a different conception of the soul. Consider, he says, a lyre made out of wood and strings, which is tuned by the tension of the strings. A living human body may be compared to a lyre in tune, and a dead body to a lyre out of tune. It would be absurd to argue that because attunement is not a material thing like wood and strings, it could survive the smashing of the lyre. When the strings of the body lose their tone through injury or disease, the soul must perish like the tunefulness of a broken lyre (84c–86e).

Cebes, too, has an objection to make. He agrees that the soul is tougher than the body and need not come to an end when the body does; in the normal course of life, the body suffers frequent wear and tear and needs constant repair by the soul. But a soul might be immortal, in the sense that it can survive death, without being imperishable, in the sense that it will live for ever. Even if it transmigrates from body to body, perhaps one day it will pass away, just as a weaver, who has made and worn out many coats in his lifetime, one day meets his death and leaves a coat behind (86e–88b).

Socrates produces several reasons for rejecting Simmias' analogy. Being in tune admits of degrees; but no soul can be more or less a soul than another. It is the tension of the strings that causes the lyre to be in tune, but in the human case the relationship goes in the other direction: it is the soul that keeps the body in order (92a–95e).

In response to Cebes, Socrates introduces a distinction between what later philosophers would call the necessary and contingent properties of things. Human beings may or may not be tall: tallness is a contingent property of humans. The number three, however, cannot but be odd, and snow cannot but be cold: these properties are necessary to them and not just contingent. Coldness cannot turn into heat, and consequently snow, which is necessarily cold, must either retire or perish at the approach of heat (103a–105c).

We can generalize: not only will opposites not receive opposites, but nothing that necessarily brings with it an opposite will admit the opposite of what it brings. Now the soul brings life, just as snow brings cold. But death is the opposite of life, so that the soul can no more admit death than snow can admit heat. But what cannot admit death is immortal, and so the soul is immortal. Unlike the snow, it does not perish, but retires to another world (105c–107a).

Socrates' arguments convince Simmias and Cebes in the dialogue, but surely they should not have done so. Is it true that opposites always come from opposites? And even when opposites do come from opposites, must the cycle continue for ever? Even if sleeping has to follow waking, may not one last waking be followed (as the Socrates of the *Apology* surmised) by everlasting sleep? And however true it may be that the soul cannot abide death, why must it retire elsewhere when the body dies, rather than perish like the melted snow?

The Anatomy of the Soul

In the *Phaedo* the soul is treated as a single, unified entity. Elsewhere, Plato offers us accounts of the soul in which it has different parts with different functions. In the *Phaedrus*, having offered a brief proof, reminiscent of Alcmaeon, that soul must be immortal because it is self-moving, Plato turns to describing its structure. Think of it, he says, as a triad: a charioteer with a pair of horses, one good and one bad, driving towards a heavenly banquet (246b). The good horse strives upwards, while the bad horse constantly pulls the chariot downwards. The horses are clearly meant to represent two different parts of the soul, but their exact functions are never made clear. Plato applies his analogy mainly in the course of setting out the lineaments of his ideal philosophical type of homoerotic love. When we reach the point where we have a man and a boy and four horses all in bed together, the metaphor has obviously got quite out of hand (256a).

The anatomy of the soul is more soberly described in the *Republic*. In book 4 Socrates suggests that the soul contains three elements, just as his imaginary state contains three classes. 'Do we learn things with one part,' he asks, 'feel anger with another, and with yet a third desire the pleasures of food and sex and the like? Or when we have such impulses are we operating with our whole soul?' (436a–b). He finds his answer by attending to the phenomena of mental conflict. A man may be thirsty and yet unwilling to drink (perhaps because of doctor's orders): this shows that there is one part of the soul that reflects and a different one that feels bodily desires. The first can be called reason (*to logistikon*) and the second appetite (*to epithymetikon*; 439d). Now anger cannot be attributed to either of these elements: not to appetite, for we may feel disgust at our own perverted desires; not to reason, because children have tantrums before they reach the age of discretion. Since anger can conflict with reason and appetite, we have to attribute it to a third element in the soul, which we can call temper (*to thymoeides*; 441b). Justice in the soul is the harmony of these three elements.

We meet the tripartite soul again in book 9 of the *Republic*. The lowest element in it can be called the avaricious element, since money is the principal means of satisfying the desires of appetite. Temper seeks power, victory, and repute, and so may be called the honour-loving or ambitious part of the soul. Reason pursues knowledge of truth: its love is learning. In each man's soul one or other of these elements may be dominant: he can be classed accordingly as avaricious, ambitious, or academic. Each type of person will claim their own life is the best life: the avaricious man will praise the life of business, the ambitious man will praise a political career, and the academic man will praise knowledge and understanding and the life of learning. Naturally, Plato awards the palm to the philosopher: he has the broadest experience and the soundest judgement, and the objects to which he devotes his life are much more real than the illusory pleasures pursued by his competitors (587a).

There are differences, it will be seen, between the accounts of the soul in book 4 and in book 9. In the meantime Plato has introduced the Theory of Ideas and has set out his plan of education for philosopher kings. Reason's task is no longer just to take care of the body: it is exercised in the ascending scale of mental states and activities described in the Line: imagination, belief, and knowledge. At the end of book 9 we bid farewell to the tripartite soul with a vivid picture. Appetite is a many-headed beast, constantly sprouting heads of tame and wild animals; temper is like a lion, and reason like a man. The beast is larger than the other two, and all three are stowed away within a human being. We have come a long way from the humble spider of Heraclitus.

The tripartite soul is not Plato's last word in the *Republic*. In book 10 he makes a contrast between different elements in the reasoning part: one that is confused by optical illusions, and another that measures, counts, and weighs. Whereas in the earlier books the parts of the soul were distinguished by their desires, we now have a difference of cognitive power presented as a basis for distinguishing parts.

In the same book Socrates offers a new proof of immortality. Each thing is destroyed by its characteristic disease: eyes by ophthalmia, and iron by rust. Vice is the characteristic disease of the soul: but it does not destroy the soul. If the soul's own disease cannot kill it, then it cannot be killed by bodily disease and must be immortal (609d). But what is immortal cannot be an uneasily composite entity like the threefold soul. Such a soul is like a statue in the sea covered with barnacles. The element of the soul that loves wisdom and has a passion for the divine must be stripped of extraneous elements if we are to see it in all its loveliness. Whether the soul seen in its true nature would prove manifold or simple is left an open question (611b ff., 612a3).

In the *Timaeus*, however, the tripartite soul reappears, and its parts are given corporeal locations. Reason sits in the head, the other two parts are placed in the body, with the neck as an isthmus to keep the divine and the mortal elements of the soul apart from each other. Temper is located around the heart, and appetite in the belly, with the midriff separating the two like the partition between the men's and women's quarters in a house. The heart is the guardroom from which commands can be transmitted around the body, via the circulating blood, when reason for some purpose or other orders combat stations. The lowest part of the soul is kept under control by the liver, which is particularly susceptible to the influence of mind. The coiling of the bowels has the function of preventing appetites from becoming insatiable (69c–73b).

Plato on Sense-Perception

While the *Timaeus*, like the earlier books of the *Republic*, anatomizes the soul on the basis of desire rather than cognition, the dialogue does deal at some length with the mechanisms of perception. The status of sense-perception also attracted Plato's attention in the *Theaetetus* in the course of the discussion of Protagoras' thesis that whatever seems to a particular person is true for that person. Behind Protagoras Plato detects Heraclitus' doctrine of universal flux.

If everything in the world is in constant change, then the colours we see and the qualities we detect with our other senses cannot be stable, objective realities. Rather, each of them is a meeting between one of our senses and some appropriate transitory item in the universal maelstrom. When the eye, for instance, comes into contact with a suitable visible counterpart, the eye begins to see whiteness, and the object begins to look white. The whiteness itself is generated by the intercourse between these two parents, the eye and the object. The eye and its object are themselves subject to perpetual change, but their motion is slow by comparison with the speed with which the sense-impressions come and go. The eye's seeing of the white object, and the whiteness of the object itself, are two twins which are born and can die together (156a–157b).

A similar tale can be told of other senses: but it is not clear how seriously Plato means us to take this account of sensation. It occurs, after all, in the course of a *reductio ad absurdum* argument against the Heraclitean thesis that everything is always changing both in quality and in place. If something stayed put, Socrates argues, we could describe how it looked, and if we had a patch of constant colour, we could describe how it moved from place to place. But if both kinds of change are taking place simultaneously, we are reduced to speechlessness: we cannot say *what* is moving, or *what* is changing colour. Each episode of seeing will turn instantly into an episode of non-seeing, and perception becomes impossible (182b–e).

Nonetheless, the principle that seeing is an encounter between eye and object is stated by Plato on his own account in the *Timaeus* and an explanation is there offered of the mechanism of vision. Within our heads there is a gentle fire, akin to daylight: this fire flows through our eyes and makes a uniform column with the surrounding light: when this strikes an object, shivers are sent back along the column, through the eyes, and into the body to produce the sensation we call sight (45d). Colours are a kind of flame that streams off bodies and is composed of particles so proportioned to our sight as to yield sensation. These flames travel towards the eye using the original light column as a kind of carrier wave. Individual colours are the product of different mixtures of particles of four basic kinds: black, white, red, and bright (67b–68d).

Aristotle's Philosophical Psychology

Plato's philosophy of mind has to be pieced together from fragments of various dialogues, largely concerned with ethical and metaphysical issues. The case is very different when we come to Aristotle's philosophical psychology. Here, in addition to material from ethical writings, we have a systematic treatise on the nature of the soul (*de Anima*) and a number of minor monographs on topics such as sense-perception, memory, sleep, and dreams. Aristotle took over and developed some of Plato's ideas, such as the division of the soul into parts and faculties and the philosophical analysis of sensation as encounter, but his fundamental approach differs by being rooted in the study of biology. The way in which he structured the soul and its faculties influenced not only philosophy but science for nearly two millennia.

For Aristotle the biologist the soul is not, as in the *Phaedo*, an exile from a better world ill-housed in a base body. The soul's very essence is defined by its relationship to an organic structure. Not only humans, but beasts and plants have souls— not second-hand souls, transmigrants paying the penalty of earlier misdeeds, but intrinsic principles of animal and vegetable life. A soul, Aristotle says, is 'the actuality of a body that has life', where life means the capacity for self-sustenance, growth, and decay. If we regard a living substance as a composite of matter and form, then the soul is the form of a natural, or as Aristotle sometimes says, organic, body (*de An.* 2.1. 412^{a}20,^{b}5–6).

Aristotle gives several definitions of 'soul' which have seemed to some scholars inconsistent with each other.[1] But the differences between the definitions arise not from an incoherent notion of soul, but from an ambiguity in Aristotle's use of the Greek word for 'body'. Sometimes the word means the living compound substance: in that sense, the soul is the form of a body that is alive, a self-moving body (2.1. 412^{b}17). Sometimes the word means the appropriate kind of matter to be informed by a soul: in that sense, the soul is the form of a body that *potentially* has life (2. 1. 412^{a}22; 2. 2. 414^{a}15–29). The soul is the form of an organic body, a body that has organs, that is to say parts which have specific functions, such as the mouths of mammals and the roots of trees.

The Greek word 'organon' means a tool, and Aristotle illustrates his notion of soul by comparison both with inanimate tools and with bodily organs. If an axe were a living body, its power to cut would be its soul; if an eye were a whole animal, its power to see would be its soul. A soul is an actuality, Aristotle tells us, but he makes a distinction between first and second actuality. When the axe is actually cutting, and the eye is actually seeing, that is second actuality. But an axe in a sheath, and the eye of a sleeper, retain a power that they are not actually exercising: that active power is a first actuality. It is that kind of actuality that the soul is: the first actuality of a living body. The exercise of this actuality is the totality of the vital operations of the organism (2. 1. 412^{b}11–413^{a}3).

The soul is not only the form, or formal cause, of the living body: it is also the origin of change and motion in the body, and above all it is also the final cause that gives the body its teleological orientation. Reproduction is one of the most fundamental vital operations. Each living thing strives 'to reproduce its kind, an animal producing an animal, and a plant a plant, in order that they may have a share in the everlasting and the divine so far as they can' (2. 4. 415^{a}26–9, ^{b}16–20).

---

[1] On this see J. Barnes, 'Aristotle's Concept of Mind' (*Proceedings of the Aristotelian Society* (1972), 101–14); J. L. Ackrill, 'Aristotle's Definitions of *Psyche*' (*Proceedings of the Aristotelian Society* (1973), 119).

The souls of living beings can be ordered in a hierarchy. Plants have a vegetative or nutritive soul, which consists of the powers of growth, nutrition, and reproduction (2. 4. 415^{a}23–6). Animals have in addition the powers of perception, and locomotion: they possess a sensitive soul, and every animal has at least one sense-faculty, touch being the most universal. Whatever can feel at all can feel pleasure: and hence animals, who have senses, also have desires. Humans in addition have the power of reason and thought (*logismos kai dianoia*), which we may call a rational soul.

Aristotle's theoretical concept of soul differs from that of Plato before him and Descartes after him. A soul, for him, is not an interior, immaterial agent acting on a body. 'We should not ask whether body and soul are one thing, any more than we should ask that question about the wax and the seal imprinted on it, or about the matter of anything and that of which it is the matter' (2. 1. 412^{b}6–7). A soul need not have parts in the way that a body does: perhaps they are no more distinct than concave and convex in the circumference of a circle (*NE* 1. 13. 1102^{a}30–2). When we talk of parts of the soul we are talking of faculties: and these are distinguished from each other by their operations and their objects. The power of growth is distinct from the power of sensation because growing and feeling are two different activities; and the sense of sight differs from the sense of hearing not because eyes are different from ears, but because colours are different from sounds (*de An.* 2. 4. 415^{a}14–24).

The objects of sense come in two kinds: those that are proper to particular senses, such as colour, sound, taste, and smell, and those that are perceptible by more than one sense, such as motion, number, shape, and size. You can tell, for instance, if something is moving either by watching it or by feeling it, and so motion is a 'common sensible' (2. 6. 418^{a}7–20). We do not have a special organ for detecting common sensibles, but Aristotle says that we do have a faculty which he calls *koine aisthesis*, literally 'common sense', but better translated, because of English idiom, 'general sense' (3.1. 425^{a}27). When we encounter a horse, we may see, hear, feel, and smell it: it is the general sense that unifies these as perceptions of a single object (though the knowledge that this object is a horse is, for Aristotle, a function of intellect rather than sense). The general sense is given by Aristotle several other functions: for instance, it is by the general sense that we perceive that we are using the particular senses (3. 1. 425^{b}13 ff.), and it is by the general sense that we tell the difference between sense objects proper to different senses (e.g. between white and sweet) (3. 4. 429^{b}16–19). This last move seems ill-judged: telling the difference between white and sweet is surely not an act of sensory discrimination like telling the difference between red and pink. What would it be like to mistake white for sweet?

Aristotle's most interesting thesis about the operation of the individual senses is that a sense-faculty in operation is identical with a sense-object in action: the actuality of the sense-object is one and the same as the actuality of the

193

sense-faculty (3. 2. 425^{b}26–7, 426^{a}16). Aristotle explains his thesis by using sound and hearing as an example; because of differences between Greek and English idiom I will try to explain what he means in the case of the sense of taste.[2] The sweetness of a cup of tea is a sense-object, something that can be tasted. My ability to taste is a sense-faculty. The operation of the sense of taste upon the object of taste is the same thing as the action of the object upon my sense. That is to say, the tea's tasting sweet to me is one and the same event as my tasting the sweetness of the tea.

Aristotle is applying to the case of sensation his scheme of layers of potentiality and actuality (2. 5. 417^{a}22–30, ^{b}28–418^{a}6). The tea is actually sweet, whereas before the sugar was put in, it was only potentially sweet. The sweetness of the tea in the cup is a first actuality: the tea's actually tasting sweet to me is a second actuality. Sweetness is nothing other than the power to taste sweet to suitable tasters; and the faculty of taste is nothing other than the power to taste such things as the sweetness of sweet objects. Thus we can agree that the sensible property in operation is the same thing as the faculty in operation, though of course the power to taste and the power to be tasted are two different things, one in an animal and the other in a substance.

This seems a sound and important philosophical analysis of the concept of sensation: it enables one to dispense with the notion, which has misled many philosophers, that sensation involves a transaction between the mind and some *representation* of what is sensed. Aristotle's detailed explanations of the chemical vehicles of sensory properties and the mechanism of the organs of sensation are very different matters, speculative theories long since superannuated. Though Aristotle is very critical of his predecessors in this area, such as Democritus and the Plato of the *Timaeus*, his own accounts are no less distant than theirs from the truth as discovered by the progress of science.

Besides the five senses and the general sense, Aristotle recognizes other faculties which later came to be grouped together as the 'inner senses': notably imagination (*phantasia*) (*de An.* 3. 3. 427^{b}28–429^{a}9), and memory, to which he devoted an entire opuscule (*de Memoria*). Corresponding to the senses at the cognitive level, there is an affective part of the soul, the locus of spontaneous felt emotion. This is introduced in the *Nicomachean Ethics* as part of the soul that is basically irrational but which is, unlike the vegetative soul, capable of being controlled by the reason. It is the part of the soul for desire and passion, corresponding to appetite and temper in the Platonic tripartite soul. When brought under the sway of reason it is the home of the moral virtues such as courage and temperance (1. 13. 1102^{a}26–1103^{a}3).

---

[2] Aristotle complains that Greek lacks a word for what an object does to us when we taste it (3. 2. 426^{a}17). English does not, but it does lack a single word corresponding to the Greek word for what a sound does to us when it makes us hear it.

For Aristotle as for Plato the highest part of the soul is occupied by mind or reason, the locus of thought and understanding. Thought differs from sense-perception, and is restricted—on earth at least—to human beings (de An. 3. 3. 427^{a}18–^{b}8). Thought, like sensation, is a matter of making judgements; but sensation concerns particulars, while intellectual knowledge is of universals (2. 5. 417^{b}23). Aristotle makes a distinction between practical reasoning and theoretical reasoning, and makes a corresponding division of faculties within the mind. There is a deliberative part of the rational soul (logistikon) which is concerned with human affairs, and there is a scientific part (epistemonikon) that is concerned with eternal truths (NE 6. 1. 1139^{a}16; 12. 1144^{a}2–3). This distinction is easy enough to understand; but in a famous passage of the de Anima Aristotle introduces a different distinction between two kinds of mind (nous) which is very difficult to grasp. Everywhere in nature, he says, we find a material element, which is potentially anything and everything, and there is also a creative element that works upon the matter. So it is too with mind.

There is a mind of such a kind as to become everything, and another for making all things, a positive state like light—for in a certain manner light makes potential colours into actual colours. This mind is separable, impassible, and unmixed, being in essence actuality; for the agent is always superior to the patient, and the principle to the matter. Knowledge in actuality is the very same thing as the object of knowledge. (de An. 3. 5. 430^{a}14–21)

In antiquity and the Middle Ages this passage was the subject of sharply different interpretations. Some—particularly among Arabic commentators—identified the separable, active agent, the light of the mind, with God or with some other superhuman intelligence. Others—particularly among Latin commentators—took Aristotle to be identifying two different faculties within the human mind: an active intellect, which formed concepts, and a passive intellect, which was a storehouse of ideas and beliefs.

The theorem of the identity in actuality of knowledge and its object—parallel to the corresponding thesis about sense-perception—was understood, on the second interpretation, in the following manner. The objects we encounter in experience are only potentially, not actually, thinkable, just as colours in the dark are only potentially, not actually, visible. The active intellect creates concepts—actually thinkable objects—by abstracting universal forms from particular experience. These matterless forms exist only in the mind: their actuality is simply to be thought. Thinking itself consists of nothing else but being busy about such universals. Thus the actualization of the object of thought, and the operation of the thinker of the thought, are one and the same.

If the second interpretation is correct, then Aristotle is here recognizing a part of the human soul that is separable from the body and immortal. In a similar vein, in the Generation of Animals (2. 3. 736^{b}27) Aristotle says that reason enters the body 'from out of doors', being the sole divine element in the soul and being unconnected with any bodily activity. These passages remind us that in addition to the official, biological notion of the soul that we have been studying, there is detectable from time to time in Aristotle a Platonic residue of thought according to which the intellect is a distinct entity separable from the body.

This line of thought is nowhere more prominent than in the final book of the *Nicomachean Ethics*. Whereas in the *Eudemian Ethics* and in the books that are common to the two treatises, the theoretical intellect is clearly a faculty of the soul, and there is no suggestion that it is transcendent or immortal, in book 10 of the *Nicomachean Ethics* the life of intellect is described as superhuman and is contrasted with that of the *syntheton*, or body–soul compound. The moral virtues and practical wisdom are virtues of the compound, but the excellence of intellect is capable of separate existence (10. 7. 1177^{a}14, ^{b}26–9; 1178^{a}14–20). It is in this activity of the separable intellect that, for the *Nicomachean Ethics*, human happiness supremely consists.

It is difficult to reconcile the biological and the transcendent strains in Aristotle's thought. No theory of chronological development has succeeded in doing so. The *de Anima* itself, as we have seen, contains a passage that strongly suggests an immortal element in the human soul; and in the very section of the work that sets out most clearly the theory of the soul as the form of an organic body, Aristotle tells us that it is an open question whether the soul is in the body as a sailor in a ship (2. 1. 413^{a}9). But that is a classic formulation of the dualist conception of the relation of soul to body.

Hellenistic Philosophy of Mind

No ancient author between Aristotle and Augustine formulated a comparably rich philosophy of mind. The philosophical psychology of Epicurus shows little advance on that of Democritus. For him the soul, like everything else, consists of atoms, which differ from other atoms only in being smaller and subtler, more finely structured even than those that constitute the winds. It is nonsense to say that the soul is incorporeal: whatever is not body is merely empty void. The soul has the major responsibility for sensation, but only through its position in the body–soul compound. At death its atoms are dispersed and cease to be capable of sensation because they no longer occupy their appropriate place in a body (LS 14B).

The third book of Lucretius' great poem *On the Nature of Things* is devoted to psychology. He distinguishes initially between a*nimus* and *anima* (34–5). The *animus*, or mind, is a part of the body just like a hand or foot; this is shown by the fact that a body becomes inert once it has breathed its last breath. The mind is a part of the *anima*, or soul; it is the dominant part, located in the heart. The rest of soul is spread throughout the body and moves at the behest of mind. Mind, soul, and body are closely interwoven, as we see when fear causes the body to tremble and bodily wounds cause the mind to grieve. Mind and soul must be corporeal or they could not move the body—to move it they must touch it, and how could they touch it unless they were themselves bodily (160–7)? Mind is very light and fine textured, like the bouquet of wine—a dead body, after all, weighs little less than a live one. It is composed of fire, air, wind, and a fourth nameless element. Mind is more important than soul; once mind goes, soul follows soon after, but mind can survive great damage to soul (402–5).

Some say that the body does not perceive or sense anything, but only the soul, conceived as an inner homunculus. Lucretius argues ingeniously against this primitive view. If the eyes are not doing any seeing, but are merely doors through which the mind sees, then we ought to be able to see more clearly if our eyes have been torn out, because a man in a house can see out much better if doors and doorposts are removed (367–9).

The goal of Lucretius' discussion of mind and soul is to prove that they are both mortal, and thus to take away the grounds on which people fear death. Water flows out of a smashed vessel: how much faster must soul's tenuous fluid leak away once the body is broken! The mind develops with the body and will decay with the body. The mind suffers when the body is sick, and is cured by physical medicine. These are all clear marks of mortality.

> What has this bugbear, death, to frighten man,
> If souls can die, as well as bodies can?
> For, as before our birth we felt no pain,
> When Punic arms infested land and main,
> When heaven and earth were in confusion hurled,
> For the debated empire of the world,
> Which awed with dreadful expectation lay,
> Sure to be slaves, uncertain who should sway:
> So, when our mortal frame shall be disjoined,
> The lifeless lump uncoupled from the mind,
> From sense of grief and pain we shall be free;
> We shall not feel, because we shall not be.
>
> (3.830–40, trans. Dryden)

We are only we, Lucretius says in conclusion, while souls and bodies in one frame agree.

The Epicureans gave an atomistic account of sense-perception, in particular of vision. Bodies in the world throw off thin films of the atoms of which they are made, which retain their original shape and thus serve as images (*eidola*). These fly around the world with astonishing speed, and perception occurs when they make contact with atoms in the soul. When we see mental images, this is the result of even more tenuous filaments joining together in the air, like spider's web or gold leaf. Thus, the image of a centaur is the result of the interweaving of a human image and a horse image; it can enter the mind during sleep as well as when awake. We are always surrounded by countless such fine images, but we are only aware of those on which the mind turns the beam of its attention (Lucretius 4. 722–85).

The Stoics, like the Epicureans, had a materialist concept of soul. We live to the extent that we breathe, Chrysippus argued; soul is what makes us live, and breath is what makes us breathe, so soul and breath are identical (LS 53G). The heart is the seat of the soul: there resides the soul *par excellence*, the master-faculty (*hegemonikon*) which sends out the senses to bring back reports on the environment for it to evaluate. Sense-perception itself takes place exclusively within the master-faculty (LS 53M). The master-faculty is material like the rest of the soul, but it is capable of surviving, at least temporarily, separation from the body at death (LS 53w). There is not, however, any real personal immortality for the Stoics: at best, the souls of the wise after death can be absorbed into the divine World Soul that permeates and governs the universe.

Some Stoics compared the human soul to an octopus: eight tentacles sprouted out from the master-faculty into the body, five of them being the senses, one being a motor agent to effect the movement of the limbs, one controlling the organs of speech, and the final one a tube to carry semen to the generative organs. Each of these tentacles was made out of breath (LS 53H, L).

It will be noted that of the eight tentacles five are afferent, and three efferent. This reflects an important clarification the Stoics introduced into philosophical psychology. Plato and Aristotle had been principally interested in dividing faculties of the soul hierarchically, on the basis of the cognitive or ethical value of the objects of the faculty: thus intellect came above sensation, and rational choice above animal desire. The Stoics were well aware of the difference between the capacities of rational language users and dumb animals (LS 53T) but they regarded as equally important a division of faculties that is vertical rather than horizontal. The distinction is thus stated by Cicero, quoting Panaetius:

Minds' movements are of two kinds: some belong to thought, and some to appetition. Thought is principally concerned with the investigation of truth and appetition is a drive to action. (Off 1. 132).

The distinction between cognitive and appetitive faculties cuts across the distinction between sensory and intellectual faculties. In later antiquity and in the Middle Ages philosophers came to accept the following scheme:

Intellect   Will

Sensation   Desire

This combines the Aristotelian distinction between the rational and the animal level, with the Stoic distinction between the cognitive and appetitive dimension.

Will, Mind, and Soul in Late Antiquity

It is often said that in classical philosophy there is no concept of the will. Some have gone so far as to say that in Aristotle's psychology the will does not occur at all, and the concept was invented only after eleven further centuries of philosophical reflection. Certainly, it is undeniable that there is no Aristotelian expression that exactly corresponds to the English expression 'freedom of the will', and scholars have concluded that he had no real grasp of the issue.

This criticism of Aristotle depends on a certain view of the nature of the will. In modern times philosophers have often thought of the will as a phenomenon of introspective consciousness. Acts of the will, or volitions, are mental events that precede and cause certain human actions; their presence or absence make the difference between voluntary and involuntary actions. The freedom of the will is to be located in the indeterminacy of these introspectible volitions.

It is not clear how far the Epicureans and Stoics shared this conception of the causation of human action, but it is certain that this concept of the will is not to be found in Aristotle. But this is to his credit, for the concept is radically flawed and has been discredited in recent times. A satisfactory philosophical account of the will must relate human action to ability, desire, and belief. It must contain a treatment of voluntariness, a treatment of intentionality, and a treatment of rationality. Aristotle's treatises contain ample material relevant to the study of the will thus understood, even though his concepts do not exactly coincide with those that it would nowadays be natural to employ.

Aristotle defined voluntariness as follows: something was voluntary if it was originated by an agent free from compulsion or error (*NE* 3. 1. 1110^{a}1 ff.). In his moral system an important role was also played by the concept of *prohairesis*, or purposive choice: the choice of an action as part of an overall plan of life (*NE* 3. 2. 1111^{b}4 ff.). His concept of the voluntary was too clumsily defined, and his concept of *prohairesis* too narrowly defined, to demarcate the everyday moral choices that make up our lives. The fact that there is no English word corresponding to 'prohairesis' is itself a mark of the awkwardness of the concept: most of Aristotle's moral terminology has been naturalized into all European languages.

Though he has a rich and perceptive account of practical reasoning, Aristotle has no technical concept corresponding to our concept of intention: that is to say, of doing A *in order to* bring about B, of choosing means to ends as well as pursuing ends for their own sake. Voluntariness is a broader concept than intention: it includes whatever we bring about knowingly but unintentionally, as an undesired consequence of action. *Prohairesis* is a narrower concept: it restricts the goal of the intention to the enactment of a grand pattern of life.

These defects in Aristotle's treatment of the appetitive side of human life are the truth behind the exaggerated claim that he had no concept of the will. It was, indeed, the reflection of Latin philosophers which led to the full development of the concept, and this reflection can be seen in copious form in the writings of Augustine.

In the second and third centuries further developments called for modification of Aristotelian philosophy of mind. The physician Galen (129–99) discovered that for the operation of the muscles nerves arising from the brain and spinal cord have to be active. Thus the brain, rather than the heart, should be regarded as the principal seat of the soul. But like the Stoics, Galen distinguished between a sensory soul and a motor soul, the former associated with afferent nerves travelling to the brain, the latter with motor nerves originating in the spinal cord.[3]

The peripatetic commentator Alexander of Aphrodisias, who flourished in the first decades of the third century, identified the Active Intellect of the *de Anima* with the unmoved mover of *Metaphysics* Λ. Alexander thus began a long tradition of interpretation which flourished, in different forms, among later commentators, especially in the Arab world. A human being at birth, he maintained, had only a material or physical intellect; true intelligence is acquired only under the influence of the supreme divine mind. In consequence, the human soul is not immortal: the best it can do is to think immortal thoughts by meditating on the Motionless Mover (*de An*. 90. 11–91. 6).

In reaction to the mortalism of the Epicureans, Stoics, and later Peripatetics, Plotinus set out, in Plato's footsteps, to prove that the individual soul is immortal. He sets out his case in one of his earliest writings, Ennead 4. 7 (2), *On the Immortality of the Soul*. If the soul is the principle of life in living beings, it cannot itself be bodily in nature. If it is a body, it must be either one of the four elements, earth, air, fire, and water, or a compound of one or more of them. But the elements are themselves lifeless. If a compound has life, this must be due to a particular proportion of the elements in the compound: but this must have been conferred by something else, the cause that provides the recipe for and combines the ingredients of the mixture. This something else is soul (4. 7. 2).

Plotinus argues that none of the functions of life, from the lowliest form of nutrition and growth to the highest forms of imagination and thought, could be carried out by something that was merely bodily. Bodies undergo change at every instant: how could something in such perpetual flux remember anything from moment to moment? Bodies are divided into parts and spread out in space: how could such a scattered entity provide the unified focus of which we are aware in perception? We can think of abstract entities, like beauty and justice: how can what is bodily grasp what is non-bodily? (4. 7. 5–8). The soul must belong, not to the world of becoming, but to the world of Being (4. 8. 5).

[3] M. R. Bennett and P. M. S. Hacker, *Philosophical Foundations of Neuroscience* (Oxford: Blackwell, 2003), 20.

Plotinus is aware that there are those who say that the soul, though not a body itself, nonetheless is dependent on body for its existence. He recalls Simmias' contention in the *Phaedo* that the soul is nothing more than an attunement of the body's sinews. He neatly turns the tables on that argument. When a musician plucks the strings of a lyre, he says, it is the strings, not the melody that he acts upon; but the strings would not be plucked unless the melody called for it (3. 6. 4. 49–80; 4. 7. 8).

Plotinus clearly maintains the personal immortality of individuals. It would be absurd to suggest that Socrates will cease to be Socrates when he goes from hence to a better world hereafter. Minds will survive in that better world, because nothing that has real being ever perishes (4. 3. 5). However, the exact significance of this claim is unclear, since Plotinus also maintains that all souls form a unity, bound together in a superior World-Soul, from which they have originated and to which they return (3. 5. 4). We shall learn more about this World-Soul in Chapter 9, when we come to discuss Plotinus' theology.

One of those who learnt most from Plotinus' speculations was the young Augustine. His own original contribution to philosophy of mind, however, is to be found in his writing on freedom. In his *de Libero Arbitrio*, written in the year of his conversion to Christianity, he defends a form of libertarianism that differs both from the compatibilism we saw in an earlier chapter when considering Chrysippus, and from the predestinarianism for which the later, Christian, Augustine is notorious.

In the third book the question is raised whether the soul sins by necessity. We have to distinguish, we are told, three senses of 'necessity': nature, certainty, and compulsion. Nature and compulsion are incompatible with voluntariness, and only voluntary acts are blameable. If a sinner sins by nature or by compulsion, the sin is not voluntary. But certainty is compatible with voluntariness: it may be certain that X will sin, and yet X will sin voluntarily and will rightly be blamed.

Consider first the necessity of nature. The soul does not sin by necessity in the way that a stone falls by necessity of nature: the soul's action in sinning is voluntary. Both the soul and the stone are agents, but the soul is a voluntary and not a natural agent. The difference is this: 'it is not in the stone's power to arrest its downward motion, but unless the soul is willing it does not so act as to abandon what is higher for what is lower' (III. 2).

As we saw in considering Chrysippus, voluntariness can be defined by reference to the power to do otherwise (liberty of indifference) or by reference to the power to do what one wants (liberty of spontaneity). In the *de Libero Arbitrio* Augustine combines the two approaches. The soul's motions are voluntary, because the soul is doing what it wants. 'I do not know what I can call my own', Augustine says, 'if the will by which I want or reject is not my own.' But the power to want is itself a two-way power. 'The motion by which the will turns in this or that direction would not be praiseworthy unless it was voluntary and placed within our power.'

Nor could the sinner be blamed when he turns the hinge (*cardo*) of the will towards the nether regions (III. 3).

Augustine offers to prove that wanting is in our power. The exact lines of his proof are not clear. On one interpretation it goes like this. Doing X is in our power if we do X whenever we want. But whenever we want, we want. Therefore wanting is in our power. This seems too easy: surely the first premiss is incomplete. It should read: Doing X is in our power if we do X whenever we want to do X. The second premiss would then have to read: Whenever we want to want to do X we want to do X. This would give us Augustine's conclusion: whatever X is, wanting X is in our power. But one may question the second premiss. May we not have a second-order want to want something, without having the first-order want itself? When Augustine wanted to be chaste, but not yet, was he really wanting to be chaste, or only wanting to want to be chaste?

If it is in my power to do X, in the sense earlier outlined by Augustine, then it must be in my power not to do X. This weakens his argument to show that wanting is in our power. For whatever plausibility there is in the claim that if I want to want something I want it, there is none in the claim that if I want not to want something then I do not want it. I may very sincerely want to give up smoking: that does not prevent my passionate want for a cigarette at this moment.

No doubt Augustine can respond by making distinctions between different kinds of wanting: but in the present context it would not be profitable to follow further his analysis of volition. The part of the *de Libero Arbitrio* most relevant to the issue of determinism and freedom is his consideration of the foreknowledge of God. Augustine believed that at any moment God foreknew all future events. He can then construct the following argument against the possibility of voluntary sin.

(1) God foreknew that Adam was going to sin.
(2) If God foreknew that Adam was going to sin, necessarily Adam was going to sin.
(3) If Adam was necessarily going to sin, then Adam sinned necessarily.
(4) If Adam sinned necessarily, Adam did not sin of his own free will.
(5) Adam did not sin of his own free will.

The line of argument here is clearly the Christian heir to the discussion of the sea-battle in Aristotle and the Master Argument of Diodorus: in each case, in different ways, the necessity of a past state or event is used as a starting point from which to derive the necessity of a future event. In the Greeks the starting premiss is logical, here it is theological.

Augustine proposes to disarm the argument by the distinction between certainty, on the one hand, and natural causation or compulsion, on the other. I can know something without causing it (as when I know it because I remember it). I can be certain that someone is about to do something without in any way compelling him to do it. Accordingly, we can distinguish the senses of 'necessity' in the argument above. In the second premiss, and the antecedent of the third premiss 'necessarily' must be taken as 'certainly'. In the fourth premiss and the consequent of the third premiss 'necessarily' must be taken as 'under compulsion'. Because of the resulting equivocation in the third premiss, the argument fails.

Augustine's response does not wholly convince: there is surely no exact analogy between conjectural human knowledge of the future and omnitemporal divine omniscience. The difficulties that his treatment leaves unsolved were taken up by many future generations of Christian theologians; but his discussion can fittingly be taken as representative of the final stage of reflection on determinism in antiquity.

8

How to Live:
Ethics

Among the sayings attributed to the earliest Greek philosophers, many have a moral content. Thales, for instance, is credited with an early version of 'Do as you would be done by': asked how we could best live, he replied, 'if we do not ourselves do what we blame others for doing'. In more ambiguous vein, when asked by an adulterer if he should swear he was innocent, he replied, 'Well, perjury is no worse than adultery' (D.L. 1. 37). Oracular utterances of a similar kind are to be found in Heraclitus: 'It is not good for men to get all they want' (DK 22 B110); 'a man's character is his destiny' (DK 22 B117). Other philosophers took stances on particular moral issues: thus Empedocles attacked meat-eating and animal sacrifice (DK 31 B128, 139). But it is not until Democritus that we find any sign of a philosopher with a moral system.

Democritus the Moralist

Democritus was eloquent on ethical topics: sixty pages of his fragments, as recorded in Diels–Kranz, are devoted to moral counsel. Much of it is of a homespun, agony-aunt type: don't take on tasks above your power, don't be envious of the rich and famous: think of all the people who are worse off than you are, and be contented with your lot (DK 68 B91). Do not try to know everything, or you will end up knowing nothing (DK 68 B69). Don't blame bad luck when things go wrong through your own fault: you can avoid drowning by learning to swim (DK 68 B119, 172). Accept favours only if you plan to do greater favours in return (DK 68 B92). A remark that has been garbled at many a wedding breakfast is fragment 272: 'One who is lucky in his son-in-law gains a son, one who is unlucky loses a daughter.'

Sometimes Democritus' advice is more controversial. It is better not to have any children: to bring them up well takes great trouble and care, and seeing them grow up badly is the cruellest of all pains (DK 68 B275). If you must have children, adopt them from your friends rather than beget them yourselves. That way, you can choose the kind of child you want, whereas in the normal way you have to put up with what you get (DK 68 B277).

From Plato onwards there have been moral philosophers who have despised the body as a corrupter of the soul. Democritus took just the opposite view. If a body, at the end of life, were to sue the soul for the pains and ills it had suffered, a fair judge would find for the body. If some parts of the body have been damaged by neglect or ruined by debauchery, that is the soul's fault. Maybe you think that the body is no more than a tool used by the soul: well and good, but if a tool is in a bad shape you blame not the tool but its owner (DK 68 B159).

Democritus' moral views have come down to us as a series of aphorisms, but there is some evidence that he developed a systematic ethics, though it is obscure what relation, if any, it had to his atomism. He wrote a treatise on the purpose of life and inquired into the nature of happiness (*eudaimonia*): it was to be found not in riches but in the goods of the soul, and one should not take pleasure in mortal things (DK 68 B37, 171, 189). The hopes of the educated, he put it, were better than the riches of the ignorant (DK 68 B285). But the goods of the soul in which happiness was to be found do not seem to have been of any exalted mystical kind: rather, his ideal was a life of cheerfulness and quiet contentment (DK 68 B188). For this reason he was known to later ages as the laughing philosopher. He praised temperance, but was not an ascetic. Thrift and fasting were good, he said, but so was banqueting; the difficulty was judging the right time for each. A life without feasting was like a highway without inns (DK 68 B229, 230).

In some ways Democritus set an agenda for succeeding Greek thinkers. In placing the quest for happiness in the centre of moral philosophy he was followed by almost every moralist of antiquity. When he said, 'the cause of sin is ignorance of what is better' (DK 68 B83), he formulated an idea that was to be central in Socratic moral thought. Again, when he said that you are better off being wronged than doing wrong (DK 68 B45), he uttered a thought that was developed by Socrates into the principle that it is better to suffer wrong than to inflict wrong—a principle incompatible with the influential moral systems that encourage one to judge actions only by their consequences and not by the identity of their agents. Others of his offhand remarks, if taken seriously, are sufficient to overturn whole ethical systems. For instance, when he says that a good person not only refrains from wrongdoing but does not even want to do wrong (DK 68 B62), he sets himself against the often held view that virtue is at its highest when it triumphs over conflicting passion.

Democritus did not explore, however, the most important concept of all for ancient ethics: that is, *arete*, or virtue. The Greek word does not match precisely any single English word, and in recent scholarly writing the traditional translation 'virtue' is often replaced by 'excellence'. 'Arete' is the abstract noun corresponding to the adjective 'agathos', the most general word for 'good'. Whatever is good of its kind has the corresponding *arete*. It is archaic in English to speak of the virtue of a horse or a knife, which is no doubt one reason for preferring the translation 'excellence'; and some of the *aretai* of human beings, such as scientific expertise, fit uncomfortably into the description 'intellectual virtue'. But it is perhaps equally odd to call a character trait like gentleness an 'excellence'; so I shall make use of the traditional translation of *arete*, having given fair warning that it is far from a perfect fit. The matter is not merely one of idiom: it reveals a conceptual difference between ancient Greeks and modern Westerners about the appropriate way to group together different desirable properties of human beings. The difference between the two conceptual structures both accounts for the difficulty, and provides a great deal of the value, of the study of ancient moral philosophy.

Socrates on Virtue

It was Socrates who initiated systematic inquiry into the nature of virtue; he placed it in the centre of moral philosophy, and indeed of philosophy as a whole. In the *Crito* his own acceptance of death is presented as a martyrdom to justice and piety (54b). In the Socratic dialogues particular virtues are subjected to detailed examination: piety (*hosiotes*) in the *Euthyphro*, temperance (*sophrosyne*) in the *Charmides*, fortitude (*andreia*) in the *Laches*, and justice in the first book of the *Republic* (which most probably began existence as a separate dialogue, *Thrasymachus*). Each of these dialogues follows a similar pattern. Socrates seeks a definition of the respective virtue, and the other characters in the dialogue offer definitions in response. Cross-examination (*elenchus*) forces each of the protagonists to admit that their definitions are inadequate. Socrates, however, is no better able than his opponents to offer a satisfactory definition, and each dialogue ends inconclusively.

The pattern can be illustrated from the first book of the *Republic*, where the virtue to be defined is justice. The aged Cephalus proposes that justice is telling the truth and returning what one has borrowed. Socrates refutes this by asking whether it is just to return a borrowed weapon to a friend who has gone mad. It is agreed that it is not just, because it cannot be just to harm a friend (331d). The next proposal, from Cephalus' son Polemarchus, is that justice is doing good to one's friends and harm to one's enemies. This is rejected on the grounds that it is not just to harm anyone: justice is a virtue and it cannot be an exercise of virtue to make anyone, friend or foe, worse rather than better (335d).

Another character in the dialogue, Thrasymachus, now questions whether justice is a virtue at all. It cannot be a virtue, he argues, for it is not in anyone's interest to possess it. On the contrary, justice is simply what is to the advantage of the powerful; law and morality are systems to protect their interests. By complicated, and often dubious, arguments Thrasymachus is eventually brought to concede that the just man will have a better life than the unjust man, so that justice is in the interest of the person who possesses it (353e). Yet the dialogue closes on an agnostic note. 'The upshot of the discussion in my case', says Socrates, 'is that I have learned nothing. Since I don't know what justice is, I will hardly know whether it is a virtue or not, and whether its possessor is happy or unhappy' (354c).

The profession of ignorance which Plato places in Socrates' mouth in these dialogues does not mean that Socrates has no convictions about moral virtue: it means rather that a very high threshold is being set for something to count as knowledge. In these dialogues Socrates and his interlocutors can often agree whether particular actions would or would not count as instances of the virtue in question: what is lacking is a formula that would cover all and only acts of the relevant virtue. Moreover, Socrates, in the course of discussion, defends a number of substantive theses both about virtues in particular (e.g. that it is never just to harm anyone) and about virtue in general (e.g. that it must always be a benefit to its possessor).

In inquiring into the nature of a virtue, Socrates' regular practice is to compare it with a technical skill or craft, such as carpentry, navigation, or medicine, or with a science such as arithmetic or geometry. Many readers, ancient and modern, find the comparison bizarre. Surely knowledge and virtue are two totally different things, one is a matter of the intellect and another a matter of the will. In response to this two things can be said. First, if we make a sharp distinction between the intellect and the will, that is because we are the heirs to many generations of philosophical reflection to which the initial impetus was given by Socrates and Plato. Secondly, there are indeed important similarities between virtues and forms of expertise. Both, unlike other properties and characteristics of mankind, are acquired rather than innate. Both are valued features of human beings: we admire people both for their skills and for their virtues. Both, Socrates claims, are beneficial to their possessors: we are better off the more skills we possess and the more virtuous we are.

But in important respects skills and virtues are unlike each other, at least prima facie. Socrates is well aware of this, and one reason for his constant recourse to the analogy between the two is to contrast them as well as to compare them. He is anxious to test how significant are the differences. One difference is that arts and sciences are transmitted through teaching by experts: but there do not seem to be any experts who can teach virtue. There are not, at any rate, genuine experts, though some sophists falsely hold themselves out to be such (*Prt.* 319a–320b; *Men.* 89e–91b). Another difference is this. Suppose someone goes wrong: we may ask whether he did it on purpose or not, and whether, if he did, that makes things better or worse. If the going wrong was making a mistake in the exercise of a skill— e.g. playing a false note on the flute, or missing the mark in archery—then it is better if it was done on purpose: that is to say, a deliberate mistake is not a reflection on one's skill. But things seem different when the going wrong is a failure in virtue: it is odd to say that someone who violates my rights on purpose is less unjust than someone who violates them unwittingly (*Hp. Mi.* 373d–376b).

Socrates believes he can deal with both of these objections to assimilating virtue to expertise. In response to the second point, he flatly denies that there are people who sin against virtue on purpose (*Prt.* 358b–c). If a man goes wrong in this way he does so through ignorance, through lack of knowledge of what is best for him. We all wish to do well and be happy: it is for this reason that people want things like health, wealth, power, and honour. But these things are only good if we know how to use them well; in the absence of this knowledge they can do us more harm than good. This knowledge of how best to use what one possesses is wisdom (*phronesis*) and it is the only thing that is truly good (*Euthd.* 278e–282e). Wisdom is the science of what is good and what is bad, and it is identical with virtue—with all the virtues.

The reason why there are no teachers of virtue is not that virtue is not a science, but that it is a science impossibly difficult to master. This is because of the way in which the virtues intertwine and form a unity. Actions that exhibit courage are of course different actions from those that exhibit temperance; but what they express is a single, indivisible state of soul. If we say that courage is the science of what is good and bad in respect of future dangers, we have to agree that such a science is only possible as part of an overall science of good and evil (*La.* 199c). The individual virtues are parts of this science, but it can only be possessed as a whole. No one, not even Socrates, is in possession of this science.[1]

We are, however, given an account of what it would look like, and it is rather a surprising account. Socrates asks Protagoras, in the dialogue named after him, to accept the premiss that goodness is identical with pleasure and evil is identical with pain. From this premiss he offers to prove his contention that no one does evil willingly. People are often said to have done evil in the knowledge that it was evil because they yielded to temptation and were overcome by pleasure. But if 'pleasure' and 'good' mean the same, then they must have done evil because they were overcome by goodness. Is not that absurd (354c–5d)?

Knowledge is a powerful thing, and the knowledge that something is evil cannot be pushed about like a slave. Given the premiss that Protagoras has accepted, knowledge that an action is evil must be knowledge that, taken with its consequences, the action will lead to an excess of pain over pleasure. No one with such knowledge is going to undertake such an action; hence the person acting wrongly must lack the knowledge. Nearby objects seem larger to vision than distant ones, and something similar happens in mental vision. The wrongdoer

---

[1] Here I am indebted to a number of articles by Terry Penner, summed up in his essay 'Socrates and the Early Dialogues', in R. Kraut (ed.), *The Cambridge Companion to Plato* (Cambridge: Cambridge University Press, 1992).

is suffering from the illusion that the present pleasure outweighs the consequent pain. What is needed is a science that measures the relative sizes of pleasures and pains, present and future, 'since our salvation in life has turned out to lie in the correct choice of pleasure and pain' (356d–357b). This is the science of good and evil that is identical with each of the virtues, justice, temperance, and courage (361b).

Plato on Justice and Pleasure

Scholars are not agreed whether Socrates seriously thought that the hedonic calculus was the answer to 'What is virtue?' Whether Socrates did so or not, Plato certainly did not, and in the *Republic* we are given a different account of justice—indeed, more than one different account. The main body of the dialogue begins in book 2 with two challenges set by Plato's brothers Glaucon and Adeimantus. Glaucon wants to be shown that justice is not just a method of avoiding evils, but something worthwhile for its own sake (358b–362c). Adeimantus wants to be shown that quite apart from any rewards or sanctions attached to it, justice is as preferable to injustice as sight is to blindness and health is to sickness (362d–367d).

The Socrates of the dialogue introduces his answer by setting out the analogy between the soul and the city. In his imagined city the virtues are allotted to the different classes of the state: the city's wisdom is the wisdom of its rulers, its courage is the courage of its soldiers, and its temperance is the obedience of the artisans to the ruling class. Justice is the harmony of the three classes: it consists in each citizen, and each class, doing that for which they are most suited. The three parts of the soul correspond to the three classes in the state, and the virtues in the soul are distributed like the virtues in the state (441c–442d). Courage belongs to temper, temperance is the subservience of the lower elements, wisdom is located in reason, which rules and looks after the whole soul. Justice is the harmony of the psychic elements. 'Each of us will be a just person, fulfilling his proper function, only if the several parts of our soul fulfil theirs' (441e).

If injustice is the hierarchical harmony of the soul's elements, injustice and all manner of vice occur when the inferior elements rebel against this hierarchy (443b). Justice and injustice in the soul are like health and disease in the body. Accordingly, it is absurd to ask whether it is more profitable to live justly or to do wrong. All the wealth and power in the world cannot make life worth living when the body is ravaged by disease. Can it be any more worth living when the soul, the principle of life, is deranged and corrupted (445b)?

That is the first account of justice and virtue given in answer to Glaucon and Adeimantus. It differs from the account in the *Protagoras* in several ways. The thesis of the unity of virtue has been abandoned, or at least modified, as a result of the tripartition of the soul. Pleasure appears not as the object of virtue, but as the crony of the lowest part of the soul. The conclusion that justice benefits its possessor, however, is common ground both to the *Republic* and to the earlier Socratic dialogues. Moreover, if justice is psychic health, then everyone must really want to be just, since everyone wants to be healthy. This rides well with the Socratic thesis that no one does wrong on purpose, and that vice is fundamentally ignorance.

However, the conclusion drawn at the end of *Republic* 4 is only a provisional one, for it makes no reference to the great Platonic innovation: the Theory of Ideas. After the role of the Ideas has been expounded in the middle books of the dialogue, we are given a revised account of the relation between justice and happiness. The just man is happier than the unjust, not only because his soul is in concord, but because it is more delightful to fill the soul with understanding than to feed fat the desires of appetite. Reason is no longer the faculty that takes care of the person, it is akin to the unchanging and immortal world of truth (585c).

Humans can be classified as avaricious, ambitious, or academic, according to whether the dominant element in their soul is appetite, temper, or reason. Men of each type will claim that their own life is best: the avaricious man will praise the life of business, the ambitious man will praise a political career, and the academic man will praise knowledge and understanding. It is the academic, the philosopher, whose judgement is to be preferred: he has the advantage over the others in experience, insight, and reasoning (580d–583b). Moreover, the objects to which the philosopher devotes his life are so much more real than the objects pursued by the others that their pleasures seem illusory by comparison (583c–587a). Plato has not altogether said goodbye to the hedonic calculus: he works out for us that the philosopher king lives 729 times more pleasantly than his evil opposite number (587e).

Plato returns to the topic of happiness and pleasure in the mature dialogue *Philebus*. One character, Protarchus, argues that pleasure is the greatest good; Socrates counters that wisdom is superior to pleasure and more conducive to happiness (11a–12b). The dialogue gives an opportunity for a wide-ranging discussion of different kinds of pleasure, very different from the *Protagoras* treatment of pleasure as a single class of commensurable items. At the end of the discussion Socrates wins his point against Protarchus: on a well-considered grading of goods even the best of pleasures come out below wisdom (66b–c).

The most interesting part of the dialogue, however, is an argument to the effect that neither pleasure nor wisdom can be the essence of a happy life, but that only a mixed life that has both pleasure and wisdom in it would really be worth choosing. Someone who had every pleasure from moment to moment, but was devoid of reason, would not be happy because he would be able neither to remember nor to anticipate any pleasure other than the present: he would be living not a human life but the life of a mollusc (21a–d). But a purely intellectual life without any pleasure would equally be intolerable (21e). Neither life would be 'sufficient, perfect, or worthy of choice'. The final good consists in a harmonious proportion between pleasure and wisdom (63c–65a).

Aristotle on Eudaimonia

The criteria for a good life set out in the *Philebus* reappear in Aristotle's account of the good life. The good we are looking for, he says, at the beginning of the *Nicomachean Ethics*, must be perfect by comparison with other ends—that is, it must be something sought always for its own sake and never for the sake of something else; and it must be self-sufficient, that is, it must be something which taken on its own makes life worthwhile and lacking in nothing. These, he goes on, are the properties of happiness (*eudaimonia*) (*NE* 1. 7. 1097^{a}15–^{b}21).

In all Aristotle's ethical treatises the notion of happiness plays a central role. This is brought out more clearly, however, in the *Eudemian Ethics*, and in my exposition I will begin by following this rather than the more familiar text of the *Nicomachean Ethics*. The treatise begins with the inquiry: what is a good life and how is it to be acquired? (*EE* 1. 1. 1214^{a}15). We are offered five candidate answers to the second question (by nature, by learning, by discipline, by divine favour, and by luck) and seven candidate answers to the first (wisdom, virtue, pleasure, honour, reputation, riches, and culture) (1. 1. 1214^{a}32, ^{b}9). Aristotle immediately eliminates some answers to the second question: if happiness comes purely by nature or by luck or by grace, then it will be beyond most people's reach and they can do nothing about it (1. 3. 1215^{a}15). But a full answer to the second question obviously depends on the answer to the first: and Aristotle works on that by asking the question: what makes life worth living?

There are some occurrences in life, e.g. sickness and pain, that make people want to give up life: clearly these do not make life worth living. There are the events of childhood: these cannot be the most choiceworthy things in life since no one in his right mind would choose to go back to childhood. In adult life there are things that we do only as means to an end; clearly these cannot, in themselves, be what makes life worth living (1. 5. 1215^{b}15–31).

If life is to be worth living, it must surely be for something that is an end in itself. One such end is pleasure. The pleasures of food and drink and sex are, on their own, too brutish to be a fitting end for human life: but if we combine them with aesthetic and intellectual pleasures we find a goal that has been seriously pursued by people of significance. Others prefer a life of virtuous action—the life of a real politician, not like the false politicians, who are only after money or power. Thirdly, there is the life of scientific contemplation, as exemplified by

Anaxagoras, who when asked why one should choose to be born rather than not replied, 'In order to admire the heavens and the order of the universe.'

Aristotle has thus reduced the possible answers to the question 'What is a good life?' to a shortlist of three: wisdom, virtue, and pleasure. All, he says, connect happiness with one or other of three forms of life, the philosophical, the political, and the voluptuary (1. 4. 1215ª27). This triad provides the key to Aristotle's ethical inquiry. Both the *Eudemian* and the *Nicomachean* treatises contain detailed analyses of the concepts of virtue, wisdom (*phronesis*), and pleasure. And when Aristotle comes to present his own account of happiness, he can claim that it incorporates the attractions of all three of the traditional forms of life.

A crucial step towards achieving this is to apply, in this ethical area, the metaphysical analysis of potentiality and actuality. Aristotle distinguishes between a state (*hexis*) and its use (*chresis*) or exercise (*energeia*).[2] Virtue and wisdom are both states, whereas happiness is an activity, and therefore cannot be simply identified with either of them (*EE* 2. 1. 1219ª39; *NE* 1. 1. 1098ª16). The activity that constitutes happiness is, however, a use or exercise of virtue. Wisdom and moral virtue, though different *hexeis*, are exercised inseparably in a single *energeia*, so that they are not competing but collaborating contributors to happiness (*NE* 10. 8. 1178ª16–18). Moreover, pleasure, Aristotle claims, is identical with the unimpeded exercise of an appropriate state: so that happiness, considered as the unimpeded exercise of these two states, is simultaneously the life of virtue, wisdom, and pleasure (*EE* 7. 15. 1249ª21; *NE* 10. 7. 1177ª23).

To reach this conclusion takes many pages of analysis and argument. First, Aristotle must show that happiness is activity in accordance with virtue. This derives from a consideration of the function or characteristic activity (*ergon*) of human beings. Man must have a function, the *Nicomachean Ethics* argues, because particular types of men (e.g. sculptors) do, and parts and organs of human beings do. What is this function? Not growth and nourishment, for this is shared by plants, nor the life of the senses, for this is shared by animals. It must be a life of reason concerned with action: the activity of soul in accordance with reason. So human good will be good human functioning, namely, activity of soul in accordance with virtue (*NE* 1. 7. 1098ª16). Virtue unexercised is not happiness, because that would be compatible with a life passed in sleep, which no one would call happy (1. 8. 1099ª1).

Secondly, Aristotle must analyse the concept of virtue. Human virtues are classified in accordance with the division of the parts of the soul outlined in the previous chapter. Any virtue of the vegetative part of the soul, such as soundness of digestion, is irrelevant to ethics, which is concerned with specifically human virtue. The part of the soul concerned with desire and passion is specifically human in that it is under the

---

[2] The *EE* prefers the distinction in the form: virtue–use of virtue; the *NE* prefers it in the form: virtue–activity in accord with virtue (*energeia kat'areten*).

control of reason: it has its own virtues, the moral virtues such as courage and temperance. The rational part of the soul is the seat of the intellectual virtues.

Aristotle on Moral and Intellectual Virtue

The moral virtues are dealt with in books 2 to 5 of the *Nicomachean Ethics* and in the second and third books of the *Eudemian*. These virtues are not innate, but acquired by practice and lost by disuse: thus they differ from faculties like intelligence or memory. They are abiding states, and thus differ from momentary passions like anger and pity. What makes a person good or bad, praiseworthy or blameworthy, is neither the simple possession of faculties or the simple occurrence of passions. It is rather a state of character which is expressed both in purpose (*prohairesis*) and in action (*praxis*) (*NE* 2. 1. 1103^{a}11–^{b}25; 4. 1105^{a}19–1106^{a}13; *EE* 2. 2. 1220^{b}1–20).

Virtue is expressed in good purpose, that is to say, a prescription for action in accordance with a good plan of life. The actions which express moral virtue will, Aristotle tells us, avoid excess and defect. A temperate person, for instance, will avoid eating or drinking too much; but he will also avoid eating or drinking too little. Virtue chooses the mean, or middle ground, between excess and defect, eating and drinking the right amount. Aristotle goes through a long list of virtues, beginning with the traditional ones of fortitude and temperance, but including others such as liberality, sincerity, dignity, and conviviality, and sketches out how each of them is concerned with a mean.

The doctrine of the mean is not intended as a recipe for mediocrity or an injunction to stay in the middle of the herd. Aristotle warns us that what constitutes the right amount to drink, the right amount to give away, the right amount of talking to do, may differ from person to person, in the way that the amount of food fit for an Olympic champion may not suit a novice athlete (2. 6. 1106^{b}3–4). Each of us learns what is the right amount by experience: by observing, and correcting, excess and defect in our conduct.

Virtue is concerned not only with action but with passion. We may have too many fears or too few fears, and courage will enable us to fear when fear is appropriate and be fearless when it is not. We may be excessively concerned with sex and we may be insufficiently interested in it: the temperate person will take the appropriate degree of interest and be neither lustful nor frigid (*NE* 2. 7. 1107^{b}1–9).

The virtues, besides being concerned with means of action and passion, are themselves means in the sense that they occupy a middle ground between two contrary vices. Thus courage is in the middle, flanked on one side by foolhardiness and on the other by cowardice; generosity treads the narrow path between miserliness and prodigality (*NE* 2. 7. 1107^{b}1–16; *EE* 2. 3. 1220^{b}36–1221^{a}12). But while there is a mean of action and passion, there is no mean of virtue itself: there cannot be too much of a virtue in the way that there can be too much of a particular kind of action or passion. If we feel inclined to say that someone is too courageous, what we really mean is that his actions cross the boundary between the virtue of courage and the vice of foolhardiness. And if there cannot be too much of a virtue, there cannot be too little of a vice: so that there is no mean of vice any more than there is a mean of virtue (*NE* 2. 6. 1107ª18–26).

While all moral virtues are means of action and passion, it is not the case that every kind of action and passion is capable of a virtuous mean. There are some actions of which there is no right amount, because any amount of them is too much: Aristotle gives murder and adultery as examples. There is no such thing as committing adultery with the right person at the right time in the right way. Similarly, there are passions that are excluded from the application of the mean: there is no right amount of envy or spite (*NE* 2. 6. 1107ª8–17).

Aristotle's account of virtue as a mean seems to many readers truistic. In fact, it is a distinctive ethical theory that contrasts with other influential systems of various kinds. Moral systems such as traditional Jewish or Christian doctrine give the concept of a moral law (natural or revealed) a central role. This leads to an emphasis on the prohibitive aspect of morality, the listing of actions to be altogether avoided: most of the commands of the Decalogue, for instance, begin with 'Thou shalt not'. Aristotle does believe that there are some actions that are altogether ruled out, as we have just seen; but he stresses not the minimum necessary for moral decency but rather the conditions of achieving moral excellence (that is, after all, what *ethike arete* means). He is, we might say, writing a text for an honours degree, rather than a pass degree, in morality.

But it is not only religious systems that contrast with Aristotle's treatment of the mean. For a utilitarian, or any kind of consequentialist, there is no class of actions to be ruled out in advance. On a utilitarian view, since the morality of an action is to be judged by its consequences there can, in a particular case, be the right amount of adultery or murder. On the other hand, some secular ascetic systems have ruled out whole classes of actions: for a vegetarian, for instance, there can be no right amount of the eating of meat. We might say that from Aristotle's point of view utilitarians go to excess in their application of the mean, whereas vegetarians are guilty of defect in its application. Aristotelianism, naturally, hits the happy mean in application of the doctrine.

Aristotle sums up his account of moral virtue by saying that it is a state of character expressed in choice, lying in the appropriate mean, determined by the prescription that a wise person would lay down. In order to complete this account, he has to explain what wisdom is, and how the wise person's prescriptions are reached. This he does in a book that is common to both ethics (*NE* 6; *EE* 5) in which he treats of the intellectual virtue.

Wisdom is not the only intellectual virtue, as he explains at the beginning of the book. The virtue of anything depends on its *ergon*, its function or job. The job of the reason is the production of true and false judgements, and when it is doing its job well it produces true judgements (6. 2. 1139ᵃ29). The intellectual virtues are then excellences that make reason come out with truth. There are five states, Aristotle says, that have this effect: skill (*techne*), science (*episteme*), wisdom (*phronesis*), understanding (*sophia*), and intuition (*nous*) (6. 3. 1139ᵇ17). These states contrast with other mental states such as belief or opinion (*doxa*) which may be true or false. There are, then, five candidates for being intellectual virtues.

Techne, however, the skill exhibited by craftsmen and experts such as architects and doctors, is not treated by Aristotle as an intellectual virtue. As we have seen, Socrates and Plato delighted in assimilating virtues to skills; but Aristotle emphasizes the important differences between the two. Skills have products that are distinct from their exercises—whether the product is concrete, like the house built by an architect, or abstract, like the health produced by the doctor (6. 4. 1140ᵃ1–23). The exercise of a skill is evaluated by the excellence of its product, not by the motive of the practitioner: if the doctor's cures are successful and the architect's houses are splendid, we do not need to inquire into their motives for practising their arts. Virtues are not like this: virtues are exercised in actions that need not have any further outcome, and an action, however objectively irreproachable, is not virtuous unless it is done for the right motive, that is to say, chosen as part of a worthwhile way of life (*NE* 2. 4. 1105ᵃ26–ᵇ8). It need not count against a person's skill that he exercises it reluctantly; but a really virtuous person, Aristotle maintains, must enjoy doing what is good, not just grudgingly perform a duty (*NE* 2. 3. 1104ᵇ4). Finally, though the possessor of a skill must know how it should be exercised, a particular exercise of a skill may be a deliberate mistake—a teacher, perhaps, showing a pupil how a particular task should *not* be performed. No one, by contrast, could exercise the virtue of temperance by, say, drinking himself comatose.

It turns out that the other four intellectual virtues can be reduced to two. *Sophia*, the overall understanding of eternal truths that is the goal of the philosopher's quest, turns out to be an amalgam of intuition (*nous*) and science (*episteme*) (6. 7. 1141ᵃ19–20). Wisdom (*phronesis*) is concerned not with unchanging and eternal matters, but with human affairs and matters that can be objects of deliberation (6. 7. 1141ᵇ9–13). Because of the different objects with which they are concerned, understanding and wisdom are virtues of two different parts of the rational soul. Understanding is the virtue of the theoretical part (the *epistemonikon*), which is concerned with the eternal truths; wisdom is the virtue of the practical part (the *logistikon*), which deliberates about human affairs. All other intellectual virtues are either parts of, or can be reduced to, these two virtues of the theoretical and the practical reason.

The intellectual virtue of practical reason is inseparably linked with the moral virtues of the affective part of the soul. It is impossible, Aristotle tells us, to be really good without wisdom, or to be really wise without moral virtue (6. 13. 1144ᵇ30–2). This follows from the nature of the kind of truth that is the concern of practical reason.

What affirmation and negation are in thinking, pursuit and avoidance are in desire: so that since moral virtue is a state which finds expression in purpose, and purpose is deliberative desire, therefore, both the reasoning must be true and the desire right, if the purpose is to be good, and the desire must pursue what the thought prescribes. This is the kind of reasoning and the kind of truth that is practical. (6. 2. 1139^{a}21–7)

Virtuous action must be based on virtuous purpose. Purpose is reasoned desire, so that if purpose is to be good both the reasoning and the desire must be good. It is wisdom that makes the reasoning good, and moral virtue that makes the desire good. Aristotle admits the possibility of correct reasoning in the absence of moral virtue: this he calls 'intelligence' (*deinotes*) (6. 12. 1144^{a}23). He also admits the possibility of right desire in the absence of correct reasoning: such are the naturally virtuous impulses of children (6. 13. 1144^{b}1–6). But it is only when correct reasoning and right desire come together that we get truly virtuous action (*NE* 10. 8. 1178^{a}16–18). The wedding of the two makes intelligence into wisdom and natural virtue into moral virtue.

Practical reasoning is conceived by Aristotle as a process starting from a general conception of human well-being, going on to consider the circumstances of a particular case, and concluding with a prescription for action.[3] In the deliberations of the wise person, all three of these stages will be correct and exhibit practical truth (6. 9. 1142^{b}34; 13. 1144^{b}28). The first, general, premiss is one for which moral virtue is essential; without it we shall have a perverted and deluded grasp of the ultimate grounds of action (6. 12. 1144^{a}9, 35).

Aristotle does not give a systematic account of practical reasoning comparable to the syllogistic he constructed for theoretical reasoning. Indeed, it is difficult to find in his writings a single virtuous practical syllogism fully worked out. The clearest examples he gives all concern reasonings that are in some way morally defective. Practical reasoning may be followed by bad conduct (*a*) because of a faulty general premiss, (*b*) because of a defect concerning the particular premiss or premisses, (*c*) because of a failure to draw, or act upon, the conclusion. Aristotle illustrates this by considering a case of gluttony.

We are to imagine someone presented with a delicious sweet from which temperance (for some reason which is not made clear) commands abstention. Failure to abstain will be due to a faulty general premiss if the glutton is someone who, instead of the life-plan of temperance, adopts a regular policy of pursuing every pleasure that offers itself. Such a person Aristotle calls 'intemperate'. But someone may subscribe to a general principle of temperance, thus possessing the appropriate general premiss, and yet fail to abstain on this occasion through the overwhelming force of gluttonous desire. Aristotle calls such a person not 'intemperate' but 'incontinent', and he explains how such incontinence (*akrasia*) takes

---

[3] See A. Kenny, *Aristotle's Theory of the Will* (London: Duckworth, 1979), 111–54.

different forms in accordance with the various ways in which the later stages of the practical reasoning break down (7. 3. 1147^{a}24–^{b}12).

From time to time in his discussion of the relation of wisdom and virtue Aristotle pauses to compare and contrast his teaching with that of Socrates. Socrates was correct, he said, to regard wisdom as essential for moral virtue, but he was wrong simply to identify virtue with wisdom (*NE* 6. 13. 1144^{b}17–21). Again, Socrates had denied the possibility of doing what one knows to be wrong, on the grounds that knowledge could not be dragged about like a slave. He was correct about the power of knowledge, Aristotle says, but wrong to conclude that incontinence is impossible. Incontinence arises from deficiencies concerning the minor premises or the conclusion of practical reasoning, and does not prejudice the status of the universal major premise which alone deserves the name 'knowledge' (*NE* 7. 3. 1147^{b}13–19).

Pleasure and Happiness

The pleasures that are the domain of temperance, intemperance, and incontinence are pleasures of a particular kind: the familiar bodily pleasures of food, drink, and sex. If Aristotle is to carry out his plan of explicating the relationship between pleasure and happiness, he has to give a more general account of the nature of pleasure. This he does in two passages, in *NE* 7 = *EE* 6 (1152^{b}1–54^{b}31) and in *NE* 10. 1–5 (1172^{a}16–1176^{a}29). The two passages differ in style and method, but their fundamental content is the same.[4]

In each treatise Aristotle offers a fivefold classification of pleasure. First of all, there are the pleasures of those who are sick (either in body or soul); these are really only pseudo-pleasures (1153^{b}33, 1173^{b}22). Next, there are the pleasures of food and drink and sex as enjoyed by the gourmand and the lecher (1152^{b}35 ff., 1173^{b}8–15). Next up the hierarchy are two classes of aesthetic sense-pleasures: the pleasures of the inferior senses of touch and taste, on the one hand, and on the other the pleasures of the superior senses of sight, hearing, and smell (1153^{b}26, 1174^{b}14–1175^{a}10). Finally, at the top of the scale, are the pleasures of the mind (1153^{a}1–20, 1173^{b}17).

Different though these pleasures are, a common account can be given of the nature of each genuine pleasure.

Each sense has a corresponding pleasure, and so does thought and contemplation. Each activity is pleasantest when it is most perfect, and it is most perfect when the organ is in good condition and when it is directed to the most excellent of its objects; and the pleasure

---

[4] See A. Kenny, *The Aristotelian Ethics* (Oxford: Clarendon Press, 1978), 233–7.

perfects the activity. The pleasure does not however perfect the activity in the same way as the object and the sense, if good, perfect it; just as health and the physician are not in the same way the cause of someone's being in good health. (*NE* 10. 4. 1174^{b}23–32)

The doctrine that pleasure perfects activity is presented in different terms in another passage in which pleasure is defined as the unimpeded activity of a disposition in accordance with nature (*NE* 7. 12. 1153^{a}14).

To see what Aristotle had in mind, consider the aesthetic pleasures of taste. You are at a tasting of mature wines; you are free from colds, and undistracted by background music; then if you do not enjoy the wine either you have a bad palate ('the organ is not in good condition') or it is a bad wine ('it is not directed to the most excellent of its objects'). There is no third alternative. Pleasure 'perfects' activity in the sense that it causes the activity—in this case a tasting—to be a good one of its kind. The organ and the object—in this case the palate and the wine—are the efficient cause of the activity. If they are both good, they will be the efficient cause of a good activity, and therefore they too will 'perfect' activity, i.e. make it be a good specimen of such activity. But pleasure causes activity not as efficient cause, but as final cause: like health, not like the doctor.

After this analysis, Aristotle is in a position to consider the relation between pleasure and goodness. The question 'Is pleasure good or bad?' is too simple: it can only be answered after pleasures have been distinguished and classified. Pleasure is not to be thought of as a good or bad thing in itself: the pleasure proper to good activities is good and the pleasure proper to bad activities is bad (*NE* 10. 5. 1175^{b}27).

If certain pleasures are bad, that does not prevent the best thing from being some pleasure—just as knowledge might be, thought certain kinds of knowledge are bad. Perhaps it is even necessary, if each state has unimpeded activities, that the activity (if unimpeded) of all or one of them should be happiness. This then would be the most worthwhile thing of all; and it would be a pleasure. (*NE* 7. 13. 1153^{b}7–11)

In this way, it could turn out that pleasure (of a certain kind) was the best of all human goods. If happiness consists in the exercise of the highest form of virtue, and if the unimpeded exercise of a virtue constitutes a pleasure, then happiness and that pleasure are one and the same thing.

Plato, in the *Philebus*, proposed the question whether pleasure or *phronesis* constituted the best life. Aristotle's answer is that properly understood the two are not in competition with each other as candidates for happiness. The exercise of the highest form of *phronesis* is the very same thing as the truest form of pleasure; each is identical with the other and with happiness. In Plato's usage, however, 'phronesis' covers the whole range of intellectual virtue that Aristotle distinguishes into wisdom (*phronesis*) and understanding (*sophia*). If we ask whether happiness is to be identified with the pleasure of wisdom, or with the pleasure of understanding, we get different answers in Aristotle's two ethical treatises.

The *Nicomachean Ethics* identifies happiness with the pleasurable exercise of understanding. Happiness, we were told earlier, is the activity of soul in accordance with virtue, and if there are several virtues, in accordance with the best and most perfect virtue. We have, in the course of the treatise, learnt that there are both moral and intellectual virtues, and that the latter are superior; and among the intellectual virtues, understanding, the scientific grasp of eternal truths, is superior to wisdom, which concerns human affairs. Supreme happiness, therefore, is activity in accordance with understanding, an activity which Aristotle calls 'contemplation'. We are told that contemplation is related to philosophy as knowing is to seeking: in some way, which remains obscure, it consists in the enjoyment of the fruits of philosophical inquiry (*NE* 10. 7. 1177^{a}12–^{b}26).

In the *Eudemian Ethics* happiness is identified not with the exercise of a single dominant virtue but with the exercise of all the virtues, including not only understanding but also the moral virtues linked with wisdom (*EE* 2. 1. 1219^{a}35–9). Activity in accordance with these virtues is pleasant, and so the truly happy man will also have the most pleasant life (*EE* 7. 25. 1249^{a}18–21). For the virtuous person, the concepts 'good' and 'pleasant' coincide in their application; if the two do not yet coincide then a person is not virtuous but incontinent (7. 2. 1237^{a}8–9). The bringing about of this coincidence is the task of ethics (7. 2. 1237^{a}3).

Though the *Eudemian Ethics* does not identify happiness with philosophical contemplation it does, like the *Nicomachean Ethics*, give it a dominant position in the life of the happy person. The exercise of the moral virtues, as well as intellectual ones, is, in the *Eudemian Ethics*, included as part of happiness; but the standard for their exercise is set by their relationship to contemplation—which is here defined in theological rather than philosophical terms.

Whatever choice or possession of natural goods—health and strength, wealth, friends, and the like—will most conduce to the contemplation of God is best: this is the finest criterion. But any standard of living which either through excess or defect hinders the service and contemplation of God is bad. (*EE* 7. 15. 1249^{b}15–20)

The *Eudemian* ideal of happiness, therefore, given the role it assigns to contemplation, to the moral virtues, and to pleasure, can claim, as Aristotle promised, to combine the features of the traditional three lives, the life of the philosopher, the life of the politician, and the life of the pleasure-seeker. The happy man will value contemplation above all, but part of his happy life will be the exercise of political virtues and the enjoyment in moderation of natural human pleasures of body as well as of soul.

The Hedonism of Epicurus

In making an identification between the supreme good and the supreme pleasure, Aristotle entitles himself to be called a hedonist: but he is a hedonist of a very unusual kind, and stands at a great distance from the most famous hedonist in ancient Greece, namely Epicurus. Epicurus' treatment of pleasure is less sophisticated, but also more easily intelligible, than Aristotle's. He is willing to place a value on pleasure that is independent of the value of the activity enjoyed: all pleasure is, as such, good. His ethical hedonism resembles that of Democritus or of Plato's *Protagoras* rather than that of either Aristotelian ethical treatise.

For Epicurus, pleasure is the final end of life and the criterion of goodness in choice. This is something that needs no argument: we all feel it in our bones (LS 21A).

We maintain that pleasure is the beginning and end of a blessed life. We recognize it as our primary and natural good. Pleasure is our starting point whenever we choose or avoid anything and it is this we make our aim, using feeling as the criterion by which we judge of every good thing. (D.L. 10. 128–9)

This does not mean that Epicurus, like Aristotle's intemperate man, makes it his policy to pursue every pleasure that offers. If pleasure is the greatest good, pain is the greatest evil, and it is best to pass a pleasure by if it would lead to long-term suffering. Equally, it is worth putting up with pain if it will bring great pleasure in the long run (D.L. 10. 129).

These qualifications mean that Epicurus' hedonism is far from being an invitation to lead the life of a voluptuary. It is not drinking and carousing, nor tables laden with delicacies, nor promiscuous intercourse with boys and women, that produce the pleasant life, but sobriety, honour, justice, and wisdom (D.L. 10. 132). A simple vegetarian diet and the company of a few friends in a modest garden suffice for Epicurean happiness.

What enables Epicurus to combine theoretical hedonism with practical asceticism is his understanding of pleasure as being essentially the satisfaction of desire. The strongest and most fundamental of our desires is the desire for the removal of pain (D.L. 10. 127). Hence, the mere absence of pain is itself a fundamental pleasure (LS 21A). Among our desires some are natural and some are futile, and it is the natural desires to which the most important pleasures correspond. We have natural desires for the removal of the painful states of hunger, thirst, and cold, and the satisfaction of these desires is naturally pleasant. But there are two kinds of pleasure involved, for which Epicurus framed technical terms: there is the kinetic pleasure of quenching one's thirst, and the static pleasure that supervenes when one's thirst has been quenched (LS 21Q). Both kinds of pleasure are natural: but among the kinetic pleasures some are necessary (the pleasure in eating and drinking enough to satisfy hunger and thirst) and others are unnecessary (the pleasures of the gourmet) (LS 21I, J).

Unnecessary natural pleasures are not greater than, but merely variations on, necessary natural pleasures: hunger is the best sauce, and eating simple food when hungry is pleasanter than stuffing oneself with luxuries when satiated. But of all natural pleasures, it is the static pleasures that really count. 'The cry of the flesh is not to be hungry, not to be thirsty, not to be cold. Someone who is not any of these states, and has good hope of remaining so, could rival even Zeus in happiness' (LS 21G).

Sexual desires are classed by Epicurus as unnecessary, on the grounds that their non-fulfilment is not accompanied by pain. This may be surprising, since unrequited love can cause anguish. But the intensity of such desire, Epicurus claimed, was due not to the nature of sex but to the romantic imagination of the lover (LS 21E). Epicurus was not opposed to the fulfilment of unnecessary natural desires, provided they did no harm—which of course was to be measured by their capacity for producing pain (LS 21F). Sexual pleasure, he said, could be taken in any way one wished, provided one respected law and convention, distressed no one, and did no damage to one's body or one's essential resources. However, these qualifications added up to substantial constraint, and even when sex did no harm, it did no good either (LS 21G).

Epicurus is more critical of the fulfilment of desires that are futile: these are desires that are not natural and, like unnecessary natural desires, do not cause pain if not fulfilled. Examples are the desire for wealth and the desire for civic honours and acclaim (LS 21G, I). But so too are desires for the pleasures of science and philosophy: 'Hoist sail', he told a favourite pupil 'and steer clear of all culture' (D.L. 10. 5). Aristotle had made it a point in favour of philosophy that its pleasures, unlike the pleasures of the senses, were unmixed with pain (cf. *NE* 10. 7. 1177^{a}25); now it is made a reason for downgrading the pleasures of philosophy that there is no pain in being a non-philosopher. For Epicurus the mind does play an important part in the happy life: but its function is to anticipate and recollect the pleasures of the senses (LS 21L, T).

On the basis of the surviving texts we can judge that Epicurus' hedonism, if philistine, is far from being licentious. But from time to time he expressed himself in terms that were, perhaps deliberately, shocking to many. 'For my part I have no conception of the good if I take away the pleasures of taste and sex and music and beauty' (D.L. 10. 6). 'The pleasure of the stomach is the beginning and root of all good' (LS 21M). Expressions such as these laid the ground for his posthumous reputation as a gourmand and a libertine. The legend, indeed, was started in his lifetime by a dissident pupil, Timocrates, who loved to tell stories of his midnight orgies and twice-daily vomitings (D.L. 10. 6–7).

More serious criticism focused on his teaching that the virtues were merely means of securing pleasure. The Stoic Cleanthes used to ask his pupils to imagine pleasure as a queen on a throne surrounded by the virtues. On the Epicurean view of ethics, he said, these were handmaids totally dedicated to her service, merely whispering warnings, from time to time, against incautiously giving offence or causing pain. Epicureans did not demur: Diogenes of Oenoanda agreed with the Stoics that the virtues were productive of happiness, but he denied that they were part of happiness itself. Virtues were a means, not an end. 'I affirm now and always, at the top of my voice, that for all, whether Greek or barbarian, pleasure is the goal of the best way of life' (LS 21P).

Stoic Ethics

In support of the central role they assigned to pleasure, Epicureans argued that as soon as every animal was born it sought after pleasure and enjoyed it as the greatest good while rejecting pain as the greatest evil. The Stoic Chrysippus, on the contrary, argued that the first impulse of an animal was not towards pleasure, but towards self-preservation. Consciousness begins with awareness of what the Stoics called, coining a new word, one's own *constitution* (LS 57A). An animal accepted what assisted, and rejected what hampered, the development of this constitution: thus a baby would strive to stand unsupported, even at the cost of falls and tears (Seneca, Ep. 121, 15 LS 57B). This drive towards the preservation and progress of the constitution is something more primitive than the desire for pleasure, since it occurs in plants as well as animals, and even in humans is often exercised without consciousness (D.L. 8. 86 LS 57A). To care for one's own constitution is nature's first lesson.

Stoic ethics attaches great importance to Nature. Whereas Aristotle spoke often of the nature of individual things and species, it is the Stoics who were responsible for introducing the notion of 'Nature', with a capital 'N', as a single cosmic order exhibited in the structure and activities of things of many different kinds. According to Diogenes Laertius (D.L. 7. 87), Zeno stated that the end of life was 'to live in agreement with Nature.' Nature teaches us to take care of ourselves through life, as our constitution changes from babyhood through youth to age; but self-love is not Nature's only teaching. Just as there is a natural impulse to procreate, there is a natural impulse to take care of one's offspring; just as we have a natural inclination to learn, so we have a natural inclination to share with others the knowledge we acquire (Cicero, *Fin.* 3. 65 LS 57E). These impulses to benefit those nearest to us should, according to the Stoics, be extended outward to the wider world.

Each of us, according to Hierocles, a Stoic of the time of Hadrian, stands at the centre of a series of concentric circles. The first circle surrounding my individual mind contains my body and its needs. The second contains my immediate family, and the third and fourth contain extensions of my family. Then come circles of neighbours, at varying distances, plus the circle that contains all my co-nationals. The outermost and largest circle encompasses the whole human race. If I am virtuous I will try to draw these circles closer together, treating cousins as if they were brothers, and constantly transferring people from outer circles to inner ones (LS 57G).

The Stoics coined a special word for the process thus picturesquely described: 'oikeiosis', literally 'homification'. A Stoic, adapting himself to cosmic nature, is making himself at home in the world he lives in. *Oikeiosis* is the converse of this: it is making other people at home with oneself, taking them into one's domestic circle. The universalism is impressive, but its limitations were soon noted. It is unrealistic to think that, however virtuous, a person can bestow the same affection on the most distant foreigner as one can on one's own family. *Oikeiosis* begins at home, and even within the very first circle we are more troubled by the loss of an eye than by the loss of a nail. But if the benevolence of *oikeiosis* is not universally uniform, it cannot provide a foundation for the obligation of justice to treat all human beings equally (LS 57H). Moreover, the Stoics believed that it was praiseworthy to die for one's country: but is not that preferring an outer circle to an inner one?

Again, the universe of nature contains more than the human beings who inhabit the concentric circles: what is the right attitude to those who share the cosmos with us? Stoics, in some moods, described the universe as a city or state shared by men with gods, and it was to this that they appealed in order to justify the self-sacrifice of the individual for the sake of the community. In their practical ethical teaching there is little concern with non-human agents. Animals, certainly, have no rights against mankind: Chrysippus was sure that humans can make beasts serve their needs without violating justice (Cicero, *Fin.* 3. 67 LS 57G).

The cosmic order does, however, provide not only the context but the model for human ethical behaviour. 'Living in agreement with nature' does not mean only 'living in accordance with human nature'. Chrysippus said that we should live as taught by experience of natural events, because our individual natures were part of the nature of the universe. Consequently, Stoic teaching about the end of life can be summed up thus:

We are to follow nature, living our lives in accordance with our own nature and that of the cosmos, doing no act that is forbidden by the universal law, that is to say the right reason that pervades all things, which is none other than Zeus, who presides over the administration of all that exists. (D.L. 7. 87)

The life of a virtuous person will run tranquilly beneath the uniform motion of the heavens, and the moral law within will mirror the starry skies above.

Living in agreement with nature was, for the Stoics, equivalent to living according to virtue. Their best-known, and most frequently criticized, moral tenet was that virtue alone was necessary and sufficient for happiness. Virtue was not only the final end and the supreme good: it was also the only real good.

Among the things there are, some are good, some are evil, and some are neither the one nor the other. The things that are good are the virtues: wisdom, justice, fortitude, temperance, and so on. The things that are evil are the opposites of these: folly, injustice, and so on. The things that are neither one nor the other are all those things that neither help nor harm: for instance, life, health, pleasure, beauty, strength, wealth, fame, good birth, and their opposites, death, disease, pain, ugliness, weakness, poverty, disrepute, and low birth. (D.L. 7.101 LS 58A)

The items in the long list of 'things that neither help nor harm' were called by the Stoics 'indifferent matters' (*adiaphora*). The Stoics accepted that these were not matters of indifference like whether the number of hairs on one's head was odd or even: they were matters that aroused in people strong desire and revulsion. But they were indifferent in the sense that they were irrelevant to a well-structured life: it was possible to be perfectly happy with or without them (D.L. 7. 104–5 LS 58B–C).

Like the Stoics, Aristotle placed happiness in virtue and its exercise, and counted fame and riches no part of the happiness of a happy person. But he thought that it was a necessary condition for happiness to have a sufficient endowment of external goods (*NE* 1. 10. 1101^{a}14–17; *EE* 1. 1. 1214^{b}16). Moreover, he believed that even a virtuous man could cease to be happy if disaster overtook himself and his family, as happened to Priam (*NE* 1. 10. 1101^{a}8). By contrast, the Stoics, with the sole exception of Chrysippus, thought that happiness, once possessed, could never be lost, and even Chrysippus thought it could be terminated only by something like madness (D.L. 7. 127).

Indifferent matters, the Stoics conceded, were not all on the same level as each other. Some were popular (*proegmena*) and others unpopular (*apoproegmena*). More importantly, some went with nature and some went against nature: those that went with nature had value (*axia*) and those that went against nature had disvalue (*apaxia*). Among the things that have value are talents and skills, health, beauty, and wealth; the opposites of these have disvalue (D.L. 7. 105–6). It seems clear that, according to the Stoics, all things that have value are also popular; it is not so clear whether everything that is popular also has value. Virtue itself did not come within the class of the popular, just as a king is not a nobleman like his courtiers, but something superior to a nobleman (LS 58E). Chrysippus was willing to allow that it was permissible, in ordinary usage, to call 'good' what strictly was only popular (LS 58H); and in matters of practical choice between indifferent matters, the Stoics in effect encouraged people to opt for the popular (LS 58C).

An action may fall short of being a virtuous action (*katorthoma*) and yet be a decent action (*kathekon*). An action is decent or fitting if it is appropriate to one's nature and state of life (LS 59B). It is decent to honour one's parents and one's country, and the neglect of parents and failure to be patriotic is something indecent. (Some things, like picking up a twig, or going into the country, are neither decent nor indecent.) Virtuous actions are, a fortiori, decent actions: what virtue adds to mere decency is first of all purity of motive and secondly stability in practice (LS 59G, H, I). Here Stoic doctrine is close to Aristotle's teaching that in order to act virtuously a person must not only judge correctly what is to be done, but choose it for its own sake and exhibit constancy of character (*NE* 2. 6. 1105ᵃ30–ᵇ1). Some actions, according to the Stoics, are not only indecent but sinful (*hamartemata*) (LS 59M). The difference between these two kinds of badness is not made clear: perhaps a Stoic sinner is like Aristotle's intemperate man, while mere indecency may be parallel to incontinence. For while the Stoics, implausibly, said that all sinful actions were equally bad, they did regard those that arose from a hardened and incurable character as having badness of a special kind (LS 59o).

The Stoic account of incontinence, however, differs from Aristotle in an important respect. They regard it not as arising from a struggle between different parts of the soul but rather as the result of intellectual error. Incontinence is the result of passion, which is irrational and unnatural motion of the soul. Passions come in four kinds: fears, desires, pain, and pleasure. According to Chrysippus passions were simply mistaken judgements about good and evil; according to earlier Stoics they were perturbations arising from such mistaken judgements (LS 65G, K). But all agreed that the path of moral progress lay in the correction of the mistaken beliefs (LS 65A, K). Because the beliefs are false, the passions must be eliminated, not just moderated as on the Aristotelian model of the mean.

Desire is rooted in a mistaken belief that something is approaching that will do us good; fear is rooted in a mistaken belief that something is approaching that will do us harm. These beliefs are accompanied by a further belief in the appropriate-ness of an emotional response, of yearning or shrinking as the case may be. Since according to Stoic theory, nothing can do us good except virtue, and nothing can do us harm except vice, beliefs of the kind exhibited in desire and fear are always unjustified, and that is why the passions are to be eradicated. It is not that emotional responses are always inappropriate: there can be legitimate joy and justified apprehension. But if the responses are appropriate, then they do not count as passions (LS 65F). Again, even the wise man is not exempt from irregular bodily arousals of various kinds: but as long as he does not consent to them, they are not passions (Seneca, *de Ira* 2. 3. 1).

When Chrysippus says that passions are beliefs, there is no need to regard him as presenting the passions, implausibly, as calm intellectual assessments: on the contrary he is pointing out that the assents to propositions that set a high value on things are themselves tumultuous events. When I lose a loved one, it appears to me that an irreplaceable value has left my life. Full assent to this proposition involves violent internal upheaval. But if we are ever to be happy, we must never allow ourselves to attach such supreme value to anything that is outside our control.[5]

---

[5] Here I am indebted to an unpublished paper by Martha Nussbaum.

The weakness in the Stoic position is, in fact, its refusal to come to terms with the fragility of happiness. We have met a parallel temptation in classical epistemology: the refusal to come to terms with the fallibility of judgement. The epistemological temptation is embodied in the fallacious argument from 'Necessarily, if I know that p, then p' to 'If I know that p, then necessarily p'. The parallel temptation in ethics is to argue from 'Necessarily, if I am happy, I have X' to 'If I am happy, I have X necessarily'. This argument, if successful, leads to the denial that happiness can be constituted by any contingent good that is capable of being lost (Cicero, *Tusc.* 5. 41). Given the frail, contingent natures of human beings as we know ourselves to be, the denial that contingent goods can constitute happiness is tantamount to the claim that only superhuman beings can be happy.

The Stoics in effect accepted this conclusion, in their idealization of the man of wisdom. Happiness lies in virtue, and there are no degrees of virtue, so that a person is either perfectly virtuous or not virtuous at all. The most perfect virtue is wisdom, and the wise man has all the virtues, since the virtues are inseparable (LS 61F). Like Socrates, the Stoics thought of the virtues as being sciences, and all of them as making up a single science (LS 61H). One Stoic went so far as to say that to distinguish between courage and justice was like regarding the faculty for seeing white as different from the faculty of seeing black (LS 61B). The wise man is totally free from passion, and is in possession of all worthwhile knowledge: his virtue is the same as that of a god (LS 61J, 63F).

The wise man whom we seek is the happy man who can think no human experience painful enough to cast him down nor joyful enough to raise his spirits. For what can seem important in human affairs to one who is familiar with all eternity and the vastness of the entire universe? (Cicero, *Tusc.* 4. 37).

The wise man is rich, and owns all things, since he alone knows how to use things well; he alone is truly handsome, since the mind's face is more beautiful than the body's; he alone is free, even if he is in prison, since he is a slave to no appetite (Cicero, *Fin* 3. 75). It was unsurprising, after all this, that the Stoics admitted that a wise man was harder to find than a phoenix (LS 61N). They thus purchase the invulnerability of happiness only at the cost of making it unattainable.

Since a wise man is not to be found, and there are no degrees of virtue, the whole human race consists of fools. Shall we say, then, that the wise man is a mythical ideal held up for our admiration and imitation (LS 66A)? Hardly, because however much we progress towards this unattainable goal, we have still come no nearer to salvation. Someone who is only two feet from the surface is drowning as much as anyone who is 500 fathoms deep in the ocean (LS 61T).

The Stoics' doctrine of wisdom and happiness, then, offers us little encouragement to strive for virtue. However, later Stoics made a distinction between doctrine (*decreta*) and precepts (*praecepta*), the one being general and the other particular (Seneca, Ep. 94, 1–4). While the doctrine is austere and Olympian, the precepts, by an amiable inconsistency, are often quite liberal and practical. Stoics were willing to give advice on the conduct of marriage, the right time for singing, the best type of joke, and many other details of daily life (Epictetus, discourses 4. 12. 16). The distinction between doctrine and precepts is matched by a distinction between choice and selection: virtue alone was good and choiceworthy (D.L. 7. 89), but among indifferent matters some could be selected in preference to others. Smart clothes, for instance, were in themselves worthless; but there could be good in the selection of smart clothes (Seneca, Ep. 92, 12). Critics said that a selection could be good only if what was selected was good (LS 64c). Sometimes, again, Stoics spoke as if the end of life was not so much the actual attainment of virtue as doing one's best to attain virtue. At this point critics complained that the Stoics could not make up their minds whether the end of life was the unattainable target itself, or simply ineffective assiduousness in target practice (LS 64F, c).

One of the best-known and most controversial of Stoic precepts was that suicide could sometimes be permissible. The Stoics 'say that the wise man may reasonably make his own exit from life, for the sake of his country or dear ones, or if he suffer intolerable pain, handicap, or disease' (D.L. 7. 130). It is difficult to see how this can be reconciled with the Stoic picture of the wise man. No amount of pain or suffering can impair the wise man's happiness, we have been told; and indeed when recommending reasonable suicide the Stoics agree that it will be the suicide of a happy man (Cicero, *Fin*, 3. 60). But then what can be the motive that provides the reason for leaving life, since virtue and happiness are supposed to be that for the sake of which everything is to be chosen?

Given that the Stoic wise man is an idealization, it is an academic issue whether his suicide would be a virtuous act. What is of practical importance is whether, for the rest of us, suicide can be a decent act. Many in antiquity believed that the Stoics taught this principle and some famous Stoics seem to have acted on it. However, it is oddly difficult to find the principle stated in our sources in a clear and unambiguous way. The most famous Stoic suicide, that of Seneca, was not a matter of his choice, but the execution of the death sentence of a tyrant.

9

God

In Homer's poems gods and goddesses figure prominently among the cast of characters. Zeus, the king of the gods, with his consort, Hera, and ten members of their extended family, including his daughter Athena, Aphrodite the goddess of love, and Poseidon the sea-god, all live together in a blissful abode on Mount Olympus. They take a keen partisan interest in the doings of the human heroes of the *Iliad* and the *Odyssey*. These gods and goddesses are simply human beings writ large, with all the emotions and vices of human beings. They interact both mentally and physically with ordinary humans, often with disastrous results. The only fundamental difference between gods and men is that men die while gods are immortal.

Xenophanes' Natural Theology

This conception of the divine was attacked by the first philosopher of religion, Xenophanes. Xenophanes savaged Homeric theology in satirical verses of which only fragments remain. Homer's stories, he complained, attributed to the gods theft, adultery, deception, and everything that, among humans, would be considered a shame and a reproach (KRS 166). But even if Homer's gods had behaved honourably, they would still resemble humans too much to be credible. Men fashion gods in their own image: Ethiopians believe in gods that are dark and snub-nosed, while the gods worshipped by the Thracians have red hair and blue eyes (KRS 168). 'If cows and horses or lions had hands and could draw, then horses would draw the forms of gods like horses, cows like cows, making their bodies similar in shape to their own' (KRS 169).

Instead of this childish anthropomorphism, Xenophanes offered a sophisticated monotheism.

He believed in

> One god, lord over gods and human kind,
> Like mortals neither in body nor in mind.   (DK 24 B23)

There could be only one God, because God is the most powerful of all things; if there were more than one god, none of them could be more powerful than the others, and none of them would be able to do whatever he wished. God must always have existed: he could not come into being from something like himself (for there cannot be anything equal to him), nor could he come into being from something unlike himself (for the greater cannot be brought into being by the lesser) (Aristotle, *MXG* 976^{b}14–36). God is a living being, but not an organic being like humans and animals: there are no parts in God, and 'he sees as a whole, he thinks as a whole, and he hears as a whole' (DK 21 B24). He has no physical contact with anything in the world, but 'remote and effortless, with his mind alone he governs all there is' (DK 21 B25).

Though he is willing to state and argue for such substantive theses about God, Xenophanes' theology is largely negative. He finds it difficult to accept either that God is finite, or that he is infinite. Similarly, when he asks whether God is changing or changeless, he finds equally balanced arguments on each side. Some of our sources leave it obscure whether his God is really transcendent or is to be identified in some mysterious way with the entire Eleatic universe. 'The clear truth about the gods no man has ever seen nor any man will ever know' (DK 21 B34).

Xenophanes was not, of course, the first monotheist. He had been anticipated much earlier in Egypt by Akhenaten and more recently in Israel by the Hebrew prophets. But he presents his monotheism not as an oracular revelation, but as the result of rational argument. In terms of a distinction not drawn until centuries later, the prophets proclaimed a revealed religion, while Xenophanes was a natural theologian.

Socrates and Plato on Piety

Plato, in the *Republic*, follows up Xenophanes' attack on the disgusting stories of the gods told by Homer and Hesiod. The stories must be eliminated from the educational curriculum, because they are false in themselves and encourage evil behaviour in their readers. Children must be told no tales of battles between the gods, or of gods changing shapes and taking human and animal form (377e–381d). God is good, and does no harm to anyone. Only the goods things in life come from God, and if the gods punish people that is for their own benefit (379c–380b). Again, God is unchanging, and does not deceive others by falsehood or disguise (382e).

Plato's assault on Homer and the poets often seems exaggerated to a modern reader. It can only be understood if we recall the centrality of the *Iliad* and the *Odyssey* in Greek education, and the importance of religion in Greek everyday life. It is true that the Greeks were never a 'people of the book', and the Homeric poems never commanded in Greek life and religion an authority similar to that which has been exercised by the Hebrew Bible, the Gospels, and the Koran. None the less, the stories of Homer and Hesiod exercised an influence in education much more powerful than that of fairy stories and children's books in our society. In that context, Plato's polemic is understandable. It must also have taken courage: after all, Socrates had been put to death on a charge of teaching the young not to believe in the gods in whom the city believes (*Apol.* 26b).

Socrates was also charged with introducing new divinities. This must be a reference to his *daimon*, an inner divine voice which, he claimed, used to warn him off wrongdoing (*Apol.* 40b). Otherwise he seems to have been respectful of conventional Greek religion. Of course he claimed not to know what piety was, just as he claimed not to know what any other virtue was. But the Socratic dialogue *Euthyphro* contains an interesting discussion of a proposed definition of piety or holiness as 'that which the gods love'.

Socrates puts the question: do the gods love what is holy because it is holy, or is it holy because the gods love it? Euthyphro responds that the holy is not so called because the gods love it; rather, the gods love what is holy because it is holy. Socrates then offers 'godly' as an abbreviation for 'what is loved by the gods'. Accordingly, Euthyphro's thesis can be stated in the following terms, substituting 'godly' for 'holy':

(A) The godly is loved by the gods because it is godly.

On the other hand, it seems clear that

(B) The godly is godly because it is loved by the gods

since 'godly' was introduced as a synonym for 'loved by the gods'. So Socrates claims to have reduced Euthyphro to inconsistency, and urges him to give up the claim that holiness is what the gods love (10a–11b).

However, there is no real inconsistency between A and B: 'because' is used in two different senses in the two theses. In (A) it introduces the gods' motive; in (B) it recalls our stipulation about meaning. A parallel point can be made in English by pointing out that it is true both that

(C) A judge judges because he is a judge

(i.e. he does it because it is his job); and also that

(D) A judge is a judge because he judges

(that is why he is called a judge).

Euthyphro, however, gives up his proposed definition and offers another: holiness is justice in the service of the gods. This too is shot down: what service can we render the gods? Socrates mocks at the idea of sacrifice as a form of trading with the gods when we have nothing worthwhile to offer them in exchange for the favours we ask them (14e–15a). If Plato's *Euthyphro* gives a realistic picture of

Socrates' methods of cross-examination, we can understand why religious folk in Athens might regard him as a purveyor of impiety and a danger to the young.

Another Socratic dialogue (this time probably not by Plato), *Second Alcibiades*, contains a deflationary discussion of the practice of prayer. When we pray for something that we want, we may be asking for something that will harm us: an answer to prayer may be a disaster. Since we lack the knowledge of what is best for us, it is better not to ask for anything; or, like the Spartans, simply to pray for what is good and noble, without specifying further (148c). In terms of sacrifice and worship the Athenians are far more religious than the Spartans, and yet the Spartans always come off better in battle. Is this surprising? 'It would be a strange and sorry thing if the gods took more account of our gifts and sacrifices than of our souls and whether there is holiness and justice to be found in them' (150a).

Plato's Evolving Theology

Plato's own attitude to religion evolved along with his other metaphysical beliefs. In the central part of the *Republic* the summit of the universe is occupied not by a personal God but by the Idea of the Good, which plays the part in the ideal world of Being that is played by the sun in our everyday world of becoming (508c–e). Everything ultimately owes its being to this absolute goodness, which is itself beyond and superior to being (509b). In the *Symposium* it is the Idea of Beauty that is supreme, and the priestess Diotima describes to Socrates, in terms appropriate to the religious initiation of mystery cults, the soul's ascent to the lofty raptures of its vision. Humans crave immortality: this craving drives them to procreate and cherish their offspring, to strive for exploits that will go down in history, and to create works of art of everlasting value. But these are only the lesser mysteries of love. To reach the greatest mysteries, the candidate should rise above beautiful bodies, above beautiful souls, above the beauty of sciences and institutions, to reach an eternal and unchanging absolute beauty. The most noble life consists in the intellectual contemplation of beauty divine, absolute, and unalloyed. These rites of love will make the initiate as immortal as any human being can be (206b 212a).

Despite the religious context and phraseology, the Idea of Beauty in the *Symposium* is no more personal than the Idea of the Good in the *Republic*. But in the *Sophist* this very fact is given as a reason for a substantial overhaul of the Theory of Ideas. 'Shall we be easily persuaded', asks the Eleatic Visitor, 'that change and life and soul and wisdom do not belong to the most perfect being, and that it neither lives nor thinks, but remains motionless and stately and sacred but mindless?' (248e).

By the time he wrote the *Timaeus* Plato had reached a conception of God close to that of the major monotheistic religions. The topic of the dialogue is the origin of the world we live in: did it always exist, or did it come into being? Because it is visible and tangible it must have come into being; but it is no easy task 'to find the maker and father of this universe' (28c). Why should such a one have brought it into being? 'He was good, and what is good has no particle of jealousy in it; and so, being free of jealousy, he wanted all things to be as much like himself as possible' (29e).[1] God is not conceived by Plato as the creator of the universe out of nothing; rather, he established the cosmos by bringing order out of chaos. 'God, therefore, wishing that all things should be good, and nothing any less perfect than was necessary, finding the visible universe not at rest but in discordant and disorderly motion, brought it from a state of disorder into one of order, an order that he judged altogether better' (30a). The dialogue then takes us through the stages of this ordering: first soul was created and then matter, with soul incarnate in the visible body of the heavens (34e, 36e). Within the universe there are four kinds of living beings: gods, birds, fish, and animals (40a). Gods, we are told, come in two kinds: visible and invisible. The visible gods are the fixed stars, living beings divine and eternal; invisible gods appear to humans from time to time at their own discretion (40b, 41a). The father of the universe delegates to these created but immortal beings the task of making the inferior living things. In the case of human beings, he himself made the immortal soul, leaving it to the lesser gods to encase this in a skull and add the rest of the body below it (69c–d). The dialogue ends by describing the visible universe as being itself a perceptible god, the image of the God who is known only by the mind (92c).

In the last of Plato's dialogues, *The Laws*, religion is prominent, and the whole of the tenth book is devoted to it. In the ideal city of Magnesia atheism is prohibited under severe penalties. The fifty-eighth of the city's laws instructs officials to bring before a court any act of impiety that is brought to their notice. Those convicted of impiety should be sent to a penitentiary for five years' solitary confinement; anyone who relapses after release is to be punished by death. Aggravated impiety, which is atheism accompanied by fraudulent claims to supernatural powers, is to be punished by life imprisonment (907e–909c).

The legislators for Magnesia believe that it is preferable to use argument and persuasion rather than sanctions to ensure compliance with the laws, and accordingly they preface these severe prohibitions with the following preamble:

No one who believes in gods as directed by law ever voluntarily commits an act of impiety or utters any lawless word. If he does so it is due to one of three possible errors. Either he does not believe that gods exist; or he believes that they exist but have no interest in the human race; or he believes that they can be won round by sacrifice and prayer. (885b)

The lawgivers accept an obligation to cure people of these errors by offering proofs of the three truths that contradict them.

---

[1] Cf. Kretzmann, *The Metaphysics of Creation* (Oxford: Oxford University Press, 1999), 101–4.

To prove the existence of gods it is not enough to point to the wonders of the universe or the order of the seasons. Atheists will say that the sun and moon and stars are only unfeeling earth and stones, and that elements and their compounds owe their existence to nature and chance (886d, 889a). Nor can one appeal to the unanimous agreement of Greeks and barbarians that gods exist: such beliefs, the atheists maintain, are simply the result of indoctrination from childhood, and in any case there is no unanimity about the nature of the gods (887c, 889e).

A refutation of atheism must take a longer way round. The fundamental error of those who think that random evolution produced the furniture of the world is that they have not grasped the priority of soul over body. Soul was created long before any bodies, and it is soul that causes the development and transformation of physical things (892a). The priority of soul is proved by an analysis of the different possible kinds of motion. There are ten such kinds, but the most important of them are just two: (*a*) one that imparts motion to other things, itself being moved by something else; and (*b*) one that imparts motion to itself as well as to other things. Obviously, a motion of the former type could not be the origin of motion in the world: motion in the universe must begin with self-generating motion. But self-generating motion is equivalent to soul: for 'that which moves itself' is a definition of 'living thing' (894c–896a).

Soul, then, is prior to body, and it is soul, or rather souls, that control the heavens. If we ask how soul controls the sun, there seem to be three possible answers: either the sun itself has a soul, which resides in its globe in the way that our souls reside in our bodies; or there is a soul with a different body of its own, which is in contact with the sun and impels it on its course; or the soul is entirely immaterial, and guides the sun on its path by some spiritual force. However it does it, the soul is clearly a god of some kind, and Thales was right that the world is full of gods (898e–899b).

It remains to be proved both that the gods care for mankind and that they are not to be swayed by prayers or gifts. The main reason for doubting their care is that they seem to allow scoundrels to prosper in spite of their wickedness. But we cannot doubt that the gods that watch over the universe possess the virtues of wisdom, temperance, and courage; they cannot be conceived as being lazy or self-indulgent. Moreover, they know and see and hear everything, and they can do whatever is in the power of mortals or immortals. If they neglect our needs it must be either because they do not know about them, or because they have allowed temptation to distract them from the knowledge. But this is absurd: after all, taking care of our tiny affairs is child's play compared with the creation of the universe (899d–903a).

The prosperity of the wicked is only temporary and apparent. It has its place in the grand divine design: but no one will forever escape punishment for misdeeds, whether he flies to heaven or hides in hell (905a). Those who say that punishment can be bought off by gifts and prayers are treating the gods as if they were sheepdogs who would yield to bribery by the wolf (906b).

GOD

Aristotle's Unmoved Movers

Plato's argument for the priority of soul over body was the progenitor of a long series of arguments for the existence of God based on an analysis of motion and change. One of the earliest and most elaborate is the argument for the existence of a cosmic unmoved mover in the last two books of Aristotle's *Physics*, which is given a highly theological interpretation in his *Metaphysics Λ*.

The basic principle of Aristotle's argument is that everything that is in motion is moved by something else. At the beginning of book 7 of the *Physics* he presents a *reductio ad absurdum* of the idea of self-movement. A self-moving object must (*a*) have parts, in order to be in motion at all; (*b*) be in motion as a whole, and not just in one of its parts; and (*c*) originate its own motion. But this is impossible. From (*b*) it follows that if any part of the body is at rest, the whole of it is at rest. But if the whole body's being at rest depends upon a part's being at rest, then the motion of the whole body depends upon the motion of the part; and thus it does not originate its own motion. So that which was supposed to be moved by itself is not moved by itself (*Ph*. 8. 241^{b}34–242^{a}49).[2]

This argument contains two fallacies. The first is represented in my paraphrase by an equivocation in the expression 'depends on'. The motion of the whole is logically dependent on the motion of the part, but it is not necessarily causally dependent on it.[3] Moreover, there is a confusion between necessary and sufficient conditions. The part's being at rest is a sufficient condition for the whole's being at rest; but from this it follows only that the motion of the part is a necessary condition for the motion of the whole. The argument fails to prove that the motion of the alleged self-mover must have something else, namely the motion of the part, as a causally sufficient condition.

Aristotle goes on to derive from the premiss that everything in motion must be moved by something else the conclusion that there must be a first mover. Rather than consider immediately his argument against an infinite regress, it is more profitable to examine the fuller argument against self-movement which is presented in the subsequent, and final, book of the *Physics*. Here Aristotle observes at

[2] There is a problem with translating Aristotle's writings on motion. 'Move' in English may be transitive or intransitive: I may move someone out of my way, or move out of her way. The corresponding Greek verb has only a transitive sense, and to express the intransitive sense Greek uses the passive form of the verb. It is often therefore difficult to tell whether a particular sentence means 'X is moving' or 'X is being moved'—an ambiguity which is obviously crucial in a discussion of unmoved movement. To avoid the ambiguity in my discussion I use 'X is in motion' for the intransitive sense, and reserve 'X moves' for the transitive case in which an object could be supplied. Similarly with 'motion' and 'movement'. See my *The Five Ways* (London: Routledge, 1969), 8–9.

[3] See Sir David Ross, *Aristotle's Physics* (Oxford: Clarendon Press, 1936), 669.

234

the outset that it appears that some things in the world are self-moving, namely living beings (*empsycha*).

It sometimes happens that when there is no motion in us, from a state of rest we go into motion, that is to say motion originates in us from ourselves without any external agent moving us. This never happens with inanimate beings: it is always some other external thing that moves them; but an animal, we say, moves itself. Therefore, if an animal is ever completely at rest, we have a case of something motionless in which motion comes into being from the thing itself and not from without. Now if this can occur in an animal, why should not the same thing happen with the universe as a whole? (252^{b}18–25)

Aristotle goes on to offer a detailed and complicated argument to show that it cannot.

He offers a proof by cases that everything that is in motion is moved by something else. Motion may be divided into motion *per accidens* and motion per se. (If something is in motion because it is located in something else, like a sleeping man in a travelling ship, then its motion is *per accidens*. Another case of motion *per accidens* is where only a part of a thing is in motion, as when a man waves his hands.)

Motion *per accidens*, he seems to take for granted, is not self-movement (254^{b}7–11). Things that are in per se motion may be in motion of themselves, or because of other things; in the former case their motion is natural while in the latter it may be either natural (e.g. the upward motion of fire) or violent (the upward movement of a stone). It is clear, Aristotle believes, that violent motion must be derived from elsewhere than the thing itself. We may agree right away that a stone will not rise unless somebody throws it; but it is not obvious that once thrown it does not continue in motion of itself. Not so, Aristotle says; a thrower imparts motion not only to a projectile, but to the surrounding air, and in addition he imparts to the air a quasi-magnetic power of carrying the projectile further (266^{b}28–267^{a}3). It is clear, he thinks, that not only the violent but also the natural motions of inanimate bodies cannot be caused by those bodies themselves: if a falling stone was the cause of its own motion, it could stop itself falling (255^{a}5–8). There are two ways in which heavy and light bodies owe their natural motions to a moving agent. First, they rise and fall because that is their nature, and so they owe their motion to whatever gave them their nature; they are moved, he says, by their 'generator'. Thus, when fire heats water, a heavy substance, it turns it into steam, which is light, and being light, naturally rises; and thus the fire is the cause of the natural motion of the steam and can be said to move it. The steam, however, might be prevented from rising by an obstacle, e.g. the lid of a kettle. Someone who lifted the lid would be a different kind of mover, a *removens prohibens*, which we might call a 'liberator' (255^{b}31–256^{a}2).

But what about the natural motions of an animal: are they not a case of self-movement? All such cases seem to be explained by Aristotle as the action of one

GOD

part of the animal on another. If a whole animal moved its whole self, this, he implies, would be as absurd as someone being both the teacher and the learner of the same lesson, or the healer being identical with the person healed (257^{b}5). (But is this so absurd: may not the physician sometimes heal himself?) 'When a thing moves itself it is one part of it that is the mover and another part that is moved' (257^{b}13–14). But in the case of an animal, which part is the mover and which the moved? Presumably, the soul and the body.[4]

Having established to his satisfaction that nothing is in motion without being moved by something else, Aristotle has a number of arguments to show that there cannot be an infinite series of moved movers: we have to come to a halt with a first unmoved mover which is itself motionless. If it is true that when A is in motion there must be some B that moves A, then if B is itself in motion there must be some C moving B and so on. This series cannot go on for ever and so we must come to some X which moves without being in motion (7. 242^{a}54–^{b}54, 256^{a}4–29).

The details of Aristotle's long arguments are obscure and difficult to follow, but the most serious problem with his course of reasoning is to discover what kind of series he has in mind. The example he most often gives—a man using his hands to push a spade to turn a stone—suggests a series of simultaneous movers and moved. We may agree that there must be a first term of any such series if motion is ever to take place: but it is hard to see why this should lead us to a single cosmic unmoved mover, rather than to a multitude of human shakers and movers.[5] But Aristotle might, I suppose, respond that a human digger is himself in motion, and therefore must be moved by something else. But his earlier arguments did not show that whatever is in motion is *simultaneously* being moved by something else: the generators and liberators that were allowed in as causes of motion may have long since ceased to operate, and perhaps ceased to exist, while the motion they cause is still continuing.

Is the argument from the impossibility of infinite regress, then, meant to apply to a series of causes of motion stretching back through time? It is hard to see how Aristotle, who believed that the world had no beginning, can contest the impossibility of an infinite series of causes of motion in an everlasting universe perpetually changing. So whichever series we start from, we fail to reach any unchanging, wholly simple, cosmic mover such as Aristotle holds out as resembling the great Mind of Anaxagoras (256^{b}28).

It is such a being that Aristotle, in *Metaphysics* Λ, describes in theological terms. There must, he says, be an eternal motionless substance, to cause everlasting motion. This must lack matter—it cannot come into existence or go out of

---

[4] See S. Waterlow, *Nature, Change, and Agency in Aristotle's Physics* (Oxford: Clarendon Press, 1982), 66.
[5] Aristotle himself at one point seems to agree with this objection, and to treat a human digger as a self-mover (256^{a}8).

existence by turning into anything else—and it must lack potentiality—for the mere *power* to cause change would not ensure the sempiternity of motion. It must be simply actuality (*energeia*) (1071^{b}3–22). The revolving heavens, for Aristotle, lack the possibility of substantial change, but they possess potentiality, because each point of the heavens has the power to move elsewhere in its diurnal round. Since they are in motion, they need a mover; and this is a motionless mover. Such a mover could not act as an efficient cause, because that would involve a change in itself; but it can act as a final cause, an object of love, because being loved does not involve any change in the beloved, and so the mover can remain without motion. For this to be the case, of course, the heavenly bodies must have souls capable of feeling love for the ultimate mover. 'On such a principle', Aristotle says, 'depend the heavens and the world of nature' (1072^b).

What is the nature of the motionless mover? Its life must be like the very best in our life: and the best thing in our life is intellectual thought. The delight which we reach in moments of sublime contemplation is a perpetual state in the unmoved mover—which Aristotle is now prepared to call 'God' (1072^{b}15–25). 'Life, too, belongs to God; for the actuality of mind is life, and God is that actuality, and his essential actuality is the best and eternal life. We profess then that God is a living being, eternal and most good, so that life and continuous and eternal duration belong to God. That is what God is' (1072^{b}13–30). Aristotle is surprisingly insouciant about how many divine beings there are: sometimes (as above) he talks as if there was a single God; elsewhere he talks of gods in the plural, and often of 'the divine' in the neuter singular. Because of the intimate link between the celestial motions and the motionless mover(s) postulated to explain them, he seems to have regarded the question of the number of movers as a matter of astronomy rather than theology, and he was prepared to entertain the possibility of as many as forty-seven (1074^{a}13). This is far distant from the reasoned monotheism of Xenophanes.

Like Xenophanes, however, Aristotle was interested in the nature of the divine mind. A famous chapter (Λ 9) addresses the question: what does God think of? He must think of something, otherwise he is no better than a sleeping human; and whatever he is thinking of, he must think of throughout, otherwise he will be undergoing change, and contain potentiality, whereas we know he is pure actuality. Either he thinks of himself, or he thinks of something else. But the value of a thought is dictated by the value of what is thought of ; so if God were thinking of anything else than himself, he would be degraded to the level of what he is thinking of. So he must be thinking of himself, the supreme being, and his thinking is a thinking of thinking (*noesis noeseos*) (1074^b).

This conclusion has been much debated. Some have regarded it as a sublime truth about the divine nature; others have thought it a piece of exquisite nonsense. Among those who have taken the latter view, some have thought it the supreme absurdity of Aristotle's theology, others have thought that Aristotle himself intended it as a *reductio ad absurdum* of a fallacious line of argument, preparatory to showing that the object of divine thought was something quite different.[6]

Is it nonsense? If every thought must be a thought of something, and God can think only of thinking, then a thinking of a thinking would have to be a thinking of a thinking of, and that would have to be a thinking of a thinking of a thinking of . . . ad infinitum. That surely leads to a regress more vicious than any that led Aristotle to posit a motionless mover in the first place. But perhaps it is unfair to translate the Greek 'noesis' as 'thinking of'; it can equally well mean 'thinking that'. Surely there is nothing nonsensical about the thought 'I am thinking'; indeed Descartes built his whole philosophy upon it. So why should God not be thinking that he is thinking? Only, if that is his only thought, then he seems to be nothing very grand, to use Aristotle's words about the hypothetical God who thinks of nothing at all.

Whatever the truth about the object of thought of the motionless mover, it seems clear that it does not include the contingent affairs of the likes of us. On the basis of this chapter, then, it seems that if Aristotle had lived in Plato's Magnesia, he would have been condemned as one of the second class of atheists, those who believe that the gods exist but deny that they have any care for human beings.

The Gods of Epicurus and the Stoics

Someone who certainly fell into this class was Epicurus. In the letter to Menoecus he wrote:

Think of God as a living being, imperishable and blessed, along the main lines of the common idea of him, but attach to him nothing that is alien to imperishability or incompatible with blessedness. Believe about him everything that can preserve this imperishable bliss. There are indeed gods—the knowledge of them is obvious—but they are not such as most people believe them to be, because popular beliefs do not preserve them in bliss. The impious man is not he who denies the gods of the many, but he who fastens on the gods the beliefs of the many. (D.L. 123 LS 23B)

The belief that endangers the gods' imperishable bliss is precisely the belief that they take an interest in human affairs. To favour some human beings, to be angry with others, would interrupt the gods' life of happy tranquillity (Letter to Herodotus, D.L. 10. 76; Cicero, ND 1. 45). It is folly to think that the gods created the world for the sake of human beings. What profit could they take from our gratitude? What urge for novelty could tempt them to venture on creation after aeons of happy tranquillity (Cicero, ND 1. 21–3; Lucretius, RN 5. 165–9)? Does the world look, the Epicurean Lucretius asks, as if it had been created for the benefit of humans? Most

---

[6] See G. E. M. Anscombe, in Anscombe and P. T. Geach, *Three Philosophers* (Oxford: Blackwell, 1961), 59.

parts of the world have such inhospitable climates that they are uninhabitable, and the habitable parts yield crops only because of human toil. Disease and death carry off many before their time: no wonder that a newborn babe wails on entering this woeful world, in which wild beasts are more at home than human beings.

> Thus, like a sailor by the tempest hurled
> Ashore, the babe is shipwrecked on the world.
> Naked he lies, and ready to expire,
> Helpless of all that human wants require;
> Exposed upon unhospitable earth,
> From the first moment of his hapless birth.
> Straight with foreboding cries he fills the room
> (Too true presages of his future doom).
> But flocks and herds, and every savage beast,
> By more indulgent nature are increased:
> They want no rattles for their froward mood,
> Nor nurse to reconcile them to their food,
> With broken words; nor winter blasts they fear,
> Nor change their habits with the changing year;
> Nor, for their safety, citadels prepare,
> Nor forge the wicked instruments of war;
> Unlaboured earth her bounteous treasure grants,
> And nature's lavish hands supply their common wants.
>
> (*RN* 5. 195–228, trans. Dryden)

The sorry lot of humans is made worse, not better, by popular beliefs about the gods. Impressed by the vastness of the cosmos and the splendour of the heavenly bodies, terrified by thunderbolts and earthquakes, we imagine that nature is controlled by a race of vengeful celestial beings bent on punishing us for our misdeeds. We cower with terror, live in fear of death, and debase ourselves by prayer, prostration, and sacrifice (*RN* 5. 1194–1225).

Epicurus accepted the existence of gods because of the consensus of the human race: a belief so widespread and so basic must be implanted by nature and therefore be true. The substance of the consensus, he maintained, is that the gods are blessed and immortal, and therefore free from toil, anger, or favour. This knowledge is enough to enable human beings to worship with piety and without superstition. However, human curiosity wishes to go further and to find out what the gods look like, what they think, and how they live (Cicero, *ND* 1. 43–5).

The way in which nature imparts a conception of the gods, according to Epicurus, is this. Human beings had dreams, and sometimes saw visions, in which grand, handsome, and powerful beings appeared in human shape. These were then idealized, endowed with sensation, and conceived as immortal, blessed, and effortless (Lucretius, *RN* 1161–82). But even as idealized the gods retain human form, because that is the most beautiful of all animate shapes, and the only one in which reason is possible. The gods are not, however, beings of flesh and blood like us; they are made of tenuous quasi-flesh and quasi-blood. They are not tangible or visible, but perceptible only by the mind; and they do not live in any region of our world. Nonetheless, there are exactly as many immortals as there are mortals (Cicero, *ND* 1. 46–9; Lucretius, *RN* 5. 146–55).

It is not easy to harmonize all the elements of Epicurus' theology. One recent study attempts to do so by treating Epicurean gods as thought-constructs, the product of streams of images that by converging on our minds become our gods. The idealized concepts that result provide ethical paradigms for imitation; but there are no biologically immortal beings anywhere in the universe. On this interpretation, Epicurus would be an ancient anticipation of nineteenth-century thinkers such as George Eliot and Matthew Arnold, whose professed theism proves on inspection to be an essentially moral theory.[7] Ingenious and attractive though this interpretation is, it is clearly not how the matter was seen by either Lucretius or the Epicurean spokesman in Cicero's *On the Nature of the Gods*, who between them provide most of our information about his theology. These admirers both took Epicurus' repudiation of atheism at face value.

Undeniably, however, there were those in classical times who took the Epicurean system as tantamount to atheism, notably the Stoics (Cicero, *ND* 2. 25). Stoic piety itself, however, like Epicurean piety, was at some distance from popular polytheistic religion. From the point of view of the great monotheistic religions Epicureans and Stoics both err in theology: Epicureans by making God too distant from the real world and Stoics by making God too close to it. For the controlling thought of Stoic theology is the identification of God with providence, that is to say, the rationality of natural processes. This is an anticipation of Spinoza's *Deus sive Natura*.

Like the Epicureans, the Stoics began by appealing to the consensus of the human race that gods exist. The two schools also agree that one origin of popular belief in gods is terror of the violence of nature. From that point, however, the two theologies diverge. The Stoics, unlike the Epicureans, offered proofs of the existence of God, and sometimes the starting points of those proofs are the same as the starting point of Epicurean arguments against the operation of divine providence. Thus Cleanthes said that what brought the concept of God into men's minds was the benefit we gain from temperate climate and the earth's fertility (Cicero, *ND* 2. 12–13). Chrysippus, again, takes as a premiss that the fruits of the earth exist for the sake of animals, and animals exist for the sake of humans (*ND* 2. 37).

The most popular argument the Stoics offered was the one that later became known as the Argument from Design. The heavens move with regularity, and the sun and moon are beautiful as well as useful. Anyone entering a house, a gymnasium, or a forum, said Cleanthes, and seeing it functioning in good order, would know that there was someone in charge. A fortiori, the ordered progression

---

[7] See LS, i. 145–9.

of bodies so many and so great must be under the governance of some mind (*ND* 2. 15). The Stoics anticipated Paley's comparison of the world to a watch that calls for a watchmaker. The Stoic Posidonius had recently constructed a wondrous armillary sphere, modelling the movement of the sun and moon and the planets. If this was brought even to primitive Britain, no one there would doubt it was the product of reason. Surely the original thus modelled proclaims even more loudly that it is the product of a divine mind. Anyone who believes that the world is the result of chance might as well believe that if you threw enough letters of the alphabet into an urn and shook them out onto the ground you would produce a copy of the Annals of Ennius. So spoke Cicero's Stoic spokesman Balbus, centuries before anyone had though of the possibility of the works of Shakespeare being produced by battalions of typing monkeys (*ND* 2. 88).

Zeno, the founder of the Stoic school, was fertile in the production of arguments for the existence of God, or at least for the rationality of the world. 'The rational is superior to the non-rational. But nothing is superior to the world. Therefore the world is rational.' 'Nothing inanimate can generate something that is animate. But the world generates things that are animate; therefore the world is animate.' If an olive tree sprouted flutes playing in tune, he said, you would have to attribute a knowledge of music to the tree: why not then attribute wisdom to the universe which produces creatures that possess wisdom? (*ND* 2. 22).

One of Zeno's most original, if least convincing, arguments went like this. 'You may reasonably honour the gods. But you may not reasonably honour what does not exist. Therefore gods exist.' This recalls an argument I once came across in a discussion of the logic of imperatives: 'Go to church. If God does not exist, do not go to church. Therefore, God exists.' We are used to hearing prohibitions on deriving an 'ought' from an 'is'. It is less usual to find philosophers seeking to derive an 'is' from an 'ought'. However, throughout the ages philosophers have been eager to derive an 'is not' from an 'ought not': those who have propounded the problem of evil have been in effect arguing that the world ought not to be as it is, and therefore there is no God.

This problem was of particular interest to the Stoics. On the one hand, the doctrine of divine providence played an important part in their system, and providence may seem incompatible with the existence of evil. On the other hand, since for the Stoics vice is the only real evil, the problem seems more restricted in scope for them than it does for theists of other schools. But even so limited, it calls for a solution, and this Chrysippus found by appealing to a principle that contraries can exist only in coexistence with each other: justice with injustice, courage with cowardice, temperance with intemperance, and wisdom with folly (LS 54Q). The principle (adapted from one of Plato's arguments for immortality in the *Phaedo*) seems faulty: no doubt the concept of an individual virtue may be inseparable from the concept of the corresponding vice, but that does not show that both of the concepts must be instantiated.

The Stoics offered other less metaphysical responses to the problem of evil. Because they were determinists, the Stoics could not offer the freewill defence which has been a mainstay of Christian treatments of the topic. Instead, they offered two principal lines of defence: either the alleged evils were not really evil (even from a non-Stoic point of view) or they were unintended but unavoidable consequences of beneficent providential action. Along the first line, Chrysippus pointed out that bedbugs were useful for making us rise promptly, and mice are helpful in encouraging us to be tidy. Along the second he argued (borrowing once again from Plato) that in order to be a fit receptacle for reason, the human skull had to be very thin, which had the inevitable consequence that it would also be fragile (LS 54o, Q). Sometimes Chrysippus falls back on the argument that even in the best-regulated households a certain amount of dirt accumulates (LS 54s).

Whatever pains and inconveniences we suffer, Chrysippus maintained, the world exists for the sake of human beings. The gods made us for our own and each other's sakes, and animals for our sakes. Horses help us in war, and dogs in hunting, while bears and lions give us opportunities for courage. Other animals are there to feed us: the purpose of the pig is to produce pork. Some creatures exist simply so that we can admire their beauty: the peacock, for instance, was created for the sake of his tail (LS 54o, P).

Divine providence was extolled by Cleanthes in his majestic hymn to Zeus.

> O King of Kings
> Through ceaseless ages, God, whose purpose brings
> To birth, whate'er on land or in the sea
> Is wrought, or in high heaven's immensity;
> Save what the sinner works infatuate.
> Nay, but thou knowest to make the crooked straight:
> Chaos to thee is order: in thine eyes
> The unloved is lovely, who didst harmonise
> Things evil with things good, that there should be
> One Word through all things everlastingly.
>
> (LS 54I, trans. James Adam)

Cleanthes addresses Zeus in terms that would be appropriate enough for a devout Jew or Christian praying to the Lord God. But the underlying Stoic conception of God is very different from that of the monotheistic religions. God, according to the Stoics, is material, himself a constituent of the cosmos, fuelling it and ordering it from within as a 'designing fire'. God's life is identical with the history of the universe, as it evolves and develops.

The doctrine of Chrysippus is thus described by Cicero:

He says that divine power resides in reason, and in the soul and mind of the whole of nature. He calls the world itself god, and the all-pervasive World-Soul, or the dominant part of that soul that is located in mind and reason. He also calls god the universal, all-embracing, common nature of things, and also the power of fate and the necessity of future events. (*ND* 1. 39)

God can be identified with the elements of earth, water, air, and fire, and in these forms he can be called by the names of the traditional gods of Olympus. As earth, he is Demeter; as water and air, Poseidon; as fire or ether, he is Zeus, who is also identified with the everlasting law that is the guide of our life and the governess of our duties (*ND* 1. 40). As described by Cicero, Chrysippus' religion is neither monotheism nor polytheism: it is polymorphous pantheism.

On Divination and Astrology

One doctrine of the Stoics that Cicero vigorously contested was their belief in divination. His dialogue *On Divination* takes the form of a conversation between his brother and himself, with Quintus Cicero defending divination and claiming that religion stands or falls with the belief in it, while Marcus Cicero denies the equivalence and denounces divination as puerile superstition. Quintus draws some of his material from Chrysippus, who wrote two books on divination, and collected lists of veridical oracles and dreams (*D* 1. 6), while Marcus is indebted for many of his arguments to the Academic sceptic Carneades.

Divination—the attempt to predict future events which on the face of them are fortuitous—was practised in Rome in many ways: by the study of the stars, the observation of the flight of birds, by the inspection of the entrails of sacrificed animals, by the interpretation of dreams, and by the consultation of oracles. Not all of these modes of divination are fashionable in the modern world, but Cicero's consideration of astrology is still, sadly, relevant.

Quintus heaps up anecdotes of remarkable predictions by augurs, soothsayers, and the like, and argues that in principle they are acting no differently from the rest of us when we predict the weather from the behaviour of birds and frogs or the copiousness of berries on bushes. In both cases we do not know the reason that links sign and signified, but we do know that there is one, just as when someone throws double sixes a hundred times in succession we know it is not pure chance. Not all soothsayers' predictions come true: but then doctors too make mistakes from time to time. We may not understand how they make their predictions, but then we don't understand the operation of the magnet either (*D* 1. 86).

Quintus confirms his empirical evidence with an a priori argument drawn from the Stoics. If the gods know the future, and do not tell it to us, then they do not love us, or they think such knowledge will be useless, or they are powerless to communicate with us. But each of these alternatives is absurd. They must know the future, since the future is what they themselves decree. So they must communicate the future to us, and they must give us the power to understand the communication: and that power is the art of divination (*D* 1. 82–3). Belief in divination is not superstitious but scientific, because it goes hand in hand with the acceptance of a single united series of interconnected causes. It is that series that the Stoics call Fate (*D* 1. 125–6).

Marcus Cicero begins his reply in a down-to-earth manner. If you want to know what colour a thing is, you had better ask somebody sighted rather than a blind seer like Tiresias. If you are sick, call a doctor, not a soothsayer. If you want cosmology, you should go to a physicist, and if you want moral advice, seek a philosopher, not a diviner. If you want a weather forecast trust a pilot rather than a prophet.

If an event is a genuine matter of chance, then it cannot be foretold, for in chance cases there is no equivalent of the causal series that enables astronomers to predict eclipses (*D* 2. 15). On the other hand, if future events are fated, then foreknowledge of a future disaster will not enable one to avoid it, and the gods are kinder to keep such knowledge from us. Julius Caesar would not have enjoyed a preview of his own body stabbed and untended at the foot of Pompey's statue. The predictions that divines offer us contradict each other: as Cato said, it is a wonder that when one soothsayer meets another they can keep a straight face (*D* 2. 52).

To match Quintus' list of prophecies, Marcus compiles a dossier of cases where the advice of divines was falsified or disastrous: both Pompey and Caesar, for instance, had happy deaths foretold to them. Cicero treats portents rather as Humeans were later to treat miracles. 'It can be argued against all portents that whatever was impossible to happen never in fact happened; and if what happened was something possible, it is no cause for wonder' (*D* 2. 49). Mere rarity does not make a portent: a wise man is harder to find than a mule in foal.

The best astronomers, Cicero says, avoid astrological prediction. The belief that men's careers are predictable from the position of stars at their birth is worse than folly: it is unbelievable madness. Twins often differ in career and fortune. The observations on which predictions are based are quite erratic: astrologers have no real idea of the distances between heavenly bodies. The rising and setting of stars is something that is relative to an observer: so how can it affect alike all those born at the same time? A person's ancestry is a better predictor of character than anything in the stars. If astrology was sound, why did not all the people born at the same moment as Homer write an *Iliad*? Did all the Romans who fell in battle at Cannae have the same horoscope (*D* 2. 94, 97)?

Finally, Cicero ridicules the idea that dreams may foretell the future. We sleep every night and almost every night we dream: is it any wonder that dreams sometimes come true? It would be foolish of the gods to send messages by dreams, even if they had time to flit about our beds. Most dreams turn out false, and so sensible people pay no attention to them. Since we possess no key to interpret dreams, for the gods to speak to us through them would be like an ambassador addressing the Senate in an African dialect.

With surprisingly little embarrassment, Cicero admits that he himself has acted as an augur—but only, he says, 'out of respect for the opinion of the masses and in the course of service to the state'. He would have sympathized with the atheist bishops of Enlightenment France. But he concludes by insisting that he is not himself an atheist: it is not only respect for tradition, but the order of the heavens and the beauty of the universe that makes him confess that there is a sublime eternal being that humans must look up to and admire. But true religion is best served by rooting out superstition (*D* 2. 149).

The Trinity of Plotinus

Philosophical theology in the ancient world culminates in the system of Plotinus. It is thus summed up by Bertrand Russell: 'The metaphysics of Plotinus begins with a Holy Trinity: The One, Spirit and Soul. These three are not equal, like the Persons of the Christian Trinity; the One is supreme, Spirit comes next, and Soul last.'[8] The comparison with the Christian Trinity is inescapable; and indeed Plotinus, who died before the church councils of Nicaea and Constantinople gave a definitive statement of the relationships between the three divine persons, undoubtedly had an influence on the thought of some of the Church fathers. But for the understanding of his own thought it is more rewarding to look backwards. With some qualification it can be said that the One is a Platonic God, Intellect (a more appropriate translation for *nous* than 'spirit') is an Aristotelian God, and Soul is a Stoic God.

The One is a descendant of the One of the *Parmenides* and the Idea of Good in the *Republic*. The paradoxes of the *Parmenides* are taken as adumbrations of an ultimately ineffable reality, which is, like the Idea of the Good, 'beyond being in power and dignity'. 'The One', it should be stressed, is not, for Plato and Plotinus, a name for the first of the natural number series: rather, it means that which is utterly simple and undivided, all of a piece, and utterly unique (Ennead 6, 9. 1 and 6). In saying that the One and the Good (Plotinus uses both names, e.g. 6. 9. 3) is beyond being he does not mean that it does not exist: on the contrary it is the most real thing there is. He means that no predicates can be applied to it: we cannot say that it *is* this, or it *is* that. The reason for this is that if any predicate was true of it, then there would have to be a distinction within it corresponding to the distinction between the subject and the predicate of the true sentence. But that would derogate from the One's sublime simplicity (5. 3. 13).

Being has a kind of shape of being, but the One has no shape, not even intelligible shape. For since its nature is generative of all things, the One is none of them. It is not of any kind, has no size or quality, is not intellect or soul. It is neither moving nor stationary, and it is in

---

[8] *A History of Western Philosophy* (London: Allen & Unwin, 1961), 292.

neither place nor time; in Plato's words it is 'by itself alone and uniform'—or rather formless and prior to form as it is prior to motion and rest. For all these are properties of being, making it manifold. (6. 9. 3. 38–45)

If no predicates can be asserted of the One, it is not surprising if we enmesh ourselves in contradiction when we try to do so. Being, for a Platonist, is the realm of what we can truly know—as against Becoming, which is the object of mere belief. But if the One is beyond being, it is also beyond knowledge. 'Our awareness of it is not through science or understanding, as with other intelligible objects, but by way of a presence superior to knowledge.' Such awareness is a mystical vision like the rapture of a lover in the presence of his beloved (6. 9. 4. 3 ff.).

Because the One is unknowable, it is also ineffable. How then can we talk about it, and what is Plotinus doing writing about it? Plotinus puts the question to himself in Ennead 5, 3. 14, and gives a rather puzzling answer.

We have no knowledge or concept of it, and we do not say it, but we say something about it. How then do we speak about it, if we do not grasp it? Does our having no knowledge of it mean that we do not grasp it at all? We do grasp it, but not in such a way as to say it, only to speak about it.

The distinction between saying and speaking about is puzzling. Could what Plotinus says here about the One be said about some perfectly ordinary thing like a cabbage? I cannot say or utter a cabbage; I can only talk about it. What is meant here by 'say', I think, is something like 'call by a name' or 'attribute predicates to'. This I can do with a cabbage, but not with the One. And the Greek word whose standard translation is 'about' can also mean 'around'. Plotinus elsewhere says that we cannot even call the One 'it' or say that it 'is'; we have to circle around it from outside (6. 3. 9. 55).

Any statement about the One is really a statement about its creatures. We are well aware of our own frailty: our lack of self-sufficiency and our shortfall from perfection (6. 9. 6. 15–35). In knowing this we can grasp the One in the way that one can tell the shape of a missing piece in a jigsaw puzzle by knowing the shape of the surrounding pieces. Or, to use a metaphor closer to Plotinus' own, when we in thought circle around the One we grasp it as an invisible centre of gravity. Most picturesquely, Plotinus says:

It is like a choral dance. The choir circles round the conductor, sometimes facing him and sometimes looking the other way; it is when they are facing him that they sing most beautifully. So too, we are always around him—if we were not we would completely vanish and no longer exist—but we are not always facing him. When we do look to him in our divine dance around him, then we reach our goal and take our rest and sing in perfect tune. (6. 9. 38–45)

We turn from the One to the second element of the Plotinian trinity, Intellect (*nous*). Like Aristotle's God, Intellect is pure activity, and cannot think of anything outside itself, since this would involve potentiality. But its activity is not a mere thinking of thinking—whether or not that was Aristotle's doctrine—it is a thinking of all the Platonic Ideas (5. 9. 6). These are not external entities: as Aristotle himself had laid down as a universal rule, the actuality of intellect and the actuality of intellect's object is one and the same. So the life of the Ideas is none other than the activity of Intellect. Intellect is the intelligible universe, containing forms not only of universals but also of individuals (5. 9. 9; 5. 7).

Despite the identity of the thinker and the thought, the multiplicity of the Ideas means that Intellect does not possess the total simplicity which belongs to the One. Indeed, it is this complexity of Intellect that convinced Plotinus that there must be something else prior to it and superior to it. For, he believed, every form of complexity must ultimately depend on something totally simple.[9]

The intellectual cosmos is, indeed, boundlessly rich.

> In that world there is no stinting nor poverty, but everything is full of life, boiling over with life. Everything flows from a single fount, not some special kind of breath or warmth, but rather a single quality containing unspoilt all qualities, sweetness of taste and smell, wine on the palate and the essence of every aroma, visions of colours and every tangible feeling, and every melody and every rhythm that hearing can absorb. (6. 7. 12. 22–30)

This is the world of Being, Thought, and Life; and though it is the world of Intellect, it also contains desire as an essential element. Thinking is indeed itself desire, as looking is a desire of seeing (5. 6. 5. 8–10). Knowledge too is desire, but satisfied desire, the consummation of a quest (5. 3. 10. 49–50). In the Intellect desire is 'always desiring and always attaining its desire' (3. 8. 11. 23–4).

How does Intellect originate? Undoubtedly Intellect derives its being from the One: the One neither is too jealous to procreate, nor loses anything by what it gives away. But beyond that Plotinus' text suggests two rather different accounts. In some places he says that Intellect emanates from the One in the way that sweet odours are given off by perfume, or that light emanates from the sun. This will remind Christian readers of the Nicene Creed's proclamation that the Son of God is light from light (4. 8. 6. 10). But elsewhere Plotinus speaks of Intellect as 'daring to apostatize from the One' (6. 9. 5. 30). This makes Intellect seem less like the Word of the Christian Trinity, and more like Milton's Lucifer.

From Intellect proceeds the third element, Soul. Here too Plotinus talks of a revolt or falling away, an arrogant desire for independence, which took the form of a craving for metabolism (5. 1. 1. 3–5). Soul's original sin is well described thus by A. H. Armstrong:

> It is a desire for a life different from that of Intellect. The life of Intellect is a life at rest in eternity, a life of thought in eternal, immediate, and simultaneous possession of all possible

---

[9] Dominic O'Meara, to whose *Plotinus: An Introduction to the Enneads* (Oxford: Clarendon Press, 1993) I am much indebted, calls this the Principle of Prior Simplicity (p. 45).

objects. So the only way of being different which is left for Soul is to pass from eternal life to a life in which, instead of all things being present at once, one thing comes after another, and there is a succession, a continuous series, of thoughts and actions.[10]

This continuous, restless, succession is time: time is the life of the soul in its transitory passage from one episode of living to the next (3. 7. 11. 43–5).

Soul is the immanent, controlling element in the universe of nature, just as God was in the Stoic system, but unlike the Stoic God Soul is incorporeal. Intellect was the maker of the universe, like the Demiurge of the *Timaeus*, but Soul is intellect's agent in managing its development. Soul links the intelligible world with the world of the senses, having an inner element that looks upwards to Intellect and an external element that looks downwards to Nature (3. 8. 3). Nature is the immanent principle of development in the material world: Soul, looking at it, sees there its own reflection. The physical world that Nature weaves is a thing of wonder and beauty even though its substance is such as dreams are made of (3. 8. 4).

Plotinus' theological system is undoubtedly impressive: but we may wonder whatever kind of argument he can offer to persuade us to accept it. To understand this, we have to explore the system from the bottom up, instead of looking from the top down: we must start not with the One, but with matter, the outermost limit of reality. Plotinus takes his start from widely accepted Platonic and Aristotelian principles. He understands Aristotle as having argued that the ultimate substratum of change must be something which possesses none of the properties of the changeable bodies we see and handle. But a matter which possesses no material properties, Plotinus argued, is inconceivable.

If we dispense with Aristotelian matter, we are left with Aristotelian forms. The most important such forms were souls, and it is natural to think that there are as many souls as there are individual people. But here Plotinus appeals to another Aristotelian thesis: the principle that forms are individuated by matter. If we have given up matter, we have to conclude that there is only a single soul.

To prove that this soul is prior to and independent of body, Plotinus uses very much the same arguments as Plato used in the *Phaedo*. He neatly reverses the argument of those who claim that soul is dependent on body because it is nothing more than an attunement of the body's sinews. When a musician plucks the strings of a lyre, he says, it is the strings, not the melody, that he acts on: but the strings would not be plucked unless the melody called for it.

How can an incorruptible World-Soul be in any way present to individual corruptible bodies? Plotinus, who liked marine metaphors, explained this in two different ways. The World-Soul he once compared to a man standing up in the sea, with half his body in the water and half in the air. But he thought that we should

[10] A. H. Armstrong (ed.), *The Cambridge History of Later Greek and Early Medieval Philosophy* (Cambridge: Cambridge University Press, 1970), 251.

really ask not how soul is in body, but how body is in soul. Body floats in soul, as a net floats in the sea (4. 3. 9. 36–42). Without metaphor, we can say that body is in soul by depending upon it for its organization and continued existence.

Soul governs the world wisely and well, but the wisdom that it exercises in the governance of the world is not native to it, but must come from outside. It cannot come from the material world, since that is what it shapes; it must come from something that is by nature linked to the Ideas that are the models or patterns for intelligent activity. This can only be a world-mind or Intellect.

We have already encountered the arguments whereby Plotinus shows that Intellect cannot be the ultimate reality because of the duality of subject and object and because of the multiplicity of the Ideas. Thus, at the end of our journey, we reach the one and only One.

Plotinus' theology continued to be taught, with modifications, until Western pagan philosophy came to an end with the closure of the school of Athens. But his influence lived on, and lives on, unacknowledged, through the ideas that were absorbed and transmitted by his first Christian readers. Most important of these was Augustine, who read him as a young man in the translation of Marius Victorinus. The reading set him on the course which led to his conversion to Christianity, and his *Confessions* and *On the Trinity* contain echoes of Plotinus on many a page. In the last days of his life, we are told, when the Vandals were besieging Hippo, he consoled himself with a quotation from the Enneads: 'How can a man be taken seriously if he attaches importance to the collapse of wood and stones, or to the death—God help us—of mortal creatures?' (1. 4. 7. 24–5).

Part Two

Medieval Philosophy

CONTENTS OF PART TWO

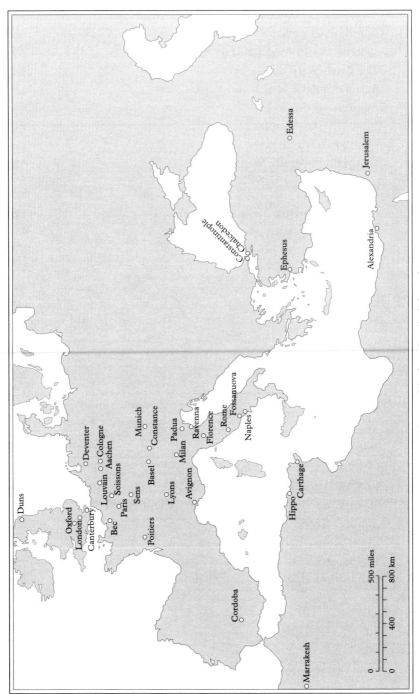

The world of medieval philosophy

INTRODUCTION TO PART TWO

Not so long ago, in many universities, courses in the history of philosophy went straight from Aristotle to Descartes, leaping over late antiquity and the Middle Ages. There was a widespread belief in academic circles that medieval philosophy was not worth studying. This belief was not usually based on any close acquaintance with the relevant texts: it was more likely to be an unexamined inheritance of religious or humanist prejudice.

There were, however, many genuine obstacles that made medieval philosophy less accessible than the philosophy of any other age. We may identify three significant barriers that have to be surmounted if one is to come to grips with the thought of the philosophers of the Middle Ages: the linguistic, the professional, and the confessional or the parochial.

The philosophy of the high Middle Ages is written in Latin that even those well trained in classical Latin find very difficult to comprehend. Even Thomas Aquinas presents initial difficulties to a reader brought up on Livy and Cicero, and Aquinas is a model of simple lucidity by comparison with most of his colleagues and successors. It is only in recent years that translations into English of medieval writers have become widely available, and the task of translation is not a trivial one. Scholastic Latin is full of technical neologisms that are hard to render into other languages without cumbrous paraphrase. It is true that many of these neologisms, transliterated, survive into modern languages, and often into everyday use (for example, 'intelligence', 'evidence', 'voluntary', 'supposition'). But the modern use is never an exact equivalent of the scholastic use, and often differs from it widely. 'Subjective' and 'objective', for instance, are two terms that have virtually reversed their meanings since medieval times.

This first, linguistic, problem is closely connected with the second problem of professionalism. The study of philosophy was more professionalized during the Middle Ages than at any other time before the present—hence the term 'scholastic'. Philosophy was the province of tight university communities sharing a common curriculum, a common patrimony of texts, and a common arsenal of technical terms. Most of the works that have come down to us are, in one way or another, the product of university lectures, exercises, or debates, and those who produced them could expect in their hearers or readers a familiarity with a complicated jargon and an ability to pick up erudite allusion. There was hardly any philosophy written for the general reader. Those who wrote or read it were overwhelmingly male, clerical, and celibate. An appendix to the *Cambridge History of Later Medieval Philosophy* gives brief biographies of the sixty-six most significant figures in medieval thought. None of them is a woman, and only two are laymen.

The third problem, again, is related to the second. Because most of the great medieval philosophers were members of the Catholic Church, their philosophy has often been regarded as a branch of theology or apologetics. This is unfair: they were all aware of the distinction between philosophical argument and dogmatic evangelism. But it is true that, since most of them concluded their academic career in the faculty of divinity, much of their best philosophical work is actually contained in their theological works, and it takes some experience to locate it.

Moreover, most of the thinkers were members of religious orders, who have often been possessive of their heritage. There have been long periods when it seemed that all and only Dominicans studied St Thomas, and all and only Franciscans studied Bonaventure and Scotus. (Some scholastics were hardly studied because they belonged to no order. John Wyclif, for instance, had as his spiritual heirs only the rather small class consisting of secular clergy who had got into trouble with the Church.) After Pope Leo XIII gave Aquinas special status as a Catholic theologian, his works were studied by many who had no connection with the Dominican order. But this elevation only reinforced the view of secular philosophers that he was an essentially ecclesiastical spokesman. Moreover, within the realm of Catholic scholarship it fostered the view that only Aquinas was worth taking seriously as a philosopher. The gradual abandonment of some of his teaching in the later Middle Aages was seen as a key factor in the decline of the church that led to the Reformation. A philosophical debate between Scotus and Ockham, from this perspective, was like a wresting match between two men standing on the edge of a cliff from which they were both about to fall to their doom.

One effect of the professionalism and confessionalism of scholastic philosophy is that, by comparison with earlier and later writers, medieval philosophers appear as rather anonymous figures. It is not just that in some cases we have very little external information about their lives: it is that their own writings betray comparatively little of their own personalities. They produce few original monographs; most of their effort goes into commenting on, and continuing, the work of their predecessors in their order or in the Church. The whole edifice of scholasticism is like a medieval cathedral: the creation of many different craftsmen who, however individually gifted, took little pains to identify which parts of the overall structure were their own unaided work. Often it is only in the spontaneous disputations called *quodlibets* that we feel we can come close to a living individual in action.

This generalization, of course, applies only to the high Middle Ages under the dominance of scholasticism. In the pre-scholastic period we meet philosophers who are highly colourful personalities, not constructed out of any template. Augustine, Abelard, and even Anselm are closer to the romantic paradigm of the philosopher as a solitary genius than they are to any ideal of a humble operative adding his stone to the communal cairn.

My own training in philosophy began at the Gregorian University in Rome, which, in the 1950s, still aimed to teach philosophy *ad mentem Sancti Thomae* in accordance with the instructions of recent popes. I was grateful to two of my professors there, Fr Bernard Lonergan and Fr Frederick Copleston, for teaching me that St Thomas's own writings were much more worth reading than popular Thomists' textbooks, and that St Thomas was not the only medieval thinker who deserved attentive study.

After studying at the Gregorian, I did graduate work in philosophy at Oxford in the heyday of ordinary language philosophy. I found this much more congenial than Roman scholasticism, but I was fortunate to meet Professor Peter Geach and Fr Herbert McCabe OP, who showed me that many of the problems exercising philosophers in the analytic tradition at that time were very similar to those studied, often with no less sophistication, by medieval philosophers and logicians.

In many ways, indeed, the keen interest in the logical analysis of ordinary language that was characteristic of Oxford in the latter part of the twentieth century brought it closer to medieval methods and concerns than any other era of post-Renaissance philosophy. But this was still not widely appreciated. William Kneale, for instance, an Oxford professor of logic who wrote a well-informed and sympathetic survey of medieval logic, had this to say about the development of medieval philosophy between 1200 and 1400:

We shall not try to decide here whether the result justified the great intellectual effort that produced it. Perhaps the systems of St Thomas Aquinas and John Duns the Scot deserve only the reluctant admiration we give to the pyramids of Egypt and the palace of Versailles. And it may be that the thousands of young men who wrestled with subtle abstractions at the medieval universities would have been better employed in the literary studies which were then thought fit only for grammar schools.[1]

It was, in fact, in the area of logic that it was first appreciated that the study of medieval texts had much to offer. Medieval logicians had addressed questions that had fallen into oblivion after the Renaissance, and many of their insights had to be rediscovered during the twentieth-century rebirth of logic. The *Cambridge History of Later Medieval Philosophy* brought this to the attention of a wide public, and inaugurated a new phase in the reception of medieval philosophy in the general, secular, academic world.

The person most responsible for the growth of interest in medieval philosophy in the last decades of the twentieth century was the principal editor of that volume, Norman Kretzmann. Kretzmann's teaching in the Sage School at Cornell bred up a brilliant group of younger scholars who in recent years have published widely and well on many topics of medieval philosophy. Paradoxically, one effect

---

[1] W. Kneale and M. Kneale, *The Development of Logic* (Oxford: Oxford University Press, 1962), 226.

of the new medieval interest was a downgrading of Thomas Aquinas. In the *Cambridge History*, for example, his index entry is not as long as the entry for *sophismata*. Kretzmann came to realize and remedy this defect, and spent the last years of his life writing two magisterial books on St Thomas's *Summa contra Gentiles*.

Aquinas, in my view, retains the right to be classed as the greatest philosopher of the high Middle Ages. But he is an outstanding peak in a mountain range that has several other resplendent summits. Medieval philosophy is above all a continuum, and when one reads an individual philosopher, whether Abelard, Aquinas, or Ockham, one is taking a sounding of an ongoing process. And one soon learns that between every two major peaks there are minor ones that are not negligible: between Aquinas and Scotus, for instance, stands Henry of Ghent, and between Scotus and Ockham stands Henry of Harclay.

A historian of the ancient world can read, without too great exhaustion, the entire surviving corpus of philosophical writing. Such a feat would be well beyond the powers of even the most conscientious historian of medieval philosophy. Augustine, Abelard, and the great Scholastics were such copious writers that it takes decades to master the entire output of even a single one of them. Consequently, anyone who undertakes a work such as the present must be heavily dependent on secondary sources, even if only for drawing attention to the best way to take soundings of the primary sources. I here acknowledge my own debt to the writers listed in my bibliography, from my teacher Fr Copleston (whose history of philosophy still bears comparison with many works written since) to the most recent monographs written by colleagues and pupils of Norman Kretzmann. My debt to others is particularly heavy in the area of Islamic philosophy, since I do not know Arabic. In the course of writing this I had cause to regret deeply that it is only in Latin that I can read the work of Avicenna, whose genius and influence I have come to realize ever more.

1

Philosophy and Faith: Augustine to Maimonides

In the first part of this history we traced the development of philosophy in the ancient world up to the conversion of St Augustine at the end of the fourth century of our era. The life of Augustine marks an epoch in the history of ideas. In his early life he imbibed from several sources philosophical ideas of various traditions, but especially the Platonic tradition, whether in the sceptical version of the New Academy or in the metaphysical version of Neoplatonism. After his conversion to Christianity he developed, in a number of massive treatises, a synthesis of Jewish, Greek, and Christian ideas that was to provide the backdrop for the next millennium of Western philosophical thought.

From a philosophical point of view, the most fertile period of Augustine's life was the period just before and just after his baptism as a Christian at Easter 387. Between his conversion and his baptism he spent several months in private preparation with friends and members of his family at Cassiciacum, a country villa north of Milan. This period produced a number of works that resemble verbatim transcripts of live discussions, notably the *Contra Academicos*, which seeks to sift the true from the false in scepticism.

Augustine also invented a new art-form to which he gave the name 'Soliloquies'. He wrote a dialogue with himself in which the two characters are named Augustine and Reason. Reason asks Augustine what he wishes to know. 'I want to know God and the soul,' Augustine replies. 'Nothing more?' 'Nothing at all' (*S* 1. 2. 7).

Reason promises to make God appear as clearly to his mind as the sun does to his eyes. For this purpose the eyes of the soul must be cleansed of all desire for mortal things. Augustine in the dialogue renounces the pursuit of riches, honour, and sexual pleasure (this last renunciation vividly described). Reason does not yet keep the promise to display God, but it does offer Augustine a proof of the immortality of his soul. Consider the notion of truth. True things may pass away, but truth itself is everlasting. Even if the world ceased to exist, it would still be true that the world has ceased to exist. But truth has its home in the soul, so the soul, like truth, must be immortal (*S* 1. 15. 28, 2. 15. 28).

After his baptism Augustine remained in Italy for a year and a half. In this period he wrote a further brief tract on the immortality of the soul, and a more substantial work, *On the Freedom of the Will*, which we encountered in the first part of this history. In 388 he returned to Africa and for the next few years lived the life of a private gentleman in his home town of Tagaste. In 391 he found his final vocation and was ordained priest, becoming soon after bishop of Hippo in Algeria, where he resided until his death in 430.

The great majority of his works were written during this final period of his life. He was a copious writer, and has left behind some 5 million words. Much of his output consists of sermons, Bible commentaries, and controversial tracts about theology or Church discipline. He no longer wrote philosophical pieces comparable to those of the years of his conversion. But a number of his major works contain material of high philosophical interest.

In 397 Augustine wrote a work entitled *Confessions*: a prayerful dialogue with God tracing the course of his life from childhood to conversion. It is not an autobiography of the normal kind, though it is the foundation specimen of the genre. Besides being the main source of our knowledge of Augustine's pre-episcopal life, it contains many incidental philosophical reflections and concludes with a full-fledged monograph on the nature of time.[1] Its enchanting style has always made it the most popular of Augustine's works.

Between 400 and 417 Augustine worked on another masterpiece, fifteen books entitled *On the Trinity*. The earlier books of the treatise are largely concerned with the analysis of biblical and ecclesiastical texts concerning the mystery of three persons in one God. Philosophers find matter of much greater interest in the subtle portrayal of human psychology employed in the later books in the course of a search for an analogy of the heavenly Trinity in the hearts and minds of men and women.[2]

Augustine on History

The most massive and most laborious of Augustine's works was *The City of God*, on which he worked from 413 to 426. Written at a time when the Roman Empire was under threat from successive barbarian invasions, it was the first great synthesis of classical and Christian thought. This is implicit in the very title of the work. The Christian gospels have much to say about the Kingdom of God; but for Greece and Rome the paradigm political institution was not the kingdom but the city. Even emperors liked to think of themselves as the first citizens of a city; and the

---

[1] See Ch. 5 below.   [2] See Ch. 7 below.

philosophical emperor Marcus Aurelius thought the city we should love above all was the city of Zeus. *The City of God* sets Jesus, the crucified King of the Jews, at the apex of the idealized city-state of pagan philosophy.

Like Aristotle in his *Metaphysics*, Augustine surveys the history of philosophy from the distant days of Thales, showing how earlier philosophers approximated to, but fell short of, the truth that he now presents. But whereas Aristotle was mainly interested in the physical theories of his predecessors, Augustine is concerned above all with their philosophical theology—their 'natural' theology, as he called it, giving currency to an expression with a long history ahead of it (*DCD* VIII. 1–9). Throughout the work Augustine sets Christian teaching side by side with the best of ancient philosophy, and especially with the writing of his favourites, the Neoplatonists, whom he regarded as almost-Christians (*DCD* VIII. 8–9). An engaging instance is the following:

Plotinus uses the beauty of flowers and leaves to show that the providence of God—whose beauty is beyond words and visible only to the mind—extends even to lowly and earthly things. These castaways, he argues, doomed to swift decay, could not display such delicate patterns if they did not draw their shapes from a realm in which a mental and unchangeable form holds them all together in a unity. And this is what the Lord Jesus tells us when he says 'Consider the lilies of the field, how they grow; they toil not, neither do they spin: and yet I say unto you that even Solomon in all his glory was not arrayed like one of these. Wherefore, if God so clothe the grass of the field, which today is, and tomorrow is cast into the oven, shall he not much more clothe you, o ye of little faith?' (*DCD* X. 14; cf. Plotinus, *Enneads* 3. 2. 13; Matt. 6: 28–9).

But while Augustine is prepared to read Platonism into the Sermon on the Mount, he has little sympathy with attempts to give philosophical and allegorical interpretations of traditional Roman religion. The original impetus for the composition of *The City of God*—which took thirteen years to complete—came from the sack of Rome by Gothic invaders. Pagans blamed this disaster on the Christians' abolition of the worship of the city's gods, who had therefore abandoned it in its hour of need. Augustine devoted the first books of his treatise to showing that the gods of classical Rome were vicious and impotent and that their worship was disgusting and depraving.

The Romans had long identified their senior gods—Jupiter, Juno, Venus, and the like—with the characters of the Homeric pantheon, such as Zeus, Hera, and Aphrodite. Augustine follows Plato and Cicero in denouncing as blasphemous the myths that represent such deities as engaged in arbitrary, cruel, and indecent behaviour. He mocks too at the proliferation of lesser gods in popular Roman superstition: is heaven so bureaucratized, he asks, so that while to look after a house a single human porter suffices, we need no less than three gods: Forculus to guard the doors, Cardea for the hinges, and Limentinus for the threshold? (*DCD* IV. 18). The identification and individuation of these minor divinities raise a number of philosophical problems, which Augustine illustrates. More often he uses against late Roman paganism the weapon of erudite sarcasm that Gibbon, thirteen centuries later, was to deploy so teasingly against historic Christianity.

A brief, eloquent, survey of the history of the Roman Republic suffices to show that the worship of the ancient Gods does not guarantee security from disasters. The eventual unparalleled greatness of the Roman Empire, Augustine says, was the reward given by the one true God to the virtues of the best among the citizens. 'They placed no value on their own wealth in comparison with the common-wealth and the public purse; they shunned avarice and gave freely of themselves to the fatherland; they were guilty of no breach of law or licentious conduct. Thus by a sure way they strove towards honour, power, and glory' (DCD V. 15). The reward which they sought has come to them: they were able to impose their law on many nations and they are renowned in the annals of many people. But they have no part in the heavenly city, for they did not worship the one true God, and they aimed only at self-glorification.

A large part of Augustine's attack on Roman religion focuses on the degrading nature of the public spectacles held in honour of the gods. No doubt many a modern liberal would be no less disgusted than Augustine at much of what went on in Roman theatres and amphitheatres. She would probably be more shocked by the cruelty of Roman entertainment than by its indecency; with Augustine it appears to have been the other way round.

Augustine does not regard the gods of pagan myth as complete fictions. On the contrary, he thinks that they are wicked spirits who take advantage of human superstition to divert to themselves worship that is due only to the one true God (DCD VII. 33). Several Platonists had spoken of a threefold classification of rational beings: gods, men, and *daimones* (demons). Gods dwelt in heaven, men on earth, and demons in the air between. Demons were like gods in being immortal, but like men in being subject to passions. Many demons are bad, but some are good, such as the *daimon* who was the familiar of Socrates.[3] Good demons, these Platonists thought, could be of service as intermediaries between men and gods (DCD VIII. 14, IX. 8, X. 9).

Augustine does not reject the idea that the air is full of demons, but he does not accept that any of them are good, still less that they can mediate between God and man. In many ways they are inferior to human beings. 'They are utterly malevolent spirits, totally indifferent to justice, swollen with pride, green with envy, cunning in deception. They do indeed live in the air, suitably imprisoned there after having been cast down from the heights of the upper heaven because of their irreparable crime' (DCD VIII. 22). In other words, Augustine identifies the Platonic *daimones* with the fallen angels whom most English readers first encounter in Milton's *Paradise Lost*. It was indeed Augustine who fastened onto the imagination

---

[3] See above, p. 40.

of Christianity the story that before creating human beings of flesh and blood God created orders of wholly spiritual beings, some of whom took part in a pre-cosmic rebellion that led to their eternal damnation.

Augustine admits that the Bible is uninformative about the early history of angels. Genesis does not mention them in the seven days of creation, and we have to turn to Psalms or Job to learn that angels are indeed God's creatures. If we are to fit them into the Genesis story, we should conclude that they were created on the first day: on that day God created light and the angels as the first partakers of divine illumination (*DCD* XI. 9). On the same day, the Bible tells us, God divided the light from the darkness: and here Augustine sees divine foresight at work. 'Only He could foresee, before it happened, that some angels would fall and be deprived of the light of truth and left for ever in the darkness of their pride' (*DCD* XI. 19). 'There are two societies of angels, contrasted and opposed: one good by nature and upright of will, one good by nature, but perverted of will. These are shown by more explicit testimonies elsewhere but indicated here in Genesis by the words "Light" and "Darkness"' (*DCD* XI. 34). These two cohorts of angels are the origin of the two cities that are the ostensible theme of the entire work, even though their history is not taken up in detail until the twelfth book. There are good and bad angels, and good and bad humans: but we do not have to think that there are four cities; men and angels can unite in the same communities.

Between the creation of angels and the creation of humans, Augustine tells us, came the creation of animals. All animals, whether solitary like wolves or gregarious like deer, were created by God in multiple specimens simultaneously. But the human race was created in a single individual, Adam: from him came Eve, and from this first pair came all other humans. This unique creation did not imply that man was an unsocial animal; just the contrary. 'The point was to emphasize the unity of human society, and to stress the bonds of human concord, if human beings were bound together not merely by similarity of nature but also by the affection of kinship' (*DCD* XII. 22). The human race, Augustine says, is, by nature, more sociable than any other species. But—he goes on to add—it is also, through ill will, more quarrelsome than any other (*DCD* XII. 28).

Human beings stand in the middle between angels and dumb animals: they share intellect with angels, but they have bodies as the beasts do. However, in the original divine plan they would have had a greater kinship with the angels, because they would have been immortal. After a life of obedience to God they would have passed into fellowship with the angels without death intervening. It was because of Adam's sin in Paradise that humans became mortal, subject to the bodily death that had always been natural for beasts. After the Fall death would be the common lot of all humans; but after death some, by God's grace, would be rewarded by admission to the company of the good angels, while others would be punished by damnation alongside the evil angels—a second death more grievous than the first (*DCD* XIII. 12, XIV. 1).

When Plato described the origin of the cosmos in the *Timaeus*, he attributed the creation of humans not to the supreme being who fashioned the world, but to lesser gods, creatures of his, who were his agents (*Tim.* 41c). Augustine does not deny the existence of such august divine servants: he simply treats Plato's word 'gods' as a misnomer for angels. But he is resolutely opposed to the idea that such superior executives can be called creators. Bringing things into existence out of nothing is a prerogative of the one true God, and whatever service an angel may render to God in the development of lesser creatures, he is no more a creator than is a gardener or a farmer who produces a crop (*DCD* XII. 26).

The contrast between the biblical and the Platonic conception of the human creature comes into sharp relief if we ask the question: Is death—the separation of soul and body—a good thing or a bad thing? For Genesis, death is an evil: it is a punishment for sin. In a world of innocence body and soul would remain forever united (*DCD* XIII. 6). For many Platonists, however, and for Plato himself in some of his writings, the soul is only happy when stripped of the body and naked before God (*DCD* XIII. 16 and 19; cf. *Phaedo* 108c; *Phaedr.* 248c). Again, it is a common Platonic theme that souls after death may be forced to return into bodies (other human bodies, perhaps, or even animal bodies) as a punishment for sins in their previous life. According to the prophets of the Old and New Testament, however, the souls of the virtuous will in the end return to their own bodies, and this reunion of body and soul will be a source of everlasting happiness (*DCD* XIII. 17 and 22, XXII. 19).

Augustine does not deny—indeed he emphasizes—that bodily desires and passions can impede spiritual progress; he quotes the book of Wisdom: 'the corruptible body weighs down the soul'. But this is true only of the body of fallen humans in their mortal life. The human body in Paradise had no disturbing emotions and no unruly desires. Adam and Eve lived without pain or fear, for they enjoyed perfect health and were never in physical danger; their bodies were incapable of injury, and childbirth, but for the Fall, would have been painless. They ate only what was necessary for the preservation of their bodies, and their sexual organs were under the entire control of cool reason, to be used only for procreation (*DCD* XIII. 23, XIV. 26). But though they lived without passion, they were not without love. 'The couple, living in true and loyal partnership, shared an untroubled love for God and for each other. This was a source of immense joy, since the beloved one was always present for enjoyment' (*DCD* XIV. 10).

Augustine's Two Cities

Augustine traces the history of the human race from its origins in Adam and Eve, fitting it into the template of his master narrative, the two cities. 'Though there are many great nations throughout the world living under different systems of religion and ethics, and diversified by language, arms, and dress, nonetheless it has come to pass that there are only two principal divisions of human society, which scripture allows us to call two cities' (*DCD* XIV. 1). One city lives according to the flesh, another according to the spirit; one is created by self-love, the other by the love of God; one glories in itself, the other is given glory by God (*DCD* XIV. 280). One is predestined to join the Devil in final punishment which will destroy it as a city; the other is predestined to reign with God for ever and ever (*DCD* XV. 1 and 4).

The division between the two cities begins with the children of the primal pair. 'Cain was the first son born to the two parents of the human race, and he belonged to the city of man; Abel, their younger son, belonged to the city of God' (*DCD* XV. 2). The enmity of the two cities is first expressed in Cain's slaughter of Abel; and Cain's fratricidal example was followed by Romulus, the founder of Rome, who slew his brother Remus (*DCD* XV. 5).

In the fifteenth and sixteenth books of *The City of God* Augustine traces the early history of the City of God, following the narrative of Genesis and seeing the City as incarnate in the Hebrew Patriarchs, through Noah, Abraham, Isaac, Jacob, Joseph, and Moses. The seventeenth book seeks illumination about the City of God from the writings of the prophets and psalmists. The prophecies that exalt the kingdom of David and the Jewish priesthood and promise them everlasting duration must have their true fulfilment elsewhere since the institutions of Israel no longer exist (*DCD* XVII. 7).

We return to secular history with the eighteenth book, which narrates the rise and fall of a series of pagan empires: Assyria, Egypt, Argos, and Rome. Augustine is anxious to reconcile biblical and secular chronologies, assigning the Mosaic exodus to the time of the mythical king Cecrops of Athens and placing the fall of Troy in the period of the judges in Israel. He treats as simultaneous the foundation of Rome, the beginnings of philosophy in Ionia, and the deportation of Israel. The destruction of the temple in Jerusalem, he tells us, happened in the reign of Tarquinius Priscus in Rome; the Babylonian captivity of the Jews ended at the same time as the expulsion of the kings and the foundation of the Roman Republic. One of the purposes of his rather dizzying chronology is to emphasize that the teaching of the Hebrew prophets antedated the researches of the Greek philosophers (XVIII. 37).

In Augustine's narrative Jerusalem becomes the emblem of the City of God and Babylon becomes the emblem of the city of the world. Babylon was the city of confusion, where God had shattered the original unity of human language in order to frustrate the building of the tower of Babel (Gen. 11: 1–9). In the city of the world philosophers speak with as many different tongues as the builders of Babel. Some say there is only one world; some say there are many; some say this world is everlasting, others say that it will perish. Some say it is controlled by a divine mind, others that it is the plaything of chance. Some say the soul is immortal, others that it perishes with the body. Some place the supreme good in the soul, others in the body, others in external goods. Some say the senses are to be trusted, others that they are to be treated with contempt. In the secular city there is no authority to decide between these conflicting views: Babylon embraces all alike, without discrimination and without adjudication (*DCD* XVIII. 42). How different in the City of God, where all accept the authority of canonical Scripture!

The most important disputations among philosophers are those that concern the ultimate good and the ultimate evil. The ultimate good is that for which other things are desirable, while it is itself desirable for its own sake. Philosophers have sought to place the ultimate good in the present life: some hold that it is pleasure, some that it is virtue, some that it is tranquillity, others that it is in the enjoyment of the basic goods with which nature has endowed us. Many sects regard the ultimate good as constituted by one or other combination of these. But the City of God knows that eternal life is the supreme good, and eternal death the supreme evil, and that it is only by faith and grace that the supreme good can be achieved and the supreme evil avoided (*DCD* XIX. 1–4).

It is clear from Augustine's description of the two cities that one cannot simply identify Babylon with the pagan empire and Jerusalem with the Christian empire. The city of God was already a community long before the birth of Christ, and longer before the conversion of Constantine. The Christian empire contains sinners as well as saints, as Augustine illustrates with the example of the emperor Theodosius, whom St Ambrose forced to do penance for the brutality with which he suppressed a rebellion at Thessalonica in 391 (*DCD* V. 26). Nor is the City of God to be identified with the Church on earth, even though in later ages Augustine's book was sometimes taken to be a guide to relations between Church and State. The nature of the two cities is not fully understood until we consider their final state, which Augustine does in the last three books of *The City of God*.

Augustine combs the sayings of the prophets, the sermons of Jesus, the epistles of the Apostles, and the book of Revelation, for information about the future of the world. Between the resurrection of Jesus and the end of history there is a period of a thousand years as described in the book of Revelation (*DCD* XX. 1–6). During this period the saints are reigning with Christ. Their thousand-year reign evolves in two stages: during their lives on earth the saints are the dominant members of a Church that includes sinners, and after their death they are still in some mysterious way in communion with the Church that is the kingdom of God (*DCD* XX. 9). Augustine is contemptuous of any interpretation of Revelation that looks forward to a thousand-year orgy of wassail for the saints after the end of history. Whether we interpret John's millennium literally, or take the number 1,000 as a symbol of perfection, we are already in the middle of the saints' reign (*DCD* XX. 7).

Augustine tells us that the final drama, after the numbered years have passed, will play itself out in seven acts. First the prophet Elijah will come and convert the

Jewish people to Christ (XX. 29). Secondly, Satan will be unloosed and for three and a half years Antichrist will persecute the faithful, using as his agents the nations of Gog and Magog. The saints will endure their sufferings until the onslaughts of Gog and Magog have burnt themselves out (*DCD* XX. 11–12. 19). Thirdly, Jesus will return to earth to judge the living and the dead. Fourthly, in order to be judged, the souls of the dead will return from their resting place and be reunited with their bodies. Fifthly, the judgement will separate the virtuous from the vicious, with the saints assigned to eternal bliss and the wicked to eternal damnation (*DCD* XX. 22, 27). Sixthly, the present world will be destroyed in a cosmic conflagration, and a new heaven and a new earth will be created (*DCD* XX. 16–18). Seventhly, the blessed and the damned will take up the everlasting abode that has been assigned to them in heaven and in hell (*DCD* XX. 30). The heavenly Jerusalem above and the unquenchable fires below are the consummation of the two cities of Augustine's narrative.

Augustine realizes that his predictions are not easy to accept, and he singles out as the most difficult of all the idea that the wicked will suffer eternal bodily punishment. Bodies are surely consumed by fire, it is objected, and whatever can suffer pain must sooner or later suffer death. Augustine replies that salamanders thrive in fire, and Etna burns for ever. Souls no less than bodies can suffer pain, and yet philosophers agree that souls are immortal. There are many wonders in the natural world—Augustine gives a long list, including the properties of lime, of diamonds, of magnets, and of Dead Sea fruit—that make it entirely credible that an omnipotent creator can keep alive for ever a human body in appalling pain (*DCD* XXI. 3–7).

Most people are concerned less about the physical mechanism than about the moral justification for eternal damnation. How can any crime in a brief life deserve a punishment that lasts for ever? Even in human jurisprudence, Augustine responds, there is no necessary temporal proportion between crime and punishment. A man may be flogged for hours to punish a brief adulterous kiss; a slave may spend years in prison for a momentary insult to his master (*DCD* XXI. 11). It is false sentimentality to believe, out of compassion, that the pains of hell will ever have an end. If you are tempted by that thought, you may end up believing, like the heretic Origen, that one day even the Devil will be converted (*DCD* XXI. 17)!

Step by step Augustine seeks to show not only that eternal punishment is possible and justified, but that it is extremely difficult to avoid it. A virtuous life is not enough, for the virtues of pagans without the true faith are only splendid vices. Being baptized is not enough, for the baptized may fall into heresy. Orthodox belief is not enough, for even the most staunch Catholics may fall into sin. Devotion to the sacraments is not enough: no one knows whether he is receiving them in such a spirit as to qualify for Jesus' promises of eternal life (*DCD* XXI. 19–25). Philanthropy is not enough: Augustine devotes pages to explaining away the passage in St Matthew's Gospel in which the Son of Man separates the sheep from the goats on the basis of their performance or neglect of works of mercy to their fellow men (Matt. 25: 31–46; *DCD* XXI. 27).

And so at last, in the twenty-second book of *The City of God*, we come to the everlasting bliss of the saints in the New Jerusalem. To those who doubt whether earthly bodies could ever dwell in heaven, Augustine offers the following highly Platonic reply:

Suppose we were purely souls, spirits without any bodies, and lived in heaven without any contact with terrestrial animals. If someone said to us that we were destined to be joined to bodies by some mysterious link in order to give life to them, would we not refuse to believe it, arguing that nature does not allow an incorporeal entity to be bound by a corporeal tie? Why then cannot a terrestrial body be raised to a heavenly body by the will of God who made the human animal? (*DCD* XXII. 4)

No Christian can refuse to believe in the possibility of a celestial human body, since all accept that Jesus rose from the dead and ascended into heaven. The life everlasting promised to the blessed is no more incredible than the story of Christ's resurrection.

It is incredible that Christ rose in the flesh and went up into heaven with his flesh. It is incredible that the world believed so incredible a story, and it is incredible that a few men without birth or position or experience should have been able to persuade so effectively the world and the learned world. Our adversaries refuse to believe the first of these three incredible things, but they cannot ignore the second, and they cannot account for it unless they accept the third. (*DCD* XXII. 5)

To show that all these incredible things are in fact credible, Augustine appeals to divine omnipotence, as exhibited in a series of miracles that have been observed by himself or eyewitnesses among his friends. But he accepts that he has to answer difficulties raised by philosophical adversaries against the whole concept of a bodily resurrection.

How can human bodies, made of heavy elements, exist in the ethereal sublimity of heaven? No more problem, says Augustine, than birds flying in air or fire breaking out on earth. Will resurrected bodies all be male? No: women will keep their sex, though their organs will no longer serve for intercourse and childbirth, since in heaven there will no longer be marriage. Will resurrected bodies all have the same size and shape? No: everyone will be given the stature they had at maturity (if they died in old age) or the stature they would have had at maturity (if they died young). What of those who died as infants? They will reach maturity instantaneously on rising.

All resurrected bodies will be perfect and beautiful: the resurrection will involve cosmetic surgery on a cosmic scale. Deformities and blemishes will be removed; amputated limbs will be restored to amputees. Shorn hair and nail clippings will return to form part of the body of their original owners, though not in the form of hair and nails. 'Fat people and thin people need not fear that in that world they will be the kind of people that they would have preferred not to be while in this world' (*DCD* XXII. 19).

Augustine raises a problem that continued to trouble believers in every century in which belief in a final resurrection was taken seriously. Suppose that a starving man relieves his hunger by cannibalism: to whose body, at the resurrection, will the digested human flesh belong? Augustine gives a carefully thought-out answer. Before A gets so hungry that he eats the body of B, A must have lost a lot of weight—bits of his body must have been exhaled into the air. At the resurrection this material will be transformed back into flesh, to give A the appropriate avoirdupois, and the digested flesh will be restored to B. The whole transaction should be looked on as parallel to the borrowing of a sum of money, to be returned in due time (*DCD* XXII. 30).

But what will the blessed *do* with these splendid risen bodies? Augustine confesses, 'to tell the truth, I do not know what will be the nature of their activity—or rather of their rest and leisure'. The Bible tells us that they will see God: and this sets Augustine another problem. If the blessed cannot open and shut their eyes at will, they are worse off than we are. But how could anyone shut their eyes upon God? His reply is subtle. In that blessed state God will indeed be visible, to the eyes of the body and not just to the eyes of the mind; but he will not be an extra object of vision. Rather we will see God by observing his governance of the bodies that make up the material scheme of things around us, just as we see the life of our fellow men by observing their behaviour. Life is not an extra body that we see, and yet when we see the motions of living beings we do not just believe they are alive, we *see* they are alive. So in the City of God we will observe the work of God bringing harmony and beauty everywhere (*DCD* XXII. 30).

Though it is dependent on the Bible on almost every page, *The City of God* deserves a significant place in the history of philosophy, for two reasons. In the first place, Augustine constantly strives to place his religious world-view into the philosophical tradition of Greece and Rome: where possible he tries to harmonize the Bible with Plato and Cicero; where this is not possible he feels obliged to recite and refute philosophical anti-Christian arguments. Secondly, the narrative Augustine constructed out of biblical and classical elements provided the framework for philosophical discussion in the Latin world up to and beyond the Renaissance and the Reformation.

Augustine was one of the most interesting human beings ever to have written philosophy. He had a keen and lively analytic mind and at his best he wrote vividly, wittily, and movingly. Unlike the philosophers of the high Middle Ages, he takes pains to illustrate his philosophical points with concrete imagery, and the examples he gives are never stale and ossified as they too often are in the texts of the great scholastics. In the service of philosophy he can employ anecdote, epigram, and paradox, and he can detect deep philosophical problems beneath the smooth surface of language. He falls short of the very greatest rank in philosophy because he remains too much a rhetorician: to the end of his life he could never really tell the difference between genuine logical analysis and mere linguistic pirouette. But then once he was a bishop his aims were never purely philosophical: both rhetoric and logic were merely instruments for the spreading of Christ's gospel.

The Consolations of Boethius

In the fifth century the Roman Empire experienced an age of foreign invasion (principally in the West) and of theological disputation (principally in the East). Augustine's *City of God* had been occasioned by the sack of Rome by the Visigoths in 410; in 430, when he died in Hippo, the Vandals were at the gates of the city. Augustine's death prevented him from accepting an invitation to attend a Church council in Ephesus. The Council had been called by the emperor Theodosius II because the patriarchates of Constantinople and Alexandria disagreed violently about how to formulate the doctrine of the divine sonship of the man Jesus Christ.

In the course of the century the Goths and the Vandals were succeeded by an even more fearsome group of invaders, the Huns, under their king Attila. Attila conquered vast areas from China to the Rhine before being fought to a standstill in Gaul in 451 by a Roman general in alliance with a Gothic king. In the following year he invaded Italy, and Rome was saved from occupation only by the efforts of Pope Leo the Great, using a mixture of eloquence and bribery.

The Council of Ephesus in 431 condemned Nestorius, the bishop of Constantinople, because he taught that Mary, the mother of Jesus, was not the mother of God. How could he hold this, the Alexandrian bishop Cyril argued, if he really believed that Jesus was God? The right way to formulate the doctrine of the Incarnation, the Council decided, was to say that Christ, a single person, had two distinct natures, one divine and one human. But the Council did not go far enough for some Alexandrians, who believed that the incarnate Son of God possessed only a single nature. These extremists arranged a second council at Ephesus, which proclaimed the doctrine of the single nature ('monophysitism'). Pope Leo, who had submitted written evidence in favour of the dual nature, denounced the Council as a den of robbers.

Heartened by the support of Rome, Constantinople struck back at Alexandria, and at a council at Chalcedon in 451 the doctrine of the dual nature was affirmed. Christ was perfect God and perfect man, with a human body and a human soul, sharing divinity with his Father and sharing humanity with us. The decisions of Chalcedon and first Ephesus henceforth provided the test of orthodoxy for the great majority of Christians, though in eastern parts of the empire substantial communities of Nestorian and monophysite Christians remained, some of which have survived to this day. In the history of thought the importance of these fifth-century councils is that they hammered out technical meanings for terms such as 'nature' and 'person' in a manner that influenced philosophy for centuries to come.

After the repulse of Attila the western Roman Empire survived a further quarter of a century, though power in Italy had largely passed to barbarian army commanders. One of these, Odoacer, in 476, decided to become ruler in name and not just in fact. He sent off the last fainéant emperor, Romulus Augustulus, to exile near Naples. For the next half-century Italy became a Gothic province. Its kings, though Christians, took little interest in the recent Christo-logical debates: they subscribed to a form of Christianity, namely Arianism, that had been condemned as long ago as the time of Constantine I. Arianism took various forms, all of which denied that Jesus, the Son of God, shared the same essence or substance with God the Father. The most vigorous of the Gothic kings, Theodoric (reigned 493–526), established a tolerant regime in which Arians, Jews, and Orthodox Catholics lived together in tranquillity and in which art and culture thrived.

One of Theodoric's ministers was Manlius Severinus Boethius, a member of a powerful Roman senatorial family. Born shortly after the end of the Western Empire, he lost his father in childhood and was adopted into the family of the consul Symmachus, whose daughter he later married. He himself became consul in 510 and saw his two sons become consuls in 522. In that year Boethius moved from Rome to Theodoric's capital at Ravenna, to become 'master of offices', a very senior administrative post which he held with integrity and distinction.

As a young man Boethius had written handbooks on music and mathematics, drawn from Greek sources, and he had projected, but never completed, a translation into Latin of the entire works of Plato and Aristotle. He wrote commentaries on some of Aristotle's logical works, showing some acquaintance with Stoic logic. He wrote four theological tractates dealing with the doctrines of the Trinity and the Incarnation, showing the influence both of Augustine and of the fifth-century Christological debates. His career appeared to be a model for those who wished to combine the contemplative and active lives. Gibbon, who could rarely bring himself to praise a philosopher, wrote of him, 'Prosperous in his fame and fortunes, in his public honours and private alliances, in the cultivation of science and the consciousness of virtue, Boethius might have been styled happy, if that precarious epithet could be safely applied before the last term of the life of man' (*Decline and Fall*, ch. 19).

Boethius, however, did not hold his honourable office for long, because he fell under suspicion of being implicated, as a Catholic, in treasonable correspondence urging the emperor Justin at Constantinople to invade Italy and end Arian rule. He was imprisoned in a tower in Pavia and condemned to death by the senate in Rome. It was while he was in prison, under sentence of death, that he wrote the work for which he is most remembered, *On the Consolation of Philosophy*. The work has been admired for its literary beauty as well as for its philosophical acumen; it has been translated many times into many languages, notably by King Alfred and by Chaucer. It contains a subtle discussion of the problems of relating human freedom to divine foreknowledge; but it is not quite the kind of work that might be expected from a devout Catholic facing possible martyrdom. It dwells on the comfort offered by pagan philosophy, but there is no reference to the consolations held out by the Christian religion.

At the beginning of the work Boethius describes how he was visited in prison by a tall woman, elderly in years but fair in complexion, clothed in an exquisitely woven but sadly tattered garment: this was the Lady Philosophy. On her dress was woven a ladder, with the Greek letter P at its foot and the Greek letter TH at its head: these meant the Practical and Theoretical divisions of Philosophy and the ladder represented the steps between the two. The lady's first act was to eject the muses of poetry, represented by Boethius' bedside books; but she was herself willing to provide verses to console the afflicted prisoner. The five books of the *Consolation* consist of alternating passages of prose and poetry. The poems vary between sublimity and doggerel; it often takes a considerable effort to detect their relevance to the developing prose narrative.

In the first book Boethius defends himself against the charges that have been brought against him. His troubles have all come upon him because he entered public office in obedience to Plato's injunction to philosophers to involve them-selves in political affairs. Lady Philosophy reminds him that he is not the first philosopher to suffer: Socrates suffered in Athens and Seneca in Rome. She herself has been subject to outrage: her dress is tattered because Epicureans and Stoics tried to kidnap her and tore her clothes, carrying off the torn-off shreds. She urges Boethius to remember that even if the wicked prosper, the world is subject not to random chance but to the governance of divine reason. The book ends with a poem that looks rather like a shred torn off by a Stoic, urging rejection of the passions.

> Joy you must banish
> Banish too fear
> All grief must vanish
> And hope bring no cheer.

The second book, too, develops a Stoic theme: matters within the province of fortune are insignificant by comparison with values within oneself. The gifts of fortune that we enjoy do not really belong to us: riches may be lost, and are most valuable when we are giving them away. A splendid household is a blessing to me only if my servants are honest, and their virtue belongs to them not me. Political power may end in murder or slavery; and even while it is possessed it is trivial. The inhabited world is only a quarter of our globe; our globe is minute in comparison with the celestial sphere; for a man to boast of his power is like a mouse crowing over other mice. The greatest of fame lasts only a few years that add up to zero in comparison with never-ending eternity. I cannot find happiness in wealth, power, or fame, but only in my most precious possession, myself. Boethius has no real ground of complaint against fortune: she has given him many good things and he must accept also the evil which she sends. Indeed, ill fortune is better for men than good fortune. Good fortune is deceitful, constant only in her inconstancy; bad fortune brings men self-knowledge and teaches them who are their true friends, the most precious of all kinds of riches.

The message that true happiness is not to be found in external goods is reinforced in the third book, developing material from Plato and Aristotle:

happiness (*beatitudo*) is the good which, once achieved, leaves nothing further to be desired. It is the highest of all goods, containing all goods with itself; if any good was lacking to it, it could not be the highest good since there would be something left over to be desired. So happiness is a state which is made perfect by the accumulation of all the goods there are. (*DCP* 3. 2)

Wealth, honour, power, glory do not fulfil these conditions, nor do the pleasures of the body. Some bodies are very beautiful, but if we had X-ray eyes we would find them disgusting. Marriage and its pleasures may be a fine thing, but children are little tormentors. We must cease to look to the things of this world for happiness. God, Lady Philosophy argues, is the best and most perfect of all good things; but the perfect good is true happiness; therefore, true happiness is to be found only in God. All the values that are sought separately by humans in their pursuit of mistaken forms of happiness—self-sufficiency, power, respect, pleasure—are found united in the single goodness of God. God's perfection is extolled in the ninth poem of the third book, *O qui perpetua*: a hymn often admired by Christians, though almost all its thoughts are taken from Plato's *Timaeus* and a Neoplatonic commentary thereon.[4] Because all goodness resides in God, humans can only become happy if, in some way, they become gods. 'Every happy man is a god. Though by nature God is one only; but nothing prevents his divinity from being shared by many' (*DCP* 3. 10).

In the fourth book Boethius asks Lady Philosophy to answer the question 'Why do the wicked prosper?' The universe, he agrees, is governed by an ideal ruler, God; but it looks like a house in which the worthless vessels are well looked after while the precious ones are left to grow filthy. Philosophy draws arguments from Plato's *Gorgias* to show that the prosperity of the wicked is only apparent. The will to do

---

[4] In Chaucer's (prose) translation it commences: 'O thou father, creator of heaven and of earth, that governest this world by perdurable reason, that commandest the times to go from since that age had its beginning: thou that dwellest thyself aye steadfast and stable, and givest all other things to be moved...'.

evil is itself a misfortune, and success in doing so is a worse disaster. Worse still is to go unpunished for one's misdeeds. While a good man can aspire to divinity, a bad man turns into a beast: avarice makes you a wolf, quarrelsomeness makes you a dog, cheating a fox, anger a lion, fear a deer, sloth an ass, and lust a pig.

All things are ruled by God's providence: does this mean that everything happens by fate? Lady Philosophy makes a distinction. Providence is the divine reason that binds all things together, while fate is what organizes the motions of things scattered in place and time; the complicated arrangements of fate proceed from the simplicity of providence. We can see only the apparent disorder of the operation of fate; if we could see the overall scheme as designed by providence, we would realize that whatever happens happens justly, and whatever is, is right.

Throughout the first four books Lady Philosophy has had much to say about Lady Luck. The fifth book addresses the question 'In a world governed by divine providence, can there be any such thing as luck or chance?' There cannot be purely random chance, if philosophy is to be believed; but human choice is something different from chance. Free choice, however, even if not random, is difficult to reconcile with the existence of a God who foresees everything that is to happen. 'If God foresees all and cannot in any way be mistaken, then that must necessarily happen which in his providence he foresees will be.' The reply offered is that God is outside time, and so it is a mistake to speak of providence as involving *fore*knowledge at all. This subtle but mysterious answer was to be much studied and developed in later ages.[5]

It is to be hoped that Boethius found consolation in his philosophical writing, because he was brutally tortured, a cord being fastened round his head and tightened until his eyes started from their sockets. He was finally executed by being beaten with clubs. Many Christians regarded him as a martyr, and some churches venerated him as St Severinus. The humanist Lorenzo Valla in the fifteenth century called him 'the last of the Romans, the first of the scholastics', and Gibbon says that he was 'the last of the Romans whom Cato or Tully could have acknowledged for their countryman'.

Boethius was not only the last philosopher of the old Latin philosophical tradition: his *Consolation* can be read as an anthology of all that he valued in classical Greek philosophy. It was perhaps as a compliment to the pagan thinkers from whom he had learnt that he eliminated from his philosophical testament any Christian element. Even the treatment of the relation between divine foreknowledge and human freedom, so influential during the Christian centuries, is couched within the framework of the Stoic discussion of the relation between providence and fate.

---

[5] Boethius' argument is analysed in detail in Ch. 9 below.

The Greek Philosophy of Late Antiquity

Pagan Greek philosophy, however, had not quite come to an end at the time when Boethius met his death: the schools of Athens and Alexandria were still active. The head of the Athens school in the previous century had been the industrious and erudite Proclus, who was said to have been capable of producing, each working day, five lectures and 700 lines of philosophical prose. Proclus wrote commentaries on several of Plato's dialogues and an encyclopedic work on Plotinus' *Enneads*. His *Elements of Theology* has served, even in modern times, as a convenient compendium of Neoplatonism.

Proclus' system is based on Plotinus' trinity of One, Mind, and Soul, but he develops Plotinus' ideas by a multiplication of triads, and a general theory of their operation (*ET* 25–39). Within each triad there is a developmental process. From the originating element of the triad there emerges a new element which shares its nature but which yet differs from it. This new element both resides in its origin, proceeds beyond it, and returns back towards it. This law of development governs a massive proliferation of triads. From the initial One there proceed a number of divine Units (henads) (*ET* 113–65). The Henads, collectively, beget the world of Mind, which is divided into the spheres of Being, Life, and Thought. In the next, lower, world, that of Soul, Proclus provides a habitation for the traditional gods of the pagan pantheon. The visible world we live in is the work of these divine souls, which guide it providentially.

Human beings, for Proclus, straddle the three worlds of Soul, Mind, and One (*ET* 190–7). As united to our animal body, the human soul expresses itself in Eros, focused on earthly beauty. But it has also an imperishable, ethereal body made out of light. Thus it passes beyond love of beauty in search of Truth, a pursuit that brings it into contact with the ideal realities of the world of Mind. But it has a faculty higher than that of thought, and that brings it, by mystical ecstasy, into union with the One.

The theory of triads bears some resemblance to the Christian doctrine of the Trinity, but in fact Proclus, though a devotee of many superstitions, was bitterly hostile to Christianity. He was, indeed, reputed to have written eighteen separate refutations of the Christian doctrine of creation. Nonetheless, many of his ideas entered the mainstream of Christian thought by indirect routes. Boethius himself made frequent, if unacknowledged, use of his work. A contemporary Christian Neoplatonist wrote a series of treatises inspired by Proclus, passing them off as the work of Dionysius the Areopagite, who was an associate of St Paul in Athens (Acts 17). Another channel by which Proclus' ideas flowed into medieval philosophy was a book known as the *Liber de Causis*, which circulated under the name of Aristotle. Even Thomas Aquinas, who was aware that the book was not authentic, treated it with great respect.

In fifth-century Alexandria, where there was a powerful Christian patriarch, it was more difficult than in Athens for pagan philosophy to flourish. Hypatia, a female Neoplatonist mathematician and astronomer, stands out in a man's world of philosophy in the same way as Sappho stands out in a man's world of poetry. While Augustine was writing *The City of God* in Hippo, Hypatia was torn to pieces in Alexandria by a fanatical Christian mob (AD 415).[6] The most important philosopher of the school of Alexandria in its last days was Ammonius, an elder contemporary of Boethius. He was more effective as a teacher than a writer, and owes his fame to the distinction of his two most famous pupils, Simplicius and Philoponus.

Both these philosophers lived in the reign of the emperor Justinian, who succeeded to the purple in 527, two or three years after the execution of Boethius. Justinian was the most celebrated of the Byzantine emperors, renowned both as a conqueror and as a legislator. His generals conquered large portions of the former Western Empire and united them for a while under the rule of Constantinople. His jurists collected and rationalized into a single code all the extant imperial edicts and statutes, and appended a digest of legal commentaries. The Code of Civil Law that was handed down in the course of his reign influenced most European countries until modern times.

Justinian's reign was not, however, as favourable to philosophy as it was to jurisprudence. The school of Athens continued the anti-Christian Neoplatonic tradition of Proclus, which brought it into imperial disfavour. Simplicius was one of the last group of scholars to adorn the school. He devoted great effort and erudition to the writing of commentaries on Aristotle, whose teachings he was anxious to reconcile with the thought of Plato as interpreted in late antiquity. Scholars of later generations are in his debt because in the course of this enterprise he quoted extensively from his predecessors as far back as the Presocratics, and is our source for many of their surviving fragments. Simplicius was still working there when, in the year 529, Justinian closed down the school because of its anti-Christian tendency. His edict, in the words of Gibbon, 'imposed a perpetual silence on the schools of Athens and excited the grief and indignation of the few remaining votaries of Grecian science and superstition' (*Decline and Fall*, ch. 40).

Philoponus, too, suffered under Justinian, but for different reasons. While Simplicius was a pagan philosopher based in Athens, Philoponus was a Christian philosopher based in Alexandria. While Simplicius was the most ardent admirer of Aristotle in antiquity, Philoponus was his severest critic. Whereas previous philosophers had either ignored Aristotle (like the Epicureans and Stoics) or interpreted him irenically (like the Neoplatonists), Philoponus knew him very well and attacked him head-on.

---

[6] Sadly, very little is known of Hypatia. Charles Kingsley made the most of what there is in his novel *Hypatia* (1853).

As a Christian, Philoponus rejected the doctrine of the eternity of the world, and demolished the arguments of Aristotle and Proclus to the effect that the world had no beginning. He carried his attack throughout the whole of Aristotle's physics, rejecting the theories of natural motion and natural place, and denying that the heavenly bodies were governed by physical principles different from those obtaining here below.[7] It was congenial to his Christian piety to demolish the notion that the world of the sun and moon and stars was something supernatural, standing in a relation to God different from that of the earth on which his human creatures live.

Philoponus wrote treatises on Christian doctrine as well as commentaries on Aristotle. They were not well received by the orthodox, who thought his treatment of the doctrine of the Trinity laid him open to the charge of believing in three Gods. Surprisingly, he accepted the Platonic belief in the existence of human souls prior to conception; even more surprisingly, this belief of his does not seem to have troubled his Christian brethren. But like many previous Alexandrian Christians, he was a monophysite, believing that in the incarnate Christ there was only a single nature, not, as defined by the Council of Chalcedon, two natures, human and divine. He was summoned to Constantinople by the emperor to defend his views on the Incarnation, but failed to answer the summons. Philoponus outlived Justinian by a few years, but was condemned after his death for his heretical teaching about the Trinity. He was the last significant philosopher of the ancient world, and after his death philosophy went into hibernation for two centuries.

Between 600 and 800 the former Roman Empire shrank to little more than Greece, the Balkans, and part of Asia Minor. Intellectual talent was expended mainly on theological disputation. The monophysite church to which John Philoponus belonged had been excluded from communion by the orthodox, who believed that Christ had not just one, but two, natures, human and divine. During the seventh century attempts were made by emperors and patriarchs to reunite the Christian communions by agreeing that even if Christ had two natures, nonetheless he had only one will; or that even if he had two wills, one human and one divine, these two were united in a single activity of willing, a single actuality, or *enerqeia*. Any concession of this kind was strongly resisted by a retired imperial officer called Maximus, who wrote copiously against 'monothelitism', the doctrine of the single will.

Maximus (known as 'the Confessor') succeeded in having the doctrines of the single will and the single actuality condemned at a council in Rome in 649, later endorsed in Constantinople in 681. Christ's human will and the divine will were always in perfect agreement, but they were two separate entities. In persuading the

---

[7] Philoponus' physics is discussed in detail in Ch. 5 below.

guardians of orthodoxy of this teaching, Maximus was obliged to investigate in detail the concepts of *will* and *actuality*. The English word 'will' and its equivalents and their cognates in Greek (*thelesis/thelema*) and Latin (*voluntas*) can refer to a faculty (as in 'Human beings have free will, animals do not'), a disposition of the will (e.g. a willingness to be martyred), an act (e.g. 'I will' in a marriage ceremony), or an object willed (as in 'Thy will be done'). Maximus analysed these concepts carefully and with a degree of originality: but he was not so original as to deserve to be credited, as some have done, with being the inventor of the concept of the will *tout court* (PG 90).[8]

Philosophy in the Carolingian Empire

Outside the Roman Empire the world was transformed beyond recognition. The life of the prophet Muhammad came to an end in 633, and within ten years of his death the religion of Islam had spread by conquest from its native Arabia throughout the neighbouring Persian Empire and the Roman provinces of Syria, Palestine, and Egypt. In 698 the Muslims captured Carthage, and ten years later they were masters of all North Africa. In 711 they crossed the Straits of Gibraltar, easily defeated the Gothic Christians, and flooded through Spain. Their advance into northern Europe was halted only in 732, when they were defeated at Poitiers by the Frankish leader Charles Martel.

Charles Martel's grandson Charlemagne, who became king of the Franks in 768, drove the Muslims back to the Pyrenees, but did no more than nibble at their Spanish dominions. To the east, however, he conquered Lombardy, Bavaria, and Saxony, and had his son proclaimed king of Italy. When Pope Leo III was driven out of Rome by a revolution, Charlemagne restored him to his see. In gratitude the Pope crowned him as Roman emperor in St Peter's on Christmas Day 800—a date which, if not the most memorable in history, is at least the easiest to remember. Thus began the Holy Roman Empire, which at Charlemagne's death in 814 included almost all the Christian inhabitants of continental western Europe.

Charlemagne was anxious to improve standards of education and culture in his dominions, and he collected scholars from various parts of Europe to form a 'Palatine School' at his capital, Aachen. One of the most distinguished of these was Alcuin of York, who took a keen interest in Aristotle's *Categories*. The logic textbook which he wrote, *Dialectica*, takes the form of a dialogue in which the

---

[8] The great theological debate of the succeeding century concerned the worship of images or icons. It might have been expected that the iconoclastic controversy would have thrown up interesting contributions to semiotics, the philosophical theory of signs. But this hope appears, from a brief survey of the literature, to be vain.

pupil Charlemagne asks questions and the teacher Alcuin gives answers. Alcuin retired in the last years of his life to run a small school in the abbey of St Martin of Tours, of which he later became abbot. He spent his time, he told the emperor, dispensing to his pupils the honey of Scripture, the wine of classical literature, and the apples of grammar. To a privileged few he displayed the treasures of astronomy—Charlemagne's favourite hobby.

When philosophy revived between the ninth and eleventh centuries, it did so not within the old Roman Empire of Byzantium, but in the Frankish Empire of Charlemagne's successors and in the Abbasid court of Muslim Baghdad. The leading philosophers of the revival were, in the West, John the Scot, and in the East, Ibn Sina (Avicenna).

John was born in Ireland in the first decades of the ninth century. He is not to be mistaken for the more famous John Duns Scotus, who flourished in the fourteenth century. It is undoubtedly confusing that there are two medieval philosophers with the name John the Scot. What makes it doubly confusing is that one of them was an Irishman, and the other was for all practical purposes an Englishman. The ninth-century philosopher, for the avoidance of doubt, gave himself the surname Eriugena, which means Son of Erin.

By 851 Eriugena had migrated from Ireland to the court of Charles the Bald, the grandson of Charlemagne. This was probably at Compiègne, which Charles thought of renaming Carlopolis, on the model of Constantinople. Charles was a lover of things Greek, and the astonishingly learned Eriugena, who had mastered Greek (no one knows where), won his favour and wrote him flattering poems in that language. He taught liberal arts at the court for a while, but his interests began to turn towards philosophy. Once, commenting on a text on the borderline between grammar and logic, he wrote 'no one enters heaven except through philosophy'.[9]

Eriugena first engaged in philosophy in 851 when invited by Hincmar, the archbishop of Reims, to write a refutation of the ideas of a learned and pessimistic monk, Gottschalk. Gottschalk had taken up the problem of predestination where Augustine had left off. He was reported to have deduced from the texts of Augustine something that was generally there left implicit, namely that predestination affected sinners as well as saints. It was, he taught, not only the blessed in heaven whose ultimate fate had been predestined, the damned also had been predestined to hell before they were ever conceived. This doctrine of double predestination seemed to Archbishop Hincmar to be heretical. At the very least, like the monks of Augustine's time, he regarded it as a doctrine inimical to good monastic discipline: sinners might conclude that, since their fate had been sealed

---

[9] See J. J. O'Meara, *Eriugena* (Oxford: Clarendon Press, 1988), chs. 1 and 2.

long ago, there was no point in giving up sinning. Hence his invitation to Eriugena to put Gottschalk down (PL 125. 84–5).

Whether or not Gottschalk had been accurately reported, Eriugena's refutation of his alleged heresy was, from Hincmar's point of view, worse than the disease. Eriugena's arguments were weak, and in attacking the predestination of the damned, he emasculated the predestination of the blessed. There could not be a double predestination, he said, because God was simple and undivided; and there was no such thing as *predestination* because God was eternal. The first argument is unconvincing because if a double predestination threatens God's simplicity, so too does the distinction between predestination and foreknowledge, which was the favoured solution of Gottschalk's opponents. The second argument does not provide the desired incentive to the sinner to repent, because whatever temporal qualification we give to the divine determining of our fate, it is certainly, on the Augustinian view, independent of any choice of ours (CCCM 50. 12).

The Frankish kingdom was torn by doctrinal strife, and both Gottschalk and Eriugena found themselves condemned by Church councils. The Council of Quierzy in 853—the third of a series—defined, against Gottschalk, that while God predestined the blessed to heaven, he did not predestine others to sin: he merely left them in the human mass of perdition and predestined only their punishment, not their guilt. The condemnation of Eriugena, at Valence in 855, affirmed that there was indeed a predestination of the impious to death no less than a predestination of the elect to life. The difference was this: that in the election of those to be saved the mercy of God preceded all merit, whereas in the damnation of those who were to perish evil desert preceded just judgement. The Council fathers were not above vulgar abuse, saying that Eriugena had defiled the purity of the faith with nauseating Irish porridge.

Despite his condemnation, Eriugena remained in favour with Charles the Bald and was commissioned by him in 858 to translate into Latin three treatises of Dionysius the Areopagite: the *Divine Names*, the *Celestial Hierarchy*, and the *Ecclesiastical Hierarchy*. He found the Neoplatonic ideas of Dionysius congenial and went on to construct his own system on somewhat similar lines, in a work of five volumes called *On the Division of Nature*—or, to give it its Greek title, *Periphyseon*.

There are, according to Eriugena, four great divisions of nature: nature creating and uncreated, nature created and creating, nature created and uncreating, and nature uncreating and uncreated (1. 1). The first such nature is God. The second is the intellectual world of Platonic ideas, which creates the third nature, the world of material objects. The fourth is God again, conceived not as creator but as the end to which things return.

Eriugena tells us that the most important distinction within nature is that between the things that are and the things that are not. It is disconcerting to be told that God is among the things that are not; however, Eriugena does not mean that there is no God, but rather that God does not fit into any of Aristotle's ten categories of being (2. 15). God is above being, and what he is doing is something better than existing. One name that we can give to the ineffable and incomprehensible brilliance of the divine goodness is 'Nothing'.[10]

Eriugena's third division, the material world, is the easiest to comprehend (3. 3). Like Philoponus, he believes that heaven and earth are made out of the same elements; there is no special quintessence for the heavenly bodies. The cosmos, he tells us, consists of three spheres: the earth in the centre, next to it the sphere of the sun (which is roughly 45,000 miles away), and outermost the sphere of the moon and the stars (roughly 90,000 miles away). While Eriugena thinks that the sun revolves around the world, he takes some steps towards a heliocentric system: Jupiter, Mars, Venus, and Mercury, he believed, were planets of the sun, revolving around it.

Where do human beings fit into Eriugena's fourfold scheme? They seem to straddle the second and third division. As animals, we belong in the third division, and yet we transcend the other animals. We can say with equal propriety that man is an animal and that he is not an animal. He shares reason, mind, and interior sense with the celestial essences, but he shares his flesh, his outward self, with other animals. Man was created twice over: once from the earth, with the animals, but once with the intellectual creatures of the second division of nature. Does this mean that we have two souls? No, each of us has a single, undivided, soul: wholly life, wholly mind, wholly reason, wholly memory. This soul creates the body, acting as the agent of God, who does not himself create anything mortal. Even when soul and body are separated at death, the soul continues to govern the body scattered throughout the elements (4. 8).

As the creator of the body, the soul belongs to that division of nature which is both created and creative. This second division consists of what Eriugena calls 'the primordial causes of things', which he identifies with the Platonic Ideas (2. 2). These were pre-formed by God the Father in his eternal Word. The Idea of Man is that in accordance with which man is made in the image of God. But that image is deformed in fallen humans. Had God not foreseen that Adam would fall, humans would not have been divided into male and female; they would have propagated as angels do. Their bodies would have been celestial and would have lacked metabolism. After the resurrection, our bodies will resume their sexless and ethereal form. When the world finally ends, place and time will disappear, and all creatures will find salvation in the nature that is uncreated and uncreating.

Eriugena was one of the most original and imaginative thinkers of the Middle Ages and built the ideas of his Greek sources into a system that was uniquely his own. Reading him is not easy, but his text can cast a fascinating spell on the reader. He has a fanatical love of paradox: whenever he writes a sentence he can hardly

---

[10] Eriugena's theology is discussed at greater length in Ch. 9 below.

bear not to follow it with its contradictory. He often displays great subtlety and ingenuity in showing that the two apparent contradictions can be interpreted in such a way as to reconcile them. But sometimes his wayward intellect leads him into sheer nonsense, as when he writes 'In unity itself all numbers are at once together, and no number precedes or follows another, since all are one' (3. 66).

Though Eriugena constantly quotes the Bible, his system is closer to pagan Neoplatonism than to traditional Christian thought, and it is unsurprising that *On the Division of Nature* was eventually condemned by ecclesiastical authority. In 1225 Pope Honorius III ordered all surviving copies of the work to be sent to Rome to be burned. But legend was kind to his memory. The story was often told of Charles the Bald asking him, over dinner, what separates a Scot from a sot, and being given the answer 'only this table'. And at one time the University of Oxford implausibly venerated him as its founder.[11]

Muslim and Jewish Philosophers

The Christian Eriugena was a much less important precursor of Western medieval philosophy than a series of Muslim thinkers in the countries that are now Iraq and Iran. Besides being significant philosophers in their own right, these Muslims provided the roundabout route through which much Greek learning was eventually made available to the Latin West.

In the fourth century there was, at Edessa in Mesopotamia, a school of Syrian Christians who made a serious study of Greek philosophy and medicine. These Christians did not accept the condemnation of Nestorius at the Council of Ephesus in 431, and they were not reconciled by the Council of Chalcedon in 451. Accordingly, their school was closed by the emperor Zeno in 489. The scholars migrated to Persia, where they continued the work they had begun at Edessa of translating the logical works of Aristotle from Greek into Syriac.

After the Muslim conquest of Persia and Syria, scholars from this school were invited to the court of Baghdad in the era of the enlightened caliphs of the *Arabian Nights*. Between 750 and 900 these Syrians translated into Arabic much of the Aristotelian corpus, as well as Plato's *Republic* and *Laws*. They also made available to the Muslim world the scientific and medical works of Euclid, Archimedes, Hippocrates, and Galen. At the same time mathematical and astronomical works were translated from Indian sources. The 'arabic' numerals that we use today, which were enormously more convenient for arithmetical purposes than the Roman and Byzantine numerals that they superseded, were imported from India in the same period.

[11] See O'Meara, *Eriugena*, 214–16.

The introduction of Greek, and especially Aristotelian, philosophy had a very significant effect on Muslim thought. Islamic theology (*kalam*) had already developed a rudimentary philosophical vocabulary and was initially—and subsequently—hostile to this foreign system of ideas (*falsafa*). For instance, the thinkers of *kalam* (known as Mutakallimun) deployed a series of proofs to show that the world had had a beginning in time; the new philosophers produced Aristotelian arguments to prove that it had always existed.[12] Whereas for Western thinkers like Augustine the vulgar Latin of Bible translations had made Christianity initially distasteful, for the *kalam* scholars of the Quran it was the broken Arabic of the Aristotelian translations that proved a stumbling block to the acceptance of philosophy. For a while they resisted the idea that logic had universal validity, treating it rather as an obscure branch of Greek grammar.

The person traditionally regarded as the father of Muslim philosophy is al-Kindi (*c*.801–66), a contemporary of Eriugena, who occupied a middle ground between *kalam* and *falsafa*. He wrote a treatise called *The Art of Dispelling Sorrows*, which bears a resemblance to Boethius' *Consolation*. More important is his treatise on First Philosophy, which develops in a highly formal way the *kalam* argument for the finitude of the world in time.[13] He is also remembered for his writings on human understanding, in one of which he suggests that our intellect is brought into operation by a single cosmic intelligence, perhaps to be identified with the Mind, which occupies second place in the Neoplatonic trinity of One, Mind, and Soul. This idea was taken up by a later philosopher, al-Farabi, a member of the school of Baghdad who died in 950. He used it to explain the baffling passage in Aristotle's *De Anima* which speaks of two minds, a mind to make things, and a mind to become things.[14]

Al-Farabi made a clear distinction between grammar and logic, which he regarded as a preparatory tool for philosophy. Philosophy proper, for him, had three divisions: physics, metaphysics, and ethics. Psychology was a part of physics, and theology was a quite separate discipline that studied the attributes of God as rewarder and punisher. One could, however, use philosophical arguments to prove the existence of God as first mover and necessary being. Al-Farabi was a member of the mystical sect of the Sufis and stressed that the task of humans was to seek enlightenment from God and return to him from whom we originally emanated.

A contemporary of al-Farabi was Saadiah Gaon (882–942), the first Jewish philosopher of the Middle Ages, who was born in Egypt and moved to Babylon, where he became head of the school of biblical studies. He translated the Bible into Arabic and wrote widely on Jewish liturgy and tradition. He was anxious

---

[12] See William Lane Craig, *The Kalam Cosmological Argument* (London: Macmillan, 1979).

[13] This is set out in detail in Ch. 5 below.

[14] See above, p. 195.

to reconcile biblical doctrine with rational philosophy, which he conceived as being two twigs from the same branch. In this task he drew on Neoplatonic sources and on material taken from the *kalam*. His most influential book was entitled *The Book of Doctrines and Beliefs*.

Human certainties, Saadiah says, arise from three sources: sense, reason, and tradition. Reason is of two kinds: rational intuition, which provides the truths of logic and knowledge of good and evil, and rational inference, which derives truths by argument from the premises provided by sense and intuition. It is by rational inference that we know that humans possess a soul and that the universe has a cause. The tradition of the Jewish people, of which the most important element is the Bible, is a further source of knowledge, whose validity is certified by the prophets' performance of miracles. This is an independent source, but it has to be interpreted judiciously in the light of information obtained from other sources.

The senses, Saadiah says, cannot tell us whether the world had a beginning or has existed for ever, so we must look to reason. He offers four proofs that the world was created in time: (1) everything in the universe is finite in size, so the force that holds it together must be finite and cannot have existed for ever; (2) the elements of the cosmos are complex but fit each other admirably, so they must be the work of a skilful creator; (3) all substances in the natural world are contingent, and need a necessary creator; (4) an infinite series cannot be grasped or traversed, so time must be finite. Some of these arguments go back as far as Philoponus, and some of them had a long future ahead of them (*PMA* 344–50).

Avicenna and his Successors

The greatest of all Muslim philosophers was Ibn Sina, known in the West as Avicenna (980–1037). He was a Persian, born near Bokhara (in present-day Uzbekistan), who was educated in Arabic and wrote most of his works in that language. He is reputed to have mastered logic, mathematics, physics, and medicine in his teens. He began to practise as a doctor when he was 16. In his autobiography, edited by his pupil Juzjani, he describes how he then took up philosophy:

For a year and a half, I devoted myself to study. I resumed the study of logic and all parts of philosophy. During this time I never slept the whole night through and did nothing but study all day long. Whenever I was puzzled by a problem ... I would go to the mosque, pray, and beg the Creator of All to reveal to me that which was hidden from me and to make easy for me that which was difficult. Then at night I would return home, put a lamp in front of me, and set to work reading and writing.[15]

---

[15] Quoted in J. L. Esposito, *Islam: The Straight Path* (New York: Oxford University Press, 1991), 57.

Thus, he tells us, he had mastered all the sciences by the time he was 18. At the age of 20 he published an encyclopedia—the first of five in the course of his life, four in Arabic and one in Persian.

Avicenna's medical skill was much in demand; he was summoned to treat the sultan of Bokhara and made full use of his splendid library. Between 1015 and 1022 he was both court physician and vizier to the ruler of Hamadan. Later he occupied a similar position in the court of Isfahan. He left behind about 200 works, of which more than 100 have survived. His *Canon of Medicine* summarizes much classical clinical material and adds observations of his own; it was used by practitioners in Europe until the seventeenth century.

Avicenna's main philosophical encyclopedia was called in Arabic *Kitab-al-Shifa*, or 'Book of Healing'. It is divided into four parts, of which the first three treat of logic, physics, and mathematics respectively. The second part includes a development of Aristotle's *De Anima*. The fourth part, whose Arabic name means 'Of Divine Things', was known in the medieval West as his *Metaphysics*. When translated into Latin in Toledo around 1150 it had an enormous influence on the Latin philosophy of the Middle Ages.

Avicenna said that he had read Aristotle's metaphysics forty times and had learnt it by heart without understanding it—only when he came across a commentary by al-Farabi did he understand what was meant by the theory of being *qua* being.[16] His own *Metaphysics* is much more than a commentary on Aristotle; it is a thoroughly thought-out original system. The book, in ten treatises, falls into two parts: the first five books treat of ontology, the science of being in general; the remaining books are devoted principally to natural theology. In the early books Avicenna deals with the notions of substance, matter and form, potentiality and actuality, and the problem of universals. In the later books he examines the nature of the first cause and the concept of necessary being, and the way in which creatures, human beings in particular, derive their being and nature from God.

As an illustration of the way in which Avicenna modifies Aristotelian concepts we may take the doctrine of matter and form. Any bodily entity, he maintains, consists of matter under a substantial form, a form of corporeality, which made it a body. All bodily creatures belong to particular species, but any such creature, e.g. a dog, has not just one but many substantial forms: as well as corporeality, it has the forms of animality and caninity. Since souls, for an Aristotelian, are forms, human beings, on this theory, have three souls: a vegetative soul (responsible for nutrition, growth, and reproduction), an animal soul (responsible for movement and perception), and a rational soul (responsible for intellectual thought). None of the souls exist prior to the body, but while the two inferior souls are mortal, the

---

[16] Avicenna, *The Life of Ibn Sina*, trans. W. E. Gohlman (Albany: State University of New York Press, 1974).

superior one is immortal and survives death in a condition either of bliss or of frustration, in accordance with the merits of the life it has led. Avicenna followed al-Farabi's interpretation of Aristotle on the intellect, and accepted, in addition to the receptive human mind that absorbs information routed through the senses, a single superhuman active intellect that gives humans the ability to grasp universal concepts and principles.[17]

In describing the unique nature of God, Avicenna introduced a novel idea that occupied a central role in all succeeding metaphysics: the distinction between essence and existence.[18] In all creatures essence and existence are distinct: not even the fullest investigation into *what kind* of thing a particular species is will show *that* any individuals of that species exist. But God is quite different: in his case, and only in his case, essence entails existence. God is the only necessary being, and all others are contingent. Since God's existence depends only in his essence, his existence is eternal; and so too, Avicenna concluded, is the world that emanates from him.[19]

Though he was irregular and unobservant in practice, Avicenna was a sincere Muslim, and took care to reconcile his philosophical scheme with the Prophet's teaching and commands, which he regarded as a unique enlightenment from the Active Intellect. But his systematic treatment of religion in the second part of his *Metaphysics* makes no special appeal to the authority of the Quran. It gives rationalistic justifications for Islamic ritual and social practices (including polygamy and the subordination of women), but it is based on religious principles of a general and philosophical kind. It was this that made it possible for his writing to be influential among the Catholic philosophers of the Latin West; but it also brought his work under suspicion among conservative Muslims. Owing to the favour of princes, however, he escaped serious persecution. He met his end in Hamadan in 1037 during a campaign against that city led by the ruler of Isfahan. He took a poison, we are told, misprescribed as a medication for an ailment brought on by his dissolute life.

A younger contemporary of Avicenna, Solomon Ibn Gabirol (c.1021–1058), made a distinctive contribution to metaphysics. Though a devout Jew and a liturgical poet, Ibn Gabirol wrote a philosophical work, *The Fountain of Life*, which betrays no trace of its Jewish origin—so much so that when it was translated into Latin in the mid-twelfth century, it was thought to be the work of a Muslim, to whom Westerners gave the name Avicebron.

Ibn Gabirol's system is fundamentally Neoplatonic, but it contains one neo-Aristotelian element. All created substances, he maintained, whether corporeal or spiritual, whether earthly or heavenly, are composed of matter and form. There is

---

[17] The philosophy of mind of al-Farabi and of Avicenna is discussed in detail in Ch. 7 below.

[18] Some writers have claimed that the distinction goes back to Aristotle, but this is doubtful (see above, p. 178).

[19] Avicenna's metaphysics is discussed in detail in Ch. 6 below.

spiritual matter as well as corporeal matter: the universe is a pyramid with the immaterial godhead at the summit and formless prime matter at the base. Since one can no longer equate 'material' with 'bodily' in his system, Ibn Gabirol has to introduce, like Avicenna, a form of corporeality to make bodies bodies. Ibn Gabirol's universal hylomorphism was to have a considerable influence on thirteenth-century Latin Aristotelianism (*PMA* 359–67).

Meanwhile, both in Christianity and in Islam, the eleventh century saw a reaction against philosophy on the part of conservative theologians. St Peter Damiani (1007–72), angered by philosophical criticisms of Catholic beliefs about the Eucharist, trumpeted that God had not chosen to save his people by means of dialectic. He did, however, himself make use of philosophical reasoning when discussing divine attributes, and it led him to some strange conclusions. If these fell foul of the principle of contradiction, so be it: logic was not the mistress, but the maidservant, of theology.[20]

Towards the end of the century the Persian philosopher and mystic al-Ghazali (1058–1111) wrote a work, *Tahafut al-falasifa* ('The Incoherence of the Philosophers'), in which he sought to show not only that Muslim philosophers, in particular Avicenna, were heretical to Islam, but also that they were fallible and incoherent by their own philosophical lights. His criticisms of Avicenna's arguments for the existence of God and for the immortality of the soul were often well taken. But he is now best remembered because his *Incoherence* provoked a reply from a twelfth-century philosopher of greater weight, Averroes.

Anselm of Canterbury

Despite these clashes between dialecticians and conservatives, the eleventh century produced one thinker who was both an original philosopher in his own right and a theologian sufficiently orthodox to be canonized: St Anselm of Canterbury (1033–1109). Born in Aosta he became, at the age of 27, a monk at the abbey of Bec. There he studied the works of Augustine under its abbot Lanfranc, himself a highly competent scholar, who later became the first archbishop of Canterbury after the Norman conquest of England. As a monk, prior, and finally abbot of Bec, Anselm wrote a series of brief philosophical and meditative works.

The *Monologion*, dedicated to Lanfranc, has as its purpose to teach students how to meditate upon the nature of God. The greater part of it (sections 29–80) is concerned with the Christian doctrine of the Trinity, but the initial sections present arguments for the existence of God—from the degrees of perfection to be found in creatures, and from dependent versus independent being. It is in a

---

[20] Damiani's unusual views on omnipotence are discussed below in Ch. 9.

slightly later work, the *Proslogion*, that he puts forward his celebrated argument for the existence of God as that than which nothing greater can be conceived. It is on this argument (commonly called the 'ontological argument') that his philosophical fame principally rests.[21] The *Proslogion*, a brief address to God in the style of Augustine's *Confessions*, shares with that work an engaging literary charm that has made it an enduring classic of philosophical literature.

Anselm, as said earlier, was distinguished both as a philosopher and as a theologian, and in his writing he does not make a sharp distinction between the two disciplines. When treating of God he does not make a systematic distinction, as later scholastics were to do, between natural theology (what can be discovered of God by unaided reason) and dogmatic theology (what can be learnt only from revelation). He sums up his own attitude in a passage at the beginning of the *Proslogion* (c. 1).

I do not aim, Lord, to penetrate your profundity, because I know my intellect is no kind of match for it; but I want to understand in some small measure that truth of yours that my heart believes and loves. For I do not seek to understand that I may believe; but I believe that I may understand. For I believe this too, that unless I believe, I shall not understand. (Isa. 7: 9)

So he treats both the existence of God and the mystery of the Trinity in the same manner, as truths that he believes from the outset, but which he wishes to understand more fully. If, in the course of this, he discovers philosophical arguments that may be used to influence also the unbeliever, that is a bonus rather than the purpose of his inquiry.

Several treatises thus straddle philosophy and theology. *On Truth* analyses different applications of the word 'true'—to sentences, to thoughts, to sense-perceptions, to actions, and to things. It concludes that there is only a single truth in all things, which is identical with justice. *On Free Will* explores to what extent human beings are capable of avoiding sin. *On the Fall of the Devil* deals with one of the most excruciating versions of the problem of evil: how could initially good angels, supremely intelligent and with no carnal temptations, turn away from God, the only true source of happiness?

While at Bec, Anselm did write one purely philosophical work. *On the Grammarian* reflects on the interface between grammar and logic, and on the relation between signifiers and signified. Against the background of Aristotle's categories Anselm analysed the contrasts between nouns and adjectives, concrete and abstract terms, substances and qualities; and he related these contrasts to each other.

In 1093 Anselm succeeded Lanfranc as archbishop of Canterbury, an office which he held until his death. His last years were much occupied with disputes over jurisdiction between the king (William II) and the Pope (Urban II). But he

---

[21] Anselm's arguments for the existence of God are analysed in Ch. 9 below.

found time to write an original justification for the Christian doctrine of the Incarnation under the title *Why did God Become Man?* Justice demands, he says, that where there is an offence, there must be satisfaction: the offender must offer a recompense that is equal and opposite to the offence. In feudal style, he argues that the magnitude of an offence is judged by the importance of the person offended, while the magnitude of a recompense is judged by the importance of the person making it. Human sin is infinite offence, since it is offence against God; human recompense is only finite, since it is made by a creature. Unaided, therefore, the human race is incapable of making satisfaction for the sins of Adam and his heirs. Satisfaction can only be adequate if it is made by one who is human (and therefore an heir of Adam) and also divine (and therefore capable of making infinite recompense). Hence the necessity of the Incarnation. In the history of philosophy this treatise of Anselm's is important because of its concept of satisfaction, which, along with deterrence and retribution, long figured in philosophical justifications of punishment in the political as well as the theological context.

Just before becoming archbishop, Anselm had become embroiled in a dispute with a pugnacious theologian, Roscelin of Compiègne (c.1050–1120). Roscelin is famous for his place in a quarrel that had a long history ahead of it: the debate over the nature of universals. In a sentence such as 'Peter is human' what does the universal term 'human' stand for? Philosophers down the ages came to be divided into realists, who thought that such a predicate stood for some extra-mental reality, and nominalists, who thought that no entity corresponded to such a word in the way that the man Peter corresponds to the name 'Peter'. Roscelin is often treated in the history of philosophy as the founder of 'nominalism', but his views were in fact more extreme than those of most nominalists. He claimed not just that universal predicates were mere names, but that they were mere puffs of breath. If this theory is applied to the doctrine of the Trinity, it raises a problem. Father, Son, and Holy Ghost are each God. But if the predicate 'God' is a mere word, then the three persons of the Trinity have nothing in common. Anselm had Roscelin condemned at a council in 1092 on a charge of tritheism, the heresy that there are three separate Gods.

Abelard

No logical work survives that can be confidently ascribed to Roscelin. All that we can be sure came from his pen is a letter to his most famous pupil, Abelard. Abelard was born into a knightly family in Brittany in 1079 and came to study under Roscelin shortly after he had been condemned. About 1100 he moved to Paris and joined the school attached to the Cathedral of Notre Dame. The teacher there was William of Champeaux, who espoused a realist theory of universals at the opposite extreme from Roscelin's nominalism. The universal nature of man, he maintained, is wholly present in each individual at one and the same time. Abelard found William's doctrine no more congenial than that of his former master, and left Paris to set up a school at Melun. He wrote the earliest of his surviving works, word-by-word commentaries on logical works of Aristotle, Porphyry, and Boethius.

Later he returned to Paris and founded a school in competition to William, whom in 1113 he succeeded as master of the Notre Dame school. While teaching there he lodged with one of the canons of the cathedral, Fulbert, and became tutor to his 16-year-old niece Héloïse. He became her lover, probably in 1116, and when she became pregnant married her secretly. Héloïse had been reluctant to marry, lest she interfere with Abelard's career, and she retired to a convent shortly after the wedding and the birth of her son. Her outraged uncle Fulbert sent to her husband's room by night a pair of thugs who castrated him. Abelard became a monk at St Denis, while Héloïse took the veil at the convent of Argenteuil.

Abelard supported Héloïse out of his tutorial earnings and the pair renewed their relationship by means of edifying correspondence. One of Abelard's longest letters, written some years later, is called *History of my Calamities*. It is the main source of our knowledge of his life up to this point, and is the liveliest piece of autobiography between Augustine's *Confessions* and the diary of Samuel Pepys.

While at St Denis, Abelard continued to teach, and began to write theological treatises. The first one, *Theology of the Highest Good*, addressed the problem that set Anselm and Roscelin at odds: the nature of the distinction between the three divine persons in the Trinity, and the relationship in the Godhead between the triad 'power, wisdom, goodness' and the triad 'Father, Son, and Spirit'. Like Roscelin, Abelard got into trouble with the Church; his work was condemned as unsound by a synod at Soissons in 1121. He had to burn the treatise with his own hand and he was briefly imprisoned in a correctional monastery.

On his return to St Denis, Abelard was soon in trouble again for denying that the abbey's patron had ever been bishop of Athens. He was forced to leave, and set up a country school in an oratory that he built in Champagne and dedicated to the Paraclete (the Holy Spirit). From 1125 to 1132 or thereabouts he was abbot of St Gildas, a corrupt and boisterous abbey in Brittany, where his attempts at reform were met with threats of murder. Héloïse meanwhile had become prioress of Argenteuil. When she and her nuns were made homeless in 1129, Abelard installed them in the Paraclete oratory.

Some time early in the 1130s Abelard returned to Paris, teaching again on the Mont Ste Geneviève. He spent most of the rest of his working life there, lecturing on logic and theology and writing copiously. He wrote a commentary on the Epistle to the Romans, and an ethical treatise with the Socratic title *Know Thyself*. He continued to assemble a collection of authoritative texts on important theological topics, grouping them in contradictory pairs under the title *Sic et Non* ('Yes and No'). He developed the ideas of his *Theology of the Supreme Good* in several succeeding versions, of which the definitive one was *The Theology of the Scholars*, which was finished in the mid-1130s.

This book brought him into conflict with St Bernard, abbot of Clairvaux and second founder of the Cistercian order, later to be the preacher of the Second Crusade. Bernard took out of the book (sometimes fairly, sometimes unfairly) a list of nineteen heresies, and had them condemned at a council at Sens in 1140. Among the condemned propositions were some that were quite inflammatory, for example, 'God should not and cannot prevent evil' and 'The power of binding and losing was given only to the Apostles and not to their successors' (DB 375, 379). Abelard appealed to Rome against the condemnation, but the only result was that the Pope condemned him to perpetual silence. He had by now retired to the abbey of Cluny, where he died two years later; his peaceful death was described by the abbot, Peter the Venerable, in a letter to Héloïse.

Of all medieval thinkers, Abelard is undoubtedly one of the most famous; but to the world at large he is more famous as a tragic lover than as an original philosopher. Nonetheless, he has an important place in the history of philosophy, for two reasons especially: for his contribution to logic and for his influence upon scholastic method.

Three logical treatises survive. The first two are both called 'Logic' and are distinguished from each other by reference to the first words of their Latin text: one is the *Logica Ingredientibus* and the other the *Logica Nostrorum Petitioni*. The third is entitled *Dialectica*. It used to be the common opinion of scholars that the third treatise was the definitive one, dating from the last years of Abelard's life. Some recent scholars have suggested, on the other hand, that it dates from a much earlier period, partly on the uncompelling ground that examples like 'May my girlfriend kiss me' and 'Peter loves his girl' are unlikely to have been included in a textbook written after the affair with Héloïse.[22] When Abelard wrote, very few of Aristotle's logical works were available in Latin, and to that extent he was at a disadvantage compared with later writers in succeeding centuries. It is, therefore, all the more to the credit of his own insight and originality that he contributed to the subject in a way that marks him out as one of the greatest of medieval logicians.

One of Abelard's works that had the greatest subsequent influence was his *Sic et Non*, which places in opposition to each other texts on the same topic by different scriptural or patristic authorities. This collection was not made with sceptical intent, in order to cast doubt on the authority of the sacred and ecclesiastical

---

[22] On the dating of Abelard's logical works, see John Marenbon, *The Philosophy of Peter Abelard* (Cambridge: Cambridge University Press, 1997), 36–53.

writers; rather, the paired texts were set out in a systematic pattern in order to stimulate his own, and others', reflection on the points at issue.

Later, in the heyday of medieval universities, a favourite teaching method was the academic disputation. A teacher would put up one of his pupils, a senior student, plus one or more juniors, to dispute an issue. The senior pupil would have the duty to defend some particular thesis—for instance, that the world was created in time; or, for that matter, that the world was not created in time. This thesis would be attacked, and the opposite thesis would be presented, by other pupils. The instructor would then settle the dispute, trying to bring out what was true in what had been said by the one and what was sound in the criticisms made by the others. Many of the most famous masterpieces of medieval philosophy— the great majority of the writings of Thomas Aquinas, for example—observe, on the written page, the pattern of these oral disputations.

Abelard's *Sic et Non* is the ancestor of these medieval disputations. The main textbook of medieval theology, Peter Lombard's *Sentences*, bore a structure similar to Abelard's work, and promoted the kind of debate standard in the schools. Thus it can be argued that it was ultimately due to Abelard that the structure of philosophical discussion took a form that was adversarial rather than inquisitorial, with pupils in the role of advocates and the teacher in the role of a judge. Though never himself more than a schoolmaster, Abelard imposed a style of thought on academic professors right up to the Renaissance.

Averroes

Several of Abelard's Christian contemporaries made contributions to philosophy. Most of them belonged to schools in or around Paris. At Chartres a group of scholars promoted a revival of interest in Plato: William of Conches commented on the *Timaeus* and Gilbert of Poitiers sponsored a moderate version of realism. The Abbey of St Victor produced two notable thinkers: a German, Hugh, and a Scotsman, Richard, both of whom combined a taste for mysticism with energetic attempts to discover a rational proof of God's existence. In the capital itself Peter Lombard, the bishop of Paris, wrote a work on the model of Abelard's *Sic et Non*, called the *Sentences*. This was a compilation of authoritative passages drawn from the Old and New Testaments, Church councils, and Church Fathers, grouped topic by topic, for and against particular theological theses. This became a standard university textbook.

However, the only twelfth-century philosophers to approach Abelard in philosophical talent came from outside Christendom. Both were born in Cordoba, within a decade of each other, the Muslim Averroes (whose real name was Ibn Rushd) and the Jew Maimonides (whose real name was Moses ben Maimon).

Cordoba was the foremost centre of artistic and literary culture in the whole of Europe, and Muslim Spain, until it was overrun by the fanatical Almohads, provided a tolerant environment in which Christians and Jews lived peaceably with Arabs.

Averroes (1126–98) was a judge, and the son and grandson of judges. He was also learned in medicine, and wrote a compendium for physicians called *Kulliyat* 'General Principles'. He entered the court of the sultan at Marrakesh; while there he caught sight of a star not visible in Spain, and this convinced him of the truth of Aristotle's claim that the world was round. Back in Spain he was commissioned in 1168 by the caliph, Abu Yakub, to provide a summary of Aristotle's works. In 1182 he was appointed court physician in addition to his judgeship, and he combined these offices with his Aristotelian scholarship until, in 1195, he fell into disfavour with the caliph al-Mansur. He was briefly placed under house arrest, and his books were burnt. He returned to Morocco and died at Marrakesh in 1198.

Throughout his life Averroes had to defend philosophy against attacks from conservative Muslims. In response to al-Ghazali's *Incoherence of the Philosophers* he wrote a book called *The Incoherence of the Incoherence*, defending the right of human reason to investigate matters of theology. He also wrote a treatise, *The Harmony of Philosophy and Religion*. Is the study of philosophy, he asks, allowed or prohibited by Islamic law? His answer is that it is prohibited to the simple faithful, but for those with the appropriate intellectual powers, it is positively obligatory, provided they keep it to themselves and do not communicate it to others (*HPR* 65).

Averroes' teaching in the *Incoherence* was misinterpreted by some of his followers and critics as a doctrine of double truth: the doctrine that something can be true in philosophy which is not true in religion, and vice versa. But his intention was merely to distinguish between different levels of access to a single truth, levels appropriate to different degrees of talent and training.

Al-Ghazali's diatribe had been directed especially against the philosophy of Avicenna. In his response to al-Ghazali, Averroes is not an uncritical defender of Avicenna; his own position is often somewhere between that of the two opponents. Like Avicenna, he believes in the eternity of the world: he argues that this belief is not incompatible with belief in creation, and he seeks to refute the arguments derived from Philoponus to show that eternal motion is impossible. On the other hand, Averroes gradually abandoned Avicenna's scheme of the emanation from God of a series of celestial intelligences, and he rejected the dichotomy of essence and existence which Avicenna had put forward as the key distinction between creatures and creator. He came to deny also Avicenna's thesis that the agent intellect produced the natural forms of the visible world. Against al-Ghazali, Averroes insisted that there is genuine causation in the created cosmos: natural causes produce their own effects, and are not mere triggers for the exercise of divine omnipotence. But in the case of human intelligence he reduced the role of natural causation further even than Avicenna had done: he maintained that the passive intellect, no less than the active, was a single, superhuman, incorporeal substance (*PMA* 324–34).[23]

Averroes' most important contribution to the development of philosophy was the series of commentaries—thirty-eight in all—that he wrote on the works of Aristotle. These come in three sizes: short, intermediate, and long. For some of Aristotle's works (e.g. *De Anima* and *Metaphysics*) all three commentaries are extant, for some two, and for some only one. Some of the commentaries survive in the original Arabic, some only in translations into Hebrew or Latin. The short commentaries, or 'epitomes', are essentially summaries or digests of the arguments of Aristotle and his successors. The long commentaries are dense works, quoting Aristotle in full and commenting on every sentence; the intermediate ones may be intended as more popular versions of these highly professional texts.

Averroes knew the work of Plato, but he did not have the same admiration for him as he had for Aristotle, whose genius he regarded as the supreme expression of the human intellect. He did write a paraphrase of Plato's *Republic*—perhaps as a *faute de mieux* for Aristotle's *Politics*, which was then unavailable in Spain. He omitted some of the principal passages about Platonic Ideas, and he tweaked the book to make it closer to the *Nicomachean Ethics*. In general, he saw it as one of his tasks as a commentator to free Aristotle from Neoplatonic overlay, even though in fact he preserved more Platonic elements than he realized.

Averroes made little mark on his fellow Muslims, among whom his type of philosophy rapidly fell into disfavour. But his encyclopedic work was to prove the vehicle through which the interpretation of Aristotle was mediated to the Latin Middle Ages, and he set the agenda for some of the major thinkers of the thirteenth century. Dante gave him an honoured place in Limbo, and placed his Christian follower Siger of Brabant in heaven flanking St Thomas Aquinas. For Thomas himself, and for generations of Aristotelian scholars, Averroes was *the* Commentator.

Maimonides

Many features of Averroes' life are repeated in those of Maimonides (1138–1204). Both were born in Cordoba as sons of religious judges, both were learned in law and medicine, and both lived a wandering life, dependent on the favour of princes and the vagaries of toleration. Driven from Cordoba by the fundamentalist Almohads when he was 13, Maimonides migrated with his parents to Fez and then to Acre, and finally settled in Cairo. There he was for five years president of

---

[23] Averroes' teaching on the intellect is described in detail in Ch. 7 below.

the Jewish community, and from 1185 he was a court physician to the vizier of Saladin.

In his lifetime his fame was due principally to his rabbinic studies: he wrote a digest of the Torah, and drew up a definitive list of divine commandments (totalling not ten, but 613). But his lasting influence worldwide has been due to a book he wrote in Arabic late in life, the *Guide of the Perplexed*. This was designed to reconcile the apparent contradictions between philosophy and religion, which troubled educated believers. Biblical teaching and philosophical learning complement each other, he maintained; true knowledge of philosophy is necessary if one is to have full understanding of the Bible. Where the two appear to contradict each other, difficulties can be resolved by an allegorical interpretation of the sacred text.

Maimonides was candid in avowing his debt to Muslim and pagan philosophers. His interest in philosophy awoke early, and at the age of 16 he compiled a logical vocabulary under the influence of al-Farabi. Avicenna, too, he read, but found him less impressive. His greatest debt was to Aristotle, whose genius he regarded as the summit of purely human intelligence. But it was impossible to understand Aristotle, he wrote, without the help of the series of commentaries culminating in those of Averroes.

Maimonides' project for reconciling philosophy and religion depends on his heavily agnostic view of the nature of theology. We cannot say anything positive about God, since he has nothing in common with people like us: lacking matter and totally actual, immune from change and devoid of qualities, God is infinitely distant from creatures. He is a simple unity, and does not have distinct attributes such as justice and wisdom. When we attach predicates to the divine name, as when we say 'God is wise', we are really saying what God is *not*: we mean that God is not foolish. To seek to praise God by attaching laudatory human epithets to his name is like praising for his silver collection a monarch whose treasury is all gold.

The meaning of 'knowledge', the meaning of 'purpose' and the meaning of 'providence', when ascribed to us, are different from the meanings of these terms when ascribed to Him. When the two providences or knowledges or purposes are taken to have one and the same meaning, difficulties and doubts arise. When, on the other hand, it is known that everything that is ascribed to us is different from everything that is ascribed to him, truth becomes manifest. (*Guide*, 3. 20)[24]

We have no way of describing God, Maimonides maintained, except through negation. If we are not to fall into idolatry, we must explain as metaphor or allegory every anthropomorphic text in the Bible.

If religion and Aristotelianism are to be reconciled, concessions have to be made on both sides. To illustrate the way in which Maimonides carries out his reconciling project we may consider two instances: the doctrine of creation and

---

[24] Trans. S. Pines, 2 vols. (Chicago: Chicago University Press, 1963).

the doctrine of providence. In the case of creation, it is Aristotle's cosmology that has to give way; in the case of providence, traditional piety must be taught sobriety.

As a believer in the Jewish doctrine that the world was created in time, Maimonides rejected Aristotle's conception of an eternal universe, and offered criticisms of philosophical arguments to show that time could have no beginning. But he did not believe that unaided reason could establish the truth of creation. Human beings cannot deduce the origin of the world from the world as it now is, any more than a man who had never met a female could work out how humans come into existence. Maimonides rejected Aristotle's view that the world consisted of fixed and necessary species. It is disgraceful to think, he says, that God could not lengthen the wing of a fly.

On the other hand, we should not think that God's governance of the universe is concerned with every individual event in the world: his providence concerns human beings individually, but it concerns other creatures only in general.

Divine providence watches only over the individuals belonging to the human species, and in this species alone all the circumstances of the individuals and the good and evil that befall them are consequent upon their deserts. But regarding all the other animals and, all the more, the plants and other things, my opinion is that of Aristotle. For I do not at all believe that this particular leaf has fallen because of a providence watching over it; nor that this spider has devoured this fly because God has now decreed and willed something concerning individuals. . . . For all this is in my opinion due to pure chance, just as Aristotle holds. (*Guide*, 3. 17)

Nonetheless, Maimonides' intention was orthodox and indeed devout. The aim of life, he insists, is to know, love, and imitate God. The prophet can learn more swiftly than the philosopher what little there is to be known about God. Knowledge should lead to love—a love that is expressed in the passionless imitation of divine action to be found in the lives of biblical prophets and lawgivers. Those who are neither prophets nor philosophers must be cajoled into well doing by stories that are less than true, such as that God answers prayers and is angered by sin.

Like Averroes, Maimonides fell foul of conservative believers who thought his interpretation of sacred texts blasphemous. Indeed some Jews in France tried to enlist the support of the Inquisition in trying to stamp out his heresies. But unlike Averroes, Maimonides after his death retained the interest and respect of his co-religionists as well as that of Latin Christians.

2

The Schoolmen: From the Twelfth Century to the Renaissance

In the twelfth century a series of devoted translators made a contribution to philosophy no less significant than that of the century's original thinkers. At the beginning of the century the only works of Aristotle known in Latin were the *Categories* and *De Interpretatione* in the translations of Boethius. Some twenty years later Boethius' translations of Aristotle's other logical works were recovered from virtual oblivion, and James of Venice translated the *Posterior Analytics* to complete the Latin *Organon*. By the middle of the century James had translated also the *Physics, De Anima*, and the early books of the *Metaphysics*, the rest of which was translated, with the exception of book 11, by an anonymous scholar. Only a portion of the *Nicomachean Ethics*, books 2 and 3 (the 'old Ethics'), was translated in the twelfth century.

In the second half of the century important philosophical texts were translated from the Arabic: works of al-Kindi, al-Farabi, al-Ghazali, and Ibn Gabirol, and substantial portions of Avicenna's great *Kitab-al-Shifa*. A number of other treatises also circulated in translation, often Neoplatonic works, under the name of Aristotle. Most important for the future history of Latin Aristotelianism was the translation of the major commentaries of Averroes into Latin, a gigantic task undertaken by Michael Scot from about 1220.

Early in the thirteenth century, therefore, philosophers had available to them a very substantial corpus of Aristotelian text and commentary. Many of these early translations were superseded by the work of later translators, particularly William of Moerbeke, who worked between 1260 and 1280 and whose versions were given canonical status through their use by Thomas Aquinas and other great scholastics. But already from the earliest decades of the century the influence of Aristotle was the dominant stimulus to the development of philosophy.

The thirteenth century was a time of uncommon intellectual energy and excitement. The context for this ferment of ideas was created by two innovations that occurred early in the century: the new universities and the new religious orders.

Bologna and Salerno have claims to be the oldest universities in Europe. Bologna celebrated its nine-hundredth anniversary in 1988 and Salerno was a flourishing institution in the mid-twelfth century. But Bologna had no permanent university buildings until 1565 and Salerno's academic glory quickly faded; moreover, both were specialized schools, concentrating on law and medicine respectively. It was at Paris and Oxford that the institution really took root, Paris receiving its charter in 1215 and Oxford having its status confirmed by a papal legate one year earlier.

The university is, in essentials, a thirteenth-century innovation, if by 'university' we mean a corporation of people engaged professionally, full-time, in the teaching and expansion of a corpus of knowledge in various subjects, handing it on to their pupils, with an agreed syllabus, agreed methods of teaching, and agreed professional standards. Universities and parliaments came into existence at roughly the same time, and have proved themselves the most long-lived of all medieval inventions.

A typical medieval university consisted of four faculties: the universal undergraduate faculty of arts, and the three higher faculties, linked to professions, of theology, law, and medicine. Students in the faculties learnt both by listening to lectures from their seniors and, as they progressed, by giving lectures to their juniors. A teacher licensed in one university could teach in any university, and graduates migrated freely in an age when all academics used Latin as a common language.

The teaching programme in the faculties was organized around set texts. It took some time to settle the canon in the arts faculty: in 1210 an edict at the University of Paris forbade any lectures on Aristotle's natural philosophy and ordered his texts to be burnt. But though reinforced by papal bulls, the condemnation seems to have quickly become a dead letter, and by 1255 not only Aristotle's physics, but his metaphysics and ethics, and indeed all his known works, became compulsory parts of the syllabus. In theology the text on which lectures were based, in addition to the Bible, was the *Sentences* of Peter Lombard. The lawyers took as their core text Justinian's codification of Roman law or Gratian's *Decretals*. In the medical faculties the set texts varied from university to university. The boundaries between the faculties are not necessarily what someone familiar with modern universities would expect. Material which we would nowadays consider philosophical is as likely to be found in the writings of medieval theologians as in the lectures that survive from the arts faculty.

For the intellectual life of the age, the foundation of the religious orders of mendicant friars, the Franciscans and the Dominicans, was no less important than the creation of the universities. St Francis of Assisi secured papal approval in 1210 for the rule he had laid down for his small community of poor, wandering preachers. St Dominic, a tireless fighter for orthodoxy, founded convents of nuns to pray and friars to preach against heresy: his order was approved by the Pope in 1216. Like the Franciscans ('Friars Minor', 'Grey Friars'), the Dominicans ('Friars Preachers', 'Black Friars') were to live on alms, but at the outset their ethos was less romantic and more scholarly than that of the Franciscans. However, after the first generation of wholly other-worldly friars, the Franciscans became just as success-ful academically as the Dominicans. By 1219 both orders were established in the University of Paris. The Black Friars arrived in Oxford in 1221 and the Grey Friars in 1224. By 1230 each order had founded a school there.

The roll-call of the great philosophers in the high Middle Ages is largely drawn from these two orders. Five of the most distinguished thinkers are St Albert, St Thomas Aquinas, St Bonaventure, John Duns Scotus, and William Ockham. Of these the first two are Dominicans and the last three Franciscans. Only in the fourteenth century, with John Wyclif, do we meet a philosopher of comparable talent who was a member of the secular (parish) clergy rather than a friar. Wyclif's eventual lapse from orthodoxy made him, in the minds of ecclesiastical historians of philosophy, a doubtful exception to the rule that it was thinkers of the religious orders who enjoyed pre-eminence.

Robert Grosseteste and Albert the Great

The three innovating impulses of the thirteenth century—the reception of Aristotle, the development of the universities, and the influence of the mendicant orders—can all be seen at work in the career of a remarkable Englishman, Robert Grosseteste (1170?–1253), who became bishop of Lincoln in 1235. He studied at Oxford and was one of the first chancellors of that university. From 1225 to 1230 he taught in the Oxford schools. In 1230 he moved to the newly founded Franciscan house and was lecturer there for five years before his appointment to the episcopate. Besides writing a number of original philosophical and scientific works, he composed the first commentary on the Latin version of Aristotle's *Posterior Analytics*, and comparatively late in life he learnt Greek and made his own translation of the *Nicomachean Ethics*.

Grosseteste belonged to a generation earlier than the great thirteenth-century scholastics, and in the opinion of many scholars he holds a more important place in the history of science than in the history of philosophy. In working on the *Analytics* he became aware of difficulties with the Aristotelian concept of science as a corpus of demonstrated necessary truths. Among Aristotle's favourite topics are eclipses of the moon. How can there be necessary truths about them, since they are comparatively rare events? Grosseteste replies that the necessary truths are of a conditional form—if the sun and the earth are in such-and-such positions, then there will be an eclipse. More importantly, he suggests that some of these conditional truths are established by experiment, not by deduction. You observe that eating the root of a certain type of convolvulus is followed by the passing of red bile. To establish with certainty that this plant really is a purgative, you have to feed it repeatedly to patients while screening out other possible purgatives (*CPA* 214–15, 252–71).

On the basis of this and other passages, Grosseteste has been hailed as the father of experimental science in western Europe. Undoubtedly he had considerable scientific curiosity, which he displays in discussing phenomena that occur in Aristotle's text only as examples—the falling of autumn leaves, the twinkling of the stars, the cause of thunder, the flooding of the Nile. He also wrote independent treatises on astronomy and meteorology (*The Sphere*, *On Comets*), and in his theological commentary on Genesis (*Hexaemeron*) he takes many opportunities to display knowledge of natural history. Medieval legend, indeed, credited him with magical powers, such as making a robot that could answer difficult questions, and riding a horse to Rome in a single night. Both the medieval gossip and the modern plaudits seem exaggerated. In his overall view of the nature of human scientific endeavour, as laid out in his commentary on the *Analytics*, Grosseteste was closer to Augustine than to either Paracelsus or Francis Bacon.

There are, he says, five types of universal with which human knowledge is concerned. The first are eternal reasons in the mind of God. (Plato called these 'Ideas', but the notion that they are separate substances is a misbegotten error.) Secondly, there are forms that God impresses on the minds of angels: these, like Platonic Ideas, serve as paradigms, or examples, for creaturely activity. Thirdly, objects on earth have *rationes causales* in the heavenly spheres: stellar and planetary forms operate in causal fashion to bring about sublunar effects. Fourthly, there are the forms that belong to earthly substances, collocating them in their species and genera. Fifthly, there are the accidental forms of objects, which provide information about the substances in which they inhere (*CPA* 224, 142–8).

The close interweaving of science and metaphysics is displayed clearly in one of Grosseteste's most original contributions, his theory of light, expounded in the *Hexaemeron* and also in a separate treatise, *On Light*. Light, he maintained, was the first corporeal form to be created: it unites with prime matter to form a simple dimensionless substance. In the first moment of time this simple substance spread instantaneously to the furthest bounds of the universe, creating tridimensionality. From the outermost sphere, the firmament, it returned inward, creating one after the other nine celestial spheres, of which the ninth is the sphere of the moon. From this sphere light travelled earthward, and produced four terrestrial spheres of fire, air, water, and earth as it moved to our world, where it produced the four familiar elements.

So far we have a physical theory; but Grosseteste at once moves into theology. Light is the natural essence that most closely imitates the divine nature: like God it can create, unaided, from within itself; like God it can fill the universe from a single point (*Hex.* 8. 4. 7). Of all creatures it is the closest to being pure form and pure act (*Hex.* 11. 2. 4). Indeed God himself is eternal light, and the angels are incorporeal lights; God is a universal form of everything, not by uniting with matter, but as the exemplar of all forms. It is only by the light of God, the supreme Truth, that the human intellect can attain to truth of any kind.

Metaphysics and science are intermingled also in the work of Albert the Great, the first German philosopher. In his work, however, science occupies a more substantial proportion. Born in Swabia in the first years of the thirteenth century, Albert studied arts in Padua and became a Dominican in 1223. He taught theology at Paris from 1245 to 1248, having among his pupils the young Thomas Aquinas, whom he took with him to Cologne in 1248 to establish a new house of studies. Thenceforth Cologne was his principal base until his death in 1280, though he moved around as provincial of the German Dominicans (1254–7), bishop of Ratisbon (1260–2), and preacher of St Louis IX's crusade.

Albert was the first of the scholastics to give a wholehearted welcome to the newly translated works of Aristotle. After commenting, as a theologian, on Lombard's *Sentences*, he wrote commentaries on Aristotle's *Ethics*, *De Anima*, and *Metaphysics*—lengthy paraphrases in the manner of Avicenna, rather than line-by-line exegesis in the style of Averroes. He was the author of the first Latin commentary on Aristotle's *Politics*. Albert was a copious writer and the critical edition of his works is still in progress; the previous complete edition extended to thirty-eight volumes. He read widely in Greek, Arabic, and Jewish authors, and acquired an encyclopedic knowledge of previous learning. His mind was capacious rather than precise, and—despite the warnings of his pupil Aquinas—he accepted as genuine several pseudo-Aristotelian works, such as the *Liber de Causis*, which meant that his Aristotelianism retained a Neoplatonic tinge.

Unlike later medieval Aristotelians, Albert shared Aristotle's own interest in the empirical and experimental observation of nature. He wrote treatises on vegetables, plants, and animals, and a geographical text entitled *On the Nature of Places*. His enthusiasm for scientific inquiry, uncommon among his peers, led to his acquiring—like Grosseteste—a posthumous reputation as an alchemist and magician. A number of spurious and curious works were attributed to him, such as *The Secrets of Women* and *The Secrets of the Egyptians*.

St Bonaventure

Just as the Franciscan order had initially been more mystical and less scholastic than the Dominican order, so the first great Franciscan philosopher was more Augustinian and less Aristotelian than the Dominican Albert. John of Fidanza, the son of an Italian physician, was born near Viterbo in 1221. As a young child he fell ill, and when he recovered his cure was attributed by his family to St Francis. His name was changed to Bonaventure and he joined the Franciscans around 1240.

In 1243 Bonaventure went to Paris, and studied under Alexander of Hales, an English secular priest who had joined the Franciscans while already a professor. Alexander became the first head of the Franciscan school, and it was he who first introduced the *Sentences* of Peter Lombard as the standard theological textbook. He composed himself, with considerable assistance from his pupils, a vast *Summa Halesiana*, a theological synthesis that exhibits knowledge of the whole Aristotelian corpus; it was itself often used as a textbook by later Franciscans after his death in 1245.

Bonaventure received his licence to teach in 1248 and wrote his own commentary on the *Sentences*; he became head of the Paris Franciscans in 1253, though troubles in the university made it difficult for him to exercise his office. During this period he wrote a textbook of theology called *Breviloquium*. Four years later he was made minister-general of the whole order, and was faced with the delicate task of reconciling the different factions who, since St Francis' death, claimed to be the true perpetuators of the Franciscan spirit. He reunited and reorganized the order and wrote two lives of St Francis, one of which he imposed as the sole official biography, ordering all others to be destroyed. Not every Franciscan, of course, welcomed his reforms: 'Paris, you destroy Assisi', objected one dissident. But it would be quite wrong to see Bonaventure as primarily an academic and an administrator. In the middle of his troubles as minister-general he wrote a devout mystical treatise, *The Journey of the Mind to God*, the book by which he is nowadays best known. It presents itself as an interpretation of the vision of St Francis on Monte Alvernia, where he received the stigmata, the impression of the wounds of Christ.

Bonaventure's administrative gifts were widely admired, and in 1265 he was chosen by the Pope to be archbishop of York. He begged to be excused, thus depriving that see of its chance to compete in the history of philosophy with St Anselm's Canterbury. He was unable, however, to decline appointment in 1273 as cardinal bishop of Albano. In that year he wrote his last work, *Collationes in Hexameron*, dealing with the biblical account of creation. A year later he died at the Council of Lyons, having preached there the sermon that marked the (short-lived) reunion of the Churches of East and West.

In his writings Bonaventure, unusually for the Latin Middle Ages, presents himself explicitly as a Platonist. Aristotle's criticisms of Plato's Theory of Ideas, he believes, are quite easily refuted. From the initial error of rejecting the Ideas there follow all the other erroneous theses of Aristotelianism: that there is no providence, that the world is eternal, that there is only a single intellect, that there is no personal immortality, and therefore no heaven and no hell (*CH*, vision III. 7). Bonaventure did not, however, believe that Ideas existed outside the divine mind; they were 'eternal reasons', exemplars on which creaturely existence was patterned. These, and not the material objects in the natural world, are the primary objects of human knowledge.

In Bonaventure's writing, as in Grosseteste's, the notion of light plays a central role. There are four different lights that illumine the soul. The first, inferior, light consists in mechanical skill. This appears to be 'light' only in metaphor. Next, there is the light of sense-perception: and here we go beyond metaphor. Each sense is a recipient of light at a different degree of intensity: sight takes it in pure, hearing takes it in mixed with air, taste takes it in mixed with fluid, and so on. Thirdly, there is the light that guides us in the search of intellectual truth: this light illumines the three domains of philosophy: logic, physics, and ethics. Finally, the supreme light enables the mind to understand saving truth: this is the light of Scripture. Like Augustine, Bonaventure is fond of number symbolism, and he points out that if one counts each branch of philosophy as a separate light, then the number of these lights adds up to six, which corresponds to the six days of creation. 'There are in this life six illuminations, and each has its twilight, for all science will be destroyed: for that reason too there follows a seventh day of rest, a day which knows no evening, the illumination of glory' (*PMA* 461–7).

Only in another life, when the blessed see God face to face, will the human mind be directly acquainted with the eternal reasons, the Ideas in the mind of God. But in the present life we acquire knowledge of necessary and eternal truths through their reflected light, just as our eyes see everything by the light of the sun though they cannot look on the sun itself. We do acquire knowledge of a kind through the senses and experience, but the created light of the human intellect is not sufficient to reach any certainty about things. To attain the real truth about anything whatever we need in addition a special divine illumination (II *Sent*. 30. 1; Sermo IV. 10. V). Knowledge and faith can reside alongside each other in the same person.[1]

Bonaventure is familiar with the work of Aristotle, but he engages with him principally in order to refute his errors. It was impossible, he thought, to accept both that the world was created and that it had existed from all eternity: accordingly, he proposed a series of arguments, similar to those used by Philoponus and the Kalam theologians, to prove that the world had a beginning in time (II *Sent*. 1. 1. 1. 2. 1–3). Bonaventure accepted Aristotle's distinction between the agent and the receptive intellect but maintained that each of these were faculties of the individual human being. The tasks which Aristotle's Arabic commentators had assigned to the unique separate agent intellect are performed, in Bonaventure's system, by God's direct illumination. Since each human person has an individual intellectual capacity, each of us is personally immortal and will be held responsible after our death for our deeds in this life.

---

[1] Bonaventure's teaching on the relation between faith and reason is described in more detail below in Ch. 4.

Bonaventure accepted Aristotelian hylomorphism and accepted that the human soul was the form of the human body. He uses this as an argument against Arabic monopsychism: 'since human bodies are distinct, the rational souls that inform those bodies will also be distinct' (*Brev.* 2. 9). Unlike Aristotle, however, and like Ibn Gabirol, he applies the structure of hylomorphism to the soul itself. Everything other than God, he maintained, is composed of matter and form; even angelic spirits who lack bodies contain 'spiritual matter'. Because Bonaventure accepted that the soul contained matter, he was able to reconcile the survival of individual disembodied souls with the commonly accepted thesis that matter was the principle of individuation. He thus avoided a difficulty that faced those, like Aquinas, who maintained that a disembodied soul was wholly immaterial; on the other hand, it is clear that the notion of 'spiritual matter' needs very careful explanation if it is not to be a plain contradiction in terms.

Thomas Aquinas

Thomas Aquinas was born into the feudal nobility of Italy at Roccasecca, probably in 1225. As a 5-year-old he was sent by his father to be brought up by the Benedictine monks of the great abbey of Monte Cassino. The abbey was on the borders between the Papal States and the Neapolitan kingdom of the emperor Frederick II, and Thomas' elementary studies came to an end in 1239 when its premises were occupied by troops in the course of a quarrel between Pope and emperor. After a period at home he studied the liberal arts at the newly founded University of Naples. Here he was introduced to Aristotelian logic and physics, studying under one Peter of Ireland.[2]

In 1244 Thomas became a Dominican friar, to the irritation of his family, who had hoped he would follow the more socially acceptable vocation of a Benedictine monk. He hoped to escape from family pressure by migrating to Paris, but was kidnapped on the way and kept under house arrest for more than a year in one or other family castle. He employed his time in prison composing two brief logical treatises, a handbook on fallacies, and a fragment on modal propositions.

The Aquino family failed to dent his resolve to be a friar. An attempt to seduce him by placing a prostitute in his cell only reinforced his determination to live a life of chastity: henceforth, his biographer tells us, he avoided women as a man avoids snakes. At length he was released, and he continued his journey to Paris. There he became a student of Albert the Great. The family made one more

---

[2] My account of Aquinas' life depends heavily on J. Weisheipl, *Friar Thomas d'Aquino* (Oxford: Blackwell, 1974) and on J. P. Torrell, *Saint Thomas Aquinas*, i (Washington: Catholic University of America Press, 1996).

attempt to set him on a career path of their choice: they procured an offer from the Pope to allow him to be abbot of Monte Cassino while remaining a Dominican. Thomas refused and followed Albert to Cologne, where he listened to his lectures on Aristotle. As a student his taciturnity and corpulence earned him the nickname 'the dumb ox'. Albert quickly appreciated his astonishing talents, and predicted that the dumb ox would fill the whole world with his bellowing.

In 1252 Aquinas moved to Paris and began studying for the mastership in theology. As a bachelor he lectured on the Bible and on the *Sentences* of Peter Lombard. His commentary on the *Sentences* is the first of his major surviving works, and already displays his original genius. In the same period he wrote a pamphlet on Aristotelian metaphysics, much influenced by Avicenna, with the title *De Ente et Essentia* ('On Being and Essence'), which was to have an influence quite out of proportion to its size. He proceeded as master in theology in the year 1256.

The Dominican order controlled two of the twelve chairs of theology in Paris. Friars were unpopular with the traditional clergy, and the university had tried to suppress one of their chairs in 1252. In the ensuing controversy many professors went on strike, and Aquinas' first lectures as bachelor were given as a blackleg. But the chair survived, and Aquinas was appointed to it shortly after becoming master. At the time of his inaugural lecture anti-Dominican feeling was so high that the priory needed a permanent guard of royal troops. St Bonaventure and his Franciscans suffered similarly during the same period.

Aquinas remained in Paris for three years, lecturing on the book of Isaiah and the Gospel of St Matthew. As a professor it was his duty to oversee the formal disputations of the bachelors, and we possess the text of the disputations over which he presided, called, after the topic of the first of them, *Quaestiones Disputatae de Veritate* ('Disputed Questions on Truth'). In fact they range over many different topics: truth and the knowledge of truth in God, angels, and men; providence and predestination; grace and justification; reason, conscience, and free will; emotion, trances, prophecy, education, and many other topics. The collection consists of 253 individual disputations, called 'articles' in the editions, and grouped by themes into twenty-nine 'questions'. The text of the series amounts to over half a million words.

In addition to these structured disputations the medieval curriculum imposed on masters the duty of undertaking a number of 'quodlibetical' disputations. These were impromptu discussions in which any member of the audience could raise a question on any topic. They were held in Advent and Lent: no doubt they were a penitential experience for the master. Of the quodlibets that survive from Aquinas' Paris period, some concern topical issues related to the controversy over the mendicant orders: for instance, the question 'Are friars obliged to perform manual labour?' Others are of less immediate impact, such as 'Are there real worms in hell?' A final legacy of this time is an unfinished commentary on Boethius' *On the Trinity*, which discusses the relationship between natural science, mathematics, and metaphysics, ranging these disciplines in a hierarchy of increasing abstraction from matter.

In 1259 Aquinas gave up his Paris professorship and spent some time in Italy. When Urban IV became pope in 1261, the papal court moved to Orvieto, and St Thomas went there too. During the early 1260s he was to be found teaching at Orvieto, Rome, and Viterbo, and mingling with the scholars, diplomats, and missionaries in attendance on the Pope. At the court of Urban IV he met William of Moerbeke, the most accurate of the translators of Aristotle, and began a fruitful association which was to result in a magnificent series of commentaries on the philosopher's major works. The saint was also employed by Pope Urban as a writer of prayers and hymns, especially for the liturgy of the new feast of Corpus Christi. This was instituted in 1264 in honour of the sacrament of the Eucharist, in which, according to Catholic belief, bread and wine were changed into the body and blood of Christ. The hymns which St Thomas wrote for the office remain popular among Catholics, and the sequence of the Mass, *Lauda Sion*, renders the doctrine of transubstantiation into surprisingly lively and singable verse.

The most important achievement of this middle period of St Thomas' life was the *Summa contra Gentiles*, begun just before the departure from Paris, and completed at Orvieto in 1265. Its title, literally translated, means 'Summary, or Synopsis, against Unbelievers'; its most frequently used English translation bears the title *On the Truth of the Catholic Faith*. According to a fourteenth-century tradition, now often discounted by scholars, the book was a missionary manual, written at the request of the Spanish Dominican Raymond of Penafort, who was evangelizing non-Christians in Spain and North Africa.

Whatever the truth of this story, the book differs from St Thomas' other major treatises in taking its initial stand (throughout the first three of its four books) not on Christian doctrine, but on philosophical premises that could be accepted by Jewish and Muslim thinkers versed in Aristotelian philosophy. Thomas explains his method thus:

Muslims and pagans do not agree with us in accepting the authority of any Scripture we might use in refuting them, in the way in which we can dispute against Jews by appeal to the Old Testament and against heretics by appeal to the New. These people accept neither. Hence we must have recourse to natural reason, to which all men are forced to assent. (*ScG* 1. 2)

Thus, the text is not a work of revealed theology, but of natural theology, which is a branch of philosophy.

The *Summa contra Gentiles* is a treatise, not a record of disputations; it is in four books of a hundred or so chapters each, amounting in total to some 300,000 words. The first book is about the nature of God, in so far as this is held to be knowable by reason unaided by revelation. The second concerns the created world and its production by God. The third expounds the way in which rational creatures are to find their happiness in God, and thus ranges widely over ethical matters. The fourth is devoted to specifically Christian doctrines such as the Trinity, the Incarnation, the sacraments, and the final resurrection of the saints through the power of Christ. In the first three books Aquinas is scrupulous to use biblical or ecclesiastical texts only as illustrations, never as premises from which the arguments start.

After the completion of the *Summa contra Gentiles* Aquinas went to Rome to establish a Dominican institute attached to the Church of Sta Sabina on the Aventine. While acting as regent master there it was once again his duty to preside over disputations. There are three groups of these, ten entitled *On the Power of God* (1265–6), and shorter series, *On Evil* (1266–7) and *On Spiritual Creatures*. These questions are in general less profound in content than the earlier ones entitled *On Truth*: this presumably reflects the fact that the students at a small house in Rome were not as sharp as those at the University of Paris. But the third of the questions on power, consisting of nineteen articles on the topic of creation, contains material of the highest interest. During the same period Thomas started, but never finished, a compendium of theology structured around the virtues of faith, hope, and charity.

It was in Rome that Aquinas began his magisterial series of commentaries on the works of Aristotle. The first was on the *De Anima*; after many further centuries of Aristotelian scholarship it is still regarded by experts as worth consulting. This was followed, at an uncertain date, by a commentary on the *Physics*. But the most important development of the Roman regency, which probably grew out of teaching experience there, was the commencement of Aquinas' masterpiece, the *Summa Theologiae*.

The *Summa Theologiae* is an immense work, of over 2 million words, divided into three parts; most of the first was probably written at Sta Sabina. In style, it falls between the *Summa contra Gentiles* and the *Disputed Questions*: it is not a record of live scholastic disputation, but it is, like a disputation, divided into questions and articles, not into chapters. However, the multiple arguments for and against a particular thesis that introduce a genuine disputation are replaced by an introductory set (usually a triad) of difficulties against the position that Aquinas intends to take up in the body of the article. This initial section is the *Videtur quod non* ('It seems not'). These objections are followed by a single consideration on the other side—usually the citation of an authoritative text—beginning with the words 'Sed contra' ('On the other hand'). After this, in the main body of the article, Aquinas sets out his own position with the reasons that support it. Each article then concludes with the solution of the difficulties set out in the introductory objections.

The method, while initially puzzling to a modern reader, provides a powerful intellectual discipline to prevent a philosopher from taking things for granted. By adopting it, St Thomas imposed on himself the question 'Whom have I got to convince of what, and what are the strongest things that can be said on the other side?'

To illustrate the structure of the *Summa* I quote one of its shortest articles, the tenth article of question nineteen of the First Part, which poses the question 'Does God have free will?'

It seems that God does not have free will.

1. St Jerome says, in his homily on the Prodigal Son, 'God is the only one who is not, and cannot be, involved in sin; all other things, since they have free will, can turn either way.'

2. Moreover, free will is the power of reason and will by which good and evil are chosen. But God, as has been said, never wills evil. Therefore, there is no free will in God.

But on the other hand, St Ambrose, in his book on Faith, says this: 'The Holy Spirit makes his gifts to individuals as he wills, in accordance with the choice of his free will, and not in observance of any necessity.'

I reply that it must be said that we have free will in regard to those things which we do not will by necessity or natural instinct. Our willing to be happy, for instance, is not a matter of free will but of natural instinct. For this reason, other animals, which are driven in certain directions by natural instinct, are not said to be directed by free will. Now God, as has been shown above, wills his own goodness of necessity, but other things not of necessity; hence, with regard to those things which he does not will of necessity, he enjoys free will.

To the first objection it must be said that St Jerome wants to exclude from God not free will altogether, but only the freedom which includes falling into sin.

To the second objection it must be said that since, as has been shown, moral evil is defined in terms of aversion from the divine goodness in respect of which God wills everything, it is clear that it is impossible for him to will moral evil. Nonetheless, he has an option between opposites, in so far as he can will something to be or not to be, just as we, without sinning, can decide to sit down or decide not to sit down. (*ST* 1. 19. 10)

In its own fashion, the *Summa Theologiae* is a masterpiece of philosophical writing. Once one has become accustomed to the syntax of medieval Latin and the technicalities of scholastic jargon one finds the style smooth, lucid, civil, and judicious. The work is almost entirely free from rhetoric, and Thomas never lets his own ego obtrude.

The First Part of the *Summa Theologiae* covers much of the same ground as the first two books of the *Summa contra Gentiles*. The first forty-three questions are concerned with the existence and nature of God. Since Thomas is writing for Catholic theology students rather than for a possibly infidel philosophical audience, he can present the doctrine of the Trinity immediately after listing the divine attributes, without having to segregate it in a special book on the mysteries of faith. But he remains careful to distinguish between truths discoverable by reason and truths available only through revelation. Five dense questions follow, dealing with the metaphysics of creation, and these are followed by fifteen questions on the nature of angels. The section on human nature (qq. 75–102) is, for a modern reader, the most rewarding part of the book.[3] It is fuller and more systematic than the corresponding section in the second book of the earlier work, and it is less heavily loaded with criticisms of Arabian exegesis of Aristotle's psychology.

While writing the First Part of the *Summa* St Thomas began a political treatise, *On Kingship*, laying down principles for the guidance of secular governments in a way that leaves no doubt that kings are subject to priests and that the pope enjoys a secular as well as a spiritual supremacy. Unfinished when Aquinas died, it was completed by the historian Tolomeo of Lucca.

In 1268, having declined an invitation to become archbishop of Naples, Aquinas was called back to Paris, where the mendicant orders were again an object of hostility. More importantly, Aristotelian ideas were being brought into disrepute by a group of arts professors, the 'Latin Averroists', who followed Arabic commentators to conclusions incompatible with Catholic orthodoxy. Aquinas wrote two polemical pamphlets, *On the Single Intellect:—Against the Averroists*, and *On the Eternity of the World:—Against the Grumblers*. He restated his long-held positions that both the agent and the receptive intellect are faculties of the individual person, and that the beginning of the world in time can be neither established nor refuted by philosophical argument. In this last treatise he was fighting on two fronts: both against the Averroists, who thought that creation in time could be disproved, and against Franciscan theologians, who thought it could be proved.

The controversies convinced Thomas that the best antidote to heterodox Aristotelianism was a thorough knowledge of the entire Aristotelian system, so he continued with his task of providing commentaries. Probably during this period he wrote line-by-line commentaries on two of Aristotle's logical works, on the entire *Nicomachean Ethics*, and on twelve books of the *Metaphysics*. Though based on an imperfect translation of defective manuscripts, these commentaries are still found valuable by modern interpreters of Aristotle.

But the most important of Aquinas' works during this second Paris regency was the Second Part of the *Summa Theologiae*. This, much the longest of the three parts, is always further divided in editions: the first part of the Second Part (*Prima Secundae*, cited as 1a 2ae) and the second part of the Second Part (*Secunda Secundae*, cited as 2a 2ae) This corresponds in subject matter to the third book of the *Summa contra Gentiles*, but it is very much fuller and owes much more to Aristotle's *Nicomachean Ethics*, on which Aquinas was simultaneously writing his commentary.[4]

The *Prima Secundae* begins, like Aristotle's treatise, by considering the ultimate end or goal of human life. Like Aristotle, Aquinas identifies the ultimate end with happiness, and like him he thinks that happiness cannot be equated with pleasure,

---

[3] Aquinas' account of the human mind is described in detail in Ch. 6.

[4] Aquinas' ethical teaching is described in detail in Ch. 8.

riches, honour, or any bodily good, but must consist in activity in accordance with virtue, especially intellectual virtue. The intellectual activity that satisfies the Aristotelian requirements for happiness is to be found perfectly only in contemplation of the essence of God; happiness in the ordinary conditions of the present life must remain imperfect. True happiness, then, even in Aristotle's terms, is to be found only in the souls of the blessed in heaven. The saints will in due course receive a bonus of happiness, undreamt of by Aristotle, in the resurrection of the body in glory.

Virtue, according to Aristotle, was a psychic disposition that found expression in both action and emotion. Aquinas, accordingly, prefaces his account of virtue with a treatise on human action (qq. 6–21) and human emotion (qq. 22–48). He also offers a general study of the concept of disposition (*habitus*): an original philosophical investigation of a topic whose importance was lost sight of when philosophy became impoverished at the Renaissance. The account of the nature of virtue itself, of the distinction between moral and intellectual virtues, and of the relation between virtue and emotion, is modelled closely on Aristotle. But Aquinas adds to Aristotle's list of virtues some Christian virtues—the 'theological' virtues of faith, hope, and charity, listed as a trio in a famous passage of St Paul. Aquinas links Aristotelian virtues with the gifts of character prized by Christians, and connects Aristotelian vices with biblical concepts of sin.

The two final sections of the *Prima Secundae* concern law and grace. Questions 90–108 constitute a treatise on jurisprudence: the nature of law; the distinction between natural and positive law; the source and extent of the powers of human legislators; the contrast between the laws of the Old and New Testament. In questions 109–14 Aquinas treats of the relation between nature and grace, and the justification and salvation of sinners: topics that were to be the focus of much controversy at the time of the Reformation. The position he adopts on these issues stands somewhere between those later taken up by Catholic and Protestant controversialists.

The *Prima Secundae* is the General Part of Aquinas' ethics, while the *Secunda Secundae* contains his detailed teaching on individual moral topics. Each virtue is analysed in turn, and the sins listed that conflict with it. First come the theological virtues: thus faith is contrasted with the sins of unbelief, heresy, and apostasy. It is in the course of this section that Aquinas sets out his views on the persecution of heretics. The virtue of charity is contrasted with the sins of hatred, envy, discord, and sedition; in treating of these sins Aquinas sets out the conditions under which he believes the making of war is justified.

The other virtues are treated within the overarching framework of the four 'cardinal' virtues, prudence, justice, fortitude, and temperance, a quartet dating back to the early dialogues of Plato. The treatise on justice covers the topics that would nowadays appear in a textbook of criminal law; but one of the special branches of justice is piety, the virtue of giving God his due. Here Aquinas ranges widely over many topics, from tithe-paying to necromancy. The discussion of fortitude provides an opportunity to treat of martyrdom, magnanimity, and magnificence. The final cardinal virtue is temperance, the heading under which Aquinas treats of moral questions concerned with food, drink, and sex.

Aquinas' list of virtues does not altogether tally with Aristotle's, though he works hard to Christianize some of the more pagan characters who figure in the *Ethics*. Aristotle's ideal man is great-souled, that is to say, he is a highly superior being who is very conscious of his own superiority to others. How can this be reconciled with the Christian virtue of humility, according to which each should esteem others better than himself? By a remarkable piece of intellectual legerdemain, Aquinas makes magnanimity not only compatible with humility but part of the very same virtue. There is a virtue, he says, that is the moderation of ambition, a virtue based on a just appreciation of one's own gifts and defects. Humility is the aspect that ensures that one's ambitions are based on a just assessment of one's defects, magnanimity is the aspect that ensures that they are based on a just assessment of one's gifts.

The *Secunda Secundae* concludes, as did the *Nicomachean Ethics*, with a comparison between the active and the contemplative life, to the advantage of the latter. But the whole is, of course, transposed into a Christian key, and when Aquinas comes to discuss the religious orders he gives the Aristotelian theme a special Dominican twist. Whereas the purely contemplative life is to be preferred to the purely active life, the best life of all for a religious is a life of contemplation that includes teaching and preaching. 'Just as it is better to light up others than to shine alone, it is better to share the fruits of one's contemplation with others than to contemplate in solitude.'

Aquinas' second Paris regency was a period of amazing productivity. The Second Part and the Commentary on the *Metaphysics* are each nearly a million words in length. When one reviews the sheer bulk of Aquinas' output between 1269 and 1272 one can believe the testimony of his chief secretary that it was his habit to dictate, like a grand master at a chess tournament, to three or four secretaries simultaneously. The learned world can be grateful that the pressure of business forced him to compose by dictation, because his own autographs are quite illegible to any but the most highly trained specialists.

In 1272 Thomas left Paris for the last time. The Dominican order assigned him the task of setting up a new house of studies in Italy; he chose to attach it to the Priory of San Domenico in Naples. His lectures there were sponsored by the king of Naples, Charles of Anjou, whose brother St Louis IX had taken the measure of his genius in Paris. He continued to work on his Aristotle commentaries and began the Third Part of the *Summa*. This concerns strictly theological topics: the Incarnation, the Virgin Mary, the life of Christ, the sacraments of baptism, confirmation, Eucharist, and penance. But reflection on these topics gave Aquinas opportunity to discuss many philosophical issues, such as personal identity and individuation and the logic of predication. The treatise on the Eucharist, in particular, called for discussion of the doctrine of transubstantiation and thus for a final presentation of Aquinas' thought on the nature of material substance and substantial change.

The *Summa* was never completed. Though not yet 50, Aquinas became subject to ever more serious fits of abstraction, and in December 1273, while saying Mass, he had a mysterious experience—perhaps a mental breakdown, or, as he himself believed, a supernatural vision—which put an end to his academic activity. He could not continue to write or dictate, and when his secretary Reginald of Piperno urged him to continue with the *Summa*, he replied, 'I cannot, because all that I have written now seems like straw.' Reginald and his colleagues, after Aquinas' death, completed the *Summa* with a supplement, drawn from earlier writings, covering the topics left untreated: the remaining sacraments and the 'four last things', death, judgement, heaven, and hell.

In 1274 Pope Gregory X called a council of the Church at Lyons, hoping to reunite the Greek and Latin Churches. St Thomas was invited to attend, and in spite of his poor condition he set out northwards, but his health deteriorated further and he was forced to stop at his niece's castle near Fossanova. After some weeks he was carried into the nearby Cistercian monastery, where he died on 7 March 1274.

The Afterlife of Aquinas

In the centuries since his death Aquinas' reputation has fluctuated spectacularly. A few years after he died several of his opinions were condemned by the universities of Paris and Oxford. An English friar who travelled to Rome to appeal against the sentence was condemned to perpetual silence. It was some fifty years before Aquinas' writings were generally regarded as theologically sound.

In 1316, however, Pope John XXII began a process of canonization. It was hard to find suitable accounts of miracles. The best that could be found concerned a deathbed scene. At Fossanova the sick man, long unable to eat, expressed a wish for herrings. These were not to be found in the Mediterranean: but surprisingly, in the next consignment of sardines, a batch of fish turned up which Thomas was happy to accept as delicious herrings. The Pope's judges did not find this a sufficiently impressive miracle. But the canonization went ahead. 'There are as many miracles as there are articles of the *Summa*,' the Pope is reported to have said; and he declared Thomas a saint in 1323.

Paris, rather belatedly, revoked the condemnation of his works in 1325. Oxford, however, seems to have taken no academic notice of the canonization, and throughout the Middle Ages Aquinas did not enjoy, outside his own order, the special prestige among Catholic theologians that he was to enjoy in the twentieth century. Tradition has it that the *Summa* was set in a place of honour, beside the Bible, during the deliberations of the Council of Trent; but it was not until the encyclical letter *Aeterni Patris* of Pope Leo XIII in 1879 that he was made, as it were, the official theologian of the whole Roman Catholic Church.

All those who study Aquinas are indebted to Pope Leo for the stimulus which his encyclical gave to the production of scholarly editions of the *Summa* and of other works. But the promotion of the saint as the official philosopher of the Church had also a negative effect. It closed off the philosophical study of St Thomas by non-Catholic philosophers, who were repelled by someone whom they came to think of as simply the spokesman of a particular ecclesiastical system. The problem was aggravated when in 1914 Pius X singled out twenty-four theses of Thomist philosophy to be taught in Catholic institutions.

The secular reaction to the canonization of St Thomas' philosophy was summed up by Bertrand Russell in his *History of Western Philosophy*. 'There was little of the true philosophical spirit in Aquinas: he could not, like Socrates, follow an argument wherever it might lead, since he knew the truth in advance, all declared in the Catholic faith. The finding of arguments for a conclusion given in advance is not philosophy but special pleading.'

It is not in fact a serious charge against a philosopher to say that he is looking for good reasons for what he already believes in. Descartes, sitting beside his fire, wearing his dressing gown, sought reasons for judging that that was what he was doing, and took a long time to find them. Russell himself spent much energy seeking proofs of what he already believed: *Principia Mathematica* takes hundreds of pages to prove that 1 and 1 make 2.

We judge a philosopher by whether his reasonings are sound or unsound, not by where he first lighted on his premises or how he first came to believe his conclusions. Hostility to Aquinas on the basis of his official position in Catholicism is thus unjustified, however understandable, even for secular philosophers. But there were more serious ways in which the actions of Leo XIII and Pius X did a disservice to Thomas' philosophical reputation in non-Catholic circles.

The official respect accorded to Aquinas by the Church meant that his insights and arguments were frequently presented in crude ways by admirers who failed to appreciate his philosophical sophistication. Even in seminaries and universities the Thomism introduced by Leo XIII often took the form of textbooks and epitomes *ad mentem Thomae* rather than a study of the text of the saint himself.

Since the Second Vatican Council, St Thomas seems to have lost the pre-eminent favour he enjoyed in ecclesiastical circles, and to have been superseded, in the reading lists of ordinands, by lesser, more recent authors. This state of affairs is deplored by Pope John Paul in *Fides et Ratio*, the most recent papal encyclical devoted to Aquinas. On the other hand, the devaluation of St Thomas within the bounds of Catholicism has been accompanied by a re-evaluation of the saint in secular universities in various parts of the world. In the first years of the twenty-first century it is not too much to speak of a renaissance of Thomism—not a confessional Thomism, but a study of Thomas that transcends the limits not only of the Catholic Church but of Christianity itself.

The new interest in Aquinas is both more varied and more critical than the earlier, denominational reception of his work. The possibility of very divergent interpretations is inherent in the nature of Aquinas' *Nachlass*. The saint's output was vast—well over 8 million words—so that any modern study of his work is bound to concentrate only on a small portion of the surviving corpus. Even if one concentrates—as scholars commonly do—on one or other of the great *Summae*, the interpretation of any portion of these works will depend in part on which of many parallel passages in other works one chooses to cast light on the text under study. Especially now that the whole corpus is searchable by computer, there is great scope for selectivity here.

Secondly, though Aquinas' Latin is in itself marvellously lucid, the translation of it into English is not a trivial or uncontroversial matter. Aquinas' Latin terms have English equivalents that are common terms in contemporary philosophy; but the meanings of the Latin terms and their English equivalents are often very different.[5] Not only have the English words come to us after centuries of independent history, they entered the language from Latin at a date when their philosophical usage had been influenced by theories opposed to Aquinas' own. We must be wary of assuming, for instance, that 'actus' means 'act' or that 'objectum' means 'object', or that 'habitus' means 'habit'.

Thirdly, in the case of a writer such as Plato or Aristotle, it is often possible for an interpreter to clear up ambiguities in discussion by concentrating on the concrete examples offered to illustrate the philosophical point. But Aquinas—in common with other great medieval scholastics—is very sparing with illustrative examples, and when he does offer them they are often second-hand or worn out. A commentator, therefore, in order to render the text intelligible to a modern reader, has to provide her own examples, and the choice of examples involves a substantial degree of interpretation.

Finally, any admirer of Aquinas' genius wishes to present his work to a modern audience in the best possible light. But what it is for an interpreter to do his best for Aquinas depends upon what he himself regards as particularly valuable in philosophy. In particular, there is a fundamental ambiguity in Aquinas' thinking that lies at the root of the philosophical disagreements among his commentators. Aquinas is best known as the man who reconciled Christianity with Aristotelianism; but, as we shall see in later chapters, there are considerable elements of Platonism to be found in his writings. Many modern

[5] This is a point well emphasized by Eleonore Stump in her *Aquinas* (London: Routledge, 2003), 35.

commentators take Aquinas' Aristotelianism seriously and disown the Platonic residues, but there are those who side with the Platonic Thomas against the Aristotelian Thomas. The motive for this may be theological: such an approach makes it easier to accept the doctrines that the soul survives the death of the body, that angels are pure forms, and that God is pure actuality. Aquinas himself, in fact, was an Aristotelian on earth, but a Platonist in heaven.

For those who are more interested in philosophy than in history, the variety of interpretations of Aquinas on offer is something to be welcomed. His own approach to the writings of his predecessors was in general extremely irenic: rather than attack a proposition that on the face of it was quite erroneous, he sought to tease out of it—by 'benign interpretation' often beyond the bounds of historical probability—a thesis that was true or a sentiment that was correct. His capacious welcome to a motley of Greek, Jewish, and Muslim texts both opens to his successors the possibility of widely divergent interpretations of his work, and encourages them to follow his example in valuing the ecumenical pursuit of philosophical truth higher than utter fidelity to critical plausibility.

Siger of Brabant and Roger Bacon

In the decades immediately after his death, Aquinas had few faithful followers. Late in life he had devoted much energy to combating a radical form of Aristotelianism in the arts faculty at Paris. These philosophers maintained that the world had always existed and that there was only a single intellect in all human beings. The former was undoubtedly a fundamental part of the cosmology of Aristotle; the latter was the interpretation of his psychology favoured by his most authoritative commentator, Averroes. For this reason the school has often been called 'Latin Averroism': its leading spokesman was Siger of Brabant (1235–82). The characteristic teachings of these Parisian scholastics were difficult to reconcile with the Christian doctrines of a creation at a date in time and a future life for individual human souls. Some claimed merely to be reporting, without commitment, the teaching of Aristotle; Siger himself seems to have taught at one time that some propositions of Aristotle and Averroes are provable in philosophy, though faith teaches the opposite.

In 1270 the archbishop of Paris condemned a list of thirteen doctrines beginning with the proposition 'the intellect of all men is one and numerically the same' and 'there never was a first man'. The condemnation may have been the result partly of the two monographs that Aquinas had written against Siger's characteristic doctrines. But despite this dispute between them, the two thinkers were often grouped together in the minds of their younger contemporaries. On the one hand, sets of propositions were condemned in Paris and Oxford in 1277 that included theses drawn from both Siger and Aquinas. On the other hand, Dante places the two of them side by side in Paradise and makes St Thomas praise Siger for the eternal light that is cast by the profundity of his thought. This compliment has puzzled commentators; but perhaps Dante thought of Siger as a representative of the contribution made by pagan and Muslim thinkers to the Thomist synthesis, a Christian thinker standing in for the unbelieving philosophers who were barred from Paradise.

Dante himself, though professionally untrained, was well versed in philosophy, and the *Divina Commedia* often renders scholastic doctrines into exquisite verse. For instance, the account of the gradual development of the human soul in *Purgatorio* 25 is extremely close to the account given in Aquinas' *Summa Theologiae*. Dante's own most substantive contribution to philosophy is his book *On Monarchy*. This argues that human intellectual development can only take place in conditions of peace, which, in a world of national rivalries, can only be achieved under a supranational authority. This, he argues, should not be the pope, but the Holy Roman emperor.

An older contemporary of Dante was Roger Bacon, who outlived Siger by some ten years. Born in Ilchester about 1210, he studied and taught in the Oxford arts faculty until about 1247. He then migrated to Paris, and in the next decade joined the Franciscan order. He disliked Paris and compared the Parisian doctors Alexander of Hales and Albert the Great unfavourably with his Oxford teacher Robert Grosseteste. The only Parisian doctor he admired was one Peter of Maricourt, who taught him the importance of experiment in scientific research, and led him to believe that mathematics was 'the door and key' to certainty in philosophy. For reasons unknown, in 1257 he was forbidden by his Franciscan superiors to teach; but he was allowed to continue to write and in 1266 the Pope, no less, asked him to send him his writings. Sadly, this pope, Clement IV, did not live long enough to read the texts, and Bacon was condemned in 1278 for heretical views on astrology, and lived out most of the rest of his life in prison, dying in 1292.

Roger Bacon is often considered a precursor of his seventeenth-century namesake Francis Bacon in his emphasis on the role of experiment in philosophy. In his main work, the *opus maius*, Roger, like Francis, attacks the sources of error: deference to authority, blind habit, popular prejudice, and pretence to superior wisdom. There are two essential preliminaries, he says, to scientific research. One is a serious study of the languages of the ancients—the current Latin translations of Aristotle and the Bible are seriously defective. The other is a real knowledge of mathematics, without which no progress can be made in sciences like astronomy. Bacon's own contribution to science focused on optics, where he followed up some of the insights of Grosseteste. It was, indeed, at one time believed that he was the first inventor of the telescope.

Bacon identifies a distinct kind of science, *scientia experimentalis*. A priori reasoning may lead us to a correct conclusion, he says, but only experience gives us certainty.

Aristotelian physics may teach that fire burns, but it is the child that is actually burnt that dreads the fire. Experiment can also take us beyond the demonstrated conclusions of the scientific disciplines, as we can see if we consider the pharmacopoeia built up by the experience of practical physicians. Constructing a model of the heavens, like an astrolabe, can teach us more things about them than deductive science can.

Though Bacon believed in the possibility of the alchemical transmutation of baser metals into gold, and saw the ability to foretell the future and to work wonders as being one of the rewards of scientific research, he made a sharp distinction between science and magic. Indeed he thought that one reason for taking up science was in order to refute the false claims made for the magical arts. But before one salutes him as a protagonist in any war between science and mysticism, it is important to remember that among the 'experience' to which he attached such importance in philosophy he includes religious visions and mystical states of rapture.

Roger Bacon was one of a distinguished trio of Franciscan thinkers who graced Oxford in the thirteenth and fourteenth centuries, the other two being John Duns Scotus and William Ockham. The three are very different from each other, as we shall see, so that it would be quite wrong to think of Oxford as the home of a particular Franciscan school of thought. But all three of them had an influence that was to extend far beyond Oxford or England.

Duns Scotus

Of all the great philosophers, John Duns Scotus is the one whose life is least known and whose biography rests almost entirely on conjecture. Any account of his career has to be based on just four firm dates for which there is documentary evidence: on 17 March 1291 he was ordained priest at Northampton; on 26 July 1300 he was at Oxford, as a Franciscan friar, unsuccessfully seeking a licence to hear confessions; on 18 November 1304 he was commended by the Franciscan minister-general for a position of authority in Paris; on 30 February 1308 he was a lector in theology at Cologne. Even the date of his death is uncertain; the date traditionally given is 8 November 1308.

From these fragments of evidence scholars have built up skeleton biographies: what follows is only one of several possible reconstructions.[6] John was born, we are told, at Duns, a town on the Scottish border a few miles inland from Berwick upon Tweed. Working back from his ordination, we can guess a birth date of early 1266. Some time in his teens he seems to have become a novice in the Franciscan house

---

[6] My account of Scotus' life owes much to a detailed study, sadly still unpublished, by Antoon Vos.

at Dumfries, under his uncle Elias Duns, head of the Scottish friars who had recently achieved a degree of self-government under the English branch of the order. During the 1280s he was sent to Oxford, where he studied philosophy in the Franciscan house, Greyfriars, which was already large enough to contain some seventy students. Scotus began theological studies in the university in 1288: the course lasted thirteen years and culminated with three years of obligatory lecturing, two on the *Sentences* of Peter Lombard and one on the Bible. In 1300–1 he obtained his baccalaureate in theology, a status equivalent to that of assistant professor.

For reasons that can only be guessed, the Franciscan authorities decided that instead of taking an Oxford doctorate Scotus should go as a bachelor to Paris. Possibly he had shown such brilliance as a lecturer that they felt he should be given a chance to shine in the premier university of the age—one with which Oxford was only just now catching up. However, the Franciscan convent in Paris, home of Alexander of Hales and Bonaventure, did not provide a peaceful environment. After a year of lecturing on the *Sentences*, Scotus, along with eighty other friars, was banished from France for supporting the papal side in the dispute between Philip the Fair and Boniface VIII.[7] He left in June 1303, and returned to England, spending some time at Cambridge, where there was a Franciscan graduate house.

After the death of Pope Boniface in late 1303 relations between the Holy See and the French kingdom improved, and the ban on the Franciscans was revoked. Scotus returned to Paris, completed his lecture series on the *Sentences*, proceeded to his doctorate, and was regent master during the year 1306–7. Once again he was forced to leave Paris at a time of political unrest, and he spent the last year of his life—the forty-second—at Cologne. He died there and was buried in the Franciscan church with the epitaph 'Scotland bore me | England taught me | France received me | Cologne now keeps me'. He was beatified by Pope John Paul II in 1993.

Many manuscripts of Scotus' writings survive, but their nature and order present as much of an enigma as the details of his biography. Most of them were in a fragmentary and incomplete form at the time of his death, and they were collected and polished by the devoted labours of disciples over several generations. The canon thus established was published in twelve volumes by Luke Wadding in 1639, an edition republished in 1891–5 by the Paris firm of Vives. The centrepieces of this edition were two commentaries on the *Sentences*, entitled *Opus Oxoniense* and *Reportata Parisiensia*; the collection also contained a series of commentaries on Aristotle, a set of quodlibetical questions, and a number of monographs, notably *De Rerum Principio*, *De Primo Principio*, and *Grammatica Speculativa*. Scholars

---

[7] Perhaps best known through Dante's account of the French mistreatment of Boniface in Anagni (*Purgatorio*, 20).

were dependent on the Vives–Wadding edition until the latter part of the twentieth century, and it still provides the only printed text for a number of Scotus' works.

The work of scholars in the twentieth century, however, has completely refashioned the canon. Most of the commentaries on Aristotle turned out to be the work of other, later, hands. There remain, as authentic, commentaries on the *Categories*, the *De Interpretatione*, and the *Sophistici Elenchi*, plus a commentary on Porphyry. These logical works most probably date from Scotus' first period in Oxford in the early 1290s.[8] So too do a set of questions on Aristotle's *De Anima*, and probably a commentary on the *Metaphysics*, though this appears to have undergone revision quite late in Scotus' career. Two of the most heavily studied monographs in the Vives–Wadding edition, the *De Rerum Principio* and the *Grammatica Speculativa*, turned out, on critical inspection, to be inauthentic.

In the mid-1920s manuscripts were discovered of a text which, after some controversy, is now accepted as Scotus' own notes for his lectures on the first two books of the *Sentences* in Oxford in the years 1298–1300. In 1938 the Franciscan order set up a scholarly commission in Rome to produce a critical edition of Scotus' works, and between 1950 and 1993 this important text was published by the Vatican Press under the title *Lectura I–II*. *Lectura III*, published in 2003, is most probably the course given by Scotus during his period in Oxford during exile from Paris in 1303. The text previously known as the *Opus Oxoniense* is now seen as consisting of elements from an ongoing revision of this course, which continued throughout the Paris years. The *Reportata Parisiensia* bears testimony to a late stage of the revision from the hands of students attending the lectures. The definitive form of a medieval lecture course was attained when the lecturer compared his own drafts with his students' notes, and incorporated the material into a single, approved, text known as an *Ordinatio*. The publication of the *Ordinatio*—never finally retouched by Scotus himself—has been the major task of the Scotist Commission. Between 1950 and 2001 seven volumes of this critical edition appeared, completing the commentary on *Sentences I–II*. For *Ordinatio III* and *IV* scholars still rely on the last two books of the *Opus Oxoniense* as printed by Wadding.

The Vatican editions of the *Lectura* and *Ordinatio* are the main point of reference for the study of Scotus by present-day philosophers and theologians. But two works of uncontested authenticity provide evidence of Scotus' mature thought. The quodlibetical questions undoubtedly belong to the brief period when Scotus was regent master in Paris, in 1306 or 1307. The brief monograph *De Primo Principio*, published in several editions since 1941, belongs to the last period of his life, and some scholars believe that it was written in Cologne in the year of his death.

---

[8] The philosophical works of Scotus are being published, since 1999, in a critical edition by a team of editors operating first in St Bonaventure, NY, and later at the Catholic University of America in Washington DC.

Finally, the genuineness of a work entitled *Theoremata* is still the object of scholarly dispute. The balance of opinion now seems in favour of authenticity, but if the work is genuine it testifies to a remarkable volte-face by Scotus on an important topic, the question whether God's existence can be proved by the natural light of reason.

Scotus is not an easy author to read. His language is crabbed, technical, and unaccommodating, and the structure of his arguments is often difficult to discern. He had, however, one of the sharpest minds ever to have engaged in philosophy, and he well deserved his sobriquet 'the subtle doctor'. In his brief academic career he altered the direction of philosophical thinking in many areas and set it on new courses to be followed for centuries.

On many major issues Scotus took the opposite side to Aquinas. In his own mind, if not in the light of history, equal importance attached to his disagreements with another of his seniors, Henry of Ghent. Henry taught at Paris from 1276 to 1292 and defended many of the ideas of Augustinian Neoplatonism against the radical Aristotelianism of some of the arts faculty. Scotus often situated his own positions in relation to Henry's stance, and it was through Henry's eyes that he viewed many of his predecessors.

Scotus broke with the Aristotelian tradition by maintaining that the concepts of being and of other universally applicable predicates such as 'good' were not analogous but univocal, and could be used about God in exactly the same sense as about creatures.[9] Metaphysics was the science that studied the univocal concept of being and its fundamental properties. Aristotle had defined metaphysics as the science that studies Being *qua* being. Scotus makes great use of this definition, but he understands it in a highly personal way and broadens its scope immeasurably by including within Being the infinite Christian God. Whatever belongs to any of Aristotle's categories—substance or accident—is part of Being; but Being is much greater than this, for whatever falls within the categories is finite, and Being contains the infinite. The most important division to be made within the realm of Being was the division between finite and infinite being.[10]

The existence of an infinite being is something that, for Scotus, can be philosophically proved. In this he agrees with Aquinas and the great majority of medieval thinkers. But he rejects the proofs of God's existence offered by Aquinas on the ground that they are too dependent on Aristotelian physics, and he offers an elaborate metaphysical proof of his own to establish the existence of God as first efficient cause, ultimate final cause, and most excellent of all beings. Unlike Aquinas, he thinks that divine attributes such as omniscience and omnipotence can be known only by revelation and cannot be established by natural reason alone.[11]

---

[9] Scotus' theory of univocity is discussed in Ch. 3 below.

[10] Scotus' metaphysics is treated in more detail in Ch. 5 below.

[11] Scotus' natural theology is discussed in Ch. 9 below.

Scotus makes use of the apparatus of Aristotelian hylomorphism, using familiar terms like 'matter', 'form', 'substance', and 'accident'. But he gives many of these terms a new and radical interpretation. In particular he recasts the Aristotelian concepts of actuality and potentiality, treating potential beings as if they are entities that possess all the detailed individuality of actual beings. This comes out, for instance, in his treatment of place and time: unlike Aristotle he held that there can be vacuous space and motionless time. Where, for Aristotle, the presence of a body is needed in order to create a space, for Scotus the mere possibility of a body is enough to keep the walls of a vacuum apart. Where, for Aristotle, there must be motion if there is to be time, since time is the measure of motion, for Scotus there can be time without motion, time that measures the mere potential for motion.[12] In treating possibilities as shadowy, but definite, individuals, Scotus betrays the influence of Avicenna; but he explores the area with a degree of elaboration that entitles him to be regarded as the begetter of the philosophy of possible worlds.

In Aristotelian tradition matter was the principle of individuation: two humans, Peter and Paul, were distinct from each other not on account of their form but on account of their matter. Scotus rejected this: it was not matter that made the difference between Peter and Paul, but a unique identifying feature that each alone possessed, a *haecceitas*, or thisness. Thus, in an individual such as Socrates there was both a common human nature and an individuating principle. The common nature and the individual difference were, he maintained, really identical, but distinguished from each other by a distinction of a special kind, the 'formal distinction'. By this means Scotus hoped to preserve the validity of universal terms without falling into Platonism: the common nature was real enough, and was not merely created by the human intellect, but it could never occur in reality except in company with an individuating element.

By comparison with Aquinas, Scotus extended the scope of the human intellect in two directions. Aquinas had held that there was no purely intellectual knowledge of individuals, because an immaterial faculty could not grasp matter, which was the principle of individuation. For Scotus, each thing has within it an intelligible principle of individuality, and therefore the intellect can grasp the individual in its singularity. Aquinas maintained that the proper object of the intellect, in this life, was the knowledge of the nature of material things. Scotus said that if we were to take the future as well as the present life into consideration, we must say that the proper object of the intellect was as wide as Being itself. To define the object of the intellect as Aquinas had, he maintained, was like defining the object of sight as what could be seen by candlelight.

Scotus definitively rejected the thesis—dear to the Augustinian tradition and revived by Henry of Ghent—that a special divine illumination was needed to

---

[12] See N. Lewis, 'Space and Time', in *CCDS*.

enable the human intellect to grasp universals. God, however, is not totally excluded from his epistemology. God's power is absolute: he can do anything that does not involve contradiction. Accordingly, God could create in a human mind a conviction of the presence of an individual entity without that entity being present. Fortunately, while having absolute power, God acts only in accordance with his orderly power, power guided by wisdom. Hence, he would not exercise the absolute power that would deceive us in the manner suggested. Here Scotus, like Descartes centuries later, can exclude radical scepticism only by appealing to the doctrine that the good God is no deceiver.

In philosophy of mind Scotus innovated in his description of the relationship between the intellect and the will. Whereas for Aquinas the will was essentially a rational appetite which derived its freedom from the flexible nature of practical reasoning, Scotus saw the will as a sovereign power whose activity could not be caused by anything except its own self-determination. The will was indeed a rational power, a power capable of being exercised in more than one way, but this did not mean that its exercise was under the direction of reason. The intellect, by contrast, was a natural power, a power which, given the appropriate natural conditions for its operation, could act only in one way. Whereas for most Aristotelian scholastics the ultimate end of human beings is an intellectual operation, the beatific vision of God, for Scotus the union of the blessed with God in heaven consists essentially in a free act of the will.[13]

In both humans and in God, Scotus assigns to the will a much broader scope than any of his predecessors had done. The human will is a power for opposites, not just in the sense that it can will different things at different times, but that at the very time of willing one thing it retains a power for willing its opposite at the same time. A created will that existed only for a single moment could still make a free choice between opposites. Again, the divine will, for Scotus, enjoys a freedom far wider than that attributed to it by previous theologians. God was free, for instance, to dispense with or cancel many of the moral precepts commonly believed to belong to the natural law.

Duns Scotus is important in the history of philosophy not so much for founding a school—though there have been devoted Scotists in every generation up to the present—but because many of his philosophical innovations came to be accepted as unquestioned principles by thinkers in later generations who had never read a word of his works. The Reformation debates between Luther and Calvin and their Catholic adversaries took place against a backcloth of fundamentally Scotist assumptions. The framework within which Descartes laid out the foundations of modern philosophy was in all its essentials a construction erected in Oxford around the year 1300. The quarter of a century that separated Aquinas'

---

[13] Scotus' philosophy of mind is discussed in Ch. 7 below.

Summa Theologiae from Scotus' *Lectura* was one of the most momentous periods in the history of philosophy.

Scotus is not widely read outside professional circles: he is a philosophers' philosopher. But one of those who had the most vivid appreciation of his genius was the Victorian poet Gerard Manley Hopkins. In his poem 'Duns Scotus' Oxford' Hopkins placed him on a pedestal above Aquinas, Plato, and Aristotle, saluting him as

> Of realty the rarest-veined unraveller; a not
> rivalled insight, be rival Italy or Greece.

What most impressed Hopkins was the concept of haecceity, which he took as anticipating his own concept of inscape, the unique characteristic of each individual, which he celebrated in many of his poems, notably 'As kingfishers catch fire'.

> Each mortal thing does one thing and the same:
> Deals out that being indoors each one dwells;
> Selves—goes itself; *myself* it speaks and spells,
> Crying *What I do is me: for that I came.*

In the decades immediately after his death Scotus did not receive such applause in Oxford, and even among his fellow Franciscans there was strong opposition to his views.

William Ockham

William Ockham arrived in Oxford shortly after Scotus had left it for the last time. He took his surname from his birthplace, the village of Ockham in Surrey. He was born in the late 1280s and joined the Franciscan order around 1302. It was probably at Greyfriars in London that he received his philosophical training. At the end of the decade he went to Oxford to commence the study of theology. By the time of his lectures on the *Sentences* in 1317–19 a school of Scotists was building up in Oxford, and Ockham defined his own position partly in contrast to them. He was soon criticized by fellow Franciscans, and also regarded with suspicion by the university's chancellor, Thomas Lutterell, who was a Thomist. He left Oxford without proceeding to the doctorate, and lived in London in the early 1320s, probably again at Greyfriars.[14] He became a lecturer in philosophy and held a

---

[14] Ockham's premature departure from Oxford without a doctorate may be the reason why his medieval nickname was *venerabilis inceptor*—'the venerable beginner'. This seems more likely than the alternative explanation, that he was regarded as an admirable innovator. But at all events, the title involves complicated wordplay, since 'incept' was, in medieval jargon, the word for actually taking the doctorate, something that Ockham never did. His other title, 'the invincible doctor', needs less explanation.

number of quodlibetal disputations. He also wrote up his Oxford lectures, composed a systematic textbook of logic, a number of commentaries on the logical and physical works of Aristotle, and an influential treatise on predestination and future contingents. He is best remembered for something he never said, namely 'Entities are not to be multiplied beyond necessity', the famous 'Ockham's razor'.

In his works Ockham took up a number of positions in logic and metaphysics either in development of, or in opposition to, Scotus. Though his thought is less sophisticated than Scotus', his language is mercifully much clearer. Like Scotus, he treated 'being' as a univocal term, applicable to God and creatures in the same sense. He sharply reduced, however, the number of created beings, reducing the ten Aristotelian categories to two, namely substances and qualities. Ockham's most significant disagreement with Scotus concerned the nature of universals. He rejected outright the idea that there was a common nature existing in the many individuals we call by a common name. No universal exists outside the mind; everything in the world is singular. Universals are not things but signs, simple signs representing many things.

According to Ockham, there are two kinds of signs: natural signs and conventional signs. Natural signs are the thoughts in our minds, and conventional signs are the words that we coin to express these thoughts. The concepts in our minds form a language system, a language common to all humans and prior to all the different spoken languages such as English and Latin. Ockham's denial of real universals is often called 'nominalism': but the names which, according to him, are the only true universals are not only spoken and written names, but also the inward names of our mental language. Accordingly, when we are making a contrast between Ockham's teaching and the realism of his opponents it would be more apt to call him a conceptualist than a nominalist.[15]

At different times Ockham gave different accounts of the way in which the names of mental language are related to objects in the world. According to his earlier theory, the mind fashioned mental images, or 'fictions', that resembled real things, and that provided the terms of mental propositions, as proxies for the corresponding realities. Fictions were universals in the sense of having an equal likeness to many different things in the world. Later, partly as a result of criticism by his Franciscan colleague Walter Chatton, Ockham gave up belief in fictions. Names in mental language, he came to think, were simply acts of thinking, items in an individual person's mental history.

Ockham accepted Scotus' distinction between intuitive and abstractive knowledge; it is only by intuitive knowledge that we can know whether a contingent fact obtains or not. However, Ockham makes explicit a consequence of the theory that is only implicit in Scotus. By his almighty power, Ockham maintains, God can do

---

[15] Ockham's nominalism is discussed in Ch. 3 below.

directly whatever he currently does by means of secondary causes. In the ordinary way, God makes me know that a wall is white by making the white wall meet my eye; but if he normally acts thus via normal sensory causation, he can make me have the same belief in the whiteness of the wall without there being any white wall there at all. This thesis obviously opens wider the breach in epistemology that had been opened by Scotus, and broadens the road to scepticism.[16]

These and other views of Ockham quickly gave rise to concern among his Franciscan brethren, and in 1323 he was asked to explain to a provincial chapter of the order his teaching about the Aristotelian categories. A year later, in response to a denunciation from Oxford, Ockham had to face a commission at the papal court in Avignon set up to examine his *Sentences* for heresy. The commission, which consisted mainly of Thomists, and included the former Oxford chancellor Lutterell, failed, after many months of work, to produce a convincing case against him.

However, Ockham's stay in Avignon did give his philosophical career a wholly new turn. The pope of the time, John XXII, was in conflict with the Franciscan order on two issues concerning poverty: the historical question whether Christ and his Apostles had lived in absolute poverty, and the practical question whether the Franciscan order could legitimately own any property. St Francis had held up an extreme ideal of poverty: the friars were to own nothing, never touch money, and depend on alms for food, clothing, and shelter. St Bonaventure, the reforming general of the order, made a distinction between ownership (*dominium*, or lordship) and use (*usus*). Franciscans could use property, but they could not own it, whether as individuals or collectively as a religious order. In 1279 Pope Nicholas III relieved the Franciscan order of the ownership of all the property made use of by the friars, and assumed it into the patrimony of the papacy.

At the end of 1322 John XXII overturned this compromise, denouncing the distinction between ownership and use—so far as concerned consumables, at least—as a hypocritical fudge. In the following year he also rejected the Franciscan teaching that Jesus and the Apostles had renounced all ownership during their lives. Ockham was asked by Michael of Cesena, the head of the Franciscan order, who was also in Avignon, to study the papal decrees containing these denunciations. He came to the conclusion that they were immoral, absurd, and heretical, and publicly denounced them. With Michael he fled from Avignon in 1328, shortly before a papal bull was issued condemning their doctrines as heretical. The pair escaped to Munich, where they came under the protection of Ludwig of Bavaria, an enemy of John XXII, who had opposed his election as emperor.

Ludwig, excommunicated in 1324, had appealed to a general council, using the quarrel with the Franciscans as a reason for denouncing the Pope as a heretic. In 1328 he entered Rome, had himself crowned as emperor, burnt John in effigy, and installed an antipope. In Rome, Ludwig was joined by another philosophical ally,

---

[16] Ockham's epistemology is discussed in Ch. 4 below.

Marsilius of Padua, former rector of the University of Paris. Marsilius had been forced, like Ockham, to flee to the protection of Ludwig because he had written a book containing a sustained attack, not just on John XXII but on the papacy as an institution.

The work, *Defensor Pacis* ('The Defender of the Peace', 1324), became a classic text of political philosophy. It begins with a denunciation of papal interference in the affairs of secular polities. The disorder, corruption, and warfare endemic in Italy, Marsilius maintains, are all the result of papal arrogance and ambition. In the course of the work he moves from local issues to general principle.

The state is a 'perfect' society, that is to say, one that is both supreme and self-sufficient within its own sphere. There are two types of government: rule by the consent of the ruler's subjects, and rule against their will. Only the former is legitimate and the latter is a form of tyranny. The laws of the state derive their legitimacy neither from the will of the ruler nor directly from God: they are given authority by the citizens themselves. The actual task of legislation may be delegated to particular bodies and institutions, which may reasonably differ from state to state. The prince is the executive head of state: the citizens' consent to his rule is best expressed if he is chosen by election, but there are other systems by which consent may legitimately be manifested. An irregular or incompetent prince should be removed from office by the legislature.

Marsilius' book was extraordinarily influential. No writer on the papal side was able to counter it at a similar level of philosophical sophistication. It influenced Orthodox Catholics and heretics alike, right up to the Lutheran reformation. Ockham was among the first philosophers to exhibit its influence, in a series of political treatises that he wrote during the 1330s. These works are less systematic, and also less radical, than the *Defensor Pacis*.

The first was the *Work of Ninety Days*, a lengthy tract written in haste in 1332. This was later followed by a *Letter to the Franciscans* and a set of *Dialogues* on the relations between Church and State. Though polemical in intent, these works are 'recitative', that is to say, they state ('recite') arguments used by papal opponents in a manner that does not necessarily commit Ockham himself to agreement with their conclusions. But by comparing them with other works written in the first person ('assertive' works) we can piece together Ockham's own opinions.

The philosophical core of Ockham's position on Franciscan poverty is a theory of natural rights. He distinguishes between two classes of rights: those that may be legitimately renounced (such as the right to private property) and those that are inalienable (such as the right to one's own life). In the garden of Eden there was no such thing as property; after the fall property rights were established by human law. Private ownership is not in itself wrong, but, *pace* Pope John, it must be distinguished from use. A host allows his guests to use the food and drink at his table, but he does not confer the ownership of these things on his guests. The Franciscans have a right to use the necessities of life, but this does not involve them in any ownership, because it is only a moral right, not enforceable in any court of law (*OND* 6. 260–71).

While Marsilius' conceptions of government were shaped by conditions in the Italian city-states of his time, Ockham's are more influenced by the structure of the Holy Roman Empire. The emperor, he says, derives his power not from the pope, but from the people via the college of imperial electors. The right to choose one's ruler is one of the natural rights of human beings. These rights can be exercised by setting up a hereditary monarchy; but the tenure of a hereditary monarch depends on good conduct, and if he abuses his power the people are entitled to depose him.

Despite his quarrel with Pope John XXII, Ockham was much less hostile than Marsilius to the papacy as an institution. However tyrannically they behaved in practice, the popes, he maintained, did have a supremacy deriving from divine law. They should, however, be regarded as constitutional, not absolute, monarchs. They were answerable to general councils, which should themselves be constituted by locally elected churchmen.

Ockham was never reconciled with the papacy of his time. In 1331 John XXII, in his late eighties, began to preach a doctrine that was universally regarded as heretical: namely, that the souls of those who depart life in good standing do not enjoy the beatific vision of God until they rejoin their bodies after the Last Judgement. This, of course, placed a new weapon in the hands of his Franciscan opponents, and the Pope was forced to recant on his deathbed in 1334. The new pope, Benedict XII, defined that the souls of the just, as soon as they die, or after a period in purgatory, see God face to face. But Benedict did not repeal the condemnation of the dissident Franciscans, and Ockham died during the Black Death, still under the ban of the Church, in Munich in 1349.

The Reception of Ockham

Paris and Oxford were the two great universities of the high Middle Ages. While Paris was undoubtedly the senior partner in the thirteenth century, Oxford took the lead in the fourteenth century. It is a matter of scholarly dispute how far Ockham's influence was felt in either university. Certainly it is an exaggeration to say that there was ever, even in Oxford, an Ockhamist school, but on the other hand a number of Parisian thinkers followed up and developed specific themes from his writings.

Gregory of Rimini, for instance, an Augustinian friar who taught in Paris in the 1340s, accepted Ockham's natural philosophy while dissenting from his logic. Jean Buridan, a member of the arts faculty who was rector of the Sorbonne in 1328 and 1340, shared Ockham's nominalism, but he was much more confident than

Ockham that progress could be made in the scientific exploration of the world. He reintroduced Philoponus' theory of impetus, and was the teacher of a distinguished generation of philosophical physicists, including Nicole Oresme, who explored, without endorsing, the hypothesis that the earth revolved daily on its axis. Like Ockham, Buridan is best known for something he never said. In discussing the freedom of the will to choose between alternatives he is alleged to have said that a donkey faced between two equally attractive bales of hay would be unable to eat either: hence 'Buridan's Ass' became a byword for indecision.

Two other French thinkers were much influenced by Ockham's epistemology: the Cistercian John of Mirecourt, and a secular canon Nicholas of Autrecourt, both of whom lectured in Paris in the 1340s, and both of whom incurred academic and ecclesiastical censure for their radical opinions. In 1347 forty-one propositions taken from John's writings were condemned by the chancellor of the Sorbonne, and more than fifty of Nicholas' theses were condemned by the papal legate. John defended his writings in an apology; Nicholas recanted and continued his career.

John of Mirecourt's epistemology was based on a development of Ockham's theory of assent. Assents may be evident or they may be given with fear of error. Central truths of logic enjoy a supreme degree of evidence, but there is also natural evidence, based on experience of the world. Natural evidence cannot produce absolute certainty, except in the case of one's own existence, which cannot be denied without self-contradiction. One cannot attain similar certainty about the existence of any other entity. Even God's existence cannot be proved with certainty, since the arguments for his existence are based on facts in the world involving only natural evidence. Moreover, even if nothing other than myself existed, God could, by a miracle, make it appear that there is a real world out there.

It will be seen that John came very close, in anticipation, to the position Descartes reached at the beginning of his Second Meditation. Nicholas of Autrecourt adopted an even more radical form of scepticism. If we define intuitive awareness as involving a 'judgement that a thing exists, whether or not it does exist', then we can never be certain that what appears to the senses is true. We cannot be certain of the existence of the objects of the five senses. One of the condemned propositions that he was made to recant ran thus: 'virtually no certainty can be obtained about things by natural appearances'. However, Nicholas qualified this sceptical claim with the remark that a modicum of certainty could be achieved in a short time if only people turned their mind to things themselves and not to the reading of Aristotle and his commentators (DB 553 ff.).

Unlike John, Nicholas did not see 'I think, therefore I am' as offering a way out of the sceptical impasse—it certainly did not prove the existence of any substantive ego. Even 'Here is an intellectual thought: therefore some intellect exists' was, he said, a far from evident argument. No form of causal argument could bring certainty of the existence of anything of any kind. Only the principle of non-contradiction, Nicholas concluded, will provide a solid basis for knowledge: and such a basis will not let one get very far in philosophy. 'The existence of one thing', ran one of his condemned propositions, 'can never be inferred or proved with the appropriate degree of evidence from the existence of some other thing, nor can the non-existence of one thing from the non-existence of another.' Here it is not Descartes, but Hume, who is brought to the mind of a reader of modern philosophy.

Rightly or wrongly, the scepticism of Nicholas of Autrecourt was often held up in later ages as an example of the horrible excess to which the teaching of Ockham could lead. With equally dubious justice, he was sometimes hailed by twentieth-century logical positivists as a distinguished predecessor.

The immediate reception of Ockham in England was not uniformly favourable. Even his close associates, such as Adam Wodeham and Walter Chatton, adapted his teachings to make them more conformable to mainstream scholasticism. Walter Burley, whose career overlapped with that of Ockham, was one of the most significant English thinkers of the time. He took his MA at Oxford in 1301 and his doctorate in theology at the Sorbonne in the early 1320s; he was a fellow of Merton and a diplomat in the service of Edward III. He is best remembered for his treatise *The Pure Art of Logic* (1328), which was one of the finest logical texts to survive from the medieval period. In that work he defended the traditional view of signification and supposition against the criticisms of Ockham.[17]

The Oxford Calculators

The second quarter of the fourteenth century saw the development among Oxford philosophers of a school that had a remarkable influence on the history of physics. Foremost among the school was Thomas Bradwardine (1295–1349), who was a fellow successively of Balliol and Merton colleges, later confessor to Edward III, and eventually archbishop of Canterbury. Other members of the school, such as William Heytesbury and Richard Swineshead, were, like Bradwardine, fellows of Merton, so that members of the group are sometimes known as the Mertonians. They shared a taste for solving philosophical and theological problems by mathematical methods, and so they are also called the Oxford Calculators, after a treatise by Swineshead called the *Liber Calculationum* (1350).

Bradwardine, in 1328, published a work entitled *De Proportionibus Velocitatum in Motibus* ('On Proportions of Velocity in Motions'). In it he developed a theory of ratios which he used to present a theory of how forces, resistances, and velocities were to be correlated in motion. This theory quickly superseded Aristotle's laws of motion, and it was influential not only in Oxford, but also in Paris, where it was adopted by Oresme. Other Calculators, too, produced work of importance for

[17] See Ch. 3 below.

natural philosophy, but they devoted their mathematical talents to the solution of logical and theological problems rather than to physical research. Questions about maxima and minima, for instance, were the germ of development towards the differential calculus; but they were first raised in connection with the question what was the minimum, and what the maximum, length of time to be spent in prayer to fulfil a command to pray night and day. The question of how to measure non-quantitative qualities, such as heat and cold, was first worked out in the analysis of the growth of grace in the souls of the faithful and in measuring the capacity for happiness of souls in heaven.

Many of the developments in physics originated as solutions to logical puzzles, or *sophismata*. These were propositions whose content was ambiguous or paradoxical, set as problems to be resolved by logic students, and solved, or determined, by masters in the arts faculty. One of the most ingenious sets of these *sophismata* was produced, around 1328, by Richard Kilvington, not himself a Mertonian, but closely associated with the other Calculators as part of a research group assembled by Richard of Bury, bishop of Durham and lord chancellor. Kilvington was not himself a mathematician, but his *sophismata* were quickly given a mathematical form by Heytesbury in his *Regulae Solvendi Sophismata* (1335), in which he worked out the theory of uniform acceleration.

Sophismata fell into disrepute at the Renaissance, but they came into fashion again in the twentieth century. At a time when France was a republic, Bertrand Russell inquired about the truth-value of 'The king of France is bald'. His investigation led to a very influential logical analysis of definite descriptions. Similarly, Kilvington in his *sophismata* sets out a scenario, for instance, that Socrates is as white as it is possible to be, and that Plato, hitherto not white, is at this moment beginning to be white. He then inquires into the truth-value of 'Socrates is whiter than Plato begins to be white'. A natural reaction might be to say that this sentence, so far from being either true or false, is not even well-formed; but Kilvington patiently spells out what one might mean by it, and in the course of expounding it and similar puzzle questions offers an analysis of concepts of degree, ratio, and proportion.

The doyen of the Calculators, Thomas Bradwardine, was also a heavyweight theologian. He was the leading representative of another Oxford fourteenth-century tendency, a revival of Augustinianism. Of course, throughout the whole medieval period Augustine had been an authority to be treated with reverence and quoted no less frequently than Aristotle. But these neo-Augustinians like Bradwardine and his Irish contemporary Richard Fitzralph (chancellor of Oxford in 1333 and later archbishop of Armagh) began to pay more attention to the historical context of Augustine's work and to take greater interest in his later writings against the Pelagians. Bradwardine, in his massive *De Causa Dei*, presented an Augustinian treatment of the issues surrounding divine foreknowledge, future contingent propositions, and human freedom.

John Wyclif

The most distinguished figure of this Augustinian renaissance was John Wyclif (1330?–1384), who was also a leader of the realist reaction against the nominalism of the Ockhamists. In the middle years of the century he was by far the most prominent figure in the university. His life exhibited a pattern that recurs in the history of Oxford and is illustrated also by John Wesley and John Henry Newman. In the middle of the fourteenth, the eighteenth, and the nineteenth centuries the most significant event in the religious history of the university was the defection of a favourite son from the religious establishment.[18]

Like Wesley and Newman, Wyclif was a fine flower of the Oxford schools, a man who stood out among his contemporaries for learning and austerity of life. Like them, he formed around himself a group of disciples, and seemed likely to dominate, by his personal influence and reputation, the course of the university's thought and practice. Like them, he took a doctrinal step which alienated his closest theological allies and vindicated the suspicions of his critics. Exiled from Oxford as they were exiled, he carried on his religious mission elsewhere, casting only a rare nostalgic glance at the distant spires of the home of his youth and promise.

Wyclif went to Oxford in the 1350s and though from time to time distracted by public service—at one time engaged in an embassy, at another offering an expert opinion to parliament—he spent his life mainly in teaching, preaching, and writing. Between 1360, when he was master of Balliol, and 1372, when he took his DD, he produced a philosophical *Summa* whose most important volume is a treatise on universals, designed to vindicate realism against nominalist sophistry. In his maturity he wrote a theological *Summa* which began with two books of banal orthodoxy, moved through several books of hardy innovation, passed into overt heresy, and ended in barren polemic. The volumes of this work covered the whole range of medieval theology. Three of them dealt with issues of law and property, and proposed the controversial theses that evil clerics should be disendowed and that even laymen, if sinners, had no right to ownership of property. Several other volumes, on Church, king, and papacy, analysed the structure of the Christian Church and society, castigated abuses, and proposed reforms. In one of his latest works, on the Eucharist, he presented a novel interpretation of the Mass, the centre of medieval spirituality.

One of Wyclif's most startling innovations was his proposal for communism, based on his theory of *dominium*, or ownership. He argued thus. On the one hand, someone who is in sin has no right to property. You can only possess something justly if you can use it justly; but no sinner can use anything justly because all his actions are sinful. On the other hand, if you are in a state of grace, as an adoptive

---

[18] See R. A. Knox, *Enthusiasm* (Oxford: Oxford University Press, 1948), 66.

son of God you inherit the whole realm of God. But if each Christian in grace is lord of all, he must share his lordship with all other Christians in grace.

All the goods of God should be common. This is proved thus. Every man should be in a state of grace; and if he is in a state of grace, he is lord of the world and all it contains. So every man should be lord of the universe. But this is not consistent with there being a number of men, unless they ought to have everything in common. Therefore all things should be in common.

Surprisingly, Wyclif's writings on dominion, radical though they were, did not seem to have caused him trouble with the authorities during his lifetime. The secular authorities used them in support of the taxation of the clergy, and ignored their implications with regard to the laity.

However, the increasing hardihood of Wyclif's speculations made his position in Oxford less and less tenable. When he denounced the popes and questioned papal claims, he could find sympathizers—at a time when a disgraceful schism was splitting Christendom in two—even among the higher clergy. When he, a secular priest enjoying several benefices, called for the disendowment of the Church, many laymen and begging friars found his words congenial. But when, in 1379, he denounced the doctrine of transubstantiation, and said that the bread and wine at Mass were Christ's body only in the same way that paper and ink in the Bible were God's Word, then friars, noblemen, and bishops all turned against him. He was condemned by a provincial synod and expelled from Oxford. He ended his life, at liberty but in disgrace, in a country living at Lutterworth in Northamptonshire.

Wyclif's influence after his death was greater than in his life. In subsequent decades his English followers, the Lollards, were disseminating a vernacular version of the Bible over his name. It is a matter of dispute how far he had himself been involved in the translation, but it is for that Bible, rightly or wrongly, that he has been most famous up to recent times. Abroad, in Bohemia, his memory was kept green by the followers of Jan Hus. The official Church, once the schism had finally ended at the Council of Constance in 1415, burnt Hus as a heretic, and condemned 260 propositions attributed to Wyclif. At home his body was exhumed and burnt.

Because of his association with the Lollard Bible, and because of his attacks on transubstantiation and the papacy, Wyclif was hailed by Protestant hagiographers as the Morning Star of the Reformation. His works have not been much read by philosophers: Protestant thinkers were repelled by the scholasticism from which the Reformation, it was believed, had delivered us all, while Catholic scholars felt they could ignore the texts of a heretic when there were holy men of genius still awaiting critical editions. But in recent years philosophers who have looked at his work have come to realize that he is a considerable thinker, worthy to make a third to his two great Oxford predecessors: the Evening Star, in fact, of scholasticism.

Beyond Paris and Oxford

Wyclif's career coincided with a period when Oxford became more isolated from the rest of Europe. Scotus and Ockham were both well known in Paris as well as in Oxford, and lived long periods on the Continent. Wyclif remained in England except for one brief visit abroad. Latin continued in use as the medium of academic exchange, but vernacular literature began to thrive in all the countries of Europe and Latin was no longer the chosen medium of the best writers among Wyclif's contemporaries, such as Chaucer and Langland. The Hundred Years' War between England and France placed a barrier between Oxford and Paris. The two universities went on their separate ways, impoverished.

By the end of the fourteenth century, however, new universities had begun to flourish in various parts of Europe. The Charles University of Prague dated its foundation to 1347; by 1402 the debates in its schools between Ockhamists and Wycliffites were reverberating throughout Europe. The University of Heidelberg was founded by papal bull in 1385, with a former rector of Paris, Marsilius of Inghen, as its first rector. In 1399 the University of Padua received its first buildings. In 1400 the Jagiellonian University was chartered at Cracow. St Andrews, the oldest Scottish university, was founded in 1410, at a time when Scotland and England belonged to the allegiances of two different schismatic popes. The first university in the Low Countries was Louvain, founded in 1425.

Replacing the old close partnership of Paris and Oxford a new international network of universities grew up. In the decades around 1500, for instance, a group of Scottish scholars, of whom the central figure was John Major or Mair, later principal of the University of Glasgow, studied together at the University of Paris. They made significant contributions to logic and epistemology which one recent scholar has not hesitated to compare to the Scottish Enlightenment of the eighteenth century.[19]

Simultaneously, a quite different kind of philosophizing was being practised outside the universities. The split between two styles of philosophy was to have serious long-term consequences for the non-academic world. In Paris in the early years of the fourteenth century, while Duns Scotus was lecturing, lectures were also being given by another philosopher of genius, the German Dominican Meister Eckhardt. Eckhardt went on to acquire a great reputation as a preacher and lecturer in the University of Cologne; and if Scotus can be seen as the first protagonist of the analytic tradition of philosophizing in the fourteenth century, Eckhardt can be regarded as the founding father of an alternative, mystical tradition.

---

[19] See A. Broadie, *The Circle of John Mair* (Oxford: Oxford University Press, 1985) and *Notion and Object* (Oxford: Oxford University Press, 1989).

The devotional writings of the thinkers of this tradition—the *Devotio Moderna* of Eckhardt's pupils John Tauler and Henry Suso—are not part of the history of philosophy. What does concern the historian of philosophy is the anti-intellectual attitude that became associated with the school. A Dutchman called Gerard Groote (1340–84) founded, in Deventer, a pious association named The Brotherhood of the Common Life. The rules that he drew up for the confraternity included an attack on the entire academic system. Only a libertine could be happy in a university, and disputations and degrees served only to foster vainglory.

The Deventer brotherhood gave birth to a new congregation of canons regular, based at Windesheim. The best known of the Windesheim canons is Thomas à Kempis, who is in all probability the author of *The Imitation of Christ*, one of the best-known classics of Christian devotion, written around the time of Wyclif's posthumous condemnation. This work contains a fierce denunciation of scholastic philosophy and theology.

What doth it profit thee to discuss the deep mystery of the Trinity, if thou art from thy lack of humility displeasing to the Trinity.... I would rather choose to feel compunction than to know its definition.... Vanity of vanities, all is vanity save to love God and serve him only ... Have no wish to know the depths of things, but rather to acknowledge thy own lack of knowledge.

The tradition of Deventer and Windesheim thrived well into the sixteenth century, and it was one of the forces that led, in that century, to the downgrading of scholasticism. The young Erasmus was a pupil of the Brothers of the Common Life, and for a while a reluctant canon of the Windesheim congregation. Luther, too, was influenced by this mystical anti-intellectualism, and it helped to fuel his attacks on medieval Aristotelianism.

One person, in the fifteenth century, straddles the analytical–sceptical tradition and the mystical–fideistic tradition. This is Nicholas of Cusa (1401–64). He was born at Kues, near Koblenz on the Moselle. He too was a pupil of the Deventer community, and subsequently studied at Heidelberg and Padua. He was a delegate to the Council of Basel in 1432, which marked the high point of the assertion of the authority of general councils against the ecclesiastical supremacy of the pope. Later, he adhered to the papal party and became a diplomat in the service of Pope Eugenius IV. Created a cardinal in 1448, he was papal legate in Germany in 1451–2. He died at Todi, in Umbria, in 1464.

Nicholas was a pious and charitable man, a dedicated Church reformer and a devoted ecumenist. Throughout his life he sought reconciliation: between the conciliarists and the papalists within the Roman obedience, between the Latin Church and the Greek Church, between scholastic and mystical theology, and between Christian and pagan thought. He held that the names that Jews, Greeks, Latins, Turks, and Saracens applied to God were equivalent to each other, reconcilable in the Tetragrammaton which was the name God himself had revealed (Sermo 1. 6. 14).

Like the Oxford Calculators, Nicholas wrote on mathematical subjects, but his best-known philosophical work, and also his earliest, was the *De Docta Ignorantia* ('On Learned Ignorance') of 1440. The leading idea of this work is that God is the *coincidentia oppositorum*, a supreme and infinite synthesis of opposites. Whenever we apply a predicate to God we can with equal propriety attach its opposite. If God is the greatest being, he is also the least being: he is both maximum and minimum, because nothing can be greater than him, but he also lacks any size or volume. The fact that opposites coincide in God shows how impossible it is for us to have any real knowledge of him. Rational attempts to reach the ultimate truth are like a polygon inscribed in a circle: however many sides we add to the polygon, it will never coincide with the circumference, however closely it approaches it.[20]

Renaissance Platonism

Nicholas of Cusa is often described as a transitional figure between the Middle Ages and the Renaissance. The composition of *On Learned Ignorance* did indeed coincide with one of the seminal events of the Renaissance: the Council of Florence of 1439. The Byzantine Greek Empire of Constantinople, threatened by the overwhelming military power of the Ottoman Turks, sought help from Western Christians. The Pope, the Venetian Eugenius IV, made theological unity a condition of a crusade, and the emperor John VIII and the patriarch of Constantinople attended a council in Ferrara and Florence in order to reunite the Latin and Greek Churches. Their presence in Florence has been immortalized by Benozzo Gozzoli's frescoes of the adoration of the Magi in the Palazzo Medici-Ricardi, which contains portraits of the main participants. The union between the Churches, proclaimed in the decree *Laetentur Caeli*, agreed by Pope, emperor, and patriarch in 1439, proved as short-lived as its predecessor of 1274. But the effects of the Council on the history of philosophy were more long-lasting.

Florence was already home to a revival of ancient classical learning: of 'humanism', not in the sense of a concern with the human race, but in the sense of a devotion to 'humane letters'. One of the earliest manifestations of this was an admiration for the style of classical Roman authors and a corresponding distaste for scholastic Latin. Leonardo Bruni, a senior Florentine civil servant in the 1430s, retranslated important texts of Aristotle into more elegant Latin. Along with a desire for new translations of Greek classics, many educated men felt a hunger to learn Greek itself and to read Plato, Aristotle, and other ancient thinkers in the original language. From 1396 Greek had been regularly taught in Florence to a select few.

[20] Nicholas' theology is studied in Ch. 9 below.

The presence of Eastern scholars at the Council of Florence gave a fillip to this movement. Those in attendance at the Council included Georgios Gemistos Plethon (1360–1452), a leading Platonist, his pupil Bessarion (1403–72), and the Aristotelian George of Trebizond (1395–1484). Of this trio only Plethon, an opponent of Church union, returned to Greece after the Council: the others stayed in Rome, George becoming a papal secretary and Bessarion a cardinal.

During the Council, Plethon lectured on the comparative merits of Plato and Aristotle. Latin philosophers, he said, greatly overvalued Aristotle. Plato was much to be preferred: he believed in a creator God, not just a prime mover; and he believed in a truly immortal soul. Aristotle was wrong about Ideas, wrong in thinking virtue was a mean, and wrong in equating happiness with contemplation.

Plethon's onslaught drew replies from both Greeks and Latins. George Scholarios, an admirer of Aquinas and a supporter of union at Florence, later became disillusioned and returned to Constantinople, where he eventually became patriarch. In 1445 he wrote a *Defence of Aristotle* against those who preferred Plato. Though Aristotle thought the world was eternal, nonetheless he did think God was its efficient cause; he believed that the human soul was immortal and indestructible. He was a much clearer and more systematic philosopher than Plato. Scholarios believed—perhaps rightly—that Plethon was not a Christian at all, but a Neoplatonist pagan, and after he died he had his works publicly burnt.

A tempestuous defence of Aristotle was made by George of Trebizond, who was at this time translating, for Pope Nicholas V, works of both Plato and Aristotle as well as many Greek Fathers. His *Comparison of Plato and Aristotle* (1458) makes Aristotle a Christian hero and Plato a heretical villain. George claims that Aristotle believed in creation out of nothing, in divine providence, and in a Trinity of divine persons. Plato, on the other hand, propounded disgusting doctrines such as the beauty of pederasty and the transmigration of souls into animals, and encouraged gymnastics for both sexes together in the nude. Devotion to Plato had led the Greek Church into heresy and schism; Latin Aristotelians had combined philosophy with orthodoxy. Only scholars who were more concerned with style than content could prefer Plato to Aristotle.

Two cardinals entered the debate to redress the balance. Nicholas of Cusa, for whom George had translated Plato's *Parmenides*, wrote a dialogue, *On the Not Other*, in which he stressed the limitations of both Aristotelian logic and Platonic metaphysics, while endeavouring to build on both of them in attaining knowledge of God, the divine Not-Other. More soberly, Bessarion wrote a treatise, published in both Greek and Latin, entitled *Against the Calumniator of Plato*. He pointed out that many Christian saints had been admirers of Plato. While neither Plato nor Aristotle agreed at all fully with Christian doctrine, the points of conflict between them were few, and there were as many points of similarity between Plato and Aristotle as between Aristotle and Christianity.

Aristotle, he said, *pace* George of Trebizond, did not believe that God freely created the world out of nothing, and Plato was much closer to the Christian belief in divine providence. Aristotle, again, did not prove that individual human souls were immortal. The way in which Aristotle explains concept-formation by the influence of the agent intellect is very close to Plato's theory of human links to the Ideas in recollection. Bessarion balances George's citation of licentious passages from the dialogues with others in which Plato exhorts to continence and virtue. Both Plato and Aristotle were outstanding thinkers, sent by providence to bring humans to the truth by different paths. Plato's anthropology, Bessarion maintains, is closer to what life would have been without original sin; Aristotle gives a more realistic account of fallen humanity.

By the 1460s it was universally accepted that the study of Plato was appropriate for Catholic scholars in the West. The fall of Constantinople to the Turks in 1453 led to an influx of refugees, bringing with them not only their own knowledge of classical Greek but also precious manuscripts of ancient authors. These were welcomed both in Rome and in Florence. Cosimo de' Medici commissioned his court philosopher, Marsilio Ficino, to translate the entire works of Plato. The work was completed around 1469, when Cosimo's grandson Lorenzo the Magnificent succeeded as head of the Medici clan. Lorenzo collected Greek manuscripts in his new Laurenziana library, just as Pope Nicholas V and his successors had been doing in the refounded Vatican library.

Marsilio Ficino gathered round him, at Careggi near Florence, a group of wealthy students of Plato, whom he called his Academy. He translated, in addition to Plato, works of Proclus and Plotinus, and the *Corpus Hermeticum*, a collection of ancient alchemical and astrological writings. He wrote commentaries on four major dialogues of Plato and on the *Enneads* of Plotinus. He also wrote a number of short treatises himself, and one major work, the *Theologia Platonica* (1474), in which he set out his own Neoplatonic account of the soul and its origin and destiny. His aim was to combine the Platonic element in the scholastic tradition with a literary and historical appreciation of its origins in the ancient world. He regarded the pagan Platonic tradition as itself divinely inspired, and believed that its incorporation in theological teaching was essential if the Christian religion was to be made palatable to the new humanistic intelligentsia. Thus he equated the charity which St Paul speaks of in 1 Corinthians with the Eros of the *Phaedrus*, and identified the Christian God with the *Republic*'s Idea of the Good.

The most distinguished of Ficino's Platonic associates was Giovanni Pico, count of Mirandola (1463–94). Well educated in Latin and Greek, Pico learnt Greek and Hebrew at an early age, and in addition to the Hermetic Corpus he made a serious study of the Jewish mystical cabbala. He wanted to combine Greek, Hebrew, Muslim, and Christian thought into a great eclectic Platonic synthesis. He spelt this out in 900 theses and invited all interested scholars to discuss these with him in a public disputation in Rome in 1487. Pope Innocent VIII forbade the disputation, and appointed a committee to examine the theses for heresy. Among the propositions condemned was 'there is no branch of science which gives us more certainty of Christ's divinity than magic and cabbala'.

The oration which Pico prepared to introduce the aborted disputation survives under the title *On the Dignity of Man*. Pico draws equally on Genesis and on Plato's *Timaeus* in describing the creation, and imagines God as addressing the newly created human being in the following terms:

The nature of other beings is limited and constrained within the bounds of laws prescribed by Us. Thou, constrained by no limits, in accordance with thine own free will, in whose hand We have placed thee, shalt ordain for thyself the limits of thy nature. We have set thee at the world's centre that thou mayest from thence more easily observe whatever is in the world. We have made thee neither of heaven nor of earth, neither mortal nor immortal, so that with freedom of choice and with honour, as though the maker and moulder of thyself, thou mayest fashion thyself in whatever shape thou shalt prefer. Thou shalt have the power to degenerate into the lower forms of life, which are brutish. Thou shalt have the power, out of thy soul's judgement, to be reborn into the higher forms, which are divine.[21]

Pico sees the human, at birth, as a totipotential being, containing the seeds of many forms of life. Depending on which seed you cultivate, you may become a vegetable, a brute, a rational spirit, or a son of God. You may even withdraw into yourself and become one with God in solitary darkness.

Pico's consistent aim in his writings was to exalt the powers of human nature. To this end he defended the use of alchemy and symbolic rituals: these were legitimate magic, to be sharply distinguished from the black magic that invoked the aid of demons. But not all the scientific claims of the ancients were to be believed. Pico wrote twelve books against astrology: the heavenly bodies could affect men's bodies but not their minds, and no one could know the stars' movements and powers well enough to cast a horoscope. Astrology was to be opposed because the determinism it proclaimed limited human freedom; white magic was to be pursued because it made man the 'prince and master' of creation.

Pico's evocation of human dignity was an ancestor of Hamlet's paean:

What a piece of work is a man, how noble in reason, how infinite in faculty, in form and moving how express and admirable, in action how like an angel, in apprehension how like a god—the beauty of the world, the paragon of animals.

In spite of his unorthodox views and difficulties with the Church authorities, Pico was much admired by St Thomas More, who as a young man wrote a life of him, holding him up as a model of piety for the layman. Pico did, indeed, make a pious end. When, after the Medici had been expelled from Florence, Savonarola

---

[21] E. Cassirer *et al.*, *The Renaissance Philosophy of Man* (Chicago: Chicago University Press, 1959), 225.

turned the city into a religious republic, Pico became one of his followers, and considered becoming a friar. But before he could carry out this plan, he died at the age of 31. At his death he was working on a volume reconciling Platonic and Aristotelian metaphysics.

Renaissance Aristotelianism

In the 1490s, while the Platonists were showing an irenic spirit towards Aristotle, a vigorous revival of Aristotelianism was under way at Padua. This took two forms, Averroist and Thomist. In 1486 the Dominican order had replaced the *Sentences* of Peter Lombard with the *Summa Theologiae* of St Thomas as the basic text to be lectured on in their schools, and this initiated a Renaissance revival of Thomism. But at Padua, initially, the Averroist faction was dominant. The two leading lecturers, Nicoletto Vernia (d. 1499) and his pupil Agostino Nifo (1473–1538), both produced editions of Averroes' commentary, and maintained the Averroist position that there is only a single immortal intellect for all individual human beings. In 1491, however, there arrived in Padua one of the greatest Thomists of all time: the Dominican Thomas de Vio, known always as Cajetan, from the Latin form of Gaeta, the town where he was born and of which he later became bishop.

Cajetan commented on several works of Aristotle, including the *De Anima*, but he is best known for his commentaries on St Thomas, beginning with one on the *De Ente et Essentia* written at Padua in the early 1590s, and including a commentary on the whole *Summa Theologiae*. Though not always easy to read, these are highly valued by Thomists to this day. Particularly influential was a small tract on analogy, which systematized and classified the different kinds of analogy to be found in scattered remarks in Aristotle and St Thomas. Between 1495 and 1497 Cajetan held the post of professor of Thomist metaphysics at Padua.[22] Though a sympathetic commentator, Cajetan was not afraid to disagree with St Thomas, and he came to believe that Aristotle did not maintain individual immortality, and that such immortality could not be known by natural reason alone.[23]

Such was also the view of the cultured and erudite scholar who emerged as the head of the Paduan Aristotelians, Pietro Pomponazzi. He was the author of a work, *De Immortalitate Animae*, which argued that if one took seriously the Aristotelian doctrine that the human soul was the form of the human body, it was impossible

---

[22] A chair of Scotism had also been founded in Padua, held at this time by the Franciscan Antonio Trombetta.

[23] Cajetan was called to Rome in 1501, and became successively head of the Dominican order, cardinal, and papal legate to Germany, in which capacity he held a famous debate with Luther at Augsburg in 1518.

to believe that it could survive death.[24] Pomponazzi considered himself a Christian, and was prepared to accept personal immortality as an article of faith: but he and his Paduan associates soon found themselves the object of ecclesiastical hostility.

In 1512 the warrior pope Julius II, battered in conflict and ailing in health, summoned a general council to meet at the Lateran, with a view to the emendation of a Church by now universally agreed to be in great need of reform. Shortly after the summoning of the Council, Julius died and was replaced by the Medici pope Leo X. Leo showed little enthusiasm for reformation, and the Council achieved almost nothing in practical terms apart from a useful decree declaring that those who ran pawnshops were not necessarily guilty of the sin of usury. Some ecclesiastical abuses were prohibited, but the decrees remained a dead letter, until the issues were brought back by Luther to haunt the papacy. In the meantime, Pope Leo found it helpful to turn the minds of the Council members to less embarrassing issues of philosophy, such as the Paduan teaching on immortality.

A bull issued in December 1513 lamented that the devil had recently sown a pernicious error in the field of the Lord, namely, the belief that the rational soul was either mortal or single in all men, and that some rash philosophers had asserted that this was true 'at least in philosophy'. It proclaimed, on the contrary that the soul, by itself and essentially, was the form of the human body, that it was immortal, and that it was multiplied in proportion to the multitude of the bodies into which it was infused by God. Moreover, since truth could not contradict truth, any assertion contrary to the revealed truth was damned as heretical.

The immortality of the soul had been Christian teaching for many centuries, and the religious teaching had already been combined with Aristotelian hylomorphism at the Council of Vienna in 1311. What is noteworthy about the Lateran Council's declaration is its insistence on the relationship between revealed and philosophical truth, and its claim that the immortality of the soul is not only true, but provable by reason. The Church, for the first time, was laying down the law not just on religious truth, but also on religious epistemology. This decree, like the reforming decrees, seems to have had little practical effect. A couple of years later Pomponazzi published his treatise on the soul: it was topped and tailed with professions of faith and submission to the Holy See, but the meat of the work consists of a battery of arguments against personal immortality.

It was while the Lateran Council was in session that Raphael painted in the Vatican, first for Pope Julius and then for Pope Leo, the Stanza della Segnatura, on whose walls and ceilings are represented the disciplines of theology, law, philosophy, and poetry. The fresco *The School of Athens* contains some of the most loving representations of philosophers and philosophical topics in the history of art. Here the reconciliation of Plato and Aristotle is given spatial and colourful form. The two philosophers, side by side, preside over a resplendent court of thinkers, Greek

---

[24] Pomponazzi's arguments are set out in greater detail in Ch. 7 below.

and Islamic. Plato, wearing the colours of the volatile elements air and fire, points heavenwards; Aristotle, clothed in watery blue and earthly green, has his feet firmly on the ground. The two are reconciled, in Raphael's vision, by being assigned different spheres of influence. Aristotle, standing under the aegis of Minerva on the side of the fresco next to the law wall, dominates a group of ethical and natural philosophers. Plato, under the patronage of Apollo, stands above a throng of mathematicians and metaphysicians. Surprisingly, perhaps, he, who banished the poets from his Republic, is given his place next to the wall dedicated to poetry and dominated by Homer. Facing, across the room, is *The Disputation of the Sacrament*, where sit the great Christian philosophers: Augustine, Bonaventure, and Aquinas. The whole is a masterpiece of reconciling genius, bringing together the two truths which, so the Lateran fathers were proclaiming, no man should put asunder.

3

Logic and Language

Augustine on Language

In his account of his childhood in his *Confessions* Augustine describes the learning of language. One passage of his account has become famous:

When they (my elders) named some object, and accordingly moved towards something, I saw this and I grasped that the thing was called by the sound they uttered when they meant to point it out. Their intention was shewn by their bodily movements, as it were the natural language of all peoples: the expression of the face, the play of the eyes, the movement of other parts of the body, and the tone of voice which expresses our state of mind in seeking, having, rejecting or avoiding something. Thus, as I heard words repeatedly used in their proper places in various sentences, I gradually learnt to understand what objects they signified, and after I had trained my mouth to form these signs, I used them to express my own desires. (*Conf.* I. 8. 13)

This passage was placed by Wittgenstein at the beginning of his *Philosophical Investigations*[1] to represent a certain fundamentally mistaken view of language: the view that naming is the foundation of language and that the meaning of a word is the object for which it stands. The passage quoted lays great stress on the role of ostension in the learning of words, and makes no distinction between different parts of speech. Despite this Augustine is a curious choice as a spokesman for the thesis attacked by Wittgenstein, since in many respects what he says resembles Wittgenstein's own views rather than the views that are Wittgenstein's target.

Like Wittgenstein, Augustine believes that the setting-up of linguistic conventions presupposes a uniformity among human beings in their natural, pre-conventional reactions to such things as pointing fingers—'the natural language of all peoples'. Ostensive definition by itself will not teach a child the meaning of a word: a child must also 'hear the words repeatedly used in their proper places in various sentences'. The whole learning process is started by the child's own efforts to

---

[1] (Oxford: Blackwell, 1953).

express its sensations and needs pre-linguistically. Just before the quoted passage he says, 'by cries and various sounds and movements of my limbs I tried to express my inner feelings and get my will obeyed'. He thus makes a point, much stressed by Wittgenstein, that 'words are connected with the primitive, the natural, expressions of a sensation and used in their place'.[2]

The account of language in the *Confessions* was preceded by a much ampler account in an early work, *On the Teacher*. The theme of the work, which is a dialogue between Augustine and his son Adeodatus, is narrower than its title suggests: it is not concerned with education in general, but focuses on the teaching and learning of the meaning of words. It begins with a lively review of the varied uses for which we employ language. We use it not solely for the communication of information, but for many other purposes also, from praying to God to singing in the bath. We can use speech without sound when we form words in our minds: in such a case we use them as means to recall to memory the objects that they signify.

Augustine does not leave unexamined the facile assumption that words are signs. He quotes a line of Vergil,

If naught of such a city is left by heav'n to stand,

and asks Adeodatus what each of the three first words signifies. What does 'if' stand for? The best Adeodatus can offer is that it expresses doubt. 'Naught' means nothing, so it cannot be true that every word means something. What of 'of'? Adeodatus proposes that it is a synonym for 'from', but Augustine suggests that this is simply replacing one sign with another—it does not take us from sign to reality (*DMg* 2. 3–4).

Ostensive definition seems to offer a way out of the impasse, at least for some words. If I ask what 'wall' means, you could point to it with your finger. Not only material objects, but colours, can be ostensively defined in this way. But there are two objections to this as a general account. First of all, words like 'of' cannot be ostensively defined; and, more fundamentally, the gesture of pointing, no less than the utterance of a word, is only a sign, not the reality signified (*DMg* 3. 5–6).

Augustine responds to these objections that there are some words, like 'walk', 'eat', and 'stand', which can be explained by producing an instance of the very thing signified: I ostensively define 'walk' by walking. But suppose I am already walking when someone asks me what 'walk' means: how do I define it? I suppose I walk a little faster, says Adeodatus. But this shows that even in this favoured case ostensive definition is incurably ambiguous: how do I know whether the meaning that is offered is that of 'walk' or of 'hurry'?

Eventually Augustine concludes from the failure of ostensive learning that the meaning of words is not something that is taught by any human teacher, but by a teacher within us whose home is in heaven (*DMg* 14. 46). This is a Christian

---

[2] *Philosophical Investigations*, I. 244.

version, in the special case of language learning, of Plato's thesis in the *Meno* that all learning is really recollection. On the way to this conclusion, however, Augustine discusses a number of important issues in philosophy of language.

First, he classifies signs in a rudimentary semiotic. All words are signs, but not all signs are words: for instance, there are letters and gestures. All names are words, but not all words are names: besides words like 'if' and 'of' there are pronouns, which stand in for nouns, and verbs, that is to say, words with tenses (*DMg* 4. 9, 5. 13).

It is important to keep in mind the distinction between a sign and what it signifies (what Augustine calls its 'significable'). No one is likely to confuse a stone with a word for a stone: but some words are words for words, and here there is a real danger of confusion between sign and significable.

In modern English we minimize the risk of such confusion by employing quotation marks. Adeodatus is human, and there are two syllables in 'human'. In antique Latin, with no quotation marks, there is no such clear distinction between the normal case when we use the word as a predicate, and the special case where we use it in order to mention itself. Adeodatus has to be on his guard to avoid the trap set by his father: you are not composed of two syllables, therefore, you are not human (*DMg* 8. 22). Augustine devotes several pages to explaining that while, at one level, not all words are names, at another level every word is a name since it can be used to name itself. Even 'verb' is a name. The problems he spells out in this dialogue were discussed at great length by the medieval scholastics who developed the theory of supposition.[3]

Augustine himself, however, made no contribution to the discipline of formal logic. He never made a serious study of Aristotle, whom he describes rather condescendingly in *The City of God* as 'a man of outstanding intellect, no match for Plato in style, but well above the common herd'. He was, for a while, very interested in the Stoics, but it was the natural and ethical, not the logical, branch of their philosophy that principally engaged him.

In his youth, indeed, Augustine had read Aristotle's *Categories*, at the bidding of his rhetoric teacher in Carthage. In the *Confessions* he boasts that he mastered the text very quickly, but complains that it did him no good. The book, he says, was very clear on the topic of substance and the items that belong to them, but it is useless from a theological perspective.

What help was this to me when the book got in my way? Thinking that everything whatever was included in the ten categories, I tried to conceive you also, my God, wonderfully simple and immutable as you are, as if you too were a subject of which magnitude and beauty are attributes. I imagined them as inhering in you as a subject like a physical body, whereas you yourself are your own magnitude and your own beauty. (*Conf.* IV. 16. 28–9)

---

[3] See below, p. 355.

Among the works traditionally attributed to Augustine, at least from the time of Alcuin, is a Latin paraphrase of the *Categories*.[4] The work, however, is not mentioned by Augustine in his *Retractationes*, an exhaustive catalogue of his *Nachlass*, and it is nowadays the universal opinion of scholars that the work is not authentic. However, the attribution to Augustine secured the attention of early medieval scholars to this part of Aristotle's logic. Another work, *De Dialectica*, long thought spurious, has recently been restored to the canon.[5] It shows signs of Stoic influence but is concerned more with grammar than with logic or philosophy of language.

The Logic of Boethius

The close connection between logic and language is emphasized by Boethius, the most significant Latin logician of the first millennium. 'The whole art of logic', he wrote, 'is concerned with speech.' Boethius translated most, perhaps all, of the books of Aristotle's logical corpus, and he prefaced his translation of the *Categories* with a commentary (indeed a pair of commentaries) on the *Isagoge*, or *Introduction*, of Porphyry (c.233–309). Porphyry, the disciple and biographer of Plotinus, had introduced the logic of Aristotle into the curriculum of the Neoplatonic schools, and his *Isagoge* became the standard introductory text. Thanks to the work of Boethius, it retained that position well into the high Middle Ages.

An important feature of Porphyry's *Isagoge* was the theory of predicables, or the kinds of relation in which a predicate might stand to a subject. He listed five heads of classification: species, genus, *differentia*, property, and accident. All of these are terms that occur in Aristotle's *Topics*, but the theory of predicables differs from Aristotle's theory of categories, though the two classifications are related to each other. 'Stigger is a Labrador' tells us the species to which Stigger belongs; 'Stigger is a dog' tells us his genus. The *differentia* indicates the feature which marks off the species within the genus, e.g. 'Stigger is golden-haired and a retriever'. Humans, it was commonly explained, formed a species of the genus *animal* marked off by the *differentia rational*.

The predicates 'human', 'animal', when used of an individual human, Socrates, are predicated in the category of substance—they indicate, wholly or partly, the basic kind of entity that Socrates is. The predicate 'rational', the *differentia*, seems to straddle the distinction between substance and accident: as part of the definition it seems to belong in the substance category, but on the other hand rationality is surely a quality, and qualities are accidents. A property (*proprium*) is an attribute

---

[4] It was edited by L. Minio-Paluello as the first volume of the *Aristoteles Latinus* (Bruges: Desclée, De Brouwer, 1953–).

[5] Edited by Darrell Jackson (Dordrecht: Reidel, 1985).

which is peculiar to a particular species, though not definitive of it: the ability to see jokes was standardly taken in medieval times to be a property of the human race. An accident is a predicate that may or may not belong to a given individual, without prejudice to that individual's existence.

The theory of predicables permits us to construct hierarchies within categories. The distinction between genus and species is relative: what is a species relative to a superior genus is a genus relative to an inferior species. But there are ultimate species that are not genera—such as the human species. And there are ultimate genera that are not species of any higher genus: such as the ten categories (which are not species of some superior genus such as 'being'). If we take the category of substance as basic, we can derive two genera from it, body and spirit, by adding the *differentia* 'material' or 'immaterial' respectively. From the genus body, we can then derive two further genera, living beings and minerals, by adding the *differentia* 'animate' or 'inanimate'. The genus of living beings will, by a similar fission, generate the genera of vegetable and animal, and the genus animal will, with the *differentia* 'rational', produce the final species human, which includes the individuals Peter, Paul, and John. A branching hierarchy of this kind, set out in a diagram, is a 'Porphyry's Tree'.

In the *Isagoge* Porphyry uses his branching strategy to pose three questions about species and genera. Species and genera are not individual entities like Peter and Paul: they are in some sense universal. Do such things, Porphyry asked, exist outside the mind, or are they merely mental? If they are outside the mind, are they corporeal or incorporeal? If they are incorporeal, do they exist in things perceptible by the senses, or are they separate from them? Porphyry left these questions unanswered; but they set an agenda for many medieval discussions. They became the canonical statement of the Problem of Universals.

Boethius himself answered these questions thus: they exist outside the mind; they are incorporeal; they are not separable except in thought from individuals. A species or a genus is a similarity abstracted from particulars, as we collect the likeness of humanity (*similitudo humanitatis*) from individual humans. This, Boethius says, was Aristotle's view; but for purposes of formal logic it is not necessary to rule out the Platonic thesis of universals existing in separation (PL 64. 835A).

Boethius wrote commentaries on Aristotle's *Categories* and *De Interpretatione*. These commentaries show that he had some acquaintance also with Stoic logic, though he never regards it as trumping Aristotle. For example, he says that the Stoics were wrong about future contingents: when p is a future-tensed proposition about a contingent matter, 'Either p or not-p' is true, but neither 'p' nor 'not-p' need be definitely true. Thus 'Either there will be a sea-battle tomorrow or there will not be a sea-battle tomorrow' is true; but neither 'There will be a sea-battle tomorrow' nor 'There will not be a sea-battle tomorrow' need be definitely true today.

Besides commenting on Porphyry and Aristotle, Boethius wrote textbooks on syllogistic reasoning, one on categorical syllogisms and one on hypothetical syllogisms. A hypothetical syllogism must contain at least one hypothetical premiss, that is to say, a molecular proposition constructed from atomic categorical propositions by means of the connectives 'if', 'or', or 'since'. Some hypothetical syllogisms contain categorical premisses as well as hypothetical ones: one example is the *modus ponens* already familiar in Stoic logic:

If it is day, the sun is shining; but it is day; therefore the sun is shining.

Boethius, however, is more interested in syllogisms where all the premisses and the conclusion too are hypothetical, such as

If it's A, it's B; if it's B it's C; so if it's A it's C.

He elaborates schemata including negative premisses as well as affirmative ones and premisses involving conjunctions other than 'if', e.g. 'Either it is day or it is night'. Hypothetical syllogisms, he maintains, are parasitic on categorical syllogisms, because hypothetical premisses have categorical premisses as their constituents, and they depend on categorical syllogisms to establish the truth of their premisses. Once again, Boethius is siding with Aristotle against the Stoics, this time about the relationship between predicate and propositional logic.

In discussing hypothetical syllogisms Boethius makes an important distinction between two different sorts of hypothetical statement. He uses 'consequentia' ('consequence') as a term for a true hypothetical; perhaps the nearest equivalent in modern English is 'implication'. In some consequences, he says, there is no necessary connection between the antecedent and the consequence: his example is 'Since fire is hot, the heavens are spherical'. This appears to be an example of what modern logicians have called 'material implication'; Boethius' expression is 'consequentia secundum accidens'. On the other hand, there are consequences where the consequent follows necessarily from the antecedent. This class includes not only the logical truths that modern logicians would call 'formal implications' but also hypothetical statements whose truth is discovered by scientific inquiry, such as 'If the earth gets in the way, there is an eclipse of the moon' (PL 64. 835ʙ).

True consequences can be derived, Boethius believes, from a set of supreme universal propositions which he calls 'loci', following Cicero's rendering of the Aristotelian Greek 'topos'. The kind of proposition he has in mind is illustrated by one of his examples: 'Things whose definitions are different are themselves different'. He wrote a treatise, *De Topicis Differentiis*, in which he offered a set of principles for classifying the supreme propositions into groups. The work, though it appears arid to a modern reader, was influential in the early Middle Ages.[6]

---

[6] *De Topicis Differentiis*, trans. Eleonore Stump (Ithaca, NY: Cornell University Press, 1978).

Abelard as Logician

Boethius' work as writer and commentator provided the background to the study of logic until the reception of the full logical corpus of Aristotle in the high Middle Ages. After that time the logic he had handed down was referred to as the 'old logic', in contrast to the new logic of the universities. The old logic culminated in the work of Abelard in the first years of the twelfth century: such was the genius of Abelard that his logic contained a number of insights that were missing from the writings of later medieval logicians.

Abelard's preferred name for logic is 'dialectic' and *Dialectica* is the title of his major logical work. He believes that logic and grammar are closely connected: logic is an *ars sermocinalis*, a linguistic discipline. Like grammar, logic deals with words—but words considered as meaningful (*sermones*) not just as sounds (*voces*). Nonetheless, if we are to have a satisfactory logic, we must begin with a satisfactory account of grammatical parts of speech, such as nouns and verbs.

Aristotle had made a distinction between nouns and verbs on the ground that the latter, but not the former, contained a time indication. Abelard rejects this: it is true that only verbs are tensed, but nouns too contain an implicit time-reference. Subject terms stand primarily for things existing at the present time: you can see this if you consider a proposition such as 'Socrates was a boy', uttered when Socrates was old. If time belonged only to the tensed verb, this sentence would mean the same as 'A boy was Socrates'; but of course that sentence is false. The true corresponding sentence is 'Something that was a boy is Socrates'. This brings out the implicit time-reference in nouns, and this could be brought out in a logically perspicuous language by replacing nouns with pronouns followed by descriptive phrases: for example, 'Water is coming in' could be rewritten 'Something that is water is coming in'.

The defining characteristic of verbs is not that they are tensed but that they make a sentence complete; without them, Abelard says, there is no completeness of sense. There can be complete sentences without nouns (e.g. 'Come here!' or 'It is raining') but no complete sentences without verbs (*D* 149). Aristotle had taken the standard form of sentence to be of the form 'S is P'; he was aware that some sentences, such as 'Socrates drinks', did not contain the copula, but he maintained such sentences could always be rewritten in the form 'Socrates is a drinker'. Abelard, on the other hand, takes the noun-verb form as canonical, and regards an occurrence of 'is' as merely making explicit the linking function that is explicit in every verb. We should take '... is a man' as a unit, a single verb (*D* 138).

The verb 'to be' can be used not only as a link between subject and predicate, but also to indicate existence. Abelard paid considerable attention to this point. The Latin verb 'est' ('is'), he says, can appear in a sentence either as attached to a subject (as in 'Socrates est', 'Socrates exists') or as third extra element (as in

'Socrates est homo', 'Socrates is human'). In the second case, the verb does not indicate existence, as we can see in sentences like 'Chimera est opinabilis' ('Chimeras are imaginable'). Any temptation to think that it does is removed if we treat an expression like '. . . is imaginable' as a single unit, rather than as composed of a predicate term 'imaginable' and the weasel word 'is'.

Abelard offers two different analyses of statements of existence. 'Socrates est', he says at one point, should be expanded into 'Socrates est ens', i.e. 'Socrates is a being'. But this is hardly satisfactory, since the ambiguity of the verb 'esse' carries over into its participle 'being'. Elsewhere—in one of his non-logical works—he was better inspired. He says that in the sentence 'A father exists' we should not take 'A father' as standing for anything; rather, the sentence is equivalent to 'Something is a father'. 'Exists' thus disappears altogether as a predicate, and is replaced by a quantifier plus a verb. In this innovation, as well as in his suggestion that expressions like '. . . is human' should be treated as a single unit, Abelard anticipated nineteenth-century insights of Gottlob Frege which are fundamental in modern logic.[7]

To Abelard's contemporaries, the logical problem which seemed most urgent was that of universals. Dissatisfied with the theories of his two first teachers, the nominalist Roscelin and the realist William of Champeaux, Abelard offered a middle way between them. On the one hand, he said, it was absurd to say that Adam and Peter had nothing in common other than the word 'human'; the noun applied to each of them in virtue of their likeness to each other, which was something objective. On the other hand, it is absurd to say that there is a substantial entity, the human species, which is present in its entirety in each and every individual; this would imply that Socrates must be identical with Plato and that he must be in two places at the same time. A resemblance is not a substantial thing like a horse or a cabbage, and only individual things exist.

When we maintain that the likeness between things is not a thing, we must avoid making it seem as if we were treating them as having nothing in common; since what in fact we say is that the one and the other resemble each other in their being human, that is, in that they are both human beings. We mean nothing more than that they are human beings and do not differ at all in this regard. (*LI* 20)

Their being human, which is not a thing but, Abelard says, a status, is the common cause of the application of the noun to the individual.

Both nominalism and realism depend on an inadequate analysis of what it is for a word to signify. Words signify in two ways: they mean things, and they express thoughts. They mean things precisely by evoking the appropriate thoughts, the concepts under which the mind brings the things in the world. We acquire these

[7] The transformation of existential propositions into quantified propositions was regarded by Bertrand Russell as a logical innovation that gave the death blow to the ontological argument for God's existence; see below, p. 479.

concepts by considering mental images, but they are something distinct from images (*D* 329). It is these concepts that enable us to talk about things, and turn vocal sounds into significant words. There is no universal *man* distinct from the universal noun 'man'—that is the degree of truth in nominalism. But, *pace* Roscelin, the noun 'man' is not a mere puff of breath—it is turned into a universal noun by our understanding. Just as a sculptor turns a piece of stone into a statue, so our intellect turns a sound into a word. In this sense we can say that universals are creations of the mind (*LNPS* 522).

Words do signify universals in that they are the expression of universal concepts. But they do not mean universals in the way that they mean individual things in the world. There are different ways in which words mean things. Abelard makes a distinction between what a word signifies and what it stands for. The word 'boy', wherever it occurs in a sentence, has the same signification: young human male. When the word stands in subject place in a sentence, as in 'A boy is running up the road', it also stands for a boy. But in 'This old man was once a boy', where it occurs as part of the predicate, it does not stand for anything. Roughly speaking, 'boy' stands for something in a given context only if it makes sense to ask 'Which boy?'

We can ask not just what individual words signify, but also what whole sentences signify. Abelard defines a proposition as 'an utterance signifying truth or falsehood'. Once again, 'signify' has a double sense. A true sentence *expresses* a true thought, and it *states* what is in fact the case (*proponit id quod in re est*). It is the second sense of 'signification' that is important when we are doing logic, for we are interested in what states of affairs follow from other states of affairs, rather than in the sequence of thoughts in anybody's mind (*D* 154). The enunciation of the state of affairs (*rerum modus habendi se*) that a proposition states to be the case is called by Abelard the *dictum* of the proposition (*LI* 275). A *dictum* is not a fact in the world, because it is something that is true or false: it is true if the relevant state of affairs obtains in the world; otherwise it is false. What is a fact is the obtaining (or not, as the case may be) of the state of affairs in question.

Abelard, unlike some other logicians, medieval and modern, made a clear distinction between predication and assertion. A subject and predicate may be put together without any assertion or statement being made. 'God loves you' is a statement; but the same subject and predicate are put together in 'If God loves you, you will go to heaven' and again in 'May God love you!' without that statement being made (*D* 160).

Abelard defines logic as the art of judging and discriminating between valid and invalid arguments or inferences (*LNPS* 506). He does not restrict inferences to syllogisms: he is interested in a more general notion of logical consequence. He does not use the Latin word 'consequentia' for this: in common with other authors he uses that word to mean 'conditional proposition'—a sentence of the form 'If *p* then *q*'. The word he uses is 'consecutio', which we can translate as 'entailment'. The two notions are related but not identical. When 'If p then q' is a logical truth, then p entails q, and q follows from p; but 'If p then q' is very often true without p entailing q.

For p to entail q it is essential that 'If p then q' be a necessary truth; but for Abelard this is not sufficient. 'If Socrates is a stone, then he is a donkey' is a necessary truth: it is impossible for Socrates to be a stone, and so impossible that he should be a stone without being a donkey (D 293). Abelard demands not just that 'If p then q' be a necessary truth, but that its necessity should derive from the content of the antecedent and the consequent. 'Inference consists in a necessity of entailment: namely, that what is meant by the consequence is determined by the sense of the antecedent' (D 253). But the necessity of entailment does not demand the existence of the things that antecedent and consequent are talking about: 'If x is a rose, x is a flower' remains true whether or not there are any roses left in the world (LI 366). It is the *dicta* that carry the entailments, and *dicta* are neither thoughts in our heads nor things in the world like roses.

In modal logic Abelard's most helpful contribution was a distinction (which he claimed to derive from Aristotle's *Sophistici Elenchi* 165^{b}26) between two different ways of predicating possibility. Consider a proposition such as 'It is possible for the king not to be king'. If we take this as saying that 'The king is not the king' is possibly true, then the proposition is obviously false. Predication in this way Abelard calls predication *de sensu* or *per compositionem*. We can take the proposition in a different way, as meaning that the king may be deposed; and so taken it may very well be true. Abelard calls this the sense de re or *per divisionem*. Later generations of philosophers were to find this distinction useful in various contexts; they usually contrasted predication *de re* not with predication *de sensu* but with predication *de dicto*.

The Thirteenth-Century Logic of Terms

In the latter half of the twelfth century the complete *Organon*, or logical corpus, of Aristotle became available in Latin and formed the core of the logical curriculum henceforth, supplemented by Porphyry's *Isagoge*, two works of Boethius, and a single medieval work—the *Liber de Sex Principiis* of an unknown twelfth-century author. This presented itself as a supplement to the *Categories*, discussing in detail those categories that Aristotle had treated only cursorily. Partly because of its novel availability, the work of Aristotle most energetically studied at this period was the *Sophistici Elenchi*. Sophisms—puzzling sentences that needed careful analysis if they were not to lead to absurd conclusions—became henceforth a staple of the medieval logical diet. Among the most studied sophisms were versions of the liar paradox: 'I am now lying', which is false if true, and true if false. These were known as *insolubilia*.

The rediscovery of Aristotle's logical texts had as one consequence that the work of Abelard, who had been unacquainted with most of the *Organon*, fell into disrepute and was neglected. This was unfortunate, because in several important features Abelardian logic was superior to Aristotelian logic. Some of his insights reappear, unattributed, in later medieval logic; others had to wait until the nineteenth century to be rediscovered independently.

In the middle of the thirteenth century there appeared two logical manuals that were to have long-lasting influence. One was the *Introductiones in Logicam* written by an Englishman at Oxford, William of Sherwood; the other was the *Tractatus*, later called *Summulae Logicales*, written by Peter of Spain, a Paris master who may or may not be identical with the man who became Pope John XXI in 1276. There was no set order in which writers dealt with logical topics, but one possible pattern corresponded to the order of treatment in the *Organon*—*Categories*, *De Interpretatione*, *Prior Analytics*. There was a certain propriety in studying in turn the logic of individual words ('the properties of terms'), of complete sentences (the semantics of propositions), and the logical relations between sentences (the theory of consequences).

Terms include not only words, written or spoken, but also the mental counterparts of these, however these are to be identified. In practice concepts are identified by the words that express them, so the medieval study of terms was essentially the study of the meanings of individual words. In the course of this study logicians developed an elaborate terminology. The most general word for 'meaning' was 'significatio', but not every word that was not meaningless had signification. Words were divided into two classes according to whether they had signification on their own (e.g. nouns) or whether they only signified in conjunction with other, significant, words. The former class were called categorematic terms, the latter were called syncategorematic (*SL* 3). Conjunctions, adverbs, and prepositions were examples of syncategorematic terms, as were words such as 'only' in 'Only Socrates is running'. Categorematic words give a sentence its content; syncategorematic words are function words that exhibit the structure of sentences and the form of arguments.

As a first approximation one can say that the signification of a word is its dictionary meaning. If we learn the meaning of a word from a dictionary, we acquire a concept that is capable of multiple application. (What constitutes the precise relation between words, concepts, and extra-mental reality will depend on what theory of universals you accept.) Categorematic terms, in addition to signification, could have a number of other semantic properties, depending on the way the words were used in particular contexts. Consider the four sentences 'A dog is scratching at the door', 'A dog has four legs', 'I will buy you a dog for Christmas', and 'The dog has just been sick'. The word 'dog' has the same signification in each of these sentences—it corresponds to a single dictionary entry—but its other semantic properties differ from sentence to sentence.

These properties were grouped by medieval logicians under the general heading of 'suppositio' (*SL* 79–89). The distinction between signification and supposition had some of the same functions as the distinction made by modern philosophers between sense and reference. The most basic kind of supposition is called by Peter of Spain 'natural supposition': this is the capacity that a significant general term has to supposit for (i.e. stand for) any item to which the term applies. The way in which this capacity is exercised in different contexts gives rise to different forms of supposition.

One important initial distinction is between simple supposition and personal supposition (*SL* 81). This distinction is easier to make in English than in Latin, because in English it corresponds to the presence or absence of an article before a noun. Thus in 'Man is mortal' there is no article and the word has simple supposition; in 'A man is knocking at the door' the word has personal supposition. But personal supposition itself comes in several different kinds, namely, discrete, determinate, distributive, and confused.

There are three different ways in which a word can occur in the subject place of a sentence: these correspond to discrete, determinate, and distributive supposition. In 'The dog has just been sick' the word 'dog' has discrete supposition: the predicate attaches to a definite single one of the items to which the word applies. This kind of supposition attaches to proper names, demonstratives, and definite descriptions. Determinate supposition is exemplified in 'A dog is scratching at the door': the predicate attaches to some one thing to which the word applies, a thing that is not further specified. In 'A dog has four legs' (or 'Every dog has four legs') the supposition is distributive: the predicate attaches to everything to which the word 'dog' applies. To distinguish determinate from distributive supposition one should ask whether the question 'Which dog?' makes sense or not.

A word can, however, have personal supposition not only when it occurs in a subject place, but also if it appears as a predicate. In 'Buffy is a dog' (or in 'A dachshund is a dog') the name 'confused' was given to the supposition of the word 'dog'. In confused supposition, as in distributive supposition, it makes no sense to ask 'Which dog?' (*SL* 82).

All the kinds of supposition we have listed—simple supposition and the various forms of personal supposition—are examples of 'formal supposition'. Formal supposition, naturally enough, contrasts with material supposition, and the underlying idea is that the sound of a word is its matter, while its meaning is its form. The Latin equivalent of ' "Dog" is a monosyllable' would be an instance of material supposition, and so is the equivalent of ' "dog" is a noun'. This is, in effect, the use of a word to refer to itself, to talk about its symbolic properties rather than about what it means or stands for. Once again, modern English speakers have the advantage over medieval Latinists. In general it takes no philosophical skill to identify material supposition, because from childhood we are taught that when we are mentioning a word, rather than using it in the normal way, we must employ quotation marks and write ' "dog" is a monosyllable'. But in more complicated cases confusion between signs and things signified continues to occur from time to time even in the works of trained philosophers.[8]

Supposition was the most important semantic property of terms, but there were others, too, recognized by medieval logicians. One was appellation, which is connected with the scope of terms and sentences. Consider the sentence 'Dinosaurs have long tails'. Is this true, now that there are no dinosaurs? If we take the view that a sentence is made true or false on the basis of the current contents of the universe, then it seems that the sentence cannot be true; and we cannot remedy this problem simply by changing the tense of the verb to 'had'. If we wish to regard the sentence as true, we shall have to regard truth as something to be determined on the basis of all the contents of the universe, past, present, and future. The medievals posed this problem as being one about the appellation of the term 'dinosaur'.

Two schools of thought adopted different approaches to the problem. One school, to which William of Sherwood belonged, held that the standard, or default, appellation of terms was only to presently existing objects. If one wishes a term to supposit for something no longer extant, one has to apply to the term a procedure called *ampliation*. The other view, to which Peter of Spain subscribed, held that the standard appellation of terms included all things to which they applied, whether present, past, or future. If one wished to restrict the supposition of a term to the current contents of the universe, one had to apply a procedure called *restriction* (*SL* 199–208). Both schools drew up complicated rules to indicate when the context imposed ampliation, or restriction, as the case may be.

Propositions and Syllogisms

If we turn from the logic of terms to the logic of propositions, we find that just as the medievals regarded nouns as expressing concepts in the mind, so they regarded sentences as expressing beliefs in the mind. Following Aristotle, they distinguished between simple thoughts (expressed in single words) and complex thoughts (expressed in combinations of words). There were, they said, again following Aristotle, two different operations of the intellect: one, the understanding of non-complexes, and the other, the composition and division of a proposition

---

[8] The reader should be warned that though most logicians made the distinctions identified above, there is considerable variation in the terminology used to make them. Moreover, in the interests of simplicity I have abbreviated some of the technical terms. What I have called 'confused supposition' should strictly be called 'merely confused' and what I have called 'distributive' should be called 'confused and distributive'. See Paul Spade in *CHLMP* 196, and W. Kneale, in *The Development of Logic* (Oxford: Oxford University Press, 1962), 252.

(cf. Aquinas, I *Sent.* 19. 5 ad 1). A proposition, we are regularly told, is a combination of words that expresses something that is either true or false.

There are a number of difficulties in reconciling these accounts of the nature of the proposition. First of all, once we have distinguished (with Abelard) between predication and assertion, it is clear that a complex consisting of a subject and predicate need not be an assertion nor express a belief. (Some medieval logicians marked the distinction by saying that not every proposition was an enunciation.)[9] Secondly, 'composition and division' in Aristotle appears to mean the same as 'positive and negative judgements'—but are not the subject and predicate put together in a single complex in a negative judgement no less than in a positive one? Thomas Aquinas offered the following answer to this problem:

If we consider what takes place in the mind by itself then there is always combination where there is truth and falsehood; for the mind cannot produce anything true or false unless it combines one simple concept with another. But if the relation to reality is taken into account, then the mind's operation is called sometimes 'combination' and sometimes 'division': 'combination' where the mind so places one concept beside another as to represent the combination or identity of the things *of* which they are the concepts; 'division' where it so places one concept beside another as to represent that the corresponding realities are distinct. We talk in the same way of sentences too: an affirmative sentence is called 'a combination' because it signifies that there is a conjunction in reality; a negative sentence is called 'a division' because it signifies that the realities are separate. (*In I Periherm.* 1. 3, p. 26)

A proposition, whether asserted or not, will be true or false; that is to say, it will, as a matter of fact, correspond or not with reality. The same is true of the corresponding thought, whether it is a belief or the mere entertainment of a conjecture. But only the speech-act of asserting, or the corresponding mental act of judging, commits the thinker or speaker to the truth of the proposition.

Against this background, we may raise the question, What do propositions signify? If we take 'signify' as equivalent to 'express', then it is easy to give an answer: spoken and written propositions express thoughts in the mind. But there is then a further question: What do mental propositions signify? Here 'signify' has to be closer to 'mean' than to 'express'. Propositions, it seems, cannot signify anything in the world, because a proposition must signify the same whether it is true or false; and if the proposition is false, there is nothing in the world to correspond to it. The most popular answer to this question in the thirteenth century was essentially that given by Abelard: it is the state of affairs which, if it obtains, makes the sentence true. Abelard had called this a *dictum*; others called it an *enuntiabile*; but most people found it difficult to give a clear account of its metaphysical status. One author said that *enuntiabilia* were neither substances nor qualities, but stood in a class of their own—not to be found in Aristotle's

---

[9] L. de Rijk, *Logica Modernorum* (Assen: van Gorcum, 1962–6), II. 1. 342.

categories. They were not tangible entities but could be grasped only by reason.[10] As we shall see, the existence of such entities was called in question in the fourteenth century.

There is a further, related, question: What kind of thing is it that is true or false? Sentences, thoughts, and *dicta* can all be called true. But which of these is the primary bearer of truth-values? The question is particularly pointed when we consider the relation between truth and time. Some philosophers believe that all that we say in natural languages by the use of tensed sentences could be said in a logical language that contained no tenses but whose sentences contained timeless verbs plus an explicit temporal reference or quantification over times. Thus, a sentence 'It will rain' uttered at time $t1$ would on this view have to be understood as expressing a proposition to the following effect: at some time t later than $t1$ it rains (timelessly). It is still a matter of debate whether such a translation of tensed sentences into timeless propositions can be carried out without loss of content.

In the Middle Ages there was little enthusiasm for such translation. Most commonly, *enuntiabilia* no less than sentences were regarded as tensed. Consequently, both sentences and *enuntiabilia* could change their truth-values. Aristotle was frequently quoted as saying that one and the same sentence 'Socrates is sitting' is true when Socrates is sitting and false when he gets up.[11] The nearest approximation to timeless propositions in the thought of medieval logicians was a disjunction of tensed propositions. Thus it was sometimes suggested that there was a single object of faith in which Hebrew prophets and Christian saints alike believed, namely, the proposition 'Christ will be born or Christ is born or Christ has been born'.[12]

The thirteenth-century logic manuals contained, in addition to discussions of terms and propositions, substantial sections on the theory of inference. The core of their treatment was Aristotle's syllogistic. The logicians provided doggerel verses to make the rules of syllogistic memorable and easy to operate. The best-known such verse is the following:

> Barbara celarent darii ferio baralipton
> Celantes dabitis fapesmo frisesomorum;
> Cesare campestres festino baroco; darapti
> Felapton disamis datisi bocardo ferison.

Each word represents a particular mood of valid syllogism, with the vowels indicating the nature of the three propositions that make it up. The letter 'a' stands for a universal affirmative proposition, and the letter 'i' a particular

---

[10] de Rijk, *Logica Modernorum*, II. 1. 357–9. There was a particular problem about the signification of tensed propositions, a problem that constantly recurred in treatments of divine foreknowledge. See Ch. 9 below.

[11] This issue was discussed particularly in connection with God's timeless knowledge of events in time; see Ch. 9 below.

[12] See G. Nuchelmans, 'The Semantics of Propositions', in *CHLMP* 202.

affirmative proposition (these letters being chosen because they are the first two vowels in 'affirmo', 'I affirm'). The letter 'e' stands for a universal negative, and 'o' for a particular negative. (The Latin for 'I deny' is 'nego': hence the choice of vowels.) Thus a syllogism in Barbara contains three universal propositions (e.g. 'All kittens are cats; all cats are animals; so all kittens are animals'). A syllogism in Celarent, by contrast, has as premisses one universal negative and one universal affirmative, with a universal negative conclusion (e.g. 'No cats are birds; all kittens are cats; so no kittens are birds').

The first four moods of syllogism were regarded as the most perspicuous forms of valid argument. Accordingly the mnemonic words for the later moods contain instructions for transforming themselves into arguments in one or other of the first four moods. The letter at the beginning of each mood's name indicates which of the four it is to be converted into. 'C' at the beginning of 'Cesare' shows that it is to be converted into a syllogism in Celarent. Other letters show how to do this: the 's' after the first 'e' in Cesare shows that the order of the terms in that premiss are to be switched. Thus 'No birds are cats; all kittens are cats; so no kittens are birds', a syllogism in Cesare, is converted, by switching the terms in the first premiss, into the syllogism in Celarent, illustrated above.

The occurrence of the letter 'c' within the body of a mnemonic word indicates that the conversion into the preferred mood has to be undertaken in a particularly complicated and difficult manner, which need not be illustrated here. But the operation left such a mark on students of logic that of the two words containing such a 'c', Baroco gave its name to a highly elaborate style of architecture while Bocardo gave its name to the prison in which delinquent Oxford students were incarcerated. Mnemonics such as these, ingenious though they are, were mocked by Renaissance writers as being, literally, barbaric; and they contributed to the disrepute of medieval logic in early modern times.

Aquinas on Thought and Language

Thomas Aquinas made little contribution to formal logic, but he reflected upon the nature of language and the relationship of language to thought: he offers various classifications of speech-acts, and of what we might call the corresponding thought-acts. He begins from a text of Aristotle which makes a distinction between two kinds of intellectual activity.

There are, as Aristotle says in the *De Anima*, two kinds of activity of our intellect. One consists in forming simple essences, such as what a man is or what an animal is: in this activity, considered in itself, neither truth nor falsehood is to be found, any more than in utterances that are non-complex. The other consists in putting together and taking apart, by affirming and denying: in this truth and falsehood are to be found, just as in the complex utterance that is its expression. (*DV* 14. 1)

The distinction between these two types of thought is linked to the difference in language between the use of individual words and the construction of complete sentences. This is brought out when Aquinas explains that any act of thinking can be regarded as the production of an inner word or inner sentence.

The 'word' of our intellect . . . is that which is the terminus of our intellectual operation. It is the thought itself, which is called an intellectual conception: which may be either a conception which can be expressed by a non-complex utterance, as when the intellect forms the essences of things, or a conception expressible by a complex utterance, as when the intellect composes and divides. (*DV* 4. 2c)

As we have seen, the notion of intellectual 'composition and division' is not a straightforward one. The paradigm example of such composition and division is the making of affirmative and negative judgements. But there are other types of complex thought. Besides judging that *p* and judging that not-*p* I may wonder whether *p*, or simply entertain the idea that *p* as part of a story. Consider any proposition, for example 'Smoking causes deafness' or 'Saudi Arabia possesses nuclear weapons'. With respect to propositions such as these a judgement, affirmative or negative, may be made or withheld; if made, it may be made truly or falsely, with or without hesitation, on the basis of argument, or on grounds of self-evidence.

Aquinas classes exercises of the intellectual powers on the basis of these different possibilities: the withholding of judgement is doubt (*dubitatio*); tentative assent, allowing for the possibility of error, is opinion (*opinio*); unquestioning assent to a truth on the basis of self-evidence is understanding (*intellectus*); giving a truth unquestioning assent on the basis of reasons is knowledge (*scientia*); unquestioning assent where there are no compelling reasons is belief or faith (*credere*, *fides*). All of these are instances of *compositio et divisio*.

What of the other intellectual activity, the conception of non-complexes? Aquinas seems, in different places, to give two different accounts of this. Sometimes he seems to equate it with the mastery of the use of a word. In that case someone would have a concept of *gold* if she knew the meaning of the word 'gold'. But in other places Aquinas equates a concept with the knowledge of the quiddity or essence of something: in this sense only a chemist, who could link the properties of gold with its atomic number and its place in the periodic table, would have a real concept of *gold* (*ST* 1a 3. 3 and 1a 77. 1 ad 3). He was well aware of the difference between the two types of concept: he points out, for instance, that we can know what the word 'God' means, but we do not and cannot know God's essence (e.g. *ST* 1a 2. 2 ad 2).

How close, for Aquinas, is the link between language and thought: what is the relationship between these varied intellectual operations and the corresponding speech-acts? Aquinas believed that any judgement that can be made can be expressed by a sentence (*DV* 2.4). It does not follow from this, nor does Aquinas maintain, that every judgement that is made *is* put into words, either publicly or in the privacy of the imagination. Again, even though every thought is expressible in language, only a small minority of thoughts are *about* language.

On the question of universals, Aquinas' starting point is a rejection of Platonism, a doctrine that he described as follows:

> Plato, to save the fact that we can have certain intellectual knowledge of the truth, posited in addition to ordinary bodily things, another class of things free of matter and change, which he called *species* or Ideas. It was by participation in these that all particular tangible objects get called 'human' or 'horse' or whatever. Accordingly, Plato held that definitions, and scientific truths, and all other things pertaining to the operation of the intellect, are not about ordinary tangible bodies, but about those immaterial things in another world. (*ST* 1a 84. 1c)

Plato was misled, Aquinas thought, by the doctrine that like can be known only by like, and so the form of what is known must be in the knower exactly as it is in the known. It is true that the objects of thought in the intellect are universal and immaterial; but universals of this kind do not exist anywhere outside an intellect.

Aquinas was prepared to agree with Plato that there are forms that make things what they are: there is, for instance, a form of humanity that makes Socrates human. But he denied that there was any such form existing apart from matter. There is not, outside the mind, any such thing as human nature as such, human nature in the absolute. There is only the human nature of individual human beings like Peter and Paul. There is no human nature that is not the nature of some individual, and there is not, in heaven or earth, such a thing as the Universal Man (*ST* 1a 79c). Human nature exists in the mind in abstraction from individuating characteristics, related uniformly to all the individual humans existing outside the mind. There is no Idea of Human, only people's ideas of humanity. Plato's Ideas are rejected in favour of Tom, Dick, and Harry's concepts (*DEE* 3. 102–7).

The humanity of an individual, as Aquinas put it, was 'thinkable' (because a form) but not 'actually thinkable' (because existing in matter). To make it actually thinkable it had to be operated upon by a special intellectual power, the 'agent intellect'. We will follow Aquinas' account of this operation when we examine his philosophy of mind; at present we may ask what are the implications of Aquinas' anti-Platonic account of universals for the semantics of names and predicates.

Aquinas spells out the consequences in respect of one kind of universal, namely, a species. The species *dog* does not exist in reality, and it is no part of being a dog to be a species, even though dogs are a species. But if being a species were part of what it was to be a dog, then Fido would be a species. When we say that dogs are a species, we are not really, if Aquinas is right, saying anything about dogs: we are making a second-order statement about our concepts. First, we are saying that the concept *dog* is universal: it is applicable to any number of dogs. Secondly, we are saying that it is a composite concept that has other concepts as constituents: for instance, *animal*. Genus and species are defined in terms of predication, and predicates are things that minds make up, in forming affirmative and negative propositions (*DEE* 3. 133–5).

One of Aquinas' best-known contributions to the logic of language is his treatment of analogical discourse. He introduces the topic most commonly when discussing the possibility of discourse about God, but it is one of wide application. Drawing on a number of cryptic passages in Aristotle, he distinguishes two different kinds of analogy. The first kind (which some scholastics called 'analogy of attribution') can be illustrated by reference to the term 'healthy'. Strictly speaking, only living things such as animals and plants can be healthy; but a diet or a complexion may naturally be described as healthy. 'We use the word "healthy" of both a diet and a complexion because both of them have some relation to health in a human, the former as a cause, the latter as a symptom' (1a 13. 5). The other kind of analogy (which some scholastics called 'analogy of proportionality') may be illustrated with reference to the analogous term 'good'. A good knife is a knife that is handy and sharp; a good strawberry is a strawberry that is soft and tasty. Clearly, goodness in knives is something quite different from goodness in strawberries; yet it does not seem to be a mere pun to call both knives and strawberries 'good', nor does one seem to be using a metaphor drawn from knives when one calls a particular batch of strawberries good.

Analogy and Univocity

Aquinas maintained that the words by which we describe God and creatures are not used in the same sense about each. Similarly, to adapt one of his examples, we do not mean quite the same thing when we call the sun 'bright' and when we call the colour of a patch of paint 'bright'. On the other hand, if we say that God is wise and that Socrates is wise, we are not making a pun or talking in metaphor. 'This way of using words', Aquinas says, 'lies somewhere between pure equivocation and simple univocity, for the word is used neither in the same sense, as with univocal usage, nor in totally different senses, as with equivocation' (*ST* 1a 13. 5).

This theory of analogy was rejected by Duns Scotus, both in itself and in its application to religious language. If it is to be possible to talk about God at all, Scotus argued, there must be some words that have the same meaning when applied to God and creatures. Not all of our theological discourse can be analogical; some of it must be univocal. Scotus focused on words such as 'good'—words that he called 'transcendental' terms, because they transcended the boundaries of the Aristotelian categories, applying across all of them. As Aristotle himself had pointed out, we can talk of good times and good places as well as good men or good qualities (*NE* 1. 5. 1096^{a}23–30). Scotus maintained that such transcendental terms were all univocal: they had a single sense whether they were applied to different kinds of creatures, or whether they were applied to creatures and to God himself. The most important transcendental term was 'ens', 'being'. Substances and accidents, creatures and creator, were all beings in exactly the same sense.

Scotus' target in his discussion of analogy and univocity was not Aquinas but Henry of Ghent. Henry had maintained that our unreflective concept of being masks two distinct concepts, one that applies to the infinite being of God, and another that applies to the creatures that fall within the different categories. Reflection reveals that there is no single, univocal, concept that applies both to God and to creatures; there is, however, a similarity between the two concepts sufficient to enable us to make analogical predications about God, describing him not just as a being, but as good, wise, and so on.

Scotus rejects the idea that there can be a half-way house between univocity and equivocation. Certainly, if we are dealing with simple concepts that have no constituent parts, there cannot be such a thing as the sense of a word being *partly* the same and *partly* different. If the terms we apply to God are equivocal—are used in a quite different sense from the one they have when applied to creatures—then we cannot draw any conclusions about God from the properties of creatures. Any attempt to use an analogical predicate as the middle term of a syllogism would be guilty of the fallacy of equivocation (*Lect.* 16. 266).

A concept is univocal, Scotus tells us, when

> it possesses sufficient unity in itself so that to affirm and deny it of one and the same thing would be a contradiction. It also has sufficient unity to serve as the middle term of a syllogism, so that whenever two extremes are united by a middle term that is one in this way, we may conclude to the union of the two extremes among themselves. (*Ord.* 3. 18)

To show that there can be a univocal concept of being that applies both to God and to creatures, Scotus argues as follows. If you can be certain that S is P while doubting whether S is Q, then P and Q must be different concepts. But you can be certain that God is a being, while doubting whether he is an infinite or a finite being. Hence the concept of being differs from that of infinite being and that of finite being—Henry's two primitive concepts—and is univocal, applying to both finite and infinite in the same sense (*Ord.* 3. 29). Concepts like 'being', 'good', 'one', and the like are thus, for Scotus, transcendental not just in transcending the boundaries of the categories, but also in transcending the gap between finite and infinite.

Scotus does not deny that there are concepts that apply analogously to God and creatures. His claim is that these are built upon, and could not exist without, more basic concepts that are univocal.

Take, for example, the formal notion of 'wisdom' or 'intellect' or 'will'. Such a notion is considered first of all simply in itself and absolutely. Because this notion includes formally no imperfection or limitation, the imperfections associated with it in creatures are removed. Retaining this same notion of 'wisdom' and 'will' we attribute these to God— but in a most perfect degree. Consequently, every inquiry regarding God is based upon the supposition that the intellect has the same univocal concept which it obtains from creatures. (*Ord.* 3. 26–7)

Perhaps the disagreement between Aquinas, Henry, and Scotus is not as sharp as it at first appears, because the notions *the same sense* and *the same concept* are themselves not sharp. Two words have different senses, we might suggest, if a dictionary would give two separate definitions of them. But when Aquinas says that 'good' is an analogous term, he need not be suggesting that every different application of 'good' creates a new lexical item. Different creatures have different good-making properties, but that does not mean that the meaning of 'good' in 'good horse' is different from the meaning of 'good' in 'good time'. Indeed, someone who did not realize that 'good' was, in Aquinas' terms, analogous, would not understand its meaning in the language at all. Scotus is right, on the other hand, that when we learn to apply 'good' to a new object, we do not learn a new vocabulary lesson.

Whether 'being' is analogous or univocal is a murky question not because of difficulties about analogy but because of the almost universal opacity of the medieval notion of *being*. If we are talking about existence, as expressed, say, in the sentence 'There is a God', then the question whether being is an analogous or univocal predicate does not arise since attributing existence to something is not a matter of attaching a predicate to a subject. But, in Scotus at least, 'to be', period, seems equivalent to a vast disjunction of predicates: 'to be a horse, or a colour, or a day, or . . . ' and so on ad infinitum. So understood, 'to be' seems clearly univocal. Suppose that there were only three items in the universe, A, B, and C. The predicate ' . . . is either A, or B, or C' seems to attach in exactly the same sense to each of the three items.

Modistic Logic

Scotus did not make any substantial contribution to formal logic, though his metaphysical ideas on the nature of power and potentiality were to have a significant long-term effect on modal logic. He was, however, long credited with an interesting work on the borders of logic and linguistics, a *Grammatica Speculativa* that the young Martin Heidegger took as the subject of his doctoral thesis. The work is now regarded as inauthentic by scholars, and attributed not to Scotus but to his little-known contemporary Thomas of Erfurt, writing about 1300.

The work is important as representative of a new approach to logic, adopted by Radulphus Brito (d. 1320) and a number of thinkers in the late thirteenth century, known as 'modistic logic' in contrast to the 'terminist logic' which we have seen in the works of Peter of Spain and William Sherwood. Rather than studying the properties of individual terms, these modist logicians studied general grammatical categories—nouns, verbs, cases, and tenses, for instance—which they called *modi significandi*, or ways of signifying.

Meaning, according to the modists, was conferred on sounds by human convention, which they called 'imposition'. The unit element of meaning was the *dictio*, 'diction'. A single diction might embrace many different verbal forms: the cases of a Latin noun, for instance, plus the adjectives and adverbs associated with it. A favourite example was the diction for *pain*, which included the noun 'dolor' in its different cases, the verb for feeling pain 'doleo', and the adverb 'dolenter', meaning 'painfully'. The basic convention setting up the diction for pain was called by the modists first imposition; further conventions, by a second imposition, established these *modi significandi* that linked different word forms to different types of use.[13]

Some *modi significandi* were more fundamental than others. The essential one defined a word as a particular part of speech—noun or verb, for example. Other accidental ones allotted to it such features as case, number, tense, or mood. Complicated rules were worked out to determine which words, with which *modi significandi*, could combine together to make a well-formed sentence.

Broadly speaking, it can be said that the study of *modi significandi* was a study of syntax, while the focus of semantics was the *ratio significandi*, or signifying relation conferred by the first imposition. The speculative grammarians did, however, seek to find a semantic element associated with the modes of signifying. The sense of an expression is fixed by the combination of *ratio* and *modi*: this was called its 'formal meaning', its meaning in virtue of language (*virtus sermonis*). In modern terminology we might call this its lexical meaning, its meaning as determined by the dictionary.

In a context of actual use, however, an expression also has a reference determined by its sense. Faced with the Latin sentence 'Homo appropinquat' we may be told that this consists of the nominative singular of the masculine noun 'homo', meaning man, plus the third-person singular of the verb 'appropinquo', meaning approach. This information is given us by the *virtus sermonis*: but we may ask, in a real-life context, *which man* is approaching; and this fact opens up a new area of inquiry. The modist logicians had various suggestions to offer here, but they were not taken up by later generations of thinkers. Instead, there was a revival of terminist logic, which had developed the theory of supposition to deal precisely with issues of the relationship between sense and reference.

---

[13] See J. Pinborg, 'Speculative Grammar', in *CHLMP* 254–69.

Ockham's Mental Language

One of the most important of the terminist logicians of the fourteenth century was William Ockham. Ockham offers a novel system: a terminist logic that is nominalist, not realist. All signs, Ockham maintained, represent individual things, because there are no such things in the world as universals for them to represent. He offers a series of metaphysical arguments against the idea that a universal is a real common nature existing in individuals. If individuals contained universals, then no individual could be created out of nothing, for the universal part of it would be already in existence. On the other hand, if God annihilated an individual, he would destroy simultaneously all other individuals of the same species by wiping out the common nature (*OPh*. 1. 15).

A universal is a singular thing, and is universal only by signification, being a single sign of many things. There are two kinds of universal: natural and conventional. A natural universal is a thought in our mind (*intentio animae*); conventional signs are universal by our voluntary decision, being words coined to express these thoughts and to signify many things. The signs in our mind are put together to make mental propositions in the same way as spoken signs are put together to make a vocal proposition (*OPh*. 1. 12).

Ockham regarded these mental concepts as forming a language system. Besides the spoken, conventional, languages like English and Latin, all human beings share a common, natural language. It is from this universal language that regional languages derive their significance. The mental language contains some, but not all, of the grammatical features studied by the modists. Thus Mental contains nouns and verbs, but not pronouns and particles. The nouns have cases and numbers, and the verbs have voices and tenses, but there are not different declensions of nouns and conjugations of verbs as in Latin grammar. If two Latin expressions, or two expressions in different languages, are synonymous with each other, then, according to Ockham, they will correspond to one, not two, elements of Mental. It follows that in Mental itself there is no such thing as synonymy.

Other logicians in later ages have from time to time endeavoured to construct ideal languages in which there is no ambiguity or redundancy. Modern formal logics can be looked at as such idealizations of certain fragments of natural language: the propositional connectives like 'and', 'or', and 'if', the quantifiers like 'all' and 'some', and various expressions concerned with tense and moods. Ockham deserves credit for being a pioneer in pointing out the idealization that is involved in applying formal logic to natural language, even if we may smile at his readiness to transfer idiomatic features of medieval Latin into the universal language of the mind.

It is one thing when a logician constructs an ideal language for a particular purpose, as an object of comparison to draw attention to features of natural languages that are ambiguous or invite confusion. It is another matter when logicians—medieval or modern—maintain that their ideal language is somehow already present in our use of natural language, and contains the ultimate explanation of the meaningfulness of the way we use words in everyday speech. If this was Ockham's intention, then his invention of Mental was futile, for it serves no such explanatory purpose.

In the first place, there is a problem about the nature of the mental entities corresponding to spoken and written nouns. Ockham himself seems to have worried about this, and to have changed his mind on the topic at least once. Initially he identified the names of mental language with mental images or representations. These were creations of the mind—'fictions' that serve as elements in mental propositions, going proxy for the things they resembled. Fictions could be universal in the sense of having an equal likeness to many different things.

What is the status of these fictions? Ockham, at this stage, maintains that they do not have real existence, but only what he calls 'objective existence', that is to say, existence as an object of thought. There are fictions, after all, not only of things that really exist in the world, but also of things like chimeras and goat-stags which are, in the ordinary modern sense, fictional. When we think a thought, there are two things to be distinguished: our act of thinking, and what we think of, that is to say, the content or object of our thought. It is the latter that is the fiction and that features as a term in a mental proposition.

Later Ockham came to regard this distinction as spurious. There is no need to postulate objects of thought: the only elements needed to support mental language are the thoughts themselves. Unlike a chimera, my-thinking-of-a-chimera is a real entity—a temporary quality of my soul, an item in my psychological history. When mental names occur in mental sentences, it is as elements in the thinking of the sentence. Ockham does not seem to have made up his mind whether they were successive stages in the thinking of the sentence, or a set of simultaneous thoughts, or a single complex thought.

There is good reason for Ockham's hesitation here, because the analogy between speech and thought breaks down when we consider temporal duration. Spoken words take time to utter, and one word comes out after another. The case is the same with mental images of words, as when one recites a poem to oneself in imagination. But thoughts are quite different: the whole content of a judgement must be present at once if a judgement is to be made at all, and there can be no question of the temporal sequence of the elements of a thought.[14]

---

[14] See P. T. Geach, *Mental Acts* (London: Routledge & Kegan Paul, n.d.), 104–5.

However mental names are conceived, in Ockham's view they all refer to, supposit for, individual objects, since in reality there are no such things as universals. These individual objects, however, may include individual thoughts. Ockham's nominalism means that he has to modify the theory of supposition that we have seen in earlier logicians such as Peter of Spain.[15] Ockham redefines the principal forms of supposition: simple supposition and personal supposition.

Simple supposition had been defined as a word standing for what it signifies; and this was taken to imply that in a sentence such as 'Man is mortal' the subject 'man' stood for a universal. But for Ockham, simple supposition occurs when a word stands for a mental entity, as in 'man is a species', in which 'man' stands for a mental term, the only kind of thing that can be a species. This is not a case of a word standing for what it signifies, for the term 'man' signifies nothing other than individual men.

In personal supposition it is indeed true that a term stands for what it signifies. In 'Every man is an animal' the word 'man' stands for what it signifies, because men are the very thing it signifies—not something that is common to them, but the very men themselves. But there can be personal supposition even when a term is not standing for a thing in the world. 'Personal supposition is where a term stands for what it signifies, whether that is an extra-mental reality, or a word, or a concept in the mind, or something written, or whatever is imaginable' (*OPh*. 1. 64).

Personal supposition is basic for Ockham, and it can apply to predicates as well as subjects. A predicate signifies, and supposits for, whatever it is true of. Thus, if Peter and Paul and John are all the men there are, then both in 'Every man is mortal' and in 'Every Apostle is a man' the word 'man' supposits for Peter, Paul, and John. This seems to mean that the first sentence is equivalent to 'Peter and Paul and John are mortal' and the second to 'Every Apostle is either Peter or Paul or John'. A general term, in other words, is equivalent to a list of proper names—a conjunctive list in the first case, and a disjunctive list in the second.

Truth and Inference in Ockham

Ockham uses the notion of supposition to define truth. A proposition like 'Socrates is human' is true if and only if the subject term 'Socrates' and the predicate term stand for the same thing. This is sometimes called a two-name theory of truth: an affirmative categorical proposition is true if it puts together, as subject and predicate, two names of the same thing. But Ockham's theory is a little more complicated than that, at least if we are thinking of names as being proper names. As we have seen, for Ockham a general term is not a proper name, but is equivalent to a list of proper names; and the truth condition he lays down in terms

---

[15] See p. 130 above.

of identity of supposition amounts to the requirement that for an affirmative categorical to be true one and the same proper name must occur in both the subject list and the predicate list.

The simple two-name theory is easily shown to break down. If 'Socrates is a philosopher' is true because Socrates can be called both 'Socrates' and 'philosopher', it is not easy to see how to explain the truth conditions of 'Socrates isn't a dog'. In order to know that 'dog' is not a name of Socrates, we have to know what it *is* a name of: and there does not seem any answer to the question 'Which dog is it that Socrates isn't?' The more complicated theory of Ockham does have an answer to this difficulty: the list corresponding to 'dog' and the (one-item) list corresponding to 'Socrates' do not have a common term. But it falls into a corresponding difficulty of its own. If every general term is an abbreviation for a list of proper names, then every proposition must be either necessarily true or necessarily false. 'Socrates is human' surely is not simply a redundant identity statement. But that is what it is if it means 'Socrates is either Socrates or Plato or Aristotle'.[16]

Ockham devoted great attention to the logical relationships between different propositions: the theory of *consequentiae*, as it came to be called in the fourteenth century. Earlier writers had used the word in the sense of 'conditional proposition'. So understood, an example of a *consequentia* would be

If Socrates is a man, Socrates is an animal,

with 'Socrates is a man' as the antecedent and 'Socrates is an animal' as the consequent.

Consequentiae, so understood, could be true or false, and could be necessary or contingent. Logicians were particularly interested in *consequentiae* that were, like the example above, necessary truths. In such cases one can construct a corresponding argument, namely,

Socrates is a man. Therefore, Socrates is an animal.

Here we have not one but two propositions, the antecedent here being a premiss and the consequent being a conclusion. Arguments are not, like propositions, true or false; they are good or bad, that is to say, valid or invalid, depending on whether the conclusion does or does not follow from the premisses.

Fourteenth-century treatises on *consequentiae* were concerned with sorting out good from bad arguments, rather than with assigning truth-values to the corresponding conditional propositions. Arguments could contain any number of premisses: Aristotelian syllogisms, which contain only two premisses, were just a single class of *consequentiae*. Premisses and conclusions could be of various forms:

---

[16] See Kneale and Kneale, *The Development of Logic*, 268.

they could include singular propositions, and not only quantified propositions such as occurred in syllogisms.

Ockham begins by distinguishing 'simple consequences' from 'consequences as of now'. A simple consequence holds if the antecedent can never be true without the consequent being true, e.g. 'No animal is running, therefore no man is running'. An as-of-now consequence holds if the antecedent cannot now be true without the consequent being true, even if at some other time that might be the case. An example would be 'Every animal is running, therefore Socrates is running', where, once Socrates is dead, the antecedent can be true without the consequent (*OPh.* III. 3. 1)

A second distinction that Ockham makes is between consequences whose validity is internal (*per medium intrinsecum*) and those whose validity is external (*per medium extrinsecum*). A consequence is valid externally if its validity does not depend on the meaning of any of the terms in the premiss and conclusion. In such a case the consequence can be stated in schematic form, using only variables: e.g. 'If only As are Bs, then all Bs are As'. A consequence is valid internally if its validity depends upon the meaning of one of the terms: e.g. the validity of 'Socrates is running, therefore a man is running' depends on the fact that Socrates is a man. There is no general principle 'If X is running, therefore an A is running' (*OPh.* III. 3. 1).

Finally, Ockham distinguishes between material and formal consequences. From the examples he gives it appears that he regards as formal consequences both those that are externally valid and those that are internally valid. In material consequences, on the other hand, the impossibility of the antecedent's being true without the consequent depends not on any connection, external or internal, between the content of the antecedent and the content of the consequent. It arises either from the antecedent's being necessarily false, or from the consequent's being necessarily true. Thus 'If a man is an ass, then God does not exist' and 'If a man is running, then God exists', are both valid material consequences (*OPh.* III. 3. 1).

The first of these is an instance of a general rule, 'Anything whatever follows from what is impossible', and the second is an instance of 'What is necessary follows from anything whatever'. Ockham formulates a set of such rules that apply to inference of very varied kinds. They include the following six:

1. What is false does not follow from what is true.
2. What is true may follow from what is false.
3. Whatever follows from the consequent follows from the antecedent.
4. Whatever entails the antecedent entails the consequent.
5. The contingent does not follow from the necessary.
6. The impossible does not follow from the possible.

Many of Ockham's rules derive from earlier philosophers, but he was the first to set them out systematically, and they were generally accepted by later logicians.

Walter Burley and John Wyclif

In *The Pure Art of Logic* of Walter Burley the theory of consequences is given even more prominence, and Aristotelian syllogistic is treated perfunctorily. A very wide variety of inferences is brought under the rubric of 'hypothetical consequences'. The premisses of such inferences include not only conditional sentences (containing 'if... then') but also conjunctive and disjunctive sentences (with 'and' or 'or') and exclusive and exceptive sentences (e.g. 'Only Peter is running' and 'Everyone is running except Peter'). An important class, studied also by Burley's colleagues among the Oxford Calculators, were sentences of the form 'A begins to φ' and 'A ceases to φ'.

Burley accepts Ockham's distinctions between different types of consequence, and adds further subdivisions of his own. In all this, he is continuing, sympathetically, work begun by Ockham. But when we turn from the theory of consequences to the more old-fashioned topic of the properties of terms, the picture is very different. Burley rejects the nominalism that Ockham had built into his logic, and restates the theory of signification and supposition in a manner closer to its traditional realist form.

First, he rejects Ockham's claim that a noun signifies all the things to which it applies.

This noun 'man' has a primary signification, and its primary signification is not Socrates or Plato. If that were so, someone hearing the word and knowing what it signified would have a determinate and distinct thought of Socrates, which is false. Therefore this noun 'man' does not have anything singular as its primary signification. So its primary signification is something common, and that common thing is the species. Whether this common thing is something outside the soul, or is a concept in the soul, I do not much mind at this point. (*PAL.* 7)

With 'signification' thus defined, Burley can restore the traditional definition of simple supposition: a term stands for what it signifies. The final sentence of the quoted paragraph leaves it open for his definition to coincide in practice with Ockham's definition of simple supposition, namely that in simple supposition a term stood for a concept in the mind.

Burley not only defended, but also extended, the traditional theory of supposition. As Ockham had done before him, he identified well-formed sentences that were not covered by the types of personal supposition listed by Peter of Spain and William Sherwood. One such sentence was 'Every man loves himself': the classification hitherto devised would not bring out the fact that this entails 'Socrates loves Socrates'. Burley said that in such a sentence 'himself' had a special form of personal supposition, half-way between confused and distributive supposition, to which he gave a new and complicated technical name. Another sentence which was ill served by the traditional apparatus is 'A horse has been promised to you'. In order to distinguish between the case where you have been promised a particular horse and the case where any old horse will be a fulfilment of the promise, Walter had again to introduce new modes of supposition to assign to the word 'horse' here.

As a critic of Ockham's nominalism, Burley was soon outpaced by John Wyclif, whose treatise *On Universals* is a sustained defence of realism. The key to understanding universals, Wyclif believed, is a grasp of the nature of predication. The most obvious form of predication is that in which subject and predicate are linguistic items, parts of sentences. This is the most discussed form of predication, and modern writers think there is no other. In fact, Wyclif said, it is modelled on a different kind of predication, real predication, which is 'being shared by or said of many things in common' (*U* 1. 35).

Real predication is not a relation between terms—like the relation between 'Banquo' and 'lives' in 'Banquo lives'—but a relation between realities, namely Banquo, and whatever in the world corresponds to 'lives'. But what is the extramental entity that corresponds to 'lives'? Indeed *is* there anything in the world that corresponds to predicates? Wyclif's answer to the second question is that, if not, then there is no difference between true and false sentences. His answer to the first question is his theory of universals.

His argument for realism is simple. Anyone who believes in objective truth, he maintains, is already committed to belief in real universals. Suppose that one individual A is perceived to resemble another individual B. There must be some respect C in which A resembles B. But seeing that A resembles B in respect of C is the same thing as seeing the C-ness of A and B; and that involves conceiving C-ness, a universal common to A and B. So anyone who can make judgements of likeness automatically knows what a universal is.

Consider, as examples of universals, the species *dog* and the genus *animal*. A realist can define genus simply as what is predicated of many things that are different in species. A nominalist has to entangle himself in some circumlocution such as this: 'A genus is a term that is predicable, or whose counterpart is predicable, of many terms that signify things that are specifically distinct'. He cannot say that it is essential to a term to be actually predicated: perhaps there is no one around to do any verbal predicating. He cannot say that any particular term—any particular sound or image or mark on papers—has to be predicable; most signs do not last long enough for multiple predication. That is why he has to talk of counterparts, other signs that are of the same kind. He cannot say that the term is predicated of terms differing in species: the *word* 'dog' does not differ in species from the *word* 'cat'—they are both English nouns on this page. So the nominalist has to say that the terms signify things that differ specifically. But of course in doing this he gives the game away: he is making specific difference something on the side of the things signified, not something belonging purely to the signs. So the nominalist's gobbledygook does not really help him at all.

Wyclif's argument is clearly directed at a nominalist of a much more radical type than Ockham. The 'names' of Ockham's system were not uttered sounds or marks on paper: they were terms in a mental language. But Wyclif's attack does hit at Ockham's weakest point: namely, the failure to give any explicit account of the relation between the terms of his imagined mental language and actual signs in the real world. Ockham seems to have felt that he explained the features of Latin grammar by postulating a mental counterpart; but the only reason for thinking Mental has any explanatory force is that its operations occur in the ghostly medium of the mind. Wyclif, by forcing the conversation on to flesh and blood sounds and pen and ink marks, was anticipating Wittgenstein's method of philosophizing by turning latent nonsense into patent nonsense.

Three-Valued Logic at Louvain

One final medieval development was the adumbration of a three-valued logic. The possibility of a third value between truth and false is aired in a number of discussions of Aristotle's treatment of the sea-battle. In one case, however, the issue aroused a quarrel that reverberated across Europe.

In 1465 a member of the arts faculty at the young University of Louvain, Peter de Rivo, was asked by his students to discuss the question: after Christ had said to St Peter 'Thou wilt deny me thrice', was it still in Peter's power not to deny Christ? Yes it was, said Peter de Rivo, but that is not compatible with accepting that what Christ said was true at the time he said it. We must instead maintain that such predictions were neither true nor false, but had instead a third truth-value, neutral.

The theology faculty reacted strongly. Scripture, they said, was full of future-tensed propositions abut singular events, namely prophecies. It was no good saying that these were going to come true at a later date: unless they were already true when made, the prophets were liars. Peter responded by saying that anyone who denied the possibility of a third truth-value must fall into the heresy of determinism. He was backed up by the university authorities at Louvain.

The theologians sought advice from friends in Rome. A Franciscan logician, Francesco della Rovere, worked out some of the logical relationships involved in a system of three-valued logic. The contradictory of a true proposition, obviously enough, is a false proposition; but the contradictory of a neutral proposition, he maintained, is not false but is itself neutral. However, those who denied future-tensed articles of the Creed could only be fairly condemned as heretics if they were uttering a falsehood. Hence, the articles they contradicted must be true, not neutral.

Fortified by this advice, the theologians delated to the Vatican the following propositions:

For a proposition about the future to be true, it is not enough that what it says should be the case: it must be unpreventably the case. We must say one of two things: either there is no present and actual truth in the articles of faith about the future, or what they say is something that not even divine power can prevent.

The propositions were condemned by the Pope in 1474.

It was not until the twentieth century that the notion of three-valued logic was seriously explored by logicians. But the episode illustrates how impossible it is, in the history of philosophy, to draw a sharp line between the Middle Ages and the Renaissance. For the logician who intervened in this eminently scholastic debate was none other than the Pope who issued the condemnation of 1474: the paradigmatically Renaissance figure of Sixtus IV, who gave his name to the Sistine Chapel.

4

Knowledge

Augustine on Scepticism, Faith, and Knowledge

During the time prior to his conversion to Christianity, Augustine, under the influence of Cicero, took an interest in the sceptical arguments of the New Academy. The first of the philosophical treatises that he wrote at Cassiciacum was *Contra Academicos*, in which he defended the possibility of attaining knowledge of various kinds. We know logical truths, such as the principle of excluded middle, namely, that either *p* or not *p* (*CA* 3. 10. 23). We also know truths about immediate appearance. The sceptic cannot refute a person who says 'I know this thing seems white, this sound is delightful, this smell is pleasant, this tastes sweet, that feels cold' (*CA* 3. 11. 26). Such claims cannot be erroneous. But don't the senses deceive us, as when a straight oar looks bent in water? There is no deceit here: rather, if the oar in the water looked straight, that would be a case of my eyes deceiving me. But of course an oar's looking bent to me is not at all the same as my making a judgement that it is bent.

There are many propositions, however, that stand somewhere between truths of logic and immediate reports of experience, and throughout his life Augustine returned to the classification and evaluation of such propositions. One of his fullest defences of the possibility of certainty occurs in a late work, *De Trinitate* ('On the Trinity'). Here he is prepared to admit, for the sake of argument, that the senses may be deceived, when the eye sees the oar as bent or navigators see landmarks in apparent motion. But I cannot be in error when I say 'I am alive'—a judgement not of the senses, but of the mind. 'Perhaps you are dreaming.' But even if I am asleep, I am alive. 'Perhaps you are insane.' But even if I am insane I am alive. Moreover, if I know that I am alive, I know that I know that I am alive, and so on ad infinitum. Sceptics may babble against the things that the mind perceives through the senses, but not against those that it perceives independently. 'I know that I am alive' is an instance of the second kind (*DT* 15. 12. 21).

Those who have read Descartes cannot help being reminded here of the Second Meditation; and indeed arguments akin to 'I think, therefore I am' are found in several of Augustine's works. In *The City of God*, for instance, in response to the Academic query 'May you not be in error?', Augustine replies, 'If I am in error, I exist.' What does not exist cannot be in error; therefore if I am in error, I exist (*DCD* IX. 26). Each of us knows not only our own existence, but other facts too about ourselves. 'I want to be happy' is also something I know, and so is 'I do not want to be in error'.

But the mature Augustine accepts the truth of many propositions besides the Cartesian certainties. We should not doubt the truth of what we have perceived through sense; it is through them that we have learnt about the heavens and the earth and their contents. A vast amount of our information is derived from the testimony of others—the existence of the ocean, for instance, and of distant lands; the lives of the heroes of history and even our own birthplace and parentage (*DUC* 12. 26). Throughout his life Augustine gave a place of honour to the truths of mathematics, which he classes as 'inward rules of truth': no one says that seven and three ought to be ten, we just know that they *are* ten (*DLA* 2. 12. 34).

Whence and how do we acquire our knowledge of mathematics, and our knowledge of the true nature of the creatures that surround us? In the *Confessions* Augustine emphasizes that knowledge of the essences of things cannot come from the senses.

My eyes say 'if they are coloured, we told you of them'. My ears say 'if they made a noise, we passed it on'. My nose says 'if they had a smell, they came my way'. My mouth says 'if they have no taste, don't ask me'. Touch says 'if it is not bodily, I had no contact with it, and so I had nothing to say'. The same holds of the numbers of arithmetic: they have no colour or odour, give out no sound, and cannot be tasted or touched. The geometer's line is quite different from a line in an architect's blueprint, even if that is drawn thinner than the threads of a spider's web. Yet I have in my mind ideas of pure numbers and geometrical lines. Where have they come from? (*Conf.* X. 11. 17–19)

Plato, in his *Meno*, had sought to show that our knowledge of geometry must date from a life before conception: what looks like learning geometry is in fact recalling our buried memories of what we have always known. Early in life Augustine was tempted by this explanation (cf. *Ep.* 7. 1. 2), but in his mature writings he cools to the idea that the soul pre-existed the formation of the body. Even if there were such a previous life, he argues in *On the Trinity*, it would not explain the learning of geometry, because we can hardly suppose that every one of us was a geometer in a previous life.

We ought rather to believe that the nature of the intellectual mind was so formed that by means of a unique kind of incorporeal light it sees the intelligible realities to which, in the natural order, it is subordinate—just as the eye of the flesh sees the things that surround it in this corporeal light. (*DT* 12. 15. 24)

What Augustine here calls 'intelligible realities' he elsewhere calls 'incorporeal and eternal reasons'. They are unchangeable, and are therefore superior to the human mind; and yet they are in some way linked to the mind, because otherwise it would not be able to employ them as standards to judge of bodily things (*DT* 12. 2. 2).

We employ them in this way when, for example, we decide that a particular cartwheel is not a perfect circle, or if we apply Pythagoras' theorem when measuring a field. But it is not only arithmetical and geometrical standards that we apply in this way: there are also intellectual canons of beauty. Augustine recalled a particular traceried arch he had seen in Carthage. His judgement that this was aesthetically pleasing was, he tells us, based on a form of eternal truth that he perceived through the eye of the rational mind (*DT* 9. 6. 11).

Augustine's 'intelligible realities' are clearly very close to Plato's Ideas. In rejecting the account of the *Meno*, Augustine is disagreeing not about the existence of eternal standards, but about the nature of human access to them. Following the lead of Neoplatonic thinkers such as Plotinus,[1] he locates the Ideas in the divine mind.

Augustine's Christianization of Plato is most explicit in the treatise *De Ideis*, which is the forty-sixth question in his *Eighty-Three Different Questions*. He offers three Latin words for Ideas: 'formae', 'species', and 'rationes'. The Ideas cannot be thought to exist anywhere but in the mind of the creator. If creation was a work of intelligence, it must have been in accord with eternal reasons. But it is blasphemous to think that God, in creating the world in accordance with Ideas, looked up to anything outside himself. Hence, the unique, eternal, unchanging Ideas have their existence in the unique, eternal, unchanging Mind of God. 'Ideas are archetypal forms, stable and immutable essences of things, not created but eternally and unchangeably existent within the divine intellect' (*83Q* 46. 2).

Augustine on Divine Illumination

Human beings acquire their own ideas not by recollection (as Plato thought) nor by abstraction (as Aristotle thought) but by divine illumination. 'Illuminated by God with intelligible light, the soul sees, by means not of bodily eyes but of the intellect which is its crowning excellence, the reasons whose vision constitutes its ultimate bliss' (*83Q* 46, end).

---

[1] See above, p. 247.

Much has been written about Augustine's theory of illumination. Is illumination necessary for all knowledge, or only for the a priori knowledge of logic and mathematics? If Ideas are the contents of the divine mind, how can a finite mind come in contact with them without seeing God himself? How is the vision of God which on this account is necessary for the basic understanding of geometry to be distinguished from the vision of God which is the final and exclusive prerogative of the blessed in heaven?

In my view, such discussions are unrewarding. Augustine does not have a thought-out theory of illumination, such as some of his medieval followers later developed. He is simply using a metaphor, which even as a metaphor is never worked out in a coherent and systematic manner.

Representing intellectual operation in terms of bodily operations is a natural and universal feature of human languages. In English we speak of *grasping* a concept, or of a proposition as *ringing true* or *smelling fishy*; but of all our bodily senses it is vision with which the action of the intellect is most often compared. When we assent to a proposition without being led to it by argument or persuasion, we may say that we simply *see* it to be true: using the same metaphor, we speak of *intuitive* knowledge. Augustine can speak quite naturally in this way of intellectual vision or of the eye of reason.

Talk of illumination, however, adds an extra feature to this natural metaphor. It implies that when we understand, there is some medium through which we understand, just as light is the medium of our vision when we see colours. It implies that there is a source from which this medium originates, in the way that the sun and lesser luminaries are the source of the light by which we see. And it implies that there are objects of vision that may be concealed by darkness as well as revealed by light.

It is hard to flesh out Augustine's account of illumination in a way that gives a coherent set of counterparts to the items involved in the metaphor. The clearest element, of course, is that God is the source of intellectual illumination, just as the sun is the source of visible light. This divine illumination is supposed to explain how we humans possess ideas corresponding to the Platonic archetypes. But the Ideas are not shady entities that need lighting up: they are supposed to be the most luminous entities there are. If we accept that there are such things as Ideas, why is any medium needed to access them? Why not say—as Descartes was later to say— that God simply creates replicas of them within our minds when he brings our minds into existence?

In evaluating Augustine's account, let us forget what we know, or think we know, of the physics of light; let us simply consider the banal facts of (literal) illumination, facts that were as familiar to him as they are to us. Light helps us to see things when light shines on the object to be seen. Light shining directly in our eyes—above all the light of the sun—does not help but hinders vision. Yet the divine illumination, as represented by Augustine, shines not upon the objects of intellectual vision, but on the eyes of our reason. Intellectual inquiry, as this metaphor represents it, seems as hopeless a venture as driving a car at night with the headlights turned backward to shine through the windscreen.

The language of illumination also throws into confusion the distinction, so important for later Christian philosophers, between faith and reason. It became customary to distinguish between what could be known about God in this life by unaided natural reason, and what could only be believed about him, in response to revelation and supernatural grace. Illumination, in Augustine, is clearly intended to be something distinct from creation, which makes it appear to be supernatural rather than natural. On the other hand, illumination seems to be necessary to enable the mind to grasp not only mysteries like the Trinity but also the most basic truths of everyday experience.

Augustine has much to say about faith (*fides*) but he does not restrict the word to the later, technical, use in which it means belief in a proposition on the basis of the revealed word of God. At one point he offers a definition of faith as 'thinking with assent' (*DPS* 2. 5). This definition became classical, but it seems inadequate in two ways. First of all, we think with assent whenever we call to mind a belief on any topic, whether religious or not. Secondly, as Augustine himself often points out, at any moment there are many things we believe even though we are not thinking about them at all. A thought, that is to say a thinking (*cogitatio*), is a dateable event in our mental life; belief (including the special kind of belief that is faith) is something different, a disposition rather than an episode.

When Augustine talks of faith, he is less concerned to expound its epistemic status than to emphasize its nature as a gratuitous virtue, one of the Pauline triad of faith, hope, and charity, infused in us by God. And when he is most eloquent in expounding its role, his language once again uses the metaphor of light, but in a manner that goes contrary to his explanation of our knowledge of eternal truths. Thus, we read in *The City of God*, 'The human mind, the natural seat of reason and understanding, is enfeebled by the darkening effect of inveterate vice. It is too weak to bear, let alone to embrace and enjoy, the changeless light. To be capable of such bliss it needs daily medication and renovation. It must submit to be cleansed by faith' (*DCD* IX. 2).

Bonaventure on Illumination

The relation of faith to reason occupied a principal place in the epistemology of Augustine's successors in the high Middle Ages. St Bonaventure, like Augustine, preferred Plato's philosophy to that of Aristotle, but he believed that even Plato's greatest successors, Cicero and Plotinus, were grievously in error about the true nature of human happiness. Without faith, no one can learn the mystery of the

Trinity or the supernatural fate that awaits humans after death (I *Sent.* 3. 4). But, for Bonaventure, the philosopher, however gifted, is in a position worse than that of mere ignorance: he is in positive error about the most important things there are to know. 'Philosophical science is the way to other sciences; but he who wishes to stop there, falls into darkness' (*De Donis*, 3. 12).

A Christian philosopher, enlightened by the grace of faith, can make good use of the arguments of philosophers to broaden his understanding of saving truth. This Bonaventure himself does, offering various proofs of the existence of God: defective being implies perfect being, he argues, dependent being implies independent being, mobile being implies immobile being, and so on. These proofs he interprets, in Platonic manner, as being mere stimuli to bring to full consciousness a knowledge of God's existence that is implanted by nature in the human mind (*Itin.*, c. 1). He offers his own version of Anselm's ontological argument to show that nothing more than reflection on what is already in our minds is needed to produce an explicit awareness of God's existence.[2] Reflection on the desire for happiness, which every human being has, will show that it is a desire that cannot be satisfied without possession of the supreme Good, which is God (*De Myst. Trin.* 1. 17, *conclusio*).

For Bonaventure, the inborn notion of God was a special case. He did not believe, in general, that our ideas were innate; he agreed with Aristotle that the mind was initially a tabula rasa, and that even the most general intellectual principles were only acquired subsequent to sense-experience (II *Sent.* 24. 1. 2. 4). The notion of God was, uniquely, innate because the mind itself was an image of God, a mirror in which God's features could be dimly seen (*De Myst. Trin.* 1. 1). Somewhere between the inborn knowledge of God and the acquired knowledge of intellectual principles stands our knowledge of virtue: not an innate idea nor an abstraction from the senses, but a natural capacity to tell right from wrong (I *Sent.* 17. 1).

The knowledge acquired from the changeable and perishable objects of sense-perception is itself subject to doubt and error. If we are to acquire stable certainties, we need assistance from the unchangeable truth which is God. The Ideas in God's mind, the 'eternal reasons', are not, in this life, visible to us; but they exercise an invisible, causal, influence on our thought. This is the divine illumination that enables us to grasp the stable essences that underlie the fleeting phenomena of the world (*Itin.* 2. 9).

Aquinas on Concept-Formation

So, following a long line of predecessors, Bonaventure appeals to the supernatural to explain how the human mind works. His contemporary, Aquinas, rejects this approach. Aquinas does use the metaphor of light to explain the working of the

---

[2] See Ch. 9 below.

intellect: the agent intellect provides light, which turns potentially thinkable individual objects in the world into actually thinkable objects in the mind. But Aquinas insists that the agent intellect is a natural faculty within the individual human being, not—as in the tradition of Avicenna and Averroes—a supernatural entity operating on the mind from outside.[3]

In the *Summa Theologiae* 1a 79. 3–4 Aquinas states with great emphasis that the agent intellect is something in the human soul. To be sure, there is an intellect superior to the human intellect, namely the divine intellect; but for human thought there needs to be a human power derived from that superior intellect. God enlightens every man coming into the world, as St John says, but only as the universal cause who gives the human soul its characteristic powers (4 ad 1).

Aquinas sets out his attitude to theories such as Bonaventure's in question 84 of the First Part, where he asks whether the intellectual soul knows material things 'in their eternal natures' (*in rationibus aeternis*). In the *Sed contra* we are told:

Augustine says: If we both see that what you say is true, and we both see that what I say is true, then where do we see that? Not I in you, nor you in me, but both of us in that unalterable truth that is above our minds (*Conf.* XIII. 25. 35). But the unalterable truth is in the eternal natures. Therefore the intellectual soul knows all things in their eternal natures.

In his usual courteous style, Aquinas in the sequel rejects the doctrine of divine illumination, but phrases his rejection in such a way as not to criticize St Augustine more than is absolutely necessary.[4]

There is no doubt that Aquinas is not an empiricist: that is to say, he denies that sensory experience is sufficient by itself for intellectual thought (*ST* 1a 84. 6c). In addition to sense-experience, there is needed the action of the agent intellect. But if Aquinas is not an empiricist, he is not an illuminist either. The agent intellect by itself is insufficient for the acquisition of intellectual knowledge. 'Beside the intellectual light within us, there is a need for thinkable species taken from outward things, if we are to have knowledge of material things' (*ST* 1a 84. 6c). The human intellect, in this life, is a faculty for the understanding of material objects. Without the senses no object would be given to us; without the agent intellect no object would be thinkable. Thoughts without phantasms are empty; phantasms without species are darkness to the mind.

The agent intellect is not, for Aquinas, something supernatural: it is part of human nature. When he discusses the nature of teaching (*ST* 1a 111. 1), Aquinas says: 'There is within each human being a principle of knowledge, namely the light of the agent intellect, by means of which from the beginning there are known certain universal principles of all sciences.' Aquinas compares the role of the agent

---

[3] See Ch. 7 below.

[4] I am here taking issue with the account in R. Pasnau, *Thomas Aquinas on Human Nature* (Cambridge: Cambridge University Press, 2001), from which I have learnt much.

intellect in teaching to the role of our bodily nature in medicine. The doctor's art imitates nature, which heals a patient by temperature control, by digestion, and by the expulsion of noxious matter. When a pupil is learning, the teacher is assisting him to make use of his intellect's natural light in order to progress to new knowledge. The analogy is telling: the action of the agent intellect is no more supernatural than the action of the digestive system. Both of them, equally, are products of the creator God; but if being a creature of God makes something supernatural, then the whole world is supernatural, and the distinction between nature and supernature loses its point.

But does not God, as creator of the agent intellect, infuse a special insight in a way in which he does not in creating other things? In the *Summa contra Gentiles* 3. 47 Aquinas distinguishes between the likeness of God that is present in every creature and the special likeness in the intellect because of its capacity for the knowledge of truth. There are some truths on which all human beings agree, the first principles of speculative and practical reasoning. It is the presence of these truths in the mind that makes the mind an image of God. These truths are not inborn, nor are they acquired from experience or induction. What is inborn is the faculty for recognizing them when experience presents us with their instances.

The agent intellect is essentially a concept-forming capacity, which operates upon phantasms. It turns the potentially thinkable data of sense-experience into the actually thinkable species. The formation of concepts involves the application of principles such as that of non-contradiction: possession of the concept of X involves the ability to distinguish what is X from what is not X. In that sense the agent intellect can be said to be aware of such principles: but of course, by itself without any sensory input, such an awareness contributes nothing to the knowledge of the essence of material objects which is the intellect's proper task in our present life.

It is the agent intellect itself that is the reflection, the mirroring, of the uncreated light of the divine intellect. When the agent intellect employs its principles in forming concepts out of sense-experience, it needs no further divine illumination, as Thomas emphasizes.

In all awareness of the truth, the human mind needs the divine operation. But in the case of things known naturally it does not need any new light, but only divine movement and direction (*IBT* 1. 1c).

St Thomas did, of course, believe that there was a supervenient, supernatural divine illumination of the human mind: this was the grace that produced faith in those fortunate enough to possess it. But he carefully distinguishes this from the innate, natural light that is the agent intellect. 'Whatever we understand and judge, we understand and judge in the light of the primary truth, in so far as any light of our intellect—whether it be the product of nature or of grace—is an impression of the primary truth' (*ST* 1a 88. 3 ad 1).

Aquinas on Faith, Knowledge, and Science

A sharp distinction between truths knowable by natural light, and those accessible only by the supernatural light of faith, is indeed one of St Thomas' principal contributions to medieval epistemology. Natural reason, he believed, was capable of reaching a limited number of truths about God: that he existed, was omniscient, omnipotent, benevolent, and so on. Doctrines such as the Trinity and the Incarnation were known only by revelation and unprovable by unaided reason. Faith, in the theological sense, is belief in something on the word of God. Faith is different from the kind of belief in the existence of God which a successful philosophical proof would produce. The faithful believer takes God's word for many things, but one cannot take God's word for it that he exists. Belief in God, in this sense, is not part of faith, but is presupposed by it. Thomas calls it a 'preamble' of faith.

Truths about God that are reached by natural reason are the province of natural theology; the mysteries of faith are the subject of revealed theology. But there is an ambiguity in the expression 'unaided reason'. It may mean that in arguing for its conclusions, natural theology rests only on premises derived from experience or reflection, and that it has no need to call in aid any premises derived from sacred texts or special revelation. In another sense it may mean that the natural theologian reaches his conclusions without the aid of divine grace. When we talk about 'unaided reason' in the first sense, we are talking about the premises from which reason reaches its conclusion, and we are talking about logical relationships. On the other hand, when we contrast unaided reason with the aid of grace, we have moved from the realm of reasons to that of causes: we are talking about the causal, not the logical, antecedents of the reasoning process.

Even those truths that are in principle open to reason, such as the existence of God and the immortality of the soul, must, according to Aquinas, in practice be accepted by many people on authority. To establish them by philosophical argument demands more intelligence, leisure, and energy than can be expected from the majority of humankind. In setting out the structure of natural theology, St Thomas makes a distinction between the beliefs of the learned and the beliefs of the simple. The simple believer need not be capable of following proofs such as the Five Ways which, in the philosopher, produce (if successful) knowledge that God exists. The simple believer only *believes* that there is a God. This belief is not faith, for the reason given; it is a belief on human, not divine, authority. But it is perfectly reasonable, provided that arguments for the existence of God are available to the believing community, even if intelligible only to the learned members of it (*ScG* 1. 3–6).

Aquinas' distinction between faith and reason and between natural and revealed theology marked a turning point in medieval epistemology. Epistemology is the philosophical discipline that studies knowledge and belief: what kinds of things we can know, and how we can know them; what kinds of things we should believe, and why we should believe them. Aquinas' work sharpened the distinction between knowledge and belief; more than any of his predecessors he emphasized that a Christian's grasp of the mystery of the Trinity was a matter not of knowledge or understanding, but of faith. Within the realm of belief he made a distinction between faith and opinion on the basis of degrees of certitude: faith, but not opinion, involves a commitment to the truth of the proposition believed parallel to that of knowledge. Corresponding to this difference of certitude, there is a difference in the type of justification: faith depends on supernatural testimony, opinion rests on everyday evidence.

Having distinguished it from faith, Aquinas gives an account of knowledge (*scientia*) that is heavily influenced by the ideal of a deductive science that Aristotle set out in his *Posterior Analytics*. Every truth that is capable of being strictly known, he maintained, is a conclusion that can be reached by syllogistic reasoning from self-evident premisses. There are some propositions that have only to be understood in order to command assent: such are the law of non-contradiction and other similar primary principles. The ability to grasp and exercise these principles is the fundamental endowment of the intellect: it is called *intellectus* in the strictest sense. The human intellect also has the power to deduce conclusions from these self-evident principles by syllogistic processes: this is called the *ratio*, or reasoning faculty. First principles are related to the conclusions of reason as axioms to theorems. The grasp of first principles is called the *habitus principiorum*; the knowledge of theorems deduced from them is the *habitus scientiae* (*ST* 1a 2ae. 57. 2).

St Thomas nowhere gives a list of the self-evident principles that are the premisses of all scientific knowledge, nor does he try, like Spinoza, to exhibit his own philosophical theses as conclusions from self-evident axioms. But he tells us that the findings of any scientific discipline constitute an ordered set of theorems in a deductive system whose axioms are either theorems of a higher science or the self-evident principles themselves. A theorem may be provable in more than one system: that the earth is round, for instance, can be shown both by the astronomer and by the physicist. Sciences differ from each other if they have different formal objects: the astronomer and the geometer, we might say, know about a single material object, the sun, under two different formal descriptions: *qua* heavenly body or *qua* spherical solid. Conclusions derivable from different sciences will be deduced from syllogisms with different middle terms. More than one chain of reasoning may lead from the first principles to a particular theorem; but from any theorem at least one chain must lead back to the axioms. The ideal of science thus set out seemed most obviously realized by Euclid's formalization of geometry.

Such a theory of *scientia* is clearly inadequate as a general epistemology. In the first place, many of the things that we are commonly, and rightly, said to know are not propositions of any deductive system. It may be claimed that this point is simply an issue of translation: the Latin verb 'scire' and the noun 'scientia' are concerned not with knowledge but with science. In fact, Aquinas often uses the verb as equivalent simply to 'know'; but it is true that he has a pair of terms, the verb 'cognoscere' and the noun 'cognitio' which have a much broader and less technical scope. These words are used in a variety of contexts to refer to very different things: sense-perception as well as intellectual understanding; knowledge by description as well as knowledge by acquaintance; acquiring concepts as well as making use of them. Careful attention to context is needed to find the appropriate translation in different contexts. Sadly, some medievalists in recent years have abandoned translation for transliteration, which not only produces ugly English but leads to intellectual confusion. The pseudo-verb 'cognize' looks like an episode verb; and so all kinds of different cognitive states, activities, and acts are made to look as if they referred to a momentary event of which there could be a mental snapshot. But it remains true that if we are to look for a rewarding epistemology in Aquinas we should examine his practice with 'cognitio' rather than his theory of *scientia*.

However, let us look for a moment at Aquinas' theory as an account of science, rather than as a general epistemology. It is important to realize that it is not intended as an account of scientific method: we are not meant to understand that the scientist starts with self-evident principles and proceeds to conclusions about the world by rolling out a priori deductions. The procedure goes in the opposite direction: the scientist starts with a phenomenon—an eclipse of the moon, say—and looks for the cause of it. Finding the cause is the same thing as finding the middle term in a syllogism which will have as its conclusion the occurrence of the eclipse. The task of science is only completed when this syllogism, in turn, is traced back, through other syllogisms, to arrive at first principles. But the first principle thus arrived at forms the conclusion, not the starting point, of the scientific inquiry.[5] The chain of deduction is not the vehicle, but the output, of the venture.

The serious problem with Aquinas' theory is that it leaves quite unclear what is the role of experience and experiment in science. True, 'scientia' is broad enough to include mathematics and metaphysics; but it is clear from Aquinas' examples that his account is meant to cover disciplines such as astronomy and medicine. *Scientia*, he tells us, concerns universal and necessary truths: but how can the fluctuating world we encounter in sense-experience provide any such truths? How can it be that—as Aquinas himself says (*ST* 1a 101. 1)—human beings depend on the senses for the acquisition of *scientia*?

---

[5] Aquinas clearly distinguishes the two procedures in *ST* 1a 79. 8, but rather confusingly he calls the deductive process 'inquiry' and the process of inquiry 'judgement'. But in his commentary on the *Posterior Analytics* he makes clear that that work is concerned with 'judgement'. See Eleonore Stump, *Aquinas* (London: Routledge, 2003), 525, to which I am much indebted.

The role that Aquinas assigns to the senses in the scientific enterprise concerns the acquisition of concepts and the understanding of principles, rather than the establishment of any contingent laws of nature. He describes how the deliverances of the senses are necessary for the abstraction of universal concepts, and he shows how we grasp universal principles by reflecting on particular instances of them. In each case he used the word 'inductio' to describe this process (*CPA* 1. 30, 2. 30). But the word, like so many of Aquinas' Latin technical terms, is a false friend. In *inductio* individual instances provide an illustration of, not an argument for, a proposition which, once clearly understood, is self-evidently true. This is something quite different from induction as understood since the time of Bacon, in which instances provide statistical support for a scientific generalization.

Since early modern times, epistemology has often taken the form of a response to scepticism: what reasons do we have for relying on the evidence of our senses, for accepting the existence of an external world, for believing in the existence of other minds? Aquinas shows very little interest in epistemology as thus understood. He accepts the general reliability of our senses, regards the nature of material objects as the proper object of the human intellect as we know it, and argues about the nature and number, rather than the existence, of human and superhuman minds. In the intellectual climate of his time there was not a clear distinction to be drawn between psychology and epistemology, that is to say between the description and the vindication of the activities of our mental faculties. Aquinas himself did not seek to develop such a distinction, in a manner parallel to the way in which he sharpened the dichotomy between faith and reason. A reader, therefore, who wishes to follow further his discussion of the operation of the senses and the intellect should turn to the chapter on philosophy of mind (Chapter 7).

The Epistemology of Duns Scotus

It is arguable that epistemology, as understood in modern times, makes its first appearance in the writings of Duns Scotus. This may seem a surprising claim. At first sight, Scotus is much further removed than Aquinas is from any concern with scepticism. Whereas Aquinas thought that the proper object of the intellect, in this life, was the nature of material objects, Scotus believed the intellect was powerful enough to include all things in heaven and earth, ranging over the full scale of being, infinite as well as finite. Moreover, while Aquinas believed that material individuals were the subject of sensory rather than intellectual knowledge, Scotus was willing to attribute to the intellect a direct knowledge of individuals in themselves (*Quodl.* 13 p. 32). But while Scotus thus extended the scope of the intellect, he diminished the degree of certainty it could attain.

A particular individual, Scotus argues in his commentary on the *De Anima* (22. 3), is something capable of being grasped by the human intellect, even in the present life when its faculties are dimmed by sin. If it were not, we would never be able to attain knowledge of universals by induction, and we would not be able to have a rational love for a human individual. But our knowledge of individuals is obscure and incomplete. If two individuals did not differ at all in their sensory properties, the intellect would not be able to tell one from the other, even though they would have two different haecceities and thus be two different individuals. This obscurity in our knowledge of individuals must carry with it also a clouding of our knowledge of universals; for 'it is impossible to abstract universals from the singular without previous knowledge of the singular; for in this case the intellect would abstract without knowing from what it was abstracting' (ibid.).

For Scotus, knowledge involves the presence in the mind of a representation of its object. Like Aquinas, he describes knowledge in terms of the presence of a species or idea in the knowing subject. But whereas for Aquinas the species was a concept, that is to say an ability of the intellect in question, for Scotus it is the immediate object of knowledge. For knowledge, he says, 'the real presence of the object in itself is not required, but something is required in which the object is represented. The species is of such a nature that the object to be known is present in it not effectively or really, but by way of being displayed.' (*Ord.* 3. 366).

For Aquinas the object of the intellect was itself really present, because it was a universal, whose only existence was exactly such presence in the mind. But Scotus, because he believes in intellectual knowledge of the individual, conceives of intellectual knowledge on the model of sensory awareness. When I see a white wall, the whiteness of the wall has an effect on my sight and my mind, but it cannot itself be present in my eye or my mind; only some representation of it.

Scotus made a distinction between intuitive and abstractive cognition. 'We should know that there can be two kinds of awareness and intellection in the intellect: one intellection can be in the intellect inasmuch as it abstracts from all existence; the other intellection can be of a thing in so far as it is present in its existence' (*Lect.* 2. 285). The distinction between intuitive and abstractive cognition is not the same as that between sense and intellect—the word 'abstractive' should not mislead us, even though Scotus did believe that intellectual knowledge, in the present life, depends on abstraction. There can be both intellectual and sensory intuitive knowledge; and the imagination, which is a sensory faculty, can have abstractive knowledge (*Quodl.* 13, p. 27). Scotus makes a further distinction between perfect and imperfect intuitive knowledge: perfect intuitive knowledge is of an existing object as present, imperfect intuitive knowledge is of an existing object as future or past.

Abstractive knowledge is knowledge of the essence of an object which leaves in suspense the question whether the object exists or not (*Quodl.* 7, p. 8). Remember that, for Scotus, essences include individual essences; so that abstractive knowledge is not just knowledge of abstract truths. The notion is a difficult one: there cannot, surely, be knowledge that *p* if *p* is not the case. Perhaps we can get round this by insisting that 'knowledge' is not the right translation of 'cognitio'. We are, however, left with a state of mind, the *cognitio* that *p*, which (*a*) shares the psychological status of the knowledge that *p* and (*b*) is compatible with *p*'s not being the case. Moreover, the question arises how we can tell whether, in any particular case, our state of mind is one of intuitive or abstractive cognition. Are the two distinguishable by some infallible inner mark? If so, what is it? If not, how can we ever be sure we really know something?

Intuitive and Abstractive Knowledge in Ockham

These problems with the notion of abstractive knowledge open a road to scepticism, which troubled Scotus himself (*Lect.* 2. 285). Because the distinction between two kinds of knowledge was extremely influential in the years succeeding Scotus' death, the road which it opened was travelled, to ever greater lengths, by his successors. We may begin with William Ockham.

In introducing the notions of intuitive and abstractive knowledge Ockham makes a distinction between apprehension and judgement. We apprehend single terms and propositions of all kinds; but we assent only to complex thoughts. We can think a complex thought without assenting to it, that is to say without judging that it is true. On the other hand, we cannot make a judgement without apprehending the content of the judgement. Knowledge involves both apprehension and judgement; and both apprehension and judgement involve knowledge of the simple terms entering into the complex thought in question (*OTh.* 1. 16–21).

Knowledge of a non-complex may be abstractive or intuitive. If it is abstractive, it abstracts from whether or not the thing exists and whatever contingent properties it may have. Intuitive knowledge is defined as follows by Ockham: 'Intuitive knowledge is knowledge of such a kind as to enable one to know whether a thing exists or not, so that if the thing does exist, the intellect immediately judges that it exists, and has evident awareness of its existence, unless perchance it is impeded because of some imperfection in that knowledge' (*OTh.* 1. 31). Intuitive existence can concern not only the existence but the properties of things. If Socrates is white, my intuitive knowledge of Socrates and of whiteness can give me evident awareness that Socrates is white. Intuitive knowledge is fundamental for any knowledge of contingent truths; no contingent truth can be known by abstractive knowledge (*OTh.* 1. 32).

On first reading, one is inclined to think that by 'intuitive knowledge' Ockham means sensory awareness. It is then natural to take his thesis that contingent truths can be known only by intuitive knowledge to be a forthright statement of empiricism, the doctrine that all knowledge of facts is derived from the senses. But Ockham insists that there is a purely intellectual form of intuitive knowledge. Mere sensation, he says, is incapable of causing a judgement in the intellect (*OTh*. 1. 22). Moreover, there are many contingent truths about our own minds— our thoughts, affections, pleasures, and pains—that are not perceptible by the senses. Nonetheless, we know these truths: it must be by an intellectual intuitive knowledge (*OTh*. 1. 28).

In the natural order of things, intuitive knowledge of objects is caused by the objects themselves. When I look at the sky and see the stars, the stars cause in me both a sensory and an intellectual awareness of their existence. But a star and my awareness of it are two different things, and God could destroy one of them without destroying the other. Whatever God does through secondary causes, he can do directly by his own power. So the awareness normally caused by the stars could be caused by him in the absence of the stars.

However, Ockham says, such knowledge would not be *evident* knowledge. 'God cannot cause in us knowledge of such a kind as to make it appear evidently to us that a thing is present when in fact it is absent, because that involves a contradiction. Evident knowledge implies that matters are in reality as stated by the proposition to which assent is given' (*OTh*. 9. 499). Whereas, for most writers, only what is true can be known, for Ockham, it seems, one can know truly or falsely; but only what is true can be *evidently* known. If God makes me judge that something is present when it is absent, Ockham says, then my knowledge is not intuitive, but abstractive. But that seems to imply that I cannot even tell (short of a divine revelation) which bits of my knowledge are intuitive and which are abstractive.[6]

If intuitive knowledge is our only route to empirical truth, and intuitive knowledge is compatible with falsehood, how can we ever be sure of empirical truths? To be sure, my deception about the existence of the star could only come about by a miracle; and Ockham adds that God could work a further miracle, suspending the normal link between intuitive knowledge and assent, so that I could refrain from the false judgement that there is a star in sight (*OTh*. 9. 499). But that seems little comfort for the revelation that I never have any way of telling whether a piece of intuitive knowledge is evident or not, or even whether a piece of knowledge is intuitive or abstractive.

It is to be remarked that Ockham's position is quite different from that of some later empiricists who have sought to preserve the link between knowledge and truth by saying that the immediate object of intuitive awareness is

---

[6] The relation in Ockham between intuitive knowledge, assent, and truth is a matter of much current controversy. For two contrasting opinions, see Eleonore Stump, 'The Mechanisms of Cognition', and E. Karger, 'Ockham's Misunderstood Theory of Intuitive and Abstractive Cognition', in *CCO*.

not any external object, but something private, such as a sense-datum. Ockham says explicitly that if the sensory vision of a colour were preserved by God in the absence of the colour, the immediate object both of the sensory and of the intellectual vision would be the colour itself, non-existent though it was (*OTh.* 1. 39).

5

Physics

Augustine on Time

In the eleventh book of the *Confessions* there is a celebrated inquiry into the
nature of time. The peg on which the discussion hangs is the question of an
objector: what was God doing before the world began? Augustine toys with, but
rejects, the answer 'Preparing hell for people who look too curiously into deep
matters' (*Conf.* XI. 12. 14). The difficulty is serious: if first God was idle and then
creative, surely that involves a change in the unchangeable one? The answer
Augustine develops is that before heaven and earth were created there was no
such thing as time, and without time there can be no change. It is folly to say
that innumerable ages passed before God created anything; because God is the
creator of ages, so there were no ages before creation. 'You made time itself, so
no time could pass before you made time. But if before heaven and earth there
was no such thing as time, why do people ask what you were doing then? When
there was no time, there was no "then"' (*Conf.* XI. 13. 15). Equally, we cannot
ask why the world was not created sooner, for before the world there was no
sooner. It is misleading to say even of God that he existed at a time earlier than
the world's creation, for there is no succession in God. In him today does not
replace yesterday, nor give way to tomorrow; there is only a single eternal
present.

In treating time as a creature, it may seem as if Augustine is treating time as a
solid entity comparable to the items that make up the universe. But as his
argument develops, it turns out that he regards time as fundamentally unreal.
'What *is* time?' he asks. 'If no one asks me, I know; if I wish to explain to an
inquirer, I know not.' Time is made up of past, present, and future. But the past is

no longer, and the future has not yet come. So the only real time is the present: but a present that is nothing but present is not time, but eternity (*Conf*. XI. 14. 17).

We speak of longer and shorter times: ten days ago is a short time back, and a hundred years is a long time ahead. But neither past nor future are in existence, so how can they be long or short? How can we measure time? Suppose we say of a past period that it was long: do we mean that it was long when it was past, or long when it was present? Only the latter makes sense, but how can anything be long in the present, since the present is instantaneous? A hundred years is a long time: but how can a hundred years be present? During any year of the century, some years will be in the past and some in the future. Perhaps we are in the last year of the century: but even that year is not present, since some months of it are past and some future. The same argument can be used about days and hours: an hour itself is made up of fugitive moments. The only thing that can really be called 'present' is an indivisible atom of time, flying instantly from future into past. But something that is not divisible into past and future has no duration (*Conf*. XI. 15. 20).

No collection of instants can add up to more than an instant. The stages of any period of time never coexist; how then can they be added up to form a whole? Any measurement we make must be made in the present: but how can we measure what has already gone by or has not yet arrived?

Augustine's solution to the perplexities he has raised is to say that time is really only in the mind. His past boyhood exists now, in his memory. Tomorrow's sunrise exists now, in his prediction. The past is not, but we behold it in the present when it is, at the moment, in memory. The future is not; all that there is our present foreseeing. Instead of saying that there are three times, past, present, and future, we should say that there is a present of things past (which is memory), a present of things present (which is sight), and a present of things future (which is anticipation). A length of time is not really a length of time, but a length of memory, or a length of anticipation. Present consciousness is what I measure when I measure periods of time (*Conf*. XI. 27. 36).

This is surely not a satisfactory response to the paradoxes Augustine so eloquently constructed. Consider my present memory of a childhood event. Does my remembering occupy only an instant? In which case it lasts no time and cannot be measured. Does it take time? In which case, some of it must be past and some of it future—and in either case, therefore, unmeasurable. If we waive these points, we can still ask how a current memory can be used to measure a past event. Surely we can have a brief memory of a long, boring event in the past, and on the other hand we can dwell long in memory on some momentary but traumatic past event.

Augustine's own text reveals that he was not happy with his solution. Our memories and anticipations are signs of past and future events; but, he says, that which we remember and anticipate is something different from these signs and is not present (*Conf*. XI. 23. 24). The way to deal with his paradoxes is not to put forward a subjective theory of time, but rather to untangle the knots which went into their knitting. Our concept of time makes use of two different temporal series: one that is constructed by means of the concepts of earlier and later, and another that is constructed by means of the concepts of past and future. Augustine's paradoxes arise through weaving together threads from the two systems, and can only be dissolved by untangling the threads. It took philosophers many centuries to do so, and some indeed believe that the task has not yet been satisfactorily completed.[1]

Augustine's interest in time was directed by his concern to elucidate the Christian doctrine of creation. 'Some people', he wrote, 'agree that the world is created by God, but refuse to admit that it began in time, allowing it a beginning only in the sense that it is being perpetually created' (DCD IX. 4). He has some sympathy with these people: they want to avoid attributing to God any sudden impetuous action, and it is certainly conceivable that something could lack a beginning and yet be causally dependent. He quotes them as saying 'If a foot had been planted from all eternity in dust, the footprint would always be beneath it; but no one would doubt that it was the footprint that was caused by the foot, though there was no temporal priority of one over the other' (DCD X. 31).

Those who say that the world has existed for ever are *almost* right, on Augustine's view. If all they mean is that there was no time when there was no created world, they are correct, for time and creation began together. It is as wrong to think that there was time before the world began as it is to think that there is space beyond where the world ends. So we cannot say that God made the world after so and so many ages had passed. This does not mean that we cannot set a date for creation, but we have to do so by counting backwards from the present, not, impossibly, counting forward from the first moment of eternity. Scripture tells us, in fact, that the world was created less than six thousand years ago (DCD IX. 4, 12. 11).

Philoponus, Critic of Aristotle

There was a well-known series of arguments, deriving from Aristotle, to the effect that the universe cannot have had a beginning. Augustine was aware of some of these arguments, and attempts to counter them, but a definitive attack on Aristotle's reasoning was first made by John Philoponus.

Philoponus' work *Against Aristotle, On the Eternity of the World* survives only in quotations gleaned from the commentaries of his adversary Simplicius, but the fragments are substantial enough to enable his argumentation to be reconstructed

---

[1] See A. N. Prior, 'Changes in Events and Changes in Things', in his *Papers on Time and Tense* (Oxford: Oxford University Press, 1968).

with confidence.[2] The first part of the work is an attack on Aristotle's theory of the quintessence, namely the belief that in addition to the four elements of earth, air, fire, and water with their natural motions upward and downward, there is a fifth element, ether, whose natural motion is circular. The heavenly and sublunar regions of the universe, he argues, are essentially of the same nature, composed of the same elements (books 1–3).

Aristotle had argued that the heavens must be eternal because all things that come into being do so out of a contrary, and the quintessence has no contrary because there is no contrary to a circular motion (*De Caelo* 1. 3. 270^a 12–22). Philoponus pointed out that the complexity of planetary motions could not be explained simply by appealing to a tendency of celestial substance to travel in a circle. More importantly, he denied that everything comes into being from a contrary. Creation is bringing something into being out of nothing; but that does not mean that non-being is the material out of which creatures are constructed, in the way that timber is the material out of which ships are constructed. It simply means that there is no thing out of which it is created. The eternity of the world, Philoponus says, is inconsistent not only with the Christian doctrine of creation, but also with Aristotle's own opinion that nothing could traverse through more than a finite number of temporal periods. For if the world had no beginning, then it must have endured through an infinite number of years, and worse still, through 365 times an infinite number of days (book 5, frag. 132).

In his commentary on Aristotle's *Physics* (641. 13 ff.) Philoponus attacked the dynamics of natural and violent motion. Aristotle encountered a difficulty in explaining the movement of projectiles. If I throw a stone, what makes it move upwards and onwards when it leaves my hand? Its natural motion is downwards, and my hand is no longer in contact with it to impart its violent motion upwards. Aristotle's answer was that the stone was pushed on, at any particular point, by the air immediately behind it; an answer that Philoponus subjected to justified ridicule. Philoponus' own answer was that the continued motion was due to a force within the projectile itself—an immaterial kinetic force impressed upon it by the thrower, to which later physicists gave the technical term 'impetus'. The theory of impetus remained influential until Galileo and Newton proposed the startling principle that *no* moving cause, external or internal, was needed to explain the continued motion of a moving body.

Philoponus applied his theory of impetus throughout the cosmos. The heavenly bodies, for instance, travel in their orbits not because they have souls, but because God gave them the appropriate impetus when he created them. Though the notion of impetus has been superannuated by the discovery of inertia, it was

---

[2] The reconstruction has been carried out by Christian Wildberg, who has translated the reconstructed text as *Philoponus: Against Aristotle on the Eternity of the World* (London: Duckworth, 1987).

itself a great improvement on its Aristotelian predecessor. It enabled Philoponus to dispense with the odd mixture of physics and psychology in Aristotle's astronomy.

Natural Philosophy in the Thirteenth Century

Nonetheless, Aristotle's natural philosophy remained influential for centuries to come. Both in Islamic and in Latin philosophy the study of nature was carried out within the framework of commentaries on Aristotle's works, especially the *Physics*. Individuals such as Robert Grosseteste and Albert the Great extended Aristotelian science with detailed studies of particular scientific topics; but the general conceptual framework remained Aristotelian until the fourteenth century. We may illustrate this by considering the concepts of motion, time, and causation.

Aristotle had defined motion as 'the actuality of what is in potentiality, in so far as it is in potentiality'.[3] Arabic commentators struggled to relate this definition to the system of categories. Avicenna placed motion in the category of *passio*: all changes in nature were due to the action of the heavenly intelligences, who as it were stirred the forms around in the broth of the natural world. Averroes emphasized the variety of types of change covered by Aristotle's term 'motion': there was local motion, which was change in place, growth, which was change in size, and there were qualitative changes of many kinds. Any instance of motion belonged in the same category as its terminus: location, quantity, or quality. So far from being the passive result of the operation of the heavenly intelligences, any change in a natural body, animate or inanimate, was the action of an internal agent (a *motor conjunctus*).

Albert the Great, with support from Aristotelian texts, sought to combine the two Islamic accounts: a motion was simultaneously an action of an agent and a *passio* of a recipient: when a gardener turns the soil, the turning of the soil is at one and the same time an action of the gardener and an event that happens to the soil. He agreed with Averroes that motion was an analogical term, which ranged across several categories; but he thought that Averroes had not fully grasped Aristotle's distinction between perfect and imperfect actualities. A movable body at point A has a potentiality to be at point B. Arrival at B is the perfect actuality of this potentiality; but motion towards B is the imperfect actuality, when the moving body is not yet at B but only on the way to B. Albert maintains that Aristotle's broad definition of motion—the actuality of what is in potentiality in so far as it is in potentiality—can be applied, extending its analogical sense to generation (substantial change) and to creation (bringing into being out of nothing).[4]

---

[3] See above, p. 147.

[4] See J. Weisheipl, 'The Interpretation of Aristotle's *Physics*', in *CHLMP* 526–9.

For Aristotle time and motion are closely linked: time is the measure of motion, and time derives its continuity from the continuity of motion. The question whether motion and time had a beginning was a subject of keen debate among Christian philosophers in the thirteenth century in connection with the provability of God's existence. Following al-Kindi and the *kalam* philosophers, and utilizing arguments from Philoponus, some theologians thought that philosophy could prove that the natural world had a beginning, and therefore there was needed a supernatural agent, God, to bring it into existence. Others thought that the beginning of the world, though taught in Genesis, was not something that could be established by pure philosophical reasoning.

Aquinas, who took the second view, sums up the arguments on both sides in the forty-sixth question of the First Part of the *Summa Theologiae*. In the first article he presents ten arguments that purport to show that the world ('the universe of creatures') has existed for ever; in the second he presents eight arguments to show that it had a beginning. He offers a refutation of each of the arguments on either side, and concludes that while the world did have a beginning, that is not something that can be proved or scientifically known, but is purely an article of faith.

Here is a sample argument to show that the world must have existed for ever: it takes the form of a *reductio ad absurdum*.

Whatever begins to be, was, before it existed, possible to be; otherwise it would have been impossible for it to come into being. So if the world began to be, before it began, it was possible for it to be. But what has the possibility of being is matter, which is in potentiality both to being (through form) and to non-being (through deprivation of form). So, then, if the world began to be, there was matter before the world began. But matter cannot exist without form; but the matter of the world, plus form, is the world. So the world already was before it began to be; which is impossible. (46. 1, obj. 1)

To which Aquinas replies that before the world existed, its possibility was not the passive possibility that constitutes matter. The pre-existent possibility consisted of two elements: the logical possibility of the existence of a world, plus the active power of the omnipotent God.

One of Aquinas' arguments on the other side is one that had already had a long history: 'If the world has always existed, then an infinite number of days has preceded today. But it is not possible to traverse anything infinite. Therefore today could never have been reached; which is obviously false' (46. 2, obj. 6). His answer is brief, but decisive. A traverse has to be from one terminus to another. But whatever earlier day you designate as the *terminus a quo* of the traverse is only a finite number of days ago. The objection assumes that you can designate a pair of termini with an infinite number of days between them.

In addition to answering individual arguments for and against the world's having existed for ever, Aquinas offers general reasons why we can never know, by pure reason, whether it had a beginning. We reason about the world by the use of universal concepts, and universals abstract from times and places, and so they cannot tell us about beginnings and endings. Reasoning about God will not help either: reason may teach us necessary truths about him, but not the inscrutable decrees of his sovereign freedom (46. 2c).

While admirably agnostic about the limits of philosophical cosmogony, Aquinas was unduly credulous about the causal structure of the universe as it actually exists. On the one hand, he accepted the Aristotelian theory that the heavenly bodies were quite different in nature from anything to be found on earth; on the other hand, he believed that the same heavenly bodies were directly causally responsible for the natural activities of all complex entities here below. The four elements, and their physical properties such as heat and cold, he maintained, were quite insufficient to explain the rich variety of natural phenomena on earth. Accordingly, he says, citing Aristotle's *De Generatione*,

we must posit some active principle in motion, which by its presence and absence causes the variations in generation and corruption of bodies on earth. Such a principle is provided by the heavenly bodies. So whatever brings into existence others of its kind on earth operates as the instrument of a heavenly body. Thus it is said in the second book of the *Physics* that man and the sun beget man. (1a 115a 3 ad 2)

In a later article Aquinas spells out how he understands this obscure Aristotelian dictum. Semen, he says, has an active power, derived from the soul of the man producing it. The active power has as its vehicle the froth in the semen, which has a special heat of its own, derived not from the soul of the male, but from the action of the heavenly bodies. Thus, in the earliest stage of the generation of a human being, there is a concurrence of the human power and the heavenly power (1a 118. 1 ad 2).

Despite his belief in the intimate involvement of heavenly bodies in earthly processes, Aquinas does not believe in all the claims made by astrologers. He does not deny that the heavenly bodies may affect human conduct—after all, a hot sun may make me take off my overcoat—but he insists that they do not do so in such a way as to determine human choice and make astrological prediction possible. If the human intellect and will were purely bodily faculties, then the stars would indeed be able to act on them directly; but since these faculties are spiritual, they escape their fatal influence. To those who claim that astrologers are successful in predicting the outcome of wars, Aquinas replies that this is because the majority of humans fail to exercise their free will and yield instead to their bodily passions. Hence astrologers can make statistically reliable predictions, but they cannot foretell the fate of an individual. Astrologers themselves admit, he says, that the wise man can overcome the stars (1a 115. 4).

Actual and Potential Infinity

Most medieval philosophers accepted the position of Aristotle that the notion of an actually infinite number was incoherent. Matter, he maintained, was divisible to infinity: but this meant, not that matter had infinitely many parts, but that however often it had been divided it could always be divided further. The infinite, he maintained, had only a potential existence.

Aristotle himself objected only to a synchronic actual infinite. The universe, he believed, had existed for ever, and that must mean that an infinite number of periods of time had already passed. However, his theorem was applied by medieval philosophers not only to the divisibility of the continuum, but also to the duration of the created universe.

Those who wished to prove that the world had been created in time often argued that belief in an eternal universe entailed belief in an actual infinite. Thus Bonaventure argues as follows:

It is impossible for any addition to be made to what is infinite. This is clear, because whatever is added to becomes greater, but nothing is greater than the infinite. But if the world had no beginning, it has lasted for infinity; therefore, no addition can be made to its duration. But it is clear that this is false; every day a new solar revolution is added to all the past revolutions. Perhaps you will say that it is infinite with respect to the past, but actually finite with respect to the present that now obtains, and it is only with respect to the current, finite, part that one can find something greater. But we can show that with respect to the past a greater can be found. It is an unquestionable truth that if the world is eternal, there have been infinite revolutions of the sun, and moreover that there have been twelve revolutions of the moon for every one of the sun. Hence, the moon has gone round more often than the sun. But the sun has gone round an infinite number of times; therefore it is possible to find something exceeding what is infinite in the very respect in which it is infinite. But this is impossible.[5]

If there were actual infinities, even if not synchronic, they would be countable, in the way that years and months are countable. But if there were countable infinities, there would be unequal infinities, and surely this was a scandal.

Medieval philosophers responded to the scandal in different ways. Some denied that 'equal to' and 'greater than' applied to infinite numbers at all. Others accepted that there could be equal and unequal infinities, but denied that the axiom 'the whole is greater than its part' applied to infinite numbers.

The infinitely divisible continuum, as envisaged by Aristotle, did not raise the problem of unequal infinities, because the parts of the continuum were only potentially distinct from each other, and potential entities were not countable in the same way as actual entities. In the fourteenth century, however, some thinkers

---

[5] II *Sent.* 1. 1. 1. 2; cited by J. Murdoch, 'Infinity and Continuity', in *CHLMP* 570.

began to argue that the continuum was composed of indivisible atoms, which were infinite in number. Notable among these was Henry of Harclay, who was chancellor of Oxford University in 1312.

Aristotle had argued that a continuum could not be composed of points that lacked magnitude. Since a point has no parts, it cannot have a boundary distinct from itself; two points therefore could not touch each other without becoming a single point. But Henry tried to argue that they could touch—they would indeed touch whole to whole, but they could differ from each other in position, and thus add to each other. This theory was difficult to understand, and Bradwardine was able to show that it made nonsense of Euclidean geometry. If you take a square and draw parallel lines from each atom on one side to each atom on the opposite side, these will meet the diagonal in exactly as many atoms as they meet the sides. But this is incompatible with the diagonal's being incommensurable with the sides.

Ockham took a much more radical stance against Henry. As part of his general reductionist programme, he argued that points had no absolute existence. Not even God could make a point exist in independence from all other entities. So far from a line being constructed out of points, as it was for Henry, a point was nothing other than a limit or cut in a line.

A point is not an absolute thing distinct from substance and quality and the other quantities listed by modern writers, because if it was, it would be something other than a line. But this is false. Is it part of a line, or not? Not a part, because, as Aristotle tries to show, a line is not made up out of points. If it is not part of a line—and a line is manifestly not part of a point—then they are two wholly distinct things, neither a part of the other. (*OPh.* 2. 207)

Ockham agrees with Aristotle about the impossibility of an actual infinite, and uses the theorem to show that a point is not an indivisible entity really distinct from anything divisible. If points were such atoms, there would be infinitely many of them actually existing. In any piece of wood you can designate any number of lines, each ending in a point. If the points are real, then there will be infinitely many actually existing entities, which is impossible and contrary to all philosophy (*OPh.* 2. 209–10).

Fourteenth-century logicians and natural philosophers took an interest not only in the spatial continuum, but in the continua of time and motion. One of Richard Kilvington's *sophismata* (no. 13) sets a problem about traversing a distance. When Socrates traverses a distance A, should we say that he traverses it at any time he is in the process of traversing, or only when he has completed the process? There seems a problem either way. If we take the second option, then Socrates is only traversing A when he has ceased to do so; if we take the first option, then Socrates traverses A infinitely many times, since the motion is infinitely divisible; yet he only traverses it once.

Kilvington deals with his puzzle sentence 'Socrates will traverse distance A' by drawing a distinction between two ways of spelling out the verb 'will traverse'.

In one way it is expounded as follows: 'Socrates will traverse distance A'—that is, 'Socrates will be in the process of traversing distance A'. And in this way the sophisma is true. Moreover, the last conclusion—that in this way infinitely often will Socrates traverse distance A—is granted; for infinitely often will Socrates be in the process of traversing distance A. The sophisma can be expounded in another way as follows: 'Socrates will traverse distance A'—that is, 'Distance A will have been traversed by Socrates'. Speaking in this way, before C [the moment of reaching the terminus] Socrates will not traverse distance A. (*Sophismata*, 328[6])

The method of 'expounding' verbs had been popular with logicians since the time of Peter of Spain. Favourite 'exponible' verbs were 'begin' ('incipere') and 'cease' ('desinere'). Kilvington and his colleagues offered to expound such verbs in order to deal with such problems as whether there were first and last moments of motion. The common answer was that there were not: only a last moment before a motion began, and a first moment after motion ceased.

Walter Burley wrote a whole treatise *On the First and Last Instant*, dividing up entities and processes of various kinds, some of which had a first instant and no last instant, others no first instant but a last instant, and so forth. He also extended the notions of continuity and divisibility to changes in quality as well as in quantity. His book *On the Intension and Remission of Forms* discussed the nature and measurement of continuous change in properties such as heat and colour.

Scholastic philosophers discussing the heating of bodies customarily took one of two positions. On one view, when a body grew hotter, it was by the addition of an element of heat. On another view, change in temperature was to be explained as an admixture of heat and cold. Burley introduced a third alternative: he introduced the notion of degrees of heat, on a single scale which he called a 'latitude'. Heat and cold were to be considered not two qualities, but a single quality. At one end of the latitude would be maximum heat, and at the other end maximum cold. He thus introduced our modern concept of temperature and laid the foundation for important developments in physics.

[6] Introd., trans., and comm. Norman Kretzmann and Barbara Ensign Kretzmann (Cambridge: Cambridge University Press, 1990).

6

Metaphysics

In the writings of the late Neoplatonists and of Augustine there is no lack of metaphysical thinking. However, in their work it is so bound up with consideration of the divine nature that it is difficult to disentangle from their natural theology, and in this volume it is considered in the chapter on God. This situation changes dramatically when we come to the philosophy of Avicenna, who was beyond doubt the greatest metaphysician of the first millennium AD.

Aristotle, it will be recalled, gives two definitions of first philosophy: one, that it was the science of divine substance, the other that it was the science that theorizes about being *qua* being. Both definitions, I have argued, coincide. The second describes metaphysics in terms of the field it is to explain, namely whatever there is. The first describes metaphysics in terms of the principle of explanation it offers: reference to the divine unmoved mover. Thus theology and the science of being *qua* being are one and the same first philosophy.[1]

Avicenna on Being, Essence, and Existence

Commentators on Aristotle, however, have commonly taken the two definitions as offering different, competing, accounts of the nature of metaphysics. Avicenna accepts the thesis that metaphysics studies being *qua* being, but rejects the idea that the object of metaphysics is God. The reason he gives is this. No science can demonstrate the existence of its own subject matter. But metaphysics, and only metaphysics, demonstrates the existence of God. So God cannot be the subject matter of metaphysics (*Metaph.* 1. 5–6).

---

[1] See above, p. 181.

Being, the object of metaphysics, is something whose existence does not have to be proved. Metaphysics studies being as such, not particular types of being, such as material objects. It studies items in the Aristotelian categories, which are as it were species of being. It treats of topics such as the one and the many, potentiality and actuality, universal and particular, the possible and the necessary—topics that transcend the boundaries between natural, mathematical, and ethical disciplines. It is called a divine science because it treats of 'things that are separate from matter in their definition and being' (*Metaph.* 1. 13–15).

According to Avicenna, the first ideas that are impressed on the soul are *thing*, *being*, and *necessary*; these cannot be explained by any ideas that are better known, and to attempt to do so involves a vicious circle. Every thing has its own reality which makes it what it is—a triangle has a reality that makes it a triangle, whiteness has a reality that makes it whiteness: this can be called its being, but a more appropriate technical term is its 'quiddity'.[2] This is a better word because 'being' also has the other sense of 'existence'.

The most important division between types of being is that between necessary being and possible being (there is no such thing as impossible being). Possible being is that which, considered in itself, has no necessity to be; necessary being is that which, considered in itself, will be necessary to be. What is necessary of itself has no cause; what is of itself possible has a cause. A being which had a cause would be, considered in abstraction from that cause, no longer necessary; hence it would not be that which is necessary of itself.

Whatever, considered in itself, is possible has a cause both of its being and its not being. When it has being, it has acquired a being distinct from non-being. But when it has ceased to be, it has a non-being distinct from being. It cannot be otherwise than that each of these is acquired either from something other than itself or not from something other than itself. If it is acquired from something other than itself, that other thing is its cause. If it is not acquired from something other than itself, then it must be derived from its own quiddity. If the quiddity is sufficient on its own for the acquisition, then it is not a possible but a necessary being. If the quiddity is not sufficient, but needs external aid, then that external element is the real cause of the being or not being of the possible being. (*Metaph.* 1. 38)

Avicenna makes use of this argument to show the existence of a first cause that is necessary of itself, and goes on to list the attributes of this necessary being: it is uncaused, incomparable, unique, and so on. But it is important to pause here and reflect on the passage just cited.

The passage supposes that there can be a subject, one and the same subject, that first possesses non-being and then, at a later stage, possesses being: an X such that

---

[2] The Arabic term is derived from the interrogative 'What?'; the Latin translators formed a corresponding word, 'quiddity', to indicate that which answers the question 'What (*quid*) is an X?' One could form an English term 'whatness', but 'quiddity' has become sufficiently Anglicized over the centuries.

first X does not exist and then X exists. This is obviously something quite different from an underlying matter that first has one form and then another, as when, in the Aristotelian system, a piece of clay takes different forms or one element is transmuted into another (cf. *Metaph.* 1. 73). But exactly what kind of metaphysical entity we are being offered is unclear. Is the subject that passes from non-being to being (and vice versa) the universe, or a species, or an individual? When we read this passage, does Avicenna want us to have in mind 'Once the universe did not exist' or 'There used to be dinosaurs, but now there aren't' or 'First there wasn't Socrates, but then there was'? Each of these thoughts raises metaphysical problems, but let us concentrate on the last of the three, which is both the clearest and the most problematic.

Surely, before Socrates existed, there was no such subject to have predicates attached to it, or, if you like, there was no Socrates around to be doing the non-existing. It seems difficult to talk about non-existent individuals, because of the impossibility of individuating what does not exist. Well, how do we individuate what *does* exist? Aristotle believed that one individual of a particular species was distinct from another because it was a different parcel of matter. But what does not exist is not a part of the material universe and hence cannot be individuated by matter. But need Avicenna accept that matter is the sole individuating feature?

To answer this, we need to look at what Avicenna tells us about the relationship between universals and particulars. A concept can be universal, he says, in different ways. It can be something that is, in actual fact, truly predicated of many things, such as *human*. It may be something that it is logically possible to predicate of many things, but which in fact is not truly predicated of many things. Here there are two possible cases. The concept *heptagonal house*, he tells us, is not truly predicated of anything, but there is nothing to stop that universal being instantiated many times. The concept *sun*, however, is truly predicated of only one thing, and cannot be truly predicated of more than one thing; but this impossibility, he says, is a matter of physics, not of logic. Individuals are quite different. 'An individual is something that cannot be conceived as being predicated of more than one thing, like the essence of Zayd here, which cannot be conceived as belonging to anything other than himself' (*Metaph.* 5. 196).

Consider the concept *horse*. We can consider this in three ways: we can consider it as it has being in individuals, or in respect of the being it has in the mind, or we can consider it absolutely, in the abstract, without reference to either being.

The definition of *horseness* bypasses the definition of *universal*, and universality is not contained in the definition of horseness. Horseness has a definition which has no need of universality; universality is something extra. Horseness is itself nothing but horseness; in itself it is neither one nor many, in itself it does not exist either in perceptible individuals nor in the soul . . . Horseness is common, in that many things share its definition; but if you take it with particular properties and designated accidents, it is individual. But horseness in itself is nothing but horseness. (*Metaph.* 5. 196)

Avicenna is not saying, in Platonic style, that there exists such a thing as horseness in itself, apart from any individual horse. Horseness is something that occurs in individual horses, Bellerophon or Eclipse, and we can study it by examining it in these individuals. We can consider also the concept as it occurs in the mind: as when we say that the concept *horse* is a concept easily attained. But we can also consider in the abstract what is involved in being a horse, and this is considering horseness in itself (*Metaph.* 5. 207).

Horseness in an individual horse, and humanity in a particular human, will be accompanied by 'particular properties and designated accidents', Avicenna says. For Aristotle, it would be these designated accidents—the ones that mark out a particular parcel of matter—that would be what individuated Socrates. But for Avicenna the humanity in an individual human is itself individuated. Though the humanity of Zayd and the humanity of Amr do not differ from each other, it is quite wrong to think that they are numerically the same: they are not one but two humanities. For Avicenna, there are individual as well as generic essences.

The invention of individual essences holds out the possibility of the individuation of non-existent entities. Just as the coming into existence of steam out of water can be looked on as the addition of the form of steam to the pre-existent matter that was previously water, so the coming into being of Socrates can be looked upon as the addition of existence to an essence that previously lacked it. The pre-existent essence can be regarded as a potentiality whose actuality is existence. Thus essence and existence appear as a third potentiality–actuality pair alongside matter–form and substance–accident. Existence, Avicenna sometimes seems to say, is an accident added to essence.[3]

In the case of a being that is necessary of itself, there is no question of having being after non-being, and so the distinction between essence and existence does not arise. But in all other entities, on Avicenna's view, the two are distinct. Since Avicenna's time some philosophers have agreed that in all cases except that of God there is a real distinction between essence and existence; other philosophers have denied this, but all have treated the issue as important. But the significance of the issue depends on whether, in this context, 'essence' means generic essence or individual essence.

If we take 'essence' in the generic sense, then the distinction between existence and essence corresponds to the distinction between the question 'Are there Xs?' and 'What are Xs?' That there are quarks is not at all the same thing as what quarks are. If this is what the distinction amounts to, then it is undeniable.[4] But if we take the distinction to be one about individual essences, then it seems to entail

---

[3] So at least he was often understood in the Latin Middle Ages; see *CHLMP* 393.

[4] Though if this interpretation is accepted, then the doctrine that in God essence and existence are not distinct amounts to saying that the answer to the question 'What is God?' is 'There is one'. Some theologians appear happy to accept this.

the possibility of individual essences not united to any existence; individual essences of possible, but non-existent individuals. The essence of Adam, say, is there from all eternity; when God creates Adam, he confers actuality on this already present potentiality.

The postulation of individual essences, though it was to be influential down to the present day, was a recipe for philosophical confusion. Let us ask how an individual humanity—say the humanity of Abraham—is itself individuated. It is not individuated *qua* humanity: that is something shared by all humans. It is not individuated by belonging to Abraham: *ex hypothesi*, it could exist, and be the same individual, even if Abraham had never been created but remained a perpetual possibility. It can only be identified, as Avicenna says, by the properties and accidents that accompany it—that is to say, by everything that was true of the actual Abraham—that he migrated from Ur of the Chaldees, obeyed a divine command to sacrifice his son, and so on. Of course, since Abraham's essence was there before Abraham existed, it could not be individuated by the actuality of these things, but only by their possibility.

But, prior to Abraham's conception, there was no one and nothing to be the subject of these possibilities. There was only the abstract possibility that there should be *an* individual who migrated from Ur, sacrificed his son, and so on; it was not the possibility of *this* individual. Similarly, before Noah was conceived, there was not the possibility that *he* would build the Ark, but only the possibility that *someone* would build an Ark. Avicenna rightly insisted against Plato that there was no actualization without individuation—there were no actual universals in existence. It was a pity that he did not accept the converse principle that there can be no individuation without actualization.

Aquinas on Actuality and Potentiality

The ideas of Avicenna were powerful throughout the high Middle Ages. Traces of his thought are often to be found in the work of Thomas Aquinas, whose early metaphysical manifesto *On Being and Essence* begins with a quotation from Avicenna to the effect that being and essence are the first things grasped by the intellect. As his thought matured, Aquinas developed his own version of Aristotelian metaphysics, but he never wholly shook off Avicenna's influence.

The key concepts in Aquinas' metaphysics are those of actuality and potentiality. He derives the notions, obviously, from Aristotle and from Aristotle's commentators; but he applies them in new areas and with new degrees of sophistication. Already in Aristotle the simple pairing of the concepts had been modified by a distinction between first and second actuality: Aquinas developed this distinction into a stratification of levels of potentiality and actuality, in particular making a systematic study of the notion of *habitus*, or disposition. In Aristotle the two principal instances of the potentiality–actuality structure are the relationships of subject to accident and matter to form. Aquinas accepts and elaborates Avicenna's addition of a third instantiation of the dichotomy: essence and being.

Aquinas devoted five questions of the *Summa Theologiae, Prima Secundae*, to the notion of *habitus*. The immediate purpose of this treatise (which, though Aristotelian in spirit, is largely original work) is to introduce the notion of virtue. But the concept of *habitus* has much wider application: indeed it is an essential element in the characterization of peculiarly human behaviour and experience, even though great philosophers have sometimes seemed almost unaware of this fact. Aquinas has the merit of having grasped the importance of the concept and of having been the first great philosopher to attempt a full-scale analysis of it.

Examples of *habitus* include—as well as virtues like temperance and charity—sickness and health, beauty and toughness, knowledge of logic and science, beliefs of any kind, and the possession of concepts. The variety of examples shows that the word 'habit' will not do as a translation; the nearest contemporary philosophical term is 'disposition'. The notion of *disposition* is best approached via the notions of *capacity* and *action*. Human beings have many capacities that animals lack: the capacity to learn languages, for instance, and the capacity for generosity. These capacities are realized in action when particular human beings speak particular languages or perform generous actions. But between capacity and action there is an intermediate state possible. When we say that a man can speak French, we mean neither that he is actually speaking French, nor that his speaking French is a mere logical possibility. When we call a man generous, we mean more than that he has a capacity for generosity in common with the rest of the human race; but we need not mean that he is currently doing something generous. States such as knowing French and being generous are dispositions. A disposition, Aquinas says, is half-way between a capacity and an action, between pure potentiality and full actuality (*ST* 1a 2ae 50. 4).

Not every activity, for Aquinas, is an exercise of a disposition. God's thought and the motion of planets are activities that spring from no dispositions. Natural agents need no dispositions in order to perform their natural activities. By nature fire heats and water wets: these are the natural activities of fire and water and the only activities for which they have capacities. Where capacity and activity are identical as in God, or where capacity can be realized only in a single activity, as with the planets and natural agents, there is no room for a third term between capacity and activity.

Dispositions are qualities: they fall into one of the nine Aristotelian categories of *accident*. Accidents inhere in substances, and that goes also for dispositions. All attributes, Aquinas stresses, are in the last analysis attributes of substances, and all a person's dispositions are dispositions of a human being. What believes, or is generous, or is healthy is, strictly speaking, a man and not his mind or his heart or his body (1a 2ae 50. 2). Still, it is not senseless to ask, say, whether skill in writing history is principally a gift of memory or of imagination. To ask whether something is a disposition of mind or of body is to ask whether it belongs to a human being *qua* intelligent being or *qua* animal of a particular constitution.

Once again, in attaching dispositions to particular faculties as well as to the substance in which as accidents they ultimately inhere, Aquinas is applying a network of stratification to the original Aristotelian dichotomy of actuality and potentiality. The results are sometimes surprising. No human activity, he maintains, issues from a purely bodily disposition. Bodily activities are either subject to voluntary control or they are not. If they are not, then they are natural activities and as such need no disposition to account for them. If they are, then the dispositions that account for them must be located primarily in the soul. Thus, for Aquinas, the ability to run a marathon is a disposition of the soul no less than the ability to read Hebrew (1ae 2ae 50. 1).

In general, Aquinas' treatment of the relation between substance and accident is a natural development of his Aristotelian original. But one highly innovative application of the concepts is Aquinas' account of the Eucharist, the sacrament in which Catholics believed that bread and wine were changed, by the words of the priest at Mass, into Christ's body and blood. The substance of bread, he maintained, gave way to the substance of Christ's body—that was *transubstantiation*—and what remained, visible and tangible on the altar, were the mere accidents of bread and wine. The shape, colour, and so on of the bread remain without a substance to inhere in (*ST* 3a 75–7).

It is hard to decide whether the concept of accidents inherent in no substance is a coherent one. On the one hand, the idea of the Cheshire cat's grin without the cat seems absurd; on the other hand, the blue of the sky is not the blue of anything real and so perhaps is an accident without a substance. But St Thomas' account seems to fail in its purpose of explaining the presence of Christ on the altar: for one of the Aristotelian accidents is location, and so 'is on the altar', like 'is white and round', simply records the presence of an accident inhering in no substance and tells us nothing about the location of Christ. At all events, this particular application of the concepts of substance and accident would certainly have taken Aristotle by surprise.

But if Aristotle would be unlikely to countenance accidental forms existing apart from a substance, he left his followers in some doubt about the possibility of substantial forms existing apart from matter. Aquinas, like Aristotle, frequently objects to Plato's postulation of separated forms; but, unlike Bonaventure, he rejects universal hylomorphism and regards angels as pure forms. Unlike the Ideal Bed or the Idea of Good, angels such as Michael and Gabriel are living, intelligent beings; but so far as metaphysical status goes, there seems little difference between

Plato's Forms and Aquinas' angels. Typical of the ambiguity in Aquinas' position is the following passage from his treatment of creation:

Creation is one way of coming into being. What coming into being amounts to depends on what being is. So those things properly come into being and are created, which properly have being. And those are subsistent objects.... That to which being properly belongs, is that which has being—and that is a subsistent thing with its own being. Forms, and accidents, and the like, are called beings not because they themselves are, but because by them something else is what it is. Thus whiteness is only called a being because by it something *is* white. That is why Aristotle says that an accident not so much *is* but *is of*. So, accidents and forms and the like, which do not subsist, are rather coexistent than existent, and likewise they should be called concreated rather than created. What really gets created are subsistent entities. (*ST* 1a. 45. 4c)

The passage as quoted is admirable as a statement of forthright Aristotelianism against any Platonic reification of forms, whether substantial or accidental. But in that very passage, in a sentence that I deliberately omitted, Aquinas divides the subsistent entities, which alone really have being and are created, into two classes: hylomorphic material substances on the one hand, and separated substances on the other. But separated substances—angelic spirits and the like—are, as understood by Aquinas, forms that are not forms *of* anything, and his way of conceiving them seems open to all the objections an Aristotelian would make against a Platonist. It seems difficult to render Aquinas' teaching coherent on this topic, other than by saying that he is an Aristotelian on earth, but a Platonist in heaven.

The most important way in which Aquinas, for better or worse, amplifies the Aristotelian system of potentiality and actuality is by applying it to the pair of concepts *essence* and *existence*, which he took over from Avicenna. For Aquinas, as for Avicenna, there are not just generic essences, such as *humanity*, but also the individual humanities of Peter and Paul. There are also two different kinds of existence, or two different senses of 'esse', the Latin verb 'to be' when it is used as equivalent to 'exist'. There is, first, generic existence, the existence of a kind of thing: as in 'Angels exist' or 'There are angels'. There is also the individual existence of particular objects as in 'The Great Pyramid still exists, but the Pharos of Alexandria does not'. (In Latin the use of 'est' and 'non est' is quite natural in such contexts; but in English 'Rome is, but Troy is not' has an archaic flavour.) Generic existence is the kind of existence that philosophers, since Kant, have insisted 'is not a predicate'; it is expressed in modern logic by the use of the particular quantifier (for some x, x is an angel). Individual existence, on the other hand, is a perfectly genuine predicate.[5]

With regard to generic existence, Aquinas' teaching is quite clear. A classic text is from *De Ente et Essentia*:

[5] In my book *Aquinas on Being* (Oxford: Oxford University Press, 2002) I have listed twelve different senses of 'esse' in Aquinas.

Whatever [belongs to a thing and] is not part of the concept of an essence or quiddity is something that arrives from outside and is added to the essence; because no essence can be conceived without the elements which are parts of the essence. But every essence or quiddity can be conceived without anything being understood with respect to its existence; for I can understand what a human being is, or what a phoenix is, and yet be ignorant whether they have existence in the nature of things. Hence it is clear that existence is different from essence or quiddity . . . (*DEE* 4. 94–105)

Whether there are things of a certain kind is quite a different issue from what things of that kind are: whether there are any angels is not at all the same question as what 'angel' means. If this is what is meant by saying that essence and existence are really distinct, then the doctrine is undoubtedly correct.

It is not so easy to work out what, for Aquinas, is the relation between individual essences and individual existence. Is there a real distinction between Peter's existence and Peter's essence—or between either of these and Peter himself? Surely not: it seems that Peter, Peter's humanity, and Peter's existence all have exactly the same duration; they all begin, roughly speaking, a few months before Peter's birth and end with Peter's death.

But perhaps one could argue for a real distinction between essence and existence in the following way. While it is true that any creature's existence persists for exactly the same length of time as its essence, there is this difference, that its existence at one time does not have consequences for its existence at a later time in the way that its essence at one time may have consequences for its existence at a later time. A human being tends to go on living for a certain time; a radioactive element tends to go out of existence at a certain rate. These tendencies are part of the relevant essences: it is because of the kind of thing they are that these creatures tend to continue or to cease to exist. Essence, therefore, would be distinct from existence, as a cause—a formal cause, in this case—is distinct from its effect.

Aquinas' teaching on the relation of essence and existence is obscure partly because the word 'esse', in addition to meaning 'existence' in both of its senses, has a variety of meanings in which it corresponds to the word 'being'. Sometimes, for instance, St Thomas tells us that all the things of different kinds in the universe—mice and men, storms and seasons, virtues and vices, times and places—have it in common that they *are*. Being in this sense is a very thin and universal predicate. (Gilbert Ryle once characterized it as 'like breathing, only quieter'.) At other times the verb 'to be' is used to mark a transition from potentiality to actuality. A caterpillar has the capacity to become a butterfly, but as long as it remains a caterpillar it *is* not a butterfly. Only when the magic day comes can we say: now it *is* a butterfly.

These senses of 'be' are important in Aquinas' system only when he uses them in order to clarify his thesis that in God, unlike creatures, there is no distinction between being and essence. God is, he claims, pure Being. Not only the distinction between essence and existence, but also the distinctions between other forms of potentiality and actuality—substance and accident, matter and form—have no place when we want to give an account of God, for he is pure actuality. These doctrines will be analysed in the final chapter of Part Two, on philosophy of religion.

The Metaphysics of Duns Scotus

In the system of Duns Scotus, metaphysics occupies a fundamental place. It is a metaphysics stated in Aristotelian terms, but given a very personal interpretation. Like Aristotle, Scotus defines metaphysics as the science that studies being *qua* being; but whereas in Aristotle, to study something *qua being* was a special way of studying, in Scotus, being *qua* being is a special object for study. Being *qua* being is indeed the broadest possible object of study, including finite and infinite being, actual and possible being.

In Scotus as in Aquinas it is a principal concern of metaphysics to establish the existence and attributes of God, so that natural theology is a branch of the discipline. But for Scotus the scope of natural theology, and therefore of metaphysics, is both broader and narrower than it is for Aquinas. It is broader, because Scotus believed that the terms that signify the fundamental properties of being *qua* being—such as 'good', 'true', 'one', and so on—applied not just analogously, but univocally to God as well as to creatures. But it is narrower, because many truths about God that Aquinas had treated as accessible to natural reason are regarded by Scotus as graspable only by faith. Aquinas had thought that reason could prove that God was omnipotent, immense, omnipresent, and so on. Scotus, on the contrary, thought that reason was impotent to prove that God was omnipotent. A Christian, he argued, knows that among the powers of an omnipotent God is the power to beget a Son; but this is not a power that pure reason can show God to possess. Thus many topics that, for Aquinas, were within the scope of the metaphysician are by Scotus assigned to the dogmatic theologian.

It was commonplace among scholastics to say that 'being' was a transcendental term that applied across the Aristotelian categories, and to say further that every being of every kind had properties like goodness and unity. Scotus' innovation in this respect was the claim that transcendental predicates such as 'being' and 'good' were univocal, not analogical.[6] But there is a different kind of transcendental to which Scotus attached great importance: the transcendental disjunction. He drew up a list of pairs of terms of which one or other must apply to whatever there is: every being must be either actual or potential, finite or infinite, necessary or contingent. 'Necessary' is not a term that applies to every being: but the disjunction 'necessary or contingent' does apply, right across the board (*Ord.* 3. 207).

---

[6] See Ch. 3 above.

Not only did Scotus lay a new emphasis on the necessary–contingent disjunction, he introduced a fundamentally new notion of contingency. It was generally believed by scholastics that many matters of fact were contingent. It is contingent that I am sitting down, because it is possible for me to stand up—a possibility that I can exemplify by standing up at the very next moment. Scotus, like other scholastics, accepted such a possibility: but he went further and claimed that at the very moment when I am sitting down there exists a possibility of my standing up at that same moment. This involves a new, more radical, form of contingency, which has been aptly named 'synchronic contingency' (*Lect.* 17. 496–7).

Of course, Scotus is not claiming that at one and the same moment I can be both sitting down and standing up. But he makes a distinction between 'moments of time' and 'moments of nature'. At a single moment of time there can be more than one moment of nature. At this moment of time I am sitting down: but at this same moment of time there is another moment of nature in which I am standing up. Moments of nature are synchronic possibilities.

Scotus is not talking about mere logical possibility: an instant of nature is a real possibility that is distinct from mere logical coherence. It is something that could be possible while the nature of the physical world remains the same. Synchronic possibilities need not be compatible with each other, as in the case just discussed; they are possible, a modern philosopher might say, in different possible worlds, not in the same possible world.

Scotus' instants of nature are indeed the ancestor of the contemporary philosophical concept of a possible world. His own account of the origin of the world sees God as choosing to actualize one among an infinite number of possible universes. Later philosophers separated the notion of possible worlds from the notion of creation, and began to take the word 'world' in a more abstract way, so that any totality of compossible situations constitutes a possible world. This abstract notion then came to be used as a means of explicating every kind of power and possibility. Credit for the introduction of the notion is often given to Leibniz, but, for better or worse, it belongs to Scotus.

The introduction of the notion of synchronic contingency involves a radical refashioning of the Aristotelian concepts of potentiality and actuality. For Scotus, unlike Aristotle or Aquinas, but like Avicenna, non-existent items can possess a potentiality to exist: a potentiality that Scotus calls *objective* potentiality, to contrast it with the Aristotelian potentiality, which he calls subjective potentiality.

There are two ways in which something can be called a being in potentiality. In one way it is the terminus of a power, that to which the power is directed—and this is called being in potentiality objectively. Thus Antichrist is now said to be in potentiality, and other things can be said to be in potentiality such as a whiteness that is to be brought into existence. In the other way something is said to be in potentiality as the subject of the power, or that in which the power inheres. In that way something is said to be in potentiality subjectively, because it is in potentiality to something but is not yet perfected by it (like a surface that is about to be whitened). (*Lect.* 19. 80)

Non-existent items, Scotus explains, are individuated by their objective potentiality: non-existent A differs from non-existent B because if and when they do exist A and B differ from each other.

Other terms of the Aristotelian metaphysical arsenal are likewise reinterpreted. The relationship between matter and form, for instance, is expounded by Scotus in a novel way. For Aristotle, matter was a fundamental item in the analysis of substantial change. Substantial change is the kind of change exemplified when one element changes into another—e.g. water into steam (air)—or a living being comes into or goes out of existence—e.g. when a dog dies and its corpse decays. When a substance of one kind changes into one or more substances of another kind, there is, for Aristotle, a form that determines the nature of the substance that precedes the change, and a different form or forms determining the nature of the substance(s) subsequent to the change. The element that remains constant throughout the change is matter: matter, as such, is not one kind of substance rather than another, and has, as such, no properties. While form determines what *kind* of thing a substance is, it is matter that determines *which thing* of that kind a substance is. Matter is the principle of individuation, and form, we might say, is the principle of specification.

Scotus rejects both the notion of matter lacking properties and the thesis that matter is the principle of individuation. Matter, according to him, has properties such as quantity, and further, prior to such properties, it has an essence of its own, even if it is virtually impossible for human beings to know what this essence is (*Lect.* 19. 101). Matter, indeed, can exist without any form at all. Matter and form are really distinct, and it is well within the power of God to create and conserve both immaterial form and formless matter, each of them individuated in their own right.

Actual material substances are composed of both matter and form: here Scotus agrees with Aristotle and Aquinas. Socrates, for instance, is a human individual, composed of individual matter and an individual form of humanity. Scotus gives a novel account, however, of the way in which the individual substance and its matter and form are themselves individuated. For Aquinas, the form of humanity is an individual form because it is the human form *of Socrates*, and Socrates is individuated by his matter, which in turn is individuated by being designated, or marked off as a particular parcel of matter (*materia signata*). For Scotus, on the other hand, the form is an individual in its own right, independently of the matter of Socrates and the substance Socrates (*Ord.* 7. 483).

What individuates Socrates is neither his matter nor his form but a third thing, which is sometimes called his haecceitas, or *thisness*. In each thing, Scotus tells us, there is an *entitas individualis*. 'This entity is neither matter nor form nor the composite thing, in so far as any of these is a nature; but it is the ultimate reality of the being which is matter or form or a composite thing' (*Ord.* 7. 393).

According to Aristotelian orthodoxy, forms themselves neither come into existence nor go out of existence: it is substances, not forms, that are the subjects of generation and corruption. Strictly speaking we should not say that the wisdom of Socrates comes into existence: that is only a complicated way of saying that Socrates becomes wise. With regard to the independently individuated substantial forms, in Scotus' system, by contrast, one can raise the question how they come into existence, and whether they come out of nothing. Are they created, or do they evolve from something pre-existing? Scotus rejects both these options. Forms do not evolve from embryonic forms, or *rationes seminales*, as Augustine, followed by Bonaventure, had thought. Postulating such entities does not answer the question of the origin of forms, since the question would simply rearise concerning whatever is the new element that distinguishes a fully fledged form from an embryonic one. On the other hand, we do not want to say that forms are created; but we can avoid saying that if we redefine 'creation' not as bringing something into existence out of nothing, but as bringing something into existence in the absence of any precondition (*Lect.* 19. 174).

Aquinas had maintained that in all material substances, including human beings, there was only a single substantial form. Scotus denied this: and in this denial he had, for once, the majority of medieval scholastics on his side. He agreed with Aquinas that non-living entities had only a single substantial form: a chemical compound did not retain the forms of the elements of which they were composed. But living bodies—plants, animals, and humans—possessed, in addition to the specific forms belonging to their kinds, a common form of corporeality that made them all bodies. He argued for this on the basis that a human body immediately after death is the same body as it was immediately before death, even though it is no longer an ensouled human being. Similar considerations hold with regard to animals and plants.

Though Scotus held that the soul is not the only substantial form of humans, he did not, like some of his predecessors, believe that there were three different souls coexisting in each human being, an intellectual, sensitive, and vegetative soul. If there were any forms in human beings other than the soul and the form of corporeality, they were forms of individual human organs—a possibility that Scotus once considered.[7] But in addition to the matter and the forms in a substance there is another item which is neither matter nor form, the haecceity that makes it the individual it is. For the individuality of the matter and the individuality of the form are between them not sufficient to individuate the composite substance (*Lect.* 17. 500).

---

[7] See R. Cross, *The Physics of Duns Scotus: The Scientific Context of a Theological Vision* (Oxford: Clarendon Press, 1998), 68.

How do all these items—matter, forms, haecceity—fit together in the concrete material substance? It is wrong to think of a material substance as being an aggregate of which all these items are parts; for the parts could, on Scotus' account, all exist separately. Moreover, the whole substance has properties that are different from any of the properties of the parts listed: for instance, the property of being a unified whole. In addition to those parts, Scotus believed, we had to add an extra item: the relationship between them—something which he is prepared to look on as yet another part. But even after we have added this, we have to say that an individual material substance is an independent entity distinct from its matter, forms, and relations (or any pair or triple of these items) (*Oxon.* 3. 2. 2 n. 8).

How are these different entities—the whole and its several parts—distinguished from each other? Scotus maintains that there is a real distinction between the substance and its matter and form and the relationship between them. By saying that these items are really distinct he means that it is at least logically possible for any of them to exist without any of the others. He adds, for good measure, that if we say that the essence or quiddity of a substance equals its matter plus its form, we must say that the essence, no less than the substance itself, is really distinct from its components.

What is the relation, we may ask, between the essence and the haecceity—are these, too, really distinct from each other? In an individual such as Socrates we have, according to Scotus, both a common human nature and an individuating principle. The human nature is a real thing that is common to both Socrates and Plato; if it were not real, Socrates would not be any more like Plato than he is like a line scratched on a blackboard. Equally, the individuating principle must be a real thing, otherwise Socrates and Plato would be identical. The nature and the individuating principle must be united to each other, and neither can exist in reality apart from each other: we cannot encounter in the world a human nature that is not anyone's nature, nor can we meet an individual that is not an individual of some kind or other. Yet we cannot identify the nature with the haecceitas: if the nature of donkey were identical with the thisness of the donkey Brownie, then every donkey would be Brownie.

To solve this enigma, Scotus introduces a new complication. Any created essence, he says, has two features: replicability and individuality. My essence as a human being is replicable: there can be, and are, other human beings, essentially the same as myself. But it is also individual: it is *my* essence, because it includes an individuating haecceity. The distinction (*Ord.* 2. 345–6) between the essence and the haecceity is not a real distinction, but it is not a mere fiction or creation of the mind. It is, Scotus says, a special kind of formal distinction, a *distinctio formalis a parte rei*, a formal distinction 'on the side of reality'. The essence and the haecceity are not really distinct, in the way in which Socrates and Plato are distinct, or in the way in which my two hands are distinct. Nor are they merely distinct in thought, as Socrates and the teacher of Plato are. Prior to any thought about them, they are, he says, formally distinct: they are two distinct formalities in the same thing. It is not clear to me, as it was not to many of Scotus' successors, how the introduction of this terminology clarifies the problem it was meant to solve. One of the problems about understanding exactly how Scotus meant his distinction to be understood is that the illustrations he gives of its meaning, and the contexts in which he applies it, are all themselves drawn from areas of great obscurity: the relationships between the different divine attributes, and the distinction between the vegetative, sensitive, and rational souls in human beings.

Ockham's Reductive Programme

William Ockham was one of the first to reject Scotus' formal distinction on the side of reality. He argued:

Where there is a distinction or non-identity, there must be some contradictories true of the items in question. But it is impossible that contradictories can be true of any items unless they—or the items for which they supposit—are distinct things, or distinct concepts, or distinct *entia rationis*, or a thing and a concept. But if the distinction is from the nature of things, then they are not distinct concepts, nor a pair of a thing plus a concept: therefore they are distinct things. (*OTh.* 2. 14)

But this assumes that the only candidates for being the terms of a distinction are (*a*) things, (*b*) *entia rationis*, (*c*) concepts. This begs the question against Scotus, who accepted a much less restricted ontology. But the move is characteristic of Ockham's reductionist drive.

'Entia non sunt multiplicanda praeter necessitatem'—'Entities are not to be multiplied beyond necessity.' This is the famous 'Ockham's razor', designed to shave off philosophers' superfluous woolliness. The remark is not, in fact, to be found in his surviving writings.[8] He did say similar things such as 'it is futile to do with many what can be done with few' and 'plurality is not to be assumed without necessity', but he was not the first person to make such remarks. However, the slogan does sum up his reductionist attitude towards the technical philosophical developments of his predecessors.

One of the first superfluous entities to be subjected to the razor are Scotus' haecceities, or individuating principles. Scotus had argued that in addition to the human nature of Socrates there must be something to make it *this* nature; because if his human nature were itself *this*, then every human nature would be *this*, that is to say would be the nature of Socrates. Ockham believed neither in the common

---

[8] It seems to have been attributed to him first in a footnote to the Wadding edition of Scotus in 1639.

nature nor in the individuating principle. All that exists in reality are individuals, and they just are individual—they need no extra principle to individuate them. It is not individuality, but universality, that needs explaining—indeed, explaining away.

But Ockham's nominalism is only part of his programme of metaphysical deflation. In addition to universals, Ockham wanted to shave off large classes of individuals. For his medieval predecessors there were individuals in every category—not only individual substances like Socrates and Brownie the donkey, but individual accidents of many kinds, such as Brownie's whereabouts and Socrates' relationship to Plato. Ockham reduced the ten Aristotelian categories to two. Only substances and qualities were real.

Belief in individuals of other kinds, Ockham maintained, was due to a naive assumption that to every word there corresponded an entity in the world (*OTh.* 9. 565). This was what led people to invent 'when-nesses' and 'wherenesses'—they might as well, he says, have invented also 'andnesses' and 'butnesses'. Medieval philosophers did not, in fact, have a great deal invested in some of the later categories of the Aristotelian catalogue. What was serious in Ockham's innovation was the denial of the reality of the categories of quantity and of relation.

Ockham was not denying the distinction between the different categories: what he was denying was that the distinction was more than a conceptual one.

Substance, quality and quantity are distinct categories, even though they do not signify an absolute reality distinct from substance and quality, because they are distinct concepts and words signifying the same things but in a different manner. They are not synonymous names, because 'substance' signifies all the things it signifies in one manner of signifying, namely directly; 'quantity' signifies the same things but in a different manner of signifying, signifying substance directly and its parts obliquely; for it signifies a whole substance and connotes that it has parts distant from other parts. (*OTh.* 9. 436)

Ockham's principal philosophical argument against the reality of quantity is derived from the phenomena of expansion and contraction, rarefaction and condensation. If a piece of metal is heated and expands from being 80 cm long to being 90 cm long, then, on the theory he is attacking, it changes from possessing an accident of 80-cm-longhood to possessing another accident of 90-cm-longhood. Ockham argues that it is difficult to give a convincing account of where the second accident has come from, and what has become of the first accident. Moreover, if the change is a continuous one, so that the metal has expanded through lengths of 81 cm to 82 cm and so on, then there will be an infinite number of fleeting accidents coming into and going out of existence. This, Ockham claims, strains our credulity. The local motion by which one part moves away from another part is quite sufficient to explain such phenomena. Accordingly, real accidents of quantity are quite superfluous, and should be eliminated from philosophical consideration.

One might think that similar considerations might be used to show that qualities, too, were not real accidents. Aristotle had listed four kinds of quality: (*a*) dispositions like virtue and health, (*b*) inborn capacities, (*c*) sensory properties like colour, taste, heat, (*d*) shapes. Ockham was willing to eliminate some of the qualities in the first class, like health and beauty, and he applied his razor very explicitly to qualities in the fourth class.

When a proposition is true of reality, if one thing is sufficient to make it true, it is superfluous to posit two. But propositions like 'this substance is square' 'this substance is round' are true of reality; and a substance disposed in such and such a way is quite sufficient for its truth. If the parts of a substance are laid out along straight lines and are not moved locally and do not grow or shrink, then it is contradictory that it should be first square and then round. So squareness and roundness add nothing to a substance and its parts. (*OTh.* 9. 707)

But he maintained that other qualities, notably colour, were different.

It is impossible for something to pass from one contradictory to another without gaining or losing something real, in cases where this is not accounted for by the passage of time or by change of place. But a man is first non-white, and afterwards white, and this change is not accounted for by change of place or the passage of time. Therefore, the whiteness is really distinct from the man. (*OTh.* 9. 706)

One might think, however, that a gradual change of colour was quite parallel to a gradual change of size: the implausibility of an infinite series of fleeting accidents can be urged in this case too. What makes the difference between the two cases, for Ockham, seems to be simply whether local motion can be called in to explain the change to be explained.

Ockham's arguments on the topic of relations are more powerful than his arguments against real quantity. If a relation were a real entity distinct from the terms of the relation, it would be capable of existing even if the terms were not. Suppose Socrates is the father of Plato, and Plato is the son of Socrates. Then there is a relation of paternity between Socrates and Plato. It is absurd to say either that this relation could exist without Socrates ever having begotten Plato, or that, Socrates having begotten Plato, God could remove from Socrates the relation of paternity (*OTh.* 4. 368).

The relation of likeness is an important one for Ockham, because of its connection with real qualities: everything that has a certain real quality P is like everything else that has that quality. A white wall is like every other white wall. A painter who paints a wall white in Rome makes it like each of the white walls in London. But if the relation of likeness was a real thing, then the painter in Rome would be bringing into existence numerous entities in London. Indeed if God made a thousand worlds and an agent produced whiteness in one of them, he would produce likenesses in each one of them (*OTh.* 1. 291, 9. 614). What is true of likeness is true of position. If I move my finger, its position is changed in relation to everything else in the world. If relations of position are real things, then by moving my finger I create a gigantic number of converse relations throughout the universe.

Ockham is not saying that a relation is identical with its foundation. 'I do not say that a relation is really the same as its foundation; but I say that a relation is not the foundation but only an intention or concept in the soul, signifying several absolute things' (*Ord.* 1. 301). Relative terms signify the absolute things that are the bearers of the relation, but they are connotative terms that signify one term of the relation, connote the other, and connote the way in which the two exist. Thus, when we say that A is next to B, we are not talking about a real entity of 'nextness'; we are signifying A, connoting B, and saying that there is nothing getting in the way between them (*OTh.* 4. 285, 312).

This, Ockham says, is what natural reason teaches: that there are no such entities as relations. But, rather ignominiously, he is prepared to accept the existence of such relations in certain cases because he believes that certain Christian doctrines—the Trinity, the Incarnation, the Eucharist—demand the existence of such relations. This naturally led to the suspicion that he was a proponent of a double truth: that something could be true in theology that was false in philosophy.

Wyclif and Determinism

In the generation after Ockham, as we have seen, there was a reaction against his nominalism and his general reductive programme. In Oxford this took the form of a revival of Augustinianism, which in turn led to a renewed interest in problems of predestination and determinism. John Wyclif was a leader of the realist reaction. After his death Wyclif acquired the reputation of being a thoroughgoing determinist. One of the propositions attributed to him and condemned at the Council of Constance was 'All things happen by absolute necessity'.

In fact, at least in his youth, Wyclif developed a highly subtle and nuanced theory of the relationship between different types of necessity and contingency. He distinguished no less than seven types of necessity, which we may crudely catalogue as: logical necessity, natural necessity, eternal truth, sempiternal truth, inevitable truth, duress, and irresistible impulses. He insisted that there were some events—e.g. human choices—that were exempt from every one of these types of necessity.

In defending this, Wyclif had to deal with the following difficulty that he puts to himself:

Just as no one can prevent the world's having been, so no one can prevent any effect coming to be at the appropriate time. For the following argument is valid: God ordains

A; therefore A will necessarily come to pass at the appropriate time. The antecedent is outside any created power and is accordingly altogether unpreventable. Therefore, so is everything which formally follows from it. (*U* XIV. 322–7)

Wyclif's solution to this is to propose that the relationship between the divine volition and events in the world is a two-way one: if God's volition causes things to happen here below, so, in a sense, events here below cause God's volition.

On this it is to be noted that the volition of God, with respect to the existence of a creature, can be understood as a relationship, a mental entity with its basis in God's willing the thing to be in accordance with its mental being—which is something absolutely necessary—and with its terminus in the existence of the creature in its own kind. And such a relationship depends on each of the terms, since if God is to will that Peter or some other creature should be it is requisite that it should in fact be. And thus the existence of the creature, even though it is temporal, causes in God an eternal mental relationship, which is always in process of being caused, and yet is always completely caused. (*U* XIV. 328–44)

The objection that if God's ordaining is outside our power, then all that follows from his ordaining is outside our power, is answered in a dramatic fashion. Wyclif simply denies the antecedent: God's ordaining is not outside our power.

It cannot be said that Wyclif's solution resolves the problem of the relationship between determinism and freedom. When he distinguished God's decrees into complex relational volitions, one simply wants to restate the objection in terms of the absolute mental volitions that are one element of the complex, an element that seems quite beyond human control. But no other medieval theologian succeeded in giving a satisfactory answer to the antinomy of divine power and earthly contingency, and perhaps no satisfactory answer will ever be possible. But it is clear that it is a great mistake to regard Wyclif as the arch-determinist. Where he departs from his colleagues is not in imputing extra necessity to human actions, but in assigning unusual contingency to divine volitions.

7

Mind and Soul

Philosophers of mind, throughout history, can be grouped into two main classes: introvert and extrovert. Introvert philosophers believe that the way to understand the nature of the human mind is to look within oneself and to pay close attention to the phenomena of introspective consciousness. Extrovert philosophers start from the observable behaviour of human beings and inquire into the criteria by which we ascribe to others mental capacities, states, and activities. In the second millennium we could point to Descartes and Hume as paradigms of the introvert school, and Aquinas and Wittgenstein as illustrating, in different degrees, the extrovert approach. Extroverts look, in the ancient world, to Aristotle as their champion; the introvert school can claim Augustine as its founding father, and to this day one of its most eloquent members.

Augustine on the Inner Life

Augustine often speaks of the 'inward man' and the 'outward man'. This is not to be confused with the distinction between soul and body. Not only the body, but certain aspects of our soul, belong to the outward man, namely, whatever we have in common with dumb animals, such as the senses and the sensory memory. The inward man is our better part: the mind, whose tasks include recollection and imagination, as well as rational judgement and intellectual contemplation (*DT* 12. 1–3).

The outward man perceives bodies with the five senses of sight, hearing, smell, taste, and touch. Augustine takes vision as the paradigm sense. When we see something—a rock, or a flame—there are three things to be taken into consideration: the object seen, the seeing of the object, and a third item that Augustine calls 'intentio animi', namely, our mental focus on the object. This third element, Augustine tells us, is something proper to the mind alone—sight is called a sense of the body only because the eyes are part of the body (*DT* 11. 2). The mental element can remain, as a striving to see, when vision itself is not possible.

Vision is the product both of the object and the sense: the body when seen impresses a form upon the sense, and that is called vision. This is a likeness of the thing seen.

We do not, by the same sense, make any distinction between the form of the body that we see, and the form that comes into existence from it in the sense of the one who sees, because the connection between them is so close that there is no room for distinguishing them. But by our reason we conclude that it would have been utterly impossible for us to perceive anything, unless some likeness of the body that was seen came into existence in our sense. (*DT* 11. 2. 3)

The image is different from the body, even though it does not remain when the body is removed; just as if a ring is placed in liquid, the displacement of the fluid is something different from the shape of the ring, even if it disappears once the ring is removed. After-images testify to the distinction between the shape of the object seen and the impression it makes on the eye; so too does the possibility of producing double vision by pressing on the eyeball. The impressed form 'is so closely united with the species of the thing which we saw that it could not be discerned at all, and this was vision itself' (*DT* 11. 2. 3).

It is a matter of debate among commentators whether this thesis commits Augustine to a representational theory of sense-perception. Most likely it does not, if a 'representational theory' is one according to which the immediate object of perception is an image or sense-datum. The image formed is not, according to Augustine, at all obvious; its existence has to be proved by argument. Probably Augustine postulates it as something that is necessary to explain the causation of memory by sensation (*DT* 11. 9. 16).[1]

The senses are sources of information about objects in the world; but of course they are not the only way in which we acquire such information. A blind man cannot see, but can find out, by asking others, the things that they have learnt by sight. What makes the difference between sense-perception and information-gathering? In answer to this question, Aristotle long ago invoked the concept of pleasure: 'Where there is sense-perception there is also both pain and pleasure, and where they occur there is also of necessity desire' (*De An.* 2. 413^{b}23). The information acquired through the senses, and the discriminations performed with their aid, may be acquired and performed by means other than the senses, and indeed by agents other than human beings. We can obtain through optical instruments visual information to classify different human beings, and catalogue

---

[1] See Gareth Matthew, 'Knowledge and Illumination', in *CCA* 176. For an opposite view, see Paul Spade in *IHWP* 63–4.

visual features of lunar landscapes through distant probes. Such operations are not sense-perception because they occur without pleasure or pain: the human beings inventoried with their statistics are not perceived as beautiful or ugly, the landscapes strike neither terror nor awe.

Augustine shows himself well aware of this dual aspect of our concept of sense, and indeed emphasizes the hedonic rather than the epistemic component of sense-perception. In *On Free Will* he remarks that 'pleasure and pain fall within the jurisdiction of the bodily senses'. Sight judges whether colours are harmonious or clash with each other, and hearing judges whether voices are melodious or harsh (*DLA* 2. 5. 12. 49). In book X of the *Confessions* he gives a colourful listing of the different types of sensual pleasure that may offer us temptation. We must distinguish, he says, between two different employments of the senses: to bring pleasure and to satisfy curiosity. The second element too, of course, can bring temptation: we can sin through the lust for experience and knowledge (*Conf.* X. 35. 54).

Among the objects of the outer senses, Augustine makes the usual distinction between those that can be perceived by one sense only (e.g. colour and sound) and those that can be perceived by more than one sense (e.g. size and shape). Besides the five outward senses, Augustine believes that there is an inner sense. In the case of animals, he says, the sense of sight is a different thing from the sense to shun or to seek what is seen, and so with the other senses, whose objects are sometimes accepted with pleasure and sometimes shunned with disgust. This sense cannot be identified with any one of the five senses, but must be some other sense that presides over all the other senses. While it is only by reasoning that we identify this separate faculty, it is not itself a part of reason, because it is possessed not only by rational humans but also by irrational beasts (*DLA* 2. 2. 8).

In his description of our mental faculties, Augustine dwells longest on the memory, and indeed he often uses 'memory' in a very broad sense, almost equivalent to 'mind' itself. He describes some of memory's powers in *Confessions* X. 13. Even in darkness and silence I can produce colours at will in my memory, and distinguish between white and black. With tongue motionless and throat silent, I can sing whatever song I wish.

Memory is something we take for granted: Augustine urges us to remind ourselves what a very remarkable faculty it is. People gaze with wonder on mountain peaks, towering waves, and broad waterfalls, on the encompassing ocean and the rotating starry skies. But they take no notice of themselves and of their memory, which contains sky, sea, and land and much else besides. I could not speak, Augustine says, of any of the wonders of nature unless I could see inwardly the mountains and waves and rivers and stars—and even the ocean that I have never seen but know about only from the tales of others. 'I see them inwardly with dimensions just as great as if I saw them in the outer world' (*Conf.* X. 8. 15).

Augustine describes memory as a huge cavern, full of dark and mysterious nooks and crannies: true to the introvert tradition he imagines the inward man exploring this vast storehouse. Within it, I can call for an item that I want to recall; fetching it may take a shorter or longer time.

Some memories rush out to crowd the mind, and while I am looking and asking for something quite different, they leap out in front of me saying 'Are we what you want?' With the hand of my heart I chase them away from the face of my memory until what I want is freed from the murk and comes out of its hiding place. (*Conf.* X. 8. 12)

Augustine has a gift for vivid phenomenological description of experiences of calling to mind and forgetting—remembering the face but not the name, being unable to recall a letter read absent-mindedly, being obsessed with an unwelcome memory one would prefer to forget (*DT* 11. 5. 9). When he comes to give a philosophical analysis of memory, it is modelled very closely on his account of outer vision. Just as when we see there is the object seen, the seeing itself, and the mental focus, so, when we remember, there is the memory recalled, the actual recalling, and the gaze of thought. The difference between a merely dispositional memory (something that we have learnt and not forgotten) and an episode of remembering is treated by Augustine as parallel to that between an object out of sight and object in full view (*DT* 11. 8). Remembering is treated very literally as inward seeing, and in the case of both inner and outer vision Augustine lays great stress on the voluntary nature of the activity. In talking of mental focus, and the gaze of thought, Augustine is thinking of the operation of the will (*DT* 11. 2. 3).

The will can choose whether to concentrate on the outer or inner eye. If it makes the latter choice, it can produce likenesses of bodies so vivid 'that not even reason itself can distinguish whether a body itself is seen without, or something similar thought within'. Terrifying imaginations can make one cry out, and sexual fantasies can cause erections. But not all such experiences are under voluntary control: in sleep and in frenzy images can force themselves upon the mental gaze by some secret force 'through certain spiritual mixings of a spiritual substance' (*DT* 11. 4. 7).

I can remember only what I have seen; but I can think of many more things. Thus I can remember only one sun, but I can think of two or three suns. I can think of the sun as larger or smaller than it is; I can think of it standing still or travelling to anywhere I will. I can think of it as square and green. Augustine clearly regards thoughts of this kind as inner seeings: he insists that what we actually see with our inner eye is derived from our memory of the one and only sun. But what of when we listen to another person's narrative? We cannot then turn our mind's eye back to memory. What happens is that we follow the story by calling up the ideas corresponding to the words of his story. But this too depends on memory.

I would never have been able to understand a storyteller the first time I had heard his words put together, unless I had remembered generically the individual things that he described. A man who describes to me a mountain rising out of a forest and clothed with olive trees is speaking to one who remembers mountains, forests, and olives. If I had forgotten them, I should not at all know what he was saying, and so could never have followed his narrative. (*DT* 11. 8. 14)

What is true of listening to another's narrative is true of inventing a story for oneself. I can combine remembered images with others and say 'O that this or that were so'. Whatever we imagine is constructed out of elements supplied by memory: thus Augustine models his idea of the walls of Alexandria, which he has never seen, on his memory of the walls of Carthage, which are familiar to him. No doubt anyone who really knew Alexandria, if they could look into Augustine's mind and see his image of it, would find it highly inadequate (*DT* 8. 6. 9). Anticipating later empiricist philosophers, Augustine says that it is impossible to have any idea of a colour one has never seen, a sound one has never heard, or a flavour one has never tasted.

The loftiest part of the mind, the reason or intellectual soul, has, for Augustine, two elements. The superior part of reason is concerned with the eternal truths, accessible to intellect alone. The inferior part controls our dealings with temporal and bodily things. It is, Augustine says, a deputy of the superior reason: a minister for contingent affairs, as it were. Both inferior and superior reason belong to the inward man (*DT* 13. 1). When God created Adam, he found among the beasts no fit companion for him; so too, in the human soul, those parts that we have in common with dumb animals are not enough to make the intellect at home in the world we live in. So God has endowed us with a faculty of practical reason, formed out of rational substance just as Eve was formed from Adam's body, intimately united with the superior reason just as Adam and Eve were two in one flesh (*DT* 12. 3).

The operation of the lower reason is called by Augustine 'scientia', which he defines as 'the cognition of temporal and changeable things that is necessary for managing the affairs of this life' (*DT* 12. 12. 17). The functions of this reason are very close to those assigned by Aristotle to *phronesis*, or practical wisdom, and the translation 'science' would give a very misleading impression of what is meant. Science, as we understand it, hardly figures in Augustine's catalogue of mental activities, and from time to time he makes disparaging remarks about the pursuit of knowledge for its own sake. *Scientia*, like *phronesis*, is indispensable if we are to possess moral virtues (*DT* 14. 22).

The superior reason's function is called 'sapientia'. Once again, the obvious translation, 'wisdom', would be misleading, since the English word is more appropriate to the virtue of practical reason than to the virtue of theoretical reason. *Sapientia*, we are told, is contemplation: the contemplation of eternal truths in this life and the contemplation of God in the life of the blessed (*DT* 12. 14).

Contemplation is not for the sake of action, but is pursued for its own sake. Augustine goes out of his way to tell us that the part of the human mind that is concerned with the consideration of eternal reasons is something 'which, as is evident, not only men but also women possess' (*DT* 12. 7. 12).

Augustine on the Will

Augustine devoted much of *On the Trinity* to seeking, in human beings, replicas of the divine trinity of Father, Son, and Holy Spirit. He identified many different triads, but the supreme image of God is in the trinity of memory, intellect, and will (9. 12, 15. 3). How is this to be related to the anatomy of the mind we have just summarized? When he is most concerned to draw the theological parallel, Augustine presents his human trinity as consisting of the mind's existence, its knowledge of itself, and its love of itself (9. 12). But he uses the terms of his mental trinity in a broad variety of contexts, which we can summarize as follows. The memory is the ability to think thoughts of all kinds; the intellect (whose activity is *sapientia*) is the ability to assent to theoretical thoughts as true; the will is the ability to consent to thoughts as plans of action.

Augustine makes great play with the notion of the will, and some commentators have alleged that in doing so he was inventing a concept that was lacking in the ancient world. The allegation can only be made by a philosopher starting from an introspective stance on philosophy of mind. Philosophical discussion of the will may start by considering it as an introspectible phenomenon, an item of consciousness that makes the difference between voluntary and involuntary actions. Or it may start with the observable behaviour of agents and ask for external criteria by which we distinguish between the voluntary and involuntary actions of others. In the ancient world Augustine is the outstanding exponent of the introspective approach; Aristotle, on the other hand, had adopted an extrovert stance, which has led introvert philosophers to deny that he had any concept of the will at all.[2]

In fact, there are considerable similarities between the two philosophers. For Augustine as for Aristotle, all fully human choice originates in the pursuit of happiness, and for both of them individual decisions are to be seen as the selection of means to that end. Suppose, Augustine says, I want to see a scar as evidence of a wound, or look through a window in order to see the passers-by. 'All these and other such acts of the will have their own proper ends, which are referred to the end of that will, by which we wish to live happily and arrive at that life which is not referred to anything else, but is sufficient in itself for the

---

[2] See A. Kenny, *Aristotle's Theory of the Will* (London: Duckworth, 1979).

lover.' This is quite parallel to Aristotle's account of practical reasoning (*NE* 1112[b] 18 ff.; *EE* 1. 1218[b]8–24).

Both Aristotle and Augustine imagine the will, or practical reason, as an issuer of commands, and both of them are keenly interested in the possibility of disobedience to these commands, in the sinner (Augustine) or in the incontinent person (Aristotle, *NE* 1147[a]32). But Augustine exploits the analogy much more fully. He regards every voluntary motion of the body as an obedience to a command of the will; and he is fascinated by the possibility of second-order volition, where the will is issuing commands to itself.

The mind (*animus*) commands the body, and obedience is instant; the mind commands itself and meets resistance. The mind tells the hand to move, and all goes so smoothly that it is hard to distinguish the command from its execution. Yet the mind is the mind, and the hand is a body. The mind tells the mind to will; one is the same as the other, and yet it does not do what it is told. (*Conf.* VIII. 9. 21)

What is really happening in such a case, when, for instance, a man wants to will to be chaste and yet does not really will to be chaste? How can the will command itself and yet not obey? The command to will, Augustine says, is half-hearted: if it were wholehearted, the will to be chaste would already be there. In his own case, he says, while he was hesitating about the service of God 'I who was willing to serve was the same I who was unwilling; I was neither wholly willing nor wholly unwilling'. Such self-conflict, such inner dissociation, is possible only because we are the descendants of Adam, inheriting his sin.

It is the consideration of Adam that leads Augustine to differ significantly from Aristotle on an important point. Aristotle accepted that a man may act against the dictates of the rational will, but he envisaged this as happening through the stress of animal passion. But Adam fell into sin in Eden, at a time when he had no disordered passions; again, Lucifer and his angels fell into sin, though they had no animal bodies. So Augustine is led to postulate uncaused acts of evil will. 'If you look for an efficient cause of such an evil volition, you will find nothing. What is it that makes a will evil, when it is doing an evil deed? The evil will is the efficient cause of the evil deed, but of an evil will there is no efficient cause' (*DCD* XII. 6). However one tries to trace back the cause of an evil action, sooner or later one will arrive at a sheer act of evil will. Suppose that we imagine two people alike in mind and body, each hitherto innocent, and each subjected to the same temptation. One gives in, the other does not. What is the cause of the sinner's sin? We cannot say it is the sinner himself: *ex hypothesi* both people were equally good up to this point. We have to say that it is a causeless evil choice (*DCD* XII. 6). Thus Augustine expounds what was later to be called 'contra-causal freedom'—which, paradoxically, he combines with a strong version of determinism, as we shall see in a later chapter when we consider his theory of predestination.

The Agent Intellect in Islamic Thought

During the latter part of the first millennium the most interesting developments in philosophy of mind concerned not the will but the intellect, and took place not in Christendom but in the Muslim schools of Baghdad. Al-Kindi and al-Farabi both devoted themselves to the elucidation of the puzzling passage in Aristotle's *De Anima* which tells us that there are two different intellects: an agent intellect 'for making things' and a receptive intellect 'for becoming things'.

Al-Farabi, following al-Kindi, explained this in terms of his own version of Aristotelian astronomy. Each of the nine celestial spheres, he believed, had a rational soul; it was moved by its own incorporeal mover, which acted upon it as an object of desire. These incorporeal movers, or intelligences, emanated one from another, in a series originating ultimately from the Prime Mover, or God. From the ninth intelligence (which governs the moon) there emanates a tenth intelligence; and this is nothing other than the agent intellect, the one that Aristotle says is what it is by virtue of making all things.

The agent intellect, according to al-Farabi, is needed in order to explain how the human intellect passes from potentiality to actuality. In his account of human psychology we find in fact three intellects, or three stages of intellect. First there is the receptive or potential intellect, the inborn capacity for thought. Under the influence of the external agent intellect, this disposition is exercised in actual thinking, and the human intellect thus becomes an intellect in actuality ('the actual passive intellect'). Finally, Al-Farabi tells us, a human being 'perfects his receptive intellect with all intelligible thoughts'. The intellect thus perfected is called the acquired intellect.[3]

Can we separate al-Farabi's psychology from its antiquated astronomical context? We may begin to make sense of it if we ask why anyone should think that an agent intellect was required at all. The Aristotelian answer would be that the material objects of the world we live in are not, in themselves, fit objects for intellectual understanding. The nature and characteristics of the objects we see and feel are all embedded in matter: they are transitory and not stable, individual and not universal. They are, in Aristotelian terms, only potentially thinkable or intelligible, not actually so. To make them actually thinkable, it is required that abstraction be made from the corruptible and individuating matter, and concepts be created that are actually thinkable objects. That is the function of the agent intellect.

Al-Farabi compares the action of the agent intellect upon the data of sensory experience to the action of the sun on colours. Colours, which are only potentially visible in the dark, are made actually visible by the sunlight. Similarly, sense-data that are stored in our imagination are turned by the active intellect into actually

---

[3] See H. A. Davidson, *Alfarabi, Avicenna and Averroes on Intellect* (Oxford: Oxford University Press, 1992), ch. 3.

intelligible thoughts. The agent intellect structures them within a framework of universal principles, common to all humans. (Al-Farabi gives as an instance 'two things equal to a third are equal to one another'.) Thus far al-Farabi's account seems philosophically plausible. The difficult point—and one that was to be debated for centuries—is whether the agent intellect is to be identified with some separate, superhuman entity, or whether it should simply be regarded as a species-specific faculty that differentiates humans from non-language-using animals.

Al-Farabi's Muslim successors emphasized, to an ever greater degree, the super-human element in intellectual thought. For Avicenna, as for al-Farabi, the First Cause is at the summit of a series of ten incorporeal intelligences, each giving rise to the next in the series by a process of emanation, of which the tenth is the agent intellect. The agent intellect, however, has for Avicenna a much more elaborate function than it has for al-Farabi: it is a veritable demigod. First it produces by emanation the matter of the sublunar world, a task that al-Farabi had assigned to the celestial spheres; that is to say, it is responsible for the existence of the four elements. Next, the agent intellect produces the more complex forms in this world, including the souls of plants, animals, and humans. Indeed the 'giver of forms' is one of Avicenna's favourite titles for the agent intellect. Once again, we encounter emanation: forms that are undifferentiated within the agent intellect are transmitted, by necessity, into the world of matter. Only at a third stage does the agent intellect exercise the function that it had in al-Farabi, of being the cause that brings the human intellect from potentiality into actuality.[4]

Avicenna on Intellect and Imagination

According to Avicenna, when a piece of matter has developed to a state in which it is apt to receive a human soul, the agent intellect, the giver of forms, infuses such a soul into it. The soul, however, is something more than the form of the human body. To show this Avicenna uses an original argument, which was later to be reinvented by Descartes.

Let someone imagine himself as wholly created in a single moment, with his sight veiled so that he cannot see any external object. Imagine also that he is created falling through the air, or in a vacuum, so that he would not feel any pressure from the air. Suppose too that his limbs are parted from each other so that they neither meet nor touch. Let him reflect whether, in such a case, he will affirm his own existence. He will not hesitate to affirm that he himself exists, but in so doing he will not be affirming the existence of any limb, or external or internal organ such as heart or brain, or any external object. He will be affirming the existence of himself without ascribing to it any length, breadth, or depth.

---

[4] See Davidson, *Alfarabi, Avicenna, and Averroes on Intellect*, 74–83.

If in this state he were able to imagine a hand or some other bodily part, he would not imagine it being a part of himself or a condition for his own existence. (*CCMP* 110)

Avicenna argues that since intellectual thoughts do not have parts, they must belong to something that is indivisible and incorporeal. Hence he concludes that the soul is an incorporeal substance that cannot be regarded simply as a form or faculty of the body.

Avicenna distinguishes four different possible conditions of the human intellect. When a human baby is born, it has an intellect that is empty of thoughts, the soul's mere capacity for thought. In the second state, the intellect has been furnished with the basic intellectual equipment: it understands the principle of contradiction, and general principles such as that the whole is greater than the part. Avicenna compares this to a boy who has learnt how to use pen and ink and can write individual letters. In the third state, the person has accumulated a stock of concepts and beliefs, but does not actually have them present in thought. This is like an accomplished scribe, who is capable of writing any text at will. All these three states are potentialities, but each of them nearer to actuality than the previous one: the third state is called by Avicenna 'perfect potentiality'. The fourth state is when the thinker is actually thinking a particular thought (one at a time)—this is like the scribe actually writing down a sentence.

In each of these transitions from potentiality towards actuality there is, for Avicenna, a direct causal influence exercised on the human intellect by the superhuman agent intellect. Experience, he argues, cannot be the source either of the first principles or the universal scientific conclusions reached by the intellect. Experience can provide only inductive generalizations such as 'All animals move their lower jaw to chew', and such generalizations are always falsifiable (as that one is falsified by the crocodile). So first principle and universal laws must be infused in us from outside the natural world.

It is hard to conceive exactly how this causality operates; it appears to be something like involuntary telepathy. Perhaps, to use a metaphor unavailable to Avicenna, the agent intellect is like a radio station perpetually broadcasting, on different wavelengths, all the thoughts that there are. The human intellect's movement from potentiality to act is the result of its being tuned in on an appropriate wavelength. To explain how a human being does the tuning in, Avicenna presents an elaborate theory of interior sensation.

In addition to the five familiar external senses, Avicenna believed that we have five internal senses:

(1) the common sense, which collects impressions from the five exterior senses;
(2) the retentive imagination, which stores the images thus collected;
(3) the compositive imagination, which deploys these images;

(4) the estimative power, which makes instinctive judgements, e.g. of pleasure or danger;

(5) the recollective power, which stores the intuitions of the estimative power.

We have met some of these faculties in Aristotle and in Augustine,[5] but Avicenna treats them in a much more detailed and systematic fashion. They are faculties that are common to humans and animals, and they have specific locations in ventricles of the brain.

Now while the brain is an appropriate storehouse for the deliveries of outer and inner sense (including, for example, the sheep's instinctive knowledge that the wolf is dangerous), it cannot be regarded as the repository of intellectual thoughts. When I am not actually thinking them, the thoughts I think are available only outside myself, in the agent intellect; my memory of those thoughts, my ability to recall them, is my ability to tune in, at will, to the ever-continuing transmission of the agent intellect.[6]

The exercise of the ability to acquire or retain intellectual thoughts does involve the senses, but only in a way parallel to that in which the development of matter in the embryo triggers the infusion of the soul. The role of the compositive imagination is here crucial: when it is preparing the human soul for intellectual thought it is called by Avicenna the 'cogitative faculty'. This faculty works on images retained in memory, combining and dividing them into new configurations: when these are in appropriate focus for a particular thought, the human intellect makes contact with the agent intellect and thinks that very thought.

Avicenna describes the interplay between imagination and intellect in the case of syllogistic reasoning. A human intellect wishes to know whether all As are B. His cogitative power rummages among images and produces an image of C, which is an appropriate middle term to prove the desired conclusion. Stimulated by this image, the human intellect contacts the agent intellect and acquires the thought of C. The acquisition of this thought from the agent intellect is an *insight*; and Avicenna explains that in favoured cases the intellect may have an insight—see the solution to an intellectual problem—without having to go through the elaborate introspectible process of cogitation.

Avicenna calls the state of somebody actually thinking an intellectual thought 'acquired intellection'. The term is appropriate, since for him every intellectual thought, even of the most everyday kind, is not the work of the human thinker,

[5] See pp. 194 and 422 above.

[6] Avicenna embellishes his already elaborate structure with a detailed analysis of the situation where a person is certain he can answer a question he has never answered before—a discussion that is interestingly parallel with Wittgenstein's discussion of the 'Now I know how to go on' phenomenon in *Philosophical Investigations*, I. 151.

430

but a gift from the agent intellect. However, he also uses a very similar term for an intellect that has achieved the possession of all scientific truth, and the ability to call it to mind at will. This might perhaps be more appropriately called 'perfected intellect'. For one who has reached such a stage, the senses are no longer necessary; they are a distraction. They are like a horse that has brought one to the desired destination and should now be let loose.

Is such a perfect state possible in this life—and if not, is there any afterlife? Avicenna's answer to the first question is unclear, but he has much to tell us in answer to the second. The destruction of the body does not entail the destruction of the soul, and the soul as a whole, not just the intellect, is immortal. Souls cease to make use of some of their faculties once they are separated from their bodies, but they remain individuated, and they do not transmigrate into other bodies.

Immortal souls, after death, achieve very different grades of well-being. One who has achieved perfect intellection so far as that is possible in this life enters into the company of celestial beings and enjoys perfect happiness. Those who fall short of this, but have achieved reasonable competence in science and metaphysics, will enjoy happiness of a decent but more modest kind. Those who are qualified for philosophical inquiry but have failed to take the opportunity for it in this life will suffer the most terrible misery. They will indeed suffer much greater misery than those philosophers who (like Avicenna himself) have over-indulged their bodily appetites. For the unfulfilled bodily appetites, when the soul survives alone, will soon wither away and lose their capacity to tease, whereas the pain of unfulfilled philosophical desire never comes to an end because intellectual curiosity is of the essence of the soul (*PMA* 259–62).

So much for the afterlife of intellectuals. But many people are what Avicenna calls 'simple souls', who have no notion of intellectual desire or intellectual satisfaction. After death these will neither enjoy the pleasures of satisfied intellect nor suffer the pains of intellect dissatisfied. They will live for all eternity in a kind of peace. If in their earthly life they have been led to believe that they will be rewarded for virtue by sensual pleasure (e.g. in a garden with dark-eyed maidens) or be punished for vice by bodily pains (e.g. in a hellish fire), then at death they will go into the appropriate dream, which will seem just as vivid to them as the reality.

Like al-Farabi, Avicenna in his psychological system assigns a significant role to prophecy. At the highest level, prophecy is the supreme level of insight, in which the human mind makes contact with the agent intellect without effort, and grasps conclusions without having to reason them out. At a lower level, the compositive imagination of a prophet recasts the prophetic knowledge in figurative form, which makes it suitable for communication to unlearned people. The ability to work miracles is, for Avicenna, a sub-category of prophecy: the prophet has a specially powerful motive faculty in his body which enables him to bring about material effects, such as the healing of the sick and the bringing of rain, by sheer operation of the will.

What are we to make of Avicenna's philosophy of mind? Taken as a system, it is clearly quite incredible. Leaving aside its link with antiquated astronomy, it contains a number of internal inconsistencies. How can the whole soul be immortal when the interior senses are shared with brute beasts? How can a disembodied soul dream when dreaming is an activity of the brain? Examples could be multiplied.

Nonetheless, Avicenna's philosophical psychology is important in the history of philosophy because he was the original begetter of many concepts and structures that played a part in the systems of more sober philosophers. Many others accepted his anatomy of the interior senses; those who disagreed with him about the nature of the agent intellect agreed in their description of the tasks it was needed to perform. Others, of various faiths, have been happy to accept (wittingly or not) his rationalization of the delights and sorrows held out by religion in the afterlife.

The Psychology of Averroes

At the beginning of his philosophical career Averroes accepted a theory of intellect quite close to Avicenna's. Each individual human, he believed, had a material or receptive intellect that was generated by congress between the inborn human disposition for thought and the activity of the transcendent agent intellect. After a period of lengthy reflection, however, Averroes put forward a radically different view. He reached the conclusion that neither the agent intellect nor the receptive intellect is a faculty of individual human beings. The receptive intellect, no less than the agent intellect, is a single, eternal, incorporeal substance.

He argues for this conclusion as follows. Aristotle told us that the receptive intellect receives all material forms. But it cannot do this if in itself it possesses any material form. Accordingly it cannot be a body nor can it be in any way mixed with matter. Since it is immaterial, it must be indestructible, since matter is the basis of corruption, and it must be single and not multiple, since matter is the principle of multiplication. The receptive intellect is the lowest in the hierarchy of incorporeal intelligences, located one rung below the agent intellect. Paradoxically, though itself incorporeal, it is related to the incorporeal agent intellect in a manner similar to that in which the matter of a body is related to the form of a body; and so it can be called the material intellect.

How then can my thoughts be *my* thoughts if they reside in a superhuman intellect? Averroes replies that thoughts belong to not one, but two, subjects. The eternal receptive intellect is one subject: the other is my imagination. Each of us possesses our own individual, corporeal, imagination, and it is only because of the role played in our thinking by this individual imagination that you and I can claim any thoughts as our own.

The method by which the superhuman intellect is involved in the mental life of human individuals is highly mysterious. Though it is an entity far superior to humankind, it appears to be to some extent under the control of mortal men. The initiative in any given thought rests with the imagination, not with the receptive intellect. The process has been well described as follows:

The eternity of the material intellect's thought of the physical world is, accordingly, not a single continuous fiber, nor does it spring from the material intellect. It is wholly dependent on the ratiocination and consciousness of individual men, the complete body of possible thoughts of the physical world being supplied at any given moment by individuals living at that moment, and the continuity of the material intellect's thought through infinite time being spun from the thoughts of individuals alive at various moments.[7]

Averroes' psychology strikes any modern reader as bizarre: and yet philosophers in the twentieth century have held positions that were not wholly unrelated. There is good reason for thinking that the contents of the imagination possess a degree of privacy and individuality that the contents of the intellect do not, though it is usually in the social rather than in the celestial realm that the reason for this is sought by modern philosophers. And all of us are inclined to talk, with a degree of awe, of Science as containing a body of coherent and lasting truth which cannot possibly all be within the mind of any mortal scientist.

Because, for Averroes, the truly intellectual element in thought is non-personal, there is not, he believed, any personal immortality for individual humans. After death, souls merge with each other. Averroes argues for this as follows:

Zaid and Amr are numerically different but identical in form. If, for example, the soul of Zaid were numerically different from the soul of Amr in the way Zaid is numerically different from Amr, the soul of Zaid and the soul of Amr would be numerically two, but one in their form, and the soul would possess another form. The necessary conclusion is therefore that the soul of Zaid and the soul of Amr are identical in their form. An identical form inheres in a numerical, i.e. a divisible multiplicity, only through the multiplicity of matter. If then the soul does not die when the body dies, or if it possesses an immortal element it must, when it has left the body, form a numerical unity.

At death the soul passes into the universal intelligence like a drop of water into the sea.

One of the first and severest critics of Averroes' philosophy of mind was Albert the Great. In a special treatise he listed thirty Averroist arguments in favour of the single agent intellect, and answered each in turn; on the other side he offered thirty-six arguments of his own. He insisted that both the receptive intellect and the agent intellect were faculties of the individual soul: there were as many agent intellects as there were human beings. Otherwise the intellectual soul would not

[7] Davidson, *Alfarabi, Avicenna and Averroes on Intellect*, 292–3.

be the form of the body and our thoughts would not be our own. The role of the human agent intellect is to complete the abstraction of a universal concept from the data of sense.

There are, for Albert, four grades of abstraction. There is already a degree of abstraction in sensation itself, even though the object is present, for instead of the material form of what is perceived, there is a separate *intentio* in our sense-faculty. The second grade of abstraction is when the *intentio* thus acquired is retained in our imagination, now divorced from the presence of the object, but still in all its particularity. The image of the man will retain the same posture, colour, age, and so on as the original. The third degree takes place in the phantasy, which Albert distinguishes from the imagination: one would expect this to be an image which is vague enough to represent more than one thing, but Albert tells us that it includes some non-sensible properties of the individual, such as whether he is good company or not, and who his father was. The fourth degree is the operation of the agent intellect producing a universal concept, applicable to all instances of a kind (*CHLMP* 603–4; *De An.* 2. 3. 4).

In keeping with his interest in empirical science, Albert is keen to locate these different activities in particular parts of the brain. The internal senses, such as the imagination and the phantasy, are located in pockets of animal spirits, or fluids, which vary in subtlety in accordance with the degrees of abstraction associated with them.

However, while emphasizing the material vehicle of all but the most intellectual forms of thought, Albert retains a vestige of the theories of Avicenna and Averroes in that he does recognize a direct divine causal influence on human intelligence. If the universal concepts and beliefs that are the work of our agent intellect are to be retained in the form of knowledge in our receptive intellect, there is need of a special light emanating from the uncreated agent intellect. Such illumination is especially necessary if we are to have knowledge of immaterial objects such as angels and God: here phantasms and abstraction are of no help.

Aquinas on the Senses and the Intellect

Aquinas rejected the need for a special divine illumination to explain normal human concept-formation and the pursuit of natural science.[8] For him the intellect—both the agent intellect and the receptive intellect—are faculties of the individual human being, standing at the summit of the hierarchy of capacities and abilities that constitute the human soul.

---

[8] See Ch. 4 above.

Following Aristotle, Aquinas accepts three different kinds of soul: a vegetative soul in plants, a sensitive soul in animals, and a rational soul in human beings. In human beings there is only one soul, the rational soul, but this soul, in addition to its own special intellectual powers, has powers that correspond to those of the other two souls: vegetative powers to grow and reproduce, and sensory and locomotive powers such as animals have. At the animal and rational level there are two kinds of powers, cognitive or information-gathering powers, and appetitive or goal-oriented powers. At the animal level there is the power to perceive and the power to desire; at the rational level there is the power to think and the power to will (*ST* 1a 78. 1 and 2).

In studying Aquinas' philosophy of mind it is important to remember that he does not, as many modern philosophers have done, identify the mind with consciousness. For him the mind was essentially the faculty, or set of faculties, that set off human beings from other animals. Dumb animals and human beings can all see and hear and feel, but only human beings can think abstract thoughts and take rational decisions. It is the possession of intellect and will that set them off from animals, and it is these two faculties that essentially constitute the mind, the rational soul.

Nonetheless, to understand Aquinas' account of the mind it is important to consider what he says about the senses, for on his view the activity of the two faculties, rational and sensory, are tightly interwoven. The operation of the senses is essential for both the origin and the exercise of intellectual concepts. Moreover, much of what a modern philosopher would consider as mental activity is, for Aquinas, the operation of a sense of a particular kind, namely, the imagination, which is one of the inner senses.

Aquinas accepted the traditional list of five outer senses: sight, hearing, touch, taste, and smell. Senses are distinguished from each other not by having different organs but by having different objects: sight and hearing differ not because eyes differ from ears, but because colours differ from sounds. Senses are essentially discriminatory powers, such as the power to tell hot from cold, black from white, and so on. Each sense has its proper object, an object that only it can detect; but there are also objects common to more than one sense, such as shape, which can be both seen and felt (*ST* 1a 78. 3. 3).

A sense, according to Aquinas, is a capacity to undergo a special kind of change caused by an external object. When we see, the form of colour is received in the eye without the eye becoming coloured. Normally, when the form of F is received by a material object, the object becomes F, as when a stone receives the form of heat and becomes hot. That is the standard form of change, material change. To the kind of change that takes place when a colour is seen, Aquinas gives the name 'intentional' change. The form of colour exists intentionally in the eye, or, as he sometimes says, the intention (*intentio* or *species*) of colour is in the eye (1a 84. 1).

An *intentio* is not a representation, even though Aquinas sometimes calls it a likeness, or *similitudo*, of the object perceived. Some philosophers believe that in sense-experience we do not directly observe objects or properties in the external world, but rather perceive private sense-data from which we infer the nature of external objects and properties. In Aquinas there are no such intermediaries between perceiver and perceived. In sensation the faculty does not come into contact with a likeness of the object; it becomes itself like the object by taking on its form. This is summed up in the slogan taken over from Aristotle: the sense-faculty in operation is identical with the sense-object in action (*sensus in actu est sensibile in actu*).[9]

Aquinas' teaching on intentionality is not meant to offer an arcane mechanism as a theory to explain sensation. It is meant to be a philosophical truism to help us to see clearly what is happening. The Aristotelian slogan means no more than this: if I pop a sweet in my mouth, my tasting its sweetness (the operation of my sense-faculty: *sensus in actu*) is one and the same thing as its tasting sweet to me (the operation of the sensory property: *sensibile in actu*). The importance of the truism is precisely to rule out the naive representationalism that is tempting in this area.

In addition to the five outer senses, Aquinas believed that there were inner senses, and took over a list of them from Avicenna: the general sense, the memory, the imagination, and a fourth faculty, which in animals is called the *vis aestimativa* and in humans the *vis cogitativa*. The *vis aestimativa* seems to correspond to our notion of 'instinct': animals' inborn appreciation of what is useful or dangerous, expressed in such activities as nest-building or fleeing from predators. Aquinas does not succeed in making clear what he regards as the equivalent human capacity (*ST* 1a 78. 4).

Many philosophers besides Aquinas have classified memory and imagination as inner senses. They have regarded these faculties as senses because they saw their function as the production of imagery; they regarded them as inner because their activity, unlike that of the outer senses, was not controlled by external stimuli. Aquinas, indeed, thought that the inner senses, like the outer ones, had organs—organs that were located in different parts of the brain.

It seems to be a mistake to regard the imagination as an inner sense. It has no organ in the sense in which sight has an organ: there is no part of the body which can be voluntarily moved so that we can imagine better, in the way that the eyes can be voluntarily moved so that we can see better. Moreover, it is not possible to be mistaken about what one imagines in the way that one can be mistaken about what one sees: others cannot check up on what I say I imagine as they can check up on what I claim to see. These are crucial differences between imagination and genuine senses.

Fortunately much of what Aquinas has to say about the role of the imagination and its relation to the intellect is unaffected by this excessive assimilation to the

---

[9] See above, p. 193.

five senses. Calling it a sense—and therefore, for Aquinas, a faculty wholly within the realm of the material—has the great advantage of distinguishing it from the intellect. Many philosophers have conceived the mind as an immaterial and private world, the locus of our secret thoughts, the auditorium of our interior monologues. This is a profound mistake. Of course it is undeniable that human beings can keep their thoughts secret and talk to themselves without making any noise and call images before their mind's eye. But this ability, for Aquinas, is not the mind: it is not the intellect but the imagination.

'Intellectus' is one of the few technical terms in Aquinas that means roughly the same as its English equivalent, 'intellect'. The cognate verb 'intelligere', however, does not have an equivalent 'intellege' and fortunately no medievalist has had the idea of coining such a word to match 'cognize'. The Latin verb is often translated 'understand', but in Aquinas' use it has a very broad sense, rather like the English 'think'. We have seen that Aquinas divides the acts of the intellect into two classes: the grasp of non-complexes, on the one hand, and composition and division on the other.[10] These correspond to two kinds of thought: thoughts *of* (such as the thought of a hawk), and thoughts *that* (such as the thought that a hawk is not a handsaw). It is not quite faithful to Aquinas, however, to equate the intellect with the capacity for thought, because he believed that animals, who do not have intellects, could have simple thoughts. It is more accurate to identify the intellect with the capacity for the kind of thought that only language-users can have.

For Aquinas, the intellect thinks in universals, and a grasp of universals is not within the capacity of animals: a universal can neither be sensed nor imagined. Nonetheless, Aquinas believed that in human beings the operation of sense and imagination was essential both for the acquisition and for the exercise of universal concepts. In the present life, he maintained, the proper object of the human intellect was the essence, or quiddity, of material objects; and this, he said, the intellect understood by abstraction from phantasms (*phantasmata*). By 'phantasms' Aquinas means the deliverances of sense and imagination, and without them Aquinas thinks that intellectual thought is impossible. But he does not believe, as empiricist philosophers have believed, that ideas are derived from sense-experience by abstraction from, or selective inattention to, features of that experience. If that were so, then animals no less than humans would be able to frame universal concepts, whereas Aquinas believed that such conceptualization demanded a species-specific human faculty, the agent intellect. On the other hand, Aquinas does not believe, as rationalist philosophers have believed, that there are individual ideas inborn in every human being. The human intellect, at birth, is for him a tabula rasa. (*ST* 1a 85).

---

[10] See Ch. 3 above.

The human intellect, for Aquinas, consists of two powers with a double function. Beside the agent intellect, which is the capacity to abstract universal ideas from particular sense-experience, there is in humans a receptive intellect, which is the storehouse of ideas abstracted from sense and beliefs acquired from experience. At birth this storehouse is empty: the receptive intellect is the initially blank page on which the agent intellect writes. But phantasms, Aquinas maintains, are necessary not only for the acquisition of concepts, but also for their exercise: not only to place ideas in the mental storehouse, but also to take them out again and put them to use (*ST* 1a 79).

This latter thesis is important when we consider the application of universal ideas to individuals in the world. Some philosophers have thought that an object could be individuated by listing the totality of its properties, that is to say, by listing the universals under which it falls. But Aquinas rejected this: however long a list we draw up, it is always possible that it might apply to more than one individual. Given that the intellect thinks in universals, it is therefore impossible for there to be purely intellectual knowledge of individuals.

It is only indirectly, and by a certain kind of reflection, that the intellect can know an individual. Even after it has abstracted ideas it cannot make use of them in intellectual operation unless it turns towards the phantasms in which it grasps the intellectual idea, as Aristotle says. Thus, what the intellect grasps directly by the intellectual idea is the universal; but indirectly it grasps individuals to which phantasms belong. And that is how it forms the proposition 'Socrates is human'. (*ST* 1a 86c)

If I know someone well there will be many descriptions I can give of him; but unless I bring in reference to particular times and places there may be no description that could not in theory be satisfied by someone else. Only by pointing, or taking you to see him, or reminding you of an occasion when you met, can I make clear to you which person I have in mind; and pointing and vision and memory are outside the realm of pure intellectual thought.

The indirect nature of intellectual thought about individuals follows from two theses that Aquinas held: first, that matter is the principle of individuation, and secondly, that the immediate object of all knowledge is form. The senses perceive accidental forms such as colour and shape; the intellect grasps substantial forms, such as humanity. Both thought and sensation are cases of the intentional occurrence of forms; but whereas in sensation the forms are individual (the smell of *this rose*), in thought the form is universal (the idea of *a rose*). It is because of this conception of the nature of thought that to this day we speak of being *informed* about a matter and call the gaining of knowledge the acquisition of *information*.

The intentionality of the intellect, like the intentionality of sensation, is expressed in a slogan: *Intellectus in actu est intelligibile in actu*: 'The actuality of the power of thinking is the very same thing as the actuality of the object of thought'.

When I have a universal thought, my thinking the universal idea is one and the same thing as the idea occurring to my mind. On the one hand, the intellect just is the capacity for thinking universal ideas; and on the other hand, the universal as such, the object of thought, is something whose only existence is its occurrence in thoughts.

Aquinas on the Will

Besides the intellect, in Aquinas' system, the other great power of the mind is the will. The intellect is a cognitive power of a specifically human kind; the will is an appetitive power of a specifically human kind. It is the power to have wants that only the intellect can frame. The will is the highest form of appetition, the topmost point on a scale whose lower rungs are the teleological tendencies of inanimate bodies (e.g. the tendency of fire to rise) and the conscious, but non-rational, desires of animals (e.g. the desire of a dog for a bone). Humans share these tendencies—*qua* heavy bodies they tend to fall if not supported; *qua* animals they want food and sleep—but they also have specifically human wants, paradigmatically the desire for happiness and for the means to happiness. In humans, moreover, even the animal wants are subject to the control of the intellectual part of the soul, the will.

In other animals the appetite of desire or aggression is acted upon immediately: thus a sheep, in fear of a wolf, runs away immediately, for it has no higher appetite to intervene. But a human being does not react immediately in response to an aggressive or impulsive drive, but waits for the command of a higher appetite, the will. (*ST* 1a 81. 3)

Aquinas frequently compares the performance of a voluntary action to obedience to an interior command. There are, he says, two sorts of acts of will. There are immediate acts (*actus eliciti*): acts such as enjoying, intending, choosing, deliberating, and consenting (1a 2ae 1. 1 ad 2); and there are commanded acts (*actus imperati*), voluntary motions of the body such as walking and speaking, whose execution involves the exercise of some other power in addition to the will.

There is no need to think that Aquinas is teaching that every time I go for a walk I utter to myself under my breath the command 'Go for a walk!' nor that there are such things as interior acts of pure willing. The Latin word 'actus' need not mean any sort of action: an act of the will is in fact standardly a tendency, not an episode (1a 2ae 6. 4). A tendency can be operative without being present to consciousness, as one's desire to reach a destination can govern one's behaviour on a journey without being constantly in one's thoughts.

For Aquinas voluntary action is action that issues from a rational consideration of the action. The minimum of rational consideration seems to be that the action should issue from a consideration of it as answering to a certain linguistic description—e.g. jumping out of the way when someone shouts 'Get out of my way'. But the kind of case Aquinas is more interested in is when we have reasons for action: when the action can be presented as the conclusion of a piece of practical reasoning. The reasons for an action need not have been consciously rehearsed before acting; but if an act is to be fully voluntary one should, on request, be able to give reasons—which might take the form of showing the goodness of the act itself or of showing that it was a means to a desirable end. In calling voluntary behaviour 'commanded action' Aquinas is drawing attention to the analogy between the logical relationship between command and execution and the relationship of willing to acting.

A volition, in the case of human beings, is a state of mind that is defined by the linguistic description of the action or state of affairs that would fulfil it. I want it to be the case that p. The proposition p both specifies my state of mind and demarcates the state of affairs that stands to it in the relationship of fulfilment to want. But suppose that instead of my wanting it to be the case that p, you command me to bring it about that p: the proposition has an analogous role. The metaphor of the will issuing commands is appropriate and fruitful.[11]

Practical reasoning is a difficult topic, and its logic has to this day not been fully worked out. One way in which it differs from theoretical reasoning is that it is, in the lawyer's jargon, *defeasible*. What that means is this. In theoretical deductive reasoning, if a conclusion follows from a given set of premisses it follows also from any larger set containing those premisses: the argument cannot be defeated by the addition of an extra premiss. But with practical reasoning it is different. A pattern of reasoning that would justify a certain course of action on the basis of certain wants and beliefs may well cease to justify it if further wants and beliefs are brought into consideration.

Aquinas recognized the defeasibility of practical reasoning, and indeed he saw it as the underlying ground of the freedom of the will. In human beings, unlike animals, he says,

Because a particular practical evaluation is not a matter of inborn instinct, but a result of weighing reasons, a human being acts upon free judgement, and is capable of going various ways. In contingent matters reason can go either way . . . and what to do in particular situations is a contingent matter. So in such cases the judgement of reason is open to alternatives and is not determined to any one course. Hence, humans enjoy free decision, from the very fact of being rational. (*ST* 1a 83. 1c)

When we look at a piece of practical reasoning—reasoning about what to do— we find, where the analogy of theoretical reasoning would lead us to expect

---

[11] The analogies are very close, as I have tried to spell out in my book *Will, Freedom and Power* (Oxford: Blackwell, 1975).

necessitation, merely contingent and defeasible connections between one step and another. Aquinas believed that this contingency was the fundamental ground of human freedom.

Aquinas does not generally employ a Latin expression corresponding to our 'freedom of the will': he talks instead of the will (*voluntas*) and of 'free choice' (*liberum arbitrium*). Choice is an expression of both the intellect and the will: it is an exercise of the intellect because it is the fruit of reasoning; it is an exercise of the will because it is a form of appetition. Following Aristotle, Aquinas tells us that it is both appetitive intelligence, and ratiocinative appetite (*ST* 1a 83c).

Intellect and will are the two great powers of the rational soul, the soul that is peculiar to human beings. Besides being the soul that only human beings have, it is the only soul that human beings have. Against those contemporaries who thought that humans had also animal and vegetable souls, plus a form of corporeality, Aquinas maintained that the rational soul was the one and only substantial form of a human being. If there had been a plurality of forms, he argued, one could not say that it was one and the same human being who thought, loved, saw, heard, drank, slept, and had a certain weight and size.

Aquinas believed that the human soul was immaterial and immortal. The argument that the soul is pure form, uncontaminated with matter, is presented thus:

The principle of the operation of the intellect, which we call the human soul, must be said to be an incorporeal and subsistent principle. For it is plain that by his intellect a human being can know the nature of all corporeal things. But to be able to know things, a knower must have nothing of their nature in his own nature. If it did, what it had in its nature would hinder it from knowing other things, as a sick person's tongue, infected with a bilious and bitter humour, cannot taste anything sweet because everything tastes sour to it. If, then, the intellectual principle had in itself the nature of any corporeal thing, it would not be able to know all corporeal things. (*ST* 1a 75. 2)

The thesis of the immateriality of the soul goes hand in hand with the thesis of the intentional existence of the objects of thought. 'Prime matter receives individual forms, the intellect receives pure forms,' Aquinas says. That is to say, the shape of the Great Pyramid is *its* shape, and not the shape of any other pyramidal object; but the intellectual idea of a pyramid in my mind is the idea purely of pyramid and not the idea of any particular pyramid. But if the mind had any matter in it, the idea would become individual, not universal (1a 75. 5c).

This argument, if successful, shows that the soul does not contain matter. But does it mean that it can exist in separation from matter—in separation, for instance, from the body of the person whose soul it is? Aquinas believes that it does. Intellectual thought is an activity in which the body has no share; but nothing can act on its own unless it exists on its own; for only what is actually existent can act, and the way it acts depends on the way it exists. 'Hence we do not say that heat heats, but that a hot body heats. So the human soul, which is called the intellect or mind, is something non-bodily and subsistent' (1a 75. 2c).

One problem with this argument is that elsewhere Aquinas insists that just as it is strictly incorrect to say that heat heats, so it is strictly incorrect to say that the soul, or the mind, thinks. Aristotle had said, 'It is better not to say that the soul pities, or learns, or thinks, but that it is the human being that does these things with his soul' (*De An.* 408^{b}15), and Aquinas echoes this when he says, 'It can be said that the soul thinks, just as the eye sees, but it is better to say that the human being thinks with the soul.' If we take this comparison seriously, we must say that just as an eye, outside a body, is not really an eye at all any more, so a soul, separated from a body, is not really a soul any more.

Aquinas goes some way to accepting this, but he does not treat it as a *reductio ad absurdum*. He agrees that a person's disembodied soul is not the same thing as the person whose soul it is. St Paul wrote, 'if in this life only we have hope in Christ we are of all men most miserable' (1 Cor. 15: 19). St Thomas, in commenting on this passage, wrote: 'A human being naturally desires his own salvation; but the soul, since it is part of the body of a human being, is not a whole human being, and my soul is not I; so even if a soul gains salvation in another life, that is not I or any human being.' Whether or not Aquinas' belief in the possibility of disembodied souls is coherent, it is remarkable that he refuses to identify such a soul, even if beatified, with any self or ego. He refuses to identify an individual with an individual's soul, as many theologians before him, and many philosophers after him, were willing to do.

Scotus versus Aquinas

Duns Scotus' philosophy of mind differed profoundly from that of Aquinas, in accordance with the differences in their metaphysical systems. Aquinas believed that there was no purely intellectual knowledge of individuals, because individuation was by matter, and intellectual thought was free of matter. But for Scotus there exists an individual element, or *haecceitas*, which is an object of knowledge: it is not quite a form, but is sufficiently like a form to be present in the intellect. And because each thing has within it a formal, intelligible, principle, the ground is cut beneath the basis on which Aquinas rested the need for a species-specific agent intellect in human beings.

Individuals, unlike universals, are things that come into and go out of existence. If the proper objects of the intellect include not only universals but individual items like a *haecceitas*, then there is a possibility of such an object being in the intellect without existing in reality. The possibility that one and the same object might be in the intellect and not exist in reality was the possibility that Aquinas' intentionality theory was careful to avoid. An individual form, for Scotus, may exist in the mind and yet the corresponding individual not exist. Hence the individual form present in the intellect can be only a representation of, and not identical with, the object whose knowledge it embodies. Hence a window is opened at the level of the highest intellectual knowledge, a window to permit the entry of the epistemological problems that have been familiar to us since Descartes.

The differences between Aquinas and Scotus, so far as concerns the intellect, are not so much a matter of explicit rejection by Scotus of positions taken up by Aquinas. It is rather that a consideration of the Scotist position leads one to reflect on its incompatibility at a deep level with the Thomist anthropology. But when we turn from the intellect to the will, things are very different. Here Scotus is consciously rejecting the tradition that precedes him; he is innovating in full self-awareness. He regards Aquinas as having misrepresented the nature of human freedom and the relation between the intellect and the will.

For Aquinas, the root of human freedom was the will's dependence on the practical reason. For Scotus, the will is autonomous and sovereign. He puts the question whether anything other than the will effectively causes the act of willing in the will. He replies, nothing other than the will is the total cause of volition. What is contingent must come from an undetermined cause, which can only be the will itself, and he argues against the position which he attributes to 'an older doctor' that the indetermination of the will is the result of an indetermination on the part of the intellect.

You say: this indetermination is on the part of the intellect, in so representing the object to the will, as it will be, or will not be. To the contrary: the intellect cannot determine the will indifferently to either of contradictories (for instance, this will be or will not be), except by demonstrating one, and constructing a paralogism or sophistical syllogism regarding the other, so that in drawing the conclusion it is deceived. Therefore, if that contingency by which this can be or not be was from the intellect, dictating in this way by means of opposite conclusions, then nothing would happen contingently by the will of God, or by God, because he does not construct paralogism, nor is he deceived. But this is false. (*Oxon.* 2. 25)

Scotus' criticism of the idea that the indeterminism of the will arises from an indeterminism in the intellect is based on a misunderstanding of the theory that he is attacking. The intellect in dictating to the reason does not say 'This will be' or 'This will not be', but rather 'This is to be' or 'This is not to be', 'This is good' or 'This is not good'. If what is in question is a non-necessary means to a chosen goal, it is possible for the intellect, without error, to dictate both that something is good and that its opposite is good. Moreover, in making the will the cause of its own freedom, Scotus' theory runs the danger of leading to an infinite regress of free choices, where the freedom of a choice depends on a previous free choice, whose freedom depends on a previous one, and so on for ever.

Scotus was not unaware of this danger, and in opposition to the position he attacks, he develops his own elaborate analysis of the structure of human freedom, in a way that he believes holds out the possibility of avoiding the regress. In any case of free action, he says, there must be some kind of power to opposites. One such power is obvious: it is the will's power to will after not willing, or its power to enact a succession of opposite acts. Of course, the will can have no power to will and not will at the same time—that would be nonsense—but while A is willing X at time t, A has the power to not will X at time $t + 1$.

But beside this obvious power, Scotus maintains, there is another, non-obvious power, which is not a matter of temporal succession (*alia, non ita manifesta, absque omni successione*). He illustrates this kind of power by imagining a case in which a created will existed only for a single moment. In that moment it could only have a single volition, but even that volition would not be necessary, but would be free. Now while the lack of succession involved in freedom is plainest in the case of the imagined momentary will, it is there in every case of free action. That is, that while A is willing X at t, not only does A have the power to not will X at $t + 1$, but A also has the power to not will X at t, at that very moment. The power, of course, is not exercised, but it is there all the same. It is quite distinct from mere logical possibility—the fact that there would be no contradiction in A's not willing X at this very moment—it is something over and above: a real active power. It is this power that, for Scotus, is the heart of human freedom.[12]

In defending the coherence of the concept of this non-manifest power, Scotus makes use of a logical distinction that can be traced back to Abelard. Consider the sentence 'This will, which is willing X at t, can not will X at t'. It can be taken in two ways. Taken one way ('in a composite sense') it means that 'This will, which is willing X at t, is not willing X at t' is possibly true. Taken in that way the sentence is false, and indeed necessarily false. Taken in another way ('in a divided sense') it means that it is possible that *not-willing X at time t* might have inhered in this will which is actually willing X at time t. Taken in this sense, Scotus maintains, the sentence can well be true (*Ord.* 4. 417–18).

Ockham versus Scotus

Ockham rejected the non-manifest power that Scotus had introduced. It was not a genuine power, he said, because it was totally incapable of actualization without contradiction. The power not to sit at time t should be regarded as a power existing not at t (when I am actually sitting) but at time $t - 1$, the last moment at which it was still open to me to be standing up at t.

---

[12] See the discussion of synchronic contingency in Ch. 6 above.

Like Ockham, I find Scotus' occult powers incomprehensible. But Ockham's rejection of them is not sufficiently wholehearted. Scotus' mistake was to regard a power as being a datable event just like the exercise of a power. Ockham accepts the notion of a power for an instant, and simply antedates the temporal location of the power. But having a power is a state; it is not a momentary episode like an action.

It may be true, at *t*, that I have the power to do X, without that entailing that I have the power to do-X-at-*t*. Of course, it may be true that I can do X at *t*, but in order to analyse such a statement we must distinguish between power and opportunity. For it to be true that I can swim now it is necessary not only that I should now have the power to swim (i.e. know how to swim) but also have the opportunity to swim (e.g. that there should be a sufficient amount of water about). Scotus and Ockham fail to make the appropriate distinction, and their temporarily qualified powers are an amalgam of the two notions of power and opportunity. But an opportunity is not an occult power of mine: it is a matter of the states and powers of other things, and the compossibility of those states and powers with the exercise of my power.[13]

In spite of their disagreements about the precise nature of freedom, Ockham is at one with Scotus in stressing the autonomy of the will. The will's action is not determined either by a natural desire for happiness, nor by any command of the intellect, nor by any habit in the sensitive appetite: it always remains free to choose between opposites.

On the cognitive side of the soul, Ockham regularly writes as if he recognizes the three sets of powers traditional in Aristotelian philosophy: outer sense (the familiar five senses), inner sense (the imagination), and intellect. However, when he discusses the intellect it is not at all clear that he is talking about the same faculty that Aristotle and Aquinas described. For Aquinas, the intellect was distinguished from the senses because its object was universal while theirs was particular; and the individual was directly knowable only by the senses. But for Ockham, both particular and universal can be known directly by both senses and intellect.

For Aquinas, a human mind's knowledge of a particular horse would be subsequent to the acquisition of the universal idea (*species*) of horse, formed out of sense-experience by the creative activity of a faculty peculiar to human beings, the agent intellect. Once this idea has been acquired, it can be applied to individuals only by a reflective activity of the intellect, reverting to sensory experience. Ockham regards all this apparatus as superfluous.

We can suppose that the intellect can be brought to the knowledge of an individual by the same process as it is led to the knowledge of a universal. If it is brought to knowledge of the universal by the agent intellect on its own, then the agent intellect on its own—we may suppose—can equally easily bring it to the knowledge of an individual. And as it can be

---

[13] See my *Will, Freedom and Power*, ch. 8.

directed by the intelligible species or by the phantasm to think of one universal rather than another, so too we can suppose that it can be directed by the intelligible species to think of this individual and not another. In whatever way after the acquisition of the universal concept the mind can be directed to think of one individual rather than another (even though the knowledge of the universal concerns all individuals equally) in just the same way it can be directed, even before the acquisition of the universal, to think of this individual rather than another. (*OTh*. 1. 493)

When Ockham claims that the intellect can know the individual, he is not basing his claim on the existence of a formal element of individuation, like the Scotist *haecceitas*. He rejected any such principle and denied the need for it. Whatever exists in the real world just is individual, and needs no principle to individuate it. His point in the quoted passage is that whatever philosophical account you give of the acquisition and employment of knowledge of the universal, exactly the same account can be given of the acquisition and employment of knowledge of the individual. If that is so, then it seems a violation of Ockham's razor to postulate two different faculties with exactly the same function.

In fact Ockham does distinguish between the senses and the intellect, but whenever he describes the operation of the intellect, it seems to be a mere double of either the inner or the outer sense. The very same object that we sense is intuitively grasped by the intellect under exactly the same description; the intellect's grasp of the object sensed is parallel to the imagination's representation of the object senses (*OTh*. 1. 494). Seeing a white object, imagining a white object, and thinking of a white object are, for Ockham, mental operations of a similar kind. The one feature which seems to be peculiar to the intellect is the act of judging that there is a white object. This judgement is an act not of the senses, nor of the will, but of the intellect alone (*OTh*. 6. 85–6).

Just as he was unconvinced by the traditional arguments for God's existence, so Ockham was unconvinced by the arguments of medieval Aristotelians to prove the immortality of the soul. If a soul is an immaterial and incorruptible form, he said,

it cannot be known evidently either by argument or by experience that there is any such form in us. Nor can it be known that thinking in us belongs to such a substance, nor that such a soul is a form of the body. I do not care what Aristotle thought of this, because he always seems to speak hesitantly. But these three things are simply objects of faith. (*OTh*. 9. 63–4)

Pomponazzi on the Soul

As the Middle Ages drew to an end, this scepticism about philosophical proofs of immortality became more widespread. The arguments for and against the immortality of individual human beings are set out in Pietro Pomponazzi's pamphlet of

1516, *On the Immortality of the Soul*. Pomponazzi begins by considering the opinion that there is a single, immortal, intellectual human soul, while each individual human being has only a mortal soul. This opinion, which he attributes to Averroes and Themistius, is, he tells us, 'widely held in our time and by almost all is confidently taken to be that of Aristotle'. In fact, he says, it is false, unintelligible, monstrous, and quite foreign to Aristotle.

To show that the opinion is false, Pomponazzi refers the reader to arguments used by St Thomas Aquinas in his *De Unitate Intellectus*. To show that it is un-Aristotelian he appeals to the teaching of the *De Anima* that, in order to operate, the intellect always needs a phantasm, which is something material. Our intellectual soul is an act of a physical and organic body. There may be types of intelligence that do not need an organ to operate, but the human intellect is not one of them.

A body, however, can function as a subject or object. Our senses need bodies in both ways: their organs are bodily and their objects are bodily. The intellect, however, does not need a body as subject, and it can perform operations (such as reflecting upon itself) which no bodily organ can do: the mind can think of itself, while the eye cannot see itself. But this does not mean that the intellect can operate entirely independently from the body.

Aquinas is again invoked in order to refute another opinion, the Platonic view that while every human has an individual immortal soul, this soul is related to his body only as mover to moved—like an ox to a plough, say. Like Aquinas, Pomponazzi appeals to experience:

I who am writing these words am beset with many bodily pains, which are the function of the sensitive soul; and the same I who am tortured run over their medical causes in order to remove these pains, which cannot be done save by the intellect. But if the essence by which I feel were different from that by which I think, how could it possibly be that I who feel am the same as I who think? (c. 6, p. 298[14])

We must conclude that the intellectual soul and the sensitive soul are one and the same in man.

In this, Pomponazzi is in agreement with St Thomas: but at this point he parts company with him. Thomas, he said, believed that this single soul was properly immortal, and only mortal in a manner of speaking (*secundum quid*). But he, Pomponazzi, will now set out to show that the soul is properly mortal, and only immortal in a manner of speaking. He continues to speak of Aquinas with great respect. 'As the authority of so learned a Doctor is very great with me, not only in divinity but also in interpretation of Aristotle, I would not dare to affirm anything against him: I only advance what I say in the way of doubt' (c. 8, p. 302).

---

[14] In E. Cassirer *et al.* (eds.), *The Renaissance Philosophy of Man* (Chicago: University of Chicago Press, 1959).

By nature man's being is more sensuous than intellective, more mortal than immortal. We have more vegetative and sensory powers than intellectual powers, and many more people devote themselves to the exercise of those powers than to the cultivation of the intellect. The great majority of men are irrational rather than rational animals. More seriously, the soul can only be separable if it has an operation independent of the body. But both Aristotle and Aquinas maintain that the phantasm is essential for any exercise of thought: hence the soul needs the body, as object if not as subject. Souls can only be individuated by the matter of the bodies they inform: it will not do to say that souls, separate from their bodies, are individuated by an abiding aptitude for informing a particular body.

Did Aristotle believe in immortality? In the *Ethics* he seems to assert that there is no happiness after death, and when he says that it is possible to wish for the impossible, the example he gives of such a wish is the wish for immortality. St Thomas asks why, if Aristotle thought there was no survival of death, he should want people to die rather than to live in evil ways. But the only immortal intelligence Aristotle seems to accept is one that precedes, as well as survives, the death of the individual human. However, Pomponazzi says, he has no desire to seek a quarrel with Aristotle: what is a flea against an elephant? (c. 8, p. 313; c. 10, p. 334).

The Aristotelian conclusion which Pomponazzi finally accepts is this: the human soul is both intellective and sensitive, and strictly speaking it is mortal, and immortal only *secundum quid*. In all its operations the human intellect is the actuality of an organic body, and always depends on the body as its object. The human soul is what makes a human individual, but it is not itself a subsistent individual (c. 9, p. 321). This position 'agrees with reason and experience, it maintains nothing mythical, nothing dependent on Faith'. The intellect that, according to Aristotle, survives death is no human intellect. When we call the soul immortal it is only like calling grey 'white' when it is compared to a black background.

The immortality of the soul, Pomponazzi concludes, is an issue like the eternity of the world. Philosophy cannot settle either way whether the world ever had a beginning; it is equally impotent to settle whether the soul will ever have an end. His last word—sincere or not—is this. We must assert beyond doubt that the soul is immortal: but this is an act of faith, not a philosophical conclusion.

8

Ethics

Augustine on How to be Happy

Like most moralists in the ancient world, Augustine bases his ethical teaching on the premiss that everyone wants to be happy, and that it is the task of philosophy to define what this supreme good is and how it is to be achieved. If you ask two people whether they want to join the army, he says in the *Confessions*, one may say yes and the other no. But if you ask them whether they want to be happy, they will both say yes without any hesitation. The only reason they differ about serving in the army is that one believes, while the other does not, that that will make him happy (*Conf.* X. 21. 31).

In *On the Trinity* (*DT* 13. 3. 6) Augustine tells the story of a stage player who promised to tell his audience, at his next appearance, what was in each of their minds. When they returned he told them 'Each of you wants to buy cheap and sell dear'. This was smart, Augustine says, but not really correct—and he gives a list of possible counter-examples. But if the actor had said 'Each of you wants to be happy, and none of you wants to be miserable', then he would have hit the mark perfectly.

The branch of philosophy that Greeks call 'ethics' and which Latins call 'moral philosophy', Augustine says, is an inquiry into the supreme good. This is the good that provides the standard for all our actions; it is sought for its own sake and not as a means to an end. Once we attain it, we lack nothing that is necessary for happiness (*DCD* VIII. 8). So far, Augustine is saying nothing that had not been said by classical moralists: and he is following precedent too in rejecting riches, honour, and sensual pleasure as candidates for supreme goodness. The Stoics, among others, held out a similar renunciation, and maintained that happiness lay in the virtues of the mind. They were mistaken, however, both in thinking that virtue alone was sufficient for happiness, and in thinking that virtue was achievable by unaided human effort. Augustine takes a step beyond all his pagan predecessors in claiming that happiness is truly possible only in the vision of God in an afterlife.

First, he argues that anyone who wants to be happy must want to be immortal. How can we hold that a happy life is to come to an end at death? If a man is unwilling to lose his life, how can he be happy with this prospect before him? On the other hand, if his life is something he is willing to part with, how can it have been truly happy? But if immortality is necessary for happiness, it is not sufficient. Pagan philosophers who have claimed to prove that the soul is immortal have also held out the prospect of a miserable cycle of reincarnation. Only the Christian faith promises everlasting happiness for the entire human being, soul and body alike (*DT* 13. 8. 11–9. 12).

The supreme good of the City of God is eternal and perfect peace, not in our mortal transit from birth to death, but in our immortal freedom from all adversity. This is the happiest life—who can deny it?—and in comparison with it our life on earth, however blessed with external prosperity or goods of soul and body, is utterly miserable. Nonetheless, whoever accepts it and makes use of it as a means to that other life that he longs for and hopes for, may not unreasonably be called happy even now—happy in hope rather than in reality. (*DCD* XIX. 20)

Virtue in the present life, therefore, is not equivalent to happiness: it is merely a necessary means to an end that is ultimately other-worldly. Moreover, however hard we try, we are unable to avoid vice without grace, that is to say without special divine assistance, which is given only to those selected for salvation through Christ. The virtues of the great pagan heroes, celebrated from time to time in *The City of God*, were really only splendid vices, which received their reward in Rome's glorious history, but did not qualify for the one true happiness of heaven.

Many classical theorists upheld the view that the moral virtues were insepar-able: whoever possesses one such virtue truly possesses them all, and whoever lacks one virtue lacks every virtue. As a corollary, some moralists held that there are no degrees of virtue and vice, and that all sins are of equal gravity. Augustine rejects this view.[1]

A woman...who remains faithful to her husband, if she does so because of the commandment and promise of God and is faithful to him above all, has chastity. I don't know how I could say that such chastity is not a virtue or only an insignificant one. So too with a husband who remains faithful to his wife. Yet there are many such people, none of whom I would say is without some sin, and certainly that sin, whatever it is, comes from vice. Hence conjugal chastity in devout men and women is without doubt a virtue—for it is neither nothing nor a vice, and yet it does not have all the virtues with it. (*Ep.* 167. 3. 10)

We are all sinners, even the most devout Christians among us; yet not everything that we do is sinful. We are all vicious in one way or another, but not every one of our character traits is a vice.

---

[1] See Bonnie Kent, 'Augustine's Ethics', in *CCA* 226–9.

In Augustine's moral teaching, however, there is an element that has many of the same consequences as the pagan thesis of the inseparability of the moral virtues. This is the doctrine that the moral virtues are inseparable from the theological virtues. That is to say, someone who lacks the virtues of faith, hope, and charity cannot truly possess virtues such as wisdom, temperance, or courage (*DT* 13. 20. 26). An act that is not done from the love of God must be sinful; and without orthodox faith one cannot have true love of God (*DCG* 14. 45).

Augustine often says that the virtues of pagans are nothing but splendid vices: an evil tree cannot bear good fruit. Sometimes he is willing to concede that someone who lacks faith can perform individual good acts, so that not every act of an infidel is a sin. But even if pagans can do the occasional good deed, this will not help them to achieve ultimate happiness: the best they can hope for is that their everlasting punishment will be less unbearable than that of others.

Through the long history of Christianity many were to accept Augustine's picture of the dreadful future that awaits the great majority of the human race. After the disruption of the Reformation, Calvin in the Protestant camp and Jansenius in the Catholic camp were to offer visions of even darker gloom; and in the nineteenth century Kierkegaard and Newman stressed, like Augustine, how narrow was the gate that gave entry to the supreme good of final bliss. The breezy optimism that characterized many Christians in the twentieth century had little backing from tradition. But that is a matter for the history of theology, not philosophy.

Augustine on Lying, Murder, and Sex

From a philosophical point of view Augustine's contributions to particular ethical debates are of greater interest than his overall view of the nature of morality. He wrote much that repays study concerning the interpretation of three of the Ten Commandments: 'Thou shalt not kill', 'Thou shalt not commit adultery', 'Thou shalt not bear false witness against thy neighbour'.

In *The City of God* Augustine defined for future generations the way in which Christians should interpret the biblical command 'Thou shalt not kill'. In the first place, the prohibition does not extend to the killing of non-human creatures.

When we read 'thou shalt not kill' we do not take this to apply to bushes, which feel nothing, nor to the irrational animals that fly or swim or walk or crawl since they are not part of our rational society. They have not been endowed with reason as we have, and so it is by a just ordinance of the creator that their life and death is subordinate to our needs. (*DCD* I. 20)

In the second place, it is not always wrong for one human being deliberately to take the life of another human being. Augustine accepts that a public magistrate may be justified in inflicting the death penalty on a wrongdoer, provided that the sentence is imposed and carried out in accordance with the laws of the state. Moreover, he says, the commandment against killing is not broken 'by those who have waged war on the authority of God' (*DCD* I. 21).

But how is one to tell when a war is waged with God's authority? Augustine is not one to glorify war: it is an evil, to be undertaken only to prevent a greater evil. All creatures long for peace, and even war is waged only for the sake of peace: for victory is nothing but peace with glory. 'Everyone seeks peace while making war, but no one seeks war while making peace' (*DCD* XIX. 10). On the other hand, Augustine is not a pacifist, as some of his Christian predecessors had been, on the basis of the Gospel command to 'turn the other cheek'. Soldiers may take part, indeed are obliged to take part, in wars that are waged by states in self-defence or in order to rectify serious injustice. Augustine does not spell out these conditions in the way that his medieval and early modern successors did in developing the theory of the just war. He is clear, however, that even in a just war at least one side is acting sinfully (*DCD* XIX. 7). And only a state in which justice prevails has the right to order its soldiers to kill. 'Remove justice, and what are kingdoms but criminal gangs writ large'? (*DCD* IV. 4). Nonetheless, he is willing to give historical examples of wars that he considers divinely sanctioned: for instance, the defence of northern Italy against the Ostrogoths, which ended with the spectacular victory of the imperial general Stilicho at Fiesole in 405 (*DCD* V. 23).

What of killing by private citizens, in self-defence or in defence of the life of a third party? Augustine does not seem to have made up his mind whether this was legitimate, and passages in his letters can be quoted in both senses. But on one topic much contested in Hellenistic philosophy Augustine is quite firm: suicide is unlawful. The command 'Thou shalt not kill' applies to oneself as much as to other human beings (*DCD* I. 20).

The issue was topical when Augustine began writing *The City of God* because during the sack of Rome in 410 many Christian men and women killed themselves to avoid rape or enslavement. Augustine maintains that no reason can ever justify suicide. Suicide in the face of material deprivation is a mark of weakness, not greatness of soul. Suicide to avoid dishonour—such as that of the Roman Cato, unwilling to bow to the tyranny of Julius Caesar—brings only greater dishonour (*DCD* I. 23–4). Suicide to escape temptation to sin, though the least reprehensible form of suicide, is nonetheless unworthy of a Christian who trusts in God. Suicide to escape rape—an action which some other Christians, such as Ambrose, regarded as heroic—falls even more firmly under Augustine's condemnation, because to be raped is no sin and should bring no shame on an unconsenting victim (*DCD* I. 19).

Augustine is less forthright in defence of human rights other than the right to life. He asks whether a magistrate does well to torture witnesses in order to extract evidence. He spells out eloquently the evils inherent in the practice: a third-party witness suffers, though not himself a wrongdoer; an innocent accused may plead guilty to avoid torture, and even when the victim of torture is actually guilty, he may lie nonetheless and escape punishment. Overall, the pain of torture is certain while its evidential value is dubious. Nonetheless, Augustine says finally, a wise man cannot refuse to carry out the duties of a magistrate, however unsavoury. He was perhaps unaware that torture had been condemned by a synod of bishops at Rome in 384.

What of slavery? Unlike Aristotle, Augustine does not think that slavery is something natural. It is, he says, the result of sin: and to illustrate this he gives the example of a kind of slavery which Aristotle too regarded as immoral, namely the enslavement of the vanquished by the victors in an unjust war. However, he falls short of an outright condemnation, in this sinful world, of slavery as an institution: he is deterred from doing so by the example of the Old Testament patriarchs, and by Paul's injunctions in the New Testament to slaves to obey their masters. 'Penal slavery is ordained by the same law as enjoins the preservation of the order of nature.' As often when faced with an intractable social or political problem, Augustine takes refuge in an internalization of the issue: it is better to be slave to a good master than to one's own evil lusts, so slaves should make the best of their lot and masters should treat their slaves kindly, punishing them only for their own good (*DCD* XIX. 15–16).

It was in matters of sexual ethics that Augustine's influence on later Christian thinkers was most profound. His teaching on sex and marriage became, with little modification, the standard doctrine of medieval moral philosophers. Among the major philosophers of the Latin Middle Ages, Augustine was the only one to have had sexual experience—if we except Abelard, whose sexual history was fortunately untypical. In modern times Augustine has acquired among non-Christians a reputation as a misogynist with a hatred of sex. Recent scholarship has shown that this reputation needs re-examination.[2]

It is true that Augustine is author of the strict Christian tradition that regards sex as permissible only in marriage, that treats procreation as the principal purpose of marriage, and that sets consequential limits on the types of sexual activity lawful between husband and wife.[3] But Augustine's teaching is much less hostile to sex than that of many of his contemporaries and predecessors. Christians like Ambrose and Jerome thought that marriage was a consequence of the Fall, and that there would have been no sex in the Garden of Eden. Augustine maintained that marriage was part of God's original plan for unfallen man and that Adam and

---

[2] See esp. Peter Brown, *The Body and Society* (New York: Columbia University Press, 1988), 387–427.

[3] Mark D. Jordan, *The Ethics of Sex* (Oxford: Blackwell, 2002), 110, points out that the principal New Testament text on marriage, 1 Cor. 7, makes no link between marital ethics and procreation: marriage is presented as a concession to the strength of sexual desire.

Eve, even had they remained innocent, would have procreated by sexual union (*DCD* XIV. 18). (It is true that such union, on his account, would have lacked all the elements of passion that make sex fun: in his Eden, copulation would have been as clinical as inoculation; *DCD* XIV. 26.) Against ascetics who regarded virginity as the only decent option for a Christian, Augustine wrote a treatise defending marriage as a legitimate and honourable estate, *De Bono Conjugali*, written in 401.

Marriage, he says, is not sinful; it is a genuine good, and not just a lesser evil than fornication. Christians may enter into it in order to beget children and also to enjoy the special companionship that links husband and wife. Marriage must be mono-gamous, and it must be stable; divorce is not permissible and only death can part the couple (*DBC* 3. 3, 5. 5). Since the purpose of procreation is what makes marriage honourable, husband and wife must not take any steps to prevent conception. Husband and wife must honour each other's reasonable requests for sexual inter-course, unless the request is for something unnatural (*DBC* 4. 4, 11. 12). But once the need for procreation has been satisfied, husbands and wives do well to refrain from intercourse and limit themselves to continent companionship (*DBC* 3. 3). Indeed, since there is no longer a need to expand the human race—as there was in the days of the polygamous Hebrew patriarchs—lifelong celibacy, though not obligatory, is a higher state than matrimony (*DBC* 10. 10).

Marriage, for Augustine, is an institution joining unequal partners: the husband is the head of the family, and the wife must obey. He could hardly think otherwise, given the clear teaching of St Paul. He also believed that the male companionship provided by an academic or monastic community was preferable to companion-ship between men and women even in the intimacy of marriage. But in judging sexual morality he does not operate with a double standard biased in favour of the male. Suppose, he says, a man takes a temporary mistress while waiting for an advantageous marriage. Such a man commits adultery, not against the future wife, but against the present partner. The female partner, however, is not guilty of any adultery, and indeed 'she is better than many married mothers if in her sexual relations she did her best to have children but was reluctantly forced into contra-ception' (*DBC* 5. 5). Augustine was also sensitive to female property rights: he cannot think of a more unjust law, he tells us, than the Roman Lex Voconia, which forbade a woman to inherit, even if she was an only daughter (*DCD* III. 21).

Since procreation is the divine purpose for sex, it goes almost without saying that only heterosexual intercourse is permissible. 'Shameful acts against nature, like those of the Sodomites, are to be detested and punished in every place and every time. Even if all peoples should do them, they would still incur the same guilt by divine law, which did not make human beings to use each other in that way' (*Conf.* III. 8. 15). Quite recently, the emperor Theodosius had decreed the public burning of male prostitutes.

The commandment 'Thou shalt not bear false witness against thy neighbour' was often extended in Christian commentary into a more general prohibition, but it was a matter of dispute whether lying was forbidden in all circumstances. Just as

Augustine opposed those Christians who justified suicide to avoid rape, so he took a rigorous line against those who justified lying in a good cause (e.g. to hide the mysteries of the faith from inquisitive pagans). He wrote two treatises on lying, which he defines as 'uttering one thing by words or signs, while having another thing in one's mind' (*DM* 3. 3). He denies that such lying, with intention to deceive, is ever permissible. Naturally he has to deal with cases in which it seems prima facie that a good person might do well to tell a lie. Suppose there is, hidden in your house, an innocent person unjustly condemned. May you lie to protect him? Augustine agrees that you may try to throw the persecutors off the scent, but you may not tell a deliberate lie. 'Since by lying you lose an eternal life, you may not ever lie to save an earthly life' (*DM* 6. 9).

Though all lies are wrong, for Augustine, not all lies are equally wrong. A lie that helps someone else without doing any harm is the most venial, a lie that leads someone into religious error is the most wicked. A false story told to amuse, without any intention to deceive, is not really a lie at all—though it may indicate a regrettable degree of frivolity (*DM* 2. 2, 25).

Abelard's Ethic of Intention

Augustine's moral teaching lays great emphasis on the importance of the motive, or the overarching desire, with which actions are performed. But among Christian moralists the one who went to the greatest length in attaching importance to intention in morals was Abelard. In his *Ethics*, entitled *Know Thyself*, he objected to the common teaching that killing people or committing adultery was wrong. What is wrong, he said, is not the action, but the state of mind in which it is done. 'It is not what is done, but with what mind it is done, that God weighs; the desert and praise of the agent rests not in his action but in his intention' (AE, c. 3).

Abelard distinguishes between 'will' (*voluntas*) and 'intention' (*intentio, consensus*). Will, strictly speaking, is the desire of something for its own sake; and sin lies not in willing but in consenting. There can be sin without will (as when a fugitive kills in self-defence) and bad will without sin (as in lustful desires that one cannot help). If we take 'will' in a broader sense, then we can agree that all sins are voluntary, in the sense that they are not unavoidable and that they are the result of some volition or other—e.g. the fugitive's desire to escape (AE 17). Intention, or consent, appears to be a state of mind that is more related to knowledge than to desire. Thus, Abelard argues that since one can perform a prohibited act innocently—e.g. marry one's sister when unaware that she is one's sister—the evil must be not in the act, but in the intention or consent.

Thus, a bad intention may ruin a good act. A criminal may be hanged justly, but if the judge condemns him not out of a zeal for justice, but out of inveterate hatred, he sins. More controversially, Abelard maintained that a good intention might justify a prohibited action. The Gospel tells us that those who were cured by Jesus disobeyed his command to keep their cures secret. They did well, because their motive in publicizing the miracles was a good one. God himself, when he ordered Abraham to kill Isaac, ordered something which it was bad to do, and ordering an evil deed is itself evil. But God's intention was a good one, to test his faith; and 'this intention of God was right in an act which was not right' (AE 31).

A good intention not carried out may be as praiseworthy as a good action. Two men both resolve to build an almshouse. One succeeds, but the second is robbed of his money before he can carry out his plan. Each is as deserving as the other: otherwise we must say that one man may be more virtuous than another simply because he is richer or luckier (AE 49).

Similarly, bad intentions are as blameworthy as bad actions. Why then punish actions rather than intentions? Abelard was an early proponent of the doctrine of strict liability, the doctrine that *mens rea* is not required for an offence. Human punishment, he says, may be justified where there is no guilt. Suppose a woman, while asleep, turns over and crushes to death the infant lying beside her. There is no sin there, since she did not know what she was doing; but she may justly be punished in order to make others more careful. The reason we punish actions rather than intentions is that human frailty regards a more manifest evil as worse than a hidden one. But at the Last Judgement God will not judge thus.

Does it follow that those who persecute Christians in the belief that they serve God thereby act praiseworthily? Not necessarily, Abelard says, but they are no more guilty than a man who kills a fellow man by mistake for an animal while hunting in a forest. However, in order to have a good intention, it is not sufficient that a man should believe that he is doing well. 'The intention of the persecutors is erroneous, and their eye is not simple.'

Abelard makes no clear distinction between the persecutors' erroneous opinion about the desirability of killing Christians and their virtuous purpose in the killing, namely to serve God. Consequently, it is not clear whether his doctrine of justification by intention means that an erroneous conscience excuses from guilt, or that a good end justifies means known to be evil. Abelard never clearly distinguished between the volitional and the cognitive element in intention.

Abelard's doctrine came close to the slogan of 1960s hippies, 'It doesn't matter what you do as long as you're sincere', and it is not surprising that it was found shocking by his contemporaries, even though he believed that our grasp of natural law set a limit to the possibilities of sincere moral error. The Council of Sens condemned the teaching that those who killed Christ in good faith were free from sin; and also among the condemned propositions was 'A man does not become better or worse on account of the works he does' (DB 380).

Aquinas' Ethical System

Aquinas, like Abelard, attached considerable importance to the role of intention in ethics. However, he located the concept of intention within a much richer account of the nature of human action, in which he drew on, and improved on, the account given by Aristotle in his *Nicomachean Ethics*. Aristotle in describing human action makes use of two key concepts: that of voluntariness and that of purpose. For him, something is voluntary if it is originated by an agent free from compulsion or error; it is a purpose (*prohairesis*) if chosen as part of an overall plan of life. His concept of the voluntary was too broad and his concept of purpose too narrow to demarcate most of the moral choices of everyday life. While retaining and refining Aristotle's concepts, Aquinas introduced the concept of intention to fill the gap between the two of them.

He explains the concept as follows. There are three types of action: those that are ends in themselves, those that are means to ends, and those that we do, perhaps reluctantly, as unavoidable accompaniments of actions of the first two kinds. It is in actions of the middle kind that we exhibit intention: we intend to achieve the end by the means. Actions of the third kind are not intentional, but merely voluntary. Voluntariness, then, is the broadest category; whatever is intentional is voluntary, but not vice versa. Intention itself, while not as broad as voluntariness, is a broader concept than Aristotle's purpose (*ST* 1a 2ae 12).

Human acts, according to Aquinas, may again be divided into three categories, this time in respect of moral evaluation. Some kinds of act are good (e.g. almsgiving), some are bad (e.g. rape), and some are indifferent (e.g. taking a country walk). Each individual action in the concrete will be performed in particular circumstances with a particular end in view. For an individual action to be morally good, it must belong to a class of acts that is not bad, it must take place in appropriate circumstances, and it must be done with a virtuous intention. If any of these elements is missing, it is a bad act. Consequently, a bad intention can spoil a good act (almsgiving out of vainglory), but a good intention cannot redeem a bad act (stealing to give to the poor). We may not do evil that good may come (*ST* 1a 2ae 19–20).

Aquinas agrees with Abelard that the goodness of a good action derives from the good will with which it is performed; but he says that the will can only be good if it is willing an action of a kind reason can approve. We may have a false belief about the goodness or badness of an action; such a belief is called by Aquinas an erroneous conscience. We must follow our conscience, even if erroneous; but though an erroneous conscience always binds us, it does not always excuse us. While an error about a fact (e.g. whether this woman is or is not married to someone else) may, if not the result of negligence, excuse from guilt, an error about divine law (e.g. the belief that adultery is not sinful) does not excuse. Again, against Abelard, Aquinas insists that good will cannot be fully genuine unless it is put into action when opportunity arises. Only involuntary failure will excuse non-execution. Thus Aquinas avoids the paradoxes that brought Abelard's theory of intention into disrepute (*ST* 1a 2ae 19. 5–6).

Aquinas uses his concept of intention when discussing how the morality of an action may be affected by its consequences. For him, foresight is not the same thing as intention: a consequence may be foreseen without being intended. 'A man, crossing a field the more easily to fornicate, may damage what is sown in the field; knowingly, but without a mind to do any damage.' In a case such as this, where it is a bad deed with bad consequences, the distinction is morally unimportant since in each case the wrongdoing is aggravated by the consequences. However, the distinction is important when we are dealing with the bad consequences of otherwise good acts. In discussing the lawfulness of killing in self-defence, Aquinas explains that the act of a person defending himself may have two effects, one the preservation of his own life, the other the death of the attacker. The use of reasonable violence in self-defence is permitted, even if death results as an unintended consequence; but it is never lawful for a private citizen actually to intend to kill (1a 2ae 20. 5).

Among both his admirers and his detractors, Aquinas has a reputation as a proponent of the doctrine of natural law. The reputation is not wholly accurate. Though he was writing within a Judaeo-Christian tradition which gives prominence to divine commandments as setting the standard by which acts are to be judged lawful or sinful, Aquinas' ethical theory gives pride of place not to the biblical concept of law but to the Aristotelian concept of virtue. In the *Prima Secundae* there are twenty questions on virtue to eighteen on law, while the *Secunda Secundae* is structured almost entirely around the virtues, pagan and Christian. But though Aquinas showed comparatively little interest in law as a key to morality, he did give an important place in his moral thinking to the notion of nature.

It has been common for centuries to think of Nature as a single universal force, more or less personified according to mood and context. Such was not Aquinas' notion. As an Aristotelian he starts from the fact that humans, animals, and other living beings reproduce their kind; and the nature of each thing that lives is what makes it belong to a particular natural kind. Generative processes end with the reproduction of a nature, that is to say, the bringing into being of another specimen of the same species. The nature of a thing is the same as its essence, but its essence considered as a source of activity and reproduction.

The reproduction of a nature, which is the result of the process of generation, is also the point and purpose of that process. St Thomas believed that each nature had itself a point no less than the process that reproduced it. This must be so, it might well seem, if reproduction itself were to serve any purpose. Bringing humans into being would have no point unless being a human had some point other than bringing other humans into being. 'The nature of a thing,' St Thomas wrote, 'which is the goal of its production, is itself directed to another goal, which is either an action, or the product of an action' (*ST* 1a 49. 3). Thus it might be that the point of being a glow-worm was to shine, and the point of being a bee was to make honey. Obviously, it is a matter of great importance, if this line of reasoning is correct, to have a correct view of what is the point of being a human.

All creatures, Aquinas teaches, exist for the sake of God; intelligent and non-intelligent creatures alike, in so far as they develop in accordance with their natures, mirror divine goodness. But intelligent creatures mirror God in a special way: they find their fulfilment in the understanding and contemplation of God. Human happiness is not to be found in sensual pleasures, in honour, glory, riches, or worldly power, nor even in the exercise of skill or moral virtue: it is to be found in the knowledge of God, not as he can be known in this life by human conjecture, tradition, or argument, but in the vision of the divine essence which Aquinas believes he can show to be possible in another life by means of supernatural divine enlightenment.

In all this, Aquinas draws heavily on Aristotle's *Ethics*. In the tenth book of that work Aristotle teaches that human happiness is to be found in philosophical contemplation, but he gives inconsistent reasons for doing so. He says that the intellect is what is most human in us, but also that it is superhuman and divine. Aquinas, in 1a 2ae 5. 5, resolves this ambiguity. A full understanding of human nature shows, he maintains, that humans' deepest needs and aspirations cannot be satisfied in the human activities—even the highest philosophical activities—that are natural for a rational animal. Human beings can be perfectly happy only if they can share the superhuman activities of the divine, and for that they need the supernatural assistance of divine grace. Instead of having a natural capacity for supreme happiness, human beings have free will, by which they can turn to God, who alone can make them happy.

The nature and point of each of the virtues is to be seen in the light of this overarching goal of human existence. Because the goal is supernatural we need, besides moral virtues such as fortitude and temperance, and besides intellectual virtues such as wisdom and understanding, the theological virtues of faith, hope, and charity. Only those who share in St Thomas' faith in the beatific vision as the culmination of a virtuous life can enter fully into the moral system that he presents. But thanks largely to the Aristotelian underpinning of his moral thinking, much of his thinking on individual moral topics is highly instructive also for the secular philosopher.

Aquinas seeks to reconcile Aristotelian with biblical ethics in the following manner. For Aristotle it is reason that sets the goal of action, and provides the standard by which actions are to be regarded as virtuous or vicious; in the Bible the standard is set by a code of laws. There is no conflict, Aquinas maintains, because law is a product of reason. Reflection on the essence of human action and choice, as described by Aristotle, leads to the formation of a set of ultimate practical principles to guide the activity of virtue in which human flourishing consists. Among these ultimate principles is the biblical injunction to love one's neighbour as oneself: a principle that Aquinas regarded as the first and common precept of human nature, self-evident to human reason.[4]

Human legislators, the political community or its delegates, use their reason to devise laws for the general good of particular states. But the world as a whole is ruled by the reason of God. The eternal plan of providential government, which exists in God as ruler of the universe, is a law in the true sense. It is a natural law, inborn in all rational creatures in the form of a natural tendency to pursue the behaviour and goals appropriate to them. It is this tendency that becomes articulate in the ultimate principles of practical reason. This natural law is simply the sharing, by rational creatures, in the eternal law of God. It obliges us to love God and to love our neighbour as ourselves. It is by the application of this principle that we reach specific moral rules to govern action in areas such as homicide, sexual relations, and private property.

Aquinas as Moralist

In each of the areas identified above Aquinas laid down norms that are issues of controversy at the present time, and to illustrate his approach to moral issues we may consider examples from each in turn.

On the topic of warfare, Aquinas puts himself the question 'Is soldiering always a sin?' (2a 2ae 40. 1). Following Augustine,[5] Aquinas answers in the negative, but lays down specific conditions for war-making to be lawful (2a 2ae 40. 1). The first is authority: only a prince may lawfully make war: a private citizen should take his grievances to court. Secondly, there must be a just cause: the enemy must be guilty of fault—not necessarily military aggression, but some violation of the rights of one's community or one's allies. Thirdly, the intention of those making war must be right: they must intend to promote good or to avoid evil. This appears to mean that the forceful redress of an injury must not do more harm than leaving the injuries unaddressed. Developed by later thinkers, in particular Grotius, the theory of the just war is still influential in both theoretical and practical international debate.

Aquinas accepted the legitimacy of capital punishment, imposed by lawful authority. This is a teaching that even some of his most devoted followers find difficult to accept, claiming that it is a violation of the principle that one may not

---

[4] All this is very well explained in J. Finnis, *Aquinas: Moral, Political, and Legal Theory* (Oxford: Oxford University Press, 1998).

[5] And also Alexander of Hales, one of the fullest early medieval theorists of the just war. See Barnes, 'The Just War', in *CHLMP* 771–84.

do evil that good may come. But anyone who is not a pacifist must accept that the deliberate taking of human life may sometimes be lawful. If a national community may in a just war lawfully take the life of citizens of other states, it is hard to see why it is absolutely prohibited from taking the life of one of its own citizens.

When we turn to sexual ethics we find that Aquinas' thought is much conditioned by the Aristotelian biology that he accepted. For much of his life he believed that in biological generation the female merely provided nutrition for an active principle provided by the male. Since like begets like, a female is, on this view, an anomalous or defective male. Aquinas combined this theory of the transmission of human nature with the biblical account of the creation of the first pair to provide a basis for the subordination of women in medieval Christian society. The following passage shows what he would have thought of the ordination of women:

St Paul says it is not for women to utter publicly before the whole church: partly because the female sex was made submissive to the male, as Genesis says, and public instruction and persuasion is a task for leaders not subjects; partly lest men's sexual desires be aroused and partly since women generally haven't the fullness of wisdom required for public instruction. The grace of prophecy enlightens the mind, and knows no difference of male or female, as St Paul says; but utterance concerns public instruction of others, and there sex is relevant. Women exercise what wisdom or knowledge they have in private instruction of their children, not in public teaching.

Aquinas is often invoked in contemporary discussions of the morality of contraception and abortion. In fact, he had very little to say on either topic. Contraception is discussed, along with masturbation, in a question in the *Summa contra Gentiles* concerning 'the disordered emission of semen'. Aquinas maintains that this is a crime against humanity, second only to homicide. This claim rests on the belief that only the male provides the active element in conception, so that the sperm has an individual history continuous with the embryo, the fetus, and the infant. In fact, of course, male and female gametes contribute equally to the genetic constitution of the eventual human being. An embryo, unlike the father's sperm or semen, is the same individual organism as an infant at birth. For Aquinas, the emission of semen in circumstances unsuitable for conception was the same kind of thing, on a minor scale of course, as the exposure or starvation of an individual infant. That is why he thought masturbation a poor man's version of homicide.[6]

On the topic of abortion, Aquinas has remarkably little to say directly, mentioning it at most thrice in the vast expanse of his corpus. But the relevance of his teaching to the contemporary debate centres on his teaching about the beginning

---

[6] In *ST* 1a 118 and 119 Aquinas presents a more complicated account of the development of the fetus, according to which the mother originates the vegetative soul, the father originates the sensitive soul, and God creates the intellectual soul. But he does not seem to have applied this schema to reproductive ethics.

of human life. He is not an ally of those at the present time who claim that human life begins at conception. The developing human fetus does not count as a human being until it possesses a human soul, and this does not occur at conception, but after pregnancy is considerably advanced. For Aquinas the first substance independent of the mother is the embryo living a plant-like life with a vegetative soul. That substance disappears and is succeeded by a substance with an animal soul, capable of nutrition and sensation. Only at a later stage is the rational soul infused by God, changing this animate substance into a human being. Aquinas clearly believed that late abortion (even if caused unintentionally) was homicide. A person who strikes a pregnant woman, he says, will not be excused from homicide (1a 2ae 64. 8). But at an earlier stage, abortion, on Aquinas' account, though wrong, is wrong only for the same reason as masturbation and contraception: it is the destruction of an individual that is potentially a human being.

The theory of three successive entities at different stages of pregnancy does not seem entitled to any great respect. It is too closely linked to the idea that only the male is the active cause of the human generative process, and to the theory that the intellectual soul is immaterial and must therefore be divinely infused. The theory obscures the fact that there is an uninterrupted history of development linking conception with the eventual life of an adult. However, there are reasons quite different from Aquinas' for denying that the life of each human individual originates at conception. The line of development from conception to fetal life is not the uninterrupted history *of an individual*. In its early days a single zygote may turn into something that is not a human being at all, or something that is one human being, or something that is two people or more. Fetus, child, and adult have a continuous individual development which gamete and zygote do not have.

If this is correct, the destruction of an embryo at an early stage is not necessarily a form of homicide. It is no easy matter to decide exactly at what point an embryo becomes a human being, and this is not the place to attempt to decide such a difficult issue. But it seems clear that much abortion in practice takes place at a point after this stage has been reached, and therefore involves—as contraception does not—the destruction of an individual human being. Aquinas' superannuated biology is one of the ancestors of the common modern opinion which places contraception and abortion on the same moral plane. This is an error whether it leads to the denunciation of contraception no less than abortion as a serious sin, or whether it leads to the defence of abortion, no less than contraception, as a fundamental right of women.

Though he was a member of an order that held all its property in common, Aquinas did not believe in communism outside religious communities. So far from property being theft, the theft of someone else's property was a serious sin. Moreover, there is nothing wrong with doing business for the sake of profit, provided that one intends to make a good use of the profit obtained (2a 2ae 77. 4). However, Aquinas cannot be regarded as an enthusiastic supporter of capitalism:

the right to acquire and retain private property is, for him, severely limited, and the making of money is subject to strict rules.

First of all, it is sinful to accumulate more property than one needs to support oneself, relatively to one's condition in life and the number of dependants one has. Secondly, if one has money to spare one has a duty—as a matter of natural justice, and not of benevolence—to give alms to those in need. Thirdly, if you fail to relieve the poor, then they may, in urgent need, legitimately take your property without your leave. 'In cases of need, all things are common. So it does not seem to be a sin if someone takes someone else's property, for it has been made common because of the state of need' (2a 2ae 66. 7). Thomas adds a Robin Hood clause: in similar cases, one may take someone else's property to succour an indigent third party (ad 3).

Aquinas was strongly opposed to usury, that is to say, the taking of interest, however small, on money lent. He bases his opposition both on Old Testament texts and on Aristotelian principles. Some things, he says, are consumed when they are used: the use of wine, for instance, is to drink it, and once drunk it no longer exists. Other things can be used without being consumed: one can live in a house without destroying it. If you tried to charge separately for the wine and its use, you would be selling the same thing twice; but you can rent the house out without selling the house itself. But because money is used by being spent, money is like wine, not like a house; if someone gives you back a sum of money you lent him, you cannot charge him for the use he made of it in the meanwhile (2a 2ae 78).

The profits of usury, Aquinas said, must be returned to those who have been wrongly charged interest. The duchess of Brabant asked him whether it would be lawful for her to confiscate from the Jews in her realm the money that they had made usuriously. Certainly, Aquinas replied: but in the style of Portia he added that if she did so, it would be wrong for her, no less than the Jews, to keep such ill-gotten gains. She should try to trace the unfortunate people who had fallen into the hands of moneylenders, and restore to them the interest they had paid (*DRI* 1. 278).

Scotus on Divine Law

Murder, abortion, usury were all, for Aquinas, violations of the natural law of God. But he structured his ethical system not around the concept of law, but around the concept of virtue as the route to self-fulfilment in happiness. It is Duns Scotus who gave the theory of divine law the central place that it was to occupy in the thought of Christian moralists henceforth. Scotus agrees with Aristotle and Aquinas that human beings have a natural tendency to pursue happiness (which he calls the *affectio commodi*); but, in addition, he postulates a natural tendency to pursue justice (an *affectio iustitiae*). The natural appetite for justice is a tendency to obey the moral law no matter what the consequences may be for our own welfare.

Human freedom consists in the power to weigh in the balance the conflicting demands of morality and happiness.[7]

In denying that humans seek happiness in all their choices, Scotus is turning his back not only on Aquinas but on a long tradition of eudaimonistic ethics, with roots going back to Plato and Aristotle. Scotus is surely right to maintain that one's own happiness is not the only possible aim in life. A person may map out his life in the service of someone else's happiness, or for the furtherance of some cause which may perhaps be unlikely to triumph during his lifetime. A daughter may forgo the prospect of marriage and congenial company and a creative career in order to nurse a bedridden parent. It is unconvincing to say that such people are seeking their own happiness in so far as they are doing what they want to do.

In the eudaimonistic tradition freedom is conceived as the ability to choose between different possible means to happiness; and wrongdoing is represented as the outcome of a failure to apprehend the appropriate means. For Scotus, freedom extends not just to the choice of means to a predetermined end, but to a choice between independent and possibly competing ultimate goals. The blame for wrongdoing is placed less on a defective understanding, more on the waywardness of an autonomous will.

The rightness or wrongness of the will's choice is determined by whether it accords or does not accord with the divine law. All medieval thinkers saw wrongdoing as a violation of divine law, but for Scotus the relationship between the morality of an action and the contents of divine commands was much more direct than it was for his predecessors. According to theologians in the eudaimonist tradition, certain actions were wrong because they were in conflict with the necessary conditions for human happiness as truly understood, and it was precisely because they were obstacles to happiness that God had forbidden them. For Scotus, on the other hand, an action could be wrong simply because God had forbidden it, whether or not it had any relevance to the fulfilment or non-fulfilment of human nature.

Just as Scotus' theory extends the degree of choice available to the human will subject to the divine law, so it extends the degree of freedom possessed by God in issuing commands to the human will. Scotus explores this topic in treating of the relation between the natural law and the explicitly formulated commands of the Decalogue (*Ord* 3. d 37). St Thomas had held that all of the Ten Commandments belonged to the natural law: it followed that God could not dispense from them, could not give permission for humans to act against them. Scotus agreed that no exceptions could be permitted to commandments belonging to the natural law; but he disagreed that all ten Commandments formed part of that law.

There are, indeed, some commands that God could not possibly give: he could not, for instance, command anyone to hate him, or blaspheme against him.

---

[7] See R. Cross, *Duns Scotus* (Oxford: Oxford University Press, 1999), 88.

Truths such as 'God must be loved above all things' are necessarily true, prior to any decision of God's will. God cannot dispense from such a law, and laws of this kind are the kernel of morality, the true natural law. In maintaining this, Scotus shows that he did not accept what is sometimes called the divine command theory of morality, according to which the moral value of any action whatever consists in nothing other than its prescription or prohibition by God. But it is only commands that have God himself as their object that strictly belong to the natural law.

Scotus does, indeed, accept the divine command theory for a limited number of cases. Beyond the provisions of the basic natural law, God's freedom to command is absolute. He can dispense from the law against killing human beings: when he ordered Abraham to sacrifice Isaac, he was replacing the original universal prohibition with a new, more specific, rule. Further, God was free, in principle, never to have enacted at all the command 'Thou shalt not kill'. And God can give commands, such as the prohibition on eating the fruit of the tree in Eden, where the action commanded or prohibited has no intrinsic rightness or wrongness. In such cases the moral value of the action does consist in nothing other than its relationship to the content of the divine command.

The laws of the second part of the Decalogue, for Scotus, fall between these arbitrary commands and the commands that are part of the basic natural law. It is true, quite apart from any divine command, that murder is a bad action, but this is a contingent, not a necessary, truth. The principles that find expression in the later Commandments can be said to belong to the law of nature only in an extended sense. In giving these commands, God exhibits justice towards his creatures: but he can override them, when necessary, in the interests of a higher justice—as when he permitted polygamy to the Old Testament patriarchs. Moreover, God is under no necessity to treat his creatures justly at all: the infinite owes no obligation to the finite. The will expressed in his commands is a free will; without any contradiction he could command murder, adultery, theft, and lying (*Oxon.* 4. 4. 6. 1). The only limit on the power to command is that placed by the principle of contradiction itself: even divine commands may not be inconsistent with each other. So the totality of commands in force must make up a coherent system.

Two important consequences follow from Scotus' ethical theory. The first is a limitation on human capacity for moral reasoning; the second is an externalization of the notion of sin. The natural law is the moral law that is capable of being discovered by natural reason: but if those principles that concern human beings' relationships to each other are not part of the natural law, then, however plausibly they can be argued for, we can only be certain of them in virtue of revelation. An act in breach of divine law places one in a state of sin; but this does not, according to Scotus, effect any internal change in the sinner. Guilt is not an intrinsic property of the human offender: it is simply the external fact that God has resolved on punishment. Both of these Scotist theses were to become fundamental issues of controversy at the time of the Reformation.

The Ethics of Ockham

Ockham's ethical theory is very similar to that of Scotus, despite the disagreements between the two philosophers on metaphysical issues. Though his analysis of freedom was different from Scotus', Ockham agrees that freedom is the fundamental feature of human beings, and that the will is independent of reason. 'Every man experiences that however much reason may dictate a thing, his will can either will it or fail to will it or will its opposite' (*OTh*. 9. 88). Even the choice of the ultimate end is free: a man may refuse to make happiness his goal, in the belief that it is a state unattainable by the kind of human beings we find ourselves to be (*OTh*. 1. 443).

Like Scotus, Ockham places law, not virtue, in the centre of ethical theory. He goes further than Scotus, however, in emphasizing the absolute freedom of God in laying down the divine law. Whereas Scotus accepted that some precepts (e.g. the command to love God) were part of a natural law, and derived their force not from the free decision of God but from his very nature, Ockham taught that the moral value of human acts derived entirely from God's sovereign, unfettered, will. God, in his absolute power, could command adultery or theft, and if he did so such acts would not only cease to be sinful but become obligatory (II *Sent*. 15. 353).

Obligation is a central ethical concept for Ockham. Evil is defined as being an action performed under an obligation to do the opposite. Humans are obliged by the divine commands; but God is under no obligation to human beings. God would not be violating any obligation if he were to order a human being to hate God himself. By the very fact that God wills something, it is right for it to be done. He would not be doing anything wrong even if he directly caused such an act of hatred in a person's will. Neither God nor the human person would sin; God because he is not under any obligation, the human because the act would not be a free one and only free actions are blamable (IV *Sent*. 9).

Ockham, like his Aristotelian predecessors, says from time to time that what makes an act virtuous is that it should be in accordance with correct rational judgement and that it should be performed precisely for that reason. Again, he follows tradition in saying that a person must act in accordance with their conscience (i.e. their rational moral judgement) even if it is in error. But these Aristotelian remarks are not in conflict with the fundamentally authoritarian nature of his ethic. If we are to follow reason and conscience, this is because God has commanded us to do so (III *Sent*. 13). Presumably, God in his absolute power could order us to disobey our consciences just as he can order us to hate the divine goodness.

If God's commands are arbitrary, can the content of the divine law be known without revelation? Ockham puts the question whether in moral matters there can be a demonstrative science. In answer he makes a distinction between two kinds of moral teaching. There is positive moral theory, which contains laws, divine and human, which concern actions that are good and evil only because they are commanded or prohibited by the relevant legislator. But there is also another kind of moral theory—the kind that Aristotle talks about—that deals with ethical principles. Positive moral theory, Ockham tells us, is not deductive; but the other kind does allow conclusions to be demonstrated (*OTh.* 9. 176–7).

One might wonder, given Ockham's general theory, whether any specific conclusion could be drawn that went beyond 'Obey God's commands'. But he tells us that there are principles that rule out particular kinds of acts (II. *Sent.* 15. 352). Murder, theft, and adultery, he tells us, are by definition, not to be done. 'Murder' denotes killing, and connotes that the killer is obliged by divine command to do the opposite. This may enable one to conclude that murder is wrong; but it will not enable one to tell, without revelation, whether a particular killing—e.g. the killing of Abel by Cain—was or was not murder.

It turns out, moreover, that for Ockham, the true subject matter of morality are not public actions like murder and adultery, but rather private, interior, acts of willing. No external act can have, in itself, a moral value, because any external act is capable of being performed by a madman, who is incapable of virtuous action. An action carried out in conformity with a virtuous will has no moral value additional to the moral value of the willing. The very same act of walking to church is virtuous if done out of piety, vicious if done for vainglory. A suicide who throws himself off a cliff, but repents while falling, passes from a vicious state to a virtuous one without any change in external behaviour.

We have already met, in Abelard's moral teaching, a similar privileging of interior as against exterior action. What is remarkable in Ockham is the complete severance that is made between the interior and the exterior life. A human's willing to perform an action is an independent action only contingently connected with the actual performance of the action. Of course an external action of mine can conform, or fail to conform, to my will—but so can the actions of causes quite outside my control. My will can just as well 'command' that a candle should burn in church, or that a donkey should shit in church (*OTh.* 9. 102).

9

God

The God of Augustine

In the second book of *On Free Will* Augustine raises the question 'How do we know that we derive our origin from God?' and in answer he develops a structured argument for God's existence. His interlocutor in the dialogue, Evodius, starts from the position of a simple believer who accepts the existence of God as taught in the Bible. Augustine wants to change this position of mere belief to one of knowledge (*DLA* 2. 1. 5). His strategy is to build up a hierarchy of beings of different kinds.

We can divide the things we find in the world into three classes: lifeless things that merely exist, such as stocks and stones, living things that have sensation and not intelligence, such as dumb animals, and things that have existence, life, and intelligence, such as the rational human beings. We share with the animals the five outward senses, and we share with them also an inner sense. By this sense animals are aware of the operation of the other senses and by it they feel pleasure and pain. But the highest thing in us is 'a kind of head or eye of our soul'.

We grade these different faculties in a hierarchy—inner sense is superior to outer senses, reason is superior to inner sense—on the basis that if A makes judgements about B, then A is superior to B. Within us, nothing is superior to reason. But if we find something outside ourselves superior to reason, Augustine asks, shall we call that God? To be God, Evodius replies, it is not enough to be superior to human reason. God is that than which nothing is superior (*DLA* 2. 6. 14).

Among the highest things in the human mind are knowledge of numbers and judgements of value. The truths of arithmetic are unchangeable, unlike fragile human bodies, and they are common to all educated people, unlike the private objects of sensation. Seven and three make ten, for ever and for everyone. Our knowledge of arithmetic is not derived from the experience of counting: on the contrary, we use the rules of addition and subtraction to point out when someone has counted wrong. We are aware of rules that apply throughout the unending series of numbers, a collection more numerous than we could ever encounter in experience (*DLA* 2. 8. 22–4).

Like arithmetical truths, there are ethical truths that are the common property of all humans. Wisdom is knowledge about the supreme good: everyone wishes to be happy, and so everyone wishes to be wise, since that is indispensable for happiness. Though people may disagree about the nature of the supreme good, they all agree on such judgements as that we ought to live justly, that the worse should be subject to the better, and that each man should be given his due (2. 10. 28). These 'rules and guiding lights of virtue', Augustine says, are true and unchangeable and available for the common contemplation of every mind and reason.

What is it that unites arithmetic and wisdom? After all, some mathematicians are very unwise, and some wise men are quite ignorant of mathematics. Augustine's response is surprising.

Far be it from me to suggest that compared with numbers wisdom is inferior. Both are the same thing, but wisdom requires an eye fit to see it. From one fire light and heat are felt as if they were 'consubstantial' so to speak. They cannot be separated one from the other. And yet the heat reaches those things which are brought near to the fire, while the light is diffused far and wide. So the potency of intellect which indwells wisdom causes things nearer to it to be warm, such as rational souls. Things further away, such as bodies, it does not affect with the warmth of wisdom, but it pours over them the light of numbers. (*DLA* 2. 11. 32)

What arithmetic and wisdom have in common is that both are true and unchangeably true and contained in a single unchangeable truth.

This truth is not the property of any human individual: it is shareable by everyone. Now is this truth superior to, or equal to, or inferior to our minds? If it were inferior to our minds, we would pass judgements about it, as we may judge that a wall is not as white as it should be, or that a box is not as square as it should be. If it were equal to our minds, we would likewise pass judgement on it: we say, for instance, that we understand less than we ought. But we do not pass judgement on the rules of virtue or the truths of arithmetic: we say that the eternal *is* superior to the temporal, and that seven and three *are* ten. We do not say these things *ought* to be so. So the immutable truth is not inferior to our minds or equal to them: it is superior to them and sets the standard by which we judge them (*DLA* 2. 12. 34).

So we have found something superior to the human mind and reason. Is this God? Only if there is nothing that is superior to it. If there is anything more excellent than truth, then that is God; if not, then truth itself is God. Whether there is or is not such a higher thing, we must agree that God exists (*DLA* 2. 15. 39). Thus we have turned our initial faith in God into a form of knowledge, however tenuous, of his existence.

Can philosophy tell us more of his nature? For Augustine one of the most important things we can know about God is that he is *simple*. In a passage of *The City of God* he explains what he means by 'simple'.

A nature is called simple when there is nothing that it has that it can lose, and when there is no difference between what it is and what it has. A vessel contains liquid, a body has a colour, the atmosphere has light and heat, a soul has wisdom. The vessel is not the same as the liquid, a body is not the same as its colour, the atmosphere is not the same as its light and heat, the soul is not its wisdom. Such things can lose what they have, and change, gaining different qualities and attributes: the vessel can be emptied of its liquid, the body may lose its colour, the atmosphere become dark and cold, and the soul become foolish. (*DCD* XI. 10)

If a being is simple, then, whatever is true of it at any time is true of it at any time. But for perfect simplicity, to be unchangeable is not enough. A simple being must not only be exempt from change, it must also lack contemporaneous parts. As a young man Augustine had believed that God was corporeal: a boundless ocean, he imagined, completely permeating the created world as if it was a sponge (*Conf.* VII. 5. 7). But anything that is corporeal is extended, having parts that are spatially distinct from each other. The one simple God cannot be corporeal, cannot be extended in space.

We can go further. Something might be immutable and unextended and yet not be simple if it had a set of distinct everlasting attributes. In God, Augustine believed, all the divine attributes are in some way identical with each other and with the divine substance in which they inhere (*DCD* XI. 10).

What then is the divine substance or essence? Augustine seizes on a text of Exodus (3: 14), God's message through Moses, 'I am who am', in order to reconcile Platonic metaphysics with biblical teaching. God is he who is: that is to say, he is supreme essence, he supremely is.

To the creatures he made out of nothing he gave being; but he did not give them supreme being like his own. To some he gave to be to a greater extent, and to others less, and thus he arranged a scale of essences among natures. 'Essence' is derived from the Latin verb 'esse', to be, just as 'sapientia' (wisdom) is the noun from the verb *sapere*. (*DCD* XII. 2)

'Essentia', Augustine tells us, is a new Latin word, recently coined to correspond to the Greek 'ousia'.

God's essence is identical with his attributes: and one of the most important of his attributes is his goodness. Just as God gives being to his creatures, so too he gives them goodness. All that he created is good by nature. Where then does evil come from? In his youth Augustine had subscribed to the Manichaean view that there were two supreme principles controlling the universe, one good and one evil, in conflict with each other. As a Christian he gave up belief in the evil principle, but this did not mean that he believed that the good God was the cause of evil. Evil is only a privation of good, it is not a positive reality and does not need a causal principle. Any evil in creatures is simply a loss of good—of integrity, beauty, health, or virtue (*DCD* XII. 3).

God does not create anything evil, but he does create some good things that are better than other good things, and they remain better than other things even if they are themselves defective. Thus a runaway horse is better than a stationary stone, and a drunkard is better than the fine wine he drinks (*DLA* 3. 2. 15). There is nothing to be regretted in one creature's being less well endowed than another: the variety of endowment adds to the beauty of the universe, and God owes no debt to anyone (*DLA* 3. 15. 45).

But what of the evil of an evil will? As we have seen, when discussing the nature of the mind[1] Augustine believes that an evil human choice has no cause. The freedom of the will is of course a gift of God, and the freedom of the will carries with it the possibility of the misuse of that freedom. But nothing forces or necessitates any individual case of such misuse. That was true at least of human nature as first created by God.

Human freedom operated unhindered before the Fall: that is one reason for the gravity of Adam's sin. But when Adam fell, his sin brought with it not only liability to death, disease, and pain, but in addition massive moral debilitation. We children of Adam inherit not only mortality but also sinfulness. Corrupt humans tainted with original sin have no freedom to live well without help: each temptation, as it comes, we may be free to resist, but our resistance cannot be prolonged from day to day. We need God's grace not only to gain heaven but to avoid a life of continual sin (*DCG* 7).

The grace that enables human beings to avoid sin is allotted to some people rather than others not on the basis of any merit of theirs, whether actual or foreseen. It is awarded simply by the inscrutable good pleasure of God. No one can be saved without being predestined. The choice of those who are to be saved, and implicitly also of those who are to be damned, was made by God long before they had come into existence or done any deeds good or bad.

The relation between divine predestination and human virtue and vice was a topic that occupied Augustine's last years. A British ascetic named Pelagius, who came first to Rome, and then after its sack to Africa, preached a view of human freedom quite in conflict with Augustine's. The sin of Adam, he taught, had not damaged his heirs except by setting them a bad example; human beings, throughout their history, retained full freedom of the will. Death was not a punishment for sin but a natural necessity, and even pagans who had lived virtuously enjoyed a happy afterlife. Christians had received the special grace of baptism, which entitled them to the superior happiness of heaven. Such special graces were allotted by God to those he foresaw would deserve them.

[1] See Ch. 7 above.

Augustine secured the condemnation of Pelagius at a council at Carthage in 418 (DB 101–8) but that was not the end of the matter. Devout ascetics in monasteries in Africa and France complained that if Augustine's account of freedom was correct, then exhortation and rebuke were vain and the whole monastic discipline was pointless. Why should an abbot rebuke an erring monk? If the monk was predestined to be better, then God would make him so; if not, the monk would continue in sin no matter what the abbot said. In response, Augustine insisted that not only the initial call to Christianity, the first stirring of faith, was a matter of sheer grace; so too was the perseverance in virtue of the most devout Christian approaching death (*DCG* 7; *DDP*).

If grace was necessary for salvation, was it also sufficient? If you are offered grace, can you resist it? If so, then there would be some scope for freedom in human destiny. While some would end up in hell because they had never been offered grace, hell would also contain those who had been offered grace and turned it down. In the course of controversy Augustine's position continually hardened, and in the end he denied even this vestige of human choice: grace cannot be declined, cannot be overcome. There are only two classes of people: those who have been given grace and those who have not, the predestined and the reprobate. We can give no reason why any individual falls in one class rather than another.

If we take two babies, equally in the bonds of original sin, and ask why one is taken and the other left; if we take two sinful adults, and ask why one is called and the other not; in each case the judgements of God are inscrutable. If we take two holy men, and ask why the gift of perseverance to the end is given to one and not to the other, the judgements of God are even more inscrutable. (*DDP* 66)

The crabbed crusader of predestination in the monastery at Hippo is very different from the youthful defender of human freedom in the gardens of Cassiciacum. It was the former, and not the latter, whose influence was powerful after his death and cast a shadow over centuries to come.

Boethius on Divine Foreknowledge

The problem that faced Augustine in reconciling human freedom with the power of God can be solved if one is willing to jettison the doctrine of predestination. But for all those who believe that God is omniscient there remains a problem about divine foreknowledge: this concerns not God's *willing* humans to act virtuously and be saved, but simply God's *knowing* what humans will or will not do. This problem was discussed in a clear and energetic fashion in the fifth book of Boethius' *Consolation of Philosophy*.

The book addresses the question: in a world governed by divine providence, can there be any such thing as luck or chance? Lady Philosophy says that if by chance we mean an event produced by random motion without any chain of causes, then there is no such thing as chance. The only kind of chance is that defined by Aristotle as the unexpected effect of coinciding causes (*DCP* 5. 1). In that case, Boethius asks, does the causal network leave any room for free human choice or does the chain of fate bind even the motions of our minds? The difficulty is this. If God foresees all, and cannot be in error, then what he foresees must happen of necessity. For if it is possible for our deeds and desires to turn out in any way other than God has foreseen, then it is possible for God to be in error. Even if in fact all turns out as he foresaw, his foresight can only have been conjecture, not true knowledge.

Boethius admits that knowledge does not, in itself, cause what is known. You may know that I am sitting, but it is my sitting that causes your knowledge, not your knowledge that causes my sitting. But necessity is different from causality; and 'If you know that I am sitting, then I am sitting' is a necessary truth. So, too, 'If God knows that I will sin, I will sin' is a necessary truth. Surely that is enough to destroy our free will, and with it all justification for reward or punishment for human actions. On the other hand, if it is still possible for me not to sin, and God thinks that I will inevitably sin, then he is in error—a blasphemous suggestion!

Lady Philosophy accepts that a genuinely free action cannot be foreseen with certainty. But we can observe, without any room for doubt, something happening in the present. When we watch a charioteer steering his horses round a racetrack, neither our vision nor anything else necessitates his skilful management of his team. God's knowledge of our future actions is like our knowledge of others' present actions: he is outside time, and his seeing is not really a *foreseeing*. 'The same future event, when it is related to divine knowledge, is necessary; but when it is considered in its own nature can be seen to be utterly free and unconditioned . . . God beholds as present those future events that happen because of free will' (*DCP* 5. 6).

There are two kinds of necessity: plain straightforward necessity, as in 'Necessarily all men are mortal', and conditional necessity as in 'Necessarily if you know that I am walking, I am walking'. Conditional necessity does not bring with it plain necessity: we cannot infer 'If you know I am walking, necessarily I am walking'. Accordingly, the future events that God sees as present are conditionally necessary, but they are not necessary in the straightforward sense that matters when we are talking of the freedom of the will (*DCP* 5. 6).

While explaining that God is outside time, Boethius produced a definition of eternity that became canonical. 'Eternity is the whole and perfect possession, all at once, of endless life' (*DCP* 5. 6). We who live in time proceed from the past into the future; we have already lost yesterday and we have not yet reached tomorrow. But

God possesses the whole of his life simultaneously; none of it has flowed into the past and none of it is still waiting in the wings.

Boethius' treatment of freedom, foreknowledge, and eternity became the classical account for much of the Middle Ages. But problems remain with his solution of the dilemma he posed with such unparalleled clarity. Surely, matters really are as God sees them; so if God sees tomorrow's sea-battle as present, then it really is present already. Again, the notion of eternity raises more problems than it solves. If Boethius' imprisonment is simultaneous with God's eternity, and God's eternity is simultaneous with the sack of Troy, does that not mean that Boethius was imprisoned while Troy was burning? We cannot say that the imprisonment is simultaneous with one part of eternity, and the sack with another part, because eternity has no parts but, on the Lady Philosophy's account, happens all at once.[2]

Negative Theology in Eriugena

Scotus Eriugena, two centuries later, returned to the Augustinian problem of predestination,[3] but his principal contribution to philosophical theology lay in the extremely restrictive account which he gives of the use of language about God. God is not in any of Aristotle's categories, so all the things that are can be denied of him—that is, negative ('apophatic') theology. On the other hand, God is the cause of all the things that are, so they can all be affirmed of him: we can say that God is goodness, light, etc.—that is, positive ('cataphatic') theology. But all the terms that we apply to God are applied to him only improperly and metaphorically. This applies just as much to words like 'good' and 'just' as to more obviously metaphorical descriptions of God as a rock or a lion. We can see this when we reflect that such predicates have an opposite, but God has no opposite. Because affirmative theology is merely metaphorical it is not in conflict with negative theology, which is literally true.

According to Eriugena, God is not good but more than good, not wise but more than wise, not eternal but more than eternal. This language, of course, does not really add anything, except a tone of awe, to the denial that any of these predicates are literally true of God. Eriugena even goes as far as to say that God is not God but more than God. So too with the individual persons of the Trinity: the Father is not a Father except metaphorically.

Among the Aristotelian categories that, according to Eriugena, are to be denied of God are those of action and passion. God neither acts nor is acted upon, except metaphorically: strictly he neither moves nor is moved, neither loves nor is loved.

[2] See my *The God of the Philosophers* (Oxford: Clarendon Press, 1979), 38–48.
[3] See above, p. 471.

The Bible tells us that God loves and is loved, but that has to be interpreted in the light of reason. Reason is superior to authority; authority is derived from reason and not vice versa; reason does not require any confirmation from authority. Reason tells us that the Bible is not using nouns and verbs in their proper sense, but using allegories and metaphors to go to meet our childish intelligence. 'Nothing can be said properly about God, since he surpasses every intellect, who is better known by not knowing, of whom ignorance is the true knowledge, who is more truly and faithfully denied in all things than affirmed' (*Periphyseon*, 1).

Our knowledge of God, such as it is, is derived both from the metaphorical statements of theology and from 'theophanies', or manifestations of God to particular persons, such as the visions of the prophets. God's essence is unknown to men and angels: indeed, it is unknown to God himself. Just as I, a human being, know *that* I am, but not *what* I am, so God does not know what he is. If he did, he would be able to define himself; but the infinite cannot be defined. It is no insult to God to say that he does not know what he is; for he is not a *what* (*Periphyseon*, 2).

In describing the relation between God and his creatures Eriugena uses language which is easily interpreted as a form of pantheism, and it was this that led to his condemnation by a Pope three and a half centuries later. God, he says, may be said to be created in creatures, to be made in the things he makes, and to begin to be in the things that begin to be (*Periphyseon*, 1. 12). Just as our intellect creates its own life by engaging in actual thinking, so too God, in giving life to creatures, is making a life for himself. To those who regarded such statements as flatly incompatible with Christian orthodoxy, Eriugena could no doubt have replied that, like all other positive statements about God, they were only metaphors.

Eriugena took his ideas of negative and positive theology from pseudo-Dionysius, but he developed those ideas in a novel and adventurous way. His work reaches a level of agnosticism not to be paralleled among Christian philosophers for centuries to come. His manner of approaching the realm of religious mystery will not be seen again in the history of philosophy until we encounter Nicholas of Cusa in the fifteenth century.

Islamic Arguments for God's Existence

Meanwhile, in the Islamic world philosophers were taking a more robust attitude to natural theology. Eriugena's contemporary al-Kindi was prepared to offer a series of elaborate and systematic proofs for the existence of God, based on establishing the finite nature of the world we live in. In his *First Philosophy*, drawing on some of the arguments of John Philoponus, known to Arabs as Yahya al-Nahwi, al-Kindi proceeds as follows.

Suppose that the physical world were infinite in quantity. If we take out of it a finite quantity, is what is left finite or infinite? If finite, then if we restore what has been taken out, we have only a finite quantity, since the addition of two finite quantities cannot make an infinite one. If infinite, then if we restore what has been taken out, we will have two infinite bodies, one (the original) smaller than the other (the restored whole). But this is absurd. So the universe must be finite in space.

Similar considerations show that the universe is finite in time. Time is quantitative, and an actually infinite quantity cannot exist. If time were infinite, then an infinite number of prior times must have preceded the present moment. But an infinite number cannot be traversed; so if time were infinite we would never have got to the present moment, which is absurd.

If time is finite, then the universe must have had a beginning in time; for the universe cannot exist without time. But if the universe had a beginning, then it must have had a cause other than itself. This cause must be the cause of the multiplicity to be found in the universe, and this al-Kindi calls the True One. This, he tells us is the cause of the beginning of coming to be in the universe, and is the cause of the unity that holds each creature together. 'The True One is therefore the First, the Creator who holds everything he has created, and whatever is freed from his hold and power reverts and perishes.'[4]

Christians as well as Muslims found it convenient that philosophical arguments could be offered for the creation of the world in time, so that the believer did not need to take this simply on faith, on the authority of Genesis or the Quran. The arguments which al-Kindi brought into Islam from Philoponus returned into the Christian world in the high Middle Ages, and their validity, as we shall see, became a matter of debate among the major scholastics.

Not all Muslim philosophers agreed that the world was created in time. Avicenna believed that God created by necessity: he is absolute goodness, and goodness by its nature radiates outwards. But if God is necessarily a creator, then creation must be eternal just as God is eternal. But though the material world is coeternal with God, it is nonetheless caused by God—not directly, but via the successive emanation of intelligences that culminates in the tenth intelligence that is the creator of matter and the giver of forms.[5]

Though the world is eternal, it is still possible to prove the existence of God by a consideration of contingency and necessity. For Avicenna there is a sense in which all things are necessary, since everything is a necessary creation of an eternal God. But there is an important distinction to be made between things that exist necessarily of themselves and those that, considered in themselves, are contingent. Starting with this distinction, Avicenna offers a proof that there must be at least one thing that is necessarily existent of itself.

[4] See William Lane Craig, *The Kalam Cosmological Argument* (London: Macmillan, 1979), 19–36.

[5] See above, p. 428.

Start with any entity you choose—it can be anything in heaven or on earth. If this is necessarily existent of itself, then our thesis is proved. If it is contingently existent of itself, then it is necessarily existent through something else. This second entity is necessarily existent either of itself, or through something else. If through something else, then there is a third entity, and so on. However long the series is, it cannot end with something that is of itself contingent; for that, and thus the whole series, would need a cause to explain its existence. Even if the complete causal series is infinite, it must contain at least one cause that is necessarily existent of itself, because if it contained only contingent causes it would need an external cause and thus not be complete.

To show that a being necessarily existent of itself is God, Avicenna has to prove that such a being (which he henceforth calls, for short, 'necessary being') must possess the defining attributes of divinity. In the seventh section of the first tractate of his *Metaphysics* Avicenna argues that there can be at most one necessary being; in the eighth tractate he develops the other attributes of the unique necessary being. It is perfect, it is pure goodness, it is truth, it is pure intelligence; it is the source of everything else's beauty and splendour (*Metaph.* 8. 368).

The most important feature of the necessary being is that it does not have an essence which is other than its existence.[6] If it did, there would have to be a cause to unite the essence with the existence, and the necessary being would be not necessary but caused. Since it has no essence other than its existence, we can say that it does not have an essence at all, but is pure being. And if it does not have an essence, then it does not belong in any genus: God and creatures have nothing in common and 'being' cannot be applied to necessary and contingent being in the same sense. Since essence and quiddity are the same, the supreme being does not have a quiddity: that is to say, there is no answer to the question 'What is God?' (*Metaph.* 8. 344–7).

Anselm's Proof of God

Avicenna's natural theology was enormously fertile: theories to be found in philosophers of religion during the succeeding ten centuries can often to be shown to be (often unwitting) developments of ideas that are first found in his writings. But one theologian whose ideas bear a remarkable resemblance to his had certainly never read him. This was Anselm, who was born four years before

[6] The Arabic word for existence, 'anniya', is translated into Latin as 'anitas'—it is what answers to the question 'An est' = 'Is there a ...?' just as *quidditas* is what answers to 'Quid est' = 'What is a ...?' 'Anity' has never taken out English citizenship as 'Quiddity' has; if one wanted to coin a word it would have to be 'ifness'—what tells us *if* there is a God.

Avicenna's death, and who died forty years before Avicenna's works were translated into Latin.

On the face of it, Avicenna's proof of the existence of a necessary being, and Anselm's 'ontological' argument for the existence of God, are very different from each other. But from a philosophical point of view they have a common structure: that is to say, they operate by straddling between the world we live in and some other kind of world. Avicenna argues from a consideration of possible worlds and argues that God must exist in the actual world; Anselm starts from a consideration of imaginary worlds and argues that God must exist in the real world. Both of them assume that an entity can be identified as one and the same entity whether or not it actually exists: they believe in what has been called, centuries later, transworld identity. Both of them, therefore, violate the principle that there is no individuation without actualization.

The ontological argument is thus stated by Anselm:

We believe that thou art something than which nothing greater can be conceived. Suppose there is no such nature, according to what the fool says in his heart *There is no God* (Ps. 14. 1). But at any rate this very fool, when he hears what I am saying—something than which nothing greater can be conceived—understands what he hears. What he understands is in his understanding, even if he does not understand that it exists. For, it is one thing for an object to be in the understanding, and another to understand that that object exists . . . Even the fool, then, is bound to agree that there exists, if only in the understanding, something than which nothing greater can be conceived; because he hears this and understands it, and whatever is understood is in the understanding. But for sure, that than which nothing greater can be conceived cannot exist in the understanding alone. For suppose it exists in the understanding alone: then it can be thought to exist in reality, which is greater. Therefore, if that than which nothing greater can be conceived exists in the understanding alone, that very thing than which nothing greater can be conceived is a thing than which something greater can be conceived. But this is impossible. Therefore it is beyond doubt that there exists, both in the understanding and in reality, a being than which nothing greater can be conceived. (*Proslogion*, c. 2)

In presenting this argument Anselm says that he prefers it to the arguments he put forward earlier in his *Monologion* because it is much more immediate. His earlier argument—to the effect that beings dependent on other beings must depend ultimately on a single independent being—bore a certain resemblance to Avicenna's argument from contingency and necessity. But the argument of the *Proslogion* marks an advance on Avicenna's natural theology. Whereas Avicenna said that God's *essence* entailed his existence, Anselm argues that the very *concept* of God makes manifest that he exists. An opponent of Avicenna can deny the reality of both God and God's essence; but someone who denies the existence of Anselm's God seems clearly enmeshed in confusion. If he does not have the concept of God, then he does not know what he is denying; if he has the concept of God, then he is contradicting himself.

From Anselm's day to the present time, his readers have debated whether the *Proslogion* argument is valid; and highly intelligent philosophers have found it difficult to make up their mind. Bertrand Russell tells us in his autobiography that as a young man a sudden conviction of the validity of the ontological argument struck him with such force that he nearly fell off the bicycle he was riding at the time. Later, Russell would quote the refutation of the ontological argument as one of the few incontrovertible instances of progress in philosophy. 'This [argument] was invented by Anselm, rejected by Thomas Aquinas, accepted by Descartes, refuted by Kant, and reinstated by Hegel. I think it may be said quite decisively that, as a result of analysis of the concept "existence", modern logic has proved this argument invalid.'[7] But the argument was not as definitively settled as Russell thought. When a later generation of logicians developed the modal logic of possible worlds, theistic philosophers made use of this logic to resurrect the ontological argument.[8]

Criticism of Anselm's proof began in his lifetime. A monk from a neighbouring monastery, Gaunilo by name, said that if the argument was sound one could prove by the same route that the most fabulously beautiful island must exist, since otherwise one would be able to imagine one more fabulously beautiful. Anselm answered that the cases were different. The most beautiful imaginable island can be conceived not to exist, since there is no contradiction in supposing it to go out of existence. But God cannot in that way be conceived not to exist: anything, however grand and sublime, that passed out of existence would not be God.

The weak element in Anselm's argument is the one that seems most innocuous: his definition of God. How does he know that 'something than which no greater can be conceived' expresses a coherent notion? May the expression not be as misbegotten as 'a natural number than which no greater can be found'? Of course we understand each of the words that goes into his definition, and there seems nothing wrong with its syntax. But that is not enough to ensure that the description expresses an intelligible thought. Philosophers in the twentieth century have discussed the expression 'the least natural number not nameable in fewer than twenty-two syllables'. This sounds like a readily intelligible designation of a number—until the paradox dawns on us that the expression itself names the number in twenty-one syllables.

Anselm himself seems to have sensed a problem here. He is at pains to point out that his definition does not imply that God is the greatest conceivable thing. Indeed, God is *not* conceivable: he is greater than anything that can be conceived. So far, so good: there is nothing contradictory in saying that than which no greater can be conceived is itself too great for conception. A Boeing 747 is

[7] B. Russell, *History of Western Philosophy* (London: Allen & Unwin, 1961), 752.
[8] See A. Plantinga, *The Nature of Necessity* (Oxford: Oxford University Press, 1974).

something than which nothing larger can fit into my garage. That does not mean that a Boeing 747 will fit into my garage—it is far too large to do so.

The real problem for Anselm is in explaining how something that cannot be conceived can be in the understanding at all. In response to this difficulty, he distinguishes, in chapter 4 of the *Proslogion*, different ways in which we can think of, or conceive, a thing. We think of a thing in one way, he says, when we think of an expression signifying it; we think of it in a different way when we understand what the thing really is in itself. The fool, he implies, is only thinking of the words; the believer is thinking of God in himself. But this is not his last word, because he goes on to say that not only the fool, but every human being, fails to understand the reality that lies behind the words 'that than which nothing greater can be thought'.

Anselm's last word on this topic comes in the ninth chapter of the reply that he wrote to Gaunilo's objection:

Even if it were true that that than which no greater can be conceived cannot itself be conceived or understood, it would not follow that it would be false that 'that than which no greater can be thought' could be thought and understood. Nothing prevents something being called ineffable, even though that which is ineffable cannot itself be said; and likewise the unthinkable can be thought, even though what is rightly called unthinkable cannot be thought. So, when 'that than which no greater can be conceived' is spoken of, there is no doubt that what is heard can be conceived and understood, even though the thing itself, than which no greater can be conceived, cannot itself be conceived or understood.

Subtle as this defence is, it is in fact tantamount to surrender. The fundamental premiss of the ontological argument was that God himself existed in the fool's understanding. But if, as we now learn, all that is in the understanding of the fool (or indeed of any of us) is a set of words, then the argument cannot get started.

Omnipotence in Damiani and Abelard

A topic that exercised philosophers and theologians in the eleventh and twelfth centuries was the nature of divine omnipotence. At first, it seems easy enough to define what it means to say that God is omnipotent: it means that he can do everything. But difficulties quickly crowd in. Can he sin? Can he make contradictories true together? Can he undo the past? The discussion ranged between extremes. Peter Damiani in the eleventh century extended omnipotence as broadly as possible; Abelard in the twelfth defined it very narrowly.

St Jerome once wrote to the nun Eustochium, 'God who can do everything cannot restore a virgin after she has fallen.' In his treatise *On Divine Omnipotence*

Damiani objects to this. In a discussion over dinner, he tells us, his friend Desiderio of Cassino had defended Jerome, saying that the only reason God could not restore virgins was that he did not want to. This, Damiani says, will not do. 'If God cannot do any of the things that he does not want to do, since he never does anything except what he wants to do, it follows that he cannot do anything at all except what he does. As a result we shall have to say frankly that God is not making it rain today because he cannot.' God cannot do bad things, like lying; but making a virgin out of a non-virgin is not a bad thing, so there is no reason why God cannot do it.

Damiani was taken by many to be arguing that God could change the past, to bring about (for instance) that Rome had never been built. This, it was objected, was tantamount to attributing to God the ability to make contradictories true together: Rome was built, and Rome was not built. It is possible, however, that in attributing to God the power to restore a virgin what Damiani had in mind was a physical operation rather than any genuine undoing of the past. The reason why God does not restore the marks of virginity to those who have lost them, he says, is to deter lecherous young men and women by making their sins easy to detect. He rejects the idea that God's power extends to contradiction. 'Nothing can both be and not be; but what is not in the nature of things is undoubtedly nothing: you are a hard master, trying to make God bring about what is not his, namely nothing.' But though God cannot change the past, he can bring about the past. He cannot change the present or the future either: what is, is, and what will be, will be. That does not prevent many things from being contingent, such as that the weather today will be fine or rainy (PL 145, 595 ff.).

Abelard pursued the topic further. He raised the question whether God can make more things, or better things, than the things he has made, and whether he can refrain from acting as he does. The question, he said, seems difficult to answer yes or no. If God can make more and better things than he has, is it not mean of him not to do so? After all, it costs him no effort. Whatever he does, or refrains from doing, is done or left undone for the best possible reasons, however hidden from us these may be. So it seems that God cannot act except in the way he has in fact acted. On the other hand, if we take any sinner on his way to damnation, it is clear that he could be better than he is; for if not, he is not to be blamed, still less to be damned, for his sins. But if he could be better, then God could make him better; so is something that God could make better than he has (*Theologia Scholarium*, 516).

Abelard opts for the first horn of the dilemma. Suppose it is now not raining: this must be because God so wills. That must mean that now is not a good time for rain. So if we say that God could now make it rain, we are attributing to God the power to do something foolish. Whatever God wants to do, he can, but if he doesn't want to, then he can't. It is true that we poor creatures can act otherwise than we do; but this is not something to be proud of, it is a mark of our infirmity, like our ability to walk, eat, and sin. We would be better off without the ability to do what we ought not to do.

In answer to the argument that sinners must be capable of salvation if they are to be justly punished, Abelard rejects the step from 'This sinner can be saved by God' to 'God can save this sinner'. The underlying logical principle—that 'p if and only if q' entails 'possibly p if and only if possibly q'—is invalid, he claims, and encounters many counter-examples. A sound is heard if and only if somebody hears it; but a sound may be audible without there being anyone able to hear it. One might object that God would deserve no gratitude from men if he cannot do otherwise than he does. But Abelard has an answer. God is not acting under compulsion: his will is identical with the goodness that necessitates him to act as he does.

Abelard's discussion—here only briefly summarized—is a remarkable example of dialectical brilliance, introducing or reinventing a number of distinctions of importance in many contexts of modal logic. However, it can hardly be said to amount to a convincing analysis or defence of the concept of omnipotence, and it certainly did not satisfy his contemporaries, in particular St Bernard. One of the propositions condemned at Sens ran: God can act and refrain from acting only in the manner and at the time that he actually does act and refrain from acting, and in no other way (DB 374).

Grosseteste on Omniscience

In the thirteenth century attention shifted from the problems of divine omnipotence to those of divine omniscience. Robert Grosseteste wrote a short but subtle tract on the freedom of the will, *De Libero Arbitrio*, which begins by setting out the following problem. Consider the argument 'Whatever is known by God either is or was or will be. A (some future contingent) is known by God. Therefore A is or was or will be. But it is not and it was not, therefore it will be.' Both premisses are necessary; therefore the conclusion is necessary, since what follows from necessary premisses is itself necessary. So A itself must be necessary, and there is no real contingency in the world.

How are we to deal with this argument? There is no doubt, Grosseteste says, that the major premiss is necessary. But is the minor a necessary truth? Some have argued that it is false on the ground that God knows only universals. But this is impious. Others have argued that it is false because knowledge is only of what is, but future contingents are not there to be known. But this would make

God's knowledge subject to change: there will be things that he does not know now but will know later.

Shall we say, then, that the minor is true but contingent? If so, then there will be a case where God knows that p, but can fail to know that p. But once again, if God were able to pass from a state of knowing that p to not knowing that p, then his knowledge would be subject to variation. One might argue that it is indeed variable, in the following way: 'God knows that I will sit. Once I have sat he will no longer know that I sit, but that I have sat. So he now knows something that he will later not know' (*De Lib. Arb.* 160).

Grosseteste dismisses this sophism. It does not show that God's knowledge varies in relation to the essences of things themselves; it shows only the vicissitudes of human tenses. We must say that whatever God now knows he cannot later not know, and this is so no matter whether the object of his knowledge is now in existence or not. Neither 'Antichrist will come' nor 'God knows that antichrist will come' can change from true to false. Suppose 'Antichrist will come' now changed from being true to being false. If it is now false, it must always have been false, which conflicts with the hypothesis that it has changed. Hence it cannot change in any way other than by its coming true; and the same applies to 'God knows that antichrist will come' (*De Lib. Arb.* 165).

Considering the same question, whether God always knows what he ever knows, Peter Lombard in his *Sentences* gave a similar answer. The prophets who foretold that Christ was to be born, and the Christians who now celebrate the fact that Christ has been born, he says, are dealing with the same truth.

What was then future is now past, so the words used to designate it need to be changed, just as at different times, when speaking of one and the same day, we designate it when it is still in the future as 'tomorrow', and when it is present as 'today', and when it is past as 'yesterday'...As Augustine says, the times have varied and so the words have been changed, but not our faith. (I *Sent.* 41. 3)

This, however, leaves Grosseteste's initial problem unresolved. In ancient Israel, for instance, someone might argue 'Isaiah has foreseen the captivity of the Jews. So he cannot not have foreseen the captivity of the Jews. So the captivity of the Jews cannot not take place.' Must we say therefore either that everything happens of necessity, or that what is necessarily entailed by necessary truths is itself merely contingent?

The solution, for Grosseteste, lies in distinguishing between two kinds of necessity. It is strongly necessary that p if it is not possible that it should ever have been the case that not-p. It is weakly necessary that p if it is not possible that it should henceforth become the case that not-p. In our argument, the minor and the conclusion are weakly necessary, but not strongly necessary. Weak necessity is compatible with freedom, so the argument does not destroy free will. On the other hand, we preserve the principle that what follows from what is necessary is itself necessary, but necessary only in the same sense as its premisses are (*De Lib. Arb.* 168).

Aquinas on God's Eternal Knowledge and Power

Grosseteste's solution, subtle though it is, did not satisfy later medieval thinkers. Thomas Aquinas rejected the view, common to Grosseteste and Lombard, that 'Christ will be born' and 'Christ has been born' were one and the same proposition. He describes the supporters of this view as 'Ancient nominalists'.

The ancient nominalists said that 'Christ is born', 'Christ will be born' and 'Christ has been born' were one and the same proposition (*enuntiabile*) because the same reality is signified by all three, namely, the birth of Christ. They deduced from this that God now knows whatever he has known, because he now knows Christ born, which has the same signification as 'Christ will be born'. But this view is false, for two reasons. First of all, if the parts of speech in a sentence differ, then the proposition differs. Second, it would follow that any proposition that was once true would be forever true, which goes against Aristotle's dictum that the very same sentence 'Socrates is sitting' is true when he sits and false when he gets up. (*ST* 1a 14. 15)

So if we take the object of God's knowledge to be propositional, it is not true that whatever God once knew he now knows. But this does not mean that God's knowledge is fickle: it simply means that his knowledge is not exercised through propositions in the way that our knowledge is.

Aquinas' own solution to the problem of reconciling divine foreknowledge with contingency is presented in two stages. The first stage, which has been common currency since Boethius, appeals to two different ways in which modal propositions can be analysed.[9] The proposition 'Whatever is known by God is necessarily true' is ambiguous: it may mean (A) or (B):

(A) 'Whatever is known by God is true' is a necessary truth.
(B) Whatever is known by God is a necessary truth.

(A), in Aquinas' terminology, is a proposition *de dicto*: it takes the original statement as a meta-statement about the status of the proposition in quotation marks. (B), on the other hand, is a proposition *de re*, a first-order statement. According to Aquinas (A) is true and (B) is false; but only (B) is incompatible with God's knowing contingent truths.

So far, so good. But Aquinas realizes that he faces a more serious difficulty in reconciling divine foreknowledge with contingency in the world. In any true conditional proposition, if the antecedent is necessarily true, then the consequent

[9] See on Abelard, p. 353 above.

is also necessarily true. 'If it has come to God's knowledge that such and such a thing will happen, then such and such a thing will happen' is a necessary truth. The antecedent, if true, is necessarily true, for it is in the past tense, and what is past cannot be changed. Therefore, the consequent is also a necessary truth; so the future thing, whatever it is, will happen of necessity.

Aquinas' solution to this difficulty depends on the thesis that God is outside time: his life is measured not by time, but by eternity. Eternity, which has no parts, overlaps the whole of time; consequently, the things that happen at different times are all present together to God. An event is known *as future* only when there is a relation of future to past between the knowledge of the knower and the happening of the event. But the relation between God's knowledge and any event in time is always one of simultaneity. A contingent event, as it comes to God's knowledge, is not future but present; and as present it is necessary; for what is the case is the case and is beyond anyone's power to alter (*ST* 1a 14. 13).

Aquinas' solution is essentially the same as Boethius', and he uses the same illustration to explain how God's knowledge is above time. 'A man who is walking along a road cannot see those who are coming after him; but a man who looks down from a hill upon the whole length of the road can see at the same time all those who are travelling along it.' Aquinas' solution is open to the same objection as Boethius': the notion of eternity as simultaneous with every point in time collapses temporal distinctions, on earth as well as in heaven, and makes time unreal. Aquinas cannot be said to have succeeded in reconciling contingency, and human freedom in particular, with divine omniscience.

Aquinas was more successful in defending the coherence of the notion of a different divine attribute, omnipotence. His first attempt at a definition is to say that God is omnipotent because he can do everything that is logically possible. This will not do, because there are many counter-examples that Aquinas himself would have accepted. It is logically possible that Troy did not fall, but Aquinas (unlike Grosseteste) did not think that there was any sense in which God could change the past. In fact, Aquinas preferred the formulation 'God's power is infinite' to the formulation 'God is omnipotent'. 'God possesses every logically possible power' is more coherent than the earlier formulation, but it is still only an approximation to a correct definition, because some logically possible powers—such as the power to weaken, sicken, and die—clash with other divine attributes.

Can God do evil? Can God do better than he does? Aquinas answers that God can only do what is fitting and just to do; but because of the condemnation of Abelard, he has to accept that God can do other than he does. He explains how the two propositions are to be reconciled.

The words 'fitting and just' can be understood in two senses. In the first sense 'fitting and just' is taken in primary conjunction with the verb 'is', and is thus restricted in reference to what is the case at present, and is assigned to God's power in this restricted sense. So restricted, the proposition is false: for its sense is this: 'God can only do what is fitting and just as things are'. But if 'fitting and just' is taken in primary conjunction with the verb 'can', which has an amplificatory force, and only subsequently in conjunction with the verb 'is', then the reference will be to a non-specific present, and the proposition will be true, understood in this sense: 'God can only do what, if He did it, would be fitting and just'. (1a 25. 5. 2)

If we prefer the idiom of possible worlds to the idiom of powers, we could make Aquinas' point as follows. In every possible world, what God does is fitting and just; it does not follow, nor is it true, that whatever God does is something that is fitting and just in every possible world.

Could God have made the world better? He could not have made it by any better method than he did; he made it in the wisest and best possible way. Could he have made men better? He could not have made human nature better than it is; creatures better by nature than we are would not be humans at all. But of any individual human, it is true that God could have made him better. And given any actual creature, however exalted, it is within God's power to make something better. There is no such thing as the best of all possible creatures, let alone the best of all possible worlds.

Aquinas' Proofs of God's Existence

In philosophical theology Aquinas is most often remembered not for his treatment of divine attributes such as omniscience and omnipotence, but for his endeavour to establish, by purely philosophical methods, the actual existence of God. Proofs of divine existence are to be met with in many places in his works: in the *De Potentia*, for instance, he takes, as the starting point of his proof, the taste of pepper and ginger. Wherever, he says, causes whose proper effects are diverse produce also a common effect, the additional common effect must be produced in virtue of some superior cause of which it is the proper effect. For example, pepper and ginger, besides producing their own proper effects, have it in common that they produce heat: they do this in virtue of the causality of fire, of which heat is the proper effect.

All created causes, while having their own proper effects that distinguish them one from another, also share in a single common effect which is being. Heat causes things to be hot, and a builder causes there to be a house. They have in common therefore that they cause being, and differ in that fire causes fire and a builder causes a house. There must, therefore, be some superior cause whose proper effect is being and in virtue of which everything else causes being. And this cause is God. (*DP* 7. 2c)

Better known are the Five Ways which are placed near the beginning of the *Summa Theologiae*: (1) motion in the world is only explicable if there is a first motionless mover; (2) the series of efficient causes in the world must lead to an uncaused cause; (3) contingent and corruptible beings must depend on an independent and incorruptible being; (4) the varying degrees of reality and goodness in the world must be approximations to a subsistent maximum of reality and goodness; (5) the ordinary teleology of non-conscious agents in the universe entails the existence of an intelligent universal orderer.[10]

None of the Five Ways is successful as a proof of God's existence: each one contains either a fallacy, or a premiss that is false or disputable. The first way depends on the premiss that whatever is in motion is moved by something else: a principle universally rejected since Newton. The series mentioned in the second way is not a series of causes through time (which Aquinas himself admitted could reach backwards for ever), but a series of simultaneous causes, like a man moving a stone by moving a crowbar; there is no reason why the first cause in such a series should be God rather than an ordinary human being. The third way contains a fallacious inference from 'Every thing has some time at which it does not exist' to 'There is some time at which nothing exists'. The fourth way depends on a Platonic, and ultimately incoherent, notion of Being. The fifth way is much the most persuasive of the arguments, but its key premiss, 'Things that lack awareness do not tend towards a goal unless directed by something with awareness and intelligence, like an arrow by an archer', needs, since Darwin, more supporting argument than we are given.

Many attempts have been made, and no doubt will be made, to restate the Five Ways in a manner that eliminates false premisses and fallacious reasoning. But one of the most promising recent attempts to reinstate Aquinas' proofs of God's existence takes its start not from the *Summa Theologiae* but from the *Summa contra Gentiles*.[11]

The argument runs thus. Every existing thing has a reason for its existence, either in the necessity of its own nature, or in the causal efficacy of some other beings. We would never, in the case of an ordinary existent, tolerate a blithe announcement that there was simply no reason for its existence; and it is irrational to abandon this principle when the existing thing in question is all-pervasive, like the universe.

Suppose that A is an existing natural thing, a member of a (perhaps beginningless) series of causes and effects that in its own nature is disposed indifferently to either existence or non-existence. The reason for A's existing must be in the causal efficacy of other beings. However many beings may be contributing to A's present existence, they could not be the reason for it if there were not some first cause at

---

[10] For a detailed treatment of the Five Ways, see my book *The Five Ways* (London: Routledge, 1969).

[11] See Norman Kretzmann, *The Metaphysics of Creation* (Oxford: Clarendon Press, 1999), 84–138.

the head of the series—something such that everything other than it must be traced back to it as the cause of its being.

Persuasive as it is, this argument contains a key weakness. What is meant by saying that A is 'disposed indifferently to either existence or non-existence'? If it means 'disposed indifferently to going on existing or not', then the contingent beings of the everyday world, from which the argument starts, do not fit the bill. Contingent things aren't of their nature equally disposed to exist or not: on the contrary, most things naturally tend to remain in existence. On the other hand, if it means 'disposed indifferently to come into existence or not', then we lapse into absurdity: before A exists there isn't any such thing as a non-existing A to have, or to lack, a tendency to come into existence.

Duns Scotus' Metaphysical Proof of an Infinite Being

Flaws in Aquinas' proofs of God's existence were pointed out very shortly after his death. Among his critics was Duns Scotus, who offered his own proofs in their place. The one closest to the argument of the *Summa contra Gentiles* makes use of the concept of causality to prove the existence of a first cause. Suppose that we have something capable of being brought into existence. What could bring it into existence? It must be something, because nothing cannot cause anything. It must be something other than itself, for nothing can cause itself. Let us call that something else A. Is A itself caused? If not, it is a first cause, which is what we were looking for. If it is caused, let its cause be B. We can repeat the same argument with B. Then either we go on for ever, which is impossible, or we reach an absolute first cause.

Scotus, like Aquinas, makes a distinction between two kinds of causal series, one of which he calls 'essentially ordered', and the other 'accidentally ordered'. He does not deny the possibility of an unending regress of accidentally ordered causes, such as the series of human beings, each begotten by an earlier human. Such a series is only accidentally ordered. A father may be the cause of his son, but he is not the cause of his son's begetting his grandson. In an essentially ordered series, A not only causes B, which is the cause of C, but actually causes B to cause C. It is only in the case of essentially ordered series—e.g. a gardener moving earth by moving a spade—that an infinite regress is ruled out. An accidentally ordered series is, as it were, a horizontal series of causes; an essentially ordered series is a vertical hierarchy; and Scotus tells us, 'infinity is impossible in the ascending order' (*DPP* 4, p. 22).

Even after the two kinds of series have been distinguished, there seem several weaknesses in Scotus' argument, considered as a proof of the existence of God. In the first place, it seems, like the proof of the *Summa contra Gentiles* on one interpretation, to assume that it is sensible to talk of something non-existing as having, or lacking, the power of coming into existence.[12] In the second place, it is not clear why instead of a single infinite first cause the argument does not lead to a number of finite first causes.

Scotus in fact admits that he has not produced a proof of God; but the reason he gives is not either of the above. Unlike Aquinas, who took as his starting point the actual existence of causal sequences in the world, Scotus began simply with the mere possibility of causation. He did so deliberately, because he preferred to base his proof not on contingent facts of nature, but on purely abstract possibilities. If you start from mere physics, he believed, you will never get beyond the finite cosmos.

But the consequence of this is that the argument, up to this point, has proved only the possibility of a first cause: we still need to prove that it actually exists. Scotus in fact goes one better and offers to prove that it *must* exist. A first cause, by definition, cannot be brought into existence by anything else; so either it just exists or it does not. If it does not exist, why does it not? If its existence is possible at all, there is nothing that could cause its non-existence. But we have shown that it is possible; therefore it must exist. Moreover, it must be infinite; because there cannot be anything that could limit its power. Scotus accepts that an infinite being is possible only if there is no incoherence in the notion of such an entity. It is a weakness, he thinks, in Anselm's argument that he does not show that 'that than which no greater can be thought' is a coherent concept. But if there were any incoherence between the notions of being and infinity, Scotus claims, it would long ago have been detected. The ear can quickly detect a discord, and the intellect even more easily detects incompatibilities (*Ord.* 4. 162–3).

Even if we concede to Scotus that the notion of God is coherent, his argument seems to fail, by trading on different senses of 'possible': logical possibility, epistemic possibility, and real possibility. From the mere logical possibility of God's existence, nothing follows about whether he actually exists. An agnostic may admit that perhaps, for all we know, there is a God: that is what is meant by 'epistemic possibility'. But from logical possibility and epistemic possibility, nothing follows about real possibility, still less about actuality. 'It is possible that there is a God' is not the same as 'It is possible for God to come into being'.[13] Since the concept of godhead includes everlasting existence, nothing has the power to bring any god into existence. If God exists, he must always have existed. Nor does anything have the power to prevent a god from existing, or to terminate the existence of a god. Such powers are all conceptually impossible, because of the nature of the concept *God*. But the absence of such powers shows nothing at all about whether that concept is or is not instantiated.

---

[12] See p. 411 above on objective possibility.

[13] The difference between the two statements is much more obvious in English than in the medieval Latin equivalent.

For Scotus, the most important element in the concept of God is infinity. The notion of infinity is simpler, more basic, than other concepts such as goodness: it is constitutive of divine being, not just an attribute of divinity. Infinity is the defining characteristic of all the divine attributes: divine goodness is infinite goodness, divine truth is infinite truth, and so on. Each divine perfection 'has its formal perfection from the infinity of the essence as its root and foundation' (*Oxon.* 4. 3. 1. 32). Scotus proves the existence of God by proving the existence of an infinite first principle; only after establishing the infinity of God does he proceed to derive other divine attributes such as that of uniqueness and simplicity.

Scotus did not believe that all the divine attributes could be proved by natural reason. Reason could show that God was infinite, unique, simple, excellent, and perfect. Reason could not, however, show that God was omnipotent, because revelation had shown that God had the power to do things that reason could never have guessed at (e.g. beget a son). Reason could, however, show that God had the power to create a world out of nothing, and that in so creating he enjoyed absolute freedom.

The infinite God, reflecting on his own essence, sees it as capable of being reproduced or imitated in various possible partial ways: it is this that, before all creation, produces the essences of things, existing in the form of divine ideas. This reflection is an exercise of the divine intellect; it is not a free action of the divine will.

The divine intellect, as, in some way, that is, logically prior to the act of the divine will, produces those objects in their intelligible being and so in respect of them it seems to be a merely natural cause, since God is not a free cause in respect of anything but that which presupposes in some way his will or an act of his will. (*Ord* 1. 163)

The essences in the divine mind, as Scotus conceives them, are in themselves neither single nor multiple, neither universal nor particular. They resemble—and not by accident—Avicenna's *horseness*, which was not identical either with any of the many individual horses, nor with the universal concept of horse in the human mind. By a sovereign and unaccountable act of will, God decrees that some of these essences should be instantiated; and thus the world is created. The decree of his will is eternal, unchangeable; but the execution of the decree takes place in time (*Ord.* 1. 566). We cannot look for any reason for God's creative decree: he does not create for the sake of any good, since all good in creatures is the consequence of his creation.

Scotus, Ockham, and Valla on Divine Foreknowledge

God's knowledge of what is possible, as we have seen, precedes the act of will by which he brings chosen possible entities into existence; but his knowledge of what is actual depends solely on his knowledge of his own will. Scotus rejects Aquinas' view that God is omniscient because he sees the whole of time as present to him all at once. Anything that is present to God, Scotus argues, cannot be genuinely past or future; the way things appear to God is the way they really are. For Scotus, God knows what has been the case, what is the case, and what will be the case, because he is aware of his own decree determining what has been, what is, and what will be. It may well be thought that such an explanation of divine omniscience, and in particular of divine foreknowledge, leaves no room for the exercise of human free will. Scotus takes this complaint very seriously, but in the end rejects it.

Consider, he says, the following argument: 'God believes I will sit tomorrow; but I will not sit tomorrow; therefore God is mistaken'. This argument is clearly valid. We must surely therefore say that the following variation on the argument is also valid: 'God believes I will sit tomorrow; but it is possible that I will not sit tomorrow; therefore God can be mistaken'. We are simply employing the schema: If p and q entail r, then p and *possibly* q entail *possibly* r. Since God cannot be mistaken, the argument seems to show that it is not possible for me to do anything other than what God has foreseen I will in fact do.

Scotus' solution to this argument is to deny the validity of the schema involved. He gives a counter-example, which can be rendered as follows. Suppose there are two suitcases A and B, each of which I can carry. But suppose further that I am carrying my suitcase A. In these circumstances, to carry your suitcase B would be to carry both A and B, which is beyond my strength. 'I am carrying A and I am carrying B' obviously entails 'I am carrying A and B'. But 'I am carrying A' and 'I can carry B' do not between them entail 'I can carry A and B' (*Lect.* 17. 509).

Scotus' response is effective, and it is applicable in many contexts other than the theological one. There are many cases where I can do some action X but will not. In such cases, there will be descriptions of doing X that will describe it in terms of the fact that I am not, in fact, going to do X. Thus, let us suppose that I am going to eat my cake. I can, if I want, have my cake, but I am not going to have my cake, I am going to eat it. Given the facts of the case, to have my cake would be to have it and eat it too. But I can, if I want, have it. So, if the principle is valid, I can have my cake and eat it too. Scotus' demolition of the principle in order to show that human freedom is compatible with divine decrees provides the essential under-pinning for any form of compatibilism, that is to say, the attempt to show that freedom and determinism are not the contradictory opposites that they appear at first sight to be.

Ockham rejected Scotus' method of reconciling divine foreknowledge with human freedom, just as Scotus had rejected Aquinas'. God, Scotus says, foresees future events by being aware of his own intentions, and future events are contingent, not necessary, because God's decrees about the world are themselves contingent. This, Ockham replies, may be sufficient to preserve contingency, but it does not suffice to leave the decisions of creatures free while establishing, at the same time, a basis for foreknowledge of them.[14]

Ockham's criticism of Scotus' position is forceful, but he does not himself offer in its place any solution to the problem of divine foreknowledge and human freedom. He makes clear, in fact, that he sympathizes with the position (which he wrongly attributes to Aristotle) that statements about future contingents lack a truth-value. But unless they are already true, future contingent propositions cannot be known, even by God. In spite of this philosophical reasoning, Ockham says, we are obliged to hold that God evidently knows all future contingents. A treatise exclusively devoted to the problem, *Tractatus de Praedestinatione et de Praescientia*, concludes, 'I say that it is impossible to express clearly the way in which God knows future contingent events. However, it must be held that he does know them, but contingently.'[15]

This was just one instance of the combination of devout fideism with philosophical agnosticism that is characteristic of Ockham's theology. He is critical of the arguments for God's existence to be found in Aquinas and Scotus. He agrees with Scotus that without a univocal concept of being, it would be impossible even to conceive of God (III *Sent.* 9, R); but he agrees with Aquinas that the primary object of the human mind is not being, but the nature of material substance (I *Sent.* 3. 1d).

Philosophical reason cannot prove that God is the first efficient cause of everything. There must, indeed, be a first cause, if there is not to be an infinite causal regress; but it need not be God, it could be a heavenly body or some finite spirit (*Quodl.* 2, p. 1; *OTh.* 6. 108). But even the impossibility of an infinite causal regress is open to question—why should there not be a series of begotten and begetter stretching forever backwards? Instead of asking what brings something into existence we might do better to ask what keeps it in existence; and Ockham agrees that it is implausible to think that there is an infinite series of simultaneous entities currently keeping us in existence. This can be shown, he thinks, not with absolute certainty, but by arguments that are reasonable enough (I *Sent.* 2. 10).

This is as far as Ockham is prepared to go in allowing the possibility of a proof of God's existence; and even this, he maintains, is insufficient to establish that there is only one God. A fortiori we cannot prove by natural reason that God is infinite, eternal, omnipotent, and creator of heaven and earth. With regard to God's knowledge, we cannot prove philosophically that God knows actual things other than himself, let alone their future free actions. All these truths about God have to be accepted as matters of faith.

The reconciliation of freedom and providence was a problem that occupied humanist thinkers no less than scholastics. Lorenzo Valla, Nicholas V's court

---

[14] Ockham also rejected Scotus' non-manifest power. See p. 443 above.

[15] Trans. Norman Kretzmann and Marilyn Adams (Chicago: Appleton-Century-Crofts, 1969).

philologist, wrote in 1439 a dialogue on free will, critical of Boethius' *Consolation*. It starts from a well-worn problem: 'If God foresees that Judas will be a traitor, it is impossible for him not to become a traitor'. For most of its length the dialogue follows moves and counter-moves familiar from scholastic discussions: it reads like a child's version of Scotus. But, near the end, two surprising moves are made.

First, Valla introduces two pagan gods into the discussion. Apollo predicted to the Roman king Tarquin that he would suffer exile and death. In response to Tarquin's complaints, Apollo said that he wished his prophecy were happier, but he merely predicted, he did not decide, Tarquin's fate. Any recriminations should be addressed to Jupiter. The introduction of the gods is not just a humanist flourish: it enables Valla, without blasphemy, to separate out the two attributes of omniscient wisdom and irresistible will which, in Christian theology, are inseparable in the one God.

The second surprise is that when the going gets really tough, Valla takes refuge in Scripture quotation. He turns to the passage in Paul's Epistle to the Romans about the predestination of Jacob and the reprobation of Esau. 'O the depth of the riches both of the wisdom and knowledge of God! How unsearchable are his judgements and his ways past finding out.' Rather than offer a philosophical reconciliation between divine providence and human freedom, Valla ends with a denunciation of the philosophers and above all of Aristotle. On this crucial topic of natural theology, both nominalist scholasticism and humanist scholarship reach the same dead end.

The Informed Ignorance of Nicholas of Cusa

Late medieval thought reaches a climax of agnosticism in Nicholas of Cusa's *De Docta Ignorantia*. No one since Socrates had emphasized so strongly that wisdom consists in awareness of the limits of one's knowledge. Brute ignorance is no virtue: but the process of learning is a gradually increasing awareness of how much one does not know. Truth is real enough: but we humans can only approach it asymptotically.

Truth does not admit of more or less, but stands absolute. Nothing other than truth itself can measure it with accuracy, just as a non-circle cannot measure a circle in its absolute being. Our intellect, which is not truth, can never comprehend truth so accurately that there does not remain the possibility of infinitely more accurate comprehension. Our intellect is related to the truth in the way that a polygon is to a circle: the more angles it contains, the more like a circle it is, but it never equates to the circle even if its angles are multiplied to infinity. (*DDI* 9)

What is true of the intellect's approach to truth in general is a fortiori true of its approach to the truth about God.

Cusa's paradigm of rational inquiry is measurement: we approach the unknown by measuring it against what we already know. But we cannot hope to measure the infinite, because there is no proportion between what is infinite and any finite thing. Every attempt we make to learn more about God reveals a new infinite gap between what we think and what God really is.

Our reason, guided by the principle of non-contradiction, proceeds by making distinctions. We distinguish, for instance, between great and small. But these distinctions are useless in inquiry about God. We may think, for instance, that God is the greatest of all things, the maximum. Certainly, God is something than which nothing can be greater. But God, who has no size at all, is also something than which nothing can be lesser. He is the minimum as well as the maximum. This is but one instance of a general principle: God is the union and coincidence of opposites (*DDI* 1. 4).

One of the pairs of opposites that coincide in God is the pair being–non-being. The maximum 'no more is than is not whatever is conceived to be. And it no more is not than is whatever is conceived not to be. It is one thing in such a way as to be all things, and it is all things in such a way as to be no thing. And it is maximally thus in such a way as to be also minimally thus' (*DDI* 1. 4). No doubt this all sounds very irrational. Cusa praises those philosophers who have distinguished between reason and intellect, regarding intellect as an intuitive faculty that can transcend the contradictions detected by reason. Literal language is incapable of grasping divine mystery: we must make use of metaphor and symbol. Cusa's preferred metaphors were mathematical. If we take a finite circle and gradually increase its diameter, the curvature of the circumference decreases. When the diameter reaches infinity, the circumference becomes absolutely straight. Thus a straight line (the maximum of straightness) is identical with an infinite circle (the minimum of curvature).

Other metaphors are used to describe the relation between God and the universe. All creatures are enfolded (*complicata*) in God; God is unfolded (*explicatus*) in all creatures. A creature stands in the same relation to God as my image in a mirror image is related to me—except that, with God and creatures, there is no mirror other than the image itself. Each creature not only mirrors God but images every other creature. Different creatures are closer or more distant images of God (*DDI* 2. 3).

Cusa, obviously, belongs in the tradition of the *via negativa*, going back to Dionysius the Areopagite. But his agnosticism goes further than that of his predecessors such as Eriugena. Cusa regards negative predicates as no less misleading than positive ones if they are applied to God. No name is apt for God. We cannot even call him 'the One', because for us oneness excludes otherness and plurality. If we exclude that exclusion, when calling God 'the One' what are we left with? We are still infinitely distant from naming God (*DDI* 1. 24). If we really come to grips with this reality, our informed ignorance will become sacred ignorance. That is the best that we humans can hope for here.

Part Three

The Rise of Modern Philosophy

CONTENTS OF PART THREE

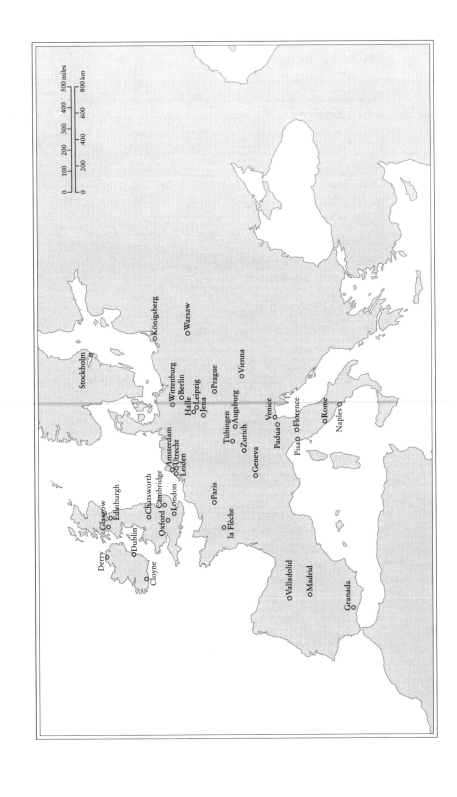

INTRODUCTION TO PART THREE

To someone approaching the early modern period of philosophy from an ancient and medieval background the most striking feature of the age is the absence of Aristotle from the philosophic scene. To be sure, in the period covered by Part Three the study of Aristotle continued in the academic establishment, and in Oxford University there has never been a time since its foundation when Aristotle was not taught. But the other striking characteristic of this period, which marks it off from both the Middle Ages and the twentieth century, is that it was a time when philosophy was most energetically pursued not within universities but outside them. Of all the great thinkers to be considered in the chapters of this book, none before Wolff and Kant held academic posts in philosophy.

Both good and evil consequences resulted when philosophy turned its back on Aristotle. For philosophy in the broad sense—philosophy as it was understood during most of our period, to include the physical sciences as 'natural philosophy'—the removal of Aristotle's dead hand was a great boon. Aristotle's physics was hopelessly erroneous, and had been shown to be so as early as the sixth century of our era; the deference that was paid to it during the Middle Ages was a great brake on scientific progress. But for philosophy in the narrow sense—philosophy as it is now practised as a distinct discipline in universities—there were losses as well as gains resulting from the abandonment of Aristotle.

Our period is dominated by two philosophical giants, one at its beginning and one at its end, Descartes and Kant. Descartes was a standard-bearer for the rebellion against Aristotle. In metaphysics he rejected the notions of potentiality and actuality, and in philosophical psychology he substituted consciousness for rationality as the mark of the mental. Hobbes and Locke founded a school of British empiricism in reaction to Cartesian rationalism, but the assumptions they shared with Descartes were more important than the issues that separated them. It took the genius of Kant to bring together, in the philosophy of human understanding, the different contributions of the senses and the intellect that had been divided and distorted by both empiricists and rationalists.

The hallmark of Cartesian dualism was the separation between mind and matter, conceived as the separation of consciousness from clockwork. This opened an abyss that hampered the metaphysical enterprise during the period of Part Three. On the one hand, speculative thinkers erected systems that placed ever greater strains on the credulity of the common reader. Whatever may be the defects of Aristotle's hylomorphism, his substances—things like cats and cabbages—did at least have the advantage of undoubted existence in the everyday world, unlike unknowable substrata, monads, noumena, and the Absolute. On the other hand, thinkers of a more sceptical turn deconstructed not only Aristotelian substantial forms, but primary and secondary qualities, material substances, and eventually the human mind itself.

In the introduction to his *Lectures on the History of Philosophy* Hegel warns against dull histories in which the succession of systems are represented simply as a number of opinons, errors, and freaks of thought. In such works, he says, 'the whole of the history of Philosophy becomes a battlefield covered with the bones of the dead; it is a kingdom not merely formed of dead and lifeless individuals, but of refuted and spiritually dead systems, since each has killed and buried the other' (*LHP* 17).

Though I try to record faithfully the opinions of the successive philosophers of my period, I hope that this volume will not fall under Hegel's censure. I believe that, despite handicapping themselves by throwing away some of the most valuable tools that philosophy had forged for itself in antiquity and the Middle Ages, the philosophers of this period made many contributions of permanent value, which are identified and described in the thematic chapters. In the course of Part Three I hope to trace the graph of both the gains and the losses. There is much to be learnt, I believe, from studying even the vagaries of those whom Hegel calls 'heroes of thought'. Great philosophers in every age have engendered great errors: it is no disrespect to them to try to expose some of the confusions to which they appear to have succumbed.

The division into themes in Part Three differs from that in the previous parts in two ways. First, there is no special chapter devoted to logic and language, since philosophers in our period made no contribution in these areas at all comparable to that of the Middle Ages or that of the nineteenth and twentieth centuries. (It is true that the period contains one logician of genius, Leibniz: but his logical work had little impact until the nineteenth century). Second, there is for the first time a chapter devoted to political philosophy. It is only from the time of Machiavelli and More that the political institutions of the age begin to bear sufficient similarity to those under which we live now for the insights of political philosophers to be relevant to contemporary discussions. The chapter on physics is briefer than in previous parts, because with Newton the history of physics becomes part of the history of science rather than the history of philosophy, leaving to philosophers, for a while at least, the abstract treatment of the notions of space and time.

1

Sixteenth-Century Philosophy

Humanism and Reform

The decade beginning in 1511 can well be regarded as the high point of the Renaissance. In the Vatican Raphael was frescoing the walls of the papal apartments, while Michelangelo covered the ceiling of the Sistine Chapel with his paintings. In Florence the Medici family, exiled since the time of the reformer Savonarola, returned to power and patronage. One of the officers of the former republic, Niccolò Machiavelli, now under house arrest, used his enforced leisure to produce a classic text of political philosophy, *The Prince*, which offered rulers frank advice on the acquisition and retention of power. Renaissance art and Renaissance ideas travelled northward as far as Germany and England. A colleague of Michelangelo's designed Henry VII's tomb in Westminster Abbey and the foremost scholar of the age, the Dutchman Desiderius Erasmus, lectured at Cambridge early in the reign of his son Henry VIII. Erasmus was a frequent guest at the house of Thomas More, a lawyer about to begin a political career that would make him, briefly, the most powerful man in England after the king.

Erasmus and More and their friends propounded in Northern Europe the humanist ideas that had taken root in Italy in the previous century. 'Humanism' at that time did not mean a desire to replace religious values with secular human ones: Erasmus was a priest who wrote best-selling works of piety, and More was later martyred for his religious beliefs. Humanists, rather, were people who believed in the educational value of the 'humane letters' (*literae humaniores*) of the Greek and Latin classics. They studied and imitated the style of classical authors, many of whose texts had been recently rediscovered and were being published thanks to the newly developed art of printing. They believed that their scholarship, applied to ancient pagan texts, would restore to Europe long-neglected arts and sciences, and, applied to the Bible and to ancient Church writers, would help Christendom to a purer and more authentic understanding of Christian truth.

Humanists valued grammar, philology, and rhetoric more highly than the technical philosophical studies that had preoccupied scholars during the Middle Ages. They despised the Latin that had been the lingua franca of medieval universities, far removed in style from the works of Cicero and Livy. Erasmus had been unhappy studying at the Sorbonne, and More mocked the logic he had been taught at Oxford. In philosophy, both of them looked back to Plato rather than to Aristotle and his many medieval admirers.

More paid a compliment to Plato by publishing, in 1516, a fictional blueprint for an ideal commonwealth. In More's *Utopia*, as in Plato's *Republic*, property is held in common and women serve alongside men in the army. More, writing in an age of exploration and discovery, pretended that his state actually existed on an island across the ocean. Like Plato, however, he was using the description of a fictional nation as a vehicle for theoretical political philosophy and for criticism of contemporary society.[1]

Erasmus was more sceptical about Plato as a guide to politics. In the teasing *Praise of Folly* that he dedicated to More in 1511 he mocks Plato's claim that the happiest state will be ruled by philosopher kings. History tells us, he says, 'that no state has been so plagued by its rulers as when power has fallen into the hands of some dabbler in philosophy' (M, 100). But when, in the same year as *Utopia*, he published his *Instruction to a Christian Prince*, he did little but repeat ideas to be found in Plato and Aristotle. For this reason his treatise of political philosophy has never achieved the renown of Machiavelli's or of More's.

Erasmus was more interested in divinity than in philosophy, and he cared more for biblical studies than for speculative theology. Scholastics like Scotus and Ockham, he complained, merely choked with brambles paths that had been made plain by earlier thinkers. Among the great Christian teachers of the past his favourite was St Jerome, who had translated the Bible from Hebrew and Greek into Latin. Erasmus worked for some years annotating the Latin New Testament, and then decided to produce a Latin version of his own to amend corruptions which had crept into the accepted text ('the Vulgate') and, where necessary, to improve on Jerome himself. In 1516 he published his new Latin version along with his annotations, and almost as an appendix, he added a Greek text of the New Testament—the first one ever to be printed. In his Latin version, in striving for fidelity to the Greek original, he did not hesitate to alter even the most beloved and solemn texts. The first words of the fourth Gospel, *In principio erat verbum*, became *In principio erat sermo*: what was in the beginning was not 'the Word' but 'the Saying'.

Erasmus' Latin version was not generally adopted, though passages of it can still be read in the chapel windows of King's College Cambridge. However, the Greek text he published was the foundation for the great vernacular testaments of the

---

[1] The political philosophy of Machiavelli and More is discussed at length in Ch. 9 below.

504

sixteenth century, beginning with the monumental German version published in 1522 by Martin Luther.

Luther was an Augustinian monk, as Erasmus had been until released by papal dispensation from his monastic commitments. Like Erasmus, Luther had made a close study of St Paul's Epistle to the Romans. This had made him question fundamentally the ethos of Renaissance Catholicism. The year after the publication of Erasmus' New Testament Luther issued, in the University of Wittenberg, a public denunciation of abuses of papal authority, in particular of a scandalously promoted offer of an indulgence (remission of punishment due to sin) in return for contributions to the building of the great new church of St Peter's in Rome.

Erasmus and More shared Luther's concern about the corruption of many of the higher clergy: they had both denounced it in print, Erasmus pungently in a satire on Pope Julius II, More with ironic circumspection in *Utopia*. But both were alienated when Luther went on to denounce large parts of the Catholic sacramental system and to teach that the one thing needful for salvation is faith, or trust in the merits of Christ. In 1520 Pope Leo X condemned forty-one articles taken from Luther's teaching, and followed this up with an excommunication after Luther had burnt the Bull of Condemnation. King Henry VIII, with some help from More, published an *Assertion of the Seven Sacraments*, which earned him the papal title 'Defender of the Faith'.

Erasmus strove in vain to dampen down the controversy. He tried to persuade Luther to moderate his language, and to submit his opinions for judgement to an impartial jury of scholars. On the other hand, he questioned the authenticity of the papal bull of condemnation and he persuaded the emperor Charles V to give Luther a hearing at the Diet of Worms in 1521. But Luther refused to recant and was placed under the ban of the empire. Pope Leo died and was succeeded by a Dutch schoolfriend of Erasmus, who took the name Adrian VI. The new pope urged Erasmus to take up his pen against the reformers. Very reluctantly, Erasmus agreed, but his book against Luther did not appear until 1524, by which time Pope Adrian was dead.

Sin, Grace, and Freedom

The ground Erasmus chose for battle was Luther's position on the freedom of the will. This had been the subject of one of the theses which had been nailed to the door at Wittenberg in 1517. Among the propositions condemned by Leo X was 'free will after sin is merely an empty title'. In response, Luther reinforced his assertion. 'Free will is really a fiction and a label without reality, because it is in no man's power to plan any evil or good' (WA VII. 91).

In his *Diatribe de Libero Arbitrio* Erasmus piles up texts from the Old and New Testament and from Church doctors and decrees to show that human beings have free will. His constant theme is that all the exhortations, promises, commands, threats, reproaches, and curses to be found in the Scriptures would lose all point if it was necessity, and not free will, that determined good or evil acts. Questions of Bible interpretation dominate both Erasmus' book and Luther's much longer reply, *De Servo Arbitrio*.

Philosophically, Erasmus is unsubtle. He refers to, but does not improve upon, Valla's dialogue on free will. He repeats commonplaces of centuries of scholastic debate which are inadequate responses to the problem of reconciling divine foreknowledge with human freedom—he insists, for instance, that even humans know many things that will happen in the future, such as eclipses of the sun. A theory of free will that leaves us no freer than the stars in their courses is not a very robust answer to Luther. But Erasmus is anxious to avoid philosophical complications. It is a piece of irreligious curiosity to inquire, as the scholastics did, whether God's foreknowledge is contingent or necessary.

Luther, though no friend to the scholastics, finds this outrageous. 'If this is irreligious, curious, and superfluous,' he asks, 'what, then, is religious, serious and useful knowledge?' God, Luther maintains, foresees nothing contingently. 'He foresees, purposes, and does all things according to His immutable, eternal, and infallible will. This thunderbolt throws free will flat and utterly dashes it to pieces' (WA VII. 615).

Luther endorses the opinion that the Council of Constance ascribed to Wyclif: that everything happens of necessity. He distinguishes, however, between two senses of 'necessity'. The human will is subject to 'necessity of immutability': it has no power to change itself from its innate desire for evil. But it is not subject to another form of necessity, namely compulsion: a human being lacking grace does evil spontaneously and willingly. The human will is like a beast of burden: if God rides it, it wills and goes where God wills; if Satan rides it, it goes where Satan wills. It has no freedom to choose its rider.

Luther prefers to abandon altogether the term 'free will'; other writers, before and after, have regarded the spontaneity that he accepts as being the only thing that can genuinely be meant by the term.[2] Luther's principal concern was to deny free will in matters that make the difference between salvation and damnation. In other cases he seems to allow the possibility of genuine choice between alternative courses of action. Humans have free will in respect not of what is above them, but in respect of what is below them. The sinner, for instance, can make his choice between a variety of sins (WA VII. 638).

The Bible, as Erasmus had copiously shown, contains many passages that imply that human choices are free, and also many passages that proclaim that the fate of humans is determined by God. Over the centuries, scholastic theologians had sought to reconcile these contradictory messages by making careful distinctions.

---

[2] See above, p. 159, on the distinction between liberty of spontaneity and liberty of indifference.

'Much toil and labour has been devoted to excusing the goodness of God,' Luther says, 'and to accusing the will of man. Here those distinctions have been invented between the ordinary will of God and the absolute will of God, between the necessity of consequence and the necessity of the consequent, and many others. But nothing has been achieved by these means beyond imposing upon the unlearned.' We should not waste time, Luther believes, in trying to resolve the contradiction between different Bible texts: we should go to extremes, deny free will altogether, and ascribe everything to God.

Distaste for scholastic subtlety was not peculiar to Luther: it was shared by Erasmus, and also by More. More himself entered the debate on free will in his controversy with Luther's English admirer, the Bible translator William Tyndale. To counter Lutheran determinism More uses a strategy which goes back to discussions of fate in Stoic philosophy:

One of their sect was served in a good turn in Almayne, which when he had robbed a man and was brought before the judges, he would not deny the deed, but said it was his destiny to do it, and therefore they might not blame him; they answered him, after his own doctrines, that if it were his destiny to steal and that therefore they must hold him excused, then it was also their destiny to hang him, and therefore he must as well hold them excused again. (More 1931: 196)

The claim that if determinism is true everything is excusable would no doubt be rejected by Luther, since he believed that God justly punished sinners who could not do otherwise than sin.

From a philosophical point of view these early Reformation debates on freedom and determinism do no more than rehearse arguments which were commonplaces of ancient and medieval philosophy. They illustrate, however, the negative side of humanist education. Scholastic debates, if sometimes arid, had commonly been sober and courteous. Thomas Aquinas, for instance, was always anxious to put the best possible interpretation on the theses of those he disagreed with. Erasmus shared something of Aquinas' eirenic spirit; but More and Luther attack each other with bitter vituperation made only the more vulgar by the elegant Latin in which it is phrased. The pugnacious conventions of humanist debate were a factor which led to the hardening of positions on either side of the Reformation divide.

Authority and Conscience

The debate on free will continued and ramified through and beyond the sixteenth century, and, as we shall see in later chapters, more sophisticated controversialists were to bring new subtlety into the philosophical treatment of the topic. For the present the most important new element introduced into the debate by Luther was a general hostility not just to scholasticism but to philosophy itself. He denounced Aristotle, and in particular his *Ethics*, as 'the vilest enemy of grace'. His contempt for the powers of unaided reason was the outcome of his belief that in Adam's Fall human nature had become totally corrupt and impotent.

In one way, Luther's scepticism about philosophical speculation was a continuation of a tendency already strong in late medieval scholasticism. Since the time of Scotus philosophers had become ever more reluctant to claim that reason alone could establish the nature of the divine attributes, the content of divine commands, or the immortality of the human soul.[3] The counterweight to their increasing philosophical scepticism had been their acceptance of the authority of the Church, expressed in Christian tradition and the pronouncements of popes and councils. This attitude found expression at the beginning of Erasmus' treatise: 'So great is my dislike of assertions that I prefer the views of the sceptics wherever the inviolable authority of the Scriptures and the decision of the Church permit' (*E*, 6).

The Lutheran Reformation, by taking away this counterweight, gave new impetus to the sceptical trend. To be sure, the Bible was retained and indeed emphasized as a decisive authority: with respect to the teaching of the Scriptures, Luther insisted, the Christian had no liberty to be a sceptic (WA VII. 604). But the content of the Bible was no longer to be subjected to professional scrutiny by philosophically trained theologians. Every Christian, Luther said, had the power of discerning and judging what was right or wrong in matters of faith. Tyndale boasted that his translation would make a boy driving the plough understand the Bible better than the most learned divine. Pessimism about the moral capacity of the trained intellect unaided by grace went hand in hand with optimism about the intellectual ability of the untrained mind illumined by faith. Squeezed between the two, philosophy found its role greatly diminished among devout Protestants.

The problem for Luther was that individual consciences, unconstrained by universal authority, and unwilling to submit faith to rational arbitrament, began to produce a great diversity of beliefs. French and Swiss reformers, such as Jean Calvin and Ulrich Zwingli, agreed with Luther in rejecting papal authority but differed from him in their understanding of the presence of Christ in the Eucharist and of the decrees through which God chose the elect. Calvin, like Luther, placed the ultimate criterion of religious truth within the individual soul: every faithful Christian experienced within himself a marvellous conviction of heavenly revelation which was more reassuring than any reasoning could ever be. But how could one tell who were faithful Christians? If one counted only the reformed, then Calvin's criterion was question-begging; on the other hand, if one counted all those who had been baptized, it led to an anarchy of belief.

---

[3] See above, pp. 446, 465.

Protestants argued that the Church could not be the ultimate authority because its claims rested on biblical texts. Catholics, quoting Augustine, claimed that the only reason for accepting the Bible was that it had been given us by the Church. The questions at issue in Europe at the Reformation were in the end settled neither by rational argument nor by interior enlightenment. In country after country conflicting answers were imposed by force of arms or by penal legislation. In England Henry VIII, irked by Vatican refusal to free him from a tedious marriage, broke with Rome and executed More for his loyalty to the pope. The country then lurched from his schismatic version of Catholicism to Calvinism under his son Edward VI, to Counter-Reformation Catholicism under his daughter Mary, and finally to an Anglican compromise under her sister Elizabeth. This chequered history produced hundreds of martyrs, both Protestant and Catholic; but England was spared the sanguinary wars of religion which raged for many decades in continental Europe.

By the mid-sixteenth century doctrinal positions had hardened into a form that they were to retain for some 400 years. Luther's lieutenant Melancthon formulated at Augsburg in 1530 a confession of faith to provide the test of orthodoxy. A concordat agreed in the same city in 1555 provided that the ruler of each state within the Holy Roman Empire could decide whether his subjects were to be Lutheran or Catholic: the principle later known as *cuius regio, eius religio*. Calvin's *Institutes of the Christian Religion* (1536) provided the standard for Protestants in Switzerland, France, and later Scotland. In Rome Pope Paul III (1534–9) promoted a Counter-Reformation, instituting a new religious order of Jesuits, and convening a Council at Trent to reform Church discipline. The council condemned the Lutheran doctrine of justification by faith alone, and the Calvinist doctrine that God predestined the wicked to hell prior to any sin. Free will, it insisted, had not been extinguished by Adam's Fall. It reaffirmed the doctrine of transubstantiation and the traditional seven sacraments. By the time the council had finished its work, in 1563, Luther was dead and Calvin was dying.

The division of Christendom was an unnecessary tragedy. The theological issues which separated Luther and Calvin from their Catholic opponents had been debated many times in the Middle Ages without leading to sectarian warfare; and few twenty-first-century Catholics and Protestants, if not professionally trained in theology, are aware of the real nature of the differences between the contrasting theories of the Eucharist, of grace, and of predestination which in the sixteenth century led to anathema and bloodshed. Questions of authority, of course, are easier to understand and more difficult to arbitrate than questions of doctrine. But the unity of Christendom could have been maintained under a constitutional papacy subject to general councils, such as Ockham had suggested, such as had been the practice in the fifteenth century, and such as even Thomas More, for the greater part of his life, believed to be the divine design for the Church.

The Decline of Logic

The combined effects of the Renaissance and the Reformation made the sixteenth century a barren one in most areas of philosophy. Logic was perhaps the branch of philosophy that suffered most severely. Logic did continue to be taught in the universities, but humanist scholars were impatient of it, regarding its terminology as barbarous and its complexities as pettifogging. Rabelais spoke for them when in *Pantagruel* (1532) he mocked logicians for inquiring whether a chimera bombinating in a vacuum could devour second intentions. Most of the advances in the subject that had been made by Stoic and medieval logicians were lost for four centuries. Instead, a bowdlerized version of Aristotle was taught at an elementary level in popular textbooks.

In the mid-century these began to be published in vernacular languages. The first in English was Thomas Wilson's *The Rule of Reason*, dedicated to Edward VI in 1551: he was the first to use the English words that are now the common terms of logic, such as 'proposition'. Others rejected such Latinisms and did their best to invent a solid Anglo-Saxon terminology. Ralphe Lever thought that logic should be called 'Witcraft'; and when he wanted to explain in his textbook that a contradictory proposition consisted of two propositions, one affirmative and one negative, with similar subject, predicate and verb, he produced the following: 'Gaynsaying shewsayes are two shewsayes, the one a yeasaye and the other a naysaye, changing neither foreset, backset nor verbe.'[4]

These English logic texts left little mark. Matters were different in France: Peter Ramus (Pierre de la Ramée, 1515–72) achieved lasting fame quite out of proportion to his actual merits as a logician. Legend has it that for his master's degree he defended the thesis that everything Aristotle had ever taught was false. Certainly he went on to publish a short anti-Aristotelian treatise, and after his appointment as professor at the Collège Royale he followed this up with twenty books of Animadversions on Aristotle. His *Dialectic*, which was published in French in 1555, in Latin in 1556, and in English in 1574, was meant to supersede all previous logic texts. For the first time, he maintained, it set out the laws which governed people's natural thinking.

Logic, he tells us, is the art which teaches how to dispute well. It is divided into two parts: invention and judgement, to each of which a book of his text is devoted. Treating of 'invention', he lists nine places or topics to which one may look to find arguments to support a conclusion one wishes to defend. They are cause, effect, subject, adjunct, opposite, comparative, name, division, and definition. He illustrates each of these topics with copious quotations from classical authors, which take up nearly half of his short first book. For instance, Ramus defines 'adjunct' as 'that which has a subject to which it is adjoined, as virtue and vice are called the

---

[4] W. and M. Kneale, *The Development of Logic* (1979), p. 299.

adjuncts of the body or soul; and to be short all things that do chance to the subject, beside the essence, is called the adjunct'. He then illustrates this with a long quotation from a speech of Cicero's, beginning:

Doth not his very head and over brow altogether shaven and scraped so clean signify that he is malicious and savoureth of knavery? Do they not utter and cry that he is a crafty fox? (*L*, 33)

Despite his official contempt for Aristotle, most of the topics for argument that he lists are taken from various places in the Aristotelian corpus and defined in similar ways. The only novelty is the discussion, at the end of the book, of what he calls 'inartificial' arguments, examples of which are the pronouncements of divine oracles and human testimony in a court of law.

The second book comes closer to the traditional subject matter of logic. Once again Ramus draws heavily on Aristotle in his classification of different kinds of statement and his analysis of syllogisms of different forms. His main innovation is that he devotes much more attention than Aristotle did to arguments containing proper names, such as 'Caesar oppresseth his native country; Tullius oppresseth not his native country; Tullius therefore is not Caesar' (*L*, 37).

Modern historians of logic can find little merit or originality in Ramus' work, but for long after his death debates raged between Aristotelians and Ramists, and there were even groups of semi-Ramists campaigning for compromise. Ramus became a Calvinist in 1561 and was killed in the massacre of Protestants on St Bartholomew's Day in 1572. His status as a martyr gave his writings a prestige they could never have earned in their own right, and his influence lasted through the centuries. John Milton, for instance, published a volume of Ramist Logic five years after the completion of *Paradise Lost*. The popularity of Ramist works impoverished logic for a long period. No further progress was made in formalizing the logic of modality and counterfactuality that had fascinated medieval logicians, and much of their own work passed into oblivion.

Scepticism, Sacred and Profane

It was not only Catholics who killed heretics. In 1553 Michael Servetus, a Spanish physician who had discovered the pulmonary circulation of the blood, was burnt in Calvin's Geneva for denying the Trinity and the divinity of Jesus. A French classicist teaching at Basel, named Sebastian Castellio, was shocked at the execution of Servetus and wrote a treatise *Whether Heretics are to be Persecuted* (Magdeburg, 1554) in which he pleaded in favour of toleration. His arguments are mainly quotations of authoritative texts or appeals to the example of Christ. 'O Christ, when thou didst live upon earth, none was more gentle, more merciful, more patient of wrong...Art thou now so changed?...If thou, O Christ, hast commanded these executions and tortures, what hast thou left for the devil to do?'[5] But in a later work, *The Art of Doubting*, Castellio developed more epistemological arguments. The difficulty of interpreting Scripture, and the variety of opinions among Christian sects, should make us very cautious in laying down the law on religious matters. To be sure, there are some truths that are beyond doubt, such as the existence and goodness of God; but on other religious topics no one can be sufficiently certain so as to be justified in killing another man as a heretic. Castellio, in his time, was a lone voice; but later supporters of toleration looked back to him as a forerunner.

Some contemporaries who regarded Castellio as excessively sceptical about religion began to feel the attractions of scepticism in non-religious areas. This was greatly reinforced when, in mid-century, the works of the ancient Greek sceptic, Sextus Empiricus, were rediscovered after total oblivion in the medieval period. Sextus' sceptical arguments were made popular by the French nobleman Michel Eyquem de Montaigne (1533–92) in an essay which is nominally a commentary on a century-old work of natural theology translated by him at the request of his father. The *Apology for Raimond Sebond* (1569), written in clear and witty French prose, became the classic modern statement of scepticism.[6]

The *Apology* contains much more than a rehearsal of ancient sceptical arguments. Prior to presenting them, Montaigne works hard to induce in his reader a proper degree of intellectual humility. Human beings are inclined to regard themselves as being at the summit of creation; but are men really superior to the other animals who share the earth with them? 'When I play with my cat,' Montaigne asks, 'who knows whether she is passing her time with me no less than I am passing my time with her?' (ME, 2, 119).

Animals of different kinds have individual senses sharper than ours; they can acquire by swift intuition information that humans have to work out laboriously. They have the same needs and emotions as we have, and they display, often to a more remarkable extent, the same traits and virtues that humans take pride in. Montaigne piles up stories of faithful and magnanimous dogs and grateful and gentle lions, to contrast with the cruelty and treachery of human beings. Most of his examples of beasts' ingenuity are drawn from Greek and Latin texts, such as the legendary logical dog, who while following a scent reaches a crossroads, and sniffs out two of the routes, and on drawing a blank charges immediately down the third route without further sniffing. But Montaigne also draws on his own experience, for instance of guide-dogs leading the blind, and some of his examples of animal tool-usage would not look out of place in papers discussed at present-day associations for the advancement of science.

---

[5] Quoted by O. Chadwick, *The Reformation* (Harmondsworth: Penguin, 1964), p. 402.

[6] Montaigne's sceptical arguments will be considered in Ch. 4 below. See above, p. 141.

Montaigne was particularly impressed by the skills of migratory birds and fishes:

The swallows which we see exploring all the nooks of our houses when spring returns: do they search without judgement, and choose without discretion, that one of a thousand places which is the most commodious for their residence? In the course of building their wonderful and beautiful nests they choose square shapes rather than round, obtuse angles rather than right angles: can they do that without knowing the appropriate conditions and effects? (ME, 2, 121)

Tuna fish, Montaigne assures us, not only compete with humans in geometry and arithmetic, but are actually superior to them in astronomy. They swim in battalions formed into a perfect cube, and at the winter solstice they stop dead where they are and do not move again until the spring equinox (ME, 146).

Montaigne believes that the skilful performances of animals prove that the same thoughts go through their heads as through ours. A fox will cock his ear to listen in order to find the safest way over a frozen river. 'Surely we have therefore reason to judge that there passes through his head the same discourse as would run through ours, reasoning from sensation to conclusion: what makes a noise, moves; what moves, is not frozen; what is not frozen is liquid; what is liquid gives way' (ME, 127).

The two spheres in which above all humans plume themselves on their unique gifts are religion and philosophy. Montaigne makes a gallant attempt to prove that we are not alone in our capacity for worship by describing the funeral rites of ants and the sun-worship liturgy of elephants. He is more persuasive when he shows that humans can take little pride in their theological beliefs and activities, given the variety of contradictory doctrines on offer, and given the often debasing nature of religious practices. As for philosophy, he has no difficulty at all in showing that there has never been a philosopher whose system has been able to withstand the criticism of other philosophers. Like many another after him, he presses into service a dictum of Cicero: 'It is impossible to say anything so absurd that it has not been said already by some philosopher or other' (ME, 211).

Montaigne's deflation of human nature in *Raimond Sebond* is the antithesis of the glorification of mankind in Pico della Mirandola's 1486 *On the Dignity of Man*.[7] The optimism generated by the rediscovery of classical texts and the exuberance of the visual arts in Renaissance Florence gave way to the pessimism natural in a Counter-Reformation France torn by sectarian warfare. Montaigne contrasted the educated and civilized citizens of European states, to their disadvantage, with the simplicity and nobility of the inhabitants of the recently discovered New World.

However, Montaigne's emphasis on the limits of the human intellect does not prevent him from claiming to be quite certain of the truth of Catholic Christianity. On the contrary, he can claim that in his scepticism about philosophy he is

---

[7] See above, p. 340.

following in the footsteps of St Paul in First Corinthians: 'Hath not God made foolish the wisdom of this world? For after that in the wisdom of God the world by wisdom knew not God, it pleased God by the foolishness of preaching to save them that believe.' Pauline texts such as these were painted on the beams of Montaigne's study along with quotations from Sextus such as 'all that is certain is that nothing is certain'.

To reconcile his scepticism with his orthodoxy, Montaigne emphasizes that what he has been attacking are the pretensions of the human intellect to achieve truth by its own efforts. But faith is not an achievement, it is a free gift of God:

It is not by reasoning or understanding that we have received our religion, it is by authority and command from above. The weakness of our judgement is more help than its strength, and our blindness is more help than our clear sight. It is through ignorance, not through knowledge that we become wise with divine wisdom. (ME, 166)

Counter-Reformation Philosophy

Montaigne's exaltation of revelation to the exclusion of reason—'fideism' as it came to be called—was not typical of the Counter-Reformation. In reaction against Luther's insistence that the human intellect and will had been totally corrupted by the sin of Adam, Catholic controversialists tended to emphasize that basic religious truths were within the scope of unaided human intellect, and that faith itself needed the support and defence of reason.

In the forefront of this optimistic thrust of the Counter-Reformation were the Jesuits, the members of the new Society of Jesus. This order was founded by the Spanish ex-soldier Ignatius Loyola and was approved by Pope Paul III in 1540. In addition to the vows of poverty, chastity, and obedience taken by all members of religious orders, the Jesuits took a further vow of unquestioning loyalty to the papacy. Its members soon distinguished themselves in educational and missionary work in many parts of the world. In Europe they were happy to risk martyrdom in the Counter-Reformation cause; in America, India, and China they showed more sympathy with indigenous religions than many other Christian proselytizers, Catholic or Protestant. In philosophy and theology in the universities they were soon able to compete with the long-established religious orders such as the Franciscans and Dominicans. They promoted a new and, as they saw it, improved version of scholasticism.

Whereas medieval scholastics had based their university lectures upon canonical texts such as the works of Aristotle and the Sentences of Peter Lombard,[8] Jesuits in universities began to replace commentaries with self-standing courses in philosophy

---

[8] See above, p. 300.

and theology. By the early seventeenth century this pattern was adopted by Dominicans and Franciscans, and this led to a sharper distinction between philosophy and theology than had been common earlier. The pioneer of this movement to reform philosophy into independent textbook form was the Spanish Jesuit Francisco Suarez, whose *Disputationes Metaphysicae* (1597) were the first such systematic treatment of scholastic metaphysics.

Born in Granada in 1548, Suarez joined the Society of Jesus in 1564 and spent the whole of his professional life as a university professor, lecturing at six different universities in Spain and in the Jesuit college in Rome. He was a devout and erudite man, and in terms of sheer intellectual power he has a strong claim to be the most formidable philosopher of the sixteenth century. In the history of philosophy, however, he does not have a place commensurate to his gifts, for two reasons. First, most of his work is a restatement and refinement of medieval themes, rather than an exploration of new territory. Second, as a writer he was not only prolific, leaving behind a corpus that fills twenty-eight volumes, but also prolix and tedious. In so far as he had an influence on subsequent philosophy, it was through the writings of lesser but more readable imitators.

The two areas in which he was, indeed, influential were metaphysics and political philosophy. He had a great reverence for St Thomas Aquinas, but as a metaphysician he followed in the footsteps of Avicenna and Duns Scotus rather than those of Aquinas himself. Paradoxically, much that was to pass for Thomism during the seventeenth, eighteenth, and nineteenth centuries was closer to Suarezian metaphysics than to the *Summa Contra Gentiles*. In political philosophy Suarez's contribution was the *De Legibus* of 1621, which was the unacknowledged source of many of the ideas of better-known thinkers. In his own day he was most famous for his controversy with King James I about the divine right of kings, in which he attacked the theory that temporal monarchs derived their sovereignty directly from God. King James had his book publicly burnt.[9]

Of the philosophical issues dividing the Catholic and Protestant camps in the sixteenth century none was more thorny than human free will, which had been proclaimed at the Council of Trent in opposition to Lutheran determinism and Calvinist predestinarianism. The Jesuits made themselves champions of the libertarian account of human freedom. Suarez and his Jesuit colleague Luis de Molina offered a definition of free agency in terms of the availability of alternative courses of action—'liberty of indifference' as it came to be known. 'That agent is called free which in the presence of all necessary conditions for action can act and refrain from action or can do one thing while being able to do its opposite.'

Such a definition did ample justice to humans' consciousness of their own choices and their attribution of responsibility to others. But by comparison with more restrictive accounts of freedom, it made it very difficult to account for God's

---

[9] Suarez's metaphysics is discussed at greater length in Ch. 6 and his political theory in Ch. 9.

foreknowledge of free human actions, to which both Catholics and Protestants were committed. Molina, in his famous *Concordia* (1589), presented an elaborate solution to the problem, in terms of God's comprehensive knowledge of the actions of every possible human being in every possible world.[10] Ingenious though it was, Molina's solution was unpopular not only among Protestants but also among his Catholic co-religionists.

Dominican theologians, of whom the most vociferous was the Thomist Domingo Banez (1528–1604), thought that the Jesuit theologians were excessively exalting human freedom and derogating from divine power. The dispute between the two religious orders became so bitter that in 1605 Pope Clement VIII, without resolving the question at issue, imposed silence on both sides. Ironically, within the reformed camp, a Leiden divine named Arminius propounded views which were similar to, if less sophisticated than, those of Molina. The Synod of Dort in 1619 declared them incompatible with Calvinist orthodoxy.

Giordano Bruno

The most colourful philosopher of the latter part of the sixteenth century operated far outside the bounds of orthodoxy, whether Catholic or Protestant. Giordano Bruno (1548–1600) was born near Naples and became a Dominican there in 1565. By 1576 he was already suspected of heresy and expelled from the order. He fled northwards to Geneva, but there became equally unpopular with the Calvinists. He had better success in France, studying and lecturing in Toulouse and Paris and enjoying, for a time, the favour of King Henri III.

Bruno's first major work, *On the Shadows of Ideas*, combined an elaborate Neoplatonic metaphysical system with practical advice on the art of memory. There is a hierarchy of ideas with human ideas at the lowest level and at the topmost level the divine Ideas forming a unity in God's mind. These are, in themselves, impenetrable to us; but they are expressed in Nature, which is the universal effect of God. Images of the celestial world are closer to God than images of our sublunar world; hence, if we wish to organize our knowledge in such a way that we can recall it systematically we should mentally dispose our thoughts within the pattern of the signs of the zodiac.

In 1583 Bruno moved to England and visited Oxford, where he gave some lectures. His stay there was not a success. He was not to be the last continental philosopher to visit the university and find himself treated as a charlatan, and in his turn to regard his philosophical hosts as more interested in words than in ideas. He expressed his disdain for Oxford pedantry, along with ideas of more universal philosophical concern, in a series of dialogues in 1584 beginning with *Supper on Ash*

---

[10] Molina's theory of 'middle knowledge' is reported in detail in Ch. 10.

Wednesday (*La cena de le ceneri*). He seems to have written these while acting as a double agent in London for both the French and the English secret services.

Bruno's dialogues are not easy reading. They are peopled by beings of grand but mysterious status, like Wagner's gods and Tolkien's creatures, with powers of uncertain limits and motives of slender intelligibility. Although bearing the names of classical deities, they operate at some distance from Homer and Vergil. The Latin Mercury, for instance, corresponds not only to the Greek Hermes, but to the Egyptian god Thoth: he represents often the teachings of the fashionable Hermetic cult. This was based on recently discovered documents believed to go back to the Egypt of Moses' time. Hermetism, in Bruno's view, was superior to Christianity and was destined to supersede it.

In the system propounded in the dialogues, the phenomena we observe are the effects of a world-soul which animates nature and makes it into a single organism. The world of nature is infinite, with no edge, surface, or limit. But the world's infinity is not the same as God's infinity because the world has parts that are not infinite, whereas God is wholly in the whole world and wholly in each of its parts. This difference perhaps suffices to distinguish Bruno's position from pantheism, but the relation between God and the world remains obscure. It is not really clarified by Bruno's august formulation that God is the Nature making Nature (*natura naturans*) while the universe is the Nature made by Nature (*natura naturata*).

Two features of Bruno's system have caught the attention of historians and scientists: his adoption of the Copernican hypothesis, and his postulation of multiple universes. Bruno accepted that it was the earth that went round the sun, and not the sun that went round the earth. He went on to develop Copernicus' ideas in a bold and dramatic manner. The earth was not the centre of the universe: but neither was the sun. Our sun is just one star among others, and in boundless space there are many solar systems. No sun or star can be called the centre of the universe, because all positions are relative.

Our earth and our solar system enjoy no unique privilege. For all we know, there may be intelligent life at other times and places within the universe. Particular solar systems come and go, temporary phases in the life of the single infinite organism whose soul is the world-soul. Within the universe each intelligent being is a conscious, immortal atom, mirroring in itself the whole of creation. If in his interfusing of God and Nature Bruno anticipated Spinoza, in his account of rational atoms he anticipated Leibniz.

Bruno's championship of Hermetism and his theory of multiple universes challenged the orthodox teaching that God was incarnate uniquely in Jesus and that Christianity was the definitive divine revelation. Nonetheless, after leaving England he was accepted for a while as a Lutheran at Wittenberg and in 1591 was lecturing in Zurich. Unwisely, he accepted an invitation from the Doge of Venice, and found himself in the prison of the local Inquisition in 1592. A year later he was passed on to the Roman Inquisition, and after a trial that dragged on for nearly seven years in 1600 he was burned as a heretic in the Campo dei Fiori, where his statue now stands.

There is no doubt that the ideas expressed in Bruno's writings were unorthodox. The remarkable things about his trial are that he showed such constancy in defending his ideas and that it took his inquisitors so long to find him guilty of heresy. But although theories of multiple universes are once again popular with cosmologists today, it is a mistake to think of Bruno as a martyr to science. His speculations were based not on observation or experiment but on occult traditions and on *a priori* philosophizing. He was condemned not because he supported the Copernican system, but because he practised magic and denied the divinity of Christ.

Galileo

Matters are very different when we turn to another Italian philosopher who suffered at the hands of the Inquisition, Galileo Galilei. Galileo, twelve years younger than Bruno and an exact contemporary of Shakespeare, was born in Pisa and studied at the university there, eventually becoming professor of mathematics in 1589. In 1592 he moved to Padua, and held a professorship there for eighteen years, which he would recall as the happiest period of his life.

Already as a young man Galileo had begun to criticize the still dominant physics of Aristotle, not, like Bruno, on the basis of Neoplatonic metaphysics, but as a result of observation and experiment. His years at Pisa became famous for one observation that he made and one experiment that he probably did not make. Observing the motion of a chandelier in the cathedral he discovered that the length of time taken by the swing of a pendulum depends only on its own length, not on its weight or the scope of its swing. He almost certainly did not, as legend tells, drop balls of different weights from the cathedral's leaning tower to prove that Aristotle was wrong to say that heavier bodies fell faster than light ones. His contemporary Aristotelian opponents, however, did carry out such an experiment, and their results were closer to his prediction than to Aristotle's: a 100 lb ball hit the ground very little sooner than a 1 lb ball.

It was in Padua that Galileo did confirm by experiment—with balls rolling down inclined planes—that bodies of different weight, in the absence of resistance, take the same time to fall a given distance, and that they accelerate at the same uniform rate. His experiments also tended to show the falsity of the principle, fundamental to Aristotelian physics, that nothing moves unless acted on by an external source of motion. On the contrary, he maintained, a body in motion will continue to move unless acted on by a contrary force, such as friction. This thesis enabled him to dispense with the notion of impetus, which earlier critics of

Aristotle such as Philoponus had invoked to explain the continued motion of projectiles.[11] It prepared the way for the principle of inertia stated later by Descartes and Newton, that any moving object, unless acted on from outside, tends to move in a straight line at a constant speed. Galileo himself did not quite arrive at this principle, since in order to explain the orbits of the planets, he postulated that inertial motion was basically circular.

On its own, Galileo's work in mechanics would entitle him to a place among the great scientists, and he also made important discoveries in hydrostatics. But it was his research into astronomy that brought him fame and tribulation. Using the newly invented telescope, which he himself substantially improved, he was able to observe four moons of Jupiter, which he named 'Medicean Stars' in honour of Grand Duke Cosimo II of Tuscany. He discovered the mountains of the moon and the variable spots on the sun; discoveries which showed that he heavenly bodies were not, as Aristotle thought, made out of a uniform crystalline quintessence, but consisted of the same sort of material as our own earth. These discoveries were published in 1610 in a book entitled *A Messenger from the Stars* (*Sidereus Nuncius*). The book was dedicated to Duke Cosimo, who forthwith gave him a lifetime appointment as philosopher and mathematician to the court of Tuscany.

Shortly afterwards, Galileo observed that the planet Venus went through phases similar to the phases of the moon. This could only be explained, he concluded, if Venus was orbiting the sun and not the earth: it provided a powerful argument in favour of the Copernican hypothesis. The discovery of the moons that revolved around Jupiter in its planetary orbit had already disposed of one of the strongest arguments urged against heliocentrism, namely that the moon would only be able to orbit the earth if the earth itself was stationary.

Galileo was initially cautious in publicly expressing the conclusions he drew from his astronomical discoveries. However, after an ecclesiastical commission in Rome had taken official notice of his major observations, he began to propagate heliocentric ideas to a wide circle of friends, and in 1613, in an appendix to a book on sunspots, he declared his adherence to Copernicus. A Dominican friar in Florence, in a sermon on Acts 1: 11 ('Ye Galileans, why stand ye gazing up to heaven?') denounced heliocentrism as being in conflict with biblical texts, such as the one in which Joshua tells the sun to stand still so that the Israelites may complete their victory over the Philistines. Galileo decided to travel to Rome to clarify his theological status.

In advance he wrote to the powerful Jesuit cardinal, St Robert Bellarmine, urging that the sacred authors who spoke of the sun as moving were merely using popular idiom and were not intending to teach geometry. Bellarmine referred the matter to a committee of the Inquisition who determined that the opinion that

---

[11] See above, p. 394.

the sun was the centre of the cosmos was heretical, and the opinion that the earth moved was at the least erroneous. On the instructions of Pope Paul V, Bellarmine instructed Galileo that he must not hold or defend either of these opinions. If there was a real proof of heliocentrism, he told one of Galileo's friends, then we would have to re-examine the biblical texts which appeared to contradict it; but as matters stood, Copernicus' theory was only an unproved hypothesis. And indeed, Galileo's own heliocentric system, though it fitted the phenomena better, was almost as complicated as the geocentric system of his opponents, demanding constant appeal to epicycles.[12] The evidence he had discovered did not justify the degree of certainty with which he maintained his thesis.

It is often said that in this exchange Bellarmine showed a sounder grasp of the philosophy of science than the age's greatest scientist and Galileo showed a sounder grasp of biblical exegesis than the age's most famous theologian. The paradox is an agreeable one, but it is not really a fair representation of the debate on either side. And whatever the merits of the case, the upshot was that while Galileo's writings were not condemned, he was silenced for several years to come.

In 1624 Galileo travelled to Rome once more. Paul V and Bellarmine were now dead, and there was a different pope wearing the tiara: Urban VIII, who as Cardinal Barberini had shown himself an admirer of Galileo's astronomical discoveries. Galileo was given permission to write a systematic treatment of the Ptolemaic and the Copernican models, on condition that he presented them both impartially without favouring heliocentrism.

In 1632 Galileo published, with the approval of the papal censor, *Dialogue on the Two Chief World Systems*. In the book one character, Salviati, presents the Copernican system, and another, Simplicius, defends the traditional one. 'Simplicius' was an appropriate name for the defender of Aristotelianism, since it had been borne by the greatest of Aristotle's Greek commentators. However, it could also be interpreted as meaning 'simpleton' and the pope was furious when he found some of his own words placed in the mouth of Simplicius. He concluded that Galileo had presented the Copernican system in a more favourable light than its opponent, and had therefore deviated from the terms of his licence to publish. In 1633 Galileo was summoned to Rome, tried by the Inquisition, and under the threat of torture forced to abjure heliocentrism. He was condemned to life imprisonment, a sentence that he served out until his death in 1642, in confinement in the houses of distinguished friends and eventually in his own home at Bellosguardo outside Florence.

While under house arrest he was allowed to receive visitors. Among them was John Milton, who in *Areopagitica* recorded: 'I found and visited the famous Galileo grown old, a prisoner of the Inquisition, for thinking in Astronomy otherwise

---

[12] Galileo did not incorporate Kepler's discovery of the elliptical orbits of the planets, which was needed to achieve the appropriate simplification of heliocentrism.

than the Franciscan and Dominican licensers thought.' The newly founded college at Harvard in the commonwealth of Massachusetts made an offer of a visiting professorship, which was politely declined. Even though going blind, Galileo continued to write, and incorporated the fruit of his lifetime's work in *Discourses and Mathematical Demonstrations Concerning Two New Sciences*. This was published in Leiden in 1638 and became the most widely influential of his works.

Galileo was treated more humanely than Bruno and many another prisoner of the Inquisition, but the evil effects of his condemnation were felt throughout Europe. Scientific investigation in Italy went into decline: 'nothing has been there written now these many years,' Milton could complain, 'but flattery and fustian.' Even in Protestant Holland, Descartes was for many years deterred by Galileo's fate from publishing his own scientific cosmology. When in 1992 Pope John Paul II publicly acknowledged the injustice the Church had done to Galileo, the apology came 350 years too late.

Bacon

An English contemporary of Galileo, Francis Bacon, shared his antipathy to Aristotle, but was more interested in the theory than in the practice of scientific method. Born in London in 1561, Bacon was educated at Trinity College, Cambridge, and studied law at Gray's Inn. He entered Parliament in 1584 and later became a client of Queen Elizabeth's favourite, the Earl of Essex. When, in 1598, Essex plotted an insurrection, Bacon took a leading part in his prosecution for treason. On the accession of James I he became solicitor-general and was knighted. In 1606 he published the first of his major philosophical writings, *The Advancement of Learning*, a systematic classification of scientific disciplines.

The climax of Bacon's career was his appointment in 1618 as Lord Chancellor with the title Lord Verulam. He planned a massive work, the *Instauratio Magna* (*The Great Instauration*), which was to take all knowledge for its province. Only two parts of this were completed: the first was a revision of *The Advancement of Learning*, and the second was the *Novum Organum* which was his principal work on scientific method. In 1621, in the course of a parliamentary inquiry, he pleaded guilty to charges of accepting bribes, and was disgraced and briefly imprisoned. He wrote other scientific and historical works and also the essays for which he is nowadays best remembered. He died at Highgate in 1626. Legend represents him as a martyr to science, offering his life in the cause of experimental refrigeration; for he died, it is said, from a chill caught stuffing a hen with snow to see whether the cold would preserve the meat.

'The parts of human learning', Bacon says in Book Two of *The Advancement*, 'have reference to the three parts of Man's Understanding, which is the seat of learning:

History to his Memory, Poesy to his Imagination, and Philosophy to his reason' (*AL*, 177). Poesy, which includes not only poetry but prose fiction, is treated only perfunctorily by Bacon: the kind of poesy he most admires is a story with a moral message, like Aesop's fables. But history and philosophy are addressed at length, and given further subdivisions.

The most important parts of history are Natural and Civil. 'Civil history' is what we would nowadays call history: Bacon himself contributed to it a narrative of the reign of Henry VII. 'Natural history' is a discipline of broad scope with three subdivisions: the history of 'nature in course, of nature erring or varying, and of nature altered or wrought'. It will include, then, treatises of natural science, records of extraordinary marvels, and manuals of technology. Bacon's own contribution to natural history consisted of two compilations of research material, a History of the Winds, and a History of Life and Death. The 'history of nature erring', he thought, should include records of superstitious narrations of sorceries and witchcrafts, in order to ascertain how far effects attributed to superstition could be attributed to natural causes. But the third subdivision, 'history mechanical', was the most fundamental and useful for natural philosophy, whose value, according to Bacon, was above all in its practical application and utility.

In his classification of philosophy, Bacon first puts on one side 'divine philosophy' or natural theology: it suffices, he tells us, to refute atheism but not to inform religion. He then divides philosophy into natural and human. Natural philosophy may be speculative or operative: the speculative kind includes both physics and metaphysics, and the operative kind includes both mechanics and magic. Mechanics is the practical application of physics, and magic is the practical application of metaphysics.

This brisk and provocative anatomy of philosophy is not as neat as it seems, and many of the names Bacon gives to the various disciplines are employed in idiosyncratic ways. His 'natural magic', he tells us, must be sharply distinguished from the 'credulous and superstitious conceits' of alchemy and astrology. It is not at all clear what he has in mind: the one thing he seems to offer as an example is the mariner's compass. Why, we may ask, is this a matter of 'magic' rather than 'mechanics'?

An answer suggests itself when we read that physics deals with the efficient and material causes of things, while metaphysics deals with the final and formal causes. So the sail, which gives the boat its motion, operates in the realm of physics, while the compass, which guides the boat's direction, operates in the realm of metaphysics. Bacon admits candidly that he is using 'metaphysics' in a novel way. What others call metaphysics he calls 'first philosophy' or 'summary philosophy': it is a receptacle, he tells us, for all the universal principles that are not exclusive to particular disciplines. (An example is 'If equals be added to unequals the result will be unequal,' an axiom which he believes applies in law as well as in mathematics.)

But the distinction made between physics and metaphysics on the basis of the Aristotelian four causes is itself misleading. Bacon's scheme for natural magic leaves no real room for teleology: 'inquiry into final causes', he tells us, 'is sterile, and like a virgin consecrated to God, produces nothing.' And when he speaks of 'forms' he is not thinking of Aristotle's substantial forms—such as the form of a lion, or of water—because these, he believes, are too varied and complicated to be discovered. Instead of studying these, we should look rather for the simpler forms which go into their composition, in the way that letters go to make up words. The task of metaphysics is to investigate the simpler forms which correspond to individual letters:

To enquire the forms of sense, of voluntary motion, of vegetation, of colours, of gravity and levity, of density, of tenuity, of heat and of cold, and all other natures and qualities, which like an alphabet are not many, and which the essences (upheld by matter) of all creatures do now consist. (*AL*, 196)

Bacon's elementary forms are obscure characters in comparison with the mathematical shapes and symbols which Galileo declared to be the alphabet in which the book of the world is written. But most probably when he talked of forms he had in mind hidden material structures underlying the overt appearance and behaviour of things.

So much for natural philosophy. Human philosophy, the other great branch of the subject, has two parts, Bacon tells us, one which considers 'man segregate' and another which considers 'man congregate'. The first part corresponds to anatomy, physiology, and psychology, and the second embraces what would nowadays be called the social sciences. The detailed subdivisions Bacon enumerates appear arbitrary and haphazard. The sciences of the body include medicine, 'cosmetic', 'athletic', and the 'Arts Voluptuary', which include practical joking. The study of the nature of the soul is a matter for theology, but there is a human science which studies the operations of the soul. These fall into two classes, one set belonging to the understanding or reason, whose function is judgement, and the other set belonging to the will or appetite, whose function is action or execution. What of the imagination, which had a privileged place in Bacon's initial classification of human faculties?

The Imagination is an agent or *nuncius* in both provinces, both the judicial and the ministerial. For sense sendeth over to Imagination before Reason have judged: and Reason sendeth over to Imagination before the Decree can be acted; for Imagination ever precedeth Voluntary Motion: saving that this Janus of Imagination hath differing faces; for the face towards Reason hath the print of Truth, but the face towards Action hath the print of Good. (*AL*, 217)

But imagination is no mere servant of the other faculties, Bacon insists: it can triumph over reason, and that is what happens in the case of religious belief.

It is clear that Bacon envisioned the mind as a kind of internal society, with the different faculties enshrined in a constitution respecting the separation of powers. When he comes to treat of the social sciences themselves he offers another threefold division, corresponding to associations for friendship, for business, and for government. Political theory is a part of civil philosophy, that branch of human philosophy that concerns the benefits that humans derive from living in society.

Having finished his classification, Bacon can boast 'I have made as it were a small globe of the intellectual world' (*AL*, 299). The various sciences which appear in his voluminous catalogue are not all at similar stages of development. Some, he thinks, have achieved a degree of perfection, but others are deficient, and some are almost non-existent. One of the most deficient is logic, and the defects of logic weaken other sciences also. The problem is that logic lacks a theory of scientific discovery:

Like as the West-Indies had never been discovered if the use of the mariner's needle had not been first discovered, though the one be vast regions and the other a small motion; so it cannot be found strange if sciences be no further discovered if the art itself of invention and discovery hath been passed over. (*AL*, 219).

Bacon set out to remedy this lack and to provide a compass to guide scientific researchers. This was the task of his *Novum Organum*.

Bacon's project of introducing discipline into research had a negative and a positive component. The researcher's first, negative, task is to be on his guard against the factors that can introduce bias into his observations. Bacon lists four of these, and calls them 'idols' because they are fetishes which can divert us from the pursuit of truth: there are the idols of the tribe, the idols of the den, the idols of the marketplace, and the idols of the theatre. The idols of the tribe are temptations endemic in the whole human race, such as the tendency to judge things by superficial appearances, the tendency to go along with popular belief, and the tendency to interpret nature anthropomorphically. The idols of the den, or cave, are features of individual temperaments which hamper objectivity: some people, for instance, are too conservative, others too ready to seize on novelties. Each person has 'a certain individual cavern of his own, which breaks and distorts the light of nature'. The idols of the marketplace (or perhaps 'idols of the courts'— *idola fori*) are snares lurking in the language we use, which contains meaningless, ambiguous, and ill-defined words. Finally the idols of the theatre are false systems of philosophy which are no more than stage plays, whether 'sophistical', like Aristotle's, or 'empirical', like contemporary alchemists, or 'superstitious' like the Neoplatonists who confuse philosophy with theology.

The positive task of the researcher is *induction*, the discovery of scientific laws by the systematic examination of particular cases. If this is not to be rash generalization from inadequate sampling of nature, we need a carefully schematized procedure, showing us how to mount gradually from particular instances to axioms of gradually increasing generality. Bacon offers a series of detailed rules to guide this process:

Suppose that we have some phenomenon X and we wish to discover its true form or explanation. We must first make a table of presences—that is to say, we list the items A, B, C, D...which are present when X is present. Then we make a table of absences, listing items E, F, G, H...which are present when X is absent. Thirdly, we make a table of degrees, recording that J, K, L, M...are present to a greater degree when X is present to a greater degree, and present to a lesser degree when X is present to a lesser degree.

This is only the preparatory step in the method. The real work of induction comes when we start the process of eliminating candidates for being the form of X. To be successful a candidate must be present in every case occurring in the table of presences, and absent in every case occurring in the table of absences. Bacon illustrates his method with the example of heat. We list cases when heat is present (e.g. the rays of the sun and the sparks of a flint) and cases in which it is absent (e.g. in the rays of the moon and the stars). Since light is present in cases listed in the table of absence, we can eliminate light as being the form of heat. After some further eliminative moves, and making use also of the table of degrees (e.g. that the more exercise animals take the hotter they get), Bacon concludes that heat is a special kind of motion ('an expansive motion held in check and pushing its way through tiny particles').

Bacon never completed the series of guidelines that he set out to present in the *Novum Organum*, and it cannot be said that his system adds up to a 'logic of induction'. However, he did establish the important point that negative instances are more significant, in the process of establishing laws, than positive ones. Twentieth-century philosophers have been willing to give him credit for being the first person to point out that laws of nature cannot be conclusively verified, but can be conclusively falsified.

Bacon's insistence on the importance of precise and repeated observations went hand in hand with an appreciation that natural science could make progress only by a massive cooperative endeavour. In the *New Atlantis*, an unfinished fragment published posthumously, a ship's crew in the South Seas land on an island containing a remarkable institution known as Salomon's House. This turns out to be a research establishment, where scientists work together to embody Bacon's utilitarian ideal of science as the extension of men's power over nature for the betterment of the human race. Their projects include plans for telephones, submarines, and aeroplanes. The president of the institute described its purpose thus:

The End of our Foundation is the knowledge of Causes, and secret motions of things, and the enlarging of the bound of Human Empire, to the effecting of all things possible. (*B*, 480)

Salomon's House was a Utopian fantasy; but it was given a counterpart in the real world when, thirty-five years after the *New Atlantis*, Bacon's compatriots of the next generation founded the Royal Society of London.

2

Descartes to Berkeley

Descartes

The seventeenth century, unlike the sixteenth century, was fertile in the production of philosophers of genius. The man who is often considered the father of modern philosophy is René Descartes. He was born in 1596, about the time when Shakespeare was writing *Hamlet*, in a village in Touraine which is now called after him La-Haye-Descartes. A sickly child, he was exempted at school from morning exercises and acquired a lifelong habit of meditating in bed. From his eleventh to his nineteenth year he studied classics and philosophy at the Jesuit college of La Flèche. He remained a Catholic throughout his life, but chose to spend most of his adult life in Protestant Holland.

In 1616, having taken a degree in law at Poitiers, Descartes gave up his studies for a while. In the wars of religion that divided Europe, he enlisted in both camps. First, he was an unpaid volunteer in the army of the Protestant Prince of Orange; later he served in the army of the Catholic Duke Maximilian of Bavaria, who was then at war with the Palatine Elector Frederick, son-in-law of King James I of Britain. After he left the army he did not adopt a profession. Unlike the great philosophers of the Middle Ages he was a layman in both the ecclesiastical and the academic sense. He never lectured in a university, and he lived a private life as a gentleman of means. He wrote his most famous work not in the Latin of the learned world, but in good plain French, so that it could be understood, as he put it, 'even by women'.

While serving in the army, Descartes acquired a conviction that he had a call to philosophy. He spent a winter's day of 1619 huddled beside a stove, engrossed in meditation. He conceived the idea of undertaking, single-handed, a reform of human learning that would display all disciplines as branches of a single wonderful science. His conviction of vocation was reinforced when, that night, he had three dreams that he regarded as prophetic. But it was not until some years later that he settled permanently to philosophical studies.

From 1620 to 1625 he travelled in Germany, Holland, and Italy, and from 1625 to 1627 he mixed in society in Paris, gambling heavily and becoming involved in a duel over a love affair. His surviving early writings show his interest in mechanical and mathematical problems, and include a brief treatise on music. In 1627 he intervened impressively in the discussion of a grand public lecture in Paris: a cardinal who was present exhorted him to devote himself to the reform of philosophy.

A year later Descartes left for Holland, where he lived until 1649, shortly before his death. He chose the country for its climate and its reputation for tolerance: he looked forward to a life free from the distractions of the city and from morning callers. He dwelt in thirteen different houses during his twenty-year sojourn and kept his address secret from all but close friends. Amid Protestant surroundings, he continued to practise as a Catholic.

Descartes kept in touch with the learned world by letter. His principal correspondent was a Franciscan friar, Father Marin Mersenne, who was the centre of an erudite international network. Mersenne acted as Descartes' literary agent, handling the publication of his works and keeping him informed of recent scientific discoveries. Of the ten volumes of the standard edition of Descartes' works, five are taken up by his letters, which are a highly important source for the development of his thought.

In Holland Descartes lived comfortably and quietly; he was not wholly without company, and in 1635 he had an illegitimate daughter, Francine, who lived only five years. He brought a few books with him from Paris, including the *Summa Theologiae* of Thomas Aquinas. He claimed that he spent very little time reading: he had no great admiration for classical languages and he boasted that he had not opened a scholastic textbook once in twenty years. When a stranger asked to see his library, he pointed to a half-dissected calf. Besides purchasing carcasses from the butcher for dissection, he ground his own lenses in order to make experiments in optics. He trusted experiment rather than learning, but more than either he trusted his own philosophical reflection.

During his first years in Holland his work was mainly mathematical and physical. He laid the foundations of analytical geometry: the Cartesian coordinates that every schoolchild learns about derive their name from the Latin form of his surname, Cartesius. He studied refraction and propounded the law of sines, the result of careful theoretical and experimental work on the nature of light and of the eye. He also worked on meteorology, trying to ascertain the true nature of rainbows.

By 1632 Descartes had in mind to publish a substantial volume which would explain 'the nature of light, the sun and the fixed stars which emit it; the heavens which transmit it; the planets, the comets and the earth which reflect it; all the terrestrial bodies which are either coloured or transparent or luminous; and Man its spectator'. The system that it propounded was a heliocentric one: the earth was a planet, moving around the sun.

The treatise was entitled *The World* and it was ready for the press when Descartes learned that Galileo had been condemned for upholding the Copernican system. Anxious to avoid conflict with ecclesiastical authority, he returned the treatise to his desk. It was never published in his lifetime, although much of its material was incorporated twelve years later in a textbook called *Principles of Philosophy*.

Instead of publishing his system, in 1637 Descartes decided to make public 'some specimens of his method': his dioptrics, his geometry, and his meteorolgy. He prefaced them with 'a discourse on the right way to use one's reason and seek truth in the sciences'. The three scientific treatises are nowadays read only by specialists in the history of science, but the *Discourse on Method* has a claim to be the most popular of all philosophical classics. In significance it compares with Plato's *Republic* and with Kant's *Critique of Pure Reason*, but it has the advantage of being much briefer and more readable than either.

Among other things, the *Discourse* is a witty and urbane piece of autobiography, as the following extracts illustrate:

Good sense is the most fairly distributed thing in the world; for everyone thinks himself so well supplied with it, that even those who are hardest to satisfy in every other way do not usually desire more of it than they already have. . . .

As soon as my age allowed me to pass from under the control of my instructors, I entirely abandoned the study of letters, and resolved not to seek after any science but what might be found within myself or in the great book of the world. . . . I spent nine years in roaming about the world, aiming to be a spectator rather than an actor in all the comedies of life.

Amidst a great and populous nation, extremely industrious and more concerned with their own business than curious about other people's, while I do not lack any conveniences of the most frequented cities, I have been able to live a life as solitary and retired as though I were in the most remote deserts. (AT VI. 2, 9, 31; *CSMK* I. 111, 115, 126)

But the *Discourse* is much more than Descartes' intellectual autobiography: it presents in minature a summary of his philosophical system and his scientific method. Descartes had an extraordinary gift for presenting complicated philosophical doctrines so elegantly that they appear fully intelligible on first reading and yet can provide material for reflection to the most expert philosophers. He prided himself that his works could be read 'just like novels'.

There are two key ideas that are presented in the *Discourse* and elaborated in later works. First: human beings are thinking substances. Second: matter is extension in motion. Everything in his system is to be explained in terms of this dualism of mind and matter. If we nowadays tend naturally to think of mind and matter as the two great mutually exclusive and mutually exhaustive divisions of the universe we inhabit, that is because of Descartes.

Descartes reaches these conclusions by the application of a method of systematic doubt. To prevent being ensnared in falsehood, the philosopher must begin by doubting whatever can be doubted. The senses sometimes deceive us; mathematicians sometimes make mistakes; we can never be certain whether we are awake or asleep. Accordingly:

I decided to feign that everything that had entered my mind hitherto was no more true than the illusions of dreams. But immediately upon this I noticed that while I was trying to think everything false, it must needs be that I, who was thinking this, was something. And observing that this truth 'I am thinking, therefore I exist' was so solid and secure that the most extravagant suppositions of sceptics could not overthrow it, I judged that I need not scruple to accept it as the first principle of philosophy that I was seeking. (AT VI. 32; *CSMK* I. 127)

This is the famous *Cogito, ergo sum*, which achieves the second task of the philosopher, that of preventing the systematic doubt from leading to scepticism. But from it Descartes goes on to derive the principles of his system. If I were not thinking, I would have no reason to believe that I existed; hence I am a substance whose whole essence is to think; being a body is no part of my essence. The same goes for every other human being. So Descartes' first main thesis is established.

What assures me that the *Cogito* is correct? Only that I see clearly that it is true. Whenever I conceive something clearly and distinctly, I am assured of its truth. But when we turn to material objects, we find that of all their properties the only ones we clearly and distinctly perceive are shape, size, and movement. So Descartes gains his second main thesis, that matter is extension in motion.

But what guarantees the principle that whatever I see clearly and distinctly is true? Only the truthful nature of the God to whom I owe my existence as a thinking thing. So establishing the existence of God is a necessary part of Descartes' system. He offers two proofs that there is a God. First, I have in myself the idea of a perfect being, and this idea cannot be caused in me by anything less than a being that is itself perfect. Second, to be perfect a being must include in itself all perfections; but existence is a perfection, and therefore a perfect being must exist.[1]

Like Bacon, Descartes compared knowledge to a tree, but for him the tree's roots were metaphysics, its trunk was physics, and its fruitful branches were the moral and useful sciences. His own writings, after the *Discourse*, followed the order thus suggested. In 1641 he wrote his metaphysical *Meditations*, in 1644 his *Principles of Philosophy*, which is a pruned version of the physical system of *The World*, and in 1649 a *Treatise on the Passions*, which is largely an ethical treatise.

The *Meditations* contain a full statement of the system sketched in the *Discourse*. Before publication the text was sent to Mersenne to circulate for comment to a number of scholars and thinkers. Six sets of objections were received. They were printed, with replies from Descartes, in a long appendix to the first edition of 1641, which thus became the first peer-reviewed work in history. The objectors were a

---

[1] Descartes' natural theology is considered in detail in Ch. 10.

varied and distinguished group: apart from Mersenne himself they included a scholastic neighbour in Holland, an Augustinian theologian from Paris, Antoine Arnauld, plus the atomist philosopher Pierre Gassendi, and the English materialist and nominalist, Thomas Hobbes.

Criticisms of the *Meditations* continued to come in after publication, and critical reaction was not only literary. The rector of Utrecht University, Gisbert Voetius, denounced Descartes to the magistrates as a dangerous propagator of atheism, and the University of Leiden accused him of the Pelagian heresy. Descartes wrote two tracts, which survive, to defend his orthodoxy; but it was really the intervention of influential friends that prevented him from being arrested and having his books burnt.

One of his most supportive friends was Princess Elizabeth, the daughter of the Elector Frederick against whom he had once soldiered. He corresponded with her from 1643 until his death, answering (and sometimes failing to answer) her acute criticisms of his writings. He gave her much medical and moral advice, and consoled her on the execution of her uncle King Charles I. It was to her that he dedicated *The Principles of Philosophy*. The first part of that book summarizes the metaphysics of the *Meditations* and its three remaining parts deal with physical science, propounding laws of motion and explaining the nature of weight, heat, and light. The account given of the solar system is disguisedly heliocentric and discreetly evolutionary. Descartes explains that he is describing not how the world was actually made, but how God might have made it otherwise, if he had so pleased.

Descartes' correspondence with Princess Elizabeth led him to reflect further on the relationship between the body and the soul, and to construct an ethical system resembling ancient Stoicism. He developed these reflections into *The Passions of the Soul*. When the treatise was published, however, it was dedicated not to Elizabeth, but to another royal lady who had interested herself in philosophy, Queen Christina of Sweden. The queen was so impressed that she invited Descartes to be her court philosopher, sending an admiral with a battleship to fetch him from Holland. Descartes was reluctant to sacrifice his solitude and the appointment proved disastrous. He felt lonely and out of place: he was employed in writing a ballet and forced to rise at 5 a.m. to instruct the queen in philosophy.

Descartes had immense confidence in his own abilities, and still more in the method he had discovered. Given a few more years of life, he thought, and given sufficient research funding, he would be able to solve all the outstanding problems of physiology and learn thereby the cures of all diseases. At this point he fell a victim to the rigours of the Swedish winter. While nursing a sick friend he caught pneumonia, and died on 11 February 1650. There was an ironic fittingness about the motto which he had chosen for himself as an epitaph:

> No man is harmed by death, save he
> Who, known too well by all the world,
> Has not yet learnt to know himself.

Descartes was a man of extraordinary and versatile genius. His ideas on physiology, physics, and astronomy were superseded within a century: they enjoyed a much shorter currency than the Aristotelian system they were designed to replace. But his work in algebra and geometry entered into the abiding patrimony of mathematics; and his philosophical ideas remain—for better or worse—enormously influential to the present day. No one can question his claim to rank among the greatest philosophers of all time.

We should not, however, take him altogether at his own valuation. In the *Discourse* he insists that systems created by an individual are to be preferred to those created by communities:

> As a rule there is not such great perfection in works composed of several parts, and proceeding from the hands of various artists, as in those on which one man has worked alone. Thus we see the buildings undertaken and carried out by a single architect are generally more seemly and better arranged than those that several hands have sought to adapt, making use of old walls that were built for other purposes. Again, those ancient cities which were originally mere boroughs, and have become towns in process of time, are as a rule badly laid out, as compared with those towns of regular pattern that are laid out by a designer on an open plan to suit his fancy. (AT VI. 11; *CSMK* I. 116)

This is not merely the expression of a taste for classical rather than Gothic architecture: laws too, Descartes goes on, are better if devised by a single legislator in a single code. Similarly, he thought, a true system of philosophy would be the creation of a single mind; and he believed himself to be uniquely qualified to be its creator.

It is true that Descartes initiated a new, individualistic, style of philosophizing. Medieval philosophers had seen themselves as principally engaged in transmitting a corpus of knowledge; in the course of transmission they might offer improvements, but these must remain within the bounds set by tradition. Renaissance philosophers had seen themselves as rediscovering and republicizing the lost wisdom of ancient times. It was Descartes who was the first philosopher since Antiquity to offer himself as a total innovator; as the person who had the privilege of setting out the truth about man and his universe for the very first time. Where Descartes trod, others followed: Locke, Hume, and Kant each offered their philosophies as new creations, constructed for the first time on sound scientific principles. 'Read my work, and discard my predecessors' is a constant theme of seventeenth- and eighteenth-century thinkers and writers.

With medieval philosophers like Aquinas, Scotus, and Ockham, a student has to read the texts closely to realize the great degree of innovation that is going on: the new wine is always decanted so carefully into the old bottles. With Descartes and his successors, the difficulty is the opposite: one has to look outside the text to realize that much that is presented as original insight is in fact to be found stated in earlier authors. There is no need to doubt the sincerity of Descartes' repeated statements that he owed nothing to his scholastic predecessors. He was not a plagiarist, but he had no appreciation of how much he had imbibed from the intellectual atmosphere in which he grew up.

When Descartes tried to doubt everything, the one thing he did not call into question was the meaning of the words he was using in his solitary meditation. Had he done so, he would have had to realize that even the words we use in soliloquy derive their meaning from the social community which is the home of our language, and that therefore it was not, in fact, possible to build up his philosophy from solitary private ideas. Again, Descartes thought that it was not possible to call into question propositions that he was taught by natural light—the clear and distinct perceptions that form the basic building blocks of his system. But in fact, as we shall see in detail in later chapters, too often when he tells us that something is taught by the natural light in our souls, he produces a doctrine that he had imbibed from the Jesuits at La Flèche.

There is no doubt of the enormous influence Descartes has exercised from his own day to ours. But his relation to modern philosophy is not that of father to son, nor of architect to palace, nor of planner to city. Rather, in the history of philosophy his position is like that of the waist of an hourglass. As the sand in the upper chamber of such a glass reaches its lower chamber only through the slender passage between the two, so too ideas that had their origin in the Middle Ages have reached the modern world through a narrow filter: the compressing genius of Descartes.

Hobbes

Of those who had been invited to comment on Descartes' *Meditations* in 1641, the most distinguished was Thomas Hobbes, the foremost English philosopher of the age. At that time Hobbes was fifty-three years old, having been born in 1588, the year of the Spanish Armada. He had been educated at Oxford and had served as a tutor to the Cavendish family and as an amanuensis to Francis Bacon. In 1629 he had published an English translation of Thucydides' *History of the Peloponnesian War*. During a visit to Paris in the 1630s he had met Descartes' Franciscan friend Marin Mersenne, whom he described as 'an outstanding exponent of all branches of philosophy'. In 1640 he had written a treatise in English, *Elements of Law, Natural and Political*, which contained in essence the principles of his philosophy of human nature and human society. He fled in the same year to Paris, anticipating the Civil War which was heralded by the activities of the Long Parliament. He remained there more than ten years, and was, for a period, tutor to the exiled heir to the throne, the future King Charles II. In 1642 he presented a number of the ideas of the *Elements of Law* in a Latin treatise, *De Cive*, which established his reputation in France.

Hobbes' comments on Descartes show little comprehension of the *Meditations*, and the two thinkers have traditionally been regarded as standing at opposite poles of philosophy. In fact they resembled each other in several ways. Both, for instance, were fired by a passion for mathematics. Hobbes' most lively biographer, the gossipy John Aubrey, described his first encounter with geometry:

He was 40 years old before he looked on geometry; which happened accidentally. Being in a gentleman's library, Euclid's *Elements* lay open, and 'twas the 47th Element at Book I. He read the proposition. 'By G —' said he, 'this is impossible!' So he reads the demonstration of it, which referred him back to such a proposition; which proposition he read. *Et sic deinceps* [and so on], that at last he was demonstratively convinced of that truth. This made him in love with geometry. (Aubrey 1975: 158)

He did not, however, grasp the importance of Descartes' analytic geometry, which he thought 'lacked bite'. He thought even more poorly of his philosophy, in particular his physics or natural philosophy. 'Mr Hobbes was wont to say,' Aubrey tells us, 'that had Des Cartes kept himself wholly to Geometrie that he had been the best Geometer in the world, but that his head did not lye for Philosophy.' There is an irony here. When, later in life, Hobbes betook himself to the serious study of geometry, he wasted years debating with the mathematical professors of Oxford in a futile attempt to square the circle.

Descartes and Hobbes had much in common. They shared a contempt for Aristotle and the Aristotelian establishment in the universities. Both were solitary thinkers who spent significant parts of their lives in exile—each, for a time, beholden to banished Stuart courts. Both of them had very modest libraries, and were contemptuous of book-learning. Those who rely on reading, Hobbes said, 'spend time in fluttering over their books; as birds that entering by the chimney, and finding themselves enclosed in a chamber, flutter at the false light of a glass window, for want of wit to consider which way they came in' (*L*, 24). Hobbes, like Descartes, was a master of vernacular prose, and wrote for popular reading as well as for the learned world.

The most significant philosophical agreement between the two men was that each of them was convinced that the material world was to be explained solely in terms of motion. 'The causes of universal things (of those, at least, that have any cause) are manifest of themselves, or (as they say commonly) known to nature; so that they need no method at all; for they have all but one universal cause, which is motion,' wrote Hobbes (*De Corpore* VI.5). Like Descartes, Hobbes denied the objective reality of secondary qualities such as colour, sound, and heat, and indeed of all real accidents. 'Whatseover accidents or qualities our senses make us think there be in the world, they are not there, but are seemings and apparitions only. The things that really are in the world without us, are those motions by which these seemings are caused' (*Elements of Law* I.10). Like Descartes, Hobbes regarded the science of optics as being a key to the understanding of the true nature of sensation.

However, while Hobbes was close to one half of Descartes' philosophy, his philosophy of matter, he was strongly opposed to the other half, his philosophy of mind. Indeed he denied the existence of mind in the sense in which Descartes understood it. There was, for Hobbes, no such thing as a non-bodily substance, unextended and unmoving. There were no incorporeal spirits, human, angelic, or divine. The very expression 'incorporeal substance', he said, was as absurd as 'round quadrangle'. Historians disagree whether Hobbes' materialism involved a denial of the existence of God, or implied that God was a body of some infinite and invisible kind. It is unlikely that he was an atheist; but he certainly denied the dualism of mind and matter in human beings.

Hobbes' materialism justifies his reputation as a great opponent of Descartes, despite the many attitudes and prejudices they shared. But in addition to the metaphysical contrast between materialism and dualism, the two are often treated by historians of philosophy as founders of opposing schools of epistemology: British empiricism and continental rationalism. In Chapter 4 I will argue that the difference between these two schools is not as great as it appears on the surface.

Hobbes outlived Descartes by nearly thirty years, but he did not remain long in France after Descartes' death in 1650. He found the position of a Protestant in Paris uncomfortable: he had resisted Mersenne's attempts to convert him to Catholicism, and when suffering from a life-threatening illness he had insisted on receiving the sacrament according to the Anglican rite. In his last years in Paris he wrote the work that was to give him immortality, *Leviathan, or the Matter, Form and Power of a Commonwealth Ecclesiastical and Civil.*

Starting from the premiss that in a state of nature, outside any commonwealth, there would be nothing but a mere war of all against all, Hobbes argues that principles of rational self-interest would urge men to give up some of their unfettered liberty in return for equal concessions by others. Such principles would lead them to transfer their rights, save that of self-defence, to a central power able to enforce laws by punishment. A covenant of every man with every man sets up a supreme sovereign, himself not a party to the covenant and therefore incapable of breaching it. Such a sovereign is the source of law and property rights, and it is his function to enforce, not just the original covenant that constitutes the state, but individual covenants that his subjects make with each other.[2]

Leviathan was published in London in 1651. Despite its eloquent presentation of the case for absolute sovereignty, the work was not well received by Charles II's entourage when copies were brought across the Channel. Banished from court and deprived by death of his best Catholic friends, Hobbes decided to return to England, now, since the execution of Charles I, a commonwealth under a Protector.

---

[2] Hobbes' political philosophy is considered in detail in Ch. 9 below.

During the Protectorate Hobbes lived quietly in London and wrote no political philosophy. He published his physical philosophy under the title *De Corpore* (*On Body*) in Latin in 1655 and in English in 1656. He engaged in controversy with Bishop Bramhall of Derry on the topics that Milton tells us engaged the devils of *Paradise Lost,* 'Providence, Foreknowledge, Will and Fate, / Fixed Fate free will, foreknowledge absolute'. The disputation was inconclusive, like that of the devils 'who found no end, in wand'ring mazes lost'. In 1658 he published a Latin work, *De Homine*, which, like the earlier *De Cive*, presented for an international readership some of the ideas of *The Elements of Law*.

Hobbes was reinstated in the favour of Charles II on his restoration to the throne in 1660. He was awarded a pension and made welcome at court, though much teased by the courtiers. 'Here comes the bear to be baited,' the King is reported to have said on seeing him; but he was able, we are told, to give as good as he got in wit and drollery. *Leviathan*, however, remained an object of suspicion. 'There was a report,' Aubrey tells us, 'that in Parliament, not long after the King was settled, some of the bishops made a motion to have the good old gentleman burn't for a heretic.'

From 1660 to his death Hobbes lived mainly at the houses of the Earl of Devonshire in London and at Chatsworth and Hardwick. He wrote no more philosophy, but translated the *Iliad* and the *Odyssey*, and wrote a history of the Civil War entitled *Behemoth* which, at the request of the King, he withheld from publication. He died at Hardwick Hall in December 1679, at the age of ninety-one, full of energy to the last in spite of Parkinson's disease. He attributed his vigorous old age to three things: regular tennis until the age of seventy-five, abstinence from wine from the age of sixty, and the continued exercise of the voice in singing. 'At night,' Aubrey tells us, 'when he was abed, and the doors made fast, and was sure nobody heard him, he sang aloud (not that he had a very good voice) but for his health's sake: he did believe it did his lungs good and conduced much to prolong his life.'

Hobbes' fame in the history of philosophy rests above all on his contribution to political philosophy. He himself, however, attached great importance to his philosophy of language. The invention of printing, he observes, was no great matter compared with the invention of writing, and that in its turn is insignificant compared to the invention of speech, which is what marks us off from beasts and makes us capable of pursuing science. Without words 'there had been amongst men, neither commonwealth, nor society, nor contract, nor peace, no more than amongst lions, bears, and wolves' (*L*, 20).

The purpose of speech is to transfer the train of our thoughts into a train of words, and it has four uses:

First, to register, what by cogitation we find to be the cause of any thing, present or past; and what we find things present or past may produce, or effect: which in sum, is aquiring of arts. Secondly, to show to others that knowledge which we have attained; which is, to counsel and teach one another. Thirdly, to make known to others our wills and purposes, that we may have the mutual help of one another. Fourthly, to please and delight ourselves, and others, by playing with our words, for pleasure or ornament, innocently. (*L*, 21)

There are four abuses corresponding to the four uses of words, and great pains are needed to avoid such abuses. 'For words are wise men's counters, they do but reckon by them; but they are the money of fools' (*L*, 21).

Hobbes is a thoroughgoing nominalist: all words are names, and names refer only to individuals. Names may be proper, such as 'Peter', or common, such as 'horse'; and they may also be abstract, such as 'life' or 'length'. They may even be descriptions (which Hobbes calls 'circumlocutions'), such as 'he that writ the Iliad'. But whatever form a name takes, it never names anything other than one or more individuals. Universal names like 'man' and 'tree' do not name any universal thing in the world or any idea in the mind, but name many individuals, 'there being nothing in the word Universall but Names; for the things named, are every one of them Individual and Singular'.

For Hobbes, names are put together to make sentences. If we say 'Socrates is just', the semantic relationship of the word 'just' to the man Socrates is exactly the same as the relationship of the word 'Socrates': both are names, and the predicate term in the sentence signifies in the same way as the subject tem does. Sentences are true when the two names they contain are both names of the same thing. 'A man is a living creature' is true because 'living creature' is a name of everything that is signified by 'man'. 'Every man is just' is false because 'just' is not a name of every man, the greater part of mankind deserving the name 'unjust' (*L*, 23; G, 38).

The two-name theory is a naive piece of semantics which would not survive serious logical criticism such as it had received in the medieval period and as it was to receive in the nineteenth century in the work of Gottlob Frege. Hobbes' version of the theory is a particularly crude one by comparison with that of its leading medieval proponent, William Ockham.[3] It remained influential, however, among the British empiricists whom many have seen as the heirs of the tradition of Ockham and Hobbes.

The Cambridge Platonists

A group of half a dozen English philosophers in the mid-seventeenth century occupied a position at odds with both Hobbes and Descartes. Five of them, of whom the most important was Ralph Cudworth (1617–88), were graduates of

---

[3] See above, pp. 368–9.

Emmanuel College, Cambridge, and one of them, Henry More (1614–87), was a graduate of Christ's College, Cambridge, of which Cudworth was for thirty years master. All of them shared an admiration for Plato, Plotinus, and their followers among the early Church Fathers. Hence the group is commonly called the 'Cambridge Platonists'.

Despite their Cambridge affiliation, the members of the group were hostile to the Puritanism that prevailed in that town and university during the Civil War. They rejected Calvinist doctrines of predestination, affirmed human freedom, and preached the merits of religious toleration. Their toleration, however, did not extend to atheists, and the focus of their hostility was Hobbes, whose materialism they regarded as tantamount to atheism. During the reign of Charles I Puritan hostility to the Anglican hierarchy had been followed by the deposition and execution of the king. For the Cambridge Platonists the political slogan 'No Bishop, No King' had a philosophical counterpart: 'No Spirit, no God'. One could not be a materialist and a theist at the same time.

Up to this point, the Cambridge Platonists sided with Descartes against Hobbes in emphasizing the distinction of mind from matter. They devoted themselves to proving the immortality of the human soul and the existence of a spiritual God in such treatises as More's *Antidote Against Atheism* and *The Immortality of the Soul*, and Cudworth's *True Intellectual System of the Universe*. For More, a human being is 'a created spirit endowed with sense and reason, and a power of organizing terrestrial matter into human shape'.[4] Like Descartes, Cudworth argues that God's existence can be proved by the presence in us of the idea of God: 'Were there no God, the idea of an absolutely or infinitely perfect Being could never have been made or feigned, neither by politicians, nor by poets, nor philosophers, nor any other.' The idea of God is a coherent one, 'therefore must it needs have some kind of entity or other, either an actual or a possible one; but God, if he be not, is not possible to be, therefore he doth actually exist.'[5]

Like Descartes, the Cambridge Platonists believed in innate ideas: the mind is not a blank page on which the senses write, but a closed book, which the senses merely open. Innate ideas, More said, are present in our minds in the way that melodies are present in the mind of a musician while he is sleeping upon the grass (*Antidote*, 17). Among the innate ideas immediately evident to the human mind are fundamental and undeniable moral principles, of which More was prepared to list, in a handbook of 1668, no fewer than twenty-three. Hobbes, Cudworth maintained, was quite wrong to think that justice and injustice arose as a result of a merely human compact. There was no way in which individual humans could confer upon a sovereign a power of life and death which they did not themselves possess.

---

[4] *The Immortality of the Soul* (1659), bk 1, ch. 8.
[5] *The True Intellectual System of the Universe* (1678), II. 537, III. 49–50.

The Cambridge Platonists parted company with Descartes when they came to explain the basis of fundamental ethical principles. It was quite wrong, Cudworth complained, to say that moral and other eternal truths depended on the omnipotent will of God and were therefore in principle variable. 'Virtue and holiness in creatures', he told the House of Commons in a 1647 sermon, 'are not therefore Good because God loves them, and will have them be accounted such; but rather, God therefore loves them because they are in themselves simply good.'[6]

The Platonists' disagreement with Descartes was much sharper when they came to consider his account of the material world. They were not opposed to new developments in science—both Cudworth and More were members of the Royal Society—but they denied that the phenomena could be accounted for mechanistically in terms of matter and motion. Unlike Descartes, they believed that animals had consciousness and sensitive souls; and even the fall of a heavy body, they believed, needed to be explained by the action of an immaterial principle. This did not mean that God did everything directly, as it were with his own hands, but rather that he had entrusted the physical world to an intermediary, 'a plastic nature' akin to a world-soul, that acted regularly and teleologically. Those like Descartes who rejected teleology were mere 'mechanic theists' and were little better than the materialist Hobbes.

Locke

Hobbes was a pioneer of modern empiricism, but his fame has been eclipsed by that of a more polished practitioner, John Locke. Locke was born in Somerset in 1632, the son of a minor gentleman who fought in the parliamentary cavalry. He was educated at Westminster School, not only in Greek and Latin but also in Hebrew, and went on to a closed studentship at Christ Church, Oxford, whence he took his MA in 1658. After the restoration of Charles II in 1660 he wrote several Latin pamphlets in defence of Anglican orthodoxy, taught Greek in the university, became a college tutor, and held a number of college offices. He became interested in chemistry and physiology, and spent seven years studying to qualify in medicine.

In 1667 Locke left Oxford to become physician and political adviser to Anthony Ashley Cooper, a member of Charles II's inner cabinet, shortly to become the Earl of Shaftesbury. Soon after arriving in London he wrote a brief *Essay on Toleration* advocating, in contradiction to his earlier tracts, the removal of doctrinal constraints on all except Roman Catholics. The years 1676–8 he spent in France, meeting a number of followers of Descartes and making a serious study of his philosophy.

---

[6] Quoted in C. Taliaferro, *Evidence and Faith* (Cambridge: Cambridge University Press, 2005), 11.

As his reign progressed, Charles II became unpopular, particularly after the conversion to Catholicism of his brother and heir, James, Duke of York. Protestant dissatisfaction came to a head in 1679 when many Catholics were tried and executed for alleged complicity in an imaginary popish plot to kill the king and place his brother on the throne. Shaftesbury became leader of the Whig Party, which sought to exclude James from the succession; his attempts to secure the passing of an Exclusion Bill were defeated when Charles dissolved Parliament in 1681. After being implicated in a plot against the royal brothers in 1682, Shaftesbury had to flee to Holland, where he died in 1683.

Locke was sufficiently identified with Shaftesbury's projects to find it necessary to go into exile during the Tory revival at the end of Charles II's life and during the short reign of his brother James II (1685–8). Around the time of the popish plot and the exclusion crisis he had written *Two Treatises on Government*. In the first he made a devastating attack on a work by Sir Robert Filmer in defence of the divine right of kings. In the second he presented an account of the state of nature—a much more optimistic one than Hobbes'—and argued that governments and commonwealths are created by a social contract in order to protect the property of individuals. He argued that if a government acts arbitrarily, or if one branch of government usurps the role of another, the government is dissolved and rebellion is justified.[7]

While in Holland, Locke worked on the composition of his greatest philosophical work, the *Essay Concerning Human Understanding*. Notes for this work date back to his early days in London, but it was not published until 1690, after which it went through four editions during Locke's lifetime.

The *Essay* consists of four books. The first and shortest, entitled 'Of Innate Notions', argues that there are no innate principles in our minds, whether speculative or practical. All our ideas are derived, either directly or by combination or reflection, from experience. Even in the case of *a priori* disciplines such as geometry, the ideas that we employ are not innate. The thirty-three chapters of the second book treat exhaustively of ideas, 'idea' being the catch-all term that Locke employs to characterize our mental skills and the concepts of our minds:

Every Man being conscious to himself, That he thinks, and that which his Mind is employ'd about whilst thinking, being the Ideas that are there, 'tis past doubt, that Men have in their Minds several ideas, such as those expressed by the words *Whiteness, Hardness, Sweetness, Thinking, Motion, Man, Elephant, Army, Drunkenness*, and others. (*E*, 104)

Locke classified ideas in various ways: there are simple ideas and complex ideas; there are clear and distinct and obscure and confused ideas; there are ideas of sensation and ideas of reflection. In dealing with simple ideas, Locke divides the qualities to be found in bodies into two categories, primary qualities such as solidity,

---

[7] Locke's political philosophy is considered in detail in Ch. 9.

motion, and figure, which are in bodies 'whether we perceive them or no', and secondary qualities such as colours, which 'are nothing in the objects themselves, but powers to produce various sensations in us by their primary qualities'. Among the ideas of reflection the first and most important is the idea of perception, for this is the first exercise of the mind upon ideas. Perception is a purely passive experience, and everyone knows what it is by looking within himself. The passive experiences of perception are the bedrock on which Locke builds his philosophy.

The second book of the *Essay* presents an empiricist philosophy of mind and will, but it contains much else: reflections on time, space, and number, for instance, and a catalogue of human passions. It deals with causal and other relations, and it contains an elaborate and highly influential discussion of the nature of personal identity.

Although Locke believes that we can recognize simple ideas within ourselves unaided, and that if we cannot recognize them no words will help us to do so, he does in practice identify the ideas that he is talking about by means of the words that express them. He admits that 'our abstract ideas, and general words, have so constant a relation one to another, that it is impossible to speak clearly and distinctly of our Knowledge, which all consists in propositions, without considering, first, the Nature, Use and Signification of Language' (*E*, 401).

To that topic, then, he devotes his third book. The most famous sections of this book are the discussion of abstract ideas and the theory of substance. The mind, Locke says, observing likenesses among natural objects, sorts them under abstract general ideas, to which it attaches general names. These general ideas have, he tells us, remarkable properties: the general idea of a triangle, for instance 'must be neither oblique nor rectangle, neither equilateral, equicrural nor scalenon, but all and none of these at once'. Substances in the world possess various qualities and powers which we make use of when we define things of different kinds; but the definitions we give them do not reveal their real essences, but only a 'nominal essence'. Of substance in general the only idea we have is of 'something we know not what' in which properties inhere.

Epistemological considerations are ubiquitous throughout the *Essay*, but it is the fourth book that is officially devoted to the topic of knowledge. Because the real essences of things are unknown to us, we cannot have true science about items in the natural world, but only probable belief. We can have genuine knowledge of our own existence and of the existence of God; and provided we keep within the bounds of actual sensation, we can have knowledge of the existence of other things. The love of truth should prevent us from entertaining any proposition with greater assurance than the evidence we have for it: 'Whoever goes beyond this measure of assent, it is plain, receives not truth in the love of it, loves not truth for truth's sake, but for some other by end' (*E*, 697).

During his exile, perhaps in 1685 when King Louis XIV revoked the Edict of Nantes which had hitherto given toleration to French Protestants, Locke wrote a

Latin letter on toleration (*Epistola de Tolerantia*) advocating to a European audience, as he had earlier done to an English one, the acceptance by Christians of a wide variety of doctrinal beliefs. When, in 1688, the 'Glorious Revolution' drove out James II and replaced him with the Dutch Protestant William of Orange, the English monarchy was placed on a new legal basis, with a Bill of Rights and a much enhanced role for Parliament. The way was now free for Locke to return and to publish works which it had hitherto been too dangerous to print. In 1689 and 1690 there appeared *Two Treatises on Government*, the first edition of the *Essay*, and an English version of the letter on tolerance. In response to controversy Locke published two further letters concerning toleration, the third of which appeared in 1692.

Locke had been deprived of his studentship at Christ Church by Charles II in 1684 and on his return from exile he spent much of his time in London. He held a number of posts in the civil service, notably as a commissioner of the Board of Trade. He found time to write *Some Thoughts on Education* (1693), two papers on the nature of money (1691 and 1695), and *The Reasonableness of Christianity* (1695). The form of Christianity which Locke considered reasonable was a very liberal one, and he had to defend himself against conservative critics in two *Vindications* of his treatise (1695 and 1697). Between 1696 and 1698 he was engaged in controversy with Bishop Stillingfleet of Worcester, who regarded the *Essay* as too rationalistic for the comfort of religion. Most of these controversial works were published anonymously; of Locke's principal works only the *Essay* appeared under his own name in his lifetime.

Since 1691 Locke had been given accommodation at Oates, the Essex manor house of Sir Francis Masham, who had married Damaris, the daughter of the Cambridge Platonist Ralph Cudworth. As the years went on Locke spent more and more time at Oates, and from 1700 until his death in 1704 it was his home. He spent the last years of his life, partly incapacitated by ill health, in writing a devout, if critical, commentary on the Epistles of St Paul. He died on 28 October 1704, while Lady Masham was reading the Psalms to him.

Pascal

Hobbes and Locke saw themselves as opponents of Descartes, one during his lifetime and one after his death. In fact, as I have tried to show in the present and in later chapters, both of them shared many of his fundamental assumptions. The same is true of the French philosophers of the generation after Descartes, whether they presented themselves as critics or continuators of his work. The most distinguished of the former group was Blaise Pascal; the most distinguished of the latter was Nicholas Malebranche.

Born in 1632, Pascal was the son of a royal official in the Auvergne. A precocious child, educated at home, he was already publishing on the geometry of conic sections at the age of sixteen, and he invented a rudimentary computer to assist his father in tax assessment. He inspired a series of experiments which proved the empirical possibility of a vacuum, which had been denied *a priori* by Descartes. Later in life he took a significant part in the development of the mathematical study of probability, and he can claim to be one of the founders of game theory.

In his own mind, his work in mathematics and physics came to seem a matter of secondary importance. In 1654 he had a religious experience which led him to make devotion and theology his main concern. He became a close associate of a group of ascetics which centred on the convent of Port Royal, where his sister Jacqueline had become a nun in 1652. Members of the group were called 'Jansenists' because they revered the memory of the Dutch Bishop Jansenius who had written a famous treatise on St Augustine, which defended a pessimistic and rigorist version of Catholicism. Jansenism stressed the corruption of fallen human nature, and held out hope of salvation only to a small minority of the human race. In our present state, some divine commands were impossible for human beings to obey, even with the best will in the world. There was little scope for free will: on the one hand, sin was unavoidable, and on the other hand, grace was irresistible.

Such teaching was condemned by Pope Innocent X in 1653, but the Jansenists fought a long rearguard battle, and their influence on Pascal remained profound. In accord with their devaluation of the powers of fallen human nature, Pascal was sceptical of the power of philosophy, especially in relation to knowledge of God. 'The true way to philosophise', he once wrote, 'is to have no time for philosophy'; as for Descartes, he was 'useless and uncertain' (*P*, 445, 671). Because the Jansenists took a poor view of the freedom of the will, they were constantly at war with its principal Catholic defenders, the Jesuits. Pascal joined the battle by writing a book, *The Provincial Letters*, in which he attacked Jesuit moral theology as excessively lax and indulgent to sinners.[8] When he died in 1662 a paper was found stitched into his coat with the words 'God of Abraham, God of Isaac, God of Jacob, not of the philosophers and scholars'.

At his death Pascal left behind a series of brief remarks which were published in 1670 as *Pensées* (thoughts). He was a master of aphorism, and many of his sayings have become familiar quotations: 'The eternal silence of the infinite spaces terrifies me'; 'Had Cleopatra's nose been shorter, the whole face of the world would have been changed', 'We die alone'. One of the most striking is this:

Man is only a reed, the frailest thing in nature; but he is a thinking reed. To crush him it does not take the whole universe in arms: a breath of wind, a drop of water is enough to kill him. But were the universe to crush him, man would still be nobler than his killer. For he

---

[8] The moral philosophy of the *Provincial Letters* is discussed in Ch. 10 below.

knows that he is dying and that the universe has the better of him. But the universe knows nothing of this. (*P*, 231)

Many of the remarks were designed to form part of an apology for the Christian religion, and to convert unbelievers and reform worldly believers. The project, however, was never completed and no consensus has been reached among scholars about the form it was intended to take. Two themes, however, recur in the surviving fragments: the misery of humanity without God, and the happiness promised by the religious life:

The wretchedness of our condition is made clear by the philosophical debate between sceptics and rationalists. The sceptics are right that we cannot even be certain whether we are awake or asleep; the rationalists are right that there are some natural principles we cannot doubt. But whether these principles are true or not, depends on whether we come from a good God or from an evil demon. And we cannot know, without faith, whether there is a God: nature offers no satisfactory proof that he exists. The best we can do, if we do not accept revelation, is to bet on his existence.[9] (*P*, 38, 42)

Human nature as we know it is a mass of contradiction. We have an ideal of truth, and yet we possess only untruth. We have a yearning for happiness, and we cannot achieve it. Humanity is something monstrous: 'Chaotic, contradictory and prodigious; judge of everything and mindless earth—worm, storehouse of truth and cesspool of error; the glory and refuse of the universe.' Pascal anticipates Pope's *Essay on Man*:

> Chaos of thought and passion, all confused;
> Still by himself abused or disabused;
> Created half to rise and half to fall;
> Great lord of all things, yet a prey to all;
> Sole judge of truth, in endless error hurled—
> The glory, jest, and riddle of the world!   (*P* II, 13)

The solution to this riddle is contained in the Christian doctrine of the Fall. It is as clear as day that the human condition is twofold. If humans had never been corrupted they would have enjoyed in their innocent state both truth and happiness. If they had never been other than corrupted, they would never have any notion of either truth or happiness. But the Fall, which is the key to understanding of ourselves, is of all Christian teachings the one most shocking to reason:

What is more contrary to the laws of our wretched justice than eternally to damn a child with no will of its own for a sin in which the child had so small a part to play that it was committed six thousand years before the child came into existence? Certainly, nothing

---

[9] Pascal's wager is considered in Ch. 10 below.

shocks us more deeply than this doctrine. Nevertheless without this most incomprehensible of all mysteries we are incomprehensible to ourselves. (*P*, 164)

But if reason revolts at the idea of the Fall, reason can also establish the idea's truth. The starting point is nothing other than human misery:

The greatness of man is so evident that it can be inferred even from his wretchedness. For that which is nature in animals we call wretchedness in man. And by this we recognize that his nature being now like that of the animals, he is fallen from a better nature which formerly was his. For who is unhappy at not being a king, except a deposed king? (Ibid.)

Although Pascal believed that only faith could lead us to saving truth and that only grace could give us lasting happiness, in his philosophical writing he was not the enemy of reason that he is often made out to be. His best-known aphorism, of course, is 'the heart has its reasons of which reason knows nothing'. But if we study his use of the word 'heart' we can see that he is not placing feeling above rationality, but contrasting intuitive with deductive reasoning—rather as we speak of learning mathematical tables 'by heart'. We can see this when he tells us that it is the heart that teaches us the foundations of geometry. In this he was not at all at odds with Cartesian rationalism.

Malebranche

Nicolas Malebranche, the son of one of Louis XIV's secretaries, was born in 1638, the year in which Descartes published *The Discourse on Method*. At the age of twenty-six, in 1664, he was ordained a priest of the French Oratory, founded by Descartes' patron Cardinal Bérulle, and in the same year he came across the posthumously published *Treatise on Man*. He was so ravished by this book, his biographer tells us, that he felt 'such violent palpitations of the heart that he was obliged to leave the book at frequent intervals'. He became the most enthusiastic of all Cartesians, and devoted his life to the pursuit of clear and distinct ideas.

In 1674–5 Malebranche published his most significant philosophical work, *The Search after Truth* (*De la recherche de la Vérité*), and in 1688 he summarized his system in *Entretiens sur la Metaphysique*. Most of his other writings were works of theological controversy, beginning with his *Treatise on Nature and Grace* of 1680. He fell foul of many of the leading theologians of the age, quarrelling with Arnauld about grace and with Fénelon about the right way to love God: his *Treatise* was placed on the index in 1690. Shortly before his death in 1715 he found himself the target of a posthumously published polemic of John Locke.

The account of sensation, imagination, intellect, and will presented in Malebranche's works is essentially the same as that of Descartes. The main new item is an explanation of the association of ideas in terms of networks of fibres in the brain. Some of these networks are inborn: from birth, for instance, the brain fibre corresponding to the idea of a steep cliff is linked to the brain fibre corresponding to the idea of death. Other networks are created by experience: if you attend some historic event, for instance, a brain network will be created linking together ever afterward the persons, times, and places involved (*R de V* 2. 1, 5).

Malebranche accepted Cartesian dualism: minds were thinking substances and the essence of matter was extension. But he tried to improve upon Descartes' account of the relationship between mind and body, long recognized as the weakest point in the Cartesian system. More consistently than Descartes, Malebranche argued that if mind was pure thought, and matter was pure extension, neither could act upon the other. Mind and body run parallel, but do not interact. 'It seems to me quite certain that the will of spiritual beings is incapable of moving the smallest body in the world. It is evident, for example, that there is no necessary connection between our will to move our arm and our arm's movement.' Sure, my arm moves *when* I will, but not *because* I will. If it was really myself moving my arm, I would know how I do it; but I cannot even explain how I wiggle my finger.

If I do not move my arm, who does? God does, answers Malebranche. God is the only true cause. From all eternity he has willed all that is to happen and when it is to happen. So he has willed the act of my will and the simultaneous movement of my arm. My willing is not the cause, but only provides an occasion for God to do the causing. (For this reason, Malebranche's system is called 'occasionalism'.) Not only can minds not act on body; neither can bodies act on bodies. If bodies collide and move away from each other, what really happens is that God wills each of them to be in the appropriate places at the appropriate moments. 'There is a contradiction in saying that one body can move another' (*EM*. 7, 10).

If minds cannot act on bodies, and bodies cannot act on bodies, can bodies act on minds? Normally we imagine that our minds are constantly being fed information from the world via our senses. Malebranche denies that our ideas come from the bodies they represent, or that they are created by ourselves. They come directly from God, who alone is capable of acting causally on our intellects. If I prick my finger with a needle, the pain does not come from the needle: it is directly caused by God (*EM*, 6). We see all things in God: God is the environment in which minds live, just as space is the environment in which bodies are located. It was this teaching which particularly aroused the indignation of John Locke.

Many Christian thinkers, from St Augustine onwards, had held that human beings see the eternal truths and the moral laws by contemplating, in some manner, ideas in the mind of God. In making this claim Malebranche could claim august authority. But it was a novelty to say that our knowledge of changeable material objects depends on immediate divine illumination. God, after all, is not himself material or changeable: all there is to be seen in God is the pure idea of intelligible extension. How does contemplation of the eternal divine archetype of extension convey to us any knowledge of the contingent history of bodies moving and changing in the world about us?

The answer that Malebranche gives is that in seeing the archetype of extension we are also made aware of all the laws of Cartesian physics that govern the behaviour of the material world. If this is to be sufficient to predict the actual course of the universe the laws must fulfil two conditions: they must be simple laws and they must be general laws. This is the theme of Malebranche's *Treatise on Nature and Grace*:

God, discovering in the infinite treasures of his wisdom an infinity of possible worlds (as the necessary consequences of the laws of motion which he can establish) determines himself to create that world which could have been produced and preserved by the simplest laws, and which ought to be the most perfect, with respect to the simplicity of the ways necessary to its production or to its conservation. (*TNG*, 116)

Two simple laws of motion, according to Malebranche, suffice to explain all physical phenomena—the first, that bodies in motion tend to continue their motion in a straight line; the second, that when two bodies collide, their motion is distributed in both in proportion to their size.

Malebranche's belief in the simplicity and generality of fundamental laws not only solves the epistemological problem about our knowledge of the external world, but also the moral problem of the presence of evil among the creatures of a good God. God could have made a world more perfect than ours; he might have made it such that rain, which makes the earth fruitful, fell more regularly on cultivated ground than on the sea, where it serves no purpose. But to do that he would have had to alter the simplicity of the laws. Moreover, once God has established laws it is beneath his dignity to tinker with them; laws must be general not only for all places but for all times:

If rain falls on certain lands, and if the sun roasts others; if weather favourable for crops is followed by hail that destroys them; if a child comes into the world with a malformed and useless head growing from his breast, it is not that God has willed these things by particular wills; it is because he has established laws for the communication of motion, of which these effects are necessary consequences. (*TNG*, 118)

It is not that God loves monsters or devises the laws of nature to engender them: it is simply that he was not able, by equally simple laws, to make a more perfect world. The key to the problem of evil is to realize that God acts by general laws and not by particular volitions.

Once again, we have ideas that were later summarized in Pope's *Essay on Man*. We are tempted, Pope says, to see nature as designed for our individual benefit. But here we meet an objection, and receive an answer:

> But errs not nature from this gracious end,
> From burning suns when livid deaths descend

When earthquakes swallow, or when tempests sweep
Towns to one grave, whole nations to the deep?
'No' ('tis replied) 'the first almighty cause
Acts not by partial, but by general laws.'   (I. 140–5)

Malebranche's teaching that God acts by general laws of nature, rather than by particular acts of providence, was what angered the theologians, who regarded it as incompatible with biblical and traditional accounts of the occurrence of miracles. The error was regarded as sufficiently wicked to be denounced by the greatest preacher of the age, Bishop Bossuet, in his funeral oration for Queen Maria Theresa of France in 1683.

Spinoza

Meanwhile, in Protestant Holland, a Jewish philosopher had developed Descartes' ideas in a way even more adventurous than that of Malebranche. Baruch Spinoza was born in Amsterdam in 1632, into a prosperous merchant family which had migrated from Portugal at the end of the previous century. His father, Michael Spinoza, a respected member of the Jewish community, ensured that he acquired a knowledge of Hebrew and a familiarity with the Bible and the Talmud at the local rabbinic school. When Michael died in 1654 Baruch took over the commercial firm in partnership with his brother, but he took much greater interest in philosophical and theological speculation. Having spoken Portuguese, Spanish, and Dutch from childhood, he now learnt Latin from a Christian physician, Francis Van den Enden, who introduced him to the writings of Descartes and had a considerable influence on the development of his thought.

By his teens, Spinoza had become sceptical of Jewish theology and on becoming an adult he gave up much of Jewish practice. In 1656 he was excommunicated from the synagogue and devout Jews were forbidden to talk to him, to write to him, or to stay under the same roof as him. He trained himself to grind lenses, and manufactured spectacles and other optical instruments. This profession gave him leisure and opportunity for scientific reflection and research; it also made him the first philosopher since Antiquity to have earned his living by the work of his hands.

In 1660 he moved from Amsterdam to the village of Rijnsburg near Leiden. In the same year the Royal Society was founded in London, and shortly after its foundation its secretary, Henry Oldenburg, wrote to Spinoza inviting him to enter into a philosophical correspondence about the Cartesian and Baconian systems. The Royal Society, he told him, was a philosophical college in which 'we devote ourselves as energetically as we can to making experiments and observations, and are much occupied with putting together a History of Mechanical Arts' (*Ep*, 3).

A Dutch traveller who visited Rijnsburg in 1661 reported that in the village there lived:

somebody who had become a Christian from a Jew and now was nearly an atheist. He does not care about the Old Testament. The New Testament, the Koran and the fables of Aesop would have the same weight according to him. But for the rest this man behaves quite sincerely and lives without doing harm to other people, and he occupies himself with the construction of telescopes and microscopes.[10]

There is no evidence that Spinoza ever became a Christian after his excommunication by the Jews, but in his writings on religion he does give Jesus a place above the Hebrew prophets.

At this time Spinoza had already begun to write his first work, a treatise on the improvement of the understanding (*Tractatus de intellectus emendatione*) which he did not complete and which was not published until after his death. This resembled Descartes' *Discourse on Method* in recounting an intellectual conversion and setting out a research agenda. It was probably also in this period that Spinoza wrote a Dutch treatise for private circulation, a *Short Treatise on God, Man, and Happiness*, which was not discovered until 1851.

In 1663 Spinoza published a solemn exposition 'in geometrical form' of Descartes' *Principles of Philosophy*. Descartes himself had praised the merits of the geometrical method of deducing truths from definitions and axioms, and in his response to the second set of objections to his *Meditations* he had set out ten definitions, five postulates, and ten axioms, from which he proved four propositions establishing the existence of God and the real distinction between mind and body (AT VII. 160–70; *CSMK* II. 113–19). Spinoza had taken this project further in teaching Cartesian philosophy to a private pupil, and at the request of a friend, Dr Lodewijk Meyer of Leiden University, he worked up his dictation notes into a complete formalization of the first two books of the *Principles*.

Spinoza took over and enlarged Descartes' set of definitions and axioms, and proved fifty-eight propositions, of which the first is 'We can be absolutely certain of nothing, so long as we do not know that we ourselves exist', and of which the last is 'If a particular body A can be moved in any direction by a force however small, it is necessarily surrounded by bodies all moving with an equal speed.' The exposition is generally very faithful to the *Principles*, but in a preface to the publication Meyer warned the reader against thinking that Spinoza's own views coincided in all respects with those of Descartes. Spinoza, for instance, had already departed from Descartes' philosophy of mind: he did not believe that the intellect and the will were distinct from each other, and he did not believe that human beings enjoyed the degree of freedom which Descartes attributed to them (*Ep*, 8). A number of salient points of Spinoza's own developing philosophy were expounded in an appendix to the geometrical exposition, entitled 'Thoughts on Metaphysics'.

In 1663 Spinoza moved to Voorburg near The Hague, where he was visited in 1665 by the astronomer Christiaan Huygens, with whom he discussed microscopes

---

[10] Quoted by W. N. A. Klever in *CCS*, p. 25.

and telescopes and made observations of the planet Jupiter. In 1665 he decided to write an apologia justifying his departure from Judaism: this grew into a much more general work of biblical criticism and political theory, the *Tractatus Theologico-Politicus*, which was published anonymously in 1670.

The *Tractatus* concludes from a careful examination of the texts that the Hebrew Bible as we have it is a compilation, from more ancient material, made no earlier than the fifth century BC. There was no canon of sacred books earlier than the time of the Maccabees, and it is foolish to regard Moses as the author of the Pentateuch or David as the author of all the Psalms (*E* I. 126, 146). It is clear that the sacred writers were ignorant human beings, children of their time and place, and full of prejudices of various sorts. If a prophet was a peasant he saw visions of oxen; if a courtier, he saw a throne. 'God has no particular style in speaking, but according to the learning and capacity of the prophet he is cultivated, compressed, severe, untutored, prolix, or obscure' (*E* I. 31).

The defects of the prophets did not hinder them from carrying out their task, which was not to teach us truth but to encourage us to obedience. It is absurd to look to the Bible for scientific information; anyone who does so will believe that the sun revolves round the earth, and that the value of π is 3. Science and Scripture have different functions, and neither is superior to the other; theology is not bound to serve reason, nor reason theology (*E* I. 190). How a passage in the Bible is intended must be determined only by examining the biblical context itself: one cannot argue from the fact that a statement is unreasonable that therefore it must be meant metaphorically. God is the author of the Bible only in the sense that its fundamental message—to love God above all things and one's neighbour as oneself—is the true religion, common to both Old and New Testaments. The Jews were God's chosen people only while they lived in Israel under a special form of government: at the present time 'there is absolutely nothing which the Jews can arrogate to themselves beyond other people' (*E* I. 55).

If you believe all the stories in the Bible but miss its message, you might as well be reading Sophocles or the Koran. On the other hand, a man who lives a true and upright life, however ignorant he is of the Bible, 'is absolutely blessed and truly possesses in himself the spirit of Christ' (*E* I. 79). But the Bible should not be a stumbling block, once one understands how to read it. Jews, Spinoza says, do not mention secondary causes, but refer all things to the Deity; for instance, if they make money by a transaction, they say God gave it to them. So when the Bible says that God opened the windows of heaven, it only means that it rained very hard; and when God tells Noah that he will set his bow in the cloud, 'this is but another way of expressing the refraction and reflection which the rays of the sun are subjected to in drops of water' (*E* I. 90).

The *Tractatus* is carefully argued and courteously expressed, and in drawing critical attention to the literary genres of Scripture, Spinoza was merely anticipating what devout Protestants were to say in the nineteenth century ('the Bible must be read like any other book') and what devout Catholics were to say in the twentieth century (the interpreter of the Bible must 'go back in spirit to those remote centuries of the East'). Nonetheless, the book's liberal interpretation of the Old Testament drew a storm of protest not only from Jews but from the Dutch Calvinists, who condemned the work in several synods. Other contemporaries, however, admired the book and when its authorship became generally known it gave Spinoza an international reputation.

This led, in 1673, to an offer from the Elector Palatine of a chair in philosophy at Heidelberg University. 'You will have', the Elector's secretary promised, 'the most ample freedom in philosophical teaching, which the prince is confident you will not misuse to disturb the religion publicly established.' But Spinoza was wary, and politely declined the offer:

I think, in the first place, that I should abandon philosophical research if I consented to find time for teaching young students. I think, in the second place, that I do not know the limits within which the freedom of my philosophical teaching would be confined, if I am to avoid all appearance of disturbing the publicly established religion. (*Ep*, 48)

Spinoza never occupied an academic post, and never married. He continued to live a retired but comfortable life, welcoming from time to time visiting scholars who came to pay their respects, such as G. W. Leibniz in 1676. He worked quietly on his major work, *Ethics Demonstrated according to the Geometrical Order*. He had it finished by 1675 and took the text to Amsterdam with the intention of having it printed; but he was warned by friends that he might risk persecution as an atheist if he did so. He returned the book to his desk and began work on a *Political Treatise*; but it, like several of his other projects, remained incomplete at his death. He died in 1667 of phthisis, due in part to the inhalation of glass dust, an occupational hazard for a lens-grinder. A volume of posthumous works—including the *Ethics*, the *Political Treatise*, plus the early *Improvement of the Intellect* and a number of letters—was published in the year of his death. Within a year the volume was banned by the States of Holland.

The *Ethics* sets out Spinoza's own system in the way he had earlier set out Descartes, on the model of Euclid's geometry. It is in five parts: 'Of God'; 'Of the Nature and Origin of the Mind'; 'Of the Origin and Nature of the Passions'; 'Of Human Bondage'; and 'Of Human Freedom'. Each part begins with a set of definitions and axioms and proceeds to offer formal proofs of numbered propositions, each containing, we are to believe, nothing that does not follow from the axioms and definitions, and concluding with QED. The geometrical method cannot be regarded as a successful method of presentation. The proofs often offer little understanding of the conclusions, and provide at best a set of hypertext links to other passages of the *Ethics*. The philosophical meat is often packed into scholia, corollaries, and appendices.

There is no doubt, however, that Spinoza was doing his best to make his philosophy utterly transparent, with no hidden assumptions and none but logical connections between one proposition and the next. If the Euclidean clothing often wears thin, the work remains geometrical in a more profound sense: it tries to explain the entire universe in terms of concepts and relationships that can be mastered by the student of elementary geometry. If the project ultimately fails, it is not the fault of the philosopher but of the nature of philosophy itself.

As the titles of the different parts show, the treatise deals with many other things besides ethics. The first book is a treatise of metaphysics and also a treatise of natural theology: it expounds a theory of the nature of substance which is at the same time an ontological argument for the existence of God. Whereas for Descartes there were two fundamental kinds of substance, mental and material, for Spinoza there is only a single substance (which may be called either 'God' or 'Nature') which possesses both the attribute of thought and the attribute of extension. The human mind and the human body, therefore, do not belong in two different worlds: the mind, as is explained in the second book, is man considered as a mode of the attribute of thought, and the body is man considered as a mode of the attribute of extension. Mind and body are inseparable: the human mind is in fact simply the idea of the human body. On this foundation, Spinoza builds up an epistemological theory of three levels of knowledge: imagination, reason, and intuition.[11]

It is in the third book that we approach the topic of the book's title. Human beings, like all other beings, strive to maintain themselves in existence and to repel whatever threatens their destruction. The consciousness of this drive in humans is desire, and when the drive operates freely we feel pleasure, and when it is impeded we feel pain. All the complex emotions of humans are derived from these basic passions of desire, pleasure, and pain. Our judgements of good and evil, and therefore our actions, are determined by our desires and aversions; but the last two books of the *Ethics* teach us how to avoid being enslaved by our passions (human bondage) by an intellectual understanding of them (human freedom).

The key to this is the distinction between active and passive emotions. Passive emotions, like fear and anger, are generated by external forces; active emotions arise from the mind's own understanding of the human condition. Once we have a clear and distinct idea of a passive emotion it becomes an active emotion; and the replacement of passive emotions by active ones is the path of liberation. In particular we must give up the passion of fear, and especially the fear of death. 'A free man thinks of nothing less than death; and his wisdom is a meditation not on death but on life' (*Eth*, 151).

Moral liberation depends, paradoxically, on the appreciation of the necessity of all things. We will cease to feel hatred for others when we realize that their acts are determined by nature. Returning hatred only increases it; but reciprocating it with

---

[11] Spinoza's metaphysics is considered in detail in Ch. 6, his natural theology in Ch. 10, and his epistemology in Ch. 4.

love vanquishes it. What we must do is to take a God's eye view of the whole necessary natural scheme of things, seeing it 'in the light of eternity'.[12]

Spinoza's unique system can be looked at historically in several different ways. We can, if we wish, situate his theory of substance in relation to Locke's. Both Locke and Spinoza eliminate the Aristotelian notion of substance: for Locke, individual substances vanish to a virtual zero, for Spinoza substance expands so far that a single substance encompasses the universe. But if we take Descartes as our point of comparison, we can say that in drawing out the implications of Cartesian assumptions Spinoza overtook Malebranche. Malebranche drew the conclusion that God was the only agent in the universe; Spinoza went further and claimed that he was the only substance. But when Spinoza says that this single substance is 'God or Nature', does this mean that he is a pantheist or an atheist? He has been taken with equal justification to be alleging that 'God' is just a code word for the order of the natural universe, and to be claiming that when scientists speak of 'Nature' they are all the time talking of God.

In philosophy the seventeenth century is the age of the revolt against Aristotle. This revolt is carried to its ultimate length by Spinoza. The hallmarks of Aristotelian scholasticism are the distinctions it makes and the pairs of concepts with which it operates to explain human beings and the material world: actuality and potentiality; form and matter; disposition and activity; intellect and will; natural and rational powers; final and formal causes. All these distinctions are collapsed by Spinoza. Of Aristotle's repertoire we are left with the distinction between substance and accident, and of the scholastic apparatus we are left with the distinction between essence and existence. These are applied once, and once only, by Spinoza in order to mark the relation between finite and infinite being. Spinoza's system is at the furthest point from the medieval Aristotelianism of an Aquinas.

Paradoxically, Spinoza and Aristotle meet at just one point—the highest of all. The intellectual love of God that Spinoza presents in the last book of his *Ethics* as the highest human activity is very similar to the joyful contemplation of the divine that Aristotle holds out, in the tenth book of his *Ethics*, as the supreme constituent of human well-being. In each case, the beatific activity to which we are invited has seemed elusive to most subsequent philosophers.

Spinoza's philosophy is often regarded as the most extravagant form of rationalism. He spelt out his system in Euclidean terms not just to elucidate the logical relations between its various theses: for him logical sequences were what held the universe together. He made no distinction between logical and causal connections: for him, the order and connection of ideas are the same as the order and connection of things. Yet this arch-rationalist exercised great influence during the Romantic era. It was the German Romantic poet Novalis who proclaimed him a 'God-intoxicated man' and thus endeared him, later, to Kierkegaard. Wordsworth

---

[12] Spinoza's ethics is considered in detail in Ch. 8.

and Coleridge used to discuss his philosophy together in Somerset in 1797 and were nearly arrested for their pains: a government informer sent to investigate whether the two poets were French revolutionary agents was perturbed to overhear them referring to Spy Nozy.[13]

Spinoza's identification of God and Nature left a mark on the verse of both poets at this period. Wordsworth described himself as a worshipper of Nature, and in his 1798 'Lines above Tintern Abbey' he famously wrote:

> I have felt
> A presence that disturbs me with the joy
> Of elevated thoughts; a sense sublime
> Of something far more deeply interfused
> Whose dwelling is the light of setting suns,
> And the round ocean, and the living air,
> And the blue sky, and in the mind of man,
> A motion and a spirit, that impels
> All thinking things, all objects of all thought
> And rolls through all things.

In the same year Coleridge, in 'Frost at Midnight', predicts for his baby son a life amid the beauties of sandy lakes and mountain crags, and tells him:

> So shalt thou see and hear
> The lovely shapes and sounds intelligible
> Of that eternal language, which thy God
> Utters, who from eternity doth teach
> Himself in all, and all things in himself.

Leibniz

Gottfried Wilhelm Leibniz straddles the boundary between the seventeenth and eighteenth centuries. Fifty-four of the seventy years of his life were passed in the seventeenth, but his principal philosophical works were composed and published in the eighteenth. Indeed, many of his most significant texts were not published until after his death, sometimes long afterwards. He was not a systematic writer, and historians of philosophy have struggled to construct a coherent and comprehensive system out of brief pamphlets, occasional pieces, and fragmentary notes. But the power of his intellect has never been questioned, and many subsequent philosophers have acknowledged themselves to be in his debt.

Leibniz was the son of a professor of philosophy at Leipzig, who died in 1652, when he was six. He spent much of his childhood in the library left by his father, reading precociously and voraciously. In adult life he showed himself to be one of the best-read philosophers ever to have lived. His interests were wide, including

---

[13] Coleridge, *Biographia Literaria*, Ch. 10.

literature, history, law, mathematics, physics, chemistry, and theology. From the age of thirteen, however, logic and philosophy had become his dominant passion. Already in his early teens, he tells us, he found Suarez as easy to read as a novel, and while hiking he would balance in his mind the rival merits of Aristotelianism and Cartesianism.

In 1661 Leibniz entered Leipzig University. After being awarded the baccalaureate in 1663 for a scholastic dissertation on the principle of individuation (G IV. 15–26), he migrated first to Jena to study mathematics, and then to Altdorf to study law. As a sideline, at the age of nineteen he published a small logical treatise, *De Arte Combinatoria*, in which he offered some improvements to standard Aristotelian syllogistic and proposed a method of representing geometrical notions by an arithmetical code. His method of resolving complex terms into simple ones would, he hoped, produce a deductive logic of discovery, something that had so far eluded logicians (G IV. 27–102).

Leibniz took his doctorate at Altdorf in 1667, writing a thesis on 'Hard Cases in Law'. He was offered a chair, but preferred to pursue a career as a courtier and diplomat. He entered the service of the Archbishop of Mainz, one of the electors of the Holy Roman Empire. He dedicated his next academic publications to the archbishop: proposals for the rationalization of German law and a new method of teaching jurisprudence. At the archbishop's suggestion he republished a forgotten fifteenth-century treatise denouncing scholastic philosophy; but he accompanied it with his own defence of Aristotle against Descartes (G I. 15–27, 129–76). A Protestant in a Catholic court, he wrote a number of theological works of an ecumenical cast, concentrating on doctrines that were held in common by all Christian denominations (G IV. 105–36).

In 1672 Leibniz was sent on a mission to Paris, to persuade Louis XIV to lead a crusade into Egypt. Diplomatically his trip was abortive, but philosophically it was fruitful. He met Arnauld and Malebranche, and began a serious reading of Descartes and Gassendi. He was briefly attracted by Gassendi's atomism and materialism, a flirtation that he later regretted. 'When I was a youth,' he wrote in 1716, 'I too fell into the snare of atoms and the void, but reason brought me back' (G VII. 377).

On a further diplomatic visit in the following year, this time to London, Leibniz was introduced to Boyle and Oldenburg. He exhibited a model of a calculating machine to the other members of the Royal Society, who were sufficiently impressed to make him a Fellow. He returned to Paris and remained there until 1676, in which year he invented the infinitesimal calculus, unaware of Newton's earlier but as yet unpublished discoveries. On his way back to Germany he visited Spinoza in Amsterdam, and studied the *Ethics* in manuscript, writing substantial comments. But after the *Ethics* had been published, and Spinoza was a target of general obloquy, Leibniz played down their former intimacy.

From 1676 until his death Leibniz was a courtier to successive rulers of Hanover, employed in many capacities, from librarian to mining engineer. He resumed the ecumenical endeavours he had started at Mainz, and began writing a book of non-sectarian Christian apologetic, for which he sought advice from Arnauld and approval from the Vatican. In 1677 he wrote under an alias a book which claimed, *inter alia*, that the Christian states of Europe made up a single commonwealth of which the emperor was the temporal head and the pope the spiritual head.

This ecumenical project stalled when the duke who sponsored it died in 1680. Leibniz's new employer was Duke Ernst August of Brunswick, whose wife Sophia was the granddaughter of King James I and the sister of Descartes' Princess Elizabeth. He set Leibniz to compile the history of his ducal house, an endeavour which involved archival searches throughout Germany, Austria, and Italy. Leibniz took the task very seriously, tracing the history of the region back to prehistoric times. The only part of the work that was finished at his death was a prefatory description of the soil and minerals of Saxony, a work of geology rather than genealogy.

It was in the winter of 1685 that Leibniz wrote the first of his works which became lastingly popular, *The Discourse on Metaphysics*. As soon as he had written it he sent a summary to Arnauld, who gave it a frosty welcome; perhaps for this reason he did not publish any of it for ten years. He regarded it as the first statement of his mature philosophical position. Brief and lucid, it serves to this day as the best introduction to Leibniz's philosophical system, and contains many of his characteristic doctrines.

The first of these is that we live in the best of all possible worlds, a world freely chosen by God who always acts in an orderly manner according to reason. God is not, as Spinoza thought, the only substance: there are also created individuals. Each individual through its history has many predicates true of it, predicates whose totality defines it as the substance it is. Each such substance, we are told, 'expresses the universe after its own manner', encapsulating the world from a particular viewpoint. Human beings are substances of this kind: their actions are contingent, not necessary, and depending on free will. Our choices have reasons, but not necessitating causes. Created substances do not directly act upon each other, but God has so arranged matters that what happens to one substance corresponds to what happens to all the others. Consequently, each substance is like a world apart, independent of any other thing save God.

The human mind contains, from its origin, the ideas of all things; no external object, other than God, can act upon our souls. Our ideas, however, are our own ideas and not God's. So too are the acts of our will, which God inclines without necessitating. God conserves us continually in being, but our thoughts occur spontaneously and freely. Soul and body do not interact with each other, but thoughts and bodily events occur in correspondence because they are placed in liaison by the loving providence of God. God has so ordered things that spirits, the most precious items in the universe, live for ever in full self-consciousness; and for those that love him he has prepared unimaginable felicity.

It will be seen from this brief summary that the *Discourse* embeds itself in Aristotelian metaphysics and traditional Christianity, and that it includes elements from recent continental philosophers carefully modified to cohere with each other. Its main ideas were published in a learned journal in 1695 under the title *New System of Nature and of the Interaction of Substances*. Many savants published criticisms of it, to which Leibniz responded with vigorous rebuttals. In 1698 he followed up with another journal article, 'On Nature itself', which clearly marked out his own system in contrast to those of Descartes, Malebranche, and Spinoza, on which he had drawn for his synthesis.

Having failed to bring together Catholics and Protestants (in spite of his *Systema Theologicum* of 1686, which set out common ground between the various confessions), Leibniz set himself the potentially easier task of achieving a reconciliation between Calvinist Protestants and Lutheran Protestants. This again proved beyond his powers of argument and persuasion. So too was his grandiose project of a European confederation of Christian states, in which he tried in vain to interest successively Louis XIV of France and Peter the Great of Russia. But his passion for ecumenism was undiminished, and in the last year of his life he was encouraging those Jesuits who were seeking an accommodation between Catholic Christianity and the traditional beliefs and rituals of Chinese Confucians. He remained a Protestant himself until his death, although he sometimes carried a rosary, which on one occasion prevented him being thrown overboard as a heretical Jonah during a storm on an Adriatic crossing.

Locke's rejection of innate ideas in his *Essay concerning Human Understanding* provoked Leibniz into an all-out attack on empiricism. This was completed by 1704 but in that year Locke died, and Leibniz decided not to publish. It saw the light some fifty years after his own death, under the title *New Essays on Human Understanding*. The longest work published during Leibniz's lifetime was *Essays in Theodicy*, a vindication of divine justice in the face of the evils of the world, dedicated to Queen Charlotte of Prussia. 'Theodicy' is a pseudo-Greek word coined to express the project of justifying the works of God to man. The book argues that in spite of appearances we do indeed live in the best of all possible worlds. Its message was summed up by Alexander Pope in his *Essay on Man*:

> Of Systems possible, if 'tis confest
> That Wisdom infinite must form the best....
> Respecting Man, whatever wrong we call,
> May, must be, right, as relative to all...
> All Nature is but Art, unknown to thee:
> All Chance, Direction which thou canst not see;
> All Discord, Harmony, not understood;
> All partial Evil, universal Good:

> And, spite of Pride, in erring Reason's spite,
> One truth is clear, 'Whatever is, is RIGHT'.

Pope wrote that in 1734. A quarter of a century later Voltaire, shocked out of optimism of this kind by the disaster of the Lisbon earthquake, responded with his satirical *Candide*. In that novel the Leibnizian Dr Pangloss responds to a series of miseries and catastrophes with the incantation: 'All is for the best in the best of all possible worlds.' Candide replies: 'If this is the best, what must the others be like?'

In 1714 two of Leibniz's most important short treatises appeared: the *Monadology* and *The Principles of Nature and of Grace*. The *Monadology* contains a developed and polished form of the system adumbrated in the *Discourse*. Whatever is complex, it argues, is made up of what is simple, and whatever is simple is unextended, for if it were extended it could be further divided. But whatever is material is extended, hence there must be simple immaterial elements. These soul-like entities Leibniz called monads—these are the 'worlds apart' of the *Discourse*. Whereas for Spinoza there was only one substance, with the attributes of both mind and extension, for Leibniz there are infinitely many substances, with the properties only of souls.

Like Malebranche, Leibniz denied that creatures could be causally affected by other creatures. 'Monads', he said, 'have no windows, by which anything could come in or go out.' Their life is a succession of mental states or perceptions, but these are not caused by the external world. A monad mirrors the world, not because the world shines into it, but because God has programmed it to change in synchrony with the world. A good clockmaker can construct two clocks which will keep such perfect time that they forever strike the hours at the same moment. In relation to all his creatures, God is such a clockmaker: at the very beginning of things he pre-established the harmony of the universe.

In the same year as Leibniz wrote the *Monadology*, Queen Anne of Britain died. The British Act of Settlement of 1701 had settled the succession on the heirs of Sophie, the Electress of Hanover, and her son, the Elector Georg Ludwig, became King George I of England. Leibniz did not follow his employer to London but was left behind in Hanover. He might well have been unwelcome in England, because of his quarrel with Newton over the ownership of the infinitesimal calculus. The Royal Society had intervened in the dispute and awarded the priority to Newton in 1712.

Leibniz died in 1716, leaving behind a mass of unpublished papers and a number of incomplete projects, the most ambitious of which was a comprehensive encyclopedia of human knowledge. This was to be the combined work of religious orders, such as the Benedictines and the Jesuits, and the recently founded learned societies, such as the Royal Society, the Académie des Sciences in Paris, and the Prusssian Academy of which Leibniz had himself been the first president. Nothing came of the project, and now, nearly 300 years later, the German Academy is still not halfway through the programme, begun in 1923, of a complete publication of Leibniz's own works.

Berkeley

During the last years of Leibniz's life several works were published which marked the appearance of a gifted young thinker. George Berkeley was born near Kilkenny in Ireland in 1685, the most talented philosopher from that island since John Scotus Eriugena in the ninth century.[14] When fifteen he entered Trinity College, Dublin, and having taken his BA in 1704 he was made a Fellow of the College on the strength of two mathematical papers. Unlike Leibniz, he wrote his best philosophical works when young, between the ages of twenty-four and twenty-eight.

An Essay towards a New Theory of Vision appeared in 1709. This offered an account of how we judge the distance, and size, of seen objects. Distance, it is argued, is not itself visible, being 'a line endwise to the eye': we judge it by the degree of distinctness of a visual appearance, and by the feelings we experience as we adjust our eyes for optimum vision. When we consider the visual perception of size, we have to distinguish between visible magnitude and tangible magnitude. 'There are two sorts of objects apprehended by sight, each whereof has its distinct magnitude or extension—the one properly tangible, i.e. to be perceived and measured by touch, and not immediately falling under the sense of seeing; the other, properly and immediately visible, by mediation of which the former is brought into view.' The visible magnitude of the moon, for instance, varies in accordance with its distance from the horizon; but its tangible magnitude remains constant. It is, however, by means of visual magnitude that we normally judge tangible magnitude. In the case both of size and distance Berkeley's discussion leads to an empiricist conclusion: our visual judgements are based on the experience of connections between sensations:

As we see distance, so we see magnitude. And we see both in the same way that we see shame or anger in the looks of a man. Those passions are themselves invisible, they are nevertheless let in by the eye along with colours and alterations of countenance, which are the immediate object of vision: and which signify them for no other reason than barely because they have been observed to accompany them. Without experience we should no more have taken blushing for a sign of shame than of gladness. (*BPW*, 309)

The connection between shape as judged by vision and shape as judged by touch is something learnt only by experience. Intrinsically, seen roundness and felt roundness have nothing in common. A man born blind, who had learnt to tell a cube from a sphere by touch, would not, if his sight were suddenly restored, be able to tell by looking alone which of two objects on a table in front of him was a cube and which was a sphere. So Berkeley affirmed, following Locke.

It will be seen that the *New Theory* was a contribution to experimental psychology as well as to philosophy of mind. The thesis just stated, for instance,

---

[14] See above, pp. 281–4.

is not a piece of conceptual analysis, but a thesis which could be tested by experiment.[15]

Berkeley's next work, the *Principles of Human Knowledge* of 1710, was something very different: it presented and ingeniously defended the astonishing thesis that there is no such thing as matter. Even Leibniz, who read the book as soon as it appeared, was a little shocked. 'Many things that are here seem right to me,' he wrote in a review. 'But they are expressed rather paradoxically. For there is no need to say that matter is nothing. It is sufficient to say that it is a phenomenon like a rainbow.'[16]

Berkeley's immaterialism was presented again in 1713 in *Three Dialogues between Hylas and Philonous*, a brief work which is one of the most charming pieces of philosophy to be written in English. In the dialogue Philonous, the lover of mind, debates with Hylas, the patron of matter, and emerges triumphant. The argument proceeds in four stages. First, it is argued that all sensible qualities are ideas. Second, the notion of inert matter is tested to destruction. Third, a proof is offered of the existence of God. Finally, ordinary language is reinterpreted to match an immaterialist metaphysics. In the end, Hylas agrees that trees and chairs are nothing but bundles of ideas, produced in our minds by God, whose own perception of them is the only thing that keeps them in continuous existence.

Berkeley's final work of theoretical philosophy was a Latin treatise on motion, published in 1712. By that time he had been for two years a priest of the Protestant Church of Ireland. From time to time he visited London, where he became a friend of Alexander Pope and was presented at court by Jonathan Swift. In 1714 he made a grand tour of the continent, taking the Alpine route in the middle of winter in an open chair; he was suitably terrified by Mont Cenis, 'high, craggy and steep enough to cause the heart of the most valiant man to melt within him'.

In 1724 he became Dean of Derry, and resigned his Fellowship of Trinity. Shortly afterwards he conceived the plan of founding a college in Bermuda to educate and give religious instruction to the sons of British colonists from mainland America alongside native Americans. He foresaw that the leadership of the civilized world would one day pass to America, and in a poem 'On the Prospect of Planting Arts and Learning in America' he wrote:

> Westward the course of empire takes its way
> The four first acts already past
> A fifth shall close the drama with the day:
> Time's noblest offspring is the last.

---

[15] And indeed, when tested in 1963, was found to be false: a man who recovered his sight after a corneal graft was immediately able, from experience of feeling the hands of his pocket watch, to tell the time visually. R. L. Gregory, *The Oxford Companion to the Mind* (Oxford: Oxford University Press, 1987), p. 95.

[16] Written in Leibniz's copy of the *Principles*; quoted in S. Brown, *Leibniz* (Brighton: Harvester Press, 1984), p. 42.

Berkeley obtained a charter for his college and the promise of a parliamentary grant of £20,000. He set sail across the Atlantic in 1728. Having reached Newport, Rhode Island, he soon determined that this would be a more suitable venue for his academy. But the promised grant did not in the end materialize, and he returned to England in 1731 without having achieved anything. The citizens of the United States, however, did not forget his care for the education of their ancestors, and named after him a college at Yale and a university town in California.

In 1734 Berkeley was appointed Bishop of Cloyne. Although he was a conscientious bishop, his pastoral task was not a heavy one, and he devoted himself to propagating the virtues of tar-water, which he advertised as a panacea for most human diseases. Tar-water was a concoction from the bark of pine trees which Berkeley had seen used in America as a remedy for smallpox. It is, he wrote in his treatise *Siris*, 'of a nature so mild and benign and proportioned to the human constitution, as to warm without heating, to cheer but not inebriate'. His words were later purloined by the poet Cowper and used in praise of tea.

In 1749 Berkeley wrote *A Word to the Wise* in which he exhorts the Roman Catholic clergy in his diocese to join with him in endeavouring to stir their countrymen out of their hereditary laziness and to improve the wretched economic condition of Ireland. Three years later the government offered him a more lucrative Irish see, but he refused the offer and retired to Oxford. He spent the last year of his life in a modest house in Holywell Street. He died at the beginning of 1753, while listening to his wife reading from the Bible; he was buried in Christ Church Cathedral where his monument may still be seen.

Berkeley was long remembered, and not only in philosophical circles, for his paradoxical thesis that matter does not exist and that so-called material objects are only ideas that God shares with us, from time to time. His slogan *esse est percipi*—to be is to be perceived—was widely quoted and widely mocked. Some people, such as Dr Samuel Johnson, thought the doctrine was incredible; others, such as the poet Arthur Hugh Clough, thought that it made no real difference to life.

James Boswell describes how he discussed Berkeley's immaterialism with Johnson in a churchyard. 'I observed, that though we are satisfied his doctrine is not true, it is impossible to refute it. I never shall forget the alacrity with which Johnson answered, striking his foot with mighty force against a large stone, till he rebounded from it, "I refute it *thus*."

In Clough's *Dipsychus* the young hero professes an austere ideal of lonely communion with God. His interlocutor, the voice of worldly wisdom, finds this hard to take seriously:

> To these remarks so sage and clerkly,
>> Worthy of Malebranche or Berkeley
> I trust it won't be deemed a sin

DESCARTES TO BERKELEY

If I too answer with a grin.
These juicy meats, this flashing wine,
　May be an unreal mere appearance;
Only—for my inside, in fine,
　They have a singular coherence.
This lovely creature's glowing charms
　Are gross illusion, I don't doubt that;
But when I pressed her in my arms
　I somehow didn't think about that.

(*Poems* (Oxford: Oxford University Press, 1974), p. 241)

3

Hume to Hegel

Hume

Shortly after Berkeley, in Dublin, gave the world his empiricist metaphysics, there was born in Edinburgh a philosopher who was to take empiricist principles to an anti-metaphysical extreme, David Hume. Hume was born in 1711 into a junior branch of a noble Scottish family. As the younger son of a mother widowed early he had to make his own way in the world. Between twelve and fifteen he studied literature and philosophy at Edinburgh University, falling in love, he tells us, with both subjects. He then set out to prepare himself for a legal profession, but soon gave up because, in his own words, he found 'an insurmountable Aversion to anything but the pursuits of Philosophy and General Learning'.

Despite this, he did attempt a commercial career with a sugar firm in Bristol; but four months of clerking there convinced him that a life in business was not for him. He decided to live frugally on his small inheritance, and went across to France where life in a country town need not be expensive. From 1734–7 he lived at La Flèche in Anjou, where Descartes had been educated at the Jesuit college. Making use of the college library, Hume wrote his first work, a substantial *Treatise of Human Nature*.

On returning to England he found some difficulty in getting this work published, and when it appeared he was disappointed by its reception. 'Never Literary Attempt was more unfortunate than my Treatise,' he wrote in his autobiography. 'It fell *dead-born from the Press*.' After his death, however, it was to achieve enormous fame. German idealists in the eighteenth century and British idealists in the nineteenth took it as the target of their criticisms of empiricism: they detested it, but at the same time they revered it. British empiricists in the twentieth century extolled it as the greatest work of philosophy in the English language. Certainly the book, along with Hume's later more popular presentations of its ideas, came to exercise a greater influence than the work of any philosopher since Descartes. The town of La Flèche can be proud of its contribution to philosophy.

The *Treatise* was published in three volumes, the first two ('Of the Understanding' and 'Of the Passions') in 1739, and the third ('Of Morals') in 1740. The aim of the work was stated in the subtitle of the first edition, *An Attempt to introduce the experimental method of reasoning into Moral Subjects.* Hume saw himself as doing for psychology what Newton had done for physics, by applying the experimental method to moral subjects. He set out to provide an account of the relationships between ideas which would be a counterpart of the gravitational attraction between bodies. Notions like causation and obligation, which had been obfuscated by the metaphysicians, would for the first time be brought into clear light. All the sciences would benefit: instead of taking small forts on the frontiers of knowledge, we would now be able to 'march up directly to the capital or centre of these sciences, to human nature itself' (*T*).

The first book of the *Treatise* begins by setting out an empiricist classification of the contents of the mind ('perceptions'). This covers much of the same ground as Locke and Berkeley's epistemology, but Hume divides perceptions into two classes, impressions and ideas. Impressions are more forceful, more vivid, than ideas. Impressions include sensations and emotions; ideas are perceptions involved in thinking and reasoning. Hume treats in detail ideas of memory and imagination, and the association between them. He endorses and reinforces Berkeley's criticism of Locke's abstract ideas.

After a second part devoted to the ideas of space and time[1] Hume presents, in a section entitled 'Of Knowledge and Probability', his most original and influential thoughts. All knowledge that extends beyond the immediate deliveries of the senses, Hume argues, depends upon the notions of cause and effect: it is through those ideas that we discover what happened in the past and conjecture what will happen in the future. We must therefore examine closely the origin of these ideas.

The idea of causation, he says, cannot arise from any inherent quality of objects, because objects of the most different kinds can be causes and effects. We must look, instead, for relationships between objects; and we find that causes and effects must be contiguous to each other, and that causes must be prior to their effects. Moreover, contiguity and succession are not enough for us to pronounce two objects to be cause and effect, unless we see that objects of the two kinds are found in constant conjunction. But that is not enough: if we are to infer an effect from its cause, we feel, there must be a necessary connection between a cause and its effect.

After many pages of artful argument, Hume leads us to an astonishing conclusion: it is not our inference that depends on the necessary connection between cause and effect, but the necessary connection that depends on the inference we

---

[1] See Ch. 4 below.

draw from one to the other. Our belief in necessary connection is not a matter of reasoning, but of custom; and to wean us from the contrary doctrine Hume presents his own analysis of the relationship between reason and belief. He rounds off the book on understanding with a Part that places his novel scepticism in the context of other versions of scepticism, ancient and modern. The Part ends with a celebrated section in which Hume denies the existence of the self as conceived by philosophers.[2]

In devoting the second book of the *Treatise* to a disquisition on the passions or emotions, Hume was following in the footsteps of Descartes and Spinoza. But the topic is much more important for him than it was for those rationalist thinkers, since his philosophy of mind attributes to the passions many of the operations which they regarded as activities of reason—causal inference being only the most striking example of many.

Passions, Hume tells us, are a special kind of impression. Having divided perceptions into impressions and ideas, he makes a further division between original and secondary impressions: sense impressions and physical pains and pleasures are the original impressions, and the secondary impressions are the passions which form the topic of the book. Particular passions, such as pride and humility, or love and hatred, are discussed in quaint detail. The book's most striking conclusion is that the much discussed conflict between passion and reason is a metaphysician's myth. Reason itself, we are told, is impotent to produce any action: all voluntary behaviour is motivated by passion. Passion can never be overcome by reason, but only by a contrary passion. This thesis should not perturb us: 'reason is and ought only to be the slave of the passions, and can never pretend to any other office than to serve and obey them' (*T* II. 3. 3).

By the end of Book Two it is already clear that Hume's ethical system is going to be something rather different from any traditional moral philosophy. Since reason cannot move us to action, moral judgements cannot be the product of reason because the whole purpose of such judgements is to guide our behaviour. Reason is concerned either with relations of ideas or with matters of fact, but neither of these leads on to action. Only the passions can do that, and reason can neither cause nor judge our passions. ' 'Tis not contrary to reason to prefer the destruction of the whole world to the scratching of my finger.' All that reason can do is to determine the feasibility of the objects sought by the passions and the best methods of achieving them. Hume concludes his remarks on reason and passion with a famous paragraph:

In every system of morality, which I have hitherto met with, I have always remark'd that the author proceeds for some time in the ordinary way of reasoning, and establishes the being of a God, or makes observations concerning human affairs; when of a sudden I am surpriz'd to

---

[2] Hume's treatment of causation is discussed in detail in Ch. 6 and his treatment of the self in Ch. 7.

find, that instead of the usual copulations of propositions, *is*, and *is not*, I meet with no proposition that is not connected with an *ought* or *ought not*. The change is imperceptible; but is, however, of the last consequence. (*T* III.1.1)

An 'ought' cannot be derived from an 'is' and the conclusion we must draw is that distinctions between good and evil, right and wrong, are the product not of reason but of a moral sense.

From this basis Hume goes on in the second part of the book to discuss justice and injustice, and in the third book other natural virtues such as benevolence and greatness of mind. He concludes that the chief source of moral distinctions is the feeling of sympathy with others. Justice is approved of because it tends to the public good; and the public good is indifferent to us, except in so far as sympathy interests us in it. 'Virtue is consider'd as a means to an end. Means to an end are only valued so far as the end is valued. But the happiness of strangers affects us by sympathy alone' (*T* III. 3.6).

The *Treatise of Human Nature* is a very remarkable achievement for a man in his twenties, and it was no wonder that Hume was disappointed by its reception. He recovered from his initial depression, and decided that the faults in the book were a matter of presentation rather than substance. Accordingly, in 1740 he published anonymously a brief abstract of the work, especially its theory of causation. After two further anonymous volumes, *Essays Moral and Political* (1741–2), which were well received, he rewrote in popular form much of the content of the *Treatise*. *An Enquiry Concerning Human Understanding*, corresponding to the first volume, appeared (under a slightly different title) in 1748 and (in a definitive edition) in 1751. This omitted the earlier consideration of space and time, but included a chapter on miracles which gave great offence to orthodox readers of the Bible. Also in 1751 Hume published *An Enquiry Concerning the Principles of Morals*, which was an abridged and revised version of the third part of the *Treatise*.

In 1745 Hume had applied for a philosophy professorship at Edinburgh. He was unsuccessful, but he did obtain a post as tutor to the young Marquis of Annandale. Next he was taken into the entourage of a distant cousin, General St Clair, under whom he served on a naval expedition to Brittany during the War of the Austrian Succession. Towards the end of that war, in 1747, he accompanied the general on diplomatic missions to Vienna and Turin. At last he began to taste prosperity: he boasted that he had amassed savings of £1,000 and he was described by a contemporary as resembling 'A Turtle Eating Alderman'. In 1751 he was made librarian to the Faculty of Advocates in Edinburgh, and set up house in the city with his sister.

In the 1750s Hume's philosophical works began to sell well and to achieve fame or at least notoriety. 'Answers by Reverends and Right Reverends', he tells us, 'came out two or three in a year.' But his own work took a new turn. Between 1754 and 1761 he wrote a six-volume history of England with a strong Tory bias. During his lifetime, indeed, he was much better known as a historian than as a philosopher.

In 1763, at the end of the Seven Years War, Hume became secretary to the British Embassy in Paris, and during a six-month period between one ambassador and another he served as *chargé d'affaires*. He found the environment most congenial, consorting with philosophers such as Diderot and d'Alembert, and engaging in an elegant flirtation with the Comtesse de Boufflers, continued in a series of love letters after his return to Britain. He brought back with him to London the Swiss philosopher, Jean-Jacques Rousseau, who feared persecution on the continent. Rousseau's difficult temperament was proof against Hume's kindly efforts to befriend and protect him, and in 1767 the two philosophers parted after a well-publicized quarrel.

Hume's career in government service ended with two years as under-secretary for the northern department from 1767–9 in the administration of the Duke of Grafton. He retired to Edinburgh where he lived until his death in 1776. He spent some time revising a set of *Dialogues Concerning Natural Religion*, a philosophical attack on natural theology, which was published posthumously in 1779. To the disappointment of James Boswell (who recorded his final illness in detail) he died serenely, having declined the consolations of religion. He left a brief autobiography which was brought out in 1777 by his friend Adam Smith, the economist. Smith himself wrote of Hume: 'Upon the whole, I have always considered him, both in his life-time and since his death, as approaching as nearly to the idea of a perfectly wise and virtuous man, as perhaps the nature of human frailty will admit.'

Smith and Reid

Adam Smith's own place is in the history of economics rather than that of philosophy, but he did hold chairs of logic and moral philosophy at Glasgow University, and in 1759 he published a *Theory of Moral Sentiments*. In this work he carried further Hume's emphasis on the role of sympathy as a fundamental element in our moral judgements, presenting a more complex analysis of sympathy itself and of its relationship to morality. Whereas, for Hume, sympathy was essentially a sharing of pleasure or pain with another, for Smith sympathy has a broader scope and can arise from the sharing of any passion. Thus, our concern for justice arises from sympathy with a victim's resentment of harm. Our approval of benevolence arises from sympathy both with the benefactor's generosity and with the beneficiary's gratitude. Because of the role of sympathy in generating moral judgement, the motive of an action matters more to us than outcome; hence utility, though of the first importance in economics, is not the ultimate criterion for morality. 'The usefulness of any disposition of mind is seldom the first ground of our approbation, and the sentiment of approbation always involves in it a sense of propriety quite distinct from the perception of utility' (*TMS*, 189).

Moral judgement, he insists, is essentially a social enterprise: a person brought up on a desert island 'could no more think of his own character, of the propriety or demerit of his own sentiments and conduct, of the beauty or deformity of his own mind than of the beauty or deformity of his own face' (*TMS*, 110). We need the mirror of society to show us ourselves: we cannot form any judgement of our own sentiments or motives unless we can somehow distance ourselves from them. Hence:

I divide myself, as it were, into two persons... The first is the spectator, whose sentiments with regard to my own conduct I endeavour to enter into, by placing myself in his situation, and by considering how it would appear to me, when seen from that particular point of view. The second is the agent, the person whom I properly call myself, and of whose conduct, under the character of a spectator, I was endeavouring to form some opinion. (*TMS*, 113)

This character, the impartial spectator whom Smith thus introduces into ethics, was to make a frequent appearance in the pages of subsequent moral philosophers.

While Adam Smith admired Hume and developed some of his philosophical ideas in an amicable manner, his successor at Glasgow as professor of moral philosophy, Thomas Reid (1710–96), was one of the earliest and fiercest critics not only of Hume but of the whole tradition to which he belonged. In 1764 he published an *Inquiry into the Human Mind on the Principles of Common Sense* in response to Hume's *Treatise*, and he followed this up in the 1780s with two essays on the intellectual and active powers of man. The paradoxical conclusions to which Hume's investigations led made Reid call in question the basic principles from which he began, and in particular the system of ideas common to both the British empiricists and the continental Cartesians:

When we find the gravest philosophers, from Des Cartes down to Bishop Berkeley, mustering up arguments to prove the existence of a material world, and unable to find any that will bear examination; when we find Bishop Berkeley and Mr Hume, the acutest metaphysicians of the age, maintaining that there is no such thing as matter in the universe—that sun, moon, and stars, the earth which we inhabit, our own bodies, and those of our friends, are only ideas in our minds, and have no existence but in thought; when we find the last maintaining that there is neither body nor mind—nothing in nature but ideas and impressions—that there is no certainty, nor indeed probability, even in mathematical axioms: I say, when we consider such extravagancies of many of the most acute writers on this subject, we may be apt to think the whole to be only a dream of fanciful men, who have entangled themselves in cobwebs spun our of their own brain.

The whole of recent philosophy, Reid maintains, shows how even the most intelligent people can go wrong if they start from a false first principle.

Reid puts his finger accurately on the basic error of Descartes and Locke, arising from the ambiguity of the word 'idea'. In ordinary language 'idea' means an act of mind; to have an idea of something is to conceive it, to have a concept of it. But philosophers have given it a different meaning, Reid says, according to which 'it does not signify that act of the mind which we call thought or conception, but some object of thought'. Ideas which are first introduced as humble images or proxies of things end up by supplanting what they represent and undermine everything but themselves: 'Ideas seem to have something in their nature unfriendly to other existences.'

Ideas in the philosophical sense—postulated intermediaries between the mind and the world—are, in Reid's view, mere fictions. We do of course, have conceptions of many things, but conceptions are not images, and in any case it is not conceptions that are the basic building blocks of knowledge, but propositions. Followers of Locke think that knowledge begins with bare conceptions ('simple apprehensions'), which we then put together to form beliefs and judgements. But that is the wrong way of looking at things. 'Instead of saying that the belief or knowledge is got by putting together and comparing the simple apprehensions, we ought rather to say that the simple apprehension is performed by resolving and analysing a natural and original judgement' (*I. 2, 4*). This thesis that concepts are logically subsequent to propositions, and result from their analysis, was an anticipation of a doctrine popular with some analytic philosophers in the twentieth century.

When I see a tree, Reid argues, I do not receive a mere idea of a tree; my vision of the tree involves the judgement that it exists with a certain shape, size, and position. The initial furniture of the mind is not a set of disconnected ideas, but a set of 'original and natural judgements'. These make up what Reid calls 'the common sense of mankind'. 'Common sense', before Reid, was commonly used by philosophers as the name of an alleged inner sense which discriminated between, and brought together, sense-data from different exterior senses. It was Reid who gave the expression the meaning which it has borne in modern times, as a repository of commonly shared unreasoned principles. In the greatest part of mankind, Reid says, no higher degree of reason is to be found, but it is a universal gift of heaven.

Among the common principles that Reid regards as the foundation of reasoning are a number that had been called in question by the British empiricists. Against Berkeley, he insists that size, shape, and motion inhere in material substances. Against Locke, he insists that secondary qualities also are real qualities of bodies: a colour I see is not identical with my sensation of it, but is that sensation's cause. Against Hume, he insists that our conscious thoughts 'must have a subject which we call mind'. And he reaffirms the principle that whatever begins to exist must have a cause which produced it (*Essays on the Active Powers of the Human Mind*, 8.3, 6).

Hume often wrote with a degree of contempt about the beliefs of 'the vulgar'— the belief, for instance, that objects continue to exist unperceived. Reid believes that philosophers despise the vulgar at their peril, and that they can discount their beliefs only because they have surreptitiously changed the meaning of words. 'The vulgar have undoubted right to give names to things which they are daily conversant about; and philosophers seem justly chargeable with an abuse of language, when they change the meaning of a common word, without giving warning.'

Reid said that 'in the unequal contest betwixt common sense and philosophy the latter will always come off both with dishonour and loss' (*I*. 1, 4). These should not be taken as the words of a philistine Luddite opposed to science and technology. Like the ordinary language philosophers of whom he was a precursor, he thought that it was only with respect to the meaning of words, not with respect to the truth or falsehood of propositions, that the man in the street had the final say. And when he talks of 'common sense' he does not mean popular beliefs about nature, or old wives' gossip, but rather the self-evident principles which other philosophers presented as intuitions of reason. Science itself was not a matter of simple common sense, but rather of rational inquiry conducted in the light of common sense; and the outcome of scientific investigation may well trump individual prejudices of the vulgar.

Reid himself was an experimental scientist, who produced original results in the geometry of visible objects, some of them anticipating the development of non-Euclidean geometries. What he wanted to show in his philosophy was that the realism of the common man was at least as compatible with the pursuit of science as the sophisticated and sophistical philosophy of the rationalists and the empiricists.

The Enlightenment

Adam Smith and Thomas Reid were two distinguished ornaments of what later came to be known as the Scottish Enlightenment. Throughout the Europe of the eighteenth century members of the intelligentsia saw themselves as bringing the light of reason into regions darkened by ignorance and superstition, but it was France which was seen by itself and others as the home of the Enlightenment *par excellence*. The high point of the French enlightenment was the publication in the 1750s and 1760s of the seventeen volumes of the *Encyclopédie, ou Dictionannaire raisonné des arts et des métiers*, edited by Denis Diderot and Jean d'Alembert. But the ground for this manifesto had been prepared for more than half a century by other French thinkers.

Pierre Bayle (1647–1706) had brought out a *Dictionnaire Historique et Critique* in which he showed, by detailed studies of biblical and historical personages, the inconsistency and incoherence of much of natural and revealed theology. The moral of his *tour d'horizon* was that religious faith was only tenable if accompanied by general toleration, and that the teaching of ethics should be made independent of religious instruction. Belief in human immortality, or in the existence of God, was not something necessary for virtuous living.

Bayle's scepticism was controverted by many, most notably by Leibniz in his *Theodicy*. But his negative attitude to religious authority set the tone for Enlightenment thinkers in Germany as well as in France. The positive element in the Enlightenment—the attempt to achieve a scientific understanding of the human social and political condition—owed more to another, more systematic thinker, Charles de Secondat, Baron de Montesquieu (1689–1755).

Montesquieu's great work was *The Spirit of the Laws* (1748), which built up a theory of the nature of the state upon a mass of historical and sociological erudition. This work, which took many years to write, had been preceded by two shorter works—the *Persian Letters* of 1721, a satire on French society, and a more ponderous treatise on the causes of the greatness and decadence of the ancient Romans (1734).[3]

Montesquieu spent a period in England and acquired a great admiration for the English Constitution. His Anglophile passion was shared by later Enlightenment philosophers, who saw themselves as heirs of Bacon, Locke, and Newton rather than of Descartes, Spinoza, and Leibniz. The first philosophical publication of Voltaire (born in 1694 as François Marie Arouet), the *Philosophical Letters* of 1734, is full of enthusiasm for the comparative freedom and moderation of English political and ecclesiastical institutions. His admiration for British tolerance was all the more sincere, since before being exiled to England in 1726 he had already been imprisoned twice in the Bastille in punishment for libellous pamphlets about senior noblemen.

Locke, Voltaire says in his thirteenth letter, is the first philosopher to have given a sober account of the human soul in place of the romantic fantasies woven by earlier philosophers. 'He has displayed to mankind the human reason just like a good anatomist explaining the machinery of the human body.' In the years before the appearance of the *Encyclopédie* Voltaire made himself a lively publicist for English science and philosophy, publishing in 1738 his *Philosophy of Newton*. The very idea of an encyclopedia came from England, where in 1728 one Ephraim Chambers had produced, in two volumes *Cyclopaedia; or, an Universal Dictionary of Arts and Sciences*.

The two editors of the *Encyclopédie* were men of different talents and temperaments. D'Alembert was a gifted mathematician with original work in fluid dynamics to his credit. He aimed to bring to all the sciences the clarity and accuracy of arithmetic and geometry. He was an early proponent of the ideal of a single great unified science. 'The Universe', he wrote in the introduction to the *Encyclopédie*, 'would be only one fact and one great truth for whoever knew how to embrace it from a single point of view.' Diderot was more interested in the biological and social sciences than in physics, and while d'Alembert was being fêted by academies, he spent a term in prison because of a *Letter on the Blind* which questioned the existence of design in the universe. The two men shared a faith in the inevitability of scientific progress, a belief that the Christian religion was a great obstacle to human betterment, and a fundamentally materialist view of human

---

[3] Montesquieu's political philosophy is treated in detail in Ch. 9.

nature. They gathered a group of like-minded thinkers as contributors to the *Encyclopédie*, including, besides Montesquieu and Voltaire, Julien de La Mettrie, a medical doctor who had recently published *L'Homme Machine*, the Baron d'Holbach, an atheist who presided over a lavish philosophical salon, and Claude Helvétius, a determinist psychologist who became notorious for a book arguing that human beings had no intellectual powers distinct from the senses.

While the Enlightenment philosophers were all anti-clerical, they were not all atheists. Voltaire, for instance, thought that the world as explained by Newton manifested the existence of God just as much as a watch shows the existence of a watchmaker. When he published his own *Philosophical Dictionary* in 1764 he wrote, in the entry on atheism:

Atheism is a monstrous evil in those who govern; and also in learned men even if their lives are innocent, because from their studies they can affect those who hold office; and that, even if not as baleful as fanaticism, it is nearly always fatal to virtue...Unphilosophical mathematicians have rejected final causes, but true philosophers accept them; and as a well-known author has said, a catechism announces God to children, and Newton demonstrates him to wise men. (*PD*, 38)

If God did not exist, Voltaire famously said, it would be necessary to invent him—otherwise the moral law would carry no weight. But he did not himself believe in a God who had freely created the world. Such a God would have to bear responsibility for catastrophic evils similar to the earthquake which struck Lisbon in 1755. The world was not a free creation, but a necessary, eternal, consequence of God's existence. To reject any accusation of atheism, Voltaire called himself a 'theist', but the standard philosophical term for those who believe in his type of divinity is 'deist'.

Although they are often seen as precursors of the French Revolution, the *philosophes* were not necessarily radical or even democratic. Diderot accepted the patronage of Catherine the Great of Russia, and Voltaire was for three years a chamberlain to Frederick II of Prussia. Their ideas of liberty resembled those of the English revolutionaries of 1688 more than those of the French revolutionaries of 1789. Freedom of expression was the freedom they most treasured, and they had no objection in principle to autocracy, although each of them was to find that their chosen despots were less enlightened than they had hoped. At home, both men were willing to take risks in protesting against abuses by government, but they did not call for any fundamental political changes. Least of all did they want an empowerment of the common people—the 'rabble', to use Voltaire's favourite term.

Rousseau

One encyclopedist was willing to go much further—Jean-Jacques Rousseau, who had contributed several articles on musical topics. Born in Geneva in 1712, the son of a watchmaker, Rousseau was brought up a Calvinist, but at the age of sixteen, a runaway apprentice, he became a Catholic in Turin. This was at the instigation of the Baronne de Warens, with whom he lived on and off between 1729 and 1740. After short spells as a singing master and a household tutor, he obtained a post as secretary to the French ambassador in Venice in 1743. Dismissed for insubordination, he went to Paris where he became close to Diderot, whom he visited regularly during his imprisonment. He was also for a while on good terms with d'Alembert and Voltaire. But he shocked the *philosophes* when in 1750 he published a prize essay which gave a negative answer to the question whether the progress of the arts and sciences had had a beneficial effect on morality. He followed this up four years later by a *Discourse on the Origin and Foundation of Inequality among Men*. The theme of both works was that humanity was naturally good, and corrupted by social institutions. The ideal human being was the 'noble savage' whose simple goodness put civilized man to shame. All this was, of course, at the opposite pole from the encyclopedists' faith in scientific and social progress: Voltaire called the *Discourse* 'a book against the human race'.

Rousseau exhibited his contempt for social convention in a practical form by a long-standing liason with a washerwoman, Therese Levasseur. By her he had five children whom he dumped, one after the other, in a foundling hospital. Having written an opera, *Le Devin du village*, which was performed before Louis XV at Fontainebleau, he returned to Geneva in 1754 and became a Calvinist again, in order to regain his citizenship there. Voltaire had returned from Berlin and was now settled in the Geneva region, but the two philosophers were not destined to be good neighbours: their mutual distaste became public with Rousseau's *Letter on Providence*, published in 1756. When, in 1757, d'Alembert published an encyclopedia article on Geneva in which he deplored the city's refusal to allow the peformance of comedies, Rousseau published in reply a *Letter to d'Alembert* in which he discoursed, in the style of Plato's *Republic*, on the morally corrupting influence of theatrical peformances. Rousseau had already quarrelled with Diderot for leaking an amatory confidence, and his break with the *philosophes* was complete when he published his *Lettres Morales* of 1861.

The period 1758 to 1761 was very productive for Rousseau, who spent the years in retirement in a small French country house. He wrote a novel, *La Nouvelle Héloïse*, which was an immediate best-seller when it appeared in Paris in 1761 He wrote also two philosophical treaties, one on education entitled *Émile*, and one on political philosophy, *The Social Contract*. *Émile* narrated the life of a child educated apart from other children, as an experiment; *The Social Contract* began with the memorable words 'Man is born free, and is everywhere in chains.'[4] These two works were published in 1762 and immediately caused an uproar because of their inflammatory doctrines. *Émile* was condemned by the Archbishop and Parliament

---

[4] Rousseau's political philosophy is discussed in detail in Ch. 9.

of Paris and it and *The Social Contract* were burnt in Geneva. With a warrant out for his arrest in both cities, Rousseau fled to Switzerland (of which Geneva was not at that time a part). After seeking refuge in various continental cities he was given sanctuary in England through the good offices of David Hume, who secured him a pension from King George III. But his paranoid ingratitude turned Hume against him, and he returned to France, spending the last years of his life (1770–78) in Paris. The main achievement of this period was a book of autobiographical *Confessions*, which was published some years after his death.

The year 1778 was also the time of Voltaire's death. In his later years his writings had become more explicitly anti-Christian. From his safe haven at Ferney, near Geneva, he published his irreverent *Pocket Philosophical Dictionary* (1765) and *The Profession of Faith of Theists* in 1768. He wrote also historical works and dramas, and he died just after returning to Paris for the triumphant first night of his play *Irène*. Rousseau and Voltaire, enemies in life, now lie side by side in the crypt of the Pantheon, the mausoleum in Paris dedicated to the great men of France.

The philosophers of the French Enlightenment, and Rousseau especially, have been regarded by many as responsible for the revolutionary convulsions into which France and Europe were plunged soon after their deaths. Thomas Carlyle, author of *The French Revolution*, was once reproached by a businessman for being too interested in mere ideas. 'There was once a man called Rousseau', Carlyle replied, 'who wrote a book containing nothing but ideas. The second edition was bound in the skins of those who laughed at the first.'[5]

Wolff and Lessing

In Germany, the Enlightenment took a form that was less threatening to the existing establishment—partly, no doubt, because it enjoyed for a while the patronage of Frederick the Great, King of Prussia from 1740 to 1786. In the first half of the eighteenth century the leading German philosopher was Christian Wolff (1679–1754), who began his career as a professor of mathematics at Halle, a post he was offered on the recommendation of Leibniz. When he first ventured into philosophy he aroused the hostility of devout Lutherans, who influenced the then monarch to deprive him of his chair and banish him from Prussia. Such an experience of persecution was almost the only thing Wolff had in common with the *philosophes*; unlike them, he was solemn, academic, systematic, and accurately erudite. His rationalism was at the opposite pole from Rousseau's romanticism.

Wolff taught for seventeen years in a Calvinist university in Marburg, but when Frederick the Great came to the throne he was restored to his chair in Halle, which

---

[5] Quoted in Alasdair MacIntyre, *A Short History of Ethics* (London: Routledge, 1976), p. 182.

he held until his death. Later, he became vice-chancellor of the university and was made a baron of the Holy Roman Empire. His philosophical system was eclectic and capacious, embracing elements from classical Aristotelianism, Latin scholasticism, Cartesian rationalism, and Leibnizian metaphysics. He took over from Leibniz the principle of sufficient reason, which he regarded as the fundamental basis of metaphysics in conjunction with the principle of identity. The sufficient reason for the existence of the world is to be found in a transcendent God, whose existence can be established by the traditional ontological and cosmological arguments. The world we live in is the best of all possible worlds, freely chosen by God's wisdom.

There was little that was original in Wolff, except for the system which he imposed upon his borrowings from earlier authors. He perceived it as his task, for instance, to impose order on what he saw as the chaos of Aristotle's metaphysics. He regimented the different branches of philosophy, popularizing such distinctions as those between natural theology and general metaphysics ('ontology'), which had been absent from medieval discussion. His definition of ontology as 'the science of all possible things insofar as they are possible', with its emphasis on possible essences rather than actual existents, was a continuation of a line begun by Avicenna and Duns Scotus. He introduced a novel distinction between physics (the experimental study of the contingent natural laws of this world) and cosmology (an *a priori* investigation of every possible material world).

Like Descartes, Wolff accepted the existence of a human soul that was a simple substance available to self-consciousness; but the relation between this soul and the body he explained by appeal to a Leibnizian pre-established harmony. In Wolff's ethical system the key notion is that of perfection. Good is what increases perfection, and evil what diminishes it. The fundamental human motivation is self-perfection, which includes the promotion of the common good and the service of God's honour. Although living bodies, including human bodies, are machines, nonetheless we enjoy free will: rational choice can, and should, overcome all the pressures of sensibility.

Wolff is nowadays hardly ever read by English readers. His importance in the history of philosophy is that his system became accepted in Germany as the paradigm of a rationalist metaphysics, and that later writers defined their own positions in relation to his. This is particularly true of Immanuel Kant, who in his magisterial critique of metaphysics often has Wolff's doctrines immediately in his sights.

A thinker who was much closer to the Enlightenment as understood in France and Britain was Gotthold Ephraim Lessing (1729–81). The son of a Lutheran pastor, he was initially destined for the Church, but he abandoned theology for a literary career, in which he supported himself by acting as librarian to the Duke of Brunswick. Like the *philosophes* he expressed his thoughts in essays and dramas in preference to academic textbooks. His first publication was an essay written jointly with the Jewish philosopher Moses Mendelssohn entitled '*Pope a Metaphysician!*', which was partly an attack on the Leibnizian views expressed in Pope's *Essay on Man*, but also a plea for a sharp separation between philosophy and poetry as two quite different spiritual activities. In *Laocoon* of 1776 he pleaded for a similar separation between poetry and the visual arts: the artistic effect of Virgil's description of the death of Laocoon is quite different, he argued, from that of the famous classical statue in the Vatican. In each case Lessing, taking as his starting point Aristotle's *Poetics* ('as much an infallible work as the *Elements of Euclid*'), delineated a special, semi-prophetic role for the poet. In doing so he foreshadowed one of the principal themes of Romanticism.

Like the Romantics, Lessing admired Spinoza. He regarded the world as a single unified system whose components were identical with ideas in the mind of God. He was willing to accept that determinism was true and that freedom was an illusion; on the other hand, he was willing to admit contingency in the world, with the consequence that some among God's ideas were contingent also. He praised Spinoza for realizing that liberation from anxiety is only to be achieved by accepting the inevitability of destiny. 'I thank my God', he said, 'that I am under necessity, that the best must be.'

Lessing's most important philosophical work was *The Education of the Human Race* (1780). The human race, like the human individual, passes through different stages, to which different kinds of instruction are appropriate. The upbringing of a child is a matter of physical rewards and punishment: the childhood of the human race was the era of the Old Testament. In our youth, educators offer us more spiritual rewards for good conduct; eternal rewards and punishments for an immortal soul. This corresponds to the period of history dominated by the Christian religion. However, as Lessing endeavoured to show in a number of critical studies of the New Testament, the evidence for the divine origin of Christianity is uncompelling. Even the strongest historical evidence about contingent facts, Lessing went on to argue, cannot justify any conclusion to necessary truths about matters of divinity.

The Christian religion, therefore, can be no more than a stage in the education of the human race, and its dogmas can have no more than symbolic value. Human nature, come of age, must extract from Christianity a belief in the universal brotherhood of man, and must pursue moral values for their own sake, not for the sake of any reward here or hereafter (although Lessing toys with the idea of a transmigration of souls into a new incarnation after death). Like the leaders of the French Enlightenment, Lessing was a passionate advocate of religious toleration; he gave fullest expression to this advocacy in his drama *Nathan the Wise* (1779). One reason for toleration that Lessing offers is that the worth of a person does not depend on whether his beliefs are true, but on how much trouble he has taken to attain the truth. This novel argument was presented in a vivid paragraph often quoted since:

If God held all truth in his right hand and in his left the everlasting striving after truth, so that I should always and everlastingly be mistaken, and said to me, Choose, with humility I would pick on the left hand and say, Father, grant me that; absolute truth is for thee alone. (*Gesammelte Werke*, ed. Lachmann and Muncker, XIII. 23)

Kant

One man who devoted his whole life to the pursuit of absolute truth was Immanuel Kant: indeed, apart from this pursuit, there is little to tell about his biography. Born in 1724 in Königsberg, which was then in the eastern part of Prussia, he lived all his life in the town of his birth. From 1755 until 1770 he was a *Privatdozent* or lecturer in Königsberg University, and from 1770 until his death in 1804 he held the professorship of logic and metaphysics there. He never travelled or married or held public office, and the story of his life is the story of his ideas.

Kant was brought up in a devout Lutheran family, but he later became liberal in his theological views, though perforce regular in religious observance. He was always a man of strict life and constant habit, notorious for exact punctuality, rising at five and retiring at ten, lecturing in the morning from seven to eight, and then writing until a late and ample luncheon. The citizens of Königsberg used to joke that they could set their watches by his appearance for his afternoon constitutional. As a university student he was taught by a disciple of Wolff, but his own early interests were more scientific than philosophical, and as a *Privatdozent* he lectured not only on logic and metaphysics but on subjects as diverse as anthropology, geography, and mineralogy. His first books, too, were written on scientific subjects, most notably the *General History of Nature and Theory of the Heavens* of 1755.

From 1760 onwards he began to devote himself seriously to philosophy, but for the next twenty years the works he published were of a cautious and conventional kind. In 1762 he wrote a short and rather superficial essay on the traditional syllogistic, criticizing the unnecessary subtlety ('Die falsche Spitzfindigkeit', as the essay's title has it) of its customary presentation. In the same year he wrote *The Only Possible Ground for a Demonstration of God's Existence*, in which, while rejecting three of the standard proofs of God's existence, he argued, in the spirit of Wolff and Duns Scotus, that if there are any possible beings at all there must be a perfect being to provide the ground of this possibility.

In 1763 the Berlin Academy set as a prize question 'whether metaphysical truths can be demonstrated with the same certainty as truths of geometry'. Kant's (unsuccessful) entry for the prize underlined a number of crucial distinctions between mathematical and philosophical method. Mathematicians start from clear definitions which create concepts which they then go on to develop; philosophers start from confused concepts and analyse them in order to reach a definition. Metaphysicians rather than aping mathematicians should follow Newtonian methods, by applying them not to the physical world but to the phenomena of inner experience.

The programme that Kant lays out here for the philosopher closely resembles that which Hume had set himself, and later Kant was to credit Hume with having woken him from the 'dogmatic slumber' of the years when he accepted the philosophy of Leibniz and Wolff. It is not certain when Kant began the serious study of Hume, but during the 1760s he became increasingly sceptical of the possibility of a scientific metaphysics. The anonymous, skittish *Dreams of a Ghost Seer* of 1766 compared metaphysical speculations with the esoteric fantasies of the visionary Immanuel Swedenborg. Among other things, Kant emphasized, in the wake of Hume, that causal relations could be known only through experience and were never matters of logical necessity. However, his inaugural dissertation as professor in 1770 (*On the Form and Principles of the Sensible and Intelligible World*) still shows the strong influence of Leibniz.

The first eleven years of his professorship were spent by Kant in developing his own original system, which was published in 1781 in *The Critique of Pure Reason*, a work which at once put his pre-critical works in the shade and established him as one of the greatest philosophers of the modern age. He followed it up with a briefer and more popular exposition of its ideas, the *Prolegomena to any Future Metaphysics* (1783), and republished it in a second edition in 1787.

Kant's aim in his critical philosophy was to make philosophy, for the first time, fully scientific. Mathematics had been scientific for many centuries, and scientific physics had come of age. But metaphysics, the oldest discipline, the one which 'would survive even if all the rest were swallowed up in the abyss of an all-destroying barbarism', was still far from maturity. Metaphysical curiosity was inherent in human nature: human beings could not but be interested in the three main objects of metaphysics, namely, God, freedom, and immortality. But could metaphysics become a true science?

Hume and others, as we have seen, had tried to do for the philosophy of mind what Newton had done for the philosophy of bodies, making the association of ideas the psychic counterpart of gravitational attraction between bodies. Kant's programme for rendering metaphysics scientific was on a more ambitious scale. Philosophy, he believed, needed a revolution like that of Copernicus who had moved the earth from the centre of the universe to put the sun in its place. Copernicus had shown that when we think we are observing the motion of the sun round the earth what we see is the consequence of the rotation of our own earth. Kant's Copernican revolution will do for our reason what Copernicus did for our sight. Instead of asking how our knowledge can conform to its objects, we must start from the supposition that objects must conform to our knowledge. Only in this way can we justify the claim of metaphysics to possess knowledge that is necessary and universal.

Kant distinguishes between two modes of knowledge: knowledge *a priori* and knowledge *a posteriori*. We know a truth *a posteriori* if we know it through experience; we know it *a priori* if we know it independently of all experience. Kant agreed with Locke that all our knowledge begins with experience, but he did not believe that it all arose from experience. There are some things that we know *a priori*, fundamental truths that are not mere generalizations from experience. Among the judgements that we make *a priori* some, Kant says, are analytic, and some are synthetic. In an analytic judgement, such as 'all bodies are extended', we are merely making explicit in the predicate something that is already contained in the concept of the subject. But in a synthetic judgement the predicate adds something to the content of the subject: Kant's example is 'all bodies are heavy'. All *a posteriori* propositions are synthetic, and all analytic propositions are *a priori*. Can there be propositions that are synthetic, and yet *a priori*? Kant believes that there are. For him, mathematics offers examples of synthetic *a priori* truths. Most importantly, there must be propositions that are both *a priori* and synthetic if it is ever going to be possible to make a genuine science out of metaphysics.

The philosopher's first task is to make plain the nature and limits of the powers of the mind. Like medieval and rationalist philosophers before him, Kant distinguishes sharply between the senses and the intellect; but within the intellect he makes a new distinction of his own between understanding (*Verstand*) and reason (*Vernunft*). The understanding operates in combination with the senses in order to provide human knowledge: through the senses, objects are given us; through the understanding, they are made thinkable. Experience has a content, provided by the senses, and a structure, determined by the understanding. Reason, by contrast with understanding, is the intellect's endeavour to go beyond what understanding can achieve. When divorced from experience it is 'pure reason', and it is this which is the target of Kant's criticism.

Before addressing pure reason, Kant's *Critique* makes a systematic study of the senses and the understanding. The senses are studied in a section entitled 'Transcendental Aesthetic', and the understanding in a section entitled 'Transcendental Logic'. 'Transcendental' is a favourite word of Kant's; he used it with several meanings, but common to all of them is the notion of something which (for better or worse) goes beyond and behind the deliverances of actual experience.

The transcendental aesthetic is largely devoted to the study of space and time. Sensations, Kant says, have a matter (or content) and a form. Space is the form of the outer senses, and time is the form of the inner sense. Space and time are not entities in the world discovered by the mind: they are the pattern into which the senses mould experience. In expounding his transcendental aesthetic, Kant offers his own novel solution to the age-old question 'Are space and time real?'[6]

---

[6] Kant's account of space and time is considered at greater length in Ch. 5.

When we move from the transcendental aesthetic to the transcendental logic we again encounter a twofold division. The logic consists of two major enterprises, which Kant calls the *transcendental analytic* and the *transcendental dialectic*. The analytic sets out the criteria for the valid empirical employment of the understanding; the dialectic exposes the illusions that arise when reason tries to operate outside the limits set by the analytic. In his analytic Kant lays out a set of *a priori* concepts which he calls 'categories', and a set of *a priori* judgements which he calls 'principles'. Accordingly, the analytic is again subdivided, into two main sections, containing 'The Deduction of the Categories' and 'The System of Principles'.

The first section presents the deduction, or legitimation, of the categories. Categories are concepts of a particularly fundamental kind: Kant gives as instances the concepts of 'cause' and 'substance'. Without these categories, he argues, we could not conceptualize or understand even the most fragmentary and disordered experience. His aim here is to meet the empiricist's challenge on the empiricist's own ground. He agrees with the empiricist that all our knowledge begins with experience, but he denies that all of it arises from experience. He seeks to show that without the metaphysical concepts that Hume sought to dismantle, Hume's own basic items of experience, impressions, and ideas would themselves disintegrate.

The second section of the analytic, the system of principles, contains a number of synthetic *a priori* propositions about experience. Experiences, Kant maintains, must possess two kinds of magnitude—extensive magnitude (of which an instance is the distance between two points) and intensive magnitude (of which an instance is a particular degree of heat). Moreover, Kant maintains, experience is only possible if necessary connections are to be found among our perceptions. Hume was wrong to think that we first perceive temporal succession between events, and then go on to regard one as cause and another as effect. On the contrary, we could not establish an objective time sequence unless we had already established relationships between causes and effects.[7]

While Kant is hostile to empiricism, he attacks rationalism no less vigorously. At the end of his analytic he insists that the categories cannot determine their own applicability, the principles cannot establish their own truth. Understanding alone cannot establish that there is any such thing as a substance, or that every change has a cause. All that one can establish *a priori* is that if experience is to be possible, certain conditions must hold. But whether experience is possible cannot be established in advance: the possibility of experience is shown only by the actual occurrence of experience itself.

The analytic shows that there cannot be a world of mere appearances, mere objects of sense that do not fall under any categories or instantiate any rules. But we cannot conclude from this that there is a non-sensible world that is established by the intellect alone. To accept the existence of extra-sensible objects that can be

---

[7] Kant's account of the relation between time and causation is discussed in Chapter 6.

studied by the use of pure reason is to enter a realm of illusion, and in his 'transcendental dialectic' Kant explores this world of enchantment.

'Transcendental', as has been said, means something that goes beyond and behind the deliverances of actual experience, and in his dialectic Kant has three principal targets: metaphysical psychology, metaphysical cosmology, and metaphysical theology. 'Pure reason', he tells us, 'furnished the idea for a transcendental doctrine of the soul, for a transcendental science of the world, and finally for a transcendental knowledge of God.' In turn he tests to destruction the three notions of an immaterial immortal soul, of a surveyable cosmic whole, and of an absolutely necessary being.

Rationalist psychology, as practised by Descartes, started with the premiss 'I think' and concluded to the existence of a substance that was immaterial, incorruptible, personal, and immortal. Kant argues that this line of argument is littered with fallacies—he lists four of them which he calls 'the paralogisms of pure reason'. These paralogisms are not accidental: in principle, any attempt to go beyond empirical psychology must be guilty of fallacy.

In order to dismantle *a priori* cosmology, Kant sets up four antinomies. An antinomy is a pair of contrasting arguments which lead to contradictory conclusions (a thesis and an antithesis). The first of the four antinomies has as its thesis 'The world has a beginning in time and is limited in space,' and as antithesis 'The world has no beginning in time and no limits in space.' Kant offers proofs of both these propositions. He does not, of course, mean us to conclude that both contradictories are true: the moral is that reason has no right to talk at all about 'the world' as a whole.

In each of the antinomies the thesis states that a certain series comes to a full stop and the antithesis states that it continues for ever. The second antinomy concerns divisibility, the third concerns causation, and the fourth concerns contingency. In each case Kant presents the series as a series of entities that are conditioned by something else—an effect, for instance, is in his terms 'conditioned' by its cause. In each of the antinomies, the thesis of the argument concludes to an unconditioned absolute. Both sides of each antinomy, Kant believes, are in error: the thesis is the error of dogmatism and the antithesis the error of empiricism. The point of constructing the antinomies is to exhibit the mismatch between the scope of empirical inquiry and the pretensions of pure reason. The thesis represents the world as smaller than thought (we can think beyond it); the antithesis represents it as larger than thought (we cannot think to the end of it). We must match thought and the world by trimming our cosmic ideas to fit the empirical inquiry.[8]

In his fourth antinomy Kant proposes arguments for and against the existence of a necessary being, and then in a later section of the *Critique* he goes on to consider the concept of God as held out by natural theology. He classifies

---

[8] A further account of the antinomies will be found in Ch. 5.

arguments for God's existence into three fundamental types, and shows how arguments of every type must fail. If God is to have a place in our thought and life, he believed, it is not as an entity whose existence is established by rational proof.

The Critique of Pure Reason is not an easy book to read, and not all the difficulty is due to the profundity of its subject matter or the originality of its thought. Kant (as must already be apparent) was excessively fond of inventing technical terms and (as will appear elsewhere in this book) was too anxious to force ideas into rigid schematisms. But any reader who perseveres through the difficult text will enjoy a rich philosophical reward.

In his sixties, Kant turned his attention to ethics and aesthetics in three seminal works: *Fundamental Principles of the Metaphysics of Morals* (1785); *The Critique of Practical Reason* (1788); and *The Critique of Judgement* (1790). In the first two of these he aimed to set out critically the synthetic *a priori* principles of practical reason just as he had, in his first *Critique*, set out the synthetic *a priori* principles of theoretical reason.

The starting point of Kant's moral theory is that the only thing that is good without qualification is a good will. Talents, character, and fortune can be used to bad ends and even happiness can be corrupting. It is not what a good will achieves that matters; good will, even if frustrated in its efforts, is good in itself alone. What makes a will good is that it is motivated by duty: to act from duty is to exhibit good will in the face of difficulty. Some people may enjoy doing good, or profit from doing good, but worth of character is shown only when someone does good not from inclination, but for duty's sake.

To act from duty is to act out of reverence for the moral law, to act in obedience to a moral imperative. There are two sorts of imperative, hypothetical and categorical. A hypothetical imperative says: if you wish to achieve a certain end, act in such-and-such a way. The categorical imperative says: no matter what end you wish to achieve, act in such-and-such a way. There are as many sets of hypothetical imperatives as there are different ends that human beings may set themselves, but there is only one categorical imperative which is this: 'Act only according to a maxim by which you can at the same time will that it shall become a universal law.' Whenever you are inclined to act in a certain way—for instance, to borrow money without any intention of paying it back—you must always ask yourself what it would be like if everyone acted in that way.

Kant offers another formulation of the categorical imperative: 'Act in such a way that you always treat humanity, whether in your own person or in the person of any other, never simply as a means, but always at the same time as an end.' As a human being, Kant says, I am not only an end in myself, I am a member of a kingdom of ends, a union of rational beings under common laws. In the kingdom of ends, we are all both legislators and subjects. A rational being 'is subject only to laws which are made by himself and yet are universal'.[9]

---

[9] Kants's moral philosophy is discussed at length in Ch. 8.

In his third critique, the *Critique of Judgement,* Kant sought to apply to aesthetic notions such as beauty and sublimity the kind of analysis that in the earlier critiques he had applied to scientific and ethical concepts. Judgements of aesthetic taste rest on feeling, and yet they claim universal validity. But it is a mistake to think that they concern some objective universal, Kant argues: what can be universally shared is rather the particular internal relationship between the imagination and the understanding which is characteristic of a contemplative judgement of taste.

In the 1890s, with his critical philosophy firmly established, Kant ventured into areas that were not just philosophically adventurous. In 1793 he published a semi-theological work, entitled *Religion within the Bounds of Reason Alone,* which offered a reinterpretation of several Christian doctrines, and in 1795, in the midst of the French revolutionary wars, he wrote a pamphlet *On Perpetual Peace.* The first of these works gave offence to Frederick William II, who saw it as an unjustified attack on the authority of the Bible. Kant refused to recant his views, but agreed not to write or lecture further on religious topics. He kept this promise until 1798, after the king's death, when he published *The Conflict of the Faculties* on the relationship between theology and philosophy. In 1797 he amplified his moral system in *The Metaphysic of Morals.* This was divided into two parts, one treating of individual virtue and the other of legal theory. It was a more substantial but much less influential treatise than the earlier *Groundwork.*

Kant died in 1804. On his tombstone was inscribed a sentence from the conclusion of his *Critique of Practical Reason.* 'Two things fill the mind with ever new and increasing admiration and awe, the more often and steadily we reflect upon them: the starry heavens above me and the moral law within me.'

Fichte and Schelling

Until his last days Kant was working on an ambitious philosophical project that was published only after his death (the *Opus Postumum*). This shows that in his last days he had begun to have some misgivings about some aspects of the system of the first *Critique.* These were occasioned by criticisms aired by some of his own most devoted admirers and pupils. Foremost among these was Johann Gottlieb Fichte, who was forty-two in the year of Kant's death, and at the apogee of his own philosophical career.

Fichte was born into a poor family and was employed at an early age to herd geese. His intellectual gifts caught the attention of a philanthropic baron, and he was able to study theology at the University of Jena, where he came to admire Lessing, Spinoza, and Kant. His first publication was a *Critique of All Revelations* (1792), written in the style of Kant so successfully that for a while it passed as the master's own composition. Kant denied authorship, but reviewed the work very favourably.

582

Partly through the influence of Goethe, Fichte was appointed to a professorship at Jena in 1794, where the great poet and dramatist Friedrich Schiller was among his colleagues.

Fichte's lectures were initially popular, but soon they were criticized by the students for being too puritanical and by the faculty for being insufficiently religious. He was forced to leave the university in 1799, and was without a tenured academic post until in 1810 he became dean of the philosophy faculty in the new University of Berlin. He was much involved in the resurgence of German nationalism during Napoleon's European hegemony. His *Addresses to the German Nation*, in 1808, rebuked the Germans for the disunity that led to their defeat by Napoleon at the battle of Jena, and he served as a volunteer in the army of resistance in 1812. He died of typhus in 1814, caught from his wife who was a military nurse.

Fichte's philosophical reputation rests on his *Wissenschaftslehre* of 1804. He saw the task of philosophy in Kantian terms as providing a transcendental account of the possibility of experience. Such an account could start either from pure objectivity (the thing in itself) or free subjectivity ('the I'). The former would be the path of dogmatism, and the latter the path of idealism. Fichte rejected the Kantian solution to the Kantian problem, and abandoned any notion of a thing-in-itself. He sought to derive the whole of consciousness from the free experience of the thinking subject. Thus he made himself the uncompromising originator of German idealism.

What is this I from which all things flow? Is it revealed by introspection? 'I cannot take a pace, I cannot move hand or foot, without the intellectual intuition of my self-consciousness in these actions,' Fichte said. If the theory is that the individual self can create the whole material world, we seem to be faced with an unconvincing and unappetizing solipsism. But this, Fichte insisted, is a misinterpretation. 'It is not the individual but the one immediate spiritual Life which is the creator of all phenomena, including phenomenal individuals' (*Sämmtliche Werke*, ed. I. H. Fichte (Berlin, 1845–6), II. 607).

This sounds rather like God, and in his later, popular works Fichte went so far as to say: 'It is not the finite self that exists, it is the divine Idea that is the foundation of all philosophy; everything that man does of himself is null and void. All existence is living and active in itself, and there is no other life than Being, and no other Being than God.' But elsewhere he said that it was superstitious to believe in any divine being that was anything more than a moral order. Clearly, he was more of a pantheist than a theist.

Fichte's philosophy of religion resembles that of Spinoza, as was pointed out by the most devoted of his disciples, F. W. J. Schelling, who had become his colleague on appointment to a professorship in Jena in 1798, at the age of twenty-three. Fichte's philosophy was the critical form, Schelling maintained, of the teaching that Spinoza had presented in dogmatic form. Schelling went on to develop his own less uncompromising form of idealism, a 'Nature Philosophy', according to which an initial absolute gives rise to two co-equal principles existing side by side: a spiritual consciousness and a physical nature. Here too we meet the ghost of Spinoza: the initial absolute is *Natura Naturans*, the system of material nature is *Natura Naturata*.

Schelling's system is rich but difficult, and his works are not much read nowadays in anglophone countries. He is perhaps best known in England because of the influence he exercised on Samuel Taylor Coleridge, who admired and imitated him to the extent of being accused of plagiarizing his works.[10] In most histories of philosophy Schelling is presented as a bridge between the idealism of Fichte and that of G. W. F. Hegel, who collaborated with him as editor of a philosophical journal at Jena in 1802–3.

Hegel

Hegel's first book, indeed, had been a comparison between the philosophies of Fichte and Schelling (1801). Born in 1770, he had studied theology at the University of Tübingen; he became a colleague of the two philosophers when he obtained a post at the University of Jena in 1801. He taught there until Jena's university was closed down after Napoleon's crushing victory over the Prussian army there in 1806. Shortly afterwards Hegel, now almost destitute, published his monumental *Phenomenology of Spirit* (*Die Phänomenologie des Geistes*).

It was not until 1816 that Hegel became a professor, at the University of Heidelberg; by that time he had published his major work, *The Science of Logic*. A year later he published an encyclopedia of the philosophical sciences—logic, philosophy of nature, and philosophy of spirit. In 1818 he was called to a chair in Berlin, which he held until his death from cholera in 1831. During these years he published little, but his lecture courses were published posthumously. In addition to covering the history of philosophy, they treat of aesthetics, philosophy of

---

[10] Coleridge was not, however, an admirer of Fichte, whose idealism he burlesqued in a poem containing the following lines:

> I, I! I, itself I!
> The form and the substance, the what and the why
> The when and the where, and the low and the high,
> The inside and outside, the earth and the sky,
> I, you, and he, and he, you and I,
> All souls and all bodies are I itself I!
>> All I itself I!
>> (Fools! A truce with this starting!)
>> All my I! all my I!
> He's a heretic dog who but adds Betty Martin!

> (*Biographia Literaria*, Ch. 9)

religion, and philosophy of history. More readable than his difficult official publications, they exhibit an enormously original and capacious mind at work.

Hegel's greatest contribution to thought was his introduction of a historical element into philosophy. He was not the first historian of philosophy: that honour is Aristotle's. Nor was he the first philosopher of history: when he wrote there were already two classic contributions to that discipline, the *Scienza Nuova* of Giambattista Vico (1725) and the *Ideen zur Philosophie der Geschichte der Menschheit* of J. G. Herder (1784), both of which reflected on historical method and emphasized the developmental evolution of human institutions. But it was Hegel who gave history a special place in philosophy, and the philosopher a special place in historiography.

Hegel believed that the philosopher had a special insight into history that ordinary historians lacked. Only the philosopher really understands that reason is the sovereign of the world, and that the history of the world is a rational process. There are two ways of reaching this understanding: either by the investigation of a metaphysical system, or by induction from the study of history itself. The belief that history is the unfolding of reason corresponds to the religious faith in divine providence; but the metaphysical understanding is deeper than the theological one, because a general providence is inadequate to account for the concrete nature of history. Only the philosopher knows the ultimate destiny of the world, and how it is to be realized.

Cosmic history, according to Hegel, consists in the life story of spirit (*Geist*). The internal development of spirit manifests itself in concrete reality. 'Everything that from eternity has happened in heaven and earth, the life of God and all the deeds of time are simply the struggles of Spirit to know itself and to find itself' (*LHP* I. 23). Spirit is not something given in advance in all its fullness: it proceeds from potentiality to actuality, and the motive force of history is spirit's drive to actualize its potential. Universal history is 'the exhibition of Spirit in the process of working out the knowledge of that which it is potentially.'

Hegel claims that the existence of spirit is a matter of logic, but he uses the word 'logic' in a special sense of his own. Just as he sees history as a manifestation of logic, so he tends to see logic in historical, indeed martial, terms. If two propositions are contradictories, Hegel will describe this as a conflict between them: propositions do battle with one another and will emerge victorious or suffer defeat. This is called 'dialectic', the process by which one proposition (the 'thesis') fights with another (the 'antithesis') and both are finally overcome by a third ('the synthesis').

We pass through two stages of dialectic in order to reach spirit. We begin with the absolute, the totality of reality, akin to the Being of earlier philosophers. Our first thesis is that the absolute is pure Being. But pure Being without any qualities is nothing, so we are led to the antithesis, 'The absolute is Nothing'. Thesis and antithesis are overcome by synthesis: the union of Being and Unbeing is Becoming, and so we say 'The absolute is Becoming'.

The becoming, the life, of the absolute provides the second stage of dialectic. We begin by considering the absolute as a subject of thought, a universal thinker: Hegel calls this 'The Concept', by which he means the totality of the concepts that the intellect brings to bear in thinking. We then consider the absolute as an object of thought: Hegel calls this 'Nature', by which he means the totality of the objects that can be studied by the intellect. Concept and nature are brought together when the absolute becomes conscious of itself, being thus both subject and object of thought. This synthesis of self-consciousness is spirit.

Hegel's notion of spirit is baffling on first acquaintance. An attempt at an explanation will be given in later chapters, but we must try to get an initial feel for what he means. We may wonder whether the spirit is perhaps God—identified perhaps with Nature, à la Spinoza. Or we may guess that 'Spirit' is a misleadingly grand way of talking about individual human minds, in the way in which medical textbooks speak of 'the liver' rather than of individual livers. Neither suggestion is quite right.

A better place to start is by reflection on the way we all talk about the human race. Without any particular metaphysical theory in mind, we are happy to say such things as that the human race has progressed, or is in decline, or has learnt much of which it was once ignorant. When Hegel uses the word 'Spirit' he is using the same kind of language, but he is adding two layers of metaphysical commit-ment. First, he is talking not just about human history, but about the history of the whole universe; and, second, he is viewing that universe as an organic whole which has a life cycle mapped out for it.

Hegel invites us to look on the universe as we look on specific organisms in nature. A plant passes through stages of development, producing twigs, leaves, blossom, and fruit; it does so in accordance with a pattern specific to its own kind. Hegel, with a deliberate bow to Plato, calls this the Idea of the plant. A plant, of course, is not conscious of its own Idea. But a human child, as its bodily powers develop, and as its intellectual skills emerge, gradually grows into consciousness of itself and its nature or Idea (*LHP* I. 29). The progress of spirit reproduces this development on a cosmic scale:

Spirit is not to be considered only as individual, finite, consciousness, but as that Spirit which is universal and concrete within itself . . . Spirit's intelligent comprehension of itself is at the same time the progression of the total evolving reality. This progression is not one that takes its course through the thought of an individual and exhibits itself in a single consciousness, for it shows itself to be universal Spirit presenting itself in the history of the world in all the richness of its form. (*LHP* I. 33)

Thus the history of the world is the history of the ever-growing self-consciousness of spirit. Different stages in the cosmic Idea present themselves at different times to different races. Spirit progresses in consciousness of freedom *pari passu* with the growth of awareness of freedom among human beings. Those who lived under oriental despots did not know that they were free beings. The Greeks and Romans knew that they themselves were free, but their acceptance of slavery showed that they did not know that man as such was free. 'The German nations, under the influence of Christianity, were the first to attain the consciousness that man, as man, is free: that it is the freedom of Spirit that constitutes its essence.'

The freedom of spirit is what marks it off from matter, which is bound by the necessity of laws such as that of universal attraction. The destiny of the world is spirit's expansion of its freedom and of its consciousness of its freedom. Self-interested individuals and nations are the unconscious instruments of spirit working out its destiny: they become conscious of their role in the cosmic drama at the point at which they are formed into a national state. The state is 'the realization of Freedom, i.e. of the absolute final aim, and it exists for its own sake.' The state does not exist for the sake of its citizens; on the contrary, the citizen possesses worth only as a member of the state—just as an eye only has any value as part of a living body.

Different states will have different characteristics corresponding to the folk-spirit of the nation which they incorporate. At different times different folk-spirits will be the primary manifestation of the progress of the world-spirit, and the people to which it belongs will be, for one epoch, the dominant people in the world. For each nation, the hour strikes once and only once, and Hegel believed that in his time the hour had struck for the German nation. The Prussian monarchy was the nearest thing on earth to the realization of an ideal state.[11]

The most important manifestation of spirit, however, was not to be found in political institutions, but in philosophy itself. The self-awareness of the absolute is brought into existence by the philosophical reflection of human beings; the history of philosophy brings the absolute face to face with itself. Hegel firmly believed that philosophy made progress: 'the latest, most modern and newest philosophy is the most developed, richest and deepest', he tells us (*LHP* I. 41). In his lectures on the history of philosophy he displays earlier philosophies as succumbing, one by one, to a dialectical advance marching steadily in the direction of German idealism.

---

[11] Hegel's political philosophy is considered in detail in Ch. 9.

4

Knowledge

Montaigne's Scepticism

In the sixteenth century, several factors contributed to make scepticism enjoy a new popularity. The clash between different Christian sects in Europe, and the discovery of peoples across oceans with different cultures and different religions, had as an immediate effect a surge of proselytizing and persecution; but these encounters also caused some reflective thinkers to question the claim of any human system of belief to hold unique possession of the truth. The rediscovery of ancient sceptical works, such as those of Sextus Empiricus, brought to the attention of the learned a battery of arguments against the reliability of human cognitive faculties. The most eloquent presentation of the new scepticism is to be found in Montaigne's *Apology for Raimond Sebond*.

Montaigne, like Sextus, favoured an extreme form of scepticism, called Pyrrhonian scepticism after its (half-legendary) founder Pyrrho of Elis, who in the time of Alexander the Great had taught that nothing at all could be known. Many of the examples that Montaigne uses to urge the fallibility of the senses and the intellect are drawn from Sextus' works, but the classical quotations that he uses in the course of his argument are taken not from Sextus, but from the great poem *On the Nature of Things* by Lucretius, a Latin follower of Epicurus, itself another great Renaissance rediscovery.

The two most influential philosophies of the classical Latin period were the Epicureans and the Stoics. The Epicureans, Montaigne tells us, maintain that if the senses are not reliable, then there is no such thing as knowledge. The Stoics tell us that if there is any such thing as knowledge it cannot come from the senses, because they are totally unreliable. Montaigne, like Sextus, uses Stoic arguments to show the fallibility of the senses, and Epicurean arguments to show the impossibility of non-empirical knowledge. Using the negative arguments of each sect, he aims to show against both of them that there is no such thing as real knowledge.

Montaigne rehearses familiar arguments to show that the senses mislead us. Square towers look round from a distance, vision is distorted by pressure on the eyeball, jaundice makes us see things yellow, mountains seem to travel past us when we look at them from shipboard, and so on. When two senses contradict each other, there is no way of resolving the difference. Montaigne quotes a famous passage of Lucretius:

> Can ears deliver verdict on the eyes?
> Can touch convict the ears, or taste the touch, of lies?

But he does not go on to conclude, with Lucretius, that the senses are infallible. Lucretius wrote:

> If what the senses tell us is not true
> Then reason's self is naught but falsehood too.[1]

Montaigne accepts this conditional; but he concludes, not that the senses tell us true, but rather that reason is equally false (*ME* II. 253).

Sense and reason, so far from cooperating to produce knowledge, each work on the other to produce falsehood. Terrified sense, when we look down, prevents us from crossing a narrow plank across a chasm, although reason tells us the plank is quite broad enough for walking. On the other hand, passions in our will can affect what we perceive with our senses: rage and love can make us see things that are not there. 'When we are asleep,' Montaigne maintains, 'our soul is alive and active and exercises all its powers neither more nor less than when it is awake.' The difference between sleep and waking is less than that between daylight and darkness (*ME* II. 260–1).

We need some criterion to distinguish between our varying and conflicting impressions and beliefs, but no such criterion is possible. Just as we cannot find an impartial arbiter to adjudicate the differences between Catholic and Protestant, since any competent judge would already be one or the other, similarly no human being could set out to settle the conflicts between the experiences of the young and the old, the healthy and the sick, the asleep and the awake:

To judge of the appearances that we receive from objects we need some judging instrument; to calibrate such an instrument, we would need an experiment; to verify the experiment, we would need some instrument. we are going round in a circle. (*ME* II. 265)

Montaigne adds some original material to the arsenal of ancient scepticism. Reverting to one of his favourite themes, he points out that some animals and birds have sharper senses than we do. Perhaps they even have senses which we totally lack. (Is it such a sense that tells the cock when to crow?) Our five senses are

---

[1] *De Rerum Natura* 4. 484–7; see above, p. 134.

perhaps only a small number of those that it is possible to have. If so, our view of the universe, compared with a true view, is no less deficient than the view of a man born blind by comparison with that of a sighted person.

Descartes' Response

Descartes, in his *Meditations*, set himself the task of liberating philosophy from the threat of scepticism that had developed in the preceding century. In order to do so, first he had to exhibit the sceptical position that he wanted to refute. In the first of the *Meditations*, he follows in Montaigne's footsteps, but sets out the arguments in brisker and neater form. The deliverances of the senses are called into question initially by considerations drawn from sense-deception, and then by the argument from dreaming:

What I have so far accepted as true *par excellence*, I have got either from the senses or by means of the senses. Now I have sometime caught the senses deceiving me; and a wise man never entirely trusts those who have once cheated him.

But although the senses may sometimes deceive us about some minute and remote objects, yet there are many other facts as to which doubt is plainly impossible, although these are gathered from the same source: e.g. that I am here, sitting by the fire, wearing a winter cloak, holding this paper in my hands and so on . . .

A fine argument! As though I were not a man who habitually sleeps at night and has the same impressions (or even wilder ones) in sleep as these men do when awake! How often, in the still of the night, I have the familiar conviction that I am here, wearing a cloak, sitting by the fire—when really I am undressed and lying in bed! (AT VII. 19; *CSMK* II. 13)

But surely even dreams are made up of elements drawn from reality:

Suppose I am dreaming, and these particulars, that I open my eyes, shake my head, put out my hand, are incorrect; suppose even that I have no such hand, no such body; at any rate it has to be admitted that the things that appear in sleep are like painted representations, which cannot have been formed except in the likeness of real objects. So at least these general kinds of things, eyes, head, hands, body must not be imaginary but real objects. (AT VII. 20; *CSMK* II. 14)

Perhaps these, in their turn, are imaginary complexes; but then the simpler elements out of which these bodies are composed—extension, shape, size, number, place, time—must surely be real. And if so we can trust the sciences of arithmetic and geometry which deal with these objects. 'Whether I am awake or asleep, two and three add up to five, and a square has only four sides; and it seems impossible for such obvious truths to fall under a suspicion of being false' (ibid.).

Even mathematics, however, is not immune to Cartesian doubt. It is not just that mathematicians sometimes make mistakes: it may be that the whole discipline itself is a delusion. God is omnipotent, and for all we know he can make us go wrong whenever we add two and three, or count the sides of a square. But surely a good God would not do that! Well, then:

I will suppose not that there is a supremely good God, the source of truth; but that there is an evil spirit, who is supremely powerful and intelligent, and does his utmost to deceive me. I will suppose that sky, air, earth, colours, shapes, sounds, and all external objects are mere delusive dreams, by means of which he lays snares for my credulity. I will consider myself as having no hands, no eyes, no flesh, no blood, no senses, but just having a false belief that I have all these things. (AT VII. 23; *CSMK* II. 15)

The second *Meditation* brings these doubts to an end by producing the *Cogito*, the famous argument by which Descartes proves his own existence. However the evil genius may deceive him, he cannot trick him into thinking he exists when he does not:

Undoubtedly I exist if he deceives me; let him deceive me as much as he can, he will never bring it about that I am nothing while I am thinking that I am something. The thought 'I exist' cannot but be true when I think it; but I cannot doubt it without thinking of it. Hence, it is not only true but indubitable, because whenever I try to doubt it I see its truth.

The *Cogito* is the rock on which Descartes' epistemology is built. From his day to ours, critics have questioned whether it is as solid as it looks. 'I am thinking, therefore I exist' is undoubtedly a valid argument, whose validity can be taken in at a single mental glance. But so too is 'I am walking, therefore I exist': so what is special abut the *Cogito*? Descartes responded that the premiss 'I am walking' could be doubted (perhaps I have no body), but the premiss 'I am thinking' cannot be doubted, for to doubt is itself to think. On the other hand, 'I think I am walking, therefore I exist' is a perfectly acceptable form of the *cogito*: the thinking referred to in the premiss can be a thought of any kind, not just the self-reflexive thought that I exist.

A more serious question concerns the 'I' in 'I am thinking'. In ordinary life the first-person pronoun gets its meaning in connection with the body that gives its utterance. Is someone who doubts whether he has a body entitled to use 'I' in soliloquy? Perhaps Descartes was entitled only to say: 'There is thinking going on.' Similar questions can be raised about the 'I' in 'I exist'. Perhaps the conclusion should only have been 'Existing is going on.' Critics have argued that the doubting Descartes has no right to draw the conclusion that there is an enduring, substantial self. Perhaps he should have concluded rather to a fleeting subject for a transient thought, or perhaps even that there can be thoughts with no owners. Is it certain that the 'I' revealed by the methodical doubt is the same person who, unpurified by doubt, answered to the name 'René Descartes'?

Even on its own terms, the *Cogito* does not prove the existence of Descartes as a whole human being. By itself, it proves only the existence of his mind. After the

Cogito Descartes continues to doubt whether he has a body, and it is only after considerable further reasoning that he concludes that he does indeed possess one. What he is aware of at all times are the contents of his mind, and it is from these that he must rebuild science. From the *Cogito*, Decartes derives much else besides his own existence: his own essence; the existence of God; the criterion of truth. But for our present purposes what is important is to see how he proceeds from this Archimidean point to re-establish the cognitive system that the sceptical arguments appear to have overthrown.

Cartesian Consciousness

The contents of our minds are thoughts. 'Thought' is used by Descartes very widely: a piece of mental arithmetic, a sexual fantasy, a severe toothache, a view of the Matterhorn, or a taste of a vintage port are all, in his terminology, thoughts. Thinking, for Descartes, includes not only intellectual meditation, but also volition, emotion, pain, pleasure, mental images, and sensations. The feature which all such elements have in common, which makes them thoughts, is the fact that they are items of consciousness. 'I use this term to include everything that is within us in such a way that we are immediately conscious of it. Thus, all the operations of the will, the intellect, the imagination and the senses are thoughts' (AT VII. 160; *CSMK* II. 113). 'Even if the external objects of sense and imagination are non-existent, yet the modes of thought that I call sensations and images, in so far as they are merely modes of thought, do, I am certain, exist in me' (AT VII. 35; *CSMK* II. 34). These thoughts, then, are the basic data of Descartes' epistemology.

One passage brings out very strikingly how the word 'thought' for Descartes applies to conscious experience of any kind:

It is I who have sensations, or who perceive corporeal objects as it were by the senses. Thus, I am now seeing light, hearing a noise, feeling heat. These objects are unreal, for I am asleep; but at least I seem to see, to hear, to be warmed. This cannot be unreal, and this is what is properly called my sensation; further, sensation, precisely so regarded, is nothing but an act of thought. (AT VII. 29; *CSMK* II. 19)

These apparent sensations, possible in the absence of a body, are what later philosophers were to call 'sense-data'. The viability of the Cartesian system depends on whether a coherent signification can be given to such a notion.[2]

In the third *Meditation* Descartes singles out an important class of thoughts, and gives them the name 'ideas': 'Some of my thoughts are as it were pictures of objects, and these alone are properly called "ideas"—for instance, when I think of

---

[2] See Ch. 8 below.

a man, or a chimera, or the sky, or an angel, or God' (AT VII. 37). The word 'idea' is now at home in ordinary language, but it was a new departure to use it systematically, as Descartes did, for the contents of a human mind: hitherto philosophers had commonly used it to refer to Plato's Forms, or to archetypes in the Mind of God. Crudely, we can say that, for Descartes, ideas are the mental counterpart of words. 'I cannot express anything in words, provided that I understand what I say, without its thereby being certain that there is within me the idea of what is signified by the words in question' (AT VII. 160).

Descartes divides ideas into three classes: 'Of my ideas, some seem to be innate, some acquired, and some devised by myself.' As examples of innate ideas, Descartes offers the ideas of *thing*, *truth*, and *thought*. The ideas that occur when Descartes seems to hear a noise, or to see the sun, or to feel the heat of a fire, appear to originate in external objects. Ideas of sirens and hippogriffs, on the other hand, seem to be creations of Descartes himself. At this stage of the epistemological journey, all this can only be a *prima facie* classification: as yet Descartes knows nothing about the origin of these ideas that occur in his mind. In particular he cannot be sure that the 'acquired' ideas originate in external objects. Even if they do so, he cannot be sure that the objects that cause the ideas also resemble the ideas.

There is, however, one idea that can be shown to originate outside Descartes' own mind. He has an idea of God, 'eternal, infinite, omniscient, almighty, and creator of all that exists beside himself'. While most of his ideas—such as the ideas of thought, substance, duration, number—may well have originated in himself, the attributes of infinity, independence, supreme intelligence, and power cannot be drawn from reflection on a limited, dependent, ignorant, impotent creature like himself. The perfections which are united in his idea of God are so much superior to anything that he can find in himself that the idea cannot be a fiction of his own creation. But the cause of an idea must be no less real than the idea itself. Accordingly, Descartes can conclude that he is not alone in the universe: there is also, in reality, a God corresponding to his idea. God himself is the source of this idea, having implanted it in Descartes from birth:

The whole force of the argument lies in this: I realise that I could not possibly exist with the nature I actually have, that is, one endowed with the idea of God, unless there really is a God; the very God, I mean of whom I have an idea; and he must possess all the perfections of which I can attain any notion, although I cannot comprehend them; and he must be liable to no defects. (AT VII. 52; *CSMK* II. 35)

God, then, is the first entity outside his own mind that Descartes recognizes; and God plays an essential role in the subsequent rebuilding of the edifice of science. Because God has no defects, Descartes argues, he cannot be deceitful, because fraud or deceit always depends on some defect in the deceiver. The principle that God is no deceiver is the thread that will enable Descartes to lead us out of the mazes of scepticism.

There are some truths which are so clear and distinct that whenever the mind focuses on them they cannot be doubted. But we cannot keep our minds fixed for long on any one topic; and often we merely remember having clearly and distinctly perceived a particular proposition. But now that we know that God is no deceiver, we can conclude that everything we clearly and distinctly perceive is true. Hence we are entitled to be certain, not just of momentary intuitions such as that of our immediate existence, but of whole *a priori* sciences such as arithmetic and geometry. These remain true and evident to us, Descartes claims, whether we are awake or asleep. So he can count these sciences among his cognitive assets even while he is still, in theory, uncertain whether he has a body and whether there is an external world. He can know a great deal about triangles, without yet knowing whether there is anything in the world that has a triangular shape (AT VII. 70; *CSMK* II. 48).

It is not until the sixth meditation that Descartes establishes to his own satisfaction that there are material things and that he does have a body. He calls our attention to the difference between intellect and imagination. Geometry is the work of the intellect, and by geometry we can establish, for instance, the difference between a polygon with a thousand sides and a polygon with a million sides. We cannot, though, by any effort of the imagination, call up a distinct mental picture of either a chiliagon or a myriagon in the way that we can call up a picture of a triangle or a pentagon. The power of imagination appears to be an optional extra to the power of intellect, which alone is essential to the mind. One way of explaining the existence of this extra power would be to postulate some bodily entity in close association with the mind. The difference between imagination and pure understanding would be this: 'in the act of understanding the mind turns as it were towards itself, and contemplates one of the ideas contained in itself; in the act of imagining, it turns to the body, and contemplates something in it resembling an idea understood by the mind itself.' But this, for the moment, is no more than a probable hypothesis (AT VII. 73; *CSMK* II. 50).

What is it that establishes the existence of bodies? Descartes finds in himself a passive power of receiving sense-impressions. Corresponding to this passive power, there must be an active power to produce or make these impressions. In theory these could be produced by God himself, but there is not the slightest clue to suggest this:

God has given me no faculty at all to detect their origin; on the other hand, he has given me a strong inclination to believe that these ideas proceed from corporeal objects; so I do not see how it would make sense to say that God is not deceitful, if in fact they proceed from elsewhere, not from corporeal objects. Therefore corporeal objects must exist. (AT VII. 80; *CSMK*, II. 55)

Since God is the author of nature, and God is no deceiver, whatever nature teaches is true. There are two principal things that nature teaches us:

There is no more explicit lesson of nature than that I have a body; that it is being injured when I feel pain; that it needs food, or drink, when I suffer from hunger, or thirst, and so on . . .

Moreover, nature teaches me that my body has an environment of other bodies, some of which must be sought for and others shunned. And from the wide variety of colours, sounds, odours, favours, degrees of hardness and so on, of which I have sensations, I certainly have the right to infer that in the bodies from which these various sense-peceptions arise there is corresponding, though not similar, variety.

Not everything, however, that appears natural to us is actually taught by nature and so guaranteed by the veracity of God—hence the caveat 'though not similar' in the last sentence of the quotation. Only what we clearly and distinctly perceive is really taught us by nature, and if we wish to achieve truth we must carefully restrict our beliefs within those limits. Only thus will a sound science of material objects be built up to replace the superannuated physics of the Aristotelian establishment.

Many philosophers nowadays find Descartes' epistemology quite unconvincing because they regard the existence of God as much more problematic than the everyday and scientific truths that he is called on to guarantee. None of his contemporary critics was willing to question the existence of God, although each was happy to challenge his method of proving it. But there were two different fundamental objections which Descartes had to meet if he was to defend his method of erecting the edifice of science on the basis of God's veracity.

First, if God is no deceiver, how is it that I constantly fall into error? The faculties that I have are given me by the truthful God; how then can they lead me astray? The answer Descartes gives is that, if properly used, our faculties do not ever lead us astray. I have one faculty, the intellect, which offers perceptions of things and of truths; I have a different faculty, the will, by which I judge whether a proposition is true or false. If I restrict the judgements of the will to cases in which the intellect presents a clear and distinct perception, then I will never go astray. Error only arises when I make a precipitate judgement in advance of clear and distinct perception. The whole intellectual exercise of the *Meditations* is designed precisely to give the reader practice in suspending judgement in the absence of clarity and distinctness.

The second objection to Descartes' method became famous under the title 'The Cartesian Circle'. It was Antoine Arnauld, author of the fourth objections, who was the first to point out an apparent circularity in Descartes' appeal to God as the guarantor of clear and distinct perceptions. 'We can be sure that God exists, only because we clearly and distinctly perceive that he does; therefore, prior to being certain that God exists, we need to be certain that whatever we clearly and evidently perceive is true' (AT VII. 245; *CSMK* II. 170).

Descartes has an answer to this objection, which depends on a distinction between particular clear and distinct perceptions, on the one hand, and the general principle, on the other, that whatever we clearly and distinctly perceive is true. No appeal to God's veracity is necessary to bring conviction of the truth of individual perceptions. Intuitions such as that I exist, or that two and three make five, cannot be doubted as long as I continue clearly and distinctly to perceive them. But although I cannot doubt something I am here and now clearly and distinctly perceiving, I can—prior to establishing God's existence—doubt the general proposition that whatever I clearly and distinctly perceive is true. Again, individual intuitions can be doubted once they are in the past. I can wonder, after the event, whether there is any truth in what I clearly and distinctly perceived while reading the second *Meditation*.

Since simple intuitions cannot be doubted while they are before the mind, no argument is needed to establish them; indeed Descartes regarded intuition as superior to argument as a method of attaining truth. Individual intuitions can only be doubted in the roundabout way I have just illustrated: they cannot be doubted in any way that involves advertence to their content. It is only in connection with the general principle, and in connection with the roundabout doubt of particular perceptions, that the appeal to God's truthfulness is necessary. Hence there is no circularity in Descartes' argument. Undoubtedly, however, in the *Meditations* the mind is *used* to validate itself. But that kind of circularity is unavoidable and harmless.

The Empiricism of Hobbes

Historians of philosophy often contrast British and continental philosophy in the seventeenth and eighteenth centuries: the continentals were rationalists, trusting to the speculations of reason, and the British were empiricists, basing knowledge on the experience of the senses. In order to assess the real degree of difference between British and continental epistemology we should look more closely at the teaching of Hobbes, who has a fair claim to be the founder of British empiricism.

Hobbes' *Leviathan* begins with a chapter 'Of Sense' and offers a resounding manifesto: 'There is no conception in a man's mind, which hath not at first, totally, or by parts, been begotten upon the organs of sense. The rest are derived from that original' (*L*, 9). Other operations of the mind, such as memory, imagination, and reasoning, are wholly dependent on sensation. Imagination and memory are the same thing, namely decaying sense:

For as at a great distance of place, that which we look at, appears dim, and without distinction of the smaller parts; and as voices grow weak, and inarticulate: so also after great distance of time, our imagination of the past is weak; and we lose (for example) of cities we have seen, many particular streets; and of actions, many particular circumstances. (*L*, 66)

Reasoning, Hobbes says, is nothing but reckoning the consequences of general names agreed upon for the marking and signifying of our thoughts; and thoughts are always, for him, mental images (of names or things) derived from sensation. 'They are every one a representation or appearance of some quality, or other accident of a body without us' (*L*, 66).

There are, according to Hobbes, two kinds of knowledge: knowledge of fact, and knowledge of consequence. Knowledge of consequence is the knowledge of what follows from what: the knowledge that keeps order in the constant succession or train of our thoughts. It is expressed in language by conditional laws, of the form 'If A then B.' Knowledge of fact—the kind of knowledge that we require from a witness—is given by sense and memory. Mere reasoning, or discourse, can never end in absolute knowledge of fact, past or to come (*L*, 42).

It is true, as empiricists claim, that we can never acquire information about the world around us, directly or indirectly, without at some stage exercising our powers of sense-perception. The weakness of British empiricism lies in its naive and unsatisfactory account of what sense-perception actually consists in. Thinkers in the Aristotelian tradition, which Hobbes specifically rejected, had emphasized that our senses are powers to discriminate: the power to tell one colour from another, to distinguish between different sounds and tastes, and so on. They had empha-sized that the senses had an active role in experience: any particular episode of sensing (e.g. tasting the sweetness of a piece of sugar) was a transaction between an item in the world (a property of the sugar) and a faculty of a perceiver (the power of taste). For Hobbes and his successors, by contrast, sensation is a passive affair: the occurrence of an image or fancy in the mind.

There is indeed, according to Hobbes, an active element in sensation; however, it is not a matter of making discriminations between genuine qualities in the real world, but rather of projecting on to the world items that are illusory fancies:

The cause of sense, is the external body, or object, which presseth the organ proper to each sense, either immediately, as in the taste and touch; or mediately, as in seeing, hearing, and smelling: which pressure, by the mediation of the nerves, and other strings, and mem-branes of the body, continued inwards to the brain and heart, causeth there a resistance, or counter-pressure, or endeavour of the heart, to deliver itself: which endeavour because *outward*, seemeth to be some matter without. And this *seeming* or *fancy*, is that which men call *sense*; and consisteth, as to the eye, in a light or colour figured; to the ear, in a *sound*; to the nostril, in an *odour*; to the tongue and palate, in a *savour*, and to the rest of the body in *heat*, *cold*, *hardness*, *softness*, and such other qualities, as we discern by *feeling*. All which qualities called *sensible*, are in the object that causeth them, but so many several motions of the matter, by which it presseth our organs diversely. (*L*, 9)

The account of sensation in the empiricist Hobbes turns out to be exactly the same as that of the rationalist Descartes. For both of them, qualities such as colour and taste are nothing more than deceptive experiences, items of private consciousness:

'fancies' for Hobbes; '*cogitationes*' for Descartes. Hobbes uses arguments similar to those of Descartes to urge the subjectivity of such secondary qualities: we see colours in reflections; a bang upon the eye makes us see stars; and so on. For Hobbes as for Descartes, there is no intrinsic difference between our sensory experience and our mental imagery and our dreams. Just as Descartes argued that he could be certain of the content of his thoughts even if he had no body and there was no external world, so Hobbes argues that all our images would remain the same even though the world were annihilated (*L*, 22).

A common error underlies the Descartes–Hobbes attack on the objectivity of sensory qualities: a confusion between relativity and subjectivity. It is true that sensory qualities are relative; that is to say, they are defined by their relationships to sensory perceivers. For a substance to have a certain taste is for it to have the ability to produce a certain effect on a human being or other animal; and the particular effect it produces will vary according to a number of conditions. But the fact that taste is a relative property does not mean that it is not an objective property. 'Being larger than the earth' is a relative property; yet it is an objective fact that the sun is larger than the earth.

Where Hobbes differs from Descartes is that he fails to make any serious distinction between the imagination and the intellect. If the intellect is, roughly, the capacity to use and understand language, then it is something quite different from the flow of images in the mind. Descartes made clear the difference between intellect and imagination in a luminous passage of the sixth *Meditation*:

When I imagine a triangle, I do not just understand that it is a figure enclosed in three lines; I also at the same time see the three lines present before my mind's eye, and this is what I call imagining them. Now if I want to think of a chiliagon, I understand just as well that it is a figure of a thousand sides as I do that a triangle is a figure of three sides; but I do not in the same way imagine the thousand sides, or see them as presented to me. (AT VII. 71; *CSMK* II. 50)

Hobbes nowhere makes a similar distinction, and systematically identifies the mind with what Descartes calls the imagination. Hobbes was, indeed, aware of the role of language in intellectual activity, and saw its possession as the main privilege that set mankind above other animals. He wrote, for instance:

By the advantage of names it is that we are capable of science, which beasts, for want of them, are not: nor man, without the use of them: for as a beast misseth not one or two out of her many young ones, for want of those names of order, one, two, three &c, which we call number; so neither would a man, without repeating orally, or mentally, the words of number, know how many pieces of money or other things lie before him. (*L*, 35–6)

He writes, however, as if the fact that a series of images passing through the mind consists of images of names rather than things is sufficient to turn a flow of fancy into an operation of the intellect. But in fact no explanation in terms of mental images can account for our knowledge even of simple arithmetic, Hobbes' favourite paradigm of reasoning. If I want to add 97 to 62, I cannot call upon any mental image of either number; and the mental image of the numerals themselves will be no help either, unless I have been through the long and tedious process of learning to do mental arithmetic. The occurrence of the images does nothing to explain that process, and it is only as a consequence of that process that the images are useful for arithmetical purposes.

Locke's Ideas

Empiricism is not often defended in the crude and blunt form in which it is put forward by Hobbes, so it is time to turn to the better-known and more generally admired presentation by John Locke. Locke and Descartes are often contrasted as the prime exponents of two different philosophical schools, but in fact they share a number of common assumptions. Locke bases his system on 'ideas', and his 'ideas' turn out to be very similar to Descartes' 'thoughts'. Both philosophers make an initial appeal to immediate consciousness: ideas and thoughts are what we meet when we look within ourselves. Both philosophers fail to clear up a fatal ambiguity in their key terms, and this cripples their epistemology and philosophy of mind.

In Locke, for instance, it is often difficult to tell whether by 'idea' is meant an object (what is being perceived or thought about) or an action (the act of perceiving or thinking). Locke says that an idea is 'whatever it is which the mind can be employed about in thinking'. The crucial ambiguity is in the phrase 'what the mind is employed about', which can mean either what the mind is thinking of (the object) or what the mind is engaged in (the action). The ambiguity is damaging when Locke considers such questions as whether greenness is an object in the world or a creation of the mind.

Although Locke often takes issue with Descartes, he adopts much of his philosophical agenda from Descartes, and asks many of the same questions. Are animals machines? Does the soul always think? Can there be space without matter? Are there innate ideas?

This last question is often taken as a deciding issue: the answer a philosopher gives shows whether she is a rationalist or an empiricist. But the question is not a simple one. If we break it down into the different meanings it may have, we find that there is no great gulf fixed between the positions of Locke and Descartes.

First, we may ask: 'Do infants in the womb think thoughts?' Locke, as well as Descartes, believed that unborn infants had simple thoughts or ideas, such as pains and feelings of warmth. Locke mocks the idea that a child who knows that an apple is not a fire will give assent to the principle of non-contradiction (*E*, 61). But Descartes did not believe any more than Locke did that infants had complicated thoughts of a philosophical kind. A child has an innate idea of self-evident principles only in the same way as it may have an inherited propensity to gout (AT VIII. 357; *CSMK* I. 303).

In the light of this, we may take the question to concern not the activity of thinking, but the mere capacity for thought. Is there an inborn, general capacity for understanding which is specific to human beings? Both Descartes and Locke believe that there is. The *Essay* begins with the statement that it is the understanding that sets man above the rest of sensible beings (*E*, 43).

Locke focuses not on the general faculty of understanding, but on assent to certain particular propositions, e.g. 'one and two are equal to three' and 'it is impossible for the same thing to be, and not to be'. Does our assent to such truths depend on experience? No, says Descartes, they are innate principles we recognize. But Locke does not think they depend on experience; he claims that experience is necessary to provide us with the concepts that make up the propositions, not in order to secure our assent to them once formed. 'Men never fail, after they have once understood the Words, to acknowledge them for undoubted Truths' (*E*, 56). Descartes, on the other hand, does not maintain that all innate ideas are principles assented to as soon as understood: some of them become clear and distinct, and command assent, only after laborious meditation.

Locke devotes much of his treatment of innate ideas to the question whether there are any principles, whether theoretical or practical, which command universal assent. He denies that there are any theoretical principles which are held by all human beings, including children and savages. Turning to practical principles, he enjoys himself piling up examples of violations, in various cultures, of moral maxims which seem fundamental to all civilized Christians—including the most basic: 'Parents preserve and cherish your children' (*E*, 65–84). Even if there were truths universally acknowledged, this would not be sufficient to prove innateness, since the explanation might be a common process of learning.

Descartes, however, can agree that universal consent does not entail innateness, and he can also retort that innateness does not entail universal consent either. It is a fundamental presupposition of his method that some people, indeed most people, may be prevented by prejudice and laziness from assenting to innate principles that are latent in their minds.

On the topic of innate ideas, the arguments of Locke and Descartes largely pass each other by. Descartes argues that experience without an innate element is an insufficient basis for scientific knowledge; Locke insists that innate concepts without experience cannot account for the knowledge we have of the world. Both contentions may well be correct.

Locke claimed that the arguments of the rationalists would lead one 'to suppose all our ideas of colours, sounds, taste, figure etc. innate, than which there cannot be anything more opposite to reason and experience' (*E*, 58). Descartes did not believe that our knowledge of the colour or taste of a particular apple was something innate; but he found nothing absurd in the general idea of redness or sweetness being innate—and that for a reason that Locke himself accepted, namely, that our ideas of such qualities are entirely subjective. Once again the surface dispute between rationalism and empiricism masks a fundamental agreement.

Locke's argument for the subjectivity of qualities like colours and tastes begins with a division between those ideas 'which come into our minds by one sense only', and those 'that convey themselves into the mind by more senses than one'. Sounds, tastes, and smells are examples of the first kind; so too 'Colours, as white, red, yellow, blue; with their several Degrees or Shades and Mixtures, as Green, Scarlet, Purple, Sea-green and the rest'. As examples of ideas that we get by more than one sense, Locke gives extension, shape, motion, and rest—items we can detect both by seeing and by feeling.

Corresponding to this distinction between two kinds of ideas is a distinction between qualities to be found in bodies. We should distinguish ideas, as they are perceptions in the mind, and as they are modifications of matter in the bodies that cause these perceptions; and we should not take it for granted that our ideas are exact images of something in the bodies that cause them. The powers to produce ideas in us are called by Locke 'Qualities'. Qualities perceptible by more than one sense he calls 'primary qualities', and qualities perceptible only by a single sense he calls 'secondary qualities'. This distinction was no innovation: it had been customary since Aristotle to distinguish between 'common sensibles' (= primary qualities) and 'proper sensibles' (= secondary qualities) (E, 134–5). Where Locke departed from Aristotle was in denying the objectivity of proper sensibles. In this he had been anticipated by Descartes, who argued that in giving a scientific account of perception only primary qualities needed to be invoked. Heat, colours, and tastes were strictly speaking only mental entities, and it was a mistake to think that in a hot body there was something like my idea of heat, or in a green body there was the same greenness as in my sensation (AT VII. 82; CSMK, II. 56). The bodily events that cause us to see or hear or taste are nothing more than motions of shaped matter. In support of this conclusion Locke offers some of the same considerations as Descartes, but presents a more sustained line of argument.

First, Locke claims that only primary qualities are inseparable from their possessors: a body may lack a smell or a taste, but there cannot be a body without a shape or a size. If you take a grain of wheat and divide it over and over again, it may lose its colour or taste, but it will retain extension, shape, and mobility. Descartes had used a similar argument, taking not wheat but stone as his example, to prove that only extension was part of the essence of a body.

We have only to attend to our idea of some body, e.g. a stone, and remove from it whatever we know is not entailed by the very nature of body. We first reject hardness; for if the stone is melted, or divided into a very fine powder, it will lose this quality without ceasing to be a body. Again, we reject colour: we have often seen stones so transparent as to be colourless.

What are we to make of such arguments? It may be true that a body must have some shape or other, but any particular shape can be lost. As Descartes himself reminds us elsewhere, a piece of wax may cease to be cubical and become spherical. What Locke says of the secondary qualities might also be said of some of the primary qualities. Motion is a primary quality, but a body may be motionless. Indeed, if motion and rest are to be considered, as Locke considers them, as a pair of primary qualities, at any time a body must lack one or other of them.

The argument for the permanence of primary properties seems to depend on taking them generically: a body cannot cease to have some length or other; some breadth or other; some height or other. The argument for the impermanence of other qualities seems to depend on taking them specifically: a body may lose its particular colour or smell or taste. It is true that a body may be tasteless, odourless, and invisible, whereas a body cannot lack all extension. But the fact that such qualities are inessential properties of bodies does not show that they are not genuine properties of bodies, any more than the fact that a body may cease to be cubical shows that a cubical shape, while it lasts, is not a genuine property of the body.

Locke says that secondary qualities are nothing but a power to produce sensations in us. Even if we grant that this is true, or at least an approximation to the truth, it does not show that secondary qualities are merely subjective rather than being genuine properties of the objects that appear to possess them. To take a parallel case, to be poisonous is simply to have a power to produce a certain effect in a living being; but it is an objective matter, a matter of ascertainable fact, whether something is or is not poisonous to a given organism. Here, as in Descartes and Hobbes, we meet a confusion between relativity and subjectivity. A property can be relative while being perfectly objective. Whether a key fits a lock is a plain matter of fact, and as Locke's contemporary Robert Boyle remarked, the secondary qualities are keys which fit particular locks, the locks being the different human senses.

'The particular Bulk, Number, Figure, and Motion of the parts of Fire, or Snow, are really in them,' Locke says, 'whether any ones senses perceive them or no.' Light, heat, whiteness, and coldness, on the other hand, are no more really in bodies than sickness or pain is in food which may give us a stomach ache. 'Take away the sensation of them; let not the Eyes see light, or Colours, nor the Ears hear Sounds; let the Palate not Taste, nor the Nose Smell, and all Colours, Tastes, Odors and Sounds, as they are such particular ideas, vanish and cease' (*E*, 138). This argument is inconsistent with what Locke has just said, namely, that secondary qualities are powers in objects to cause sensations in us. These powers, to be sure, are only exercised in the presence of a sensing organ; but powers continue to exist even when not being exercised. (Most of us have the power to recite 'Three Blind Mice', but rarely exercise it.)

Locke claims that what produces in us the ideas of secondary qualities is nothing but the primary qualities of the object having the power. The sensation of heat, for instance, is caused by the corpuscles of some other body causing an increase or diminution of the motion of the minute parts of our bodies. But even if this were a true account of how a sensation of heat is caused, why conclude that the sensation itself is nothing but 'a sort and degree of motion in the minute particles of our nerves'? The only ground for this conclusion seems to be the archaic principle that like causes like. But to take an example of Locke's own, a substance can cause illness without itself being ill.

Locke denies that whiteness and coldness are really in objects, because he says there is no likeness between the ideas in our minds and the qualities in the bodies. This statement trades on the ambiguity we noted at the outset in the notion of an idea. If an idea of blueness is a case of the action of perceiving blueness, then there is no more reason to expect the idea to resemble the colour than there is to expect playing a violin to resemble a violin. If, on the other hand, the idea of blueness is what is perceived, then when I see a delphinium the idea is not an image of blueness, but blueness itself. Locke can deny this only by assuming what he is setting out to prove.

Locke's final argument is an analogy between perception and feeling:

He that will consider, that the same Fire, that at one distance produces in us the Sensation of Warmth, does at a nearer approach, produce in us the far different Sensation of Pain, ought to bethink himself, what Reason he has to say, that his Idea of Warmth, which was produced in him by the Fire, is actually in the Fire; and his Idea of Pain, which the same Fire produced in him the same way, is not in the Fire. (*E*, 137)

The analogy is being misapplied. The fire is painful as well as hot. In saying that it is painful, no one is claiming that it feels pain; equally, in saying that it is hot, no one is claiming that it feels heat. If Locke's argument worked it could be turned against himself. To take an example of his own, when I cut myself I feel the slash of the knife as well as the pain—does that mean that motion, too, is a secondary quality?

Locke insists, drawing on familiar examples, that the sensations produced by the same object will vary with circumstances (lukewarm water will appear hot to a cold hand and cold to a hot hand, what colours we see in porphyry depends on the intensity of the light shining on it, and so on). But the moral of this is not that secondary qualities are not objective. Grass is green, all right; but 'green' is not, as Locke thought it was, the name of a private ineffable experience, and being green is not a simple property, but a complicated one that includes such features as looking blue under certain conditions of lighting.

Spinoza on Degrees of Knowledge

In Spinoza's system epistemology is not as prominent as it is in Locke's, but it presents a number of subtle features. In his early *Improvement of the Understanding*

Spinoza describes four levels of knowledge or perception. First, there is knowledge by hearsay: the kind of knowledge I have of when I was born and who were my parents. Second, there is knowledge 'from crude experience': Spinoza is thinking of inductive conclusions such as that water puts out fire and that one day I shall die. Third, there is the kind of knowledge where 'the essence of one thing is inferred from the essence of another, but not adequately'. Spinoza illustrates this rather obscure definition by giving as an example our knowledge that the sun is larger than it looks. Finally, there is knowledge of things by their essences: an instance is the knowledge of a circle we are given by geometry. This fourth kind of knowledge is the only one which gives us an adequate, error-free, grasp of things (E II. 11). It is noteworthy that although Spinoza calls all of these forms of knowledge 'perception', raw sense-perception itself does not figure as a kind of knowledge.

In his later work, *Ethics*, Spinoza gives a threefold rather than a fourfold division of knowledge. We are told nothing more about hearsay, an important topic commonly neglected by philosophers—the honourable exceptions being Hume in the eighteenth century, Newman in the nineteenth, and Wittgenstein in the twentieth. Instead we are told of three levels of knowledge, namely, imagination, reason, and intuition. Hearsay becomes a subdivision of the level of imagination, which is the second item of the earlier classification. Reason and intuition correspond to the last two items of the earlier classification.

Like Descartes and Locke, Spinoza describes knowledge in terms of ideas in our minds, and like them he includes under the under the term 'idea' both concepts (the idea *of* a triangle) and propositions (the idea *that* a triangle has three sides). Concepts and propositions of this kind, he maintains, are inseparable. I cannot affirm that a triangle has three sides without having a concept of a triangle; and I cannot have a concept of a triangle without affirming that it has three sides (*Eth*, 63).

There is often an ambiguity when Spinoza speaks of 'the idea of X': we may wonder whether the 'of' is a subjective or objective genitive; that is to say, is the idea of X an idea belonging to X, or is it an idea whose content is X? When Spinoza tells us that the idea of God includes God's essence and everything that necessarily follows from it, he is clearly speaking of the idea that God has, God's idea, rather than the idea that you and I might have of God (*Eth*, 33). But not every reference to 'the idea of God' is similarly unambiguous. And a corresponding ambiguity attaches to Spinoza's statement that the human mind is the idea of the human body.[3]

However, Spinoza expressly excludes an ambiguity in the term 'idea' that often gives us trouble when reading Descartes and Locke:

---

[3] See Chapter 7 below.

A true idea—for we do possess such a thing—is something different from its object (*ideatum*). Thus, a circle is one thing, and the idea of a circle is another. The idea of a circle is not a thing that has a circumference and a centre, as a circle has. Again, the idea of a body is something other than the body itself. (E II. 12)

A man Peter is something real; the idea of Peter is also a real thing, but a different one. We can also have an idea of the idea of Peter, and so on indefinitely.

If we know something, Spinoza maintains, we know that we know it, and know that we know that we know it. Philosophers ask how we know when we have knowledge, and look for some criterion to distinguish knowledge from mere belief; without this, they think, we can never achieve certainty. But this, Spinoza says, is to begin at the wrong end. In order to know that we know, we must first know; and in order to achieve certainty we need no special sign beyond the possession of an adequate idea. He who has a true idea knows *eo ipso* that he has a true idea, and cannot doubt its truth (*Eth*, 58). 'How can a man be sure that his idea corresponds to its object?' philosophers ask. Spinoza replies: 'His knowledge arises simply from his having an idea that does in fact correspond to its object; in other words, truth is its own criterion' (*Eth*, 59).

The different stages of knowledge correspond to ideas with different properties. An idea may be true without being adequate, and it may be adequate without being clear and distinct. From the experience of our body coming into contact with other objects, we gather not only ideas of individuals like Peter but also general ideas such as man, horse, or dog. Spinoza explains the origin of such general ideas in the following manner:

They arise from the fact that so many images, for instance, of men are formed simultan-eously that they overpower the faculty of imagination—not entirely, but to the extent that the mind loses count of small differences between individuals (colour, size, and so on) and of their actual number. It imagines distinctly only that which the individuals have in common in so far as the body is affected by them—for that is the point in which each of the individuals principally affected it—and this the mind expresses by the name *man* and it predicates it of infinite individuals. (E II. 112)

Other ideas are formed from symbols, from our having read or heard certain words. These ideas, while they are true, are confused and unsystematic. Our repertoire of such notions constitutes our knowledge of the first kind, which we may call 'opinion' or 'imagination'.

There are some ideas, however, which are common to all human beings, which represent adequately the properties of things. Such are the ideas of extension and motion. Spinoza defines an adequate idea as 'an idea which, insofar as it is considered in itself, without relation to the object, has all the properties or intrinsic marks of a true idea' (*Eth*, 32). It is not quite clear how this is to be reconciled with his statement that a true idea needs no mark of its truth. It is tempting to think that Spinoza means merely that adequate ideas express truths that are self-evident and are not derived by deduction from other truths. But in fact adequate ideas are linked by logical connections to each other, forming a system of necessary truths. This is the province of reason (*ratio*) and constitutes knowledge of the second kind (*Eth*, 57). Both the second and third kind of knowledge, then, can give us true and adequate ideas.

Knowledge of the third kind is called by Spinoza 'intuitive knowledge', and it is clearly the form of knowledge that is most to be valued. We are offered little help, however, in understanding its nature. It is clear that reason operates step by step; intuition is an immediate mental vision. More importantly, intuition grasps the essences of things; that is to say, it understands their universal features and their place in the general causal order of the universe. Reason may tell us that the sun is larger than it looks; only intuition can give us a full grasp of why this is so. But Spinoza's formal definition of intuitive knowledge raises as many questions as it solves: 'This kind of knowledge proceeds from an adequate idea of the formal essence of certain attributes of God to the adequate knowledge of the essence of things' (*Eth*, 57). Perhaps only a complete mastery of the whole philosophical system of the *Ethics* would provide us with such knowledge.

Spinoza twice attempts to illustrate the three degrees of knowledge by inviting us to consider the problem of finding the number x which has to a given number c the same proportion as a given a has to a given b. Merchants, he says, will have no difficulty in applying the rule of three that they have gathered from experience or learnt by rote. Mathematicians will apply the nineteenth proposition of the seventh book of Euclid. This illustration distinguishes the first and second degree clearly enough; but we are left in the dark about the intuitive method of solving the problem. Perhaps Spinoza has in mind something like the achievements of Indian mathematicians who can solve such problems instantaneously without calculation.

Spinoza's epistemology has to answer one final question. In the content of any idea, he maintains, there is no positive element other than truth (*Eth*, 53). But if there is no positive element in ideas on account of which they can be called false, how is error possible at all? Descartes had explained error in the following manner: error is wrong judgement, and judgement is an act of the will, not of the intellect; error occurs when the will makes a judgement in the absence of enlightenment from the intellect. Spinoza cannot offer this explanation, since for him the will and the intellect are not distinct; he cannot, therefore, give the advice that in order to avoid error one should suspend judgement whenever the intellect fails to present a clear and distinct idea.

Spinoza's response is to say that error is not anything positive. Error—which occurs only at the first level of knowledge—consists not in the presence of any idea, but in the absence of some other idea which should be present:

Thus, when we look at the sun, and imagine that it is about two hundred feet away from us, this imagination by itself does not amount to an error; our error is rather the fact that while we thus imagine we do not know either the true distance of the sun or the cause of our fancy. (Ibid.)

As for suspension of judgement, that is possible indeed, but not by any free act of will. When we say that someone suspends judgement, we merely mean that she sees that she does not have an adequate perception of the matter in question. Even in dreams we suspend our judgement, when we dream that we dream (*Eth*, 66).

The Epistemology of Leibniz

Spinoza's epistemology consists of a series of attempts to reconcile what we naturally say and think about knowledge and experience with his metaphysical thesis that ideas in the mind and motions in the body are just two aspects of individual items in the life of the single substance which is God and nature. Leibniz's epistemology is likewise an attempt to match ordinary speech and thought to a metaphysical system—but to one diametrically opposite to Spinoza's, in which ideas and motions, so far from being substantially identical with each other, have no interaction at all and belong to two different and wholly independent series of events, linked only by the harmony pre-established in the mind of God.

Given Leibniz's official theory of monads, it is hard to see how he could have, in the normal sense, any epistemology at all. How, for instance, could he give any account of sense-perception, since there are no transactions between the mind and the external world? How could he take an interest in the debate about which of our ideas are innate and which are acquired, since for him every single idea is an internal product of the mind alone? Yet in fact one of the most substantial of Leibniz's works is a work of epistemology: *New Essays on Human Understanding*, in which he offers a detailed critique of Locke's empiricist theory of knowledge. *New Essays* is a 500-page-long debate between Philalethes, a spokesman for Locke, and Theophilus, the mouthpiece of Leibniz. Each chapter of the work corresponds to a chapter of Locke's *Essay*, and answers it point by point.

Many of the positions that Leibniz defends in the *New Essays*, and many of the arguments he employs, could in fact be adopted by a philosopher with a much more commonsensical metaphysic. Leibniz is aware of this, and defends himself by saying that for expository purposes he has a right to talk of bodies acting on minds just as a Copernican philosopher goes on talking of the sun rising and setting (G V. 67). It is indeed difficult to make everything in the *New Essays* consistent with the official metaphysical system, but this makes the book more rather than less interesting to those who are more interested in epistemology than monadology.

Empiricists claim that there is nothing in the intellect that was not in the senses. Leibniz responds by adding 'except the intellect itself'. Our soul is a being, a substance, a unity, identical with itself, a cause, and the locus of ideas and reasoning. Consequently, the ideas of being, substance and so on can be acquired by the soul's reflection on itself. Moreover, they could never be acquired from the senses (G V. 45, 100–1). These ideas, then, are innate in the fullest sense. This does not mean that a newborn child already thinks of them; but it has more than a mere ability to learn them: it has a predisposition to grasp them. If we want to think of the mind as being initially like an unpainted canvas, we can do so; but it is a canvas already pencil-marked for painting by numbers (G V. 45, 132).

Among ideas that are innate in this sense, Leibniz includes the principles of logic, arithmetic, and geometry. But what of truths such as 'red is not green' and 'sweet is not bitter'? Leibniz is prepared to say that 'sweet is not bitter' is not innate in the sense in which 'a square is not a circle' is innate. The feelings of sweet and bitter, he says, come from the senses (G V. 79). How can this be reconciled with the denial that the external world acts on the mind and the thesis that all the thoughts and actions of the soul originate internally?

To answer this, we must recall that for Leibniz the human soul is a dominant monad, situated at the top of a pyramid of monads, which are animated entities corresponding to the different parts and organs of the human body. Translated into monadese, the statement that some feelings come into the mind from the senses appears to mean that some of the ideas of the dominant monad originate from the inferior monads. Perceptions of inferior monads are brought into focus by the apperception, the self-conscious awareness of the dominant monad. Monads are windowless, Leibniz says, and let in nothing from the external world; but perhaps monad can talk to monad by a kind of telepathy.[4]

Leibniz cashes this out in a study of levels of awareness that is one of the most interesting parts of his epistemology. 'There are a thousand indications which lead us to think that there are constantly numberless perceptions in us, but without apperception and without reflection' (G V. 46). A man living by a mill or a waterfall soon ceases to notice the noise it makes. Walking by the seashore we hear the roar of the tide coming in, but we do not distinguish the crash of each individual wave. Much of our conscious experience is in this way composed of a multitude of tiny perceptions of which we have no distinct idea. The perceptions characteristic of inferior monads are confused ideas; the apperception of the dominant monad brings clarity and distinction into our ideas. It is because sense-perceptions are confused that they appear to come from outside.

Leibniz uses his distinction between levels of awareness to answer a standard objection to innate ideas, namely, that we learn individual truths long before we are aware of the fundamental laws of logic. 'General principles', he says, 'enter into

---

[4] On perception and apperception, see below, p. 676.

our thoughts and form the soul of each and the link between them. They are as necessary as muscles and tendons are necessary for walking, even though we don't think of them.' The mind relies on logic all the time, but it takes an effort to identify its laws and make them specific. The Chinese speak in articulate sounds just as Europeans do; but they have not invented an alphabet to express the recognition of this (G V. 69–70).

For Locke, the basic building blocks of knowledge were simple ideas presented by the senses. Leibniz regards the notion of a simple idea as an illusion:

I believe that one can say that the ideas of the senses appear to be simple because they are confused: they do not give the mind scope for distinguishing their content. It is like the way in which distant objects appear round, because we cannot distinguish their angles, even though we take in some confused impression of them. It is obvious, for instance, that green is made out of blue and yellow, mixed together—so you might well think that the idea of green is composed of those two ideas. And yet the idea of green appears to us as simple as those of blue or warm. So we must believe that the ideas of blue and warm are only apparently simple. (G V. 109)

Leibniz also rejected Locke's distinction between secondary qualities, such as colour, which were subjective, and primary qualities, such as shape, which were objective: he regarded both primary and secondary qualities as phenomenal. His position on this issue was to be fully developed by Berkeley (whose early works were read and approved by Leibniz).

Berkeley on Qualities and Ideas

In the first of his *Dialogues between Hylas and Philonous* Berkeley argues for the subjectivity of secondary qualities, using Locke as an ally; then he turns the tables on Locke by producing parallel arguments for the subjectivity of primary qualities. He concludes that no ideas, not even those of primary qualities, are resemblances of objects.

In the dialogue Hylas, the materialist, is hampered in his defence of matter by his acceptance without question of Locke's premiss that we do not perceive material things in themselves, but only their sensible qualities. 'By sensible things,' he says, 'I mean those only which are perceived by sense; and that in truth the senses perceive nothing which they do not perceive immediately, for they make no inferences' (*BPW*, 138). Material things may be inferred, but they are not perceived. Sensible things, in fact, are nothing else but so many sensible qualities. But these qualities are independent of the mind.

Philonous, the idealist in the dialogue, in order to undermine Hylas' belief in the objectivity of sensible qualities, takes him through Locke's argument to show the subjectivity of heat. All degrees of heat are perceived by the senses, and the greater the heat, the more sensibly it is perceived. But a great degree of heat is a great pain; material substance is incapable of feeling pain, and therefore the great heat cannot be in the material substance. All degrees of heat are equally real, and so if a great heat is not something in an external object, neither is any heat.

The argument is full of fallacies that are artfully concealed by Berkeley. The false moves are placed in the mouth of Hylas, not Philonous. Philonous simply asks leading questions, which Hylas then answers with a 'yes' or 'no' when he should be making distinctions. Let us give some instances:

Phil. Heat then is a sensible thing?

Hyl. Certainly.

Phil. Doth the reality of sensible things consist in being perceived? or is it something distinct from their being perceived, and that bears no relation to the mind?

Hyl. To exist is one thing, and to be perceived is another.

Let us accept that we are talking of heat as a perceptible quality, not as a form of energy definable in physical terms. Hylas is right to say that to exist is not the same as to be perceived: the fire in the fireplace may be hot when no one is standing near enough to feel the heat. But he should not have accepted—as he goes on to do—Philonous' equation of 'distinct from being perceived' and 'bearing no relation to the mind'. A shrewder defender of the objectivity of qualities might have admitted that they have a relation to perception, while still insisting that their existence is distinct from their actually being perceived. Another example:

Phil. Is not the most vehement and intense degree of heat a very great pain?

Hyl. No one can deny it.

Phil. And is any unperceiving thing capable of pain or pleasure?

Hyl. No certainly.

Phil. Is your material substance a senseless being, or a being endowed with sense and perception?

Hyl. It is senseless without doubt.

Phil. It cannot therefore be the subject of pain?

Hyl. By no means.

To the first question Hylas should have replied with a distinction: the maximum degree of heat *causes* great pain, agreed; the heat is itself a great pain, no. When asked if senseless things are capable of pain, he should have made a corresponding distinction: capable of *feeling* pain, no; capable of *causing* pain, yes. And he should never have admitted that material substances are senseless: some are (e.g. rocks), and some are not (e.g. cats). But here of course the blame rests with Locke for his argument that a material substance cannot have sensation because it is what *has* sensation.

It would be tedious to follow, line by line, the sleight of hand by which Hylas is tricked into denying the objectivity not only of heat, but of tastes, odours, sounds, and colours. Halfway through the dialogue, Hylas concedes that secondary qualities have no existence outside the mind. But he tries to defend Locke's position that primary qualities really exist in bodies. Philonous is now in a strong position to show that the arguments used by Locke to undermine the objectivity of secondary qualities can also be deployed against primary qualities.

Locke had argued that odours were not real properties because things that smell foul to us smell sweet to animals. Can one not equally argue that size is not a real property because what one of us can hardly discern will appear as a huge mountain to some minute animal (*BPW*, 152)? If we argue that neither heat nor cold is in water, because it can seem warm to one hand and cold to another, we can just as well argue that there are no real sizes or shapes in the world, because what looks large and angular to a nearby eye looks small and round to a distant eye (*BPW*, 153).

At the end of the first dialogue, Hylas, accepting that material objects are in themselves imperceptible, still maintains that they are perceived through our ideas. But Philonous mocks this: how can a real thing, in itself invisible, be like a colour? Hylas has to concur that nothing but an idea can be like an idea, and that no idea can exist without the mind; hence he is unable to defend the claim that ideas give us any information about anything outside the mind.

In the next chapter we will follow the course of the argument in the second and third dialogues in which Berkeley seeks to establish his metaphysical immaterialism. But to complete our account of his epistemology we have to consider what he has to say not only about the ideas of the senses, but also about the universal ideas that have traditionally been regarded as the province of the intellect. Locke had said that the ability to form general ideas was the most important difference between humans and dumb animals. Unlike animals, humans use language; and the words of language have meaning by standing for ideas, and general words, such as sortal predicates, correspond to abstract general ideas. In his *Principles of Human Knowledge* Berkeley mounted a destructive attack on Locke's theory of abstraction. Abstract ideas are said to be attained in the following manner:

The mind having observed that Peter, James and John resemble each other in certain common agreements of shape and other qualities, leaves out of the complex or compound idea it has of Peter, James, and any other particular man, that which is peculiar to each, retaining only what is common to all, and so makes an abstract idea, wherein all the particulars equally partake; abstracting entirely from and cutting off all those circumstances and differences which might determine it to any particular existence. And after this manner it is said we come by the abstract idea of *Man*. (*BPW*, 48)

Thus, the abstract idea of man contains colour, but no particular colour; stature but no particular stature; and so on.

Berkeley thinks this is absurd. 'The idea of man that I frame myself must be either of a white or a black, or a tawny, a straight, or a crooked, a tall, or a low or a middle-sized man. I cannot by any effort of thought conceive the abstract idea.' He is surely wrong about this. If by 'idea' we mean a concept, then there is no doubt that the concept 'man' applies to human beings irrespective of their colour or size, and anyone who possesses the concept knows that. If, as seems more likely, Berkeley is thinking of an idea as an image, he still seems mistaken: mental images do not need to contain all the properties of that of which they are images. My mental image of Abraham does not make him either tall or short; I have no idea which he was. Berkeley conceives mental images very much on the pattern of real images; but even allowing for this, he is mistaken. A portrait on canvas need not specify all the features of a sitter, and a dress pattern need not specify a colour, even though any actual dress must have some particular colour.

At one point Locke writes that it takes skill to form the general idea of a triangle, 'for it must be neither oblique nor rectangle, neither equicrural nor scalenon, but all and none of these at once'. Berkeley is right to say that this is a piece of nonsense. But he should really be attacking Locke for believing that the possession of images of any kind was sufficient to explain our acquisition of concepts. That is what is really wrong with Locke's theory of language, not that he has chosen the wrong images or described them in self-contradictory terms.

To use an image, or a figure, to represent an X, one must already have a concept of an X. An image does not carry on its face any determination of what it represents. An image of an oak leaf, like a drawing of an oak leaf, may represent a leaf, an oak, a tree, a boy-scout achievement, a military rank, or many other things. And concepts cannot be acquired simply by stripping off features from images. What does one strip off from an image of blue in order to use it as an image of colour? In any case there are concepts to which no image corresponds: logical concepts, for instance, such as those corresponding to 'some' or 'not' or 'if'. There are other concepts that can never be unambiguously derived from images, for instance, arithmetical concepts. One and the same image may represent four legs and one horse, or seven trees and one copse.

Berkeley was correct, against Locke, in separating the mastery of language from the possession of abstract general images. But he retained the idea that mental images were the key to language: for him, a general name signified not a single abstract image but 'indifferently a great number of particular images'. But once concept-possession has been distinguished from image-mongering, mental images become unimportant for the philosophy of language and mind. Imaging is no more essential to thinking than illustrations are to a book. It is not our images that explain our possession of concepts, but our concepts that confer meaning on our images.

Hume on Ideas and Impressions

The empiricist identification of thinking and imaging is carried to an extreme point in the philosophy of Hume. Hume does, however, attempt to improve on

Locke and Berkeley by making a distinction between two classes of perceptions, impressions and ideas, instead of calling them all 'ideas'. Everyone, Hume says, knows the difference between feeling and thinking. Feeling is a matter of impressions: sensations and emotions. Thinking involves ideas: the sort of things that come into one's head while reading the *Treatise*, for instance (*T*, 1).

It becomes quite clear that Hume's 'ideas' are mental images. They are, he says, like impressions except by being less forceful and vivid. Moreover, simple ideas are copies of impressions. This looks at first like a definition of 'idea', but Hume appeals to experience in support of it. From time to time he invites the reader to look within himself to verify the principle and challenges him to produce a counter-example. He supports the principle by telling us that a man born blind has no idea of colours. In the case of colour ideas, however, he is himself willing to produce a counter-example. Suppose that a man has encountered all colours except one particular shade of blue:

Let all the different shades of that colour, except that single one, be placed before him, descending gradually from the deepest to the lightest; it is plain that he will perceive a blank where that shade is wanting, and will be sensible that there is a greater distance in that place between the contiguous colours than any other. Now I ask, whether it be possible for him, from his own imagination, to supply this deficiency, and raise up to himself the idea of that particular shade, though it had never been conveyed to him by the senses? I believe there are few but will be of opinion that he can. (*E* II. 17)

Hume is prepared to accept this thought experiment as providing an exception to his principle that all ideas are derived from impressions. 'This instance is so singular,' he continues, 'that it is scarcely worth our observing, and does not merit that for it alone we should alter our general maxim'. This cavalier dismissal of a counter-example must call in question the genuineness of Hume's commitment to 'the experimental method' in the study of the mind. Undeterred, he puts the principle 'no idea without antecedent impression' to vigorous use whenever he wishes to attack metaphysics.

Having used vivacity as the criterion for differentiating between ideas and impressions, Hume makes a further distinction on the basis of vivacity between two different kinds of ideas: ideas of memory and ideas of imagination. ' 'Tis evident at first sight', he tells us, 'that the ideas of the memory are much more lively and strong than those of the imagination, and that the former faculty paints its objects in more distinct colours than any which are employ'd by the latter.' In accordance with his general principle, Hume says that both kinds of ideas must have been preceded by the corresponding impression, but he also notes a difference between them: the ideas of the imagination, unlike the ideas of the memory, are not tied down to the order in time and space of the original impressions.

We are given, then, two criteria for distinguishing memory from imagination: vivacity and orderliness. It is not clear, however, how these criteria are to be used.

It is, no doubt, to enable us to distinguish genuine from delusory memory ('Do I remember that I posted the letter, or am I only imagining it?'). The second criterion would make the distinction, but could never be applied in a case of doubt; the first criterion could be used by a doubter, but would be unreliable, since fantasies can be more forceful and obsessive than memories.

Hume thinks of memory as reliving in the mind a series of past events; but of course remembering the date of the Battle of Hastings, remembering how to make an omelette, or remembering the way to Oxford from London, are very different from each other. So are many other different kinds of memory. Similarly, the word 'imagination' covers much more than the free play of mental imagery: it includes misperception ('Is that a knock at the door, or am I only imagining it?'), hypothesizing ('imagine what the world would be like if everyone behaved in that way!'), and creative originality ('*The Lord of the Rings* is a work of extraordinary imagination'). Hume's treatment of memory and imagination tries to pack a great variety of mental events, capacities, activities, and errors into a single empiricist straitjacket.

There are cases which seem to fit Hume's account reasonably well. I hear a bird sing and then try to recapitulate the melody mentally; I gaze at a patterned wallpaper, and see an after-image after I have closed my eyes. But even in these cases Hume misrepresents the situation. On the face of it, the difference between the impressions and the ideas is that whereas the bird and the wallpaper are external to me, the after-image and the subvocal humming are interior events. But Hume accepts the empiricist thesis that all we ever know are our own perceptions. My hearing the bird sing is not a transaction between myself and the bird, but my encounter with a vivid bird-like sound. For Hume, everyone's life is just one introspection after another.

It has to be by introspection, then, that we tell the difference between our memories and our imaginings. The difference between the two, one might think, could best be made out in terms of *belief*. If I take myself to be remembering that *p*, then I believe that *p*; but I can imagine *p*'s being the case without any such belief. As Hume himself says, we conceive many things that we do not believe. But his classification of mental states makes it difficult for him to find a suitable place for belief.

The difference between merely having the thought that *p* and actually believing that *p* cannot be a difference of content. As Hume puts it, belief cannot consist in the addition of an extra idea to the idea or ideas which constitute *what* is believed. One argument for this is that we are free to add any ideas we like, but we cannot choose to believe whatever we please. A more convincing reason would be that if belief consisted in an extra idea, someone who believes that Caesar died in his bed and someone who does not believe that Caesar died in his bed would not be in conflict with each other because they would not be considering the same proposition (*T*, 95).

In the *Enquiry*, Hume says that belief is a conception 'attended with a feeling or sentiment, different from the loose reveries of the fancy'. But such a feeling would surely be an impression; and in an appendix to the *Treatise*, Hume argues forcefully that this would be directly contrary to experience—belief consists only of ideas. But he still insists that 'An idea assented to *feels* different from a fictitious idea,' and he offers various names to describe the feeling: 'force, vivacity, solidity, firmness, steadiness'. He ends by confessing that ''tis impossible to explain perfectly this feeling or manner of conception' (*T*, 629). But he urges us to accept his account on the implausible ground that history books (which we believe to be factual) are much more vivid to read than novels (which we are well aware are fiction) (*T*, 97).

Some of the difficulties in Hume's account of vivacity as a mark of belief are internal to his system. We observe his embarrassment at discovering a perception that is neither quite an idea nor quite an impression. We may wonder how we are to distinguish the belief that Caesar died in his bed from a memory of Caesar dying in his bed, since vivacity is the mark of each. But other difficulties are not merely internal. The crucial problem is that belief need not involve imagery at all (when I sit down, I believe the chair will support me; but no image or thought about the matter enters my mind). And when a belief does involve imagery, an obsessive fantasy (of a spouse's infidelity, for instance) may be livelier than a genuine belief.

There is something pitiable about Hume's delusion that in presenting his few scattered remarks about the association of ideas he was doing for epistemology what Newton had done for physics. But it is unfair to blame him because his philosophical psychology is so jejune: he inherited an impoverished philosophy of mind from his seventeenth-century forebears, and he is often more candid than they in admitting the gaps and incoherences in the empiricist tradition. The insights that make him great as a philosopher can be disentangled from their psychological wrapping, and continue to provoke reflection. His treatment of causation, of the self, of morality, and of religion will be treated in the appropriate chapters. His main contribution to epistemology was the presentation of a new form of scepticism.

This begins from the distinction, which we have met in several philosophers, between propositions expressing relations of ideas, and propositions expressing matters of fact. The contrary of every matter of fact is possible, Hume says, because it can never imply a contradiction. That the sun will not rise tomorrow is as intelligible and coherent as the affirmation that it will rise. Why then do we believe the latter but not the former (*E* II. 25–6)?

All our reasonings concerning matters of fact, Hume argues, are founded on the relation of cause and effect. But how do we arrive at our knowledge of causal relations? The sensible properties of objects do not reveal to us either the causes that produced them or the effects that will rise from them. Merely looking at gunpowder would never tell you that it was explosive; it takes experience to learn that fire burns things up. Even the simplest regularities of nature cannot be established *a priori*, because a cause and an effect are two totally different events and the one cannot be inferred from another. We see a billiard ball moving towards another, and we expect it to communicate its motion to the other. But why? 'May not both these balls remain at absolute rest? May not the first ball return in a straight line, or leap off from the second in any line or direction? All these suppositions are consistent and conceivable' (*E* II. 30).

The answer, obviously enough, is that we learn the regularities of nature from experience. But Hume carries his probe further. Even after we have experience of the operations of cause and effect, he asks, what ground is there in reason for drawing conclusions from that experience? Experience gives us information only about past objects and occurrences: why should it be extended to future times and objects, which for aught we know resemble past objects only in appearance? Bread has nourished me in the past, but what reason does this give me for believing that it will do so in the future?

These two propositions are far from being the same, *I have found that such an object has always been attended with such an effect* and *I foresee, that other objects, which are in appearance, similar, will be attended with similar effects*. I shall allow, if you please, that the one proposition may justly be inferred from the other: I know, in fact, that it always is inferred. But if you insist that the inference is made by a chain of reasoning, I desire you to produce that reasoning. (*E* II. 34)

No demonstrative argument is possible: there is nothing at all self-contradictory in the supposition that the next time I put the kettle on the stove the water will refuse to boil. But no argument from experience is possible; for if we countenance the possibility that the course of nature may change we cannot regard experience as a reliable guide. Any argument from experience to prove that the future will resemble the past must manifestly be circular. Clearly, therefore, it is not reasoning that makes us believe that it will.

At the level of argument, then, scepticism is victorious. But Hume tells us not to be cast down by this discovery: we are led to believe in the regularity of nature by a principle stronger than reasoning. This principle is custom or habit. No one could infer causal relationship from a single experience, because causal powers are not something observable by the senses. But after we have observed similar objects or events to be constantly conjoined, we immediately infer one kind of event from the other. And yet, a hundred instances have given us no more reason to draw the conclusion than the single one did. 'After the constant conjunction of two objects—heat and flame, for instance, weight and solidity—we are determined by custom alone to expect the one from the appearance of the other' (*E* II. 43). It is custom, not reason, that is the great guide of human life.

Kant's *Synthetic* a priori

Many readers have regarded Hume's conclusion as small comfort in return for his devastating demolition of any reasoned ordering of our experience over time.

No one was more perturbed by Hume's sceptical challenge than Immanuel Kant, and no one worked harder to meet the challenge and to re-establish the function of the intellect in the ordering of our perceptions.

Just as Hume started his argument with a contrast between matters of fact and relations of ideas, Kant begins his response by making distinctions between different kinds of propositions. But instead of a single distinction, he has a pair of distinctions to make, one epistemological and one logical. First, he distinguishes between two modes of knowledge: knowledge derived from experience, which he calls *a posteriori* knowledge, and knowledge independent of all experience, which he calls *a priori* knowledge. Next, he makes a distinction between two kinds of judgement, analytic and synthetic. He explains how to decide to which kind a judgement of the form 'A is B' belongs:

Either the predicate B belongs to the subject A, as something that is contained (though covertly) in the concept A, or it lies quite outside the concept A even though it is attached to it. In the first case, I call the judgement analytic, in the second synthetic. (A, 6)

He gives as an example of an analytic judgement 'all bodies are extended', and as an example of a synthetic judgement 'all bodies are heavy'. Extension, he explains, is part of the concept 'body', whereas weight is not.

Kant's distinction between analytic and synthetic propositions is not wholly satisfactory. It is clearly intended to be universally applicable to propositions of all kinds, yet not all propositions are structured in the simple subject–predicate form he uses in his definition. The notion of 'containing' is metaphorical and although the distinction is clearly intended to be a logical one, Kant sometimes speaks of it as if it were a matter of psychology. Some later philosophers tried to tighten up the distinction, and others tried to break it down; but it retained a permanent place in subsequent philosophical discussion.

What is the relation between the epistemological distinction *a priori/a posteriori* and the logical distinction *analytic/synthetic*? The two distinctions are made on different bases, and they do not, according to Kant, coincide in their application. All analytic propositions are *a priori*, but not all *a priori* propositions are analytic. There is no contradiction in the notion of a synthetic *a priori* proposition, and indeed there are many examples of such propositions. Our knowledge of mathematics is *a priori* because mathematical truths are universal and necessary, whereas no generalization from experience can have those properties. Yet many truths of arithmetic and geometry are synthetic, not analytic. 'That a straight line between two points is the shortest one is a synthetic proposition. For my concept of *straightness* contains no notion of size, but only of quality' (B, 16). Physics, too, contains synthetic *a priori* principles, such as the law of conservation of matter. Finally, a genuine metaphysics is not possible unless we can have *a priori* knowledge of synthetic truths.

How such synthetic *a priori* judgements are possible is the principal problem for philosophy. Its solution is to be found by reflection on the way that human knowledge arises from the combined operation of the senses and the understanding. It is the senses that present us with objects; it is the understanding that makes objects thinkable. Our senses determine the content of our experience; our understanding determines its structure. To mark the contrast between content and structure, Kant uses the Aristotelian terms 'matter' and 'form'. The matter of sensation would include what makes the difference between a splash of blue and a splash of green, or the sound of a violin and the sound of a trumpet. If we isolate sensation from everything that really belongs to the understanding, we find that there are two forms of pure sensory awareness, space and time: the common structure into which our perceptions are fitted. But in real life human beings never have purely sensory awareness.

For human knowledge, both senses and understanding are necessary:

Neither of these faculties has a priority over the other. Without the senses no object would be given to us, and without the understanding no object could be thought. Thoughts without content are empty, awareness without concepts is blind . . . The understanding is aware of nothing, the senses can think nothing. Only through their union can knowledge arise. (A, 51)

In human experience any object of sense is also an object of thought: whatever is experienced is classified and codified; that is to say, it is brought by the understanding under one or more concepts.

In addition to the understanding, Kant tells us, human beings have a faculty of judgement. The understanding is the power to form concepts, and the judgement is the power to apply them. The operations of the understanding find expression in individual words, while judgements are expressed in whole sentences. A concept is nothing other than a power to make judgements of certain kinds. (To possess the concept 'plant', for instance, is to have the power to make judgements expressible by sentences containing the word 'plant' or its equivalent.)

There are many different kinds of judgement: they may, for instance, be universal or particular, affirmative or negative. More importantly, as Kant illustrates by examples, they may be categorical ('there is a perfect justice'), or hypothetical ('if there is a perfect justice, the obstinately wicked are punished'), or disjunctive ('the world exists either through blind chance, or through inner necessity, or through an external cause'). Corresponding to the different kinds of judgement there are different fundamental types of concepts.

Concepts and judgements may be empirical or *a priori*: *a priori* judgements are called principles and *a priori* concepts are called categories. In an elaborate, and not wholly convincing, 'deduction of the categories' Kant relates each category to a different kind of judgement. For instance, he relates the category of substance to categorical judgements, hypothetical judgements to the category of cause, and disjunctive judgements to the category of interaction. Whether or not we are convinced by these specific links, we cannot deny the importance of Kant's general claim that there are some concepts that are indispensable if anything is to count as the operation of understanding. Is the claim true?

It may be easier to answer the question if we put it in linguistic form. Are there any concepts that must find expression in any fully-fledged language? The answer seems to be that any genuine language-users, however alien they may be to us, need to have a concept of negation, and the ability to use quantifiers such as 'all' and 'some'. These are the concepts corresponding to Kant's distinction between affirmative and negative judgements, and his distinction between universal and particular judgements. Again, any rational language-user will need the ability to draw conclusions from premisses, and this ability is expressed in the mastery of words like 'if', 'then', and 'therefore', which are related to Kant's class of hypothetical judgements. So, whatever we think of particular details of the transcendental deduction of the categories, it seems to be correct to link concepts with judgements and to claim that certain concepts must be fundamental to all understanding.

Kant goes on to argue that not only are there *a priori* concepts that are essential if we are to make sense of experience, but there are also *a priori* judgements, the ones that he calls 'principles'. Some of these are analytic, but the principles that are really interesting are the ones that underlie synthetic judgements.

One such principle is that all experiences have extension. Whatever we experience is extended—that is to say, has parts distinct from other parts, either in space or in time. It is this principle that underpins the synthetic *a priori* axioms of geometry, such as the axiom that between two points only one straight line is possible.

Another principle is that in all appearances the object of sensation has intensive magnitude. For instance, if you feel a certain intensity of heat, you are aware that you could be feeling something hotter or less hot: what you are feeling is a point on a scale that extends in two directions. A colour, too, is of its nature located on a spectrum. When I have a sensation I know *a priori* the possibility of similar sensations at another point upon a common scale. Kant calls this 'an anticipation of perception', but the term is unfortunate—he does not mean that you can tell what feeling is going to come next; as he says himself, 'sensation is just that element which cannot be anticipated'. A better word than 'anticipation' might be 'projection'.

Realism vs Idealism

In later chapters we will explore in greater detail other categories and other principles that Kant derives in the course of his transcendental analytic. But the epistemological question that is raised by his brilliant exposition of the *a priori* elements in our experience is this: if so much of what we perceive is the creation of our own mind, can we have any genuine knowledge at all of the real, extra-mental world? A reader of the first *Critique* begins to worry about this long before the transcendental analytic, when he is told at the end of the transcendental aesthetic that space and time are empirically real, but transcendentally ideal. 'If we take away the subject,' Kant tells us there 'space and time disappear: these as phenomena cannot exist in themselves, but only in us.'

If space and time are subjective in this way, can anything be more than mere appearance? We commonly distinguish in experience, Kant explains in response, between that which holds for all human beings and that which belongs only to a single viewpoint. The rainbow in a sunny shower may be called a mere appearance, while the rain is regarded as a thing-in-itself. In this sense, we may grant that not everything is mere experience. But this distinction between appearance and reality, Kant continues, is something merely empirical. When we look more closely, we realize that 'not only are the drops of rain mere appearances, but that even their round shape, nay even the space in which they fall, are nothing in themselves, but merely modifications or fundamental forms of our sensible awareness, and that the transcendental object remains unknown to us' (A, 46).

Passages such as this make it sound as if Kant is an idealist, who believes that nothing is real except ideas in our mind. In fact, Kant is anxious to distance himself from previous idealists, whether they are, like Descartes, 'problematic idealists' ('I exist' is the only indubitable empirical assertion), or, like Berkeley, 'dogmatic idealists' (the external world is illusory). Kant fastens on the point that is common to both versions of idealism, namely, that the inner world is better known than the outer world, and that outer substances are inferred (correctly or incorrectly) from inner experiences.

In fact, Kant argues, our inner experience is only possible on the assumption of outer experience. I am aware of changing mental states, and thus I am conscious of my existence in time, that is to say, as having experiences first at one moment and then at another. But the perception of change involves the perception of something permanent: if there is to be change, as opposed to mere succession, there has to be something which is first one thing and then another. But this permanent thing is not myself: the unifying subject of my experience is not an object of experience. Hence, only if I have outer experience is it possible for me to make judgements about the past—even about my own past inner experience (B, 275–6).

Philosophers, Kant says, make a distinction between phenomena (appearances) and noumena (objects of thought). They divide the world into a world of the senses and a world of the intellect. But as the transcendental analytic has shown, there cannot be a world of mere appearances, mere sense-data that do not fall under any categories or instantiate any rules. Nor can there be, in any positive sense, pure noumena, that is to say, objects of intellectual intuition independent of sensory awareness. However, if we are to talk of appearances at all, we must think that they are appearances of *something*, a something that Kant calls 'the transcendental object'. It is, however, only an unknown X, 'of which we know, and with the present constitution of our understanding can know, nothing whatsoever'. We cannot say anything about it: to do so we would have to bring it under a category, and the categories are applicable only to sensory awareness. The concept of noumenon can only be understood in a negative sense, as a limiting concept whose function is to set the bounds of sensibility (A, 255–6; B, 307–10). But it is fundamental to Kant's claim that while he is a transcendental idealist he is, at the empirical level, a realist and not an idealist like Berkeley.

Kant took great pains to distinguish his own position from that of other philosophers in the early modern period. It may be instructive, finally, to compare his position with an earlier philosopher whom he resembles more closely than he resembles Berkeley or Descartes: St Thomas Aquinas. Kant and Aquinas agree that knowledge is possible only through a cooperation between the senses and the intellect. According to Aquinas, in order not only to acquire but also to exercise concepts the intellect must operate upon what he calls 'phantasmata', which correspond to Kant's 'sensory manifold'—the deliverances of inner and outer senses. For Aquinas, as for Kant, concepts without experience are empty, and phantasms without concepts are unintelligible.

We may ask whether, in the last analysis, Aquinas and Kant are idealists: do they believe that we never know or understand the real world, but only ideas of the mind? It is easier to give a straight answer in the case of Aquinas. For him, ideas were universals, and universals, as such, were creations of the mind; there was no such thing as a universal in the real world. But this does not mean that he was an idealist in the sense defined. Universal concepts were not the objects of intellectual knowledge: they were the tools by which the intellect acquired knowledge of the nature of the material substances of the world around us. All thought, therefore, made use of ideas, but not all thought was about ideas. Natural objects had a reality of their own, of which, through experience, we could acquire a piecemeal and partial knowledge, though the essences of much of the natural world remained unknown to us.[5]

Kant, however, can distinguish his position from that of Berkeley only by claiming that there exists a noumenon, a thing-in-itself underlying the appearances, to which we have no access either by sense or by intellect, and which cannot be described under pain of uttering nonsense. He is emphatic that it is false to say that there is nothing other than appearance; but to many of his readers it has seemed that a nothing would do just as well as a something about which nothing can be said.

[5] See above, p. 437.

Idealist Epistemology

No sooner was Kant dead than his system was subject to fundamental criticism. Fichte argued that there was a radical inconsistency in the *Critique of Pure Reason*. How could it simultaneously be true that our experience was caused by things in themselves and that the concept of cause could only be applied within the sphere of phenomena? The way to avoid this contradiction, Fichte claimed, was to abandon the idea of an unknown, mind-independent cause of phenomena, and to accept wholeheartedly the idealist position that the world of experience is the creation of a thinking subject.

Fichte convinced few of the possibility of deriving the universe from the subjectivity of the individual ego, and German idealism was given a more plausible and influential form by Hegel, who concurred in the elimination of the thing-in-itself, but who saw the creative activity of the mind occurring on a cosmic scale rather than at the level of individual consciousness.

Nonetheless, *The Phenomenology of Spirit*, however metaphysical in intent, contains some acute reflection on the nature of everyday knowledge and perception. In his customary fashion, Hegel sees human cognitive faculties as threefold, an ascending hierarchy of consciousness, self-consciousness, and reason. Consciousness in its turn proceeds through three stages: there is first sense-awareness (*Die sinnliche Gewissheit*), then there is perception (*Wahrnehmung*), and finally there is understanding (*Verstand*).

Immediate sense-awareness, the reception of crude sense-data, has seemed to many philosophers, before and after Hegel, the richest and firmest form of knowledge. Hegel shows that it is in fact the thinnest and emptiest level of consciousness. If we try to express what we experience, stripped of the categories of the understanding, we are reduced to impotent silence. We cannot even pin down our sense-datum as 'this, here, now'; all these indexical expressions are really universals, capable of being used on different occasions for quite different experiences, times, and places.

It is at the level of perception that consciousness can first claim to be knowledge. At this stage, we take the objects of sense to be things possessing properties. But this too is an illusory form of knowledge. Hegel proceeds, in Kantian style, to show that if we are to reconcile the multiplicity of sense-experience with the unity of properties in a substance we have to rise to the level of understanding, which invokes scientific, non-sensible, categories to confer order on sensory phenomena. Thus we appeal to the notion of force, and construct natural laws to regulate its operation. But reflection shows that these laws are the creation of the understanding itself, rather than some super-phenomenal objective system. Thus consciousness must return upon itself and become self-consciousness.

Consciousness and self-consciousness in their turn yield to the higher faculty of reason, which sees both the nature which is the object of consciousness and the mind which is the object of self-consciousness as manifestations of a single infinite spirit. At this point epistemology turns into metaphysics. Reason's task is no longer to observe or know the world, but to create it and fashion it. For reason is itself an episode in the life of the all-embracing spirit.

Throughout the period that we have been considering, epistemology was the discipline that occupied the centre of philosophical attention: 'What can we know, and how can we know it?' became the key philosophical question. Indeed, the major philosophical schools are given names—'empiricist' and 'rationalist'—that define them in epistemological terms. This makes an important difference between the early modern period and the ancient and medieval periods, and also between the early modern period and the post-Hegelian age. In the Hegelian tradition epistemology merged with metaphysics; in another tradition that was to become dominant in many parts of the world in the twentieth century, the study of logic and language superseded epistemology as the master philosophical discipline. This we shall see in Part Four.

5

Physics

Natural Philosophy

The period at the end of the sixteenth century and the beginning of the seventeenth was one of great importance in the philosophy of the natural world. What had been, up to this point, a single discipline of 'natural philosophy' gradually split into two different endeavours: the philosophy of natural science and the science of physics. Both disciplines share a common subject matter, but they have different purposes and operate in different ways. The philosophy of nature seeks an understanding of the concepts we employ in describing and accounting for natural phenomena: concepts such as 'space', 'time', 'motion', and 'change'. Scientific physics seeks to establish and explain the phenomena themselves, not by *a priori* reasoning or conceptual analysis, but by observation, experiment, and hypothesis. The two disciplines are not in competition, and indeed each needs the other; but it is of prime importance to keep in mind the difference between their goals and methods.

The separation of the two was achieved, in this early modern period, in the course of a battle about the authority of the natural philosophy of Aristotle, which contains elements of both disciplines indiscriminately entwined. That philosophy remained dominant in universities both Catholic and Protestant throughout the period, and its influence undoubtedly acted as a brake on the development of sciences such as mechanics and astronomy. These sciences gathered impetus only to the extent that the Aristotelian yoke was thrown off, and this was due above all to three philosophers who attacked the system from outside the academic mainstream: Galileo, Bacon, and Descartes. Sadly, the liberation of physics was accompanied by an impoverishment of philosophy. Though Aristotle's scientific physics was shown to be very largely mistaken, his conceptual scheme retained much of its value. All too often, both bad and good were thrown overboard together.

The establishment which persecuted Galileo has long been denounced by historians as hidebound, protectionist, and obscurantist. In particular, the scholastic professors have been blamed for preferring *a priori* speculation to observation and experiment. Not only were they reluctant to conduct research themselves, the charge goes, but they were unwilling to take account of the research of others. They rejected observation, even when it was handed to them, as when a Paduan professor refused to look through Galileo's telescope.

The charge is basically just, though overdrawn. Some of Galileo's Jesuit adversaries were respectable astronomers in their own right. More importantly, we must remember that the anti-empiricist bias of these latter-day Aristotelians was not typical of Aristotle himself. In a famous passage, Aristotle had affirmed the primacy of fact over speculation: 'We must trust observation rather than theory, and trust theories only if their results conform with the observed phenomena.'[1] Indeed, that passage was often quoted by Galileo's critics: heliocentrism was only a theory, but the motion of the sun was something we could see with our own eyes.

Aristotle's own works are full of original and careful observation, and it is no disgrace to him if his physics was shown to be mistaken after a lapse of eighteen centuries. It is paradoxical that one of the greatest scientists of the ancient world should have turned out to be the greatest obstacle to scientific progress in the early modern world. The explanation, however, is simple. When Aristotle's works were rediscovered in the Latin West they were introduced into a society that was predominantly text-based. Christianity, like Judaism and Islam, was a 'religion of a book'. Supreme authority rested with the Bible: the function of the Church was to preserve, proclaim, and interpret the messages contained in that book, and to promote the ideals and practices that it presented. Once Aristotle's texts secured acceptance in Latin academia, instead of being read as stimuli to further research, they were treated with the reverence appropriate to a sacred book. Hence Galileo's genuine contradictions of Aristotle caused as much scandal as his imagined contradictions of the Bible.

Scientific method, as it has been commonly understood in recent centuries, consists of four principal stages. First, systematic observation is undertaken of the phenomena to be explained. Second, a theory is proposed which would provide an explanation of these phenomena. Third, from this theory is derived a prediction of some phenomenon other than those already included in the survey. Fourth, the prediction is tested empirically: if the prediction turns out false, than the theory is to be rejected; if it comes true, then the theory is so far confirmed, and should be put to further test. At each of these stages, mathematics plays a crucial role: in the accurate measurement of the phenomena to be explained and of the result of the test experiment, and in the formulation of the appropriate hypotheses and the derivation of their expected consequences.

During our period four philosophers, through their writings, contributed features of the eventual consensus: Aristotle, Galileo, Bacon, and Descartes.

---

[1] See above, p. 62.

Each of them, however, was guilty of a failure to appreciate one or other element that was needed for the synthesis, and for most of them a key deficiency was a misunderstanding of the relationship between science and mathematics.

Aristotle, while an admirable empirical investigator in practice, presented in his *Posterior Analytics* an unrealistic model of science based on geometry, the most advanced branch of mathematics in his day. He believed that a completed science could be presented as an axiomatic *a priori* system such as was later developed by Euclid. Descartes, himself a distinguished mathematician, thought that science should imitate mathematics not by adopting its methods of ratiocination and calculation, but by looking for truths which had the immediate intuitive appeal of propositions of simple arithmetic and basic geometry.

Bacon, while devoting more care than either of these philosophers to describing procedures for the systematic collection of empirical data and the formation of appropriate hypotheses, had little appreciation of the importance of mathematics in these two tasks. He thought of mathematics as a mere appendix to science, and he complained about 'the daintiness and pride of mathematicians, who will needs have this science almost domineer over physic' (*De Augmentis*, 476).

Of our quartet only Galileo fully appreciated the essential role of mathematics. The book of the universe, he famously said, 'is written in the language of mathematics, and its characters are triangles, circles and other geometric figures, without which it is humanly impossible to understand a single word of it' (*Il Saggiatore*, 6). His weakest point was precisely the one insisted on by his Aristotelian opponents: he failed fully to appreciate that a hypothesis is only confirmed, not proved with certainty, by the success of a prediction. It is this point which was seized on by twentieth-century philosophers of science, such as Pierre Duhem and Karl Popper, who judged Bellarmine the victor in the debate on heliocentrism. They were perhaps over-generous in attributing to the cardinal a full grasp of the hypothetico-deductive method.

Cartesian Physics

Like Galileo, and unlike Bacon, Descartes thought that mathematics was the key to physics, though he did not have Galileo's grasp of the use of mathematics in the construction and verification of experiments. In the *Principles of Philosophy* he wrote:

I recognize no kind of matter in corporeal objects except that matter susceptible of every sort of division, shape, and motion which geometers call quantity and which they presuppose as the subject matter of their proofs. Further, the only properties I consider in it are those divisions, shapes and motions; and about them I accept only what can be derived from indubitable true axioms with the sort of self-evidence that belongs to a mathematical proof. All natural phenomena, as I shall show, can be explained in this way:

I therefore do not think any other principles in physics are either necessary or desirable. (AT VIII. 78; *CSMK* I. 247)

Descartes' physical system is mechanistic; that is to say it assumes that all natural phenomena can be explained by the motion of geometrical matter. It is not just a matter of seeing everything, outside the mind, as being merely clockwork. Even the simplest form of clock, as naturally explained, is not a mechanistic system, since it involves the notion of *weight*, and for Descartes weight, as distinct from motion or extension, is just one of many properties which are to be dismissed as subjective or secondary:

I observed...that colours, odours, savours and the rest of such things, were merely sensations existing in my thought, and differing no less from bodies than pain differs from the shape and motion of the instrument which inflicts it. Finally, I saw that weight, hardness, the power of heating, attraction, and of purging, and all other qualities which we experience in bodies, consisted solely in motion or its absence, and in the configuration and situation of their parts. (AT VII. 440; *CSMK* II. 397)

To prove that the essence of matter is constituted by extension, Descartes argues that a body, without ceasing to be a body, can lose any of its properties with the exception of extension. Consider our idea of a stone. Hardness is not essential to it: it may be ground into a fine powder. Colour is not essential: some stones are transparent. Weight is not essential to a body: fire is bodily but light. A stone may change from being warm to being cold and yet remain a stone. 'We may now observe that absolutely no element of our idea remains, except extension in length, breadth and depth.'

One might agree that properties such as colour and warmth are not essential to a body, and yet claim that they are genuine, objective properties. Such was the position of Descartes' scholastic predecessors, who regarded such things as 'real accidents' of substances—'real' because they were objective, and 'accidents' because they were not essential. Descartes offers several arguments against this position.

First he points out that such properties are perceived only by a single sense, unlike shape and motion which are perceived by several senses—warmth and colour are, in Aristotelian jargon, 'proper sensibles' not 'common sensibles'. This seems a poor argument. It is true that judgements, if they are to be objective, must be capable of assessment and correction, and that a judgement of a single sense cannot be corrected by the operation of any other sense. But any individual's sense-judgement can be corrected by his own further, closer, investigation by the same sense, or by the cooperation of other observers using the same faculty.

Descartes' main argument for the subjectivity of proper sensibles is a negative one: the scholastic notion of 'real accidents' is incoherent. If something is real, it must be a substance; if it is an accident, it cannot be a substance. If, *per impossibile*, there were such things as real accidents, they would have to be specially created by God from moment to moment (AT III. 505, VII. 441; *CSMK* II. 298, III. 208).

Possibly some of Descartes' scholastic contemporaries were vulnerable to this argument. But Thomas Aquinas, centuries earlier, had pointed out that the idea that accidental forms must be substances rested on a misunderstanding of language:

Many people make mistakes about forms by judging about them as they would about substances. This seems to come about because forms are spoken of in the abstract as if they were substances, as when we talk of whiteness or virtue or suchlike. So, some people, misled by ordinary usage, regard them as substances. Hence came the error of those who thought that forms must be occult and those who thought that forms must be created. (*Q. D. de Virt in Comm.*, ed. R. Pession (Turin: Marietti, 1949), 11)

Descartes saw no need for the accidents and forms of scholastic theory because he claimed to be able to explain the whole of nature in terms of motion and extension alone. Because matter and extension are identical, he argued, there cannot be any empty space or vacuum, and the only possible movement of bodies is ultimately circular, with A pushing B out of its place and B pushing C and so on, until Z moves into the place vacated by A. In the beginning God created matter along with motion and rest: He preserves the total quantity of motion in the universe as constant, but varies its distribution in accordance with the laws of nature. Descartes claims to deduce these laws *a priori* from the immutability of God. The first law says that every body, if unaffected by extraneous causes, perseveres in the same state of motion or rest; the second states that simple or elementary notion is always in a straight line. On the basis of these laws Descartes constructed an elaborate system of vortices, that is to say whirlpools of material particles varying in size and velocity. This system, he maintained, was adequate to explain all the phenomena of the natural world (AT VIII. 42–54, 61–8; *CSMK* I. 224–33; 240–5).

Descartes' physical system enjoyed a limited popularity for a period, but within a century it had been totally superseded. It was, in fact, internally incoherent, as can be shown in many ways. Inertia provides the simplest example. According to Descartes' first law everything tends, so far as it can, to remain in the same state of motion or rest in which it is. But if a moving body's tendency to continue moving is not a genuine property of a body, then it cannot explain physical effects. If, on the other hand, it is a genuine property of the body, then it is untrue that bodies have no properties except motion and geometrical properties. For a tendency to move cannot be identified with actual motion; the one may be present without the other. Descartes is badly served here by his contempt for the Aristotelian categories of potentiality and actuality.

Experimental observation during his own lifetime exhibited the weaknesses in Descartes' system. Descartes incorporated into his account of the human body the circulation of the blood recently discovered by William Harvey, but he attempted to explain it purely mechanistically in terms of rarefaction and expansion. This involved him in an account of the movement of the heart that was in total conflict with Harvey's own results, because, unlike Harvey, he believed that it was the expansion of the heart, rather than its contraction, that was responsible for the expulsion of blood.

Again, because he identified matter with extension, Descartes denied the possibility of a vacuum. If God took away all the matter inside a vessel without allowing it to be replaced, he said, then the sides of the vessel would touch each other (AT VIII.51; CSMK I. 231). Because of his rejection of the vacuum, he also opposed the atomic hypothesis. Matter, being identical with extension, must be infinitely divisible, and there was no such thing as a void for the atoms to move about in. Descartes sought to explain away the evidence for the existence of a vacuum that had been provided in 1643 by Evangelista Torricelli's invention of the barometer.

The Atomism of Gassendi

When Descartes published his *Principles*, atomism was being revived by Pierre Gassendi, on the model of the ancient theories of Democritus and Epicurus, whose ideas had recently become familiar to the learned world through the discovery and wide dissemination of Lucretius' great Epicurean poem, *De Rerum Natura*.[2] A Catholic priest, who held both a professorship of mathematics and the deanship of a cathedral, Gassendi sought to show that the philosophy of the pagan Epicurus was no more difficult to reconcile with Christianity than was the philosophy of the pagan Aristotle. Both pagan philosophers had erred in teaching that the world was eternal and uncreated; but from a philosophical point of view the explanation of physical phenomena in terms of the behaviour of atoms was to be preferred to an account in terms of substantial forms and real accidents. Gassendi attacked Aristotle in his earliest treatise, and in a series of works between 1647 and his death in 1655 Gassendi defended not only the atomism, but also the ethics and character, of Epicurus.

Natural bodies, said Gassendi, following Epicurus, are aggregates of small units of matter. These units are atoms, that is to say, they are indivisible. They possess size, shape, and weight, and solidity or impenetrability. These atoms, according to Gassendi, possess motion under the constant influence of the divine prime mover: they move in a straight line unless they collide with other atoms or get incorporated into a larger unit (which he called a 'molecule'). All bodies of whatever size are composed of molecules of atoms, and the motions of atoms are the origin and cause of all motions in nature.

---

[2] See above, pp. 144–5.

Philosophical objections against atomism, Gassendi argued, rested on a confusion between physics and metaphysics. One could accept that any magnitude must be theoretically capable of further division—no matter how short a line may be, it always makes sense to talk of a line only half as long—and yet maintain that there are some physical bodies which cannot be divided by any power short of the omnipotence of God. A distinction between the two kinds of divisibility is ruled out only if one accepts Descartes' identification of matter with extension. But Gassendi rejected this identification, and was willing to accept the Aristotelian term 'prime matter' to describe the ultimate constituents of his atoms.

Against both Aristotle and Descartes, but again following Epicurus, Gassendi maintained that there could be no motions, whether of atoms or of composite bodies, unless there was a void or vacuum for them to move through. When air is compressed, for instance, the air atoms move into the empty spaces that were hitherto between them. Empty space, he believed, would exist even if there were no bodies in existence; it existed before creation, and so too did time:

Even if there were no bodies, there would remain a steady place and a flowing time; so time and place do not seem to depend on bodies or be accidents of bodies . . . Place and time must be considered real things, or actual entities, for although they are not the kind of thing that substance and accident are commonly regarded, they do actually exist and do not depend on the mind like a chimaera, for whether mind thinks of them or not place stays put and time flows on. (1658, 182–3)

Space, according to Gassendi, is immense and immovable, and spatial regions are also incorporeal—not in the sense of being spiritual, but in the sense of being penetrable in a way that solid bodies are not.

Newton

Subsequent thinkers more often agreed with Gassendi than with Descartes about the nature of matter and the possibility of a vacuum. Nonetheless, in the mid-seventeenth century Gassendi's system was not a serious competitor to Descartes' theories. The death blow to Descartes' physics was given by the publication in 1687 of Sir Isaac Newton's *Principia Mathematica*. Newton established a universal law of gravitation, showing that bodies are attracted to each other by a force in direct proportion to their masses and in inverse proportion to the square of the distance between them. The force of gravity was something above and beyond the mere motion of extended matter which was all that was allowed in Cartesian physics. Descartes had considered the notion of attraction between bodies, but had rejected it as too like Aristotelian final causes, and as involving the attribution of consciousness to inert masses.

What is it, Newton asks, that glues together the parts of homogeneous hard bodies? Descartes tells us that it is nothing but lack of motion; Gassendi talks of the hooks and eyes of atoms. The first answer explains nothing; the second merely puts the question back. 'I had rather infer from their cohesion', Newton said, 'that their particles attract one another by some force, which in immediate contact is exceedingly strong.' It was this same power of attraction which, operating upon bodies not in immediate contact, was the force of gravity. Was this then a case of action at a distance? At first Newton denied this; but by the time of his *Opticks* (1706) he seemed to be willing to accept that gravity, magnetism, and electricity were indeed forces or powers by which the particles of bodies could act at a distance. He seems to have remained agnostic whether the laws that he had discovered could eventually be explained without appeal to action across a vacuum—e.g. by the postulation of some medium such as an aether.[3]

By accepting the existence of forces in nature which may, for all we know, have no explanation in terms of matter and motion, Newtonian physics made a complete break with the mechanism of Descartes. And by bringing under a single law not only the motion of falling bodies on earth, but also the motion of the moon round the earth and the planets round the sun, Newton put to rest for ever Aristotle's idea that terrestrial and celestial bodies were totally different from each other. His physics was quite different from the competing systems it replaced, and for the next two centuries physics simply *was* Newtonian physics.

The Labyrinth of the Continuum

The separation of physics from the philosophy of nature, set in train by Galileo, was now complete. However, Newton left one problem for philosophers to chew upon for a century or more: the nature of space. On the basis of the experiments with a vacuum, Newton believed that space was an absolute entity, not a mere set of relations between bodies. In this Newton resembled Gassendi, but he went further than him when he described space as 'the sensorium of God'. It is not quite clear what he meant by this—he probably did not wish to attribute organs to God—but undoubtedly he thought of space as some kind of divine attribute. 'God endures for ever and is present everywhere,' he wrote, 'and by existing always and everywhere he constitutes space, eternity, and infinity' (Newton 1723: 483).

These views of Newton were criticized by Leibniz in 1715 in a letter to Caroline, Princess of Wales. This led to a famous exchange of letters with Newton's admirer Samuel Clarke. Leibniz argued that space was not real, but simply ideal: 'I hold space to be something merely relative, as time is; I hold it to be an order of

---

[3] See Steven Nadler, 'Doctrines of Explanation', in *CHSCP*, pp. 342–6.

coexistences as time is an order of successions. For space denotes, in terms of possibility, an order of things which exist at the same time, considered as existing together' (A, 25–6). An empty space, he maintained, would be an attribute without a subject, and he offered many arguments against the idea that space was a substance or any kind of absolute being.

Clarke replied by reaffirming Newton's idea of time and space as belonging to God:

Space is not a Substance, but a Property . . . Space is immense, and immutable, and eternal: and so also is Duration. Yet it does not at all from hence follow, that anything is eternal hors de Dieu. For Space and Duration are not hors de Dieu, but are caused by, and are immediate and necessary consequences of his existence: And without them, his Eternity and Ubiquity (or omnipresence) would be taken away.

The identification of space with the immensity of God is not plausible, since God has no parts and it is essential to the notion of space that one part of it is distinct from another. On the other hand, Leibniz's own view contradicts not just an absolute notion of space, but denies any reality to space at all. For the only real substances in his system are monads, and these are not in any spatial relationship to each other, being each a world of its own. He adopted this position because he could see no coherent way of accepting the reality of the continuum. 'The geometers', he wrote, 'show that extension does not consist of points, but the metaphysicians claim that matter must be made up of unities or simple substances' (G II. 278).

The problem seemed to be this. Since space is infinitely divisible, bodies that occupy space must be infinitely divisible too. They must, therefore, contain an infinite number of parts. How big are these parts? If they lack any size, like a point, then even an infinite number of them will lack size too, and no body will have any extension. On the other hand, if they have size, then any body containing an infinite number of them will itself be infinite in extension.

Aristotle had long ago shown that the way to avoid this problem was to make a distinction between two senses of infinite divisibility. 'Divisible to infinity', he insisted, means 'unendingly divisible', not 'divisible into infinitely many parts'. However often a magnitude has been divided, it can always be divided further— there is no end to its divisibility. But that does not mean that the continuum has infinitely many parts: infinity is always potential, never actual.[4] Gassendi had shown that this metaphysical infinite divisibility need not conflict with the atomistic theory that some physical objects are indivisible by any physical power.

The 'labyrinth of the continuum', as Leibniz called it, is an illusion that rests on two bases: the rejection of the Aristotelian metaphysic of actuality and potentiality; and the acceptance of the Cartesian identification of matter with extension. Without the former, there is no reason to see any contradiction in the notion of infinite divisibility. Without the latter, there is no reason to believe that bodies must

[4] See above, p. 145.

be infinitely divisible because space is infinitely divisible. Matter may be atomic without extension being lumpy.

Throughout the eighteenth century, however, the continuum was regarded as one of the greatest conundrums of philosophy. David Hume took a robust way out: he simply denied the infinite divisibility of space and time, mocking it as one of the strangest and most unaccountable opinions, supported only by 'mere scholastick quibbles'. He based his argument against infinite divisibility upon the finite nature of the human mind:

Whatever is capable of being divided *in infinitum* must consist of an infinite number of parts, and 'tis impossible to set any bounds to the number of parts, without setting bounds at the same time to the division. It requires scarce any induction to conclude from hence, that the *idea*, which we form of any finite quality, is not infinitely divisible, but that by proper distinctions and separations we may run up this idea to inferior ones, which will be perfectly simple and indivisible. In rejecting the infinite capacity of the mind, we suppose it may arrive at an end in the division of its ideas; nor are there any possible means of evading the evidence of this conclusion. 'Tis therefore certain, that the imagination reaches a minimum, and may raise up to itself an idea, of which it cannot conceive any sub-division, and which cannot be diminished without a total annihilation. (*T*, 27)

What goes for ideas, goes also for impressions: 'Put a spot of ink upon paper, fix your eye upon that spot, and retire to such a distance, that at last you lose sight of it; 'tis plain, that the moment before it vanished the image or impression was perfectly indivisible' (*T*, 27).

Kant's Antinomies

Kant had a novel way of dealing with the problems of the continuum. He took over the arguments of his predecessors (for and against infinite extension of time, for and against the infinite divisibility of matter), and instead of taking sides between them he proclaimed that the impossibility of resolving the debate showed that it was a mistake to talk of the universe as a whole or to treat space and time as having reality in themselves. This is the tactic he adopted in the part of the transcendental dialectic called 'the antinomies of pure reason'

The first antinomy concerns the extension of time and space. If we leave aside space for the moment, the thesis is 'The world had a beginning in time' and the antithesis is 'The world had no beginning in time'. Both propositions had long been discussed by philosophers. Aristotle thought the antithesis could be proved, Augustine thought the thesis could be proved, and Aquinas thought that neither could be proved. Kant now proposes that both can be proved: not, of course, to show that there are two contradictory truths, but to show the impotence of reason to talk about 'the world' as a whole (A, 426–34).

The argument for the thesis is this. An infinite series is one that can never be completed, and so it cannot be the case that an infinite series of temporal states has already passed away. This argument fails, because of an ambiguity in the word 'completed'. It is true that any discrete series which has two termini cannot be infinite; but such a series may be closed at one end and go on for ever in the other. Elapsed time would then be 'completed' by having a terminus in the present, while reaching forever backward.

The argument for the antithesis is equally unconvincing. If the world had a beginning, it goes, then there was a time when the world did not exist. There is nothing to differentiate any moment of this 'void time' from any other; hence there can be no answer to the question 'why did the world begin when it did?' One may agree that it is not possible to date the beginning of the world from outside ('at such a point in void time'), while maintaining that one can locate it from within ('so many time-units before now'). Augustine and Aquinas would have agreed in rejecting the notion of void time: for them, time began when the world began.

The second antinomy concentrates not on time but on space—or rather, the spatial divisibility of substances. The thesis is: 'Every composite substance in the world is made up of simple parts'; the antithesis is: 'No composite thing in the world is made up of simple parts.' The thesis is the affirmation, and the antithesis the denial, of atomism. Once again the arguments Kant presents on each side of the antinomy are inconclusive: they fail to take full account of Aristotle's distinction between something's being divisible into infinite parts, and something's being infinitely divisible into parts.

The antinomies are designed to exhibit the general pointlessness of asking or answering questions about the world as a whole, but in the particular case of space and time Kant had already argued for their unreality earlier in the first *Critique*, in the transcendental aesthetic. He started from an inherited distinction between inner and outer senses. Space, he claimed, is the form of outer sense; it is the subjective condition of our awareness of objects outside ourselves (A, 26). Time, on the other hand, is the form of inner sense, by means of which the mind experiences its own inner states, which have no extension in space but are all ordered in time:

What, then, are space and time? Are they real existences? are they only determinations or relations of things, yet such as would belong to things even if they were not intuited? Or are space and time such that they belong only to the form of awareness, and therefore to the subjective constitution of our mind, apart from which they could not be ascribed to anything whatsoever?

A dogmatic metaphysician, Kant tells us, would say that infinite space and infinite time are presupposed by experience, and that we can imagine space and time without objects but not objects without space and time. But we may ask how it is that we can know truths about space and time which are based on awareness (because they are not analytic) and yet are *a priori* (because they are necessary and universal). Kant's answer is that the knowledge of synthetic *a priori* truths about space and time is only explicable if they are formal elements of sense-experience rather than properties of things in themselves.

Does this mean that they are unreal? Empirically, Kant replies, they are real, but transcendentally they are ideal. 'If we take away the subject, space and time disappear: these as phenomena cannot exist in themselves but only in us.' What things are in themselves, beyond the phenomena, is something that is unknown to us.

During the period covered by this Part, as we have seen, the philosophical study of the material world passed through two stages. In the first phase, the seventeenth century saw the gradual separation of the old discipline of natural philosophy into the science of physics, whose role was the empirical investigation of actual natural laws, and the philosophy of physics, whose task it was to analyse the concepts presupposed by any physical inquiry. In the second phase, philosophers examined a wide gamut of possible conceptions of space and time, ranging from the extreme realism of Newton and Clarke to the subjective idealism of Kant. In the next Part, there will not be a thematic chapter devoted to the philosophy of physics. By the nineteenth century physics was a fully mature empirical science, operating independently of philosophy; the history of physics is now quite separate from the history of philosophy. To be sure, the philosophy of physics continues on its way, as an analysis of the conceptual implications of novel physical theories. Such a discipline, however, can be pursued only by those with more knowledge of the modern science of physics itself than can be presumed in the readership of an introductory history of philosophy.

6

Metaphysics

The Metaphysics of Suarez

It was through the *Disputationes Metaphysicae* of Francisco Suarez, directly or indirectly, that the metaphysics of the medieval scholastics became known to the philosophers of the early modern age. Suarez was well acquainted with the works of his medieval predecessors, and he summarized their views, codified their positions, and built up his own system by choosing options from the menu that they offer. A summary of the main positions of the *Disputationes* accordingly provides a good starting point for a consideration of the metaphysics of our period.

Suarez starts from Aristotle's definition of the subject as the discipline that studies being qua being. He expands on this by offering a classification of different types of being, proceeding by a series of dichotomies. First there is the division between infinite being and finite being, or, as he often says, between *ens a se* (that which has being of itself) and *ens ab alio* (that which has being from elsewhere). The creaturely world of finite being is then divided first of all into substance and accident. Substances are things like stars and dogs and pebbles which subsist on their own; accidents are entities like brightness, fierceness, and hardness which exist only by inhering in substances and have no independent history. We can proceed further if we wish by subdividing substances into living and non-living, and living substances into animal and vegetable and so on; we can also identify at least nine different kinds of accidents corresponding to Aristotle's categories. But such further division will take us outside the scope of general metaphysics, which operates at the most abstract level. All these items are beings, but metaphysics is interested in studying them only *qua beings*. The study of living beings *qua living*, for instance, is for physical rather than metaphysical disciplines—biology, say, and zoology or psychology.

To Aristotle's definition Suarez adds a qualification. The subject matter of metaphysics, strictly speaking, is not any old being, but *real* being. All the items we have considered in the previous paragraph, including items like fierceness and hardness, count as real beings. If so, one might wonder, what other beings are there? In addition, Suarez says, there are creations of the reason (*entia rationis*) that have being only in the mind and not in reality. Blindness is an *ens rationis*: this does not mean that it is something unreal or fictitious; it means that it is not a positive reality, as the power of sight is, but an absence of such a power. Certain types of relation form another class of *entia rationis*: when I become a great-uncle, I acquire a new relationship but there is no real change in myself. Finally, there are the creations of the imagination: chimeras and hippogriffs. So there are three kinds of *entia rationis*: negations, relations, and fictions. These are fringe topics for the metaphysician rather than his principal concern.

Let us return then to the centre: real being. Is there a single, univocal concept of being that applies in the same sense to all the varied kinds of being? Aquinas had said no: 'being' was an analogous term, and God is not a being in the same sense as ants are beings. Scotus had said yes: 'being' could be used about God in exactly the same sense as about creatures. Suarez offers a subtle answer which he believes enables him to take sides with both Aquinas and Scotus. There is a single abstract concept of being which applies to everything alike, and Scotus is so far correct; but this is not a concept that tells us anything real or new about the objects to which it applies, and to that extent Aquinas is right. Sentences like 'this animal is a dog' or 'this dog is white' can be instructive, because the predicate carries information that is not already implicit in the subject. But the predicate '...is a being' can never be instructive in the same way: *being* is not an activity or attribute distinct from *being an animal* or *being a dog* (*DM* 2. 1, 9; 2. 3, 7).

In saying this, Suarez is touching on a dispute much ventilated in the Middle Ages, namely, whether in creatures there is a real distinction between essence and *esse*. The issue is not a clear one, and its significance depends on two decisions. First, it matters whether we take 'essence' as generic essence or individual essence (e.g. as 'humanity' or as 'Peter's humanity'). Second, it matters whether we take *esse* as equivalent to 'existence' or as the all-embracing predicate 'being'. There is one option which gives a clear answer. If we take essence in the generic sense, and *esse* as existence, then there is an undeniable difference between essence and existence: essence is what answers the question 'What is an X?' and existence is what answers the question 'Are there Xs?' The difference between the questions is so enormous that talk of a 'real distinction' seems to fail only by understatement.

Suarez in fact denies that there is a real distinction between essence and *esse*; the distinction, he says, is only mental (*tantum ratione*). We have to look closely to see which of the options he is taking. It becomes clear that by 'essence' he means individual essence; the essence of an individual person, Peter, not anything like humanity in the abstract. And by *esse* he means the all-embracing predicate which delineates the subject matter of metaphysics. In denying the real distinction he is denying that there is any real difference in Peter between *being* and *being Peter*. These are different predicates we can apply to Peter: we can say 'Peter is Peter' and (in Latin, if not idiomatically in English) 'Peter is'. But in using these two forms of speech we are not referring to two different real items in Peter, as we are when we say 'Peter is tall' and 'Peter is wise'.

Some earlier scholastics, notably Thomas Aquinas, would have said that the sentence which tells us the essence of Peter is not 'Peter is Peter' but rather 'Peter is human'. This was because Aquinas believed that the principle of individuation was matter: what makes two peas two rather than one is not any difference between their properties, but the fact that they are two different lumps of matter. According to Aquinas, in an individual human like Peter there was no extra formal element in addition to humanity which gave him his individuality. For Duns Scotus and his school, on the other hand, Peter possessed, in addition to his humanity, a further individuating feature, his *haecceitas* or 'thisness'. Once again, Suarez wants to side with both his great predecessors. 'The adequate principle of individuation is this matter and this form in union, the form being the chief principle and sufficient by itself for the composite, as an individual thing of a certain species, to be considered numerically one' (*DM* 5. 6, 15). In effect, Suarez comes down definitely on the side of Scotus. There is in Peter a real formal element, a *differentia individualis*, in addition to the specific nature of humanity, which is what makes him Peter and not Paul (*DM* 5. 2, 8–9).

Scotus, as we have just seen, adds an extra metaphysical item to the apparatus employed by Aquinas. Suarez, in his turn, adds an extra item of his own. In Peter we have not just the matter and form which all followers of Aristotle accepted, and not just the individuating element that Scotists accepted, but an extra thing, that makes Peter a substance and not an accident. Subsistence, the form of existence peculiar to substance as opposed to accident, adds to an individuated essence a *mode*, and there is a special form of composition which is that of mode-plus-thing-modified. Suarez employed his notion of mode in an attempt to illuminate the difference between a soul existing embodied and a soul existing in separation after death. But his new terminology was to be widely employed, and made popular, especially by Descartes.

Descartes on Eternal Truths

Descartes took over many of the technical terms of scholastic metaphysics—substance, mode, form, essence, and so on—but used many of them in novel ways. His most important innovation in metaphysics was one that was not fully spelt out in his published works and only became clear when his copious correspondence was made public after his death. This was his doctrine of the creation of eternal truths.

In 1630, when he was completing his treatise *The World*, Descartes wrote to Mersenne:

The mathematical truths that you call eternal have been laid down by God and depend on him entirely as much as all other creatures ... Please do not hesitate to assert and proclaim everywhere that it is God who has laid down these laws in nature just as a king lays down laws in his kingdom. (AT I. 135; *CSMK* III. 23)

As for the eternal truths, I say once more that they are true or possible only because God knows them as true or possible. They are not known as true by God in any way which would imply that they are true independently of Him ... In God willing and knowing are a single thing, in such a way that by the very fact of willing something He knows it, and it is only for this reason that such a thing is true. (AT I. 147; *CSMK* III. 13)

It was a new departure to say that the truths of logic and mathematics depended upon the will of God. Scholastic philosophers agreed that they were dependent on God, but dependent on his essence, not on his will: they did not believe, as Descartes did, that God was free to make it not be true that the three angles of a Euclidean triangle were equal to two right angles (AT IV. 110; *CSMK*. III. 151; Aquinas, *ScG* II. 25). Moreover, scholastics believed that prior to the creation of the world logical and mathematical truths had no reality independent of God; whereas for Descartes these truths were creatures, distinct from God, brought into existence from all eternity by His creative power. 'It is certain that He is no less the author of creatures' essence than he is of their existence; and this essence is nothing other than the eternal truths ... I know that God is the author of everything and that these truths are something and consequently that he is their author' (AT I. 151; *CSMK* III. 25).

For Descartes, the truths of logic and mathematics had their being neither in the material world nor in the mind of anyone, divine or human. The eternal truths were not truths about material objects: theorems about triangles could be proved even if there was not a single triangular object in existence, and geometry held true even if the external world was a complete illusion. The eternal truths were prior to, and independent of, any human minds, and though they were dependent on, they were distinct from, the mind of God. The eternal truths belonged in a third realm of their own, similar to the domain in which in Antiquity Plato had located his Ideas. St Augustine had relocated the Platonic Ideas in the mind of God, and that had been ever since the standard position among Christian philosophers right up to Suarez. Descartes' novel doctrine makes him the founder of modern Platonism.[1]

The theory of the creation of eternal truths plays a fundamental role in Descartes' metaphysics and physics. At the time when he was explaining his

---

[1] For Plato, see above, pp. 46–8. Among scholastics, Henry of Ghent (whom Descartes is most unlikely to have read) came closest to anticipating his position (see above, p. 322).

theory to Mersenne, Descartes was writing a sustained attack on the Aristotelian metaphysics of real qualities and substantial forms. Rejection of substantial forms entailed rejection also of essences, since the two are closely connected in the Aristotelian system—essence being identical with form in the case of immaterial beings, and in the case of material beings consisting of form plus the appropriate matter. Descartes did not reject the terminology of essence as firmly as he rejected that of form and quality, but he reinterpreted it drastically. Essences, as he told Mersenne, are nothing but eternal truths.

In the Aristotelian system it was the forms and essences that provided the element of stability in the flux of phenomena—the stability that was necessary for there to be universally valid scientific knowledge. Having rejected essences and forms, Descartes needed a new foundation for physics, and he found it in the eternal truths. If there are no substantial forms, then what connects one moment of a thing's history to another is nothing but the immutable will of God (AT VII. 80; AT XI. 37).

God has laid down the laws of nature, enshrined in the eternal truths. These include not only the laws of logic and mathematics, but also the law of inertia and other laws of motion. Consequently they provide the foundations of mechanistic physics. But if they are dependent on God's unfettered will, how do we know that they will not change? There can, of course, be no question of God changing his mind; but might he not have decreed from all eternity that at a certain point in time the laws should change? To rule out that possibility, Descartes once again appeals to the notion that God is no deceiver. The veracity of God, in his post-Aristotelian system, is necessary to establish the permanent validity of these clearly and distinctly perceived truths.

The doctrine of the creation of the eternal truths was, as we have said, from one point of view a gigantic innovation. But it can also be looked at as the culmination of a philosophical development which had been taking place throughout the later Middle Ages—the gradual extension of the scope of divine omnipotence. In respect to the determination of moral truths, for instance, Scotus and Ockham had allotted to the divine will a much freer scope than Aquinas had done. In the religious sphere this tendency had been taken to an extreme by Jean Calvin's doctrine of the absolute sovereignty of God, who freely and unaccountably predestines humans to salvation or damnation. Descartes' extension of divine freedom into the realm of logic and mathematics might be seen as the philosophical counterpart of Calvinist absolutism.

Three Notions of Substance

In the Aristotelian system, the notion of substance was all important: all qualities and other properties were accidents belonging to substances, and only substances were real and independent. Descartes, too, assigned to substance a fundamental role. 'Nothing has no qualities or properties,' he wrote, 'so that where we perceive some there must necessarily be a thing or substance on which they depend.' That was a step in the argument from *cogito* to *sum*, to the existence of the first discoverable substance, Descartes' own self. In his *Principles* he offered a definition of substance as 'a thing which so exists that it needs no other thing in order to exist'. Strictly speaking, he observed, only God counted as a substance by this definition, but created substances could be said to be things which need only the concurrence of God in order to exist (AT VIII. 24; *CSMK* I. 210).

For the Aristotelians, there were many different kinds of substances, each specified by a particular substantial form—humans by the form of humanity and so on. According to Descartes there were no such things as substantial forms, and there were only two kinds of substance: mind, or thinking substance, and body, or extended substance. These did not have substantial forms, but they did have essences: the essence of mind was thought and the essence of body was extension. How particular substances of these two kinds are individuated remains unclear in Descartes' system, and in the case of body he sometimes writes as if there was only one single, cosmic, substance, of which the objects we encounter are simply local fragments engaging in local transactions (AT VIII. 54, 61; *CSMK* I. 233, 240).

The Aristotelians believed that substances were visible and tangible entities, accessible to the senses, even though it took the intellect to work out the nature of each substance. When I look at a piece of gold, I am genuinely seeing a substance, though only science can tell me what gold really is. Descartes took a different view. 'We do not have immediate awareness of substances,' he wrote in the *Fourth Replies*, 'rather, from the mere fact that we perceive certain forms or attributes, which must inhere in something in order to have existence, we name the thing in which they exist a substance' (AT VII. 222; *CSMK* II. 156). So substances are not perceptible by the senses—not only their underlying nature, but their very existence, is something to be established only by intellectual inference.

Locke took much further the thesis that substances are imperceptible. The notion of substance, he says, arises from our observation that certain ideas constantly go together. If, to some idea of substance in general, we join 'the simple Idea of a certain dull whitish colour, with certain degrees of Weight, Hardness, Ductility and Fusibility, we have the Idea of Lead' The idea of any particular kind of substance always contains the notion of substance in general; but this is not a real idea, certainly not a clear and distinct one, but only a 'supposition of we know not what support of such qualities which are capable of producing simple Ideas in us; which are commonly called Accidents' (*E*, 295).

The operative part of our idea of a distinct kind of substance, then, will be a complex idea made up of a number of simple ones. The idea of the sun, for instance, is 'an aggregate of those several simple Ideas, Bright, Hot, Roundish, having a constant regular motion, at a certain distance from us, and, perhaps some other' (*E*, 299). The ideas of kinds of substance such as *horse* or *gold* are called 'sortal ideas': collections of simple co-occurent ideas plus the confused idea of the unknown substratum. Particular substances are concrete individuals belonging to these different sorts or species.

The substances of different sorts have essences: to be a man, or to be an oak, is to have the essence of man or the essence of oak. But there are, for Locke, two kinds of essence: real and nominal. The real essence is: 'The real, internal, but generally in substances, unknown constitution of things, whereon their discoverable Qualities depend.' The nominal essence is the collection of simple ideas that have been assembled and attached to names in order to rank things into sorts or species. The nominal essence gives the right to bear a particular name, and nominal essences are largely the arbitrary creation of human language.

In the case of a triangle, the real essence and the nominal essence (*three-sided figure*) are the same. Not so in the case of substances. Locke considers the gold ring on his finger:

It is the real constitution of its insensible Parts, on which depend all those Properties of Colour, Weight, Fusibility, Fixedness etc. which are to be found in it. Which Constitution we know not; and so having no particular Idea of it, have no Name that is the sign of it. But yet it is its Colour, Weight, Fusibility and Fixedness etc. which makes it to be Gold, or gives it a right to that Name, which is therefore its nominal Essence. Since nothing can be called Gold, but what has a conformity of Qualities to that abstract complex Idea, to which that Name is annexed. (*E*, 419)

The real essences of things, like the hidden constitution of gold, are generally unknown to us. Even in the case of a human being we have no more idea of his real essence than a peasant has of the wheels and springs which make a church clock strike (E 440).

Essences belong to sorts, not individuals. Individuals have neither real nor nominal essences. 'Nothing I have', Locke says, ' is essential to me. An accident or Disease, may very much alter my Colour, or Shape; a Fever, or Fall, may take away my Reason, or Memory, or both; and an Apoplexy leave neither Sense, nor Understanding no nor Life' (*E*, 440). The real Locke, it seems to follow, is the underlying, impenetrable, substratum of various properties; something quite other than a human being.

Locke maintains that substance itself is indescribable because it is propertyless. But it seems incredible that someone should argue that substance has no properties precisely because it is what *has* the properties. The thesis that individuals have no nominal essence means that one could identify an individual, A, and then go on to inquire whether that individual did or did not have the properties which would qualify it to be called 'man' or 'mountain' or 'moon'. But how is a propertyless individual to be identified in the first place?

In the Aristotelian tradition there was no such thing as a propertyless substance, a something that could be identified as a particular individual without reference to any sortal. Fido is an identifiable individual only so long as he remains a dog, so long as the sortal 'dog' can be truly applied to him. We cannot ask whether A is the same indidividual as B without asking whether A is the same individual F as B, where 'F' holds a place for some sortal: 'man', 'mountain', or whatever. Locke's confused doctrine of substance led him into insoluble difficulties about identity and individuation: we shall meet them again when we come, in Chapter 8, to consider the topic of personal identity.

Single Necessary Substance

While Locke, in England, evacuated the notion of substance of any significant content, Spinoza, in Holland, had made it the basis of his metaphysical system. One of the first definitions in the *Ethics* reads: 'By substance I mean that which is in itself, and is conceived through itself: that of which a concept can be formed independently of the concept of anything else' (*Eth*, 1). Descartes had defined substance as 'that which requires nothing but itself in order to exist'. Such a definition, Spinoza thought, could apply at most to God; finite minds and bodies, which Descartes counted as substances, needed to be created and conserved by God in order to exist.

Spinoza, like Descartes, links the notion of substance with the notions of attribute and of mode. An attribute is a property conceived to be essential to a substance; a mode is a property only conceivable by reference to a substance. Armed with these definitions, Spinoza proves that there can be at most one substance of a given kind. If there are two or more distinct substances, they must be distinguished from each other either by their attributes or by their modes. They cannot be distinguished by their modes, because substance is prior to mode and therefore any distinction between modes must follow, and cannot create, a distinction between substances. They must therefore be distinguished by their attributes, which they could not be if there were two substances having an attribute in common. Moreover, no substance can cause any other substance, because an effect must have something in common with its cause, and we have just shown that two substances would have to be totally different in kind.

The seventh proposition of Book One of the *Ethics* is 'It belongs to the nature of substance to exist', and its proof runs as follows:

A substance cannot be produced by anything other than itself; it must therefore be its own cause—that is, its essence necessarily involves existence, or it belongs to its nature to exist. (*Eth*, 4)

So far, the word 'God' has not been mentioned in the *Ethics*, except in the introductory definition where it is said to mean infinite substance. By now, however, every reader must suspect where Spinoza is leading him. In the very next proposition we are told that any substance is necessarily infinite. At this point one may feel inclined to object that now that substance has been given such august properties, we cannot take it for granted that there are any substances in existence at all. Spinoza would agree: the first few propositions of the *Ethics* are designed to show that at most one substance exists. Only at proposition 11 does he move on to show that at least one substance exists, namely, God.

Spinoza's treatment of God's existence and nature will be considered in detail in Chapter 10. Here we are concerned with the consequences that he draws for the metaphysics of finite beings. Mind and matter are not substances, for if they were they would present limitations on God and God would not be, as he is, infinite. Everything that there is is in God, and without God nothing else can exist or be conceived. Thought and extension, the defining characteristics of mind and matter, are in fact attributes of God himself, so that God is both a thinking and an extended thing: he is mental and he is bodily (*Eth*, 33). Individual minds and bodies are modes, or particular configurations, of the divine attributes of thought and extension. It is thus that the idea of any individual thing involves the thought of the eternal and infinite essence of God.

All Spinoza's contemporaries agreed that finite substances were dependent on God as their first cause. What Spinoza does is to represent the relationship between God and finite substances not in terms of physical cause and effect, but in the logical terms of subject and predicate. Any apparent statement about a finite substance is in reality a predication about God: the proper way of referring to creatures like us is to use not a noun but an adjective. Indeed the word 'creature' is not really in place: it suggests a distinction between a creator and what he creates, whereas for Spinoza there is no such distinction between God and nature.

The key element in Spinoza's monism is not the doctrine that there is only one substance; it is the collapsing of any distinction between entailment and causation. There is just a single relation of consequence: it is this which unites an effect with its causes and a conclusion with its premiss. Smoke follows from fire in just the same way as a theorem follows from axioms. The laws of nature, therefore, are as necessary and exceptionless as the laws of logic. From any given cause there necessarily follows its effect, and everything is ruled by absolute logical necessity. For most other thinkers causes had to be distinct from their effects. Not so for Spinoza, given his identification of causation with entailment. Just as a proposition entails itself, God is His own cause and He is the immanent, not the transient, cause of all things.

This system is extremely difficult to understand, and may well be ultimately incomprehensible. It is more profitable to follow another line of thought which Spinoza offers in order to explain the structure of the universe. Our bodies, he remarks, are composed of many different parts, varying in kind from each other; the parts may change and vary, and yet each individual retains its nature and identity. 'We may easily proceed thus to infinity, and conceive the whole of nature as one individual, whose parts, that is, all bodies, vary in infinite ways, without any change in the individual as a whole' (*Eth*, 43). This invites us to see the relationship between finite beings and God not in terms of effect and cause but in terms of part and whole.

We often talk of parts of our body as performing actions and undergoing changes—but it is not too difficult to see that this is an improper way of talking. It is not my eyes which see, or my liver which purifies my blood. My eyes and liver do not have a life of their own, and such activities are activities of my whole organism. Philosophers from Aristotle onwards have pointed out that it is more correct to say that I see with my eyes and that my body uses my liver to purify my blood. If we follow Spinoza's hint we will see that he is inviting us to see nature as a single organic whole, of which each of us is a particle and an instrument.

This vision of nature as a single whole, a unified system containing within itself the explanation of all of itself, is found attractive by many people. Many, too, are willing to follow Spinoza in concluding that if the universe contains its own explanation, then everything that happens is determined, and there is no possibility of any sequence of events other than the actual one. 'In nature,' Spinoza says, 'there is nothing contingent; everything is determined, by the necessity of the divine nature, to exist and operate in a certain manner' (*Eth*, 20).

Making Room for Contingency

Of all Spinoza's contemporaries, the philosopher closest to him was Malebranche. Like Spinoza, Malebranche thought that the connection between a cause and its effect must be a necessary one. 'A true cause as I understand it', he wrote, 'is one such that the mind perceives a necessary connection between it and its effects' (*R de V* 6. 2, 3). Many people, having read Hume on causation, believe that before his time it was a unanimous philosophical opinion that there must be a necessary connection between cause and effect. But, in fact, Spinoza and Malebranche were unusual in treating the following of an effect from a cause as being on a par with the following of a conclusion from a premiss. Aquinas, for instance, had insisted that relationship to a cause is no part of the definition of the thing that is caused. He considers an argument purporting to show that things can come into existence without a cause. The argument goes like this:

Nothing prevents a thing's being found without what does not belong to its concept, e.g. a man without whiteness; but the relation of caused to cause does not seem to be part of the concept of existent things: for they can be understood without that. Therefore they can exist without that. (*ST*. 1a, 44. 1)

Aquinas does not accept that things can come into existence without a cause, but he does not find fault with the minor premiss of the argument.

For Spinoza and Malebranche, on the other hand, the necessary connection between cause and effect was indeed a conceptual one. In laying this down as a condition for a true causal relation, both of them realized that they were making it more difficult to find in the world examples of genuine causal relations. Parcels of matter in motion could not be genuine causes. A body could not move itself, because the concept of body did not include that of motion, and no body could move another, for there was no logical relationship between motion in one body and motion in another body. Both Spinoza and Malebranche, in fact, came to the conclusion that there is only one genuine cause operating in the physical world, and that is God.

Malebranche's position, however, was more complicated than Spinoza's. For Spinoza, God was the only cause, not just in the physical world, but in the universe as a whole (since for him mind and extension are two aspects of the same entity). Again, for Spinoza, God is not just the only cause in the universe, but also the only substance, and his existence and his operation are all matters of logical necesssity.

Malebranche, on the other hand, allows that in addition to God and the material world there are finite spirits, which are genuine agents and enjoy a degree of freedom. Human beings, for instance, can direct their thoughts and desires in one direction rather than another. But created spirits are incapable of causing any effect in the natural world. I cannot even move my own arm. It is true that it moves when I will; however, I am not, he says, the natural cause of this movement, but only its occasional cause. That is to say, my internal act of willing provides the occasion for God to cause the movement of my arm in the external world. What goes for parts of my body goes *a fortiori* for other material objects: 'There is a contradiction in saying that you can move your armchair . . . No power can transport it where God does not transport it or place it where God does not place it' (*EM*, 7, 15).

For Malebranche, unlike Spinoza, there is contingency in the physical universe, therefore, but it derives only from the eternal free decree of God. God wills without any change or succession all that will take place in the course of time. He is not (unlike Spinoza's God) necessitated to will the course of natural history, but other than Him there are no other causal agents to introduce contingency into the material world.

Leibniz took issue here with Malebranche and Spinoza: in order to allow for divine and human freedom he wished to make room for contingency throughout the universe. In the *Monadology* Leibniz makes a distinction between truths of reason and truths of fact. Truths of reason are necessary and their opposite is impossible; truths of fact are contingent and their opposite is possible. Truths of reason are ascertained by a logical analysis parallel to the mathematicians' derivation of theorems from axioms and definitions; their ultimate basis is the principle of non-contradiction. Truths of fact are based on a different principle: the principle that nothing is the case without there being a sufficient reason why it should be thus rather than otherwise (G, 6, 612–13).

Leibniz attached great importance to the principle of sufficient reason, which was his own innovation. It is not immediately obvious how to reconcile the statement that truths of fact are contingent with the statement that they rest on the principle of sufficient reason. We discover that consistency is purchased at the price of a new, and minimalist, account of contingency.

On the face of it, human beings seem to have some properties that are necessary and others that are contingent. Antoine is necessarily human, but it is a contingent matter whether he is a bachelor or is married. It was thus that scholastic philosophers distinguished between the essential properties of a substance, and its accidental ones. But this is not at all how Leibniz saw the matter. He believed that every predicate which was, as a matter of fact, true of a particular subject was in some way part of its essence, 'so that whoever understood perfectly the notion of the subject would also judge that the predicate belongs to it' (D VIII).

Consider the history of Alexander the Great, which consists in a series of truths of fact. God, seeing the individual notion of Alexander, sees contained in it all the predicates truly attributable to him: whether he conquered Darius, whether he died a natural death, and so on. The predicate 'conqueror of Darius' must appear in a complete and perfect idea of Alexander. A person of whom that predicate was not true would not be our Alexander but somebody else (D VIII).

Leibniz tells us that necessary truths, such as the truths of geometry and arithmetic, are analytic: 'when a truth is necessary, the reason for it can be found by analysis, that is, by resolving it into simpler ideas and truths until the primary ones are reached.' As an example of how this is to be done, we may take Leibniz's proof that $2 + 2 = 4$. We start with three definitions: (i) $2 = 1 + 1$; (ii) $3 = 2 + 1$; (iii) $4 = 3 + 1$; and the axiom that if equals are substituted for equals the equality remains. We then demonstrate as follows:

$$2 + 2 = 2 + 1 + 1 (\text{df i})$$
$$= 3 + 1 (\text{df ii})$$
$$= 4 (\text{df iii})^2$$

Now truths of fact are not capable of demonstration of this kind; human beings, it seems, can discover them only by empirical investigation. But Leibniz's account of individual notions means that in every statement of fact the predicate is covertly included in the subject. Hence, statements of fact are in a sense analytic. But the analysis necessary to exhibit this would be an infinite one, which only God could complete.

---

[2] As Frege was later to point out, there is a gap in this proof: Leibniz has tacitly assumed that $2 + (1 + 1) = (2 + 1) + 1$, which depends on the associative law for addition.

But if statements of fact are from God's point of view analytic, how can they be contingent? Leibniz answers that the demonstration that their predicates belong to their subjects 'is not as absolute as those of numbers or of geometry, but that it supposes the sequence of things that God has freely chosen and which is founded on the first free decree of God, the import of which is always to do what is most perfect' (D XIII). There are two elements in this answer: first, there is no internal contradiction in the notion of an Alexander who was defeated by Darius, such as there is in the notion of a triangle with four sides. Second, the inclusion of the predicate in the notion of *our* Alexander is the result of a free decree of God to create such a person. To be sure, this makes Alexander's conquest in a sense necessary, but only by moral necessity, not metaphysical necessity. God cannot but choose the best, but this is because of his goodness, not because of any limit on his almighty power (T, 367).

The contingency that we are left with seems very slender. There is nothing contingent about the actual Alexander's possession of each of his properties and going through each event in his life. What is contingent is the existence of this particular Alexander, with this particular history, rather than any of the other possible Alexanders that God might have created. This is something that is contingent even from God's point of view: the only necessary existence is God's own existence.

There is clearly a remarkable notion of identity at work here. If I imagine myself with one hair more on my chin than I have, then on Leibniz's terms I am imagining a different person altogether. Leibniz gave considerable thought to the logic of identity, and enunciated two theorems about it. One is that if A is identical with B, then whatever is true of A is true of B, and whatever is true of B is true of A. The other is that if whatever is true of A is true of B, and vice versa, then A is identical with B. The first principle, though commonly known as 'Leibniz's law', was widely accepted both before and after his time. The second, commonly called the principle of the identity of indiscernibles, has always been more controversial: this is the thesis that no two individuals have all their properties in common. Leibniz himself, when he stated in the *Discourse* (IX) that it was not possible for two substances to resemble each other entirely and differ only numerically, described this as 'a notable paradox'.

He could, however, cite authorities in support. Scholastic Aristotelians had held that the principle of individuation, that is to say what distinguished one individual from another, was matter: two peas, however alike, were two peas and not one because they were two different pieces of matter.[3] As a consequence of this, thinkers like Aquinas had argued that if there were substances that were immaterial—angels, say—then there could be only one of each kind, since there was no matter to distinguish one member of a species from another. Leibniz's doctrine of

---

[3] Above, p. 412.

individual notions or essences forced him to generalize this: all substances, and not just Aquinas' angels, were unique specimens of their kind. He argued that if there were in nature two beings indiscernible from each other, then God would act without sufficient reason in treating one differently from the other (G VII. 393).

Is the principle of the identity of indiscernibles itself necessary or contingent? Leibniz does not seem to have made up his mind. Since, to establish it, he appeals to the principle of sufficient reason, not to that of non-contradiction, it appears contingent; and in a letter he wrote that it was possible to conceive two indiscernible substances, even though it was false to suppose they existed (G VII. 394). In his *New Essays*, however, he says that if two individuals were perfectly alike and indistinguishable there would not be any distinction between them; and he goes on to draw the conclusion that the atomic theory must be false. It was not enough to say that one atom was at a different time and place from another: there must be some internal principle of distinction or there would be only one atom, not two (G V. 214).

Berkeley's Idealism

Leibniz's philosophy is the first systematic presentation since Antiquity of idealism, the theory that reality consists ultimately of mental entities, that is to say immaterial perceivers along with their perceptions. During his lifetime another version of idealism was propounded by Bishop Berkeley. The two systems resemble each other, but there are important differences between them: Leibniz's idealism is a rationalist idealism; Berkeley's is an empiricist idealism. The differences arise from the different starting points of the two philosophers. Before comparing the systems in detail, therefore, we should follow the track of argument by which Berkeley arrives at his destination.

In the second of Berkeley's *Dialogues*, Hylas, having earlier been made to agree that primary and secondary qualities are alike only mental, nonetheless attempts to defend the concept of material substance. His arguments for the existence of matter are swiftly despatched. Matter is not perceived, because it has been agreed that only ideas are perceived. It must, therefore, be something discovered by the reason, not the sense. Shall we say then that it is the cause of ideas? But matter is inert and unthinking; so it cannot be a cause of thought. But perhaps, Hylas pleads, the motions of matter may be an instrument of the supreme cause, God. But matter, having no sensible qualities, cannot have motion or even extension; and surely God, who can act by mere willing, has no need of lifeless tools. Shall we say, as Malebranche did, that matter provides the occasion for God to act? Surely the all-wise one needs no prompting! 'Do you not at length perceive', taunts Philonous, 'that in all these different acceptations of Matter, you have been only supposing you know not what, for no manner of reason, and to no kind of use?' He sums up his argument triumphantly:

Either you perceive the being of Matter immediately or mediately. If immediately, pray inform me by which of the senses you perceive it. If mediately, let me know by what reasoning it is inferred from those things which you perceive immediately. So much for the perception. Then for the Matter itself, I ask whether it is object, *substratum*, cause, instrument or occasion? You have already pleaded for each of these, shifting your notions, and making Matter to appear sometimes in one shape, then in another. And what you have offered hath been disapproved and rejected by yourself. (*BPW*, 184)

If Hylas continues to defend the existence of matter, he does not know what he means by 'matter' or what he means by 'existence' (*BPW*, 187).

I think we must agree that Berkeley has successfully exploded the Lockean notion of substance, with which poor Hylas has been saddled. But suppose that Philonous were to debate not with Hylas but with Aristotle. What answers would he receive? Material substances, he would be told, are indeed perceived by the senses. Take a cat: I can see it, hear it, feel it, smell it, and if I feel so inclined, taste it. It is true that it is not by sense but by intellect that I know what *kind* of substance it is—I know that it is a cat because I have learnt how to classify animals—but that does not mean that I infer by reasoning that it is a cat. So much for material substance; what of matter itself? That too I perceive by the senses, in that the substances we encounter are chunks of matter, matter in this case with the form of cattishness. Prime matter, matter devoid of any form, is indeed not perceptible by any sense; but that is because there is no such thing in reality; prime matter is a philosophical abstraction for the purpose of the analysis of substantial change.[4]

It cannot, of course, be taken for granted that the Aristotelian account of substance and matter can be reconciled with, or adapted to, the progress made by seventeenth-century scientists in the analysis and explanation of motion and change. The point I wish to make here is simply that the traditional notion of substance is not disposed of by Berkeley's demolition of the quite different, internally incoherent, notion propagated by Locke.

The criticism of matter is not in fact essential to the construction of Berkeley's idealism; it merely removes an obstacle to its acceptance. Matter was fantasized in order to be the basis of our ideas. That role in Berkeley's system belongs not to matter but to God. The first premiss of the argument to that conclusion is that human beings know nothing except ideas; and that premiss is stated long before the onslaught on the notion of material substance. The first book of the *Principles* begins thus:

It is evident to any one who takes a survey of the *objects of human knowledge*, that they are either *ideas* actually imprinted on the senses; or else such as are perceived by attending to the

---

[4] See above, p. 154.

passions and operations of the mind; or lastly *ideas* formed by help of memory and imagination. (BPW, 61)

This is surely *not* evident at all. Use the word 'idea', if you wish, in such a broad sense as to make it true that whenever I perceive, remember, or think of X I have an idea of X, and that whenever I learn, believe, or know that *p* I have a corresponding idea. It still does not follow that the objects of all human knowledge are ideas. From the very broad nature of the definition it follows that any cognitive act or state will involve my having ideas; but that does not mean that every cognitive act or state is *about* those ideas, or has those ideas as its *object*. If I see a giraffe, I will, given this terminology, have an idea of a giraffe; but what I see is a giraffe, not an idea. If I think of the larch at the end of my garden, I will, again, have an idea of that tree; but what I am thinking about is the tree, not the idea. To be sure, I can also think of that idea; for instance, I can think that it is a pretty hazy one. But that is quite a different thought, a thought about an idea, not a thought about a tree. In thinking it, I am not thinking that the tree is a pretty hazy one. Ideas, if you must speak of ideas in this way, are the things we think *with*; they are not, in general, the things that we think *about*.

The opening passage quoted from the *Principles* already assumes the idealism that is supposed to be the conclusion of a long argument. Idealism is implicit in the initial confusion between mental acts and their objects. It cannot be said that Berkeley was unaware that this criticism could be levelled. Hylas, near the end of the first Dialogue, makes a distinction between object and sensation. He says:

The sensation I take to be an act of the mind perceiving; besides which, there is something perceived; and this I call the *object*. For example, there is red and yellow on that tulip. But then the act of perceiving those colours is in me only, and not in the tulip. (*BPW*, 158)

Philonous' rejection of this takes a very oblique route. He picks on the word 'act' and proceeds to argue that a sensation—e.g. smelling the tulip—is something passive, not active.

Dubious though that claim is, there is no need for Hylas to controvert it in order to defend his distinction. All he has to do is to substitute the expression 'event in the mind' for 'act of the mind'. But Philonous sails on to his conclusion by substituting the ambiguous word 'perception' for the ambiguous word 'idea', and taking it casually for granted that the object of a perception is a *part* of the perception (*BPW*, 159).

If there is nothing that we can know except ideas, and if ideas can exist only in a mind, then it is not difficult for Berkeley to reach his conclusion that everything that we can know to exist is in the mind of God:

When I deny sensible things an existence out of the mind, I do not mean my mind in particular but all minds. Now it is plain they have an existence exterior to my mind; since I find them by experience to be independent of it. There is therefore some other Mind wherein they exist, during the intervals between the times of my perceiving them: as likewise they did before my birth, and would do after my supposed annihilation. And as the same is true with regard to all other finite created spirits, it necessarily follows that there is an *omnipresent eternal Mind*, which knows and comprehends all things.[5]

In the final dialogue, Berkeley gives Philonous the task of showing that the thesis that nothing exists except ideas in a finite or infinite mind is something that is perfectly compatible with our common-sense beliefs about the world. This involves a heroic reinterpretation of ordinary language. Statements about material substances have to be translated into statements about collections of ideas: a cherry, for instance, is nothing but a congeries of sensible impressions, or ideas perceived by various senses (*BPW*, 211). It is much easier to do this, Philonous argues, than to interpret them as statements about inert Lockean substrata. 'The real things are those very things I see and feel and perceive by my senses ... A piece of sensible bread, for instance, would stay my stomach better than ten thousand times as much of that insensible, unintelligible, real bread you speak of' (A, 192). Only his own phenomenalist system, Berkeley believes, enables one to say truly that snow is white and fire is hot.

A material substance, then, is a collection of sensible ideas of various senses treated as a unit by the mind because of their constant conjunction with each other. This thesis is, according to Berkeley, perfectly consistent with the use of scientific instruments and the framing of natural laws. Such laws state relationships not between things but between phenomena, that is, ideas; and what scientific instruments do is to bring new phenomena for us to relate to the old ones. If we make a distinction between appearance and reality, what we are really doing is contrasting more vivid ideas with less vivid ideas, and comparing the different degrees of voluntary control that accompany our ideas. There is no hidden reality: everything is appearance. That is the doctrine of 'phenomenalism', to use a word which was not invented until the nineteenth century.

Both Leibniz and Berkeley are phenomenalists in the sense that they agree that the material world is a matter of appearance rather than reality. But they give different accounts of the nature of the phenomena, and different explanations of their underlying causes. For the empiricist Berkeley, ideas are not infinitely divisible, since there is a finite limit to the mind's ability to discriminate by the senses. The rationalist Leibniz, on the other hand, rejects such atomism: the phenomenal world has the properties exhibited by geometry and arithmetic. With this difference in the nature of the phenomena goes a difference in their sustaining causes. For Leibniz, the underlying reality is the infinity of animate monads; for Berkeley, it is the single all-comprehending God.

---

[5] Berkeley's proof of the existence of God is considered in detail in Ch. 10.

Hume on Causation

If neither of these two philosophies is in the end credible, this is not due to any lack of ingenuity in their inventors. Rather, the defects in each system can be traced back to a single root: the confused epistemology of ideas, which was bequeathed to rationalists by Descartes and to empiricists by Locke. The philosopher in whose work we can see most fully the consequences of such an epistemology is David Hume. His official system, according to which everything whatever is a mere collection of ideas and impressions, is nothing less than absurd. Nonetheless, Hume's genius is such that despite the distortions and constraints which his system imposed upon him, he was able to make highly significant contributions to philosophy. Nowhere is this more evident than in his treatment of causality.

Prior to Hume, the following propositions about causes were very widely held by philosophers:

1. Every contingent being must have a cause.
2. Cause and effect must resemble each other.
3. Given a cause, its effect must necessarily follow.

The first two propositions were common ground between Aristotelian philosophers and their opponents. Paradigm examples of Aristotelian efficient causes were the generation of living beings and the operation of the four elements. Every animal has parents, and parents and offspring resemble each other: dog begets dog and cat begets cat, and in general like begets like. Fire burns and water dampens: that is, a hot thing makes other things hot and a wet thing makes other things wet; once again, like causes like. Early modern philosophers offered other more subtle examples of causal relations, but they continued to subscribe to propositions (1) and (2).

The third proposition was not quite such a simple matter. Spinoza stated 'Given a determinate cause, the effect follows of necessity' (E I, 3), and Hobbes claimed that when all causal elements of a situation are present, 'it cannot be understood but that the effect is produced'. Aristotle, however, was not so determinist as Spinoza and Hobbes were, and he made a distinction between natural causes and rational causes. A natural cause, like fire, was 'determined to one thing'; a rational cause, such as a human being, had a two-way power, a power that could be exercised or not at will. Even in such a case, Aristotle was willing to link the notions of cause and necessity: the possessor of a rational power, if it has the desire to exercise it, does so of necessity.[6]

Hume sets out to demolish all three of the theses set out above. He does so by altering the standard examples of causation. For him, a typical cause is not an

---

[6] See G. E. M. Anscombe, 'Causality and Determination', in *Metaphysics and the Philosophy of Mind* (Oxford: Blackwell, 1981), pp. 133–47.

agent (like a dog or a stove) but an event (like the rolling of a billiard ball across a table). The change in paradigm is masked by his talking of causes and effects as 'objects'. Strictly speaking, the only events possible in a Humean world are occurrences of ideas and occurrences of impressions; but this rule, fortunately, is not uniformly observed in the discussion. A rule that does hold firm is this: cause and effect must be two events identifiable independently of each other.

In attacking the traditional account of causation, Hume first denies that whatever begins to exist must have a cause of existence:

As all distinct ideas are separable from each other, and as the ideas of cause and effect are evidently distinct, 'twill be easy for us to conceive any object to be non-existent this moment, and existent the next, without conjoining to it the distinct idea of a cause or productive principle. (*T*, 79)

Since the ideas can be separated, so can the objects; so there is no contradiction in there being an actual beginning of existence without a cause. To be sure, 'effect' and 'cause' are correlative terms, like 'husband' and 'wife'. Every effect must have a cause, just as every husband must have a wife. But that does not mean that every event must be caused, any more than that every man must be married.

If there is no absurdity in conceiving something coming into existence without any cause at all, there is *a fortiori* no absurdity in conceiving of it coming into existence without a cause of a particular kind. Anything, Hume says, may produce anything. There is no logical reason to believe that like must be caused by like. 'Where objects are not contrary, nothing hinders them from having that constant conjunction, on which the relation of cause and effect totally depends' (*T*, 173). Because many different effects are logically conceivable as arising from a particular cause, only experience leads us to expect the actual one. But on what basis?

Hume offers three rules by which to judge of causes and effects:

1. The cause and effect must be contiguous in space and time.
2. The cause must be prior to the effect.
3. There must be a constant union betwixt the cause and the effect. (*T*, 173)

The third rule is the most important one: 'Contiguity and succession are not sufficient to make us pronounce any two objects to be cause and effect, unless we perceive that these two relations are preserved in several instances.' But how does this take us further? If the causal relationship was not to be detected in a single instance, how can it be detected in repeated instances?

Hume's answer is that the observation of the constant conjunction produces a new impression *in the mind*. Once we have observed a sufficient number of instances of a B following an A, we feel a determination, when next we encounter an A, to pass on to B. This is the origin of the idea of necessary connection which was expressed in the third of the traditional axioms. Necessity is 'nothing but an internal impression of the mind, or a determination to carry our thoughts from one object to another'. This account enables Hume to claim that once again the thesis is verified that there is no idea without an antecedent impression. The felt expectation of the effect when the cause presents itself, an impression produced by customary conjunction, is the impression from which the idea of necessary connection is derived.

Hume sums up his discussion by offering two definitions of causation. The first is this: a cause is 'an object precedent and contiguous to another, and where all the objects resembling the former are placed in a like relation of priority and contiguity to those objects that resemble the latter'. In this definition nothing is said about necessary connection, and no reference is made to the activity of the mind. Accordingly, we are offered a second definition that makes the philosophical analysis more explicit. A cause is 'an object precedent and contiguous to another, and so united with it in the imagination that the idea of the one determines the mind to form the idea of the other, and the impression of the one to form a more lively idea of the other' (*T*, 170, 172).

There are problems with both these definitions. Take the second one first. The mind, we are told, is 'determined' to form one idea by the presence of another idea. Is there not a circularity here, since 'determination' is not very different from 'causation'? Remember that Hume's theory of necessary connection is supposed to apply to moral necessity as well as to natural necessity, to mental as well as to physical causation. If we go back to the first definition, we need to look more closely at the notion of *resemblance*. If we took Hume's definition literally we would have to deny such things as that my young son's white mouse was the cause of the disappearance of that piece of cheese in his cage; for all white things resemble my mouse, but not all white things cause cheese to disappear. It must be doubtful whether the notion of *resemblance* could be appropriately refined (e.g. by reference to natural kinds) without some tacit reference to causal concepts.

The Response of Kant

Hume's account of causation deserves, and has received, intense philosophical scrutiny. Kant attacked the idea that temporal succession could be used to define causality; rather, we make use of causal notions in order to determine temporal sequence. More recently it has been questioned whether a causeless beginning of existence is conceivable: here, too, it is arguable that we use causal notions in order to determine when things begin.[7] Nonetheless, Hume introduced a completely new approach to the philosophical discussion of causation, and the agenda for that discussion remains to this day the one that he set.

[7] See G. E. M. Anscombe, 'Times, Beginnings and Causes', in *Metaphysics and the Philosophy of Mind*, pp. 148–62.

Kant's response to Hume occurs in the system of principles in the *Critique of Pure Reason*, in a section unhelpfully entitled 'Analogies of Experience'. This section sets out to establish the following thesis: experience is only possible if necessary connections are to be found among our perceptions. There are three stages in the proof, which are called by Kant the first, second, and third analogies. The first two are as follows: (a) If I am to have experience at all I must have experience of an objective realm, and this must contain enduring substances; (b) If I am to have an experience of an objective realm, I must have experience of causally ordered substances. Each of these stages takes off from reflection on our awareness of time: time considered first as duration, and then as succession. The third analogy, which appears as something of an appendix to the argument offered in the first two, arises from a consideration of coexistence in time. Distinct objects which exist at the same time as each other must coexist in space, and if they do so they must form a system of mutual interaction.

Kant begins by pointing out that time itself cannot be perceived. In a momentary sensation considered as an independent atom of experience, there is nothing to show when it occurs, or whether it occurs before or after any other given inner event. We can only be aware of time, then, if we can relate such phenomena to some permanent substratum. Moreover, if there is to be genuine change, as opposed to mere succession, there has to be something that is first one thing and then another. But this permanent element cannot be supplied by our experience, which is itself in constant flux; it must therefore be supplied by something objective, which we may call 'substance'. 'All existence in time and all change in time have to be viewed simply as a mode of the existence of something that remains and persists' (A, 184).

The conclusion of the first analogy is not altogether clear. Does Kant think that he has shown that there must be one single permanent thing behind the flux of experience—something such as an everlasting quantity of conserved matter? Or is his conclusion simply that there must be at least some permanent things, objective entities with non-momentary duration, such as we commonly take rocks and trees to be? Only the latter, weaker, conclusion is necessary in order to refute empiricist atomism.

The second analogy is based on a simple observation, whose significance Kant was the first philosopher to see. If I stand still and watch a ship moving down a river I have a succession of different views: first of the ship upstream, then of it downstream, and so on. But, equally, if I look at a house, there will be a certain succession in my experiences: first, perhaps, I look at the roof, then at the upper and lower floors, and finally at the basement. What is it that distinguishes between a merely subjective succession of phenomena (the various glimpses of the house) and an objective observation of a change (the motion of the ship downstream)? In the one case, but not the other, it would be possible for me at will to reverse the order of perceptions. But there is no basis for making the distinction except some necessary causal regularity:

Let us suppose that there is an event which has nothing preceding it from which it follows according to a rule. All succession in perception would then be only in the apprehension, that is would be merely subjective, and there would be no way to determine which perceptions really came first and which came later. We should then have only a play of impressions relating to no object and it would be impossible in our perceptions to make temporal distinctions between one phenomenon and another. (A, 194)

This shows that there is something deeply wrong with Hume's idea that we first perceive temporal succession between events, and then go on to regard one as cause and one as effect. Matters are the other way round: without relationships between cause and effect we cannot establish order in time. Even if we could, Kant goes on, bare temporal succession is insufficient to account for causality, because cause and effect may be simultaneous. Augustine had long ago said that a foot causes a footprint, not the other way round, and Kant echoes him by saying that a ball laid on a stuffed cushion makes a hollow as soon as it is laid on it, yet the ball is the cause and the hollow is the effect. We know this because every such ball makes a dent, but not every such hollow contains a ball.

The third analogy starts from the same point as the second, but moves in the opposite direction:

I can direct my perception first to the moon and then to the earth, or, conversely, first to the earth and then to the moon; and because the perceptions of these objects can follow each other in either order I say that they are coexistent. (B, 258)

But nothing in either perception tells me that the order between them can be reversed, that is, that they coexist with each other. 'Thus,' Kant concludes, perhaps too swiftly, 'the coexistence of substances in space cannot be known in experience save on the assumption of their reciprocal interaction' (B, 258).

Whatever criticisms may be made of details of Kant's analogies, there is no doubt that they establish that the relation between time and causation is much more complicated than Hume imagined, and that Berkeley's abolition of the notion of substance demolishes along with it the ordered sequence of phenomena, held out by virtue of his idealism as the reality of the world.

Whereas Kant, in *The Critique of Pure Reason*, tried to show the futility of claims to knowledge divorced from the conditioned world of experience, Hegel, especially in *The Phenomenology of Spirit*, tried to establish the authenticity of a metaphysics which would provide unconditioned knowledge of the absolute. In one sense, Hegel's idealism marks the high point of metaphysical speculation, and opponents of metaphysics have often chosen gobbets of his text as examples to illustrate the necessary obscurity and futility of any such enterprise. Yet it is surprisingly difficult to select and present passages from his writings which display insights relevant to the topics that have been the concerns of this chapter. This is not because Hegel lacked genius; it is because of the holism that is the dominant characteristic of his thought. At every level, Hegel maintained, parts can only be understood as parts of a whole. We can have no real knowledge even of the smallest item unless we understand its relationship to the entire universe. There is no truth short of the whole truth. Some of his writings can be quarried for nuggets of golden insight, but his metaphysical system must either be taken as a whole or passed by.

The period between Descartes and Hegel was the great age of metaphysical system-building. In the medieval period there were many gifted metaphysicians, but they did not think of themselves as creating a new system; rather, they offered piecemeal improvements to a system already given by the teaching of the Church and the genius of Aristotle. Descartes, Spinoza, Kant, and Hegel, on the other hand, saw themselves as setting out, for the first time, a complete system to harmonize all the fundamental truths that could be known. It cannot be said that any of them succeeded in this gigantic task; but there is much to be learnt from their heroic failures.

In the nineteenth and twentieth centuries, when Western philosophy split into conflicting traditions on the European continent and in the anglophone world, one tradition adopted the medieval pattern and the other followed the lead of the early modern metaphysicians. In Germany and France, philosophers continued to see it as their task to create a new system which would supersede that of their predecessors. In England and the United States, most philosophers contented themselves with the attempt to clarify or amend particular elements within a framework given us by the work of the natural scientists and the language of our everyday lives. But many philosophers have resisted being judged by either paradigm; and the best way to avoid being obsessed with either is a study of philosophy's history over the long term.

7

Mind and Soul

Descartes on Mind

The area of philosophy that underwent the most significant development in the early modern period was the philosophy of mind. This was due above all to the work of Descartes. Whereas Cartesian physics had a short and inglorious life, Cartesian psychology was widely adopted and to this day its influence remains powerful in the thinking of many who have never read his work or who explicitly reject his system.

Descartes redrew the boundaries between mind and body, and introduced a new way of characterizing the mental. Since his time it has been natural for philosophers and scientists to structure psychology in a way quite different from that employed by his Aristotelian predecessors in the Middle Ages and the Renaissance.[1] This has affected even everyday thinking about human nature and about the natural world.

The Aristotelians regarded mind as the faculty, or set of faculties, that mark off human beings from other animals. Dumb animals share with us certain abilities and activities: dogs, cows, and pigs can all, like us, see and hear and feel; they have in common with us the faculty or faculties of sensation. But only human beings can think abstract thoughts and take rational decisions: they are set off from other animals by the possession of intellect and will. It was these two faculties which, for the Aristotelians, essentially constituted the mind. Intellectual activity was in a particular sense immaterial, whereas sensation was impossible without a material body.

For Descartes and those who followed him, the boundary between mind and matter was set elsewhere. It was consciousness, not intelligence or rationality, that was the defining criterion of the mental: the mind is the realm of whatever is accessible to introspection. So the mind included not only human understanding and willing, but also human seeing, hearing, feeling, pain, and pleasure. Every

---

[1] See Part Two, Ch. 8.

form of human experience, according to Descartes, included an element that was spiritual rather than material, a phenomenal component that was no more than contingently connected with bodily causes, expressions, and mechanisms.

Descartes, like his Aristotelian predecessors, believed that the mind was what distinguished human beings from other animals; but he did so for quite different reasons. For the Aristotelians, the mind was restricted to the intellectual soul, and this was something that only humans possessed. For Descartes, mind extends also to sensation, but only humans had genuine sensation. The bodily machinery that accompanies sensation in human beings may occur also in animal bodies, but in an animal a phenomenon like pain is a purely mechanical event, unaccompanied by any consciousness.

Not many people have followed Descartes in regarding animals as mere machines, but there has been very widespread acceptance of his substitution of consciousness in place of rationality as the defining characteristic of the mental. This has the consequence of making the mind appear a specially private place. The intellectual capacities characteristic of language-users are not marked by any special privacy: another person may know better than I do whether I understand quantum physics or am motivated by ambition. On the other hand, if I want to know what experiences someone is having, I have to give his utterances a special status. If you tell me what you seem to see or hear, or what you are imagining or saying to yourself, what you say cannot be mistaken. Of course it need not be true—you may be lying, or misunderstand the words you are using—but your utterance cannot be erroneous. Experiences, thus, have a certain property of indubitability, and it was this property that Descartes took as the essential feature of thought, and used as the foundation of his epistemological system.[2]

To see the way in which Descartes effects this revolutionary change, we need to go back to the second *Meditation*. Having proved to his own satisfaction that he exists, Descartes goes on to ask: '*What* am I, this I whom I know to exist?' The immediate answer is that I am a thing that thinks (*res cogitans*). 'What is a thing that thinks? It is a thing that doubts, understands, conceives, affirms, denies, wills, refuses, which also imagines and feels' (AT VII. 28; *CSMK* II. 19). As always in Descartes 'thought' is to be understood broadly: thinking is not always to think *that* something or other, and not only intellectual meditation but also volition, sensation, and emotion count as thoughts. No previous author had used the word with such a wide extension, but Descartes did not believe that he was altering the sense of the word. He applied it to unusual items because he believed that they possessed the feature which was the most important characteristic of the usual items, namely, immediate consciousness. 'I use this term to include everything that is within us in such a way that we are immediately conscious of it' (AT VII. 160; *CSMK* II. 113).

---

[2] See above, Ch. 4.

Let us examine in turn the activities that Descartes lists as characteristic of a *res cogitans*. Understanding and conception—the mastery of concepts and the formulation of articulate thoughts—are, for him as for the Aristotelians, operations of the intellect. Thoughts and perceptions that are both clear and distinct are for him operations of the intellect par excellence. The next items, affirming and denying, would have been regarded prior to Descartes as acts of the intellect; but for Descartes the making of judgements is the task not of the intellect but of the will. For instance, understanding the proposition '115 + 28 = 143' is a perception of the intellect, but making the judgement that the proposition is true, actually affirming that 115 plus 28 is 143, is an act of will. The intellect merely provides the ideas which are the content on which the will is to make a judgement (AT VII. 50; *CSMK* II. 34). The mind's consciousness of its own thoughts is not a case of judgement: simply to entertain an idea or set of ideas, without affirming or denying any relation between them and the real world, is not to make a judgement. 'Affirming and denying', then, go not with the preceding items in Descartes' list, 'understanding and conceiving', but rather with the following items, 'willing and refusing'. The will is the faculty for saying 'yes' or 'no' to propositions (about what is the case) and projects (about what to do).

The intellect, then, is the faculty of knowing (*facultas cognoscendi*) and the will is the faculty of choosing (*facultas eligendi*). In many cases the will can choose to refrain from making a judgement about the ideas that the intellect presents. Doubting, too (which comes first in Descartes' list because he is just emerging from his universal doubt), is an act of the will, not of the intellect. However, when the intellectual perception is clear and distinct, doubt is not possible. A clear and distinct perception is one that forces the will, a perception that cannot be doubted however hard one tries. Such is the perception of one's own existence produced by the *cogito*. It is possible, but wrong, for the will to make a judgement in the absence of clear and distinct perception. To avoid error one should suspend judgement until perception achieves the appropriate clarity and distinctness (AT VII. 50; *CSMK* II. 34).

Descartes believed in the freedom of the will; but to understand his teaching we have to recall the distinction between liberty of indifference (the ability to choose between alternatives) and liberty of spontaneity (the ability to follow one's desires). Descartes placed no great value on liberty of indifference: that was only possible when there was a balance of reasons for and against a particular choice. Clear and distinct perception, which left the will with no alternative to assent, took away liberty of indifference but not liberty of spontaneity: 'If we see very clearly that something is good for us it is very difficult—and on my view impossible, as long as one continues in the same thought—to stop the course of our desires.' The human mind is at its best when assenting, spontaneously but not indifferently, to the data of clear and distinct perception.

So much, then, for the faculties of intellect and will. But among the activities of a *res cogitans*, imagination and sensation are listed also. Here it is that Descartes makes his most striking innovation. For Aristotelians, sensation was impossible without a body, because it involved the operation of bodily organs. Descartes sometimes uses the verb 'sentire' in a similar way, when he has not yet weaned his readers off their Aristotelian prejudices. But within the Cartesian system sensation is strictly nothing other than a mode of thought. We have already met the passage where, striving to emerge from his doubt, he says, 'I am now seeing light, hearing a noise, feeling heat. These objects are unreal, for I am asleep; but at least I seem to see, to hear to be warmed. This cannot be unreal, and this is what is properly called my sensation.' Here he seeks to isolate an indubitable immediate experience, the seeming-to-see-a-light that cannot be mistaken, the item that is common to both veridical and hallucinatory experience. This does not involve any judgement: it is a thought that I can have, while refraining, as part of the discipline of Cartesian doubt, from making any judgements at all. But of course the thought *may* be accompanied by judgement, and a person not yet purified of Aristotelianism will indeed accompany it with the erroneous judgement that there are real things in the world which totally resemble my perceptions (AT VII. 437; *CSMK* II. 295).

Human sensation is accompanied and occasioned by motions in the body: vision, for instance, by motions in the extremities of the optic nerves. But such mechanical events are only contingently connected with the purely mental thought, and Descartes can be certain of the occurrence of his sensations at a stage when he still doubts whether he has a body and whether there is an external world. It is only after meditation on the veracity of God, and the nature of the faculties God has given him, that he is in a position to pronounce upon the mechanical element involved in the sensations occurring in an embodied mind.

The same mechanical motions may occur in the body of a non-human animal. If we like, we can call these sensations in a broad sense. But an animal cannot have thoughts, and it is thought in which sensation, strictly so called, consists. It follows that, for Descartes, an animal cannot suffer pain, though the machine of its body may cause it to react in a way which, in a human, would be the expression of a pain:

I see no argument for animals having thoughts except that fact that since they have eyes, ears, tongues and other sense-organs like ours it seems likely that they have sensations like us; and since thought is included in our mode of sensation, similar thought seems to be attributable to them. This argument, which is very obvious, has taken possession of the minds of all men from their earliest age. But there are other arguments, stronger and more numerous, but not so obvious to everyone, which strongly urge the opposite.

The doctrine that animals have no feelings and no consciousness did not seem as shocking to Descartes' contemporaries as it does to most people nowadays. But people reacted with horror when some of his followers claimed that human beings, no less than animals, were only complicated machines.

Dualism and its Discontents

In human beings, Descartes argues for a sharp distinction between mind and body. In the sixth *Meditation* he says that he knows that if he can clearly and distinctly understand one thing without another, that shows that the two things are distinct, because God at least can separate them. Since he knows that he exists, but observes nothing else as belonging to his nature other than that he is a thinking thing, he concludes that his nature or essence consists simply in being a thinking thing; he is really distinct from his body and can exist without it. In considering this argument, it is hard to avoid the conclusion that Descartes is confusing 'I can clearly and distinctly perceive A without clearly and distinctly perceiving B' with 'I can clearly and distinctly perceive A without B.'

As a matter of contingent fact, human beings in this world are, Descartes agrees, compounds of mind and body. But the nature of this composition, this 'intimate union' between mind and body, is one of the most puzzling features of the Cartesian system. The matter is made even more obscure, when we are told (AT XI. 353; *CSMK* I. 340) that the mind is not directly affected by any part of the body other than the pineal gland in the brain. All sensations and emotions consist of motions in the body which travel through the nerves to this gland and there give a signal to the mind which occasions a certain experience.

Descartes explains the mechanism of vision as follows:

If we see some animal approach us, the light reflected from its body depicts two images of it, one in each of our eyes, and these two images form two others, by means of the optic nerves, in the interior surface of the brain which faces its cavities; then from there, by means of the vital fluids with which its cavities are filled, these images so radiate towards the little gland that is surrounded by these fluids, that the movement that forms each point of one of the images tends towards the same point of the gland towards which tends the movement that forms the point of the other images which represents the same part of this animal. By this means the two images which are in the brain form but one upon the gland, which, acting immediately on the soul, causes it to see the form of this animal. (AT IX. 355; *CSMK* I. 341)

To speak of the soul as seeing, or reading off, images in the brain is to imagine the soul as a little human being or homunculus. This is a fallacy that Descartes himself warned against in his *Dioptrics* when he was describing the formation of retinal images. These images, he informed the reader, were part of the process of conveying information from the world to the brain, and they retained a degree of resemblance to the objects from which they originated. 'We must not think', he warned, 'that it is by means of this resemblance that the image makes us aware of the objects—as though we had another pair of eyes to see it, inside our brain.'

But the homunculus fallacy is no less involved in treating the transaction between the soul and the pineal gland as if it was a case of seeing or reading. The interaction between mind and matter is philosophically as puzzling a few centimetres behind the eye as it is in the eye itself. The mind–body problem is not solved, but merely miniaturized, by the introduction of the pineal gland.

Interaction between mind and matter, as conceived by Descartes, is highly mysterious. The only form of material causation in Descartes' physical system is the communication of motion, and the mind is not the kind of thing to move around in space. 'How can soul move body?' Princess Elizabeth asked. Surely, motion involves contact, and contact involves extension, and the soul is unextended. Descartes, in reply, told her to think of weight, of the heaviness of a body which pushed it downward without there being any surface contact involved. But this conception of weight, as Elizabeth was quick to point out, was one that Descartes himself regarded as a scholastic muddle. After a few more exchanges, Descartes was reduced to telling the princess not to bother her pretty head further about the problem.

Elizabeth had, in fact, located the fundamental weakness in Descartes' philosophy of mind. Descartes' system was dualist, that is to say, it was tantamount to belief in two separate worlds—the physical world containing matter, and a psychical world containing private mental events. The two worlds are defined and described in such systematically different ways that mental and physical realities can interact, if at all, only in a mysterious manner that transcends the normal rules of causality and evidence. Such dualism is a fundamentally mistaken philosophy. The incoherence spotted by Princess Elizabeth was to be pointed out with exhaustive patience in later centuries by Kant and Wittgenstein. But Cartesian dualism is still alive and well in the twenty-first century.

Determinism, Freedom, and Compatibilism

In Descartes' own time the most vociferous critic of dualism was the materialist Thomas Hobbes, who denied the existence of any non-extended, spiritual entities like the Cartesian mind. Whereas Descartes exaggerated the difference between humans and animals, Hobbes minimized it. He described human action as a particular form of animal behaviour. There are two kinds of motion in animals, he says, one called vital and one called voluntary. Vital motions include breathing, digestion, and the course of the blood. Voluntary motion is 'to go, to speak, to move any of our limbs, in such manner as is first fancied in our minds'. The operations that Descartes (and the Aristotelians before him) attributed to reason are by Hobbes assigned to the imagination, a faculty common to all animals that is purely material, all thoughts of any kind being small motions in the head. If a particular imagining is caused by words or other signs, it is called 'understanding'.

But this too is common to all animals, 'for a dog by custom will understand the call or the rating of his Master, and so will many other Beasts' (*L*, 3, 10).

The difference between animals and humans here is simply that when a man imagines a thing, he goes on to wonder what he can do with it. But this is a matter of will, not intellect. Not that the will is a faculty peculiar to humans: a will is simply a desire, the desire that comes last at the end of a train of deliberation, and 'beasts that have deliberation must necessarily also have will'. Human and animal desires are alike consequences of mechanical forces. The difference is simply that humans have a wider repertoire of wants, in the service of which they employ their imaginations. The freedom of the will is no greater in humans than in animals.

This thesis caused great offence, and led to a celebrated debate with John Bramhall, a royalist Bishop of Derry who had shared Hobbes' exile.[3] Hobbes insisted, 'Such a liberty as is free from necessity is not to be found in the will either of men or of beasts.' He claimed, however, that liberty and necessity were not necessarily incompatible:

Liberty and Necessity are Consistent: as in the water, that hath not only liberty, but a necessity of descending by the Channel; so likewise in the Actions which men voluntarily do; which, because they proceed from their will, proceed from liberty; and yet, because every act of man's will, and every desire and inclination proceedeth from some cause, and that from another cause, in a continuall chaine, whose first link is in the hand of God, first of all causes, they proceeed from necessity. (*L*, 140)

'This is a brutish liberty,' Bramhall objected, 'such a liberty as a bird hath to fly when her wings are clipped. Is not this a ridiculous liberty?' Hobbes replied that a man was free to follow his will, but was not free to will. The will to write, for instance, or the will to forbear from writing, did not come upon a person as a result of some previous will. 'He that cannot understand the difference between *free to do it if he will* and *free to will* is not fit', Hobbes snorted, 'to hear this controversy disputed, much less to be a writer in it.'

Hobbes' account of liberty gives him a claim to be the founder of the doctrine called 'compatibilism', the thesis that freedom and determinism are compatible with each other. He presents it in a crude form which, as Bramhall pointed out, fails to do justice to the obvious differences between the modes of action of inanimate agents and of rational agents like human beings. His version depends on a linear model of causation as a series of events following in sequence, each linked to the next by a causal relation. Thus my action is preceded and caused by my willing, which is preceded and caused by my deliberation, which is preceded and caused by a series of motions outside my control which terminates ultimately in the primal causation by

---

[3] Published in 1663 as *The Questions Concerning Liberty, Necessity and Chance*, from which the following quotations are taken.

God. My action is free, because the event which immediately precedes it is an act of will; it is necessitated, because it comes at the end of a series each of whose items is a necessary consequence of its predecessor.

There are problems with the notion of a series which alternates in this manner between mental and physical events. It is true that for Hobbes mental events (a thought or a will) do not take place, as they did for Descartes, in a spiritual realm outside material space; for him all the motions of the mind are actually motions in the body. But there are further problems, which later philosophers would explore, in simply identifying mental and physical events in this manner. Moreover, in many cases of voluntary behaviour, there is in advance of the action no identifiable mental event to fulfil the causal role that Hobbes' version of compatibilism requires of the will. The pros and cons of compatibilism are better evaluated in the versions developed by later, more sophisticated, thinkers such as Immanuel Kant.[4]

Locke's treatment of the will is already an improvement on Hobbes. We find in ourselves, he says, a power to begin or forbear actions of our minds and bodies 'barely by a thought or preference of the mind ordering, or as it were commanding the doing or not doing such or such a particular action'. This power is what we call the will, and the exercise of such a power—the issuing of such an order—is volition, or willing. An action in obedience to such an order is what is called voluntary. Whenever a man has a power to think, or not to think, to move or not to move, in accordance with the direction of his mind, he is so far free (E, 236–7).

Liberty or freedom requires two things: a volition to act, and a power to act or forbear. A tennis ball is not free, because it has neither of these. A man who falls from a broken bridge has a volition to stop falling, but no power to do so; his fall is not a free action. Even if I have a volition to do something, and am actually doing it, that may not be enough to make my action a free one:

Suppose a man be carried, whilst fast asleep, into a Room, where is a person he longs to see and speak with; and be there locked fast in, beyond his Power to get out: he awakes, and is glad to find himself in so desirable a Company, which he stays willingly in, i.e. prefers his stay to going away. I ask, Is not this stay voluntary? I think, no Body will doubt it: and yet being locked fast in, 'tis evident he is not at liberty not to stay, he has not freedom to be gone. (E, 238)

This shows that an action may be voluntary without being free. Freedom is the opposite of necessity, but voluntariness is compatible with necessity. A man may prefer the state he is in to its absence or change, even though necessity has made it inalterable. But although voluntariness is not a sufficient condition for freedom, it is an essential prerequisite. Agents that have no thought or volition at all are all necessary agents.

What are we to make of the question whether the human will is free or not? Locke tells us that the question is as improper as asking whether sleep is swift or virtue is

---

[4] See below, p. 683, and my *Will, Freedom and Power* (Oxford: Blackwell, 1975), pp. 145–61.

square. The will is a power, not an agent, and liberty belongs only to agents. When we talk of the will as a faculty, we should beware of personifying it. We can, if we wish, talk of a singing faculty and a dancing faculty; but it would be absurd to say that the singing faculty sings or that the dancing faculty; dances. It is no less foolish to say that the will chooses, or is free.

Here, Locke seems to be avoiding the question that preoccupied Hobbes. On Locke's own account a volition is an act of the mind directing or restraining a particular action. Can we say that the agent is free to perform or forbear such a particular act of the mind? Locke states as a general proposition, that if a particular thought is such that we have power to take it up, or lay it by, at our preference, then we are at liberty. But volition, he says, is not such a thought. 'A man in respect of willing, or the Act of Volition, when any action in his power is once proposed to his Thoughts, as presently to be done cannot be free' (*E*, 245).

It is not just that we cannot, during waking life, help willing something or other; we cannot, Locke says, help the particular volitions that we have. 'To ask whether a Man be at liberty to will either Motion or Rest; Speaking or Silence; which he pleases, is to ask, whether a man can will what he wills'—and this is a question that needs no answer. Here, Locke seems to be guilty of a fallacy which trapped other great philosophers: the invalid argument from the true premiss 'Necessarily, if I prefer X, I prefer X', to the dubious conclusion 'If I prefer X, I necessarily prefer X'.

But Locke has a positive reason for denying liberty to the choices of the will. Every choice to perform an action, he maintains, is determined by a preceding mental state: one of uneasiness at the present state of things. Uneasiness alone acts on the will and determines its choices. We are constantly beset with sundry uneasinesses, and the most pressing one of those that are removable 'determines the will successively in that train of voluntary actions which make up our lives'. The most we can do is to suspend the execution of a particular desire while we decide whether to act on it would make us happy in the long run. This, Locke says, is the source of all liberty, and this is what is called (improperly) free will. But once the pros and cons have been weighed up, the resulting desire will determine the will (*E*, 250–63).

Locke is aware that the objection can be made to his system that a man is not free at all, if he be not as free to will, as he is to act what he wills. He does not offer a direct answer to this objection; instead he considers at length what are the factors which lead people to make wrong choices. His principal explanation is the same as that given by Plato in the *Protagoras*: that, by the intellectual equivalent of an optical illusion, we misjudge the proportion between present pains and pleasures and future pains and pleasures. He illustrates this with the example of a hangover:

Were the Pleasure of Drinking accompanied, the very moment a Man takes off his Glass, with that sick Stomack, and aking Head, which in some Men are sure to follow not many hours after, I think no body, whatever Pleasure he had in his Cups, would, on these

Conditions, ever let Wine touch his Lips; which yet he daily swallows, and the evil side comes to be chosen only by the fallacy of a little difference in time. (*E*, 276)

Locke on Personal Identity

Locke's most influential contribution to the philosophical study of human beings concerned not the freedom of the will, but the nature of personal identity. In discussing identity and diversity, Locke accepts that identity is relative rather than absolute: A may be the same F as B, but not the same G as B. The criterion for the identity of a mass of matter (no particles added and no particles taken away) is not the same as the criterion for the identity of a living being:

In the state of living Creatures, their Identity depends not on a Mass of the same Particles; but on something else. For in them the variation of great parcels of Matter alters not the Identity: An Oak, growing from a Plant to a great Tree, and then lopp'd, is still the same Oak; and a Colt grown up to a Horse, sometimes fat, sometimes lean, is all the while the same Horse: though, in both these Cases, there may be a manifest change of the parts: So that truly they are not either of them the same Masses of Matter, though they be truly one of them the same Oak, and the other the same Horse. (*E*, 330)

The identity of plants and animals consists in continuous life in accordance with the characteristic metabolism of the organism. Human beings are animal organisms, and Locke offers a similar account of 'the Identity of the same *Man*'. (By 'man' of course he means a human being of either sex.) The identity of a human being consists in 'nothing but a participation of the same continued Life by constantly fleeting Particles of Matter, in succession vitally united to the same organized Body'. Only such a definition, he says, will enable us to accept that an embryo and 'one of years, mad and sober' can be one and the same man, without having to accept wildly improbable cases of identity.

So far, Locke's definition of human identity seems sound and straightforward; but it is complicated by his having to position himself with respect to ancient theories of the reincarnation and transmigration of souls, together with Christian doctrines of the survival of disembodied souls and the eventual resurrection of long-dead bodies. We cannot, Locke says, base our account of the identity of a human being on the identity of a human soul. For if souls can pass from one body to another, we cannot be sure that Socrates, Pontius Pilate, and Cesare Borgia are not the same man. Some have supposed that the souls of wicked men—such as the Roman Emperor Heliogabalus—were sent as a punishment after death into the bodies of brutes. 'But yet I think no body, could he be sure that the Soul of Heliogabalus were in one of his Hogs, would yet say that Hog were a man or Heliogabalus' (*E*, 332). A man is an animal of a certain kind, indeed of a certain shape. However rational and intelligent a parrot might turn out to be, it would still not be a man.

However, settling the question of human identity does not yet settle the nature of personal identity. Locke distinguishes the concept *man* from the concept *person*. A person is 'a thinking intelligent Being, that has reason and reflection, and can consider it self as itself, the same thinking thing in different times and places'. Self-consciousness is the mark of a person, and the identity of a person is the identity of self-consciousness. 'As far as this consciousness can be extended backwards to any past Action or Thought, so far reaches the Identity of that Person; it is the same *self* now as it was then; and 'tis by the same *self* with this present one that now reflects on it, that that Action was done' (*E*, 335).

So if we want to know whether A (at this moment) is the same person as B (some time ago) we ask whether A's consciousness extends back to the actions of B. If so, A is the same person as B; if not, not. But what is it for a consciousness to extend backward in time? It seems unobjectionable to say that my consciousness extends backwards for so long as this consciousness had a continuous history. But what makes *this* consciousness the individual consciousness it is? Locke cannot reply that *this* consciousness is the consciousness of *this* human being, because of the distinction he has made between *man* and *person*.

So it seems that Locke must say that my present consciousness extends backwards so far, and only so far, as I remember. He accepts that this means that if I remember the experiences of a human being that lived before my birth, then I am the same person as that man:

Whatever has the consciousness of present and past Actions, is the same Person to whom they both belong. Had I the same consciousness that I saw the Ark and Noah's Flood, as that I saw an overflowing of the Thames last Winter, or as that I write now, I could no more doubt that I, that write this now, that saw the Thames overflow'd last Winter, and that view'd the Flood at the general Deluge, was the same self... than that I that write this am the same *my self* now whilst I write... that I was Yesterday. (*E*, 341)

The converse of this is that my past is no longer my past if I forget it, and I can disown actions I no longer recall. I am not the same person, but only the same man, who did the actions I have forgotten.

Locke believes that punishment and reward attached not to the man, but to the person: it seems to follow that I should not be punished for actions I have forgotten. Locke seems willing to accept this, though the example he chooses to illustrate his acceptance is a very particular case, tendentiously selected. If a man has fits of madness, he says, human laws do not punish 'the mad man for the sober man's actions; nor the sober man for what the mad man did, thereby making them two persons'. But Locke seems unwilling to contemplate the further consequences of his thesis that if I erroneously think I remember being King Herod ordering the massacre of the innocents then I can be justly punished for their murder. A consequence that can be drawn from Locke's definition of a person is that very young infants, who have not yet acquired self-consciousness, are not yet persons and therefore do not enjoy the human rights and legal protections that persons enjoy. Philosophers in later ages have drawn this consequence—some treating it as a *reductio ad absurdum* of Locke's distinction between persons and humans, others treating it as a legitimation of infanticide.

It is not only ethical considerations, however, that may make one hesitate to accept Locke's identification of personality with self-consciousness. The main difficulty—ably presented in the eighteenth century by Bishop Joseph Butler—arises in connection with the role that Locke assigns to memory. If a person, call her Titia, claims to remember doing something, or being somewhere, we can check whether her memory is accurate by investigating whether she actually did the deed or was present on the appropriate occasion. We do this by tracing the history of her body. But if Locke is right, this will tell us nothing about the person Titia, but only about the human being Titia. Nor can Titia herself, from within, distinguish between genuine memories and present images of past events which offer themselves delusively as memories. Locke's account of self-consciousness makes it difficult to draw the distinction between veracious and deceptive memories at all. The distinction can only be made if we are willing to join together what Locke has put asunder and recognize that persons are human beings.

Whatever the merits of Locke's distinction between persons and humans, it does not exhaust the complication of his account of personal identity, because he includes a third category, that of spirits. According to Locke, I am at the same time a man (a human animal), a spirit (a soul or immaterial substance), and a person (a centre of self-consciousness). These three entities are all distinguishable, and Locke rings the changes on various combinations of them. The soul of Heliogabalus translated into one of his hogs gives us a case of one spirit in two bodies. One spirit might be united to two persons: Locke had a friend who thought he had inherited the soul of Socrates, though he had no memory of any of Socrates' experiences. On the other hand, if the present mayor of Queensborough had conscious recall of the life of Socrates, we would have two spirits in one person. Locke proposes more complicated combinations which we need not explore. There are many difficulties, by no means peculiar to Locke's system, in the whole notion of a soul considered as an immaterial, spiritual substance, and few of Locke's modern admirers wish to preserve this part of his theory of personal identity.

The Soul as the Idea of the Body in Spinoza

The relation between soul and body, which was problematic in Descartes and Locke, becomes more obscure than ever when we turn to Spinoza. The way in which Spinoza states it, however, sounds beautifully simple: the soul is the idea of the body. What this means is not obvious; but it is at least clear that Spinoza thinks that in order to understand the soul we have first to understand the body (*Eth*, 40). Human beings are bodies, related to and limited by other bodies; all these bodies are modes of the divine attribute of extension. Every body, and every part of every body, is represented by an idea in the mind of God; that is to say, to every item in the divine attribute of extension there corresponds an item in the divine attribute of thought. The item of divine thought that corresponds to the item of divine extension which is Peter's body is what constitutes Peter's mind. It follows, Spinoza says, that the human mind is part of the infinite intellect of God (*Eth*, 39).

What exactly is the 'correspondence' which constitutes the relationship between an individual soul and an individual body? It is, for Spinoza, nothing less than identity. Peter's soul and Peter's body are one and the same thing, looked at from two different points of view. Thinking substance and extended substance, he has told us, are one and the same substance—namely God—looked at now under one attribute, now under another (*Eth*, 35). The same goes for modes of these attributes. Peter's soul is a mode of the attribute of thinking, and Peter's body is a mode of the attribute of extension: they are both one and the same thing, expressed in two ways. This doctrine is meant to exclude the problem that bedevilled Descartes, namely, how to explain the manner in which soul and body interact. They do not interact at all, Spinoza answers: they are the very same thing.[5]

The human body is composed of a great number of parts, each of them complex and capable of modification by other bodies in various ways. The idea that constitutes the mind is likewise complex, compounded of a great number of ideas (*Eth*, 44). The mind, Spinoza says, perceives absolutely everything that takes place in the body (*Eth*, 39). This rather surprising statement is qualified by a later proposition (*Eth*, 47) which states that the human mind has no knowledge of the body, and does not know it to exist, except through the ideas of the modifications whereby the body is affected. We are left wondering why there may not be—as common sense suggests—processes in the body of which the mind is unaware. Why does there have to be an idea corresponding to every bodily event?

Spinoza does indeed agree that there is a lot that we do not know about bodies. The mind, he says, is capable of perceiving many things other than its own body, in proportion to the many ways in which the body is capable of receiving impressions. The ideas which go through my mind when I perceive involve the natures both of my own body and of other bodies. It follows, Spinoza says, that the ideas that we have of external bodies indicate rather the constitution of our own body than the nature of external bodies (*Eth*, 45). Further, the mind only knows

---

[5] It is not clear how this metaphysical thesis is to be reconciled with the epistemological thesis that the idea of X is something quite distinct from X; perhaps we have a case of the ambiguity of 'idea of X' identified above on p. 651.

itself in so far as it perceives the ideas of the modifications of the body. These ideas are not clear and distinct, and the sum of our ideas does not give us an adequate knowledge of other bodies, or of our own bodies, or of our own souls (*Eth*, 51). 'The human mind, when it perceives things after the common order of nature, has not an adequate but only a confused and fragmentary knowledge of itself, of its own body, and of external bodies' (*Eth*, 51).

Spinoza's account of the soul as the idea of the body gives rise to a question that has perplexed many a reader. What, we may wonder, is supposed to individuate the soul of Peter, and makes it the soul of Peter and not of Paul? Ideas are naturally thought to be individuated by belonging to, or inhering in, particular thinkers: my idea of the sun is distinct from your idea of the sun, simply because it is mine and not yours. But Spinoza cannot say this, since all ideas belong only to God. It must, then, be the content, not the possessor, of the idea that individuates it. But there are ideas of Peter's body in many minds other than Peter's mind: how then can the idea of Peter's body be Peter's soul?

Spinoza responds:

We clearly understand what is the difference between the idea, say, of Peter, which constitutes the essence of Peter's mind, and the idea of the same Peter, which is in another man, say Paul. The former directly expresses the essence of Peter's own body, and involves existence only as long as Peter exists; but the latter indicates the constitution of Paul's body rather than the nature of Peter, and therefore, as long as that disposition lasts, contemplates Peter as present even though Peter may not exist. (*Eth*, 46)

The crucial passage here is the statement that the idea of Peter that is Peter's soul 'involves existence only as long as Peter exists'. Does this mean that Peter's soul goes out of existence when Peter does? This would seem to follow from Spinoza's statements that a human being consists of body and soul, and that body and soul are the same thing under two different aspects. Peter, Peter's soul, and Peter's body should, on this account, come into and go out of existence together. But if we ask whether the soul is immortal, Spinoza does not give a totally unequivocal answer. On the one hand, he says 'our mind can only be said to last as long as our body lasts'—but this remark occurs in a footnote to a proposition that reads 'the human mind cannot be totally destroyed with the body, but something of it remains that is eternal' (*Eth*, 172). But this turns out really only to mean that since our soul is an idea, and all ideas are ultimately in the mind of God, and God is eternal, there never was or will be a time when our soul was totally non-existent. Our life is but an episode in the eternal life of God, and when we die that life persists. This is something very different from the personal survival in an afterlife which was the aspiration of popular piety.

In proclaiming that body and mind are a single thing, Spinoza can perhaps be said to have founded a school that persists to this day: the school that maintains that the relationship between mind and body is one of identity. But his teaching is so entwined with his more general thesis of the identity between God and nature that it is difficult to make exact comparisons between his thesis and that of later identity theorists. It is much easier to place Spinoza in connection with another fundamental thesis of his philosophy of mind, namely, psychological determinism.

Like Hobbes, Spinoza believes that every one of our thoughts and actions is predetermined by a necessity as rigid as the necessity of logical consequence. Spinoza indeed believed that the necessity of our lives *was* the necessity of logical consequence, in virtue of his general theory that the order of things and the order of ideas are one and the same. 'All things follow from the eternal decree of God by the same necessity, as it follows from the essence of a triangle, that the three angles are equal to two right angles' (*Eth*, 14). But the upshot is the same for both philosophers: freedom of the will is an illusion begotten of ignorance:

Men are mistaken in thinking themselves free; their opinion is made up of consciousness of their own actions, and ignorance of the causes by which they are determined. Their idea of freedom is simply their lack of knowledge of any cause for their actions. (*Eth*, 53)

Hobbes and many who would later follow him argued that though we are free to do what we will, we are not free to will what we will. Here again, Spinoza goes further: there is no such thing as the will:

When people say that human actions depend on the will, these are mere words to which no idea corresponds. What the will is, and how it moves the body, they none of them know; and when they go on to imagine seats and domiciles for the soul, they provoke ridicule or nausea. (*Eth*, 53)

Here Spinoza's target is Descartes, who located the soul in the pineal gland, and who placed great importance on the distinction between the intellect and the will. For Spinoza, there is no faculty of the will; there are indeed individual volitions, but these are merely ideas, caused by previous ideas, which have in their turn been determined by other ideas, and so on ad infinitum. Activities which Descartes attributed to the will—such as making or suspending judgements—are part and parcel of the series of ideas, they are perceptions or the lack thereof. A particular volition and a particular idea are one and the same thing, therefore will and understanding are one and the same (*Eth*, 63).

Leibniz's Monadology

Spinoza's amalgamation of intellect and will, and his identification of soul and body as aspects of a single substance, were among the elements of his philosophy that were unpicked by Leibniz. But Leibniz did not return to Descartes' system in which mind and matter were the two contrasting elements of a dualistic universe.

Instead, he gave mind a status of unprecedented privilege. In the Cartesian partnership of mind and matter, of course, mind had always held the senior position; but for Leibniz, matter is no more than a sleeping partner.

In the *Discourse* Leibniz takes issue with Descartes' fundamental claim that matter is extension:

> The nature of body does not consist merely in extension, that is, in size, shape, and motion, but we must necessarily recognize in body something akin to souls, something we commonly call substantial form, even though it makes no change in the phenomena, any more than do the souls of animals, if they have any. (*D*, 12)

The notions of extension and motion, Leibniz went on to argue, were not as distinct as Descartes thought: the notions of these primary qualities contained a subjective element no less than secondary qualities such as colour and heat. This was a theme later to be developed by Berkeley.[6]

Leibniz had two main arguments against the identification of matter with extension. First, if there were nothing in matter but size and shape, he argued, bodies would offer no resistance to each other. A rolling pebble colliding with a stationary boulder would put the boulder into motion without losing anything of its own force. Second, if matter was mere extension, we could never identify individual bodies at all, for extension is infinitely divisible. At whatever point we stop in our division we meet only an aggregate—and an aggregate (e.g. the pair formed by the diamond of the Great Mogul and the diamond of the Grand Duke) is only an imaginary object, not a real being. Only something resembling a soul can confer individual unity on a body and give it a power of activity (*D*, 21; G II. 97).

For these reasons Leibniz felt compelled to re-admit into philosophy the substantial forms which were so despised by fashionable philosophers, and he adopted a name for them which advertised their Aristotelian origin, namely 'entelechy'. But he differed from contemporary Aristotelians in two ways. First, he thought that while substantial forms were necessary to explain the behaviour of bodies, they were not sufficient; for the explanation of particular phenomena one must have recourse to the mathematical and mechanical theories of current corpuscular science. If asked how a clock tells the time, he said, it would be futile to say they had a horodictic faculty rather than explaining how the weights and wheels worked (*D*, 10; G V. 61). Second, he thought that in a human being there was not just one substantial form but an infinite number: each organ of the body had its own entelechy, and each organ was, he told Arnauld, 'full of an infinite number of other corporeal substances endowed with their own entelechies' (G II. 120).

The great gap which Leibniz saw in Descartes' system was the lack of the notion of *force*. 'The idea of energy or virtue,' he wrote in 1691, 'called by the Germans *Kraft* and by the French *la force*, to explain which I have projected a special science

---

[6] See above, p. 610.

of dynamics, throws a lot of light on the true understanding of substance' (G IV. 469). It was for this reason that the notion of substantial form had to be rehabilitated. Once the role of force was appreciated, it was matter, not form, that turned out to be illusory. Cartesian extension was a pure phenomenon, he told Arnauld, like a rainbow.[7]

Leibniz was, however, still trapped in Descartes' false dichotomy of mind and matter. Because force could find no place in a world of mere extension, he located it in the realm of the mental. He thought of it as a form of appetition analogous to human desire and volition. This comes out most clearly in the mature form of his philosophy presented in his *Monadology*. The monads or entelechies which are the basis of his system have the properties only of mind. The inert bodies that we see and feel around us are only phenomena, aggregates of invisible, intangible monads. They are not illusory entities—they are, in Leibniz's phrase, well-founded phenomena. But the only true substances are the monads.

Monads are independent, indivisible, and unrepeatable. Having no parts, they cannot grow or decay; they can only be created or annihilated. They can change, but only in the way that souls can change. As they have no physical properties to alter, their changes must be changes of mental states. The life of a monad, Leibniz tells us, is a series of perceptions. A perception is an internal state that is a representation of other items in the universe. This inner state will change as the environment changes, not because of the environmental change, but because of the internal drive or 'appetition' that has been programmed into them by God.

Monads are incorporeal automata; they are everywhere and there are countless millions of them:

There is a world of created beings—living things, animals, entelechies and souls—in the least part of matter. Each portion of matter may be conceived as a garden full of plants and as a pond full of fish. But every branch of each plant, every member of each animal, and every drop of their liquid parts is itself likewise a similar garden or pond. (G VI. 66)

The idea that the human body is an assemblage of cells, each living an individual life, was still a new one, though not of course peculiar to Leibniz. The monads that correspond to a human body in the Leibnizian system are like cells in having an individual life-history, but unlike cells in being immaterial and immortal.

We have come a long way from our Cartesian starting point. For Descartes, human minds were the only souls in the created universe; all else was lifeless machinery. For Leibniz, the smallest part of the smallest bug is ensouled—and it

---

[7] Here I am indebted to Daniel Garber, 'Leibniz on Body, Matter, and Extension', *PASS* (2004): 23–40.

has not only one, but myriad souls. We have indeed gone further than Aristotle, for whom only living things had souls. Now there are souls galore behind every stock and stone. What, in this pullulating maelstrom of monads, makes the human mind unique?

For Leibniz, the difference between living and non-living bodies is this. Organic bodies are not mere aggregates of monads: they have a single dominant monad which gives them an individual substantial unity. The dominant monad in a human being is the human soul. All monads have perception and appetite, but the dominant monad in a human being has a more vivid mental life and a more imperious appetition. It has not just perception, but 'apperception', which is self-consciousness, reflexive knowledge of the internal states that constitute perception. Whereas we know of the existence of other monads only by philosophical reasoning, we are aware of our own substantiality through this self-consciousness. 'We have a clear but not a distinct idea of substance,' Leibniz wrote in a letter, 'which comes, in my opinion, from the fact that we have the internal feeling of it in ourselves' (G III. 247).

The good of the soul is the goal, or final cause, not just of its own activity, but also of all the other monads that it dominates. The soul does not, however, exert any efficient causality on any of the other monads, nor any of them on any other: the good is achieved in virtue of the harmony pre-established by God in the body and in its environment and throughout the universe. Once again, Leibniz's rehabilitation of Aristotle goes further than Aristotle himself. Final causes were just one of Aristotle's quartet of causes; Descartes had expelled them from science but they are now readmitted and enthroned as the *only* finite causes operative in biology.

In all of this, is any room left for free will? In theory, Leibniz defends a full libertarian doctrine:

Absolutely speaking, our will, considered as contrasted with necessity, is in a state of indifference, and it has the power to do otherwise or to suspend its action altogether, the one and the other alternative being and remaining possible. (*D*, 30)

But human beings, like all agents, finite or infinite, need a reason for acting; that follows from the principle of sufficient reason. In the case of free agents, Leibniz maintains, the motives that provide the sufficient reason for action 'incline but do not necessitate'. But it is hard to see how he can really make room for a special kind of freedom for human beings. True, in his system, no agent of any kind is acted on from outside; all are completely self-determining. But no agent, rational or not, can step outside the life-history laid out for it in the pre-established harmony. Hence it seems that Leibniz cannot consistently accept that we enjoy the liberty of indifference that he described in the *Discourse*. All that is left is 'liberty of spontaneity'—the ability to act upon one's motives. But this, as Bramhall had argued against Hobbes, is an illusory freedom unless accompanied by liberty of indifference.

Berkeley and Hume on Spirits and Selves

In the universe of Berkeley there are only two kinds of things: spirits and ideas. 'The former', he says, 'are *active*, *indivisible substances*; the latter are *inert*, fleeting, dependent beings, which subsist not by themselves, but are supported by, or exist in minds or spiritual substances' (*BPW*, 98). Since Berkeley's metaphysical system places more weight on the notion of *spirit* than any other philosophy, one would expect that he would give us a full account of the concept; but in fact his philosophy of mind is remarkably jejune. Indeed, he tells us that we have no idea of what a spirit is.

This turns out to be less agnostic than it sounds, because Berkeley is here, as so often, using 'idea' to mean image. He concedes that we do have a notion of spirit in the sense that we understand the meaning of the word. A spirit is a real thing, which is neither an idea nor like an idea, but 'that which perceives ideas, and wills and reasons about them' (*BPW*, 120). Perhaps, for consistency, Berkeley should have said that a spirit was a congeries of ideas, just as he said a body was; but in the case of spirit, unlike body, he is willing to accept the notion of an underlying substance, distinct from ideas, in which ideas inhere. There is no distinction, in Berkeley's philosophy, between 'spirit' and 'mind'; he simply prefers the first term because it emphasizes the mind's immateriality.

How do we know that there are such things as spirits? 'We comprehend our own existence by inward feeling or reflexion, and that of other spirits by reason,' Berkeley tells us; but it is hard to see how he can consistently say either of these things. The only things that I can perceive or reflect upon are ideas; and Berkeley tells us that nothing could be more absurd than to say 'I am an idea or notion'. And the line of reasoning by which he seeks to establish the existence of other minds is broken-backed.

According to Berkeley, when I am looking at my wife, I do not see her at all. All I see is a collection of my own ideas that I have constantly observed in conjunction with each other. I know her existence and that of other people, he tells us, because 'I perceive several motions, changes, and combinations of ideas, that inform me there are certain particular agents like myself, which accompany them, and concur in their production.' But the ideas I see are my ideas, not my wife's ideas; and the ideas for which she provides the substratum are her ideas, to which I have no possible access. Berkeley cannot claim that she 'concurs in the production' of my ideas. No one other than myself or God can cause me to have an idea.

Berkeley's account of causation is minimalist. When we speak of one thing as cause and another as effect we are talking of relations between ideas. 'The connexion of ideas does not imply the relation of cause and effect, but only of a mark or sign with the thing signified. The fire which I see is not the cause of the pain I suffer on my approaching it, but the mark that forewarns me of it.' But how can the ideas which constitute my perception of my wife inform me either of her ideas, which I can never perceive, or of her spirit, which even she does not perceive? The problem of other minds was a *damnosa hereditas* which Berkeley bequeathed to following phenomenalists.

Hume, however, was to show that empiricism presents us with a problem not only about the minds of others but also about our own minds. Solipsism—the belief that only one's own self really exists—was always the logical conclusion of empiricism, implicit in the thesis that the mind knows nothing except its own perceptions. Hume drew out this implication more candidly than previous empiricists, but he went further and reached the conclusion that even the self of solipsism is an illusion.

Since Descartes and Locke, philosophers had conceived sensation not as a transaction between a perceiver and an object in the external world, but as the private perceiving by the mind of some interior perception, impression, or idea. Seeing a horse is really observing a horse-like visual sense-datum; feeling a teddy bear is really observing a teddy-like tactile sense-datum. The relation between a thinker and his thoughts is that of an inner eye to an inner art gallery. Hume follows wholeheartedly in this tradition and endeavours to give purely internal accounts of the differences between different mental activities, events, and states. This comes out particularly clearly in his account of the passions.

The relation between a passion and the mind to which it belongs is conceived by Hume as the relation of perceived to perceiver. 'Nothing', he writes, ' is ever present with the mind but its perceptions or impressions and ideas . . . To hate, to love, to think, to feel, to see; all this is nothing but to perceive' (T, 67). One might draw from the passage the idea that loving a woman is one way of perceiving a woman, just as seeing a woman is one way of perceiving a woman; but that is not what Hume means at all. What is perceived when a passion is felt is the passion itself. The mind is represented as an observer which perceives the passions which are present to it.

The self as thus conceived is essentially the subject of such inner observation: it is the eye of inner vision, the ear of inner hearing; or rather, it is supposed to be the possessor of both inner eye and inner ear and whatever other inner organs of sensation may be demanded by empiricist epistemology. It was Hume who had the courage to show that the self, as thus conceived, was a chimera. Empiricism teaches that nothing is real except what can be discovered by the senses, inner or outer. The self, as inner subject, clearly cannot be perceived by the outer senses. But can it be discovered by inward observation? Hume, after the most diligent investigation, failed to locate the self:

Whenever I enter most intimately into what I call *myself*, I always stumble on some particular perception or other, of heat or cold, light or shade, love or hatred, pain or pleasure. I never catch *myself* at any time without a perception and never can observe anything but the perception . . . If anyone upon serious and unprejudic'd reflection, thinks he has a different notion of *himself*, I must confess I can reason no longer with him. All I can allow him is, that he may well be in the right as well as I, and that we are essentially different in this particular. He may, perhaps, perceive something simple and continu'd, which he calls *himself*; though I am certain there is no such principle in me. (*T*, 252)

The imperceptibility of the self is a consequence of the concept of it as an inner sensor. We cannot taste our tongue, or see our eyes: the self is an unobservable observer, just as the eye is an invisible organ. But, as Hume shows, the empiricist self vanishes when subjected to systematic empiricist scrutiny. It is not discoverable by any sense, whether inner or outer, and therefore it is to be rejected as a metaphysical monster. Berkeley had maintained that ideas inhered in nothing outside the mind; Hume shows that there is nothing inside the mind for them to inhere in. There is no impression of the self, and no idea of the self; there are simply bundles of impressions and ideas.

Hume showed that the inner subject was illusory, but he did not expose the underlying error which led the empiricists to espouse the myth of the self. The real way out of the impasse is to reject the thesis that the mind knows nothing but its own ideas, and to accept that a thinker is not a solitary inner perceiver, but an embodied person living in a public world. Hume was right that he had no self other than himself; but he was himself not a bundle of impressions, but a portly human being in the midst of eighteenth-century society.

It might be thought that a bundle of impressions was so different from any kind of active agent that it would be idle to discuss whether or not it enjoyed free will. However, Hume goes on to address the topic of liberty and necessity, quite oblivious to his official philosophy of mind. (This is his custom when pursuing a difficult philosophical agenda—an agreeable inconsistency for which we may be grateful.) His general thesis is that human decisions and actions are necessitated by causal laws no less than the operations of lifeless natural agents, and are equally predictable:

Were a man, whom I know to be honest and opulent, and with whom I live in intimate friendship, to come into my house, where I am surrounded with my servants, I rest assured that he is not to stab me before he leaves it in order to rob me of my silver standish . . . A man who at noon leaves his purse full of gold on the pavement at Charing Cross may as well expect that it will fly away like a feather as that he will find it untouched an hour after. (*E*, 91)

Whatever we do, Hume maintains, is necessitated by causal links between motive, circumstance, and action. Class, among other things, is a great determinant of character and behaviour: 'The skin, pores, muscles and nerves of a day-labourer are different from those of a man of quality: So are his sentiments, actions and manners.' Hume's insistence on determinism leads him to some implausible conclusions: that a group of labourers should go on strike is for him as unthinkable as that an unsupported heavy body will not fall.

Although he believes that human actions are determined, Hume is willing to accept that we do enjoy a certain liberty. Like some of his successors, he was a 'compatibilist', someone who maintains that freedom and determinism are compatible with each other if rightly understood. Our natural reluctance to accept that our actions are necessitated, he believes, arises from a confusion between necessity and constraint:

Few are capable of distinguishing betwixt the liberty of *spontaneity*, as it is call'd in the schools, and the liberty of *indifference*; betwixt that which is oppos'd to violence, and that which means a negation of necessity and causes. The first is even the most common sense of the word; and as 'tis only that species of liberty, which it concerns us to preserve, our thoughts have been principally turn'd towards it, and have almost universally confounded it. (*T*, 408)

Experience exhibits our liberty of spontaneity: we often do, unconstrained, what we want to do. But experience cannot provide genuine evidence for liberty of indifference, that is, the ability to do otherwise than we in fact do. We may imagine we feel such a liberty within ourselves, 'but a spectator can commonly infer our actions from our motives and character; and even when he cannot, he concludes in general, that he might, were he perfectly acquainted with every circumstance of our situation and temper, and the most secret springs of our complexion and disposition' (*T*, 408).

Such talk of 'secret springs' of action is one indication that in discussing this issue Hume has forgotten his official theory of mind and his official theory of causation. Indeed, his very definition of the human will seems incompatible with them. 'By *the will* I mean nothing but the *internal impression we feel and are conscious of, when we knowingly give rise to any new motion of our body, or new perception of our mind*' (*T*, 399). Given his view of causation, we must wonder what right Hume has to talk of our 'giving rise' to motions and perceptions. But if we replace 'we knowingly give rise to any new motion' with 'any new motion is observed to arise', the definition no longer looks at all appropriate.

Kant's Anatomy of the Mind

The anatomy of the mind, as described by Kant, contains many traditional elements. He made a distinction between the intellect and the senses, and between inner sense and the five outer senses. These distinctions, although rejected by some philosophers, had remained commonplaces since the Middle Ages. Kant's only innovation so far was to give novel epistemological functions to traditional faculties. But he went on to draw new distinctions, and to bring new insights to bear on the philosophy of mind.

In the *Critique of Judgement* Kant divides the faculties of the human mind into: (a) cognitive powers; (b) powers of feeling pleasure and pain; and (c) powers of desire. By 'cognitive powers' are meant, in this context, intellectual powers, and here Kant makes a threefold distinction between understanding (*Verstand*), reason (*Vernunft*), and judgement (*Urteil*). Understanding is the legitimate operation of the intellect in the conceptualization of experience. That is something that we know from the first critique, where too 'Reason' is used as a technical term for the illegitimate operation of the intellect in transcendental speculation. In the second critique a positive role is given to reason as the arbiter of ethical behaviour. The function of judgement, however, is not clear from the earlier critiques. Previous philosophers had used the word (as Kant himself often does) to mean an assent to a proposition of any kind. In the third critique Kant concentrates on judgements of aesthetic taste. We thus arrive at a trinity of faculties: one (the understanding) which has truth as its object; one (the practical reason) which has goodness as its object; and one (the judgement) which has as its object the beautiful and the sublime (M, 31ff.).

All the operations of the intellect are accompanied by self-consciousness. Kant spells this out most fully in the case of the understanding. The conceptualization of experience involves the union of all the items of awareness in a single consciousness. In a difficult, but original and profound, section of the first critique entitled 'The original synthetic unity of apperception' Kant analyses what is meant by speaking of the unity of self-consciousness (B, 132–43).

It is not possible for me to *discover* that something is an item of *my* consciousness. It is absurd to think of me as being faced with an item of consciousness, then going on to wonder to whom it belongs, and then concluding upon inquiry that it belongs to none other than myself. Through reflection I may become aware of many features of my conscious experience (is it painful? is it clear? etc.) but I cannot become aware that it is *mine*. The self-conscious discoveries that one can make about one's perceptions are called by Kant 'apperceptions'. The point that one does not rely on experience to recognize one's consciousness as one's own is stated thus by Kant: one's ownership of one's own consciousness is not an empirical apperception, but a 'transcendental apperception'.

What unites my experiences in a single consciousness is not experience itself; in themselves my experiences are, as Kant says, 'many coloured and diverse'. The unity is created by the *a priori* activity of the understanding making a synthesis of intuitions, combining them into what Kant calls 'the transcendental unity of apperception'. But this does not mean that I have some transcendental self-knowledge. The original unity of apperception gives me only the concept of myself; for any actual self-awareness, experience is necessary.

Kant agrees with Descartes that the thought 'I think' must accompany every other possible thought. Self-consciousness is inseparable from thought, because self-consciousness is necessary to think of thinking, and in advance of experience we attribute to things those properties which are the necessary conditions of our thinking of them. However, Kant disagrees sharply with the conclusions that Descartes drew from his *Cogito*. In the section of the transcendental dialectic entitled 'The paralogisms of Pure Reason' he makes a sustained attack upon Cartesian psychology, and indeed upon *a priori* and rational psychology in general.

Whereas empirical psychology deals with the soul as the object of inner sense, rational psychology treats of the soul as the thinking subject. Rational psychology, Kant says, 'professes to be a science built upon the single proposition *I think*'. It purports to be a study of an unknown X, the transcendental subject of thinking, 'the I or he or it (the thing) that thinks' (A, 343–5).

Our natural drive to go beyond the limits of merely empirical psychology leads us into fallacies—Kant calls them 'paralogisms' or bogus syllogisms. He lists four paralogisms of pure reason which can be crudely summarized as follows: (1) from 'Necessarily the thinking subject is a subject' we conclude 'The thinking subject is a necessary subject'; (2) from 'Dividing up the ego makes no sense' we conclude 'The ego is an indivisible substance; (3) from 'Whenever I am conscious, it is the same I who am conscious' we conclude 'Whenever I am conscious, I am conscious of the same I'; (4) from 'I can think of myself without my body' we conclude 'Without my body I can think of myself'.

In each paralogism, a harmless analytical proposition is converted, by logical sleight of hand, into a contentious synthetic *a priori* proposition. On the basis of the paralogisms rational psychology concludes that the self is an immaterial, incorruptible, personal, immortal entity.

The rational proof of the immortality of the soul is nothing but delusion. But that does not mean that we cannot believe in a future life as a postulate of practical reason. In the present life happiness is clearly not proportioned to virtue; so if we are to be motivated to behave well, we must believe that the balance will be redressed in another life elsewhere. The refutation of rational psychology, Kant claims, is a help, not a hindrance, to faith in an afterlife. 'For the merely speculative proof has never been able to exercise any influence upon the common reason of men. It so stands upon the point of a hair, that even the schools preserve it from falling only so long as they keep it unceasingly spinning round like a top' (B, 424).

The positive element in Kant's philosophy of mind that has had the longest-lasting influence is his treatment of freedom and determinism. His contribution to this topic is placed not in the section of the first critique devoted to rational and empirical psychology, but among the antinomies that purport to show the incoherence of attempts to survey the cosmos as a whole. The third antinomy relates the idea of the world as a single determinist system to the belief in the possibility of free uncaused action. The topic of this antinomy was later eloquently laid out by Tolstoy at the end of *War and Peace*:

The problem of freewill from earliest times has occupied the best intellects of mankind and has from earliest times appeared in all its colossal significance. The problem lies in the fact that if we regard man as a subject for observation from whatever point of view—theological, historical, ethical or philosophic—we find the universal law of necessity to which he (like everything else that exists) is subject. But looking upon man from within ourselves—man as the object of our own inner consciousness—we feel ourselves to be free.

The laws of necessity taught us by reason, Tolstoy thought, forced us to renounce an illusory freedom and recognize our unconscious dependence on universal law.

Kant, on the other hand, thought that determinism and freedom could be reconciled. In the third antinomy, unlike the first two antinomies, both thesis and antithesis, if properly interpreted, are true. The thesis is that natural causality is not sufficient to explain the phenomena of the world; in addition to determining causes we must take account of freedom and spontaneity. The antithesis argues that to postulate transcendental freedom is to resign oneself to blind lawlessness. As Tolstoy was to put it, 'If one man only out of millions once in a thousand years had the power of acting freely, i.e. as he chose, it is obvious that one single free act of that man in violation of the laws would be enough to prove that laws governing all human action cannot possibly exist.'

Kant, like Tolstoy, was a determinist, although he was not a hard determinist but a soft determinist. That is to say, he believed that determinism was compatible with human freedom and spontaneity. The human will, he said, is sensuous but free: that is to say, it is affected by passion but not necessitated by passion. 'There is in man a power of self-determination, independently of any coercion through sensuous impulses.' But the exercise of this power of self-determination has two aspects: empirical (perceptible in experience); and intelligible (graspable only by the intellect). Our free agency is the intelligible cause of sensible effects; and these sensible phenomena are also part of an unbroken series that unfolds in accordance with unchangeable laws. To reconcile human freedom with deterministic nature Kant says that nature operates in time, whereas the human will belongs to a non-phenomenal self that transcends time.

Throughout the centuries theologians had sought to reconcile human freedom with the omniscience of God by saying that God's knowledge was outside time. It was a novelty for a philosopher to seek to reconcile human freedom with the omnipotence of Nature by saying that human freedom was outside time. It is indeed difficult to reconcile Kant's claim that the human will is atemporal with the examples he himself gives of free action, such as his rising from the chair at his desk. But an impressive line of philosophers up to the present day have sought, like Kant, to show that freedom and determinism are compatible with each other. It is surely correct that causal explanation ('I knocked him over because I was pushed') and explanation by reasons ('I knocked him over to teach him a lesson') are two radically different types of explanation, each irreducible to the other. Kant was surely right to emphasize this difference and to believe that it must be the basis of any reconciling project.

The reconciliation between freedom and determinism takes a baroque form in the metaphysics of Hegel. Individual human choices such as Caesar's decision to cross the Rubicon are actually determined by the world-spirit, who uses 'the cunning of Reason' to give effect to its purposes. But the necessity that operates at the level of the individual is an expression of the highest form of freedom, for freedom is the essential attribute of spirit and its ever increasing expression is the guiding force of history.

When Hegel speaks of the world-spirit his references to it are not mere metaphors for the operation of impersonal historical forces. Hegel's spirit resembles Kant's transcendental unity of apperception in being the subject of all experience, which cannot itself be an object of experience. Kant was content to assume that there will be a separate such focus in the life of each individual mind. But what ground, Hegel might ask, is there for such an assumption? Behind Kant's transcendental self stands the Cartesian ego; and one of the first critics of Descartes' *cogito* put the pertinent question: how do you know that it is you who are thinking, and not the world-soul that thinks in you? Hegel's spirit is meant to be a centre of consciousness prior to any individual consciousness. One spirit thinks severally in the thoughts of Descartes and in the thoughts of Kant, perhaps rather as I, as a single person, can simultaneously feel toothache and gout in different parts of myself. But it is difficult to accommodate within either empirical or analytic psychology a spirit whose behavioural expression is the entire universe. Rather than a philosophy of mind, Hegel offers us a Philosophy of Mind.

In respect of the philosophy of the human mind, the thinker who made the most significant contribution in our period was undoubtedly Kant. Throughout the seventeenth and eighteenth centuries, philosophy of mind was made subordinate to epistemology, in consequence of the Cartesian pursuit of certainty. In the course of this pursuit, Descartes and the rationalists undervalued the role of the senses, and the British empiricists eliminated the role of the intellect. It took the overarching genius of Kant to put together again what the partisan energies of his predecessors had shattered, and to give an account of the human mind that did justice to its various faculties. In his work epistemology and philosophical psychology once again meet together, as they had done in the best work of the Middle Ages.

8

Ethics

Histories of ethics often skim swiftly over the sixteenth century. In the high Middle Ages moral philosophy was presented in commentaries on Aristotle's *Nicomachean Ethics* and in treatises on the natural or revealed law of God. In Aquinas' *Summa Theologiae* both elements are combined, but the system is structured around the concept of virtue rather than around the concept of law. It was Aquinas' successors, from Duns Scotus onward, who gave the theory of divine law the central place in presentations of Christian morality.[1] But the medieval tradition in ethics suffered a shock, from which it never recovered, under the impact of the Reformation and the Counter-Reformation.

Both Luther and Calvin emphasized the depravity of human nature in the absence of the divine grace that was offered only through Christianity. For them, the path to human salvation and happiness lay through faith, not through moral endeavour, and there was little scope for any philosophical system of ethics. Aristotle was the enemy, not the friend, of the only possible good life. As for other ancient sages, their teaching could not lead to virtue; as Augustine had insisted, the best it could do was to add a certain splendour to vice.

Catholics did not agree that human possibilities for goodness had been totally extinguished by the Fall, and the Council of Trent declared it a heresy to say that all deeds of non-Christians were sinful. But the disciplinary regulations of that council gave Catholic moral theology a new direction which took it far away from Aquinas' synthesis of Aristotelian and Augustinian ethics. A decree of 1551, strengthening a rule of the Lateran Council of 1215, laid down that all Catholics must make regular confession to a priest. It made a distinction between two classes of sin, mortal and venial: mortal sins were more serious, and if unrepented rendered the sinner liable to the eternal punishments of hell. Under the new rule, a penitent was bound to confess all mortal sins according to their species, number, and circumstances. Henceforth, Catholic moralists focused less on

---

[1] See above, pp. 455–65.

consideration of the virtues than on the specification and individuation of different kinds of sin, and the listing of aggravating or mitigating circumstances.

Casuistry

The decree of Trent fostered a whole new ethical discipline: the science of casuistry. Casuistry in general is the application of moral principle to particular decisions; in particular to 'cases of conscience' where such principles might appear to conflict with each other. In the broad sense, any expert advice given to resolve a particular moral dilemma might count as an exercise of casuistry: for instance, the guidance given to the Emperor Charles V by a group of theologians on the treatment of his new American subjects, or the counsel given to King Charles I by Archbishop Laud on the legality of the impeachment of the Earl of Strafford. But when contemporaries and historians talked of casuistry they commonly had in mind the textbooks and manuals, produced in abundance in the sixteenth and seventeenth centuries, which dealt not with actual decisions, but with imaginary cases, as a guide to confessors and spiritual directors in their dealings with the penitent and the devout.

Although manuals of casuistry were written by theologians from many different religious orders, casuistry became and remained specially associated with the newly founded Counter-Reformation order of the Jesuits, the Society of Jesus. While the Jesuit system of training made provision for more scholarly students to study the moral system of Aquinas, those destined for non-academic work learnt their ethics through the study of cases of conscience, reading manuals of casuistry, listening to lectures from casuists, and practising pastoral care through case conferences. Jesuits were much in demand as confessors, in particular to the great and the good; in 1602 the general of the order felt obliged to issue a special instruction *On the Confession of Princes*. Thus casuistry acquired political as well as ethical importance.

During the sixteenth century the casuists had to face a number of novel moral problems. One of the most important was the relationship of Christians to the original inhabitants of the newly discovered continent of America. Were the Spanish and Portuguese colonists entitled to annex the lands of the indigenous peoples and make them their slaves? The Emperor Charles V called a conference of theologians at Valladolid in 1550 to discuss the issue. His imperial historiographer, Sepulveda, basing his theories on Aristotle's teaching that some men were better fitted to serve than to rule, and were therefore natural slaves, argued that American Indians, who lived a life of rudeness and inferiority, and were ignorant of Christianity, could justly be enslaved and forcibly converted. This position was controverted on the spot by the missionary Bartolomé de las Casas, and forcefully attacked in publications by two of the most influential Spanish theologians of the age, the Dominican Francisco de Vitoria and the Jesuit Franscisco Suarez.

In his posthumously published treatises, *De Indis* (1557), Vitoria first of all defended St Thomas' teaching that the forcible conversion of the heathen was unjust, and went on to deny that either the pope or the emperor had any jurisdiction over the Indians. The Indians, he maintained, had ownership and property rights just as if they were Christians: they constituted a genuine political society, and their civil arrangements showed that they enjoyed the full use of reason:

> There is a certain method in their affairs, for they have polities which are orderly arranged, and they have definite marriage and magistrates, overlords, laws, and work-shops, and a system of exchange, all of which call for the use of reason.[2]

He concluded that there was no justification for confiscating the land and possessions of these heathen peoples on the pretext that they had no genuine ownership of their property. The Jesuit Suarez took a similar line in his discussion of the rights and wrongs of war.[3]

The expansion of overseas exploration and international trade in the sixteenth century forced casuists to examine the ethics of the methods by which maritime ventures were financed. On the basis of certain biblical texts, and of an Aristotelian analysis of the nature of money, Thomas Aquinas had issued a severe condemnation of the taking of interest on loans.[4] There was however an important difference, recognized by Aquinas, between two ways of financing a project. One was by making a loan to an entrepreneur (to be repaid to the lender whether the venture succeeds or not); the other was by buying a share in the enterprise (where the financier bears part of the risk of failure). The first was usury, and it was wicked. The second was partnership, and it was honourable (*ST* 2. 2. 78. 2 ad 5).

The prohibition on usury was maintained throughout the Middle Ages: it was repeated by St Antoninus, who in the fifteenth century was archbishop of Florence, a city that was by then home to great banking houses such as the Medici. Antoninus did, however, allow a charge to be made upon a loan in one particular case: if delay in repayment of a loan had led to unforeseen loss to the lender (given the technical name *damnum emergens*). This was seen as compensation for damage inflicted, rather than interest on the loan itself. But this minor relaxation of the prohibition led, over the next century, to its total emasculation at the hands of the casuists.

---

[2] *De Indis Recenter Inventis*, 1. 23; quoted by Bull *et al.*, *Hugo Grotius and International Relations* (Oxford: Oxford University Press, 1990), p. 46.

[3] See below, p. 711. It is sad that the views of las Casas, Vitoria, and Suarez did not have more effect on the actual practice of Christian colonizers.

[4] See above, p. 463.

The first step was the introduction of the notion of opportunity cost. One of the things one gives up when making a loan is the possibility of making profit from an alternative use of the money. So *damnum emergens* is joined by *lucrum cessans* (cessation of gain) as a title to reimbursement. The expansion of capitalism during the sixteenth century multiplied the opportunities for alternative investment, and so casuists were able to argue that in almost every case there would be present one or other of these justifications for charging interest.

The casuists' logic was surely, on their own terms, very dubious. The money which I lend you I could indeed put to other uses: I could lend it to someone else, or I could invest it in a partnership. But on the first supposition, the only gain I am losing by lending to you is a gain which would itself be unlawful, namely, the taking of usury. And on the second supposition, it is not at all sure that I am losing anything by making you the loan. My alternative venture might go wrong and so far from making a profit, I would lose my capital as well. You may turn out to have been doing me a good turn by borrowing from me.

Nonetheless, casuists, some of them hired as consultants by the major banking houses, came out with ever more complicated schemes to circumvent the prohibition on usury. The Duke of Bavaria, in whose dominions such schemes were highly popular, proposed the following case for consideration by a commission of Jesuits in 1580. It is worth quoting in its own terms, for it is framed in the typical format of a 'case of conscience':

Titius, a German, loans Sympronius a sum of money. Sympronius is a person of means, and the money is lent to him for no specific purpose. The conditions are that Titius is to receive annually five florins for every hundred lent, and afterwards have the whole capital back. There is no danger to the capital, and Titius must get his 5%, whether or not Sympronius makes a profit.[5]

The question proposed was: is this contract lawful? The commissioners returned a highly qualified reply, but on its basis the Jesuit order declared the contract morally licit. Henceforth the prohibition on usury was a dead letter among Roman Catholics.

Mysticism and Stoicism

The heyday of casuistry was the century from 1550 to 1650. During that period volumes of casuistry were not, of course, the only guides to life that were published. On the one hand, there were many manuals of devotion which included practical

[5] Quoted by Jonsen and Toulmin, *The Abuse of Casuistry* (Berkeley: University of California Press, 1988), p. 189.

moral advice; on the other hand, some writers urged the merits of ancient ethical texts. As examples of these two tendencies we may consider St John of the Cross and René Descartes.

St John of the Cross (1542–91), the spiritual director of St Teresa of Avila, who reformed the Carmelite order, was a poet and mystic. His work *The Dark Night of the Soul* describes the long and painful ascent which leads to union with God. He describes the ecstasy of the goal in terms of incomprehensible rapture, but he makes clear that the way towards it is through suffering and self-discipline. First one must enter the dark night of the senses; but this is only a kindergarten of preparation for the dark night of the soul, which is itself only the first stage of the mystical ascent. It is thus that he sets out the first steps of the spiritual life:

Strive always to prefer, not that which is easiest, but that which is most difficult;
Not that which is most delectable, but that which is most unpleasing;
Not that which gives most pleasure, but rather that which gives least
Not that which is restful, but that which is wearisome . . .
In order to arrive at having pleasure in everything,
Desire to have pleasure in nothing.
In order to arrive at possessing everything
Desire to possess nothing.
In order to arrive at being everything,
Desire to be nothing.

St John's treatise was the most severe of sixteenth-century devotional guides, and was clearly addressed to a cloistered minority. But similar teaching, in a more emollient form, was presented by the French bishop St Francis de Sales, in his *Introduction to the Devout Life* (1608), the first manual of piety aimed at lay people living a secular life in the world.

Descartes, although an observant Catholic, drew the inspiration of his morality from quite different sources. When he was embarking on his project of all-embracing doubt, he safeguarded himself by drawing up a provisional code of morality, consisting of three principal maxims: first, to obey the laws and customs of his country; second, to be resolute in action once he had taken a decision; third, 'to try always to conquer myself rather than fortune; to change my desires, rather than the order of the world'. This, he says, 'was the secret of those philosophers of old who could withdraw from the dominion of fortune, and, amid suffering and poverty, could debate whether their Gods were as happy as they' (AT VI. 26; *CSMK* I. 124).

Observing Catholic practice appears only as a subdivision of 'obeying the laws and customs of my country': it is to ancient Stoicism that the young Descartes looks for ethical guidance. It was the same ten years later when he was corresponding with Princess Elizabeth. He repeated his three maxims, and to instruct her on the nature of true happiness, he recommended a reading of Seneca's *De Vita Beata*. In his letters of moral advice, he constantly stresses the role of reason in the moderation of the passions, which make us believe certain goods to be more desirable than they are. 'The true function of reason', he wrote, 'in the conduct of life is to examine and consider without passion the value of all perfections of body and soul that can be acquired by our conduct, so that since we are commonly obliged to deprive ourselves of some goods in order to acquire others, we shall always choose the better' (AT IV. 286; *CSMK* III. 265).

Descartes worked up some of the ideas of his correspondence with Elizabeth into a *Treatise on the Passions*. This is as much an exercise in speculative physiology as in moral philosophy: an understanding of the bodily causes of our passions, Descartes believed, was a valuable aid to our bringing them under rational control. The detailed examination of the passions, he believed, was the one area in which his own moral philosophy was superior to that of the ancients (AT XI. 327–8; *CSMK* I. 328–9).

The passion whose description brings out most fully Descartes' moral ideals is the passion of *générosité*, which defies exact translation into English. The *généreux* is no doubt generous, but he is much more than that: he is, we might say with a degree of anachronism, the perfect gentleman. Such people, Descartes tells us:

are naturally led to do great deeds, and at the same time not to undertake anything of which they do not feel themselves capable. And because they esteem nothing more highly than doing good to others and disregarding their own self-interest, they are always perfectly courteous, gracious and obliging to everyone. Moreover, they have complete command over their passions. In particular they have mastery over their desires, and over jealousy and envy, because everything they think sufficiently valuable to be worth pursuing is such that its acquisition depends solely on themselves. (AT XI. 448; *CSMK* I. 385)

Pascal against the Jesuits

Descartes' *généreux*, tranquil, aloof, and self-sufficient, lives in a different world from the penitents of the casuists, wallowing in a sea of sin and craving advice and absolution from their confessors. But by the time of *The Passions of the Soul* the casuists had brought themselves into great disrepute, which came to a climax with the publication of Pascal's *Lettres Provinciales* in 1655. There were three practices commended by casuists which Pascal was not alone in regarding as scandalous: equivocation, probabilism, and the direction of intention. We will consider each in turn.

Traditional Christian teaching strictly forbade lying: Augustine and Aquinas agreed that deliberately stating a falsehood was always sinful. It was not always obligatory to utter the whole truth, but even to save the life of an innocent person, one must never tell a lie. This doctrine appeared harsh to many in the sixteenth century. In the England of Queen Elizabeth it was a capital crime for a priest or Jesuit to enter the country, and Catholic missionaries had to move about secretly, often concealing themselves in hideaways in country mansions. If government officials raided a house in search of priests, was it lawful for the host to deny that there was a priest in the house?

In 1595 the leader of the English Jesuits, Father Henry Garnet, in an anonymous pamphlet entitled *A Treatise of Equivocation or Against Lying and Fraudulent Dissimulation*, answered this question in the affirmative. The master or mistress of the house should say 'There is no priest in the house,' and mean 'There is no priest in the house about whom anyone is bound to tell you.' This was not a lie, he argued, because a lie was a case of saying one thing while believing another. In this case, the spoken proposition did correspond to the proposition in the mind of the speaker; it was simply that the utterance revealed only part of it. But it was common ground among theologians that one did not have to tell *the whole truth* when that would damage an innocent third party. Hence, equivocation of this kind was perfectly lawful.

Garnet's version of equivocation shocked many of his fellow casuists. Others had been prepared to defend equivocation in the sense of giving an answer which contained words which were genuinely ambiguous. But it was a different matter to alter completely the natural sense of a spoken sentence by a totally private addition or subtraction of words ('mental reservation' as it came to be called). Equivocation of this kind, many felt, was worse than lying, piling hypocrisy upon deceit. After he had been tried and executed for complicity in the Gunpowder Plot of 1605, Garnet became for English Protestants the paradigm of the deceitful Jesuit. In Shakespeare's *Macbeth*, after the murder of Duncan, a drunken porter imagines he is keeper of the gates of hell. Among those who knock to be admitted:

Faith, here's an equivocator, that could swear in both the scales against either scale, who committed treason enough for God's sake, yet could not equivocate to Heaven: O, come in, equivocator. (II. iii)

Garnet's defence of mental reservation was a minority opinion even among casuists. But there was a second-order moral principle, widely held by casuists, which gave a special significance to minority opinions. Suppose that moralists disagree with each other whether a particular action is sinful or not: is it lawful to perform it? One school of thought answered that one must take the least dangerous course, and refrain; that was called 'tutiorism', from the Latin word *tutior* meaning 'safer'. Another school of thought said that one could perform the action only if a majority of authorities regarded it as lawful. This was 'probabiliorism', which maintained that one must follow the more probable opinion. But there was a third theory, popular with many casuists, which held that even a less probable opinion could lawfully be followed, provided that it was probable at all. To be 'probable' it was sufficient that the opinion was maintained by someone in a position of authority, even though he might have the majority of experts against him. This was the doctrine of 'probabilism'. It was first propounded in 1577 by a Dominican commentator on St Thomas, Bartolomeo Medina of Salamanca, who wrote 'if an opinion is probable, it is licit to follow it, even though the opposite opinion is more probable'.[6]

The use of probabilism was perhaps not so very different from the common practice in business and politics today of shopping around among lawyers until one finds one who is willing to advise that the course of action one has decided on is perfectly legal. But to thinkers like Pascal it seemed to eat away the foundation of all religious morality. The variety of opinions among moralists upon important issues, which pious people might well regard as a scandal, turns out, on the probabilists' assumptions, to be a great boon. 'I now see the purpose', he says to a fictional Jesuit, 'of the conflicts of opinion between your Doctors on every topic. One of them will always serve your turn, and the other will do you no harm' (*LP* V. 51). Some casuists went so far as to say that an opinion could be made probable by being propounded even by a single moralist, provided he was a person of weight. This meant, as Pascal saw it, that any Johnny-come-lately who had got himself a chair in moral theology could overturn the teaching of all the Fathers of the Church.

In his attack on the laxity which, he alleged, Jesuit confessors encouraged in their clients, one of the targets that Pascal singled out for attack was the practice of 'direction of intention'. The imaginary Jesuit in his book says: 'Our method of direction consists in proposing to oneself, as the end of one's actions, a permitted object. So far as we can we turn men away from forbidden things, but when we cannot prevent the action at least we purify the intention.' Thus, for instance, it is allowable to kill a man in return for an insult, even though the Bible tells us not to return evil for evil. 'All you have to do is to turn your intention from the desire for vengeance, which is criminal, to the desire to defend one's honour, which is permitted.' Duelling is prohibited, but if one is challenged one may turn up at the place designated, not with the intention of fighting a duel, but to avoid being thought a coward; and then, if threatened by one's opponent, one may of course kill him in self-defence.

Such direction of intention, obviously enough, is simply a performance in the imagination which has little to do with genuine intention, which is expressed in the means one chooses to one's ends. It was this doctrine, and Pascal's attack on it, which brought into disrepute the doctrine of double effect, according to which there is an important moral distinction between the intended and unintended effects of one's action. If the theory of double effect is combined with the practice of direction of intention, it becomes no more than a hypocritical cloak for the justification of the means by the end.

---

[6] Quoted in Jonsen and Toulmin, *The Abuse of Casuistry*, p. 164.

There was, however, hypocrisy on both sides of this controversy over casuistry. Pascal, in the *Provinicial Letters*, poses as a man of the world shocked by the excessive laxity of Jesuit confessors. In fact, as a Jansenist, he saw not only the Jesuits, but any moralists willing to make the slightest concession to human weakness, as tools of Satan. He and his friends at Port Royal saw themselves as a small privileged elect, chosen to walk on the difficult path to salvation while the great mass of mankind hurtled on its way to damnation.

There is an odd similarity between Port Royal in the seventeenth century and Bloomsbury in the twentieth century. In each case a small group of upper-class intellectuals—ascetics in the one case, hedonists in the other—saw themselves as uniquely enlightened in a world of philistines. Each group contained writers of great literary skill, and each group fostered artists of talent. On the fringe of each group there stood out a great mathematical philosopher: Bertrand Russell in the case of Bloomsbury; Blaise Pascal in the case of Port Royal. Each group flared for a while in the limelight, and then gradually faded into obscurity, leaving behind a musty odour of exquisite spiritual snobbery.

Spinoza's Ethical System

No one could ever accuse Spinoza of having belonged to a clique. A solitary thinker of great intellectual courage, he devised an elaborate, elegant, and demanding ethical system. Like Descartes, he gives an important role in ethics to the detailed examination of the passions, which occupies the third book of the *Ethics*. But both the philosophical substructure and the practical conclusions of his analysis of the emotions are very different from Descartes', so that the resulting ethical system is unlike any other of modern times.

The metaphysical basis of Spinoza's ethical system is a principle of existential inertia. Everything, so far as it can by its own power, endeavours to persevere in its own being. This self-perpetuating endeavour in each thing constitutes its very essence (*Eth*, 75). Applied to men and women, this general principle means that the fundamental motive of human action is self-preservation. Desire is defined by Spinoza as the self-conscious endeavour to preserve the existence of soul and body. We are conscious not only of this appetite for existence, but also of any increase or diminution in our powers of action: consciousness of such an increase constitutes pleasure; consciousness of diminution constitutes pain (*Eth*, 77). Desire, pleasure, and pain are the three fundamental human drives: all the other emotions, such as love, hatred, hope, and fear, are derived from them.

There are, however, two different kinds of emotions, passive and active. There are passive emotions, or passions, in which we 'toss to and fro like waves of the sea driven by contrary winds' (*Eth*, 103). In the passive emotions, modifications of the body give rise to corresponding ideas in the mind—ideas which will be inadequate and confused. But there are also active emotions arising from the mind's own endeavour to increase its understanding by conceiving clear and distinct ideas. Active emotions are derivable only from desire and pleasure; pain, which is the mark of a reduction in human power, physical and mental, cannot give rise to an active emotion. Actions arising from active emotions are expressions of strength of character (*fortitudo*). Strength of character, when it is expressed in self-perserving actions, is called 'courage' (*animositas*); when expressed in actions aiming at the good of others, it is called 'nobility' (*generositas*).

The notion of nobility, which is introduced at the end of Book Three of the *Ethics*, appears at first sight to conflict with the ruthlessly egoistical analysis of the passions which occupies most of the book. We are told, for instance, 'He who conceives that someone he hates is in pain will feel pleasure' (*Eth*, 82), and that 'if we conceive that anyone delights in an object that only one person can possess, we will try to prevent the person in question from gaining possession of it' (*Eth*, 87). Apparently cynical remarks of this kind are often shrewd: for instance, 'if a man begins to hate what he once loved but loves no more, he will regard it with greater hatred than if he had never loved it' (*Eth*, 90). But only a rare remark prepares the way for the notion of nobility: for instance, 'Hatred is increased when it is reciprocated, but hatred can be destroyed by love' (*Eth*, 93).

The reconciliation of egoism and altruism is carried out by Spinoza in the fourth and fifth books of the *Ethics*: 'On Human Bondage' and 'On Human Freedom'. The overarching theme of these books is this: we are in bondage to the extent that we feel passive emotions, and we are free to the extent that we feel active emotions. An emotion ceases to be a passion once we achieve a clear and distinct idea of it, which means an understanding of its causes. Paradoxically, the key to liberation is the appreciation of the necessity of all things. We cannot avoid being determined, but moral progress consists in the replacement of external determination by internal determination. What we need to do is to take a God's eye view of the whole necessary natural scheme of things, seeing it 'in the light of eternity'.

Not all passions can be turned into emotions, but those that cannot may be eliminated. Hatred, for instance, is a passive emotion, being a form of pain. But once I understand that the actions of others are determined, I will cease to feel hatred to those that do me harm. The passions of different people may conflict with each other, but people who are guided by reason and feel emotion rather than passion will find themselves in agreement (*Eth*, 132). Self-preservation remains the underlying drive, prior to any virtue (*Eth*, 127). Nonetheless, we ought to want virtue for its own sake, for there is nothing more useful for us which might serve as its goal. This is how egoism and altruism are to be reconciled. There is scope for nobility when self-preservation is enlightened by the realization of one's own place as a part of the great whole which is Nature:

To man there is nothing more useful than man—nothing, I repeat, more excellent for preserving their being can be wished for by man, than that all should so in all points agree that the minds and bodies of all should form, as it were, one single mind and one single body, and that all should, with one consent seek what is useful to them all. Hence, men who are governed by reason—that is, who seek what is useful to them in accord with reason—desire for themselves nothing, which they do not also desire for the rest of mankind, and consequently are just, faithful, and honourable in their conduct. (*Eth*, 125)

In 'On Human Bondage' Spinoza goes through the emotions, telling us which ones are good and which are bad ('good' and 'bad' for him, of course, simply mean what is conducive or non-conducive to self-preservation). Mirth, for instance, is a good thing, which we cannot have too much of; melancholy, however, is always bad (*Eth*, 138). (Spinoza recommends music as a cure for melancholy (*Eth*, 115).) Desires for non-competitive goods should be preferred to desires for goods that can be possessed by one person only. The highest good is one that is common to all who follow virtue, one in which all can equally rejoice. 'The mind's highest good is the knowledge of God, and the mind's highest virtue is to know God' (*Eth*, 129). God, of course, is for Spinoza the same as Nature, and the more we increase our knowledge of Nature the more we rejoice. This joy, accompanied by the thought of God as cause, is called by Spinoza 'the intellectual love of God'.

Spinoza's ideal human, a free person absorbed in the intellectual love of God, is no less subject to determinism than someone who is in bondage to the basest passions. The difference is that the free man is determined by causes that are internal, not external, and that are clearly and distinctly perceived. One of the effects of the clear and distinct perception of the human condition is that time ceases to matter. Past, present, and future are all equal to each other. We naturally think of the past as what cannot be changed, and the future as being open to alternatives. But in Spinoza's deterministic universe, the future is no less fixed than the past. The difference, therefore, between past and future should play no part in the reflections of a wise man: we should not worry about the future nor feel remorse about the past.

One passion which must altogether disappear in a free man is the passion of fear. Fear can never be a rational emotion; its object is future evil, and for Spinoza both the future and evil are ultimately unreal. The free man has only positive motives: he eats well and takes healthy exercise because he enjoys doing so, not in order to postpone his death. 'A free man thinks of death least of all things; and his wisdom is a meditation not on death but on life' (*Eth*, 151).

It is difficult not to admire the beauty of Spinoza's ethical writing; it is equally difficult to accept it as offering a real guide to living. Spinoza is a victim of his own success: he has woven his ethics so tightly to his metaphysics that it is difficult to swallow the one without the other. Bertrand Russell, who totally rejected Spinoza's metaphysics, but thought him the one really admirable human being in the history of philosophy, made a gallant effort to draw a practical moral from the *Ethics*:

Spinoza's principle of thinking about the whole, or at any rate about larger matters than your own grief, is a useful one. There are even times when it is comforting to reflect that human life, with all that it contains of evil and suffering, is an infinitesimal part of the life of the universe. Such reflections may not suffice to constitute a religion, but in a painful world they are a help towards sanity and an antidote to the paralysis of utter despair. (*HWP*, 562)

Hume on Reason, Passion, and Virtue

For Spinoza, as for Socrates in the ancient world, all wrongdoing is a result of ignorance: vicious conduct is ultimately a failure of reason. At the opposite pole stands David Hume: for him, reason has nothing at all to do with the distinction between right and wrong, between virtue and vice. Reason's only function is a technical one: to assist us in the achievement of the goals set by our passions. In the evaluation of our goals, reason has no place. ' 'Tis not contrary to reason to prefer the destruction of the whole world to the scratching of my finger. 'Tis not contrary to reason for me to chuse my total ruin, to prevent the least uneasiness of an Indian or person totally unknown to me' (*T*, 416). Reason can neither adjudicate nor control passion; a passion can be conquered only by another, stronger, passion. Why then do people—and not only philosophers—talk so much about the conflict between reason and passion? Hume's answer is that they mistake for reason what is actually a gentle, non-violent, passion:

There are certain calm desires and tendencies which, tho' they be real passions, produce little emotion in the mind, and are more known by their effects than by the immediate feeling or sensation. These desires are of two kinds; either certain instincts originally implanted in our natures, such as benevolence and resentment, the love of life, and kindness to children; or the general appetite to good, and aversion to evil, consider'd merely as such. When any of these passions are calm, and cause no disorder in the soul, they are very readily taken for the determinations of reason. (*T*, 417)

Moral judgements are calm passions of this kind: they are not ideas, but impressions. Morality is more properly felt than judged of. Virtue gives us pleasure, and vice pain: 'An action or sentiment or character is virtuous or vicious; why? because its view causes a pleasure or uneasiness of a particular kind.' But of course not every action or person or thing that gives us pleasure is virtuous: wine, women, and song may be pleasant but the pleasure they give is not the special pleasure taken by the moral sense. Well, what are the marks of the *particular* kind of pleasure involved in favourable moral judgement? Hume offers two: that it should be disinterested and that it should involve approbation. These seem insufficient to mark off moral from aesthetic judgement. Surely we need to distinguish one from the other if morality is not simply to be a matter of taste.

696

Hume offers us no general criterion adequate to differentiate moral judgement, but proceeds to investigate individual virtues. The two most important are benevolence and justice. Benevolence is universally admired: we all esteem those who relieve the distressed, comfort the afflicted, and are generous even to strangers. But in a natural state, benevolence extends only to those who in one way or another are close to us. 'There is no such passion in human minds, as the love of mankind, merely as such, independent of personal qualities, of services, or of relation to ourself' (*T*, 481). Benevolence alone, then, cannot be the foundation of justice; of our obligation to repay our debts even to strangers and enemies. We must conclude that justice is not a natural virtue, but an artificial one.

Human beings are impotent outside society; but society is unstable unless social rules are observed, in particular property rights. What we need is a convention entered into by all members of society to leave everyone in possession of the external goods acquired by their fortune and industry. Justice is founded therefore on utility, on self-interest broadly interpreted:

Instead of departing from our own interest, or from that of our nearest friends, by abstaining from the possessions of others, we cannot better consult both these interests, than by such a convention; because it is by that means we maintain society, which is so necessary to their well-being and subsistence, as well as to our own. (*T*, 489)

It is because it is based on a convention, entered into for the sake of utility, that justice is an 'artificial virtue'.

Natural virtues, such as meekness, charity, clemency, or generosity, are not based on utility, but arise from a more fundamental feature of human nature: sympathy. The passions of each human being are reflected in other human beings, as strings resonate in harmony. A difference between natural and artificial virtues is this: that individual acts of benevolence do good, whereas it is only the entire system of justice that promotes happiness. 'Judges take from a poor man to give to a rich; they bestow on the dissolute the labour of the industrious; and put into the hands of the vicious the means of harming both themselves and others. The whole scheme, however, of law and justice is advantageous to the society.' It is because of this advantage to society that we esteem justice; but justice is only a means to an end:

Now as the means to an end can only be agreeable, where the end is agreeable; and as the good of society, where our own interest is not concerned, or that of our friends, pleases only by sympathy: It follows, that sympathy is the source of the esteem which we pay to all the artificial virtues. (*T*, 577)

In an appendix to the second Enquiry, Hume takes some pains to argue against those who claim that benevolence is only a disguised form of self-love. Even animals show disinterested benevolence; so why should we doubt the genuineness of human gratitude and friendship and maternal love? In thus rejecting the long philosophical tradition of eudaimonism—the thesis that the ultimate goal of all one's actions is one's own happiness—Hume was, probably unwittingly, following in the footsteps of his compatriot Duns Scotus.[7] But whereas Scotus thought that the innate motive independent of self-love was a love of justice, Hume saw the motive of benevolence as even more deeply rooted in human nature.

Kant on Morality, Duty, and Law

Kant, although he presented a very different system of ethics, agreed with Hume in the rejection of eudaimonism. Happiness, he argues in the *Groundwork*, cannot be the ultimate purpose of morality:

Suppose now that for a being possessed of reason and will the real purpose of nature were his preservation, his welfare, or in a word his happiness. In that case nature would have hit on a very bad arrangement by choosing reason in the creature to carry out this purpose. For all the actions he has to perform with this end in view, and the whole rule of his behaviour, would have been mapped out for him far more accurately by instinct; and the end in question could have been maintained far more surely by instinct than it ever can be by reason. (*G*, 395)

The overarching concept in Kantian morality is not happiness, but duty. The function of reason in ethics is not to inform the will how best to choose means to some further end; it is to produce a will that is good in itself, and a will is good only if it is motivated by duty. Good will, for Kant, is the only thing that is good without qualification. Fortune, power, intelligence, courage, and all the traditional virtues can be used to bad ends; even happiness itself can be corrupting. It is not what it achieves that constitutes the goodness of a good will; good will is good in itself alone:

Even if, by some special disfavour of destiny, or by the niggardly endowment of step-motherly nature, this will is entirely lacking in power to carry out its intentions, if by its utmost effort it still accomplishes nothing, and only good will is left . . . even then it would still shine like a jewel for its own sake as something which has its full value in itself. (*G*, 394)

Good will is the highest good and the condition of all other goods, including happiness.

If a will is good only when motivated by duty, we must ask what it is to act out of duty. A first answer is to say that it is to act as the moral law prescribes. But this is not enough. Kant distinguishes between acting in accordance with duty, and acting from the motive of duty. A grocer who chooses honesty as the best policy,

---

[7] See above, p. 464.

or a philanthropist who takes delight in pleasing others, may do actions that are in accord with duty. Such actions conform to the moral law, but they are not motivated by reverence for it. Actions of this kind, however correct and amiable, have, according to Kant, no moral worth. Worth of character is shown only when someone does good not from inclination but from duty. A man who is wholly wretched and longs to die, but preserves his own life solely out of a sense of duty—that is Kant's paradigm of good willing (G, 398).

Happiness and duty, therefore, are for Kant not just different but conflicting motives. Aristotle had taught that people were not really virtuous as long as virtuous action went against the grain. *His* paradigm of a virtuous man was somebody who thoroughly enjoyed carrying out his virtuous endeavours. But for Kant it is the painfulness of well-doing that is the real mark of virtue. If virtue brings happiness, that must only be as a by-product. 'The more a cultivated reason concerns itself with the aim of enjoying life and happiness, the farther does man get away from true contentment' (G, 395). We should not take the Bible seriously when it tells us to love our neighbour: it is cold, unfeeling, charitable assistance that is really commanded (G, 399).

The way to test whether one is acting out of a sense of duty is to inquire into the maxim, or principle, on which one acts; that is to say, the imperative that guides one's action. An imperative may take a hypothetical form: 'If you wish to achieve so-and-so, act in such-and-such a way.' Such an imperative enjoins an action as a means to a particular end. Thus, the maxim of the honest grocer may be the hypothetical imperative: 'If you wish to keep your customers, do not overcharge them.'

A person who acts out of duty, however, is obeying not a hypothetical imperative, but a categorical imperative, which commands: 'No matter what you wish to achieve, act in such-and-such a way.' The categorical imperative of duty is an overarching imperative which discriminates between virtuous and vicious hypothetical imperatives. It is thus formulated by Kant: 'Act only according to a maxim which you can at the same time will to become a universal law.'

Kant gives several examples to illustrate the operation of the categorical imperative. Suppose that I am tempted to get out of a difficulty by making a promise I have no intention of keeping, and I then wonder whether such a lying promise can be reconciled with duty:

I have then to ask myself 'Should I really be content that my maxim (the maxim of getting out of a difficulty by a false promise) should hold as a universal law (one valid both for myself and others)? And could I really say to myself that every one may make a false promise if he finds himself in a difficulty from which he can extricate himself in no other way?' I then become aware at once that I can indeed will to lie, but I can by no means will a universal law of lying; for by such a law there could properly be no promises at all. (G, 403)

A second example is this. A well-to-do person is asked to help some others who are suffering hardship. He is tempted to respond: 'What does this matter to me? Let everyone be as happy as Heaven wills or as he can make himself. I won't do him any harm, but I won't help him either.' But when he considers the categorical imperative he comes to realize that he cannot will 'never harm but never help' as a universal maxim because in many situations he will himself need help and sympathy from others (*G*, 423).

These two examples illustrate two different ways in which the categorical imperative operates. In the first case, the vicious maxim cannot be universalized because its universalization leads to contradiction: if no one keeps promises, there is no such thing as promising. In the second case, there is nothing self-contradictory in the idea of no one ever helping anyone else; but no one could rationally *will* to bring about such a situation. Kant says that the two different kinds of case correspond to two different kinds of duties: strict duties (like that of not lying) and meritorious duties (such as that of helping the needy) (*G*, 424).

Kant argues that the categorical imperative rules out suicide. But it is not clear how it does so, in the formulation he has given. There is nothing self-contradictory in the prospect of universal suicide; and someone disgusted with the human race might well applaud the prospect. Kant has, however, a different formulation of the categorical imperative which does not appeal to universalizability: 'Act in such a way that you always treat humanity, whether in your own person or in the person of any other, never simply as a means, but always at the same time as an end.' This formulation is more effective in ruling out suicide, since it can be argued that to take one's own life is to use one's own person as a means of bringing to an end one's discomfort and distress. It also clearly rules out slavery, and in *On Perpetual Peace* Kant argues that it rules out aggressive wars. However, it is hard to see exactly what else it excludes, since we all every day make use, as means to our own ends, of other people from dustmen to solicitors. We need more enlightenment about what it is to treat people 'at the same time as an end'.

What Kant tells us is that as a human being I am not only an end in myself, but a member of a kingdom of ends. In rationally choosing my maxims, I am proposing universal laws; but so too is every other rational being. Universal law is law which is made by rational wills like mine. 'There arises', Kant tells us, 'a systematic union of rational beings under common objective laws—that is a kingdom.' A rational being is subject only to laws that are made by himself and yet are universal: the moral will is autonomous, giving to itself the laws that it obeys. In the kingdom of ends, we are all both legislators and subjects. The idea of the autonomy of the moral will is very attractive; but one wonders how Kant can be so confident that the operation of all the different rational choices of maxim will produce a single system of universal laws. Can we, as he cheerfully tells us to do, 'abstract from the personal differences between rational beings, and also from all the content of their private ends' (*G*, 433)?

'In the kingdom of ends', Kant tells us, 'everything has either a price or a worth'. If it has a price, something else can be put in its place as a fair exchange; if it is beyond price and is unexchangeable, then it has worth. There are two kinds of price: market price, which is related to the satisfaction of need, and fancy price, which is related to the satisfaction of taste. Morality is above and beyond either kind of price:

Morality, and humanity so far as it is capable of morality, is the only thing which has worth. Skill and diligence in work have a market price; wit, imagination, and humour have a fancy price; but fidelity to promises and benevolence based on principle (not on instinct) have an intrinsic worth. (*G*, 435)

Kant made room, in the kingdom of ends, for a sovereign or head who was (like the members) a legislator, but who (unlike the members) was not subject to law and did not act out of duty. This sovereign is no doubt God, but he is given no special role in the determination of the moral law. Kant's successors in later centuries, who have been attracted by the idea of the autonomous will as the moral legislator, have quietly dropped the sovereign, and turned the kingdom of ends into a republic of ends, in which no legislator is privileged over any other.

Hegel's Ethical Synthesis

We noticed earlier that Kant's ethics stood at an opposite pole from Aristotle's. For Aristotle the overarching ethical concept was that of happiness, which was the ultimate goal of every fully rational human action. Kant dethroned happiness and put in its place duty, the necessary motive of any action of moral worth. For Aristotle virtue was exhibited in the joy that a good man took in his good actions; for Kant the measure of virtue was the cost in painful effort of its exercise.

Hegel saw Aristotelian ethics and Kantian ethics as thesis and antithesis to which he should offer a synthesis. Like Aristotle he saw the foundation of ethics as a concept of human flourishing; but he defined this in terms of free self-actualization, which accorded with Kant's emphasis on the autonomy of the moral life. Unlike Kant, however, he gave pride of place in moral theory not to the notion of duty, but the notion of right: in Hegel, as in Aristotle, obedience to law takes second place to the free expression of what is best in each person's human nature.

Hegel's great innovation in moral philosophy was that he injected a social and historical element into the notion of 'human nature'. The aims and capacities which an individual can pursue and develop depend on the social institutions within which she lives, and these institutions will vary in different places and times. Rights, which are the basic elements in Hegel's ethics, are claims to exercise one's individual choice within an 'external sphere'—and this sphere is to a large extent defined by the form of the society to which one belongs. Hegel demonstrates this in a famous passage of the *Phenomenology of Spirit* which sets out how individual self-consciousness develops as a consciousness of one's role in relation to others. The example of a social relation he chooses to illustrate the point is that of master and slave.

Initially a master is fully self-conscious, but sees his slave as a mere thing. The slave is conscious of his master, but sees his own self only in his relation to the master's purposes. The master recognizes selfhood only in himself, and the slave recognizes it only in his master. However, as the slave is set to work to produce benefits for the master, the relationship changes. As his labour transforms matter into useful products, the slave becomes aware of his own power, but finds his goals still limited by the master's commands. The master, on the other hand, sees his own self-consciousness as limited through his inability to find a responsive self-consciousness in the slave. The relationship denies to each of them a full measure of self-consciousness (*PG*, 178–96).

Hegel traces through history attempts to remove the obstacles to self-consciousness set by the master–slave relationship. Stoicism encouraged people to accept their social position as a matter of cosmic necessity, to be accepted with tranquillity: both the slave Epictetus and the Emperor Marcus Aurelius embraced Stoicism. But looking within and turning one's back on society does not really resolve the contradictions implicit in the master–slave relationship. It leads on to the second form of false consciousness, the sceptical attitude which outwardly conforms to society's demands while inwardly denying the reality of the norms which society proclaims. The contrast between inner and outer attitudes becomes intolerable, and consciousness passes into a third false stage, which Hegel calls 'The Unhappy Consciousness', and which he regards as typical of medieval Christendom.

In the unhappy consciousness the contradictions of the master–slave relationship are recreated within a single individual self. A person is conscious of a gap between an ideal self and his own imperfect self, the latter a false self, the former a true but as yet unrealized self. The ideal self is then projected into another world and identified with a God of which the actual self is no part. Thus a person's consciousness is divided, and he becomes 'alienated' from it. This concept of alienation—of treating as alien something with which by rights one should identify—was to have a powerful future among Hegel's disciples.

All such forms of false consciousness represent an attempt to interiorize a problem that can only be solved by a change in social institutions. The realization of this is what accounts for the emphasis that Hegel places on rights. A person has an inalienable right to life and to freedom from slavery, and to a minimum of personal property; only societies that protect these rights can provide a context for individual human flourishing (*PR*, 46).

Rights are necessary because an individual person can only express herself as a free spirit by giving herself an external sphere of freedom. A right is an entitlement to property interpreted in a broad sense; for Hegel, a person's body, life, and liberty are his property no less than material things. Some rights, like the right to the products of one's labour, can be given up; but no one can relinquish her total freedom by accepting slavery.

Besides rights to property Hegel recognizes two other forms of right: rights of contract and rights of punishment. The former are embodied in the civil law, and the latter in the criminal law. Hegel's view of punishment is retributive: it is an annulment of wrongdoing, implicitly willed by the criminal himself since his crime was itself a violation of the universal will (PR, 99–100).

The theory of rights, important though it is for Hegel, is only one of three sections of his ethics. The other two are the theory of morality (*Moralität*) and of uprightness (*Sittlichkeit*). Morality incorporates the Kantian elements of Hegel's system, and uprightness the Aristotelian elements. Morality is defined largely in formal terms; uprightness is described in more concrete examples. Morality is related to duty, and uprightness is related to virtue.

For Hegel, morality is concerned mainly with the motives of the moral agent. Hegel distinguishes between purpose (*Absicht*) and intention (*Vorsatz*). The purpose is the overarching motive that relates an action to my welfare; the intention is the immediate end to which I choose a means. (Thus, in taking a particular medication my intention might be to lower my cholesterol level; my purpose is to keep in good health.) Intention is, for Hegel, defined in terms of knowledge: unforeseen consequences of my actions are not intentional. A good purpose is essential if an action is to be morally good.

Hegel resembles Kant in the emphasis he places on the importance of purpose, or ultimate motive. But he does not agree with him that duty is the only morally worthy purpose, and he does not appeal to the principle of universalizability as the criterion of moral acceptibility. Kant's formula of universal law, he complains, allows in some highly suspect maxims (PR, 148).

The mere belief that one's purpose is good does not suffice to render an action morally correct. Following one's conscience is indeed necessary, but not sufficient, for virtuous behaviour. Hegel stands at a distance from those subjectivists, before him and after him, who have claimed that the individual conscience is the ultimate court of appeal. Here, as elsewhere, Hegel is well aware of the social context of private judgement.

When we turn to the third section of Hegel's ethical system, uprightness, the social element becomes clearly dominant. For uprightness consists of self-harmony in one's social life; it concerns the concrete, external aspect of ethical behaviour, and this must take place in an institutional setting. This section of the *Philosophy of Right* examines the nature of three social structures in which individuals find themselves: the family, civil society, and the state. Its exposition belongs, therefore, rather to the succeeding chapter on political philosophy than to the present chapter on ethics.

The period covered by this volume is an instructive one for anyone who wishes to inquire to what extent metaphysics is a guide to ethics. Of the great seventeenth-century metaphysicians, Descartes produced an ethical system which, despite the recent respectful attention of scholars, is generally regarded as too jejune to be a key to life, while Spinoza devised an ethics which is so closely interwoven with his metaphysics that it can give guidance only to those who share his cosmic outlook. On the other hand, two great philosophers of the eighteenth century still exercise substantial influence on moral philosophy, precisely because their ethics stands at a distance from metaphysics. Hume insisted that moral prescriptions should be quite separate from any judgements of fact, whether physical or (if such were possible) metaphysical: an 'ought' never followed from an 'is'. Kant, on the other hand, though the greatest metaphysician of them all, created a moral system that demands no commitment whatever to other areas of his philosophy. Despite, or perhaps because of, this his contribution to moral philosophy went far beyond that of any other of the philosophers we have been considering. His ethics of duty remains to this day the main competitor to the eudaimonistic virtue ethics of Plato and Aristotle, and to the consequentialist utilitarian ethics that became the most influential moral system of much of the nineteenth and twentieth centuries.

9

Political Philosophy

Machiavelli's Prince

Two works of the decade 1511–20 mark the beginning of modern political philosophy: Machiavelli's *Prince* and More's *Utopia*. Both books are very different from the typical scholastic treatise which seeks to derive, from first principles, the essence of the ideal state and the qualities of a good ruler. One is a brief, stylish, how-to manual; the other is a work of romantic fantasy. The two works stand at opposite ends of the political spectrum. A Machiavellian prince is an absolute autocrat, while Utopia holds out a blueprint for democratic communism. For this reason, the two treatises can be regarded as setting out the parameters for subsequent debate in political philosophy.

It should be said, however, that *The Prince* was not Machiavelli's only political work. He also wrote discourses on Livy in which he set out recipes for republican government parallel to his recipes for monarchical rule. In the course of those discourses he enunciates the following principle:

When a decision is to be taken on which the whole safety of one's country depends, no attention should be paid either to justice or injustice, to kindness or cruelty, to praise or shame. All other considerations should be set aside, and that course adopted which will save the life and preserve the freedom of one's country.[1]

Salus populi suprema lex—'the welfare of the people is the highest law'—was not a wholly new doctrine. Cicero had proclaimed it in theory and acted on it in practice. In *The Prince*, however, it is not only the welfare of the state, but also the welfare of its ruler, which trump all other considerations. The autocratic ruler can, in the appropriate circumstances, ignore legality, morality, and public opinion.

Drawing on his experience as an official and diplomat, and on his reading of ancient history, Machiavelli describes how provinces are won and lost and how

---

[1] Quoted in Janet Coleman, *A History of Political Thought from the Middle Ages to the Renaissance* (2000), p. 248.

they can best be kept under control. If a prince is to take over a state that has been free and self-governing, he must destroy it utterly; otherwise the memory of liberty will always goad the subjects into rebellion. Once in power a prince must strive to appear, rather than to be, virtuous. He should desire to be accounted merciful rather than cruel, but in reality it is safer to be feared than to be loved.

But in order to feared, it is not necessary to make oneself hated. A prince may be feared without being hated:

so long as he does not meddle with the property or with the women of his citizens and subjects. And if constrained to put any to death, he should do so only when there is reasonable justification and manifest cause. But above all, he must abstain from the property of others. For men will sooner forget the death of their father than the loss of their patrimony. (P, ch. 17)

Nothing is more important for a prince than to appear to have the virtues of mercy, good faith, humanity, integrity, and piety, and he should never let a word leave his mouth which is not full of those estimable qualities. But in fact, in order to preserve the state, he will frequently be constrained to violate faith and to sin against charity, humanity, and religion. More people will see and hear his admirable professions than will feel the pain of his unscrupulous practice, and thus he will maintain his rule and win his subjects' praise (P, ch. 18).

In particular, a prince need not keep a promise when keeping it is hurtful to him and when the reasons for the promise have been removed. He should imitate a fox, no less than a lion, and he will never lack for plausible reasons to cloak a breach of faith. But how will anyone believe princes who constantly break their word? History shows that it is simply a matter of skill in deception. Anyone who has a mind to deceive will have no trouble finding people who are willing to be deceived.

The cool cynicism of Machiavelli's teaching is impressive. Not only does he recommend to princes absolute unscrupulousness; his advice is based on the assumption that all their subjects are gullible and guided solely by self-interest. Some have been shocked by the book's immorality; others have found its lack of humbug refreshing. Few, however, have been persuaded to admire the models held up by Machiavelli, such as Pope Alexander VI and his son Cesare Borgia. Alexander is praised as the arch dissembler: 'No man was ever more effective in making promises, or bound himself by more solemn oaths, or observed them less.' Cesare, who worked by bribery and assassination to appropriate central Italy for the Borgias, and failed to do so only through an unpredictable piece of ill-luck, is saluted as a paradigm of political skill: 'Reviewing thus all the actions of the Duke, I find nothing to blame; on the contrary it seems proper to hold him as an example to be imitated' (P, ch. 18).

The history of the papal states under the Borgia pope, or under his enemy and successor the warrior Pope Julius II, is hard to reconcile with the brief chapter of

The Prince devoted to ecclesiastical princedoms. Princes who are churchmen, Machiavelli says, have states that they do not defend and subjects that they do not govern; yet their undefended states are not taken from them, and their ungoverned subjects do not and cannot think of throwing off their allegiance. 'Accordingly, only such princedoms are secure and happy' (*P*, ch. 11).

More's Utopia

It is hard to know whether this remark was meant ironically, or was a shameless pitch to secure employment in Rome under the new Medici Pope Leo who had succeeded Julius. The passage finds a parallel in More's *Utopia*, where it is observed that treaties are always solemnly observed in Europe, partly out of reverence for the sovereign pontiffs:

Which, like as they make no promises themselves, but they do very religiously perform the same, so they exhort all princes in any wise to abide by their promises; and them that refuse or deny so to do, by their pontifical power and authority they compel thereto. (*U*, 116)

Here the intention must surely be ironical. More was willing to die in defence of the papal office; but he was not willing to deceive himself about the perfidy of some of its sixteenth-century holders.

Direct, oblique, and ironical criticism of vicious practices and institutions is a regular feature of *Utopia*. The work—a dialogue between More, just returned from a diplomatic mission to Flanders, Peter Gilles, the town clerk of Antwerp, and a fictitious navigator named Raphael Hythlodaye—is divided into two books. In the first of these, social criticism is direct and pointed; in the second, a mocking mirror is held up to reveal the distortions of contemporary society.

Hythlodaye, we are told in the first book, had been a Portuguese companion of the navigator Amerigo Vespucci, from whom the newly discovered continent of America had taken its name. Left behind by Vespucci in Brazil, he had travelled home via India and had visited many different countries, of which the most remarkable had been Utopia. More and Gilles are anxious to hear him describe it, but before doing so Hythlodaye makes some observations about practices in England. The execution of thieves, he complains, is too harsh a penalty and insufficient as a deterrent to those for whom starvation is the only alternative to robbery. It is altogether unjust that one man should suffer the loss of his life for the loss of someone else's money. Theft should be attacked by removing its cause, which is poverty. This is due to the avarice of noblemen, drones who live on the labour of others: they drive out poor farmers to enclose land for sheep-rearing, which puts up the price of both wool and food.

Hythlodaye presents two arguments against the death penalty for theft. First, it is a violation of the divine command 'Thou shalt not kill'. Second:

Everyone knows how absurd and even dangerous to the commonwealth it is that a thief and a murderer should receive the same punishment. Since the robber sees that he is in as great danger if merely condemned for theft as if he were convicted of murder as well, this reason alone impels him to murder one whom otherwise he would only have robbed... There is greater safety in putting the man out of the way and greater hope of covering up the crime if he leaves no one left to tell the tale. (U, 30)

This argument was to be repeated by reformers until the death penalty for theft was abolished by Parliament in the nineteenth century.[2] But it is the second rather than the first book of *Utopia* that was to make More famous: for it is there that we read the description of the fictitious commonwealth.

'Utopia' is a Latin transliteration of a Greek name. The Latin 'U' may represent a Greek ov, in which case the name means 'Nowhereland'. Or it may represent a Greek εv, in which case the name means 'Happyland'. The ambiguity is probably intentional.

Utopia is an island, shaped like a crescent moon, 500 miles long and 200 across at its broadest part. It contains fifty-four cities of 6,000 households apiece, each with its own agricultural hinterland. The farms are worked by the city-dwellers who are sent according to a rota, in batches of twenty, to spend two-year stints in the country. Every year each city sends three elders to meet in a senate in the capital, Amaurot. As described, Amaurot resembles More's London, with one startling difference: there is no such thing as privacy or private property. All houses are open and no door is ever locked.

Every citizen, male or female, in addition to farming learns a craft such as clothworking or carpentry. Only scholars, priests, and elected magistrates are exempt from manual labour. There are no drones, and everyone must work, but the working day is only six hours long. How do the Utopians satisfy their needs while working so few hours? It is easy to work this out if you consider how many people in Europe live in idleness:

First, almost all the women which be the half of the whole number: or else, if the women be somewhere occupied, there most commonly in their stead the men be idle. Besides this, how great and how idle a company is there of priests and religious men, as they call them; put thereto all rich men, specially all landed men, which commonly be called gentlemen and noblemen—take into this number also their servants: I mean all that flock of stout bragging swashbucklers. Join to them also sturdy and valiant beggars, cloaking their idle life under the colour of some disease or sickness. (U, 71–2)

Work in Utopia is made light not only by the many hands, but by the simplicity of the needs they serve. Buildings, being communal, are well maintained and do not need constant alteration at the whim of new owners. Clothes do not demand

---

[2] See, for instance, Macaulay's *Notes on the Indian Penal Code*, in his *Collected Works* (London, 1898), XI. 23.

great labour in their manufacture, since Utopians prefer coarse and sturdy wear of undyed cloth.

A big difference between Utopia and Plato's Republic is that the family household is the primary unit of society. Girls, when they grow up, move to the household of their husbands, but sons and grandsons remain in the same household under the rule of the oldest parent so long as he is fit to govern it. No household may contain less than ten or more than sixteen adults; excess numbers are transferred to other households who have fallen below quota. If the number of households in the city exceeds 6,000, families are transferred to smaller cities. If every city in the island is fully manned, a colony is planted overseas. If the natives there resist settlement, the Utopians will establish it by force of arms, 'for they count this the most just cause of war, when any people holdeth a piece of ground void and vacant to no good and profitable use, keeping others from the use and possession of it which, notwithstanding, by the law of nature, ought thereof to be nourished and relieved' (*U*, 76).

Each household, as has been said, is devoted to a single craft. The households' produce is placed in storehouses in the city centre from which any householder can carry away, free of charge, whatever he needs. The Utopians make no use of money; they employ gold and silver only to make chamber pots and fetters for criminals. Internal travel is regulated by passport; but any authorized traveller is warmly welcomed in other cities. But no one, wherever he may be, is fed unless he has done his daily stint of work.

The women of the households take turns in preparing meals, which are eaten in a common hall, with the men sitting with their backs to the wall facing the women on the outer benches. Nursing mothers and children under five eat apart in a nursery; the children over five wait at table. Before dinner and supper a passage is read from an edifying book; after supper there is music and spices are burnt to perfume the hall. 'For they be much inclined to this opinion: to think no kind of pleasure forbidden, whereof cometh no harm' (*U*, 81).

Utopians indeed are no ascetics, and they regard bodily mortification for its own sake as something perverse. However, they honour those who live selfless lives performing tasks that others reject as loathsome, such as road-building or sick-nursing. Some of these people practise celibacy and are vegetarians; others eat flesh and live normal family lives. The former, they say, are holier, but the latter are wiser.

Males marry at twenty-two and females at eighteen. Premarital intercourse is forbidden, but before the marriage 'a grave and honest matron showeth the woman, be she maid or widow, naked to the wooer; and likewise a sage and discreet man exhibiteth the wooer naked to the woman'. A man would not buy a colt without thorough inspection, the Utopians argue, so it is the height of foolishness to choose a partner for life without having seen more than a face (*U*, 110). In principle, marriage is lifelong, but adultery may break a marriage and in that case the innocent, but not the adulterous, spouse is allowed to remarry. Adultery is severely punished and if repeated incurs the death penalty. On rare occasions, divorce by consent is permitted.

Apart from family law, the Utopians have few laws and no lawyers. Their laws are stated simply enough to need no interpretation, and they think it better that a man should plead his own case and tell the same story to the judge that he would tell to his own attorney.

The Utopians are not pacifists, but they regard war as a matter of necessity rather than of glory: it is justified in order to repel invaders or to liberate peoples oppressed by tyranny. If a Utopian is killed or maimed anywhere, they send an embassy to determine the facts and demand the surrender of wrongdoers; if this is refused, they forthwith declare war. But they prefer to win a war by bribery or assassination rather than by battle and bloodshed; if a pitched battle abroad cannot be avoided they employ foreign mercenaries to fight it for them. In wars of defence in the homeland, husbands and wives stand in battle side by side. 'It is a great reproach and dishonesty for the husband to come home without his wife, or the wife without her husband' (U, 125).

The final chapter of Hythlodaye's account concerns Utopian religion. Most Utopians worship a 'godly power, unknown, everlasting, incomprehensible, inexplicable, far above the capacity and reach of man's wit', which they call 'the father of all'. Utopians do not impose their religious beliefs on others, and toleration is the rule. A Christian convert who proselytized with hellfire sermons was arrested, tried, and banished, 'not as a despiser of religion, but as a seditious person and raiser up of dissension among the people' (U, 133). But toleration has limits: anyone who professes that the soul perishes with the body is condemned to silence and forbidden to hold public office. Suicide on private initiative is not permitted, but the incurably and painfully sick may, after counselling, take their own lives. Reluctance to die is taken as a sign of a guilty conscience, but those who die cheerfully are cremated with songs of joy. When a good man dies 'no part of his life is so oft or gladly talked of, as his merry death'.

There are priests in Utopia—persons of extraordinary holiness 'and therefore very few'. There are thirteen, in fact, in every city, elected by popular vote in secret ballot. Women as well as men may become priests, but only if they are widows of a certain age. The male priests marry the choicest wives. Priests, male and female, take charge of the education of children, have the power to excommunicate for immoral behaviour, and serve as chaplains to the army. On great festivals they wear vestments made from birds' feathers, like those of American Indian chiefs. The service culminates in a solemn prayer in which the worshippers thank God that they belong to the happiest commonwealth and profess the truest of all religions (U, 145).

Like the Platonic Republic, Utopia alternates attractive features with repellent ones, and mixes practicable institutions with lunatic devices. Like Plato, More often leaves his readers to guess how far he is proposing serious political reforms, and how far he is simply using fantasy to castigate the follies and corruption of actual society.

Just and Unjust Wars

When discussing the Utopians' attitude to war, More states: 'Their one and only object in war is to secure that which, had it been obtained beforehand, would have prevented the declaration of war' (*U*, 120). Such a maxim would rule out all demands for unconditional surrender, and other forms of mission creep. But More, who was himself involved as a politician in more than one of Henry VIII's wars, did not work out systematically the ethical principles which make the difference between just and unjust wars. This was done later in the century by the Jesuit theologian Francisco Suarez.

Suarez, developing ideas to be found in Aquinas, summarizes the classic theory of the just war as follows:

For war to occur honourably several conditions must be observed, which can be reduced to three heads. First, it must be declared by a lawful authority; second, there must be just cause and title; third, the proper means and proportion must be observed in its inception, prosecution and victory. (*De Caritate*, 13. 1. 4)

The condition of lawful authority means, for Suarez, that wars may be waged only by sovereign governments. Individuals and groups within a state have no right to settle their differences by force of arms. The pope, however, as a supranational authority, has the right to intervene to settle disputes between Christian sovereigns.

Two kinds of just cause are recognized by Suarez. If one's country is attacked, one has the right to defend it in arms. But it can also be legitimate to wage an offensive war: a sovereign may order an attack on another state if that is the only way to remedy a grave injustice to oneself or one's allies. But hostilities may be initiated only if there is good hope of victory; otherwise the recourse to arms will fail to remedy the injustice which provided the initial ground for war.

The third condition has three elements. Before beginning war, a sovereign must offer the potential enemy the opportunity to remedy the evil complained of. Only if he fails to do so may he be attacked. In the course of the war, only such violence must be used as is necessary to achieve victory. After the war, compensation and just punishment may be exacted, and wartime wrongdoers may be executed.

The second of these elements, Suarez says, rules out deliberate attacks on innocent people. But who are the innocent? Suarez gives a definition that is narrower than that of some of his successors. Children, women, and those unable to bear arms are declared innocent by the natural law, and positive law rules out attacks on ambassadors and clerics. But all others, Suarez maintains, are legitimate targets. 'All other persons are considered guilty, for human judgement looks upon those able to take up arms as having actually done so' (13. 7. 10). Suarez accepts too that in war it is likely that some innocent people will be killed as part of the collateral damage inflicted in the course of an attack. What is ruled out is the deliberate targeting of the innocent.

Suarez sees his rules as primarily binding on sovereigns: it is they who have the duty to satisfy themselves that, on the balance of probabilities, the war they are contemplating is a just one. A regular soldier, ordered to fight, can assume that the war is just unless it is manifestly unjust; and even a mercenary volunteer can put the burden of the inquiry on to the commander of his brigade.

Suarez's teaching on the morality of warfare was taken over without acknowledgement and given much wider circulation by Hugo Grotius, a polymath Dutch lawyer and diplomat who published in 1625 a celebrated treatise, *De Iure Belli et Pacis* ('On the rights and wrongs of war and peace'). This set the doctrine of the just war in the context of a moral theory which was deliberately designed to be detachable from the notion of divine law. This did not at all mean that Grotius was an unbeliever, but his experience of the wars of religion, and the frustration of his own efforts in aid of Christian unification, led him to conclude that particular religious beliefs were an unreliable foundation for a sound international order.

Hobbes on Chaos and Sovereignty

Suarez and Grotius saw warfare as a sometimes necessary deviation from a natural order in which states would coexist harmoniously within a consensual moral framework. The most famous political philosopher of the seventeenth century, Thomas Hobbes, had a directly contrary view of the nature of politics: the natural state of free human beings was one of perpetual warfare, and it was the prime task of the moral philosopher to justify the consent of individuals to live in peaceful subjection to a government. To this he devoted his masterpiece *Leviathan*.

Hobbes draws a sombre picture of the natural condition of mankind. Men are roughly equal in their natural powers of body and mind. 'From this equality of ability, ariseth equality of hope in the attaining of our ends. And therefore if any two men desire the same thing, which nevertheless they cannot both enjoy, they become enemies.' Whether they are seeking pleasure, or aiming simply at self-preservation, men find themselves in competition with each other. Each man distrusts his competitors and fears attack, so he seeks by anticipation to overpower them. Each man seeks praise from his companions, and resents any sign of dispraise. 'So that in the nature of man, we find three principal causes of quarrel. First, competition; secondly diffidence; thirdly glory' (*L*, 82–3).

Unless and until there is a common power to keep men in awe, there will be constant quarrelsome and unregulated competition for goods, power, and glory. This can be described as a state of war: a war of every man against every man. In such conditions, Hobbes says, there can be no industry, agriculture, or commerce:

no knowledge of the face of the earth; no account of time; no arts; no letters; no society; and, which is worst of all, continual fear and danger of violent death; and the life of man, solitary, poor, nasty, brutish and short. (*L*, 84)

Some readers may think this picture too gloomy; surely there was never such a time of universal war. Perhaps not throughout the world, Hobbes admits, but we can see instances of it in contemporary America; and even in civilized countries, men are always taking precautions against their fellows. Let the reader consider that 'when taking a journey, he arms himself, and seeks to go well accompanied; when going to sleep, he locks his doors; when even in his house, he locks his chests; and this when he knows there be laws and public officers' (*L*, 84).

Hobbes insists that in describing the primeval state of war, he is not accusing human beings in their natural state of any wickedness. In the absence of laws there can be no sin, and in the absence of a sovereign there can be no law. In the state of nature, the notions of right and wrong, or justice and injustice, have no place. 'Where there is no common power, there is no law: where no law, no injustice. Force, and fraud, are in war the two cardinal virtues.' Likewise, there is no property or ownership, 'but only that to be every man's, that he can get; and for so long, as he can keep it' (*L*, 85).

Philosophers are accustomed to speak of a natural law (*lex naturalis*) and a right of nature (*ius naturale*). It is important, Hobbes insists, to distinguish between laws and rights. A right is a liberty to do or forbear doing something. A law is a command to do or forbear something. In a state of nature there are, strictly speaking, neither laws nor rights. But there are 'laws of nature': principles of rational self-interest; recipes for maximizing the chances of survival. And because there is a necessity of nature that each man desires his own good, there is a right of nature that every man may preserve his own life and limbs with all the power he has. Since he has a right to this end, he has a right to all necessary means to it, including a right to the bodies of others (*L*, 87).

As long as men retain this right, no man has security of living out his natural life. Rational self-interest, therefore, urges a man to give up some of the unfettered liberty conferred by this right in return for equal concessions by others. Thus there is a law of nature:

That a man be willing, when others are so too, as far forth, as for peace, and defence of himself he shall think it necessary, to lay down this right to all things; and be contented with so much liberty against other men, as he would allow other men against himself. (*L*, 87)

This and other laws of nature lead men to transfer all their rights, except that of basic self-defence, to a central power which is able to enforce the laws of nature by punitive sanctions.

Among the other laws of nature (Hobbes lists nineteen in all), the most important is the third 'that men keep their covenants made'. A covenant, for Hobbes, is a particular form of contract. A contract is a transfer of right to another in consideration of a reciprocal benefit. A covenant is a contract in which—unlike immediate buying and selling—there is an element of trust. At least one party to a covenant leaves the other party to perform his part of the bargain at a later time. Without the third law of nature, Hobbes says, 'covenants are in vain and but empty words; and the right of all men to all things remaining, we are still in the condition of war'. It is this law that is the foundation of the notions of justice and injustice; for injustice is precisely the failure to perform a covenant; and whatever is not unjust is just (*L*, 95–6).

But covenants do not bind where there is a fear of non-performance on either part, as there is bound to be in the state of nature. 'Therefore before the names of just, and unjust can have place, there must be some coercive power, to compel men equally to the performance of their covenants, by the terror of some punishment, greater than the benefit they expect by the breach of their covenant.' Before the establishment of a commonwealth there is no such power: 'Covenants, without the sword, are but words, and of no strength to secure a man at all' (*L*, 95–6, 111).

The only way to set up a common power is for men to 'confer all their power and strength to one man, or one assembly of men, that may reduce all their wills, by plurality of voices, unto one will'. Each man must say to every other man 'I give up my right of governing myself, to this man, or to this assembly of men, on this condition, that thou give up thy right to him and authorise all his actions in like manner.' The central authority then personifies the entire multitude, and the multitude united in a single person is called a Commonwealth. 'This is the generation of that great Leviathan, or to speak more reverently, of that mortal god, to which we owe under the immortal God our peace and defence'. The covenant made by the members of the commonwealth sets up a sovereign, and makes all the covenanting members his subjects.

There may seem to be a vicious circle in Hobbes' account. He says that there cannot be binding covenants, unless there is a sovereign to enforce them; and there cannot be a sovereign unless he is set in office by a binding covenant. To solve this difficulty, we must appreciate that the covenant and the sovereign come into existence simultaneously. The sovereign is not himself a party to the covenant, and therefore cannot be in breach of it. It is his function to enforce, not only the original covenant that constitutes the state but individual covenants that his subjects make with one another.

Although Hobbes made no secret that he was himself a royalist, he deliberately left it open in his political theory whether the sovereign should be an individual or an assembly. Had he not done so, he could hardly with consistency have returned in 1652 to an England ruled over by Parliament. But whether the sovereign authority is a monarchy, an aristocracy, or a democracy, *Leviathan* insists that its rule must be absolute. A sovereign cannot forfeit his power, and no subject can accuse his sovereign of injustice. Because the sovereign personifies the multitude, every subject is the author of every action of the sovereign, and so he cannot make any complaint about such actions. 'No man that hath sovereign power can justly be put to death, or otherwise in any manner by his subjects punished. For seeing every subject is author of the actions of his sovereign; he punisheth another, for the actions committed by himself' (*L*, 118).

The sovereign is the source of law and of property rights. He has the right to determine what means are necessary for the defence of the commonwealth, and it is his prerogative to make war and peace with other nations. He is the arbiter of all contested lawsuits, and it is for him to decide what opinions and doctrines may be maintained within the commonwealth. He alone has the power to appoint, and to reward and punish, all ministers and magistrates. If the sovereign is a monarch, he has the right to dispose of the succession to the throne (*L*, 118–20).

Finally, the sovereign is supreme in matters of religion. It is for the sovereign, and not for any presbytery or bishop, to determine which books are to be accepted as Holy Scripture and in what way they are to be interpreted. The insolent interpretations of fanatical sectaries have been the cause of civil war in England, but the greatest usurpation of sovereignty in the name of religion is to be found in Rome. 'If a man will consider the originall of this great Ecclesiastical Dominion, he will easily perceive, that the Papacy is no other, than the Ghost of the deceased Roman Empire, sitting crowned upon the grave thereof' (*L*, 463).

Under a Hobbesian sovereign, what liberty is left to the subject? Liberty is no more than the silence of the law: the subject has liberty to do whatever the sovereign has not regulated by law. Thus, a subject has liberty to buy and sell, to choose his abode, his diet, and his trade; parents have liberty to educate their children as they think fit. But does a subject ever have liberty to disobey a sovereign's command? One might expect Hobbes to answer 'Never!'—to do so would be to disobey oneself. But in fact he allows ample scope for civil disobedience:

If the sovereign command a man (though justly condemned) to kill, wound, or maim himself; or not to resist those that assault him; or to abstain from the use of food, air medicine, or any other thing, without which he cannot live; yet hath that man the liberty to disobey. (*L*, 144)

A subject cannot be compelled to incriminate himself, nor is he bound in justice to fight as a soldier at his sovereign's command. Allowance must be made, Hobbes says, for natural timorousness, not only in women but in men 'of feminine courage'. To avoid battle may be cowardly, but it is not unjust. The one occasion when military service is obligatory is when the defence of the commonwealth requires the enlistment of all who are able to bear arms. Finally, 'the obligation of subjects to the sovereign is understood to last as long, and no longer, than the power lasteth, by which he is able to protect them'. Accordingly, if the sovereign fails to fulfil his principal function, that of protecting his subjects, then their obligation to him lapses.

The theory of commonwealth presented in *Leviathan* is an original and powerful intellectual system whose structure has been reflected in the work of political philosophers from Hobbes' day to our own. The system is not totalitarian, in spite of its emphasis on absolute sovereignty, because within it the state exists for the sake of the citizens, not the other way round. Despite his loyalty to Stuart sovereigns, Hobbes did not believe in the doctrine of the divine right of kings propounded by the founder of that dynasty, King James I. For him, the rights of the sovereign derive not from God but from the rights of those individuals who renounce them to become his subjects. In this doctrine, Hobbes' closest precursor was Marsilius of Padua, who had insisted in the fourteenth century that the laws enacted by rulers derived their legitimacy, not directly from God, but only through the mediation of the citizens' consent.[3] But Hobbes is the first philosopher to derive the legitimacy of a ruler directly from a covenant of the citizens, without any authorization by God over and above his role as the ultimate cause of human nature.

Spinoza's Political Determinism

The political theory put forward by Spinoza in his *Tractatus Theologico Politicus* in 1670 resembles that of Hobbes in *Leviathan* two decades earlier. Both philosophers were determinists, and both started from a view of human nature as fundamentally egoistic. 'It is the sovereign law and right of nature', Spinoza tells us, 'that each individual should endeavour to preserve itself as it is, without regard to anything but itself.' When Spinoza talks of natural laws, he does not mean a set of commands or principles that human beings are obliged to obey: he means rather the underlying natural regularities that determine the behaviour of all things, living or inert. Fishes have natural rights no less than men, and in the context of the eternal order of nature humans are no more than a speck (E I. 200–13).

An individual's natural rights are not determined by reason but by desire and power; everyone, wise or foolish, has a right to whatever he wants and can get; nature prohibits only what no one wants and no one can achieve. However, it is better for men to live according to laws and dictates of reason, for every one is ill at ease in the midst of enmity, hatred, anger, and deceit, even though all these are

---

[3] See above, p. 328.

legitimate in the state of nature. So men must make an agreement to be guided by reason, to repress harmful desires, and to do as they would be done by.

But an agreement between one individual and another, Spinoza maintains, is only valid as long as it is useful; I can break any promise once it ceases to be to my advantage to keep it. It is necessary, therefore, to back up contracts with the threat of some greater evil than the evil which will tempt men to break it. This can only be achieved 'if each individual hands over the whole of his power to the body politic, which will then possess sovereign natural right over all things'. This power, like Hobbes' sovereign, will be bound by no laws, and everyone will be bound to obey it in all things.

But the rights of the sovereign in civil society, like the rights of the individual in a state of nature, extend only so far as his power. If he lacks the power to enforce his will, he lacks also the right. For this reason the transfer of power from individual to state can never be complete: a sovereign cannot command the inner affections of the subject (E I. 214). Here Spinoza explicitly dissociates himself from Hobbes: no man's mind can possibly lie wholly at the disposition of another, for no one can willingly transfer his natural right of free reason and judgement or be compelled to do so. In a democracy, which Spinoza believed to be the most natural form of government, 'no one transfers his natural right so absolutely that he has no further choice in affairs, he only hands it over to the majority of a society, whereof he is a unit. Thus all men remain, as they were in the state of nature, equals' (E II. 368). Moreover, Spinoza offers a more positive reason than Hobbes does for subjecting oneself to the sovereignty of the state. It is not simply for security from attack by others; it is also to provide the context for a life of full self-realization.

From his abstract theory of the state, combined with reflections upon history, especially that of the Hebrews, Spinoza derives a number of quite specific political conclusions. One is that it always leads to trouble if the clergy are given political power. Another is that good governments will allow freedom of religious belief and philosophical speculation. Everyone should be free to choose for himself his basic creed, because laws directed against mere opinion only irritate the upright without constraining any criminal. Finally, Spinoza warns that once you set up a monarchy, it is very difficult to get rid of it. In proof of this he points to the recent history of England, where the dethronement of a lawful king was followed by the rule of a much greater tyrant.

Locke on Civil Government

Spinoza was writing after the restoration of King Charles II, and it was in his reign that the theory of divine right of kings became a major issue for English philosophers. In 1680, the year after the death of Hobbes, a book called *Patriarcha, or the*

Natural Power of Kings was published. This had been written years earlier by a royalist landowner, Sir Robert Filmer, who had died during the commonwealth. It compared the monarch's power over the nation to a father's power over his family. The king's authority, it claimed, derived by patriarchal descent from the royal authority of Adam, and should be free of all restraint by elected bodies such as Parliament. Filmer's book presented an easy target for the most politically influential philosopher of the age, John Locke.

Like Hobbes, Locke in his *Two Treatises of Civil Government* takes his start from a consideration of the state of nature. Filmer's great error, he maintains, is to deny that by nature men are free and equal to each other. In the natural state, men live together without any earthly superior. 'All men', he maintains, 'are naturally in that state and remain so till by their own consents they make themselves members of some politic society' (*TG*, 2, 15).

Locke's view of the state of nature is much more optimistic than Hobbes. It is not a state of war, because everyone is aware of a natural law which teaches that all men are equal and independent, and that no one ought to harm another in his life, liberty, or possession. This law is binding prior to any earthly sovereign or civil society. It confers natural rights, notably the rights to life, self-defence, and freedom. No one can take away a right to life, whether his own or others'; and no one can take away the right to liberty by enslaving himself or another.

What of property in the state of nature? Is the whole earth the common possession of mankind, as earlier political theorists had argued, or did God assign different portions of it to different peoples and families? Or is there no such thing as private property prior to all organized society?

Locke's answer is ingenious. What gives a title to private property, even in a state of nature, is labour. My labour is undoubtedly my own; and by mixing my labour with natural goods, by drawing water, clearing forests, tilling the soil, and collecting fruit, I acquire a right to what I have worked on and what I have made of it. But my right is not unlimited: I am entitled only to such fruits of my labour as I can consume, and only to the amount of land that I can cultivate and use (*TG*, 5, 49). However, what I have thus acquired I can pass on to my children; the right of inheritance is natural and precedes any civil codification.

For Locke, then, unlike Hobbes, property rights precede and do not depend upon any covenant. However, in the state of nature men have only a precarious hold on their property. Other men, although aware of the teachings of nature, may transgress them, and there is no central authority to discipline them. Individuals have a theoretical right to punish; but they may lack power to do so, and it is unsatisfactory for everyone to be judge in his own case. It is this that leads to the institution of the state, by the only possible means, namely, by men agreeing together to give up some of their natural liberty 'to join and unite into a community for their comfortable, safe, and peaceable living one amongst another, in a secure enjoyment of their properties and a great security against any that are not of it' (*TG*, 8, 95).

Individual members of society therefore transfer whatever powers they have to enforce the law of nature to a central authority. A government has more power, and can be expected to be more impartial, in enforcing individuals' property rights than any isolated individual could hope to be. The existence of a central government, set up by consent, gives authority to two institutions whose legitimacy was doubtful in the mere state of nature: namely, the enclosure of land, and the institution of money. These institutions make it lawful to produce and enjoy more than is necessary for one's immediate subsistence, and this in turn benefits the whole of society.

The citizens hand over to a legislature the right to make laws for the common good, and to an executive the right to enforce these laws. (Locke was aware of good reasons for separating these two branches of government.) The legislature and executive may take several differen forms: it is for a majority of the citizens (or at least of the property owners) to decide which form to adopt. But a problem arises if—as Locke believed—the power of enforcing the laws includes the right to exact capital punishment. The initial contractors can hand over only what rights they have, but no one has, by the natural law, the right to commit suicide. How then can anyone confer on anyone else the right—even a conditional right—to kill him? Surely only God can confer such a right; and this was one of Filmer's arguments for deriving the authority of sovereigns directly from God.

This, however, was only one of the objections that Locke's contemporaries and successors could make to his theory of social contract. The most common was that there were no records of any such contracts ever being made. Locke offered some implausible historical examples, but more important was his distinction between explicit and implicit consent. The maintenance of any government, he insisted, depended on the continuing consent of the citizens in each generation. Such consent, he admits, is rarely explicit, but implicit consent is given by anyone who enjoys the benefits of society, whether by accepting an inheritance or merely by travelling on the highway. He can always renounce his consent by migrating to another country, or going into the wilderness to live in the state of nature.

The principal way in which Locke's social compact differs from Hobbes' convention is that the governors, unlike Hobbes' sovereign, are themselves parties to the initial contract. They hold their powers as trustees for the community, and if the government breaches the trust placed in it, the people can remove or alter it. Laws must fulfil three conditions: they must be equal for all; they must be designed for the good of the people; and they must not impose any taxation without consent. 'The supreme power cannot take from any man any part of his property without his consent.' A ruler who violates these rules, and governs in his own interest, rather than for the common good, is then at war with his subjects and rebellion is justified as a form of self-defence. When he published his *Treatises* Locke obviously had in mind the autocratic rule of the Stuart kings and the Glorious Revolution of 1688.

Locke's system is not original and is not consistent, as many later critics were to point out. It combines uneasily elements from medieval theories of natural law and post-Renaissance theories of voluntary confederation. Nonetheless, it was very influential, and its influence continued among people who had ceased to believe in theories of the state of nature and the natural law that underpinned them. The Founding Fathers of the United States drew heavily on the *Second Treatise* to argue that King George III, no less than the Stuart monarchs, had by arbitrary government and unrepresentative taxation forfeited his claim to rule and made himself the enemy of his American subjects.

Montesquieu on Law

The American Constitution also owed much to the French philosopher, Montesquieu, who was nearly sixty years Locke's junior. Montesquieu assembled a great mass of geographical, historical, and sociological data, of uneven reliability, on which to construct a theory of the nature of the state. 'Men', he tells us, 'are governed by many factors: climate, religion, law, the precepts of government, the examples of the past, customs, manners; and from the combination of such influences there arises a general spirit.' The general spirit of a particular society finds its expression in the laws appropriate for it; it creates 'the spirit of the laws', which was the title of Montesquieu's political treatise.

Montesquieu believed that there were fundamental laws of justice established by God, which preceded actual human legislation in the same way as the properties of triangles preceded their codification by geometers. But these universal principles were not in themselves sufficient to determine the appropriate structure for particular societies. It is not possible to single out a particular set of social institutions as suitable for all times and places: the government should be fitted to the climate, the wealth, and the national character of a country.

Aristotle had studied a wide variety of constitutions and classified them into three kinds: monarchy, aristocracy, and democracy.[4] Montesquieu, likewise, after his sociological inquiries, comes up with a threefold classification, but his types are republican, monarchical, and despotic. (With a bow to Aristotle, he divides republics into democratic and aristocratic republics (EL II. 1).) Each type of state is marked by a dominant characteristic: virtue, honour, and fear, respectively.

---

[4] See above, p. 71.

Such are the principles of the three governments; which does not mean that in a certain republic people are virtuous, but that they ought to be. This does not prove that in a certain monarchy people have a sense of honour, and that in particular despotic states people have a sense of fear, but that they ought to have it. Without these qualities a government will be imperfect (EL III. 2).

In a despotic state, rule is by the decree of the ruler, backed up not by law but by religion or custom. In a monarchy, government is carried on by a hierarchy of officials of varied rank and status. In a republic, all the citizens need to be educated in civic values and trained to carry out public tasks.

Republics, we are told, suit cold climates and small states; despotism suits large states and hot climates. A constitution suitable for Sicilians would not suit Scotsmen, since, *inter alia*, sea-girt islands differ from mountainous mainlands. Montesquieu's own preference, however, is for monarchy, and particularly the 'mixed monarchy' he discerned in England.

The feature that Montesquieu admired in the British Constitution, and that found its way into the American Constitution, was the principle of the separation of powers. After the revolution of 1688 Parliament had achieved sole legislative power, while leaving in practice considerable executive discretion to the king's ministers, and judges became very largely free of governmental interference. There was not—and is not to this day—to be found in British constitutional law any explicit statement that the legislative, executive, and judicial branches of government should not be combined in a single person or institution, or any formulated theory of checks and balances. Nonetheless, Montesquieu's benign interpretation of the Hanoverian system, in which the power of a sovereign's ministers essentially depended on the consent of Parliament, had a lasting influence on constitution makers in many parts of the world.

The separation of powers was important, Montesquieu believed, because it provided the best bulwark against tyranny and the best guarantee of the liberty of the subject. What, then, is liberty? 'Liberty', Montesquieu replies, 'is a right of doing whatever the laws permit' (EL XI. 3). Is that all, we may wonder; doesn't a citizen of a tyranny enjoy that much freedom? We must first remember that for Montesquieu a despot ruled not by law but by decree: only an instrument created by an independent legislature counts as a law. Secondly, in many countries, including the France of Montesquieu's own time, citizens have often been at risk of arbitrary arrest for actions that were perfectly legal but were regarded as offensive by those in power.

Montesquieu offered another, more substantial, definition of liberty. It does not consist in freedom from all restraint, but 'in the power of doing what we ought to will and in not being constrained to do what we ought not to will' (EL XI. 3). This link between liberal social institutions and an idealized form of the individual will was developed into a substantial political theory by Jean-Jacques Rousseau in his *Social Contract*.

Rousseau and the General Will

When Rousseau begins by saying 'Man is born free, and he is everywhere in chains,' those who have read his earlier works on the corrupting effect of civilization are likely to assume that the chains are those of social institutions, and that we are about to be encouraged to reject the social order. Instead, we are told that it is a sacred right which is the basis of all other rights. Social institutions, Rousseau now thinks, liberate rather than enslave.

Like Hobbes and Locke, Rousseau begins with a consideration of human beings in a state of nature. His account of such a state is, in accordance with his earlier thoughts about the noble savage, more optimistic than Hobbes'. In a state of nature men are not necessarily hostile to each other. They are motivated by self-love, to be sure, but self-love is not the same as egoism: it can be combined, in both humans and animals, with sympathy and compassion for one's fellows. In a state of nature a man has only simple, animal, desires: 'the only goods he acknowledges in the world are food, a female, and sleep; the only ills he fears are pain and hunger'. These desires are not as inherently competitive as the quest for power in more sophisticated societies.

Rousseau agrees with Hobbes, against Locke, that in a state of nature there are no property rights and therefore neither justice nor injustice. But as society develops from its primitive state, the lack of such rights begins to be felt. Economic cooperation and technical progress make it necessary to form an association for the protection of individuals' persons and possessions. How can this be done while allowing each member of the association to remain as free as he was before? The *Social Contract* provides the solution by presenting the concept of the general will.

The general will comes into existence when 'each of us puts his person and all his power in common under the supreme direction of the general will, and, in our corporate capacity, we receive each member as an indivisible part of the whole' (*SC* 1. 6). This compact creates a public person, a moral and collective body, the state or sovereign people. Every individual is both a citizen and a subject: as a citizen he shares in the sovereign authority, and as subject owes obedience to the laws of the state.

Rousseau's sovereign, unlike Hobbes' sovereign, has no existence independent of the contracting citizens who compose it. Consequently, it can have no interest independent of theirs: it expresses the general will and it cannot go wrong in its pursuit of the public good. Men lose their natural liberty to grasp whatever tempts them, but they gain civil liberty, which permits the stable ownership of property.

But what is the general will, and how is it to be ascertained? It is not the same as the unanimous will of the citizens: Rousseau distinguished between 'the general will' and 'the will of all'. An individual's will may go contrary to the general will. 'There is often considerable difference between the will of all and the general will. The latter is concerned only with the common interest, the former with interests that are partial, being itself but the sum of particular wills' (*SC* 3. 3). Should we say then that the general will should be identified with the will of the majority of the citizens? No, the deliberations of a popular assembly are by no means infallible: voters may suffer from ignorance, or be swayed by individual self-interest.

It appears to follow that even the general will is not ascertainable even by a referendum, and this seems to make it an abstraction of no practical value. But Rousseau believed that it could be determined by plebiscite on two conditions: first, that every voter was fully informed, and second, that no two voters held any communication with each other. The second condition is laid down to prevent the formation of groups smaller than the whole community. 'It is essential,' Rousseau wrote, 'if the general will is to be able to express itself, that there should be no partial society within the State, and that each citizen should think only his own thoughts' (*SC* 2. 3). So not only political parties but religious groups also must be banned if the general will is to find expression in a referendum. It is only within the context of the entire community that the differences between the self-interest of individuals will cancel out and yield the self-interest of the sovereign people as a whole.

Rousseau is no devotee in principle of the separation of powers. The sovereignty of the people, he says, is indivisible: if you separate the powers of the legislative and executive branches you make the sovereignty chimerical. However, a practical division of responsibility follows from his requirement that the sovereign people should legislate only on very general matters, leaving executive power concerning particular issues in the hands of a government which is an intermediary between subjects and sovereign. But the government must always act as a delegate of the people, and ideally a popular assembly should meet at regular intervals to confirm the constitution and to renew or terminate the mandate of the holders of public office.

The type of arrangement here proposed by Rousseau seems practicable only in a Swiss canton or a city-state like Geneva. But he insisted, like Montesquieu, that one cannot specify a single form of government as appropriate to all circumstances. However, an issue of much wider application is raised by the theory of the general will. A citizen in a Rousseauian state gives his consent to all the laws, including those that are passed in spite of his opposition (*SC* 4. 2). What, in such a polity, are the rights of dissident minorities?

Rousseau says that the social compact tacitly includes an undertaking that whoever refuses to submit to it may be constrained by his fellow citizens to conform to it. 'This means nothing other than that he shall be forced to be free.' If I vote against a measure which then triumphs in a poll, this shows that I was mistaken about where my true good, and my genuine freedom, were to be found. But the freedom that an imprisoned malefactor enjoys is only the rather rarefied freedom to be a reluctant expression of the general will.

In spite of his concern with the general will, Rousseau was not a wholehearted supporter of democracy in practice. 'If there were a people of gods, they would govern themselves democratically. But a government of such perfection is not suitable for human beings' (SC 3. 4). In a direct democracy where rule is by popular assembly, government is likely to be fractious and inefficient. Better have an elective aristocracy in which the wise govern the masses: 'there is no point in getting twenty thousand men to do what a hundred select men can do ever better' (SC 3. 4). Aristocracy demands fewer virtues in the citizens than democracy does—all that it requires is a spirit of moderation in the rich and of contentment in the poor. Naturally, the rich will do most of the governing: they have more time to spare.

This seems a tame and bourgeois conclusion to a book that began by calling mankind to throw off its chains. Nonetheless, the concept of the general will had an explosive revolutionary potential. Examined closely, the notion is theoretically incoherent and practically vacuous. It is not true as a matter of logic that if A wills A's good and B wills B's good, then A and B jointly will the good of A and B. This remains true, however well informed A and B may be, because there may be a genuine, unavoidable incompatibility between the goods of each.

It is precisely the difficulty of determining what the general will prescribes that made the notion of the general will such a powerful tool in the hands of demagogues. Robespierre at the height of the French revolutionary terror could claim that he was expressing the general will, and forcing citizens to be free. Who was in a position to contradict him? The conditions Rousseau laid down for the general will's expression were that every citizen should be fully informed and that no two citizens should be allowed to combine with each other. The first condition could never be fulfilled outside a community of gods, and the second condition of its nature demands a totally tyranny to enforce.

For better or worse, the *Social Contract* became the bible of revolutionaries, and not only in France; Rousseau's influence was enormous. Napoleon, never one to under-estimate his own importance, attributed to Rousseau an equal responsibility with himself for the gigantic changes that Europe underwent as the eighteenth century turned into the nineteenth. 'Who can tell', he asked as he approached death, 'whether the world would be a better place if Rousseau and I had never lived?'

Hegel on the Nation-State

Rousseau's notion of the general will was taken up, in different ways, by Kant and Hegel. Kant sought to give it a non-mythical form as a universal consensus of moral agents each legislating universal laws for themselves and for all others. Hegel transformed it into the freedom of the world-spirit expressing itself in the history of mankind.

There seems a vast difference, Hegel realized, between his thesis of the evolution of the spirit into ever greater freedom and self-consciousness, and the dismal spectacle presented by actual history. He accepted that nothing seemed to happen in the world except as the result of the self-interested actions of individuals; and he was willing to describe history as the slaughterhouse in which the happiness of peoples, the wisdom of states, and the virtues of individuals are sacrificed. But the gloom, he maintained, is not justified; for the self-interested actions of individuals are the only means by which the ideal destiny of the world can be realized. 'The Ideal provides the warp, and human passions the woof, of the web of history.'

Human actions are performed in social contexts, and self-interest need not be egoistic. One can find self-fulfilment in the performance of social roles: my love of my family and my pride in my profession contribute to my happiness without being forms of selfishness. Conversely, social institutions are not a restraint on my freedom: they expand my freedom by giving a wider scope to my possibilities of action. This is true of the family, and it is true also of what Hegel calls 'civil society'—voluntary organizations such as clubs and businesses. It is true above all of the state, which provides the widest scope for freedom of action, while at the same time furthering the purposes of the world-spirit (*Weltgeist*).

Ideally, a state should be so organized that the private interests of the citizens coincide with the common interests of the state. In respect of history, states and peoples themselves count among the individuals who are, unconsciously, the instruments by which the world-spirit achieves its object. There are also some unique figures, great men like Caesar or Napoleon, who have a special role in expressing the will of the world-spirit, and who see the aspects of history which are ripe for development in their time.

Such people, however, are the exception, and the normal development of the world-spirit is through the spirit of particular peoples or nations, the *Volksgeist*. That spirit shows itself in the culture, religion, and philosophy of a people, as well as in its social institutions. Nations are not necessarily identical with states— indeed, when Hegel wrote, the German nation had not yet turned itself into a German state—but only in a state does a nation become self-conscious of itself.

The creation of the state is the high object for which the world-spirit uses individuals and peoples as its instruments. A state for Hegel is not just a coercive instrument for keeping the peace or for protecting property: it is a platform for new and higher purposes which extend the liberty of individuals by giving a new dimension to their lives. The state, as the incarnation of freedom, exists for its own sake. All the worth, all the spiritual reality which the individual citizen possesses, he possesses only through the state. For only by participating in social and political life is he fully conscious of his own rationality, and of himself as a manifestation, through the folk-spirit, of the world-spirit. The state, Hegel says, is the divine Idea as it exists on earth.

The divine Idea, however, is not yet fully realized. The German spirit, Hegel believed, was the spirit of a new world in which absolute truth would be realized in unlimited freedom. But even the kingdom of Prussia was not the last word of the world-spirit. Given Hegel's constant preference for wholes over their parts, one might expect that in his scheme of things nation-states would eventually give way to a world-state. But Hegel disliked the idea of a world-state, because it would take away the opportunity for war, which was a necessary stage in the dialectic of history. War, for him, was not just a necessary evil, but had a positive value as a reminder of the contingent nature of finite existence. It was 'the condition in which we have to take seriously the vanity of temporal goods and things' (PR, 324). Accordingly, Hegel attacked Kant's quest for perpetual peace. The future of humanity, Hegel predicted, lay neither in Germany nor in a united world, but rather in America, 'where, in the ages that lie before us, the burden of the world's history shall reveal itself'—perhaps in a great continental struggle between North and South.

The history of Germany for a century and more after Hegel's death brought upon his political philosophy a barrage of obloquy. His glorification of the state as an end in itself, his belief in the cosmic role of the German people, and his positive evaluation of warfare can hardly avoid a share of the responsibility for the two World Wars that disfigured the twentieth century. It is true that the Prussian model that he commended was a constitutional monarchy, and that the nationalism he preached was at some remove from the totalitarian racism of the Nazis. Nonetheless, his philosophical career, like Rousseau's, is a reminder of the disastrous consequences that can flow from flawed metaphysics. One can believe that the state has an intrinsic value of its own only if we think of it as in some way personal, and indeed a higher form of person than an ordinary human individual. And one can rationally believe this only if one accepts some version of Hegel's metaphysical doctrine that there is a world-spirit whose life is lived through the interplay between the folk-spirits that animate the nation-states.

For those who are interested in the history of philosophy for the sake of the light it can cast on contemporary concerns, the period from Machiavelli to Hegel is the heyday of political philosophy. The political institutions of the ancient and medieval world are too distant from our own for the reflections upon them of ancient and medieval philosophers to have much to offer to contemporary political philosophy. On the other hand, as we shall see in the next Part, the political evaluations of the great philosophers of the nineteenth century owe as much to the nascent disciplines of economics and sociology as they do to the conceptual concerns that remain as the abiding core of pure political philosophy.

10

God

Molina on Omniscience and Freedom

The problem of reconciling human freedom with God's foreknowledge of human actions had baffled all the great scholastics of the Middle Ages. Thomas Aquinas maintained that God foresaw what we would do because all our actions were present to him in the single moment of eternity. Duns Scotus complained that this solution would work only if time was fundamentally unreal. Instead, he proposed that God knew creatures' actions by knowing what he himself had decreed from all eternity. Ockham objected that such knowledge would provide foreknowledge of human actions only if our actions were predetermined and therefore unfree. He himself offered no solution to the problem: divine foreknowledge was just a dogma to be blindly believed. Peter de Rivo had tried to preserve freedom while accepting divine omniscience by denying that future contingent propositions had any truth-value to be known even by God; but this was a weasel way out and was condemned by the Church. Lorenzo Valla, Erasmus, and Luther were no better able than their predecessors to reconcile liberty and omniscience. All were reduced to quoting the Pauline text with which every theologian sooner or later admits his bafflement on this topic: 'Oh, the depth of the riches both of the wisdom and knowledge of God! How unsearchable are his judgments and his ways past finding out!' (Rom 11: 35).[1]

A novel and highly ingenious solution to the problem was proposed at the end of the sixteenth century by the Jesuit Luis Molina. Molina agreed with Ockham in rejecting the accounts of Aquinas and Scotus, and he accepted the Church teaching that future contingent propositions had truth-values. His innovation was to suggest that God's knowledge of the future depended on God's knowledge of the truth-values of counterfactual propositions. God knows what any possible creature would freely do in any possible circumstances. By knowing this and by

---

[1] See above, pp. 482–5.

knowing which creatures he will create and which circumstances he will himself bring about, he knows what actual creatures will in fact do.

Molina made a distinction between three kinds of divine knowledge. First, there is God's natural knowledge, by which he knows his own nature and all the things that are possible to him either by his own action or by the action of free possible creatures. This knowledge is prior to any divine decision about creation. Then there is God's free knowledge: his knowledge of what will actually happen after the free divine decision to create certain free creatures and place them in certain particular circumstances. Between these two kinds of knowledge there is God's 'middle knowledge': that is, his knowledge of what any possible creature will do in any possible circumstances. Because middle knowledge is based on creatures' own hypothetical decisions, human autonomy is upheld; because middle knowledge is prior to the decision to create, God's omniscience about the actual world is preserved.

What Molina called 'circumstances', or 'orders of events', later philosophers have called 'possible worlds'. So Molina's theory is essentially that God's knowledge of what will happen in the actual world is based on his knowledge of all possible worlds plus his knowledge of which possible world he has decided to actualize. Before creating Adam and Eve God knew that Eve would yield to the serpent and Adam would yield to Eve. He knew this because he knew all kinds of counter-factuals about Adam and Eve: he knew what they would do in every possible world. He knew, for instance, whether Adam, if tempted by the serpent directly rather than via Eve, would still have eaten the forbidden fruit. The weak point in Molina's solution is his assumption that all counterfactual propositions—propositions of the form 'If A were to happen, B would happen'—have truth-values. Undoubtedly, some such propositions, e.g. 'if the earth were to crash into the sun, human life would cease to exist,' are true; other such propositions, e.g. 'if the Great Pyramid were hexagonal, it would have seventeen sides,' are false; but when we ascribe truth-values to such propositions we do so on the basis of logical or natural laws. Matters are different when we construct counterfactuals about free agents. There is no general principle of conditional excluded middle which runs 'Either (if A were to happen B would happen), or (if A were to happen B would not happen').

Descartes, in answer to a query from Princess Elizabeth, offered a reconciliation between divine foreknowledge and human freedom that in some ways resembles Molina's. He wrote:

Suppose that a King has forbidden duels, and knows with certainty that two gentlemen of his kingdom who live in different towns have a quarrel, and are so hostile to each other that if they meet nothing will stop them from fighting. If this King orders one of them to go on a certain day to the town where the other lives, and orders the other to go on the same day to the place where the first is, he knows with certainty that they will meet, and fight, and thus disobey his prohibition: but none the less, he does not compel them, and his knowledge, and even his will to make them act thus, does not prevent their combat when they meet being as voluntary and free as if they had met on some other occasion and he had known nothing about it. And they can be no less justly punished for disobeying the prohibition. Now what a King can do in such a case, concerning certain free actions of his subjects, God, with His infinite foresight and power does infallibly in regard to all the free actions of all men. (AT IV. 393; *CSMK* III. 282)

Descartes does not, however, say like Molina that God knows what our actions will be because he has already seen what we would do in all possible worlds; he goes on to say that God knows what we will do because he has determined what desires he will give us and what circumstances he will place us in. But this takes away the point of the parallel with the king of his parable. It is only because all the other actions of the duellists that have formed their characters are independent of the king's desires and control that he can plausibly be said not to be responsible for their final duel, and to be entitled to punish them for disobeying his prohibition. If every action of every human being is stage-managed by God just as much as the final act in the duellists' drama it is hard to see how God himself can avoid being responsible for sin.

Descartes' Rational Theology

Descartes' principal contributions to philosophical natural theology are in two different areas. First, he refashioned the traditional concept of creation. Second, he revived a version of the ontological argument of God's existence.

Theologians have commonly distinguished between creation and conservation. In the beginning, God created heaven and earth, and from day to day he keeps heaven and earth in being. But his conservation of the universe does not involve fresh acts of creation: beings, once created, have by themselves a tendency to keep on existing, unless interfered with. They have a kind of existential inertia.

Descartes rejected this, when, in the third *Meditation*, he was inquiring about his own origin:

All the course of my life may be divided into an infinite number of parts, none of which is in any way dependent on the other; and thus from the fact that I was in existence a short time ago it does not follow that I must be in existence now, unless some cause at this instant, so to speak, produces me anew. (AT VII. 50; *CSMK* II. 334)

One's life is not a continuous duration, but rather is built up out of instants, in the way in which movement in the cinema is built out of a series of stills. The cause that Descartes has in mind in this passage is, of course, God. So for him there is no distinction between creation and conservation: at each moment I am created anew by God. In physics, Descartes opposed atomism; since matter was identical with extension, and extension was infinitely divisible, there could be no indivisible parts of matter. But the doctrine of continuous creation seems to involve a certain metaphysical atomism: history is built up out of an infinite number of time slices, each of which is quite independent of its predecessor and its successor.

The passage we have been considering occurs in the third *Meditation* when Descartes was offering a proof of God's existence from the occurrence in his own mind of an idea of God.[2] But in the fifth *Meditation* he offers a different proof of God's existence, which since the time of Kant has been famous under the title 'the ontological argument'. The argument was already adumbrated in the *Discourse on Method*:

I saw quite well that, assuming a triangle, its three angles must be equal to two right angles; but for all that, I saw nothing that assured me that there was any triangle in the real world. On the other hand, going back to an examination of my idea of a perfect Being, I found that this included the existence of such a Being; in the same way as the idea of a triangle includes the equality of its three angles to two right angles ... Consequently, it is at least as certain that God, the perfect Being in question, is or exists, as any proof in geometry can be. (AT VI. 36; *CSMK* I. 129)

Expanding on this in the fifth *Meditation*, Descartes says that reflecting on the idea he has of God, a supremely perfect being, he clearly and distinctly perceives that everlasting existence belongs to God's nature. Existence can no more be taken away from the divine essence than the sum of the angles can be taken away from a Euclidean triangle. 'It is not less absurd to think of God (that is, a supremely perfect being) lacking existence (that is, lacking a certain perfection) than to think of a hill without a valley' (i.e. an uphill slope without a downhill slope).

To see that this argument is not a simple begging of the question of God's existence, we have to recall that Descartes believed in a Platonic world of essences independent both of the real world and the world of the mind.[3] 'When I imagine a triangle, it may be that no such figure exists anywhere outside my thought, or never has existed; but there certainly is its determinate nature, its essence, its form, which is unchangeable and eternal. This is no figment of mine, and does not depend on my mind.' Theorems can be proved about triangles whether or not anything in the world is triangular; similarly, therefore, theorems could be stated about God in abstraction, whether or not there exists any such being. One such theorem is that God is a totally perfect being, that is, he contains all perfections. But existence itself is a perfection; hence, God, who contains all perfections, must exist.

The vulnerable point in the argument is the claim that existence is a perfection. This was siezed upon by Pierre Gassendi, author of the fifth set of Objections to the Meditations. 'Neither in God nor in anything else is existence a perfection, but rather that without which there are no perfections ... Existence cannot be said to exist in a thing like a perfection; and if a thing lacks existence, then it is not just

[2] See p. 529 above.   [3] See p. 639 above.

imperfect or lacking perfection, it is nothing at all.' Descartes had no ultimately convincing answer to this objection, and it was later to be pressed home conclusively by Immanuel Kant and Gottlob Frege.[4]

Pascal and Spinoza on God

Continental philosophers in the century of Descartes moved on from his treatment of God's existence in two different directions. Blaise Pascal abandoned the quest for a demonstration: our natural reason was so limited and so corrupt that any such attempt must be futile. Instead, he urged informal considerations that should prompt us to believe in the absence of proof. Baruch Spinoza, on the other hand, offered his own version of the ontological argument, giving it the most thoroughly formalized presentation it had ever received.

Pascal admits that by the natural light of reason we are incapable not only of knowing what God is, but even if there is a God at all. But the believer is not left without resource. He addresses the unbeliever thus:

Either God exists or not. Which side shall we take? Reason can determine nothing here. An infinite abyss separates us, and across this infinite distance a game is being played, which will turn out heads or tails. Which will you bet? (*P*, 680)

You, the unbeliever, perhaps prefer not to wager at all. But you cannot escape: the game has already begun and all have a stake. The chances, so far as reason can show, are equal on either side. But the outcomes of the possible bets are very different. Suppose you bet your life that God exists. If you win, God exists, and you gain infinite happiness; if you lose, then God does not exist and what you lose is nothing. So the bet on God is a good one. But how much should we bet? If you were offered three lives of happiness in return for betting your present life, it would make sense to take the offer. But in fact what you are offered is not just three lifetimes but a whole eternity of happiness, so the bet must be infinitely attractive. We have been assuming that the chances of winning or losing a bet on God are fifty-fifty. But the proportion of infinite happiness, in comparison with what is on offer in the present life, is so great that the bet on God's existence is a solid proposition even if the odds against winning are enormous, so long as they are only finite.

Is it true, as Pascal assumes, that one cannot suspend judgement about the existence of God? In the absence of a convincing proof either of theism or of atheism, is not the rational position that of the agnostic, who refuses to place a bet either way? Pascal claims that this is tantamount to betting against God. That may

---

[4] See below, p. 742.

be so, if in fact there is a God who has commanded us under pain of damnation to believe in him; but that should be the conclusion, not the starting point of the discussion.

What is it, in fact, to bet one's life on the existence of God? For Pascal, it meant leading the life of an austere Jansenist. But if reason alone can tell us nothing about God, how can we be sure that that is the kind of life that he will reward with eternal happiness? Perhaps we are being invited to bet on the existence, not just of God, but of the Jansenist God. But then the game is no longer one in which there are only two possible bets: someone may ask us to bet on the Jesuit God, or the Calvinist God, or the God of Islam. Pascal's ingenious apologetic does not succeed in its task; but it does draw attention to the fact that it is possible to have good reasons for believing in a proposition that are quite separate from reasons that provide evidence for its truth. This consideration was to be developed in more elaborate ways by later philosophers of religion such as Søren Kierkegaard and John Henry Newman.

Spinoza, on the other hand, was not at all a betting man: he liked his reasons as cut and dried as possible. The existence of God, he believed, could be shown to be as plain to see as the truth of any proposition in Euclid. To show this he presented his own version of the ontological argument, set out in geometrical form, in the first book of his *Ethics*.

Proposition 11 of that book reads: 'God, a substance consisting of infinite attributes, each of which expresses an eternal and infinite essence, necessarily exists.' The description here given of God is derived from the sixth of the series of definitions set out at the beginning of the book.

The proof of proposition 11 is by *reductio ad absurdum*:

If you deny this, conceive, if you can, that God does not exist. Therefore (by Axiom 7) his essence does not involve existence. But this (by Proposition 7) is absurd. Therefore, God necessarily exists. Q.E.D. (*Eth*, 7)

If we look up Axiom 7, we find that it says that if a thing can be conceived as non-existing its essence does not involve existence. Proposition 7 is more controversial: existence is part of the nature of a substance. To prove this, Spinoza tells us that a substance cannot be produced by anything else, and so must be its own cause; that is to say, its essence must involve existence. But why cannot a substance be produced by something else—by another substance? We are referred to Proposition 5 (there cannot be two or more substances with the same attribute) and to Proposition 3 (if A is to be the cause of B, A must have something in common with B). These in turn rest on Definition 3, the initial definition of substance as 'that which is in itself and is conceived by itself, so that its concept can be formed independently of the concept of any other thing' (*Eth*, 1).

Two elements in Spinoza's argument are counterintuitive. Are we not surrounded in life by cases of substances giving rise to other substances, most conspicuously living things generating other living things? And why should we accept the claim that if B is the cause of A, then the concept of B must be part of the concept of A? It is not possible to know what lung cancer is without knowing what a lung is, but is it not possible to know what lung cancer is without knowing what the cause of lung cancer is? Spinoza is identifying causal relationships and logical relationships in a manner that is surely unwarranted. But it is not, of course, inadvertent: the equivalence of the two kinds of consequence, logical and causal, is a key element of his metaphysical system. But it is not argued for: it is smuggled in through the original definition of substance.

Spinoza's initial set of definitions includes also a novel definition of God as containing an infinite number of attributes. Since we are told that we can only know two of these attributes, namely thought and extension, these infinite attributes play little further part in the system. Once Spinoza has proved to his satisfaction the existence of God he goes on to derive a number of properties of God that belong to traditional theism: God is infinite, indivisible, unique, eternal, and all-comprehending; he is the first efficient cause of everything that can fall within his comprehension, and he is the only entity in which essence and existence are identical (*Eth*, 9–18). But he also describes God in highly unorthodox ways. Although in the *Tractatus* he had campaigned against anthropomorphic concepts of God, he nonetheless states that God is extended, and therefore is something bodily (*Eth*, 33). God is not a creator as envisaged in the Judaeo-Christian tradition: he does not choose to give existence to the universe, but everything that there is follows by necessity from the divine nature. He is free only in the sense that he is not determined by anything outside his own nature, but it was not open to him not to create or to create a world different from the one that we have (*Eth*, 21–2). He is an immanent and not a transcendent cause of things, and there is no such thing as the purpose of creation.

Spinoza's innovations in natural theology are summed up in the equation of God with Nature. Although the word was not invented until the next century, his theism can be called 'pantheism', the doctrine that God is everything and everything is God. But, like every other element in his system, 'Nature' is a subtle concept. Like Bruno, Spinoza distinguishes *Natura Naturans* (literally, 'Nature Naturing', which we may call 'active nature') and *Natura Naturata* ('Nature Natured', which we may call 'passive nature'). The infinite attributes of the single divine substance belong to active nature; the series of modes that constitute finite beings belong to passive nature. Just as the finite beings that make up the tapestry of the universe cannot exist or be conceived without God, so too God cannot exist or be conceived of without each of these threads of being. Most significantly, we are told that intellect and will belong not to active nature but to passive nature. Hence, God is not a personal God as devout Jews and Christians believed.

Does this mean that God does not love us? Spinoza, as we have seen, believed that intellectual love for God was the highest form of human activity. But he went on to say that a man who loves God should not endeavour that God should love him in return. Indeed, if you want God to love you, you want him to cease to be God (*Eth*, 169–70). However, God can be said to love himself, and our love of God can be seen as one expression of this self-love. In this sense God's love for men is exactly the same thing as men's intellectual love of God.

The Optimism of Leibniz

When Leibniz visited Spinoza in 1676 one of the topics they discussed was Descartes' ontological argument for the existence of God. Descartes had argued that God is by definition a being who possesses all perfections; but existence is a perfection, therefore God possesses existence. Leibniz thought this argument had a dubious premiss: how can we know that the idea of a being possessing all perfections is a coherent idea? He wrote a paper for Spinoza in which he tried to make good this defect. He defined a perfection as a 'simple quality which is positive and absolute'. Incompatibility, he argued, could only arise between complex qualities which, when analysed, might be shown to contain contradictory elements. But a simple quality is unanalysable. Accordingly, there is nothing impossible in the notion of a being containing all simple qualities, that is to say an *ens perfectissimum* (G VII. 261–2).

Leibniz, having added this rider, accepted the ontological argument. He did not question the idea that existence is a perfection—the premiss that, to Gassendi at the time, and to many philosophers from Kant to the present day, has seemed the really vulnerable point in Descartes' reasoning. This is surprising, for as we have seen in his own system existence is something quite different from all the predicates that attach to a subject and constitute its definition.[5]

Leibniz gives a new twist also to the cosmological proof which argues to God as the first cause of the universe. He does not assume that a series of finite causes must itself be a finite series: he says, for instance, that an infinity of shapes and movements, present and past, form part of the efficient cause of his writing the *Monadology*. But each element in this series is a contingent entity which does not have in itself a sufficient reason for its existence. The ultimate reason must be found outside the series, in a necessary being, and this we call God (G VI. 613). Clearly, this argument stands or falls with the principle of sufficient reason.

Leibniz offers two other proofs of God's existence, one traditional and one novel. One is the argument from eternal truths, which goes back to St Augustine.[6] It runs as follows. Minds are the regions in which truths dwell; but logical and mathematical truths are prior to human minds, so they must have a *locus* in an eternal divine mind.

---

[5] See above, p. 648.   [6] See above, pp. 468–70.

The second, new, argument depends on the theory of the pre-established harmony: 'This perfect harmony of so many substances that have no communication with each other can only come from a common cause' (G IV. 486). This argument, of course, will convince only those who have accepted Leibniz's system of windowless monads.

Unlike Spinoza, Leibniz believed that God was totally distinct from nature, and that he had freely created a world of free creatures. Before deciding to create, God surveys the infinite number of possible creatures. Among the possible creatures there will be many possible Julius Caesars; among these there will be one Julius Caesar who crosses the Rubicon and one who does not. Each of these possible Caesars acts for a reason, and neither of them will be necessitated to act. When, therefore, God decides to give existence to the Rubicon-crossing Caesar he is making actual a freely choosing Caesar. Hence, our Caesar crossed the Rubicon freely.

What of God's own choice to give existence to the actual world we live in, rather than the myriad other possible worlds he might have created? Leibniz answers that God, as a rational agent, chose to create the best of all possible worlds. In the eighth chapter of the first part of his *Theodicy* he says that God's supreme wisdom, conjoined with infinite goodness, could not have failed to choose the best. A lesser good is a kind of evil, just as a lesser evil is a kind of good; so God must have chosen the best world under pain of having done evil. If there were no best world, he would not have chosen to create at all. It may appear that a world without sin and suffering would have been better than ours, but that is an illusion. If the slightest existing evil were lacking in the present world, it would be a different world. The eternal truths demand that physical and moral evil are possible, and therefore many of the infinitely many possible worlds will contain them. For all we can show to the contrary, therefore, the best of all worlds is among those that contain evils of both kinds (G VI. 107 ff.).

Leibniz was not the first to claim that our world was the best possible—already in the twelfth century Abelard had maintained that God had no power to make a better world than the one he had made.[7] But Leibniz distinguished his position from Abelard's by saying that other worlds besides the actual one are possible— metaphysically possible. The necessity which obliged God to choose the best world was a moral, not a metaphysical, necessity. he was determined not by any lack of power, but by the infinity of his goodness. Thus Leibniz can claim, in the *Discourse* (D, 3), that God creates the world freely: it is the highest liberty to act perfectly, according to sovereign reason. God acts freely because although he cannot create anything but the best he need not have created at all.

Leibniz believed that his theory solved the traditional problem of evil: why does an omnipotent and loving God permit sin and suffering? He points out that not all

[7] See above, p. 481.

things that are possible in advance can be made actual together: as he puts it, A and B may each be possible, but A and B may not be compossible. Any created world is a system of compossibles, and the best possible world is the system that has the greatest surplus of good over evil. A world in which there is free will that is sometimes sinfully misused is better than a world in which there is neither freedom nor sin. Thus the existence of evil in the world provides no argument against the goodness of God.

One is inclined to make to the 'optimism' of Leibniz the kind of objection that he made to Descartes' ontological argument. How do we know that 'the best of all possible worlds' expresses a coherent notion? Leibniz himself offered a proof that there was no such thing as the fastest of all possible motions. If there is such a velocity, imagine a wheel rotating at such a rate; if you stick a nail in the wheel to project out from its circumference, the nail will rotate even faster, which shows the absurdity of the notion (G IV. 424). If the alleged best possible world contains evil E, can we not imagine a world similar in all other respects but lacking E? And if God is omnipotent, how could it be impossible for him to bring such a world into being?

The God of Berkeley

We have seen that Leibniz found much to approve in Berkeley's early writings. The admiration, however, does not seem to have been reciprocated. Berkeley was scornful of Leibniz's ontological argument for the existence of God. On the other hand he offered a new proof of his own—a 'direct and immediate demonstration' of the being of God—which could be regarded as a gigantic expansion of the argument from eternal truths borrowed by Leibniz from St Augustine. In the dialogue, having established to his satisfaction that sensible things cannot exist otherwise than in a mind or spirit, he continues:

Whence I conclude, not that they have no real existence, but that, seeing they depend not on my thought, and have an existence distinct from being perceived by me, there must be some other Mind wherein they exist. As sure, therefore, as the sensible world really exists, so sure is there an infinite omnipresent Spirit who contains and supports it. (BPW, 175)

Thus, not only do the august truths of logic and mathematics dwell as ideas in the mind of God, so does the most everyday empirical truth, such as the fact that there is a ladybird walking across my desk at this moment. Berkeley is not simply saying that God knows such humble truths—that had long been the majority opinion among theologians. He is saying that the very thing that makes such a proposition true is nothing other than a set of ideas in God's mind—God's idea of the ladybird and God's idea of my desk. This was indeed an innovation. 'Men commonly believe that all things are known or perceived by God, because they believe the being of a God, whereas I on the other side immediately and necessarily conclude the being of a God, because all sensible things must be perceived by Him' (*BPW*, 175).

If we grant to Berkeley, for the sake of argument, that the sensible world consists only of ideas, there still seems to be a flaw in his proof of God's existence. One cannot, without fallacy, pass from the premiss 'There is no finite mind in which everything exists' to the conclusion 'therefore there is an infinite mind in which everything exists'. It could be that whatever exists exists in some finite mind or other, even though no finite mind is capacious enough to hold every existent. Few would be convinced by the following parallel argument. 'All humans are citizens; there is no nation state of which everyone is a citizen; therefore there is an international state of which everyone is a citizen.'

Perhaps Berkeley is really intending to argue that if things existed only in finite minds, their existence would be patchy and intermittent. The horse in his stable would exist while he was looking at it, and again when his groom was attending to it, but would go out of existence in between whiles. Only if there is an infinite, omnipresent, omnitemporal mind will continuous existence be guaranteed. This is the theme of a famous pair of limericks in which Ronald Knox tried to summarize Berkeley's contention:

> There was a young man who said, 'God
> Must think it exceedingly odd
>   If he finds that this tree
>   Continues to be
> When there's no one about in the Quad.'

Reply:

> Dear Sir, your astonishment's odd
> *I* am always about in the Quad.
>   And that's why the tree
>   Will continue to be
> Since observed by
>   Yours faithfully,
>   GOD.

The God whose existence is allegedly proved by Berkeley's route seems different in an important respect from the God of traditional theism. If objects when perceived by no finite spirit are kept in existence by God's perceiving them, there must be in God's mind ideas of all perceptible things—not only objects like desks and ladybirds, but also colours, shapes, smells, pleasures, pains, and all kinds of sense-data. But Christian thinkers had commonly denied that God enjoyed sense-experience. The psalmist asked: 'Is the inventor of the ear unable to hear? The creator of the eye unable to see?' These rhetorical 'questions expecting the answer no' were given a 'yes' answer by Thomas Aquinas and a multitude of other theologians. Commenting on the text 'the eyes of the Lord are on the just,' Aquinas wrote, 'Parts of the body are ascribed to God in the scriptures by a metaphor drawn from their functions. Eyes, for example, see, and so when "God's eye" is spoken of, it means his power to see, even though his seeing is an intellectual and not a sensory activity' (Ia 3.1 ad 3).

For Aristotelians it was clear that God had no senses or sensory experience, because in order to see, hear, feel, taste, or otherwise sense it was essential to have a body, and God had no body. However, since Descartes had made popular the idea that the key element in human sensation was in fact a purely mental event, the matter was no longer so clear-cut. But Berkeley is anxious to avoid the conclusion that God has sense-experience.

In the third dialogue Hylas, the opposition spokesman, says that it would follow from Berkeley's theory that God, the perfect spirit, suffers pain, which is an imperfection. Berkeley's mouthpiece, Philonous, replies as follows:

> That God knows or understands all things, and that he knows, among other things, what pain is, even every sort of painful sensation, and what it is for creatures to suffer pain, I make no question. But that God, though he knows and sometimes causes painful sensations in us, can himself suffer pain, I positively deny ... No corporeal motions are attended with the sensations of pain or pleasure in His mind. To know everything knowable is certainly a perfection; but to endure or suffer or feel anything by sense is an imperfection. The former, I say, agrees to God, but not the latter. God knows, or hath, ideas; but His ideas are not conveyed to him by sense as ours are. (*BPW*, 202–3)

It is difficult to see how this is consistent with Berkeley's epistemology. Among the ideas we encounter are those of hot and cold, sweet and sour. If all ideas are ideas in the mind of God, then these ideas are somehow in the mind of God. If God nonetheless does not feel sensations, then the possession of such ideas is insufficient for sensation. But if that is so, then Berkeley's account of ordinary human sensation is quite inadequate.

Hume on Religion

Unlike Berkeley, Hume made a lasting, if negative, contribution to natural theology. His critical observations on the arguments for the existence of God, and his discussion of the role of miracles in establishing the authority of a revelation, have remained points of departure for both theist and atheist philosophers of religion. We may consider first the essay on miracles which was inserted as section ten of the *Inquiry*, having no counterpart in the earlier *Treatise*.

A miracle, for Hume, is a violation of a law of nature: he gives as examples of miracles a dead man coming back to life, or the raising of a house or ship into the air. Surprisingly, he does not deny that miracles are possible—he does not, like some of his followers, argue that if an apparently miraculous event were proved to have happened that would not show that a law had been violated, but that we had oversimplified our statement of the law. What he is really interested in is not whether miracles can be done, but whether they can be seen to be done. For his target is the use of miracles by apologists to claim supernatural authorization of a particular religious message.

The first part of the essay ends with the following statement:

> No testimony is sufficient to establish a miracle unless the testimony be of such a kind that its falsehood would be more miraculous, than the fact, which it endeavours to establish . . . When anyone tells me that he saw a dead man restored to life, I immediately consider with myself whether it be more probable that this person should either deceive or be deceived, or that the fact, which he relates, should really have happened . . . If the falsehood of his testimony would be more miraculous than the event which he relates; then, and not till then, can he pretend to command my belief or opinion. (W, 212)

Hume is not ruling out that a miracle could be proved, any more than he ruled out that a miracle could happen. Indeed, he tells us that given the appropriate unanimity of testimony, he would himself be prepared to believe what he regards as a miracle, namely, a total darkness over the whole earth for eight days. We may find this surprising. On his own definition a miracle is a violation of the laws of nature, and someone's being deceived or deceiving could never be a violation of a law of nature; therefore the evidence against a miracle must always be stronger than the evidence for it. But we must remember that according to Hume's account of the human will, a human action can be just as much a violation of a law of nature as any physical event.

Hume is surely right that if it is claimed that an event E has happened which is a violation of a law of nature, then the probability that E happened must be in inverse proportion to the evidence that if E happened it would be a violation of the law. For the evidence that if E happened it would be a violation of the law is *eo ipso* evidence that E didn't happen. But surely Hume must have overstated his case. Otherwise it would never be possible for scientists to correct a mistaken belief about a natural law. Faced with a claim by a colleague that his experiments have revealed a counter-example to the law, they should, on Hume's showing, discount the evidence on the grounds that it would be less of a miracle for the experimenter to be lying or mistaken than for the law to be violated.

In the second part of the essay Hume offers three de facto arguments to show that miracles never have been established on evidence full enough to meet his standards. First, he states categorically that no miracle has been sufficiently attested by sufficiently good witnesses who have much to lose and can be easily detected if fraudulent. Second, he evokes the credulity of the human race, as shown in the numerous imposture miracles subsequently detected. Third, he maintains that supernatural and miraculous stories abound chiefly among ignorant and barbarous nations. Each of these contentions can be, and has been, contested on straightforward historical grounds.

More interesting is his fourth argument, which is based on the undoubted fact that miracles are claimed to have been wrought in aid of religions which contradict each other. If a miracle proves a doctrine to be revealed by God, and consequently true, a miracle can never be wrought for a contrary doctrine. Hence, every story of a miracle wrought in support of one particular religion must be a piece of evidence against any story of a miracle wrought in favour of a different religion.

Hume considers three examples to illustrate his point: the cure of a blind and lame man by the emperor Vespasian, reported in Tacitus; Cardinal de Retz's account of a man who grew a second leg by rubbing an amputated stump with holy oil; and the miracles wrought at the tomb of a devout Jansenist, the Abbé Paris. The three cases are of uneven interest: the evidence for the first two miracles is no more than a few hundred words, but for the third there are volumes and volumes of authenticated testimony. Hume describes the events thus:

The curing of the sick, giving hearing to the deaf, and sight to the blind, were everywhere talked of as the usual effects of that holy sepulchre. But what is more extraordinary: many of the miracles were immediately proved on the spot, before judges of unquestioned integrity, attested by witnesses of credit and distinction, in a learned age, and on the most eminent theatre that now is in the world. (W, 220)

Hume's picture is a little overdrawn, and is not quite consistent with his earlier point that miracles are only reported in barbarous contexts. But historians of undoubted Catholic piety confirm the main lines of his account of these miracles wrought in support of a heresy that had been repeatedly condemned by the popes. It seems to me that this final argument does establish Hume's case that a miracle cannot be proved in such a way as to be the foundation of a religion. Not, of course, that theists have ever thought that it could be so, in the sense of showing that God exists; they have only claimed that if we know from elsewhere that God exists we know that he is almighty and that it is in his power to work miracles, perhaps in order to authenticate one sect rather than another.

Do we know of God from other sources—from the traditional arguments, for instance? Hume believed that there was no being whose non-existence implied a contradiction: accordingly, he had little sympathy with the ontological argument for the existence of God. But he makes no direct onslaught on it; his most relevant remarks occur in the section of the *Treatise* in which he is trying to establish the nature of belief. In arguing that belief was not an idea, he claimed that when, after conceiving something, we conceive it is existent, we add nothing to our first idea:

Thus when we affirm, that God is existent, we simply form the idea of such a being, as he is represented to us; nor is the existence, which we attribute to him, conceiv'd by a particular idea, which we join to the idea of his other qualities, and can again separate and distinguish from them ... When I think of God, when I think of him as existent, and when I believe him to be existent, my idea of him neither encreases nor diminishes. (*T*, 94)

It is correct that believing and conceiving need not differ in content: if I believe that God exists and you do not we are disagreeing, in Hume's terms, about the same idea. But having a thought about God and believing that God exists are two quite different things—an atheist who says 'if there is a God, then he is a brute or braggart' expresses, in his if-clause, the thought that God exists without assenting to it. And Hume is wrong to say that there is no concept of existence distinct from the concept of the existing thing—if that were so, how could we judge that something does *not* exist? But it is true, and important, that the concept of existence is quite a different kind of concept from the concept of God or the concept of a unicorn. To say that unicorns exist is to make a statement of a quite different logical form from the statement that unicorns are difficult to tame. Hume's insight here was given more precise and accurate form by later philosophers such as Kant and Frege, who used it in a definitive demolition of the ontological argument.

The argument from design is treated more fully and respectfully by Hume. His *Dialogues Concerning Natural Religion* feature three characters, Cleanthes, Philo, and Demea. It is a tribute to Hume's skill in composition that it is not easy to identify which of the three is the spokesman for his own views. Of the three, Demea is the character presented least sympathetically; but scholars have been willing, on both internal and external grounds, to identify both Philo and Cleanthes as mouthpieces for their author. It is remarkable that both of them take seriously the argument from design.

In the second part, Cleanthes compares the universe to a great machine divided into an infinite number of smaller machines:

All these various machines, and even their most minute parts, are adjusted to each other with an accuracy, which ravished into admiration all men, who have ever contemplated them. The curious adapting of means to ends, throughout all nature, resembles exactly, though it much exceeds, the productions of human contrivance; of human designs, thought, wisdom and intelligence. Since therefore the effects resemble each other, we are led to infer, by all the rules of analogy, that the causes also resemble; and that the Author of Nature is somewhat similar to the mind of man; though possessed of much larger faculties, proportioned to the grandeur of the work, which he has executed. (W, 116)

Philo is critical of this argument, but he too, in the final section of the dialogues, and after a detailed presentation of the problem of evil as a counterbalance to the argument from design, is willing to say that a divine being 'discovers himself to reason in the inexplicable contrivance and artifice of Nature' (W, 189). But his assent to natural theology is very guarded. He is willing to agree that the cause or causes of order in the universe probably bear some remote analogy to human intelligence; but his agreement is hedged about with conditions. However, provided: (1) that 'this proposition be not capable of extension, variation or more particular explication'; (2) that 'it afford no inference that affects human life or can be the source of any action or forbearance'; and (3) that 'the analogy, imperfect as it is, can be carried no farther than to the human intelligence', then he is prepared to accept the conclusion of the argument from design. 'What can the most inquisitive, contemplative, and religious man do more than give a plain, philosophical assent to the proposition as often as it occurs; and believe that the arguments on which it is established exceed the objections which lie against it' (W, 203).

This probably represents Hume's own position. It is clear that Hume enjoyed annoying the clergy, and that he detested Christianity itself, despite the ironical compliments to it which he scatters throughout his works. But with respect to the existence of God he was an agnostic, not an atheist. It was not until the triumph of Darwinism in the next century that an atheist could feel confident that he had an effective antidote to the argument from design.

Kant's Theological Dialectic

The third chapter of Kant's transcendental dialectic is entitled 'The Ideal of Pure Reason': its principal topic is a critique of rational theology, the attempt to establish by pure reason the existence of a transcendent God. Kant begins with the claim that all possible proofs of God's existence must fall into one of three classes. There are ontological arguments, which take their start from the *a priori* concept of a supreme being; there are cosmological proofs, which argue from the general nature of the empirical world; and there are proofs based on particular natural phenomena, which we may call 'physico-theological proofs'. In every kind of proof, Kant says, reason 'stretches its wings in vain, to soar beyond the world of sense by the mere might of speculative thought' (M, 346).

The ontological argument, as Kant sets it out, begins with a definition of God as an absolutely necessary being. Such a being is a thing whose non-existence is impossible. But can we really make sense, he asks, of such a definition? Necessity really belongs to propositions, not to things; and we cannot transfer the logical necessity of a proposition such as 'a triangle has three angles' and make it a property of a real being. Logical necessity is only conditional necessity; nothing is absolutely necessary:

To suppose the existence of a triangle and not that of its three angles is self-contradictory; but to suppose the non-existence of both triangle and angles is perfectly admissible. The same holds true of the concept of an absolutely necessary being. If you think away its existence, you think away the thing itself with all its predicates, and there is no question of any contradiction. (M, 348)

If the ontological argument is valid, then 'God exists' is an analytic proposition: 'exist' is a predicate that is tacitly contained in the subject 'God'. But Kant insists that all statements of real existence are synthetic: we cannot derive actual reality from pure concepts. We might object that we can at least argue from concepts to non-existence: it is because we grasp the concepts *square* and *circle* that we know there are no square circles. If 'square circles do not exist' is analytic, why not 'there is a necessary being'?

Kant's real objection to the ontological argument is not that 'God exists' is a synthetic proposition, but that it is not a subject–predicate proposition at all. 'God is omnipotent' contains two concepts linked by the copula 'is'. But:

If I take the subject, God, with all its predicates including omnipotence and say 'God is' or 'There is a God' I add no new predicate to the concept of God, I merely posit or affirm the existence of the subject with all its predicates: I posit the object corresponding to my concept. (M, 350)

Existential propositions do not, in fact, always 'posit', because they may occur as subclauses in a larger sentence (as in 'If there is a God, sinners will be punished'). But it is true that neither the affirmation nor the supposition of God's existence adds anything to the predicates that make up the concept of God. This point is correct whether or not any particular concept of God is coherent or not (as Kant thought *necessary being* was not). Even if we allow that God is possible, there remains the point that Kant memorably expressed by saying that a hundred real dollars contain no more than a hundred possible dollars.

Echoing Hume, Kant says: 'By however many predicates we may think a thing—even if we completely determine it—we do not make the least addition to the thing when we further declare that this thing *is*. Otherwise it would not be exactly the same thing that exists, but something more than we had thought in the concept; and we could not, therefore, say that the exact object of my concept exists' (M, 350). It must always be illegitimate to try to build existence—even possible existence—into the concept of a thing. Existence is not a predicate that can enter into such a concept.

Abelard in the twelfth century, and Frege in the nineteenth century, urged us to rephrase statements of existence so that 'exists' does not even look like a predicate. 'Angels exist' should be formulated as 'Some things are angels'. This has the advantage that it does not make it appear that when we say 'Angels do not exist' we are first positing angels and then rejecting them. But it does not settle the issues surrounding the ontological argument, because the problems about arguing from possibility to actuality return as questions about what counts as 'something': are we including in our consideration possible as well as actual objects? Thus some recent philosophers have tried to restate the ontological argument in a novel way, by including possible objects within the range of discussion. A necessary being, they argue, is one that exists in all possible worlds. So defined, a necessary being must exist in our world, the actual world. Our world would not exist unless it were possible; so if God exists in every possible world he must exist in ours.

Kant is surely right to insist that whether there is something in reality corresponding to my concept of a thing cannot itself be part of my concept. A concept has to be determined prior to being compared to reality, otherwise we would not know *which* concept was being compared and found to correspond, or maybe not correspond, to reality. *That* there is a God cannot be part of what we mean by 'God'; hence, 'there is a God' cannot be an analytic proposition and the ontological argument must fail.

However, Kant overestimated the force of his criticism. He maintained that the refutation of the ontological argument carried with it the defeat of the much more popular proof of God's existence from the contingency of the world. That argument is briskly set out by Kant:

> If anything exists, an absolutely necessary being must also exist. Now I, at least, exist. Therefore an absolutely necessary being exists. The minor premise contains an experience, the major premise the inference from their being any experience at all to the existence of the necessary. The proof therefore really begins with experience and is not wholly *a priori* ontological. For this reason, and because the object of all possible experience is called the world, it is entitled the *cosmological* proof. (A, 605)

Kant argues that the appeal to experience here is illusory; the force of the cosmological derives only from the ontological argument. For what is meant by 'necessary being'? Surely, a being in whom essence involves existence, that is to say, a being whose existence can be established by the ontological argument. But here Kant ignores the possibility of a different definition of 'necessary being' as meaning a being which can neither come into nor go out of existence, and which cannot suffer change of any kind. Such in fact was the standard account of necessary being given by medieval philosophers who, like Kant, rejected the ontological argument. Such a being may well be regarded as sufficiently different from the caused, variable, and contingent items in the world of experience to provide the necessary stable grounding for our fragile and fleeting cosmos.

However, Kant has a further criticism of the cosmological argument which is independent of his claim that it is the ontological argument in disguise. All forms of the cosmological argument seek to show that a series of contingent causes, however prolonged, can be completed only by a necessary cause. But if we ask whether the necessary cause is, or is not, part of the chain of causes, we are faced with a dilemma. If it is part of the chain, then we can ask, in its case as in others, why it exists. But we cannot imagine a supreme being saying to itself 'I am from eternity to eternity, and outside me there is nothing save what is through my will, *but whence then am I?*' (A, 613). On the other hand, if the necessary being is not part of the chain of causation, how can it account for the links in the chain that end with the existence of myself?

The argument for God's existence that Kant treats most gently is the physico-theological proof, which he says must always be mentioned with respect and which he himself states with great eloquence:

This world presents to us such an immeasurable spectacle of variety, order, purpose and beauty, shown alike in its infinite extent and in the unlimited divisibility of its parts, that even with such knowledge as our weak understanding can acquire we encounter so many marvels immeasurably great that all speech loses its force, all numbers their power to measure, our thoughts lose all precision, and our judgement of the whole dissolves into an amazement whose very silence speaks with eloquence. Everywhere we see a chain of effects and causes, of ends and means, regularity in coming into and going out of existence. Nothing has of itself come into the condition into which we find it, but always points behind itself to something else as its cause; and this in its turn obliges us to make the same inquiry. The whole universe would thus sink into the abyss of nothingness unless over and above this infinite chain of contingencies one assumed something to support it—something that is original and independently self-subsistent, and which not only caused the origin of the universe but also secures its continuance. (A, 622)

The argument thus presented seems to combine several of the traditional proofs of God's existence—the argument to a first cause, for instance, as well as the argument from design. There is no doubt that everywhere in the world we find signs of order, in accordance with a determinate purpose, apparently carried out with great wisdom. Since this order is alien to the individual things which constitute the world, we must conclude that it must have been imposed by one or more sublime wise causes, operating not blindly as nature does, but freely as humans do. Kant raises various difficulties about the analogies that the argument draws between the operation of nature and the artifice of human skill; but his real criticism of the proof is not to deny its authority but to limit its scope. The most the argument can prove is the existence of 'an *architect* of the world who is always very much hampered by the adaptability of the material in which he works, not a *creator* of the world to whose idea everything is subject'. Many religious believers would be very content to have established beyond reasonable doubt the existence of such a grand architect.

However, Kant did not say his last word about God in the *Critique of Pure Reason*. In his second critique he sets out a number of postulates of practical reason; assumptions that must be made if obedience to the moral law is to be made a rational activity. The postulates turn out to be the same as the traditional topics of natural metaphysics: God, freedom, and immortality. We have an obligation to pursue perfect goodness, which includes both virtue and happiness. We can only have an obligation to pursue something if it is possible of achievement: '*Ought*', Kant said memorably, 'implies *can*.' But only an all-powerful, omniscient God could ensure that virtue and happiness can coincide—and even such a God can do so only if there is a life after the present one. Hence, it is morally necessary to assume the existence of God.

Kant insists that there is no inconsistency between this claim and his denial in the first critique that speculative reason could prove the existence and attributes of God. The postulation of God's existence demanded by the moral life is an act of faith. Already in a preface to the first Critique Kant had marked out the difference between the two approaches to theology, and claimed that his critical approach to metaphysics was actually a necessary condition of a morally valuable belief in God's existence:

I cannot even assume God, freedom and immortality for the sake of the necessary practical use of my reason unless I simultaneously deprive speculative reason of its pretension to extravagant insights . . . Thus I have to deny knowledge in order to make room for faith. The dogmatism of metaphysics—the idea that it is possible to make progress in the subject without criticizing pure reason—is the true source of that dogmatic unbelief which is at odds with morality. (B, XXX)

Kant's postulation of God as a condition of moral behaviour is an elaboration of a strategy first laid out by Pascal, namely, that we should believe that God exists not because we have reason to think that 'God exists' is true, but because it is a proposition that is good for us to believe.

The Absolute of Hegel

Hegel was fond of using Christian language. For instance, he divides the history of Germany into three periods: the period up to Charlemagne, which he calls the Kingdom of the Father; the period from Charlemagne to the Reformation, which he calls the Kingdom of the Son; and finally the period from the Reformation to the Prussian monarchy, which is the Kingdom of the Holy Ghost or Spirit. From time to time he refers to the absolute as God and his statement that the absolute is the Thought that thinks itself recalls a phrase of Aristotle that was often employed by Christian thinkers as an approach to a definition of God. But on examination it turns out that the absolute is something very different from the Christian God.

God as conceived by Christian tradition is an eternal, unchanging, being whose existence is quite independent of the existence of the world and of human beings. Before Adam and Abraham existed, God already existed in the fullness of self-awareness. Hegel's absolute, on the other hand, is a spirit who lives only through the lives of human beings, and the self-awareness of the absolute is brought about by the reflection of philosophers in the everyday world. Spirit, however, is not simply reducible to the totality of human thinking; the absolute has purposes which are not those of any human thinker and which human activity unconsciously serves. But the spirit's plan of the universe is not something imposed from outside by a transcendent creator; it is an internal evolution programmed by a cosmic equivalent of DNA.

Hegel saw his system as a rational, scientific, presentation of truths conveyed symbolically by religion. Philosophy and religion covered the same area as each other:

The objects of philosophy are upon the whole the same as those of religion. In both the object is Truth, in that supreme sense in which God and God only is the Truth. Both in like manner go on to treat of the finite worlds of Nature and the human Mind, with their relation to each other and to their truth in God.

In both philosophy and religion mankind aims to make its own the universal cosmic reason: religion does this by worship; philosophy by rational reflection.

Initially, religion presents us with myths and images. Thus in classical Antiquity Homer and Hesiod created the pantheon of Greek gods and goddesses. The first reaction of philosophy to myth and image is to explode their pretensions to literal truth: thus Plato denounces the theology of the poets and the sculptors. This pattern repeats itself in other cultures. The Jewish and Christian narratives, for instance, are mocked by the philosophers of the Enlightenment. But this antagonism between religion and anti-religious philosophy is superseded in the true, Hegelian, philosophy which accepts both faith and reason as different methods of presenting a single eternal truth.

What philosophy presents in thought, religion presents in images. What appears in Hegel's system as the objectification of the concept in Nature is presented in the great monotheistic religions as the free creation of a world by a transcendent God. The Hegelian insight that the finite spirit is a moment in the life of infinite spirit is expressed in Christianity by the doctrine that in Christ God became incarnate in a human being. But philosophy does not render religion superfluous: 'The form of Religion is necessary to Mind as it is in and for itself; it is the form of truth as it is for all men, and for every mode of consciousness.' Hegel proudly proclaimed that he was a Lutheran and intended to remain one (*LHP*, I.73).

Hegel's attitude to Christian doctrines, then, was one of sympathetic condescension. So too was his attitude to traditional proofs of the existence of God. But if God is the absolute, and the absolute is all being, then God's existence hardly needs proof. That is Hegel's version of the ontological argument. 'It would be strange', he wrote, 'if the concrete totality we call God were not rich enough to include so poor a category as being, the very poorest and most abstract of all' (*Logic* 1975, 85). For him, the real proof of the existence of God is the Hegelian system itself in its entirety.

The early modern period was a testing time for natural theology. It underwent criticism not only from philosophers who became increasingly sceptical of elements of religious tradition, but also from theologians who wished to downgrade

GOD

the claims of natural religion to make room for faith. The Enlightenment philosophers sought to downgrade and perhaps eliminate the input of theological doctrines into the areas of epistemology, psychology, biology, ethics, and politics. The French Revolution and its aftermath led European thinkers to re-evaluate both traditional religion and the Enlightenment programme. In the nineteenth century, as we will observe in Part Four, this led to both an intensification of the challenge to religion from admirers of the sciences, and a reactive response from the religious intelligentsia.

Part Four

Philosophy in the Modern World

CONTENTS OF PART FOUR

INTRODUCTION TO PART FOUR

Certain themes have occupied chapters in each of the four parts of this work: epistemology, metaphysics, philosophy of mind, ethics, and philosophy of religion. Other topics have varied in importance over the centuries, and the pattern of thematic chapters has varied accordingly. The first two parts began the thematic section with a chapter on logic and language, but there was no such chapter in Part Three because logic went into hibernation at the Renaissance. In the period covered by Part Four, formal logic and the philosophy of language occupied such a central position that each topic deserves a chapter to itself. In the earlier parts, there was a chapter devoted to physics, considered as a branch of what used to be called 'natural philosophy'; however, since Newton physics has been a fully mature science independent of philosophical underpinning, and so there is no chapter on physics in Part Four. Part Three was the first to contain a chapter on political philosophy, since before the time of More and Machiavelli the political institutions of Europe were too different from those under which we live for the insights of political philosophers to be relevant to current discussions. Part Four is the first and only one to contain a chapter on aesthetics: this involves a slight overlap with the previous part, since it was in the eighteenth century that the subject began to emerge as a separate discipline.

The introductory chapters in Part Four, unlike those in previous ones, do not follow a single chronological sequence. The first chapter does indeed trace a single line from Bentham to Nietzsche, but, because of the chasm that separated English-speaking philosophy from continental philosophy in the twentieth century, the narrative diverges in the second and third chapters. The second chapter begins with Peirce, the doyen of American philosophers, and with Frege, who is commonly regarded as the founder of the analytic tradition in philosophy. The third chapter treats of a series of influential continental thinkers, commencing with a man who would hate to be regarded as a philosopher, Sigmund Freud.

I have not found it easy to decide where and how to end my history. Many of those who have philosophized in the second half of the twentieth century are people I have known personally, and several of them have been close colleagues and friends. This makes it difficult to make an objective judgement on their importance in comparison with the thinkers who have occupied the earlier parts and the earlier pages of Part Four. No doubt my choice of who should be included and who should be omitted will seem arbitrary to others no less qualified than myself to make a judgement.

In 1998 I published a *Brief History of Western Philosophy*. I decided at that time not to include in the book any person still living. That, conveniently, meant that I could finish the story with Wittgenstein, whom I considered, and consider, to be the most significant philosopher of the twentieth century. But since 1998, sadly, a number of philosophers have died whom anyone would expect to find a place in a history of modern philosophy—Quine, for instance, Anscombe, Davidson, Strawson, Rawls, and others. So I had to choose another way of drawing a *terminus ante quem*. As I approached my seventy-fifth birthday the thought occurred to me of excluding all writers who were younger than myself. But this appeared a rather egocentric cut-off point. So finally I opted for a thirty-year rule, and have excluded works written after 1975.

I must ask the reader to bear in mind that this is the final part of a history of philosophy that began with Thales. It is accordingly structured in rather a different way from a self-standing history of contemporary philosophy. I have, for instance, said nothing about twentieth-century neo-scholastics or neo-Kantians, and have said very little about several generations of neo-Hegelians. To leave these out of a book devoted to the philosophy of the last two centuries would be to leave a significant gap in the history. But the importance of these schools was to remind the modern era of the importance of the great thinkers of the past. A history that has already devoted many pages to Aquinas, Kant, and Hegel does not need to repeat such reminders.

Having in mind an audience at the level of second- or third-year undergraduate study, I have not included in the bibliography works in languages other than English, except for the original texts of writers in other languages. Since many people read philosophy not for curricular purposes, but for their own enlightenment and entertainment, I have tried to avoid jargon and to place no difficulties in the way of the reader other than those presented by the subject matter itself. But, however hard one tries, it is impossible to make the reading of philosophy an undemanding task. As has often been said, philosophy has no shallow end.

1

Bentham to Nietzsche

Bentham's Utilitarianism

Britain escaped the violent constitutional upheavals that affected most of Europe during the last years of the eighteenth, and the early years of the nineteenth, century. But in 1789, the year of the French Revolution, a book was published in England that was to have a revolutionary effect on moral and political thinking long after the death of Napoleon. This was Jeremy Bentham's *An Introduction to the Principles of Morals and Legislation*, which became the founding charter of the school of thought known as utilitarianism.

Bentham was born in 1748, the son of a prosperous London attorney. A tiny, bookish, and precocious child, he was sent to Westminster School at the age of 7 and graduated from The Queen's College, Oxford, at the age of 15. He was destined for a legal career, and was called to the Bar when 21, but he found contemporary legal practice distasteful. He had already been repelled by current legal theory when, at Oxford, he had listened to the lectures of the famous jurist William Blackstone. The English legal system, he believed, was cumbrous, artificial, and incoherent: it should be reconstructed from the ground up in the light of sound principles of jurisprudence.

The fundamental such principle, on his own account, he owed to Hume. When he read the *Treatise of Human Nature*, he tells us, scales fell from his eyes and he came to believe that utility was the test and measure of all virtue and the sole origin of justice. On the basis of an essay by the dissenting chemist Joseph Priestley, Bentham interpreted the principle of utility as meaning that the happiness of the majority of the citizens was the criterion by which the affairs of a state should be judged. More generally, the real standard of morality and the true goal of legislation was the greatest happiness of the greatest number.

During the 1770s Bentham worked on a critique of Blackstone's *Commentaries on the Laws of England*. A portion of this was published in 1776 as *A Fragment on Government*, which contained an attack on the notion of a social contract. At the same time he wrote a dissertation on punishment, drawing on the ideas of the Italian penologist Cesare Beccaria (1738–94). An analysis of the purposes and limits of punishment, along with the exposition of the principle of utility, formed the substance of the *Introduction to the Principles of Morals and Legislation*, which was completed in 1780, nine years before its eventual publication.

The *Fragment on Government* was the first public statement by Bentham of the principle that 'it is the greatest happiness of the greatest number that is the measure of right and wrong'. The book was published anonymously, but it had some influential readers, including the Earl of Shelburne, a leading Whig who was later briefly Prime Minister. When Shelburne discovered that Bentham was author of the work, he took him under his patronage, and introduced him to political circles in England and France. Most significant among Bentham's new English friends was Caroline Fox, a niece of Charles James Fox, to whom, after a long but spasmodic courtship, he made an unsuccessful proposal of marriage in 1805. Most important of the French acquaintances was Étienne Dumont, tutor to Shelburne's son, who was later to publish a number of his works in translation. For a time Bentham's reputation was greater in France than in Britain.

Bentham spent the years 1785–7 abroad, travelling across Europe and staying with his brother Samuel, who was managing estates of Prince Potemkin at Krichev in White Russia. While there he conceived the idea of a novel kind of prison, the Panopticon, a circular building with a central observation point from which the jailer could keep a permanent eye on the inmates. He returned from Russia full of enthusiasm for prison reform, and tried to persuade both the British and French governments to erect a model prison. William Pitt's government passed an Act of Parliament authorizing the scheme, but it was defeated by ducal landowners who did not want a prison near their estates, and by the personal intervention (so Bentham liked to believe) of King George III. The French National Assembly did not take up his offer to supervise the establishment of a Panopticon, but did confer on him an honorary citizenship of the Republic.

Bentham's interest in legal theory and practice extended far beyond its original focus on criminal law. Exasperated by the confused state of civil law he wrote a long treatise *Of Laws in General*, which, like so many of his works, remained unpublished until long after his death. Reflecting on the Poor Laws he proposed that a network of Panopticons should be set up to serve as workhouses for the 'burdensome poor', managed by a national joint stock company, which would pay a dividend once the inmates' labour had provided for their sustenance. No Panopticon, whether penal or commercial, was ever constructed. In 1813, however, Parliament voted Bentham the giant sum of £23,000 in compensation for his work on the scheme.

In 1808 Bentham became friends with a Scottish philosopher, James Mill, who was just starting to write a monumental *History of India*. Mill had a remarkable two-year-old son, John Stuart, and Bentham assisted in that prodigy's education. Partly because of Mill's influence Bentham, who had been working for some years on the rationale of evidence in the courts, now began to focus on political and constitutional reform rather than on criticisms of legal procedure and practice. He wrote a *Catechism of Parliamentary Reform*, which was completed in 1809, though it was not published until 1817, when it was followed up, a year or two later, with the draft of a radical reform bill. He spent years on the drafting of a constitutional code, which was unfinished when he died. By the end of his life, he had become convinced that the existing British constitution was a screen hiding a conspiracy of the rich against the poor. He therefore advocated the abolition of the monarchy and the House of Lords, the introduction of annual parliaments elected by universal suffrage, and the disestablishment of the Church of England.

Bentham's constitutional and liberal proposals extended well beyond the affairs of Britain. In 1811 he proposed to James Madison that he should draw up a constitutional code for the United States. He was active on the London Greek Committee, which sponsored the expedition on which Lord Byron met his death at Missolonghi in 1823. For a time he had hopes that his constitutional code would be implemented in Latin America by Simón Bolívar, the President of Colombia.

The group of 'philosophical radicals' who accepted the ideals of Bentham in 1823 founded the *Westminster Review* in order to promote utilitarian causes. They were enthusiasts for educational reform. Bentham devised a curriculum for secondary education which emphasized science and technology rather than Greek and Latin. He and his colleagues were active in the establishment of University College London, which opened its doors in 1828. This was the first university-level institution in Britain to admit students without religious tests. There, in accordance with his will, Bentham's remains were placed after his death in 1832, and there, clothed and topped with a wax head, they survive to this day— his 'auto-icon' as he termed it. A more appropriate memorial to his endeavours was the Great Reform Bill, widely extending the parliamentary franchise, which passed into law a few weeks before he died.

Among those who knew him well, even his greatest admirers agreed that he was a very one-sided person, powerful in intellect but deficient in feeling. John Stuart Mill described him as precise and coherent in thought, but lacking in sympathy for the most natural and strongest feelings of human beings. Karl Marx said that he took the English shopkeeper as the paradigm of a human being. 'In no time and in no country', Marx said, 'has homespun commonplace ever strutted about in so self-satisfied a way' (C 488). Bentham's knowledge of human nature was indeed very limited. 'It is wholly empirical,' Mill said, 'and the empiricism of one who has had little experience.' He never, in Mill's view, reached maturity. 'He was a boy to the last' (U 78).

The Development of John Stuart Mill

Mill himself was never allowed to be a boy. He did not go to school or mingle with other children, but was educated at home by his demanding father. He began to learn Greek at the age of three and by the age of twelve had read much of Plato in the original. At that age he began studying logic from the text of Aristotle, while helping to proofread his father's *History of India*. In the following year he was taken through a course in political economy. He was never allowed a holiday 'lest the habit of work should be broken, and a taste for idleness acquired'. But when he was fourteen he spent a year in France at the house of Bentham's brother Samuel, which gave him an opportunity to attend science lectures at Montpellier. Apart from that, he had no university education, but by the age of sixteen he was already far more well-read than most Masters of Arts.

What Mill, looking back, most valued in his extraordinary education was the degree to which his father left him to think for himself. 'Anything which could be found out by thinking I never was told, until I had exhausted my efforts to find it out for myself' (*A* 20). He reckoned that he started adult life with an advantage of a quarter of a century over his contemporaries who had been to public school and university. But his education turned him, in his own words, into 'a mere reasoning machine'. After several years spent campaigning for liberal causes alongside colleagues on the *Westminster Review*, while holding a day job as a clerk with the East India Company, Mill suffered a mental breakdown and fell victim to a deep depression in which even the most effective work for reform seemed quite pointless.

He was rescued from his crisis, on his own account, by the reading of Wordsworth in the autumn of 1828. The poems made him aware not only of natural beauty, but of aspects of human life that had found no place in Bentham's system.

They seemed to be the very culture of the feelings, which I was in quest of. In them I seemed to draw from a source of inward joy, of sympathetic and imaginative pleasure, which could be shared in by all human beings; which had no connexion with struggle or imperfection, but would be made richer by every improvement in the physical or social condition of mankind. From them I seemed to learn what would be the perennial sources of happiness, when all the greater evils of life shall have been removed. And I felt myself at once better and happier as I came under their influence. (*A* 89)

After his crisis and recovery, Mill did not cease to venerate Bentham and to regard his work as having superseded that of all previous moralists; but he became convinced that his system needed modification and supplementation in both its personal and its social aspects.

On the personal side, Mill's thought developed under the influence of English poets, of whom Coleridge soon overtook Wordsworth as the dominant presence in his mind. In mature life he was willing to pair Coleridge and Bentham as 'the two great seminal minds of England in their age'. On the social side, the new influences on Mill were French in origin—the nascent socialism of the Comte de Saint-Simon (1760–1825) and the embryonic positivism of Auguste Comte (1798–1857).

While the British utilitarians had been content to take private ownership and hereditary property as something given and indefeasible, the Saint-Simonians argued that the capital and labour of a society should be managed as a whole for the general good of the community, with each of the citizens being obliged to contribute according to their ability, and entitled to be rewarded in proportion to their contribution. Mill was unconvinced by the socialist programme, but it made him aware of the need of a justification for the institutions of private property and the free market. He admired the Saint-Simonians' idealism, and was inspired by a number of their principles—in particular their insistence on the perfect equality of men and women.

Comte had begun his philosophical career as a Saint-Simonian, but went on to develop a system of his own to which he gave the name of 'positive philosophy'. The feature of this system that made a lasting impression on Mill was the theory that human knowledge and human societies passed through three historical stages: theological, metaphysical, and positive. These stages were, in the Saint-Simonian term, 'organic', or self-contained. In the first stage, societies gave supernatural explanations of phenomena and endeavoured to bring about effects in the world by magical or religious practices. This phase, according to Comte, lasted through the feudal system up to the Reformation. In the metaphysical phase, phenomena were explained by essences and forces, which turned out to be no less occult than the supernatural factors held to operate in the theological stage. It was the French Revolution that had brought this stage to conclusion, and the world was now about to enter upon the positive, or truly scientific, stage of science and society.

What Mill took from Comte and the Saint-Simonians was the idea of Progress. Between each organic period and the next there was, so Mill understood, a critical and disruptive period, and he believed that he was living in such a period. He now began to look forward

to a future which shall unite the best qualities of the critical with the best qualities of the organic periods; unchecked liberty of thought, unbounded freedom of individual action in all modes not hurtful to others; but also, convictions as to what is right and wrong, useful and pernicious, deeply engraven on the feelings by early education and general unanimity of sentiment. (A 100)

Once that state was achieved, further progress would be unnecessary: moral convictions would be so firmly grounded in reason and necessity that they would not, like all past and present creeds, need to be periodically thrown off.

Though a prolific journalist from an early age, Mill did not publish any books until his late thirties. But his first published book, in 1843, was a work of substance which achieved immediate and lasting fame. This was *A System of Logic* in six books, on which he had been working for several years, and which went through eight editions in his lifetime.

The book covers a wide variety of topics, unified by Mill's desire to present a nineteenth-century update of the British empiricist tradition. He presented a secular version of Berkeley's theological phenomenalism: matter is no more than a permanent possibility of sensation, and the external world is 'the world of possible sensations succeeding one another according to laws'. He agreed with Hume that we have no conception of mind itself, as distinguished from its conscious manifestations in ourselves, and he regarded it as a particularly difficult problem for a philosopher to establish the existence of minds other than his own. But unlike previous empiricists, Mill had a serious interest in formal logic and the methodology of the sciences.

The *System of Logic* begins with an analysis of language, and an account of different types of name (including proper names, pronouns, descriptions, general terms, and abstract expressions). All names, according to Mill, denote things: proper names denote the things they are names of, and general terms denote the things they are true of. But besides denotation, there is connotation: that is to say, a word like 'man' will denote Socrates (among others) but will also connote attributes such as rationality and animality.

Mill gave a detailed theory of inferences, which he divided into real and verbal. Syllogistic inference is verbal rather than real, because a syllogism gives us no new knowledge. Real inference is not deductive, but inductive, as when we reason 'Peter is mortal, James is mortal, John is mortal, therefore all men are mortal'. Such induction does not, as some logicians had thought, lead us from particular cases to a general law. The general laws are merely formulae for making inferences from known particulars to unknown particulars. Mill sets out five rules, or canons, of experiment to guide inductive scientific research. The use of such canons, Mill maintains, enables empirical inquiry to proceed without any appeal to a priori truths.[1]

The *System of Logic* ranges far beyond the discussion of language and inference. Its sixth book, for instance, is entitled 'On the Logic of the Moral Sciences'. The principal such sciences are psychology, sociology, and what Mill called 'ethology', or the study of the formation of character. Social science includes the science of politics and the study of economics; but Mill's fullest treatment of these topics appeared in a different book, *Principles of Political Economy* of 1848.

In presenting his modernized empiricism Mill took one unprecedented, and important, step. The truths of mathematics have always presented a difficulty for thoroughgoing empiricists, since they seem to be among the most certain objects of our knowledge, and yet they seem to precede rather than result from experience.

---

[1] Mill's logic is discussed in detail in Ch. 4.

Mill maintained that arithmetic and geometry, no less than physics, consist of empirical hypotheses—hypotheses that have been very handsomely confirmed in experience, but hypotheses that are none the less corrigible in the light of later experience.

This thesis—implausible as it has appeared to most subsequent philosophers—was essential to Mill's overriding aim in *A System of Logic*, which was to refute a notion that he regarded as 'the great intellectual support of false doctrines and bad institutions', namely the notion that truths external to the mind may be known by intuition independent of experience. Mill indeed saw this issue as the most important in all philosophy. 'The difference between these two schools of philosophy, that of Intuition, and that of Experience and Association, is not a mere matter of abstract speculation; it is full of practical consequences, and lies at the foundation of all the greatest differences of practical opinion in an age of progress' (*A* 162).

The most aggressive campaign waged by Mill in this intellectual battle was carried out in one of his last works, *An Examination of Sir William Hamilton's Philosophy* (1865). Sir William Hamilton was a Scottish philosopher and reformer who was Professor of Logic and Metaphysics in Edinburgh from 1838 to 1856. In his lectures he attempted to present a new and improved version of the common-sense philosophy of Reid, just as Mill had tried to bring out a new and improved version of the empiricism of Hume. Mill saw in these lectures, when they were published, an ideal target at which to fire his explosive criticisms of all forms of intuitionism.

Mill's *Examination* achieved more fame than the text it was examining; but nowadays it too is not often studied. The works of Mill that have retained a large readership were, on his own account, not entirely his own work. In 1851 he married Harriet, the widow of a London merchant, John Taylor, a bluestocking with whom he had enjoyed an intimate but chaste friendship for some twenty years. The marriage lasted only seven years before Harriet died at Avignon. According to Mill she should be counted as co-author of his pamphlets *On Liberty* (published in 1859) and *The Subjection of Women* (written in 1861 and published in 1869).

On Liberty seeks to draw limits to government interference with individual freedom. Its key principle is set out thus:

The sole end for which mankind are warranted, individually or collectively, in interfering with the liberty of action of any of their number, is self-protection. The only purposes for which power can be rightfully exercised over any member of a civilised community, against his will, is to prevent harm to others. His own good, either physical or moral, is not a sufficient warrant.

Over himself, Mill says, over his own body and mind, the individual is sovereign. The essay applies this principle in various areas, most conspicuously in support of freedom of opinion and freedom of expression.

The publication of *The Subjection of Women* was the culmination of a long campaign by Mill to secure female rights and improve women's lot. When James

Mill, in his *Essay on Government*, had affirmed that women did not need a vote, because their interests coincided with that of their menfolk, young John Stuart, supported by Bentham, had dissented. In his *Thoughts on Parliamentary Reform* of 1859 he proposed that every educated householder, male or female, should be entitled to vote 'for why should the vote-collector make a distinction where the tax-gatherer makes none?' (*CW* xix. 328). In 1866 he presented a petition for female suffrage, and during the debates on the Second Reform Bill proposed an amendment—which attracted seventy-three votes—to strike out the words that restricted the franchise to males. But *The Subjection of Women* addressed issues much wider than that of the suffrage, and attacked the whole institution of marriage as interpreted by Victorian law and morality. So structured, he maintained, wedlock was simply a form of domestic servitude.

From 1865 to 1868 Mill was Member of Parliament for Westminster. In addition to feminist issues, he interested himself in Irish affairs and in electoral reform. He was critical of the British government's policy of coercion in Ireland, and published a pamphlet advocating a radical reform of the landholding system. He advocated proportional representation in parliamentary elections, as a safeguard against the exercise of tyranny by a majority against a minority. His thoughts on such matters had appeared in print in 1861 in *Considerations on Representative Government*.

During the last years of his life Mill dwelt at Avignon with his stepdaughter Helen Taylor. He died there in 1873 and was buried beside his wife. His *Autobiography* and *Three Essays on Religion* were published posthumously by his stepdaughter.

Though Mill's liberalism never ceased to have admirers, his reputation as a systematic philosopher faded rapidly after his death. His logical work was looked on with disfavour by the founders of modern symbolic logic. His empiricism was swamped by the wave of idealism that engulfed Britain in the last decades of the nineteenth century. It was only when empiricism returned to favour in the 1930s that his writings began once more to be widely read. But the utilitarian tradition was kept alive without interruption by Henry Sidgwick (1838–1900), who published his principal work, *Methods of Ethics*, in the year after Mill's death.

Sidgwick was a Fellow of Trinity College, Cambridge, who in 1869 resigned his fellowship on conscientious grounds. He became Professor of Philosophy in the university in 1883. He was at first an uncritical admirer of Mill and welcomed his system as giving him relief from the arbitrary moral rules of his upbringing. But he came to hold that there was an inconsistency between two great principles of Mill's system: psychological hedonism (everyone seeks their own happiness) and ethical hedonism (everyone should seek the general happiness). One of the main tasks he set himself in *Methods of Ethics* was to resolve this problem, which he called 'the dualism of practical reason'.

In the course of his thinking Sidgwick abandoned the principle of psychological hedonism and replaced it with an ethical principle of rational egoism, that each person has an obligation to seek his own good. This principle, he believed, was intuitively obvious. Ethical hedonism, too, he decided, could only be based on fundamental moral intuitions. Thus, his system combined utilitarianism with intuitionism, which he regarded as the common-sense approach to morality. However, the typical intuitions of common sense were, he believed, too narrow and specific; the ones that were the foundation of utilitarian morality were more abstract. One such was that future good is as important as present good, and another is that from the point of view of the universe any single person's good is of no more importance than any other person's.

The remaining difficulty is to reconcile the intuitions of utilitarianism with those of rational egoism. Sidgwick came to the conclusion that no complete solution of the conflict between my happiness and the general happiness was possible on the basis of mundane experience (*ME*, p. xix). For most people, he accepted, the connection between the individual's interest and his duty is made through belief in God and personal immortality. As he himself was unwilling to invoke God in this context, he concluded sadly that 'the prolonged effort of the human intellect to frame a perfect ideal of rational conduct is seen to have been foredoomed to inevitable failure' (*ME*, end). He consoled himself by seeking, through the work of the Society for Psychical Research, founded in 1882, empirical evidence for the survival of the individual after death.

Schopenhauer's Philosophy of the Will

In setting out his principle of utility, Bentham had contrasted it with the principle of asceticism, which approves of actions in so far as they tend to diminish happiness. Bentham's target was Christian morality, but no Christian ever held the principle of asceticism in all its fullness. Of all philosophers the one who came closest to professing such a principle was the atheist Arthur Schopenhauer, who was just one year old when Bentham published his *Introduction*.

Schopenhauer was the son of a Danzig merchant, and was brought up to follow a business career until his father's death in 1803. He then resumed a life of study, beginning in 1810 a course of philosophy at the University of Göttingen, after a false start as a medical student. His favourite philosophers were Plato and Kant, but he did not admire Kant's disciple Fichte, whose lectures he heard at Berlin in 1811. In particular he was disgusted by Fichte's nationalism, and rather than join the Prussian struggle against Napoleon he withdrew to write a work *On the Fourfold Root of the Principle of Sufficient Reason*, which he presented as a doctoral dissertation to the University of Jena in 1813.

During the years 1814–18 he wrote his major work, *The World as Will and Idea*. The work is divided into four books, the first and third devoted to the world as Idea, and the second and fourth to the world as Will. By 'idea' (*Vorstellung*, sometimes translated 'representation') Schopenhauer does not mean a concept, but a concrete experience—the kind of thing that Locke and Berkeley called by the name 'idea'. According to Schopenhauer, the world exists only as idea, only in relation to consciousness: 'The world is my idea.' For each of us our own body is the starting point of our perception of the world, and other objects are known through their effects on each other.

Schopenhauer's account of the world as idea is not very different from the system of Kant. But the second book, in which the world is presented as will, is highly original. Science, Schopenhauer says, explains the motion of bodies in terms of laws such as inertia and gravitation. But science offers no explanation of the inner nature of these forces. Indeed no such explanation could ever be offered if a human being was no more than a knowing subject. However, I am myself rooted in the world, and my body is not just one object among others, but has an active power of which I am conscious. This, and this alone, allows us to penetrate the nature of things. 'The answer to the riddle is given to the subject of knowledge, who appears as an individual, and the answer is *will*. This and this alone gives him the key to his own existence, reveals to him the significance, shows him the inner mechanism of his being, of his action, of his movements' (*WWI* 100). Each of us knows himself both as an object and as a will, and this throws light on every phenomenon in nature. The inner nature of all objects must be the same as that which in ourselves we call will. But there are many different grades of will, reaching down to gravitation and magnetism, and only the higher grades are accompanied by knowledge and self-determination. Nonetheless, the will is the real thing-in-itself for which Kant sought in vain.

Since he agrees that inanimate objects do not act on reasons or act for motives, why does Schopenhauer call their natural tendencies 'will' rather than 'appetite' like Aristotle, or 'force' like Newton? If we explain force in terms of will, Schopenhauer replies, we explain the less known by the better known. The only immediate knowledge we have of the world's inner nature is given us by our consciousness of our own will.

But what is the nature of will itself? All willing, Schopenhauer tells us, arises from want, and so from deficiency, and therefore from suffering. If a wish is granted, it is only succeeded by another; we always have many more desires than we can satisfy. If our consciousness is filled by our will, we can never have happiness or peace; our best hope is that pain and boredom will alternate with each other.

In the third and fourth book of his masterpiece Schopenhauer offers two different ways of liberation from the slavery to the will. The first way of escape is through art, through the pure, disinterested contemplation of beauty. The second way of escape is through renunciation. Only by renouncing the will to live can we be totally freed from the tyranny of the will. The will to live is to be renounced not by suicide, but by asceticism. To make real moral progress we must leave behind not just wickedness (delighting in the suffering of others) and badness (using others as means to our ends) but also mere justice (treating others on equal terms with ourselves) and even goodness (willingness to sacrifice oneself for others). We must go beyond virtue to asceticism. I must come to have such a horror of this miserable world that I will no longer think it enough to love others as myself or to give up my own pleasures when they stand in the way of others' good. To reach the ideal I must adopt chastity, poverty, and abstinence, and welcome death when it comes as a deliverance from evil.

As models of self-abnegation, Schopenhauer held out Christian, Hindu, and Buddhist saints. However, his case for asceticism did not rest on any religious premises, and he accepted that the life of most saints was full of superstition. Religious beliefs, he thought, were mythical clothings of truths unattainable by the uneducated. But his system was expressly influenced by the Maya doctrine of Indian philosophy, the doctrine that individual subjects and objects are all mere appearance, the veil of Maya.

The World as Will and Idea had little immediate influence. In 1820 Schopenhauer went to Berlin, where the dominant philosopher in the university was Hegel, for whom he had little respect, sneering at 'the narcotic effect of long-spun periods without a single idea in them'. He deliberately advertised his lectures at the same time as Hegel's, but he was unable to woo the students away. The boycott of his lectures added fuel to his dislike of the Hegelian system, which he regarded as mostly nonsense, or, as he put it, 'atrocious and extremely wearisome humbug' (*WWI* 26).

Schopenhauer did not win any public recognition of his genius until 1839, when he won a Norwegian prize for an essay *On the Freedom of the Will*. This he published in 1841, along with another essay on the foundation of ethics, under the title *The Two Fundamental Problems of Ethics*. In 1844 he published an expanded edition of *The World as Will and Idea* and in 1851 a collection of essays entitled *Parerga and Paralipomena*. These enabled a wide public to appreciate the wit and clarity of his literary style, as well as to savour, with pleasure or distaste, his irreverent and politically incorrect opinions.

The unsuccessful Continental revolutions of 1848 took place just after Schopenhauer's sixtieth birthday. In his sixties he became popular with members of a generation that had become disillusioned with political attempts to make the world a better place. He was courted by the German academic establishment that he had flagellated in his writings. He was able to enjoy the comforts of the world that he had denounced as a degrading illusion. If people complained that his own life was very different from the ascetic ideal that he proclaimed, he would reply, 'it is a strange demand upon a moralist that he should teach no other virtue than that which he himself possesses'. He died in 1860.

Ethics and Religion in Kierkegaard

While Schopenhauer, in Frankfurt, was expanding *The World as Will and Idea*, a Danish philosopher in Copenhagen was bringing out a series of treatises that presented a similar call to asceticism on a quite different metaphysical basis. This was Søren Aabye Kierkegaard, born in 1813 into a tragic family. His mother and five of his six siblings died before he reached adulthood, and his father believed himself cursed for a blasphemy uttered long ago while a shepherd boy. Sent to Copenhagen University in 1830 to study theology, Kierkegaard acquired, like Schopenhauer, a familiarity with, and a hatred for, the philosophy of Hegel. He disliked theology, but in 1838 he underwent a religious conversion, accompanied by a mystical experience 'of indescribable joy'. In 1840 he became engaged to Regine Olsen, but he broke off the engagement a year later, deciding that his own and his family's history rendered him unsuitable for marriage. Henceforth he saw himself as a man with a vocation as a philosopher.

In 1841, after completing a dissertation on Socratic irony, Kierkegaard went to Berlin and attended the lectures of Schelling. His distaste for German idealism increased; but unlike Schopenhauer, he thought that its mistake was to undervalue the concrete individual. Like Schopenhauer, though, he sketched out for his readers a spiritual career that ends with renunciation. In his version, however, each upward phase in the career, far from being a diminution of individuality, is a stage in the affirmation of one's own unique personality.

Kierkegaard's system was expounded, between 1843 and 1846, in a series of works published under different pseudonyms. *Either/Or*, of 1843, presents two different life-views, one aesthetic and one ethical. From a starting point in which the individual is an unquestioning member of a crowd, the aesthetic life is the first stage towards self-realization. The aesthetic person pursues pleasure, but does so with taste and elegance. The essential feature of his character is that he avoids taking on any commitment, whether personal, social, or official, that would limit his options for seizing whatever is immediately attractive. As time goes on, such a person may realize that his demand for instant freedom is actually a limitation on his powers. If so, he moves on to the ethical stage, in which he takes his place within social institutions and accepts the obligations that flow from them. But however hard he tries to fulfil the moral law, he finds that his powers are unequal to it. Before God he is always in the wrong.

Both aesthetic and ethical ways of life have to be transcended in an ascent to the religious sphere. This message is conveyed in different ways in further pseudonymous works: *Fear and Trembling* in 1843, *The Concept of Anxiety* in 1844, and *Stages on Life's Way* in 1845. The series reached its climax with the publication of the lengthy *Concluding Scientific Postscript* in 1846, whose message is that faith is not the outcome of any objective reasoning as the Hegelians had claimed.

The transition from the ethical to the religious sphere is vividly portrayed in *Fear and Trembling*, which takes as its text the biblical story of God's command to Abraham to kill his son Isaac in sacrifice. An ethical hero, such as Socrates, lays down his life for the sake of a universal moral law; but Abraham breaks a moral law in obedience to an individual command of God. This is what Kierkegaard calls 'the teleological suspension of the ethical'—Abraham's act transgresses the ethical order to pursue a higher end (*telos*) outside it. But if an individual feels a call to violate the moral law, no one can tell him whether this is a mere temptation or a genuine command of God. He cannot even know or prove it to himself: he has to make a decision in blind faith.

After a second mystical experience in 1848 Kierkegaard adopted a more transparent method of writing, and published, under his own name, a number of Christian discourses and works such as *Purity of Heart is to Will One Thing* (1847) and *Works of Love* (1847). But he reverted to a pseudonym for *Sickness unto Death*, which presents faith as being the only alternative to despair, and as the necessary condition for a full realization of one's authentic existence or selfhood.

Much of the latter part of Kierkegaard's life was taken up in conflict with the established Danish Church, which he regarded as Christian only in name. He was highly critical of the Primate, Bishop J. P. Mynster, and after his death in 1854 published a bitter attack on him. He founded and funded an anticlerical broadsheet, *The Moment*, which ran for nine issues, after which he collapsed in the street and died, after a few weeks' illness, in November 1855. Against his wishes, and against the protests of his nephew, he was given a church funeral.

Dialectical Materialism

Schopenhauer and Kierkegaard both derived their philosophical impetus from a reaction against the system of Hegel. But the most violent and most influential rejection of Hegelianism was that of Karl Marx, who described his own philosophical mission as 'turning Hegel upside down'. The dialectical idealism of Hegel was in his vision to be replaced by a dialectical materialism.

Marx's father was a liberal Jew who had turned Protestant shortly before his son's birth in 1816. The young Karl went to school in Trier and attended Bonn University for one year, studying law and living riotously. He then went to Berlin University for five years, where he sobered up, took to writing poetry, and switched from law to philosophy. When Marx arrived in Berlin, Hegel was already dead, but he studied Hegelian philosophy with a left-wing group known as the Young Hegelians, which included Ludwig Feuerbach and was led by Bruno Bauer. From Hegel and Bauer, Marx learnt to view history as a dialectical process. Each stage of history was determined by its predecessor according to fundamental logical or metaphysical principles in a process that had a rigour similar to that of a geometrical proof.

The Young Hegelians attached great importance to Hegel's concept of alienation, that is to say, the state in which people view as exterior to themselves something that is truly an intrinsic element of their own being. The form of alienation Hegel himself emphasized was that in which individuals, all of whom were manifestations of a single Spirit, saw each other as hostile rivals rather than elements of an underlying unity. Bauer, and still more Feuerbach, regarded religion as the supreme form of alienation, in which humans, who were the highest form of beings, projected their own life and consciousness into an unreal heaven. 'Religion is the separation of man from himself,' Feuerbach wrote; 'he sets God over against himself as an opposed being' (*W* vi. 41).

For both Hegel and Feuerbach religion was a form of false consciousness. For Hegel this was to be remedied by the translation of religious myths into idealist metaphysics. For Feuerbach, however, Hegelianism was itself a form of alienation. Religion should be eliminated, not translated, and replaced by a naturalistic, and positive, understanding of the everyday life of human beings in society. Marx agreed that religion was a form of false consciousness, but he thought that both Hegel and Feuerbach had provided only inadequate remedies for alienation. Hegel's metaphysics represented man as a mere spectator of a process that he should in fact control. Feuerbach, on the other hand, had not realized that God was not the only alien essence men worshipped. Much more important was money, which represented the alienation of men's labour. In so far as private property was the basis of the State, Marx wrote in a critique of Hegel's political philosophy, the State too was an alienation of man's true nature. Alienation was not to be removed by philosophical reflection: what was needed was nothing less than social upheaval. 'The philosophers have only interpreted the world in various ways; the point is to change it' (*TF* 11).

Having obtained a doctorate from Jena University for a thesis on Democritus and Epicurus, in 1842 Marx broke with the Young Hegelians, went to live in Cologne, and began a career as a political journalist. He edited a radical newspaper, the *Rheinische Zeitung*. In 1843 he married a woman he had known since childhood, Jenny von Westphalen, the daughter of a baron in the service of the Prussian government. Though irritable and dictatorial, Marx—unusually among great philosophers—enjoyed, until Jenny's death in 1881, a happy married life. Shortly after the wedding, the *Rheinische Zeitung* was closed down by the Prussian government, under pressure from the Tsar of Russia.

The Marxes moved to Paris, where Karl found further work as a journalist, read his way through the English classics of political economy, and made a number of radical friends. The most important of these was Friedrich Engels, who had just returned from working for his father's cotton-spinning business in Manchester, where he had written a study of the English working classes. Marx and Engels, after a meeting at the Café de Régence in Paris, began to work out together the theory of 'communism', that is to say, the abolition of private property in favour of communal ownership. The major work on which the two men collaborated was *The German Ideology*, which was completed in Brussels, whither Marx had migrated after being expelled from Paris for subversive journalism.

In this book Marx and Engels presented the materialist conception of history. Life determines consciousness, not consciousness life. The basic reality of history is the process of economic production, and to understand it one must understand the material conditions of this production. The varying modes of production give rise to the formation of social classes, to warfare between them, and eventually to the forms of political life, law, and ethics. The hand-mill, for instance, gives you a society presided over by a feudal lord, the steam mill produces a society dominated by the industrial capitalist. A dialectical process is leading the world through these various stages towards a proletarian revolution and the arrival of communism.

The German Ideology was not published until long after Marx's death, but its ideas were summarized in *The Poverty of Philosophy* of 1847 (a response to a work of P. J. Proudhon entitled *The Philosophy of Poverty*). A better-known presentation of the materialist conception of history was *The Communist Manifesto*, which Marx produced in February 1848 on the basis of drafts by Engels. This was intended as an epitome of the principles and ideals of the newly founded Communist League. The message of the *Manifesto* was summed up thus by Engels in the foreword to one of its later editions:

The whole history of mankind (since the dissolution of primitive tribal society, holding land in common ownership) has been a history of class struggles, contests between exploiting and exploited, ruling and oppressed classes; the history of these class struggles forms a series of evolutions in which, nowadays, a stage has been reached where the exploited and oppressed class—the proletariat—cannot attain its emancipation from the sway of the exploiting and ruling class—the bourgeoisie—without at the same time, and once and for all, emancipating society at large from all exploitation, oppression, class distinctions and class struggles. (*CM* 48)

The most famous sentences of the *Manifesto* were its last: 'Let the ruling classes tremble at a communistic revolution. The proletarians have nothing to lose but their chains. They have a world to win. Working men of all countries, unite!'

In the year in which the *Manifesto* was published there were armed uprisings in many cities, notably Paris, Berlin, Milan, and Rome. Marx and Engels briefly returned to Germany, urging the revolutionaries to set up a system of free state education, to nationalize transport and banking, and to impose a progressive income tax. After the collapse of the revolution, Marx was twice tried in Cologne, once on a charge of insulting the public prosecutor and once on a charge of incitement to revolt. He was acquitted on both counts but was expelled from Prussian territories. He returned briefly to Paris but was once more expelled from there. For the rest of his life he lived in London, often in abject poverty, which caused three of his six children to die of starvation.

In London, Marx worked tirelessly at developing the theory of dialectical materialism, often spending ten hours a day researching in the library of the British Museum. During the winter of 1857–8 he wrote a series of notebooks in which he summed up his economic thought of the previous decade: these were not made available to the world in general until 1953, when they appeared under the German title *Grundrisse*. On these drafts he based the *Contribution to a Critique of Political Economy* of 1859. The preface of that work contains a succinct and authoritative statement of the materialist theory of history.

Throughout his life Marx endeavoured to combine communist theory with communist practice. In 1864 he helped to found the International Working Men's Association, better known as the First International. It held six congresses in nine years, but it suffered from internal dissension, led by the anarchist Mikhail Bakunin, and fell into external disrepute because of its support for the savage and futile insurrection in Paris in 1870. It was dissolved in 1876.

Marx's writing career culminated in the massive *Capital*, which sought to explain in detail how the course of history was dictated by the forces and relations of production. The first volume of this was published in Hamburg in 1867; the second and third volumes remained unpublished when Marx died in 1883 and were posthumously published by Engels. Marx was buried beside his wife in Highgate Cemetery.

The theme of Marx's great work is that the capitalist system is in a state of terminal crisis. Capitalism, of its very nature, involves the exploitation of the working class. For the true value of any product depends upon the amount of labour put into it. But the capitalist appropriates part of this value, paying the labourer less than the product's real worth. As technology develops, and with it the labourer's productivity, a greater and greater proportion of the wealth generated by labour finds its way into the pockets of the capitalist.[2] This exploitation is bound to reach a point at which the proletariat finds it intolerable, and rises in revolt. The capitalist system will be replaced by the dictatorship of the proletariat, which will abolish private property and introduce a socialist state in which the means of production are totally under central government control. But the socialist state, in its turn, will wither away to be replaced by a communist society in which the interests of the individual will coincide with those of the community.

Marx's predictions of proletarian revolution followed by universal socialism and communism have, mercifully, been falsified by the course of history since his death. But whatever he may himself have thought, his theories are essentially philosophical and political rather than scientific; and judged from that standpoint they can claim both successes and failures. Marx erred in claiming that events are determined totally by economic factors. Even in countries that underwent socialist

---

[2] Marx's theory of surplus value will be considered in detail in Ch. 11.

revolutions of a Marxist type, the power wielded by individuals such as Lenin, Stalin, and Mao gave the lie to the theory that only impersonal forces give history its shape. But, on the other hand, no historian, not even a historian of philosophy, would nowadays dare to deny the influence of economic factors on politics and culture.

If we look back, a century and a half later, on the proposals of *The Communist Manifesto*, we find a mixture of rash draconian measures enforceable only by tyranny (e.g. abolition of inheritance and compulsory agricultural labour), institutions that advanced countries now take for granted (progressive taxation and universal education), and experiments that have been adopted with greater or less success in different times and places (nationalization of railways and banks). Considered as a prophet, Marx has been discredited; and so has his claim that ideology is merely the smokescreen of the status quo. But the most convincing refutation of the thesis that consciousness is impotent to determine life is provided by Marx's own philosophy. For the history of the world since his death has been enormously influenced, for good or ill, by his own system of ideas, considered not as a scientific theory, but as an inspiration to political activism and a guideline for political regimes.

Darwin and Natural Selection

Ten years before his death Marx sent a copy of the second edition of the first volume of *Capital* to Charles Darwin, whose *On the Origin of Species* had been published fourteen years earlier. He received a courteous acknowledgement of this gift of 'the great work', but Darwin, like many another reader, found it impossible to proceed beyond the volume's early pages. In giving Marx's funeral oration Engels described the materialist conception of history as a scientific breakthrough comparable with the discovery of evolution by natural selection. This was an exaggeration, but Marx and Darwin did turn out to be the two most influential thinkers of the nineteenth century—and the two most heavily criticized, then and now.

Charles Darwin was born in Shrewsbury in 1809 and boarded at Shrewsbury School from 1818 to 1825. He enrolled as a medical student at Edinburgh in 1825 but did not complete his studies; instead he went to Christ's College in Cambridge and took a pass BA in 1831. The Professor of Botany recommended him to Captain Fitzroy of HMS *Beagle*, who appointed him ship's naturalist. During a five-year cruise in the southern hemisphere Darwin collected a mass of geological, botanical, zoological, and anthropological material. Initially he was more interested in geology than in zoology, and made discoveries about the nature of volcanic islands and the formation of coral reefs. He published a popular account of his maritime researches in 1839 in a volume best known as *The Voyage of the Beagle*. In the same year he married Emma Wedgwood and was elected to the Royal Society.

During the 1840s and 1850s, studying the flora and fauna of his estate in Kent, he developed the theory of natural selection, producing in 1844 a sketch of his ideas for private circulation. He had in mind to present the theory in a vast volume, to be completed some time in the 1860s. However, when another zoologist, Alfred Russell Wallace, had a similar theory of the 'survival of the fittest' presented to a learned society in 1858, Darwin decided to establish the independence and priority of his own ideas, and thus rushed into print an 'abstract' of his ideas, which was *On the Origin of Species*. In 1860 at a meeting of the British Association for the Advancement of Science, Thomas Henry Huxley successfully defended Darwinism in a famous debate with Samuel Wilberforce, the Bishop of Oxford.

In later years Darwin published a number of supplementary treatises on fertilization and variations of structure and behaviour within and across species. The best known of his later books was published in 1871, *The Descent of Man and Selection in Relation to Sex*. In that book, besides developing the theory of sexual selection, which was an important supplement to the theory of natural selection, he defended the thesis that human beings shared a common ancestor with orang-utans, chimpanzees, and gorillas. He died in 1882 and was buried in Westminster Abbey.

Darwin was not the first person to propose a theory of evolution. In the ancient world, as Darwin himself acknowledged, the Sicilian philosopher Empedocles had 'shadowed forth the principle of natural selection'.[3] But Empedocles had been savaged by Aristotle, who believed that species had existed from eternity, and he was ignored by Christians, who believed that animal species had been created by God for Adam in the Garden of Eden. The great Swedish naturalist Linnaeus (1707–78), whose classification of plant and animal species was to provide the platform on which Darwin's theory was built, believed that each species had been separately created and that the resemblances and differences between them revealed the design of the creator.

Linnaeus and other taxonomists had divided the plant and animal kingdoms into genera and species, to which they gave Latin names. All lions, for instance are members of the same species, *felis leo*. The lion species is a member of the genus of cats (*felis*), which includes other species such as the tiger (*felis tigris*) and the leopard (*felis pardus*). Within a given species the characteristics of individuals may vary widely, but the defining mark of a species is that its members can breed with other members to produce offspring of the same species. Unions between members of different species, on the other hand, are commonly sterile.

Rather than appeal to the inscrutable purposes of a creator, a number of naturalists had suggested that the resemblances between different species within a genus might be explained by descent from a distant common ancestor. This was

---

[3] See above, p. 24.

proposed by Darwin's grandfather Erasmus Darwin (1731–1802), and also by the French zoologist J. B. Lamarck, who in 1815 maintained that any generation of a species might acquire a beneficial characteristic which it would then pass on to its offspring. Giraffes, stretching to reach the topmost leaves, would lengthen their necks and beget longer-necked offspring.

Darwin, by resurrecting the ancient idea of natural selection, was able to put forward a quite different explanation of the resemblances and differences between species. The fundamental bases of his theory were three. First, organisms vary greatly in the degree to which they are adapted to the environment in which they live. Second, all species are capable of reproducing at a rate that would increase their numbers from generation to generation: even a single couple of slow-breeding elephants, after a period of 500 years, could have 15 million descendants. Third, the reason that species do not increase and multiply at this rate is that in each generation only a few offspring survive to breed. All the members of each species have to fight for existence, against the climate and against competing individuals and competing species, to obtain food for themselves and to avoid becoming food for others. It is this third factor that operates the selection that is the mechanism of evolution.

Owing to this struggle for life, any variation, however slight, and from whatever cause proceeding, if it be in any degree profitable to an individual of any species in its infinitely complex relations to other organic beings and to external nature, will tend to the preservation of that individual and will generally be inherited by its offspring. The offspring, also, will thus have a better chance of surviving, for, of the many individuals of any species which are periodically born, but a small number can survive. (OS 52)

Darwin distinguished three different kinds of selection. Artificial selection had long been practised by human husbandmen who selected for breeding the specimens, whether of potatoes or racehorses, that were best adapted to their purposes. Natural selection, unlike artificial selection, was not purposive. Advantageous variations were preserved and extended simply by natural pressures on the survival and reproduction of the individuals of a species. Within natural selection Darwin made a further distinction: between natural selection in the narrow sense, which determined whether an individual survived long enough to breed, and sexual selection, which determined with whom such a surviving individual would mate. Unlike Lamarck, Darwin did not believe that the variations in adaptation were acquired by parents in their lifetime: the variations that they passed on were ones they had themselves inherited. Though it was possible to establish some laws of variability, the origin of a particular advantageous variation could well be a matter of chance.

Natural selection can easily be illustrated, and observed, in the case of characteristics within a single species. Suppose that there is a population of moths, some happening to be dark and others happening to be pale, who live on birch trees and are preyed upon by birds. While the trees retain their natural silver colour, the better-camouflaged pale moths will have a better chance of survival, and will therefore come to form the greater part of the population. If, however, the trees become blackened with soot, the odds of survival will tilt in favour of the dark moths. As they survive in more than average numbers, it will appear from the outside that the species is changing its colour, from being characteristically pale to being characteristically dark.

Darwin believed that over a long period of time natural selection could go further and create whole new species of plants and animals. This would, indeed, be a process so slow as to be in the normal sense unobservable; but recent discoveries in geology made plausible the idea that the earth had existed for a sufficient length of time for species to come into and go out of existence in this manner. Evolution could thus explain not only the likenesses and differences between existing species, but also the difference between the species now extant and defunct species from earlier ages that were being discovered in fossil form throughout the world. Even the most complex organs and instincts, Darwin claimed, could be explained by the accumulation of innumerable slight variations, each good for the individual.

To suppose that the eye, with all its inimitable contrivances for adjusting the focus to different distances, for admitting different amounts of light, and for the correction of spherical and chromatic aberration, could have been formed by natural selection, seems, I freely confess, absurd in the highest possible degree. Yet reason tells me, that if numerous gradations from a perfect and complex eye to one very imperfect and simple, each grade being useful to its possessor, can be shown to exist; if further, the eye does vary ever so slightly, and the variations be inherited, which is certainly the case; and if any variation of modification in the organ be ever useful to an animal under changing conditions of life, then the difficulty of believing that a perfect and complex eye could be formed by natural selection, though insuperable by our imagination, can hardly be considered real. (*OS* 152)

The case for Darwin's theory was greatly strengthened after his death, first when the laws of population genetics established by Gregor Mendel became generally known, and then when the identification of DNA enabled molecular geneticists to elucidate the mechanisms of heredity. The story of Darwinism belongs to the history of science, not the history of philosophy; but no history of philosophy can omit to mention Darwin, because of the implications of his biological work on philosophy of religion and on general metaphysics.[4]

John Henry Newman

Though Darwin's ideas met with opposition in some ecclesiastical circles, they were accepted with equanimity by the greatest religious writer of the Victorian

---

[4] These implications are discussed in Chs. 7 and 12.

age, John Henry Newman. Shortly after the appearance of *On the Origin of Species* Newman observed that if one were to believe in the separate creation of each species one would also have to believe in the creation of fossil-bearing rocks. 'There is as much want of simplicity in the creation of distinct species', he wrote, 'as in those of the creation of trees in full growth or of rocks with fossils in them. I mean that it is as strange that monkeys should be so like men, with no historical connexion between them, as that there should be...no history or course of facts by which fossil bones got into the rocks.'[5] He was quite prepared 'to go the whole hog with Darwin' and he took no part in any controversy between science and religion. His claim to a place in the history of philosophy lies elsewhere.

Newman was born in London in 1801, and was an undergraduate at Trinity College, Oxford, from 1817 to 1820, and a Fellow of Oriel between 1822 and 1845. In 1828 he became Vicar of St Mary's, the university church, and acquired a lasting fame as a preacher. After an evangelical upbringing he became convinced, over the years, of the truth of the Catholic interpretation of Christianity. He was one of the founders of the 'Oxford Movement', which sought to have this interpretation accepted as authoritative within the Church of England. In 1845, however, he converted to Roman Catholicism having resigned his Oriel fellowship.

As a Roman Catholic priest he founded an oratory, or community of parochial priests, in Birmingham, where he was based for most of the rest of his life. In 1850 he was appointed the first Rector of a new Catholic university in Dublin, a post which he held until 1858. The lectures and addresses which he gave in that capacity became *The Idea of a University*, which when published became a classic of the theory of education.

Newman wrote numerous theological works both before and after his conversion, but his claim to be a great writer was established for the general public by his *Apologia pro Vita Sua*, an autobiography written in response to charges against his integrity brought by the novelist Charles Kingsley. In addition to historical and devotional works he wrote one philosophical classic, *An Essay in Aid of a Grammar of Assent* of 1870, which developed epistemological ideas he had first presented in his University Sermons in St Mary's. Newman did not share the enthusiasm of Cardinal Manning, head of the Catholic Church in England, for the Vatican Council's definition of Papal Infallibility in 1870. Nonetheless, he was in 1879 made a cardinal by Pope Leo XIII. He lived a retired life until his death in 1890. One of his best-known works today is *The Dream of Gerontius*, a poetical drama and meditation on death, which was set to music by Edward Elgar in 1900.

Newman's interest in philosophy derived from his desire to prove to the world that not just belief in God, but the acceptance of a specific religious creed, was a completely rational activity. He faced squarely the question: how can religious

[5] Quoted by David Brown, *Newman: A Man for our Time* (London: SPCK, 1990), 5.

belief be justified, given that the evidence for its conclusions seems inadequate for the total commitment of faith? He did not, like Kierkegaard, demand the adoption of faith in the absence of reasons, a blind leap over a precipice. He sought to show that adhesion to a creed was itself reasonable, even if no proof could be offered of its articles. In the course of dealing with this question in *The Grammar of Assent*, Newman had much to say of general philosophical interest about the nature of belief, in secular as well as religious contexts.

The general philosophical question posed by Newman is this: is it always wrong to give assent to a proposition in the absence of adequate evidence or argument? Locke had asserted that no proposition should be entertained with greater assurance than justified by the proofs it was built on. In response, Newman pointed to the fact that many of our most solid beliefs go well beyond the flimsy evidence we could offer for them. We all believe that Great Britain is an island; but how many of us have circumnavigated it, or met people who have? If we refused ever to give assents going beyond the force of evidence, the world could not go on, and science itself could make no progress.

Religious belief, then, cannot be condemned as irrational simply on account of being based on grounds that are no more than conjectural. In fact, Newman maintained, strong evidence for the truth of the Christian religion is to be found in the history of Judaism. He agreed, however, that this evidence carried weight only for those who were already prepared to receive it, people who believed in the existence of God and the possibility of revelation. If it is asked why one should believe in God in the first place, Newman responds by appealing to the inward experience of divine power, which is to be found in the voice of conscience.

Few who were not already believers have found convincing either Newman's argument from conscience or his appeal to the testimony of history. But the general epistemological account within which he embeds his apologetics has been admired by philosophers who were far from sharing his religious faith. It is arguably the best treatment of the topics of belief and certainty between Hume and Wittgenstein.[6]

Nietzsche

Just at the time when Newman was presenting his justification of the rationality of religious belief, there was appointed to a professorship in Basel a young man who was to make the twentieth century echo to his proclamation of the death of God. Friedrich Nietzsche was born into a devout Lutheran family in Saxony in 1844. He studied at the universities of Bonn and Leipzig; his training was not in philosophy

---

[6] See Ch. 6 below.

but in classical philology, in which he displayed such facility that he became a full professor at the age of twenty-four, before he had even completed his doctorate. He taught at Basel from 1869 to 1879, with a brief interval of service in the ambulance corps during the Franco-Prussian War of 1870.

Nietzsche was profoundly influenced by two events shortly before he took up his chair. One was reading of Schopenhauer's *The World as Will and Idea*; the other was meeting Richard Wagner, whose *Tristan und Isolde* had fascinated him since he had heard it at the age of sixteen. His first published work, *The Birth of Tragedy* of 1872, showed the influence of both men. In it he drew a contrast between two aspects of the Greek psyche: the wild irrational passions personified in Dionysus, which found expression in music and tragedy, and the disciplined and harmonious beauty represented by Apollo, which found expression in epic and the plastic arts. The triumph of Greek culture was to achieve a synthesis between the two—a synthesis that was disrupted by the rationalistic incursion of Socrates. The decadence which then overtook Greece had infected contemporary Germany, which could achieve salvation only through following the lead of Wagner, to whom the book was dedicated.

Between 1873 and 1876 Nietzsche published four essays, *Untimely Meditations* (or, in another English version, *Songs out of Season*). Two were negative, one a criticism of David Strauss, author of a famous life of Jesus, the other an attack on the pretensions of scientific history. Two were positive: one in praise of Schopenhauer and the other in eulogy of Wagner. But by 1878 Nietzsche had broken with Wagner (he was disgusted with *Parsifal*) and had lost his enthusiasm for Schopenhauer (whose pessimism he now found stifling). In *Human, All too Human*, he showed himself uncharacteristically sympathetic to utilitarian morality and for once appeared to value science as superior to art. But his enduring underlying conviction that art was the supreme task of life displayed itself in the form of the work, which is poetic and aphoristic rather than argumentative or deductive.

In 1879, afflicted by psychosomatic illness, Nietzsche took early retirement from his chair at Basel and brought his academic career to an end. For the next ten years he dwelt in various places in Italy and Switzerland in pursuit of better health, spending many a summer in Sils Maria in the Engadine. He published a series of works in which he hoped to replace the pessimism of Schopenhauer with an optimistic affirmation of life. In works such as *Daybreak* in 1881 and *The Gay Science* (or *Joyful Wisdom*) in 1882 he denounced, as elements hostile to life, Christian self-denial, altruistic ethics, democratic politics, and scientific positivism. He saw it as his task 'to erect a new image and idea of the free spirit'.

As a practical expression of the freedom of his spirit, Nietzsche in 1882 joined the German materialist Paul Rée and the Russian feminist Louise von Salomé in a cohabiting 'trinity'. This love triangle, however, did not last long and from 1883 to 1885 Nietzsche devoted himself to the production of his most famous work, the oracular *Thus Spake Zarathustra*. The unhappy ending of his relationship with Lou may be part cause of the book's most famous aphorism, 'You are going among women? Do not forget the whip!' But the work contained three more important ideas that were going to be of significance in the final period of Nietzsche's life. One is the idea that men as they now are will be superseded by a race of supermen: 'higher ones, stronger ones, more triumphant ones, merrier ones, built squarely in body and soul'. The second is the idea of the transvaluation of values: a complete overturning of traditional and especially Christian moral priorities. The third is the idea of eternal recurrence: in infinite time there are periodic cycles in which all that has ever happened happens once again.

These ideas were given an exposition that was less prophetical and more discursive in the philosophically most important of Nietzsche's works, *Beyond Good and Evil* of 1886 and *The Genealogy of Morals* in 1887. These texts set out a contrast between an aristocratic master-morality which places a high value on nobility, bravery, and truthfulness, and a slave-morality or herd-morality which values submissive traits such as humility, sympathy, and benevolence. Nietzsche saw these works as prolegomena to a systematic exposition of his philosophy, on which he worked energetically but was never able to complete. Several versions extracted from his notes were posthumously published, but only the first part of the work appeared in his lifetime, under the title *The Antichrist* (published in 1895).

The year 1888 was one of feverish production. In addition to *The Antichrist* Nietzsche published a ferocious attack on Wagner (*The Case of Wagner*) and wrote *The Twilight of the Idols* (published in 1889). He also wrote a semi-autobiographical work, *Ecce Homo*, in which can be detected signs of the mental instability (probably of syphilitic origin) that led to him being institutionalized in Jena in 1889. He ended his days insane, being nursed first by his mother and later at Weimar by his sister Elizabeth, who built up an archive of his papers. Nietzsche died in 1900; his sister took control of his *Nachlass* and exercised a degree of protective control over its publication.

During the twentieth century Nietzsche had a great influence in continental Europe, especially upon Russian literature and German philosophy. His opposition to submissive morality and to democratic socialism made him popular among Nazis, who saw themselves as developing a race of superior humans. Partly for this reason, he was long neglected by English-speaking philosophers; but in the latter part of the century, ethicists in the analytic tradition came to realize that his onslaught on traditional morality needed to be answered rather than ignored.[7]

[7] Nietzsche's writings on morality are considered in detail in Ch. 9.

2

Peirce to Strawson

C. S. Peirce and Pragmatism

The thinkers whom we have considered so far in these volumes have all come from Europe, North Africa, or the Middle East. The American continent, nowadays home to many of the world's most influential philosophers, was almost barren of philosophy until the latter part of the nineteenth century. In the eighteenth century acute contributions to different areas of philosophy were made by the Calvinist theologian Jonathan Edwards (1703–58) and the Enlightenment polymath Benjamin Franklin (1706–90). Early in the nineteenth century the essayist Ralph Waldo Emerson (1803–82) presented a form of idealism, called 'transcendentalism', which was briefly fashionable in the United States. But it was with the work of Charles Sanders Peirce (1839–1914) that American philosophy really came of age.

Peirce was the son of a formidable professor of mathematics at Harvard, and he took a *summa cum laude* degree in chemistry there in 1863. For thirty years he served on the US coastal survey, and he also undertook research at Harvard Observatory. The only book he published, *Photometric Researches*, was a work of astronomy. Around 1872 he joined William James, Chauncey Wright, Oliver Wendell Holmes, and others in a discussion group known as the Metaphysical Club. He gave several lecture courses at Harvard on the history and logic of science, and from 1879 until 1884 he was a lecturer on logic at the new, research-oriented Johns Hopkins University in Baltimore. But he was a difficult colleague, impatient of academic conventions, and his marriage to Melusina Fay, a pioneering feminist, broke down in 1883. He failed to obtain tenure, and he never again held an academic post or a full-time job. During the latter part of his life he lived in poverty in Pennsylvania with his devoted second wife, Juliette.

Peirce was a highly original thinker. Like many another nineteenth-century philosopher, he took as his starting point the philosophy of Kant, whose *Critique of Pure Reason* he claimed to know almost by heart. But he regarded Kant's comprehension of formal logic as amateurish. When he set himself to repair this deficiency he found it necessary to recast substantial parts of the Kantian system, such as the theory of categories. Unusually among his contemporaries, he knew and admired the writings of the medieval scholastics, in particular the works of Duns Scotus. The feature he most praised in scholastic philosophers (as in Gothic architects) was the complete absence in their work of self-conceit. He himself had a high opinion of his own merits, regarding Aristotle and Leibniz as his only peers in logic. His work ranged widely, not only over logic in the narrow sense, but also encompassing theory of language, epistemology, and philosophy of mind. He was the originator of one of the most influential of American schools of philosophy, namely pragmatism.

During his lifetime, Peirce's philosophy was presented to the public only in a series of journal articles. In 1868 he published in the *Journal of Speculative Philosophy* two articles with the title 'Questions Concerning Certain Faculties Claimed for Man': these set out an early version of his epistemology. The results are mainly negative: we have no power of introspection, and we have no power of thinking without signs. Above all we have no power of intuition: every cognition is determined logically by some prior cognition.

More influential was a series of 'illustrations of the logic of science' which appeared in the *Popular Science Monthly* in 1877–8. In these he enunciated his principle of fallibilism, that anything that claims to be human knowledge may, in the end, turn out to be mistaken. This, he insisted, does not mean that there is no such thing as objective truth. Absolute truth is the goal of scientific inquiry, but the most we can achieve is ever-improving approximations to it. One of the 1878 articles contains the first formulation of what was later called 'the principle of pragmatism'. This was to the effect that in order to attain clearness in our thoughts of an object, we need only consider what conceivable effects of a practical kind the object may involve (*EWP* 300).

In 1884 Peirce edited a collection of *Johns Hopkins Studies in Logic*. He wrote an essay on the logic of relations, and his system of quantificational logic was presented by one of his students. The system included a novel notation for representing the syntax of relations: e.g. the compound sign 'Lij' could represent that Isaac loves Jessica, and the sign 'Gijk' could represent that Isaac gave Jessica to Kore. It also contained two signs for quantifiers, 'Σ' corresponding to 'some', and 'Π' corresponding to 'all'. The syntax of Peirce's 'General Algebra of Logic', as he called it, was equivalent to that of the system of logic that Gottlob Frege, unknown to him, had developed in Germany a few years previously.

In *The Monist* in 1891–2, 'A Guess at the Riddle', Peirce presented his metaphysics and philosophy of mind against the background of an overall evolutionary cosmology. The definitive statement of his pragmatism (which he now preferred to call 'pragmaticism', since he wished to disown some of the theses of his pragmatist disciples) was issued in a course of lectures at Harvard in 1903 and a further series of papers in *The Monist* in 1905.

In the last years of his life Peirce worked hard to develop a general theory of signs—a 'semiotic' as he called it—as a framework for the philosophy of thought and language. Many of these ideas, which some regard as his most important contribution to philosophy, were worked out between 1903 and 1912 in correspondence with an Englishwoman, Victoria Welby.

Peirce never completed the full synthesis of philosophy on which he worked for many years, and at his death left a mass of unpublished drafts, many of which were posthumously published once interest in his work blossomed in the twentieth century. His influence on other philosophers has not been in proportion to his genius. Peirce's work in logic was never presented in a fully rigorous form, and it was Frege who, through Russell, gave to the world the logical system that the two of them had independently conceived. Peirce's subtle version of pragmatism never seized the imagination of the world in the same way as the more popular version of his admirer William James. It is to the work of Frege and James, therefore, that we now turn.

The Logicism of Frege

Gottlob Frege (1848–1925) was known to few people in his lifetime, but after his death came to occupy a unique position in the history of philosophy. He was the inventor of modern mathematical logic, and an outstanding philosopher of mathematics. He is revered by many as the founder of the school of philosophy which has long been the dominant one in Anglophone universities: analytic philosophy, which focuses its concern on the analysis of meaning in language. It was his influence—mediated in Britain by Bertrand Russell and on the European mainland by Edmund Husserl—that gave philosophy the linguistic turn that characterized the twentieth century.

Frege was born into a Lutheran family of schoolteachers who lived in Wismar, on the Baltic coast of Germany. His father died when he was in his teens, and he was supported through school and university by his mother, now headmistress of the girls' school that had been founded by her husband. He entered Jena University in 1869, but after four semesters he moved to Göttingen, where he took his Ph.D., with a geometrical dissertation, in 1873. He returned to Jena as a *privatdozent*, or unsalaried lecturer, in 1874, and taught there in the mathematics faculty for forty-four years, becoming a professor in 1879. Apart from his intellectual activity his life was uneventful and secluded. Few of his colleagues troubled to read his books and articles, and for his most important work he had difficulty in finding a publisher.

Frege's productive career began in 1879 with the publication of a pamphlet entitled *Begriffsschrift* ('Concept Script'). The concept script that gave the book its title was a new symbolism designed to bring out clearly logical relationships that ordinary language obscures. Frege used it to develop a new system that has a permanent place at the heart of modern logic: the propositional calculus. This is the branch of logic that deals with those inferences that depend on the force of negation, conjunction, disjunction, etc. when applied to sentences as wholes. Its fundamental principle is to treat the truth-value (i.e. the truth or falsehood as the case may be) of sentences containing connectives such as 'and', 'if', and 'or' as being determined solely by the truth-values of the component sentences linked by the connectives. Composite sentences such as 'Snow is white and grass is green' are treated as being, in the logicians' technical term, *truth-functions* of their constituent simple propositions such as 'Snow is white' and 'Grass is green'.

Propositional logic had been studied in the ancient world by the Stoics and in the Middle Ages by Ockham and others;[1] but it was Frege who gave it its first systematic formulation. *Begriffsschrift* presents the propositional calculus in an axiomatic manner in which all the laws of propositional logic are derived, by a specified method of inference, from a number of primitive propositions. The actual symbolism that Frege invented for this purpose is difficult to print, and has long been superseded in the presentation of the calculus; but the operations that it expressed continue to be fundamental in mathematical logic.

It was not, however, the propositional calculus, but the predicate calculus, that was Frege's greatest contribution to logic. This is the branch of logic that deals with the internal structure of propositions rather than with propositions considered as atomic units. Frege invented a novel notation for quantification, that is to say, a method of symbolizing and rigorously displaying those inferences that depend for their validity on expressions such as 'all' or 'some', 'no' or 'none'. With this notation he presented a predicate calculus that greatly improved upon the Aristotelian syllogistic that had hitherto been looked upon as the be-all and end-all of logic. Frege's calculus allowed formal logic, for the first time, to cope with sentences containing multiple quantification, such as 'Nobody knows everything' and 'Every boy loves some girl'.[2]

Though *Begriffsschrift* is a classical text in the history of logic, Frege's purpose in writing it was concerned more with mathematics than with logic. He wanted to put forward a formal system of arithmetic as well as a formal system of logic, and most importantly, he wanted to show that the two systems were intimately linked. All the truths of arithmetic, he claimed, could be shown to follow from truths of logic without the need of any extra support. How this thesis (which came to be known as 'logicism') was to be demonstrated was sketched in *Begriffsschrift*, and set out more fully in two later works, *Grundlagen der Arithmetik* ('Foundations of Arithmetic') of 1884 and *Die Grundgesetze der Arithmetik* ('The Fundamental Laws of Arithmetic') of 1893 and 1903.

---

[1] See above, pp. 115, 369.   [2] See Ch. 4 below.

The most important step in Frege's logicist programme was to define arithmetical notions, such as that of number, in terms of purely logical notions, such as that of class. Frege achieves this by treating the cardinal numbers as classes of equivalent classes, that is to say, of classes with the same number of members. Thus the number two is the class of pairs, and the number three the class of trios. Such a definition at first sight appears circular, but in fact it is not since the notion of equivalence between classes can be defined without making use of the notion of number. Two classes are equivalent to each other if they can be mapped onto each other without residue. Thus, to take an example of Frege's, a waiter may know that there are as many knives as there are plates on a table without knowing how many of each there are. All he needs to do is to observe that there is a knife to the right of every plate and a plate to the left of every knife.

Thus, we could define four as the class of all classes equivalent to the class of gospel-makers. But such a definition would be useless for the logicist's purpose since the fact that there were four gospel-makers is no part of logic. Frege has to find, for each number, not only a class of the right size, but one whose size is guaranteed by logic. He does this by beginning with zero as the first of the number series. This can be defined in purely logical terms as the class of all classes equivalent to the class of objects that are not identical with themselves: a class that obviously has no members ('the null class'). We can then go on to define the number one as the class of all classes equivalent to the class whose only member is zero. In order to pass from these definitions to definitions of the other natural numbers Frege needs to define the notion of 'succeeding' in the sense in which three succeeds two, and four succeeds three, in the number series. He defines 'n immediately succeeds m' as 'There exists a concept F, and an object falling under it x, such that the number of Fs is n and the number of Fs not identical with x is m'. With the aid of this definition the other numbers can be defined without using any notions other than logical ones such as identity, class, and class-equivalence.

Begriffsschrift is a very austere and formal work. *The Foundations of Arithmetic* sets out the logicist programme much more fully, but also much more informally. Symbols appear rarely, and Frege takes great pains to relate his work to that of other philosophers. According to Kant, our knowledge of both arithmetic and geometry depended on intuition: in the *Critique of Pure Reason* he had maintained that mathematical truths were synthetic a priori, that is to say that while they were genuinely informative, they were known in advance of all experience.[3] John Stuart Mill, as we have seen, maintained that mathematical propositions were empirical generalizations, widely applicable and widely confirmed, but a posteriori nonetheless.

Frege agreed with Kant against Mill that mathematics was known a priori, and like Kant he thought that geometry rested on intuition. But his thesis that

[3] See above, p. 578.

arithmetic was a branch of logic meant that it was not synthetic, as Kant had claimed, but analytic. It was based, if Frege was right, solely upon general laws that were operative in every sphere of knowledge and needed no support from empirical facts. Arithmetic had no separate subject matter of its own any more than logic had.

In the *Foundations* there are two theses that Frege regarded as important. One is that each individual number is a self-subsistent object. The other is that the content of a statement assigning a number is an assertion about a concept. At first sight these propositions seem to conflict with each other; but once we understand what Frege means by 'concept' and 'object' we see that they do not.

In saying that a number is an object, Frege is not suggesting that it is something tangible like a bush or a box. Rather, he is denying two things. First, he is denying that a number is a property of anything: in three blind mice, threeness is not a property of any mouse in the way that blindness is. Second, he is denying that number is anything subjective, an image or idea or any property of any mental item.

Concepts, for Frege, are mind-independent, and so there is no contradiction between the claim that numbers are objective and the claim that number statements are statements about concepts. By this second claim, Frege means that a statement such as 'The earth has one moon' assigns the number one to the concept *moon of the earth*. Similarly, 'Venus has no moons' assigns the number zero to the concept *moon of Venus*. In this latter case, it is quite clear that there does not exist any moon to have a number as its property. But all statements of number are to be treated in the same way.

But if number statements of this kind are statements about concepts, what kind of object is a number itself? Frege's answer is that a number is the extension of a concept. The number that belongs to the concept *F*, he says, is the extension of the concept 'like numbered to the concept *F*'. This is tantamount to saying that it is the class of all classes that have the same number of members as the class of *F*s, as was explained above. So Frege's theory that numbers are objects depends on the possibility of taking classes as objects.

In the years after the publication of *Foundations*, Frege published a number of seminal papers on the philosophy of language. Three appeared in 1891–2: 'Function and Concept', 'Sense and Reference', 'Concept and Object'. Each of these presented original philosophical ideas of great importance with astonishing brevity and clarity. They were seen, no doubt, by Frege himself as ancillary to his concerns with the nature of mathematics, but at the present time they are regarded as founding classics of modern semantic theory.[4]

Between 1884 and 1893 Frege worked on the treatise that should have been the climax of his intellectual career, the *Grundgesetze der Arithmetik*, which was to set out in

---

[4] Frege's contribution to the philosophy of language is detailed in Ch. 5.

a complete and formal manner the logicist construction of arithmetic from logic. The task was to enunciate a set of axioms that would be recognizably truths of logic, to propound a set of undoubtedly sound rules of inference, and then from those axioms by those rules to derive, one by one, the standard truths of arithmetic. The derivation was to occupy three volumes, of which only two were completed, the first dealing with the natural numbers, and the second with negative, fractional, irrational, and complex numbers.

Frege's ambitious project aborted before it was completed. Between the publication of the first volume in 1893 and the second in 1903 Frege received a letter from an English philosopher, Bertrand Russell, pointing out that the fifth of the initial set of axioms rendered the whole system inconsistent. This axiom stated, in effect, that if every F is a G, and every G is an F, then the class of Fs is identical with the class of Gs; and vice versa. It was the axiom which, in Frege's words, allowed the transition from a concept to its extension, the transition from concepts to classes that was essential if it was to be established that numbers were logical objects.

The problem, as Russell pointed out, was that the system, with this axiom, permits without restriction the formation of classes of classes, and classes of classes of classes, and so on. Classes must themselves be classifiable. Now can a class be a member of itself? Most classes are not (the class of men is not a man) but some apparently are (e.g. the class of classes is surely a class). It seems, therefore, that we have two kinds of classes: those that are members of themselves and those that are not. But the formation of the class of all classes that are not members of themselves leads to paradox: if it is a member of itself, then it is not a member of itself, and if it is not a member of itself, then it is a member of itself. A system that leads to such a paradox cannot be logically sound.

The second volume of *Grundgesetze* was already in press when Russell's letter arrived. Utterly downcast, Frege described the paradox in an appendix, and attempted to patch the system by weakening the guilty axiom. But this revised system in its turn proved inconsistent. After retiring from Jena in 1918 Frege seems to have given up his belief that arithmetic can be derived from logic, and returned to the Kantian view that it is, like geometry, synthetic a priori.

We now know that the logicist programme can never be carried out. The path from the axioms of logic to the theorems of arithmetic is barred at two points. First, as Russell showed, the naive set theory that was part of Frege's logical basis was inconsistent in itself. Second, the notion of 'axioms of arithmetic' was itself called in question when it was later shown (by the Austrian mathematician Kurt Gödel in 1931) that it was impossible to give arithmetic a complete and consistent axiomatization.

Nonetheless, Frege's philosophical legacy was enormous. He often compared the mathematician to a geographer who maps new continents. His own career as a thinker resembled that of Christopher Columbus as an explorer. Just as Columbus failed to find a passage to India but made Europe acquainted with a whole new continent, so Frege failed to derive arithmetic from logic, but made innovations in logic and advances in philosophy that permanently changed the whole map of both subjects. Like Columbus, Frege succumbed to discouragement and depression; he was never to know that he was the founder of an influential philosophical movement. But he did not give up all hope that his work had value: leaving his papers to his son just before his death in 1925 he wrote, 'Do not despise the pieces I have written. Even if all is not gold, there is gold in them.'

Psychology and Pragmatism in William James

William James (1842–1910) was six years older than Frege, but he began his philosophical career quite late in life. He was born in New York, the son of a Swedenborgian theologian and the elder brother of the celebrated novelist Henry James. He was educated partly in America and partly in Europe, where he attended schools in France and Germany. For a while he hesitated between painting and medicine as a career, but in 1864 he enrolled in the Harvard Medical School. After taking his degree he suffered a period of ill health and depression, but after a recovery (which he attributed to reading the works of the French philosopher Charles Renouvier) he was appointed to the Harvard faculty in 1873 as an instructor in anatomy and physiology. His interests shifted towards empirical psychology, and in 1876 he established the first psychological laboratory in America. Among his pupils was the novelist Gertrude Stein. His two-volume *Principles of Psychology*, of 1890, was a racy survey of the results of the infant discipline. The task of psychology, as James saw it, was to link conditions of the brain with the varying phenomena of the stream of consciousness.

The book became a standard textbook, but by the time it was published James had left psychology and become a professor of philosophy—a subject that had fascinated him since his discussions with Peirce and others in the Metaphysical Club of 1872. Like his father, James was deeply concerned with religious issues, and was anxious to reconcile a scientific world-view with a belief in God, freedom, and immortality. His professional career as a philosophical writer was inaugurated in 1897 with the appearance of *The Will to Believe*, in which he discussed situations where we have to decide on issues in the absence of compelling theoretical evidence. In such cases, he argued, the duty to believe truth should be given equal weight with the duty to avoid error. He soon built up an international reputation, and in 1901–2 he gave the Gifford lectures in Edinburgh, which were later published as *Varieties of Religious Experience*. In that work he set himself to examine 'the feelings, acts and experiences of individual men in their solitude, so far as they apprehend themselves to stand in relation to whatever they may consider the divine.' He subjected the phenomena of mysticism and other forms of religious sentiment to empirical investigation in the hope of establishing their authenticity and validity.

It was the publication of *Pragmatism* in 1907 that established James's position as the doyen of American philosophy. Both the title and the main theme of the work were credited by James to Peirce, and in his formulation of his pragmatic principle, his debt is obvious.

To attain perfect clearness in our thoughts of an object, we need only consider what conceivable effects of a practical kind the object may involve—what sensations we are to expect from it, and what reactions we must prepare. Our conception of these effects, whether immediate or remote, is then for us the whole of our conception of the object, so far as that conception has positive significance at all. (*P* 47)

However, whereas Peirce's pragmatism was a theory of meaning, James's was a theory of truth, and whereas Peirce's pragmatism was interpersonal and objective, James's was individualist and subjective. For this reason, Peirce disowned James's theory and renamed his own 'pragmaticism'.

According to James's pragmatism, an idea is true so long as to believe it is profitable to our lives: 'The true is the name of whatever proves itself to be good in the way of belief' (*P* 42). He and his followers sometimes summed this up in the slogan, 'What is true is what works'. Critics objected that belief in a falsehood might make people happier than belief in a truth, which meant that truth could not be identified with long-term satisfactoriness. Both believers and unbelievers were shocked by James's statement, 'if the hypothesis of God works satisfactorily in the widest sense of the word, it is true' (*P* 143).

James insisted that his theory did not involve any denial of objective reality. Reality and truth are different from each other. Things have reality; it is ideas and beliefs that are true. 'Realities are not *true*, they *are*; and beliefs are true *of* them' (*T* 196). It is not by discovering whether the consequences of a belief are good that we learn whether it is true or not; but it is the consequences that assign 'the only intelligible practical *meaning* to that difference in our beliefs which our habit of calling them true or false comports' (*T* 273).

It is often said that what makes a belief true is its correspondence with reality. James is willing to accept this, but asks what in the concrete the notion of correspondence amounts to. When we speak of an idea 'pointing to' reality, or 'fitting it', or 'corresponding', or 'agreeing' with it, what we are really talking about is the processes of validation or verification that lead us from the idea to the reality. Such mediating events, James says, *make* the idea true.

In a series of essays (collected in *The Meaning of Truth*, 1909) James defended, qualified, and refined his pragmatism. But it remained unclear whether in his system the actual existence of a reality is a necessary condition of a belief in it being satisfactory (in which case he is committed to correspondence as an element of truth) or whether a belief in an object may be satisfactory without that object actually existing (in which case he is open to the charge of preferring wishful thinking to genuine inquiry).

In the same year as he published *The Meaning of Truth* James published *A Pluralistic Universe*, in which he applied pragmatism in support of a religious world-view. He spoke of our awareness of a 'wider self from which saving experiences flow in' and of a 'mother sea of consciousness'. He believed, however, that the amount of suffering in the world prevents us from believing in an infinite, absolute divinity: the superhuman consciousness is limited either in power, or in knowledge, or in both. Even God cannot determine or predict the future; whether the world will become better or worse depends on the choices of human beings in cooperation with him.

In his old age James, a genial and affable personality and a great communicator, was revered by many inside and outside the United States. Peirce, on the other hand, was isolated and destitute, and in 1907 was discovered by one of James's students nearly dead from starvation in a Cambridge lodging house. James organized a fund which supplied Peirce's basic needs until his death from cancer in 1914. James himself died of heart disease in 1910; on his deathbed in Cambridge he asked his brother Henry to remain close for six weeks to receive any messages he could send to him from beyond the grave. No messages are recorded.

James died before completing his metaphysical system, but his pragmatist programme was continued by others after his death. John Dewey (1859–1952), in a long academic career at Ann Arbor, Chicago, and Columbia in New York, applied it most particularly in the area of American education, but he also wrote influential books on many social and political topics. His constant aim was to explore how far methods of inquiry that had been so successful in physical science and in technology could be extended into other areas of human endeavour.

In England F. C. S. Schiller (1864–1937) developed a version of pragmatism that he called 'humanism'. Schiller was a graduate of Balliol College, Oxford, and taught for a while at Cornell University in upstate New York, where he met James, before returning to a fellowship at Corpus Christi College. He was a lonely figure at Oxford because in the last years of the nineteenth century, philosophy departments in the major universities of the United Kingdom were dominated by a British version of Hegelian idealism.

British Idealism and its Critics

After the death of John Stuart Mill a reaction had set in against the tradition of British empiricism of which he had been such a distinguished exponent. In 1874, a year after Mill's death, a Balliol tutor, T. H. Green (1836–82), brought out an edition of David Hume's *Treatise of Human Nature* with a substantial introduction subjecting the presuppositions of empiricism to devastating criticism. In the same year there appeared the first of a long series of English translations of the works of Hegel, which had first been introduced to Oxford in the 1840s by Benjamin Jowett (1817–93), the Master of Green's college. Two years later F. H. Bradley of Merton published *Ethical Studies*, a founding classic of British Hegelianism. In 1893 Bradley completed *Appearance and Reality*, the fullest and most magisterial statement of British idealism. Shortly afterwards at Cambridge the methods and some of the doctrines of Hegel's *Logic* were expounded in a series of treatises by the Trinity College philosopher J. M. E. McTaggart.

Green's idealism, like James's pragmatism, was partly motivated by religious concerns. 'There is one spiritual and self-conscious being of which all that is real is the activity and expression,' he wrote in *Prolegomena to Ethics*, published the year after his death in 1882; 'we are all related to this spiritual being, not merely as parts of the world which is its expression, but as partakers in some inchoate measure of the self-consciousness through which it at once constitutes itself and distinguishes itself from the world.' This participation, he maintained, was the source of morality and religion. Bradley and McTaggart, however, evacuated idealism of any remotely Christian content, and the latter went so far as to deny that there was any Absolute other than a community of finite selves.

It was common ground among the British idealists, however, that reality was essentially spiritual in nature: they rejected the dualist idea that mind and matter were two equal and independent realms of being. But Bradley's 'monism' had another fundamental aspect: the claim that reality is to be considered as a totality. Truth belongs not to individual, atomistic propositions, but only to judgements about being as a whole. In *Appearance and Reality* Bradley sought to show that if we try to conceive the universe as a complex of independent substances distinct from their relations to each other we fall into contradiction. Every item in the universe is related—internally related, by its very essence—to every other item. The objects of everyday experience, the space and time that they inhabit, and indeed the very subject of experience, the individual self—all these are mere appearances, helpful for practical purposes, but quite misleading as to the true nature of reality.

The dominance of idealism was decisively called into question at the turn of the century by two young Cambridge philosophers, G. E. Moore (1873 1958) and Bertrand Russell (1872–1970). Both were pupils of McTaggart and took their first steps in philosophy as Hegelians. But Russell found Hegel himself much less impressive than McTaggart, and was disgusted by his woolly attitude to mathematics. Moore, in 'The Nature of Judgement' (1899), rejected the fundamental thesis that reality is a creation of the mind, and replaced it with a Platonic realism: concepts are objective, independent realities, and the world consists of such concepts combined with each other into true propositions. After this attack on metaphysical idealism, Moore four years later attacked empiricist idealism. In 'The Refutation of Idealism' he rejected the claim that *esse* is *percipi*; to exist is something quite different from being perceived, and the objects of our knowledge are independent of our knowledge of them. Moreover, material objects are something we directly perceive.

Moore's revolt against idealism had a great impact on Russell. 'It was an immense excitement', he later recalled, 'after having supposed the sensible world unreal, to be able to believe again that there really were such things as tables and chairs' (*A* 135). He received a great sense of liberation from the thought that, *pace* Locke and his successors, grass really was green. Like Moore, he combined his renunciation of idealism with the affirmation of a Platonic faith in universals: every word, particular or general, stood for an objective entity. In particular, in reaction against Bradley, he attached great importance to the independent reality of relations. In a brilliant study of the philosophy of Leibniz in 1899 he went so far as to maintain that the elaborate and incredible structure of the metaphysics of monads arises from the single error of thinking that all sentences must be of subject–predicate form, instead of realizing that relational sentences are irreducible to that pattern.

Russell on Mathematics, Logic, and Language

Relations were a matter of particular interest to Russell at this time because the focus of his thought was on the nature of mathematics, in which relational statements such as '*n* is the successor of *m*' play an important role. Independently of Frege, and initially without any knowledge of his work, Russell had undertaken a logicist project of deriving mathematics from pure logic. His endeavour was indeed more ambitious than Frege's since he hoped to show that not just arithmetic, but geometry and analysis also, were derived from general logical axioms. Between 1900 and 1903, influenced in part by the Italian mathematician Giuseppe Peano, he worked out his ideas for incorporation into a substantial volume, *The Principles of Mathematics*. It was in the course of this work that he encountered the paradox that bears his name, the paradox generated by the class of all classes that are not members of themselves. As we have seen, he communicated this discovery to Frege, to whom he had been directed by Peano. Russell introduced Frege's work to an English readership in an appendix to *The Principles*. In the light of the paradox, the two great logicists saw that their project, if it was to succeed, would need considerable modification.

Russell's attempt to avoid the paradox took the form of a Theory of Types. According to this theory, it was wrong to treat classes as randomly classifiable objects. Individuals and classes belonged to different logical types, and what could be asserted of elements of one type could not be significantly asserted of another. 'The class of dogs is not a dog' was not true or false but meaningless. Similarly, what can significantly be said of classes cannot be said of classes of classes, and so on through the hierarchy of logical types. To avoid the paradox, we must observe the difference of types between different levels of the hierarchy.

But now another difficulty arises. Recall that Frege had, in effect, defined the number two as the class of all pairs, and defined all the natural numbers in a similar manner. But a pair is just a two-membered class, so the number two, on this account, is a class of classes. If we put limitations on the formation of classes of classes, how can we define the series of natural numbers? Russell retained the definition of zero as the class whose only member is the null class, but he now treated the number one as the class of all classes equivalent to the class whose members are (*a*) the members of the null class, plus (*b*) any object not a member of that class. The number two was treated in turn as the class of classes equivalent to the class whose members are (*a*) the members of the class used to define one, plus (*b*) any object not a member of that defining class. In this way the numbers can be defined one after the other, and each number is a class of classes of individuals.

However, the natural number series can be continued thus ad infinitum only if the number of objects in the universe is itself infinite. For if there are only n individuals then there will be no classes with $n + 1$ members, and so no cardinal number $n + 1$. Russell accepted this and therefore added to his axioms an axiom of infinity, i.e. the hypothesis that the number of objects in the universe is not finite. Whether or not this hypothesis is true, it is surely not a truth of pure logic, and so the need to postulate it appears to nullify the logicist project of deriving arithmetic from logic alone.

Russell's later philosophy of mathematics was presented to the world in two remarkable works. The first, more technical, presentation was written in collaboration with his former tutor A. N. Whitehead and appeared in three volumes between 1910 and 1913 under the title *Principia Mathematica*. The second, more popular work, *Introduction to Mathematical Philosophy*, was written while he was serving a prison sentence for his activities as an anti-war protester in 1917.

By this time, Russell had achieved distinction outside the philosophy of mathematics in areas that were later to become major preoccupations of British philosophers. His early work, along with that of Moore, is often said to have inaugurated a new era in British philosophy, the era of 'analytic philosophy'. Even though the impetus to the analytic style of thinking can be traced back, as Russell himself was happy to admit, to the work of Frege, it was Moore who first gave currency, in the twentieth century, to the term 'analysis' itself as the mark of a particular way of philosophizing.

'Analysis' was, first and foremost, an anti-idealist slogan: instead of accepting the necessity of understanding a whole before one could understand its parts, Moore and Russell insisted that the right road to understanding was to analyse wholes by taking them to pieces. But what was it that was to be taken to pieces—things or signs? Initially, both Moore and Russell saw themselves as analysing concepts, not language—concepts that were objective realities independent of the mind. 'Where the mind can distinguish elements', Russell wrote in 1903, 'there must *be* different elements to distinguish' (*PM* 466). Analysis would reveal the complexity of concepts, and exhibit their constituent elements. These constituents might be the subjects of further analysis, or they might be simple and unanalysable. In *Principia Ethica* (1903) Moore famously claimed that *good* was such a simple, unanalysable property.

Russell, at the time of *The Principles of Mathematics*, believed that in order to save the objectivity of concepts and judgements it was necessary to accept the existence of propositions that subsisted independently of their expression in sentences. Not only concepts, relations, and numbers had being, he believed, but also chimeras and the Homeric gods. If they had no being, it would be impossible to make propositions about them. 'Thus being is a general attribute of everything, and to mention anything is to show that it is' (*PM* 449).

It was Russell's seminal paper of 1905, 'On Denoting', that gave analysis a linguistic turn. In that paper he showed how to make sense of sentences containing expressions like 'the round square' and 'the present King of France' without maintaining that these expressions denoted some entity, however shadowy, in the world. The paper was for long regarded as a paradigm of analysis; but of course it contains no analysis of round squares or non-existent kings. Instead, it shows how to rewrite such sentences, preserving their meaning, but removing the apparent attribution of being to the non-existent. And Russell's method is explicitly linguistic: it rests on making a distinction between those symbols (such as proper names) that denote something and the world, and other symbols which he called 'incomplete symbols', of which definite descriptions such as 'the present King of France' are one instance. These symbols have no meaning on their own—they do not denote anything—but the sentences in which they occur do have a meaning, that is to say they express a proposition that is either true or false.[5]

Logical analysis, then, as practised in 'On Denoting' is a technique of substituting a logically clear form of words for another form of words which is in some way misleading. But in Russell's mind logical analysis was not only a linguistic device for the classification of sentences. He came to believe that once logic had been cast into a perspicuous form it would reveal the structure of the world.

Logic contains individual variables and propositional functions: corresponding to this, Russell believed, the world contains particulars and universals. In logic complex propositions are built up as truth-functions of simple propositions. Similarly, Russell came to believe, there were in the world independent atomic facts corresponding to the simple propositions. Atomic facts consisted either in the possession by a particular of a characteristic, or else in a relation between two or more particulars. This theory of Russell's acquired the name 'logical atomism'.

---

[5] Russell's theory of definite descriptions is presented in detail in Ch. 5.

The development of the theory can be followed in the books that Russell wrote in the years leading up to the First World War: *The Problems of Philosophy* (1912), a lastingly popular introduction to the subject, and the more professional *Our Knowledge of the External World* of 1914. The most vivid presentation was in a series of lectures in London in 1918, 'The Philosophy of Logical Atomism', published much later in *Logic and Knowledge* (1956). Russell came to believe that every proposition that we can understand must be composed wholly of items with which we are acquainted. 'Acquaintance' was his word for immediate presentation: we were acquainted, for instance, with our own sense-data, which were his equivalents of Hume's impressions or Descartes's thoughts. But direct acquaintance was also possible with the universals that lay behind the predicates of a reformed logical language; so much of Russell's early Platonism remained. Acquaintance, however, was not possible with objects distant in space and time: we could not be acquainted with Queen Victoria or even with our own past sense-data. The things that were not known by acquaintance were known by description; hence the importance of the theory of descriptions in the development of logical atomism.

Russell now applied the theory of descriptions not only to round squares and fictional objects but to many things that common sense would regard as perfectly real, such as Julius Caesar, tables, and cabbages. These, he now maintained, were logical constructions out of sense-data. In a sentence such as 'Caesar crossed the Rubicon', uttered in England now, we have a proposition in which there are no individual constituents with which we are acquainted. In order to explain how we can understand the sentence, Russell analysed the names 'Caesar' and 'Rubicon' as definite descriptions which, spelt out in full, would not include any terms referring to the objects apparently named in the sentence.

Ordinary proper names, therefore, were disguised descriptions. A fully analysed sentence would contain only logically proper names (words referring to particulars with which we are acquainted) and universal terms (words indicating characters and relations). Russell's account of what counted as logically proper names varied from time to time. In the most austere versions of the theory only pure demonstratives appeared to count as names, so that an atomic proposition would be something like '(this) red' or '(this) beside (that)'.

'The Philosophy of Logical Atomism' was far from being Russell's last word on philosophy. In 1921 he wrote *The Analysis of Mind*, which defended a version of William James's neutral monism, the theory that both mind and matter consist of a neutral material which is, for all practical purposes, nothing other than the data of internal and external senses. During the 1930s and 1940s Russell wrote many popular books on social and political topics, and he became famous for the unorthodox nature of his moral ideas and notorious for the breakdown of successive marriages. In 1940, having been appointed to a short-term professorship at the City College of New York, he was declared unfit to teach by the State

Supreme Court. In 1945 he published a brilliantly written, if often inaccurate, *History of Western Philosophy*, which led to his being awarded the Nobel Prize for literature.

Russell's last philosophical book was *Human Knowledge: Its Scope and Limits*, published in 1948, in which he attempted to provide an empiricist justification of scientific method. To his disappointment, the book received little attention. Indeed, though he became very widely known in later life, especially after he inherited an earldom, as a campaigner on social and political topics, particularly on the issue of nuclear disarmament, his reputation among professional philosophers never recovered the level of respect accorded to his works prior to 1920. Logical atomism itself, as he was the first to admit, was in large part due to the ideas of one of his former pupils, Ludwig Wittgenstein, to whose history we now turn.

Wittgenstein's Tractatus

Wittgenstein was born in Vienna in 1889 into an Austrian family of Jewish descent. The family was large and wealthy, the father a prominent steel millionaire who had nine children by his Catholic wife, and had all of them baptized as Catholics. The family was also highly artistic; Johannes Brahms was a frequent guest, and Ludwig's brother Paul was a concert pianist who achieved international fame in spite of losing an arm in the 1914–18 war. Ludwig was educated at home until he was fourteen, after which he attended for three years the *Realschule* at Linz. Among his schoolboy contemporaries was Adolf Hitler.

At school Wittgenstein, partly under the influence of Schopenhauer, ceased to be a religious believer. He studied engineering in Berlin, and later at the University of Manchester, where he designed a jet-reaction engine for aircraft. He read Russell's *Principles of Mathematics* and through it became acquainted with the work of Frege, whom he visited at Jena in 1911. On Frege's advice he went to Cambridge, and spent five terms at Trinity College, studying under Russell, who quickly recognized and generously fostered his genius.

Wittgenstein left Cambridge in 1913 and went to live as a solitary in a hut he had built himself in Norway. The notes and letters he wrote at this period exhibit the germination of the view of philosophy he was to retain throughout his life. Philosophy, he wrote, was not a deductive discipline; it could not be placed on the same footing as the natural sciences. 'Philosophy gives no pictures of reality and can neither confirm nor confute scientific investigations' (*NB* 93).

When war broke out in 1914 Wittgenstein enlisted as a volunteer in the Austrian artillery, and served with conspicuous courage on the eastern and Italian fronts. He was captured by Italian soldiers in the southern Tyrol in November 1918 and sent to a prison camp near Monte Cassino. During his military service he had written philosophical thoughts into his diary, and during his imprisonment he turned them into the only philosophical book that he published in his lifetime, *Tractatus Logico-Philosophicus*. He sent this book from the prison camp to Russell, with whom he was later able to discuss it in Holland. It was published in German in 1921 and shortly afterwards in England with an English translation by C. K. Ogden and an introduction by Russell.

The *Tractatus* is short, beautiful, and cryptic. It consists of a series of numbered paragraphs, often very brief. The first is 'The world is all that is the case' and the last is 'Whereof one cannot speak, thereof one must be silent.' The key theme of the book is the picture theory of meaning. Language, we are told, consists of propositions that picture the world. Propositions are the perceptible expressions of thoughts, and thoughts are logical pictures of facts, and the world is the totality of facts.

An English sentence, such as 'The London train leaves at 11.15' or 'Blood is thicker than water', does not look like a picture. But Wittgenstein believed that propositions and thoughts were pictures in a literal sense; if they did not look like pictures, that was because language throws a heavy disguise around thought. But even in ordinary language, he insisted, there is a perceptibly pictorial element. Take the sentence 'My fork is to the left of my knife'. This says something quite different from another sentence containing exactly the same words, namely 'My knife is to the left of my fork'. What makes the first sentence have the meaning it does is the fact that within it *the words* 'my fork' occur to the left of *the words* 'my knife', as they do not in the second sentence. So here a spatial relationship between words pictures a spatial relationship between things (*TLP* 4.102).

Few cases are as simple as this. If the sentence were spoken instead of written, it would be a temporal relation between sounds rather than a spatial relationship on the page that would represent the relationship between the items on the table. But this in turn is because the spoken sequence and the spatial array have a certain abstract structure in common. According to the *Tractatus* any picture must have something in common with what it depicts. This shared minimum Wittgenstein calls its logical form. Most propositions, unlike the untypical example above, do not have spatial form in common with the situation they depict; but any proposition must have logical form in common with what it depicts.

To reveal the pictorial structure of thought behind the disguise of ordinary language, Wittgenstein believed, we have to proceed by logical analysis along the lines suggested by Russell. In this analysis, he maintained, we will in the end come to symbols that denote entirely non-complex objects. A fully analysed proposition will consist of a combination of atomic propositions, each of which will contain names of simple objects, names related to each other in ways that will picture, truly or falsely, the relations between the objects they represent. Such an analysis may be beyond human powers, but the thought the proposition expresses already, in the mind, has the complexity of the fully analysed proposition. We express this thought in plain German or English by the unconscious operation of extremely complicated rules. The connection between language and the world is made by the correlation between the ultimate elements of these thoughts deep in the mind, and the atomic objects that constitute the essence of the world. How these correlations are made we are not told: it is a mysterious process which, it seems, each of us must manage for himself, creating as it were a private language.

Having expounded the picture theory of the proposition and the world-structure that goes with it, Wittgenstein shows how propositions of various kinds are to be analysed into combinations of atomic pictures. Science consists of propositions whose truth-value is determined by the truth-values of the atomic propositions from which they are built up. Logic consists of tautologies, that is to say, complex propositions that are true no matter what the truth-value of their constituent propositions. Not all propositions are capable of analysis into atomic propositions: there are some that reveal themselves as pseudo-propositions. Among these are propositions of ethics and theology. So too, it turns out, are the propositions of philosophy, including those of the *Tractatus* itself.

The *Tractatus*, like other metaphysical treatises, tries to describe the logical form of the world; but this is something that cannot be done. A picture must be independent of what it pictures; it must be capable of being a false picture no less than a true one. But since any proposition must contain the logical form of the world, it cannot picture it. What the metaphysician attempts to say cannot be said, but only shown. The paragraphs of the *Tractatus* are like a ladder that must be climbed and then kicked away if we are to see the world aright. Philosophy is not a theory, but an activity, the activity of clarifying non-philosophical propositions. Once clarified, the propositions will mirror the logical form of the world and thus show what the philosopher wishes to, but cannot, say.

Neither science nor philosophy can show us the meaning of life. But this does not mean that a problem is left unsolved.

Doubt can exist only where a question exists, a question only when an answer exists, and an answer only where something *can be said*. We feel that even when *all possible* scientific questions have been answered, the problems of life remain completely untouched. Of course there are then no questions left, and this itself is the answer. The solution of the problem of life is seen in the vanishing of this problem. (*TLP* 6.5–6.521)

Even if one could believe in immortality, it would not confer meaning on life; nothing is solved by surviving for ever. An eternal life would be as much a riddle as this one. 'God does not reveal himself *in* the world,' Wittgenstein wrote; 'it is not how things are in the world that is mystical, but *that* it exists' (*TLP* 6.432, 6.44).

Philosophy can do very little for us. What it can do, however, had been done once for all by the *Tractatus*—or so Wittgenstein believed. With perfect consistency, having published the book he gave up philosophy and took up a number of more humdrum jobs. On the death of Karl Wittgenstein in 1912 Ludwig like his siblings had inherited a large fortune, but on returning from the war he renounced his share, and supported himself instead as a gardener in a monastery or a school-master in rural schools. In 1926 a charge of sadistic punishment was brought against him on behalf of one of his pupils, and though he was acquitted this brought his schoolteaching career to an end.

Logical Positivism

Wittgenstein returned to Vienna, and had a hand in designing the architecture of a new house for his sister. He was introduced by her to Moritz Schlick, since 1922 Professor of the Philosophy of Science at Vienna University, with whom he resumed his philosophical inquiries. The two met on Monday evenings in 1927 and 1928, and were joined by others, including Rudolf Carnap and Friedrich Waismann. In 1929 Wittgenstein went to Cambridge to work on a philosophical manuscript (published posthumously as *Philosophische Bemerkungen*). During his absence the discussion group developed into a self-conscious philosophical move-ment and issued a manifesto, the *Wissenschaftliche Weltauffassung der Wiener Kreis*, which launched a campaign against metaphysics as an outdated system that must give way to a scientific world-view.

The anti-metaphysical programme exploited some of the ideas of Wittgenstein's *Tractatus*, and proclaimed that necessary truths were necessary only because they were tautologies. This enabled them to accept that mathematical truths were necessary while denying that they told us anything about the world. Knowledge about the world could be gained only by experience, and propositions had meaning only if they could either be verified or falsified by experience. The thesis that the meaning of a proposition was its mode of its verification, the verification principle, was the great weapon in the attack on metaphysics. If two metaphys-icians disputed over the nature of the Absolute, or the purpose of the universe, they could be silenced by the question, 'What possible experience would settle the issue between you?'

Disputes quickly broke out about the status and formulation of the verification principle. Was it itself a tautology? Was it verifiable by experience? Neither answer seemed satisfactory. Moreover, general laws of science, no less than metaphysical dogmas, seemed incapable of conclusive verification. Still, they were capable of falsification, and that would be sufficient to give them significance. Shall we then replace the verification principle with a falsification principle? But if we do, it is hard to see how assertions of existence are significant, since only an exhaustive tour of the universe could conclusively falsify them. It seemed prudent to reformulate the criterion of significance in a weaker form that laid down that a proposition was meaningful only if there were some observations that would be relevant to its truth or falsity. Wittgenstein gave only qualified assent to the verification principle, but at this time he frequently defended its a priori analogue that the sense of a mathematical proposition is the method of its proof.

The true task of philosophy, the positivists thought, was not so much to lay down universal philosophical propositions as to clarify non-philosophical statements, and in this they were at one with Wittgenstein. Their chosen method of such clarification was to show how empirical statements were built up truth-functionally from elementary, or 'protocol', statements that were direct records of experience. The words occurring in protocol statements derived their meaning from ostensive definition—that is to say, from a gesture that would point to the feature of experience for which the word stood.

This programme came up against a massive obstacle. The experiences recorded by protocols appear to be private to each individual. If meaning depends on verification, and each of us carries out verification by a process to which no one else has access, how can anyone ever understand anyone else's meaning? Schlick tried to answer this by a distinction between form and content. The content of my experience is what I enjoy or live through when, for example, I see something red or see something green. This is private and incommunicable. But the form, or structure, of experience may be common to many. When I see a tree or a sunset I cannot know whether other people have the same experiences—perhaps, when they look at a tree they see what I see when I look at a sunset. But as long as we all agree to call a tree green and a sunset red, we are able to communicate with each other and construct the language of science.

Wittgenstein was dissatisfied with this solution, and strove to give an account of meaning that would not present a threat of solipsism. He distanced himself from the Vienna Circle and returned permanently to Cambridge. Having submitted the *Tractatus* as a Ph.D. dissertation he became a Fellow of Trinity College. The Circle continued its anti-metaphysical programme, notably in a journal, *Erkenntnis*, edited by Schlick in conjunction with Hans Reichenbach of Berlin. Its ideas were given wide currency in Britain by the publication in 1936 of A. J. Ayer's *Language, Truth and Logic*. Later in the same year, however, Schlick was shot dead by a disgruntled student; and by 1939 the Circle ceased to exist, with some of its most prominent members forced into exile. The Circle's most distinguished legacy to posterity was its publication, in 1935, of *The Logic of Scientific Discovery* by Karl Popper, who was never a fully paid-up member of the group.

Wittgenstein's Later Philosophy

In the 1930s Wittgenstein became the most influential teacher of philosophy in Britain. During this period he turned epistemology and philosophy of mind upside down. Previous philosophers, from Descartes to Schlick, had striven to show how knowledge of the external public world—whether scientific or commonsensical—could be built up from the ultimate, immediate, private data of intuition or experience. Wittgenstein, in these years, showed that private experience, far from being the bedrock on which knowledge and belief is founded, was something that itself presupposed a shared public world. Even the words that we use to frame our most secret and inward thoughts derive the only sense they have from their use in our common external discourse. The problem of philosophy is not to construct the public from the private, but to do justice to the private in the context of the social.

After his return to philosophy Wittgenstein abandoned many of the theses of the *Tractatus*. He ceased to believe in logical atoms, and ceased to look for a logically articulate language cloaked in common speech. A defining doctrine of logical atomism had been that every elementary proposition is independent of every other elementary proposition. This was clearly not true of the positivists' protocol statements: the truth-value of 'This is a red patch' is not independent of the truth-value of 'This is a blue patch'. Reflection on this led Wittgenstein to question the distinction between elementary and non-elementary propositions and to give up the idea that the ultimate elements of language were names designating simple objects.

In the *Tractatus*, Wittgenstein came to believe, he had grossly oversimplified the relation between language and the world. The connection between the two was to consist in two features only: the linking of names to objects, and the match or mismatch of propositions to facts. This, he now thought, was a great mistake. Words look like each other, in the same way as a clutch looks very like a foot-brake; but words differ from each other in function as much as the mechanisms operated by the two pedals. Wittgenstein now emphasized that language was interwoven with the world in many different ways: and to refer to these tie-ups he coined the expression 'language-game'.

As examples of language-games Wittgenstein lists obeying and giving orders, describing the appearance of objects, expressing sensations, giving measurements, constructing an object from a description, reporting an event, speculating about the future, making up stories, acting plays, guessing riddles, telling jokes, asking, cursing, greeting, and praying. Each of these language-games, and many others, need to be examined if we are to understand language. We can say that the meaning of a word is its use in a language-game—but this is not a general theory of meaning, it is simply a reminder that if we wish to give an account of the meaning of a word we must look for the part it plays in our life. The use of the word 'game' is not meant to suggest that language is something trivial; the word was chosen because games exhibit the same kind of variety as linguistic activities do. There is no common feature that marks all games as games, and likewise there is no one feature that is essential to language—there are only family likenesses between the countless language-games.

Wittgenstein never abandoned his early view that philosophy is an activity, not a theory. Philosophy does not discover any new truths, and philosophical problems are solved not by the acquisition of new information, but by the rearrangement of what we already know. The function of philosophy, Wittgenstein once said, is to untie the knots in our thinking. This means that the philosopher's movements will be complicated, but his result will be as simple as a plain piece of string.

We need philosophy if we are to avoid being entrapped by our language. Embodied in the surface grammar of our language there is a philosophy that bewitches us, by disguising from us the variety of ways in which language functions as a social, interpersonal activity. Philosophical misunderstanding will not harm us if we restrict ourselves to everyday tasks, using words within the language-games that are their primitive homes. But if we start upon abstract studies—of mathematics, say, or of psychology, or of theology—then our thinking will be hampered and distorted unless we can free ourselves of philosophical confusion. Intellectual inquiry will be corrupted by mythical notions about the nature of numbers, or of the mind, or of the soul.

Like the positivists, Wittgenstein was hostile to metaphysics. But he attacked metaphysics not with a blunt instrument like the verification principle, but by the careful drawing of distinctions that enable him to disentangle the mixture of truism and nonsense within metaphysical systems. 'When philosophers use a word—"knowledge", "being", "object", "I", "proposition", "name"—and try to grasp the *essence* of the thing, one must always ask oneself: is the word ever actually used in this way in the language which is its original home? What *we* do is to bring words back from their metaphysical to their everyday use' (*PI* I, 116).[6]

While teaching at Cambridge between the wars, Wittgenstein published nothing. He wrote copiously, filling notebooks, drafting and redrafting manuscripts, and circulating substantial handouts among his pupils, who also took and preserved detailed notes of his lectures. But none of this material was published until after his death. His ideas circulated, often in garbled form, largely by word of mouth.

When Austria became part of Nazi Germany by the *Anschluss* of 1938, Wittgenstein became a British citizen. During the war he worked as a paramedic, and in 1947 he resigned his Cambridge chair, being succeeded by his Finnish pupil Georg Henrik von Wright. He continued to write philosophy and to communicate philosophical thoughts to close friends and disciples. After a period of solitary life in Ireland, he stayed in the houses of various friends in Oxford and Cambridge until his death in 1951 at the age of sixty-two.

---

[6] Wittgenstein's attitude to metaphysics is treated at length in Ch. 7.

Analytic Philosophy after Wittgenstein

In 1949 Gilbert Ryle, Professor of Metaphysics at Oxford, published a book called *The Concept of Mind*. The ideas presented in that book bore a strong resemblance to Wittgenstein's. Ryle was strongly anti-Cartesian, and indeed the first chapter of the book was entitled 'Descartes' Myth'. Ryle emphasized a distinction between 'knowing how' and 'knowing that', which may have owed something to Heidegger. His discussion of the will and the emotions annihilated the notion of internal impressions which many philosophers had inherited from the British empiricists. In a chapter on 'Dispositions and Occurrences' he brought to the attention of modern philosophers the importance of the Aristotelian distinctions between different forms of actuality and potentiality. His discussion of sensation, imagination, and intellect leaned too heavily in the direction of behaviourism to win general acceptance. Nonetheless, the book remained a classic of analytic philosophy of mind.

However, when Wittgenstein's *Philosophical Investigations* appeared posthumously in 1953 it was possible to see ideas that Ryle had displayed vividly but crudely now presented with far greater subtlety and profundity. It was, and remains, a matter of controversy how far Ryle, in the development of his ideas, had drawn on conversations with Wittgenstein and hearsay accounts of his Cambridge lectures, and how far he had reached similar conclusions by independent reflection.

Wittgenstein left the copyright of his literary remains to three of his former pupils: Georg Henrik von Wright, Elizabeth Anscombe, and Rush Rhees. The three philosophers corresponded to different facets of Wittgenstein's own personality and work. Von Wright, who held Wittgenstein's Cambridge chair from 1948 to 1951 and then returned to a career in his native Finland, resembled Wittgenstein the logician of the *Tractatus*; the books that first made his reputation were on induction, probability, and modal logic. Anscombe, an Oxford tutor who in her turn held the Cambridge chair towards the end of the century, carried forward the work of the later Wittgenstein on philosophy of mind, and with her book *Intention* inaugurated extensive discussion of practical reasoning and the theory of action. Of the three Rhees was the most sympathetic to the mystical and fideistic side of Wittgenstein's temperament, and inspired in Wales a characteristic school of philosophy of religion.

During the later decades of the twentieth century the literary executors presided over the publication of Wittgenstein's extensive *Nachlass*. Many volumes appeared, of which the most significant were *Philosophical Grammar* (1974) and *Philosophical Remarks* (1975) from the pre-war manuscripts, and *Remarks on the Foundations of Mathematics* (1978), *Remarks on the Philosophy of Psychology* (1980), plus *On Certainty* (1969) from later notebooks up until the time of Wittgenstein's death. The entire *Nachlass* was published by Oxford University Press in 1998, in transcription and facsimile, in an electronic form prepared by the University of Bergen.

After Wittgenstein's death many people regarded W. V. O. Quine (1908–2000) as the doyen of Anglophone philosophy. Having early established a reputation as a formal logician, Quine spent time with the Vienna Circle, and in Prague and Warsaw. After his return to the United States in 1936 he joined the faculty at Harvard, where he remained for the rest of his professional life with the exception of years of war service in the navy. His most important books were *From a Logical Point of View* (1953), which contained two famous essays, 'On What there Is' and 'Two Dogmas of Empiricism', and *Word and Object* (1960), which was a magisterial exposition of his system, later supplemented by a number of less influential studies.

Quine's aim in philosophy was to provide a framework for a naturalistic explanation of the world in the terms of science and especially physical science. He offered to do so by an analysis of language that is both empiricist and behaviourist. All the theories by which we explain the world (whether informal or scientific) are based on the input to our sense-receptors. All the terms and sentences occurring in the theories are to be defined in terms of the behaviour of the speakers and hearers who use them. The basic form of the meaning of an utterance is stimulus meaning: the class of all stimulations that would prompt a language-user to assent to the utterance.

In spite of his pursuit of a radically empiricist programme, Quine made his first major impact on philosophy with 'Two Dogmas of Empiricism' (written in 1951). He stated in the following terms the two targets of his attack:

> One is a belief in some fundamental cleavage between truths which are *analytic*, or grounded in meanings independently of matters of fact, and truths which are *synthetic*, or grounded in fact. The other dogma is *reductionism*: the belief that each meaningful statement is equivalent to some logical construct upon terms which refer to immediate experience. (*FLPV* 20)

Quine did not deny that there are logically true statements, statements that remain true under any interpretation of their non-logical terms—e.g. 'No unmarried man is married'. But we cannot move from such a logically true statement to the allegedly analytic statement 'No bachelor is married' because that depends on taking 'unmarried man' and 'bachelor' as synonymous. But what is synonymy? Shall we say that two expressions are synonymous if one can be substituted for the other in a sentence without affecting its truth-value? But 'creature with a heart' and 'creature with a kidney' are interchangeable in that manner, but no one supposes that 'All creatures who have hearts have kidneys' is analytic. Nor can we appeal to any notion of necessity in order to define analyticity; the explanation must go the other way round.

Shall we try, instead, to define what it is for a sentence to be synthetic, saying for instance that a sentence is synthetic if and only if it can be verified or falsified by experience? Quine argues that this move rests on a false conception of verification: it is not single sentences, but whole systems, that are verified or falsified. 'Our statements about the external world face the tribunal of sense experience not individually, but only as a corporate body' (*FLPV* 140).

The totality of our so-called knowledge or beliefs, from the most casual matters of geography and history to the profoundest laws of atomic physics or even of pure mathematics and logic, is a man-made fabric which impinges on experience only at the edges. Or, to change the figure, total science is like a field of force whose boundary conditions are experience. A conflict with experience at the periphery occasions readjustments in the interior of the field. Truth values have to be redistributed over some of our statements. Reevaluation of some statements entails reevaluation of others, because of their logical interconnections—the logical laws being in turn simply certain further statements of the system, certain further elements in the field. (*FLPV* 140)

It follows from this that it is folly to single out a class of analytic statements, which remain true whatever happens. Any statement can be held true come what may, if we make drastic adjustments elsewhere in the system. On the other hand no statement—not even a law of logic—is totally immune to revision. Science as a whole does depend both on language and on experience—but this duality cannot be traced in individual sentences.

If no sense can be given to the notions of synonymy and analyticity, then the whole notion of meaning is suspect, because there can be no criteria of identity for meaning. Certainly, Quine insisted, there are no such things as meanings that have to be interpreted by appeal to intentional concepts such as belief or understanding. Meaning must be explained purely in extensionalist terms, by mapping sensory stimuli on to verbal behaviour. Quine imagines a field linguist endeavouring to translate from a wholly alien language, using as his only data 'the forces that he sees impinging on the native's surfaces and the observable behaviour, vocal and otherwise, of the native' (*WO* 28).

The upshot of Quine's thought experiment is to identify three levels of indeterminacy. First, there is indeterminacy of individual reference. The linguist may observe that the natives use the sound 'Gavagai' only in the presence of rabbits. But—even assuming that this is an observation statement—it may equally well refer to rabbit, rabbit stage, or rabbit part. Second, there is indeterminacy at the level of the entire language: the data may support equally well two different, incompatible translation manuals. This indeterminacy is a particular example of a more general phenomenon, namely that theories, and not only theories of translation, are underdetermined by sensory inputs. More than one total scientific system, therefore, may be compatible with all the data ever available.

We must indeed give up the idea that there is any fixed furniture of the world. What exists depends upon what theory we adopt. In his early essay 'On What There Is', Quine famously said, 'To be is to be the value of a bound variable.' When he said this he was following in the footsteps of Frege and Russell, who insisted that in a scientific theory no names should be allowed that lacked a definite reference. When all dubious names have been eliminated with the aid of Russell's theory of description we are left with sentences of the form 'There is an *x* such that *x* is...' followed by a set of predicates setting out the properties by which the putative individual is to be identified. What exists, according to the theory, will be the entities over which the quantifiers range. But because different theories may be equally supported, so may different ontologies. What can be said to exist is always relative to a theory.

Wittgenstein and Quine are often regarded, especially in continental Europe, as the two leading exponents of analytical philosophy. In fact, their philosophies are very different from each other.[7] In particular the two men disagreed about the nature of philosophy. Because of his disbelief in the analytic–synthetic distinction Quine saw no sharp boundary between philosophy and empirical science. Wittgenstein, throughout his life, continued to believe what he wrote in the *Tractatus* (4. 111), 'Philosophy is not one of the natural sciences. The word "philosophy" must mean something which stands above or below, but not beside the natural sciences.' Scientism, i.e. the attempt to see philosophy as a science, was his *bête noire*. In the *Blue Book* he wrote, 'Philosophers constantly see the methods of science before their eyes, and are irresistibly tempted to answer questions in the way science does. This tendency is the real source of metaphysics, and leads the philosopher into complete darkness' (*BB* 18).

In the United States, however, the scientism introduced by Quine had come to stay. One of its most eloquent exponents was Quine's Harvard pupil Donald Davidson (1917–2003), who taught at many universities in the United States, ending, for the last twenty-two years of his life, at Berkeley. Davidson's chosen method of publication was the short paper, but many of his essays have been collected into volumes, notably *Essays on Actions and Events* (1980) and *Inquiries into Truth and Interpretation* (1984). In the philosophy of mind and action, Davidson's scientism took the form of a denial that there was a divide between philosophy and psychology; in the philosophy of language it took the form of an empirical and extensional theory of meaning.

Davidson's 1967 paper 'Truth and Meaning' begins as follows:

It is conceded by most philosophers of language, and recently by some linguists, that a satisfactory theory of meaning must give an account of how the meanings of sentences depend upon the meanings of words. Unless such an account could be supplied for a particular language, it is argued, there would be no explaining the fact that, on mastering a finite vocabulary, and a finitely stated set of rules, we are prepared to produce and to understand any of a potential infinitude of sentences. (*ITI* 17)

---

[7] The differences have been luminously detailed by P. M. S. Hacker, *Wittgenstein's Place in Twentieth Century Analytic Philosophy* (Oxford: Blackwell, 1996), 183–227.

Davidson's theory of meaning is built upon a theory of truth. A truth-theory for a language L sets out the truth-conditions for all the sentences of L. This is to be done, not by the impossible method of listing every sentence, but by showing how the component parts of sentences contribute to the truth-conditions of sentences in which they occur. Such a theory will contain a finite list of terms and a finite set of syntactical rules but it will entail as derived theses the potentially infinite set of truth-sentences of the form: ' "S" is true in L if and only if *p*'.

Like Quine, Davidson illustrates his theory by considering a case in which we encounter a community with a totally alien language. In order to interpret it, we have to build up a truth-theory for their language by seeing what sentences they assent to in what circumstances; but we avoid the threat of indeterminacy and scepticism by assuming that the natives have true and reasonable beliefs and draw conclusions and make decisions in a rational way. This is 'the principle of charity'.

The actual behaviour of people is determined by their reasons, that is to say their desires and beliefs, which Davidson construes as mental events. The relation between these mental events and the actions they 'rationalize' is a causal one: to say that an action is intentional is precisely to say it was caused by the appropriate beliefs and wants. But for Davidson the causation is oblique: we cannot form psychological laws connecting agents' beliefs and desires with the acts they cause. Instead, Davidson argues, every individual mental event is also an individual physical event, and this event is related by physical laws to the individual physical events that are identical with the actions. No psychophysiological laws can be stated, however, relating physiological events of certain kinds with psychological events of certain kinds.

Davidson's position is materialist, in that there are never any events that are not physical events. But he endeavours to take the sting out of this materialism by insisting on what he calls 'the anomalousness of the mental'. Any mental event is identical with a physical event, but different descriptions apply to the event qua mental and qua physical. As a mental event it is subject not to causal laws but to interpretation, because its identity as a mental event depends upon its position in a network of other mental events. As a mental event, but not as a physical event, it is subject to normative evaluation as rational or irrational. This makes the exact nature of mental–physical causation, as Davidson admits, deeply mysterious.

In England philosophers continued to believe that there was a gulf, and not just a fuzzy border, between science and philosophy. They maintained, like Ryle and Wittgenstein, that the goal of philosophy was not information but understanding. Peter Strawson (1919–2006) with his tutor Paul Grice, in a paper entitled 'In Defence of a Dogma', rebutted Quine's attack on the analytic–synthetic distinction. In his own philosophizing, Strawson was anything but dogmatic. At a time when Oxford philosophy was overconfident of its own value, and unwilling to learn from philosophers distant in space and time, Strawson reminded his colleagues of the value of other styles of philosophy by writing about, and to some extent modelling his work on, Kant's *Critique of Pure Reason*. At a time when 'metaphysics' was regarded by many as a dirty word, Strawson gave the subtitle 'An Essay in Descriptive Metaphysics' to his most important work, *Individuals* (1959).

Descriptive metaphysics aims to describe the actual structure of our thought about the world, with no pretension to improve that structure (such pretension is the mark of revisionary metaphysics). In *Individuals* Strawson sought to draw out the fundamental conditions for a language in which it is possible to refer to objects and reidentify them, and to make predications about them. He saw his task as one of conceptual analysis, but one of a wide and general scope. 'The structure the metaphysician seeks', Strawson wrote, 'does not readily display itself on the surface of language, but lies submerged' (*I* 10).

Strawson sought to establish that in our conceptual scheme material bodies and persons occupy a special position: particulars of these two kinds are the basic particulars. The two speech acts of referring and describing, corresponding to the subject–predicate structure of language, are only possible if we can identify and reidentify material objects, and this requires a unified spatio-temporal framework. (In a world of pure sounds, in which there is only pitch and temporal sequence, reidentification is hard to come by.) A structure of objects located in space and time and possessing properties is prior to, and presupposed by, any language that might simply record the distribution of features in various locations.

Persons, no less than material bodies, are for Strawson a fundamental logical category. A person must not be conceived in the terms of Cartesian dualism. If minds are Cartesian egos to which only private experiences can be ascribed, then the problem of how one ascribes states of consciousness to others becomes insoluble. 'It is a necessary condition of one's ascribing states of consciousness, experiences, to oneself, in the way that one does, that one should also ascribe them, or be prepared to ascribe them, to others who are not oneself' (*I* 99). One can ascribe such states to others only if one can identify other objects of experience. And one cannot identify others if one can identify them *only* as subjects of experience, possessors of states of consciousness. Hence, what is primitive is the concept not of a mind, but of a person:

What I mean by the concept of a person is the concept of a type of entity such that *both* predicates ascribing states of consciousness *and* predicates ascribing corporeal characteristics, a physical situation etc., are equally applicable to a single individual of that single type … The concept of a person is logically prior to that of an individual consciousness. The concept of a person is not to be analysed as that of an animated body or of an embodied anima. (*I* 102–3)

Nonetheless, Strawson believed, it was not impossible to conceive of one's own individual survival after bodily death. Such survival, however, would be the survival of an individual that was strictly solitary, unable to communicate with others, and unable to bring about effects in the world. In proportion as memories fade and impotence palls, the survivor's concept of himself as an individual becomes attenuated. 'At the limit of attenuation there is, *from the point of view of his survival as an individual*, no difference between the continuance of experience and its cessation. Disembodied survival, on such terms as these, may well seem unattractive. No doubt it is for this reason that the orthodox have wisely insisted on the resurrection of the body' (*I* 116).

Strawson's own death, early in 2006, marked the end of an era in English philosophy.

3

Freud to Derrida

In the nineteenth century there was a constant interchange of philosophical ideas between the countries of continental Europe and the English-speaking world. Kant and Hegel were massively influential in British universities, while the tradition of British empiricism was found attractive by many radical thinkers on the Continent. The career of William James illustrates the cosmopolitan nature of the philosophy of the time. Converted to philosophy by the reading of a French philosopher, he studied in Germany and lectured frequently in Britain, while based in the United States. Again, the young Bertrand Russell was not at all an insular philosopher: while working out his philosophy of mathematics he was in regular correspondence with the German Frege and the Italian Peano.

By the middle of the twentieth century all this had changed. Continental and Anglophone philosophers went their separate ways, hardly speaking the same language as each other. In Britain and America the analytic tradition in philosophy, which Russell had helped to found, had come to be dominant in academic circles, and had almost driven out alternative styles of philosophizing. In continental Europe existentialism was the fashionable school, led in France by Jean-Paul Sartre and in Germany by Martin Heidegger. Well-meaning attempts to bring together proponents of the different styles of philosophizing met with only limited success in the second half of the century.

Freud and Psychoanalysis

The Continental thinker who had the greatest influence on Anglo-American philosophical thought throughout the twentieth century was not a philosopher at all, but a man who regarded himself as a scientist, and indeed as the inventor of a new science: Sigmund Freud. Very few philosophers described themselves as Freudians, but all who were engaged in teaching philosophy of mind, ethics, or philosophy of religion were forced to take account of Freud's novel and exciting proposals in these areas.

Freud was born in Moravia in 1856 into an Austrian family of non-observant Jews. In 1860 the family moved to Vienna, and Freud trained as a doctor in the university there, joining the staff of the General Hospital in 1882, where he specialized initially in brain anatomy. He also collaborated with the neurologist Joseph Breuer, treating hysterical patients under hypnosis. Three years later he moved to Paris to study under the neurologist Jean-Martin Charcot, and soon after his return, in 1886, went into private medical practice. In the same year he married Martha Bernays, by whom he had six children, three girls and three boys.

In 1895, in conjunction with Breuer, Freud published a work on hysteria which presented an original analysis of mental illness. Gradually he ceased to use hypnosis as a method of treatment and replaced it with a novel form of therapy which he called psychoanalysis, consisting, as he put it himself, in nothing more than an exchange of words between patient and doctor.

The premiss underlying the new method was that the hysterical symptoms were the result of memories of a psychological trauma which had been repressed by the patient, but which could be recovered by means of a process of free association. The patient, lying on a couch, was encouraged to talk about whatever came to mind. Freud became convinced, as a result of many such sessions, that the relevant psychological traumas dated back to infancy and had a sexual content. His theories of infantile sexuality led to a breach with Breuer.

In isolation from medical colleagues, Freud continued in practice in Vienna. In 1900 he published the most important of his works, *The Interpretation of Dreams*, in which he argued that dreams no less than neurotic symptoms were a coded expression of repressed sexual desires. The theory here presented, he maintained, was applicable to normal as well as neurotic persons, and he followed it up a year later with a study entitled *The Psychopathology of Everyday Life*. These were the first of a series of highly readable books constantly modifying and refining his psychoanalytic theories. In 1902 Freud was appointed to an extraordinary chair of neuropathology at Vienna University, and he began to acquire pupils and colleagues. Prominent among these were Alfred Adler and Carl Jung, both of whom eventually broke with him and founded their own schools.

In 1923 Freud published *The Ego and the Id*, in which he presented a new and elaborate anatomy of the unconscious mind. Never deterred by controversy, he presented a deflationary account of the origin of religion in *The Future of an Illusion* (1927). He was himself an atheist, but this did not prevent him from identifying with Jewish culture or from suffering the assaults of anti-Semitism. Psychoanalysis was banned by the Nazis and when Austria was annexed by Germany in 1938 he was forced to migrate to England. He was given a warm welcome in London, where his works had been translated and published by members of the Bloomsbury group. Having suffered for sixteen years from cancer of the jaw, Freud died on 23 September 1939 of a lethal injection of morphine administered by his physician at his own request. His psychoanalytic work was continued by his youngest daughter, Anna.

In a set of introductory lectures delivered between 1915 and 1917 Freud summed up psychoanalytic theory in two fundamental theses. The first is that the greater part of our mental life, whether of feeling, thought, or volition, is unconscious. The second is that sexual impulses, broadly defined, are supremely important not only as potential causes of mental illness but also as the motor of artistic and cultural creation. If the sexual element in the work of art and culture remains to a great extent unconscious, this is because socialization demands the sacrifice of basic instincts. Such instincts become sublimated, that is to say diverted from their original goals and channelled towards socially acceptable activities. But sublimation is an unstable state, and untamed and unsatisfied instincts may take their revenge through mental illness and disorder.

The existence of the unconscious, Freud believed, is manifested in three different ways: through everyday trivial mistakes, through reports of dreams, and through the symptoms of neurosis. Dreams and neurotic symptoms, it is true, do not on their face, or as interpreted by the unaided patient, reveal the beliefs, desires, and sentiments of which the unconscious is deemed by Freud to consist. But the exercise of free association in analysis, he believed, as interpreted by the analyst, reveals the underlying pattern of the unconscious mind.

It is sexual development that is the key to this pattern. Infantile sexuality, Freud explained, begins with an oral stage, in which pleasure is focused on the mouth. This is followed by an anal stage, between the ages of one and three, and a 'phallic' stage, in which the child focuses on its own penis or clitoris. At that time, Freud maintained, a boy is sexually attracted to his mother, and resents his father's possession of her. But his hostility to his father leads him to fear that his father will retaliate by castrating him. So the boy abandons his sexual designs on his mother, and gradually identifies with his father. This is the Oedipus complex, a crucial stage in the emotional development of every boy. Neurotic characters are people who have become fixated at an early stage of their development. The recovery of Oedipal wishes, and the history of their repression, was an important part of every analysis. Freud was in no doubt that *mutatis mutandis* there was a feminine equivalent of the Oedipus complex, but it was never fully worked out in a convincing manner.

Towards the end of his life, Freud replaced the earlier dichotomy of conscious and unconscious with a threefold scheme of the mind. 'The mental apparatus', he wrote in *The Ego and the Id*, 'is composed of an *id* which is the repository of the instinctual impulses, of an *ego* which is the most superficial portion of the id and one which has been modified by the influence of the external world, and of a superego which develops out of the id, dominates the ego, and represents the inhibitions of instinct that are characteristic of man' (*SE* xx. 266).

The whole endeavour of the ego, Freud says, is to effect a reconciliation between the parts of the soul. So long as the ego is in harmony with the id and the superego, all will be well. But in the absence of such harmony mental disorders will develop. Conflicts between the ego and the id lead to neuroses; conflicts between the id and the superego lead to melancholia and depression. When the ego comes into conflict with the external world, psychoses develop.

Freud would not thank us for including him in a history of philosophy, since he regarded himself as a scientist, dedicated to discovering the rigid determinisms that underlie human illusions of freedom. In fact, most of his detailed theories, when they have been made precise enough to admit of experimental testing, have been shown to lack foundation. Medical professionals disagree how far psychoanalytic techniques are effective forms of therapy, and if they are, whence they derive their efficacy. When they do achieve success it appears to be not by uncovering deterministic mechanisms, but by expanding the self-awareness and freedom of choice of the individual. But despite all the theoretical criticisms that can be made of his work, Freud has had an enormous influence on society—in relation to sexual mores, to our understanding of mental illness, to our appreciation of art and literature, and on interpersonal relationships of many kinds.

Freud was not the first thinker to assign to the sexual impulse a place of fundamental significance in the human psyche. He had been preceded by many generations of theologians who regarded our actual human condition as having been shaped by a sin of Adam which was sexual in origin, transmission, and effect. If nineteenth-century prudery strove to conceal the ubiquity of sex, the veil was always easy to tear away. Freud loved to quote a dictum of Schopenhauer that it was the joke of life that sex, man's chief concern, should be pursued in secret. Sex was, Schopenhauer said, the true hereditary lord of the world, treating with scorn all preparations made to bind it.

Freud's contemporaries were shocked by his emphasis on infantile sexuality. But Victorian sentimentality about children was an attitude of recent origin. It was not shared, for instance, by Augustine, who wrote in his *Confessions*: 'What is innocent is not the infant's mind, but the feebleness of his limbs. I have myself watched and studied a jealous baby. He could not yet speak, and pale with jealousy and bitterness, glared at his brother sharing his mother's milk. Who is unaware of this fact of experience?' The sexual permissiveness of many modern societies is due not only to the availability of contraceptives but to a whole climate of thought which Freud did much to create. It is not that he recommended sexual licence in his published writings, but that he gave currency to an influential metaphor: the vision of sexual desire as a psychic fluid that must find an outlet through one channel or another. In the light of that metaphor, sexual abstinence appears as a dangerous damming-up of forces that will eventually break through any restraining barriers with a disastrous effect on mental health.

The very concept of mental health, as developed in modern times, may be said to date from the time when Freud, Breuer, and Charcot began to treat hysterical patients as genuine invalids instead of malingerers. This, it is often said, was more of a moral decision than a medical discovery, but most people nowadays would regard it as the right moral decision. It can be claimed that Freud redrew the boundaries between morals and medicine. Forms of behaviour that previous to his time would have been regarded as transgressions worthy of punishment have now long been seen, in the courthouse no less than in the consulting room, as maladies fit for therapy. The difficulty in making a hard and fast distinction between clinical judgement and moral evaluation is strikingly illustrated by changing attitudes to homosexual behaviour. This, having been long regarded as heinously criminal, was for nearly a century regarded as symptomatic of a psychopathological disorder, and is now regarded by many as the key element of a rationally chosen alternative lifestyle.

Freud's influence on art and literature has been great, in spite of his unflattering view of artistic creation as closely similar to neurosis. Novelists make use of associative techniques similar to those of the analyst's couch, and critics delight to interpret works of literature in Oedipal terms. Historians enjoy writing psychobiography, analysing the actions of mature public figures on the basis of real or imagined episodes in their childhood. Painters and sculptors have taken Freudian symbols out of a dream world and given them concrete form.

All of us, in fact, directly or indirectly, have imbibed a great deal of psychoanalytic theory. In discussion of our relationships with our family and friends we talk unselfconsciously of repression and sublimation, and we describe characters as anal or narcissistic. People who have never read a word of Freud can happily identify their own and others' Freudian slips. No philosopher since Aristotle has made a greater contribution to the everyday vocabulary of psychology and morality.

It is hard to fault the judgement of W. H. Auden, who mourned Freud's death in twenty-eight intricate quatrains:

> If often he was wrong, and, at times, absurd,
>   to us he is no more a person
>   now but a whole climate of opinion.

Husserl's Phenomenology

The life of Edmund Husserl resembles, at crucial points, that of Sigmund Freud. Husserl was three years younger than Freud. Like him he was born into a Jewish family in Moravia, and attended lectures in Vienna. Both men devoted the greater part of their lives to a personal project that was intended to be the first really scientific study of the human mind. At the end of their lives both men fell foul of Nazi anti-Semitism, with Freud driven out of Austria to die in exile, and Husserl's books burnt by German troops marching into Prague in 1939.

Husserl's professional life, however, was quite different from Freud's. His initial studies were in mathematics and astronomy, not in medicine. He went on to pursue an orthodox academic career in philosophy, holding posts in a succession of university departments. Though his doctorate was from Vienna, he went on for his habilitation degree to Halle, and the chairs to which he was later called were in German and not Austrian universities.

Husserl's interest in philosophy was first awakened by the lectures of Franz Brentano in Vienna between 1884 and 1886. Brentano (1838–1917) was an ex-priest, an erudite scholar who had sought to relate Aristotelian philosophy of mind to contemporary experimental inquiry in a book *Psychology from an Empirical Standpoint* (1874), which was to prove widely influential. The data of consciousness, the book explained, come in two kinds: physical and mental phenomena. Physical phenomena are such things as colours and smells; mental phenomena, such as thoughts, are characterized by having a content, or immanent object. This feature, for which Brentano reintroduced the scholastic term 'intentionality', was the key to the understanding of mental acts and life.

While influenced by Brentano's approach to psychology, Husserl continued initially to focus his attention on mathematics. His habilitation thesis at Halle was on the concept of number, and his first book, published in 1891, was the *Philosophy of Arithmetic*. This sought to explain our numerical concepts by identifying the mental acts that were their psychological origin. Our concept of plurality, for instance, was alleged to derive from a process of 'collective combination' that grouped items into aggregates. Because of his desire to find a basis for mathematics in empirical psychology, Husserl was forced into some unattractive conclusions. He denied, for instance, that zero and one were numbers, and he had to make a sharp distinction between the arithmetic of small numbers and the arithmetic of large numbers. With our mind's eye we can see only tiny groups, so only a small part of arithmetic can rest on an intuitive basis; once we deal with larger numbers, we move away from intuition into a merely symbolic realm.

Reviewers of Husserl's book, notably Frege, complained that it contained a confusion between imagination and thought. The mental events that were the subject matter of psychology, being private to the individual, could not be the foundation of a public science such as arithmetic. That must rest on thoughts that were the common property of the race. Husserl yielded to the criticism and abandoned his early psychologism. In his *Logical Investigations* of 1900–1 he argued that logic cannot be derived from psychology, and that any attempt to do so must involve a vicious circle since it will have to appeal to logic in the course of its deduction. Henceforth, like Frege, he maintained a sharp distinction between logic and psychology. But while Frege, followed by the analytic tradition, focused philosophy on the logical side of the divide, Husserl, followed by the Continental tradition, saw the psychological side as philosophy's rightful home. At this period, however, Frege and Husserl were at one in basing philosophy—whether logical or psychological—on an explicit Platonic realism.

The overall situation at the beginning of the twentieth century has been vividly, if not quite impartially, described by Gilbert Ryle:

> Husserl at the turn of the century was under many of the same intellectual pressures as were Meinong, Frege, Bradley, Peirce, G. E. Moore and Bertrand Russell. All alike were in revolt against the idea-psychology of Hume and Mill; all alike demanded the emancipation of logic from psychology; all alike found in the notion of meaning their escape-route from subjectivist theories of thinking; nearly all of them championed a Platonic theory of meanings, i.e. of concepts and propositions; all alike demarcated philosophy from natural science by allocating factual enquiries to the natural sciences and conceptual enquiries to philosophy; nearly all of them talked as if these conceptual enquiries of philosophy terminated in some super-inspections of some super-objects, as if conceptual enquiries were, after all, super-observational enquiries; all of them, however, in the actual practice of their conceptual enquiries necessarily diverged from the super-observations that their Platonising epistemology required. Husserl talked of intuiting essences somewhat as Moore talked of inspecting concepts, and as Russell talked of acquaintanceship with universals, but of course it was by their intellectual wrestlings, not by any intellectual intuitings, that they tackled their actual conceptual difficulties. (*CP* i. 180)

Ryle does well to emphasize the common starting point of the analytic and Continental traditions; but in the case of Husserl, the intellectual wrestlings were, in fact, more complicated than this brisk passage suggests.

Husserl took over from Brentano the notion of intentionality, that is to say, the idea that what is characteristic of mental, as opposed to physical, phenomena is that they are directed to objects. I think of Troy, perhaps, or I worry about my investments—intentionality is the feature indicated in the little words 'of' and 'about'. What is the relation between what is going on in my mind and a long defunct city or stock markets across the world? Husserl, and many after him, spent years wondering about the answer to that question.[1]

Two things are essential to a thought: that it should have a content and that it should have a possessor. Suppose that I think of a dragon. Two things make this the thought it is: first, that it is the thought of a dragon and not of an eagle or a horse; second, that it is my thought and not your thought or Napoleon's thought. Husserl would mark these features by saying that it was an *act* of mine with a particular *matter* (its intentional object). Other people, too, may think of dragons;

---

[1] Intentionality is nothing to do with 'intention' in the modern sense. Brentano took the word from medieval contexts, in which it was derived from the verb 'intendere', meaning to pull a bowstring in the course of aiming at a target. An intentional object is, as it were, the target of a thought.

in that case, for Husserl, we have several individual acts belonging to the same species. The concept *dragon*, in fact, is nothing other than the species to which all such acts belong.

Concepts are thus, in the *Logical Investigations*, defined on the basis of psychological items. How, then, is logic related to concepts thus understood? In the same way, Husserl now believed, as the theorems of geometry are related to empirical three-dimensional bodies. Thus he was able to disown his earlier psychologism, and make a clear distinction between psychology and logic. He now proceeded to go further, and draw a line between psychology and epistemology. He did so by a reinvention of psychology as a new discipline of 'phenomenology'.

Phenomenology was developed during the first decade of the twentieth century. In 1900 Husserl was appointed to an associate professorship at the University of Göttingen. There he had as a colleague the renowned mathematician David Hilbert, but his most enthusiastic collaborators in his new venture were a group of philosophers at Munich, who coined the phrase 'phenomenological movement'. By 1913 the movement was self-confident enough to publish a yearbook for phenomenological research. In the first issue of this appeared a book-length text of Husserl's, which was planned as the first volume of a work to be entitled *Ideas Pertaining to a Pure Phenomenology*.

The aim of phenomenology was the study of the immediate data of consciousness, without reference to anything that consciousness might tell us, or purport to tell us, about the extra-mental world. When I think of a phoenix, the intentionality of my thought is exactly the same whether or not there are any phoenixes in reality. Already, in 1901, Husserl had written, 'It makes no essential difference to an object presented and given to consciousness whether it exists, or is fictitious, or is perhaps completely absurd. I think of Jupiter as I think of Bismarck, of the tower of Babel as I think of Cologne Cathedral, of a regular thousand-sided polygon as of a regular thousand-faced solid' (*LI* ii. 99). So too, Husserl believed, when I see a table. The intentionality of my experience is just the same whether there is a real table there or if I am hallucinating. The phenomenologist should make a close study of the psychological phenomena, and place in brackets the world of extra-mental objects. His attitude to the existence of that world should be one of suspense of judgement, for which Husserl used the Greek word *epoche*. This was called 'the phenomenological reduction'. It was, as it were, philosophy drawing in its horns.

Phenomenology is not the same as phenomenalism. A phenomenalist believes that nothing exists except phenomena, and that statements about such things as material objects have to be translated into statements about appearances. Berkeley and Mill held versions of phenomenalism.[2] Husserl, on the other hand, did not assert in *Ideas* that there are no realities other than phenomena; he deliberately left

[2] See above, pp. 652 and 762.

open the possibility that there is a world of non-phenomenal objects. Only, such objects are no concern, or at least no initial concern, of the philosopher.

The reason for this is that, according to Husserl, we have infallible immediate knowledge of the objects of our own consciousness while we have only inferential and conjectural information about the external world. Husserl made a distinction between immanent perception, which was self-evident, and transcendent perception, which was fallible. Immanent perception is my immediate acquaintance with my own current mental acts and states. Transcendent perception is my perception of my own past acts and states, of physical things and events, and of the contents of other people's minds.

Immanent perception provides the subject matter of phenomenology. Immanent perception is more fundamental than transcendent perception not only because immanent perception is self-evident while transcendent perception is fallible, but because the inferences and conjectures that constitute transcendent perception are based, and have to be based, on the deliverances of immanent perception. Only consciousness has 'absolute being'; all other forms of being depend upon consciousness for their existence (*Ideas*, i. 49). Thus phenomenology is the most basic of all disciplines, because the items that are its subject matter provide the data for all other branches of philosophy and science.

Husserl projected *Ideas* as a three-volume work, but the last two volumes were published only after his death. In 1916 he moved to Freiburg and remained as a professor in the university there until he retired in 1928, having rejected in 1923 a call to the University of Berlin. At Freiburg his lectures attracted a wide international audience, and he had among his pupils some who were to become highly influential philosophers, such as Martin Heidegger and Edith Stein. In those years he developed in several directions the system presented in *Ideas I*. One the one hand he extended the phenomenological method in order to undercut some assumptions that Descartes had left unquestioned, so that his *epoche* became more radical than Cartesian doubt. On the other hand, he endeavoured to combine his methodological solipsism with a solution to the problem of intersubjectivity that would establish the existence of other minds. His final position was a transcendental idealism which he maintained was the inseparable conclusion of phenomenology (*CM* 42). Some of the results of his later reflections were published in two works that appeared in the year after his retirement: *Cartesian Meditations* and *Formal and Transcendental Logic*.

The Existentialism of Heidegger

Two years earlier one of Husserl's pupils had published a book that was to have a much greater impact on philosophy than either of these. The *Sein und Zeit* of

Martin Heidegger (1889–1976) claimed that phenomenology, up to this point, had been too half-hearted. It purported to examine the data of consciousness, but it employed notions like 'subject', 'object', 'act', and 'content' which were not items that it had discovered in consciousness, but items inherited from earlier philosophy. Most importantly, Husserl had accepted the framework of Descartes in which there were the two correlative realms of consciousness and reality. Only one of these, consciousness, was the subject matter Husserl had adopted for phenomenology. But the first task of phenomenology, Heidegger maintained, was to study the concept of Being (*Sein*) which was prior to the cleavage between consciousness and reality. The experience that leads us to contrast these two as polar opposites is the primary phenomenon to be examined.

We must therefore go back behind Descartes in order to get clear about the nature of philosophy, and take as our starting point not consciousness but Being. But it will not suffice, Heidegger warns us, simply to return to the categories of Plato and Aristotle, which already have an element of artificial sophistication. The Presocratics provide the best examples for a thoroughgoing phenomenalist to imitate, because they pre-date the formation of a professional philosophical vocabulary with all the presuppositions such a vocabulary entails. Heidegger would set himself the task of inventing a pristine vocabulary that would enable us, as it were, to philosophize in the nude.

The most important of Heidegger's coinages is *Dasein*. *Dasein* is the kind of being that is capable of asking philosophical questions, and as Heidegger expounds *Dasein* it sounds initially suspiciously like the Cartesian ego. But whereas Descartes's ego was essentially a thinking thing, a *res cogitans*, thinking is only one, and not the most fundamental, of the ways in which *Dasein* has its being. The primitive element of *Dasein* is 'being-in-the world', and thinking is only one way of engaging with the world: acting upon it and reacting to it are at least as important elements. *Dasein* is prior to the distinction between thinking and willing or theory and practice. *Dasein* is caring about (*besorgen*). *Dasein* is not a *res cogitans*, but a *res curans*: not a thinking thing, but a caring thing. Only if I have some care about, or interest in, the world will I go on to ask questions about it and give answers to those questions in the form of knowledge-claims.

Concepts and judgements can be thought of as instruments for coping with the world. But there are more primitive such instruments, things that are tools in a literal sense. A carpenter relates to the world by using a hammer. He does not need to be thinking about the hammer to be using it well; consciousness of the hammer may indeed get in the way of the concentration on his project that is his true engagement with reality. Entities that we cope with in this transparent mode are called by Heidegger 'ready-to-hand'. The distinction between what is and what is not ready-to-hand underlies our construction of the spatiality of the world.

Heidegger emphasizes the temporal nature of *Dasein*: we should think of it not as a substance but as the unfolding of a life. Our life is not a self-contained, self-developing entity: from the outset we find ourselves thrown into a physical, cultural, and historical context. This 'thrownness' (*geworfenheit*) is called by Heidegger the 'facticity' of *Dasein*. Nor is my life exhausted by what I am now and have hitherto been: I *can* be what I have not yet been, and my potentialities are as essential to my being as my achievements are. Indeed, according to Heidegger, in defining what I am the future has priority over the past and the present. *Dasein*, says Heidegger, is 'an ability to be' and what I am aiming at in my life determines the significance of my present situation and capacities. But whatever my achievements and potentialities are, they all terminate in death—but though death *terminates* them, it does not *complete* them. Any view of my life as a whole must take account of the difference between what I will be and what I might have been: hence comes guilt and anxiety.

If Heidegger is right, there is something absurd in the attempts of philosophers, from Descartes to Russell, to prove the existence of an external world. We are not observers trying, through the medium of experience, to gain knowledge of a reality from which we are detached. From the outset we are ourselves elements of the world, 'always already being-in-the-world'. We are beings among other beings, acting upon and reacting to them. And our actions and reactions need not at all be guided by consciousness. It is, in fact, only when our spontaneous actions misfire in some way that we become conscious of what we are doing. This is when the 'ready-to-hand' becomes 'unready-to-hand'.

The activity of *Dasein*, for Heidegger, has three fundamental aspects. First, there is what he calls 'attunement': the situations into which we are thrown manifest themselves as attractive, or alarming, or boring, and so on, and we respond to them with moods of various kinds. Second, *Dasein* is discursive: that is to say, it operates within a world of discourses, among entities that are articulated and interpreted for us by the language and culture that we share with others. Third, *Dasein* is 'understanding' in a special sense—that is to say, its activities are directed (not necessarily consciously) towards some goal, some 'for-the-sake-of' which will make sense of a whole life within its cultural context. These three aspects of *Dasein* correspond to the past, present, and future of time: the time that gives *Sein und Zeit* the second part of its title.

Though *Dasein* operates within a biological, social, and cultural context, there is no such thing as a human nature that gives rise to the activities of the human individual. The essence of *Dasein*, says Heidegger, is its existence. In saying this, he became the father of 'existentialism', the school of philosophy that emphasizes that individuals are not mere members of a species and are not determined by universal laws. What I essentially am is what I freely take myself to be. The ungroundedness of such a choice is alarming, and I may well take refuge in unthinking conformity. But that is an inauthentic decision, a betrayal of my *Dasein*. To be authentic I must make my own life in full awareness that there is no ground, either in human nature or in divine command, for the choices I make, and that no choice is going to bring any transcendent meaningfulness to my life.

Being and Time is a difficult book to read, and any interpreter who wishes to make its ideas seem readily intelligible has to write in a style very different from Heidegger's own. It is a matter of dispute whether Heidegger's idiosyncratic vocabulary and convoluted syntax were essential to his project or were an unnecessary piece of self-indulgence. But there is no doubt that his work was not just original but important. One of Heidegger's most pungent opponents, Gilbert Ryle, admitted at the end of a critical review of the book that he had nothing but admiration for his 'phenomenological analysis of the root workings of the human soul'.

As a work of phenomenology, *Sein und Zeit* enjoyed a greater éclat than any of the works of phenomenology's founder, Husserl. The relationship between the disciple and his master had an unhappy ending. In 1929 Heidegger succeeded Husserl as Professor of Philosophy at Freiburg and in 1933 he became Rector of the university. In a notorious inaugural address in May of that year he welcomed Nazism as the vehicle through which the German people would at last carry out its historic spiritual mission. One of his first acts as Rector was to exclude from the University Library all Jewish faculty members, including Emeritus Professor Husserl, who still had five years to live. After the war Heidegger had to do penance for his support of Hitler and was himself prevented from teaching in the university from 1945 to 1950. However, his thought remained influential up to and beyond his death in 1976.

The Existentialism of Sartre

In contrast to the right-wing existentialism of Heidegger, in France Jean-Paul Sartre, once briefly a student under him, developed a form of existentialism that moved steadily towards the political left. Born in Paris in 1905, Sartre studied at the École Normale Supérieure from 1924 to 1928 and for some years supported himself by teaching philosophy in high schools. It was, however, in Berlin and Freiburg from 1933 to 1935 that he began to develop his own philosophy, which found its first expression in two philosophical monographs published in 1936, *The Transcendence of the Ego* and *Imagination: A Psychological Critique*. These were followed by a novel, *Nausea*, in 1938 and *Sketch for a Theory of the Emotions* in 1939.

Sartre's pre-war essays are detailed studies in the philosophy of mind in the phenomenological mould. Sartre, like Heidegger, complained that Husserl had not taken the phenomenological reduction far enough. Husserl had accepted the Cartesian ego, the thinking subject, as a datum of consciousness, but in fact it is no such thing: when I am absorbed in what I am seeing or hearing I have no thought of myself. It is only by reflection that we make the self into an object, so if we are to be thorough phenomenologists we must start from pre-reflexive consciousness. The self, the thinking subject, lies outside consciousness and therefore belongs, no less than other minds, to the transcendent world.

In *Imagination* Sartre attacks the notion, widespread among philosophers but particularly explicit in Hume, that in imagination we are surveying the contents of an interior mental world. It is a mistake, Sartre showed, to think that perception and imagination both consisted in the mental presence of pictures or simulacra, the only difference between them being that in perception the images are more intense or vivid than they are in imagination. In fact, Sartre maintained, imagining relates us to extra-mental objects, not to internal images. It does so no less than perception, but in a different mode. This is most easily made out in the case where we imagine a real, but absent, person; in the cases where what we imagine does not in fact exist, what we are doing is creating an object in the world.

Emotions, too, according to Sartre, are misconceived if we think of them as passive internal sensations. Emotion is a certain manner of apprehending the world: to feel hatred towards someone, for instance, is to perceive him as hateful. But obviously emotion is not an impartial, unbiased awareness of our environment; on the contrary, Sartre goes so far as to describe it as 'a magical transformation' of the situations in which we find ourselves. When we are depressed, for instance, we as it were cast a spell over the world such as to make all efforts to cope with it appear pointless.

When war broke out in 1939 Sartre was conscripted, and in 1940 he fought in the army until captured by the Germans. Released after the armistice, he returned to Paris as a philosophy teacher, but also took part in the resistance to Nazi occupation. In 1943 he published his *magnum opus*, *Being and Nothingness*. While his pre-war essays had been Husserlian in inspiration, this work owes a great debt to Heidegger, which is acknowledged by the form of its title. Parts of *Being and Nothingness* are as difficult as anything in *Sein und Zeit*. But, as befits a novelist and playwright, Sartre had a gift, which Heidegger lacked, for illustrating philosophical points with detailed and convincing narratives. After the war Sartre returned to present the main themes of his work in a briefer and more popular manner in *Existentialism and Humanism* (1946).

Being (*l'être*), for Sartre, is what precedes and underlies all the different kinds and aspects of things that we encounter in consciousness. We sort things into kinds and classes in accordance with our interests and as instruments for our purposes. If we strip off all the distinctions that consciousness has made, we are left with pure being, being in itself, *l'en-soi*. This is opaque, massive, simple, and above all contingent. It is 'without reason, without cause, without necessity' (*BN* 619). To say that it is without cause is not to say that it is its own cause, *causa sui*; it is just simply there—'gratuitous' Sartre calls it, and sometimes 'de trop'.

The *en-soi* is one of the two key concepts of *Being and Nothingness*. The other is *le pour-soi*, the for-itself, that is to say human consciousness. How is this related to the nothingness of the title? Sartre's answer is that man is the being through whom nothingness comes into the world. Negation is the element that makes the difference between *le pour-soi* and *l'en-soi*.

Sartre is here expanding a theme of Heidegger's. While English philosophers took Heidegger's dictum 'nothing noths' (*Das Nichts nichtet*) as the quintessence of absurdity, Sartre accepts the objectification of *nothing*, and attempts to give it an important significance. When consciousness articulates the world, it does so by means of negation. If I have a concept of *red*, I divide the world into the red and the not-red. If I distinguish between chairs and tables, then I must consider chairs as not-tables and tables as not-chairs. If I want to make a distinction between consciousness and being, I must say that consciousness is not-being: 'the being by which nothingness comes into the world must be its own nothingness' (*BN* 23).

To the historian, it looks as if Sartre is reintroducing into philosophy a conundrum devised by Parmenides and solved long ago by Plato.[3] A. J. Ayer, in 1945, compared Sartre's treatment of *le néant* with the response of the King in *Alice in Wonderland* when Alice says that she sees nobody on the road: 'I only wish I had such eyes ... To be able to see Nobody! And at that distance too!' Fortunately, *Being and Nothingness*, despite its title, contains much that is of importance quite independently of Sartre's account of 'nihilification'. The most interesting idea is again taken from Heidegger. Whereas for most objects essence precedes existence, 'there is at least one being whose existence comes before his essence, a being which exists before it can be defined by any conception of it. That being is man' (*EH* 66). Human freedom precedes the essence of man and makes it possible. Whereas an oak tree has to follow a particular life pattern because that is the kind of thing it is, human beings do not belong to a kind in this way: it is for each person to decide what kind of thing to be. Human freedom creates a fissure in the world of objects.

The life of a human individual, according to Sartre, is not determined in advance, neither by a creator, nor by necessitating causes, nor by absolute moral laws. The one necessity I cannot escape is the necessity to choose. Human freedom is absolute but it is also alarming, and we try to hide it from ourselves, and adopt some predetermined role offered by morality, society, or religion. But our efforts at concealment are bound to fail, and we end up double-minded, tacitly aware of our freedom while striving to reduce ourselves to mere objects. This is the condition that Sartre calls 'bad faith'.

The alternative attitude is to accept and affirm one's freedom and accept the responsibility for one's own acts and life, unsustained by any pre-existing moral order and unconstrained by any contingent circumstances. To be sure, there will be physical limits to my possible actions, but by the adjustment of my own desires and projects it is I who confer significance on the situation in which I find myself. I must make a total choice of myself. 'I emerge alone and in dread in the face of the

---

[3] See above, pp. 161 and 171.

unique and first project which constitutes my being: all the barriers, all the railings, collapse, annihilated by the consciousness of my liberty; I have not, nor can I have, recourse to any value against the fact that it is I who maintain values in being' (*EH* 66).

In the years after the war Sartre, with Simone de Beauvoir, became the centre of the cultural and intellectual life of the left bank of Paris. He founded and edited an avant-garde monthly, *Les Temps Modernes*, and wrote a number of successful novels and plays, of which perhaps the best known was *Huis clos* ('In Camera'), which contains the often-quoted line 'Hell is other people'. In *Being and Nothingness*, in addition to the *en-soi* and the *pour-soi*, Sartre had introduced the notion of being-for-others. This is essentially the way in which I am presented to others and observed by them, becoming nothing more than an object for them, the object perhaps of their envy or contempt. The original meaning of being-for-others, he had written, is conflict. In his later work Sartre developed this theme and gave it greater importance.

On social and political views he took up positions close to those of the Communist Party, though Marxist determinism was not easy to reconcile with the absolute libertarianism that was the keynote of existentialism. In an effort to resolve this tension he wrote a *Critique of Dialectical Reason* in 1960. In 1964 he declined the Nobel Prize for literature and in 1968 he supported the student rebellions that threatened the de Gaulle government. He died in 1980.

Jacques Derrida

For a brief period in the 1960s it looked as if there might be a rapprochement between Continental and Anglophone philosophy. In 1962 a thirty-two-year-old philosopher, of Algerian Jewish parentage, called Jacques Derrida published a doctoral thesis on Husserl and geometry. In the same year there was posthumously published a set of lectures by the Oxford philosopher J. L. Austin (1911–60), entitled *How to Do Things with Words*, which contained a theory of the different kinds of speech acts. In 1967 Derrida published three highly original works (*Writing and Difference*, *Speech and Phenomena*, and *Of Grammatology*) which bore clear marks of Austin's influence.

The two philosophers, however, treated the same topic in very different ways. Austin started, as early as 1946, from a distinction between two kinds of speech, constative and performative. A constative sentence is used to state how things are as a matter of fact: 'It is raining', 'The train is approaching'. Performative utterances, however, were not statements that could be judged and found true or false by comparison with the facts; they were speech acts that changed things rather than reported on them. Examples are 'I name this ship the *Queen Elizabeth*', 'I promise to meet you at ten o'clock', 'I bequeath my watch to my brother'.

Austin went on to classify many different kinds of performative utterances, such as bets, appointments, vetoes, apologies, and curses, and to identify concealed performative elements in apparently straightforward statements. In its developed stage his theory made room, in speech acts, for three elements: the locutionary, the illocutionary, and the perlocutionary force. Suppose someone says to me 'Shoot her!' The locutionary act is defined by specifying the sense of 'shoot' and the reference of 'her'. The illocutionary act is one of ordering, or urging, etc. The perlocutionary act (which takes place only if the illocutionary act achieves its goal) would be described by, for example, 'He made me shoot her'.

Austin introduced many new technical terms to bring out distinctions between different kinds of speech acts and elements within them. Each term, as introduced, is defined in lucid terms and is illuminated by examples. The overall effect is to bring clarity, at a microscopic level, into a vast and important field of the philosophy of language.

Derrida's method is quite different. He, too, introduces technical terms in great profusion: for instance, 'gram', 'reserve', 'incision', 'trace', 'spacing', 'blank', 'supplement', 'pharmakon', and many others. But he is much less willing to offer definitions of them, and often seems to reject the very request for a definition as somehow improper. The relevance of his illustrative examples is rarely clear, so that even banal features of language take on an air of mystery.

In treating of speech acts, Austin was not particularly interested in the distinction between what is spoken (as in an oral promise) and what is written (as in a will); the philosophical points he makes apply in general to both kinds of language use. Derrida, on the other hand, attached great important to the distinction, attacking what he calls 'phonocentrism', the alleged overemphasis in Western civilization on the spoken word. Given the emphasis placed by both law and business on getting things in writing, and the enormous efforts modern societies have put into making their citizens literate, Derrida's charge of phonocentrism has to be based on a number of eccentric texts starting with an ironic passage in Plato's *Phaedrus*.

Among performative speech acts promising is a paradigm case that interested both Austin and Derrida. Austin listed, in an instructive way, the different kinds of infelicity that may affect a promise, from insincerity to incapacity. Derrida was principally impressed by the fact that one may die before fulfilling a promise, a circumstance which he expresses by saying that every performative is haunted by death. But, *pace* Derrida, since we are all, always, mortal, the possibility of death tells us nothing about performatives in particular. Cycling to work, no less than making a promise, is something that may be interrupted by death. Of course, in a promise death may actually be mentioned, as when bride and groom vow fidelity 'till death do us part'. But in that case, a promise is not in fact broken, or left unfulfilled, when one of the spouses dies.

Derrida's hostility to phonocentrism was part of an attack on what he called 'the metaphysics of presence', the notion that the basis of claims to meaning and truth is something intimate given in consciousness. The prime target of his attack was Husserl, but the empiricist notion of sense-data lies open to similar criticism. Speech was given primacy over writing in Western tradition, he claims, because speech is closer than writing to the thinking that is idealized as the ultimate, transcendental object of signification. Derrida 'deconstructs' the opposition between speech and writing and gives the privileged position to the written text, the one furthest from the control of its author, the one most capable of diverse and superseding interpretations. Some have seen Derrida's attack on the metaphysics of presence as an enterprise, in a very different key, parallel to Wittgenstein's demolition of the notion of a private language.

Derrida in his early works showed evidence of great philosophical acumen; but after 1967 his thinking and writing moved further and further away from that of Austin and Wittgenstein. As his career developed, his style of operation moved far away not only from current analytic philosophy, but from philosophy as understood by the great philosophers from Aristotle to Husserl. It has always been seen as a task of philosophers to draw distinctions between concepts that may be confused with each other, and if necessary to invent or adapt terms to mark these distinctions. Derrida, by contrast, introduced new terms whose effect was to confuse ideas that are perfectly distinct.

Consider the notion of 'deferrence' (*différance*), in which Derrida took great pride.[4] Deferrence is supposed to combine the notions of deferring (putting off) and difference (being distinct). 'Deferrence', he tells us, 'is to be conceived prior to the separation between deferring as delay and differing as the actual work of difference' (*SP* 88). It is not clear how these two contrasting notions can be combined in this way, and the explications and paraphrases offered by Derrida are not altogether helpful:

Deferrence is what makes the movement of signification possible only if each so-called present element, each element appearing on the scene of presence, is related to something other than itself, thereby keeping within itself the mark of a past element, and already letting itself be vitiated by the mark of its relation to a future element, this trace being related no less to what is called the future than to what is called the past, and constituting what is called the present by means of this very relation to what it is not, to what it absolutely is not: that is, not even to a past or a future as a modified present. (*Diff.* 13)

One can see what he means. If I say to the breakfast waiter 'bacon and eggs', the meaning of what I say depends on the fact that at the moment when I utter the word 'and' the word 'bacon' is in the past, but remains related to it; moreover

---

[4] The word 'différance' is often translated by 'differance', but my translation corresponds more exactly to the construction of the French word. I must, however, ask the reader to pronounce it exactly like 'difference', out of deference to Derrida, who attached importance to the equivalent French words sounding alike.

the 'and' is also related to the word 'eggs' that has not yet been uttered, but is about to be related to it. Very true. And if that is what deferrence means, then what Derrida says of it is perfectly correct: 'it is not the name of an *object*, not the name of some "being" that could be present. And for that reason it is not a concept either.' But that cannot be all 'deferrence' means, because we know that some of Derrida's readers have taken it to be a name of God—though Derrida reassures us that it 'blocks every relationship to theology' (*P* 40). The various paraphrases we find of 'deferrence' in his texts are perhaps themselves an instance of deferrence: IOUs that are quite distinct from a definition and which put off to an indefinite future an actual conferment of sense.

Derrida devised a method of dealing with authors, a technique that can be nicknamed the nosegay method. To assemble a nosegay, one collects a number of texts that contain the same word (or often just the same phoneme). One then snips them out of context and date, discards utterer or voice, and modifies the natural sense by italicization, omission, or truncation. One gathers them together and presents them as a nosegay with some striking or provocative thesis tied around it. The nosegay technique became popular in some departments of literature, since it demands considerably less effort than more traditional methods of literary criticism.

The later Derrida maintains the reader's attention by the deft deployment of rhetoric. A particularly successful device might be named 'the irrefutable paradox'. One of the most often quoted lines in *Grammatology*—underlined by the author himself—is 'There is nothing outside the text.' An arresting, even shocking, remark! Surely the Black Death and the Holocaust were not textual events in the way that a new edition of Johnson's *Lives of the Poets* is a textual event. But later Derrida kindly explains that by text he does not mean a corpus of writing, but something that overruns the limits of the world, of the real, of history.[5] Well, if what we are being told is simply that there is nothing outside the universe, it would be rash to contradict. And an injunction to try to see things in context is surely sound advice.

Like the skilful rhetorician that he is, Derrida keeps his readers awake by bringing in sex and death. We have already met death haunting the performatives; we meet sex in equally irrelevant places. Talking to oneself, we are told, stands in the same relation to talking aloud as masturbation stands to copulation. No doubt it does. A no less apt comparison would have been with solitaire vs. whist; but that would not have tickled the reader in quite the same way. Again, at the end of the book of Revelation, we read: 'And the Spirit and the bride say Come! And let him that heareth say Come!' (22: 17). Derrida has written at length on this text, making great play with the double entendre that attaches, in French as in English, to the

---

[5] 'Living On', in Harold Bloomfield (ed.), *Deconstruction and Criticism* (New York: Seabury Press, 1979).

word 'come'. If one were churlish enough to point out that the Greek word translated 'come' cannot possibly have the sense of 'achieve orgasm', one would no doubt be told that one had missed the whole thrust of the exercise.

It may appear unseemly to criticize Derrida in the manner just illustrated. The reason for doing so is that such a parody of fair comment is precisely the method he adopted in his own later work: his philosophical weapons are the pun, the bawdy, the sneer, and the snigger. Normally, the historian tries to identify some of the major doctrines of a philosopher, present them as clearly as he can, and then perhaps add a word of evaluation. In the later Derrida there are no doctrines to present. It is not just that an unsympathetic reader may fail to identify or understand them; Derrida himself rejects the idea that his work can be encapsulated in theses. Indeed, sometimes he even disclaims the ambition to be a philosopher.

Is it not unfair, then, to include Derrida, whether for blame or praise, in a history such as this? I think not. Whatever he himself may say, he has been taken by many people to be a serious philosopher, and he should be evaluated as such. But it is unsurprising that his fame has been less in philosophy departments than in departments of literature, whose members have had less practice in discerning genuine from counterfeit philosophy.

4

Logic

Mill's Empiricist Logic

John Stuart Mill's *System of Logic* falls into two principal parts. The first two books present a system of formal logic; the remainder of the work deals with the methodology of the natural and social sciences. He begins the first part with an analysis of language, and in particular with a theory of naming.

Mill was the first British empiricist to take formal logic seriously, and from the start he is anxious to dissociate himself from the nominalism that had been associated with empiricism since the time of Hobbes. By 'nominalism' he means the two-name theory of the proposition: the theory that a proposition is true if and only if subject and predicate are names of the same thing. The Hobbesian account, Mill says, fits only those propositions where both predicate and subject are proper names, such as 'Tully is Cicero'. But it is a sadly inadequate theory of any other propositions.

Mill uses the word 'name' very broadly. Not only proper names like 'Socrates' and pronouns like 'this', but also definite descriptions like 'the king who succeeded William the Conqueror', count as names for him. So too do general terms like 'man' and 'wise', and abstract nouns like 'wisdom'. All names, whether particular or general, whether abstract or concrete, denote things; proper names denote the things they name and general terms denote the things they are true of: thus not only 'Socrates' but also 'man' and 'wise' denote Socrates. General terms, in addition to having a denotation in this way, also have a connotation: there are items they connote as well as items they denote. What they connote are the attributes they signify, that is to say, what would be specified in a dictionary definition of them. In logic, connotation is prior to denotation: 'when mankind fixed the word wise they were not thinking of Socrates' (*SL* 1. 2. 5. 2).

Since 'name' covers such a multitude of terms, Mill can accept the nominalist view that every proposition is a conjunction of names. But this does not commit him to the Hobbesian view since, unlike Hobbes, he can appeal to connotation in setting out the truth-conditions of propositions. A sentence joining two conno-tative terms, such as 'all men are mortal', tells us that certain attributes (those, say, of animality and rationality) are always accompanied by the attribute of mortality.

In his second book, Mill discusses inference, of which he distinguished two kinds, real and verbal. Verbal inference brings us no new knowledge about the world; knowledge of the language alone is sufficient to enable us to derive the conclusion from the premiss. As an example of a verbal inference, Mill gives the inference from 'No great general is a rash man' to 'No rash man is a great general': both premiss and conclusion, he tells us, say the same thing. There is real inference when we infer to a truth, in the conclusion, which is not contained in the premisses.

Mill found it very difficult to explain how new truths could be discovered by general reasoning. He accepted that all reasoning was syllogistic, and he claimed that in every syllogism the conclusion is actually contained and implied in the premisses. Take the argument from the premisses 'All men are mortal, and Socrates is a man' to the conclusion 'Socrates is mortal'. If this syllogism is to be deductively valid, then surely the proposition 'Socrates is mortal' must be pre-supposed in the more general assumption 'All men are mortal'. On the other hand if we substitute for 'Socrates' the name of someone not yet dead (Mill's example was 'the Duke of Wellington') then the conclusion does give us new information, but it is not justified by the evidence summarized in the first premiss. Hence the syllogism is not a genuine inference:

All inference is from particulars to particulars. General propositions are merely registers of such inferences already made, and short formulae for making more. The major premise of a syllogism, consequently, is a formula of this description; and the conclusion is not an inference drawn *from* the formula, but an inference drawn *according to* the formula; the real logical antecedent or premise being the particular facts from which the general proposition was collected by induction. (*SL* 3. 3. 4)

'Induction' was a name that had long been given by logicians to the process of deriving a general truth from particular instances. But there is more than one kind of induction. Suppose I state 'Peter is a Jew, James is a Jew, John is a Jew...' and then go on to enumerate all the Apostles. I may go on to conclude 'All the Apostles are Jews', but if I do so, Mill says, I am not really moving from particular to general: the conclusion is merely an abridged notation for the particular facts enunciated in the premiss. Matters are very different when we make a generalization on the basis only of an incomplete survey of the items to which it applies—as when we conclude from previous human deaths that all humans of all times will die.

Mill's criticism of deductive argument involves a confusion between logic and epistemology. An inference may be, as he says, deductively valid without being informative: validity is a necessary but not a sufficient condition for an argument to produce true information. But syllogism is not the only form of inference, and there are many valid non-syllogistic arguments (e.g. arguments of the form 'A = B', 'B = C', therefore 'A = C') which are quite capable of conveying information. Even in the case of syllogism, it is possible to give an account that makes it a real inference if we interpret 'All men are mortal' not as saying that 'mortal' is a name of every member of the class of men but—in accordance with Mill's own account of naming—as saying that there is a connection between the attributes connoted by 'man' and by 'mortal'.

Mill would no doubt respond by asking how we could ever know such a connection, if not by induction; and the most interesting part of his Logic is his attempt to set out the rules of inductive discovery. He set out five rules, or canons, of experimental inquiry to guide researchers in the inductive discovery of causes and effects. We may consider as illustrations the first two of these canons.

The first is called the method of agreement. It states that if a phenomenon F appears in the conjunction of the circumstances A, B, and C, and also in the conjunction of the circumstances C, D, and E, then we are to conclude that C, the only common feature, is causally related to F.

The second, the method of disagreement, states that if F occurs in the presence of A, B, and C, but not in the presence of A, B, and D, then we are to conclude that C, the only feature differentiating the two cases, is causally related to F.

Mill maintains that we are always, though not necessarily consciously, applying his canons in daily life and in the courts of law. Thus, to illustrate the second canon he says, 'When a man is shot through the heart, it is by this method we know that it was the gunshot which killed him: for he was in the fullness of life immediately before, all circumstances being the same, except the wound.'

Mill's methods of agreement and disagreement are a sophistication of Bacon's tables of presence and absence.[1] Like Bacon's, Mill's methods seem to assume the constancy of general laws. Mill says explicitly, 'The proposition that the course of Nature is uniform, is the fundamental principle, or general axiom, of Induction.' But where does this general axiom come from? As a thoroughgoing empiricist, Mill treats it as being itself a generalization from experience: it would be rash, he says, to assume that the law of causation applied on distant stars. But if this very general principle is the basis of induction, it is difficult to see how it can itself be established by induction. But then Mill was prepared to affirm that not only the fundamental laws of physics, but those of arithmetic and logic, including the very principle of non-contradiction itself, were nothing more than very well-confirmed generalizations from experience.[2]

---

[1] See above, pp. 524–5.   [2] See Ch. 6 below.

Frege's Refoundation of Logic

On these matters Frege occupied the opposite pole from Mill. While for Mill propositions of every kind were known a posteriori, for Frege arithmetic no less than logic was not only a priori but also analytic. In order to establish this, Frege had to investigate and systematize logic to a degree that neither Mill nor any of his predecessors had achieved. He organized logic in a wholly new way, and became in effect the second founder of the discipline first established by Aristotle.

One way to define logic is to say that it is the discipline that sorts out good inferences from bad. In the centuries preceding Frege the most important part of logic had been the study of the validity and invalidity of a particular form of inference, namely the syllogism. Elaborate rules had been drawn up to distinguish between valid inferences such as

All Germans are Europeans.
Some Germans are blonde.
Therefore, Some Europeans are blonde.

and invalid inferences such as

All cows are mammals.
Some mammals are quadrupeds.
Therefore, All cows are quadrupeds.

Though both these inferences have true conclusions, only the first is valid, that is to say, only the first is an inference of a form that will never lead from true premisses to a false conclusion.

Syllogistic, in fact, covers only a small proportion of the forms of valid reasoning. In Anthony Trollope's *The Prime Minister* the Duchess of Omnium is anxious to place a favourite of hers as Member of Parliament for the borough of Silverbridge, which has traditionally been in the gift of the Dukes of Omnium. He tells us that she 'had a little syllogism in her head as to the Duke ruling the borough, the Duke's wife ruling the Duke, and therefore the Duke's wife ruling the borough'. The Duchess's reasoning is perfectly valid, but it is not a syllogism, and cannot be formulated as one. This is because her reasoning depends on the fact that 'rules' is a transitive relation (if A rules B and B rules C, then A does indeed rule C), while syllogistic is a system designed to deal only with subject–predicate sentences, and not rich enough to cope with relational statements.

A further weakness of syllogistic was that it could not cope with inferences in which words like 'all' or 'some' occurred not in the subject place but somewhere in the grammatical predicate. The rules would not determine the validity of inferences that contained premisses such as 'All politicians tell some lies' or

'Nobody can speak every language' in cases where the inference turned on the word 'some' in the first sentence or the word 'every' in the second.

Frege devised a system to overcome these difficulties, which he expounded first in his *Begriffsschrift*. The first step was to replace the grammatical notions of *subject* and *predicate* with new logical notions, which Frege called 'argument' and 'function'. In the sentence 'Wellington defeated Napoleon' grammarians would say (or used to say) that 'Wellington' was the subject and 'defeated Napoleon' the predicate. Frege's introduction of the notions of *argument* and *function* offers a more flexible method of analysing the sentence.

This is how it works. Suppose that we take our sentence 'Wellington defeated Napoleon' and put into it, in place of the name 'Napoleon', the name 'Nelson'. Clearly this alters the content of the sentence, and indeed it turns it from a true sentence into a false sentence. We can think of the sentence as in this way consisting of a constant component, 'Wellington defeated . . .', and a replaceable element, 'Napoleon'. Frege calls the first, fixed component a function, and the second component the argument of the function. The sentence 'Wellington defeated Napoleon' is, as Frege would put it, the value of the function 'Wellington defeated . . .' for the argument 'Napoleon' and the sentence 'Wellington defeated Nelson' is the value of the same function for the argument 'Nelson'.

We could also analyse the sentence in a different way. 'Wellington defeated Napoleon' is also the value of the function ' . . . defeated Napoleon' for the argument 'Wellington'. We can go further, and say that the sentence is the value of the function ' . . . defeated . . .' for the arguments 'Wellington' and 'Napoleon' (taken in that order). In Frege's terminology, 'Wellington defeated . . .' and ' . . . defeated Napoleon' are functions of a single argument; ' . . . defeated . . .' is a function of two arguments.[3]

It will be seen that in comparison with the subject–predicate distinction the function–argument dichotomy provides a much more flexible method of bringing out logically relevant similarities between sentences. Subject–predicate analysis is sufficient to mark the similarity between 'Caesar conquered Gaul' and 'Caesar defeated Pompey', but it is blind to the similarity between 'Caesar conquered Gaul' and 'Pompey avoided Gaul'. This becomes a matter of logical importance when we deal with sentences such as those occurring in syllogisms that contain not proper names like 'Caesar' and 'Gaul', but quantified expressions such as 'all Romans' or 'some province'.

Having introduced these notions of function and argument, Frege's next step is to introduce a new notation to express the kind of generality expressed by a word

---

[3] As I have explained them above, following *Begriffsschrift*, functions and arguments and their values are all bits of language: names and sentences, with or without gaps. In his later writings Frege applied the notions more often not to linguistic items, but to the items that language is used to express and talk about. I will discuss this in the chapter on metaphysics (Ch. 7).

like 'all' no matter where it occurs in a sentence. If 'Socrates is mortal' is a true sentence, we can say that the function '... is mortal' holds true for the argument 'Socrates'. To express generality we need a symbol to indicate that a certain function holds true no matter what its argument is. Adapting the notation that Frege introduced, logicians write

$(x)(x$ is mortal$)$

to signify that no matter what name is attached as an argument to the function '... is mortal', the function holds true. The notation can be read as 'For all x, x is mortal' and it is equivalent to the statement that everything whatever is mortal.

This notation for generality can be applied in all the different ways in which sentences can be analysed into function and argument. Thus '(x)(God is greater than x)' is equivalent to 'God is greater than everything'. It can be combined with a sign for negation ('$\sim$') to produce notations equivalent to sentences containing 'no' and 'none'. Thus '$(x)\sim(x$ is immortal$)$' = 'For all x, it is not the case that x is immortal' = 'Nothing is immortal'. To render a sentence containing expressions like 'some' Frege exploited the equivalence, long accepted by logicians, between (for example) 'Some Romans were cowards' and 'Not all Romans were not cowards'. Thus 'Some things are mortal' = 'It is not the case that nothing is mortal' = '$\sim(x)\sim(x$ is mortal$)$'. For convenience his followers used, for 'some', a sign '(Ex)' as equivalent to '$\sim(x)\sim$'. Frege's notation, and its abbreviation, can be used to make statements about the existence of things of different kinds. '$(Ex)(x$ is a horse$)$', for instance, is tantamount to 'There are horses' (provided, as Frege notes, that this sentence is understood as covering also the case where there is only one horse).

Frege believed that objects of all kinds were nameable—numbers, for instance, were named by numerals—and the argument places in his logical notation can be filled with the name of anything whatever. Consequently '$(x)(x$ is mortal$)$' means not just that everyone is mortal, but that everything whatever is mortal. So understood, it is a false proposition, because, for instance, the number ten is not mortal.

It is rare, in fact, for us to want to make statements of such unrestricted generality. It is much more common for us to want to say that everything *of a certain kind* has a certain property, or that everything that has a certain given property also has a certain other property. 'All men are mortal' or 'What goes up must come down' are examples of typical universal sentences of ordinary language. In order to express such sentences in Frege's system one must graft his predicate calculus (the theory of quantifiers such as 'some' and 'all') on to a propositional calculus (the theory of connectives between sentences, such as 'if' and 'and').

In Frege's system of propositional logic the most important element is a sign for conditionality, roughly corresponding to 'if' in ordinary language. The Stoic logician Philo, in ancient times, had defined 'If p then q' by saying that it was a proposition that was false in the case in which p was true and q false, and true in the three other possible cases.[4] Frege defined his sign for conditionality (which we may render '→') in a similar manner. He warned that it did not altogether correspond to 'if…then' in ordinary language. If we take '$p \rightarrow q$' as equivalent to 'If p then q' then propositions such as 'If the sun is shining, $3 \times 7 = 21$' and 'If perpetual motion is possible, then pigs can fly' turn out true—simply because the consequent of the first proposition is true, and the antecedent of the second proposition is false. 'If' behaves differently in ordinary language; the use of it that is closest to '→' is in sentences such as 'If those curtains match that sofa, then I'm a Dutchman'. Frege's sign can be looked on as a stripped-down version of the word 'if', designed to capture just that aspect of its meaning that is necessary for the formulation of rigorous proofs containing it.

In Frege's terminology, '$\ldots \rightarrow \ldots$' is a function that takes sentences as its arguments: its values, too, are sentences. Whether the sentences that are its values (sentences of the form '$p \rightarrow q$') are true or false will depend only on whether the sentences that are its arguments ('p' and 'q') are true or false. We may call functions of this kind 'truth-functions'. The conditional is not the only truth-function in Frege's system. So too is negation, represented by the sign '~', since a negated sentence is true just in case the sentence negated is false, and vice versa.

With the aid of these two symbols Frege built up a complete system of propositional logic, deriving all the truths of that logic from a limited set of primitive truths or axioms, such as '$(q \rightarrow p) \rightarrow ({\sim}p \rightarrow {\sim}q)$' and '${\sim}{\sim}p \rightarrow p$'. Connectives other than 'if', such as 'and' and 'or', are defined in terms of conditionality and negation. Thus, '${\sim}q \rightarrow p$' rules out the case in which p is false and ${\sim}q$ is true: it means that p and q are not both false, and therefore is equivalent to 'p or q' (in modern symbols, '$p \vee q$'). 'p and q' ('$p \& q$'), on the other hand, is rendered by Frege as '${\sim}(q \rightarrow {\sim}p)$'. As Frege realized, a different system would be possible in which conjunction was primitive, and conditionality was defined in terms of conjunction and negation. But in logic, he maintained, deduction is more important than conjunction, and that is why 'if' and not 'and' is taken as primitive.

Earlier logicians had drawn up a number of rules of inference, rules for passing from one proposition to another. One of the best known was called *modus ponens*: 'From "p" and "If p then q" infer "q"'. In his system Frege claims to prove all the laws of logic using this as a single rule of inference. The other rules are either axioms of his system or theorems proved from them. Thus the rule traditionally called contraposition, which allows the inference from

> If John is snoring, John is asleep

to

> If John is not asleep, John is not snoring,

is justified by the first of the axioms quoted above.

[4] See above, p. 112.

When we put together Frege's propositional calculus and his predicate calculus we can symbolize the universal sentences of ordinary language, making use of both the sign of generality and the sign of conditionality. The expression

$$(x)(Fx \rightarrow Gx)$$

can be read

For all x, if Fx then Gx,

which means that whatever x may be, if 'Fx' is true then 'Gx' is true.

If we substitute 'is a man' for 'F' and 'is mortal' for 'G' then we obtain 'For all x, if x is a man, x is mortal', which is what Frege offers as the translation of 'All men are mortal'. The contradictory of this, 'Some men are not mortal', comes out as '$\sim(x)(x$ is a man $\rightarrow x$ is mortal)' and its contrary, 'No man is mortal', comes out as '$(x)(x$ is a man $\rightarrow \sim x$ is mortal)'. By the use of these translations, Frege is able to prove as part of his system theorems corresponding to the entire corpus of Aristotelian syllogistic.

Frege's logical calculus is not just more systematic than Aristotle's; it is also more comprehensive. His symbolism is able, for instance, to mark the difference between

Every boy loves some girl $= (x)(x$ is a boy $\rightarrow Ey(y$ is a girl $\&$ x loves $y))$

and the apparently similar (but much less plausible) passive version of the sentence

Some girl is loved by every boy $= (Ey(y$ is a girl $\&$ $(x)(x$ is a boy $\rightarrow x$ loves $y))$.

Aristotelian logicians in earlier ages had sought in vain to find a simple and conspicuous way of bringing out such differences of meaning in ambiguous sentences of ordinary language. A final subtlety of Frege's system must be mentioned. The sentence 'Socrates is mortal', as we have seen, can be analysed as having 'Socrates' for argument, and '...is mortal' as function. But the function '...is mortal' can itself be regarded as an argument of a different function, a function operating at a higher level. This is what happens when we complete the function '...is mortal' not with a determinate argument, but with a quantifier, as in '$(x)(x$ is mortal)'. The quantifier '$(x)(x...)$' can then be regarded as a second-level function of the first-level function '...is mortal'. The initial function, Frege always emphasizes, is incomplete; but it may be completed in two ways, either by having an argument inserted in its argument place, or by itself becoming the argument of a second-level function. This is what happens when the ellipsis in '...is mortal' is filled with a quantifier such as 'Everything'.

Induction and Abduction in Peirce

A number of Frege's innovations in logic occurred, quite independently, to C. S. Peirce; but Peirce was never able to incorporate his results into a rigorous system, much less to publish them in a definitive form. Peirce's importance in the history of logic derives rather from his investigations into the structure of scientific inquiry. Deductive logic assists us in organizing our knowledge; but the kind of reasoning that extends our knowledge ('ampliative inference' as Peirce calls it) is of three kinds: induction, hypothesis, and analogy. All of these inferences, Peirce claimed, depend essentially on sampling. Any account, therefore, of non-deductive inference must be related to the mathematical theory of probability (*EWP* 177).

Scientists frame hypotheses, make predictions on the bases of these hypotheses, and then make observations with a view to confirming or refuting their hypotheses. These three stages of inquiry are called by Peirce abduction, deduction, and induction. In the abductive phase the inquirer selects a theory for consideration. In the deductive phase he formulates a method to test it. In the inductive phase he evaluates the results of the test.

How does a scientist decide which hypotheses are worth inductive testing? Indefinitely many different theories might explain the phenomena he wishes to investigate. If he is not to waste his time, his energy, and his research funding, the scientist needs some guidance about which theories to explore. This guidance is given by the rules of the logic of abduction. The theory must, if true, be genuinely explanatory; it must be empirically testable; it should be simple and natural and cohere with existing knowledge, though not necessarily with our subjective opinions about antecedent likelihood. (*P* 7. 220–1)

Rules of abduction, however, do not by themselves explain the success of scientists in their choice of hypotheses. We have to believe that in their investigation of nature they are assisted by nature herself.

Science presupposes that we have a capacity for 'guessing' right. We shall do better to abandon the whole attempt to learn the truth ... unless we can trust to the human mind's having such a power of guessing right that before very many hypotheses shall have been tried, intelligent guessing may be expected to lead us to the one which will support all tests. (*P* 6. 530).

This trust has to be presupposed at the outset, even though it may rest on no evidence. But in fact the history of science shows such trust to be well founded: 'it has seldom been necessary to try more than two or three hypotheses made by clear genius before the right one was found' (*P* 7. 220).

Once the theory has been chosen, abduction is succeeded by deduction. Consequences are derived from the hypothesis, experimental predictions that is, which will come out true if the hypothesis is correct. In deduction, Peirce maintained, the mind is under the dominion of habit: a general idea will suggest a particular case. It is by verifying or falsifying the predictions of the particular instantiations that the scientist will confirm, or as the case may be refute, the hypothesis under test.

It is induction that is the all-important element in the testing, and induction is essentially a matter of sampling.

Suppose a ship arrives in Liverpool laden with wheat in bulk. Suppose that by some machinery the whole cargo be stirred up with great thoroughness. Suppose that twenty-seven thimblefuls be taken equally from the forward, midships, and aft parts, from the starboard, center and larboard parts, and from the top, half depth and lower parts of her hold, and that these being mixed and the grains counted, four-fifths of the latter are found to be of quality A. Then we infer, experientially and provisionally, that approximately four fifths of all the grain in the cargo is of the same quality. (*EWP* 177)

By saying that we draw the inference provisionally, Peirce means that if our experience be indefinitely extended, and every correction that presents itself be duly applied, then our approximation will become indefinitely close in the long run. Inference of this kind, Peirce claims, rests on no postulation of matter of fact, but only on the mathematics of probability.

Induction thus described is quantitative induction: an inference from the proportion of a sample to the proportion of a population. But there is another kind of induction that is important not only in science but in everyday life. That is qualitative induction, when we infer from one or more observed qualities of an individual to other, unobserved qualities. To illustrate this Peirce introduces us to the concept of the *mugwump*. A mugwump, he tells us, has certain characteristics:

He has a high self-respect and places great value upon social distinction. He laments the great part that rowdyism and unrefined good-fellowship play in the dealings of American politicians with their constituency.... He holds that monetary considerations should usually be the decisive ones in questions of public policy. He respects the principle of individualism and of *laissez-faire* as the greatest agency of civilisation. These views, among others, I know to be the obtrusive marks of a 'mugwump'. Now, suppose I casually meet a man in a railway train and falling into conversation find that he holds opinions of this sort; I am naturally led to suppose that he is 'mugwump'. That is hypothetic inference. That is to say, a number of readily verifiable a marks of a mugwump being selected, I find this man has these, and infer that he has all the other characters that go to make a thinker of that stripe. (*EWP* 210)

This homespun example illustrates the three stages of scientific inquiry as described by Peirce. My fellow passenger deplores the plebeian vulgarity of his congressman. I frame the hypothesis that he is a mugwump. I conclude that he is likely to oppose government regulation of business. I ask him his opinion on a recent measure in restraint of trade, and my hypothesis is confirmed by his vehement denunciation. It remains, however, no more than probable, in spite of further conversation, for the train journey is, mercifully, only finitely long.

The Saga of Principia Mathematica

Peirce's logical investigations left little mark on the development of logic in the early twentieth century. It was rather the work of Frege that was carried forward, in particular by the work of Russell and Whitehead, his successors in the quest for the logicist grail. The three volumes of *Principia Mathematica* contain a systematization of logic that soon became much better known than that presented in Frege's own works.

One reason for the greater popularity of *Principia* is that it replaces Frege's ingenious but cumbersome symbolism with a much more convenient notation, which Russell and Whitehead took over from its inventor, the Italian mathematician Giuseppe Peano. Whereas Frege's system was two-dimensional, and called for complicated typesetting, the Peano system is linear, and calls only for a few special signs in addition to letters of the alphabet. Thus the tilde sign '∼' was used for negation, the sign 'V' for disjunction, and the horseshoe sign '⊃' for the truth-functional 'if'. These signs for logical connectives are still in common use, though we use in this text instead of the horseshoe the sign '→', which is nowadays preferred. For conjunction Russell and Whitehead used a simple point, as in 'p.q'; nowadays the ampersand, as in 'p & q', is commonly used instead. Russell and Whitehead expressed universal quantification thus: '$(x)F(x)$'; and existential quantification thus: '$(Ex)F(x)$'. These symbols, too, are now in common use; the 'E' in existential quantification is sometimes printed in reverse.

The system of *Principia* is, like Frege's, an axiomatic system in which logical truths are derived by rule from a handful of axioms. The initial set of axioms, however, differs from Frege's set, and whereas Frege had taken 'if' and 'not' as primitive connectives from which the others could be defined, Russell and Whitehead took 'or' and 'not' (which they called 'logical constants') as basic. In fact many other sets of axioms are possible, with different primitive constants, and they were studied by logicians in the next decades.

But it soon came to be realized that axiomatic systems were not the only way, or even necessarily the best way, to give logic a rigorous form. This was shown by Wittgenstein, who invented a formal device which, like many of those of Frege, passed into the logic textbooks, namely the truth-table.

It is possible to define the propositional connectives by setting out in a table the truth-conditions of propositions containing them. Thus the table

p	q	$p \& q$
T	T	T
F	T	F
T	F	F
F	F	F

represents that '*p* & *q*' is true in the case in which '*p*' and '*q*' are both true, and false in the three other possible cases, namely (*a*) when '*p*' is false and '*q*' is true, (*b*) when '*p*' is true and '*q*' is false, (*c*) when '*p*' and '*q*' are both false. The truth-value of '*p* & *q*', as the table brings out, is determined by the truth-values of the component propositions '*p*' and '*q*'; the compound proposition, we may say, is a *truth-function* of its constituents, and the possible combinations of the truth-values of the constituents set out the *truth-conditions* for the compound proposition.

Similar tables can be set out for the other logical constants, such as 'or' and 'if'. 'If *p* then *q*' is written as '*p* → *q*' and is interpreted as a truth-functional condition that is true in all cases except where '*p*' is true and '*q*' is false. The simplest truth-table is the one for 'not':

p	$\sim p$
T	F
F	T

This shows that a proposition is true when its negation is false, and vice versa.

Propositions of great length and complexity may be built up by repeated use of the logical constants, but however complex they are their truth-value can always be determined from the truth-values of the simple propositions that make them up (Wittgenstein, *TLP* 5. 31). Consider the following proposition:

> If *p* and *q*, then not-*p* and *q*.

This is a truth-function of '*p*' and '*q*' as shown in the following table:

p	*q*	*p* & *q*	→	$\sim p$ & *q*
T	T	T T T	F	F T F T
F	T	F F T	T	T F T T
T	F	T F F	T	F T F F
F	F	F F F	T	T F F F

This table is constructed in the following manner. First the columns under each occurrence of the single propositional variables are filled in by copying out the values given in the two left-hand columns, which represent a conventional arrangement to ensure that all possible combinations of truth-values are covered (*TLP* 4. 31). Then in the fourth column from the right the truth-value of 'not-*p*' is filled in under the '$\sim$' sign by reversing the truth-value of '*p*'. Then the columns under the '&'s are filled in by deriving the truth-value of the conjunct propositions via the table given earlier. Finally the '→' column is computed, the truth-values being derived from the truth-functional definition of 'if . . . then'. This column shows the value of the whole complex formula for every possible combination of truth-values of its constituents. It turns out to be false if '*p* & *q*' is true, and to be true in all other cases.

When we construct truth-tables for complex propositions in this manner, we sometimes find that they take the same truth-value for every possible truth-value of the elementary propositions. Thus, the proposition 'p or not p' is true whether 'p' is true or false, as we see thus:

p	p V $\sim p$
T	T T FT
F	F T TF

On the other hand, the proposition 'p and not-p' is false whatever 'p' may be:

p	p & $\sim p$
T	T F FT
F	F F TF

A proposition that is true for all truth-possibilities of its elementary propositions is called a *tautology*; a proposition that is false for all truth-possibilities is called a *contradiction* (*TLP* 4. 46). The tautology set out above corresponds to the law of excluded middle. The tautology that is the negation of the contradiction set out above corresponds to the law of non-contradiction. These two laws were two of the three traditional laws of thought.

In this way the study of tautologies links with old-fashioned logics, but it also marks an advance on Frege's handling of propositional logic. It can be shown that all formulae that are tautologous by Wittgenstein's test are either axioms or theorems of Frege's system, and conversely that anything that can be proved from Frege's axioms will be a tautology. The truth-table method and the axiomatic system thus turn out to be two devices for handling the same material, namely the logical truisms of the propositional calculus. But the truth-table method has several advantages over the axiomatic method.

First, it represents all logical truths as on a level with each other, whereas Frege's system and the system of *Principia* privilege an arbitrarily chosen set of them as axioms. Second, there is no need to appeal to any self-evidence in logic: the truth-table method is entirely mechanical, in the sense that it can be carried out by a machine. Finally, given a formula of the propositional calculus we can always settle, by the use of a truth-table, whether or not it is a tautology. An axiomatic system offers nothing comparable. To be sure, if we discover a proof we know the formula is a theorem; but if we fail to discover a proof this may exhibit nothing more than the limits of our own ingenuity. If we are asked 'Is p a tautology or not?', Wittgenstein's method gives us a foolproof method of answering the question not only with a 'yes' but with a 'no'. The axiomatic method does not offer a similar *decision procedure* (to use the term that became standard among logicians).

The classical propositional calculus, as formulated in different ways by Frege, Russell, and Wittgenstein, was criticized by a school of logicians, founded by L. E. J. Brouwer, who deplored the use in mathematics of the principle of excluded middle. These logicians, called 'intuitionists', conceived mathematics as a construction of the human mind, and therefore they assigned truth only to such mathematical propositions as were capable of demonstration. On this basis it would be wrong to affirm 'p' without independent proof, simply because one had refuted 'not-p'. Intuitionists devised systems of logic that lacked not only '$p \lor \sim p$' but other familiar theorems such as '$\sim\sim p \to p$'.

Logicians in the 1920s and 1930s showed that there were many different ways in which the propositional and predicate calculus could be formalized. Besides axiomatic systems containing one or other set of axioms plus a number of rules of inference, one could have a system with no rules but an infinite set of axioms, or a system with no axioms and a limited number of rules. A system of the latter kind was devised by Georg Gentzen in 1934: it consisted of seven rules for the introduction of the logical constants and quantifiers, and eight rules for their elimination. Formal logic, if presented in this manner, resembles non-formal arguments in everyday life more closely than any axiomatic system does. Systems of this kind, accordingly, were called systems of 'natural deduction'. They were appropriate not only for classical but also for intuitionist logic.

Besides devising a variety of methods of systematizing logic, logicians interested themselves in establishing second-order truths about the properties of various systems. One property that it is desirable, indeed essential, for a system of logic to possess is the property of consistency. Given a set of axioms and rules, for instance, we need to show that from those axioms, by those rules, it will never be possible to derive two propositions that contradict each other. Another property, which is desirable but not essential, is that of independence: we wish to show that no axiom of the system is derivable by the rules from the remaining axioms of the system. The logician Paul Bernays in 1926 showed that the propositional system of *Principia Mathematica* was consistent, and that four of its axioms were independent of each other, but the fifth was deducible as a thesis from the remaining four.

The method of proving consistency and independence depends upon treating the axioms and theorems of a deductive system simply as abstract formulae, and treating the rules of the system simply as mechanical procedures for obtaining one formula from another. The properties of the system are then explored by offering a set of objects as a model, or interpretation, of the abstract calculus. The elements of the system are mapped on to the objects and their relations in such a way as to satisfy, or bring out true, the formulae of the system. A formula P will entail a formula Q if and only if all interpretations that satisfy P also satisfy Q. This model-theoretic approach to logic gradually assumed an importance equal to that of the earlier approach that had focused on the notion of proof.

A third property of deductive systems that was explored by logicians in the inter-war years was that of completeness. An axiomatic presentation of the propositional calculus is complete if and only if every truth-table tautology is provable within the system. Hilbert and Ackermann in 1928 offered a proof that the propositional calculus of *Principia Mathematica* was in this sense complete. Indeed, it was complete also in the stronger sense that if we add any non-tautologous formula as an axiom, we reach a contradiction. In 1930 Kurt Gödel proved that first-order predicate calculus, the logic of quantification, was complete in the weaker, but not the stronger, sense.

The question now arose: was arithmetic, like general logic, a complete system? Frege, Russell, and Whitehead had hoped that they had established that arithmetic was a branch of logic. Russell wrote, 'If there are still those who do not admit the identity of logic and mathematics, we may challenge them to indicate at what point, in the successive definitions and deductions of *Principia Mathematica*, they consider that logic ends and mathematics begins' (*IMP* 194–5). If arithmetic was a branch of logic, and if logic was complete, then arithmetic should be a complete system too.

Gödel, in an epoch-making paper of 1931, showed that it was not, and could not be turned into one. By an ingenious device he constructed a formula within the system of *Principia* that can be shown to be true and yet is not provable within the system: a formula that in effect says of itself that it is unprovable. He did this by showing how to turn formulae of the logical system into statements of arithmetic by associating the signs of *Principia* with natural numbers, in such a way that every relationship between two formulae of the logical system corresponds to a relation between the numbers thus associated. In particular, if a set of formulae A, B, C is a proof of a formula D, then there will be a specific numerical relationship between the Gödel numbers of the four formulae. He then went on to construct a formula that could only have a proof in the system if the relevant Gödel numbers violated the laws of arithmetic. The formula must therefore be unprovable; yet Gödel could show, from outside the system, that it was a true formula. We might think to remedy this problem by adding the unprovable formula as an axiom to the system; but this will enable another, different, unprovable formula to be constructed, and so on ad infinitum. We have to conclude that arithmetic is incomplete and incompletable.

Even if a system is complete, it does not follow that there will always be a way of deciding whether or not a particular formula is valid. Production of a proof will of course prove that it is; but failure to produce a proof does not prove that it is invalid. For propositional calculus, there is such a decision procedure: the truth-table method will show whether something is or is not a tautology. Arithmetic, being incompletable, a fortiori is undecidable. But between propositional logic and arithmetic, what of first-order predicate logic, which Gödel had shown to be complete: is there a decision procedure there? The painstaking work of logicians showed that parts of the system were decidable, but that there can be no decision procedure for the entire calculus, nor can we give a satisfactory rubric to determine which parts are decidable and which are not.

Modern Modal Logic

Meanwhile, other logicians were studying a branch of logic that had been neglected since the Middle Ages, modal logic. Modal logic is the logic of the notions of necessity and possibility. Its study in modern times dates from the work of C. I. Lewis in 1918, who approached it via the theory of implication. What is it for a proposition *p* to imply a proposition *q*? Russell and Whitehead treated their horseshoe sign (the truth-functional 'if') as a sign of implication, on the grounds that 'If *p* and *p* → *q* then *q*' was a valid inference. But they realized that it was an odd form of implication—it entails, for instance, that any false proposition implies every proposition—and so they gave it the name of 'material implication'. Lewis insisted that the only genuine implication was strict implication: *p* implies *q* only if it is *impossible* that *p* should be true and *q* false. '*p* strictly implies *q*', he maintained, was equivalent to '*q* follows logically from *p*'. He drew up axiomatic systems in which the sign for material implication was replaced by a new sign to represent strict implication, and these systems were the first formal systems of modal logic. Strict implication struck many critics as being hardly less paradoxical than material implication, since an impossible proposition strictly implies every proposition, so that 'If cats are dogs then pigs can fly' comes out true.

Lewis's modal researches, however, were interesting in their own right. He offered five different axiom systems, which he numbered S1 to S5, and showed that each of the axiom sets was consistent and independent. They vary in strength. S1, for instance, does not allow a proof of 'If *p*&*q* is possible, then *p* is possible and *q* is possible' (which seems very plausible), while S5 contains 'If *p* is possible, then *p* is necessarily possible' (which seems rather dubious). In some ways the most interesting system is S4, which Gödel showed was equivalent to the logic of *Principia Mathematica* with the following additional axioms (reading 'if' as material, not strict, implication):

(1) If necessarily *p*, then *p*.
(2) If necessarily *p*, then (if necessarily [if *p* then *q*] then necessarily *q*).
(3) If necessarily *p*, then necessarily necessarily *p*.

He added also a rule, that if '*p*' was any thesis of the system, we can add also 'necessarily *p*'. The system exploits the interdefinability of necessity (which he represented by the symbol □) and possibility (represented by ◇). As was well known in antiquity and the Middle Ages, 'necessarily' can be defined as 'not possibly not' and 'possibly' as 'not necessarily not'.

There are many statements that can be formulated within modal logic about whose truth-value there is no consensus among logicians. The most contentious ones are those in which modal operators are iterated. The system that Gödel axiomatized, S4, contains as derivable theses the two following formulae:

If possibly possibly p, then possibly p
If necessarily p, then necessarily necessarily p

It does not, however, contain these two:

If possibly p, then necessarily possibly p
If possibly necessarily p, then necessarily p

which are provable in S5 and are characteristic features of that system. The relative merits of S4 and S5 as systems of modal logic remain a matter of debate today, and not only among logicians. Some philosophers of religion, for instance, have argued that if it is possible that a necessary being (i.e. God) exists, then a necessary being does exist. This involves a tacit appeal to the second of the S5 theses listed above.

There are a number of parallels between modal operators and the quantifiers of predicate logic. The interdefinability of 'necessary' and 'possible' parallels the interdefinability of 'all' and 'some'. Just as 'For all x, Fx' entails 'Fa', so 'Necessarily p' entails 'p', and just as 'Fa' entails 'For some x, Fx', so 'p' entails 'possibly p'. There are laws of distribution in modal logic that are the analogues of those in quantification theory: thus it is necessary that p and q if and only if it is both necessary that p and necessary that q, and it is possible that p or q if and only if it is either possible that p or it is possible that q. Because of this, if we introduce quantification into modal logic, and use modal operators and quantifiers together, we have a system that resembles double quantification.

In quantified modal logic it is important to mark the order in which the operators and quantifiers are placed. It is easily seen that 'For all x, x is possibly F' is not the same as 'It is possible that for all x, x is F': in a fair lottery, everyone has a chance of being the winner, but there is no chance that everyone is the winner. Likewise we must distinguish between 'There is something that necessarily Φs' and 'Necessarily, there is something that Φs'. It is true that of necessity there is someone than whom no one is more obese. However, that person is not necessarily so obese: it is perfectly possible for him to slim and cease to be a champion fatty. Sentences in which the modal operator precedes the quantifier (as in the second of each of the two pairs above) were called in the Middle Ages modals *de dicto*, and sentences in which the quantifier comes earlier (as in the first of each of the two pairs above) were called modals *de re*. These terms have been revived by modern modal logicians to make very similar distinctions.

Despite the parallels between modal logic and quantification theory there is also an important difference, once we introduce into the system the notion of identity. In the technical term introduced by Quine, modal logics are referentially opaque, whereas quantificational contexts are not. Referential opacity is defined as follows. Let E be a sentence of the form A = B (where A and B are referring expressions). Then if P is a sentence containing A, and Q is a sentence resembling P in all respects except that it contains B where P contains A, then P is referentially opaque if P and E do not together imply Q.

Modal contexts are easily seen to be opaque in this way. When Quine wrote, the number of planets was nine, but whereas 'Necessarily, 9 is greater than 7' is true, 'Necessarily, the number of planets is greater than 7' is not. Because of this opacity some logicians, notably Quine, rejected modal logic altogether. But the work of a number of logicians in the early 1960s—notably Føllesdal, Kripke, and Hintikka—made modal logic respectable.

The key idea of modern modal logic is to exploit the similarities between quantification and modality by defining necessity as truth in all possible worlds, and possibility as truth in some possible world. Plain truth is then thought of as truth in the actual world, which is one among all possible worlds. Talk of possible worlds need not involve any metaphysical implications: for the purposes of modal semantics any model with the appropriate formal structure will suffice.

To illustrate how the semantics is set out, consider a universe in which there are just two objects, *a* and *b*, and three predicates, *F*, *G*, and *H*, and let us suppose that there are three possible worlds in that universe of which world 2 is the actual one, which we may call alpha.

World 1	*Fa*	~*Ga*	~*Ha*	~*Fb*	*Gb*	*Hb*
World 2	*Fa*	~*Ga*	*Ha*	~*Fb*	*Gb*	~*Hb*
World 3	*Fa*	*Ga*	~*Ha*	*Fb*	*Gb*	*Hb*

If necessity is truth in all possible worlds, we have in this universe 'Necessarily *Fa*' and 'Necessarily *Gb*'. The thesis 'If necessarily *p*, then *p*' is exemplified by the truth of *Fa* and *Gb* in alpha, the actual world. If possibility is truth in some possible world we have, for example, 'Possibly *Fb*' and 'Possibly *Ga*', even though '*Fb*' and '*Ga*' are false in alpha.

The iteration of modalities, which as we saw gave rise to problems, is now explained in terms of a relationship to be defined between different possible worlds. One possible world may or may not be *accessible* from another. When we use a single operator, as in 'possibly *p*', we can be taken to be saying 'In some world beta, accessible from alpha, *p* is the case'. If we iterate, and say 'possibly possibly *p*', we mean 'In some world gamma, accessible from beta, which is accessible from alpha, *p* is the case'. It cannot be taken for granted that every world accessible from beta is also accessible from alpha: whether this is the case will depend on how the accessibility relation is defined. This, in turn, will determine which system—which, for instance, of Lewis's S1–S5—is the appropriate one for our purposes.

If the notions that we wish to capture in our modal logic are those of logical necessity and possibility, then every possible world will be accessible from every other possible world, since logic is universal and transcendent. But there are other forms of necessity and possibility. There is, for instance, epistemic necessity and possibility, where 'possibly *p*' means 'For all I know to the contrary, *p*'. Philosophers have also extended the notion of modality into many different contexts, where there are pairs of operators that behave in ways that resemble the paradigmatic modal operators. In the logic of time, for instance, 'always' corresponds to 'necessary' and 'sometimes' to 'possible', both pairs of operators being interdefinable with the aid of negation. In deontic logic, the logic of obligation, 'obligatory' is the necessity operator, and 'permitted' is the possibility operator. In these and other cases the accessibility relationship will need careful definition: in a logic of tenses, for instance, future worlds, but not past worlds, will be accessible from the actual (i.e. the present) world.[5]

The problem of referential opacity arises in all these broadly modal contexts. It can be dealt with by making a distinction between two different kinds of reference. To be a genuine name, a term must be, in the terminology of Kripke, a rigid designator: that is to say, it must have the same reference in every possible world. There are other expressions whose reference is determined by their sense (e.g. 'the discoverer of oxygen') and therefore may change from one possible world to another. Once this distinction has been made, it is easy to accept that a statement such as '9 = the number of the planets' is not a genuine identity statement linking two names. '9' is indeed a rigid designator that keeps its reference across possible worlds; but 'the number of the planets' is a description that in different worlds may refer to different numbers.

---

[5] The logic of time and tense was first studied systematically by A. N. Prior in *Time and Modality* (Oxford: Oxford University Press, 1957) and deontic logic by G. H. von Wright in *An Essay on Deontic Logic* (Amsterdam: North-Holland, 1968).

5

Language

In the course of the nineteenth century, philosophers turned their attention ever more intensely on the topic of meaning. What do words and sentences signify? How do they signify and do they all signify in the same way? What is the relationship between meaning and truth? These questions were now asked with an urgency that had not been felt since the Middle Ages.[1]

Frege on Sense and Reference

A seminal work in the theory of meaning was Frege's paper of 1892, 'Sense and Reference'. That paper starts from a question about statements of identity. Is identity a relation? If it is a relation, is it a relation between signs or between what signs stand for? It seems that it cannot be a relation between objects that signs stand for, because if so, when '$a = b$' is true then '$a = a$' cannot differ from '$a = b$'. On the other hand, it seems that it cannot be a relationship between signs, because names are arbitrary, and if a sentence of the form '$a = b$' expressed a relationship between symbols it could not express any fact about the extra-linguistic world. Yet a sentence such as 'The morning star is identical with the evening star' expresses not a linguistic tautology, but an astronomical discovery.

Frege solved this problem by distinguishing between two different kinds of signification. Where other philosophers talk of meaning, Frege introduces a distinction between the *reference* of an expression (the object to which it refers, as the planet Venus is the reference of 'the morning star') and the *sense* of an expression (the particular mode in which a sign presents what it designates). 'The evening star' differs in sense from 'the morning star' even though it has been discovered that both expressions refer to Venus. Frege says, in general, that an identity statement will be true and informative if the sign of identity is

---

[1] For medieval theories of meaning, see above, pp. 355–6, 367–8.

flanked by two names with the same reference but different senses. The word 'name' is, as the example shows, used by Frege in a broad sense to include complex designations of objects. He is prepared to call all such designations 'proper names' (*CP* 157–8).

Frege applies the distinction between sense and reference to sentences of all kinds. In his account of meaning there are items at three levels: signs, their senses, and their references. By using signs we express a sense and denote a reference (*CP* 161). In a well-regulated language, Frege believed, every sign would have a sense and only one sense. In natural languages words like 'bank' and 'port' are ambiguous, and a name like 'Aristotle' can be paraphrased in many different ways; we have to be content if the same word has the same sense in the same context. On the other hand, there is no requirement, even in an ideal language, that every sense should have only one sign. The same sense may be expressed by different signs in different languages or even in the same language. In a good translation, the sense of the original text is preserved. What is lost in translation is what Frege calls 'the colour' of the text. Colour is important for poetry but not for logic; it is not objective in the way that sense is.

The sense of a word is what we grasp when we understand the word. It is quite different from a mental image, even though, if a sign refers to a tangible object, I may well have a mental image associated with it. Images are subjective and vary from person to person; an image is *my* image or *your* image. The sense of a sign, on the other hand, is something that is the common property of all users of the language. It is because senses are public in this way that thoughts can be passed on from one generation to another.

For Frege, it is not only proper names—simple or complex—that have senses and references. What of entire sentences, which express thoughts? Is the thought, that is to say the content of the sentence, its sense or its reference?

> Let us assume for the time being that the sentence has reference. If we now replace one word of the sentence by another having the same reference, but a different sense, this can have no bearing upon the reference of the sentence. Yet we can see that in such a case the thought changes; since e.g. the thought in the sentence 'The morning star is a body illuminated by the Sun' differs from that in the sentence 'The evening star is a body illuminated by the Sun'. Anybody who did not know that the evening star is the morning star might hold the one thought to be true, the other false. The thought, accordingly, cannot be the reference of the sentence, but must rather be considered as the sense. (*CP* 162)

If the thought expressed by a sentence is not its reference, does the sentence have a reference at all? Frege agrees that there can be sentences lacking reference: sentences occurring in works of fiction such as the *Odyssey*. But the reason these sentences lack a reference is that they contain names that lack a reference, such as 'Odysseus'. Other sentences do have a reference; and consideration of fictional sentences will enable us to determine just what that reference is.

We must expect that the reference of a sentence is determined by the reference of the parts of a sentence. Let us inquire, therefore, what is missing from a sentence if one of its parts lacks a reference. If a name lacks a reference, that does not affect the thought, since that is determined only by the sense of its constituent parts, not by their reference. It is only if we treat the *Odyssey* as science rather than myth, if we want seriously to take the sentences it contains as true or false, that we need to ascribe a reference to 'Odysseus'. 'Why do we want every proper name to have not only a sense, but also a reference? Why is the thought not enough for us? Because, and to the extent that, we are concerned with its truth-value' (*CP* 163). We are, Frege says, driven into accepting as the reference of a sentence its truth-value, the True, or as the case may be, the False. Every seriously propounded indicative sentence is a name of one or other of these objects. All true sentences have the same reference as each other, and so do all false sentences.

The relation, then, between a sentence and its truth-value is the same as that between a name and its reference. This is a surprising conclusion: surely, to assert that pigs have wings is to do something quite different from naming anything. Frege would agree; but that is because asserting a sentence is something quite different from putting a sentence together out of subject and predicate. 'Subject and predicate (understood in the logical sense) are indeed elements of thought; they stand on the same level as items for comprehension. By combining subject and predicate one reaches only a thought, never passes from sense to reference, never from a thought to its truth value' (*CP* 164). Sentences can occur unasserted, perhaps as a clause in a conditional, such as 'If pigs have wings, then pigs can fly'. Though every serious sentence names a truth-value (in this case the False) the mere use of a sentence does not commit the user to specifying its truth-value. Only if we assert a sentence do we *say that* it is a name of the True.

Many philosophers since Frege have made use of his distinction between sense and reference, and have accepted that there is an important difference between predication and assertion; but almost all have rejected the notion that complete sentences have a reference of any kind. Indeed, in his own later writings Frege himself seems to have given up the idea that there were two grand objects, the True and the False; instead, he came to accept that truth was not an object but a property, albeit one of an indefinable, *sui generis* kind (*CP* 353).

Towards the end of his life Frege became more interested in aspects of language that were not captured by his system of logic—the 'colouring' in the expression of thoughts. Scientific language as it were presents thoughts in black and white; but in humane disciplines sentences may clothe thoughts in colourful garb, with expressions of feeling. We interject words and phrases like 'Alas!' or 'Thank God!' and we use charged words like 'cur' instead of plain words like 'dog'. Such features of sentences are not concerns of logic because they do not affect their truth-value. A statement containing the word 'cur' in place of 'dog' does not become false merely because the person uttering it does not feel the hostility that the word expresses (*PW* 140).

In his paper 'The Thought' Frege considered the features of language represented by the tenses of verbs, and by indexical expressions such as 'today', 'here', and 'I'. If a sentence contains a present-tense verb, as in 'It is snowing', then in order to grasp the thought expressed you need to know when the sentence was uttered. Something similar happens with the use of the first-person pronoun. 'I am hungry' said by Peter expresses a different thought than is expressed by 'I am hungry' said by Paul. One thought may be true and the other false. So one and the same sentence may, in different contexts, express a different thought. The opposite may also happen, according to Frege. If on 9 December I say 'It was snowing yesterday' I express the same thought as if on 8 December I say 'It is snowing today'. It was left to logicians of a later generation to try to incorporate such complications into formal systems.

The Pragmatists on Language and Truth

Charles Sanders Peirce, who had developed quantificational theory independently of Frege, likewise expressed, in a different terminology, many of Frege's insights into philosophy of language. Both philosophers rejected the traditional way of distinguishing between subject and predicate, and analysed propositions into elements of two kinds, one a complete symbol (the *arguments* in Frege's *Begriffsschrift*) and the other an incomplete, or unsaturated, symbol (the *functions* of *Begriffsschrift*). The proper names that Frege called 'arguments' Peirce called 'indices', and Frege's concept expressions or functions were called by Peirce 'icons'. For Peirce a particularly important class of icons was expressions for relations. 'In the statement of a relationship,' he wrote, 'the designations of the correlates ought to be considered as so many logical subjects and the relative itself as the predicate.' In his treatment of sentences concerning two-place relationships such as 'John loves Mary' Peirce differed little from Frege. However, he extended the notion of relationship in two directions, by considering what he called the 'valency' (i.e. the number of arguments) of different relations. He was interested in particular in three-place relationships (such as 'John gave Fido to Mary'); and in addition to 'polyadic' relationships with two or more subjects, he introduced the term 'monadic relationship' for ordinary one-place predicates such as '... is wise' He was even willing to call a complete proposition a 'medadic relation'—that is, a relative proposition with zero (in Greek *meden*) unsaturated places.

Peirce's logic and theory of language was embedded in a general theory of signs, which he called 'semiotics', and to which he attached great importance. A sign stands for an object by being understood or interpreted by an intelligent being; the interpretation is itself a further sign. Peirce calls the external sign a 'representamen' and the sign as understood 'the interpretant'. The semiotic function of signs is a triadic relation between representamen, object, and interpretant.

Peirce classified signs into three classes. There are natural signs: clouds, for instance, are a natural sign of rain, and stripped bark on a tree may be a sign of the presence of deer. Next, there are iconic signs, which signify by resembling their objects. Naturalistic paintings and sculptures are the most obvious examples, but there are others such as maps. Two features are essential to an iconic sign: (1) it should share with its object some feature that each could have if the other did not exist; (2) the method of interpreting this feature should be fixed by convention. Finally, there are symbols, of which words are the most important example, but which include such things as uniforms and traffic signals. These, like iconic signs, are determined by convention, but unlike iconic signs they do not operate by exploiting any resemblance to their objects.

Since Peirce, theorists have divided semiotics into three disciplines: syntactics, the study of grammar and whatever may underlie grammatical structure; semantics, the study of the relationship between language and reality; and pragmatics, the study of the social context and the purposes and consequences of communication. Peirce's own work operated at the interface of all three disciplines; but in the work of his followers, despite their school title of 'pragmatists', discussion focused upon two key concepts of semantics, namely meaning and truth.

Peirce and James explained meaning in similar ways: in order to discover what an utterance meant you had to explore what would be the practical consequences of its being true, and if there was no difference between the consequences of two different beliefs then they were in effect the same belief. But James maintained that the truth of a belief, and not just its meaning, depended on its consequences, or rather on the consequences of believing it. If my believing that p is something that pays in the long run, something whose overall consequence is profitable for my life, then p is true for me. The pragmatist's claim, he tells us, is this:

Truth, concretely considered, is an attribute of our beliefs, and these are attitudes that follow satisfactions. The ideas around which the satisfactions cluster are primarily only hypotheses that challenge or summon a belief to come and take its stand upon them. The pragmatist's idea of truth is just such a challenge. He finds it ultra-satisfactory to accept it, and takes his own stand accordingly. (T 199)

Pragmatism, he claimed, was not at all inconsistent with realism. Truth and reality are not the same as each other; truth is something known, thought, or said about the reality. Indeed, the notion of a reality independent of any believer, James said, was at the base of the pragmatist definition of truth. Any statement, to be counted true, must agree with some such reality.

Pragmatism defines 'agreeing' to mean certain ways of 'working', be they actual or potential. Thus, for my statement 'the desk exists' to be true of a desk recognized as real by you, it must be able to lead me to shake your desk, to explain myself by words that suggest that desk to your mind, to make a drawing that is like the desk you see, etc. Only in such ways as this is there sense in saying it agrees with *that* reality, only thus does it gain for me the satisfaction of hearing you corroborate me. (*T* 218)

Passages like this suggest that pragmatism adds to, rather than subtracts from, the common-sense notion of truth. For '*p*' to be true, it appears, not only must it be the case that *p*, but it must actually have been verified, or at least verifiable, that *p* is the case. To an objector who protested that when a belief is true, its object does exist, James retorted, 'it is *bound* to exist, on sound pragmatic principles'. How is the world made different for me, he asked, by my conceiving an opinion of mine as true? 'First, an object must be findable there (or sure signs of such an object must be found) which shall agree with the opinion. Second, such an opinion must not be contradicted by anything else I am aware of' (*T* 275).

But in spite of his bluff, sleeves-rolled-up, manner of speech, James was rather a slippery writer, and it is quite difficult to pin him down on the question whether a proposition can be true without any fact to correspond to it. He tries to avoid the question by making the notion of truth a relative one. In human life, he tells us, the word 'truth' can only be used 'relatively to some particular trower'. Critics objected that there were some truths (say, about the pre-human past) that nobody would ever know; to which James replied that these, though never actual objects of knowledge, were always possible objects of knowledge, and in defining truth we should surely give priority to the real over the merely virtual. But there is another, more serious, objection to his claim that truth is relative to the truth-claimer. Surely if I hold that *p* is true, and you hold that not-*p* is true, it is a genuine question which of us is in the right.

Russell's Theory of Descriptions

One of James's earliest and most trenchant critics was Bertrand Russell, who attacked the pragmatist account of truth in an article of 1908 entitled 'Transatlantic Truth'. 'According to the pragmatists', he wrote, 'to say "it is true that other people exist" means "it is useful to believe that other people exist". But if so, then these two phrases are merely different words for the same proposition; therefore when I believe the one I believe the other' (James, *T* 278). But, Russell claimed, one proposition could be true and the other false; and in general it was often much easier in practice to find out whether *p* was true than whether it was good to believe that *p*. 'It is far easier', Russell wrote, 'to settle the plain question of fact "Have popes always been infallible?" than to settle the question whether the effects of thinking them infallible are on the whole good' (James, *T* 273).

In the years leading up to *Principia Mathematica*, however, Russell's philosophical interests were focused less on the nature of truth than on the different kinds of meaning that words and phrases might have, and also the possible ways in which they might turn out to lack meaning. When he wrote *The Principles of Mathematics* he had a very simple view of meaning which led to a very catholic view of being, reminiscent of Parmenides.[2]

Being is that which belongs to every conceivable term, to every possible object of thought—in short to everything that can possibly occur in any proposition, true or false, and to all such propositions themselves. . . . 'A is not' must always be either false or meaningless. For if A were nothing it could not be said not to be; 'A is not' implies that there is a term A whose being is denied, and hence that A is. Thus, unless 'A is not' be an empty sound, it must be false—whatever A may be, it certainly is. Numbers, the Homeric gods, relations, chimeras and four-dimensional spaces all have being, for if they were not entities of a kind, we could make no propositions about them. Thus being is a general attribute of everything, and to mention anything is to show that it is. (*PM* 449)

It was not long before he began to believe that a system that made distinctions between different ways in which signs might signify was more credible than one in which the world contained a profusion of different kinds of object all related to symbols by a single simple relation of denotation. He soon, for instance, adopted Frege's method of dealing with assertions and denials of existence. As he was to put it in *Principia Mathematica*:

Suppose we say 'The round square does not exist'. It seems plain that this is a true proposition, yet we cannot regard it as denying the existence of a certain object called 'the round square'. For if there were such an object, it would exist: we cannot first assume that there is a certain object, and then proceed to deny that there is such an object. Whenever the grammatical subject of a proposition can be supposed not to exist without rendering the proposition meaningless, it is plain that the grammatical subject is not a proper name, i.e. not a name directly representing some object. Thus in all such cases the proposition must be capable of being so analysed that what was the grammatical subject shall have disappeared. Thus when we say 'The round square does not exist' we may, as a first attempt at such analysis, substitute 'it is false that there is an object x which is both round and square'. (*PM*, 2nd edn., 66)

Russell continued to believe that any genuine proper name must stand for something, must 'directly represent some object'. But he thought that not all apparent names were genuine names. For instance, he thought that Frege was wrong to treat 'Aristotle' and 'the tutor of Alexander' as being the same kind of symbol, each a name with a sense and a reference. If 'Aristotle' was a genuine proper name, he maintained, it did not have a sense, but had meaning solely by having a reference. On the other hand an expression like 'the tutor of Alexander' was not a name at all, because unlike a genuine name it had parts that were symbols in their own right. Russell's positive account of such expressions is called his *theory of definite descriptions*; it was first put forward in his paper 'On Denoting' of 1905.

---

[2] See above, pp. 161–5.

Consider the sentence 'The author of *Hamlet* was a genius'. For this to be true, it must be the case that one and only one individual wrote *Hamlet* (otherwise no one has the right to be called '*the* author of *Hamlet*'). So Russell proposed to analyse the sentence into three elements, thus:

For some *x*, (1) *x* wrote *Hamlet*
  and (2) For all *y*, if *y* wrote *Hamlet*, *y* is identical with *x*
  and (3) *x* was a genius.

The first element says that at least one individual wrote *Hamlet*, and the second that at most one individual wrote *Hamlet*. Having thus established that exactly one individual wrote *Hamlet*, the analysed sentence uses the third element to go on to say that that unique individual was a genius. In the unanalysed sentence 'the author of *Hamlet*' looks like a complex name, and would have been treated as one in Frege's system. As analysed by Russell no such nominal expression appears, and instead we have a combination of predicates and quantifiers. The analysis is meant to apply not only when—as in this case—there actually is an object that answers to the definite description, but also when the description is a vacuous one, such as 'the present King of France'. A sentence such as 'The King of France is bald', when analysed along Russellian lines, turns out to be false.

Consider the following two sentences:

(1) The sovereign of the United Kingdom is male.
(2) The sovereign of the United States is male.

Neither of these sentences is true, but the reason differs in the two cases. The first sentence is plain false, because though there is a sovereign of the United Kingdom she is female; the second fails to be true because the United States has no sovereign ruler. On Russell's analysis this sentence is not just untrue but positively false, and accordingly its negation, 'It is not the case that the sovereign of the United States is male', is true. (On the other hand 'The sovereign of the United States is not male' comes out, like the second sentence above, positively false.)

What is the point of this complicated analysis? It is natural to think that since there is no sovereign of the United States, sentence (2) is not so much false as misleading; the question of its truth-value does not arise. This is no doubt true of our use of such definite descriptions in ordinary language, but Frege and Russell aimed to construct a language that would be a more precise instrument than ordinary language for the purposes of logic and mathematics. They both regarded it as essential that such a language should contain only expressions with a definite sense, by which they meant that all sentences containing the expressions should have a truth-value. If we allow into our system sentences lacking a truth-value, then inference and deduction become impossible.

Frege proposed to avoid truth-value gaps by various arbitrary stipulations. Russell's analysis, whereby 'the sovereign of X' is in no case a referring expression at all, achieves the definiteness that he and Frege both sought, and does so by far less artificial means. It is easy enough to recognize that 'the round square' denotes nothing, because it is an obviously self-contradictory expression. But prior to investigation it may not be at all clear whether some complicated mathematical formula contains a hidden contradiction. And if it does so, we shall not be able to discover this by logical investigation (e.g. by deriving a *reductio ad absurdum*) unless sentences containing it are assured of a truth-value.

The Picture Theory of the Proposition

In the *Tractatus Logico-Philosophicus* Wittgenstein built upon Russell's theory of descriptions in order to analyse the descriptions of complex objects. 'Every statement about complexes', he wrote, 'can be resolved into a statement about their constituents and into the propositions that describe the complexes completely.' Consider the following sentence (not one of Wittgenstein's own examples):

Austria-Hungary is allied to Russia.

That sentence was untrue when Wittgenstein wrote the *Tractatus* because Austria-Hungary was at war with Russia. It is not true now for a quite different reason, because the political unit called 'Austria-Hungary' no longer exists. If we follow the lead of Russell, we will say that in both cases the sentence is meaningful but false. The two possibilities of falsehood are clearly parallel to those for 'The sovereign of X is male'. 'Austria-Hungary' can be looked on as a definite description, roughly, 'the union of Austria and Hungary'.

If we follow Wittgenstein and analyse the sentence on the lines of Russell's theory, we get:

For some x and some y, $x =$ Austria
and $y =$ Hungary
and x is united to y
and x is allied to Russia
and y is allied to Russia.

Or more simply we can say that 'Austria-Hungary is allied to Russia' means 'Austria is allied to Russia and Hungary is allied to Russia, and Austria is united to Hungary'. In the *Tractatus* Wittgenstein built a great deal of metaphysics on the possibility of analysis of this kind. But in philosophy of language, he wrote,

'Russell's merit is to have shown that the apparent logical form of a proposition need not be its real form.'

When he wrote the *Tractatus* Wittgenstein believed that language disguised the structure of thought beyond recognition. It was the task of philosophy to uncover, by analysis, the naked form of thought beneath the drapery of ordinary language. Complex propositions were to be reduced to elementary propositions, and elementary propositions would be revealed as pictures of reality. Wittgenstein recorded in his diary on 29 September 1914 how the idea first dawned on him that propositions were essentially pictorial in nature:

The general concept of the proposition carries with it a quite general concept of the coordination of proposition and situation. The solution to all my questions must be extremely simple. In a proposition a world is as it were put together experimentally. (As when in the law-court in Paris a motor-car accident is represented by means of dolls, etc.) This must yield the nature of truth straight away. (*NB* 7)

The thesis that a proposition is a picture is not so implausible when we realize that Wittgenstein counted as pictures not only paintings, drawings, and photographs, and not only three-dimensional models, but also such things as maps, musical scores, and gramophone records. His picture theory is perhaps best regarded as a theory of representation in general.

In any representation there are two things to consider: (*a*) what it is a representation *of*; (*b*) whether it represents it correctly or incorrectly. The distinction between these two features of a representation, in the case of a proposition, is the distinction between what the proposition *means*, and whether what it means is true or false—the distinction between sense and truth-value.

If, in a law court, a toy lorry and a toy pram are to represent a collision between a lorry and a pram, several things are necessary. First, the toy lorry must go proxy for the real lorry, and the toy pram for the real pram: the elements of the model must stand in for the elements of the situation to be represented. This is called by Wittgenstein the pictorial relationship that makes the picture a picture (*TLP* 2. 1514). Second, the elements of the model must be related to each other in a particular way. The positioning of the toy lorry and the toy pram represents the spatial relationship at the time of the accident, in a way in which it would not if the toys had simply been stowed away together in a cupboard. This, for Wittgenstein, is the *structure* of the picture (*TLP* 2. 15). Every picture, then, consists of structure plus pictorial relationship.

The relationship between the toys in court is a fact, and this led Wittgenstein to say that a picture, a proposition, is a fact and not a mere collection of objects or names. It is a fact that could have been otherwise. The possibility of structure—in the case of the toys in court, their three-dimensionality—is called by Wittgenstein pictorial form. Pictorial form is what pictures have in common with what they picture, the common element that enables one to be a picture of the other at all. Thus, a picture represents a possibility in the real world (*TLP* 2. 161).

How does the picture connect with the reality it represents? This is done by the choice of an object qua object with a certain pictorial form. If I select a set of toys as three-dimensional proxies for three-dimensional objects, I at the same time make their three-dimensional properties the pictorial form of the picture. I make the connection with reality by making the correlation between the elements of the picture and the elements of the situation it is to represent. How do I make this correlation? When he wrote the *Tractatus* Wittgenstein thought this was an empirical matter of no importance to philosophy.

Pictures can be more or less abstract, more or less like what they picture: their pictorial form can be more or less rich. The minimum that is necessary if a picture is to be able to portray a situation is called by Wittgenstein logical form (*TLP* 2. 18). The elements of the picture must be capable of combining with each other in a pattern corresponding to the relationship of the elements of what is pictured. Thus, for instance, in a musical score the ordering of the notes on the page from left to right represents the ordering of the sounds in time. The spatial arrangements of the notes is not part of the pictorial form, since the sounds are not in space; but the ordering is common to both, and that is what is logical form.

Wittgenstein applied his general theory of representation to thoughts and to propositions. A logical picture of a fact, he said, is a thought, and in the proposition a thought is expressed in a manner perceptible to the senses (*TLP* 3. 32). Though, in the *Tractatus*, thoughts are prior to propositions and give life to propositions, Wittgenstein has much less to tell us about thoughts than about propositions, and in order to understand him it is better to focus on propositions as pictures than on thoughts as pictures. If we ask what are the elements of thoughts, for instance, we are given no clear answer; but if we ask what are the elements of propositions an answer immediately presents itself: names.

Indeed the picture theory of the propositions grew out of Wittgenstein's reflections on the difference between propositions and names. For Frege names and propositions alike had both sense and reference, the reference of a proposition being a truth-value. But, as Wittgenstein came to see, there is an important contrast between the relation between names and what they refer to, on the one hand, and propositions and what they refer to, on the other. To understand a proper name, like 'Bismarck', I must know to whom or what it refers; but I can understand a proposition without knowing whether it is true or false. What we understand, when we understand a proposition, is not its reference but its sense. A name can have only one relationship to reality: it either names something or it is not a significant symbol at all. But a proposition has a two-way relation: it does not cease to have a meaning when it ceases to be true (*TLP* 3. 144).

So, to understand a name is to grasp its reference; to understand a proposition is to grasp its sense. There is a further difference between names and propositions consequent on this first difference. The reference of a name has to be explained to one; but to understand the sense of a proposition no explanation is necessary. A proposition can communicate a new sense with old words: we can understand a proposition that we have never heard before and whose truth-value we do not know. It is this fact to which Wittgenstein appeals when he asserts that a proposition is a picture.

What Wittgenstein meant by calling a proposition a picture can be summed up in nine theses:

(1) A proposition, unlike a name, is essentially composite. (*TLP* 4. 032)
(2) The elements of a proposition are correlated by human decision with elements of reality. (*TLP* 3. 315)
(3) The combination of these elements into a proposition presents—without further human intervention—a possible situation or state of affairs. (*TLP* 4. 026)
(4) A proposition stands in an essential relation to the possible situation it represents: it shares its logical structure. (*TLP* 4. 03)
(5) This relationship can only be shown, but not said, because logical form can only be mirrored, not represented. (*TLP* 4. 022)
(6) Every proposition is bipolar: it is either true or false. (*TLP* 3. 144)
(7) A proposition is true or false by agreeing or disagreeing with reality: it is true if the possible situation it depicts obtains in fact, and false if it does not. (*TLP* 4. 023)
(8) A proposition must be independent of the actual situation, which, if it obtains, makes it true; otherwise it could never be false. (*TLP* 3. 13)
(9) No proposition is a priori true. (*TLP* 3. 05)

In stating these theses I have not used the word 'picture', because the theory is interesting and important whether or not it is misleading to encapsulate it in the slogan 'A proposition is a picture'. Wittgenstein did in fact believe that all the theorems remain true if for 'proposition' one substitutes the word 'picture'. He was also well aware that propositions do not look like pictures. But he believed that if a proposition were fully articulated and written out in an ideal language, then to each element of the propositional sign would correspond a single object in the world. Thus its pictorial nature would leap to the eye (*TLP* 3. 2).

We should not think, however, that there is anything wrong with the unanalysed sentences we utter in ordinary life. Wittgenstein insists that all the propositions of our everyday language, just as they stand, are in perfect logical order (*TLP* 5. 5563). That is because the full analysis of them is already present in the thought of any of us who understand them, although of course we are no more conscious of how our words symbolize than we are of how our sounds are produced (*TLP* 4. 002).

Not all sentences produced by English speakers, however, are genuine propositions: many are only pseudo-propositions which analysis would reveal to lack sense. The last seventeen pages of the *Tractatus* are devoted to a brisk demonstration of how the propositions of logic (6. 1 ff.), mathematics (6. 2 ff.), a priori science (6. 3 ff.), ethics and aesthetics (6. 4 ff.), and finally philosophy (6. 5 ff.) are all in different ways pseudo-propositions.

The only propositions that deserve a place in logic books are tautologies, which say nothing themselves but simply exhibit the logical properties of genuine propositions, which do say things (*TLP* 6. 121). Mathematics consists of equations, but equations are concerned not with reality but only with the substitutability of signs. In real life we make use of mathematical propositions only in passing from one non-mathematical proposition to another (*TLP* 6. 2–3). In science, propositions such as the axioms of Newtonian mechanics are not really propositions; rather, they are expressions of insights into the forms in which genuine scientific propositions can be cast (*TLP* 6. 32 ff.).

In ethics and aesthetics, likewise, there are no genuine propositions. No proposition can express the meaning of the world or of life, because all propositions are contingent—they have true–false poles—and no genuine value can be a contingent matter (*TLP* 6. 41). Finally, the propositions of philosophy itself fall under the axe. Philosophy is not a corpus of propositions but an activity, the activity of analysis. Applied to the propositions of everyday life, philosophy gives them a clear meaning; applied to pseudo-propositions it reveals them as nonsensical. The propositions of the *Tractatus* itself are meaningless because they are attempts to say what can only be shown. This, however, does not make them useless, because their very failure is instructive.

My propositions serve as elucidations in the following way: anyone who understands me eventually recognizes them as nonsensical, when he has used them as steps to climb up beyond them. (He must, so to speak, throw away the ladder after he has climbed up it.) He must transcend these propositions, and then he will see the world aright. (*TLP* 6. 54)

Language-Games and Private Languages

When he returned to philosophy in the 1920s and 1930s, Wittgenstein retained the idea that philosophy was an activity, not a theory, and that philosophical pronouncements were not propositions in the same sense as statements of everyday language. But he came to have a very different view of how ordinary propositions had meaning. Early and late, he believed that ordinary language was in order just as it stood. At the time of the *Tractatus*, however, he believed this because he thought ordinary language was underpinned by a perfect language articulated into logical atoms. From the *Philosophische Grammatik* onwards he believed this because he thought ordinary language was embedded in the social activities and structures that he called 'language-games'.

What is it, he asked in the *Grammatik*, that gives significance to the sounds and marks on paper that make up language? By themselves the symbols seem inert and dead; what is it that gives them life (*PG* 40, 107; *PI* 1. 430)? The obvious answer is that they become alive by being meant by speakers and writers and understood by hearers and readers. This obvious answer is the true one; but we must get clear what meaning and understanding are. They are not, as one might think, mental processes that accompany spoken sentences. If you are tempted to think this, try to perform that process without the speaking. 'Make the following experiment,' says Wittgenstein; '*say* "It's cold here" and *mean* "it's warm here". Can you do it? and what are you doing as you do it?' (*PI* 1. 332, 510).

If you try to perform an act of meaning without uttering the appropriate sentence, you are likely to find yourself reciting the sentence itself under your breath. But of course it would be absurd to suggest that simultaneously with every public utterance of a sentence there is also a *sotto voce* one. It would take skill to ensure that the two processes were exactly in synchrony—and how disastrous it would be if they got out of step so that the meaning of a word got wrongly attached to its neighbour!

It is true that when we hear a sentence in a language we know, there are mental events—feelings, images, etc.—that differ from those that occur when we hear a sentence in a language we do not know. But these experiences will vary from case to case, and cannot be regarded as themselves constituting the understanding. Understanding cannot really be thought of as a process at all. Wittgenstein asks:

When do we understand a sentence? When we have uttered the whole of it? Or while we are uttering it? Is the understanding an articulated process like the speaking of the sentence; and does its articulation correspond to the articulation of the sentence? Or is it non-articulated, accompanying the sentence in the way in which a pedal point accompanies a melody? (*PG* 50)

Understanding language, like knowing how to play chess, is a state rather than a process; but we should not think of it as a state of some hidden mental mechanism.

Sometimes we are tempted to think that the conscious operations of our mind are the outcome of a mental process at a level lower than that of introspection. Perhaps, we think, our mental mechanism operates too swiftly for us to be able to follow all its movements, like the pistons of a steam engine or the blades of a lawn mower. If only we could sharpen our faculty for introspection, or get the machinery to run in slow motion, we might then be able actually to observe the processes of meaning and understanding.

According to one version of the mental-mechanism doctrine, to understand the meaning of a word is to call up an appropriate image in connection with it. I am told 'Bring me a red flower' and according to this story I have to have a red image in my mind, and ascertain what colour flower to bring by comparing it with this image. But that cannot be right: otherwise how could one obey the order 'Imagine a red patch'? The theory sets us off on an endless regress (*BB* 3; *PG* 96).

Suppose we replace the alleged inspection of an image with the actual inspection of a red bit of paper. Surely, the greater vividness of the sample will make it even more explanatory! But no: if it is to be explained how someone knows what 'red' means it is equally to be explained how he knows that his sample—whether mental or physical—is red. 'As soon as you think', Wittgenstein says, 'of replacing the mental image by, say, a painted one, and as soon as the image thereby loses its occult character, it ceases to seem to impart any life to the sentence at all' (*BB* 5). Of course, it is true that often as we talk mental images pass through our minds. But it is not they that confer meanings on the words we use. It is rather the other way round: the images are like the pictures illuminating a written text in a book.

One of the most important versions of the mistaken theory that meaning is a mental process is the thesis that naming is a mental act. This idea is the target of one of the most important sections of the *Philosophical Investigations*: the attack on the notion of a private language, or more precisely, of the notion of private ostensive definition.

In the epistemology of Russell and the logical positivists, ostensive definition played a crucial role: it was where language linked up with knowledge by acquaintance. But Wittgenstein insists that acquaintance with the object for which a word stands is not the same thing as knowledge of the word's meaning. Acquaintance with the object will not suffice without a grasp of the role in language of the word to be defined. Suppose I explain the word 'tove' by pointing to a pencil and saying 'This is called "tove"'. The explanation would be quite inadequate, because I may be taken to mean 'This is a pencil' or 'This is round' or 'This is wood' and so on (*PG* 60; *BB* 2). To name something it is not sufficient to confront it and to utter a sound: the asking and giving of names is something that can be done only in the context of a language-game.

This is so even in the relatively simple case of naming a colour or a material object; matters are much more complicated when we consider the names of mental events and states, such as sensations and thoughts. Consider the way in which the word 'pain' functions as the name of a sensation. We are tempted to think that for each person 'pain' acquires its meaning by being correlated by him with his own private, incommunicable sensation. But Wittgenstein showed that no word could acquire meaning in this way. One of his arguments runs as follows.

Suppose that I want to keep a diary about the occurrence of a certain sensation, and that I associate the sensation with the sign 'S'. It is essential to the supposition that no definition of the sign can be given in terms of our ordinary language, because otherwise the language would not be a private one. The sign must be defined for me alone, and this by a private ostensive definition. 'I speak, or write the sign down and at the same time I concentrate my attention on the sensation . . . in this way I impress on myself the connection between the sign and the sensation' (*PI* I. 258).

Wittgenstein argues that no such ceremony could establish an appropriate connection. When next I call something 'S', how will I know what I mean by 'S'? The problem is not that I may misremember and call something 'S' which is not S; the trouble goes deeper. Even to think *falsely* that something is S, I must know the meaning of 'S', and this, Wittgenstein argues, is impossible in a private language. But can I not appeal to memory to settle the meaning? No, for to do so I must call up the right memory, the memory of S, and in order to do that I must already know what 'S' means. There is in the end no way of making out a difference between correct and incorrect use of 'S', and that means that talk of 'correctness' is out of place. The private definition I have given to myself is no real definition.

The upshot of Wittgenstein's argument is that there cannot be a language whose words refer to what can only be known to the individual speaker of the language. The English word 'pain' is not a word in a private language because, whatever philosophers may say, other people can very often know when a person is in pain. It is not by private ostensive definition that 'pain' becomes the name of a sensation; pain-language is grafted on to the pre-linguistic expression of pain when the parents teach a baby to replace her initial cries with a conventional, learned expression through language.

What is the point of the private language argument, and who is it directed against? Wittgenstein once wrote that philosophical therapy is directed against the philosopher in each of us. It is quite plausible to propose that each of us, when we begin to philosophize, implicitly believe in a private language. Certainly, many first-year students are tempted by the sceptical suggestion. 'For all we know, what I call "red" you call "green" and vice versa.' This suggestion was at the root of Schlick's distinction between form and content in protocol sentences, and the whole edifice of logical positivism tumbles down if a private language is impossible. So too do the epistemologies of Russell and of the earlier Wittgenstein himself.

But the scope of the private language argument extends much further back in the history of philosophy. Descartes, in expressing his philosophical doubt, assumes that my language has meaning while the existence of my own and other bodies remains uncertain. Hume thought it possible for thoughts and experiences to be recognized and classified while the existence of the external world is held in suspense. Mill and Schopenhauer, in different ways, thought that a man could express the contents of his mind in language while questioning the existence of other minds. All of these suppositions are essential to the structure of the philosophy in question, and all of them require the possibility of a private language.

Both empiricism and idealism entail that the mind has no direct knowledge of anything but its own contents. The history of both movements shows that they lead in the direction of solipsism, the doctrine 'Only I exist'. Wittgenstein's attack on private definition undercuts solipsism by showing that the possibility of the very language in which it is expressed depends on the existence of the public and social world. The destruction of solipsism carries over into a refutation of the empiricism and idealism that inexorably involve it.

Wittgenstein's demolition of the notion of a private language was the most significant event in the philosophy of language in the twentieth century. After his death, philosophy of language took a different turn because of differing conceptions of the nature of philosophy itself. Wittgenstein had made a sharp distinction between science, which is concerned with the acquisition of new information, and philosophy, which sought to provide understanding of what we already know. But Quine's attack on the traditional distinction between analytic and synthetic propositions led many philosophers, particularly in the United States, to question whether there was a sharp boundary between philosophy and empirical science.

In particular, there was a drive to amalgamate the philosophy of language with psychology and linguistics. This was spearheaded from the philosophical side by Donald Davidson in the quest of a systematic theory of meaning for natural languages, and from the side of linguistics by Noam Chomsky with successive theories postulating hidden mechanisms underlying the acquisition of everyday grammar. In my view, Wittgenstein was correct in seeing the task of philosophy as completely different from that of empirical science, and many developments in the philosophy of language in the latter part of the twentieth century served to obscure, rather than to enrich, the insights that had been gained in its earlier decades.

6

Epistemology

Two Eloquent Empiricists

Mill described his *System of Logic* as a textbook of the doctrine that derives all knowledge from experience. He was, therefore, a proponent of empiricism, though he did not like the term. Indeed, in an important respect, he was one of the most resolute empiricists there have ever been. He went beyond his predecessors in claiming that not only all science, but also all mathematics, derived from experience. The axioms of geometry and the first principles of mathematics are, he says, 'notwithstanding all appearances to the contrary, results of observations and experiences, founded, in short, on the evidence of the senses' (*SL* 3. 24. 4).

The definition of each number, Mill maintained, involves the assertion of a physical fact.

Each of the numbers two, three, four &c., denotes physical phenomena, and connotes a physical property of those phenomena. Two, for instance, denotes all pairs of things, and twelve all dozens of things, connoting what makes them pairs or dozens; and that which makes them so is something physical; since it cannot be denied that two apples are physically distinguishable from three apples, two horses from one horse, and so forth: that they are a different visible and tangible phenomenon. (*SL* 3. 24. 5)

He does not make clear exactly what the property is that is connoted by the name of a number, and he admits that the senses find some difficulty in distinguishing between 102 horses and 103 horses, however easy it may be to tell two horses from three. Nonetheless, there is a property connoted by numbers, namely, the characteristic manner in which the agglomeration is made up, and may be separated into parts. For instance, collections of objects exist, which while they impress the senses thus ∴ may be separated into two parts thus .. .'This proposition being granted, we term all such parcels Threes' (*SL* 2. 6. 2).

Critics of Mill were to observe that it was a mercy that not everything in the world is nailed down; for if it were, we should not be able to separate parts, and two and one would not be three. It does not, on sober reflection, seem that there is any physical fact that is asserted in the definition of a number like 777,864. But Mill's thesis that arithmetic is essentially an empirical science does not stand or fall with his account of the definition of numbers.

He claims, for instance, that a principle such as 'The sums of equals are equals' is an inductive truth or law of nature of the highest order. Inductive truths are generalizations based on individual experiences. Assertions of such truths must always be to some extent tentative or hypothetical; and so it is in this case. The principle 'is never accurately true, for one actual pound weight is not exactly equal to another, nor one measured mile's length to another; a nice balance, or more accurate measuring instruments, would always detect some difference' (*SL* 2. 6. 3).

Here critics said that Mill was confusing arithmetic with its applications. But it was important for Mill to maintain that arithmetic was an empirical science, because the alternative, that it was an a priori discipline, was the source of infinite harm. 'The notion that truths external to the mind may be known by intuition or consciousness, independently of observation and experience is, I am persuaded, in these times the great intellectual support of false doctrines and bad institutions' (*A* 134). To avoid this mischief Mill was willing to pay a high price, and entertain the possibility that at some future time, in some distant galaxy, it might turn out that two and two made not four but five.

Considered as a philosopher, John Henry Newman belonged to the same empiricist tradition as John Stuart Mill. He disliked the German metaphysics that was beginning to infiltrate Oxford during his time there. 'What a vain system of words without ideas such men seem to be piling up,' he remarked. After his conversion to Rome he was equally ill at ease with the scholastic philosophy favoured by his Catholic confrères. The only direct acquaintance we have with things outside ourselves, he asserted, comes through our senses; to think that we have faculties for direct knowledge of immaterial things is mere superstition. Even our senses convey us but a little way out of ourselves: we have to be near things to touch them; we can neither see nor hear nor touch things past or future. But though a staunch empiricist, Newman gives a more exalted role to reason than it was granted by the idealist Kant:

Now reason is that faculty of mind by which this deficiency [of the senses] is supplied: by which knowledge of things external to us, of beings, facts, and events, is attained beyond the range of sense. It ascertains for us not natural things only, or immaterial only, or present only, or past or future; but even if limited in its power, it is unlimited in its range ... It reaches to the ends of the universe, and to the throne of God beyond them; it brings us knowledge, whether real or uncertain, still knowledge, in whatever degree of perfection, from every side; but at the same time, with this characteristic that it obtains it indirectly, not directly. (*US* 199)

Reason does not actually perceive anything: it is a faculty for proceeding from things that are perceived to things that are not. The exercise of reason is to assert one thing on the grounds of some other thing.

Newman identifies two different operations of the intellect that are exercised when we reason: inference (from premises) and assent (to a conclusion). It is important to keep in mind that these two are quite distinct from each other. We often assent to a proposition when we have forgotten the reasons for assent; on the other hand assent may be given without argument, or on the basis of bad arguments. Arguments may be better or worse, but assent either exists or not. It is true that some arguments are so compelling that assent immediately follows inference. But even in the cases of mathematical proof there is a distinction between the two intellectual operations. A mathematician who has just hit upon a complex proof would not assent to its conclusion without going over his work and seeking corroboration from others.

Assent, as has been said, may be given without adequate evidence or argument. This often leads to error; but is it always wrong? Locke maintained that it was: he gave, as a mark of the love of truth, the not entertaining any proposition with greater assurance than the proofs it is built on will warrant. 'Whoever goes beyond this measure of assent, it is plain receives not truth in the love of it, loves not truth for truth-sake, but for some other by-end' (*Essay concerning Human Understanding*, IV. xvi). Locke maintained that there can be no demonstrable truth in concrete matters, and therefore assent to a concrete proposition must be conditional and fall short of certitude. Absolute assent has no legitimate exercise except as ratifying acts of intuition or demonstration.

Newman disagrees. There are no such things as degrees of assent, he maintains, though there is room for opinion without the assent that is necessary for knowledge.

Every day, as it comes, brings with it opportunities for us to enlarge our circle of assents. We read the newspapers; we look through debates in Parliament, pleadings in the law courts, leading articles, letters of correspondents, reviews of books, criticisms in the fine arts, and we either form no opinion at all upon the subjects discussed, as lying out of our line, or at most we have only an opinion about them . . . we never say that we give [a proposition] a degree of assent. We might as well talk of degrees of truth as degrees of assent. (*GA* 115)

Nonetheless, Newman argues, assent on evidence short of intuition or demon-stration may well be legitimate, and frequently is so.

We are sure beyond all hazard of a mistake, that our own self is not the only being existing; that there is an external world; that it is a system with parts and a whole, a universe carried on by laws; and that the future is affected by the past. We accept and hold with an unqualified assent, that the earth, considered as a phenomenon, is a globe; that all its regions see the sun by turns; that there are vast tracts on it of land and water; that there are really existing cities on definite sites, which go by the names of London, Paris, Florence and Madrid. We are sure that Paris or London, unless suddenly swallowed up by an earthquake or burned to the ground, is today just what it was yesterday, when we left it. (*GA* 117)

Each of us is certain that we shall all one day die. But if we are asked for evidence of this, all that we can offer is circuitous argument or *reductio ad absurdum*.

We laugh to scorn the idea that we had no parents though we have no memory of our birth; that we shall never depart this life, though we can have no experience of the future; that we are able to live without food, though we have never tried; that a world of men did not live before our time, or that that world has no history: that there has been no rise and fall of states, no great men, no wars, no revolutions, no art, no science, no literature, no religion. (*GA* 117)

On all these truths, Newman sums up, we have an immediate and unhesitating hold, and we do not think ourselves guilty of not loving truth for truth's sake because we cannot reach them by a proof consisting of a series of intuitive propositions. None of us can think or act without accepting some truths 'not intuitive, not demonstrated, yet sovereign'.

Though he denies that there are degrees of assent, Newman makes a distinction between simple assent and complex assent or certitude. Simple assent may be unconscious, it may be rash, it may be no more than a fancy. Complex assent involves three elements: it must follow on proof, it must be accompanied by a specific sense of intellectual contentment, and it must be irreversible. The feeling of satisfaction and self-gratulation characteristic of certitude attaches not to knowledge itself, but to the consciousness of possessing knowledge.

One difference between knowledge and certitude that is commonly agreed among philosophers is this: If I know p, then p is true; but I may be certain that p and p be false. Newman is not quite consistent on this issue. Sometimes he talks as if there is such a thing as false certitude; at other times he suggests that a conviction can only be a certitude if the proposition in question is objectively true (*GA* 128). But whether or not certitude entails truth, it is undeniable that to be certain of something involves believing in its truth. It follows that if I am certain of a thing, I believe it will remain what I now hold it to be, even if my mind should have the bad fortune to let my belief drop. If we are certain of a belief, we resolve to maintain it and we spontaneously reject as idle any objections to it. If someone is sure of something, if he has such a conviction, say, that Ireland is to the west of England, if he would be consistent, he has no alternative but to adopt 'magisterial intolerance of any contrary assertion'. Of course, despite one's initial resolution, one may in the event give up one's conviction. Newman maintains that anyone who loses his conviction on any point is thereby proved never to have been certain of it.

How do we tell, then, at any given moment, what our certitudes are? No line, Newman thinks, can be drawn between such real certitudes as have truth for their object, and merely apparent certitudes. What looks like a certitude always is exposed to the chance of turning out to be a mistake. There is no interior, immediate test sufficient to distinguish genuine from false certitudes (*GA* 145).

Newman correctly distinguishes certainty from infallibility. My memory is not infallible: I remember for certain what I did yesterday but that does not mean that I never misremember. I am quite clear that two and two make four, but I often make mistakes in long additions. Certitude concerns a particular proposition, infallibility is a faculty or gift. It was possible for Newman to be certain that Victoria was queen without claiming to possess any general infallibility.

But how can I rest in certainty when I know that in the past I have thought myself certain of an untruth? Surely what happened once may happen again.

Suppose I am walking out in the moonlight, and see dimly the outlines of some figure among the trees;—it is a man. I draw nearer, it is still a man; nearer still, and all hesitation is at an end.—I am certain it is a man. But he neither moves nor speaks when I address him; and then I ask myself what can be his purpose in hiding among the trees at such an hour. I come quite close to him and put out my arm. Then I find for certain that what I took for a man is but a singular shadow, formed by the falling of the moonlight on the interstices of some branches or their foliage. Am I not to indulge my second certitude, because I was wrong in my first? Does not any objection, which lies against my second from the failure of my first, fade away before the evidence on which my second is founded? (*GA* 151)

The sense of certitude is, as it were, the bell of the intellect, and sometimes it strikes when it should not. But we do not dispense with clocks because on occasions they tell the wrong time.

No general rules can be set out that will prevent us from ever going wrong in a specific piece of concrete reasoning. Aristotle in his *Ethics* told us that no code of laws, or moral treatise, could map out in advance the path of individual virtue: we need a virtue of practical wisdom (*phronesis*) to determine what to do from moment to moment. So too with theoretical reasoning, Newman says: the logic of language will take us only so far, and we need a special intellectual virtue, which he calls 'the illative sense', to tell us the appropriate conclusion to draw in the particular case.

In no class of concrete reasonings, whether in experimental science, historical research, or theology, is there any ultimate test of truth and error in our inferences besides the trustworthiness of the Illative Sense that gives them its sanction; just as there is no sufficient test of poetical excellence, heroic action, or gentleman-like conduct, other than the particular mental sense, be it genius, taste, sense of propriety, or the moral sense, to which those subject matters are severally committed. (*GA* 231–2)

Newman's epistemology has not been much studied by subsequent philosophers because of the religious purpose that was his overarching aim in developing it. But the treatment of belief, knowledge, and certainty in *The Grammar of Assent* has merits that are quite independent of the theological context, and which bear comparison with classical texts of the empiricist tradition from Locke to Russell.

Peirce on the Methods of Science

Within the decade after the publication of Newman's *Grammar*, C. S. Peirce, in America, was endeavouring to devise an epistemology appropriate to an age of scientific inquiry. He presented it in a series of articles in the *Popular Science Monthly* entitled 'Illustrations of the Logic of Science'. The most famous of the series are the two first articles, 'The Fixation of Belief' and 'How to Make our Ideas Clear' (*CP* 5. 358 ff., 388 ff.).

In the first essay Peirce observes that inquiry always originates in doubt, and ends in belief.

The irritation of doubt is the only immediate motive for the struggle to obtain belief. It is certainly best for us that our beliefs should be such as may truly guide our actions so as to satisfy our desires; and this reflection will make us reject any belief that does not seem to have been so formed as to insure this result. But it will only do so by creating a doubt in the place of that belief. With the doubt, therefore, the struggle begins, and with the cessation of doubt it ends. Hence, the sole object of inquiry is the settlement of opinion. (*EWP* 126)

In order to settle our opinions and fix our beliefs, Peirce says, four different methods are commonly used. They are, he tells us, the method of tenacity, the method of authority, the a priori method, and the scientific method.

We may take a proposition and repeat it to ourselves, dwelling on all that supports it and turning away from anything that might disturb it. Thus, some people read only newspapers that confirm their political beliefs, and a religious person may say 'Oh, I could not believe so-and-so, because I should be wretched if I did'. This is the method of tenacity, and it has the advantage of providing comfort and peace of mind. It may be true, Peirce says, that death is annihilation, but a man who believes he will go straight to heaven when he dies 'has a cheap pleasure that will not be followed by the least disappointment'.

The problem you meet if you adopt the method of tenacity is that you may find your beliefs in conflict with those of other equally tenacious believers. The remedy for this is provided by the second method, that of authority. 'Let an institution be created that shall have for its object to keep correct doctrines before the attention of the people, to reiterate them perpetually, and to teach them to the young; having at the same time power to prevent contrary doctrines from being taught, advocated, or expressed.' This method had been most perfectly practised in Rome, from the days of Numa Pompilius to Pio Nono, but throughout the world, from Egypt to Siam, it has left majestic relics in stone of a sublimity comparable to the greatest works of nature.

There are two disadvantages to the method of authority. First, it is always accompanied by cruelty. If the burning and massacre of heretics is frowned upon in modern states, nonetheless a kind of moral terrorism enforces uniformity of opinion. 'Let it be known that you seriously hold a tabooed belief and you may be perfectly sure of being treated with a cruelty less brutal but more refined than hunting you like a wolf.' Second, no institution can regulate opinion on every subject, and there will always be some independent thinkers who, by comparing their own culture with others, will see that the doctrines inculcated by authority arise only from accident and custom.

Such thinkers may adopt a third method, attempting, by a priori meditation, to produce a universally valid metaphysics. This is more intellectually respectable than the other two methods, but it has manifestly failed to produce a fixation of beliefs. From earliest times to latest, the pendulum has swung between idealist and materialist metaphysics without ever coming to rest.

We must therefore adopt the fourth method, the method of science. The first postulate of this method is the existence of a reality independent of our minds.

There are real things, whose characters are entirely independent of our opinions about them; those realities affect our senses according to regular laws, and, though our sensations are as different as our relations to the objects, yet, by taking advantage of the laws of perception, we can ascertain by reasoning how things really are, and any man, if he has sufficient experience and reason enough about it, will be led to the one true conclusion. (*EWP* 133)

The task of logic is to provide us with guiding principles to enable us to find out, on the basis of what we know, something we do not know, and thus to approximate ever more closely to this ultimate reality.

Though Peirce insisted that doubt was the origin of inquiry, he rejected Descartes's principle that true philosophy must begin from universal, methodical scepticism. Genuine doubt must be doubt of a particular proposition, for a particular reason. Cartesian doubt was no more than a futile pretence, and the Cartesian endeavour to regain certainty by private meditation was even more pernicious. 'We individually cannot reasonably hope to attain the ultimate philosophy we pursue; we can only seek it, therefore, for the *community* of philosophers' (*EWP* 87).

Descartes was right that the first task in philosophy is to clarify our ideas; but he failed to give an adequate account of what he meant by clear and distinct ideas. If an idea is to be distinct, it must sustain the test of dialectical examination. Processes of investigation, if pushed far enough, will give one certain solution to every question to which they can be applied. Scientists may study a problem—e.g. that of the velocity of light—by many different methods. They may at first obtain different results, but as each perfects his method and his processes, the results will move steadily together towards a destined centre. It is at that centre that truth is to be found.

Does this conflict with the thesis that reality is independent of thought? Peirce's answer to this is complex and subtle.

On the one hand, reality is independent, not necessarily of thought in general, but only of what you or I or any finite number of men may think about it...on the other hand, though the object of the final opinion depends on what that opinion is, yet what that opinion is does not depend on what you or I or any man thinks. Our perversity and that of others may indefinitely postpone the settlement of opinion; it might even conceivably cause an arbitrary proposition to be universally accepted as long as the human race should last. (*EWP* 155)

It is possible, therefore, that *p* should be true even though every human being believes it to be false. Peirce offers two ways of making room for this possibility. On the one hand, he says, another race might succeed the extinction of ours, and the true opinion would be the one they ultimately came to. But he also says that 'the catholic consent that constitutes the truth is by no means to be limited to men in this earthly life or to the human race, but extends to the whole communion of minds to which we belong' (*EWP* 60).

It is important to be clear about the content of the beliefs that we attain in the course of this communal, unceasing pursuit of truth. Belief, Peirce says, has three properties: first, it is something we are aware of; second, it appeases the irritation of doubt; third, it involves the establishment in our nature of a rule of action, that is to say, a habit. Different beliefs are distinguished by the different modes of action to which they give rise. 'If beliefs do not differ in this respect, if they appease the same doubt by producing the same rule of action, then no mere differences in the manner of consciousness of them can make them different beliefs.'

To illustrate this point Peirce uses a religious example. Protestants say that after the words of consecration have been said the offerings on the altar are bread and wine; Catholics say they are not. But members of the two sects do not differ from each other in the expectations they have of the sensible effects of the sacrament. 'We can mean nothing by wine but what has certain effects, direct or indirect, upon our senses; and to talk of something as having all the sensible characters of wine, yet being in reality blood, is senseless jargon' (*EWP* 146).

It is in this context that Peirce first put forward his principle of pragmatism, which he presents as the rule for attaining the maximum clearness about our ideas. 'Consider what effects, that might conceivably have practical bearings, we conceive the object of our conception to have. Then, our conception of these effects is the whole of our conception of the object' (*EWP* 146). It is important to note that Peirce's pragmatism is a theory not of truth, but of meaning; and as such it anticipates the verification theory of meaning later put forward by the logical positivists. He applies the principle to the concepts of hardness, weight, freedom, and force, and concludes, in the latter case, 'if we know what the effects of force are, we are acquainted with every fact that is implied in saying that a force exists, and there is nothing more to know' (*EWP* 151).

In Peirce's writing it is not always clear how he sees the relationship between logic and psychology. At the beginning of his essays to illustrate the logic of science he writes thus:

The object of reasoning is to find out, from the consideration of what we already know, something else that we do not know. Consequently, reasoning is good if it be such as to give a true conclusion from true premises and not otherwise. Thus the question of its validity is purely one of fact and not of thinking. (*EWP* 122)

On the other hand, Peirce sometimes writes as if logical truths were laws of mental behaviour. Thus, having told us that the three main classes of logical inference are deduction, induction, and hypothesis, he goes on to say, 'In deduction the mind is under the dominion of a habit or association by virtue of which a general idea suggests in each case a corresponding reaction' (*EWP* 209). Perhaps the two statements are to be reconciled in this way: reasoning, whether good or bad, is a matter of habit; but it is a matter of fact, not of thought, whether a particular piece of reasoning is valid or not.

Frege on Logic, Psychology, and Epistemology

In the writings of Frege, there is no lack of explicit discrimination between logic and psychology. While he was writing his logicist works, from *Begriffsschrift* onwards, Frege was not interested in epistemology for its own sake, but he was concerned to set out the relationship between epistemology and other related disciplines. In the tradition of Descartes, Frege believed, epistemology had been given a fundamental role in philosophy that should really be assigned to logic. On the other hand, philosophers in the empiricist tradition had confused logic with psychology. In working out his logical system Frege was anxious to show the difference in nature and role between logic and these two other branches of study.

Frege took over, and adapted for his own purposes, Kant's distinction between a priori and a posteriori knowledge. To ensure that talk of a priori knowledge involves no confusion between psychology and logic, he reminds us that it is possible to discover the content of a proposition before we hit on a proof of it. We must distinguish, therefore, between how we first come to believe a proposition, and how we would eventually justify it. There must *be* a justification, if we are to talk of knowledge at all, for knowledge is belief that is both true and justified. It is absurd to talk of an a priori mistake, because one can only know what is true.

When a proposition is called *a posteriori* or analytic in my sense, this is not a judgement about the conditions, psychological, physiological and physical, which have made it possible to represent the content of the proposition in consciousness. Nor is it a judgement about the possibly defective method by which some other person has come to believe it true. Rather, it is a judgement about the fundamental ground which provides the justification for believing it to be true. (*FA* 3)

If the proposition is a mathematical one, its justification must be mathematical; it cannot be a psychological matter of processes in the mathematician's mind. To be sure, mathematicians have sensations and mental images, and these may play a part in the thoughts of someone who is calculating. But these images and thoughts are not what arithmetic is about. Different mathematicians associate different images with the same number: in operating with the number one hundred, one person may think of '100' and another of 'C'. Even if psychology could give a causal explanation of the occurrence of the thought that ten squared is one hundred, it would still be totally different from arithmetic, for arithmetic is concerned with the truth of such propositions, psychology with their occurrence in thought. A proposition may be thought of without being true, and a proposition may be true without being thought of.

Psychology is interested in the cause of our thinking, mathematics in the proof of our thoughts. Cause and proof are quite different things. Without an appropriate ration of phosphorus in his brain, no doubt, Pythagoras would have been unable to prove his famous theorem; but that does not mean that a statement of the phosphorus content of his brain should occur as a line in the proof. If humans have evolved, no doubt there has been evolution in human consciousness; so if mathematics was a matter of sensations and ideas, we would need to warn astronomers against drawing conclusions about events in the distant past. Frege brings out the absurdity of this position in an ironic passage:

You reckon that $2 \times 2 = 4$; but the idea of number has a history, an evolution. It may be doubted whether it had yet progressed so far. How do you know that in that distant past that proposition already existed? Might not the creatures then alive have held the proposition $2 \times 2 = 5$? Perhaps it was only later that natural selection, in the struggle for existence, evolved the proposition $2 \times 2 = 4$, and perhaps that in its turn is destined to develop into $2 \times 2 = 3$. (*FA*, pp. vi–vii)

Throughout his life, Frege continued to maintain a sharp distinction between logic and psychology. In his late essay 'Thoughts' he warned against the ambiguity inherent in the statement that logic deals with the laws of thought. If, by 'laws of thought', we mean psychological laws that relate mental events to their causes, then they are not laws of logic because they would make no distinction between true and false thoughts, since error and superstition have causes no less than sound belief. Logical laws are 'laws of thought' only in the same sense as moral laws are laws of behaviour. Actual thinking does not always obey the laws of logic any more than actual behaviour always obeys the moral law.

However, in his late 'Thoughts' Frege ventures into epistemology in a manner that tends to blur the distinctions he had so resolutely defended. He inquires about the sense, or mode of presentation, of the first-person pronoun 'I', which he treats as a proper name that has its user as its reference. Everyone, Frege says, 'is presented to himself in a special and primary way, in which he is presented to no one else'. Suppose that Horatio has the thought that he has been wounded. Only he can grasp the sense of that thought, since it is only to himself that he is presented in this special way.

He cannot communicate a thought he alone can grasp. Therefore, if he now says 'I have been wounded' he must use 'I' in a sense which can be grasped by others, perhaps in the sense of 'the person who is now speaking to you'. In doing so he makes the circumstances of his utterance serve the expression of the thought. (*CP* 360)

This seems to contradict Frege's hitherto consistent claim that whereas mental images might be private, thoughts were the common property of us all. On his own principles an incommunicable thought about a private ego would not be a thought at all. But instead of rejecting the idea that 'I' is a proper name and discarding the whole notion of the Cartesian ego, Frege went on to present in highly Cartesian terms a full-blown doctrine of two separate worlds, one interior and private and the other exterior and public. Perceptible things of the physical world, he said, are accessible to us all: we can all see the same houses and touch the same trees. But in addition, he claimed, there is an inner world of sense-impressions, images and feelings, of desires and wishes—items which, for present purposes, we may call 'ideas'.

Anyone who maintains, as Frege did in this essay, that our mental life takes place within an inner private world must at some time face the question: what reason is there for believing that there is any such thing as an outer world? Descartes, in his *Meditations*, used sceptical arguments to purify the reader, temporarily, from belief in anything beyond the private realm; he then endeavoured to restore the reader's faith in the external world by appealing to the truthfulness of God. Frege here accepts the Cartesian distinction between matter (the world of things) and mind (the world of ideas). Like Descartes, he accepted the need to provide an answer to idealist scepticism, the thesis that nothing exists except ideas.

What if everything were only a dream, a play performed upon the stage of my consciousness (*CP* 363)? I seem to be walking in a green field with a companion; but perhaps the realm of things is empty, and all I have is ideas of which I myself am the owner. If only what is my idea can be the object of my awareness, then for all I know there is no green field (for a field is not an idea, and there are no green ideas) and no companion (for human beings are not ideas). For all I know there are not even any ideas other than my own (for I can know of no one else to own them). Frege concludes: 'Either the thesis that only what is my idea can be the object of my awareness is false, or all my knowledge and perception is restricted to the range of my ideas, to the stage of my self-consciousness. In this case I should have only an inner world and I should know nothing of other people' (*CP* 364). Indeed, does not this train of sceptical reasoning lead to the conclusion that I am myself an idea? Lying in a deckchair, I have a range of visual impressions, from the toes of my shoes to the blurred outline of my nose. By what right do I pick out one of my ideas and set it up as owner of the others? Why have an owner for ideas at all?

Here we come to a full stop. If there is no owner of ideas, there are no ideas either; there cannot be an experience without someone to experience. A pain is necessarily *felt*, and what is felt must have someone feeling it. If so, there *is* something that is not yet my idea, and yet can be an object of my thought, namely myself. Frege, like Descartes, brings scepticism to an end with a *cogito, ergo sum*. But whereas Descartes's ego was a non-ideal *subject* of thinking, Frege's ego is a non-ideal *object* of thought. Its existence refutes the thesis that only what is part of the content of my consciousness can be the object of my thought.

If there is to be such a thing as science, Frege maintained, 'a third realm must be recognized'—a world in addition to the world of things and the world of ideas. The ego, as the owner of ideas, is the first citizen of this third realm. The third realm is the realm of objective thought. The denizens of this realm share with ideas the property of being imperceptible by the senses, and share with physical objects the property of being independent of an owner. Pythagoras' theorem is timelessly true and needs no owner; it does not begin to be true when it is first thought of or proved (*CP* 362).

Other people, Frege says, can grasp thoughts no less than I; we are not owners of our thoughts as we are owners of our ideas. We do not *have* thoughts; thoughts are what we *grasp*. What is grasped is already there and all we do is take possession of it. Our grasping a thought has no more effect on the thought itself than our observing it affects the new moon. Thoughts do not change or come and go; they are not causally active or passive in the way in which objects are in the physical world. In that world, one thing acts on another and changes it; it is itself acted upon and itself changes. This is not so in the timeless world that Pythagoras' theorem inhabits (*PW* 138).

Few who have followed Frege down the path of Cartesian scepticism will follow him in the route he offers out of the maze. His response to the challenge is no more convincing than Descartes's own. Both philosophers, having accepted a division between a public world of physical things and a private world of human consciousness, seek to rejoin what they have separated by appealing to a third world: the divine mind in the case of Descartes, and the world of thoughts in the case of Frege. In each case the fatal mistake was the acceptance of the initial dichotomy. There are not two worlds, but a single one to which there belong not just inert physical objects but also conscious rational animals. Frege was wrong, and sinned against his own cardinal principle of separating thoughts from ideas, in accepting that consciousness provides us with incommunicable contents and unshareable certainties.

Knowledge by Acquaintance and Knowledge by Description

Six years before Frege published his articles on the nature of thought, Bertrand Russell had written his brief *Problems of Philosophy*, a book that was to give many generations of philosophy students their first introduction to epistemology. Russell was a godson of John Stuart Mill, and for a great part of his life he endeavoured to be faithful to the British empiricist tradition of which Mill had been such an intrepid exponent. But Russell could not accept Mill's view of mathematics as an empirical science, and so his empiricism was always blended with an element of the Platonism that he shared with Frege. His starting point in *Problems* is the systematic doubt of Descartes.

It seems to me that I am now sitting in a chair, at a table of a certain shape, on which I see sheets of paper with writing or print. By turning my head I see out of the window buildings and clouds and the sun. I believe that the sun is about ninety-three million miles from the earth; that it is a hot globe many times bigger than the earth; that, owing to the earth's rotation, it rises every morning, and will continue to do so for an indefinite time in the future. (*PP* 7–8)

However evident this seems, Russell tells us, it may all be reasonably doubted. The table looks different and feels different from different angles and to different people in different circumstances. The real table is not what we immediately experience, but is an inference from what is immediately known. What is immediately known in sensation is something quite different from any real table.

Let us give the name of 'sense data' to the things that are immediately known in sensation: such things as colours, sounds, smells, hardnesses, roughnesses, and so on. We shall give the name 'sensation' to the experience of being immediately aware of these things. Thus, whenever we see a colour, we have a sensation *of* the colour, but the colour itself is a sense-datum, not a sensation. The colour is that *of* which we are immediately aware, and the awareness itself is the sensation. (*PP* 12)

Sense-data are the only things of which we can be really certain. Descartes brought his own doubt to an end with the *cogito*, 'I think, therefore I am'. But this, Russell warns us, says something more than what is certain: sense-data bring no assurance of an abiding self, and what is really certain is not 'I am seeing a brown colour' but 'a brown colour is being seen'. Sense-data are private and personal: is there any reason to believe in public neutral objects such as we imagine tables to be? If there is not, then a fortiori there is no reason to believe in persons other than myself, since it is only through their bodies that I have any access to others' minds.

Russell concedes that there is no actual proof that the whole of life is not just a dream. Our belief in an independent external world is instinctive rather than reflective, but this does not mean that there is any good reason to reject it. If we agree provisionally that there are physical objects as well as sense-data, should we say that these objects are the causes of the sense-data? If we do, we must immediately add that there is no reason to think that these causes are *like* sense-data—e.g. that they are coloured. Common sense leaves us quite in the dark about their true nature.

In order to clarify the relationship between sense-data and the objects that cause them, Russell introduces his celebrated distinction between knowledge by acquaintance and knowledge by description.

> We shall say that we have *acquaintance* with anything of which we are directly aware, without the intermediary of any process of inference or any knowledge of truths. Thus in the presence of my table I am acquainted with the sense-data that make up the appearance of my table—its colour, shape, hardness, smoothness, etc. . . . My knowledge of the table as a physical object, on the contrary, is not direct knowledge. Such as it is, it is obtained through acquaintance with the sense-data that make up the appearance of the table. We have seen that it is possible, without absurdity, to doubt whether there is a table at all, whereas it is not possible to doubt the sense-data. My knowledge of the table is of the kind which we shall call 'knowledge by description'. The table is 'the physical object which causes such-and-such sense-data'. This *describes* the table by means of the sense-data. (*PP* 46–7)

Sense-data are not the only things with which we have acquaintance. Introspection gives us acquaintance with our own thoughts, feelings, and desires. Memory gives us acquaintance with past data of the inner or outer senses. We may even, though this is a matter of doubt, have acquaintance with our own selves. We do not have acquaintance with physical objects or other minds. But we do have acquaintance with rather more rarefied entities: namely, universal concepts, such as *whiteness*, *brotherhood*, and so on.

Like Plato, Russell thought that universals belonged to a supra-sensible world, the world of being. The world of being was unchangeable, rigid, perfect, and dead. It was the world of existence that contained thoughts, feelings, and sense-data. By temperament some people preferred one world, and others preferred the other. But 'both are real, and both are important to the metaphysician' (*PP* 100).

Every proposition that we can understand, Russell maintained, must be composed wholly of constituents with which we are acquainted. How then can we make statements about Bismarck, whom we have never seen, or Europe, which is far too big to be taken in by a sense-datum? Russell's answer is that any judgement about Bismarck or Europe really contains a nested series of definite descriptions, and all knowledge about them is ultimately reducible to knowledge of what is known by acquaintance. Only in this way can we have any knowledge of things that we have never experienced.

When he came to write *Our Knowledge of the External World* (1914) Russell described the relationship between physical objects and sense-data by saying that the former were logical constructions out of the latter. Whereas in *Problems* he though that objects *caused* sense-data, but were distinct from them, he now came to believe that statements about the objects of everyday life, and scientific statements also, were reducible by analysis into statements about sensory experiences. But this too turned out to be a temporary phase in his thinking, and in his last philosophical work, *Human Knowledge: Its Scope and Limits* (1948), he returned to a causal theory of perception. In the meantime much had happened to call in question the whole basis and method of his epistemology.

Husserl's Epoche

Husserl was the last great philosopher in the Cartesian tradition. He saw the phenomenological reduction, and in particular the programme of *epoche*, or suspension of judgement about the existence of extra-mental reality, as a refinement of Descartes's methodological doubt. In several ways he sought to be more radical than Descartes in cutting away from the foundations of philosophy whatever it is possible to doubt. First of all, he denied the indubitability of the *cogito* if that is supposed to affirm the existence of an enduring self rather than just the subject of my present sensations. Second, he thought that Descartes took the data of consciousness at their face value, without distinguishing within them between what was actually given in sensation, and what in them was the result of a metaphysical interpretation that tacitly presupposed the existence of an external world, spread out in space and time and subject to a principle of causality (*LI* 16).

The differences that separate Husserl from Descartes are, however, unimportant in comparison with the similarities that bind the two together. Both philosophers saw epistemology as the basic discipline, which is prior to all other parts of philosophy and to all empirical sciences. Husserl, like Descartes, never doubted two things: the certainty of his own mental states and processes, and the language that he uses to report these phenomena. These certainties, they both believe, can survive any doubt about the external world.

Descartes believed that God could have created my mind, just as it is, without there being any such thing as matter. Husserl argued that our awareness of external objects consists in our partial glimpses and contacts with them our 'adumbrations' of them, as he puts it. But unless these adumbrations exhibited the order they do, we could not in any way construct objects out of them. However, it is perfectly conceivable that this order might be shattered, leaving only a chaotic series of sensations. If so, we would cease to perceive physical objects, and our world would be destroyed. But consciousness, Husserl argued, would survive such a destruction of the world (*Ideas*, 49).

If my own consciousness is indubitably certain, while the world of matter is essentially dubious, nothing could seem more judicious than to suspend judgement about the latter while concentrating on the accurate description and analysis of the former. But Husserl's *epoche*, or suspension of judgement, is not the neutral starting point that it appears to be between realism and idealism. For the assumption that consciousness can be given expression in a purely private world begs the question against realism from the start. Because they separate the content of consciousness from any non-contingent link with its expression in language and its objects in the external world, both Husserl and Descartes find themselves trapped into a form of solipsism, from which Descartes tries to escape by appeal to the veracity of God, and Husserl, in his later years, by postulating a transcendental consciousness.

The line of argument that drove Husserl to become a transcendental idealist went as follows. His starting point was the natural one that consciousness is part of the world, with physical causes. But if one is to avoid having to postulate, like Kant, a *Ding an Sich* which is unattainable by experience, one must say that the physical world is itself a creation of consciousness. But if the consciousness that creates it is our own ordinary psychological consciousness, then we are confronted by paradox: the world as a whole is constituted by one of its elements, human consciousness. The only way to avoid the paradox is to say that the consciousness that constitutes the world is no part of the world but is transcendental.[1]

The world that consciousness creates, however, is shaped not only by our own experiences but by the culture and fundamental assumptions in which we live: what Husserl calls 'the life-world'. The life-world is not a set of judgements based on evidence, but rather an unexamined substrate underlying all evidence and all judgement. However, it is not something ultimate and immutable. Our life-world is affected by developments in science just as science is rooted in our life-world. Hypotheses get their meaning through their connection with the life-world, but in their turn they gradually change it. In a paper first published in 1939, *Experience and Judgement*, Husserl wrote:

everything which contemporary natural science has furnished as determinations of what exists also belongs to us, to the world, as this world is pregiven to the adults of our time. And even if we are not personally interested in natural science, and even if we know nothing of its results, still, what exists is pregiven to us in advance as determined in such a way that we at least grasp it as being in principle scientifically determinable.

It is not easy to see how to reconcile these late thoughts with the earlier stages of Husserl's thinking. Similarly, readers of Wittgenstein's latest writings find him exploring new and disquieting ideas on the nature of the ultimate justification of knowledge and belief.[2]

---

[1] Here I am indebted to Herman Philipse's article 'Transcendental Idealism' in *CCH* 239–319.
[2] The similarity between the two is pointed out by Dagfinn Føllesdal in his paper 'Ultimate Justification in Husserl and Wittgenstein', in M. E. Reicher and J. C. Marek (eds.), *Experience and Analysis* (Vienna: ÖBT & HPT, 2005), to which I am indebted for the quotation in the above paragraph.

Wittgenstein on Certainty

Descartes's scepticism has had a more enduring effect than his rationalism: philosophers have been more impressed by the difficulties raised in his First and Third Meditations than by the replies to those difficulties in the Fourth and Sixth Meditations. Husserl's transcendental idealism is only the last of a long series of unsuccessful attempts to respond to Cartesian scepticism about the external world while accepting the Cartesian picture of the internal world. Wittgenstein's private language argument, which showed that there was no way of identifying items of consciousness without reference to the public world, cut the ground beneath the whole notion of Cartesian consciousness. But it was only in the last years of his life, in the epistemological writings published posthumously as *On Certainty*, that Wittgenstein addressed Cartesian scepticism head-on.

In response to sceptical doubt of the kind presented in the First Meditation, Wittgenstein makes two initial points. First, doubt needs grounds (*OC* 323, 458). Second, a genuine doubt must make a difference in someone's behaviour: someone is not really doubting whether he has a pair of hands if he uses his hands as we all do (*OC* 428). In reply, Descartes could agree with the first point; that is why he invented the evil genius, to provide a ground for suspicion of our intuitions. The second point he would answer with a distinction: the doubt he is recommending is a theoretical, methodological doubt, not a practical one.

Wittgenstein's next criticism is much more substantial. A doubt, he claims, presupposes the mastery of a language-game. In order to express the doubt that *p* one must understand what is meant by saying *p*. Radical Cartesian doubt destroys itself because it is bound to call in question the meaning of the words used to express it (*OC* 369, 456). If the evil genius is deceiving me totally, then he is deceiving me about the meaning of the word 'deceive'. So 'The evil genius is deceiving me totally' does not express the total doubt that it was intended to.

Even within the language-game, there must be some propositions that cannot be doubted. 'Our doubts depend on the fact that some propositions are exempt from doubt, are as it were the hinges on which those turn' (*OC* 341). But if there are propositions about which we cannot doubt, are these also propositions about which we cannot be mistaken? Wittgenstein distinguished between mistake and other forms of false belief. If someone were to imagine that he had just been living for a long time somewhere other than where he had in fact been living, this would not be a mistake, but a mental disturbance; it was something one would try to cure him of, not to reason him out of. The difference between madness and mistake is that whereas mistake involves false judgement, in madness no real judgement is made at all, true or false. So too with dreaming: the argument 'I may be dreaming' is senseless, because if I am dreaming this remark is being dreamt as well, and indeed it is also being dreamt that these words have any meaning (*OC* 383).

Wittgenstein's purpose in *On Certainty* is not just to establish the reality of the external world against Cartesian scepticism. His concern, as he acknowledged, was much closer to that of Newman in *The Grammar of Assent*: he wanted to inquire how it was possible to have unshakeable certainty that is not based on evidence. The existence of external objects was certain, but it was not something that could be proved, or that was an object of knowledge. Its location in our world-picture (*Weltbild*) was far deeper than that.

In the last months of his life Wittgenstein sought to clarify the status of a set of propositions that have a special position in the structure of our epistemology, propositions which, as he put it, 'stand fast' for us (*OC* 116). Propositions such as 'Mont Blanc has existed for a long time' and 'One cannot fly to the moon by flapping one's arms' look like empirical propositions. But they are 'empirical' propositions in a special way: they are not the results of inquiry, but the foundations of research; they are fossilized empirical propositions that form channels for the ordinary, fluid propositions. They are propositions that make up our world-picture, and a world-picture is not learnt by experience; it is the inherited background against which I distinguish between true and false. Children do not learn them; they as it were swallow them down with what they do learn (*OC* 94, 476).

It is quite sure that motor cars don't grow out of the earth. We feel that if someone could believe the contrary he could believe *everything* we say is untrue, and could question everything that we hold to be sure.

But how does this *one* belief hang together with all the rest? We would like to say that someone who could believe that does not accept our whole system of verification. The system is something that a human being acquires by means of observation and instruction. I intentionally do not say 'learns'. (*OC* 279)

When we first begin to believe anything, we believe not a single proposition but a whole system: light dawns gradually over the whole.

Though these propositions give the foundations of our language-games, they do not provide grounds, or premisses for language-games. 'Giving grounds', Wittgenstein said, 'justifying the evidence, comes to an end; but the end is not certain propositions striking us immediately as true, i.e. it is not a kind of *seeing* in our part; it is our acting, which lies at the bottom of the language game.' (*OC* 204).

Epistemology in the twentieth century went through parallel stages of development in different climates of thought. In each case from an initial concentration on the individual consciousness epistemologists moved towards an appreciation of the role of social communities in the build-up of the web of belief. Likewise, they moved from a concentration on the purely cognitive aspect of experience to an emphasis on its affective and practical element. This development took place both within different schools of philosophy (Continental and analytic) and also within the thought of individual philosophers such as Husserl and Wittgenstein. In each case the development brought enrichment to a field of philosophy that had initially been cramped by excessive individualism.

7

Metaphysics

Varieties of Idealism

I n the first part of the nineteenth century the most significant philosophers were all idealists of one kind or another. The period was the heyday of transcendental idealism in Germany, with Fichte, Schelling, and Hegel working towards a theory of the universe as the developing history of an absolute consciousness. But even those who were most critical of absolute idealism owed allegiance to a different form of idealism, the empiricist idealism of Berkeley according to which to be is to be perceived. John Stuart Mill in England and Arthur Schopenhauer in Germany both take as their starting point Berkeley's thesis that the world of experience consists of nothing but ideas, and both try to detach Berkeley's theory of matter from its theological underpinning.[1]

According to Mill, our belief that physical objects persist in existence when they are not perceived amounts to no more than our continuing expectation of further perceptions in the future. He defines matter as 'a permanent possibility of sensation'; he tells us that the external world is the world of possible sensations succeeding one another in a lawful manner.

Right at the start of his *World as Will and Idea* Schopenhauer tells us, 'The world is my idea.' Everything in the world exists only as an object for a subject, exists only in relation to consciousness. To achieve philosophical wisdom a man must accept that 'he has no knowledge of a sun and of an earth, but only of an eye that sees the sun and a hand that feels the earth' (*WWI* 3). The subject, Schopenhauer says, is that which knows all things and is known by none; it is therefore the bearer of the world.

Schopenhauer accepts from Kant that space, time, and causality are necessary and universal forms of every object, intuited in our consciousness prior to any experience. Space and time are a priori forms of sensibility, and causality is an a priori form of understanding. Understanding (*Verstand*) is not peculiar to

[1] See above, pp. 558, 736.

humans, because other animals are aware of relations between cause and effect. Understanding is what turns raw sensation into perception, just as the rising sun brings colour into the landscape. The faculty that is peculiar to humans is reason (*Vernunft*), that is to say the ability to form abstract concepts and link them to each other. Reason confers on humans the possibility of speech, deliberation, and science; but it does not increase knowledge, it only transforms it. All our knowledge comes from our perceptions, which are what constitute the world.

The thesis that the world exists only for a subject leads to paradox. Schopenhauer accepted an evolutionary account of history: animals existed before men, fishes before land animals, and plants before fishes. A long series of changes took place before the first eye ever opened. Yet, according to the thesis that the world is idea, the existence of this whole world is forever dependent on that first eye, even if it was only that of an insect.

Thus we see, on the one hand, the existence of the whole world necessarily dependent on the first knowing [conscious] being, however imperfect it be; on the other hand, this first knowing animal just as necessarily dependent on a long chain of causes and effects which has preceded it, and in which it itself appears as a small link. (*WWI* 30)

This antinomy can be resolved only if we move from consideration of the world as idea to the world as will.

The second book of *The World as Will and Idea* begins with a consideration of the natural sciences. Some of these, such as botany and zoology, deal with the permanent forms of individuals; others, such as mechanics and physics, promise explanations of change. These offer laws of nature, such as those of inertia and gravitation, which determine the position of phenomena in time and space. But these laws offer no information about the inner nature of the forces of nature—matter, weight, inertia, and so on—that are invoked in order to account for their constancy. 'The force on account of which a stone falls to the ground or one body repels another is, in its inner nature, not less strange and mysterious than that which produces the movements and the growth of an animal' (*WWI* 97).

Scientific inquiry, so long as it restricts its concern to ideas, leaves us unsatisfied. 'We wish to know the significance of these ideas; we ask whether this world is merely idea; in which case it would pass by us like an empty dream or a baseless vision, not worth our notice; or whether it is also something else, something more than idea, and if so what' (*WWI* 99). We would never be able to get any further if we were mere knowing subjects—winged cherubs without a body. But each of us is rooted in the world because of our embodiment. My knowledge of the world is given me through my body, but my body is not just a medium of information, one object among others; it is an active agent of whose power I am directly conscious. It is my will that gives me the key to my own existence and shows me the inner mechanism of my actions.

The movements of my body are not effects of which my will is the cause: the act and the will are identical. 'Every true act of a man's will is also at once and without exception a movement of his body.' Conversely, impressions upon the body are also impacts on the will—pleasant, if in accordance with the will, painful if contrary to the will. Each of us knows himself both as an object and as a will; and this is the key to the understanding of the essence of every phenomenon in nature.

[We shall] judge of all objects which are not our own bodies, and are consequently not given to our consciousness in a double way but only as ideas, according to the analogy of our own bodies, and shall therefore assume that as in one aspect they are idea, just like our bodies, and in this respect are analogous to them, so in another aspect, what remains of objects when we set aside their existence as idea of the subject must in its inner nature be the same as that in us which we call *will*. For what other kind of existence or reality should we attribute to the rest of the material world? Whence should we take the elements out of which we construct such a world? Besides will and idea nothing is known to us or thinkable. (*WWI* 105)

The force by which the crystal is formed, the force by which the magnet turns to the pole, the force which germinates and vegetates in the plant—all these forces, so different in their phenomenal existence, are identical in their inner nature with that which in us is the will. Phenomenal existence is mere idea, but the will is a thing in itself. The word 'will' is like a magic spell that discloses to us the inmost being of everything in nature.

This does not mean—Schopenhauer quickly insists—that a falling stone has consciousness or desires. Deliberation about motives is only the form that will takes in human beings; it is not part of the essence of will, which comes in many different grades, only the higher of which are accompanied by knowledge and self-determination. Why, we may wonder, should we say that natural forces are lower grades of will, rather than saying that the human will is the highest grade of force? Schopenhauer's reply to this is that our concept of force is an abstraction from the phenomenal world of cause and effect, whereas will is something of which we have immediate consciousness. To explain will in terms of force would be to explain the better known by the less known, and to renounce the only immediate knowledge we have of the world's inner nature.

Will is groundless: it is outside the realm of cause and effect. It is wrong, therefore, to ask for the cause of original forces such as gravity or electricity. To be sure, the expressions of these forces take place in accordance with the laws of cause and effect; but it is not gravity that causes a stone to fall, but rather the proximity of the earth. The force of gravity itself is no part of the causal chain, because it lies outside time. So do all other forces.

Through thousands of years chemical forces slumber in matter till the contact with the reagents sets them free; then they appear; but time exists only for the phenomena, not for the forces themselves. For thousands of years galvanism slumbered in copper and zinc, and they lay quietly beside silver, which will inevitably be consumed in flame as soon as all three are brought together under the required conditions. (*WWI* 136)

This account of the operation of causality in the world has some features in common with the occasionalism of Malebranche, and Schopenhauer draws attention to the resemblance.[2] 'Malebranche is right: every natural cause is only an occasional cause.' But whereas for Malebranche God was the true cause of every natural effect, for Schopenhauer the true cause is the universal will. A natural cause, he tells us,

only gives opportunity or occasion for the manifestation of the one indivisible will which is the 'in-itself' of all things, and whose graduated objectification is the whole visible world. Only the appearance, the becoming visible in this place, at this time, is brought about by the cause and is so far dependent on it, but not the whole of the phenomenon, nor its inner nature. (*WWI* 138)

The universal will is objectified at many different levels. The principal difference between the higher and lower grades of will lies in the role of individuality. In the higher grades individuality is prominent: no two humans are alike, and there are marked differences between individual animals of higher species. But the further down we go, the more completely individual character is lost in the common character of the species. Plants have hardly any individual qualities, and in the inorganic world all individuality disappears. A force like electricity must show itself in precisely the same way in all its million phenomena. This is the reason why it is easier to predict the phenomena the further down we go in the hierarchy of will.

Throughout the world of nature will is expressed in conflict. There is conflict between different grades of will, as when a magnet lifts a piece of iron, which is the victory of a higher form of will (electricity) over a lower (gravitation). When a person raises an arm, that is a triumph of human will over gravity, and in every healthy animal we see the conscious organism winning a victory over the physical and chemical laws that operate on the constituents of the body. It is this perpetual conflict that makes physical life burdensome and brings the necessity of sleep and eventually of death. 'At last these subdued forces of nature, assisted by circumstances, win back from the organism, wearied even by the constant victory, the matter it took from them, and attain to an unimpeded expression of their being' (*WWI* 146). At the bottom end of the scale, similarly, we see the universal essential conflict that manifests will. The earth's revolution around the sun is kept going by the constant tension between centrifugal and centripetal force. Matter itself is kept in being by attractive and repulsive forces, gravitation and impenetrability.

---

[2] See above, p. 545.

This constant pressure and resistance is the objectivity of will in its very lowest grade, and even there, as a mere blind urge, it expresses its character as will.

The will, in Schopenhauer's system, occupies the same position as the thing-in-itself in Kant's. Considered apart from its phenomenal activities, it is outside time and space. Since time and space are the necessary conditions for multiplicity, the will must be single; it remains indivisible, in spite of the plurality of things in space and time. The will is objectified in a higher way in a human than in a stone; but this does not mean that there is a larger part of will in the human and a smaller part in the stone, because the relation of part and whole belongs only to space. So too does plurality: 'the will reveals itself just as completely in one oak as in millions' (*WWI* 128).

The different grades of objectification of the will are identified by Schopenhauer with the Ideas of Plato. These too, like the will itself, are outside space and time.

Those different grades of the will's objectification, expressed in innumerable individuals, exist as the unattained patterns of these, or as the eternal forms of things. Not themselves entering into time and space, the medium of individuals, they remain fixed, subject to no change, always being, never having become. The particular things, however, arise and pass away; they are always becoming and never are. (*WWI* 129)

The combination of Platonic idealism with Indian mysticism gives Schopenhauer's system a uniquely metaphysical quality. However much they admired his style, or admitted his influence, few philosophers felt able to follow him all the way. There has never been a school of Schopenhauerians as there have been schools of Kantians and Hegelians. The one person who was willing to declare himself a disciple of Schopenhauer was the Wagner of *Tristan und Isolde*.

Metaphysics and Teleology

It is a far cry from Schopenhauer's mystical idealism to Darwin's evolutionary naturalism, and indeed it may seem odd to mention a biologist at all in a chapter on metaphysics. But Darwin's theories had implications, which went beyond his immediate interests, for the general theory of causation. Aristotle, who was the first to systematize metaphysics, did so in terms of four kinds of causes: material, formal, efficient, and final. The final cause was the goal or end of a structure or activity. Explanations in terms of final causes were called 'teleological' after the Greek word for end, *telos*. For Aristotle teleological explanations were operative at every level, from the burrowing of an earthworm to the rotation of the heavens. Since Darwin, many thinkers have claimed, there is no longer any room at all for teleological explanation in any scientific discipline.

Aristotelian teleological explanations of activities and structures have two features: they explain things in terms of their ends, not their beginnings, and they invoke the notion of goodness. Thus, an activity will be explained by reference not to its starting point but to its terminus; and arrival at the terminus will be exhibited as some kind of good for the agent whose activity is to be explained. Thus, the downward motion of heavy bodies on earth was explained by Aristotle as a movement towards their natural place, the place where it was best for them to be, and the circular motion of the heavens was to be explained by love of a supreme being. Similarly, teleological explanation of the development of organic structures showed how the organ, in its perfected state, conferred a benefit on the complete organism. Thus, ducks grow webbed feet so that they can swim.

Descartes rejected the use of teleological explanation in physics or biology. Final causation, he maintained, implied in the agent a knowledge of the end to be pursued; but such knowledge could only exist in minds. The explanation of every physical movement and activity must be mechanistic; that is, it must be given in terms of initial, not final, conditions, and those conditions must be stated in descriptive, not evaluative, terms. Descartes offered no good argument for his contention, and his thesis ruled out straightforward gravitational attraction no less than the Aristotelian cosmic ballet. Moreover, Descartes was wrong to think that teleological explanation must involve conscious purpose: whatever Aristotle may have thought about the heavenly bodies, he never believed that an earthworm, let alone a falling pebble, was in possession of a mind.

It was not Descartes, but Newton and Darwin, who dealt the serious blows to Aristotelian teleology, by undermining, in different ways, its two constituent elements. Newtonian gravity, no less than Aristotelian motion, provides an explanation by reference to a terminus: gravity is a centripetal force, a force 'by which bodies are drawn, or impelled, or in any way tend, towards a point as to a centre'. But Newton's explanation is fundamentally different from Aristotle's in that it involves no suggestion that it is in any way good for a body to arrive at the centre to which it tends.

Darwinian explanations in terms of natural selection, on the other hand, resemble Aristotle's in demanding that the terminus of the process to be explained, or the complexity of the structure to be accounted for, shall be something that is beneficial to the relevant organism. But unlike Aristotle, Darwin explains the processes and the structures, not in terms of a pull by the final state or perfected structure, but in terms of the pressure of the initial conditions of the system and its environment. The red teeth and red claws involved in the struggle for existence were, of course, in pursuit of a good, namely the survival of the individual organism to which they belonged; but they were not in pursuit of the ultimate good that is to be explained by selection, namely, the survival of the fittest species. It is thus that the emergence of particular species in the course of evolution could be explained not only without appeal to a conscious designer, but without evoking teleology at all.

It is, of course, only at one particular level that Darwin's system offers to render teleology superfluous. Human beings, such as husbandmen, act for the sake of goals not only in breeding improved stock, but in human life and business in general. Others among the higher animals not only act on instinct, but pursue goals learnt by experience. Moreover, Darwinian scientists have not given up the search for final causes. Indeed, contemporary biologists are much more adept at discerning the function of structures and behaviours than their predecessors in the period between Descartes and Darwin. What Darwin did was to make teleological explanation respectable by offering a general recipe for translating it into an explanation of a mechanistic form. His successors thus feel able freely to use such explanations, without offering more than a promissory note about how they are to be reduced to mechanism in any particular case. Once they have identified the benefit, G, that an activity or structure confers on an organism, they feel entitled to say without further ado that 'the organism evolved in such a way that G'.

Two great questions about teleology are left unanswered by the work of Darwin. First, are the free and conscious decisions of human beings irreducibly teleological, or can they be given an explanation in mechanistic terms? There are those who believe that when more is known about the human brain it will be possible to show that every human thought and action is the outcome of mechanistic physical processes. This belief, however, is an act of faith; it is not the result of any scientific discovery or of any philosophical analysis.

Second, if we assume that broadly Darwinian explanations can be found for the existence of the teleological organisms we see around us, does our investigation rest there? Or can the universe itself be regarded as a system that operates, through mechanistic means, to the goal of producing species of organisms, in the way that a refrigerator works through mechanistic means to the goal of a uniform temperature? Is the universe itself one huge machine, a goal-directed system?

Biologists are divided whether evolution itself has a direction. Some believe that it has an inbuilt tendency to produce organisms of ever greater complexity and ever higher consciousness. Others claim that there is no scientific evidence that evolution has any kind of privileged axis. Either way, the question remains whether it is teleological explanation or mechanistic explanation that is the one that operates at a fundamental level of the universe. If God created the world, then mechanistic explanation is underpinned by teleological explanation; the fundamental explanation of the existence and operation of any creature is the purpose of the creator. If there is no God, but the universe is due to the operation of necessary laws upon blind chance, then it is the mechanistic level of explanation that is fundamental. So far as I know, no one, whether scientist or philosopher, has provided a definitive answer to this question.

Realism vs. Nominalism

Throughout the history of philosophy one metaphysical problem recurs again and again, presented in different terms. This is the question whether, if we are to make sense of the world we live in, there must exist, outside the mind, entities of a quite different kind from the fleeting individuals that we meet in everyday existence. In the ancient world, Plato and Aristotle discussed whether or not there were Ideas or Forms existing independently of matter and material objects. Throughout the Middle Ages, realist and nominalist philosophers disputed whether universals were realities or mere symbols. In the modern era philosophers of mathematics have conducted a parallel debate about the nature of mathematical objects, with formalists identifying numbers with numerals, and realists asserting that numbers have an independent reality, constituting a third world separate from the world of mind and the world of matter.

The most vociferous defender of realism in modern times is Frege. In a lecture entitled 'Formal Theories of Arithmetic' (*CP* 112–21) he attacks the idea that signs for numbers, like '½' and 'π', are merely empty signs designating nothing. Even calling them 'signs', he says, already suggests that they do signify something. A resolute formalist should call them 'shapes'. If we took seriously the contention that '½' does not designate anything, then it is merely a splash of printer's ink or a splurge of chalk, with various physical and chemical properties. How can it possibly have the property that if added to itself it yields 1? Shall we say that it is given this property by definition? A definition serves to connect a sense with a word; but this sign was supposed to have no content. Sure, it is up to us to give a signification to a sign, and therefore it is partly dependent on human choice what properties the content of a sign has. But these properties are properties of the content, not of the sign itself, and hence, according to the formalist, they will not be properties of the number. What we cannot do is to give things properties merely by definition.

In the *Grundgesetze* Frege uses against the formalists the kind of argument that Wyclif used against the nominalists of the Middle Ages.[3]

One cannot by pure definition magically conjure into a thing a property that in fact it does not possess—save that of now being called by the name with which one has named it. That an oval figure produced on paper with ink should by a definition acquire the property of yielding one when added to one, I can only regard as a scientific superstition. One could just as well by a pure definition make a lazy pupil diligent. (*BLA* 11)

For Frege, not only numbers but functions too were mind-independent realities. Consider an expression such as '$2x^2 + x$'. This expression splits into two parts, a sign for an argument and an expression for a function. In the expressions

---

[3] See above, pp. 372–3.

$$(2 \times 1^2) + 1$$
$$(2 \times 4^2) + 4$$
$$(2 \times 5^2) + 5$$

we can recognize the same function occurring over and over again, but with different arguments, namely 1, 4, and 5. The content that is common to these expressions is what the function is. It can be represented by '$2(\ )^2 + (\ )$', that is, by what is left of '$2x^2 + x$' if we leave the xs out. The argument is not part of the function, rather it combines with the function to make a complete whole. A function must be distinguished from its value for a particular argument: the value of a mathematical function is always a number, as the number 3 is the value of our function for the argument 1, so that '$(2 \times 1^2) + 1$' names the number 3. A function itself, unlike the numbers that are its arguments and its values, is something incomplete, or 'unsaturated' as Frege calls it. That is why it is best represented, symbolically, by a sign containing gaps. In itself, it is not a sign but a reality lying behind the sign.

It was not only in mathematics that Frege was a resolute realist. He extended the notion of function in such a way that all concepts of any kind turn out to be functions. The link between mathematical functions and predicates such as '... killed ...' or '... is lighter than ...' is made in a striking passage of 'Function and Concept' where we are invited to consider the function '$x^2 = 1$'.

The first question that arises here is what the values of this function are for different arguments. Now if we replace x successively by -1, 0, 1, 2 we get:

$$(-1)^2 = 1$$
$$0^2 = 1$$
$$1^2 = 1$$
$$2^2 = 1$$

Of these equations the first and third are true, the others false. I say 'the value of our function is a truth-value' and distinguish between the truth-values of what is true and what is false. (*CP* 144)

Once this move has been made, it is possible for Frege to define a concept as a function whose value for every argument is a truth-value. A concept will then be the extra-linguistic counterpart of a predicate in language: what is represented, for instance, by the predicate '... is a horse.' Concepts, like numbers, are quite independent of mind or matter: we do not create them, we discover them; but we do not discover them by the operation of our senses. They are objective, though they do not have the kind of reality (*Wirklichkeit*) that belongs to the physical world of cause and effect.

Frege's realism is often called Platonism, but there is a significant difference between Plato's Ideas and Frege's concepts. For Plato, the Ideal Horse was itself a horse: only by being itself a horse could it impart horsiness to the non-ideal horses of the everyday world.[4] Frege's concept *horse*, by contrast, is something very unlike a horse. Any actual horse is an object, and between objects and concepts there is, for Frege, a great gulf fixed. Not only is the concept *horse* not a horse, it is, Frege tells us, not a concept. This remark at first hearing brings us up short; but there is nothing really untoward about it. Prefacing '*horse*' with 'the concept' has the effect of turning a sign for a concept into a sign for an object, just as putting quotation marks round the word 'swims' turns the sign for a verb into a noun which, unlike a verb, can be the subject of a sentence. We can say truly ' "swims" is a verb', but also ' " "swims" " is a noun'. That is the clue to understanding Frege's claim that the concept *horse* is not a concept.

First, Second, and Third in Peirce

In the English-speaking world, the most original system of metaphysics devised in the nineteenth century was that of C. S. Peirce. It is true that Peirce's principle of pragmatism resembles the verification principle of the logical positivists, and that from time to time he was willing to denounce metaphysics as 'meaningless gibberish'; nonetheless, he himself constructed a system that was as abstruse and elaborate as anything to be found in the writings of German idealists.

Like Hegel, Pierce was fascinated by triads. He wrote in *The Monist* in 1891:

> Three conceptions are perpetually turning up at every point in every theory of logic, and in the most rounded systems they occur in connection with one another. They are conceptions so very broad and consequently indefinite that they are hard to seize and may be easily overlooked. I call them the conceptions of First, Second, Third. First is the conception of being or existing independent of anything else. Second is the conception of being relative to, the conception of reaction with, something else. Third is the conception of mediation, whereby a first and second are brought into relation. (*EWP* 173)

This triadic system was inspired by Peirce's research into the logic of relations. He classified predicates according to the number of items to which they relate. '... is blue' is a monadic or one-place predicate, '... is the son of ...', with two places, is dyadic, and '... gives ... to ...' is triadic. A sense-impression of a quality is an example of a 'firstness', heredity is an example of a 'secondness'. The third class of items can be exemplified by the relationship whereby a sign signifies ('mediates') an object to an interpreting mind. Universal ideas are a paradigm case of thirdness, and so are laws of nature. If a spark falls into a barrel of gunpowder (first) it causes an explosion (second) and does so according to a law that mediates between the two (third).

---

[4] See above, p. 166.

Peirce was willing to apply this triadic classification very widely, to psychology and to biology as well as to physics and chemistry. He even employed it on a cosmic scale: in one place he wrote 'Mind is First, Matter is Second, Evolution is Third' (*EWP* 173). Moreover, he offered an elaborate proof that while a scientific language must contain monadic, dyadic, and triadic predicates, there are no phenomena that require four-place predicates for their expression. Expressions containing such predicates can always be translated into expressions containing only predicates of the three basic kinds.

Thirdness, however, Peirce sees as an irreducible element of the universe, neglected by nominalist philosophers, who refused to accept the reality of universals. The aim of all scientific inquiry is to find the thirdness in the variety of our experience—to discover the patterns, regularities, and laws in the world we live in. But we should not be looking for universal, exceptionless laws that determine all that happens. The doctrine of necessity, indeed, was one of Peirce's chief targets in his criticism of the *Weltanschauung* of nineteenth-century science. He states it thus:

> The proposition in question is that the state of things existing at any time, together with certain immutable laws, completely determine the state of things at every other time (for a limitation to *future* time is indefensible). Thus, given the state of the universe in the original nebula, and given the laws of mechanics, a sufficiently powerful mind could deduce from these data the precise form of every curlicue of every letter I am now writing. (*EWP* 176)

This proposition, Peirce thought, was quite indefensible. It could be put forward neither as a postulate of reasoning nor as the outcome of observation. 'Try to verify any law of nature and you will find that the more precise your observations, the more certain they will be to show irregular departures from the law' (*EWP* 182). Peirce maintained that there was an irreducible element of chance in the universe: a thesis which he called 'tychism' from the Greek word for chance, τυχη. In support of tychism he enlisted both Aristotle and Darwin. The inclusion of chance as a possible cause, he said, was of the utmost essence of Aristotelianism; and the only way of accounting for the laws of nature was to suppose them results of evolution. 'This supposes them not to be absolute, not to be obeyed precisely. It makes an element of indeterminacy, spontaneity, or absolute chance in nature' (*EWP* 163). Thus, there was ample room for belief in the autonomy and freedom of the human will.

There were, Peirce thought, three ways of explaining the relationship between physical and psychical laws. The first was neutralism, which placed them on a par as independent of each other. The second was materialism, which regarded psychical laws as derived from physical ones. The third was idealism, which regarded psychical laws as primordial and physical laws as derivative. Neutralism, he thought, was ruled out by Ockham's razor: never look for two explanatory factors where one will do. Materialism involved the repugnant idea that a machine could feel. 'The one intelligible theory of the universe is that of objective idealism, that matter is effete mind, inveterate habits becoming physical laws' (*EWP* 168).

Peirce offered to explain the course of the universe in terms of firstness, secondness, and thirdness. 'Three elements are active in the world', he wrote; 'first, chance; second, law; and third, habit-taking' (*CP* i. 409). In the infinitely remote beginning, there was nothing but unpersonalized feeling, without any connection of regularity. Then, the germ of a generalizing tendency would arise as a sport, and would be dominant over other sports. 'Thus, the tendency to habit would be started; and from this with the other principles of evolution all the regularities of the universe would be evolved' (*EWP* 174).

Peirce's theory of cosmic evolution differs from Darwinism in several ways. First of all, he states its principle in utterly general terms, with no reference to animal or plant species:

Wherever there are large numbers of objects, having a tendency to retain certain characters unaltered, this tendency, however, not being absolute but giving room for chance variations, then, if the amount of variation is absolutely limited in certain directions by the destruction of everything that reaches these limits, there will be a gradual tendency to change in directions of departures from them. (*EWP* 164)

Second, while Darwin's doctrine of the survival of the fittest sought to eliminate the need to explain the course of nature in terms of Aristotelian final causes, Peirce, like Aristotle, saw the pursuit of an ultimate goal as the dynamic that rules the universe. Surprising as it may seem, it is love that is the driving force of cosmic history. The original slimy protoplasm has the power of growth and reproduction; it is capable of feeling and it has the property of taking habits. 'Love, recognizing germs of loveliness in the hateful, gradually warms it into life and makes it lovely.' That, for Peirce, is the secret of evolution.

Peirce distinguished three modes of evolution: evolution by fortuitous variation, evolution by mechanical necessity, and evolution by creative love. In accordance with his passion for fashioning English terms from Greek roots, he called these types of evolution tychastic, anancastic, and agapastic, from the Greek words respectively for chance, necessity, and love. Darwin's evolutionary theory was tychastic: there was, Peirce thought, little positive evidence for it, and its popularity was due to the nineteenth century's passion for heartless laissez-faire economics. 'It makes the felicity of the lambs just the damnation of the goats, transposed to the other side of the equation.' The principle of necessity that underpinned anancastic evolution had already, Peirce believed, been disposed of by his arguments. We are left with the third form of evolution, agapastic evolution. Such a form of evolution had been proposed by Lamarck: the endeavours of parents produce beneficial modifications that are inherited by their offspring. 'A genuine evolutionary philosophy,' Peirce tells us in conclusion, 'that is, one that makes the principle of growth a primordial element of the universe, is so far from being antagonistic to the idea of a personal creator, that it is really inseparable from that idea' (*EWP* 214). We have come some distance from the empiricist verificationism that seemed to be the kernel of Peirce's pragmatism.

The Metaphysics of Logical Atomism

Metaphysics goes hand in hand with logic also in Wittgenstein's *Tractatus*. Though most of the book is devoted to the nature of language, its earliest pages consist of a series of pronouncements about the nature of the world. Both historically and logically the theses about the world are dependent upon Wittgenstein's thesis about language; but they amount to a metaphysical system that merits consideration in its own right.

According to the *Tractatus*, to each pair of contradictory propositions there corresponds one and only one fact: the fact that makes one of them true and the other false. The totality of such facts is the world. Facts may be positive or negative: a positive fact is the existence of a state of affairs, a negative fact is the non-existence of a state of affairs. A state of affairs, or situation (*Sachverhalt*), is a combination of objects. An object is essentially a possible constituent of a state of affairs, and its possibility of occurring in combination with other objects in states of affairs is its nature. Since every object contains within its nature all the possibilities of its combination with other objects, it follows that if any object is given all objects are given (*TLP* 1. 1–2. 011).

Objects are simple and lack parts, but they can combine into complexes. They are ungenerable and indestructible, because any possible world must contain the same objects as this one; change is only an alteration in the configuration of objects. Objects may differ from each other by nature, or in external properties, or they may be merely numerically distinct, indiscernible but not identical (*TLP* 2. 022–2. 02331). The objects make up the unalterable and subsistent form, substance, and content of the world.

Objects combine into states of affairs: the way in which they are connected gives the state of affairs its structure. The possibility of a structure is the form of the state of affairs. States of affairs are independent of one another: from the existence or non-existence of one of them it is impossible to infer the existence or non-existence of another. Since facts are the existence and non-existence of states of affairs, it follows that facts too are independent of each other. The totality of facts is the world.

These dense pages of the *Tractatus* are difficult to understand. No examples are given of objects that are the bedrock of the universe. Commentators have offered widely varying interpretations: for some, objects are sense-data; for others, they are universals. Possibly, both of these items would have been recognized by Wittgenstein as objects: after all, they are the same as the items that, according to Russell, were known to us by acquaintance. But the lack of examples in the *Tractatus* is not accidental. Wittgenstein believed in the existence of simple objects and atomic states of affairs not because he thought he could give instances of them, but because he thought that they must exist as the correlates in the world for the names and elementary propositions of a fully analysed language.

His reasoning to that conclusion is based on three premises. First, whether a sentence has meaning or not is a matter of logic. Second, what particular things exist is a matter of experience. Third, logic is prior to all experience. Therefore, whether a sentence has meaning or not can never depend on whether particular things exists. This conclusion lays down a condition that any system of logic must meet. To meet it, Wittgenstein thought, one must lay down that names could signify only simple objects. If 'N' is the name of a complex, then 'N' would have no meaning if the complex were broken up, and sentences containing it would be senseless. So when any such sentence is fully analysed, the name 'N' must disappear and its place be taken by names that name simples (*TLP* 3. 23, 3. 24; *PI* I. 39).

Simple objects, in the world of the *Tractatus*, are concatenated into atomic states of affairs, which correspond to elementary propositions that are concatenations of names. The world can be completely described by listing all elementary propositions, and listing which of them are true and which are false (*TLP* 4. 26). For the true elementary propositions will record all the positive facts, and the false elementary propositions will correspond to all the negative facts, and the totality of facts is the world (*TLP* 2. 06).

Bad and Good Metaphysics

The *Tractatus* is one of the most metaphysical works ever written: its likeness to Spinoza's *Ethics* is no coincidence. Yet it was taken as a bible by one of the most anti-metaphysical groups of philosophers, the Vienna Circle. The logical positivists seized on the idea that necessary truths were necessary only because they were tautologies: this enabled them, they believed, to reconcile the necessity of mathematics with a thoroughgoing empiricism. They then employed the verification principle as a weapon that enabled them to dismiss all metaphysical statements as meaningless.

Wittgenstein, throughout his life, shared the positivists' view that the removal, the dissolution, of metaphysics was one of the tasks of the philosopher. He described the task of the philosopher as 'bringing words back from their metaphysical to their everyday use'. He condemned the metaphysics that was a search for the hidden essence of language or of the world. Yet he was himself a metaphysician in his own right—and not just at the time of the *Tractatus*, whose propositions he condemned as nonsensical, but throughout his later philosophy. He recognized that there could be a legitimate attempt to understand essences, in which he was himself engaged. In our investigations, he said, 'we try to understand the essence of language, its function and construction'. What was wrong, on his view, was to consider the essence not as something that lies open to view and must merely be given a perspicuous description, but as something interior and hidden: a kind of metaphysical ectoplasm or hardware that explains the functioning of mind and language. There were in particular three kinds of metaphysics against which Wittgenstein set his face: spiritualistic metaphysics, scientistic metaphysics, and foundationalist metaphysics.

When we consider human thought, the metaphysical impulse may lead us to postulate spiritual substances, or spiritual processes. We are misled by grammar. When grammar makes us expect a physical substance, but there is not one, we invent a metaphysical substance; where it makes us expect an empirical process, but we cannot find one, we postulate an incorporeal process. This is the origin of Cartesian dualism; the Cartesian mind is a metaphysical substance and its operation upon the body is a metaphysical process. Cartesianism is metaphysical in the sense of isolating statements about mental life from any possibility of conclusive verification or falsification in the public world.

Besides dualist metaphysics, there is materialist metaphysics. 'The characteristic of a metaphysical question', he wrote, 'is that we express an unclarity about the grammar of words in the form of a scientific question' (*BB* 35). Metaphysics is philosophy masquerading as natural science, and this is the form of metaphysics particularly beloved of materialists. It is a metaphysical error to think, for instance, that exploration of the brain will help us to understand what is going on in our minds when we think and understand.

The great metaphysicians of the past have often thought of their subject as having primacy over all other parts of philosophy: Aristotle called metaphysics 'first philosophy' and Descartes thought metaphysics was the root of the tree of knowledge. Wittgenstein denied that any part of philosophy should be privileged in this way. One could start philosophizing at any point, and leave off the treatment of one philosophical problem to take up the treatment of another. Philosophy had no foundations, and did not provide foundations for other disciplines. Philosophy was not a house, nor a tree, but a web.

The real discovery is the one that makes me capable of stopping doing philosophy when I want to.
The one that gives philosophy peace, so that it is no longer tormented by questions which bring *itself* in question.

Instead, we now demonstrate a method, by examples; and the series of examples can be broken off.

Problems are solved (difficulties eliminated), not a *single* problem. (*PI* I. 133)

But while Wittgenstein, throughout his life, was hostile to scientistic and foundational metaphysics, in his later work he did in fact make substantial contributions to areas of philosophy that would traditionally have been regarded as metaphysical. Much of Aristotle's *Metaphysics* is devoted to philosophical activities that resemble quite closely Wittgenstein's own method.

The distinction between actuality and potentiality, and the classification of different kinds of potentiality, is universally recognized (by both friend and foe) as being one of Aristotle's most characteristic contributions to philosophy and in particular to the philosophy of mind. His distinctions were later systematized by scholastic philosophers in the Middle Ages. Wittgenstein undertook a prolonged investigation of the nature of potentiality in the Brown Book, where sections 58–67 are devoted to various language-games with the word 'can'. The distinctions that he draws between processes and states, and between different kinds of states, correspond to the Aristotelian distinctions between *kinesis*, *hexis*, and *energeia*. The criteria by which the two philosophers make the distinctions often coincide. The example that Wittgenstein discusses at length, to illustrate the relation between a power and its exercise, namely learning to read (*PI* I. 156 ff.), is close to the standard Aristotelian example of a mental *hexis*, namely, knowledge of grammar. We may call the systematic study of actuality and potentiality *dynamic metaphysics*, and if we do so we must say that Wittgenstein was one of the most consummate practitioners of that particular form of metaphysics.

It was not an Aristotelian type, however, but a Leibnizian one, that turned out to be the most flourishing version of metaphysics in the latter half of the twentieth century. The development of modal semantics in terms of possible worlds[5] need not, in itself, have had metaphysical implications, but a number of philosophers interpreted it in a metaphysical sense and were prepared to countenance the idea that there were identifiable individuals that had only possible and not actual existence.

In my view, this was a mistaken development. There is a difficulty in providing a criterion of identity for merely possible objects. If something is to be a subject of which we can make predications, it is essential that it shall be possible to tell in what circumstances two predications are made of *that same subject*. Otherwise we shall never be able to apply the principle that contradictory predications should not be made of the same subject. We have various complicated criteria by which we decide whether two statements are being made about the same actual man; by what criteria can we decide whether two statements are being made about the

---

[5] See p. 846 above.

same *possible* man? These difficulties were entertainingly brought out by Quine in his famous paper 'On What There Is' of 1961:

Take, for instance, the possible fat man in that doorway; and again, the possible bald man in that doorway. Are they the same possible man, or two possible men? How do we decide? How many possible men are there in that doorway? Are there more possible thin ones than fat ones? How many of them are alike? Are no *two* possible things alike? Is this the same as saying that it is impossible for two things to be alike? Or, finally, is the concept of identity simply inapplicable to unactualised possibles? But what sense can be found in talking of entities which cannot meaningfully be said to be identical with themselves and distinct from one another? (*FLPV* 666)

The questions asked by Quine seem to me unanswerable, and thus to expose the incoherence of the notion of unactualized possible individuals. But in the last decades of the century philosophers of great talent exercised themselves to answer Quine's questions and thus to solve what was called 'the problem of transworld identity'. In the light of the history recorded in these volumes it seems to me more prudent to adhere to the grand Aristotelian principle that there is no individuation without actualization—the counterpart of the cardinal anti-Platonic principle that there is no actualization without individuation.

In the English-speaking world metaphysics was flourishing at the beginning of the twentieth century, with Peirce in America extolling the principle of cosmic love, and the neo-Hegelians in Britain tracing the lineaments of the Absolute. As the century progressed philosophers became more and more hostile to metaphysics; this hostility climaxed with the positivism of the 1930s, but it continued to be influential well into the second half of the century. With the approach of the twenty-first century, metaphysics once more became respectable, but with a difference. The place once occupied by the monistic metaphysics of the British idealists is now taken by the pluralistic, indeed exuberant, metaphysics of the explorers of possible worlds. It will be interesting to see whether the twenty-first century exhibits a similar cycle of metaphysical thought.

8

Philosophy of Mind

Bentham on Intention and Motive

Bentham's *Principles of Morals and Legislation* contained a detailed analysis of human action. It devoted substantial chapters to such topics as intention and motive. Not since the Middle Ages had a great philosopher devoted such minute attention to the different cognitive and affective elements whose presence or absence may contribute to the moral character of individual actions. Bentham's approach to the topic resembles that of Aquinas, but he is much more generous in providing concrete examples to illustrate his points. More importantly, there is a significant difference between the two philosophers both in terminology and in moral evaluation.[1]

For Aquinas, an action was intentional if it was chosen as a means to an end; if an action was only an unavoidable accompaniment or consequence of such a choice it was not intentional, but only voluntary. Bentham disliked the word 'voluntary'; it was misleading, he said, because it sometimes meant *uncoerced* and sometimes meant *spontaneous*. He preferred to use the word 'intentional'. However, he made the same distinction as Aquinas, but marked it as a distinction between two kinds of intention. A consequence, he said, may be either directly intentional ('when the prospect of producing it constituted one of the links in the chain of causes by which the person was determined to act') or obliquely intentional ('when the consequence was foreseen as likely, but the prospect of producing it formed no link in the determining chain'). For Bentham, an incident that is directly intentional may be either ultimately or mediately intentional, according to whether the prospect of producing it would or would not have operated as a motive if not viewed as productive of a further event. This distinction between ultimate and mediate intention corresponds to the scholastic distinction between ends and means.

Bentham illustrated his panoply of distinctions by referring to the story of the death of King William II of England, who died while stag hunting from a wound

[1] See above, p. 458.

inflicted by one Sir Walter Tyrell. He rang the changes on the possible degrees of consciousness and intentionality in the mind of Tyrell, and assigned the appropriate classification to each imagined case: unintentional, obliquely intentional, directly intentional, mediately intentional, ultimately intentional.

The effect of Bentham's terminology was to define intention itself in purely cognitive terms: to find out what a person intended you need to ascertain what she knew, not what she wanted. What she wanted is relevant only to the subclass of intentionality involved. An act is unintentional only if its upshot was quite unforeseen; it is thus that 'you may intend to touch a man without intending to hurt him; and yet, as the consequences turn out, you may chance to hurt him'. The cognitive slant that Bentham gives to intention is of great importance, since for him intention is a key criterion for the moral and legal evaluation of actions.

We should not think, however, Bentham tells us, that intentions are good and bad in themselves. 'If [an intention] be deemed good or bad in any sense, it must be either because it is deemed to be productive of good or of bad consequences or because it is deemed to originate from a good or from a bad motive' (*P* 8. 13). Now consequences depend on circumstances, and circumstances are simply either known or unknown to the agent. So whatever is to be said of the goodness or badness of a person's intention as resulting from the consequences of his act depends on his knowledge ('consciousness') of the circumstances.

In the ninth chapter of the *Principles* Bentham classifies the different possible degrees of such consciousness. If a man is aware of a circumstance when he acts, then his act is said to have been an *advised* act, with respect to that circumstance; otherwise an *unadvised* act. Besides being unaware of circumstances that actually obtain, an agent may suppose that circumstances do obtain which in fact do not obtain; this is *missupposal* and makes an act *misadvised*. If an act is intentional, and is advised with respect to all circumstances relevant to a particular consequence, and there is no missupposal of preventive circumstances, then the consequence is intentional. 'Advisedness, with respect to the circumstances, if clear from the missupposal of any preventive circumstance, extends the intentionality from the act to the consequences' (*P* 9. 10).

Bentham makes a distinction between intentions and motives: a man's intentions may be good and his motives bad. Suppose that 'out of malice a man prosecutes you for a crime of which he believes you to be guilty, but of which in fact you are not guilty'. Here the motive is evil, and the actual consequences are mischievous; nonetheless, the intention is good, because the consequences of the man's action would have been good if they had turned out as he foresaw.

In discussing motives Bentham stresses the evaluative overtones of words such as 'lust', 'avarice', and 'cruelty'. In itself, he says, no motive is either good or bad; these words denote bad motives only in the sense that they are never properly applied except where the motives they signify happen to be bad. 'Lust', for instance, 'is the name given to sexual desire when the effects of it are regarded as bad.' It is only in individual cases that motives can be good or bad. 'A motive is good, when the intention it gives birth to is a good one; bad, when the intention is a bad one; and an emotion is good or bad according to the material consequences that are the objects of it' (*P* 10. 33).

By 'motive' Bentham means what, described in neutral terms, he would call an ultimately and directly intentional consequence. From his explanation it is clear that it does not supply a separate title of moral qualification of an act; the only mental state primarily relevant to the morality of a voluntary act is the cognitive state with regard to the consequences.

Bentham's account of motive is in accord with the general utilitarian position that moral goodness and badness in actions is to be judged in terms of their consequences with respect to pleasure and pain. His cognitive conception of intention brought his followers into conflict with the doctrine of double effect according to which there may be a moral difference between doing something on purpose and merely foreseeing it as an unwanted consequence of one's choices. These moral issues will be discussed in detail in Chapter 9.

In his *Groundwork* Kant exalted the importance of motive more than any other moral philosopher had ever done. Bentham's position stands at the opposite extreme of ethical theory. As J. S. Mill was to put it, the utilitarians 'have gone beyond almost all others in affirming that the motive has nothing to do with the morality of the action'. Not only motive, but also intention as commonly understood, is irrelevant to utilitarian moral judgement of behaviour. It is an agreeable paradox that the founder of utilitarianism should have offered a fuller analysis of the concepts of intention and motive than any previous writer had achieved.

Reason, Understanding, and Will

In continental Europe the analysis of mental concepts took a different course. The absolute idealism of a philosopher such as Hegel makes it difficult to distinguish in his work between philosophy of mind and metaphysics. Schopenhauer, however, starting from Kant's distinction between understanding (*Verstand*) and reason (*Vernunft*), offers a detailed study of the differences that mark off human from animal cognitive faculties.

Understanding, as well as sensation, is something that animals share with humans, because understanding is the capacity to grasp causal relations, which is something that animals can clearly do. Indeed, the sagacity of animals like foxes and elephants sometimes surpasses human understanding. But human beings alone possess reason, that is to say, abstract knowledge embodied in concepts. Reason is the capacity for reflection, which places humans far above animals, both in power and in suffering. Animals live in the present alone; man lives at the same time in the future and the past (*WWI* 36).

Reason confers three great gifts on humans: language, freedom, and science. The first and most essential is language.

Only by the aid of language does reason bring about its most important achievements, namely the harmonious and consistent action of several individuals, the planned cooperation of many thousands, civilization, the State; and then, science, the storing up of previous experience, the summarizing into one concept of what is common, the communication of truth, the spreading of error, thoughts and poems, dogmas and superstitions. (*WWI* 37)

The importance of abstract knowledge is that it can be retained and shared. Understanding can grasp the mode of operation of a lever, or the support of an arch; but more than understanding is needed for the construction of machines and buildings. For practical purposes, mere understanding may sometimes be preferable: 'it is of no use to me to know in the abstract the exact angle, in degrees and minutes, at which I must apply a razor, if I do not know it intuitively, that is, if I have not got the feel of it'. But when long-term planning is necessary, or when the help of others is required, abstract knowledge is essential.

Animals and humans, according to Schopenhauer, both have wills, but only humans can deliberate. It is only in the abstract that different motives can be simultaneously presented in consciousness as objects of choice. Ethical conduct must be based on principles; but principles are abstract. However, reason, though necessary for virtue, is not sufficient for virtue. 'Reason is found with great wickedness no less than with great kindness, and by its assistance gives great effectiveness to the one as to the other' (*WWI* 86).

The will, for Schopenhauer, is present and active throughout the universe, but we grasp its nature only through the human willing of which we are ourselves directly aware. All willing, Schopenhauer tells us, arises from a want, a deficiency, and therefore from suffering. A wish may be granted, but for one wish that is satisfied there are ten that are denied. Desire lasts long; fulfilment is only momentary. 'No attained object of desire can give lasting satisfaction, but merely a fleeting gratification; it is like the alms thrown to the beggar, that keeps him alive today that his misery may be prolonged till the morrow' (*WWI* 196).

As a general rule, knowledge is at the service of the will, engaged in the satisfaction of its desires. This is always the case in animals, and is symbolized by the way in which the head of a lower animal is directed towards the ground. In humans, too, for the most part knowledge is the slave of will; but humans can rise above the consideration of objects as mere instruments for the satisfaction of desire. The human stands erect, and like the Apollo Belvedere he can look into the far distance, adopting an attitude of contemplation, oblivious to the body's needs.

In this state the human mind encounters a new class of objects: not just the Lockean ideas of perception, nor just the abstract ideas of reason, but the universal

Ideas that Plato described. The way to grasp the Ideas is this: let your whole consciousness be filled with the quiet contemplation of a landscape or a building, and forget your own individuality, your own needs and desires. What you will then know will no longer be an individual, but an eternal form, a particular degree of objectification of the universal will. And you will lose yourself and become a pure, will-less, painless, timeless subject of knowledge, seeing things *sub specie aeternitatis*. 'In such contemplation the particular thing becomes at once the *Idea* of its species, and the perceiving individual becomes *pure subject of knowledge*. The individual, as such, knows only particular things; the pure subject of knowledge knows only Ideas' (*WWI* 179). In contemplation free from the servitude of the will, we lose our concern with happiness and unhappiness. Indeed, we cease to be individual: we become 'that *one* eye of the world which looks out from all knowing creatures, but which can become perfectly free from the service of will in man alone'.

Every human being has it within his power to know the Ideas in things, but a specially favoured individual may possess this knowledge more intensely and more continuously than ordinary mortals. Such a person is what we mean by a genius.

Schopenhauer spells out for us the characteristics of the genius: the genius is imaginative and restless, he dislikes mathematics, and he lives on the borderline of madness. His gift finds expression above all in works of art, and it is through works of art that those of us who are not geniuses can be introduced to the liberating effect of contemplation. Schopenhauer spells this out in a detailed consideration of the various arts. The deliverance from the tyranny of the will that is offered by art is, however, a limited and temporary one. The only way to a complete liberation is by renouncing altogether the will to live.[2]

What, in Schopenhauer's system, is the relationship between soul and body? First of all, there is a complete rejection of the dualistic idea that there are causal relations between the inner and the outer. The will and the movements of the body are not two different events linked by causality: the actions of the body are the acts of the will made perceptible. The whole body, with all its parts, Schopenhauer says, is nothing but the objectification of the will and its desires:

Teeth, throat and bowels are objectified hunger; the organs of generation are objectified sexual desire; the grasping hand, the hurrying feet, correspond to the more indirect desires of the will which they express. As the human form in general corresponds to the human will in general, so the individual bodily structure corresponds to the individually modified will, the character of the individual, and therefore it is throughout and in all its parts characteristic and full of expression. (*WWI* 108)

Schopenhauer here anticipates a famous remark of Wittgenstein's, 'The human body is the best picture of the human soul' (*PI* II. 178).

---

[2] Schopenhauer's aesthetic theory is considered in Ch. 10 and his ethical theory in Ch. 9 below.

The body is intimately involved in knowledge as well as in desire; my own body is the starting point of my perception of the world, and my knowledge of other perceptible objects depends on their effects on my body. But even when we rise above knowledge of ideas to knowledge of Ideas, the body still has a role, as Schopenhauer rather surprisingly tells us. 'Man is at once impetuous and blind striving of will (whose pole or focus lies in the genitals) and eternal, free, serene subject of pure knowledge (whose pole is the brain)' (*WWI* 203).

Is there any part of a human being that survives the death of the body, or does total extinction await us? On the one hand Schopenhauer says, 'Before us there is indeed only nothingness'; on the other hand, he can say, 'if, *per impossibile*, a single being, even the most insignificant, were entirely annihilated, the whole world would inevitably be destroyed with it' (*WWI* 129). The latter claim is derived from the metaphysical principle that the will which is the inner reality of every individual is itself single and indivisible. Interpreters have sought to reconcile the two pronouncements by suggesting that at death the human person is absorbed into the single will: it continues, therefore, to exist, but it loses all individuality.

Experimental vs. Philosophical Psychology

As the nineteenth century progressed, psychologists endeavoured to launch a new science of the mind, which would study mental phenomena by empirical and experimental methods. In Europe the first psychological laboratory was set up in 1879 at the University of Leipzig by Wilhelm Wundt, a professor of physiology, specializing in the nervous system, who five years earlier had published an influential text entitled 'Principles of Physiological Psychology'. William James, who had gone to Germany to study in this field, anticipated Wundt by setting up a psychology laboratory in Harvard, and in 1878 the first ever doctorate in psychology was awarded. James summed up the findings of the new science in his volumes *Principles of Psychology* (1890), a work described by Bertrand Russell as possessing 'the highest possible excellence'.

The task of the new psychology was to relate mental events and states to processes in the brain and nervous system. James's textbook introduced the student to the relevant physiology and reported the work of European psychologists on the reaction times of experimental subjects. It ranged widely, from the instinctive behaviour of animals to the phenomena of hypnotism. For most of the time, James was surveying the work of others; but from time to time he made his own original contribution to the subject.

James's most famous innovation in philosophical psychology was his theory of the emotions. While his contemporaries strove to find the exact relation between emotional feelings and their concomitant bodily processes, James proposed that the emotions were nothing more than the perception of these processes. In *The Principles of Psychology* he wrote:

Our natural way of thinking about coarser emotions is that the mental perception of some fact excites the mental affection called the emotion, and that this latter state of mind gives rise to the bodily expression. My theory, on the contrary, is that the bodily changes follow directly the perception of the exciting fact, and that our feeling of the same changes as they occur IS the emotion. Commonsense says, we lose our fortune, are sorry and weep; we meet a bear, are frightened and run; we are insulted by a rival, are angry and strike. The hypothesis here to be defended says that this order of sequence is incorrect, that the one mental state is not immediately induced by the other, that the bodily manifestations must first be interposed between, and that the more rational statement is that we feel sorry because we cry, angry because we strike, afraid because we tremble. (ii. 250)

In order to account for the great variety of emotional states, James insisted that there was hardly any limit to the permutations and combinations of possible minute bodily changes, and each one of these, he claimed, was felt, acutely or obscurely, the moment it occurred. But he was not able to give any independent criterion for the occurrence of such feelings.

James's theory of the emotions had been anticipated by Descartes. The influence of Descartes is, in fact, all-pervasive in his account of the human mind. Nineteenth-century psychologists were anxious to emancipate themselves from the thrall of philosophy; but while their investigations of physiological phenomena produced genuine scientific discoveries, their notion of the conscious mind was taken over, lock, stock, and barrel, from the Cartesian tradition in philosophy. This is abundantly clear in James's *Principles*, but is perhaps most candidly expressed in his early paper of 1884, 'The Function of Cognition' (*T* 1–42).

All states of consciousness, James there says, can be called 'feelings'; and by 'feeling' he means the same as Locke meant by 'idea' and Descartes meant by 'thought'. Some feelings are cognitive and some are not. In order to determine what makes the difference between cognitive and non-cognitive states, James invites us to consider a feeling of the most basic possible kind:

Let us suppose it attached to no matter, nor localized at any point in space, but left swinging *in vacuo*, as it were, by the direct creative *fiat* of a god. And let us also, to escape entanglement with difficulties about the physical or psychical nature of its 'object', not call it a feeling of fragrance or of any other determinate sort, but limit ourselves to assuming that it is a feeling of *q*. (*T* 3)

We are further invited to consider this as a feeling that constitutes the entire universe, and lasts only an infinitesimal part of a second.

James inquires what addition to this primal feeling would be needed to make it into a cognitive state. He replies (*a*) that there must be in the world another entity resembling the feeling in its quality q, and (b) the feeling must either directly or indirectly operate upon this other entity. James's account of knowledge does not appear very plausible, but it is not his conclusion but his starting point that it is important to notice. He envisages consciousness as consisting fundamentally of a series of solitary atoms devoid of any context or relation to any behaviour or to any body.

Later in his life James took a less atomistic view of the nature of feeling, believing that as a matter of empirical fact consciousness flowed in a continuous stream without sharp breaks between one item and the next. But he retained the idea of consciousness as an essentially private internal phenomenon, connected only contingently with any external manifestation in speech and behaviour, and capable in principle of existing in isolation from any body. This, of course, was precisely how Descartes had conceived of consciousness.

Physiological psychologists saw themselves as liberating themselves from philosophy by substituting experiment for introspection as the method of studying the mind. But in this they were mistaken in two ways. First, a thinker like James retains the picture of consciousness as an object of introspection: something we can *see* when we look *within*; something to which we have ourselves direct access, but which others can learn of only indirectly, by accepting our verbal testimony or making causal inferences from our physical behaviour. Second, whatever Locke and Hume may have thought, the philosophy of mind does not operate by scrupulous observation of internal phenomena but by the examination of the concepts that we make use of in expressing our experience.

The hollowness of Descartes's notion of consciousness was exposed, later in the twentieth century, by the work of Wittgenstein (who admired James as a particularly honest and candid exponent of the Cartesian tradition). But in James's own lifetime, what appeared to be the most serious challenge to the work of the experimental psychologists came from a different quarter: from the picture of the mind presented by Freudian psychoanalysis.

The Freudian Unconscious

In his *Introductory Lectures on Psychoanalysis* Freud states as one of the two main foundations of his theory that the greater part of our mental life, whether of feeling, thought, or volition, is unconscious. Before deciding whether we should accept this principle we need to look closely at what is meant by 'unconscious'. There are several possible senses of the word, and depending on which sense we take, Freud's thesis may turn out a truism or a piece of hardy speculation.

It is obvious that at any given moment only a tiny fraction of what we know and believe is present to consciousness in the sense of being an object of our immediate attention. For more than sixty years I have known the nursery rhyme 'Three Blind Mice' and have believed that the battle of Waterloo took place in 1815; but the occasions on which I have recited the rhyme or adverted to the date have been few and far between. The distinction between knowledge and its exercise was already made by Aristotle as a distinction between first and second actuality. Knowing Greek, he said, was an actuality in comparison with the simple ability to learn languages with which all humans are endowed. But knowledge of Greek was only a first actuality, an ability that is exercised only when I am speaking, hearing, reading, or thinking in Greek. That was the second actuality. A parallel distinction can be made with regard to one's wishes, plans, and intentions. You no doubt wish to have an adequate provision for your pension. But the thought of your pension does not occupy your mind all the time: only when you are worrying about it, or engaged in taking steps to make such provision, are you conscious of this wish of yours.

If this is the way in which we make the distinction between the conscious and the unconscious then Freud's statement that most of our mental life is unconscious is nothing more than a philosophical commonplace. But of course, Freud meant more than that. Knowledge, thoughts, and feelings of the kind I have described can, in appropriate circumstances, easily be brought to mind. If someone asks me the date of the battle of Waterloo I can give it; if a financial adviser asks you about your pension provision you have no difficulty in admitting that it is a matter of concern. The unconscious that Freud postulated, in contrast, is not at all so easy to bring to consciousness.

There are in fact three levels of the Freudian unconscious. To disentangle these we must recall that according to Freud there are three sets of phenomena that reveal the existence of the unconscious, namely, trivial everyday mistakes, reports of dreams, and neurotic symptoms.

We all frequently make slips of the tongue, fail to recall names, and mislay useful objects. Freud believed that such 'parapraxes', as he called them, are not as accidental as they seem and may have hidden motives. He quotes the case of a Viennese professor who in his inaugural lecture, instead of saying, according to his script, 'I have no intention of underrating the achievements of my illustrious predecessor' said 'I have every intention of underrating the achievements of my illustrious predecessor.' Freud regards the professor's slip of the tongue as a better guide to his intentions that the words he had written in his notes. But of course the professor was perfectly well aware of his true attitude to his predecessor's work: his intention was only 'unconscious' in the sense that he did not mean to *express* it so publicly. Something similar can happen in writing as well as in speech. Freud tells of a husband who, writing to his estranged wife some years after the sinking of the *Lusitania*, urged her to join him across the Atlantic with the words 'Sail on the *Lusitania*' when he meant to write 'Sail on the *Mauretania*'. Dramatists, Freud maintained, have long been aware of the significance of such parapraxes. In *The Merchant of*

Venice, when Portia is struggling between her public obligation to be neutral between her suitors and her private love for Bassanio, Shakespeare makes her say to him:

> One half of me is yours, the other half yours—
> Mine own, I would say.

That such 'Freudian slips' can be revelatory of states of mind that the utterer would prefer to conceal is now very widely accepted. But note that the mental state in question is something that can be verified in a perfectly straightforward way, by seeking a truthful confession from the person guilty of the slip. Such states are, for Freud, the superficial level of the unconscious; he sometimes called this level 'the preconscious' (*NIL* 96).

Matters are rather different when we come to the second method of tapping into the unconscious: the analysis of dream reports. The interpretation of dreams, Freud maintained, 'is the royal road to a knowledge of the unconscious activities of the mind'. But the interpretation is not something that the dreamer can casually undertake for herself; it calls for long and perhaps painful sessions with the psychoanalyst.

Dreams, Freud claimed, are almost always the fulfilment, in fantasy, of a repressed wish. True, few dreams are obvious representations of a satisfaction, and some dreams such as nightmares seem to be just the opposite. But this, according to Freud, is because we dream in code. The true, latent content of the dream is given a symbolic form by the dreamer; this is the 'dream-work', which produces the innocuous manifest content reported by the dreamer. Once stripped of its symbolic form the latent content of the dream can commonly be revealed as sexual, and indeed Oedipal. However, Freud warns us, 'the straightforward dream of sexual relations with one's mother which Jocasta alludes to in the *Oedipus Rex* is a rarity in comparison with the multiplicity of dreams which psychoanalysis must interpret in the same sense' (*SE* xix. 131 ff.).

How is a dream to be decoded and the dream-work undone? Every dream can easily be given a sexual significance if one takes every pointed object like an umbrella to represent a penis, and every capacious object like a handbag to represent the female genitals. But Freud's method was nothing like as crude as that. He did not believe that it was possible to create a universal dictionary linking symbols to what they signified. The significance of a dream item for a particular dreamer could only be discovered by finding out what the dreamer herself associated with that item. Only after such an exploration could one discover the nature of the unconscious wish whose fulfilment was fantasized in the dream.

The third (though chronologically the first) method by which Freud purported to explore the unconscious was by the examination of neurotic symptoms. A typical case is the following. One of his patients, an Austrian undergraduate, was staying at a holiday resort during the vacation. He was suddenly obsessed with the thought that he was too fat: he said to himself

'Ich bin zu dick'. Consequently, he gave up all heavy foods, and used to leap up from the table before the pudding arrived in order to run up mountains in the August heat. 'Our patient could think of no explanation of this senseless obsessional behaviour until it suddenly occurred to him that at this time his fiancée had also been stopping at the same resort in company with an attractive English cousin called Dick.' His purpose in slimming, Freud suggests, had been to get rid of this Dick (*SE* x. 183).

There is a certain circularity in Freud's procedure for discovering the deeper levels of the unconscious. The existence of these deeper levels is held to be proved by the evidence of dreams and neuroses. But dreams and neurotic symptoms do not, either on their face or as interpreted by the unaided patient, reveal the beliefs, desires, and sentiments of which the unconscious is supposed to consist. For a cure to be effective, the patient has to acknowledge the alleged latent desire. But the analyst's decoding is often rejected by the patient, and the criterion of success in decipherment is that the decoded message should accord with the analyst's notion of what the unconscious is like. But that notion was supposed to derive from, and not to precede, the exploration of dreams and symptoms.

Towards the end of his life Freud replaced the dichotomy of conscious and unconscious with a threefold scheme. 'Superego, ego and id', he said in *New Introductory Lectures* (1933), 'are the three realms, regions, or provinces into which we divide the mental apparatus of the individual' (*NIL* 97). The id is the unconscious locus of hunger and love and instinctual drives. It is ruled by the pleasure principle, and it is both more extensive and more obscure than the other parts of the soul. 'The logical laws of thought', Freud tells us, 'do not apply in the id, and this is true above all of the law of contradiction. Contrary impulses exist, side by side, without cancelling each other out or diminishing each other' (*SE* xxii. 73).

The ego, by contrast, represents reason and common sense, and it is devoted to the reality principle. It is the part of the soul most in touch with the external world perceived by the senses. The ego is the rider and the id the horse. 'The horse supplies the locomotive energy, while the rider has the privilege of deciding on the goal and of guiding the powerful animal's movement' (*SE* xx. 201). But the ego's control is not absolute: the ego is more like a constitutional monarch who has to think long and hard before vetoing any proposal of parliament. Psychoanalysis, however, can strengthen the ego's hold on the id, and assist it in its task of controlling instinctual desires, choosing harmless moments for their satisfaction or diverting their expression. Varying his metaphor, Freud speaks in hydraulic terms of the operation of the id as a flow of energy that can find a normal discharge, be channelled into alternative outlets, or be dammed up with catastrophic results.

The superego, finally, is an agency that observes, judges, and punishes the behaviour of the ego. One form of its manifestations is the utterances of conscience, forbidding actions in advance and reproaching the ego for them after the event (*NIL* 82). The superego is not present from birth; in early childhood its place is taken by parental authority. As the child develops, the superego takes over one half of the function of parents—not their loving and caring activities, but only their harshness and severity, their preventive and punitive functions. The superego is also 'the vehicle of the ego ideal by which the ego measures itself, which it emulates and whose demand for ever greater perfection it is always striving to fulfil' (*SE* xxii. 65).

Freud claimed that the modification of his earlier theory had been forced on him by the observation of the patients on his couch. Yet the mind, in this later form, closely resembles the tripartite soul of Plato's *Republic*.[3] The id corresponds to what Plato calls appetite (*epithumetikon*), the source of the desires for food and sex. The ego has much in common with Plato's reasoning power (*logistikon*): it is the part of the soul most in touch with reality and has the task of controlling instinctual desire. Finally, the superego resembles Plato's temper (*thumoeides*); both are non-rational punitive forces in the service of morality, the source of shame and self-directed anger.

The ego, as depicted by Freud, has to try to satisfy three tyrannical masters: the external world, the superego, and the id.

Goaded on by the id, hemmed in by the super-ego, and rebuffed by reality, the ego struggles to cope with its economic task of reducing the forces and influences which work in it and upon it to some kind of harmony; and we may well understand how it is that we so often cannot repress the cry 'Life is not easy'. (*NIL* 104)

Like Plato, Freud regards mental health as harmony between the parts of the soul, and mental illness as unresolved discord between them. 'So long as the ego and its relations to the id fulfil these ideal conditions (of harmonious control) there will be no neurotic disturbance' (*SE* xx. 201). The ego's whole endeavour is 'a reconciliation between its various dependent relationships' (xix. 149). In the absence of such reconciliation mental disorders develop, and Freud details the symptoms of different kinds of internal conflict.

Philosophical Psychology in the Tractatus

While Freud, in the Austrian capital, was giving his Introductory Lectures on Psychoanalysis, Wittgenstein, in the Austrian army, was constructing, in his notebooks, a different model of the mind. Wittgenstein accepted that psychology was a genuine empirical science, and he saw philosophy of mind as standing in the same relation to psychology as philosophy in general stood to the natural sciences: its task was to clarify its propositions and draw limits to its competence (*TLP* 4. 112, 4. 113). It would do this by analysing sentences reporting beliefs, judgements,

---

[3] See above, pp. 189–90, and A. Kenny, *The Anatomy of the Soul* (Oxford: Blackwell, 1974), 10–14.

perception, and the like; and above all by casting the light of logic on the nature of thought.

The first thing the *Tractatus* tells us about a thought is that it is a logical picture of facts. A logical picture is a picture whose pictorial form—that which it has in common with what it depicts—is logical form. Ordinary pictures may have more than logical form in common with what they depict, as a painting has spatial form in common with a landscape; but a thought is a picture in the mind that has in common with what it depicts nothing other than logical form.

Sometimes Wittgenstein identifies thoughts with propositions (*TLP* 4). But if we examine his use of 'proposition' closely, it is clear that there are two different elements involved. There is the propositional sign or sentence, which is the holding of a relation between written or spoken words. There is also what is expressed by this propositional sign, namely the thought, which is itself the holding of a relation between psychic elements, about whose precise nature Wittgenstein refused to commit himself, since that was a matter for empirical psychology (*TLP* 3. 1, 3. 11–12). A propositional sign can only be a proposition if projected by a thought on to the world, and conversely a relationship between mental elements can only be a thought if it is a projection on to the world of a propositional sign (*TLP* 3. 5).

'In a proposition', Wittgenstein says at 3. 2, 'a thought can be expressed in such a way that elements of the propositional sign correspond to the objects of the thought.' The 'objects of the thought' are the psychic elements whose relation to each other constitutes the thought. A proposition is fully analysed when the elements of the propositional sign correspond to the elements of the thought. An unanalysed proposition of ordinary language does not bear this relation to the thought; on the contrary, it disguises the thought. We can understand ordinary language and grasp the thought beneath its folds only because of enormously complicated tacit conventions. Wittgenstein in the *Tractatus* resembles Freud in attaching great weight to unconscious operations of the mind; the structure of the thoughts that lie behind our utterances are something of which we have not the faintest awareness.

Among our thoughts there appear to be some that are thoughts about thoughts: propositions reporting beliefs and judgements, for example. These are apparent counter-examples to the general thesis of the *Tractatus* that one proposition could occur within another only truth-functionally, because a sentence like 'A believes that p' is not a truth-function of p. Wittgenstein deals with the problem in drastic fashion: such sentences are not genuine propositions at all.

'It is clear,' we are told at 5. 542, 'that "A believes that p", "A has the thought that p", and "A says p" are of the form " 'p' says p", and this does not involve a correlation of a fact with an object, but rather the correlation of facts by means of the correlation of their objects.' ' "p" says p' is a pseudo-proposition: it is an attempt to say what can only be shown; a proposition can only show its sense and cannot state it. We may think that, according to the *Tractatus*, the fact that, say, in 'London is bigger than Paris' 'London' is to the left of 'is bigger than' and 'Paris' is to the right of 'is bigger than' that *says* that London is bigger than Paris. But it is only this fact *plus the conventions of the English language* that says any such thing. What does the saying in the sentence is what the propositional sign has in common with all other propositional signs which could achieve the same purpose; and what *this* is could only be described by—*per impossibile*—specifying and making explicit the tacit conventions of English.

Suppose I think a certain thought; my thinking that thought will consist in certain psychic elements—mental images, or internal impressions, perhaps—standing in a relation to each other. That these elements stand in such and such a relation will be a psychological fact within the purview of science. But the fact that these elements have the meaning they have will not be a fact of science. Meaning is conferred on signs by *us*, by our conventions. But where are the acts of will that confer the meaning by setting up the conventions? They cannot be in the empirical soul studied by superficial psychology: any relation between *that* will and any pair of objects would be a scientific fact and therefore incapable of the ineffable activity of conferring meaning. When I confer meaning on the symbols I use, the I that does so must be a metaphysical I, not the self that is studied by introspective psychology. Thought, unlike language, will have the appropriate complexity to depict the facts of the world. But its complexity gives it only the *possibility* of depicting. That a thought actually does depict, truly or falsely, depends on the meaning of its elements, and that is given by the extra-psychological will that gives those elements an application and a use (*TLP* 5. 631 ff.).

Intentionality

The philosophy of mind presented in the *Tractatus* is jejune and incredible. This is something that Wittgenstein was himself later to realize; but many who read the work when it first appeared must have observed that it ignored what many contemporaries regarded as the central aspect of mental acts and processes, namely intentionality. The concept of intentionality, medieval in origin, had been reintroduced to philosophy by Brentano in the nineteenth century, and given prominence in Husserl's *Logical Investigations* (1901–2) and *Ideas* (1913).

In his book *Psychology from an Empirical Standpoint* (1874) Brentano had sought to find a property that would mark off psychical from physical phenomena. He considered and rejected the suggestion that the peculiarity of psychical phenomena was that they lacked extension. He then proposed a different criterion of distinction:

Every psychical phenomenon is characterized by what the medieval scholastics called the intentional (or mental) existence of an object, and what we, not quite unambiguously, would call 'relation to a content' 'object-directedness' or 'immanent objectivity'. ('Object' here does not mean reality.) Each such phenomenon contains in itself something as an object, though not each in the same manner. In imagination something is imagined, in judgement something is accepted or rejected, in love something is loved, in hatred something is hated, in desire something is desired and so forth.

This intentional existence is a property only of psychical phenomena; no physical phenomenon displays anything similar. And so we can define psychical phenomena by saying that they are those phenomena that contain an object intentionally. (*PES* ii. 1. 5)

This famous passage is not altogether clear. It is true that where there is love something is loved, and where there is hatred something is hated—but is it not equally true that if heating takes place something is heated? Yet 'heat' is not a psychological verb. How can Brentano say that object-directedness is peculiar to psychological phenomena, when it seems to be a feature common to all grammatically transitive verbs, verbs that 'take an accusative'?

The answer becomes clear if we look to Brentano's scholastic sources, who made a distinction between two kinds of action, immanent and transient. Transient actions are actions that change their objects (heating is a transient action, which makes its object hot). Immanent actions do not change their objects, but their agents. To find out whether the doctor has cured his patient, we examine the patient; to find out whether he has fallen in love with his patient, we must observe the doctor. Brentano's distinction between psychical and physical phenomena corresponds to the distinction between immanent and transient actions.[4]

Husserl took over from Brentano the scholastic concept of intentionality and made it a centrepiece of his system, from 1901 onwards. In the fifth of the *Logical Investigations* he tells us that consciousness consists of intentional experiences or acts, and he makes a series of distinctions between different elements to be found in consciousness. The intentionality of an act is what it is *about*; it is also called the act-matter, the sense, and in later works, the *noema*. A mental item is given its intentionality by an act of meaning (*Meinen*). There are two kinds of meaning: one kind is that which gives significance to a word, and the other kind is that which gives sense to a proposition. 'Each meaning is ... either a nominal meaning or a propositional meaning, or, still more precisely, either the meaning of a complete sentence or a possible part of such a meaning' (*LI* vi. 1).

Every mental act will be an act of a certain kind, belonging to a particular species, which will be determined by its matter. Every thought of a horse, whoever's thought it is, belongs to the same species; and the concept *horse* is precisely the species to which all these thoughts belong. Similarly, whenever anyone makes the judgement that blood is thicker than water, the meaning of that judgement, the proposition *blood is thicker than water*, is precisely the species to which all such acts of judgement belong. If A agrees with the judgement of B, then while A's judgement and B's judgement are distinct individual mental events, they are, because they have the same matter,

---

[4] See e.g. Aquinas, *Summa Theologiae*, 1a 18. 3 ad 1.

instances of the same species. In his later writing Husserl called the individual act the *noesis* and the specific content the *noema*.

In addition to having matter, acts have qualities. It is not only words and sentences that have meaning, and not only the corresponding mental acts and states, such as knowing and believing. So too do perception, imagination, emotion, and volition. My seeing Rome and my imagining Rome are acts that have the same matter, or intentional object, but because seeing is different from imagining, they are acts of different quality (*LI* vi. 22).

Husserl's theory of intentionality was a fertile one, and his account of it contains many shrewd observations and valuable distinctions. But the nature of the act of meaning, which underpins the universe of mental phenomena, remains deeply mysterious. In the 1920s and 1930s some philosophers attempted to present a philosophy of mind that would dispense altogether with intentionality. Bertrand Russell, in his *Analysis of Mind*, presented an account of desire that made it definable in terms of the events that brought it to an end. 'A mental occurrence of any kind—sensation, image, belief or emotion,' he wrote,

> may be a cause of a series of actions continuing, unless interrupted, until some more or less definite state of affairs is realized. Such a series of actions we call a 'behaviour cycle'.... The property of causing such a cycle of occurrences is called 'discomfort'... the cycle ends in a condition of quiescence, or of such action as tends to preserve the *status quo*. The state of affairs in which this condition of quiescence is achieved is called the 'purpose' of the cycle, and the initial mental occurrence involving discomfort is called a 'desire' for the state of affairs that brings quiescence. A desire is called 'conscious' when it is accompanied by a true belief as to the state of affairs that will bring quiescence; otherwise it is called 'unconscious'. (*AM* 75)

Behaviour cycles, according to Russell, are causally initiated by mental events possessing the characteristic of discomfort. The nature of these events is left unclear in his system. But other philosophers and psychologists, in their accounts of desire and emotion, dispensed altogether with mental events. For the behaviourist school, particularly after Pavlov had in 1927 presented his theory of conditioned reflexes, the relation between mental and bodily events was no longer a causal one. Behaviour cycles were not the effect of mental events, they were the actual constituents of such things as desire and satisfaction. Behaviourists regarded reports of mental acts and states as disguised reports of pieces of bodily behaviour, or at best of tendencies to behave bodily in certain ways. Intentionality thus vanished from psychology.

Wittgenstein's Later Philosophy of Mind

It was in reaction to Russell's account of desire and expectation that Wittgenstein began to develop his later philosophy of mind. What was wrong with Russell's account, he said, was precisely that it ignored intentionality; and he agreed with

916

Husserl that intentionality was all-important if we were to understand language and thought. To give a correct account of it was one of the major problems of philosophy.

> That's *him* (this picture represents *him*)—that contains the whole problem of representation.
>
> What is the criterion, how is it to be verified, that this picture is the portrait of that object, i.e. that it is *meant* to represent it? It is not similarity that makes the picture a portrait (it might be a striking resemblance of one person, and yet be a portrait of someone else it resembles less) ...
>
> When I remember my friend and see him 'in my mind's eye' what is the connection between the memory image and its subject? The likeness between them? (*PG* 102)

Wittgenstein's achievement in philosophy of mind was to give an account that preserved the intentionality that the behaviourists had denied without accepting the Cartesian picture of consciousness in which Husserl's account was embedded.

One way to describe Wittgenstein's contribution to philosophy of mind is to say that he exhibited, with unparalleled sensitivity, that the human mind is not a spirit, not even an incarnate spirit. First and foremost, there is no such thing as the Cartesian ego, a self, or *moi*, that is referred to in first-person utterances. This is not because the word 'I' refers to something other than a self; it is because 'I' is not a referring expression at all. The self is a piece of philosopher's nonsense produced by misunderstanding of the reflexive pronoun.

When Descartes argued that he could doubt whether he had a body, but he could not doubt whether he existed, it was essential to his argument that it should be possible for him to use 'I' to refer to something of which his body was no part. But that was a great misunderstanding. My 'self' is not a part of myself, not even a very central part of myself; it is, obviously enough, myself. We talk of 'my body', but the possessive pronoun does not mean that there is an 'I' which is the possessor of a body that is other than myself. My body is not the body that I have, but the body that I am, just as the city of Rome is not a city that Rome has but the city that Rome is.

The second thing that is meant by saying that the mind is not a spirit is that it is not some ghostly medium or locus of mental events and processes that is accessible only by introspection. Wittgenstein frequently attacked a mythology about the nature of the mind that we are all prone to accept. We imagine a mechanism in our minds, a strange mechanism that works very well in its own mysterious medium but which, if understood as a mechanism in the ordinary sense, is quite unintelligible. Wittgenstein thought that this was a piece of hidden or latent nonsense. The way to turn latent nonsense into patent nonsense was to imagine that the mechanism really existed.

There is a temptation to think, for instance, that when you recognize somebody what you do is to consult a mental picture of her and check whether what you now see matches the picture. Wittgenstein suggests that if we have this nonsensical idea in our mind we can make ourselves see that it is nonsense, and that it in no way explains recognition. If we suppose the process to happen in the real world, with the picture as a real and not just a mental picture, our initial problem just returns. How do we recognize that this is a picture of a particular person in order to use it to recognize her? The only thing that gave the illusion of explanation in this case was the fuzzy nature of the original supposition; the fact that the process was supposed to take place in the ghostly medium of the mind.

The task of a scientific theory of the mind, according to some philosophers and psychologists, is to establish a principle of correlation between the occurrence of mental states and processes and the occurrence of states and processes in the brain. This correlation would only be a possibility if mental events (e.g. thoughts, or flashes of understanding) were themselves measurable in the way in which physical events are measurable. But thought and understanding are not processes in a psychic medium in the way in which electrolysis and oxidization are processes in a physical medium. Thought and understanding are not processes at all, as Wittgenstein showed by a painstaking analysis of uses of the words 'think' and 'understand'. The criteria by which we decide whether someone understands a sentence, for instance, are quite different from the criteria by which we decide what mental processes are going on while he is uttering or writing the sentence (*PG* 148).

Those who think of the mind as a ghostly medium, and thought and understanding as processes occurring there, regard the medium as accessible by introspection, and only by introspection. The mind, on this view, is an inner space that deserves exploration at least as much as outer space. But whereas—given enough time, money, and energy—everyone can explore the same outer space, each of us can only explore our own inner space. We do so by looking within at something to which we ourselves have direct access, but which others can learn of only indirectly, by accepting our verbal testimony or making inferences from our physical behaviour. The connection between consciousness on the one hand, and speech and behaviour on the other, is on this view a purely contingent one.

To demolish this conception was one of Wittgenstein's great merits. If the connection between consciousness and expression is merely contingent, then for all we know everything in the universe may be conscious. It is perfectly consistent with the idea that consciousness is something private, with which we make contact only in our own case, that the chair on which I am now sitting may be conscious. For all we know, may it not be in excruciating pain? Of course, if it is, we have to add the hypothesis that it is also exhibiting stoical fortitude. But why not?

If consciousness really is merely contingently connected with its expression in behaviour, can we be confident in our ascription of it to other human beings? Our only evidence that humans are conscious is that each of us, if he looks within *himself*, sees consciousness *there*. But how can a man generalize his own case so irresponsibly? He cannot look within others: it is the essence of introspection that it should be something that we all have to do for ourselves. Nor can he make a causal deduction from other people's behaviour. A correlation between other people's consciousness and their behaviour could never be established when the first term of the correlation is in principle unobservable.

'Only of a human being', Wittgenstein wrote, 'and what resembles (behaves like) a human being can one say: it has sensations; it sees; is blind; hears; is deaf; is conscious or unconscious' (*PI* I. 281). This does not mean that he is a behaviourist; he is not identifying experience with behaviour, or even with dispositions to behave. The point is that what experiences one can have depends on how one *can* behave. Only someone who can play chess can feel the desire to castle; only someone who can talk can be overcome by an impulse to swear. Only a being that can eat can be hungry, and only a being that can discriminate between light and darkness can have visual experiences.

The relation between experiences of certain kinds, and the capacity to behave in certain ways, is not a merely contingent connection. Wittgenstein made a distinction between two kinds of evidence that we may have for the obtaining of states of affairs, namely *symptoms* and *criteria*. Where the connection between a certain kind of evidence and the conclusion drawn from it is a matter of empirical discovery, through theory and induction, the evidence may be called a *symptom* of the state of affairs; where the relation between evidence and conclusion is not something discovered by empirical investigation, but is something that must be grasped by anyone who possesses the concept of the state of affairs in question, then the evidence is not a mere symptom, but a *criterion* of the event in question. A red sky at night may be a symptom of good weather the following morning, but the absence of clouds, the shining of the sun, etc. tomorrow morning are not just symptoms but criteria for the good weather. Similarly, scratching is a criterion for itching, and reciting 'Three Blind Mice' is a criterion for knowing it—though of course not everyone who itches scratches, and one can know the rhyme for years and years without ever reciting it.

Exploiting the notion of *criterion* enabled Wittgenstein to steer between the Scylla of dualism and the Charybdis of behaviourism. He agreed with dualists that particular mental events could occur without accompanying bodily behaviour; on the other hand he agreed with behaviourists that the possibility of ascribing mental acts to people depends on such acts having, in general, a behavioural expression.

If it is wrong to identify the mind with behaviour, it is even more mistaken, according to Wittgenstein, to identify the mind with the brain. Such materialism is in fact a grosser philosophical error than behaviourism because the connection between mind and behaviour is a more intimate one than that between mind and brain. The relation between mind and behaviour is a criterial one, something prior to experience; the connection between mind and brain is a contingent one, discoverable by empirical science. Any discovery of links between mind and brain must take as its starting point the everyday concepts we use in describing the mind, concepts that are grafted on to behavioural criteria.

Oddly enough, developments in the philosophy of mind since Wittgenstein have shown that it is possible to combine the errors of materialism with those of dualism. One of the most ubiquitous misunderstandings of the nature of the mind is the picture of mind's relation to body as that between a little person or homunculus on the one hand, and a tool or instrument or machine on the other. We smile when medieval painters represent the death of the Virgin Mary by showing a small-scale model virgin emerging from her mouth; but basically the same idea can be found in the most unlikely places, including the writings of cognitive scientists.

Descartes, when first he reported the occurrence of retinal images, warned us not to be misled by the resemblance between images and their objects into thinking that when we saw the object we had another pair of eyes, inside our brain, to see the images. But he himself believed that seeing was to be explained by saying that the soul encountered an image in the pineal gland. This was a particularly striking version of what has been nicknamed 'the homunculus fallacy'—the attempt to explain human experience and behaviour by postulating a little human within an ordinary human.

What is wrong with the homunculus fallacy? In itself there is nothing misguided in speaking of images in the brain, if one means patterns in the brain, observable to a neurophysiologist, that can be mapped on to features of the visible environment. What is misleading is to take these mappings as representations, to regard them as visible to the mind, and to say that seeing consists in the mind's perception of these images.

The misleading aspect is that such an account pretends to explain seeing, but the explanation reproduces exactly the puzzling features it was supposed to explain. For it is only if we think of the relation between a mind and an image in the pineal gland as being just like the relation between a human being and pictures seen in the environment that we will think that talk of an encounter between the mind and the image has any illuminating power at all. But whatever needs explaining in the human turns up grinning and unexplained in the shape of the manikin.

At the present time, when energetic efforts are being made to construct a new cognitive science of the mind, it is the brain, or parts of the brain, that are usually assigned the role of the homunculus. We may be told that our brains ask questions, solve problems, decode signals, and construct hypotheses. Those who ascribe human capabilities to parts of human beings are unmindful of Wittgenstein's warning, 'Only of a human being and what resembles (behaves like) a human being can one say: it has sensations; it sees; is blind; hears; is deaf; is conscious or unconscious.' But the same point had been made millennia ago by Aristotle, who wrote, 'To say that the soul gets angry is as if one were to say that the soul weaves or builds a house. Probably it is better not to say that the soul pities, or learns, or thinks, but that the human being does these things with its soul' (*de Anima* 408^{b}12–15).

Wittgenstein's philosophy of mind was in fact closer to that of Aristotle than it is to contemporary materialist psychology. At one point he countenanced the possibility that there may be mental activities that lack any correlate in the brain:

No supposition seems to me more natural than that there is no process in the brain correlated with associating or with thinking; so that it would be impossible to read off thought-processes from brain processes. . . . It is perfectly possible that certain psychological phenomena *cannot* be investigated physiologically, because physiologically nothing corresponds to them. I saw this man years ago: now I have seen him again, I recognize him, I remember his name. And why does there have to be a cause of this remembering in my nervous system? . . . Why should there not be a psychological regularity to which *no* physiological regularity corresponds? If this upsets our concept of causality, then it is high time it was upset. (Z 608–10)

This frontal attack on the idea that there must be physical counterparts of mental phenomena was not intended as a defence of any kind of dualism. The entity that does the associating, thinking, and remembering is not a spiritual substance, but a corporeal human being. But Wittgenstein did seem to be envisaging as a possibility an Aristotelian soul or entelechy, which operates with no material vehicle—a formal and final cause to which there corresponds no mechanistic efficient cause.

9

Ethics

The Greatest Happiness of the Greatest Number

In most systems of morality, happiness is a concept of great importance. A long series of moral philosophers, tracing their ancestry back to Plato and Aristotle, had treated happiness as the supreme good, and some ethicists went so far as to affirm that human beings seek happiness in all their choices.[1] In challenging the primacy of happiness, Kant was unusual. In his *Groundwork* he proclaimed that duty, not happiness, was the supreme ethical motive. At first sight, therefore, when Bentham declared that every action should be evaluated in accordance with the tendency it appears to have to augment or diminish happiness, he was just reaffirming a long-standing consensus. But on closer inspection Bentham's greatest happiness principle is very different from traditional eudaimonism.

In the first place, Bentham identifies happiness with pleasure: it is pleasure that is the supreme spring of action. The *Introduction to the Principles of Morals and Legislation* famously begins:

Nature has placed mankind under the governance of two sovereign masters, pain and pleasure. It is for them alone to point out what we ought to do, as well as to determine what we shall do. On the one hand, the standard of right and wrong, on the other the chain of causes and effects, are fastened to their throne. They govern us in all we do, in all we say, in all we think: every effort we can make to throw off our subjection, will serve but to demonstrate and confirm it. (*P* 1. 1)

To maximize happiness, therefore, for Bentham, is the same thing as to maximize pleasure. Utilitarians could cite Plato as a forebear, since in his *Protagoras* he had offered for discussion the thesis that virtue consists in the correct choice of pleasure and pain.[2] Aristotle, on the other hand, made a distinction between happiness and pleasure, and in particular refused to identify happiness with the pleasures of the senses. Bentham by contrast not only treated happiness as

---

[1] See above, pp. 69, 462. [2] See above, p. 208.

equivalent to pleasure, but regarded pleasure itself as simply a sensation. 'In this matter we want no refinement, no metaphysics. It is not necessary to consult Plato, nor Aristotle. Pain and pleasure are what everybody feels to be such.'

Bentham was careful to point out that pleasure was a sensation that could be caused not only by eating and drinking and sex, but also by a multitude of other things, as varied as the acquisition of wealth, kindness to animals, or belief in the favour of a Supreme Being. So critics who regarded Bentham's hedonism as a call to sensuality were quite mistaken. However, whereas for a thinker like Aristotle pleasure was to be identified with the activity enjoyed, for Bentham the relation between an activity and its pleasure was one of cause and effect. Whereas for Aristotle the value of a pleasure was the same as the value of the activity enjoyed, for Bentham the value of each and every pleasure was the same, no matter how it was caused. 'Quantity of pleasure being equal', he wrote, 'push-pin is as good as poetry.' What went for pleasure went for pain, too: the quantity of pain, and not its cause, is the measure of its disvalue.

It is the quantification of pleasure and pain, therefore, that is of prime importance for a utilitarian: in deciding on an action or a policy we need to estimate the amount of pleasure and the amount of pain likely to ensue. Bentham was aware that such quantification was no trivial task, and he offered recipes for the measurement of pleasures and pains. Pleasure A counts more than pleasure B if it is more intense, or if it lasts longer, or if it is more certain, or if it is more immediate. In the 'felicific calculus' these different factors must be taken into account and weighed against each other. In judging pleasure-producing actions we must also consider fecundity and purity: a pleasurable action is fecund if it is likely to produce a subsequent series of pleasures, and it is pure if it is unlikely to produce a subsequent series of pains. All these factors are to be taken into account when we are operating the calculus with respect to our own affairs; if we are considering public policy, we must further consider another factor, which Bentham calls 'extension'—that is, how widely the pains and pleasures will be spread across the population.

Bentham offered a mnemonic rhyme to aid in operating the calculus:

> Intense, long, certain, speedy, fruitful, pure—
> Such marks in pleasures and in pains endure.
> Such pleasures seek if private be thy end;
> If it be public, wide let them extend.
> Such pains avoid, whichever be thy view
> If pains must come, let them extend to few.   (P 4. 2)

In using the felicific calculus for purposes of determining public policy, extension is the crucial factor. 'The greatest happiness of the greatest number' is an impressive slogan; but when probed it turns out to be riddled with ambiguity.

The first question to be raised is 'greatest number of *what*?' Should we add 'voters' or 'citizens' or 'males' or 'human beings' or 'sentient beings'? It makes a huge difference which answer we give. Throughout the two centuries of utilitarianism's history most of its devotees would probably give the answer 'human beings', and this is most likely the answer that Bentham would have given. He did not advocate women's suffrage, but only because he thought that to do so would provoke outrage; in principle he thought that on the basis of the greatest happiness principle 'the claim of [the female] sex is, if not still better, at least altogether as good as that of the other' (B ix. 108–9).

In recent years many utilitarians have extended the happiness principle beyond humankind to other sentient beings, claiming that animals have equal claims with human beings. Though a great lover of animals (especially cats) Bentham himself did not go as far as this, and he would have rejected the idea that animals have rights, because he did not believe in natural rights of any kind. But by making the supreme moral criterion a matter of sensation he made it appropriate to consider animals as belonging to the same moral community as ourselves since animals as well as humans feel pleasure and pain. This, in the long term, proved to be one of the most significant consequences of Bentham's break with the classical and Christian moral tradition, which placed supreme moral value in activities not of the sense but of the reason, and regarded non-rational animals as standing outside the moral community.

A second question about the principle of utility is this: should individuals, or politicians, in following the greatest happiness principle attempt to control the number of candidates for happiness (however these are defined)? Does the extension of happiness to a greater number mean that we should try to bring more people (or animals) into existence? What answer we give to this is linked to a third, even more difficult, question: when we are measuring the happiness of a population, do we consider only total happiness, or should we also consider average happiness? Should we take account of the distribution of happiness as well as of its quantity? If so, then we have to strike a difficult balance between quantity of happiness and quantity of people.

This issue is a problem rather for political philosophy than for moral philosophy. But even if we restrict our consideration to matters of individual morality, there remains a problem raised by the initial passage of the *Introduction* quoted above. The hedonism there proclaimed is twofold: there is a psychological hedonism (pleasure determines all our actions) and an ethical hedonism (pleasure is the standard of right and wrong). But the pleasure cited in psychological hedonism is the pleasure of the individual person; the pleasure invoked in ethical hedonism is the pleasure (however quantified) of the total moral community. If I am, in fact, predetermined in every action to aim at maximizing my own pleasure, what point is there in telling me that I am obliged to maximize the common good? This was a problem that was to exercise some of Bentham's successors in the utilitarian tradition.

Bentham commended utilitarianism by contrasting it with other ethical systems. The second chapter of the *Introduction* is entitled 'Of Principles Adverse to that of Utility'. He lists two such principles, the first being the principle of asceticism, and the second the principle of sympathy and antipathy. The principle of asceticism is the mirror image of the principle of utility, approving of actions to the extent that they tend to diminish the quantity of happiness. A man who accepts the principle of sympathy and antipathy, on the other hand, judges actions as good or bad to the extent that they accord or not with his own feelings (*P* 2. 2).

Bentham's principle of asceticism set up a straw man. Religious traditions have indeed set a high value on self-denial and mortification of the flesh; but even among religious teachers it is rare to find one who makes the infliction of suffering upon oneself the overarching principle of every action.[3] No one, religious or secular, had ever proposed a policy of pursuing the greatest misery of the greatest number. Bentham himself admits, 'The principle of asceticism never was, nor ever can be, consistently pursued by any living creature' (*P* 2. 10).

The principle of sympathy and antipathy is a catch-all that includes moral systems of very different kinds. Sympathy and antipathy, Bentham says, may be given various fancy names: moral sense, common sense, understanding, rule of right, fitness of things, law of nature, right reason, and so on. Moral systems that present themselves under such banners, Bentham believes, are all simply placing a grandiose screen in front of an appeal to individual subjective feeling. 'They consist all of them in so many contrivances for avoiding the obligation of appealing to any external standard, and for prevailing upon the reader to accept of the author's sentiment or opinion as a reason for itself' (*P* 2. 14). We cannot appeal to the will of God to settle whether something is right; we have to know first whether it is right in order to decide whether it is conformable to God's will. 'What is called the pleasure of God is, and must necessarily be (revelation apart) neither more nor less than the good pleasure of the person, whoever he be, who is pronouncing what he believes, or pretends, to be God's pleasure' (*P* 2. 18).

Bentham does not bring out what is the really significant difference between utilitarianism and other moral systems. We may divide moral philosophers into absolutists and consequentialists. Absolutists believe that there are some kinds of action that are intrinsically wrong, and should never be done, irrespective of any consideration of the consequences. Consequentialists believe that the morality of actions should be judged by their consequences, and that there is no category of act that may not, in special circumstances, be justified by its consequences. Prior to Bentham most philosophers were absolutists, because they believed in a natural law, or natural rights. If there are natural rights and a natural law, then some kinds of action, actions that violate those rights or conflict with that law, are wrong, no matter what the consequences.

Bentham rejected the notion of natural law, on the grounds that no two people could agree what it was. He was scornful of natural rights, believing that real rights

---

[3] One such is St John of the Cross, but even he sees this as a means to eventual superabundant happiness; see above, p. 689.

could only be conferred by positive law; and his greatest scorn was directed to the idea that natural rights could not be overridden. 'Natural rights is simple nonsense: natural and imprescriptible rights, rhetorical nonsense—nonsense upon stilts' (B ii. 501). If there is no natural law and no natural rights, then no class of actions can be ruled out in advance of the consideration of the consequences of such an action in a particular case.

This difference between Bentham and previous moralists is highly significant, as can be easily illustrated. Aristotle, Aquinas, and almost all Christian moralists believed that adultery was always wrong. Not so for Bentham: the consequences foreseen by a particular adulterer must be taken into account before making a moral judgement. A believer in natural law, told that some Herod or Nero has killed 5,000 citizens guilty of no crime, will say without further ado, 'That was a wicked act'. A thoroughgoing consequentialist, before making such a judgement, must ask further questions. What were the consequences of the massacre? What did the monarch foresee? What would have happened if he had allowed the 5,000 to live?

Modifications of Utilitarianism

John Stuart Mill was, like Bentham, a consequentialist. But in other ways he toned down aspects of Bentham's teaching that had been found most offensive. In his treatise *Utilitarianism*, written in his late fifties, he acknowledges that many people have thought that the idea that life has no higher end than pleasure was a doctrine worthy only of swine. He replies that it is foolish to deny that humans have faculties that are higher than the ones they share with animals. This allows us to make distinctions between different pleasures not only in quantity but also in quality. 'It is quite compatible with the principle of utility to recognise the fact that some *kinds* of pleasure are more desirable and more valuable than others' (U 258).

How then do we grade the different kinds of pleasure? 'Of two pleasures', Mill tells us, 'if there be one to which all or almost all who have experience of both give a decided preference, irrespective of any feeling of moral obligation to prefer it, that is the more desirable pleasure.' Armed with this distinction a utilitarian can put a distance between himself and the swine. Few humans would wish to be changed into a lower animal even if promised a cornucopia of bestial pleasures. 'It is better to be a human being dissatisfied than a pig satisfied.' Again, no intelligent, educated person would wish, at any price, to become a foolish ignoramus. It is 'better to be Socrates dissatisfied than a fool satisfied' (U 260).

Happiness, according to Mill, involves not just contentment, but also a sense of dignity; any amount of the lower pleasures, without this, would not amount to happiness. Accordingly, the greatest happiness principle needs to be restated:

The ultimate end, with reference to and for the sake of which all other things are desirable (whether we are considering our own good or that of other people), is an existence exempt as far as possible from pain, and as rich as possible in enjoyments, both in point of quantity and quality; the test of quality, and the rule for measuring it against quantity, being the preference felt by those who in their opportunities of experience, to which must be added their habits of self-consciousness and self-observation, are best furnished with the means of comparison. (*U* 262)

Suppose, then, that a critic grants to Mill that utilitarianism need not be swinish. Still, he may insist, it does not appeal to the best in human nature. Virtue is more important than happiness, and acts of renunciation and self-sacrifice are the most splendid of human deeds. Mill agrees that it is noble to be capable of resigning one's own happiness for the sake of others—but would the hero or martyr's sacrifice be made if he did not believe that it would increase the amount of happiness in the world? A person who denies himself the enjoyment of life for any other purpose 'is no more deserving of admiration than the ascetic mounted on his pillar'.

Objections to utilitarianism come in two different forms. As a moral code, it may be thought to be too strict, or it may be thought to be too lax. Those who complain that it is too strict say that to insist that in every single action one should take account not just of one's own but of universal happiness is to demand a degree of altruism beyond the range of all but saints. Indeed, even to work out what is the most felicific of the choices available at any given moment calls for superhuman powers of calculation. Those who regard utilitarianism as too lax say that its abolition of absolute prohibitions on kinds of action opens a door for moral agents to persuade themselves whenever they feel like it that they are in the special circumstances that would justify an otherwise outrageous act. They could quote words that Mill himself wrote to Harriet Taylor soon after they met:

Where there exists a genuine and strong desire to do that which is most for the happiness of all, general rules are merely aids to prudence, in the choice of means; not peremptory obligations. Let but the desires be right, and the 'imagination lofty and refined'; & provided there be disdain of all false seeming, 'to the pure all things are pure'.[4]

In *Utilitarianism* Mill offers a defence on both fronts. Against the allegation of excessive rigour, he urges us to distinguish between a moral standard and a motive of action: utilitarianism, while offering universal happiness as the ultimate moral standard, does not require it to be the aim of every action. Moreover, there is no need to run through a felicific calculus in every case: it is absurd to talk 'as if, at the moment when some man feels tempted to meddle with the property or life of another, he had to begin considering for the first time whether murder and theft are injurious to human happiness' (*U* 275). To those who allege laxity, he responds with a *tu quoque*: all moral systems have to make room for conflicting obligations,

[4] F. A. Hayek, *John Stuart Mill and Harriet Taylor* (London: Routledge, 1957), 59.

and utility is not the only creed 'which is able to furnish us with excuses for evil doing, and means of cheating our own conscience' (*U* 277).

The difficulty about utilitarianism that Mill himself takes most seriously is the allegation that it is a recipe for preferring expedience to justice. Mill responds that the dictates of justice do indeed form part of the field of general expediency, but that nonetheless there is a difference between what is expedient, what is moral, and what is just. If something is expedient (in the sense of conducing to the general happiness) then, on utilitarian grounds, it should be done, but there need not be any question of duty involved. If something is not just expedient but also moral, then a duty arises; and it is part of the notion of a duty that a person may be rightly compelled to fulfil it. Not all duties, however, create correlative rights in other persons, and it is this extra element that makes the difference between morality in general and justice in particular: 'Justice implies something which is not only right to do, and wrong not to do, but which some individual person can claim from us as his moral right' (*U* 301). It is important, for Mill, to mark the connection between justice and *moral* rights: because he emphasizes that there can be legal rights that are unjust, and just claims that conflict with law.

Mill explains how various notions connected with justice—desert, impartiality, equality—are to be reconciled with the utilitarian principle of expediency. With regard to equality, he cites a maxim of Bentham's, 'everybody to count for one, nobody for more than one'—each person's happiness is counted for exactly as much as another's. But he does not really address the problem inherent in the greatest happiness principle, that it leaves room for the misery of an individual to be discounted in order to increase the overall total of happiness in the community.

Indeed, in *Utilitarianism* Mill has little to say about distributive justice other than to note that those forms on offer vary from system to system:

Some Communists consider it unjust that the produce of the labour of the community should be shared on any other principle than that of exact equality; others think it just that those should receive most whose wants are greatest; while others hold that those who work harder, or who produce more, or whose services are more valuable to the community, may justly claim a larger quota in the division of the produce. And the sense of natural justice may be plausibly appealed to in behalf of every one of these opinions. (*U* 301)

Schopenhauer on Renunciation

The ethical teaching of Schopenhauer is closely linked to his metaphysics, and in particular to the theses that the world of experience is illusory and that the true reality, the thing-in-itself, is the universal will. We see individuals rising out of nothing, receiving their lives as a gift, and then suffering the loss of this gift in death, returning again to nothing. But if we consider life philosophically we find that the will, the thing-in-itself in all phenomena, is not at all affected by birth and death.

It is not the individual, but only the species, that Nature cares for, and for the preservation of which she so earnestly strives, providing for it with the utmost prodigality. . . . The individual, on the contrary, neither has nor can have any value for Nature, for her kingdom is infinite time and infinite space, and within these infinite multiplicity of possible individuals. Therefore she is always ready to let the individual fall, and hence it is not only exposed to destruction in a thousand ways by the most insignificant accident, but originally destined for it, and conducted towards it by Nature herself from the moment it has served its end of maintaining the species. (*WWI* 276)

We should be no more troubled by the thought that at death our individuality will be replaced by other individuals than we are troubled by the fact that in life every time we take in new food we excrete waste. Death is just a sleep in which individuality is forgotten. It is only as phenomenon that one individual is distinct from another. 'As thing-in-itself he is the will which appears in everything, and death destroys the illusion which separates his consciousness from that of the rest: this is afterlife or immortality' (*WWI* 282).

Morality is a matter of the training of character; but what this consists in can only be understood, according to Schopenhauer, if we accept Kant's reconciliation of freedom with necessity. The will, which is the thing-in-itself, is free from eternity to eternity; but everything in nature, including human nature, is determined by necessity. Just as inanimate nature acts in accordance with laws and forces, so each human being has a character, from which different motives call forth his actions necessarily. If we had a complete knowledge of a person's character and the motives that are presented to him, we would be able to calculate his future conduct just as we can predict an eclipse of the sun or moon. We believe we are free to choose between alternatives, because prior to the choice we have no knowledge of how the will is going to decide; but the belief in liberty of indifference is an illusion.

If all our ethical conduct is determined by one's character, it might seem that it is a waste of trouble to try to improve oneself, and it is better simply to gratify every inclination that presents itself. In rejecting this, Schopenhauer makes a distinction between several kinds of character. There is what he calls the intelligible character, which is the underlying reality, outside time, that determines our response to the situations presented to us in the world. There is also the empirical character; that is to say, what we and others learn, through the course of experience, of the nature of our own intelligible character. Finally, there is the acquired character, which is achieved by those who have learnt the nature and limitations of their own individual character. These are persons of character in the best sense: people who recognize their own strengths and weaknesses, and tailor their projects and ambitions accordingly.

Our wills can never change, but many degrees are possible of awareness of will. Humans, unlike other animals, possess abstract and rational knowledge. This does not exempt them from the control of conflicting motives, but it makes them aware of the conflict, and this is what constitutes choice. Repentance, for instance, never proceeds from a change of will, which is impossible, but from a change of knowledge, from greater self-awareness. 'Knowledge of our own mind and its capacities of every kind, and their unalterable limits, is the surest way to the attainment of the greatest possible contentment with ourselves' (*WWI* 306).

Even to the best of humans, Schopenhauer holds out no great hope of contentment. We are all creatures of will, and will of its nature is insatiable. The basis of all willing is need and pain, and we suffer until our needs are satisfied. But if the will, once satisfied, lacks objects of desire, then life becomes a burden of boredom. 'Thus life swings like a pendulum backwards and forwards between pain and ennui' (*WWI* 312). Walking is only constantly prevented falling; the life of our body is only ever-postponed death; the life of our mind is constantly deferred boredom. Want of food is the scourge of the working class, want of entertainment that of the world of fashion. All happiness is really and essentially negative, never positive.

The only sure way to escape the tyranny of the will is by complete renunciation. What the will wills is always life; so if we are to renounce the will we must renounce the will to live. This sounds like a recommendation to suicide; but in fact Schopenhauer condemned suicide as a false way of escape from the miseries of the world. Suicide could only be inspired by an overestimate of the individual life; it was motivated by concealed will to live.

Renunciation is renunciation of the self, and moral progress consists in the reduction of egoism, that is to say, the tendency of the individual to make itself the centre of the world and to sacrifice everything else to its own existence and well-being. All bad persons are egoists: they assert their own will to live, and deny the presence of that will in others, damaging, and perhaps destroying, the existence of others if they get in their way. There are people who are not only bad, but really wicked; they go beyond egoism, taking delight in the sufferings of others not just as a means to their own ends, but as an end in itself. Schopenhauer names Nero and Robespierre as examples of this level of cruelty.

A common or garden bad person, however, while regarding his own person as separated by a great gulf from others, nonetheless retains a dim awareness that his own will is just the phenomenal appearance of the single will to live that is active in all. He dimly sees that he is himself this whole will, and consequently he is not only the inflicter but the endurer of pain, a pain from which he is separated only by the illusive dream of space and time. This awareness finds its expression in remorse. Remorse in the bad man is the counterpart of resignation, which is the mark of the good man.

Between the bad man and the good man, there is an intermediate character: the just man. Unlike the bad man, the just man does not see individuality as being an absolute wall of partition between himself and others. Other persons, for him, are not mere masks, whose nature is quite different from his own. He is willing to recognize the will to live in others on the same level as his own, up to the point of abstaining from injury to his fellow humans.

In the really good man, the barrier of individuality is penetrated to a far greater degree, and the principle of individuation is no longer an absolute wall of partition. The good man sees that the distinction between himself and others, which to the bad man is so great a gulf, only belongs to a fleeting and illusive phenomenon. 'He is just as little likely to allow others to starve, while he himself has enough and to spare, as any one would be to suffer hunger one day in order to have more the next day than he could enjoy' (*WWI* 373).

But well doing and benevolence is not the highest ethical state, and the good man will soon be taken beyond it.

If he takes as much interest in the sufferings of other individuals as his own, and therefore is not only benevolent in the highest degree, but even ready to sacrifice his own individuality whenever such a sacrifice will save a number of other persons, then it clearly follows that such a man, who recognizes in all beings his own inmost and true self, must also regard the infinite suffering of all suffering beings as his own, and take on himself the pain of the whole world. (*WWI* 379)

This will lead him beyond virtue to asceticism. It will no longer be enough to love others as himself: he will experience a horror of the whole nature of which his own phenomenal existence is an expression. He will abandon the will to live, which is the kernel of this miserable world. He will do all he can to disown the nature of the world as expressed in his own body: he will practise complete chastity, adopt voluntary poverty, and take up fasting and self-chastisement. Schopenhauer's ideal man does indeed adopt the ascetic principle denounced by Bentham: 'he compels himself to refrain from doing all that he would like to do, and to do all that he would like not to do, even if this has no further end than that of serving to mortify his will' (*WWI* 382). Such asceticism, he says, is no vain ideal; it can be learned through suffering and it has been practised by many Christian, and still more by Hindu and Buddhist, saints.

It is true that the life of many saints has been full of the most absurd superstition. Religious systems, Schopenhauer believed, are the mythical clothing of truths which in their naked form are inaccessible to the uneducated multitude. But, he says, 'it is just as little needful that a saint should be a philosopher as that a philosopher should be a saint' (*WWI* 383)

The power of Schopenhauer's prose, and the enchantment of his metaphors, give the impress of grandeur to his ethical system. But it rests on a false metaphysic, and it leads to a self-stultifying conclusion. There is no reason to believe that the world is nothing but an illusory idea, or to accept that insatiable will is the ultimate reality. From the alternation between desire and satisfaction,

Schopenhauer decided that life was a history of suffering and boredom; from the same premiss he might with equal justification have concluded that it was a history of excitement and contentment. In order to distinguish the world of will from the world of idea, and to reach a thing-in-itself, he has to persuade each of us that our own individuality is the fundamental reality; in order to persuade us to ascend the path through virtue to asceticism, he must get us to accept that our individuality is nothing but illusion.

Schopenhauer provides no convincing reason, other than a prejudice in favour of pessimism, why we should adopt the ascetic programme with which he concludes. To be sure, the more philanthropic a person is, the more she will identify with the lives of others; but why should she identify only with their sufferings and not also with their joys? St Francis of Assisi mortified his flesh as severely as any Indian mystic, and yet his prayer was that he would replace despair, darkness, and sadness with hope, light, and rejoicing.

The complete renunciation of the will to which we are called by Schopenhauer appears to be a contradiction in terms; for if the renunciation is voluntary, it is itself an act of the will, and if it is necessary it is not a real renunciation. Schopenhauer tries to escape by appealing to the Kantian distinction between a phenomenon that is necessary and a thing-in-itself that is free. But the will that is free is outside time, while the history of any self-denying saint belongs in the world of phenomena. One and the same act of self-denial cannot be both inside and outside time.

The Moral Ascent in Kierkegaard

Kierkegaard's moral system resembles Schopenhauer's in several ways. Both philosophers take a deeply pessimistic view of the ethical condition of the average human being, and both philosophers hold out a spiritual career that leads to renunciation. But whereas Schopenhauer's system was built on an atheistic metaphysic, Kierkegaard's evolves against a background of Protestant Christianity. For him the renunciation that is the high point of the ethical life is only a preliminary to an ultimate leap of faith. Whereas Schopenhauer's programme is designed to lead to the erasure of individuality, Kierkegaard's aims to put the individual in full possession of his own personality as a unique creature of God.

The final stage of the Kierkegaardian spiritual journey will be considered in Chapter 12; our present concern is with the previous stage—the ethical, which comes between the aesthetic and the religious. Kierkegaard's aesthetic person is governed by his feelings, and blind to spiritual values; but we must not think of him as a sensual boor, a philistine glutton, or a sexual deviant. As he is portrayed as one of the two protagonists in *Either/Or* he is a cultured, law-abiding person, popular in society and not without consideration for others. What distinguishes him from a serious moral agent is that he avoids entering into any engagements that would limit his capacity for the pursuit of whatever is immediately attractive. To preserve his freedom of choice he refuses to take any public or private office; he avoids any deep friendship, and marriage above all.

The aesthetic person, Kierkegaard argues, is deluded when he thinks of his existence as one of freedom; in fact it is extremely limited.

In case one were to think of a house, consisting of cellar, ground floor, and *premier étage*, so tenanted, or rather so arranged, that it was planned for a distinction of rank between the dwellers on the several floors; and in case one were to make a comparison between such a house and what it is to be a man—then unfortunately this is the sorry and ludicrous condition of the majority of men, that in their own house they prefer to live in the cellar. The soulish–bodily synthesis in every man is planned with a view to being spirit, such is the building; but the man prefers to dwell in the cellar, that is, in the determinants of sensuousness. And not only does he prefer to dwell in the cellar; no, he loves that to such a degree that he becomes furious if anyone would propose to him to occupy the *piano nobile* which stands empty at his disposition—for in fact he is dwelling in his own house. (*SD* 176)

Such a person, Kierkegaard says, is in a state of despair. 'Despair', as used in *Sickness unto Death* and other works, does not mean a state of gloom or despondency; the aesthetic person, in fact, may well believe that he is happy. A despairing person, in Kierkegaard's terms, is a person who has no hope of anything higher than his present life. To despair is to lack awareness of the possibility of achieving a higher, spiritual self. Despair, so understood, is not a rare, but a well-nigh universal phenomenon. Most men, in Kierkegaard's expressive phrase, 'pawn themselves to the world'. 'They use their talents, accumulate money, carry on worldly affairs, calculate shrewdly etc., etc., are perhaps mentioned in history, but themselves they are not; spiritually understood they have no self, no self for whose sake they could venture everything' (*SD* 168).

The first step towards a cure is the realization that one is in despair. Already, in the hidden recesses of the aesthetic person's happiness, there dwells an anxious dread. Gradually, he may come to realize that his dissipation is a dispersal of himself. He will be faced with the choice of abandoning himself to despair, or of moving upward by committing himself to an ethical existence.

The nature of such an existence, and the necessity for undertaking it, is spelt out most fully in the correspondence of Judge Vilhelm, the fictional author of the second part of *Either/Or*. Vilhelm is himself a fully paid-up member of ethical society: he is happily married, the father of four children, and a civil court judge. Unhappily for the reader, he also has a ponderous and repetitious manner of writing, quite different from the witty and novelettish style with which Kierkegaard endowed the aesthetic author of *Either/Or*'s first part, who is now the recipient of the edifying letters.

Vilhelm goes to great lengths to express the contrast between the aesthetic and the ethical character, and sums it up in the following terms:

We said that every aesthetic life-view was despair; this was because it was built upon what may or may not be. That is not the case with the ethical life-view, for this builds life upon what has being as its essential property. The aesthetic, we said, is that in which a person is immediately what he is; the ethical is that whereby a person becomes what he becomes. (*E/O* 525)

Kierkegaard attaches great importance to the concept of the self. People often wish to have the talents or virtues of others; but they never seriously wish to be another person, to have a self other than their own (*E/O* 517). In the aesthetic stage, the self is undeveloped and undifferentiated; a morass of unrealized and conflicting possibilities: life is a hysterical series of experiments with no outcome. The aesthete is in a state of permanent pregnancy: always in travail and never giving birth to a self. To enter the ethical stage is to undertake the formation of one's true self, where 'self' means something like a freely chosen character. Instead of merely developing one's talents one follows a vocation. The ethical life is a life of duty; of duty, however, not externally imposed but internally realized. The proper development of the individual involves the internalization of universal law.

Only when the individual himself is the universal, only then can the ethical be realised. This is the secret of conscience; it is the secret the individual life shares with itself, that is at one and the same time an individual life and also the universal. . . . The person who regards life ethically sees the universal, and the person who lives ethically expresses his life in the universal; he makes himself into the universal man, not by divesting himself of his concretion, for then he would be nothing at all, but by clothing himself in it and permeating it with the universal. (*E/O* 547)

In grammars of foreign languages, some particular word is chosen as a paradigm to illustrate the way that nouns decline and verbs conjugate. The words chosen have no particular priority over any other noun and verb, but they teach us something about every noun and verb. In a similar sense, Vilhelm says, 'Everyone can, if he wants, become a paradigm man, not by wiping out his contingency but by remaining in it and ennobling it. But he ennobles it by choosing it' (*E/O* 552). The pattern that he lays out to be followed leads through the acquisition of personal virtues, through the civic virtues, and ends finally with the religious virtues. The man whom Kierkegaard most often chooses as a paradigm of the ethical person is Socrates. His life illustrates the fact that the ethical stage may make strict demands on the individual, and call for heroic self-sacrifice.

Judge Vilhelm does not offer us Kierkegaard's last word on morality, because in his system the ethical is not the highest category. Kierkegaard himself neither took a job nor got married, which are the two marks of the ethical life. Because of his own and his family's history he felt incapable of the total sharing of all secrets which he thought was essential to a good marriage. Faced with the demands made by the ethical life, Kierkegaard tells us, the individual becomes vividly conscious of human weakness; he may try to overcome it by strength of will, but find himself unable to do so. He becomes aware that his own powers are insufficient to meet the demands of the moral law. This brings him to a sense of guilt and a consciousness of sinfulness. If he is to escape from this, he must rise from the ethical sphere to this religious sphere: he must make 'the leap of faith'.[5]

Nietzsche and the Transvaluation of Values

Nietzsche agreed with Kierkegaard that a call to the Christian life was something that could not be justified by reason. But whereas Kierkegaard concluded, 'So much the worse for mere reason', Nietzsche concluded, 'So much the worse for the call of Christianity'. Not that Nietzsche spent much time in demonstrating that Christianity was irrational: his main complaint against it was rather that it was base and degrading. In works like *The Genealogy of Morals* he seeks not so much to refute the claims of Christian morality as to trace its ignoble pedigree.

History, Nietzsche says, exhibits two different kinds of morality. In the earliest times, strong, privileged aristocrats, feeling themselves to belong to a higher order than their fellows, described their own qualities—noble birth, bravery, candour, blondness, and the like—as 'good'. They regarded the characteristics of the plebeians—vulgarity, cowardice, untruthfulness, and swarthiness—as 'bad'. That is master-morality. The poor and weak, resenting the power and riches of the aristocrats, turned this system on its head. They set up their own contrasting system of values, a morality for the herd that puts a premium on traits such as humility, sympathy, and benevolence, which benefit the underdog. They saw the aristocratic type of person not just as bad (*schlecht*) but as positively evil (*böse*). The erection of this new system Nietzsche called 'a transvaluation of values', and he blamed it on the Jews.

It was the Jews who, reversing the aristocratic equation (good = noble = beautiful = happy = loved by the gods), dared with a frightening consistency to suggest the contrary equation, and to hold on to it with the teeth of the most profound hatred (the hatred of the powerless). It is they who have declared 'the wretched alone are the good; the poor, the weak, the lowly are alone good; the suffering, the needy, the sick, the hideous, are the only ones who are pious, the only ones who are blessed, for them alone is salvation. You, on the other hand, you noblemen, you men of power, you are to all eternity the evil, the cruel, the covetous, the insatiate, and the godless ones. You will be forever unblessed, accursed, and damned.' (*GM* 19)

---

[5] Kierkegaard's teaching on faith and religion is discussed in Ch. 12 below.

The revolt of the slaves, begun by the Jews, achieved its triumph with the rise of Christianity. In Rome itself, once the fatherland of aristocratic virtue, men now bow down to four Jews: Jesus, Mary, Peter, and Paul (*GM* 36).

Christianity puts itself forward as a religion of love, but in fact, according to Nietzsche, it is rooted in weakness, fear, and malice. Its dominant motive is what he calls *ressentiment*, the desire of the weak for revenge on the strong, which disguises itself as a wish to punish the sinner. Christians pose as the executors of divine commands, but this is only to cloak their own bad conscience. Christians exalt compassion as a virtue, but when they assist the afflicted it is commonly because they enjoy exercising power over them. Even when philanthropy is not hypocritical it does more harm than good, by humiliating the sufferer. Pity is a poison that infects a compassionate person with the sufferings of others (*Z* 112).

The success of Christianity has led to the degeneration of the human race. Systematic tenderness for the weak lowers the general health and strength of mankind. Modern man, as a result, is a mere dwarf, who has lost the will to be truly human. Vulgarity and mediocrity become the norm; only rarely there still flashes out an embodiment of the noble ideal.

The herd-man in Europe nowadays puts on airs as if he were the only acceptable type of human being. He glorifies the qualities that make him tame, docile, and useful to the herd as if they were the true human virtues: public spirit, benevolence, considerateness, industriousness, moderation, modesty, tolerance, compassion. But there are cases where a leader or bell-wether is felt to be indispensable; in such cases people keep trying to set up an aggregation of clever herd-men in place of real commanders: that is the origin, for instance, of all parliamentary constitutions. But what a blessing, in spite of everything, what a release from an increasingly unbearable burden is the appearance of an absolute commander for these herd-Europeans! This was demonstrated most recently by the effect of Napoleon when he appeared on the scene. The history of the impact of Napoleon can be said to be the history of the highest happiness this entire century has achieved in its most valuable men and moments. (*BGE* 86)

If the human race is to be saved from decadence, the first step must be to reverse the values of Christianity, introducing a second transvaluation of values. 'The weak and the failures shall perish: that is the first principle of *our* love of mankind,' Nietzsche wrote on the first page of his *Antichrist*. Human beings fell into two types: 'ascending' people and 'descending' people, that is to say, people who represented the upward and downward track of human evolution. It was not always easy to tell which was which—only Nietzsche himself had a perfect nose to discriminate between the two—but once detected, the descending creatures had to make way for the well-constituted, taking away from them as little space, energy, and sunshine as possible (*WP* 373).

However, it is not just Christian morality that must be overturned. We must go beyond the opposition between good and evil that is the feature of any slave

936

morality. It is not only Christians, for instance, who regard truth as a fundamental value. But we should not, Nietzsche argues, object to judgements just because they are false.

The question is rather to what extent the judgement promotes life, preserves life, preserves the species, perhaps even enhances the species. We are in principle inclined to claim that judgements that are most false—including synthetic a priori judgements—are the ones most indispensable to us. Human beings could not live without accepting logical fictions...To give up false judgements would be to give up life, to deny life. Recognizing untruth as a condition of life? What a dangerous rejection of traditional values! A philosophy that dares to do this has already placed itself beyond good and evil. (*BGE* 7)

Truth is that kind of error without which a particular living being could not survive. Life is the supreme value by which all others are to be judged. 'Whenever we speak of values', Nietzsche wrote, 'we speak under the inspiration of life and from the perspective of life. Life itself forces us to establish values; it is life that does the evaluation by means of us whenever we posit values' (*TI* 24). Human life is the highest form of life that has so far emerged, but in the contemporary world it has sunk to the level of some of the forms that preceded it. We must affirm life and bring it to a new level, a synthesis transcending the thesis and antithesis of master and slave, the Superman (*Ubermensch*).

The proclamation of the Superman is the prophetic message of Nietzsche's oracular spokesman Zarathustra. The Superman will be the highest form of life, the ultimate affirmation of the will to live. But our will to live must not be, like Schopenhauer's, one that favours the weak; it must be a will to power. The will to power is the secret of all life; every living thing seeks to discharge its force, to give full scope to its ability. Pleasure is merely the consciousness of power's exercise. Knowledge—to the extent that there can be knowledge when there is no absolute truth—is merely an instrument of power. The greatest realization of human power will be the creation of Superman.

Humanity is merely a stage on the way to Superman, who is what gives meaning to the world. 'Humanity is something that must be surpassed: man is a bridge and not a goal' (*Z* 44). Superman, however, will not come into existence through the forces of evolution, but only through the exercise of will. 'Let your will say "Superman *is to be* the meaning of the earth."'

Zarathustra says: 'You could surely create the Superman! Perhaps not you yourselves, my brothers! But you could transform yourselves into forefathers and ancestors of the Superman: and let this be your finest creation!' The arrival of Superman will be the perfection of the world and give it meaning. But because of the eternal recurrence, it will not be the end of history. Superman will have a second, and a third, and an infinite number of comings.

What will Superman be like? This is something we need to know if his character is to present any standard by which to make a judgement of human virtue and vice. But Zarathustra has very little to tell us about him, and in his later philosophical works Nietzsche no longer employed the concept. He does, however, continue to talk of 'higher human beings', and we get the impression that his ideal would be a combination of Goethe and Napoleon, each of whom, in different ways, developed a variety of talents to their maximum degree. The combination is a more plausible one than another that he once scribbled in a notebook, 'Roman Caesar with the soul of Christ'.

It is difficult to make a critical judgement about Nietzsche's ethics, since his writing is often wilfully chaotic, and it is unsurprising that scholars vary widely in their interpretation and evaluation. It is not easy, for instance, to find out where Nietzsche stands on an issue such as the morality of cruelty. When denouncing the role played by guilt in slave morality, he describes with eloquent outrage the tortures inflicted by persecuting bigots. But he is tender to the excesses of his aristocratic 'blond beasts' who 'perhaps come from a ghastly bout of murder, arson, rape, and torture, with bravado and a moral equanimity, as though some wild student's prank had been played'.

Certainly Nietzsche is an enthusiast where war is concerned. 'Renouncing war', he wrote, 'means renouncing the *great* life' (*TI* 23). War is an education in freedom, and freedom means that the manly instincts that delight in victory triumph over any other instinct, including the desire for happiness. 'The *liberated* man, and even more the liberated *spirit*, tramples underfoot the despicable kind of well-being that shopkeepers, Christians, cows, women, Englishmen, and other democrats, dream of ' (*TI* 65).

Suicide, too, in certain circumstances engages Nietzsche's admiration. Physicians should remind their patients that sick persons are parasites on society, and that a time comes when it is indecent to live longer.

Die proudly if it is no longer possible to live proudly. Death freely chosen, death at the right time, brought about cheerfully and joyfully among children and witnesses—so that a real leave-taking is still possible, when the one who is taking his leave *is still there*; a true assessment of one's achievements and ambitions, a summing up of one's life—all this in contrast to the ghastly and pitiful comedy that Christianity has made of the hour of death. (*TI* 61)

If you do away with yourself, Nietzsche concludes, you are doing what is most admirable: it almost earns you the right to live.

But is Nietzsche an ethicist at all? Is he a genuine moralist with highly unconventional views of virtue and vice, or is he a completely amoral person with no concern for right and wrong? On the one hand, he is clearly operating in the same field as some great past moralists: his ideal human being bears a resemblance to the great-souled man of Aristotle's *Nicomachean Ethics*. On the other hand, he himself professes not just to be presenting novel views of good and evil, but to be transcending those categories altogether. He calls himself an immoralist, and tells us that there are no moral facts, and he does his best to devalue two of the key concepts of most moral systems, namely justice and guilt.

The answer, I think, is that Nietzsche shares with traditional morality an ultimate concern with human flourishing, and the reason that he condemns many conventional virtues is precisely because he believes that they hinder rather than help the achievement of a worthwhile life. But in his preference for the great over the good, and for the nobleman over the gentleman, he shows himself to have a fundamentally aesthetic, rather than ethical, criterion of the good life. His ideal human being not only does not love his neighbour: he *has* no neighbour.

Analytic Ethics

As an ethicist, G. E. Moore stands at the opposite pole from Nietzsche. He placed goodness at the apex of the pyramid of moral concepts, and he was not at all interested in genealogical questions of the origin and development of the concept. In his *Principia Ethica* (1903) he sees himself as giving an answer to the question 'How is goodness to be defined?' simply by inspection of the object or idea that the word 'good' stands for. The question, he maintained, is fundamental and must be faced before we ask what kinds of actions we ought to perform. For the actions we ought to perform are those that will cause more good to exist in the universe than any possible kind of alternative.

So before we ask what things are good, we must ask what kind of property goodness itself is. The question, he maintained, could not be answered by giving any definition of goodness, because goodness was a simple, indefinable notion, like the notion of yellow. But unlike yellowness, which was a natural property of things, goodness, Moore maintained, was a non-natural quality. If we consider goodness, and any other property akin to it, such as pleasantness, we will see that 'we have two different notions before our minds'. Even if everything good were in fact pleasant, it does not follow that 'good' and 'pleasant' mean the same. To identify goodness with any property such as pleasantness was to commit a fallacy: the naturalistic fallacy, of confusing a non-natural property with a natural one.

Though Moore maintained that goodness was not a natural property, he did not deny that it could be a property of natural things. Indeed, it was a principal task of moral philosophy to determine what things possessed this non-natural property. After lengthy investigation Moore came to the conclusion that the only things that have intrinsic goodness are friendship and aesthetic experience.

The arguments in *Principia Ethica* are extraordinarily flimsy, and Moore himself was later to admit that 'I did not give any tenable explanation of what I meant by saying that "good" was not a natural property.'[6] Yet the book was remarkably

---

[6] P. A. Schilpp (ed.), *The Philosophy of G. E. Moore* (Chicago: Open Court, 1942).

influential, especially through two significant groups of admirers. The Bloomsbury group, in particular J. M. Keynes, Lytton Strachey, and E. M. Forster, held up the book as a charter for a lifestyle that threw overboard conventional notions of respectability and rectitude. In addition, professional philosophers who could not swallow the notion of goodness as a non-natural property nonetheless used the expression 'naturalistic fallacy' as a mantra to dispose of moral theories of which they disapproved.

Under the influence of logical positivism, however, some philosophers began to deny that goodness was any sort of property, natural or non-natural, and to claim that ethical utterances were not statements of fact at all. Thus A. J. Ayer maintained that if I say 'Stealing money is wrong',

> I produce a sentence which has no factual meaning—that is, expresses no proposition which can be either true or false. It is as if I had written 'Stealing money!!'—where the shape and thickness of the exclamation marks show, by a suitable convention, that a special sort of moral disapproval is the feeling which is being expressed. It is clear that there is nothing said here which can be true or false. Another man may disagree with me about the wrongness of stealing, in the sense that he may not have the same feelings about stealing as I have, and he may quarrel with me on account of my moral sentiments. But he cannot, strictly speaking, contradict me. (*LTL* 107)

This view of ethical utterances was called 'emotivism'. While Ayer laid stress on the expression of one's own emotion, other emotivists saw as the function of moral language the encouragement of feelings and attitudes in other people. But no emotivist was able to give a convincing account of the particular character of the sentiments in question, or to show in what way logic enters into moral reasoning when we use words like 'because' and 'therefore'.

R. M. Hare (1919–2002), an Oxford tutor who later became White's Professor of Moral Philosophy, was anxious to make room in ethics for logic. In *The Language of Morals* (1952) and in *Freedom and Reason* (1963) Hare pointed out that there is a logic of imperatives no less than a logic of assertion, and he drew on this to expound a theory of moral reasoning. He distinguished between prescriptive and descriptive meaning. A descriptive statement is one whose meaning is defined by the factual conditions for its truth. A prescriptive sentence is one that entails, perhaps in conjunction with descriptive statements, at least one imperative. To assent to an imperative is to prescribe action, to tell oneself or others to do this or do that. Prescriptive language comes in two forms: there are straightforward imperatives, and there are value judgements.

Value judgements may contain a word like 'good' or a word like 'ought'. To call something 'good' is to commend it; to call something a good X is to say that it is the kind of X that should be chosen by anyone who wants an X. There will be different criteria for the goodness of Xs and the goodness of Ys, but this does not amount to a difference in the meaning of the word 'good', which is exhausted by its commendatory function. 'Ought' statements—which Hare, following Hume, thought could never be derived from 'is' statements—entail imperatives. 'A ought to Φ' entails an order to Φ addressed not only to A but to anyone else in a relevantly similar situation, and the addressees include the utterer of the sentence himself. The utterer's willingness to obey the order, if the occasion arises, is the criterion of his sincerity in uttering the sentence. Ought-sentences are not just prescriptive, but unlike common or garden commands they are universalizable.

Hare distinguished between ethics and morals. Ethics is the study of the general features of moral language, of which prescriptivity and universalizability are the most important; moral judgements are prescriptions and prohibitions of specific actions. In principle, ethics is neutral between different and conflicting moral systems. But this does not mean that ethics is practically vacuous: once an understanding of ethics is combined with the desires and beliefs of an actual moral agent, it can lead to concrete and important moral judgements.

The way in which prescriptivity and universalizability enter into actual moral argument is explained thus by Hare. Though nothing other than my own choices gives authority to my moral judgements, my choices in addition to the logical properties of moral language give rise to something like a Golden Rule. Let us suppose that A owes money to B, B owes money to C, and neither is in a position to repay the debt on the due date. B may judge 'A ought to go to prison'. But since this judgement is universalizable, and B is in the same position as A, the judgement entails for B 'I ought to go to prison'—a judgement that is unlikely to command his assent. Hare maintained that considerations of this sort would lead to the adoption of a roughly utilitarian system of moral judgements, since he believed, implausibly, that only a small minority of fanatics would be content to be done by as they had done to others.

In the late 1950s Hare's prescriptivism was subjected to devastating criticism by a number of colleagues living in Oxford, notably Foot, Geach, and Anscombe.

Philippa Foot (b. 1920) in 'Moral Beliefs' (1958) and 'Goodness and Choice' (1961) attacked the distinction between descriptive and evaluative predicates by concentrating attention on the names of particular virtues and vices. She invites us to consider words like 'rude' and 'courageous'. It is not difficult to describe in purely factual terms behaviour that would merit these epithets; yet calling someone rude or courageous is clearly a matter of evaluation.

A judgement cannot be treated as moral judgement, Foot argued, simply on the basis of formal characteristics such as universalizability and prescriptivity. Merely by making the appropriate choices one cannot make clasping the hands three times in an hour into a good action, or determine that what makes a man a good man is having red hair. Moral beliefs must concern traits and actions that are beneficial or harmful to human beings. Since it is not a matter of human decision which traits and actions promote or diminish human flourishing, moral judgements likewise cannot depend simply on human choice.

In the ancient and medieval world the analysis of virtues and vices, and the investigation of their relationship to happiness, was a very substantial part of moral philosophy. It is largely due to Philippa Foot that in recent decades virtue theory, after centuries of neglect, has come to occupy a prominent part in moral philosophy.

Peter Geach (b. 1919) in 'Good and Evil' (1956) attacked the descriptive–evaluative distinction in the case also of the most general terms, such as 'good'. The important distinction, he claimed, is that between attributive and predicative terms. In the case of a predicative term like 'red' one can know what it is for an X to be red without knowing what an X is. The case is not the same with attributive terms like 'large' or 'false'. 'Good' and 'bad', Geach says, are always attributive, not predicative. If we say of an individual A that he is good *simpliciter*, we really mean that he is a good man, and if we call some behaviour good, we mean that it is a good human action. It is therefore folly to look for some property called goodness, or some activity called commending, which is always present when we call something good.

In 'Assertion' (1965) Geach showed that the meaning of 'good' could not be explained in terms of commendation, because in many contexts we use it without any intention of commending. 'Good' can be predicated, for instance, in if-clauses. Someone who says 'If contraception is a good thing, then free distribution of condoms is a good thing' need not be commending either contraception or the free distribution of condoms. Of course, 'good' may on occasion be used to commend, but this does not mean that its primary meaning is not descriptive.

Geach's wife, Elizabeth Anscombe, wrote an influential paper in 1958, 'Modern Moral Philosophy'. This was a frontal attack not only on Hare but on the whole of Anglophone moral philosophy since the time of Sidgwick. Its first paragraph proclaims a resounding thesis:

The concepts of obligation and duty—*moral* obligation and *moral* duty, that is to say—and of what is *morally* right and wrong, and of the *moral* sense of 'ought', ought to be jettisoned if this is psychologically possible; because they are survivals, or derivatives of survivals, from an earlier conception of ethics which no longer generally survives, and are only harmful without it. (*ERP* 26)

Aristotle has much to say about the virtues and vices, but he has no concept answering to our term 'moral'. It was Christianity, taking its moral notions from the Torah, that introduced a *law* conception of ethics. Conformity to the virtues and avoidance of the vices henceforth became a requirement of divine law.

Naturally it is not possible to have such a conception unless you believe in God as a lawgiver; like Jews, Stoics and Christians. But if such a conception is dominant for many centuries, and then is given up, it is a natural result that the concepts of 'obligation', of being bound or required as by a law, should remain though they had lost their root; and if the word 'ought' has become invested in certain contexts with the sense of 'obligation', it too will remain to be spoken with a special emphasis and a special feeling in these contexts. It is as if the notion 'criminal' were to remain when criminal law and criminal courts had been abolished and forgotten. (*ERP* 30)

It is true, as philosophers have said since Hume, that one cannot infer an 'ought'—a moral 'ought'—from an 'is'; but that is because this 'ought' has become a word of mere mesmeric force, once the notion of a divine lawgiver has been dropped.

The most significant practical result of this, Anscombe maintained, is that philosophers have all become consequentialists, believing that the right action is the one with the best possible consequences. Every one of the best-known English academic ethicists 'has put out a philosophy according to which, e.g. it is not possible to hold that it cannot be right to kill the innocent as a means to any end whatsoever and that someone who thinks otherwise is in error'. This means that all their philosophies are incompatible with the Hebrew–Christian ethic, which held that there are certain things forbidden whatever consequences threaten. According to Anscombe, the differences between individual philosophers since Sidgwick are, in comparison with this incompatibility, unimportant and provincial.

The notions of duty, and of moral right and wrong, Anscombe proposed, should be discarded in favour of the notions of justice and injustice, which had a genuine content. Even of these notions it remained difficult to give a clear account, until we had a satisfactory philosophical psychology. For one cannot analyse the concepts of justice and virtue unless one has a satisfactory account of such terms as 'action', 'intention', 'pleasure', and 'wanting'. Anscombe herself made a monumental contribution to this area of philosophy in her book *Intention* (1957), which was taken as a model by many later investigators.

In the latter part of the twentieth century a variety of approaches to ethics was explored by English-speaking philosophers, and in Britain no single philosopher stood out as a prime exponent of ethical theory, as for a time Hare had done. In reaction to Hare's revival of Kantian morality a number of philosophers placed a renewed focus on themes of Aristotelian ethics. Thus Philippa Foot laid emphasis on the central role of virtue in morality, inspiring a school of 'virtue ethics', and Bernard Williams reminded philosophers of the great part played by luck in determining one's moral situation.

Foot's starting point is that the virtues are characteristics that any human being needs to have both for his own sake and for that of others. They differ from other qualities necessary for flourishing—such as health and strength, intelligence and skill—in that they are not mere capacities, but they engage the will. They concern matters that are difficult for humans, and where are temptations to be resisted; but *pace* Kant moral worth is not to be measured by the difficulty of moral action. The really virtuous person is one who does good actions almost

943

effortlessly: a really charitable person, for instance, is one who finds it easy, rather than hard, to make the sacrifices that charity calls for. Without the virtues the life of a human being is stunted, in the way that the life of an animal lacking a sense-faculty is stunted.

Williams began by recalling the way in which in the classical tradition happiness had been regarded as the product of self-sufficiency: what was not in the domain of the self was not in its control and so was subject to luck and the contingent enemies of tranquillity. In more recent thought, the ideal of making the whole of life immune to luck was abandoned, but for Kant there was one supreme value, moral value, that could be regarded as immune: the successful moral life was a career open not merely to the talents but to a talent that all rational beings necessarily possess in the same degree. Williams insisted that the aim of making morality immune to luck was bound to be disappointed. There is the constitutive luck of the temperament we inherit and the culture into which we are born: this sets the conditions within which our moral dispositions, motives, and intentions must operate. There is also—and Williams developed this theme in telling detail—the incident luck that is involved in bringing any project of moral importance to a successful conclusion.

As the century progressed philosophers began to focus their attention not so much on the higher-order questions such as the nature of moral language, or the relationships between principles, character, luck, and virtue, but on specific first-order issues such as the rightness or wrongness of particular actions: lying, abortion, torture, and euthanasia, for example. Foot and Williams played a significant part in this change of emphasis, which was also reflected in universities in the growth of such courses as medical ethics and business ethics.

Both Foot and Williams taught on both sides of the Atlantic. In the United States the most significant moral philosopher of the latter part of the twentieth century was John Rawls. Like Foot and Williams, Rawls was an enemy of utilitarianism, a system that he believed provided no safeguard against many forms of unfair discrimination. His project was to derive a theory of justice from the notion of fairness, which he did by introducing a novel version of social contract theory into ethics. Since the major implications of his theory concern political institutions rather than individual morality, his work will be considered later, in Chapter 11.

10

Aesthetics

The Beautiful and the Sublime

The person generally held to be the founder of aesthetics as an independent philosophical discipline is Alexander Gottlieb Baumgarten (1714–62). Certainly it was he who coined the word 'aesthetics', in a short treatise on poetry published in 1735. For Baumgarten, the purpose of art is to produce beauty, defined in terms of the ordered relationship between the parts of a whole. The point of beauty is to give pleasure and arouse desire. The finest beauty is to be found in nature, and therefore the highest aim of art is to imitate nature.

Other eighteenth-century philosophers sought to give a more precise analysis of beauty. Hume, in the section of his *Treatise of Human Nature* entitled 'Of Beauty and Deformity', offered the following definition:

beauty is such an order and constitution of parts, as either by the *primary constitution* of our nature, by *custom*, or by *caprice*, is fitted to give a pleasure and satisfaction to the soul. This is the distinguishing character of beauty, and forms all the difference betwixt it and deformity, whose natural tendency is to produce uneasiness. Pleasure and pain, therefore, are not only necessary attendants of beauty and deformity, but constitute their very essence. (II. i. 8)

Later, Hume was dissatisfied with the idea that unexamined custom and uneducated caprice could determine beauty; he sought to make room, in aesthetic judgements, for correctness and incorrectness. In *The Standard of Taste* (1757) he argued that the criteria of judgement should be established by ascertaining which features of works of art were most highly pleasing to qualified and impartial connoisseurs.

Edmund Burke (1729–97) introduced into aesthetics, alongside the concept of beauty, that of sublimity. The sublime, as well as the beautiful, can be the aim of art: a feeling of beauty is a form of love without desire, and to feel something as sublime is to feel astonishment without fear. In *A Philosophical Inquiry into the Origin of our Ideas of the Sublime and the Beautiful* Burke sought to explain by what qualities objects inspire these feelings in us. He traced the feeling for the sublime to the fears and horrors implicit in the original instinct for self-preservation. The feeling for beauty, whose paradigm is a chaste appreciation of female perfection, derives, he maintained, from the need for social contact and ultimately from the instinct to propagate the race.

The treatise that dominated aesthetics in the nineteenth century was Kant's *Critique of Judgement* (1790). In his 'Analytic of the Beautiful' and 'Analytic of the Sublime' Kant sought to do for aesthetics what his earlier Critiques had done for epistemology and ethics. Human beings possess, in addition to theoretical under-standing and practical reason, a third faculty, the capacity for judgement (*Urteil-skraft*), the judgement of taste, which is the basis of aesthetic experience.

Agreeing with Burke, and disagreeing with Baumgarten, Kant sees disinterest-edness as fundamental to the aesthetic response. 'Taste', he says, 'is the faculty of judging of an object or a method of representing it by an *entirely disinterested* satisfaction or dissatisfaction. The object of such satisfaction is called *beautiful*' (M 45).

Kant makes a distinction between two kinds of satisfaction: he calls sensual delight 'gratification' and reserves the notion of 'pleasingness' for the disinterested enjoyment of beauty. He writes, 'What gratifies a person is called pleasurable; what merely pleases him is called beautiful; what he values is called good.' Animals enjoy pleasure, but only humans appreciate beauty. Only the taste for beauty is completely disinterested, because the practical reason that determines goodness has reference to our own well-being. To point the difference, Kant remarks that while we can distinguish between what is good in itself and what is good only as a means, we do not make any parallel distinction between what is beautiful as a means and what is beautiful as an end (M 42).

A judgement of taste, Kant tells us, does not bring an experience under a concept, in the way that an ordinary judgement does; it relates the experience directly to the disinterested pleasure. Unlike an expression of sensual pleasure, it claims universal validity. If I like the taste of Madeira, I don't go on to claim that everyone else should like it too; but if I think a poem, a building, or a symphony beautiful, I impute to others an obligation to agree with me. Judgements of taste are singular in form ('This rose is beautiful') but universal in import; they are, as Kant puts it, expressions of 'a universal voice'. Yet, because a judgement of taste does not bring its object under a concept, no reason can be given for it and no argument can constrain agreement to it.

Judgements of value are related to purpose. If I want to know whether an X is a good X, I need to know what Xs are for—that is how I tell what makes a good knife, or a good plumber, and so on. Judgements of perfection are similar: I cannot know what is a perfect X without knowing what is the function of an X. Judgements of beauty, however, cannot be quite like this, since they do not bring their objects under any concept X. However, Kant maintains that beautiful objects exhibit 'purposiveness without purpose'. By this he means perhaps that while beauty has no point, yet it invites us to linger over its contemplation.

This obscure thesis becomes clearer when Kant makes a distinction between types of beauty. There are two kinds of beauty: free beauty (*pulchritudo vaga*) and derivative beauty (*pulchritudo adhaerens*). The first presupposes no concept of what the object ought to be; the second does presuppose such a concept, and the perfection of the object in accordance therewith. The first is called the self-subsistent beauty of this or that thing; the second, as dependent upon a concept (conditioned beauty), is ascribed to objects with a particular purpose. A judgement of beauty without reference to any purpose that an object is to serve is a pure judgement of taste. A flower is Kant's regular paradigm of a free natural beauty. As for the other kind of beauty: 'Human beauty (i.e. of a man, a woman, or a child), the beauty of a horse, or a building (be it church, palace, arsenal or summer house), presupposes a concept of the purpose which determines what the thing is to be, and consequently a concept of its perfection; it is therefore derivative beauty' (M 66).

It is clear from this passage that Kant's aesthetic is much more at home with natural beauty than with the beauty of artefacts. But the problem he is mainly concerned with arises in both contexts. How can a judgement of beauty, a judgement that is not based on reason, claim universal validity? When I make such a judgement, I do not claim that everyone will agree with me, but I do claim that everyone ought to do so. This is only possible if we are all in possession of a common sensibility (*Gemeinsinn*)—a sensibility which, since it is normative, cannot derive from experience but must be transcendental.

Kant begins his 'Analytic of the Sublime' with a distinction between two kinds of sublimity, which he calls (not very happily) the mathematical and the dynamical. In each case the sublime object is vast, great, overwhelming; but in the mathematical case what is overwhelmed is our perception and in the dynamical case what is overwhelmed is our power. Whatever is mathematically sublime is too great to be taken in by any of our senses; it awakens in us the feeling of a faculty above sense which reaches out towards infinity. Whatever is dynamically sublime is something to which any resistance on our part would be vain, but which yet allows us to remain without fear in a state of security.

Bold, overhanging, and as it were threatening rocks; clouds piled up in the sky, moving with lightning flashes and thunder peals; volcanoes in all their violence of destruction; hurricanes with their track of devastation; the boundless ocean in a state of tumult; the lofty waterfall of a mighty river, and such like—these exhibit our faculty of resistance as insignificantly small in comparison with their might. But the sight of them is the more attractive, the more fearful it is, provided only that we are in security; and we willingly call these objects sublime, because they raise the energies of the soul above their accustomed height and discover in us a faculty of resistance of a quite different kind, which gives us courage to measure ourselves against the apparent almightiness of nature. (M 100–1)

Nature can be both beautiful and sublime, but art can only be beautiful. What, then, is the relation between beauty in nature and beauty in art? Kant's answer is subtle. On the one hand, nature is beautiful because it looks like art. On the other hand, if we are to admire a beautiful work of art, we must be conscious that it is artificial and not natural. Yet, Kant tells us, 'the purposiveness in its form must seem to be as free from all constraint of arbitrary rules as if it were a product of mere nature' (M 149). For the judgement of beautiful art taste is needed; for its production what is needed is genius.

The production of beauty is the purpose of art, but artificial beauty is not a beautiful thing, but a beautiful representation of a thing. Beautiful art can indeed present as beautiful things that in nature are ugly or repellent. There are three kinds of beautiful arts, each with their beautiful products. There are the arts of speech, namely rhetoric and poetry. There are what Kant calls the formative arts, namely painting and the plastic arts of sculpture and architecture. There is a third class of art which creates a play of sensations: the most important of these is music. 'Of all the arts', says Kant, '*poetry* (which owes its origin almost entirely to genius and will least be guided by precept or example) maintains the first rank' (M 170).

It is interesting to compare Kant's ideas on aesthetics with those expressed a few years later by the English Romantic poets. In treating of works of art Kant as it were starts from the consumer and works back to the producer; he begins by analysing the nature of the critic's judgement and ends by deducing the qualities that are necessary for genius (namely, imagination, understanding, spirit, and taste). The Romantics, on the other hand, start with the producer: for them, art is above all the expression of the artist's own emotions. Wordsworth, in his *Preface to Lyrical Ballads*, tells us that what distinguishes the poet from other men is that he has a greater promptness of thought and feeling without immediate external excitement, and a greater power of expressing such thoughts and feelings:

Poetry is the spontaneous overflow of powerful feelings: it takes its origin from emotion recollected in tranquillity: the emotion is contemplated till, by a species of reaction, the tranquillity gradually disappears, and an emotion, kindred to that which was before the subject of contemplation, is gradually produced and does itself actually exist in the mind.

In giving expression to this emotion in verse, the poet's fundamental obligation is to give immediate pleasure to the reader.

Coleridge agreed with this. 'A poem', he wrote, 'is that species of composition, which is opposed to works of science, by proposing for its *immediate* object pleasure, not truth.' But in describing the nature of poetic genius Coleridge improved on both Kant and Wordsworth, by identifying a special necessary gift. Whereas Kant and earlier authors had regarded the imagination as a faculty common to all human beings—the capacity to recall and reshuffle the experiences of everyday life—Coleridge preferred to call this banal, if important, capacity 'the fancy'.

The imagination, truly so called, was the special creative gift of the artist: in its primary form it was nothing less than 'the living Power and prime Agent of all human Perception, and as a representation in the finite mind of the eternal act of creation in the infinite I AM'. So Coleridge wrote in 1817 in the thirteenth chapter of his *Biographia Literaria*; and from that day to this critics and philosophers have debated the exact nature of this lofty faculty.

The Aesthetics of Schopenhauer

No philosopher has given aesthetics a more important role in his total system than Schopenhauer. The third book of *The World as Will and Idea* is largely devoted to the nature of art. Aesthetic pleasure, Schopenhauer tells us, following in Kant's footsteps, consists in the disinterested contemplation of nature or of artefacts. When we view a work of art—a nude sculpture, say—it may arouse desire in us: sexual desire perhaps, or desire to acquire the statue. If so, we are still under the influence of will, and we are not in a state of contemplation. It is only when we view something and admire its beauty without thought of our own desires and needs that we are treating it as a work of art and enjoying an aesthetic experience.

Disinterested contemplation, which liberates us from the tyranny of the will, may take one of two forms, which Schopenhauer illustrates by describing two different natural landscapes. If the scene I am contemplating absorbs my attention without effort, then it is my sense of beauty that is aroused. But if the scene is a threatening one, and I have to struggle to escape from fear and achieve a state of contemplation, then what I am encountering is something that is sublime rather than beautiful. Schopenhauer, like Kant, calls up various scenes to illustrate the sense of the sublime: foaming torrents pouring between overhanging rocks beneath a sky of thunderclouds; a storm at sea with the waves dashing against cliffs and sending spray into the air amid lightning flashes. In such cases, he says:

In the undismayed beholder, the two-fold nature of his consciousness reaches the highest degree of distinctness. He perceives himself, on the one hand, as an individual, as the frail phenomenon of will, which the slightest touch of these forces can utterly destroy, helpless against powerful nature, dependent, the victim of chance, a vanishing nothing in the presence of stupendous might; and, on the other hand, as the eternal, serene, knowing subject, who as the condition of every object is the sustainer of this whole world, the fearful strife of nature being only his own idea, and he himself free and apart from all desire and necessity in the contemplation of the Ideas. This is the full impression of the sublime. (*WWI* 205)

The impression produced in this way may be called 'the dynamical sublime'. But the same impression may be produced by calm meditation on the immensity of space and time while contemplating the starry sky at night. This impression of sublimity (which Schopenhauer, borrowing Kant's unhelpful term, calls 'the mathematical sublime') can be produced also by voluminous closed spaces such as the dome of St Peter's in Rome and by monuments of great age such as the pyramids. In each case the sense arises from the contrast between our own smallness and insignificance as individuals and a vastness that is the creation of ourselves as pure knowing subjects.

The sublime is, as it were, the upper bound of the beautiful. Its lower bound is what Schopenhauer calls 'the charming'. Whereas what is sublime makes an object of contemplation out of what is hostile to the will, the charming turns an object of contemplation into something that attracts the will. Schopenhauer gives as instances sculptures of 'naked figures, whose position, drapery, and general treatment are calculated to excite the passions of the beholder' and, less convincingly, Dutch still lifes of 'oysters, herrings, crabs, bread and butter, beer, wine, and so forth'. Such artefacts nullify the aesthetic purposes, and are altogether to be condemned (*WWI* 208).

There are two elements in every encounter with beauty: a will-less knowing subject, and an object which is the Idea known. In contemplation of natural beauty and of architecture, the pleasure is principally in the purity and painless-ness of the knowing, because the Ideas encountered are low-grade manifestations of will. But when we contemplate human beings (through the medium of tragedy, for example) the pleasure is rather in the Ideas contemplated, which are varied, rich, and significant. On the basis of this distinction, Schopenhauer proceeds to grade the fine arts.

Lowest in the scale comes architecture, which brings out low-grade Ideas such as gravity, rigidity, and light:

The beauty of a building lies in the obvious adaptation of every part . . . to the stability of the whole, to which the position, size and form of every part have so necessary a relation that if it were possible to remove some part, the whole would inevitably collapse. For only by each part bearing as much as it conveniently can, and each being supported exactly where it ought to be and to exactly the necessary extent, does this play of opposition, this conflict between rigidity and gravity, that constitutes the life of the stone and the manifestation of its will, unfold itself in the most complete visibility. (*WWI* 215)

Of course, architecture serves a practical as well as an aesthetic purpose, but the greatness of an architect shows itself in the way he achieves pure aesthetic ends in spite of having to subordinate them to the needs of his client.

The representational arts, in Schopenhauer's view, are concerned with the universal rather than the particular. Paintings or sculptures of animals, he is convinced, are obviously concerned with the species, not the individual: 'the most typical lion, wolf, horse, sheep, or ox, is always the most beautiful also'. But with representations of human beings, the matter is more complicated. It is quite wrong to think that art achieves beauty by imitating nature. How could an artist recognize the perfect sample to imitate if he did not have an a priori pattern of beauty in his mind? And has nature ever produced a human being perfectly beautiful in every respect? What the artist understands is something that nature only stammers in half-uttered speech. The sculptor 'expresses in the hard marble that beauty of form which in a thousand attempts nature failed to produce, and presents it to her as if telling her "This is what you wanted to say"' (*WWI* 222).

The general idea of humanity has to be represented by the sculptor or painter in the character of an individual, and it can be presented in individuals of various kinds. In a genre picture, it does not matter 'whether ministers discuss the fate of countries and nations over a map, or boors wrangle in a beer-house over cards and dice'. Nor does it matter whether the characters represented in a work of art are historical rather than fictional: the link with a historical personage gives a painting its nominal significance, not its real significance.

For example, Moses found by the Egyptian princess is the nominal significance of a painting; it represents a moment of the greatest importance in history; the real significance, on the other hand, that which is really given to the onlooker, is a foundling child rescued from its floating cradle by a great lady, an incident which may have happened more than once. (*WWI* 231)

Because of this, the paintings of Renaissance painters that Schopenhauer most admired were not those that represented a particular event (such as the nativity or the Crucifixion) but rather simple groups of saints alongside the Saviour, engaged in no action. In the faces and eyes of such figures we see the expression of that suppression of will which is the summit of all art.

Schopenhauer's theory of art combines elements from Plato and elements from Aristotle. The purpose of art, he believed was to represent not a particular individual, nor an abstract concept, but a Platonic Idea. But whereas Plato condemned art works as being at two removes from the Ideas, copies of material things that themselves were only imitations of Ideas, Schopenhauer thinks that the artist comes closer to the ideal than the technician or the historian. This is particularly the case with poetry and drama, the highest of the arts. History is related to poetry as portrait painting is to historical painting: the one gives us truth in the individual, and the other truth in the universal. Like Aristotle, Schopenhauer concludes that far more inner truth is to be attributed to poetry than to history. And among historical narratives, he decides rather eccentrically, the greatest value is to be attributed to autobiographies.

Kierkegaard on Music

In Kierkegaard's works, the word 'aesthetic' and its cognates occur frequently. However, for him 'aesthetic' is an ethical rather than an aesthetic category. The aesthetic character is someone who devotes his life to the pursuit of immediate pleasure; and the pleasures he pursues may be natural (such as food, drink, and sex) no less than artistic (such as painting, music, and dance). Kierkegaard's main interest in discussing the aesthetic attitude to life (notably in *Either/Or*) is to stress its superficial and fundamentally unsatisfactory nature, and to press the claims of a profounder ethical, and eventually religious, commitment. But in the course of a detailed presentation of the aesthetic life he has occasion to discuss issues that are aesthetic in the narrower sense of being concerned with the nature of art. For instance, the first part of *Either/Or* contains a long section that is subtitled 'The Musical Erotic'.

The essay, which purports to be written by an ardent exponent of aesthetic hedonism, is largely a meditation on Mozart's opera *Don Giovanni*. Don Juan is the supreme personification of erotic desire, and Mozart's opera is its uniquely perfect expression. Music, we are told, is of all the arts the one most capable of expressing sheer sensuality. The rather unexpected reason we are given for this is that music is the most abstract of the arts. Like language, it addresses the ear; like the spoken word, it unfolds in time, not in space. But while language is the vehicle of spirit, music is the vehicle of sensuality.

Kierkegaard's essayist goes on to make a surprising claim. Though religious puritans are suspicious of music, as the voice of sensuality, and prefer to listen to the word of the spirit, the development of music and the discovery of sensuality are both in fact due to Christianity. Sensual love was, of course, an element in the life of the Greeks, whether humans or gods; but it took Christianity to separate out sensuality by contrasting it with spirituality.

If I imagine the sensual erotic as a principle, as a power, as a realm characterized by spirit, that is to say characterized by being excluded by spirit, if I imagine it concentrated in a single individual, then I have the concept of the spirit of the sensual erotic. This is an idea which the Greeks did not have, which Christianity first introduced to the world, if only in an indirect sense.

   If this spirit of the sensual erotic in all its immediacy demands expression, the question is: what medium lends itself to that? What must be especially borne in mind here is that it demands expression and representation in its immediacy. In its mediate state and its reflection in something else it comes under language and becomes subject to ethical categories. In its immediacy it can only be expressed in music. (*E/O* 75)

Kierkegaard illustrates the various forms and stages of erotic pursuit by taking characters from different Mozart operas. The first awakening of sensuality takes a melancholy, diffuse form, with no specific object: this is the dreamy stage expressed by Cherubino in *The Marriage of Figaro*. The second stage is expressed in the merry, vigorous, sparkling chirping of Papageno in *The Magic Flute*: love seeking out a specific object. But these stages are no more than presentiments of Don Giovanni, who is the very incarnation of the sensual erotic. Ballads and legends represent him as an individual. 'When he is interpreted in music, on the other hand, I do not have a particular individual, I have the power of nature, the demonic, which as little tires of seducing, or is done with seducing, as the wind is tired of raging, the sea of surging, or a waterfall of cascading down from its height' (*E/O* 90).

Because Don Giovanni seduces not by stratagem, but by sheer energy of desire, he does not come within any ethical category; that is why his force can be expressed in music alone. The secret of the whole opera is that its hero is the force animating the other characters: he is the sun, the other characters mere planets, who are half in darkness, with only that side which is turned towards him illuminated. Only the Commendatore is independent; but he is outside the substance of the opera as its antecedent and consequent, and both before and after his death he is the voice of spirit.

Because music is uniquely suitable to express the immediacy of sensual desire, in *Don Giovanni* we have a perfect match of subject matter and creative form. Both matter and form are essential to a work of art, Kierkegaard says, even though philosophers overemphasize now one and now the other. It is because of this that *Don Giovanni*, even if it stood alone, was enough to make Mozart a classic composer and absolutely immortal.

Nietzsche on Tragedy

For the young Nietzsche it is not Mozart but Wagner whose operas are supreme. This is because of a shared debt to Schopenhauer. In 1854 Wagner wrote to Franz Liszt that Schopenhauer had come into his life like a gift from heaven. 'His chief idea, the final negation of the desire for life, is terribly gloomy, but it shows the only salvation possible.'[1] In his *The Birth of Tragedy* (1872) Nietzsche likewise bases his aesthetic theory on Schopenhauer's pessimistic view of life, taking as his text the Greek myth of King Midas' quest for the satyr Silenus.

When Silenus was finally in his power, the king asked him what was the best and most desirable thing for mankind. The daemon stood in silence, stiff and motionless, but when the king insisted he broke out into a shrill laugh and said 'Wretched, ephemeral race, children of misery and chance, why do you force me to say what it would be more expedient for you not to hear? The best of all things is quite beyond your reach: it is not to have been born, not to be at all, to be nothing. The next best thing is to die as soon as may be.' (*BT* 22)

Schopenhauer had held out art as the most accessible escape from the tyranny of life.

---

[1] A. Goldman, *Wagner on Music and Drama* (New York: Dutton, 1966).

Nietzsche, too, sees the origin of art in humans' need to mask life's misery from themselves. The ancient Greeks, he tells us, in order to be able to live at all 'had to interpose the radiant dream-birth of the Olympian gods between themselves and the horrors of existence' (*BT* 22). There are two kinds of escape from reality: dreaming and intoxication. In Greek mythology, according to Nietzsche, these two forms of illusion are personified in two different gods: Apollo, the god of light, and Dionysus, the god of wine. 'The development and progress of Art originates from the duality of the Apolline and the Dionysiac, just as reproduction depends on the duality of the sexes' (*BT* 14).

The prototype of the Apolline artist is Homer, the founder of epic poetry; he is the creator of the resplendent dream-world of the Olympic deities. Apollo is an ethical deity, imposing measure and order on his followers in the interests of beauty. But the Apolline magnificence is soon engulfed in a Dionysiac flood, the stream of life that breaks down barriers and constraints. The followers of Dionysus sing and dance in rapturous ecstasy, enjoying life to excess. Music is the supreme expression of the Dionysiac spirit, as epic is of the Apolline.

The glory of Greek culture is Athenian tragedy, and this is the offspring of both Apollo and Dionysus, combining music with poetry. The choruses in Greek tragedy represent the world of Dionysus, while the dialogue plays itself out in a lucid Apolline world of images. The Greek spirit found its supreme expression in the plays of Aeschylus (especially *Prometheus Vinctus*) and Sophocles (especially *Oedipus Rex*). But with the plays of the third famous tragedian, Euripides, tragedy dies by its own hand, poisoned by an injection of rationality. The blame for this must be laid at the door of Socrates, who inaugurated a new era that valued science above art.

Socrates, according to Nietzsche, was the antithesis of all that made Greece great. His instincts were entirely negative and critical, rather than positive and creative. In rejecting the Dionysiac element he destroyed the tragedians' synthesis. 'We need only consider the Socratic maxims "Virtue is knowledge, all sins arise from ignorance, the virtuous man is the happy man". In these three basic optimistic formulae lies the death of tragedy' (*BT* 69). Tragedy, in Euripides, took the death-leap into bourgeois theatre. The dying Socrates, freed by insight and reason from the fear of death, became the mystagogue of science.

Was it possible, in modern Germany, to remedy the disease inherited from Socrates, and to restore the union of Apollo and Dionysus? Nietzsche had no appreciation of the novel, which in the nineteenth century might be thought the genre most fertile of the beneficent illusion that in his view was the function of art. The novel, he thought, was essentially a Socratic art form, that subordinated poetry to philosophy. Oddly, he blamed its invention on Plato. 'The Platonic dialogue might be described as the lifeboat in which the shipwrecked older poetry and all its children escaped, crammed together in a narrow space and fearfully obeying a single pilot, Socrates . . . Plato gave posterity the model for a new art form—the novel' (*BT* 69). Nor had Nietzsche any high opinion of Italian opera, in spite of the combination of poetry and music it involved. He complained that it was ruined by the separation between recitative and aria, which privileged the verbal over the musical. Only in Germany was there hope of a rebirth of tragedy:

From the Dionysiac soil of the German spirit a power has risen that has nothing in common with the original conditions of Socratic culture: that culture can neither explain nor excuse it, but instead finds it terrifying and inexplicable, powerful and hostile—*German Music*, as we know it pre-eminently in its mighty sun-cycle from Bach to Beethoven, from Beethoven to Wagner. (*BT* 94)

The *Birth of Tragedy* peters out into a set of rapturous and incoherent programme notes to the third act of *Tristan und Isolde*. No one has condemned their weaknesses with more force than Nietzsche himself, who after he had emerged from the spell of Wagner prefaced later editions of the book with an 'Attempt at Self-Criticism'. There he recants his attempt to link the genius of Greece with a fictional 'German Spirit'. But he did not disown what he came to see as the fundamental theme of the book, namely, that art and not morality is the properly metaphysical activity of man, and that the existence of the world finds justification only as an aesthetic phenomenon.

Art and Morality

For Nietzsche, art is not only autonomous but is supreme over morality. At the opposite pole from Nietzsche stand two nineteenth-century aestheticians who saw art and morality as inextricably intertwined. One was John Ruskin (1819–1900), and the other Leo Tolstoy (1828–1910).

Ruskin regarded art as a very serious matter. In his massive work *Modern Painters* (1843) he wrote:

Art, properly so called, is no recreation; it cannot be learned at spare moments, nor pursued when we have nothing better to do. It is no handiwork for drawing-room tables, no relief of the ennui of boudoirs; it must be understood and undertaken seriously, or not at all. To advance it men's lives must be given, and to receive it their hearts.[2]

But the demands made by art could be justified only by the seriousness of its moral purpose: namely, to reveal fundamental features of the universe. Beauty is something objective, not a mere product of custom. The experience of beauty arises from a truthful perception of nature, and leads on to an apprehension of the divine. Only if an artist is himself a morally good person will he be able to deliver this revelation in an incorrupt form, and set before us the glory of God. But in a decaying society—as Ruskin believed nineteenth-century industrial society to be—both

---

[2] John Ruskin, *Selected Writings* (London: Dent, 1995).

moral and artistic purity are almost impossible to achieve. Both the imaginative faculty that creates, and the 'theoretic' faculty that appreciates, are radically corrupt. Work is degraded by the modern division of labour, and the workman deprived of his due status as a craftsman seeking perfection.

Ruskin applied his moralizing theory of art to two arts in particular: painting and architecture. Painting, for him, is essentially a form of language: technical skill is no more than mastery of the language, and the worth of a painting depends on the value of the thoughts that it expresses. Ruskin sought to bear out this contention by a close examination of the works of J. M. W. Turner. In *The Seven Lamps of Architecture* Ruskin set out the criteria by which he judged Gothic architecture superior to the architecture of the Renaissance and the baroque. The 'lamps' are predominantly moral categories: sacrifice, truth, power, obedience, and the like. For architecture, in his definition, is the art that disposes and adorns edifices so that the sight of them may contribute to man's mental health, power, and pleasure. And the essential element in mental health was a just appreciation of man's place in a divinely ordered universe.

For Tolstoy, art can be good only if it has a moral purpose. In *What is Art?* he described the price, in terms of money and hard labour, of the artistic ventures of his day, especially of opera. Such art, he maintained, could arise only upon the slavery of the masses of the people; and he asked whether the social costs involved could be morally justified. It was an art that appealed only to the sentiments of the upper classes, which extended no further than pride, sex, and ennui.

Tolstoy rejected the claims of earlier writers that the aim of art is beauty and that beauty is recognized by the enjoyment it gives. The real purpose of art was communication between human beings. While rejecting the Romantic idea that art must give pleasure, he agreed with Wordsworth that its essence was the sharing of emotion:

To take the simplest example: one man laughs, and another who hears becomes merry, or a man weeps, and another who hears feels sorrow. A man is excited or irritated, and another man seeing him is brought to a similar state of mind.... a man expresses his feelings of admiration, devotion, fear, respect or love, to certain objects, persons, or phenomena, and others are infected by the same feelings of admiration, devotion, fear, respect or love, to the same objects, persons, or phenomena. (*WA* 66)

Art in the broad sense of the world permeates our life, which is full of works of art of every kind, from lullabies, jokes, mimicry, the ornamentation of dresses, houses, and utensils, to church services and triumphal processions. But the feelings with which these works of art infect us may be good or bad. Art is only good if the emotions it injects are good; and those emotions can be good only if they are fundamentally religious and contribute to a sense of universal human brotherhood.

The emotions to be communicated by art must be emotions that can be shared by mankind in general, and not just by a pampered elite. Where this is not the case we have either bad art or pseudo art. Tolstoy is willing to accept that this judgement condemns many of the most admired works of music and literature—including his own novels. The greatest novel of the nineteenth century, he maintained, was *Uncle Tom's Cabin*, which spread the message of universal brother-hood across the boundaries of race and class.

Among the works of art Tolstoy condemned was Beethoven's Ninth Symphony. Does this transmit the highest religious feeling? No: no music can. Does it unite all men in one common feeling? No, Tolstoy replied: 'I am unable to imagine to myself a crowd of normal people who could understand anything of this long, confused, and artificial production, except short snatches which are lost in a sea of incomprehensibility.' It is true that the work's last movement is a poem of Schiller which expresses the very thought that it is feeling, in particular gladness, that unites people together. 'But though this poem is sung at the end of the symphony the music does not accord with the thought expressed in the verses; for the music is exclusive and does not unite all men, but unites only a few, dividing them off from the rest of mankind' (*WA* 249).

Art for Art's Sake

Tolstoy's moralistic view of art quickly became unfashionable in the twentieth century. The autonomy of art, if not its Nietzschean supremacy, was widely accepted: a work of art might be good art, and even great art, while being morally or politically deleterious. The artistic merit of a work was even held to redeem its ethical dubiety, and many countries repealed laws that forbade the production and publication of works of art that had a tendency to 'deprave and corrupt'.

One of the most influential of twentieth-century aestheticians was the Italian philosopher Benedetto Croce (1866–1952). In metaphysics, Croce was an idealist, and developed a Hegelian system along with Giovanni Gentile (1875–1944) until the two parted company in 1925 over the issue of Fascism. Gentile became a theoretician of Fascism, while Croce, who was a cabinet minister in both pre Fascist and post-Fascist Italian governments, was the leading intellectual opponent of Mussolini in the 1930s.

For Croce, art occupies a position between history and science. Like history it deals with particular cases rather than general laws, but its particular cases are imagined, not real, and they illustrate, as science does, universal truths. Croce himself distinguished between four phases of his aesthetic theory, from the first volume of his *Filosofia dello Spirito* in 1902 to *La Poesia* of 1936. But several themes are common to every one of the phases of his thought.

The core of art, for Croce, is intuition. Intuition is not the same as feeling, whatever positivists might say: feelings need expression, and expression is a cognitive, not just an emotional, matter. Art in human beings, unlike emotion in animals, is something spiritual, not merely sensual. On the other hand, rationalist aestheticians are wrong to see art as something intellectual: it operates through images, not through concepts. Thus Croce distances himself from Romantics on the one hand and classicists on the other.

The artistic intuition is essentially lyrical. Croce explains what this means principally by contrasts. Art is not concerned with the True (as logic is) nor the Useful (as economics is) nor with the Good (as morality is). It has its own object, the Beautiful, that stands independently on equal terms with the other three. (For Croce, the notion of the Sublime was only a pseudo-concept.) An artistic expression is lyrical only if it is concerned exclusively with the beautiful. Thus a poem like Lucretius' *de Rerum Natura*, with its heavy scientific and moral messages, is not something lyrical, but merely a piece of literature. True poetry must have no utilitarian, moral, or philosophical agenda.

Views similar to Croce's were made familiar to the English-speaking world by R. G. Collingwood (1889–1943), who translated Croce's article on aesthetics for the 1928 edition of the *Encyclopaedia Britannica*. Collingwood, a classicist and archaeologist of distinction, became Waynflete Professor of Metaphysics at Oxford in 1936. He is best known for his contributions to the philosophy of history, on which he was specially qualified to write, but his *Principles of Art* (1938) was a significant contribution to aesthetic theory.

Much of the book is taken up with explaining what art is not. Art is not mere amusement; even if much of what goes by the name of art is simply entertainment, true art is something different. Art is not a magical procedure like a war dance. By magic, Collingwood explains, he means a procedure for arousing emotion to some preconceived end, such as patriotic emotion or proletarian fervour. Most importantly, art must be distinguished from craft or technical skill. Art is not imitation or representation (*mimesis*), for that too is a craft. Of course, a great work of art will also be a work of craft, but what makes it a work of art is not what makes it a work of craft.

If art were a craft, we could distinguish in it between end and means. But if art has an end, it can only be the arousing of emotion; and this is not something that can be identified separately from the artistic activity, as a shoe can be identified separately from the act of cobbling. Art should not be seen as the activity of arousing emotion, but as the activity of expressing emotion. The true work of art is in fact the emotion in the artist himself. Successful artists conclude their success in their own imagination; the externalization of their images in a public work of art is merely a matter of craft.

The inner work, the true work of art, consists in raising something preconscious, an inarticulate feeling, into an explicit and articulate state. Following

Croce, Collingwood accepted on this basis that imagination and expression were one and the same thing. It is through language that the preconscious is transformed into the articulate; and in this sense all artistic expression, in whatever medium, is essentially linguistic.

If art is the expression of emotion, Collingwood argues, then the distinction between artist and audience disappears.

If a poet expresses, for example, a certain kind of fear, the only hearers who can understand him are those who are capable of experiencing that kind of fear themselves. Hence, when someone reads and understands a poem, he is not merely understanding the poet's expression of his, the poet's, emotions, he is expressing emotions of his own in the poet's words, which have thus become his own words. As Coleridge put it, we know a man for a poet by the fact that he makes us poets. (PA 118)

Poet and reader share and express the same emotion: the difference is that the poet can solve for himself the problem of expressing it, whereas the reader needs the poet to show him how it is done. By creating for ourselves (aided or unaided) an imaginary experience or activity, we express our emotions; and this is what we call art.

Croce and Collingwood differed from Tolstoy because they regarded art as something distinct from and independent of morality. But all three writers shared a conception of art as expression of emotion. Most twentieth-century philosophers rejected the Tolstoyan view of the function of art as the communication of emotion. Wittgenstein, for instance, wrote:

There is *much* that could be learned from Tolstoy's false theorizing that the work of art conveys a 'feeling'. And indeed you might call it, if not the expression of a particular feeling, an expression of feeling, or a felt expression. And you might say too that people who understand it to that extent 'resonate' with it, respond to it. You might say: The work of art does not seek to convey *something else*, just itself. As, if I pay someone a visit, I don't wish only to produce such and such feelings in him, but first and foremost to pay him a visit—though of course I also want to be welcome.

The real absurdity starts when it is said that the artist wants others, in reading, to feel what he felt while writing. I can indeed think that I understand a poem, for example, that is, understand it in the way its author would want it to be understood. But what *he* may have felt while writing it isn't *any* concern of mine at all. (CV 67)

The independence of a work of art from its creator became a prominent theme, both in the English-speaking world and in continental Europe. American critics denounced as 'the intentional fallacy' any attempt to reach an understanding of a text on the basis of elements in its author's biography or psychology or motivation, rather than in properties to be discerned in the text in isolation. In France, philosophers went so far as to speak of 'the death of the author'. The text, they have argued, is the primary object; the notion of an author is rather an economic

959

and legal construct. So far as interpretation goes, the reception of a text by generations of readers may be of greater significance than any item in the biography of the person who initially penned it.

The thesis of the death of the author has not been warmly welcomed in British philosophical circles. But the idea that in the interpretation of a work of art the author has no privileged status was anticipated by a nineteenth-century Englishman. The Victorian poet Arthur Hugh Clough wrote a controversial, some thought blasphemous, poem about the Resurrection, *Easter Day*. In a later poem he imagines himself questioned about its meaning: was it intended to be ironic or sarcastic? He responds:

> Interpret it I cannot. I but wrote it.

11

Political Philosophy

Utilitarianism and Liberalism

In introducing his greatest happiness principle, Bentham was less concerned to provide a criterion for individual moral choices than to offer guidance to rulers and legislators on the management of communities. But it is precisely in this area, when we have to consider not just the total quantity of happiness in a community but also its distribution, that the greatest happiness principle, on its own, fails to provide a credible decision procedure.

Suppose that, by whatever means, we have succeeded in establishing a scale for the measurement of happiness: a scale from 0 to 10 on which 0 represents maximum misery, 10 represents maximum happiness, and 5 a state of indifference. Imagine that we are devising political and legal institutions for a society, and that we have a choice between implementing two models. The result of adopting model A will be that 60 per cent of the population will score 6, and 40 per cent will score 4. The result of adopting model B will be that 80 per cent of the population will score 10 and 20 per cent will score 0. Faced with such a choice, anyone with a care for either equality or humanity will surely wish to implement model A rather than model B. Yet if we operate Bentham's felicific calculus in the obvious manner, model A scores only 520 points, while model B achieves a total of 800.

The principle that we should seek the greatest happiness of the greatest number clearly leads to different results depending on whether we opt to maximize happiness or to maximize the number of happy people. The principle needs, at the very least, to be supplemented by some limits on the amount of inequality between the best off and the worst off, and limits on the degree of misery of the worst off, if it is not to permit outcomes that are gross violations of distributive justice.

Despite the problems with his grand principle, problems that he left for his successors to struggle with, Bentham did make very substantial contributions to political philosophy. He is seen at his best when he is, in the words of J. S. Mill, 'organising and regulating the merely *business* part of social arrangements'. On such topics he can write acutely and briskly, make shrewd distinctions, expose common fallacies, and pack a weight of argument into brief and lucid paragraphs. His treatment of state-imposed punishment is an excellent example of the way in which he puts these talents to use.

What, he asks, is the purpose of the penal system?

> The immediate principal end of punishment is to control action. This action is either that of the offender, or of others: that of the offender it controls by its influence, either on his will, in which case it is said to operate in the way of *reformation*; or on his physical power, in which case it is said to operate by *disablement*; that of others it can influence no otherwise than by its influence over their wills; in which case it is said to operate in the way of *example*. (*P* 13. 1)

Punishment, being the infliction of pain, is as such an evil, so it should only be admitted in so far as it promises to exclude some greater evil. Bentham rejected the retributive theory of punishment, according to which justice demands that he who has done harm shall suffer harm. Unless the infliction of punishment has some deterrent or remedial effect either on the offender or on others, retribution is merely a rendering of evil for evil, and increases the amount of evil in the world without restoring any balance of justice.

It is true that the punishment of an offender, even if it has no deterrent or reformatory effect, may give a feeling of satisfaction to a victim, or to the law-abiding public. This, like any other pleasure, must be placed in the utilitarian scales. But no punishment, Bentham says, should be imposed merely for this vindictive purpose, because no pleasure ever produced by punishment can be equivalent to the pain.

Since the principal purpose of punishment was deterrence, punishment should not be inflicted in cases where it would have no deterrent effect, either on the offender or on others, nor should it be inflicted to any greater extent than is necessary to deter. Punishment, he says, must not be inflicted when it is inefficacious (cannot deter) or unprofitable (will cause more mischief than it prevents) or needless (where the mischief can be prevented by other means).

In the fourteenth chapter Bentham drew up a set of rules setting out the proportion between punishments and offences, based not on the retributive principle of 'an eye for an eye, a tooth for a tooth' but on the effect that the prospect of punishment will have on the reasoning of a potential offender. Bentham imagined a prospective criminal calculating the profit and loss that is likely to accrue from the offence, and regarded it as the function of the penal law to ensure that the loss will outweigh the profit. The law must therefore impose punishments that are sufficient to deter, but they should equally be no more than is necessary to deter. Punishment should, in Bentham's terms, be *frugal*.

While deterrence is the principal end of punishment, Bentham admits subsidiary purposes, such as the reformation or disablement of the offender. Reform, in the condition of most actual prisons, was and is unlikely to be achieved; but Bentham has some proposals for particular reformatory regimes. Imprisonment does have the effect of the temporary disablement of the offender, but obviously disablement is most efficaciously achieved by the death penalty. 'At the same time', Bentham observes, 'this punishment, it is evident, is in an eminent degree *unfrugal*; which forms one among the many objects there are against the use of it, in any but very extraordinary cases' (P 15. 19).

John Stuart Mill's political philosophy, like his moral philosophy, owed much to Bentham, but in this area too he felt obliged to temper the strict utilitarianism of his master. Bentham's system, with its denial of natural rights, would in principle justify, in certain circumstances, highly autocratic government and substantial intrusion on personal liberty. So too would the early forms of socialism with which Mill had flirted in his youth, which had given birth to the positivist system of Auguste Comte. In his mature years Mill attached supreme importance to setting limits to the constraints that social systems, however benevolent in principle, could place on individual independence. He described the Système de Politique Positive as a device 'by which the yoke of general opinion, wielded by an organised body of spiritual teachers and rulers, would be made supreme over every action, and as far as is in human possibility, every thought, of every member of the community'. He denounced Comte for proposing 'the completest system of spiritual and temporal despotism which ever yet emanated from a human brain'. In *On Liberty* he sought to set out a general libertarian principle that would protect the individual from illegitimate authoritarian intrusion whether motivated by utilitarianism, socialism, or positivism.

To safeguard liberty, Mill maintains, it is not sufficient to replace autocratic monarchy by responsible democracy, because within a democratic society the majority may exercise tyranny over the minority. Nor is it sufficient to place limits upon the authority of government, because society can exercise other and more subtle means of coercion.

There needs protection also against the tyranny of the prevailing opinion and feeling; against the tendency of society to impose, by other means than civil penalties, its own ideas and practices as rules of conduct on those who dissent from them; to fetter the development, and if possible, prevent the formation, of any individuality not in harmony with its ways. (L 130)

In order to place a just limit on coercion by physical force or public opinion we must affirm, as a fundamental principle, that the only part of the conduct of anyone for which he is accountable to society is that which concerns others. In the part which merely concerns himself, his independence should be absolute.

The most important application of this principle concerns liberty of thought, and the cognate liberties of speaking and writing. According to Mill, no authority, autocratic or democratic, has the right to suppress the expression of opinion. 'If all mankind minus one were of one opinion, and only one person were of the contrary opinion, mankind would be no more justified in silencing that one person than he, if he had the power, would be justified in silencing mankind' (*L* 130). This is because to suppress an opinion is to rob the whole human race. The opinion silenced may, for all we know, turn out to be true, because none of us is infallible. If it is not wholly true, it may well contain a portion of truth that would otherwise be neglected. Even an opinion that is wholly false has a value as offering a challenge to the contrary opinion and thus ensuring that the truth is not held as a mere prejudice or as a formal profession. Freedom of opinion, Mill concludes, and freedom of the expression of opinion, is essential for the mental well-being of mankind.

But freedom of opinion is not all that is needed. Men should be free to act upon their opinions, and to carry them out in their lives, without hindrance, either physical or moral, from their fellows. Of course the freedom should not extend to the right to harm others—even freedom of speech must be curtailed in circumstances where the expression of opinion amounts to an incitement to mischief. But ample scope should be given to varieties of character and to experiments in living, provided these concern only the individual's own affairs or the affairs of others 'with their free, voluntary, and undeceived consent and participation'. The individual's rule of conduct should be his or her own character, not the traditions or customs of other people. If this principle is denied, 'there is wanting one of the principal ingredients of human happiness, and quite the chief ingredient of individual and social progress' (*L* 185).

Without individuality, human beings become mere machines, conforming to a pattern imposed from without. But 'human nature is not a machine to be built after a model, and set to do exactly the work prescribed for it, but a tree, which requires to grow and develop itself on all sides' (*L* 188). If eccentricity is proscribed, damage is done not only to the individual constrained, but to society as a whole. We may all have something to learn from unconventional characters. 'There is always need of persons not only to discover new truths, and point out when what were once truths are true no longer, but also to commence new practices, and set the example of more enlightened conduct, and better taste and sense in human life' (*L* 193). Energetic and unorthodox characters are needed more than ever in an age when public opinion rules the world, and individuals are lost in the crowd. Genius must be allowed to unfold itself in practice as well as in thought.

What exactly does Mill have in mind when he commends 'experiments in living'? Sadly, he expounds his thesis by a series of eloquent metaphors rather than by offering examples of beneficial eccentricity. When he comes to offer practical applications of his principles, he confines himself to denouncing laws restricting humdrum activities of everyday people, not statutes constraining the development of genius. As examples of bad legislation, actual or hypothetical, he considers such things as prohibitions on the eating of pork and the drinking of spirituous liquors, or laws against travelling on the sabbath and restrictions on dancing and theatrical performances.

No doubt when Mill was encouraging nonconformity one example at the back of his mind was his own unconventional relationship with Harriet Taylor during the long years before their marriage. But, oddly, the one example he actually gives of an experiment in living is one of which he heartily disapproved: the Mormon sanction of polygamy. This experiment, he admitted, was in direct conflict with his libertarian principles, being 'a mere riveting of the chains of one half of the community, and emancipation of the other from reciprocity of obligation towards them' (L 224). However, since the world taught women that marriage was the one thing needful, he thought it understandable that many a woman should prefer being one of several wives to not being a wife at all. Mill was not commending polygamy; merely urging that Mormons should not be coerced into abandoning it. And it must be said that he had almost as much distaste for current English monogamy as for the institutions of Salt Lake City.

At the time of his own marriage in 1851 he wrote out a protest against the laws that conferred upon one party to the contract complete control over the person and property of the other. 'Having no means of legally divesting myself of these odious powers...I feel it my duty to put on record a formal protest against the existing law of marriage, in so far as conferring such powers, and a solemn promise never in any case or under any circumstances to use them' (CCM 396). He set out his objections to the English law of marriage at length in the pamphlet On the Subjection of Women. The legal subordination of one sex to the other was wrong in principle and a chief obstacle to human progress. A wife was simply a bond-servant to her husband; she was bound to give him lifelong obedience, and any property she acquired instantly passed to him. In some ways she was worse off than a slave. In a Christian country a slave had a right and duty to reject sexual advances from her master; but a husband can enforce upon his wife 'the lowest degradation of a human being, that of being made the instrument of an animal function contrary to her inclinations' (L 504).

The subjection of women to men had no other origin than the greater muscular strength of the male, and had been continued into a civilized age only through male self-interest. No one could say that experience had shown that the existing system of male superiority was preferable to any alternative; for no other alternative had ever been tried. Women had, by centuries of training from the earliest age, been brought to acquiesce in the system.

When we put together three things—first, the natural attraction between opposite sexes; secondly, the wife's entire dependence on the husband, every privilege or pleasure she has being either his gift, or depending entirely on his will; and lastly, that the principal object of human pursuit, consideration, and all objects of social ambition, can in general be sought or obtained by her only through him—it would be a miracle if the object of being attractive to men had not become the polar star of feminine education and formation of character. (*L* 487)

If women did wish to throw over their subjection, rebellion against their masters is harder than any rebellion against despots has ever been. Husbands have greater facilities than any monarch has ever had to prevent any uprising against their power: their subjects live under their eyes and in their very hands. It is no wonder that the tyranny of males has outlasted all other forms of unjust authority.

Kierkegaard and Schopenhauer on Women

The significance of *On the Subjection of Women* in the climate of the time can be brought out by comparing it with the treatment of marriage and womanhood in the works of two Continental philosophers, Kierkegaard and Schopenhauer. In Kierkegaard's *Either/Or* a ninety-page essay is devoted to affirming 'the aesthetic validity of marriage'—that is, to persuade the reader that entering into matrimony need not diminish, indeed may fortify, the raptures of first love. Romantic ballads and novels are quite wrong to portray love as a quest that surmounts obstacles and trials to achieve its goal in marriage: a wedding is the beginning, not the end, of truly romantic love. The essay takes the form of a letter to a romantic correspondent who has fundamental objections to the whole idea of a church marriage.

Kierkegaard imagines the objector saying:

The girl before whom I could fall down and worship, whose love I feel could snatch me out of all confusion and give me new birth, it is she I am to lead to the Lord's altar, she who is to stand there like a sinner, of whom and to whom it shall be said that it was Eve who seduced Adam. To her before whom my proud soul bows down, the only one to whom it has bowed down, to her it shall be said that I am to be her master and she subservient to her husband. The moment has come, the Church is already reaching out its arms for her and before giving her back to me it will first press a bridal kiss upon her lips, not that bridal kiss I gave the whole world for; it is already reaching out its arms to embrace her, but this embrace will cause all her beauty to fade, and then it will toss her over to me and say 'Be fruitful and multiply'. What kind of power is it that dares intrude between me and my bride, the bride I myself have chosen and who has chosen me? And this power would command her to be true to me; does she then need to be commanded? And is she to be true to me only because a third party commands it, one whom she therefore loves more than me? And it bids me be true to her; must I be bidden to that, I who belong to her with my whole soul? And this power decides our relation to each other; it says I am to ask and she is to obey; but suppose I do not want to ask, suppose I feel myself too inferior for that? (*E/O* 408)

Judge Vilhelm, whom Kierkegaard sets up as the defender of traditional marriage, urges his correspondent to accept that in marriage he cannot but be master, that his wife is no more a sinner than any other woman, and that accepting a third power means only thanking God for the love between bride and groom. At marriage the husband comes to understand that real love is daily possession throughout a lifetime, not the preternatural power of a brief infatuation; and his taking her as a gift from God, rather than as a conquest of his own, enables the wife 'to put the loved one at just enough distance for her to be able to draw breath' (*E/O* 411).

Vilhelm is emphatic that the only worthy motive for entering on marriage is love for the spouse. He lists, and rejects, other reasons why people marry or are urged to marry: that marriage is a school for character, that one has a duty to propagate the human race, that one needs a home. None of these motives are adequate, from either an aesthetic or an ethical point of view. 'Were a woman to marry', he tells us, 'so as to bear a saviour to the world, that marriage would be just as unaesthetic as immoral and irreligious' (*E/O* 417). Love is the one thing that will bring the sensual and the spiritual together into unity.

It is true that marriage, unlike romantic love, brings with it duties. But duty is not the enemy of love, but its friend. In marriage 'duty here is just one thing, truly to love, with the sincerity of the heart, and duty is as protean as love itself, declaring everything holy and good when it is of love, and denouncing everything, however pleasing and specious, when it is not of love' (*E/O* 470).

If *On the Subjection of Women* is a classic of feminism, and Judge Vilhelm's contribution to *Either/Or* was a classic defence of traditional marriage, Schopenhauer's *Essay on Women* of 1861 was a classic of male chauvinism. The natural purpose of women, the essay began, was to give birth, to care for children, and to be subject to a man, to whom she should be a patient and cheering companion. Women were better than men at nurturing children, because they were themselves childish: they lived in the present and were mentally myopic. Nature had provided women with sufficient beauty to allure a man into supporting them, but wisely took it away from them once they had produced a child or two, so that they should not be distracted from raising their families.

The fundamental defect of the female character, according to Schopenhauer, was lack of a sense of justice. As the weaker sex, they had to make their way by cunning. 'As nature has equipped the lion with claws and teeth, the elephant with tusks, the wild boar with fangs, the bull with horns and the cuttlefish with ink, so it has equipped woman with the power of dissimulation as her means of attack and defence' (*EA* 83). Women feel they are justified in deceiving individual men because their prime loyalty is not to the individual but to the species—to the propagation of the race that is their entire vocation.

Women are inferior to men not only in their powers of reasoning, but also in artistic talent and appreciation. It is not just that they chatter in the theatre at concerts (something that clearly annoyed Schopenhauer intensely); they altogether lack creative ability.

... the most eminent heads of the entire sex have proved incapable of a single truly great, genuine and original achievement in art, or indeed of creating anything at all of lasting value: this strikes one most forcibly in regard to painting, since they are just as capable of mastering the technique as we are, and indeed paint very busily, yet cannot point to a single great painting. (*EA* 86)

The worst type of woman is the *lady*, the woman who is set on a pedestal, treated with gallantry by men, and educated in arrogant haughtiness. A European lady is an unnatural creature, the object of derision in the East; and by her very existence she makes the great majority of her own sex deeply unhappy.

The law made a great mistake, Schopenhauer tells us, when it gave women equal rights with men without at the same time endowing them with masculine reasoning powers. By 'equal rights' Schopenhauer does not mean anything so outrageous as property rights or the suffrage; he simply means the institution of monogamy, which allows members of each sex to have one and only one marital partner. Polygamy, in fact, is a much more satisfactory arrangement: it makes sure that every woman is taken care of, whereas under monogamy many women are left untended as old maids or forced into hard labour or prostitution. 'There are 80,000 prostitutes in London alone: and what are they if not sacrifices on the altar of monogamy?' Polygamy is a benefit to the female sex, considered as a whole, and it regularizes the satisfaction of male desire. 'For who is really a monogamist? We all live in polygamy, at least for a time and usually for good.' Since every man needs many women, there could be nothing more just than that he should be free, indeed obliged, to support many women.

We may be grateful that it was Mill, and not Schopenhauer, whom future generations followed. Indeed, *On the Subjection of Women* has become antiquated as a result of its own success. The battle of which it was an early salvo has long been won, at least in the countries for whom Mill was writing. The marriage laws that Mill denounced have long been repealed, and in all matters of law women are now treated as in every respect the equals of men. And it has to be said that the cruel imprisonment that Victorian marriage law imposed on women is brought home with greater impact by the narrative and dialogue of novelists like Eliot and Trollope than by the ponderous earnestness of Mill's periods.

The issues discussed in Mill's *On Liberty*, by contrast, remain of the highest importance, though contemporary liberals often differ from Mill when they come to draw the line between warranted and unwarranted state interference with personal liberty. Most liberals accept parcels of legislation whose purpose is to promote an individual's own well-being rather than to protect others from harm: laws imposing compulsory insurance, or the wearing of protective headgear, for instance. If a modern liberal justifies this as designed to prevent the individual from becoming a charge on society, rather than as aiming at his own health and prosperity, it should be pointed out that the possibility of the poor and sick placing a burden on others assumes the existence of a network of social services provided at the taxpayer's expense—something for which Mill had a very limited enthusiasm.

On the other hand, Mill countenanced restrictions on liberty that most modern liberals would reject. He thought, for instance, that a government could legitimately limit the size of families, and he reconciled it with his libertarian principle on the following grounds: 'In a country either over-peopled, or threatened with being so, to produce children, beyond a very small number, with the effect of reducing the reward of labour by their competition, is a serious offence against all who live by the remuneration of their labour' (*L* 242). Many liberals share Mill's lifelong enthusiasm for population control by contraception (a cause for which he was willing to go, briefly, to prison). But when China introduced legislation to limit the size of families to a single child, most Western liberals reacted with horror.

Marx on Capital and Labour

At the same time and in the same city as Mill was writing classical works of liberal thought, Karl Marx was developing the theory of the communism that was to be for more than a century one of liberalism's greatest enemies. The basis of the theory was historical materialism: the thesis that in every epoch the prevailing mode of economic production and exchange determines the political and intellectual history of society. 'The mode of production of material life conditions the social, political, and intellectual life-process in general. It is not the consciousness of human beings that determines their being; on the contrary it is their social being that determines their consciousness' (*CPE*, p. x). There were two elements that determined the course of history: the forces and the relations of production. By the forces of production Marx meant the raw materials, the technology, and the labour that are necessary to make a finished product; as wheat, a mill, and a millworker are all needed to produce flour. The relations of production, on the other hand, are the economic arrangements governing these forces, such as the ownership of the mill and the hiring of the worker. Relations of production are not static; they alter as technology develops. In the age of the hand-mill, for instance, the worker is the serf of a feudal lord, tied to the land; in the age of the steam-mill he is the mobile employee of the capitalist. Relations of production are not matters of free choice; they are determined by the interplay of the productive forces. If, at any time, they become inappropriate to the productive forces, then a social revolution takes place.

Marx divided the past, present, and future history of the relations of production into six phases, three past, one present, and two to come. The past phases were

969

primitive communism, slavery, and feudalism. The present, critical phase was that of capitalism. After capitalism's inevitable collapse, the future would bring first socialism and ultimately communism once more.

Following Engels, Marx believed that in the earliest stages of history human beings had been organized into primitive communist tribes, holding land in common, owning no private property, and ruled by a matriarchy. In the Iron Age, however, society became patriarchal, it became possible to accumulate private wealth, and slavery was introduced.

Slavery was the dominant economic feature of classical antiquity. Society was to be divided into classes: patrician and plebeian, freemen and slaves. Thus there began the story of class antagonism which was henceforth to be the fundamental feature of human history. The splendour of the classical culture of Greece and Rome was merely an ideological superstructure built upon the relations of production between the classes.

The ancient world gave way to the feudal system, with its relationships between lord and serf, and between guildsmen and journeymen. Once again, the philosophy and religion of the Middle Ages were an ideological superstructure sustained by the economic system of the age. From the serfs of the Middle Ages sprang the chartered burghers of the earliest towns: these were the first bourgeois, a middle class between the servile labourers and the aristocratic landowners. Since the time of the French Revolution the bourgeoisie had been gaining the upper hand over the aristocrats.

> The modern bourgeois society that has sprouted from the ruins of feudal society has not done away with class antagonisms. It has but established new classes, new conditions of oppression, new forms of struggle in place of the old ones.
>
> Our epoch, the epoch of the bourgeoisie, possesses, however, this distinctive feature: it has simplified the class antagonisms. Society as a whole is more and more splitting up into two great hostile camps, into two great classes directly facing each other; Bourgeoisie and Proletariat. (*CM* 3)

Marx believed that the capitalist society in which he lived had reached a state of crisis. The opposition between bourgeoisie and proletariat would become steadily stronger and lead to a revolutionary change which would usher in the final stages, first of socialism, in which all property would pass to the state, and finally to communism, after the state had withered away. The crisis which capitalism had reached, Marx maintained, was not a contingent fact of history; it was something entailed by the nature of capitalism itself. He based this conclusion on an analysis of the nature of economic value.

How is the value of a commodity determined? As a first step, we can say that a thing's value is the rate at which it can be exchanged for other commodities: a quarter of wheat may be worth so much iron, and so on. But the real value of something must be different from the countless different rates at which it can be exchanged with innumerable other commodities. We need a method of expressing the value of commodities that is common to, but distinct from, all the different particular exchanges between them.

As the *exchangeable values* of commodities are only *social functions* of those things, and have nothing at all to do with the *natural* qualities, we must first ask: What is the common *social substance* of all commodities? It is *labour*. To produce a commodity a certain amount of labour must be bestowed upon it, or worked up in it. And I say not only *labour*, but *social labour*. A man who produces an article for his own immediate use, to consume it himself, creates a *product*, but not a commodity. As a self-sustaining producer he has nothing to do with society. But to produce a *commodity* a man must not only produce an article satisfying some *social* want, but his labour itself must form part and parcel of the total sum of labour expended by society. It must be subordinate to the *division of labour within society.* (*VPP* 30)

To value a commodity, we should look on it as a piece of crystallized labour. How is labour itself measured? By the length of time the labour lasts. A silken handkerchief is worth more than a brick because it takes longer to make than a brick does. Marx states his theory thus: 'The value of one commodity is to the value of another commodity as the quantity of labour fixed in the one is to the quantity of labour fixed in the other' (*VPP* 31).

Two qualifications must be made to this simple equation. A lazy or unskilful worker will take longer to produce a commodity than an energetic and skilful one: does this mean that his product is worth more? Of course not: when we speak of the quantity of labour fixed in a commodity we mean the time that is *necessary* for a worker of average energy and skill to produce it. Moreover, we must add into the equation the labour previously worked up into the raw material of the commodity, and into the technology employed.

For example, the value of a certain amount of cotton yarn is the crystallisation of the quantity of labour added to the cotton during the spinning process, the quantity of labour previously realised in the cotton itself, the quantity of labour realised in the coal, oil, and other auxiliary matter used, the quantity of labour fixed in the steam engine, the spindles, the factory building and so forth. (*VPP* 32)

Naturally, only a proportion of the value of the spindle will be incorporated into the value of a particular quantity of yarn: the exact proportion will depend on the average working life of a spindle.

The value of a product at any given time will depend upon the productivity prevailing at that time. If an increase in population means that less fertile soils must be cultivated, the value of agricultural products will rise because greater labour is needed to produce them. On the other hand, when the introduction of the power-loom made it twice as easy to produce a given quantity of yarn, the value of yarn sank accordingly.

971

When value is expressed in monetary terms, it is called price. Since labour itself has a price, it too must have a value. But how is this to be defined? To answer this question we must note that what the labourer sells to his employer is not his actual labour, but his labouring power. If he is paid £10 for a sixty-hour week, he is selling for £10 his labouring power for sixty hours. But how are we to reckon the value of labouring power itself?

Like that of every other commodity, its value is determined by the quantity of labour necessary to produce it. The labouring power of a man exists only in his living individuality. A certain mass of necessaries must be consumed by a man to grow up and maintain his life. But the man, like the machine, will wear out, and must be replaced by another man. Beside the mass of necessaries required for *his own* maintenance, he wants another amount of necessaries to bring up a certain quota of children that are to replace him on the labour market and to perpetuate the race of labourers. (*VPP* 39)

It follows that the value of labouring power is determined by the cost of keeping the labourer alive and well and capable of reproduction.

To show how the capitalist exploits the labourer, Marx invites us to consider a case such as described above. Suppose that it takes twenty hours to produce the means of subsistence of the labourer for one week. He would, in that case, produce a value sufficient to maintain himself by working for twenty hours. But he has sold his working power for sixty hours. So over and above the twenty hours to replace his wages he is working a further forty hours. Marx calls these hours of *surplus labour*, and the product of those hours of labour will be *surplus value*. It is the surplus value that produces the capitalist's profit. The profit is the difference between the value of the product (six days' labour) and the value of the labourer's work (two days' labour). It is, Marx says, just as if he was working two days of the week for himself and working unpaid four days of the week for his employer.

As technology develops, and productivity increases accordingly, surplus value increases and the proportion of the labourer's work that is returned to him in wages becomes smaller and smaller. The surplus value in the output of a factory is shared between the landlord who takes rent, the banker who takes interest, and the entrepreneur who takes a commercial profit. All that goes to the labourer is the ever smaller sum that is necessary to keep him alive.

The very development of modern industry must progressively turn the scale in favour of the capitalist against the working man, and consequently the general tendency of capitalistic production is not to raise, but to sink the average standard of wages, or to push the value of labour more or less to its minimum limit. (*VPP* 61)

Given the inexorable tendencies of the capitalist system, it is futile to call for 'a fair day's wages for a fair day's work'. Only the total abolition of the cash nexus between employer and employee can achieve a fair return for labour.

The systematic exploitation endemic to the wages system is bound to reach a point at which the proletariat finds it intolerable and rises in revolt. Capitalism will be replaced by the dictatorship of the proletariat, which will abolish private property, and usher in a socialist state. Under socialism the means of production will be totally under central government control. The socialist state itself, however, will be only a temporary stage of the evolution of society. Eventually it will wither away to be replaced by a communist society in which individual and common interest will coincide. Just as Christian thinkers throughout the ages have given fuller accounts of hell than of heaven, so too Marx's descriptions of the evils of nineteenth-century capitalism are more vivid than his predictions of the final beatific state of communism. All we are told is that communist society will 'make it possible for me to do one thing today and another tomorrow, to hunt in the morning, fish in the afternoon, rear cattle in the evening, and write criticism just as I have a mind, without ever becoming hunter, fisherman, shepherd or critic' (*GI* 66).

Marx's analysis of surplus value is thought-provoking and contains profound philosophical insights. But considered as a predictive scientific theory, which was how Marx wished it to be taken, it has a fatal flaw. We are offered no convincing reason why the capitalist, no matter how great his profits, should pay the labourer no more than a subsistence wage. But that claim was an essential element in the thesis that revolution was an inevitable consequence of technological development within a capitalist system. If Marx's hypothesis had been correct, revolution would have occurred soonest in those states in which technology, and therefore exploitation, was progressing fastest. In fact the first communist revolution occurred in backward Russia, and in the developed countries of western Europe employers soon began, and have since continued, to pay wages well above subsistence level. But to be fair, the improvement in the condition of the working classes would not have taken place without the heightened awareness of the wretched state of factory labourers to which the work of Marx and Engels made a significant contribution.

Among the many philosophers who wrote in the wake of Marx and Engels the most influential was V. I. Lenin, the leader of the Russian Revolution of 1917. Lenin's influence was exercised not so much through his philosophical writings, though he was the author of two works on materialism and its epistemology, as through his leadership of the Communist Party. Against other Russian communists who believed in waiting for the inevitable dissolution of capitalism, he insisted that the birth-pangs of the new order should be hastened by violent revolution. He insisted that the party should be led by an authoritarian elite, whose ideas would shape, rather than be shaped by, economic change. Soviet democracy was to be marked not so much by the rule of the majority as by the use of force, on behalf of the majority, against the minority.

Closed and Open Societies

Lenin was disappointed when other nations failed to follow Russia's example and rise up against their capitalist rulers, but he explained the failure of Marx's predictions of their economic collapse by their imperialist exploitation of colonies as an outlet for excess capital and a source of cheap labour and raw materials. Imperialism, he famously said, was the monopoly stage of capitalism. Lenin's successor, Josef Stalin, was content to see his task as the preservation of socialism in one country, and the power of the communist elite was sustained and preserved by the patriotic fervour of the nation's struggle against Nazi Germany from 1941–5.

Neither Hitler's Germany nor Mussolini's Italy produced any lasting work of political philosophy. It is a mistake, however, to class the two ideologies together under the heading 'Fascism'. True, both Hitler and Mussolini were nationalist dictators who believed in a totalitarian state, but the leading idea of Nazism was racism, while the corporatism that was a central doctrine of Italian Fascism had nothing to do with race. Corporatism was intended to be a vocational organization of society in which individuals were grouped for purposes of representation according to their social functions. The corporate state would regulate relations between capitalists, workers, the professions, and the Church in such a way as to avoid the conflicts between classes that led to revolution. This was a different kind of political creed from the idea that one race was superior to all others and should dominate or eliminate them. Of course, Hitler and Mussolini were wartime allies; but so were Stalin and Churchill.

The Second World War did, however, produce one classic of political philosophy: *The Open Society and its Enemies*, by the Austrian exile Karl Popper. If a political organization is to flourish, Popper maintained in this book, its institutions must leave maximum room for self-correction. Just as science progresses by the constant correction of inadequate hypotheses, so society will only progress if policies are treated as experiments that can be evaluated and discontinued. Two things, therefore, are important: that the ruled should have ample freedom to discuss and criticize policies proposed by their rulers; and that it should be possible without violence or bloodshed to change the rulers, if they failed to promote their citizens' welfare. These are the central features of an open society, and they are more important elements of democracy than the mere election of a government by a majority. An open society is at the opposite extreme from the centrally controlled polities of wartime Germany, Italy, and Russia.

Popper did not rule out, however, all forms of government intervention. Unbounded tolerance could lead to intolerance, and unrestrained capitalism could lead to unacceptable levels of poverty. Incitement to intolerance should therefore be considered as criminal, and the state must protect the economically weak from the economically strong.

This, of course, means that the principle of non-intervention, of an unrestrained economic system, has to be given up; if we wish freedom to be safeguarded, then we must demand that the policy of unlimited economic freedom be replaced by the planned economic intervention of the state. We must demand that unrestrained *capitalism* give way to an *economic interventionism*. (*OSE* ii. 125)

Unlimited economic freedom was in any case a contradiction in terms: unlimited freedom of the labour market could not be combined with unlimited freedom of workers to unite.

In the two volumes of his book Popper attacked two philosophers whom he saw as enemies of the open society: Plato and Marx. His detailed critique of some Platonic political institutions was perhaps no more than a useful corrective to the fatuous admiration for the *Republic* that had been fashionable in British universities since the time of Benjamin Jowett. The critique of Marx, however, was something much more effective and influential. Popper's principal target was Marx's belief that he had discovered scientific laws that determined the future of the human race, tendencies that worked with iron necessity towards inevitable results. Popper showed how the course of history since *Capital* had in fact falsified many of Marx's specific would-be scientific predictions.

Marx's determinism was only one example of a more general error that Popper pilloried in a later book, *The Poverty of Historicism* (1957): 'I mean by "historicism" an approach to the social sciences which assumes that *historical prediction* is their principal aim, and which assumes that this aim is attainable by discovering the "rhythms" or the "patterns", the "laws" or the "trends" that underlie the evolution of history.' Besides Marxism, early Christian belief in an imminent Second Coming, and Enlightenment belief in the inevitability of human progress, offer examples of historicism. All forms of historicism, Popper showed, can be refuted by a single argument. What form the future will take will depend, *inter alia*, on what form scientific progress will take. If, therefore, we are to predict the future of society we must predict the future of science. But it is logically impossible to predict the nature of a scientific discovery; to do so would entail actually making the discovery. Hence, historicism is impossible, and the only meaning we can find in history, past or future, is that given it by free, contingent, unpredictable human choices.

The most sustained attempt to set out a systematic theoretical structure for the type of liberal democracy aspired to by most Western states was made by John Rawls (1921–2002) in his book *A Theory of Justice* (1971). Utilitarianism, Rawls argued, was insufficient as a foundation for a liberal state because it placed welfare over justice, ignoring what he called 'the priority of the right over the good'. 'Each person possesses an inviolability founded on justice that even the welfare of society as a whole cannot override. Therefore, in a just society the rights secured by justice are not subject to political bargaining or the calculus of social interests' (*TJ* 66). Instead of utilitarianism, Rawls proposed as a basis for determining the inalienable freedoms a novel kind of social contract, a thought-contract like a thought-experiment.

975

Imagine that there are as yet no social institutions, but we are all initially equal. In this 'original position' we are ignorant of the facts that will determine our position in the society to be designed. We do not know our race, sex, religion, class, talents, and abilities; we do not even know how we will conceive the good life. Under this 'veil of ignorance' we are to draw up a constitution on the basis of a rational desire to further our own aims and interests, whatever they may turn out to be. Because of our ignorance of the factors that are going to distinguish us from others, we are driven, in this imaginary position, to an equal concern for the fate of everyone.

The participants in this constitution-building, Rawls maintains, would choose to abide by two principles of justice. The first principle is that each person should have the right to the most extensive basic liberty compatible with a like liberty for all. The second principle is that social and economic inequalities are to be attached to office and positions that are open to all in fair competition, and that these inequalities are justified only if they can be arranged so that they are to the benefit of the worst off. If the two principles come into conflict, the principle of equal liberty trumps the principle of equal opportunity.

Rawls sees it as obvious that no one in the original position would agree to a system that incorporated slavery, for fear that when the veil of ignorance was lifted he would find himself a slave. But he also uses his two principles to operate upon a number of more contentious issues, such as intergenerational justice and civil disobedience. In a pluralistic society, he maintains, there is little chance of achieving total unanimity in ethics; the most we can hope for is a set of shared values. But by discussion of, reflection on, and adjustment to our moral judgements Rawls hopes that we may achieve what he calls 'an overlapping consensus' on ethical issues.

The goal that Rawls holds out is a state of 'reflective equilibrium'. The initial intuitions of different citizens will clash with each other, and indeed a single individual's intuitions may be inconsistent among themselves. However, if we reflect upon these intuitions and endeavour to articulate them into defensible principles we may advance towards coherence and consensus. As we do our best to deal with intuitions that are recalcitrant to the rules we have formulated, we may hope to achieve an ever more harmonious set of moral principles for ourselves and our society.

12

God

Faith vs. Alienation

Hegel regarded his system as a sophisticated and definitive presentation of philosophical truths that had been given fluctuating and mythical expression in the world's religions. In the first half of the nineteenth century the two most important reactions to the Hegelian treatment of religion came from opposite points of the philosophical compass. While Ludwig Feuerbach (1804–72) regarded Hegel as excessively sympathetic to religion, Søren Kierkegaard (1813–55) thought him impudently disrespectful of it.

In criticizing Hegel, Feuerbach made use of the Hegelian concept of alienation, the condition in which people treat as alien something that is in fact part of themselves. The fundamental idea of his *Essence of Christianity* (1841) is that God is a projection of the human mind. Humans are the highest form of beings, but they project their own life and consciousness into an unreal heaven. Men take their own essence, imagine it freed from its limitations, project it into an imagined transcendent sphere, and then venerate it as a distinct and independent being. 'God as God, that is, as a being not finite, not human, not materially conditioned, not phenomenal, is only an object of thought' (*EC* 35).

Whatever Hegel may say about Spirit, for Feuerbach the real essence of man is that he is a material being and part of nature. 'Man', he said famously, 'is what he eats.' But man differs from other animals; and the great difference that marks him out is his possession of religion. Awareness of his dependence on nature makes man initially deify natural objects like trees and fountains. The monotheistic idea of a personal God arises when humans become conscious of themselves as possessing reason, will, and love. In religion, man contemplates his own latent nature, but as something apart from himself.

Religion is the disuniting of man from himself; he sets God before him as the antithesis of himself. God is not what man is—man is not what God is. God is the infinite, man the finite being; God is perfect, man imperfect; God eternal, man temporal; God almighty, man weak; God holy, man sinful. God and man are extremes: God is the absolutely positive, the sum of all realities; man the absolutely negative, comprehending all negations. (*EC* 33)

Feuerbach agrees with Hegel that religion represents an essential, but imperfect, stage of human self-consciousness. But Hegel's own philosophy, according to Feuerbach, is yet another form of alienation: it is the last refuge of theology. By treating nature as posited by the Idea it offers us only a disguised version of the Christian doctrine of creation. We must set Hegel on his feet, and place philosophy on the solid ground of materialism.

Like Hegel's doctrine of alienation, Feuerbach's criticism of religion and idealism had a great influence on Marx and Engels. But Marx regarded not religion but capitalism as the greatest form of alienation—it was money, not God, that was the capitalist's object of worship. Religion, said Marx, is the opium of the people. By this he did not mean that religion was a pipe-dream (though he believed that it was) but that belief in a happier afterlife was a necessary stupefacient to make labour under capitalism bearable. 'Religious suffering is at one and the same time the expression of real suffering and a protest against real suffering. Religion is the sigh of the oppressed creature, the heart of a heartless world and the soul of soulless conditions. It is the opium of the people' (*EW* 257).

While Hegel and Schopenhauer regarded traditional religious beliefs as popular allegorical or mythical presentations of philosophical truths that were accessible only to an enlightened elite, and while Feuerbach and Marx regarded them as the illusory projections of alienated consciousness, Kierkegaard always placed faith at the summit of human progress, and regarded the religious sphere as superior to the regions of science and politics. Ethics, too, he taught, must be strictly subordinated to worship.

For centuries, ever since Plato's *Euthyphro*, philosophers had debated the relationship between religion and morality. Does the moral value of an action depend simply on whether it is prescribed or prohibited by God? Or is it only because some actions are already of their own nature good or bad that God commands or forbids them? Thomas Aquinas had held that all the Ten Commandments belonged to a natural law from which not even God could offer dispensation. Duns Scotus, on the other hand, maintained that God could dispense from the law against murder and had done so when he ordered Abraham to sacrifice Isaac.[1]

In *Fear and Trembling* Kierkegaard adopted a new approach to this thorny topic. He too took the Genesis story of Abraham and Isaac as the test case for his discussion.

---

[1] See above, pp. 230–1, 464–5.

God did tempt Abraham and said unto him, Abraham: and he said, Behold here I am.

And he said, Take now thy son, thine only son Isaac, whom thou lovest, and get thee into the land of Moriah; and offer him there for a burnt offering upon one of the mountains which I will tell thee of.

And Abraham rose up early in the morning, and saddled his ass, and took two of his young men with him, and Isaac his son, and clave the wood for the burnt offering, and rose up, and went unto the place of which God had told him.

Then on the third day Abraham lifted up his eyes and saw the place afar off.

And Abraham said unto his young men, Abide ye here with the ass; and I and the lad will go yonder and worship, and come again to you.

And Abraham took the wood of the burnt offering, and laid it upon Isaac his son; and he took the fire in his hand, and a knife; and they went both of them together.

And Isaac spoke unto Abraham his father, and said My father: and he said Here am I, my son.

And he said, Behold the fire and the wood: but where is the lamb for a burnt offering?

And Abraham said, My son, God will provide himself a lamb for a burnt offering: so they went both of them together.

And they came to the place which God had told him of; and Abraham built an altar there, and laid the wood in order, and bound Isaac his son, and laid him on the altar upon the wood.

And Abraham stretched forth his hand, and took the knife to slay his son. (Gen. 22: 1–10)

There is undoubtedly something heroic in Abraham's willingness to sacrifice Isaac—the son for whom he had waited eighty years, and in whom all his hope of posterity rested. But in ethical terms, is not his conduct monstrous? He is willing to commit murder, to violate a father's duty to love his son, and in the course of it to deceive those closest to him.

Biblical and classical literature, Kierkegaard reminds us, offers other examples of parents sacrificing their children: Agamemnon offering up Iphigenia to avert the gods' curse on the Greek expedition to Troy, Jephtha giving up his daughter in fulfilment of a rash vow, Brutus condemning to death his treasonable sons. These were all sacrifices made for the greater good of a community: they were, in ethical terms, a surrender of the individual for the sake of the universal. Abraham's sacrifice was nothing of the kind: it was a transaction between himself and God. Had he been a tragic hero like the others, he would, on reaching Mount Moriah, have plunged the knife into himself rather than into Isaac. Instead, Kierkegaard tells us, he stepped outside the realm of ethics altogether, and acted for the sake of an altogether higher goal.

Such an action Kierkegaard calls 'the teleological suspension of the ethical'. Abraham's act transgressed the ethical order in view of his higher end, or *telos*, outside it. Whereas an ethical hero, such as Socrates, lays down his life for the sake of a universal moral law, Abraham's heroism lay in his obedience to an individual divine command. Moreover, his action was not just one of renunciation, like the rich young man in the gospel abandoning his wealth: a man does not have a duty to his money as he does to his son, and it was precisely in violating this duty that Abraham showed his obedience to God.

Was his act then sinful? If we think of every duty as being a duty to God, then undoubtedly it was. But such an identification of God with duty actually empties of content the notion of duty to God himself.

The whole existence of the human race is rounded off completely like a sphere, and the ethical is at once its limit and its content. God becomes an invisible vanishing point, a powerless thought, His power being only in the ethical which is the content of existence. If in any way it might occur to any man to want to love God in any other sense, he is romantic, he loves a phantom which if it had merely the power of being able to speak, would say to him 'I do not require your love. Stay where you belong'. (*FT* 78)

If there is to be a God who is more than a personification of duty, then there must be a sphere higher than the ethical. If Abraham is a hero, as the Bible portrays him, it can only be from the standpoint of faith. 'For faith is this paradox, that the particular is higher than the universal.'

Even if we accept that the demands of the unique relationship between God and an individual may override commitments arising from general laws, a crucial question remains. If an individual feels called to violate an ethical law, how is he to tell whether this is a genuine divine command or a mere temptation? Kierkegaard insists that no one else can tell him; that is why Abraham kept his plan secret from Sarah, Isaac, and his friends. The knight of faith (as Kierkegaard calls Abraham) has the terrible responsibility of solitude. But how can he even know or prove to himself what is a genuine divine command? Kierkegaard merely emphasizes that the leap of faith is taken in blindness. His failure to offer a criterion for distinguishing genuine from delusive vocation is something that cries out to us in an age when more and more people feel they have a personal divine command to sacrifice their own lives in order to kill as many innocent victims as possible.

Kierkegaard's silence at this point is not inadvertent. In his *Philosophical Fragments* and his *Concluding Unscientific Postscript* he offers a number of arguments to the effect that faith is not the outcome of any objective reasoning. The form of religious faith that he has in mind is the Christian belief that Jesus saved the human race by his death on the cross. This belief contains definite historical elements, and Kierkegaard asks, 'Is it possible to base an eternal happiness upon historical knowledge?', and he gives three arguments for a negative answer.

First, it is impossible, by objective research, to obtain certainty about any historical event; there is always some possibility of doubt, however small, and we never achieve more than an approximation. But faith leaves no room for doubt; it is a resolution to reject the possibility of error. No mere judgement of probability is sufficient for this faith which is to be the basis of eternal happiness. Hence, faith cannot be based on objective history.

Second, historical research is never definitively concluded: it is always being refined and revised, difficulties are always arising and being overcome. 'Each generation inherits from its predecessors the illusion that the method is quite impeccable, but the learned scholars have not yet achieved success.' If we are to take a historical document as the basis of our religious commitment, that commitment must be perpetually postponed.

Third, faith must be a passionate devotion of oneself, but objective inquiry involves an attitude of detachment. Because belief demands passion, Kierkegaard argues that the improbability of what is believed not only is no obstacle to faith, but is an essential element of faith. The believer must embrace risk, for without risk there is no faith. 'Faith is precisely the contradiction between the infinite passion of the individual's inwardness and the objective uncertainty.' The greater the risk of falsehood, the greater the passion involved in believing. We must throw away all rational supports of faith 'so as to permit the absurd to stand out in all its clarity, in order that the individual may believe if he wills it' (P 190).

If the improbability of a belief is the measure of the passion with which it is believed, then faith, which Kierkegaard calls 'infinite personal passion', must have as its object something that is infinitely improbable. Such was the faith of Abraham, who right up to the moment of drawing the knife on Isaac continued to believe in the divine promise of posterity. And his faith was rewarded, when God's angel held back his hand and Isaac, liberated from the pyre, went on to become the father of many nations.

Few believing Christians have been willing to accept that Christianity is infinitely improbable, and non-believers are offered by Kierkegaard no motive, not to say reason, for accepting belief. Paradoxically, his irrationalism has been most influential not among his fellow believers, but among twentieth-century atheists. Existentialist thinkers such as Karl Jaspers in Germany and Jean-Paul Sartre in France found attractive his claim that to have an authentic existence one must abandon the multitude and seize control of one's own destiny by a blind leap beyond reason.

The Theism of John Stuart Mill

In England, religious thought took a very different turn in the writings of John Stuart Mill, published some fifteen years after the *Concluding Unscientific Postscript*. Jeremy Bentham and James Mill had ensured that religious instruction should form no part of John Stuart's education. Accordingly, in his autobiography, Mill says he is 'one of the very few examples in this country of one who has, not thrown off religious belief, but never had it'. Possibly because of this, he did not feel the animus against religion that many other utilitarians have felt. In his posthumously published *Three Essays on Religion* he took a remarkably dispassionate look at the arguments for and against the existence of God, and at the positive and negative effects of religious belief.

While dismissing the ontological and causal arguments for God's existence, Mill took seriously the argument from design, the only one based upon experience. 'In the present state of our knowledge', he wrote, 'the adaptations in Nature afford a large balance of probability in favour of creation by intelligence.' He did not, however, regard the evidence as rendering even probable the existence of an omnipotent and benevolent creator. An omnipotent being would have no need of the adaptation of means to ends that provides the support of the design argument; and an omnipotent being that permitted the amount of evil we find in the world could not be benevolent. Still less can the God of traditional Christianity be so regarded. Recalling his father, Mill wrote in his autobiography:

Think (he used to say) of a being who would make a Hell—who would create the human race with the infallible foreknowledge, and therefore with the intention, that the great majority of them were to be consigned to horrible and everlasting torment. The time, I believe, is drawing near when this dreadful conception of an object of worship will be no longer identified with Christianity; and when all persons, with any sense of moral good and evil, will look upon it with the same indignation with which my father regarded it. (*A* 26)

We cannot call any being good, Mill maintained, unless he possesses the attributes that constitute goodness in our fellow creatures—'and if such a being can sentence me to hell for not so calling him, to hell I will go'.

But even if the notion of hell is discarded as mythical, the amount of evil we know to exist in this world is sufficient, Mill believes, to rule out the notion of omnipotent goodness. Mill was indeed an optimist in his judgement of the world we live in: 'all the grand sources', Mill wrote, 'of human suffering are in a great degree, many of them almost entirely, conquerable by human care and effort' (*U* 266). Nonetheless, the great majority of mankind live in misery, and if this is due largely to human incompetence and lack of goodwill, that itself counts against the idea that we are all under the rule of all-powerful goodness.

Mill's essay *Theism* concludes as follows:

These, then, are the net results of natural theology on the question of the divine attributes. A being of great but limited power, how or by what limited we cannot even conjecture; of great and perhaps unlimited intelligence, but perhaps also more narrowly limited power than this, who desires, and pays some regard to, the happiness of his creatures, but who seems to have other motives of action which he cares more for, and who can hardly be supposed to have created the universe for that purpose alone. Such is the deity whom natural religion points to, and any idea of God more captivating than this comes only from human wishes, or from the teaching of either real or imaginary revelation. (*3E* 94)

If that is the case, what can be said about the desirability or otherwise of religious belief? It cannot be disputed, Mill says, that religion has value to individuals as a source of personal satisfaction and elevated feelings. Some religions hold out the prospect of immortality as an incentive to virtuous behaviour. But this expectation rests on tenuous grounds; and as humanity makes progress it may come to seem a much less flattering prospect.

It is not only possible but probable that in a higher, and above all, a happier condition of human life, not annihilation but immortality may be the burdensome idea; and that human nature, though pleased with the present, and by no means impatient to quit it, would find comfort and not sadness in the thought that it is not chained through eternity to a conscious existence which it cannot be assured that it will always wish to preserve. (*3E* 122)

Creation and Evolution

By the time Mill's Essays were published in 1887, religious believers felt under threat more from evolutionary biology than from empiricist philosophy. *On the Origin of Species* and *The Descent of Man* were greeted with horror in some Christian circles. At the meeting of the British Association in 1860, the evolutionist T. H. Huxley, so he reported, had been asked by the Bishop of Oxford whether he claimed descent from an ape on his father's or his mother's side. Huxley— according to his own account—replied that he would rather have an ape for a grandfather than a man who misused his gifts to obstruct science by rhetoric.

The quarrel between Darwinian evolutionists and Christian fundamentalists continues today. Darwin's theory obviously clashes with a literal acceptance of the Bible account of the creation of the world in seven days. Moreover, the length of time that would be necessary for evolution to take place would be immensely longer than the 6,000 years that Christian fundamentalists believe to be the age of the universe. But a non-literal interpretation of Genesis was adopted long ago by theologians as orthodox as St Augustine, and many Christians today are content to accept that the earth may have existed for billions of years. It is more difficult to reconcile an acceptance of Darwinism with belief in original sin. If the struggle for existence had been going on for aeons before humans evolved, it is impossible to accept that it was man's first disobedience and the fruit of the forbidden tree that brought death into the world.

On the other hand, it is wrong to suggest, as is often done, that Darwin disproved the existence of God. For all Darwin showed, the whole machinery of natural selection may have been part of a creator's design for the universe. After all, belief that we humans are God's creatures has never been regarded as incompatible with our being the children of our parents; it is no more incompatible with us being, on both sides, descended from the ancestors of the apes.

At most, Darwin disposed of one argument for the existence of God: namely, the argument that the adaptation of organisms to their environment exhibits the handiwork of a benevolent creator. But even that is to overstate the case. The only argument refuted by Darwin would be one that said: wherever there is adaptation to environment we must see the immediate activity of an intelligent being. But the old argument from design did not claim this; and indeed it was an essential step in the argument that lower animals and natural agents did not have minds. The argument was only that the ultimate explanation of such adaptation must be found in intelligence; and if the argument was ever sound, then the success of Darwinism merely inserts an extra step between the phenomena to be explained and their ultimate explanation.

Darwinism leaves much to be explained. The origin of individual species from earlier species may be explained by the mechanisms of evolutionary pressure and selection. But these mechanisms cannot be used to explain the origin of species as such. For one of the starting points of explanation by natural selection is the existence of true breeding populations, namely species.

Many Darwinians claim that the origin and structure of the world and the emergence of human life and human institutions are already fully explained by science, so that no room is left for postulating the existence of activity of any non-natural agent. Darwin himself was more cautious. Though he believed that it was not necessary, in order to account for the perfection of complex organs and instincts, to appeal to 'means superior to, though analogous with, human reason', he explicitly left room, in several places in the second edition of *On the Origin of Species*, for the activity of a creator. In defending his theory from geological objections he pleads that the imperfections of the geological record 'do not overthrow the theory of descent from a few created forms with subsequent modification' (*OS* 376). 'I should infer from analogy', he tells us, 'that probably all the organic beings which have ever lived on this earth have descended from some one primordial form, into which life was first breathed by the Creator' (*OS* 391).

Indeed, Darwin claims it as a merit of his system that it is in accord with what we know of the divine mode of action:

To my mind it accords better with what we know of the laws impressed on matter by the Creator, that the production and extinction of the past and present inhabitants of the world should have been due to secondary causes, like those determining the birth and death of the individual. When I view all beings not as special creations, but as the lineal descendants of some few beings which lived long before the first bed of the Silurian system was deposited, they seem to me to become ennobled. (*OS* 395)

It was special creation, not creation, that Darwin objected to.

When neo-Darwinians claim that Darwin's insights enable us to explain the entire cosmos, philosophical difficulties arise at three main points: the origin of language, the origin of life, and the origin of the universe.

In the case of the human species there is a particular difficulty in explaining by natural selection the origin of language, given that language is a system of conventions. Explanation by natural selection of the origin of a feature in a population presupposes the occurrence of that feature in particular individuals of the population. Natural selection might favour a certain length of leg, and the long-legged individuals in the population might outbreed the others. But for this kind of explanation of features to be possible, it must be possible to conceive the occurrence of the feature in single individuals. There is no problem in describing a single individual as having legs n metres long. But there is a problem with the idea that there might be just a single human language-user.

It is not easy to explain how the human race may have begun to use language by claiming that the language-using individuals among the population were advantaged and so outbred the non-language-using individuals. This is not simply because of the difficulty of seeing how spontaneous mutation could produce a language-using individual; it is the difficulty of seeing how anyone could be described as a language-using individual at all before there was a community of language-users. Human language is a rule-governed, communal activity, totally different from the signalling systems to be found in non-humans. If we reflect on the social and conventional nature of language, we must find something odd in the idea that language may have evolved because of the advantages possessed by language-users over non-language-users. It seems almost as absurd as the idea that banks may have evolved because those born with an innate cheque-writing ability were better off than those born without it.

Language cannot be the result of trial and error learning because such learning presupposes stable goals that successive attempts realize or fail to realize (as a rat may find or fail to find a food pellet in maze). But there is no goal to which language is a means: one cannot have the goal of acquiring a language, because one needs a language to have that wish in.

If it is difficult to see how language could originate by natural selection, it is equally difficult to see how life could originate that way. However successful natural selection may be in explaining the origin of particular species of life, it clearly cannot explain how there came to be such things as species at all. Darwin never claimed that it did; he did not offer an explanation of the origin of life.

Neo-Darwinians, by contrast, often attempt to tell us how life began, speculating, say, about electrical changes in some primeval organic soup. These explanations are of a radically different kind from those that Darwin put forward to account for evolution. Neo-Darwinians try to explain life as produced by the chance interaction of non-living materials and forces subject to purely physical laws. These accounts, whatever their merits, are not explanations by natural selection.

Natural selection and intelligent design are not incompatible with each other, in the way that natural selection is incompatible with the Genesis story. But though 'intelligent design' may be used in political circles as a euphemism for biblical fundamentalism, in the sheer idea of an extra-cosmic intelligence there is nothing that commits one to a belief in the Judaeo-Christian, or any other, religious revelation. To be sure, discussion of the possibility of such an intelligence does not belong in the science classroom; if it did, the intelligence would not be an extra-cosmic one, but a part of nature. But that is no reason why philosophers should not give it serious consideration.

The most fundamental reason in favour of postulating an extra-cosmic agency of any kind is surely the need to explain the origin of the universe itself. It is wrong to say that God provides the answer to the question, 'Why is there something rather than nothing?' The question itself is ill-conceived: the proposition 'There is nothing' cannot be given a coherent sense, and therefore there is no need to ask why it is false. It is not the existence of the universe that calls for explanation, but its coming into existence. At a time when philosophers and scientists were happy to accept that the universe had existed forever, there was no question of looking for a cause of its origin, only of looking for an explanation of its nature. But when it is proposed that the universe began at a point of time measurably distant in the past, then it seems perverse simply to shrug one's shoulders and decline to seek any explanation. In the case of an ordinary existent, we would be uneasy with a blithe announcement that there was simply no reason for its coming into existence. Unless we accept a Kantian view of the limitations of reason, it seems irrational to abandon this attitude when the existing thing in question is all-pervasive, like the universe.

Newman's Philosophy of Religion

If one accepts that the origin of the universe needs some explanation outside itself, that is not of itself sufficient to amount to a belief in God as defined in the great monotheistic traditions. Nor, even according to some believers, is it necessary. So devout a philosopher as John Henry Newman could write, 'It is indeed a great question whether Atheism is not as philosophically consistent with the phenomena of the physical world, taken by themselves, as the doctrine of a creative and governing power' (US 186).

For Newman, the justification of religious faith came from quite different sources, as he explained in *The Grammar of Assent*. 'Faith', for Newman, has a quite precise sense. Faith in God is more than just belief that there is a God: Aristotle believed in a prime mover unmoved but his belief was not faith. Faith in God was not necessarily total commitment to God: Marlowe's Faustus, on the verge of damnation, still believes in redemption. Faith contrasted with reason and love; the special feature of a belief that makes it faith is that it is a belief in something as revealed by God, belief in a proposition on the word of God. Such was Newman's conception of faith. It is a Catholic conception, different from the Lutheran one that we encountered in Kierkegaard.

Faith, understood as belief rather than commitment, is an operation of the intellect, not of the will or emotions. But is it a reasonable operation of the intellect, or is it rash and irrational? Newman accepts that the testimony on which faith is based is in itself weak. It can only convince someone who has an antecedent sympathy with the content of the testimony.

Faith . . . does not demand evidence so strong as is necessary for . . . belief on the ground of Reason; and why? for this reason, because it is mainly swayed by antecedent considerations . . . previous notices, prepossessions, and (in a good sense of the word) prejudices. The mind that believes is acted upon by its own hopes, fears, and existing opinions. (*US* 179–80)

Newman is well aware that his stress on the need for preparation of the heart may well make faith appear to be no more than wishful thinking. He emphasizes, however, that the mismatch between evidence and commitment, and the importance of previous attitudes, is to be observed not only in religious faith, but in other cases of belief.

We hear a report in the streets, or read it in the public journals. We know nothing of the evidence; we do not know the witnesses, or anything about them: yet sometimes we believe implicitly, sometimes not: sometimes we believe without asking for evidence, sometimes we disbelieve till we receive it. Did a rumour circulate of a destructive earthquake in Syria or the South of Europe, we should readily credit it; both because it might easily be true, and because it was nothing to us though it were. Did the report relate to countries nearer home, we should try to trace and authenticate it. We do not call for evidence till antecedent probabilities fail. (*US* 180)

Two objections may be made to Newman's claim that faith is reasonable even though acceptance of it depends not so much on evidence as on antecedent probabilities. The first is that antecedent probabilities may be equally available for what is true and for what merely pretends to be true. They supply no intelligible rule to decide between a genuine and a counterfeit revelation:

If a claim of miracles is to be acknowledged because it happens to be advanced, why not for the miracles of India as well as for those of Palestine? If the abstract possibility of a Revelation be the measure of genuineness in a given case, why not in the case of Mahomet as well as of the Apostles? (*US* 226)

Newman, who is never more eloquent than when developing criticisms of his own position, nowhere provides a satisfactory answer to this objection.

Secondly, it may be objected that there is a difference between religious faith and the reasonable, though insufficiently grounded, beliefs to which we give assent in our daily lives. In Newman's own words, Christianity is to be 'embraced and maintained as true, on the grounds of its being divine, not as true on intrinsic grounds, nor as probably true, or partially true, but as absolutely certain knowledge, certain in a sense in which nothing else can be certain'. In the ordinary cases, we are always ready to consider evidence that tells against our beliefs; but the religious believer adopts a certitude that refuses to entertain any doubt about the articles of faith.

Newman responds that even in secular matters, it can be rational to reject objections as idle phantoms, however much they may be insisted upon by a pertinacious opponent, or present themselves through an obsessive imagination.

I certainly should be very intolerant of such a notion as that I shall one day be Emperor of the French; I should think it too absurd even to be ridiculous, and that I must be mad before I could entertain it. And did a man try to persuade me that treachery, cruelty, or ingratitude was as praiseworthy as honesty and temperance, and that a man who lived the life of a knave and died the death of a brute had nothing to fear from future retribution, I should think there was no call on me to listen to his arguments, except with the hope of converting him, though he called me a bigot and a coward for refusing to enter into his speculations.

On the other hand, a believer can certainly investigate the arguments for and against his religious position. To do so need not involve any weakening of faith. But may not a man's investigation lead to his giving up his assent to his creed? Indeed it may, but:

my vague consciousness of the possibility of a reversal of my belief in the course of my researches, as little interferes with the honesty and firmness of that belief while those researches proceed, as the recognition of the possibility of my train's oversetting is an evidence of an intention on my part of undergoing so great a calamity. (*GA* 127)

There is no need to follow in detail the arguments by which Newman does his best to show that the acceptance of the Catholic religion is the action of a reasonable person. He maintains that the enduring history of Judaism and Christianity through the vicissitudes of human affairs is a phenomenon that carries on its face the probability of a divine origin. But it does so, Newman admits, only to someone who already believes that there is a God who will judge the world.

But what reason is there in the first place to believe in God and a future judgement? In response, Newman makes his celebrated appeal to the testimony of conscience:

If, on doing wrong, we feel the same tearful, broken hearted sorrow which overwhelms us on hurting a mother; if, on doing right, we enjoy the same sunny serenity of mind, the same soothing satisfactory delight which follows on our receiving praise from a father, we certainly have within us the image of some person, to whom our love and veneration look, in whose smile we find our happiness, for whom we yearn, towards whom we direct our pleadings, in whose anger we are troubled and waste away. These feelings in us are such as require for their exciting cause an intelligent being. (*GA* 76)

It is difficult for members of a post-Freudian generation to read this passage without acute discomfort. It is not the mere existence of conscience—of moral judgements of right and wrong—that Newman regards as intimations of the existence of God. Such judgements can be explained—as they are by many Christian philosophers as well as by utilitarians—as conclusions arrived at by natural reason and common sense. It is the emotional colouring of conscience that Newman claims to be echoes of the admonitions of a Supreme Judge. The feelings that he eloquently describes may indeed be appropriate only if there is a Father in heaven. But no feelings can guarantee their own appropriateness in the absence of reason.

Earlier, we noticed parallels between the accounts of belief given by Newman and Frege. Frege himself had no great interest in philosophy of religion. There is, however, one passage in the *Foundations of Arithmetic* that is of great importance to anyone interested in the possibility of proving the existence of God. Frege sets out an analogy between existence and number. 'Affirmation of existence', he says (*FA* 65), 'is in fact nothing but denial of the number nought.' What he means is that an affirmation of existence (for example, 'Angels exist' or 'There are [such things as] angels') is an assertion that a concept (for example, *angel*) has something falling under it. And to say that a concept has something falling under it is to say that the number belonging to that concept is not zero.

It is because existence is a property of concepts and not of objects, Frege says, that the ontological argument for the existence of God breaks down. That is to say, that-there-is-a-God cannot be a component of the concept *God*, nor can it be a component of that concept that-there-is-only-one-God. If in fact there is one and only one God, that is a property, not of God, but of the concept *God*.

Frege's argument was taken by many later philosophers—including Bertrand Russell—as giving the death-blow to the ontological argument. But the matter is not so simple. Frege has not shown that it is never possible to make an inference, as the ontological argument does, from the components of a concept to its properties. Frege himself infers from the components of the concept *equilateral right-angled triangle* that it has the property of possessing the number zero. Perhaps, one may argue, there may also be cases where one can infer from the component characteristics of a concept to existence or to uniqueness. Moreover, if, as some later logicians have done, one is prepared to allow into one's ontology not only actual but also possible objects, then existence is indeed a property of objects: it is precisely what makes some of them actual and not possible.

The Death of God and the Survival of Religion

Two years before Frege published his criticism of the ontological argument, Nietzsche had announced in *The Gay Science* that God was dead, that belief in the Christian God had become incredible. He did so, however, in the tones not of a philosopher, but of an evangelist; he was not offering arguments against a thesis, but proclaiming the greatest of good news. 'At last the horizon lies free before us, even granted that it is not bright; at least, the sea, *our* sea lies open before us.' The Christian God, with his commands and prohibitions, had been hitherto the greatest obstacle to the fullness of human life. Now that he is dead we are free to express our will to live.

Nietzsche had no patience with those thinkers—particularly in England—who tried to preserve Christian morality while denying the Christian faith. He was particularly scornful of that 'moralizing little woman' George Eliot, clinging on to respectability after being emancipated from theology.

Christianity, Nietzsche says, is a system, a coherent and *complete* view of things. If you break off one of its principal concepts, the belief in God, then you shatter the whole thing; you have nothing essential left in your fingers. Christianity presupposes that man does not—*cannot*—know what is good for him, and what is evil: he believes in God, and God alone knows these things. Christian morality is an imperative; its origin is transcendental; it is beyond any criticism, any right to criticize; it is true only if God is truth—it stands and falls with the belief in God (*TI* 45).

The idea of a moral law without a lawgiver is vacuous. English people who believe that they can detect good and evil by intuition merely reveal how much they are still under the hidden influence of the Christianity they have thrown off. While a healthy morality would fulfil 'the decrees of life', conventional morality is anti-natural and fights our vital instincts. 'In saying "God looks at the heart" it says no to the lowest and highest of life's desires, and proclaims God as the enemy of life . . . The saint, in whom God is well pleased, is the ideal castrato . . . Life ends where "the kingdom of God" begins' (*TI* 23).

One person who took seriously Nietzsche's criticism of saintliness was William James. For Nietzsche, he observed, the saint represents little but sneakingness and slavishness. He is the sophisticated invalid, the degenerate par excellence, the man of insufficient vitality; his prevalence would put the human type in danger. Poor Nietzsche's antipathy, James said, was sickly enough, but the clash he describes between two ideals is real and important. 'The whole feud', James wrote, 'revolves essentially upon two pivots: Shall the seen world or the unseen world be our chief sphere of adaptation? and must our means of adaptation in this seen world be aggressiveness or non resistance?' (*VRE* 361). James devoted five of his 1902 Gifford lectures to a defence of the value of saintliness. But the defence was qualified. 'Abstractly the saint is the highest type', he concluded, 'but in the present environment it may fail, so we make ourselves saints at our peril' (*VRE* 10).

The Varieties of Religious Experience is not a work of philosophy, of whose powers in this area James was sceptical, nor of anthropology, since it is based not on fieldwork but on written sources. It is more like a Kama Sutra guide to the experiences of those who have sought release and satisfaction in religion. (Not that James welcomed any assimilation of religion to sex. 'Few conceptions are less instructive', he wrote, 'than this re-interpretation of religion as perverted sexuality'; *VRE* 33.)

Besides saintliness, James surveyed religious phenomena such as the sense of sin, the experience of conversion, and mystical states. The treatment of saintliness and conversion left unanswered the question, 'Is the sense of divine presence a sense of anything objectively true?' Mysticism, James concluded, was too private and too various to make any claim to universal authority. In the last lectures of his series he asked whether philosophy could stamp any warrant of veracity upon the religious man's sense of the divine.

James had little hope of any help from traditional proofs of God's existence, whether the argument to a first cause, or the argument from design, or the argument from morality to a lawgiver. 'The arguments for God's existence', he wrote, 'have stood for hundreds of years with the waves of unbelieving criticism breaking against them, never totally discrediting them in the ears of the faithful, but on the whole slowly and surely washing the mortar from between their joints' (*VRE* 420).

James listed the attributes of God that theologians had striven over the centuries to establish: his self-derived existence (aseity), his necessity, his unique-ness, his spirituality, his metaphysical simplicity, his immensity and omnipresence, his omniscience and omnipotence. James has a brief, no-nonsense, pragmatist's way with these conceptions of natural theology. To develop a thought's meaning, he stated, with a salute to Peirce, we need only determine what conduct it is fitted to produce, and that conduct is for us its sole significance. If we apply this principle to God's metaphysical attributes, we have to confess them destitute of all intelli-gible significance.

Take God's aseity for example; or his necessariness; his immateriality; his 'simplicity' or superiority to the kind of inner variety and succession which we find in finite beings, his indivisibility, and lack of the inner distinctions of being and activity, substance and accident, potentiality and actuality, and the rest; his repudiation of inclusion in a genus; his actualized infinity; his 'personality', apart from the moral qualities which it may comport; his relations to evil being permissive and not positive; his self-sufficiency, self-love, and absolute felicity in himself:—candidly speaking, how do such qualities as these make any definite connection with our life? And if they severally call for no distinctive adaptations of our conduct, what vital difference can it possibly make to a man's religion whether they be true or false? (*VRE* 428)

So much for God's metaphysical attributes. But what of his moral attributes, such as holiness, justice, and mercy? Surely these are, from the point of view of pragmatism, on a different footing: they positively determine fear and hope and expectations, and are foundations for the saintly life. Well, perhaps these predicates are meaningful; but dogmatic theology has never produced any convincing arguments that they do in fact belong to God. And modern idealism, James believed, has said goodbye to dogmatic theology for ever.

It is not reason, he maintained in conclusion, that is the source of religion, but feeling. Philosophical and theological formulas are secondary. All that philosophy can do is to assist in the articulation of religious experience, compare different expressions of it, eliminate local and accidental elements from these expressions, mediate between different believers, and help to bring about consensus of opinion. The theologians' enumeration of divine epithets is not worthless, but its value is aesthetic rather than scientific. 'Epithets lend an atmosphere and overtones to our devotion. They are like a hymn of praise and service of glory, and may sound the more sublime for being incomprehensible' (*VRE* 437–9).

In a world governed by science and its laws, is there any room for prayer? James distinguishes between petitionary prayer, and prayer in a wider sense. Among petitionary prayers, he makes a further distinction between prayers for better weather, and prayers for the recovery of sick people. The first are futile, but not necessarily the second. 'If any medical fact can be considered to stand firm, it is that in certain environments prayer may contribute to recovery and should be encouraged as a therapeutic measure' (*VRE* 443).

Taken in a wider sense, prayer means 'every kind of inward communion or conversation with the power recognized as divine'. This, James maintains, is untouched by scientific criticism. Indeed, the whole upshot of his investigation of religious experience is that 'religion, wherever it is an active thing, involves a belief in ideal presences and a belief that in our prayerful communion with them, work is done, and something real comes to pass'. But is this belief *true*, or is it a mere anachronistic survival from a pre-scientific age? Any science of religion is as likely to be hostile as to be favourable to the claim that the essence of religion is true.

But science, James thinks, need not necessarily have the last word. Religion is concerned with the individual and his personal destiny, science with the impersonal and general. 'The God whom science recognizes must be a God of universal laws exclusively, a God who does a wholesale, not a retail business' (*VRE* 472). But which is more real, the universal or the particular? According to James, 'so long as we deal with the cosmic and the general, we deal only with the symbols of reality, but *as soon as we deal with private and personal phenomena as such, we deal with realities in the completest sense of the term*' (*VRE* 476). It is absurd for science to claim that the egotistic elements of experience should be suppressed. 'Religion, occupying herself with personal destinies and keeping thus in contact with the only absolute realities which we know, must necessarily play an eternal part in human history' (*VRE* 480).

James is willing, in conclusion, to call the supreme reality in the universe 'God'. But his positive account of God is extremely nebulous; it is similar to Matthew Arnold's definitions of God as 'the stream of tendency by which all things seek to fulfil the law of their being' or 'an eternal power, not ourselves, that makes for righteousness'. James's woolliness of expression, however, is only to be expected, since he regarded religion as essentially a matter of feeling, and feelings as essentially inarticulate. But it disappointed many of his friends, who regarded him, on other topics, as a model of candour and precision. 'His wishes made him turn down the lights', said his old friend Oliver Wendell Holmes, Jr., 'so as to give miracle a chance.'[2]

Freud on Religious Illusion

Freud, on the other hand, wanted to turn up the lights on the dark corners of the soul in order to rid the world of enchantment. Religion, he maintained, was an illusion; and he used 'illusion' in a precise sense as a belief determined by human wishes. Illusions, for Freud, are not necessarily false beliefs, as delusions are, but they are beliefs undetermined by evidence; if they are true it is by a happy accident. 'For instance, a middle-class girl may have the illusion that a prince will come and marry her. This is possible; and a few such cases have occurred.' Freud's definition means that he can maintain that religion is an illusion while, in theory at least, leaving open the question of the truth-value of religious beliefs. It is unlikely, he thinks, that the Messiah will come and found a golden age; but religious doctrines can no more be disproved than they can be proved.

Religious ideas, Freud says in *The Future of an Illusion*, are not the result of experience or ratiocination.

They are illusions, fulfilments of the oldest, strongest and most urgent wishes of mankind. The secret of their strength lies in the strength of those wishes.... The terrifying impression of helplessness in childhood aroused the need for protection—for protection through love—which was provided by the father; and the recognition that this helplessness lasts throughout life made it necessary to cling to the existence of a father, but this time a more powerful one. Thus the benevolent rule of a divine Providence allays our fear of the dangers of life; the establishment of a moral world-order ensures the fulfilment of the demands of justice, which have so often remained unfulfilled in human civilization; and the prolongation of earthly existence in a future life provides the local and temporal framework in which these wish-fulfilments shall take place. (*FI* 47–8)

Though Freud disowns any pretension to refute religious claims, he clearly thinks it would be better for all concerned if religion withered away. Religion has rendered great service by helping to tame human instincts. But in the thousands of years it has held sway it has achieved very little. There is no evidence that men were in general happier when religious doctrines were universally accepted, and they were certainly no morally better than they are nowadays. The growth of the scientific spirit has decisively weakened the hold of religion. 'Criticism has whittled

[2] Letter of 1 Sept. 1910, quoted in Louis Menand, *The Metaphysical Club* (London: Flamingo, 2001), 436.

993

away the evidential value of religious documents, natural science has shown up the errors in them, and comparative research has been struck by the fatal resemblance between the religious ideas which we revere and the mental products of primitive people and times.' (*FI* 63).

Thus far Freud's criticism of religion, as he himself insists, owes nothing to psychoanalysis. But, ever since *Totem and Taboo* in 1913, he had propounded a psychoanalytic narrative of the origin of religious morality. In the earliest ages, he reported, humans lived in hordes, each horde being ruled by a primal father who enslaved the other men and possessed all the women. One day the men banded together and slew the primal father and established taboos against murder and incest. The primal crime left an inheritance of guilt, so that humans deified the murdered father in their imaginations and determined to respect his will henceforward. Religion, on this view, is the universal obsessional neurosis of humanity.

Like the obsessional neurosis of children it arose out of the Oedipus complex, out of the relation to the father. If this view is right, it is to be supposed that a turning-away from religion will occur with the fatal inevitability of a process of growth, and that we find ourselves at this very juncture in the middle of that phase of development. (*FI* 71)

Freud tells us that the time has come to replace the effects of repression by the results of the rational operation of the intellect. But what he is doing is not at all replacing religion with science, but substituting for the myth of Adam's fall another myth of no greater credibility as a historical narrative. His later writings diminished, rather than increased, any plausibility that *Totem and Taboo* may have possessed. In *Moses and Monotheism* he maintained that the prehistoric primal murder had been twice repeated in historic times—once when the Jewish people murdered Moses (did they, now?) and once when they murdered Jesus. Thus 'there is a real piece of historical truth in Christ's resurrection, for he was the resurrected Moses and behind him the returned primal father of the primitive horde, transfigured and, as the son, put in the place of the father' (*SE* xxiii. 89–90).

Philosophical Theology after Wittgenstein

God is hardly mentioned in Wittgenstein's *Tractatus Logico-Philosophicus*: no doubt he is among the things whereof one should keep silent. But throughout his life, Wittgenstein, though he early gave up his Catholic faith, took religion very seriously. 'To believe in God', he wrote in a notebook during the First World War, 'means to see that life has a meaning.' But believing in God was not a matter of assenting to a doctrine. The Gospels do not provide a historical basis for faith.

Christianity is not based on a historical truth: rather, it offers us a (historical) narrative and says: now believe. But not: believe this narrative with the belief appropriate to a historical narrative; rather, believe through thick and thin, which you can do only as a result of a life. Here you have a narrative; don't take the same attitude as you take to other historical narratives. Make quite a different place in your life for it. (*CV* 32)

Wittgenstein was most opposed to the idea that Christianity was reasonable, and that its reasonableness was established by a branch of philosophy called natural theology. Philosophy, he thought, could not give any meaning to life; the best it could provide would be a form of wisdom. But compared with the burning passion of faith, wisdom is only cold grey ash.

But though only faith, and not philosophy, can give meaning to life, that does not mean that philosophy has no rights within the terrain of faith. Faith may involve talking nonsense, and philosophy may point out that it is nonsense. Having in the *Tractatus* urged us to avoid nonsense by silence, Wittgenstein after his return to philosophy said, 'Don't be afraid of talking nonsense' (*CV* 56). But he went on to add: 'You must keep an eye on your nonsense.'

The logical positivists shared the view that religious language was nonsense; but they felt for it none of the paradoxical respect accorded it by Wittgenstein. A. J. Ayer, in *Language, Truth and Logic*, offered a brisk proof that religious language was meaningless and that 'God' was not a genuine name. A religious man, he tells us, would say that God was a transcendent being who could not be defined in terms of any empirical manifestations. But in that case, 'God' was a metaphysical term:

To say that 'God exists' is to make a metaphysical utterance which cannot be either true or false. And by the same criterion, no sentence which purports to describe the nature of a transcendent god can possess any literal significance.

It is important not to confuse this view of religious assertions with the view that is adopted by atheists, or agnostics. For it is characteristic of an agnostic to hold that the existence of a god is a possibility in which there is no good reason either to believe or disbelieve; and it is characteristic of an atheist to hold that it is at least probable that no god exists. And our view that all utterances about the nature of God are nonsensical, so far from being identical with, or even lending any support to, either of these familiar contentions, is actually incompatible with them. For if the assertion that there is a god is nonsensical, then the atheist's assertion that there is no god is equally nonsensical, since it is only a significant proposition that can be significantly contradicted. (*LTL* 115)

For some years, believing philosophers were alarmed by verificationist arguments against religious doctrines, and strove to defend their meaningfulness without making much effort to demonstrate their truth. Towards the end of the twentieth century, however, some natural theologians recovered confidence and were much less defensive in their attitudes. Typical of this phase is Alvin Plantinga, first of Calvin College, Grand Rapids, and later of Notre Dame University.

For instance, Plantinga has offered a sophisticated restatement of the ontological argument. In a simplified version his revision goes like this. Let us begin by defining the property of maximal excellence, a property that includes omniscience, omnipotence, and moral perfection. Obviously God, if he exists, has maximal excellence in the actual world. But maximal excellence is not sufficient for Godhead: we need to consider worlds other than this one.

Those who worship God do not think of him as a being that happens to be of surpassing excellence in *this* world but who in some other worlds is powerless or uninformed or of dubious moral character. We might make a distinction here between *greatness* and *excellence*; we might say that the *excellence* of a being in a given world W depends only upon its . . . properties in W, while its greatness in W depends not merely upon its excellence in W, but also upon its excellence in other worlds. The limiting degree of greatness, therefore, would be enjoyed in a given world W only by a being who had maximal excellence in W and in every other possible world as well.[3]

Maximal greatness therefore is maximal excellence in every possible world, and it is maximal greatness, not just maximal excellence, that is equivalent to divinity or Godhead. Anything that possesses maximal greatness must exist in every possible world, because in a world in which it does not exist it does not possess any properties. If it is possible for maximal greatness to be instantiated, then it is instantiated in every world. If so, then it is instantiated in our world, the actual world; that is to say, Godhead is instantiated and God exists.

Plantinga's argument obviously depends on the coherence of the apparatus of possible worlds, and on a solution having been found to the problem of trans-world identity. He believes that he has found such a solution, and he presents it at considerable length in his book. But it should also be remarked that in the case of a possible God, rather than of a possible human, the problem does not seem so pressing; it seems foolish to put to Plantinga the question, '*Which* God are you proving the existence of?' It remains the case, however, as Plantinga himself points out, that the whole argument depends on the truth of the premiss that it is possible for maximal greatness to be exemplified—that is to say, in his terms, that it is exemplified in some possible world.

Bertrand Russell, in his *History of Western Philosophy*, maintained that there were instances where philosophy had reached definitive answers to central questions. He gave as one example the ontological argument. 'This as we have seen was invented by Anselm, rejected by Thomas Aquinas, accepted by Descartes, refuted by Kant, and reinstated by Hegel. I think it may be said quite decisively that as a result of analysis of the concept "existence" modern logic has proved this argument invalid' (p. 752). Plantinga's reinstatement of the argument, using logical techniques more modern than any available to Russell, serves as a salutary warning of the danger that awaits any historian of logic who declares a philosophical issue definitively closed.

---

[3] Alvin Plantinga, *The Nature of Necessity* (Oxford: Clarendon Press, 1974), 214.

CHRONOLOGY

Some of these dates are approximate and others, especially in the earlier years, conjectural.

585 BC	Thales predicts an eclipse
547	Anaximander dies
530	Pythagoras migrates to Italy
525	Anaximenes dies
500	Heraclitus in mid-life
470	Xenophanes dies
	Democritus born
469	Socrates born
450	Parmenides and Zeno visit Athens
	Empedocles in mid-life
444	Protagoras writes a constitution
427	Plato born
399	Socrates executed
387	Plato's Academy founded
384	Aristotle born
347	Plato dies
336	Alexander king of Macedon
322	Aristotle dies
313	Zeno of Citium comes to Athens
306	Epicurus founds the Garden
273	Arcesilaus becomes head of the Academy
263	Cleanthes becomes head of the Stoa
232	Chrysippus succeeds as head of the Stoa
155	Carneades heads the Academy and visits Rome
106	Cicero born
55	Lucretius' *De Rerum Natura*
44	Julius Caesar assassinated
30	Augustus becomes Emperor
52 AD	St Paul preaches in Athens
65	Suicide of Seneca
161	Marcus Aurelius becomes Emperor
205	Plotinus born
387	St Augustine baptized

387	Conversion of St Augustine
430	Death of St Augustine
480	Birth of Boethius
525	Death of Boethius
529	Justinian closes Athens' schools
575	Death of John Philoponus
781	Alcuin meets Charlemagne
800	Charlemagne crowned in Rome
863	Eriugena's *Periphyseon*
980	Avicenna born
1077	Anselm's *Proslogion*
1140	Abelard condemned at Sens
1155	*Sentences* of Peter Lombard
1179	Averroes' *Harmony*
1188	Oxford's first faculties
1190	Maimonides' *Guide of the Perplexed*
1215	Paris University receives statutes
1225	Thomas Aquinas born
1248	Albert the Great at Cologne
1253	Death of Grosseteste
1266	*Summa Theologiae* begun
1274	Aquinas and Bonaventure die
1277	219 theses condemned at Paris
1300	Duns Scotus lecturing in Oxford
1307	Dante Alighieri begins *Divina Commedia*
1308	Duns Scotus dies
1318	Ockham lecturing in Oxford
1324	Marsilius' *Defensor Pacis*
1347	Black Death; Ockham dies
1360	Wyclif master of Balliol
1415	Council of Constance condemns Wyclif
1439	Council of Florence welcomes Greeks
1440	Nicholas of Cusa's *De Docta Ignorantia*
1469	Ficino begins *Theologia Platonica*
1474	Peter de Rivo condemned by Sixtus IV
1513	Lateran Council condemns Pomponazzi
1513	Machiavelli's *Prince*
1516	More's *Utopia*
1520	Papal condemnation of Luther
1540	Foundation of the Jesuits
1543	Copernicus publishes heliocentrism
1545–63	Council of Trent

1561	Murder of Ramus
1569	Montaigne's Essays
1588	Molina's *Concordia*
1600	Burning of Giordano Bruno
1605	Bacon's *Advancement of Learning*
1625	Grotius' *On War and Peace*
1638	Galileo's *Two New Sciences*
1641	Descartes' *Meditations*
1650	Death of Descartes
1651	Hobbes' *Leviathan*
1662	Death of Pascal
1677	Publication of Spinoza's *Ethics*
1686	Leibniz's *Discourse on Metaphysics*
1687	Newton's *Principia Mathematica*
1690	Locke's *Essay* and *Treatises of Civil Government*
1713	Berkeley's *Three Dialogues*
1714	Leibniz's *Monadology*
1739	Hume's *Treatise*
1750	Montesquieu's *Spirit of the Laws*
1764	Reid's *Common Sense*
1764	Rousseau's *Social Contract*
1781	Kant's *Critique of Pure Reason*
1785	Kant's *Groundwork of the Metaphysic of Morals*
1804	Fichte's *Wissenschaftslerhe*
1807	Hegel's *Phenomenology of Spirit*
1831	Death of Hegel
1757	Burke's *Enquiry into the Origin of our Ideas of the Sublime and Beautiful*
1789	Bentham's *Introduction to the Principles of Morals and Legislation*
1790	Kant's *Critique of Judgement*
1800	Wordsworth's *Preface to Lyrical Ballads*
1841	Feuerbach's *Essence of Christianity*
1843	Mill's *System of Logic*
1844	Schopenhauer's *World as Will and Idea* (2nd edn.)
1846	Kierkegaard's *Concluding Unscientific Postscript*
1848	Marx and Engels's *Communist Manifesto*
1859	Mill's *On Liberty*; Darwin's *On the Origin of Species*
1867	Marx's *Capital*, vol. I
1870	Newman's *Essay in Aid of a Grammar of Assent*
1872	Nietzsche's *Birth of Tragedy*
1874	Sidgwick's *Methods of Ethics*
1879	Frege's *Begriffsschrift*
1884	Frege's *Grundlagen der Arithmetik*

ABBREVIATIONS AND CONVENTIONS

Part One

CHHP K. Algra, J. Barnes, J. Mansfeld, and M. Schofield (eds.), *The Cambridge History of Hellenistic Philosophy* (Cambridge: Cambridge University Press, 1999)

CHLGP A. H. Armstrong (ed.), *The Cambridge History of Later Greek and Early Medieval Philosophy* (Cambridge: Cambridge University Press, 1967)

DK H. Diels and W. Kranz (eds.), *Die Fragmente der Vorsokratiker*, 6th edn., 3 vols. (Berlin: Wiedmann, 1951); cited as DK, followed by the chapter, letter, and the number of the fragment (e.g. DK 8 B115). Each chapter of this work is divided into two sections, A (which contains references in ancient authors) and B (which contains fragments that have been handed down verbatim)

D.L. Diogenes Laertius, *Lives of the Philosophers*, trans. R. D. Hicks, Loeb Classical Library, 2 vols. (Cambridge, Mass.: Harvard University Press, 1972); cited by book and paragraph (e.g. 8. 8)

Ep. Epistle

fr. fragment

KRS G. S. Kirk, J. E. Raven, and M. Schofield (eds.), *The Presocratic Philosophers*, 2nd edn. (Cambridge: Cambridge University Press, 1983); cited as KRS, followed by the number of the fragment in the single series that runs through the edition (e.g. KRS 433)

LS A. A. Long and D. N. Sedley (eds.), *The Hellenistic Philosophers*, 2 vols. (Cambridge: Cambridge University Press, 1987); cited as LS, followed by the number of the chapter and the letter corresponding to the individual text (e.g. LS 30F)

S.E. Sextus Empiricus

Alexander of Aphrodisias

de An. *de Anima*

Fat. *On Fate*

Aristotle

The standard form of reference is to the book and chapter of the individual work, followed by page, column, and line of the classic 1831 edition of Bekker (e.g. *Physics* 3. 1. 200^{b}32)

APo.	*Posterior Analytics*
APr.	*Prior Analytics*
Barnes	*The Complete Works of Aristotle*, ed. J. Barnes, Oxford Translation (Princeton: Princeton University Press, 1984)
Cael.	*On the Heavens*
Cat.	*Categories*
de An.	*On the Soul*
EE	*Eudemian Ethics*
GA	*On the Generation of Animals*
GC	*On Generation and Corruption*
HA	*History of Animals*
Int.	*de Interpretatione*
Metaph.	*Metaphysics*
Mete.	*Meteorologica*
MM	*Magna Moralia*
MXG	*de Melisso, Xenophane, et Gorgia*
NE	*Nicomachean Ethics*
PA	*On the Parts of Animals*
Ph.	*Physics*
Po.	*Poetics*
Pol.	*Politics*
Rh.	*Rhetorica*
SE	*Sophistical Refutations*
Top.	*Topics*

Cicero

Acad.	*Academica*
D.	*On Divination*
Fat.	*On Fate*
Fin.	*de Finibus*
ND	*On the Nature of the Gods*
Off.	*On Duties (de Officiis)*
Tusc.	*Tusculan Disputations*

Epictetus

Disc.	*Discourses*

Lucretius

RN	*On the Nature of Things*

1002

Plato

It is the universal custom to refer to the works of Plato by the name of the work followed by the page, section, and line of the Stephanus edition of 1578 (e.g. *Phaedo* 64a5). This numeration is preserved in all editions and most translations of Plato.

Apol.	*Apologia Socratis*
Cra.	*Cratylus*
Euthd.	*Euthydemus*
Euthphr.	*Euthyphro*
Grg.	*Gorgias*
Hp. Ma.	*Hippias Major*
Hp. Mi.	*Hippias Minor*
La.	*Laches*
Men.	*Meno*
Phd.	*Phaedo*
Phdr.	*Phaedrus*
Phlb.	*Philebus*
Prm.	*Parmenides*
Prt.	*Protagoras*
Rep.	*Republic*
Smp.	*Symposium*
Sph.	*Sophist*
Tht.	*Theaetetus*
Ti.	*Timaeus*

Plotinus

Plotinus is standardly cited according to the schema of his pupil Porphyry, who divided his works into Enneads, or groups of nine. The number of the Ennead is given, followed by the number of the work, chapter, and line (e.g. Ennead 6, 1. 5. 27; or simply 6. 1. 5. 27)

Sextus Empiricus (S.E.)

Sextus Empiricus is cited as S.E., followed by an abbreviation for the work (e.g. S.E., *M.*)

M.	*Against the Professors*
P.	*Outlines of Pyrrhonism*

Xenophon

Mem.	*Memorabilia*

Part Two

CCCM	Corpus Christianorum, Continuatio Medievalis
CCMP	A. S. McGrade, *The Cambridge Companion to Medieval Philosophy* (Cambridge: Cambridge University Press, 2003)
CCSL	Corpus Christianorum, Series Latina
CHLGP	A. H. Armstrong (ed.), *The Cambridge History of Later Greek and Early Medieval Philosophy* (Cambridge: Cambridge University Press, 1967)
CHLMP	N. Kretzmann, A. Kenny, and J. Pinborg (eds.), *The Cambridge History of Later Medieval Philosophy* (Cambridge: Cambridge University Press, 1982)
CPA	*Commentary on 'Posterior Analytics'*
CSEL	Corpus Scriptorum Ecclesiasticorum Latinorum
DB	H. Denzinger (ed.), *Enchiridion Symbolorum*, 33rd edn. (Barcelona: Herder, 1950)
IHWP	Anthony Kenny (ed.), *The Oxford Illustrated History of Western Philosophy* (Oxford: Oxford University Press, 1994)
PG	Patrologia Graeca
PL	Patrologia Latina
PMA	A. Hyman and J. J. Walsh, *Philosophy in the Middle Ages*, 2nd edn. (Indianapolis: Hackett, 1973).
Sent.	*Commentary on Lombard's 'Sentences'*; cited by book, distinction, article, and question

Abelard

AE	Abelard, *Ethics* (*Know Thyself*)
D	*Dialectica*
LI	*Logica Ingredientibus*
LNPS	*Logica Nostrorum Petitioni Scholarium*

Aquinas

DEE	*De Ente et Essentia* ('On Essence and Existence')
DP	*De Potentia* ('On Power')
DRI	*De Regimine Iudaeorum* ('On Jews and Government'); Leonine edn. vol. 42
DV	*De Veritate* ('On Truth')
IBT	*In Boethium de Trinitate* ('On Boethius' *De Trinitate*')
In I Periherm.	*In II Libros Perihermeneias Aristotelis Expositio*, ed. R. M. Spiazzi (Turin: Marietti, 1966)
ScG	*Summa contra Gentiles* ('On the Truth of the Catholic Faith'); cited by book and chapter
ST	*Summa Theologiae*; cited by part, question (q.), article, and (if appropriate) objection or answer

Aristotle

De An.	*De Anima*
EE	*Eudemian Ethics*
NE	*Nicomachean Ethics*

Augustine

References are to book, chapter, and alternative chapter number where relevant.

83Q	*De Diversis Quaestionibus LXXXIII* ('Eighty-Three Different Questions')
CA	*Contra Academicos* ('Against the Sceptics')
CCA	E. Stump and N. Kretzmann (eds.), *The Cambridge Companion to Augustine* (Cambridge: Cambridge University Press, 2001)
Conf.	*Confessiones* ('Confessions')
DBC	*De Bono Conjugali* ('On the Good of Marriage')
DCD	*De Civitate Dei* ('The City of God')
DCG	*De Correptione et Gratia* ('On Grace')
DDP	*De Dono Perseverantiae* ('On Perseverance')
DLA	*De Libero Arbitrio* ('On Free Will')
DM	*De Mendacio* ('On Lying')
DMg	*De Magistro* ('On the Teacher')
DPS	*De Praedestinatione Sanctorum* ('On Predestination')
DT	*De Trinitate* ('On the Trinity')
DUC	*De Utilitate Credendi* ('The Benefit of Belief')
Ep.	*Epistulae* ('Letters')
S	*Soliloquia* ('Soliloquies')

Averroes

HPR	*The Harmony of Philosophy and Religion*

Avicenna

Metaph.	*Metaphysics*

Boethius

DCP	*De Consolatione Philosophiae* ('On the Consolation of Philosophy')

Bonaventure

Brev.	*Breviloquium*
CH	*Collationes in Hexameron*
De Myst. Trin.	*De Mysterio Trinitatis*
Itin.	*Itinerarium Mentis in Deum*

Walter Burley

PAL	*The Pure Art of Logic*, ed. Philotheus Boehner (St Bonaventure, NY: Franciscan Institute, 1955)

Cusanus

DDI	*De Docta Ignorantia* ('On Informed Ignorance')

Duns Scotus

CCDS	T. Williams (ed.), *The Cambridge Companion to Duns Scotus* (Cambridge: Cambridge University Press, 2003)
DPP	*De Primo Principio* ('On the First Principle')
Lect.	*Lectura*, in *Opera Omnia*, ed. C. Balic *et al.* (Vatican City, 1950–), vols. 1–3: *Ordinatio* 1–2; vols. 16–20: *Lectura* 1–3; cited by volume and page
Ord.	*Ordinatio*, in *Opera Omnia*, ed. C. Balic *et al.* (Vatican City, 1950–), vols. 1–3: *Ordinatio* 1–2; vols, 16–20: *Lectura* 1–3; cited by volume and page
Oxon.	*Opus Oxoniense*
Quodl.	*God and Creatures: The Quodlibetical Questions* (Princeton: Princeton University Press, 1975)

Eriugena

References are to book and chapter.

Robert Grosseteste

De Lib. Arb.	*De Libero Arbitrio*, in *Die philosophische Werke des Robert Grosseteste*, ed. L. Baur, Beiträge zur Geschichte der Philosophie des Mittelalters 9 (Munster: Aschendorff, 1912)
Hex.	*Hexaemeron*

William Ockham

CCO	P. V. Spade (ed.), *The Cambridge Companion to Ockham* (Cambridge: Cambridge University Press, 1999)
OND	*Opus Nonaginta Dierum* ('Work of Ninety Days')
OPh.	*Opera Philosophica*; cited by part and chapter
OTh.	*Opera Theologica*; cited by volume and page

Peter of Spain

SL	Peter of Spain, *Tractatus, called afterwards Summule Logicales*, ed. L. M. de Rijk (Assen: van Gorcum, 1972)

Plato

Phaedr.	*Phaedrus*
Tim.	*Timaeus*

Proclus

ET	*Elements of Theology*

John Wyclif

U	*On Universals*, tr. A. Kenny (Oxford: Clarendon Press, 1985)

Part Three

General

HWP	Bertrand Rusell, *History of Western Philosophy*
PASS	*Supplementary Proceedings of the Aristotelian Society*
ST	Thomas Aquinas, *Summa Theologiae*, cited by part, question, and article
CHSCP	*The Cambridge History of Seventeenth-Century Philosophy*, ed. D. Garber and M. Ayers

Luther

E	*Erasmus–Luther: Discourse on Free Will*, ed. E. F. Winter (London: Constable, 1961), cited by page
WA	Weimarer Ausgabe, the standard edition of his works

Machiavelli

P	*Il Principe*, cited by chapter

Montaigne

ME	*Essais*, cited by page in the Flammarion edition of 1969

More

U	*Utopia*, cited by page in the edition of E. Surtz (New Haven, Conn.: Yale University Press, 1964)

Ramus

L	*Peter Ramus: The Logike 1574* (Menton: Scolar Press, 1970), cited by page

Suarez

DM   *Disputationes Metaphysicae* = vol. 25 of *Opera Omnia* (Hildesheim: Olms, 1965), cited by disputation, section, and article

Bacon

B   Oxford Authors *Bacon*, cited by page

Descartes

AT   The standard edition of Adam and Tannery, cited by volume and page

CSMK   The 3-volume standard English translation, cited by volume and page

Hobbes

L   *Leviathan*, cited by page in the Oxford World Classics edition, ed. J. C. A. Gaskin

G   *Human Nature and De Corpore Politico*, ed. J. C. A. Gaskin (Oxford World Classics, 1994), cited by page

Locke

E   *Essay on Human Understanding*, cited by page in the Oxford edition by P. H. Nidditch

T   *Two Treatises on Government*, cited by page in the Yale University Press edition of 2003

Pascal and Malebranche

EM   *Essai de la Metaphysique*, ibid.

LP   *Lettres Provinciales*, ed. H. F. Stewart (Manchester: Manchester University Press, 1919), cited by page

P   Pascal's *Pensées*, cited by the number in the Oxford World Classics edition

R de V   *De la Recherche de la Verité* in *Oeuvres Complètes de Malebranches*, ed. André Robinet (Paris: Vrin, 1958–84)

TNG   Malebranche's *Treatise on Nature and Grace*, cited by page of the Oxford translation of 1992

Spinoza

CPS   *The Cambridge Companion to Spinoza*, ed. D. Garett (Cambridge: Cambridge University Press, 1996)

E   References are given by page to Curley's Penguin translation of the *Ethics* (1996)

Ep   References are to the letters edited by A. Wolf

ABBREVIATIONS AND CONVENTIONS

Leibniz

A   *The Leibniz–Clarke Correspondence*, ed. H. G. Alexander (Manchester: Manchester University Press, 1956)

D   References to the *Discourse on Metaphysics* are to the Manchester edition of 1988

G   References are given by volume and page to the Gerhardt edition of the complete works

T   *Theodicy*, trs. E. M. Huggard (Lasalle, Ill.: Open Court Press, 1985)

Berkeley

BPW   References are given by page to *Berkeley's Philosophical Writings*, ed. D. A. Armstrong (New York: Collier Macmillan, 1965)

Hume

T   *Treatise of Human Nature*, ed. S. Bigge and P. H. Nidditch; references are given by book, part and, section

E   *Enquiry Concerning Human Understanding*, by the same editors; references are given by page numbers

W   *Hume on Religion*, ed. R. Wollheim (London: Collins, 1963)

Smith and Reid

I   Thomas Reid, *Inquiry and Essays*, ed. R. E. Beanblossom and K. Lehrer

TMS   Adam Smith, *Theory of Moral Sentiments* (Oxford: Oxford University Press, 1976), cited by page

The Enlightenment

PD   Voltaire, *Philosophical Dictionary*, ed T. Besterman (Harmondsworth: Penguin, 1971), cited by page

EL   Montesquieu, *Esprit des lois*, ed. G. Truc (Paris: Payot, 1945)

Rousseau

SC   References to the *Social Contract* are by chapter and paragraph

Kant

A   Reference by page number to the first edition of the *Critique of Pure Reason*

B   Reference by page number to the second edition of the *Critique of Pure Reason*

G   *Groundwork of the Metaphysics of Morals*, cited by page of the Akademie edition

M   *Critique of Judgement*, ed. J. H. Meredith (Oxford: Oxford University Press, 1978)

Hegel

LHP	*Lectures on the History of Philosophy*, trs. E. S. Haldane and F. H. Simpson, 1966
PG	*The Phenomenology of Spirit*, trs. A. V. Miller, cited by page
PR	*Philosophy of Right*, trs. H. B. Nisbet, ed. A. Wood (Cambridge: Cambridge University Press, 1991), cited by page

Part Four

Works cited are quoted by page number unless otherwise specified.

Anscombe

ERP	*Ethics, Religion and Politics* (Oxford: Blackwell, 1981)

Ayer

LTL	*Language, Truth and Logic*, 2nd edn. (London: Gollancz, 1949)

Bentham

B	*The Works of Jeremy Bentham*, ed. John Bowring, 10 vols. (New York: Russell & Russell, 1962)
P	*Introduction to the Principles of Morals and Legislation*, ed. J. H. Burns and H. L. A. Hart (London: Athlone, 1982); cited by chapter, section, and/or subsection

Brentano

PES	*Psychology from an Empirical Standpoint*, ed. Oskar Kraus, 2 vols. (Hamburg: Meiner, 1955)

Collingwood

PA	*Principles of Art* (Oxford: Clarendon Press, 1938)

Darwin

OS	*On the Origin of Species*, Oxford World's Classics (Oxford: Oxford University Press, 1996)

Davidson

EA	*Essays on Actions and Events* (Oxford: Oxford University Press, 1980)
ITI	*Inquiries into Truth and Interpretation* (Oxford: Oxford University Press, 1984)

Derrida

Diff.	*Writing and Difference*, trans. Alan Bass (London: Routledge & Kegan Paul, 1978)
G	*Of Grammatology*, trans. G. C. Spivak (Baltimore, Md.: Johns Hopkins University Press, 1976)
P	*Positions*, trans. A. Bass (Chicago: Chicago University Press, 1981)
SP	*Speech and Phenomena* (Evanston, Ill.: Northwestern University Press, 1973)

Engels

See under Marx.

Feuerbach

EC	*The Essence of Christianity*, trans. G. Eliot (New York: Harper, 1957)
W	*Sämtliche Werke*, 12 vols. (Stuttgart: Bolin, 1959–60)

Frege

BLA	*The Basic Laws of Arithmetic: Exposition of the System*, trans. Montgomery Furth (Berkeley: University of California Press, 1964)
CN	*Conceptual Notation and Related Articles*, trans. T. W. Bynum (Oxford: Oxford University Press, 1972)
CP	*Collected Papers on Mathematics, Logic and Philosophy*, ed. B. McGuinness (Oxford: Blackwell, 1984)
FA	*The Foundations of Arithmetic*, trans. J. L. Austin (Oxford: Oxford University Press, 1950, 1980)
PW	*Posthumous Writings* (Oxford: Blackwell, 1979)

Freud

EI	*The Ego and the Id* (London: Hogarth Press, 1962)
FI	*The Future of an Illusion* (Garden City, NY: Doubleday, 1964)
NIL	*New Introductory Lectures on Psychoanalysis* (London: Hogarth Press, 1949)
SE	*The Standard Edition of the Complete Psychological Works of Sigmund Freud*, 24 vols. (London: Hogarth Press, 1981)

Husserl

CCH	Barry Smith and David Woodruff Smith (eds.), *The Cambridge Companion to Husserl* (Cambridge: Cambridge University Press, 1995)
CM	*Cartesian Meditations* (Dordrecht: Kluwer, 1988)
Ideas	*Ideas Pertaining to a Pure Phenomenology*, 3 vols. (Dordrecht: Kluwer, 1980, 1982, 1989)
LI	*Logical Investigations*, ed. J. N. Findlay, 2 vols. (London: Routledge, 2001)

James

T	*The Meaning of Truth* (New York: Prometheus Books, 1997)
VRE	*Varieties of Religious Experience* (London: Fontana, 1960)

Kant

M	*Critique of Judgement*, ed. J. C. Meredith (Oxford: Oxford University Press, 1978)

Kierkegaard

E/O	*Either/Or*, trans. A. Hannay (Harmondsworth: Penguin, 1992)
FT	*Fear and Trembling*, trans. A. Hannay (Harmondsworth: Penguin, 1985)
P	*Papers and Journals: A Selection*, trans. A. Hannay (Harmondsworth: Penguin, 1996)
SD	*Sickness unto Death*, trans. A. Hannay (Harmondsworth: Penguin, 1989)

Marx

C	*Capital*, ed. D. McLellan, Oxford World's Classics (Oxford: Oxford University Press, 1995)
CM	Karl Marx and Friedrich Engels, *The Communist Manifesto*, ed. D. McLellan, Oxford World's Classics (Oxford: Oxford University Press, 1992)
CPE	*Critique of Political Economy* (Moscow: Progress, 1971)
EW	*Early Writings* (Harmondsworth: Penguin, 1975)
GI	*The German Ideology*, ed. C. J. Allen (London: Lawrence & Wishart, 1920, 2004)
TF	*Theses on Feuerbach* (New York: Prometheus Books, 1998)
VPP	*Value, Price and Profit*, ed. E. M. Aveling (New York: International Publishers, 1935)

Mill

3E	*Three Essays* (London: Longman, 1887)
A	*Autobiography*, ed. J. Stillinger (Oxford: Oxford University Press, 1969)
CCM	*The Cambridge Companion to Mill*, ed. J. Skorupski (Cambridge: Cambridge University Press, 1998)
CW	*The Collected Works of John Stuart Mill*, ed. John M. Robson, 33 vols. (Toronto: University of Toronto Press, 1963–91)
L	*On Liberty and Other Essays*, Oxford World's Classics (Oxford: Oxford University Press, 1991)
SL	*A System of Logic*; many editions; cited by book and section number
U	*Utilitarianism*, ed. M. Warnock (London: Collins, 1962)

Newman

GA	*The Grammar of Assent*, ed. I. Ker (Oxford: Oxford University Press, 1985)
US	*University Sermons* (London: Rivington, 1844)

Nietzsche

BGE	*Beyond Good and Evil*, trans. M. Faber, Oxford World's Classics (Oxford: Oxford University Press, 1998)
BT	*The Birth of Tragedy*, trans. S. Whiteside (Harmondsworth: Penguin, 1993, 2003)
GM	*The Genealogy of Morals*, trans. D. Smith, Oxford World's Classics (Oxford: Oxford University Press, 1996)
TI	*Twilight of the Idols*, trans. D. Langan, Oxford World's Classics (Oxford: Oxford University Press, 1998)
WP	*The Will to Power* (New York: Vintage, 1968)
Z	*Thus Spoke Zarathustra* (Harmondsworth: Penguin, 1961)

Peirce

CP	*Collected Papers of Charles Sanders Peirce*, 8 vols. (Cambridge, Mass.: Harvard University Press, 1931–58)
EWP	*The Essential Writings of Charles Peirce*, ed. E. C. Moore (New York: Prometheus Books, 1998)
P	*Pragmatism* (New York: Prometheus Books, 1997)

Popper

OSE	*The Open Society and its Enemies*, 2 vols. (London, 1945)

Quine

FLPV	*From a Logical Point of View* (Cambridge, Mass.: Harvard University Press, 1953)
WO	*Word and Object* (Cambridge, Mass.: MIT Press, 1960)

Rawls

TJ	*A Theory of Justice* (Cambridge, Mass.: Harvard University Press, 1971)

Russell

A	*The Autobiography of Bertrand Russell, 1872–1916* (London: Allen & Unwin, 1967)
AM	*The Analysis of Mind* (London: Allen & Unwin, 1921)
IMP	*Introduction to Mathematical Philosophy* (London: Allen & Unwin, 1917)
PM	*The Principles of Mathematics* (Cambridge: Cambridge University Press, 1903; 2nd edn., 1927)
PP	*The Problems of Philosophy* (London: Oxford University Press, 1912)

Ryle

CM	*The Concept of Mind* (London: Hutchinson, 1949)
CP	*Collected Papers*, 2 vols. (London: Hutchinson, 1949)

Sartre

BN	*Being and Nothingness*, trans. Hazel Barnes (London: Routledge, 1969)
EH	*Existentialism and Humanism* (London: Methuen, 1947)

Schopenhauer

EA	*Essays and Aphorisms*, trans. R. J. Hollingdale (London: Penguin, 2004)
WWI	*The World as Will and Representation*, trans. E. F. Payne, 2 vols. (New York: Dover, 1969); all quotations are from volume I.

Sidgwick

ME	*Methods of Ethics* (London: Macmillan, 1901)

Strawson

I	*Individuals* (London: Methuen, 1959)

Tolstoy

WA	*What is Art?* (Oxford: Oxford University Press, 1966)

Wittgenstein

BB	*The Blue and Brown Books* (Oxford: Blackwell, 1958)
CV	*Culture and Value* (Oxford: Blackwell, 1980)
NB	*Notebooks 1914–1916* (Oxford: Blackwell, 1961)
OC	*On Certainty* (Oxford: Blackwell, 1969)
PG	*Philosophical Grammar*, trans. A. Kenny (Oxford: Blackwell, 1974)
PI	*Philosophical Investigations*, trans. G. E. M. Anscombe (Oxford: Blackwell, 1953, 1997); part I cited by paragraph, part II by page
TLP	*Tractatus Logico-Philosophicus* (London: Routledge, 1921, 1961); cited by paragraph
Z	*Zettel* (Oxford: Blackwell, 1967)

BIBLIOGRAPHY

Part One

This bibliography does not contain all the works cited in footnotes, nor all the works referred to in the course of writing the text. It is a selection of works that I believe readers will find particularly helpful in pursuing their interests in ancient philosophers and in the philosophical topics they discussed. The selection is limited mainly to works in English of an accessible kind; many such works themselves contain much fuller bibliographies.

General Works

BRUNSCHWIG, J., and LLOYD, G. E. R., *Greek Thought: A Guide to Classical Knowledge* (Cambridge, Mass.: Harvard University Press, 2000).

FREDE, M., *Essays in Ancient Philosophy* (Oxford: Clarendon Press, 1987).

GOTTLIEB, A., *The Dream of Reason: A History of Western Philosophy from the Greeks to the Renaissance* (London: Allen Lane, 2000).

IRWIN, T., *Classical Philosophy*, Oxford Readers (Oxford: Oxford University Press, 1999).

OWEN, G. E. L., *Logic, Science, and Dialectic: Collected Papers in Greek Philosophy*, ed. M. Nussbaum (London: Duckworth, 1986).

Routledge History of Philosophy, i: *From the Beginning to Plato*, ed. C. C. W. Taylor; ii: *From Aristotle to Augustine*, ed. D. Furley (London: Routledge, 1997, 1999).

Presocratic Philosophers (Chapter 1)

The standard collection of the original texts of the surviving fragments of the philosophers prior to Socrates is that of H. Diels and W. Kranz, *Die Fragmente der Vorsokratiker*, 6th edn., 3 vols. (Berlin: Wiedmann, 1951). Our main source for the biographies of the Presocratics, and many other ancient philosophers, is the *Lives of the Philosophers* by Diogenes Laertius, trans. R. D. Hicks, Loeb Classical Library, 2 vols. (Cambridge, Mass.: Harvard University Press, 1972).

There is a helpful, though less complete, collection which contains English translations in addition to the original texts: G. S. Kirk, J. E. Raven, and M. Schofield (eds.), *The Presocratic Philosophers*, 2nd edn. (Cambridge: Cambridge University Press, 1983).

An excellent collection of texts in translation alone is J. Barnes, *Early Greek Philosophy* (Harmondsworth: Penguin, 1987). A more recent translation is R. Waterfield, *The First Philosophers: The Presocratics and the Sophists*, World's Classics (Oxford: Oxford University Press, 2000).

BARNES, J., *The Presocratic Philosophers*, rev. edn. (London: Routledge, 1982).

CORNFORD, F. M., *Plato and Parmenides* (London: Kegan Paul, 1939).

DE ROMILLY, JACQUELINE, *The Great Sophists in Periclean Athens* (Oxford: Clarendon Press, 1992).

DODDS, E. R. (ed.), *Plato: Gorgias*, text with introd. and comm. (Oxford: Clarendon Press, 1959).

GUTHRIE, W. K. C., *A History of Greek Philosophy*, vols. i–iii (Cambridge: Cambridge University Press, 1962–9).

INWOOD, B., *The Poem of Empedocles* (Toronto: University of Toronto Press, 1992).

KAHN, C. H., *The Verb 'Be' in Ancient Greek* (Dordrecht: Reidel, 1973).

—— *The Art and Thought of Heraclitus* (Cambridge: Cambridge University Press, 1979).

—— *Anaximander and the Origins of Greek Cosmology*, repr. of 1960 edn. (Indianapolis: Hackett, 1994).

KERFERD, G. B., *The Sophistic Movement* (Cambridge: Cambridge University Press, 1981).

MOURELATOS, A. P. D., *The Route of Parmenides* (New Haven: Yale University Press, 1970).

O'BRIEN, D., *Empedocles' Cosmic Cycle* (Cambridge: Cambridge University Press, 1969).

OSBORNE, C., *Rethinking Early Greek Philosophy: Hippolytus and the Pre-Socratics* (London: Duckworth, 1987).

SCHOFIELD, M., *An Essay on Anaxagoras* (Cambridge: Cambridge University Press, 1980).

TAYLOR, C. C. W. (ed.), *Plato: Protagoras*, trans. with notes, rev. edn. (Oxford: Clarendon Press, 1991).

Socrates and Plato (Chapter 1)

All the works of Plato in the original Greek are contained in five volumes of the series of Oxford Classical Texts (Oxford University Press) and, with an English translation on facing pages, in twelve volumes of the Loeb Classical Library (Harvard University Press). There is a convenient English single-volume edition of Plato's complete works edited by J. M. Cooper and D. S. Hutchinson (Indianapolis: Hackett, 1997).

The Clarendon Plato series (Oxford: Clarendon Press, 1973–) contains translations with notes of the major Platonic dialogues, notably *Theaetetus* (ed. J. McDowell, 1973), *Philebus* (ed. J. C. B. Gosling, 1975), and *Phaedo* (ed. D. Gallop, 1975). Many dialogues are translated in volumes of the Penguin Classics and of the Oxford World's Classics series.

The Socratic works of Xenophon appear in two volumes of the Loeb Classical Library: *Memorabilia* (trans. E. C. Marchant, London, 1923) and *Symposium and Apology* (trans. O. J. Todd, London, 1961). A good English translation is Xenophon, *Conversations of Socrates*, ed. H. Tredennick and R. Waterfield (Harmondsworth: Penguin, 1990).

ADAM, J. (ed.), *The Republic of Plato*, 2 vols. (Cambridge: Cambridge University Press, 1902).

ALLEN, R. E., *Plato's Euthyphro and the Earlier Theory of Forms* (London: Routledge & Kegan Paul, 1970).

—— (ed.), *Studies in Plato's Metaphysics* (London: Routledge & Kegan Paul, 1965).

ANNAS, J., *An Introduction to Plato's Republic* (Oxford: Oxford University Press, 1981).

BLONDELL, R., *The Play of Character in Plato's Dialogues* (Cambridge: Cambridge University Press, 2002).

BRANDWOOD, L., *The Chronology of Plato's Dialogues* (Cambridge: Cambridge University Press, 1990).

BRICKHOUSE, T. C., and SMITH, N. D., *Socrates on Trial* (Oxford: Oxford University Press, 1989).

—— —— *Plato's Socrates* (New York: Oxford University Press, 1994).

DOVER, K. (ed.), *Plato: Symposium* (Cambridge: Cambridge University Press, 1980).

GOSLING, J. C. B., *Plato* (London: Routledge & Kegan Paul, 1973).

HACKFORTH, R., *Plato's Examination of Pleasure* (Cambridge: Cambridge University Press, 1945).

IRWIN, T., *Plato's Moral Theory: The Early and Middle Dialogues* (Oxford: Clarendon Press, 1977).

KAHN, C. H., *Plato and the Socratic Dialogue* (Cambridge: Cambridge University Press, 1996).

KRAUT, R. (ed.), *The Cambridge Companion to Plato* (Cambridge: Cambridge University Press, 1992).

LEDGER, G., *Re-counting Plato: A Computer Analysis of Plato's Style* (Oxford: Clarendon Press, 1989).

MEINWALD, C. C., *Plato's Parmenides* (New York: Oxford University Press, 1991).

MORROW, GLENN R., *Plato's Epistles*, a trans. with critical essays and notes, 2nd edn. (Indianapolis: Bobbs-Merrill, 1962).

ROBINSON, R., *Plato's Earlier Dialectic* (Oxford: Clarendon Press, 1953).

ROWE, C. J. (ed.), *Plato: Phaedrus* (Warminster: Aris & Phillips, 1986).

RYLE, G., *Plato's Progress* (Cambridge: Cambridge University Press, 1966).

SAUNDERS, T. J., *Plato's Penal Code* (Oxford: Clarendon Press, 1991).

SAYRE, KENNETH M, *Plato's Late Ontology: A Riddle Resolved* (Princeton: Princeton University Press, 1983).

STONE, I. F., *The Trial of Socrates* (Boston: Little, Brown, 1988).

TAYLOR, C. C. W., *Socrates: A Very Short Introduction* (Oxford: Oxford University Press, 1998).

VLASTOS, G., *Platonic Studies*, 2nd edn. (Princeton: Princeton University Press, 1981).

—— *Socrates, Ironist and Moral Philosopher* (Cambridge: Cambridge University Press, 1991).

WHITE, N. I., *A Companion to Plato's Republic* (Indianapolis: Hackett, 1979).

Aristotle (Chapter 2)

Most of Aristotle's works appear in the original in volumes of the Oxford Classical Texts series, and many of them appear with a translation in volumes of the Loeb Classical Library. All of the surviving works are to be found in English in the two-volume Oxford Translation, edited by J. Barnes (Princeton: Princeton University Press, 1984).

The Clarendon Aristotle series (Oxford: Clarendon Press, 1963–) contains translations of selected Aristotelian texts, with detailed philosophical notes. The series includes *Categories and de Interpretatione* (ed. J. L. Ackrill, 1963), *de Anima II and III* (ed. D. W. Hamlyn, 1968), *de Generatione et Corruptione* (ed. C. J. F. Williams, 1971), *de Partibus Animalium* (ed. D. M. Balme, 1972), *Eudemian Ethics I, II, VIII* (ed. M. Woods), *Metaphysics Γ, Δ and E* (ed. C. Kirwan, 1971, 1993), *Metaphysics Z and H* (ed. D. Bostock, 1994), *Metaphysics M and N* (ed. J. Annas, 1976), *Physics I and II* (ed. W. Charlton, 1970), *Physics III and IV* (ed. E. Hussey, 1983), *Posterior Analytics* (ed. J. Barnes, 1975, 1993), *Topics 1 and 8* (ed. R. Smith, 1994).

Many of Aristotle's works are available in translation in Penguin Classics or in Oxford World's Classics.

ACKRILL, J. L., *Aristotle the Philosopher* (Oxford: Oxford University Press, 1981).

ANSCOMBE, G. E. M., and GEACH, P. T., *Three Philosophers* (Oxford: Blackwell, 1961).

BAMBROUGH, R. (ed.), *New Essays on Plato and Aristotle* (London: Routledge & Kegan Paul, 1965).

BARNES, J. (ed.), *The Cambridge Companion to Aristotle* (Cambridge: Cambridge University Press, 1995).

—— *Aristotle: A Very Short Introduction* (Oxford: Oxford University Press, 2000).

—— SCHOFIELD, M., and SORABJI, R. (eds.), *Articles on Aristotle*, i: *Science*; ii: *Ethics and Politics*; iii: *Metaphysics*; iv: *Psychology and Aesthetics* (London: Duckworth, 1975).

BROADIE, S., and ROWE, C., *Aristotle: Nicomachean Ethics*, trans., introd., and comm. (Oxford: Oxford University Press, 2002).

IRWIN, T. H., *Aristotle's First Principles* (Oxford: Oxford University Press, 1988).

JAEGER, W., *Aristotle: Fundamentals of the History of his Development*, trans. R. Robinson, 2nd edn. (Oxford: Clarendon Press, 1948).

KENNY, A., *The Aristotelian Ethics* (Oxford: Clarendon Press, 1978).

—— *Aristotle on the Perfect Life* (Oxford: Clarendon Press, 1992).

KRAUT, R., *Aristotle: Political Philosophy* (Oxford: Oxford University Press, 2002).

LEAR, J., *Aristotle and Logical Theory* (Cambridge: Cambridge University Press, 1980).

LLOYD, G. E. R., *Aristotle: The Growth and Structure of his Thought* (Cambridge: Cambridge University Press, 1968).

MEIKLE, S., *Aristotle's Economic Thought* (Oxford: Clarendon Press, 1995).

ROSS, W. D., *Aristotle's Metaphysics* (Oxford: Clarendon Press, 1924).

—— *Aristotle's Physics* (Oxford: Clarendon Press, 1936).

SORABJI, R., *Time, Creation and the Continuum* (London: Duckworth, 1983).

SORABJI, R., *Matter, Place and Motion: Theories in Antiquity and their Sequel* (London: Duckworth, 1988).

WATERLOW, S., *Passage and Possibility: A Study of Aristotle's Modal Concepts* (Oxford: Clarendon Press, 1982).

Hellenistic Philosophy (Chapter 2)

Much of our information about these philosophers derives from later writers such as Cicero, Lucretius, and Sextus Empiricus, whose works have been published as Oxford Classical Texts or in the Loeb Classical Library.

The most helpful collection of the extant fragments and of references in ancient authors is *The Hellenistic Philosophers* by A. A. Long and D. N. Sedley, 2 vols. (Cambridge: Cambridge University Press, 1987). One volume of this work gives translations of the principal sources, and another gives an annotated edition of the Greek and Latin texts.

The classic edition of surviving Stoic texts was for long J. von Arnim, *Stoicorum Veterum Fragmenta*, 3 vols. (Leipzig, 1903–5) (*SVF*). It has been superseded by K. Hulser, *Die Fragmente zur Dialektik der Stoiker* (Stuttgart: Frommann-Holzboog, 1987). For Epicureanism the fundamental collection is H. Usener, *Epicurea* (Leipzig, 1887).

ALGRA, K., BARNES, J., MANSFELD, J., and SCHOFIELD, M., *The Cambridge History of Hellenistic Philosophy* (Cambridge: Cambridge University Press, 1999).

ANNAS, J. E., and BARNES, J., *The Modes of Scepticism: Ancient Texts and Modern Interpretations* (Cambridge: Cambridge University Press, 1985).

ASMIS, E., *Epicurus' Scientific Method* (Ithaca, NY: Cornell University Press, 1984).

BARNES, J., BRUNSCHWIG, J., BURNYEAT, M., and SCHOFIELD, M., *Science and Speculation: Studies in Hellenistic Theory and Practice* (Cambridge: Cambridge University Press, 1982).

BURNYEAT, M., *The Sceptical Tradition* (Berkeley: University of California Press, 1983).

FURLEY, D. J., *Two Studies in the Greek Atomists* (Princeton: Princeton University Press, 1967).

LONG, A. A., *Hellenistic Philosophy*, 2nd edn. (Berkeley: University of California Press, 1986).

RIST, J. M., *Stoic Philosophy* (Cambridge: Cambridge University Press, 1969).

—— *Epicurus: An Introduction* (Cambridge: Cambridge University Press, 1972).

SHARPLES, R. W., *Stoics, Epicureans and Sceptics* (London: Routledge, 1994).

Roman and Imperial Philosophy

The works of Epictetus, Marcus Aurelius, and Plotinus have appeared in the Loeb Classical Library, and those of Plotinus as an Oxford Classical Text edited by P. Henry and H.-R. Schyzer, which has become the standard edition (Oxford: Oxford University Press, 1964–82).

O'DONNELL, J. J., *Augustine: Confessions*, 3 vols. (Oxford: Clarendon Press, 1992).

There are many translations of *Confessions*, notably H. Chadwick in the World's Classics series (Oxford: Oxford University Press, 1991).

ARMSTRONG, A. H. (ed.), *The Cambridge History of Later Greek and Early Medieval Philosophy* (Cambridge: Cambridge University Press, 1970).

BAILEY, C., *Titi Lucreti Cari de Rerum Natura Libri Sex*, 3 vols. (Oxford: Oxford University Press, 1947).

BARNES, J., and GRIFFIN, M., *Philosophia Togata*, vols. i and ii (Oxford: Clarendon Press, 1989, 1997).

CLARK, G., and RAJAK, T., *Philosophy and Power in the Graeco-Roman World* (Oxford: Oxford University Press, 2002).

DILLON, J., *The Middle Platonists* (Ithaca: Cornell University Press, 1977).

DODDS, E. R., *Proclus: The Elements of Theology*, ed., trans., and comm., 2nd edn. (Oxford: Clarendon Press, 1992).

GRIFFIN, M. T., *Seneca, a Philosopher in Politics* (Oxford: Oxford University Press, 1976).

LLOYD, A. C., *The Antomy of NeoPlatonism* (Oxford: Clarendon Press, 1990).

O'BRIEN, D., *Plotinus on the Origin of Matter* (Naples: Bibliopolis, 1991).

O'MEARA, D. J., *Plotinus: An Introduction to the Enneads* (Oxford: Clarendon Press, 1993).

RIST, J., *Plotinus: The Road to Reality* (Cambridge, Cambridge University Press, 1967).

SEDLEY, D., *Lucretius and the Transformation of Greek Wisdom* (Cambridge: Cambridge University Press, 1998).

STUMP, E., and KRETZMANN, N., *The Cambridge Companion to Augustine* (Cambridge: Cambridge University Press, 2001).

Logic (Chapter 3)

KNEALE, W. C., and KNEALE, M., *The Development of Logic* (Oxford: Clarendon Press, 1962).

ŁUKASIEWICZ, J., *Aristotle's Syllogistic from the Standpoint of Modern Formal Logic*, 2nd edn. (Oxford: Clarendon Press, 1957).

MATES, B., *Stoic Logic*, 2nd edn. (Berkeley: University of California Press, 1961).

NUCHELMANS, G., *Theories of the Proposition* (Amsterdam: North-Holland, 1973).

PATZIG, *Aristotle's Theory of the Syllogism* (Dordrecht: Reidel, 1968).

PRIOR, A. N., *Time and Modality* (Oxford: Clarendon Press, 1957).

Epistemology (Chapter 4)

BOSTOCK, D., *Plato's Theaetetus* (Oxford: Clarendon Press, 1988).

HANKINSON, R. J., *The Sceptics* (London: Routledge, 1994).

McKIRAHAN, R. D., *Principles and Proofs: Aristotle's Theory of Demonstrative Science* (Princeton: Princeton University Press, 1992).

SCHOFIELD, M., BURNYEAT, M., and BARNES, J., *Doubt and Dogmatism: Studies in Hellenistic Epistemology* (Oxford: Clarendon Press, 1980).

WHITE, N. P., *Plato on Knowledge and Reality* (Indianapolis: Hackett, 1976).

Philosophy of Physics (Chapter 5)

BOBZIEN, S., *Determinism and Freedom in Stoic Philosophy* (Oxford: Clarendon Press, 1998).

HANKINSON, R. J., *Cause and Explanation in Ancient Greek Thought* (Oxford: Clarendon Press, 1998).

HOENEN, P., *Cosmologia* (Rome: Pontifical Gregorian University, 1949).

SORABJI, R., *Necessity, Cause, and Blame* (London: Duckworth, 1980).

—— *Time, Creation and the Continuum* (London: Duckworth, 1983).

WATERLOW, S., *Nature, Change, and Agency in Aristotle's Physics* (Oxford: Clarendon Press, 1982).

Metaphysics (Chapter 6)

BARNES, J., and MIGNUCCI, M. (eds.), *Matter and Metaphysics* (Naples: Bibliopolis, 1988).

FINE, GAIL, *On Ideas: Aristotle's Cricitism of Plato's Theory of Forms* (Oxford: Clarendon Press, 1993).

GRAHAM, D. W., *Aristotle's Two Systems* (Oxford: Oxford University Press, 1987).

MALCOLM, J., *Plato on the Self-Predication of Forms* (Oxford: Clarendon Press, 1991).

SCALTSAS, T., *Substances and Universals in Aristotle's Metaphysics* (Ithaca: Cornell University Press, 1994).

Philosophy of Mind (Chapter 7)

ANNAS, J. E., *Hellenistic Philosophy of Mind* (Berkeley: University of California Press, 1992).

BRUNSCHWIG, J., and NUSSBAUM, M. (eds.), *Passions and Perceptions: Studies in Hellenistic Philosophy of Mind* (Cambridge: Cambridge University Press, 1993).

HICKS, R. D. (ed.), *Aristotle: De Anima*, with trans., introd., and comm. (Cambridge: Cambridge University Press, 1907).

NUSSBAUM, M. C. (ed.), *Aristotle: De Motu Animalium*, with trans., introd., and essays (Princeton: Princeton University Press, 1978).

—— and RORTY, A. O. (eds.), *Essays on Aristotle's Philosophy of Mind* (Oxford: Oxford University Press, 1992).

Ethics (Chapter 8)

ANNAS, J., *Platonic Ethics Old and New* (Ithaca: Cornell University Press, 1999).

BROADIE, S., *Ethics with Aristotle* (New York: Oxford University Press, 1991).

GOSLING, J. C. B., and TAYLOR, C. C. W., *The Greeks on Pleasure* (Oxford: Clarendon Press, 1982).

INWOOD, B., *Ethics and Human Action in Early Stoicism* (Oxford: Clarendon Press, 1985).

NUSSBAUM, M. C., *The Fragility of Goodness* (Cambridge: Cambridge University Press, 1986).

PRICE, A., *Love and Friendship in Plato and Aristotle* (Oxford: Clarendon Press, 1989).

SCHOFIELD, M., and STRIKER, G., *The Norms of Nature: Studies in Hellenistic Ethics* (Cambridge: Cambridge University Press, 1986).

Philosophy of Religion (Chapter 9)

FESTUGIERE, A. J., *Epicurus and his Gods* (Oxford: Blackwell, 1955).

KENNY, A., *The Five Ways* (London: Routledge, 1969).

KRETZMANN, NORMAN, *The Metaphysics of Theism* (Oxford: Oxford University Press, 1999).

Part Two

General

ARMSTRONG, A. H. (ed.), *The Cambridge History of Later Greek and Early Medieval Philosophy* (Cambridge: Cambridge University Press, 1967).

CATTO, J. I., *The History of the University of Oxford*, i: *The Early Oxford Schools* (Oxford: Oxford University Press, 1984).

—— and EVANS, T. A. R., *The History of the University of Oxford*, ii: *Late Medieval Oxford* (Oxford: Oxford University Press, 1992).

COPLESTON, F. C., *A History of Philosophy*, 9 vols. (London: Burnes Oates, 1947–75).

CRAIG, WILLIAM LANE, *The Problem of Divine Foreknowledge and Future Contingents from Aristotle to Suarez* (Leiden: E. J. Brill, 1988).

DENZINGER, H. (ed.), *Enchiridion Symbolorum*, 33rd edn. (Barcelona: Herder, 1950); trans. as *The Sources of Catholic Dogma* by R. J. DeFerrari (Fitzwilliam, NY: Loreto Publications, 1955). [Texts of official Church documents.]

GEACH, P. T., *Reference and Generality: An Examination of Some Medieval and Modern Theories* (Ithaca, NY: Cornell University Press, 1980).

GRACIA, J., and NOONE, T., *A Companion to Philosophy in the Middle Ages* (Oxford: Blackwell, 2003).

GRANT, E., *God and Reason in the Middle Ages* (Cambridge: Cambridge University Press, 2001).

HUGHES, PHILIP, *A History of the Church*, iii: *Aquinas to Luther* (London: Sheed & Ward, 1947).

HYMAN, A., and WALSH, J. J., *Philosophy in the Middle Ages*, 2nd edn. (Indianapolis: Hackett, 1973).

KENNY, A., *A Brief History of Western Philosophy* (Oxford: Blackwell, 1998).

—— (ed.), *The Oxford Illustrated History of Western Philosophy* (Oxford: Oxford University Press, 1994).

KNEALE, W., and KNEALE, M., *The Development of Logic* (Oxford: Oxford University Press, 1962).

KNUUTILA, S., *Modalities in Medieval Philosophy* (London: Routledge, 1993).

KRETZMANN, N., KENNY, A., and PINBORG, J., *The Cambridge History of Later Medieval Philosophy* (Cambridge: Cambridge University Press, 1982).

KRETZMANN, N., KENNY, A., STUMP, E., *et al.*, *The Cambridge Translations of Medieval Philosophical Texts*, i: *Logic and the Philosophy of Language*; ii: *Ethics and Political Philosophy*; iii: *Mind and Knowledge* (Cambridge: Cambridge University Press, 1998–).

LEFTOW, B., *Time and Eternity* (Ithaca, NY: Cornell University Press, 1991).

McGRADE, A. S., *The Cambridge Companion to Medieval Philosophy* (Cambridge: Cambridge University Press, 2003).

MARENBON, JOHN, *Later Medieval Philosophy* (London: Routledge & Kegan Paul, 1987).

——— *Early Medieval Philosophy*, rev. edn. (London: Routledge & Kegan Paul, 1988).

——— (ed.), *Aristotle in Britain during the Middle Ages* (Turnhout: Brepols, 1996).

——— (ed.), *Routledge History of Philosophy*, iii: *Medieval Philosophy* (London: Routledge, 1998).

PASNAU, ROBERT, *Theories of Cognition in the Later Middle Ages* (New York: Cambridge University Press, 1997).

SCHMITT, C. B., and SKINNER, Q., *The Cambridge History of Renaissance Philosophy* (Cambridge: Cambridge University Press, 1988).

SORABJI, R., *Time, Creation and the Continuum* (London: Duckworth, 1983).

SPADE, P. V. (ed. and trans.), *Five Texts on the Medieval Problem of Universals: Porphyry, Boethius, Abelard, Duns Scotus, Ockham* (Indianapolis: Hackett, 1994).

Augustine

The City of God, trans. H. Bettenson (Harmondsworth: Penguin, 1972).

Confessions, trans. H. Chadwick (Oxford: Oxford University Press, 1991).

Confessions, text, trans., and comm. J. J. O'Donnell, 3 vols. (Oxford: Clarendon Press, 1992).

De Bono Conjugali, CSEL 41 (Vienna: Tempsky, 1900).

De Civitate Dei, CCSL 47–8 (Turnhout: Brepols, 1955).

De Dialectica, ed. Darrell Jackson (Dordrecht: Reidel, 1985).

De Libero Arbitrio, CCSL 29 (Turnhout: Brepols, 1970).

De Trinitate, CCSL 50 (Turnhout: Brepols, 1970).

Earlier Writings, trans. John H. S. Burleigh, Library of Christian Classics (Philadelphia: Westminster Press, 1953).

On the Free Choice of the Will, trans. T. Williams (Indianapolis: Hackett, 1993).

Soliloquies, text, trans., and comm. G. Watson (Warminster: Aris & Phillips, 1990).

Treatises on Marriage and Other Subjects, trans. Roy J. Deferrari (New York: Fathers of the Church, 1955).

The Trinity, trans. S. McKenna (Washington: CUA Press, 1963).

BROWN, P., *The Body and Society* (New York: Columbia University Press, 1988).

——— *Augustine of Hippo: A Biography*, rev. edn. (London: Faber & Faber, 2000).

DIHLE, A., *The Theory of the Will in Classical Antiquity* (Berkeley: University of California Press, 1982).

JORDAN, MARK D., *The Ethics of Sex* (Oxford: Blackwell, 2002).

KIRWAN, C., *Augustine* (London: Routledge, 1989).

MARKUS, R. A., 'Augustine', in A. H. Armstrong (ed.), *The Cambridge History of Later Greek and Early Medieval Philosophy* (Cambridge: Cambridge University Press, 1967).

MATTHEWS, G. B., *The Augustinian Tradition* (Berkeley: University of California Press, 1999).

MENN, STEPHEN, *Descartes and Augustine* (Cambridge: Cambridge University Press, 1998).

SORABJI, R., *Time, Creation and the Continuum* (London: Duckworth, 1983).

STUMP, E., and KRETZMANN, N., *The Cambridge Companion to Augustine* (Cambridge: Cambridge University Press, 2001).

WILLS, GARRY, *St Augustine* (London: Weidenfeld & Nicolson, 1999).

Boethius

Boethius: The Theological Tractates and The Consolation of Philosophy, text and trans. H. J. Stewart and E. K. Rand, rev. S. J. Tester, Loeb Classical Library (Cambridge, Mass.: Harvard University Press, 1973).

CHADWICK, H., *Boethius: The Consolations of Music, Logic, Theology & Philosophy* (Oxford: Clarendon Press, 1981).

MARENBON, J., *Boethius* (Oxford: Oxford University Press, 2003).

Late Greek Philosophy

PHILOPONUS, *Against Aristotle on the Eternity of the World*, trans. Christian Wildberg (London: Duckworth, 1987).

—— *On Aristotle on the Intellect*, trans. W. Charlton (London: Duckworth, 1991).

PROCLUS, *The Elements of Theology*, ed. and trans. E. R. Dodds (Oxford: Clarendon Press, 1992).

CHADWICK, H., *East and West: The Making of a Rift in the Church* (Oxford: Oxford University Press, 2003).

SORABJI, R. (ed.), *Philoponus and the Rejection of Aristotelian Science* (London: Duckworth, 1987).

Eriugena

De Praedestinatione Divina, CCCM 50 (Turnhout: Brepols, 1978).

Periphyseon (The Division of Nature), ed. E. Jeanneau, CCSL 161–5 (Turnhout: Brepols, 1996–2003).

Periphyseon (The Division of Nature), trans. I. P. Sheldon-Williams, rev. J. J. O'Meara (Dublin: Dublin Institute for Advanced Studies, 1968–95).

MORAN, D., *The Philosophy of John Scottus Eriugena* (Cambridge: Cambridge University Press, 1989).

O'MEARA, J. J., *Eriugena* (Oxford: Clarendon Press, 1988).

Islamic Philosophy

AVICENNA, *Metafisica*, trans. O. Lizzini (Milan: Bompiani, 2002).

AVICENNA LATINUS, *Liber de Anima*, ed. S. van Riet, 2 vols. (Louvain-la-Neuve: Institut Supérieur de Philosophie, 1977–83).

AVICENNA LATINUS, *Liber de Philosophia Prima*, ed. S. van Riet, 3 vols. (Louvain-la-Neuve: Institut Supérieur de Philosophie, 1977–83).

CRAIG, WILLIAM LANE, *The Kalam Cosmological Argument* (London: Macmillan, 1979).

DAVIDSON, H. A., *Alfarabi, Avicenna and Averroes on Intellect* (New York: Oxford University Press, 1992).

ESPOSITO, J. L., *Islam: The Straight Path* (New York: Oxford University Press, 1991).

NASR, S. H., and LEAMAN, O., *History of Islamic Philosophy*, 2 vols. (London: Routledge, 1996).

PETERS, F. E., *Aristotle and the Arabs* (New York: New York University Press, 1968).

Anselm

Anselm of Canterbury:The Major Works, ed. B. Davies and G. R. Evans, World's Classics (Oxford: Oxford University Press, 1998).

Opera Omnia, ed. F. S. Schmitt, 6 vols. (Edinburgh: Thomas Nelson, 1946–61).

Proslogion, text with trans. M. J. Charlesworth (Oxford: Oxford University Press, 1965).

BARNES, JONATHAN, *The Ontological Argument* (London: Macmillan, 1975).

PLANTINGA, A., *The Nature of Necessity* (Oxford: Oxford University Press, 1974).

SOUTHERN, R. W., *St Anselm and his Biographer* (Cambridge: Cambridge University Press, 1963).

——— *Anselm: A Portrait in a Landscape* (Cambridge: Cambridge University Press, 1990).

Averroes

Commentary on Plato's Republic, ed. E. Rosenthal (Cambridge: Cambridge University Press, 1956).

The Incoherence of the Incoherence, trans. and introd. S. van den Bergh, 2 vols. (London: Luzac, 1954).

Middle Commentaries on Aristotle's Categories and De Interpretatione, trans. C. Butterworth (Princeton: Princeton University Press, 1983).

On the Harmony of Religion and Philosophy, trans. and introd. G. Hourani (London: Luzac, 1961).

LEAMAN, O., *Averroes and his Philosophy* (Oxford: Clarendon Press, 1988).

Twelfth-Century Philosophy

DRONKE, P. (ed.), *A History of Twelfth Century Western Philosophy* (Cambridge: Cambridge University Press, 1988).

SOUTHERN, R. W., *Scholastic Humanism and the Unification of Europe* (Oxford: Blackwell, 2001).

Abelard

Dialectica, ed. L. M. de Rijk (Assen: van Gorcum, 1971).

Ethics (Scito te ipsum), ed. and trans. D. Luscombe (Oxford: Oxford University Press, 1971).

Logica, in *Peter Abelards philosophische Schriften*, Beitrage zur Geschichte der Philosophie des Mittelalters 15 (Munster: Aschendorff, 1919–31). [Contains *Logica Ingredientibus* and *Logica Nostrorum Petitioni*.]

MARENBON, J., *The Philosophy of Peter Abelard* (Cambridge: Cambridge University Press, 1997).

Maimonides

The Guide of the Perplexed, trans. S. Pines, 2 vols. (Chicago: Chicago University Press, 1963).

RUDAVSKY, T. (ed.), *Divine Omniscience and Omnipotence in Medieval Philosophy* (Dordrecht: Reidel, 1982).

Grosseteste and Albert

GROSSETESTE, ROBERT, *Hexaemeron*, ed. Richard Dales and Servus Gieben (London: British Academy, 1982).

Die philosophischen Werke des Robert Grosseteste, ed. L. Bauer, Beiträge zur Geschichte der Philosophie des Mittelalters 9 (Munster: Aschendorff, 1912).

McEVOY, JAMES, *The Philosophy of Robert Grosseteste* (Oxford: Oxford University Press, 1982).

WEISHEIPL, J. (ed.), *Albertus Magnus and the Sciences* (Toronto: Pontifical Institute of Medieval Studies, 1980).

Bonaventure

—— *The Journey of the Mind to God*, ed. S. Brown (Indianapolis: Hackett, 1993).

Opera Omnia, 10 vols. (Quarracchi: Collegium S. Bonaventurae, 1882–1902).

GILSON, E., *The Philosophy of St Bonaventure*, trans. I. Trethowan and F. J. Sheed (London: Sheed & Ward, 1965).

Thirteenth-Century Logic

PETER OF SPAIN, *Tractatus, called afterwards Summule Logicales*, ed. L. M. de Rijk (Assen: van Gorcum, 1972).

Aquinas

The Leonine edition (Rome, 1882–), which will include all of Aquinas' works, is incomplete and inconvenient to use. More convenient, and commonly derived from the Leonine text, are the Marietti editions of particular works, including the following:

In II Libros Perihermeneias Aristotelis Expositio, ed. R. M. Spiazzi (Turin: Marietti, 1966).

Quaestiones Disputatae I (De Veritate), ed. R. M. Spiazzi (Turin, 1955).

Quaestiones Disputatae II (De Potentia, De Malo), ed. R. Pession *et al.* (Turin, 1949).

Summa contra Gentiles, ed. C. Pera (Turin, 1961).

Summa contra Gentiles, trans. as *On the Truth of the Catholic Faith* by A. C. Pegis *et al.* (South Bend, Ind.: Notre Dame University Press, 1975).

Summa Theologiae, Blackfriars edn., 61 vols. (London: Eyre & Spottiswoode, 1964–80). [For English-language readers, this is the best edition, with Latin and English on facing pages.]

DAVIES, BRIAN, OP, *The Thought of Thomas Aquinas* (Oxford: Clarendon Press, 1992).

FINNIS, JOHN, *Aquinas: Moral, Political, and Legal Theory* (Oxford: Oxford University Press, 1998).

GEACH, PETER, 'Aquinas', in G. E. M. Anscombe and Peter Geach, *Three Philosophers* (Oxford: Blackwell, 1961).

KENNY, ANTHONY, *The Five Ways* (London: Routledge, 1969).

—— *The God of the Philosophers* (Oxford: Clarendon Press, 1979).

—— *Aquinas* (Oxford: Oxford University Press, 1980).

—— *Aquinas on Mind* (London: Routledge, 1993).

—— *Aquinas on Being* (Oxford: Oxford University Press, 2002).

—— (ed.), *Aquinas: A Collection of Critical Essays* (London: Macmillan, 1969).

KRETZMANN, NORMAN, *The Metaphysics of Theism* (Oxford: Clarendon Press, 1997).

—— *The Metaphysics of Creation* (Oxford: Clarendon Press, 1999).

LONERGAN, BERNARD, *Verbum: Word and Idea in Aquinas* (Notre Dame, Ind.: University of Notre Dame Press, 1967).

PASNAU, R., *Thomas Aquinas on Human Nature* (Cambridge: Cambridge University Press, 2001).

STUMP, ELEONORE, *Aquinas* (London: Routledge, 2003).

TORRELL, JEAN-PIERRE, *Saint Thomas Aquinas: The Person and his Work* (Washington: Catholic University of America Press, 1996).

WEISHEIPL, JAMES A., *Friar Thomas d'Aquino* (Oxford: Blackwell, 1974).

Duns Scotus

De Primo Principio, ed. and trans. F. Roche (St Bonaventure, NY: Franciscan Institute, 1945).

God and Creatures: The Quodlibetical Questions (Princeton: Princeton University Press, 1975).

Opera Omnia, ed. C. Balic *et al.* (Vatican City, 1950   ), vols. i–iii: *Ordinatio* 1–2; vols. xvi–xx: *Lectura* 1–3.

Opus Oxoniense, ed. Luke Wadding, 12 vols. (Lyons: Durand, 1639).

Questions on the Metaphysics of Aristotle, trans. G. Etzkorn and A. Wolter, 2 vols. (St Bonaventure, NY: Franciscan Institute, 1997).

BOS, E. P. (ed.), *John Duns Scotus (1265/6–1308): Renewal of Philosophy* (Amsterdam: Rodopi, 1998).

BROADIE, A., *The Shadow of Scotus: Philosophy and Faith in Pre-Reformation Scotland* (Edinburgh: T. & T. Clark, 1995).

CROSS, RICHARD, *The Physics of Duns Scotus: The Scientific Context of a Theological Vision* (Oxford: Clarendon Press, 1998).
—— *Duns Scotus* (Oxford: Oxford University Press, 1999).
LANGSTON, DOUGLAS C., *God's Willing Knowledge: The Influence of Scotus' Analysis of Omniscience* (Philadelphia: University of Pennsylvania Press, 1986).
VOS JACZN, ANTONIE, et al., *John Duns Scotus: Contingency and Freedom* (Dordrecht: Kluwer, 1994).
WILLIAMS, T. (ed.), *The Cambridge Companion to Duns Scotus* (Cambridge: Cambridge University Press, 2003).
WOLTER, ALLAN B., *The Philosophical Theology of John Duns Scotus*, ed. M. M. Adams (Ithaca, NY: Cornell University Press, 1990).

Ockham

Opera Philosophica et Theologica, ed. Gedeon Gál et al., 17 vols. (St Bonaventure, NY: Franciscan Institute, 1985).
Opera Politica, ed. H. S. Offler et al., 4 vols. (vols. i–iii Manchester: Manchester University Press, 1956–74; vol. iv Oxford: Oxford University Press, 1997).
Philosophical Writings, trans. P. Boehner (Indianapolis: Hackett, 1990).
Quodlibetal Questions, trans. A. J. Freddoso and Francis E. Kelly, 2 vols. (New Haven: Yale University Press, 1991).
Tractatus de Praedestinatione et de Praescientia Dei, trans. Norman Kretzmann and Marilyn Adams (Chicago: Appleton-Century-Crofts, 1969).

ADAMS, MARILYN McCORD, *William Ockham*, 2 vols. (Notre Dame, Ind.: University of Notre Dame Press, 1987).
SPADE, P. V. (ed.), *The Cambridge Companion to Ockham* (Cambridge: Cambridge University Press, 1999).

Philosophy after Ockham

BURLEY, WALTER, *The Pure Art of Logic*, ed. Philotheus Boehner (St Bonaventure, NY: Franciscan Institute, 1955).
CAJETAN, THOMAS DE VIO, *Commentary on Being and Essence*, trans. L. H. Kendzierski and F. C. Wade (Milwaukee, Wis.: Marquette University Press, 1964).
KILVINGTON, RICHARD, *The Sophismata of Richard Kilvington*, introd., trans., and comm. Norman Kretzmann and Barbara Ensign Kretzmann (Cambridge: Cambridge University Press, 1990).
MARSILIUS OF PADUA, *The Defender of the Peace*, trans. A. Gewirth (Toronto: Pontifical Institute of Medieval Studies, 1980).
NICHOLAS OF CUSA, *Devotional Works*, ed. J. Doakes (Washington: Westminster Press, 1995).

CASSIRER, E., et al. (eds.), *The Renaissance Philosophy of Man* (Chicago: University of Chicago Press, 1959).

COURTENAY, WILLIAM J., *Schools and Scholars in Fourteenth Century England* (Princeton: Princeton University Press, 1987).

HUDSON, ANNE, and WILKS, MICHAEL, *From Ockham to Wyclif* (Oxford: Blackwell, 1987).

KENNY, ANTHONY, *Wyclif* (Oxford: Oxford University Press, 1985).

—— (ed.), *Wyclif in his Times* (Oxford: Oxford University Press, 1986).

KRETZMANN, NORMAN (ed.), *Infinity and Continuity in Ancient and Medieval Thought* (Ithaca, NY: Cornell University Press, 1982).

Part Three

General works

BENNETT, JONATHAN, *Locke, Berkeley, Hume: Central Themes* (Oxford: Oxford University Press, 1971).

COPLESTON, FREDERICK, *History of Philosophy*, 9 vols. (London: Burns Oates and Search Press, 1943–7).

COTTINGHAM, JOHN, *The Rationalists* (Oxford: Oxford University Press, 1988).

CRAIG, E. G., *The Mind of God and the Works of Man* (Oxford: Oxford University Press, 1987).

GARBER, DANIEL and AYERS, MICHAEL, *The Cambridge History of Seventeenth-Century Philosophy*, 2 vols. (Cambridge: Cambridge University Press, 1998).

GRIBBIN, JOHN, *Science, a History 1543–2001* (Harmondsworth: Penguin, 2002).

KENNY, ANTHONY, *The God of the Philosophers* (Oxford: Clarendon Press, 1979).

—— *The Metaphysics of Mind* (Oxford: Clarendon Press, 1989).

KNEALE, WILLIAM and KNEALE, MARTHA, *The Development of Logic* (Oxford: Clarendon Press, 1979).

POPKIN, R. H., *The History of Scepticism from Erasmus to Spinoza* (Leiden: Gorcum van Assen, 1979).

SCHMITT, CHARLES B., and SKINNER, QUENTIN, *The Cambridge History of Renaissance Philosophy* (Cambridge: Cambridge University Press, 1988).

WOOLHOUSE, R. S., *The Empiricists* (Oxford: Oxford University Press, 1988).

—— *Descartes, Spinoza, Leibniz: the Concept of Substance in Seventeenth-Century Metaphysics* (London: Routledge, 1993).

Sixteenth-Century Philosophy

COLEMAN, JANET, *A History of Political Thought from the Middle Ages to the Renaissance* (Oxford: Blackwell, 2000).

COPENHAVER, B. P. and SCHMITT, CHARLES B., *Renaissance Philosophy* (Oxford: Oxford University Press, 1992).

MCCONICA, JAMES, *Renaissance Thinkers* (Oxford: Oxford University Press, 1993).

MACHIAVELLI, NICCOLÒ, *Il Principe* (Milano: Mondadori, 1994).

MORE, THOMAS *Utopia*, ed. Edward Surtz (New Haven, Conn.: Yale University Press, 1964).

Descartes

The standard edition is that of Adam and Tannery, 12 volumes in the revised edition of Vrin/CRNS, Paris, 1964–76. The now standard English translation is that in 3 volumes published by Cambridge University Press in 1985 and 1991, the first two edited by J. Cottingham, R. Stoothoff, and D. Murdoch, and the third edited by the same and A. Kenny. A very convenient French edition is the single volume Pleiade text, ed. A. Bridoux (Paris: Gallimard, 1973). A lively English translation of selected texts is that by E. Anscombe and P. T. Geach, *Descartes, Philosophical Writings* (London: Nelson, 1969).

COTTTINGHAM, JOHN, *The Cambridge Companion to Descartes* (Cambridge: Cambridge University Press, 1992).

—— (ed.), *Descartes: Oxford Readings in Philosophy* (Oxford: Oxford University Press, 1998).

—— *Descartes* (Oxford: Blackwell, 1986).

CURLEY, EDWIN, *Descartes against the Sceptics* (Oxford: Blackwell, 1978).

DAVIES, RICHARD, *Descartes, Belief, Scepticism and Virtue* (London: Routledge, 2001).

FRANKFURT, HARRY, *Demons, Dreamers and Madmen* (Indianapolis: Bobbs-Merrill, 1970).

GARBER, DANIEL, *Descartes' Metaphysical Physics* (Chicago: University of Chicago Press, 1992).

GAUKROGER, STEPHEN, *Descartes: An Intellectual Biography* (Oxford: Clarendon Press, 1995).

KENNY, ANTHONY, *Descartes* (New York: Random House, 1968; reprinted by Thoemmes, 1993).

ROZEMOND, MARLEEN, *Descartes's Dualism* (Cambridge, Mass.: Harvard University Press, 1998).

WILLIAMS, BERNARD, *Descartes: the Project of Pure Inquiry* (Harmondsworth: Penguin, 1978).

WILSON, MARGARET, *Descartes* (London: Routledge & Kegan Paul, 1976).

Hobbes

The complete works of Hobbes were edited by W. Molesworth between 1839 and 1845, in 11 volumes of English works and 5 volumes of Latin works. Oxford University Press is producing a modern edition of his works, but so far only the following volumes have appeared: *De Cive* (1984), *Writings on Common Law and Hereditary Right* (2005), and the correspondence, edited in 2 volumes by Noel Malcolm (1994). There are convenient editions of *Leviathan* (1996) and *Human Nature and De Corpore Politico* (1999) by J. C. A. Gaskin (Oxford World Classics).

AUBREY, JOHN, *Brief Lives*, ed. Oliver Lawson Dick (Harmondsworth: Penguin, 1962; London: Folio Society, 1975).

GAUTHIER, DAVID, *The Logic of Leviathan* (Oxford: Oxford University Press, 1969).

OAKESHOTT, MICHAEL, *Hobbes on Civil Association* (Oxford: Oxford University Press, 1975).

RAPHAEL, DAVID D., *Hobbes, Morals and Politics* (London: Routledge, 1977).

SORELL, TOM, *Hobbes* (London: Routledge 1986).

—— *The Cambridge Companion to Hobbes* (Cambridge: Cambridge University Press 1996).

TUCK, RICHARD, *Hobbes* (Oxford: Oxford University Press, 1989).

WARRENDER, HOWARD, *The Political Philosophy of Hobbes* (Oxford: Oxford University Press, 1957).

Locke

The Clarendon edition of the works of John Locke is planned to occupy 30 volumes, which will include his diaries and letters. The series is approaching completion (Oxford: Oxford University Press, 1975–) and all the major works are already published. The edition of the *Essay Concerning Human Understanding* by P. H. Nidditch (1975) was brought out in paperback in 1975. A convenient paperback of *Two Treatises on Government* and *A Letter Concerning Toleration* (ed. Ian Shapiro) was produced by Yale University Press (New Haven, Conn.) in 2003.

AYERS, MICHAEL, *Locke*, 2 vols. (London: Routledge, 1991).

CHAPPELL, VERE, *The Cambridge Companion to Locke* (Cambridge: Cambridge University Press, 1994).

CRANSTON, MAURICE, *John Locke: a Biography* (Oxford: Oxford University Press, 1985).

DUNN, JOHN, *The Political Thought of John Locke* (Cambridge: Cambridge University Press, 1969).

—— *Locke* (Oxford: Oxford University Press, 1984).

MACKIE, JOHN, *Problems from Locke* (Oxford: Oxford University Press, 1976).

ROGERS, G. A. J., *Locke's Philosophy: Content and Context* (Oxford: Oxford University Press, 1974).

WOOLHOUSE, R. S., *Locke* (Brighton: Harvester, 1983).

YOLTON, JOHN, *John Locke and the Way of Ideas* (Oxford: Oxford University Press, 1956).

—— *John Locke: Problems and Perspectives* (Cambridge: Cambridge University Press, 1969).

—— *Locke, an Introduction* (Oxford: Blackwell, 1985).

—— *A Locke Dictionary* (Oxford: Blackwell, 1993).

Pascal and Malebranche

The best complete edition of the works of Pascal is *Oeuvres Complètes*, ed. Louis Lafuma (Paris: Editions du Seuil, 1963). The numbering of the *Pensées* in this edition is the one commonly used. There is an edition of *Les Provinciales* by H. F. Stewart (Manchester: Manchester University Press, 1919), and a translation by A. J. Krailsheimer (Harmondsworth: Penguin, 1967). A new translation of the *Pensées* by Honor Levi has appeared in Oxford World Classics (Oxford University Press, 1995). The standard edition of Malebranche is *Oeuvres Complètes*, ed. André Robinet, in 20 vols. (Paris: Vrin, 1958–84). There is an English translation of the *Treatise on Nature and Grace* by Patrick Riley (Oxford: Clarendon Press, 1992).

KRAILSHAIMER, ALBAN, *Pascal* (Oxford: Oxford University Press, 1980).

McCRACKEN, C. J., *Malebranche and British Philosophy* (Oxford: Oxford University Press, 1983).

MESNARD, J., *Pascal, His Life and Works* (London: Collins, 1952).

NADLER, STEVEN, *Malebranche and Ideas* (Oxford: Oxford University Press, 1992).

Spinoza

The standard edition is *Spinoza Opera*, ed. Carl Gebhardt, 4 vols. (Heidelberg: Carl Winter, 1925). A convenient 2-vol. English translation is *The Chief Works of Benedict de Spinoza*, translated by R. H. M. Elwes (New York: Dover, 1951). A new edition of the Collected Works in English is being published by Princeton University Press, edited and translated by Edwin Curley, of which the first volume appeared in 1985. A Penguin translation of the *Ethics* was published in 1996. His correspondence, edited and translated by A. Wolf, was published in 1928 and reprinted (London: Frank Cass) in 1966.

BENNETT, JONATHAN, *A Study of Spinoza's Ethics* (Indianapolis: Hackett, 1984).

CURLEY, EDWIN, *Spinoza's Metaphysics: An Essay in Interpretation* (Cambridge, Mass.: Harvard University Press, 1969).

DELAHUNTY, R. J., *Spinoza* (London: Routledge & Kegan Paul, 1985).

DONAGAN, ALAN, *Spinoza* (Chicago: Chicago University Press, 1988).

HAMPSHIRE, STUART, *Spinoza* (Harmondsworth: Penguin, 1951).

WOLFSON, HARRY A., *The Philosophy of Spinoza*, 2 vols. (Cambridge, Mass.: Harvard University Press, 1934).

Leibniz

The current standard edition of the philosophical writings is *Die Philosophischen Schriften*, in 7 vols. ed. C. I. Gerhardt (Hildesheim: Olms, 1963). In due course this will be replaced by the German Academy edition, *Samtliche Schriften und Briefe* (1923–). English editions of his writings include: *G. W. Leibniz: Philosophical Papers and Letters* (Dordrecht: Reidel, 1969); *G. W. Leibniz: Discourse on Metaphysics and related Writings*, ed. and trs. R. Martin and others (Manchester: Manchester University Press, 1988); *Leibniz: Philosophical Writings*, ed. and trs. G. H. R. Parkinson (London: Dent, 1973); *Leibniz: Logical Papers*, ed. and trs. G. H. R. Parkinson (Oxford: Clarendon Press, 1966); *Theodicy*, trs. E. M. Huggard (Lasalle, Ill.: Open Court Press, 1985); *Monadology and other Philosophical Essays*, trs. P. and A. M. Schrecker (Indianapolis: Bobbs-Merrill, 1965).

ADAMS, ROBERT, *Leibniz: Determinist, Theist, Idealist* (Oxford: Oxford University Press, 1994).

ARIEW, ROGER, *The Cambridge Companion to Leibniz* (Cambridge: Cambridge University Press, 1995).

BROWN, STUART, *Leibniz* (Brighton: Harvester Press, 1984).

ISHIGURO, HIDE, *Leibniz's Philosophy of Logic and Language* (London: Duckworth, 1972).

MATES, BENSON, *The Philosophy of Leibniz: Metaphysics and Language* (Oxford: Oxford University Press, 1986).

PARKINSON, G. H. R., *Logic and Reality in Leibniz's Metaphysics* (Oxford: Oxford University Press, 1965).

RUSSELL, BERTRAND, *A Critical Exposition of the Philosophy of Leibniz*, 2nd edn. (London: Allen and Unwin, 1937).

Berkeley

Berkeley's works have been published in 9 volumes by A. A. Luce and T. E. Jessop (Edinburgh: Thomas Nelson, 1948–57). His *Principles* and *Dialogues* have appeared in Oxford World Classics (Oxford: Oxford University Press, 1999).

BERMAN, D., *George Berkeley: Idealism and the Man* (Oxford: Clarendon Press, 1994).

MARTIN, C. B. and ARMSTRONG, D. M. eds., *Locke and Berkeley: A Collection of Critical Essays* (New York: Doubleday, 1968).

PITCHER, GEORGE, *Berkeley* (London: Routledge & Kegan Paul, 1977).

URMSON, JAMES, *Berkeley* (Oxford: Oxford University Press, 1982).

WARNOCK, GEOFFREY, *Berkeley* (Harmondsworth: Penguin, 1953).

WINKLER, K., *Berkeley, An Interpretation* (Oxford: Oxford University Press, 1989).

Hume

The most complete current edition is *The Philosophical Works of David Hume*, ed. T. H. Green and T. H. Grose (London: Longman Green, 1875). The Clarendon Press is publishing a new edition, in which the *Enquiries* are edited by Tom Beauchamp (1999, 2001) and the *Treatise* is edited by D. and M. Norton (2006). Convenient editions of the main works are *Treatise of Human Nature*, ed. L. A. Selby Bigge and P. H. Nidditch (3rd edn.; Oxford: Oxford University Press, 1978), and *Enquiry Concerning Human Understanding*, ed. L. A. Selby Bigge and P. H. Nidditch (2nd edn.; Oxford: Oxford University Press, 1978). *Hume on Religion*, ed. Richard Wollheim (London: Collins, 1963), is a useful selection, including *The Natural History of Religion* and *Dialogues Concerning Natural Religion*.

AYER, ALFRED J., *Hume* (Oxford: Oxford University Press, 1980).

FLEW, ANTONY, *Hume's Philosophy of Belief* (London: Routledge & Kegan Paul, 1961).

KEMP SMITH, NORMAN, *The Philosophy of David Hume* (London: Macmillan, 1941).

PEARS, DAVID, *Hume's System* (Oxford: Oxford University Press, 1990).

STRAWSON, GALEN, *The Secret Connexion* (Oxford: Clarendon Press, 1989).

WRIGHT, J. P., *The Sceptical Realism of David Hume* (Manchester: Manchester University Press, 1983).

Smith and Reid

A Glasgow edition of the works of Adam Smith is being produced by Oxford University Press; his *Theory of Moral Sentiments* was published in this series in 1976. *The Wealth of Nations* has appeared in Oxford World Classics, ed. K. Sutherland (Oxford: Oxford University Press, 1993). Reid's *Essays on the Intellectual Powers of Man* and *Essays on the Active Powers of the Human Mind* are available in modern reprints (Cambridge, Mass.: MIT Press).

LEHRER, KEITH, *Thomas Reid* (London: Routledge, 1989).
RAPHAEL, D. D., *Adam Smith* (Oxford: Oxford University Press, 1985).

The Enlightenment

Several of Voltaire's works are conveniently available in French in the Flammarion collection (Paris, 1964–), and in English translations in Oxford World Classics, and in Penguin Classics, which published his *Philosophical Dictionary*, ed. T. Besterman, in 1971. Rousseau's works are similarly available from Flammarion, and his *Discourse on Political Economy* and the *Social Contract* are in English in Oxford World Classics; his *Confessions* was published as a Penguin Classic in 1966. Lessing's *Laocoon* was published in a translation by E. A. McCormick in 1962, in the Library of Liberal Arts (Indianapolis: Bobbs-Merrill).

WADE, I., *The Intellectual Development of Voltaire* (Princeton, NJ: Princeton University Press).
WOKLER, R., *Rousseau* (Oxford: Oxford University Press, 1995).

Kant

The standard critical edition of Kant is the Akademie edition (*Kant's Gesammelte Schriften*), published in 29 vols. since 1900 (Berlin: Reimer/de Gruyter). A convenient German pocket edition in 12 vols. was published by Insel Verlag (Wiesbaden, 1956). A Cambridge edition of Kant's works in English was begun in 1991, with the publication of *Metaphysics of Morals* (ed. M. Gregor); the *Critique of Pure Reason*, ed. and trs. Paul Guyer and A. W. Wood, was published by Cambridge University Press in 1998. Among earlier translations still used are *The Critique of Practical Reason*, trs. Lewis White Beck (Indianapolis: Bobbs-Merrill, 1956) and *The Critique of Judgement*, trs. J. C. Meredith (Oxford: Oxford University Press, 1978)

BENNETT, JONATHAN, *Kant's Analytic* (Cambridge: Cambridge University Press, 1966).
—— *Kant's Dialectic* (Cambridge: Cambridge University Press, 1974).
CAYGILL, HOWARD, *A Kant Dictionary* (Oxford: Blackwell, 1994).
GUYER, PAUL, *Kant and the Claims of Knowledge* (Cambridge: Cambridge University Press, 1987).
—— (ed.), *The Cambridge Companion to Kant* (Cambridge: Cambridge University Press, 1992).
KITSCHER, PATRICIA, *Kant's Transcendental Psychology* (Oxford: Oxford University Press, 1990).
KÖRNER, STEPHAN, *Kant* (Harmondsworth: Penguin, 1955).

O'NEILL, ONORA, *Constructions of Reason: Explorations of Kant's Practical Philosophy* (Cambridge: Cambridge University Press, 1989).

PATON, H. J., *The Moral Law* (London: Hutchinson, 1955).

SCRUTON, ROGER, *Kant* (Oxford: Oxford University Press, 1982).

STRAWSON, PETER, *The Bounds of Sense* (London: Methuen, 1966).

WALKER, RALPH, *Kant* (London: Routledge & Kegan Paul, 1978).

WOOD, ALLEN, *Kant's Rational Theology* (Ithaca, NY: Cornell University Press, 1978).

Hegel

The Deutsche Forschungsgemeinschaft has been bringing out a critical edition of Hegel's works since 1968 (Hamburg: Meiner). The most convenient German edition to use is the *Werkausgabe* in 20 vols., ed. E. Moldenhauer and K. Michel (Frankfurt: Suhrkamp, 1969–72). Among English translations of Hegel's works are *Logic*, trs. William Wallace (Oxford: Oxford University Press, 1975); *Phenomenology of Spirit*, trs. A. V. Miller (Oxford: Oxford University Press, 1977); *Lectures on the History of Philosophy*, trs. E. S. Haldane and F. H. Simpson (3 vols. London: Routledge, 1966); *Philosophy of Right*, trs. H. B. Nisbet, ed. Allen Wood (Cambridge: Cambridge University Press, 1991).

FINDLAY, J. N., *Hegel: A Re-examination* (London: George Allen and Unwin, 1958).

INWOOD, MICHAEL, *Hegel* (London: Routledge & Kegan Paul, 1983).

KAUFMANN, WALTER, *Hegel: A Re-examination* (Garden City, NY: Doubleday, 1965).

POPPER, KARL, *The Open Society and its Enemies* (London: Routledge & Kegan Paul, 1966).

ROSEN, MICHAEL, *Hegel's Dialectic and its Criticism* (Cambridge: Cambridge University Press, 1982).

SOLOMON, ROBERT, *In the Spirit of Hegel* (Oxford: Oxford University Press, 1983).

TAYLOR, CHARLES, *Hegel* (Cambridge: Cambridge University Press, 1975).

—— *Hegel and Modern Society* (Cambridge: Cambridge University Press, 1979).

WALSH, W. H., *Hegelian Ethics* (London: Macmillan, 1969).

Part Four

General

The *Routledge History of Philosophy* contains five volumes that overlap with the period of this volume. They are volume VI, *The Age of German Idealism*, ed. Robert Solomon and Kathleen Higgins; VII, *The Nineteenth Century*, ed. C. L. Ten; VIII, *Continental Philosophy in the 20th Century*, ed. Richard Kearney; IX, *Philosophy of Science, Logic and Mathematics in the 20th Century*, ed. S. G. Shanker; and X, *Philosophy of Meaning, Knowledge and Value in the 20th Century*. The *Routledge Encyclopaedia of Philosophy* also contains many articles about the people and topics treated here.

BIBLIOGRAPHY

Titles marked 'AP' appeared in the Routledge series Arguments of the Philosophers, and titles marked 'PM' appeared in the Oxford series Past Masters.

COPLESTON, F. C., *A History of Philosophy*, vols. vii–ix (London: Burnes Oates, 1963–75)

KENNY, A., *A Brief History of Western Philosophy* (Oxford: Blackwell, 1998)

—— (ed.), *The Oxford Illustrated History of Western Philosophy* (Oxford: Oxford University Press, 1994)

KNEALE, W. and M., *The Development of Logic* (Oxford: Oxford University Press, 1962)

MACINTYRE, ALASDAIR, *A Short History of Ethics* (London: Macmillan, 1966)

—— *After Virtue: A Study in Moral Theory* (London: Duckworth, 1981)

Bentham

The Collected Works of Jeremy Bentham, ed. J. H. Burns, J. R. Dinwiddy, and F. Rosen (London: Athlone, 1968–)

Introduction to the Principles of Morals and Legislation, ed. J. H. Burns and H. L. A. Hart (London: Oxford University Press, 1982)

DINWIDDY, J. R., *Bentham* (Oxford: Oxford University Press, 1989)

HARRISON, ROSS, *Bentham* (London: 1983) (AP)

HART, H. L. A., *Essays on Jurisprudence and Political Theory* (Oxford: 1982)

Mill and Sidgwick

The Collected Works of John Stuart Mill, ed. John M. Robson, 33 vols. (Toronto: University of Toronto Press, 1963–91)

Mill, *On Liberty*, Oxford World's Classics (Oxford: Oxford University Press, 1991)

Mill, *Principles of Political Economy*, Oxford World's Classics (Oxford: Oxford University Press, 1994)

The Cambridge Companion to Mill, ed. J. Skorupski (Cambridge: Cambridge University Press, 1998)

Sidgwick, *Methods of Ethics* (1874); the most convenient edition is (London: Macmillan, 1901)

ALEXANDER, EDWARD, *Matthew Arnold and John Stuart Mill* (London: Routledge & Kegan Paul, 1965)

BERLIN, ISAIAH, *Four Essays on Liberty* (London: Oxford University Press, 1969)

CRISP, ROGER, *A Guidebook to J. S. Mill's Utilitarianism* (London: Routledge, 1997)

MACKIE, J. L., *The Cement of the Universe* (Oxford: Oxford University Press, 1973)

RYAN, ALAN, *The Philosophy of John Stuart Mill*, 2nd edn. (New York: Macmillan, 1988)

SCHULTZ, BART, *Henry Sidgwick, Eye of the Universe* (Cambridge: Cambridge University Press, 2004)

SKORUPSKI, JOHN, *John Stuart Mill* (London: Routledge, 1989) (AP)

Schopenhauer

Schopenhauer's works are available in several German editions, of which the most recent is *Werke in fünf Banden. Nach den Ausgaben letzter Hand*, ed. Ludger Lütkehaus, 5 vols. (Zurich: Haffmans Verlag, 1988).

The most convenient recent English edition of his main work is *The World as Will and Representation*, trans. E. F. Payne, 2 vols. (New York: Dover, 1969).

English translations of other works include:

Essays and Aphorisms, trans. R. J. Hollingdale (London: Penguin, 2004)
Essay on the Freedom of the Will, trans. K. Kolenda (Indianapolis: Bobbs-Merrill, 1960)
On the Fourfold Root of the Principle of Sufficient Reason, trans. E. F. Payne (La Salle, Ill.: Open Court, 1974)

The Cambridge Companion to Schopenhauer, ed. Christopher Janaway (Cambridge: Cambridge University Press, 1999)

GARDINER, PATRICK, *Schopenhauer* (Bristol: Thoemmes Press, 1997)
HAMLYN, D. W., *Schopenhauer* (London: Routledge & Kegan Paul, 1980) (AP)
MAGEE, BRYAN, *The Philosophy of Schopenhauer* (Oxford: Clarendon Press, 1997)
TANNER, MICHAEL, *Schopenhauer: Metaphysics and Art* (London: Phoenix, 1998)

Kierkegaard

There is a twenty-volume edition of Kierkegaard's works in Danish, which has gone through three editions. A complete English edition, translated by Howard V. Hong and others, is being published in twenty-six volumes by Princeton University Press. In England, Penguin have published translations of several of his works by Alastair Hannay (*Fear and Trembling* (1985); *The Sickness unto Death* (1989); *Either/Or* (1992); *Papers and Journals: A Selection* (1996))

The Cambridge Companion to Kierkegaard, ed. Alastair Hannay and Gordon D. Marino (Cambridge: Cambridge University Press, 1998)

GARDINER, PATRICK, *Kierkegaard* (Oxford: Oxford University Press, 1998) (PM)
HANNAY, ALASTAIR, *Kierkegaard* (London: Routledge, 1991) (AP)
POJMAN, LOUIS, *The Logic of Subjectivity: Kierkegaard's Philosophy of Religion* (Tuscaloosa: University of Alabama Press, 1984)
RUDD, A., *Kierkegaard and the Limits of the Ethical* (Oxford: Oxford University Press, 1993)

Marx

The first complete edition of the works of Marx and Engels in German was published by the East German authorities in 1968 (*Marx-Engels Werke*). An English translation of this edition was commenced by the London publishers Lawrence & Wishart. English translations of the major works have appeared in the Marx Library (New York: Random

House; Harmondsworth: Penguin) between 1974 and 1984. A convenient abridgement of *Capital*, edited by David McLellan, appeared in Oxford World's Classics in 1995.

The Cambridge Companion to Marx, ed. Terrell Carver (Cambridge: Cambridge University Press, 1991)

BERLIN, ISAIAH, *Karl Marx*, 4th edn. (Oxford: Oxford University Press, 1978)

KOLAKOWSKI, LESZEK, *Main Currents in Marxism*, trans. P. S. Falla, 3 vols. (Oxford: Oxford University Press, 1978)

MCLELLAN, DAVID, *Karl Marx: His Life and Thought* (New York: Harper & Row, 1973)

SINGER, PETER, *Marx* (Oxford: Oxford University Press, 1980) (PM)

WHEEN, FRANCIS, *Karl Marx* (London: Fourth Estate, 1999)

Darwin

On the Origin of Species is available in many editions, notably Oxford World's Classics and Penguin Classics. Recent philosophical discussions of his work appear in the following:

RUSE, M., *Taking Darwin Seriously: A Naturalistic Approach to Philosophy* (Oxford: Oxford University Press, 1986)

SOBER, ELLIOTT, *Philosophy of Biology* (Oxford: Oxford University Press, 1993)

Newman

Newman's major philosophical work is *An Essay in Aid of a Grammar of Assent* (ed. I. Ker (Oxford: Oxford University Press, 1985)). There is a good Past Masters biography by Owen Chadwick (Oxford: Oxford University Press, 1983).

GRAVE, S. A., *Conscience in Newman's Thought* (Oxford: Oxford University Press, 1989)

Nietzsche

The critical edition of his collected works is *Kritische Gesamtausgabe Werke*, edited by G. Colli and M. Montinari, 30 vols. in 8 parts (Berlin: de Gruyter, 1967–). A more convenient German edition is *Werke in Drei Bänden*, edited by Karl Schlechta (Munich: Carl Hansers, 1965). The following works have been translated into English by Walter Kaufmann and published in New York by Random House: *Beyond Good and Evil* (1966), *The Birth of Tragedy* (1967), *On the Genealogy of Morals* (1967), *The Gay Science* (1974). Several of Nietzsche's works, including *Thus Spake Zarathustra*, are available in Oxford World's Classics and Penguin Classics.

DANTO, ARTHUR, *Nietzsche as Philosopher: An Original Study* (New York: Columbia University Press, 1965)

HOLLINGDALE, R. J., *Nietzsche* (London: Routledge & Kegan Paul, 1973)

SCHACHT, R., *Nietzsche* (London: Routledge & Kegan Paul, 1983)

Peirce

The *Collected Papers of Charles Sanders Peirce* were published in eight volumes by Harvard University Press between 1931 and 1958. A new, chronological edition has been under way since 1982, published by Indiana University Press. Meanwhile, there are accessible collections of his main papers in the two-volume *The Essential Peirce*, edited by N. Houser and C. Kloesel (Bloomington: Indiana University Press, 1992–4) and in the one-volume *The Essential Writings*, edited by E. C. Moore (New York: Prometheus Books, 1998)

BRENT, J., *Charles Sanders Peirce: A Life* (Bloomington: Indiana University Press, 1993)
HOOKWAY, CHRISTOPHER, *Peirce* (London: Routledge, 1985) (AP)

Frege

The most widely available works of Frege in English are the following:
Conceptual Notation and Related Articles, trans. T. W. Bynum (Oxford: Oxford University Press, 1972)
The Foundations of Arithmetic, trans. J. L. Austin (Oxford: Oxford University Press, 1950, 1980)
Collected Papers on Mathematics, Logic and Philosophy, ed. B. McGuinness (Oxford: Blackwell, 1984)
The Basic Laws of Arithmetic: Exposition of the System, trans. Montgomery Furth (Berkeley: University of California Press, 1964)

DUMMETT, MICHAEL, *Frege: Philosophy of Language* (London: Duckworth, 1973)
—— *The Interpretation of Frege's Philosophy* (London: Duckworth, 1981)
—— *Frege: Philosophy of Mathematics* (London: Duckworth, 1991)
KENNY, A., *Frege* (London: Penguin, 1995; Oxford: Blackwell, 2000)

James

The Principles of Psychology of 1890 has been reissued many times: a convenient reprint is the Dover paperback (2 vols. in 1; New York, 1950). *Varieties of Religious Experience* is also available in many editions, including one by Collier Macmillan of London in 1961.

AYER, A. J., *The Origins of Pragmatism* (London: Macmillan, 1968)
BIRD, G., *William James* (London: Routledge & Kegan Paul, 1987) (AP)

British Idealists and Critics

AYER, A. J., *Language, Truth and Logic*, 2nd edn. (London: Gollancz, 1949)
BRADLEY, F. H., *Appearance and Reality* (Oxford: Oxford University Press, 1893)
—— *Ethical Studies*, 2nd edn. (Oxford: Oxford University Press, 1927)
GREEN, T. H., *Prolegomena to Ethics* (Oxford: Oxford University Press, 1883)
McTAGGART, *The Nature of Existence* (Cambridge: Cambridge University Press, 1910, 1927)
MOORE, G. E., *Principia Ethica* (Cambridge: Cambridge University Press, 1903)

BALDWIN, THOMAS, *G. E. Moore* (London: Routledge, 1990)

GEACH, PETER, *Truth, Love, and Immortality: An Introduction to McTaggart's Philosophy* (London: Methuen, 1979)

WOLLHEIM, RICHARD, *F. H. Bradley* (Harmondsworth: Penguin, 1959)

Russell

Among the more important of Russell's copious publications are *The Principles of Mathematics* (Cambridge: Cambridge University Press, 1903; 2nd edn., 1927); 'On Denoting', *Mind*, 14 (1905) (often reprinted); *The Problems of Philosophy* (Oxford: Oxford University Press, 1912); *Our Knowledge of the External World* (London: Allen & Unwin, 1914); *Introduction to Mathematical Philosophy* (London: Methuen, 1917); *The Analysis of Mind* (London: Allen & Unwin, 1921); *Human Knowledge: Its Scope and Limits* (London: Allen & Unwin, 1948)

AYER, A. J., *Bertrand Russell* (Chicago: University of Chicago Press, 1988)

PEARS, D. F., *Bertrand Russell and the British Tradition in Philosophy* (London: Fontana, 1967)

SAINSBURY, MARK, *Russell* (London: Routledge, 1979) (AP)

Wittgenstein

Wittgenstein's entire *Nachlass* is available in transcription and facsimile in electronic form, in a text established by the University of Bergen and published by Oxford University Press (Oxford, 1998). *Tractatus Logico-Philosophicus* was published by Routledge & Kegan Paul in London in 1921; a new translation by D. F. Pears and Brian McGuinness was published in 1961. Other writings of Wittgenstein were all published posthumously by Blackwell at Oxford, including *Notebooks 1914–1916* (1961); *Philosophical Investigations* (1953, 1997); *Philosophical Remarks* (1966); *Philosophical Grammar* (1974); *Culture and Value* (1980); *Remarks on the Philosophy of Psychology* (1980); *Last Writings on the Philosophy of Psychology* (1982, 1992); *On Certainty* (1969). A comprehensive and scholarly commentary on the *Philosophical Investigations* was produced by G. P. Baker and P. M. S. Hacker between 1980 and 1996. In 1994 I published with Blackwell an anthology of texts under the title *The Wittgenstein Reader*. A second edition appeared in 2006.

ANSCOMBE, G. E. M., *An Introduction to Wittgenstein's 'Tractatus'* (London: Hutchinson, 1959)

KENNY, A., *Wittgenstein* (Harmondsworth: Penguin, 1973; Oxford: Blackwell, 2006)

KRIPKE, SAUL, *Wittgenstein on Rules and Private Language* (Oxford: Blackwell, 1982)

PEARS, DAVID, *The False Prison* (Oxford: Oxford University Press, 1997, 1998)

RUNDLE, BEDE, *Wittgenstein and Contemporary Philosophy of Language* (Oxford: Blackwell, 1990)

Analytic Philosophy

An excellent overview is given by P. M. S. Hacker in *Wittgenstein's Place in Twentieth Century Analytic Philosophy* (Oxford: Blackwell, 1996). Important works by individual analytic philosophers are listed below.

ANSCOMBE, G. E. M., *Intention* (Oxford: Blackwell, 1957)

AUSTIN, J. L., *How to Do Things with Words* (Oxford: Oxford University Press, 1961)

DAVIDSON, DONALD, *Essays on Actions and Events* (Oxford: Oxford University Press, 1980)

—— *Inquiries into Truth and Interpretation* (Oxford: Oxford University Press, 1984)

FØLLESDAL, DAGFINN, *Referential Opacity and Modal Logic* (London: Routledge, 2004)

GEACH, PETER, *Mental Acts* (London: Routledge & Kegan Paul, 1958)

QUINE, W. V. O., *From a Logical Point of View* (Cambridge, Mass.: Harvard University Press, 1953)

—— *Word and Object* (Cambridge, Mass.: MIT Press, 1960)

RAWLS, JOHN, *A Theory of Justice* (Cambridge, Mass.: Harvard University Press, 1971)

RYLE, GILBERT, *The Concept of Mind* (London: Hutchinson, 1949)

—— *Collected Papers* (London: Hutchinson, 1949)

STRAWSON, P. F., *Individuals* (London: Methuen, 1959)

Freud

Freud's works are collected in German in *Gesammelte Werke*, edited by A. Freud and others (Frankfurt am Main: S. Fischer Verlag, 1960–87). In English there is *The Standard Edition of the Complete Psychological Works of Sigmund Freud*, 24 vols. (London: Hogarth Press, 1981). All the most significant works are easily accessible in *The Penguin Freud Library*, edited by A. Richards and A. Dickson.

The Cambridge Companion to Freud, ed. J. Neu (Cambridge: Cambridge University Press, 1991)

GAY, P., *Freud: A Life for our Time* (New York: Norton, 1988)

LEAR, JONATHAN, *Freud* (London: Routledge, 2005)

RIEFF, P., *Freud: The Mind of the Moralist* (Chicago: Chicago University Press, 1979)

WOLLHEIM, R., *Sigmund Freud* (Cambridge: Cambridge University Press, 1971)

—— and HOPKINS, J. (eds.), *Philosophical Essays on Freud* (Cambridge: Cambridge University Press, 1982)

Husserl

The critical edition of Husserl's works was inaugurated in 1950 with the publication of *Cartesianische Meditationen*. Since then twenty-eight volumes have appeared, edited first by Leo van Breda, and later by Samuel Ijsseling. It is now published by Kluwer (Dordrecht). The most useful English translations are *Logical Investigations*, trans. J. N. Findlay, 2nd edn. (London: Routledge, 2001); *Ideas Pertaining to a Pure Phenomenology and to a Phenomenological Philosophy*, First Book, trans. F. Kersten (The Hague: Nijhoff, 1982); Second Book, trans. R. Rojcewicz and A. Schuwer (Dordrecht: Kluwer, 1989); Third Book, trans. T. E. Klein and W. E. Phol (Dordrecht:

Kluwer, 1980); *Husserl, Shorter Works*, ed. and trans. P. McCormick and F. Elliston (Notre Dame, Ind.: University of Notre Dame Press, 1981).

The Cambridge Companion to Husserl, ed. Barry Smith and David Woodruff Smith (Cambridge: Cambridge University Press, 1995).

BELL, DAVID, *Husserl* (London: Routledge, 1989) (AP)

DREYFUS, H. L. (ed.), *Husserl, Intentionality and Cognitive Science* (Cambridge, Mass.: MIT Press, 1982)

MOHANTY, J. N., and MCKENNA, W. R. (eds.), *Husserl's Phenomenology: A Textbook* (Lanham, Md.: Centre for Advanced Research in Phenomenology, 1989)

SIMONS, PETER, *Philosophy and Logic in Central Europe from Bolzano to Tarski* (Dordrecht: Kluwer, 1992)

Heidegger

A *Gesamtausgabe* of Heidegger's works is planned in approximately 100 volumes. Some seventy have now been published by Klostermann (Frankfurt am Main). English translations of the major works include: *Being and Time*, trans J. Stambaugh (Albany, NY: SUNY Press, 1996); *Basic Writings*, ed. D. F. Krell (New York: Harper & Row, 1977); *What is Philosophy?*, trans. W. Kluback and J. T. Wilde (New Haven, Conn.: College & University Press, 1958)

The Cambridge Companion to Heidegger, ed. C. Guignon (Cambridge: Cambridge University Press, 1993)

DREYFUS, H. L., *Being-in-the-World: A Commentary on Heidegger's 'Being and Time' Division I* (Cambridge, Mass.: MIT Press, 1991)

MULHALL, STEPHEN, *On Being in the World: Wittgenstein and Heidegger on Seeing Aspects* (London: Routledge, 1990)

PÖGGLER, OTTO, *Martin Heidegger's Path of Thinking*, trans. D. Magurshak and S. Barber (Atlantic Highlands, NJ: Humanities Press, 1987)

STEINER, GEORGE, *Martin Heidegger* (Chicago: University of Chicago Press, 1987)

Sartre

La Nausée (Paris, 1938), trans. Robert Baldick as *Nausea* (Harmondsworth: Penguin, 1965)

L'Être et le néant (Paris, 1943), trans. Hazel Barnes as *Being and Nothingness* (London: Routledge, 1969)

L'Existentialisme est un humanisme (Paris, 1946), trans. Philip Mairet as *Existentialism and Humanism* (London: Methuen, 1948)

CAWS, P., *Sartre* (London: Routledge, 1979) (AP)

COOPER, DAVID, *Existentialism, a Reconstruction* (Oxford: Blackwell, 1990)

WARNOCK, MARY, *The Philosophy of Sartre* (London: Hutchinson, 1965)

Derrida

De la grammatologie (Paris, 1967), trans. G. C. Spivak as *Of Grammatology* (Baltimore: Johns Hopkins University Press, 1976)

L'Écriture et la différence (Paris, 1967), trans. Alan Bass as *Writing and Difference* (London: Routledge & Kegan Paul, 1978)

Positions, trans. Alan Bass (Chicago: University of Chicago Press, 1981)

NORRIS, CHRISTOPHER, *Derrida* (London: Routledge, 1987) (AP)

ROYLE, NICHOLAS, *Jacques Derrida* (London: Routledge, 2003)

INDEX

INDEX

INDEX